Financial
executive's
handbook

Financial executive's handbook

edited by

RICHARD F. VANCIL
Professor of Business Administration
Harvard University

1970

DOW JONES-IRWIN, INC.
Homewood, Illinois

Library of Congress Catalog Card No. 69–15541

Printed in the United States of America

CONSULTING EDITORS

CONTRIBUTING AUTHORS*

ABELY, JOSEPH F., JR. (Chapter 19*)—Vice President and Controller, General Foods Corporation

AXELSON, CHARLES F. (Chapter 57)—Controller and Assistant Treasurer, United States Gypsum Company

BELDA, BERTRAND J. (Chapter 54)—Partner in charge of Management Consulting Services, Ernst and Ernst

BROWN, HENRY L. (Chapter 65)—Vice President–Corporate Public Relations, National Distillers and Chemical Corporation

BUMP, JACK A. (Chapter 23)—Divisional Controller, Coated Abrasive & Tape Divisions, Norton Company

BURSON, HAROLD (Chapter 63*)—Chairman, Burson-Marsteller

CARROLL, R. E. (Chapter 11)—Vice President–Business Operations, Space Division, North American Rockwell Corp.

CASTLE, JOHN K. (Chapter 50)—Vice President, Donaldson, Lufkin & Jenrette

CENTER, O. D. (Chapter 6)—Vice President–Administration and Finance, Stromberg-Carlson Corporation

CHAMBERLIN, LARRY L. (Chapter 51*)—Consultant, Peat, Marwick, Mitchell & Co.

COCKRUM, WILLIAM M. (Chapter 47)—Vice President, A. G. Becker & Co. Incorporated

CONLEY, PATRICK (Chapter 21)—Vice President, The Boston Consulting Group, Inc.

CONNOR, JOSEPH E. (Chapter 60)—Partner, Price Waterhouse & Co.

CROSSEN, JOHN E. (Chapter 17)—Senior Vice President–Latin America and Pacific, H. J. Heinz Co.

DAHLE, ROBERT D. (Chapter 14*)—Manager, Analytical Support, Advanced Development Department, Xerox Corporation

DUDAS, JOHN F. (Chapter 30)—Manager, Technical Planning, Tele-Computer Center, Westinghouse Electric Corp.

FORSBERG, J. MARVIN (Chapter 22)—Manager of Long Range Forecasting and Analysis, Corporate Economic Planning, Burroughs Corporation

FOSTER, LEBARON R. (Chapter 62)—Vice President, Opinion Research Corporation

FUNARI, MARIO R. (Chapter 38)—Vice President–Controller, The Weatherhead Company

GELLEIN, OSCAR S. (Chapter 56*)—Partner, Haskins & Sells

GRELA, JOHN J. (Chapter 5)—Vice President–Organization and Management Development, Sperry Rand Corporation

HACKETT, J. T. (Chapter 40*)—Vice President–Finance, Cummins Engine Company, Inc.

HART, JOHN N. (Chapter 43)—Vice President & Controller, The B. F. Goodrich Co.

---

* Denotes co-author.

HELFERT, ERICH A. (Chapter 35)—Assistant to the President, Crown Zeller-bach Corporation

HICKS, ERNEST L. (Chapter 58)—Partner, Arthur Young & Company

HORNE, WILLIAM M., JR. (Chapter 9)—Vice President, Commercial Credit Company

HUBLER, MYRON J., JR. (Chapter 15)—Controller, Instrument Division, Reliance Electric Company

HUGHES, ANTHONY D. (Chapter 63*)—Vice President–Financial Relations, Burson-Marsteller

HUMMEL, C. RONALD (Chapter 19*)—Director, Financial Planning and Analysis, General Foods Corporation

JERRETT, ROBERT, JR. (Chapter 3)—President, Venture Resources, Inc.

JONES, DONALD P. (Chapter 24*)—Vice President, Sun Oil Company

KAY, ROBERT S. (Chapter 55)—Partner, Touche Ross and Company

KINGSTON, JOHN A. (Chapter 48)—President, Meinhard-Commercial Corporation

KNORTZ, HERBERT C. (Chapters 4 & 52)—Senior Vice President and Comptroller, International Telephone & Telegraph Corp.

KOPEL, BERNARD (Chapter 42*)—Vice President, The First National Bank of Boston

KOTCHIAN, A. CARL (Chapter 1)—President, Lockheed Aircraft Corporation

LANGDON, PAUL R. (Chapter 37)—Assistant Treasurer, Battelle Memorial Institute

LINTON, FRANK L. (Chapter 27)—Vice President (Retired), Allied Chemical Corporation

LITTLEFIELD, W. JOSEPH (Chapters 7 & 8)—Controller for Financial Analysis (Retired), Johns-Manville Corporation

LOWE, WILLIAM H. (Chapter 44)—Vice President–Finance and Chairman of the Finance Committee, Inland Steel Company

LUPER, O. L. (Chapter 53)—Vice President and Director, Humble Oil & Refining Company

LYONS, DANIEL E. (Chapter 64)—Vice President–Finance, City Investing Company

McEACHRON, WILLIAM D. (Chapter 26)—Manager, Planning & Economics, Standard Oil Co. (Indiana)

MAKELA, BENJAMIN R. (Chapter 18)—Editor, *Financial Executive Magazine*

MANN, HARRY S. (*deceased*) (Chapter 33*)—Late Vice President–Finance, Digital Equipment Corp.

MARTIN, A. S., JR. (Chapter 24*)—Coordinator of Production Accounting, Sun Oil Company

MEYER, ROBERT F. (Chapter 2)—Treasurer and Vice President, Aerosol Techniques, Inc.

MINTS, FREDERIC E. (Chapter 12*)—Manager of Internal Auditing (Retired), Lockheed-California Company

MUCK, P. F. (Chapter 25)—Controller, Mesta Machine Company

NELSON, WILLIAM G., IV (Chapter 49)—Manager, Planning and Commercial Development, Monsanto Company

---

* Denotes co-author.

PACKER, DAVID W. (Chapter 33*)—Manager, Systems and EDP, Digital Equipment Corporation

PESKE, EDGAR (Chapter 66)—Vice President and Treasurer, Illinois Bell Telephone Co.

PHILIPS, J. N. (Chapter 46*)—Executive Vice President, Eastern Gas & Fuel Associates

REID, FRANK T. (Chapter 61)—Treasurer and Assistant Secretary, Western International Hotels Company

RESNICK, CHARLES H. (Chapter 10)—Vice President, Secretary and General Counsel, Raytheon Company

RICHY, JOHN W. (Chapters 28, 29* and 31)—Manager of Technical Services, Computer and Data Communication Systems, United Air Lines

RICKARD, E. B. (Chapter 34)—Marketing Services Manager, Ford Motor Company

ROBINSON, H. G. (Chapter 56*)—Partner, Haskins & Sells

ROBINSON, WILLIAM J. (Chapter 39)—Vice President–Controller, Insurance Company of North America

SCOTT, CHARLES K. (Chapter 29*)—Operations Research Analyst, Department of Health, Education and Welfare

SENEY, WILSON (Chapter 13)—President, Wilson Seney, Inc., and Management Consultant

SINNICKSON, LLOYD (Chapter 42*)—General Credit Manager, American Cyanamid Company

SKINNER, DAVID C. (Chapter 16)—President, Logic Resources, Inc.

SMITH, JAMES S. (Chapter 51*)—Partner, Peat, Marwick, Mitchell & Co.

STILLMAN, RICHARD N. (Chapter 36)—Controller, Stauffer Chemical Company

SWAYZE, W. S. (Chapter 20)—Controller, Mobil Oil Corporation

THURSTON, G. R. (Chapter 40*)—Manager, Corporate Cash Management, Cummins Engine Company, Inc.

WALLACE, STANLEY L. (Chapter 45)—Vice President, Johnson & Higgins

WALSH, DOROTHY (Chapter 32)—Vice President, Advanced Computer Techniques Corporation

WHEELER, LINDEN E. (Chapter 41)—Vice President–Credit, Sears, Roebuck and Co.

WICK, MERLE S. (Chapter 59)—Vice President, New York Stock Exchange

WITT, HERBERT (Chapter 12*)—Regional Audit Director, Department of Health, Education, and Welfare, San Francisco Region

ZIVAN, S. M. (Chapter 14*)—Regional Controller, Xerox Corporation

---

* Denotes co-author.

Preface

The top financial executive in today's modern corporation carries an almost unbelievable range of responsibilities. This handbook is designed to help these executives meet the requirements of their demanding, challenging positions.

As Mr. Kotchian describes in his opening essay, the role of the financial executive has changed rapidly—and radically—in the last two decades. The two most important aspects of these changes are (1) a broadening of his responsibilities to embrace the entire set of corporate financial, accounting, and administrative activities, coupled with (2) an increasing sophistication in the arsenal of analytical techniques and management concepts available to assist him in fulfilling his responsibilities in a professional manner. Both of these factors impose new and continuing knowledge requirements on the financial executive, obligations which can best be met only by a heavy workload of current reading of management periodicals and new books.

A handbook is no substitute for current reading—the world is changing too fast—but a well-organized handbook does help to meet the need. As an accurate, up-to-date compendium of current knowledge, a handbook has the advantage of compact comprehensiveness; it is a convenient place for the executive to start his search for relevant concepts and techniques on any particular topic. As a codification of the state-of-the-art as of the date of publication, a handbook limits the need for further search to only the most recent publications.

Such, at least, is the purpose of this volume. This handbook is not intended as an elementary text on the duties of a financial executive. Rather, the presumption is that the reader is a mature, experienced executive with broad general knowledge of the field; he uses the handbook to review and update his understanding of specific topics as the need arises.

In order to achieve this purpose, the first editorial decision was to have all the chapters written by practicing businessmen, addressing themselves to their peers. To the extent that academic theories are practicable (as they increasingly are), they are described' and, more importantly, their translation into workable procedures and policies is documented. Nearly three dozen Consulting Editors, a third of them outstanding academicians, have served as reviewers, thus helping to insure that both good theory and good practice are properly represented.

In order to use this handbook effectively, several features of its structure should be noted. The 66 chapters have been grouped into 10 major sections, roughly attempting to parallel the way that many financial executives have organized their offices. The first two sections deal with the broad responsibilities of the financial executive as a member of the top management team and as an administrator for his own function. The next seven sections deal with major substantive matters; the groupings reflect the way that chief financial officers of large corporations frequently distribute responsibilities among their lieutenants. The final section is, again, broad in scope, covering several topics concerning the financial executive's responsibility for external relations.

Within each of the seven functional sections, the individual chapters are organized in one of two ways. One approach, as illustrated by Part III on Financial and Economic Analysis, is to use the first chapter as a general overview of the area. Chapter 14 on Systems Analysis and Simulation is a sort of "umbrella" for the specific topics treated in subsequent chapters in that section; it describes the general approach and broadly applicable techniques, thus permitting cross-references that reduce the redundancy that would otherwise be necessary if each of the following chapters attempted to be wholly self-contained. As a result, most users of the handbook will want to review the opening chapter for sections organized in this way, before turning to a specific topic. The other umbrella chapters are No. 34, Reporting to Operating Management (Part VI); No. 46, Capital Structure Determination (Part VIII); and No. 53, Nature and Objective of Financial Statements (Part IX).

The other three sections are organized with a different philosophy; the sequence of chapters is roughly chronological. In both Part IV (Planning and Budgeting) and Part V (Information Technology) the chapters use cross-references to build upon the discussion of earlier steps in the process that were covered in preceding chapters in that section. The chapters in Part VII (Asset Management and Control) use the chronology of asset liquidity as the sequencing thread.

Despite this attempt to use major sections as a device for grouping related chapters, several important topics could not be neatly pigeonholed, either because (1) the pervasiveness of the topic made it relevant to many others, or (2) various aspects of the topic related to different organizational segments of the typical financial executive's office. Topics of the first type, such as the impact of income taxes and the organization and staffing for specific activities, are thus covered in each chapter where needed; Chapters 7 and 9 deal with these topics in general terms only. Topics of the second type were subdivided into two or three chapters and then assigned to the appropriate section in the handbook. For example, three separate chapters are devoted to the topic of mergers and acquisitions: No. 18, Analysis of Potential Acquisitions; No. 51, Financial Aspects of Acquisitions and Mergers; and No. 57, Accounting for Business Combinations and Goodwill. Similarly, various aspects of international operations are dealt with in chapters 4, 52, and 60. Liberal cross-referencing between chapters of multifaceted topics is intended to help the reader find what he is looking for.

On balance, we hope that these complexities in the structure of the handbook are more than offset by the benefits that result from having a larger number of shorter, narrowly focused chapters. On the one hand, each chapter had to be kept fairly specific if it was to be written by a busy financial executive. On the other, a short chapter, if well done, is the most effective way to meet the specific informational needs of the user. We have attempted to mitigate the problems of brevity by cross-referencing, by including a bibliography at the end of those chapters where needed, and by an extensive index to the entire volume.

Speaking personally, rather than with the honest "we" used above, it has been an enormous pleasure to serve as the editor for this undertaking. Such a project could only be attempted as a group activity; no one individual—and certainly not the editor—has sufficient depth of knowledge to write definitively on these 66 topics. Thus, it would be presumptuous of me to start "thanking" various people for their help when I am but one of the team of more than one hundred who contributed in various ways. I would, however, like to insure that some of the less obvious contributions do not pass unnoticed.

All of the participants are listed, of course, and the work of each Contributing Author is readily identifiable. On the other hand, the members of the Editorial Advisory Board are the real initiators of this volume. Without their willingness to begin, and their patience and counsel during the early months, the original idea would have died aborning. In addition, 32 unsung individuals played crucial roles as Consulting Editors. Their sharp criticism of the first drafts of each chapter served to stiffen my backbone in requesting revisions and improvements from busy authors. The result, I believe, is that *we* have produced a handbook of unusually high quality; a book which we hope will be a real contribution to the profession of corporate financial management.

On behalf of all the participants, I would like to thank two people: my secretary, Mrs. Marie McCarthy, and my editorial assistant, Mr. Charles K. Scott. I know they enjoyed their labors (each on several occasions told me how well they "knew" a certain author or editor they had never met), and they share my pride—and relief—that the job is finally done.

Boston   R.F.V.
January, 1970

Contents

PART V. Information technology

loss effect. Loss reporting. Self-assumption methods: *Deductible. Disappearing deductible. Retrospective rating. Self-insurance. Captive insurance companies.* The insurance function: *Administration. Brokers, agents, and consultants. Consolidations of policies. Company policy.* Conclusion. Bibliography.

PART VIII. Financial structure

Changes in ownership interest. Ownership of common stock, preferred stock, and debt obligations of a subsidiary. Reciprocal or cross holdings. Income taxes. Minority interest. Footnotes to consolidated financial statements. Unconsolidated subsidiaries. Combined statements. Consolidating process. Summary.

PART X.   External relations

List of exhibits

Chapter 8

Chapter 11

Chapter 14

Chapter 15

Chapter 16

Chapter 19

Chapter 20

Chapter 21

Chapter 22

Chapter 23

Chapter 34

Chapter 35

Chapter 36

Chapter 38

Chapter 39

Chapter 40

PART I

The financial executive as a member of the top management team

An overview

A. Carl Kotchian*

This handbook offers the practicing financial executive a comprehensive source of information concerning almost every facet of his function. The 65 chapters that follow contain the latest financial principles and practices, techniques and tools, that can help the financial executive achieve greater effectiveness in his organization and greater success in his business career.

It occurs to me, however, that an individual could master the entire contents of this handbook, understand every detail of every financial operation in today's complex business environment, and still be an ineffectual financial executive. From the viewpoint of top management, it is not just the financial executive's knowledge that counts, rather it is the extent to which this knowledge is applied throughout the organization.

Inevitably, every management decision involves money. This means the financial executive has continuous opportunity to contribute his knowledge to the organization's decision-making process. The goal of every financial executive, therefore, should be to use these opportunities to gain the maximum adoption of sound financial management throughout the organization. How widespread the financial skills become within the organization is the yardstick top management uses in judging the performance of financial executives, and I recommend it to everyone in the finance function.

The financial executive may appear in many forms and will be different things to different people. He may, from an organization standpoint,

---

* President, Lockheed Aircraft Corporation, Burbank, California.

be the chairman of the finance committee of the board of directors, the vice president of finance, the controller, or the treasurer. Viewed externally he has different roles in the eyes of a shareholder, a credit grantor, an independent auditor, a vendor, a customer, or a tax collector. Viewed internally by his superior, peers, subordinates, or other organization associates, he is seen in many diverse roles. One thing is obvious: there is no other comparable function that places so many officers at the top level, has such a diverse range of contacts, or is so inextricably woven into the affairs of management.

An expanding role

The position enjoyed today by a financial executive was not always so. During my 30 years in industry, I have witnessed an ever increasing role for the financial executive, and each degree of expansion has brought a commensurate growth in the reliance placed upon him and in his importance to his company.

This expanding role of the financial executive has been evident almost since the early 1930's. It was in this period that the Controllers Institute, now the Financial Executives Institute, was formed and served to signal the excision of the accountant's or controller's role from that of the treasurer. But the early pace of development, which at the time seemed almost too fast, was, in contrast to today's, most pedestrian. Perhaps the intrusion of World War II served to dampen the rate of change that might otherwise have occurred, but in any event, even in the mid-1940's, the role of the financial executive fell far short of what it is today.

Even as late as 1945, the role of the financial executive in most companies included the controller's function, largely involved with the historical collection of accounting data, and the treasurer's function, largely custodial. The controller's functions concerned internal and external reporting and interpreting, evaluation of business policy, tax administration, government reporting, and protection of assets. Likewise, the treasurer's role was most circumscribed and was concerned with provisioning of capital, both long- and short-term, banking and custody, credits and collections, investments, and the procurement of insurance.

Historical financial functions

In this period, the controller's main functions were typically concerned with internal and external reporting. On the internal front, the effort was directed towards the control, measurement, reporting, and evaluation of operations. Reports were issued periodically to operating management, reporting the results for the period and in most cases comparing these with operating budgets. Assisting line management in the creation of operating budgets made possible the first advances toward assuming accounting responsibility.

Where appropriate, reports on divisional performance were presented. Reports were presented on research and development expenditures, but these were mainly concerned with a comparison of the actual level of effort compared with that which had been budgeted. Reports on manufacturing costs were presented and, because of the early industrial engineering developments, utilized relatively sophisticated cost control techniques. Reports concerning distribution and administrative costs were, as in the case of research and development expenses, concerned with matching actual with budgeted levels of expenses.

As for external reporting, because of the expanding influence of the Securities and Exchange Commission, more and more attention was being devoted to this field. Increased concern was being devoted to the adequacy and consistency of accounting policies. The importance of the income statement had come to the fore, but the residual cost or asset accounts contained in the balance sheet were in most cases presented in the same fashion as a couple of decades previously.

As noted, the treasurer's functions in this period were for the most part custodial in nature. Primary concern was devoted to asset management, mostly with respect to the working capital sector of the balance sheet. The function was also concerned with the provisioning of the necessary capital. External financing through equity or debt issues was undertaken as required. The treasurer's function was responsible for cash, banking relationships, and short-term financing. Investments in fixed assets were budgeted, but in most cases this concern was born of financial considerations related to insuring the solvency of the company. Similar concern was exercised over the levels of receivables and inventory; with respect to the former, the function had primary responsibility in matters of credit appraisal and collection. The insurance function was also under the treasurer's jurisdiction.

Looking back and comparing what constituted the financial executives' functions then with those of today, I can only wonder—in light of the business world's demonstrated capacity for change—why it took so long to develop our modern concepts of the financial executive. Perhaps some light has been shed on this by Warren Bennis. In 1966 Professor Bennis proudly pointed out that "blazing advances have been made in the areas of management education and research during the last ten years."[1] Prior to this time, business education did not compare too favorably with other disciplines. Although some of the larger universities had already developed respectable schools of business, well staffed,

---

[1] Warren G. Bennis, *Changing Organizations* (New York: McGraw-Hill Book Company, 1966), p. 181.

academically challenging, and highly research oriented, most campuses offered little more than a collection of descriptive courses covering current or even outdated business practices. Under these circumstances, business education, by and large, did not rank very high in the academic hierarchy, and the products of such training eventually occupied most of the financial management positions throughout the business community. Fortunately, as Bennis points out, "Today management education is respectable, rigorous, and rich,"[2] and the financial function owes much of its recent progress to this infusion of new knowledge from the campuses.

Impact of change

The Ford and Carnegie Foundation studies of the 1950's deserve much of the credit for the "blazing advances" we have seen in all fields of business education and research during the past decade. The impact of the better trained graduates coming into the business community cannot be minimized; however, the seeds of change for the financial function had already been sown by the changing business environment of the mid-1940's. The prospects of victory during the final phase of World War II had brought forth a plethora of post-war planning. Budgeting concepts were being extended into areas described as profit planning and management planning and control; and, as these efforts necessitated direction, we began to hear about management by objectives. First-generation computers were available and conversions from tabulating equipment had been made in some routine areas. Operations research had come upon the scene, and through managers with scientific or engineering background the operations research methodology found application to administrative and managerial problems.

Professor J. Fred Weston has succinctly described the process of change in the field of finance, enumerating in particular five major changes in the external environment that have contributed to the increasing emphasis on analytic methods:

1. The pace of technological change has increased, shortening the life cycle of individual products.

2. The pressure on profit margins overall and particularly in industries subject to the competition of new product developments has increased competitive pressures in the American economy. The penalties of being "second-best" have increased.

3. The sustained period of economic growth following World War II has increased the rewards of anticipating new opportunities and making provision for the financial means to participate in growth.

4. The continued development of large scale enterprise has resulted in firms too large to be administered by one man and has required the decentralization of a number of activities. This decentralization has increased the need

---

[2] *Ibid.*, p. 183.

for planning and control methods to maximize the contribution of individual departments to the overall performance of the enterprise.

5. The institutionalization of the flow of savings and investment has resulted in the professionalization of the investment of funds. This has stimulated analytical methods for evaluating firms, and this increased sophistication in turn has led to an expectation that the firms in which investments are made demonstrate that the funds will be utilized effectively.[3]

These environmental changes stimulated the application of tools new to financial decision making. Problems which heretofore were not quantified, or, at least, were not stated in mathematical terms, not only began to be expressed in equation form but also have by now been structured as models with premise flexibility to take advantage of computer capabilities.

In the process of structuring these problems for this more sophisticated level of analysis, relationships among functions and responsibilities within the enterprise have been identified, and improvements in decision-making effectiveness have followed.

Just as the pace of technological change had served to increase the exchange of ideas in the field of science between business and the college campuses, the new developments in the financial field both quickened and widened the dialogue between the financial executive and his campus counterparts. While the latter exchange was by no means universal, it was sufficient and diverse enough in scope to advance the concern of the financial executive with new theories and tools of analysis and the campus counterpart with the practical day-to-day problems of business.

This interchange of ideas greatly expanded and enhanced the conceptual technology applicable to run-of-the-mill business problems such as make-or-buy, capital investment, and leasing decisions. The horizons in financial and economic analysis were extended. Applications of this broadened conceptual technology became widespread, particularly in the analysis of product-line profitability and the acquisition of new businesses. The latest advance, broad-scale systems analysis, is truly a team effort of business and campus and represents an integration of the state of the art in concepts and tools into a powerful analytic methodology that shows great promise for the future.

But as the conceptual technology developed, new road blocks were encountered. As Professors Alexander A. Robichek and Stewart C. Myers point out: "Probably if we were to choose one characteristic which differentiated finance from other business fields such as marketing, production, organizational behavior, and so on, that characteristic would be time. All financial decisions require an estimate of future events, often not just what will happen next month or next year, but of all the events

---

[3] J. Fred Weston, *The Scope and Methodology of Finance*, © 1966. By permission of Prentice-Hall, Inc., Englewood Cliffs, N.J., pp. vii-viii.

at ten, twenty or more years in the future. Our knowledge of such events ranges from a fair degree of certainty to guesses we can only hope are educated."[4] Financial theory, which is subject to the constraints of time and uncertainty, was in danger of foundering on the practical seas of business uncertainty with respect to the future.

Peter Drucker has described the problem faced by the financial executive by noting:

> The financial area in a business is a peculiar area. All other areas have more information than understanding and theory. We have excellent theory of finance and we do not need new understanding. We have the conceptual tools. The trouble is that we have never been able to use them because we had no information. Our theory requires a great deal of manipulation of figures, which could never be done before. The data were not available, and the amount of work required to produce them was simply not possible to do. It would have required even more clerks than there are, and there are more than enough around already.
>
> Financial people have been particularly frustrated because their understanding has been so much greater than their ability to move, which is almost the exact opposite of any other manager. Look at the personnel people, who have no understanding of the motivation of people in groups. Their data greatly outruns their understanding.
>
> With us it is the other way around. We need the systems analyst and the computer to help us get some data to serve our understanding.[5]

With the advent of the third-generation computers, representing an infinite advance in speed and capacity, it became possible to acquire and manipulate the relevant data. Computer technology served to revolutionize the way traditional roles had been performed. Information technology was spawned and new levels of efforts were devoted to the analysis and design of information systems. Managing the data processing system became a major job. Selection of appropriate equipment for the tasks at hand and the procurement or development of software and the management thereof became major concerns.

And as the function of the financial executive has grown and expanded he has clarified his basic theory and sharpened and honed the tools of analysis. In the current financial literature there is widespread acceptance of what Professor Ezra Solomon describes as the objective of financial management: the maximization of wealth, or net present wealth, of the enterprise. Solomon also observes:

> If the scope of financial management is redefined to cover decisions about both the use and the acquisition of funds it is clear that the principal content

---

[4] Alexander A. Robichek and Stewart C. Myers, *Optimal Financial Decisions,* © 1965. By permission of Prentice-Hall, Inc., Englewood Cliffs, N.J., p. 2.

[5] Peter F. Drucker, *The Computer's Contribution to Financial Management* (The Diebold Research Program Professional Paper Series) (New York: The Diebold Group, Inc., 1968), p. 2.

of the subject should be concerned with how financial management should make judgments about whether an enterprise should hold, reduce, or increase its investment in all forms of assets that require company funds. This in turn requires a defensible basis for answering three questions:

1. What specific assets should an enterprise acquire?
2. What total volume of funds should an enterprise commit?
3. How should the funds required be financed?[6]

For the modern financial executive the tools of the function now commonly include linear programming, simulation, queuing, sampling theory, decision theory, game theory, and probability theory or risk analysis. The financial executive does not have to acquire the skills to perform these tasks himself, but he should be knowledgeable to the degree that he understands how these tools may be profitably applied to his operations. Additionally, discounted cash flow or present values are widely used to measure the relative worth of competing investment projects. With the theory and tools now at hand, the financial executive's role is today more rapidly expanding than ever.

Our financial executive of today is "future oriented." He is more than ever a member of the top management team and never before has he had such an opportunity to expand his contributions and enlarge his responsibilities. The financial executive can play an important role in such diverse areas as the establishment of overall corporate objectives and project scheduling. His counsel is vital on matters ranging from public relations to capital budgeting. And, as demonstrated in the chapters of this Handbook, he can more and more base his advice and decisions on applications of a sound and sizeable body of knowledge and analytical techniques.

The test of effectiveness

I have offered a sanguine description of the financial executive of today and of his future. But even the most cursory review of the contemporary scene readily discloses that all financial executives have not achieved the stature and position in their organization that others have succeeded in doing. The fact that they have not suggests several areas of constraint.

The role of the financial executive that I have described relates to an individual who has shown an awareness of change and has recognized the necessity of adapting his capabilities so as to accommodate the change. He has not been content to exist on his original formal training. Instead, he has dedicated himself to constant expansion of his knowledge and has remained thoroughly competent in his functional field. He has by his efforts become a beneficiary rather than a victim of change. The

---

[6] Ezra Solomon, *The Theory of Financial Management* (New York: Columbia University Press, 1963), p. 8.

fact that we speak of half-lives of original training and of obsolete executives is, to him, a challenge and not an obituary.

Where we see such a modern financial executive the chances are that he has been employed in a company whose management is thoroughly conscious of the rewards and penalties involved and has done everything possible to encourage rather than hinder self-development. I do not wish to imply that this problem is in the past. I suspect that there is much more to come. Where we stand today is not where we will stand tomorrow. The financial executive must continue his efforts to remain thoroughly modern.

A second area of concern relates to the willingness of the financial executive to be a constructive member of the management team. Financial skills are not an end unto themselves. Rather, they are a means to the fulfillment of organization objectives. Seldom are financial tools so precise that they yield unequivocal answers. Tradeoffs with objectives of a non-financial nature are often necessary as are tradeoffs between short- and long-term objectives. The financial executive can be of immeasurable assistance in these decisions. But his primary concern should be to maintain a stature such that his opinion and judgment are willingly sought. A financial executive who seeks to dominate every decision, and to have all decisions based upon financial considerations alone, will not enjoy this stature. His main concern should be the recognition of financial implications by management and, if it is necessary to insist on the dominance of the financial aspect, this should only be on major decisions.

But the area of greatest concern to me is the attitude of the financial executive toward his function. The descriptions I have used of his function and opportunities would, in a narrow sense, make him appear at least the equal if not the superior of the president. Yet, his effectiveness is determined not by his organizational authority, but rather by his knowledge. If he regards his role as that of a "no" man rather than that of a "know" man, his role will be most circumscribed.

Employee morale, motivation, and performance and reward relationships come under the purview of the industrial relations function. No one would suggest, however, that these activities were the sole responsibility of the industrial relations manager. These matters are the concern of all managers, and it is the obligation of industrial relations only to set basic policy and insure its fulfillment.

Yet, too often, we see financial executives trying to perform their entire function alone. It cannot be done this way. As in the case of industrial relations, the function will be performed best in the hands of a receptive organization that willingly applies the concepts of its financial executive, because everyone knows that in so doing he will be enhancing the value of the enterprise and of his own contribution to it.

The successful financial executive is one who knows that his effectiveness can best be achieved by obtaining the willing help of others. And he knows that this will not be achieved unless it can be demonstrated that the available financial tools will help others achieve their goals. In the final analysis, the success or failure of the financial executive can be determined by how widespread the use of sound financial skills has become within his organization.

Strategy formulation and implementation

Robert F. Meyer*

The purpose of this chapter is to describe the basic long-term goal-setting process of an enterprise in terms of strategy formulation and strategy implementation. The ideas evolved in this field are concerned with techniques but they surely can also stir the imagination on both a personal and corporate level of interest. In this introduction two central themes will be presented.

The first theme of this chapter is that the management of an enterprise amounts to more than the management of the sum of its various functional parts; that strategy as an administrative function differs from making and selling; and that for this reason the concern of top executives is often more with administration in this sense than it is with the performance of departmental work.[1] This theme should gain perspective as the chapter develops and as it becomes clear that new managerial skills must be acquired as a manager moves from lower to higher management positions.

The second theme of this chapter is that the corporate goal-setting process has historically taken place in a dynamic environment. Thus, the enormous expansion of the American economy; the increasing pace of

---

* Treasurer and Vice President, Aerosol Techniques, Incorporated, Milford, Connecticut.

[1] Alfred D. Chandler, Jr., *Strategy and Structure: Chapters in the History of the Industrial Enterprise* (Garden City, N.Y.: Doubleday & Co., Inc. Anchor Books Ed., 1966), p. 10.

technological change, the growth in population, the move to the suburban way of life, and the more complex demands of a consumer-oriented economy have all served to provide changing perspectives on the strengths and weaknesses of individual corporations and indeed on the positions of whole industries. The Brookings Institution has given substance to this theme in its analysis of the movement of America's 100 largest industrial companies in the 50 years between 1909 and 1960.[2] It has shown, for example, that of the 100 largest companies in 1909, only 31 are among the 100 largest in 1960; that just about half of 1919's new entries to the list and approximately one third of both 1929's and 1935's new entries remained on the list in 1960. Even between 1948 and 1960 only a scant two thirds of the 1948 entries remained in the top-100 chart by 1960. Clearly, many of yesterday's giants lost their prominence in a relatively short span of time, and those that have survived, such as Du Pont and General Electric, today bear little resemblance to their origins.

Moreover, this same report shows that these shifts in the patterns of success surrounding individual companies have been accompanied by comparable changes in the movement of whole industries. Thus, the iron and steel industry, which represented 29 percent—and the lion's share—of the total assets employed by the top 100 companies in 1909, tumbled to a 10 percent position by 1960. The food industry in this same period fell more than half, from a 5 to a 2 percent share of big business. Coal mining and leather companies have virtually disappeared from view. By contrast, the petroleum industry has come to dominate the top 100 companies, rising from a 13 percent share of assets in 1909 to an over-31 percent position by 1960. Similarly, both the transport and the electrical equipment industries have more than doubled their hold among the top 100 companies in the last 50 years as automobiles, airplanes, radio, and television have all become commonplace in the present day.

Strategy, then, is an identifiable activity, and it is concerned with striving for the long-term health of an enterprise within an environment in which there is no free parking. Indeed, as the Red Queen said in *Through the Looking Glass*, ". . . it takes all the running you can do to keep in the same place. If you want to get somewhere else, you must run at least twice as fast as that!"

Strategy formulation

Much of strategy's excitement and appeal comes from the opportunity it gives to formulate corporate choice. The choice itself is made by assessing the risks and opportunities in a changing and competitive environment, by identifying existing and obtainable corporate strengths,

---

[2] A. D. H. Kaplan, *Big Enterprise in a Competitive System* (rev. ed.; Washington, D.C.: The Brookings Institution, 1964), chap. 7.

and finally by determining from these data basic long-term strategic objectives.

Scanning the environment

Analyzing the environment and recognizing those key technical, economic, and social trends which are and will be important to the long-term development of an enterprise presents one of the most critical and hazardous aspects of the goal-setting process. In the course of this analysis, it is important not only to analyze overall industry trends but also to look to opportunities for profit within particular market segments.

Certainly, the comparative histories of Sears, Roebuck and Montgomery Ward provide a dramatic example of what can happen when a company fails to understand the forces at work in its environment. Thus, while General Wood of Sears, Roebuck bet on a new and expanding America, Sewell Avery of Montgomery Ward developed the notion that post-war inflation would end in a crash of 1929 proportions. As a result, General Wood continued to move Sears into the retail store business as he foresaw the decline in farm income and the rise of the city and suburban way of life, while Sewell Avery waited for an economic debacle which never came.[3] The typewriter industry provides another and more recent illustration of how important it is to distinguish correctly between those environmental trends which are due to begin and those environmental trends which are due to expire. Thus, before World War II, the old-line typewriter companies in the United States clearly dominated the world typewriter trade, exporting between one half and two thirds of the world's typewriter requirements; but by 1950 companies such as Royal and Underwood became increasingly threatened by the rise of a powerful European low-cost typewriter industry, by the rapid shift toward electric typewriters, by the development of a systems approach to information processing, and by the emergence of new selling techniques in which systems engineers were trained to solve problems the customer never knew he had. By contrast, IBM, having foreseen the systems approach to information processing in the mid-1930's, was destined to become such a dominant factor in the typewriter industry that by 1960 it was reportedly supplying between 60 and 70 percent of all office electric typewriters sold in the United States.[4]

The consequences of failing to look at individual market segments can be equally dramatic. Certainly Alfred P. Sloan's decision in 1921 to design a specific line of cars for each of several separately defined price

---

[3] "Montgomery Ward: Prosperity Is Still around the Corner," *Fortune,* November 1960.

[4] Harvard University, Typewriter Industry Case Series. Reprinted in Learned, Christensen, Andrews and Guth, *Business Policy: Text and Cases* (Homewood, Ill.: Richard D. Irwin, Inc., 1965).

categories had long-lasting effects on those automobile companies which failed to differentiate between market segments.[5] Thus, before this decision, General Motors had been on the verge of collapse while Ford, with one model, enjoyed a 60 percent share of the American car market. But within five years of the inception of this stratified product policy, General Motors became the dominant factor in the automobile business while Ford rapidly lost ground and profits trying to appeal to all potential customers with one model. On a more heroic scale, the success of American Motors' low-priced compact automobile in an overall environment guarded by Sloan's giant of 40 years later once more attests to the possibility of levering a corporate strategy on the basis of a well-defined, think-small, market niche.

But, in thinking big and thinking small, the point to be underscored is that it is important for policy makers to make explicit their understanding of the various forces that can affect the environment of their firm and industry. To this end, Learned *et al.* have suggested the following questions as a checklist to highlight changing opportunity and risk:

1. What are the essential economic and technical characteristics of the industry in which the company participates?
2. What trends suggesting future change in economic and technical characteristics are apparent?
3. What is the nature of competition both within the industry and across industries?
4. What are the requirements for success in competition in the company's industry?
5. Given the technical, economic, social, and political developments that most directly apply, what is the range of strategy available to any company in this industry?[6]

In a world that turns over every 24 hours and where yesterday's Model T can be today's white elephant, five questions to keep in touch with the environment—even though they are often extremely hard to answer—do not seem too many to bear in mind. More important, detailed answers to these questions can put some teeth into corporate long-range analysis.

Identifying corporate strengths

Although it would seem that identifying corporate strengths would offer a far more tangible base for analysis than scanning the blue horizons of the environment, the fact is that the identification of corporate strengths is as difficult as the objective assessment of personal strengths and weaknesses. Thus, there is often a level of corporate or personal ex-

---

[5] Alfred P. Sloan, *My Years with General Motors* (New York: MacFadden-Bartell Corp., 1965), chap. 4.

[6] Learned et al., *op. cit.*, pp. 172–73.

perience which is denied awareness because it is inconsistent with our corporate or personal fantasies. The problem of assessing strengths and weaknesses objectively is made particularly difficult because in so many cases failure arises out of previous success. Thus, once success has come the organization adopts those policies, practices, procedures, strategies, and techniques which brought about that success. Meanwhile, conditions go on changing and the rigid practices of the past may no longer meet the challenges that arise. In this way, simonized declarations of strengths issued in top-management memoranda often appear to be aspirational: to contain lists of qualities which create errors of strategy as competition is tackled with insufficient resources, as internal growth moves are mistimed, and as synergistic expectations from acquisitions fail to materialize.

For example, a long-established and leading textile research company decided that, because it had become an important factor in textile research, it could expand by using the strength of its textile reputation to move into lusher fields of electronic and engineering research. Unfortunately, however, the majority of the company's key personnel had been restricted to a professional background which began at textile trade school and which had ever since been solely reliant on the company's long tradition of empirical research. The company's key personnel, thus trained, turned out to be more qualified by hope than by science to enter those more exotic technical research areas where competition had already made substantial investments in highly sophisticated research personnel and laboratory equipment. As a result, the company's expansion program not only failed to produce planned profits, but it also—and this is perhaps more serious—damaged the reputation of the company as a leading high-quality textile research house.

In contrast, what the process of strategy formulation actually demands is the identification of what Selznick calls the "distinctive competence" of an organization[7]—that is, those key tasks that the organization can do particularly well in relation to its strategy, its environment, and its competition. While patents can be an underlying cause of corporate strength, there are many other opportunities for an enterprise to earn distinction. For example, the power of *Playboy*'s strategy stems at least as much from the magazine's unique technical superiority over its competition as it does from Hugh Hefner's tastes in philosophy and female beauty. No expense is spared in production, top prices are paid to famous writers, color is used lavishly, photographers are carefully chosen from many applicants nationwide, and advertisements are screened to see that they are in keeping with the aesthetic concept of the magazine. Clearly, in this case there is an effective degree of consistency between Mr.

---

[7] Philip Selznick, *Leadership in Administration* (New York: Harper & Row, 1957), p. 42.

Hefner's values and the more tangible managerial strengths that lie behind the production of his product as against the products of his competition.[8]

Since an evaluation of the distinctive competence of a company requires the organization of some systematic and objective intelligence concerning its relative strengths as compared with those of its competitors, it is important to assemble specific data on such critical corporate resources as trained management people, trained sales people, trained plant people, trained research people, capital, back-up capital, physical facilities, physical product characteristics, financial product characteristics, channels of distribution, market niche, and the like. In this way, at least some effort to be explicit can always be present as a company attempts to rank its distinctive qualities against those of its competitors and against the industry's key technical and economic conditions for success. In this process of self-appraisal, the key question is not "What do you want to be?" but rather "Why is it that you are succeeding?"

Determining basic long-term goals

Given a theory of present and future markets and given a reasoned appraisal of corporate strengths, the long-term goal-setting process can now begin.

On an analytical level alternate objectives are established, programs are defined to meet each objective, resources are identified for each program, time scales are roughed out, and a systematic analysis of the cost and inventory effects of each possibility is then determined as a basis for economic ranking. To help on this score, various mathematical devices can be brought in—such as three-dimensional diagrams, decision trees, matrices, and the like. For example, the analyst can take a grid and put headings up one side and across the top; thus, if a company is going to grow, it needs to consider "on one side" such ideas as product development, market development, market penetration, integration, diversification, and just plain old-fashioned cost cutting, and it needs to consider "across the top" such things as pay-off, time, and available capital, technology, and management. In this process of analysis, the key to consistency is the sequential screening of probable opportunity-resource combinations, and the key to success is the analysis of alternatives under extended time horizons.

But the selection of strategic alternatives means more than looking at a line wriggling through a matrix. It means in addition a recognition of the notion that managers also deal with choice on a subjective basis. Thus, as much as economic calculations define what a company might do

---

[8] Harvard University case, "HMH Publishing Company, Inc." Reprinted in Learned et al., *op. cit.*

in view of its opportunities and resources, they do not—of themselves—indicate what a company wants to do as a coalition of human interests. For example, many companies short-circuit the detailed analytical approach by simply stating that they want to continue to deal with problems they feel capable of handling. These feelings usually relate to the kind of business, the rate of growth, and the kind of risk. Thus conglomerates prefer to deal with financial problems; cigarette companies prefer to deal with product differentiation problems; and some companies prefer expansion by acquisition to internal growth, whatever the comparative return on investment statistics may indicate.

Again, while profit maximization is a common underlying value, it is not by any means the only preference available to corporate managers. A notable illustration of this is a study of the *New York Times* which indicates that the managers who run this concern value their reputation as a voice of authority and their image as a national newspaper more highly than they do their potential to increase profits through making economic modifications to the newspaper itself.[9] While it is not the purpose of this chapter to question the wide variety of preferences which are often deeply buried in strategic choice, the point can be made that these value commitments should be explicit—and should be clearly communicated both to those who formulate policy and to those who must implement policy if it is to become effective.

The formal determination of long-term goals thus offers a systematic way of thinking through a complex situation calling partly for hard economic analysis and partly for subjective judgment. The result of this effort should be an explicit statement of key corporate tasks and goals, practical enough to encourage organizational effort and visible enough to prevent day-to-day problems from siphoning management away from its long-range objectives.

Summary

To summarize, the essence of strategy formulation is in that level of consistency which exists between the emerging environment and the firm as a distinctive human and economic institution. More important, without explicit attention to the formulating of strategic goals, a company's chances for influencing the competitive environment in which it exists—and, indeed, for surviving—may rest on little more than shifting sand. Thus, looking back and looking forward, there has been and will be many a fallen Goliath, to say nothing of an occasional David who will throw his pebble—and miss.

---

[9] Harvard University case, "The *New York Times*." Reprinted in Learned et al., *op. cit.*

Strategy implementation

Strategy implementation is concerned with converting broadly stated strategic purpose into day-by-day action. This gap between purpose and action is classically bridged by building an effective organization, by creating an internal goal-setting process, by developing workable policies and procedures, and by measuring and rewarding individual members of the organization.

Designing structure

The relationship between strategy and structure is heavily influenced by two strategic themes: first, the general nature of strategic objectives, and second, the key tasks which strategy specifies.

The history of structural changes at E. I. du Pont as recorded by Alfred D. Chandler, Jr. illustrates the first theme that "structure follows strategy."[10] Thus, between 1902 and 1918, the growth of Du Pont resulted from the expansion of its explosives business and the success of a highly centralized structure which enabled Du Pont to exert a tight control over its wide-spread plants, laboratories, and personnel. By 1917, however, Du Pont was beginning to change the nature of its business as it foresaw postwar overcapacity threatening the future of the explosives industry. As a result, by 1919 Du Pont was not only in explosives but was also in chemicals, paint, pyroxylin, and artificial leathers—a strategy of product diversification which, while tied to the common base of nitrocellulose technology, plunged the company into many new and different markets. This strategy of diversification soon showed signs of placing unforeseen financial stress on the company: paints were in the red, losses became even greater as more paint was sold, and all the other new ventures were running well below expectation.

Even more serious was the strain that this strategy of diversification was placing on Du Pont's traditionally centralized and functionally departmentalized structure, since now each functional area had to coordinate several very different product lines without the benefit of being able to turn to any executive who would in fact be responsible for the profitability of each line of business. Thus, it soon became clear that the new strategy at Du Pont demanded a new structure. To meet this demand, Du Pont created in 1921 the decentralized multidivisional structure: each division would carry the responsibility for return on investment on its own line of business; the Corporate General Office would be responsible for coordinating, appraising, and planning the administration

---

[10] Chandler, *op. cit*, chap. 2.

of what had become a multiindustry enterprise. This new structure shortly became one of the keystones of Du Pont's subsequent success.

By contrast, and to give a recent example of very much less regal proportions, the largest company in America's aerosol contract loading industry, a company based on the East coast, achieved its present size by acquiring in the early 1960's three other aerosol contract loading companies strategically located across the country. For several years following these mergers each of these companies continued to operate as individual administrative units, each with its own profit responsibility and each with its own independent sales- and production-policy makers. On subsequent reappraisal it was recognized that this loose federation of administrative entities did not match the strategy of an acquisition program whose key purpose had been to capitalize on the closely related nature of the companies' markets and their scheduling and production problems. For this reason, it was decided to reshape the multidivisional structure of the company toward centralized control: first, through the establishment of uniform accounting information systems; and second, through the enlargement of the head office's administrative activities by the addition of vice presidents in charge of operations and major nationwide customers.

It would be remiss to leave the impression that there is no way of appraising the shape of an organization until it breaks down. On the contrary, these two examples point to the need for questioning the relationship between the aims of strategy and the planned design of organizational structure: Has a corporate structure simply loosely evolved, or does it strengthen the distinctive competence of the firm? Does the structure work to enable a company to contain trouble and risk? Does it provide a framework for the effective allocation of scarce resources? Does it relate to present and future needs? Needless to say, as an enterprise grows in size and complexity the need increases to ensure that the design of its formal organization provides a basis for effective corporate action.

The second theme which has an important bearing on the relationship between structure and strategy is the idea that structure must highlight those key operational tasks which are implied or defined by a company's statement of strategy. This connection between the key physical, technical, and economic product characteristics of a business and the design of a management organization is certainly a well-established tradition in view of the classic contributions made to organization theory by such men as F. W. Taylor, Alfred P. Sloan, Pierre du Pont and Donaldson Brown, who were trained engineers.

For example, in the early years of the aerosol industry, to return once more to the aerosol story, the key operational requirement for success was innovation. For this reason, the structure of the leading aerosol contract filler was sharply focused on those skills necessary to develop new aerosol products both through applied laboratory research and through research into new market concepts. In this way, perfumes for men were developed and called deodorants, lemon oil was mixed into furniture polish, pineapple was put into barbecue sauce, peppermint was sprayed into the oral cavities of the nation, and the question that was continuously lobbed over the net by the customer and within the industry was not "How cheap can you do it?" but "What's new?"

Ten years later, however, as the aerosol-product life-cycle began to mature, the key operational requirement for strategic success began to shift from the need for creativity to the need to provide aerosol production-line time flexibly and efficiently. Accordingly, the corporate focus of skills, investment, and hierarchy began to move toward the financial analysis of job output and inventory levels and toward the procurement of in-depth professional manufacturing expertise in such fields as industrial engineering, mechanical engineering, and on-line chemical instrumentation.

To summarize, the shape of an organization must be related to, and supportive of, the general demands of strategy. At the same time, the choice of a formal structure gives an enterprise an opportunity to highlight those physical, technical, and economic skills necessary to achieve the specialized operational tasks that strategy specifies. It should be noted, however, that hand in hand with these characteristics of specialization and hierarchy, which essentially symbolize the formal organization, come the problems of communication within the organization.

Establishing systems of internal communication

Since the theory of strategy implementation has so far been couched in almost exclusively impersonal terms, the question is "How should a company set about getting its loftily planned desires put into effect by live groups of people?" People, as individuals, naturally bring their own expectations to a company and exercise an influence on the goal-setting processes of their departments. It requires no feat of imagination to anticipate latent conflicts between the ideas of such departmental subgroups and the goals of other company departments. The following paragraphs show that formal goal setting and formal procedures will, at the very least, buy a bureaucratic beginning toward achieving improvement in internal communication and more effective integration of individual behavior to overall corporate purpose.

The existence of unresolved goal conflicts is a common cause for communication and implementation anguish. For example, individual goals will conflict with corporate goals, the sales group's growth goals will conflict with the financial group's profit goals, the production group's output goals will conflict with the marketing group's flexibility goals, and inventory goals will provide an ample opportunity for misunderstanding a wide assortment of production, sales, and finance objectives. In noting these difficulties, Cyert and March have described three major ways in which companies can try to reconcile and improve their individual, group, and corporate goal-setting processes. These are the bargaining process by which individuals are hired, the budgetary process by which an internal and mutual control system is established, and the adjustment process by which goals can be related to actual achievements.[11] In the first place, the hiring of personnel offers a preliminary opportunity to clarify the goals of the organization and match them to the goals of the individual. In this process the payment offered represents a critical purchase, not only of time but also of commitment to policy. Secondly, the budgetary process can provide an internal mechanism by which these initial policy commitments can be confirmed. Thus, opening commitments are elaborated and stabilized as the responsibilities for each functional area are assigned and reviewed; as the costs and revenues for each department are defined and related to the economics of other departments; and as the budget itself becomes a precedent for evaluating future levels of promised performance. Finally, projected levels of performance, when compared to actual achievement, provide a base for goal setting which can focus on both the resolution of past conflicts and the minimization of those overaspirational and overpessimistic departmental or individual assumptions which might otherwise threaten the success of the implementation plan.

Corporate procedures can provide another important teaching mechanism with which to help an organization give stability and direction to its corporate programs. These procedures can be thought of as falling into a number of categories, three of which have been described as task performance rules, recording and reporting rules, and planning rules.[12] Task performance rules simply try to establish how things are done consistently with how other things are done. For example, it can be important for the maintenance department to design its program of planned changeovers to fit into a rotating production-line schedule established for the manufacturing department by the industrial engineering group. Again, on a higher organizational level, it is important for the marketing department to price its product lines according to those task performance rules laid down by the financial department to ensure an adequate return on investment. Rules for the design and maintenance of continuing records and reports make an equally vital contribution to management control, if for no other reason than that they influence decisions that will be taken within the organization. Thus, these records highlight those critical variables through which a company interprets its environment and its performance; and, in so doing, these records moti-

[11] Cyert and March, *A Behavioral Theory of the Firm* (New York: Prentice-Hall, Inc., 1963), pp. 26–36.

[12] Cyert and March, *op. cit.*, pp. 103–13.

vate the actions of corporate managers. Finally, planning rules help to set a climate of consistency between the behavior of the individual and the strategy of the firm, not only because they prescribe the goal-setting process as such but also because their procedural aspects consciously attempt to simplify the issues confronting both the firm and the individual.

In summary, detailed attention to individual goal-setting and corporate procedures can encourage, if only in a formal way, a level of congruity between the behavior of the individual and the needs of the firm. Certainly, in the absence of such external administrative pressures, directional effort is often made toward individual preferences which may be, and usually are, detrimental to the requirements of corporate strategy.

Applying measurement and rewards

Measurement and reward systems supply the cutting edge for influencing individual behavior. Thus, the choices made concerning factors to be measured, people to be judged, and rewards to be given are the very choices which lie at the heart of corporate administrative power.

In the first place, it is clear that the choices made concerning factors to be measured present once again an opportunity to highlight those variables which are important to explaining the success or failure of a business. For example, in the automobile industry each model's physical shape and performance, each model's timing into the market, each model's planned and maximum volumes, each model's variable costs, and each model's fixed styling, tooling, and marketing expenditures represent critical variables which eventually cumulate to explain the financial success or failure of an automobile program.[13] Although critical variables of this nature often correlate smoothly to key physical, technical, and economic decisions, there are occasions when the relationships between critical variables and success are less than obvious. This difficulty seems especially common in those attempts which are made to quantify sales/profit-goal relationships. For example, in the magazine industry subscription departments are frequently measured on the basis of their *annual* subscription receipts even though subscription sales traditionally represent a far greater degree of readership loyalty than newsstand sales. On further thought, however, it is clear that a more accurate measure of a subscription department's work can be provided by calculating the present value of *all future* subscription revenue generated by a subscription department in any given year. Obviously, the point to be made is that by accounting for the whole stream of subscription revenues in this way,

---

[13] E. B. Rickard, "The Past is History . . . The Future is Planning," from *The Controller,* October, 1962. Reprinted in Anthony, Dearden, and Vancil, *Management Control Systems* (Homewood, Ill.: Richard D. Irwin, Inc., 1965).

and not just the year's subscription receipts, the formal process of selecting a critical measurement factor can help a magazine's management to better understand the economics of its business, especially in that area which calls for resolving the classic economic problem of how to efficiently allocate corporate resources—in this case, between newsstand sales and subscription sales.

In the second place, the selection of critical measurement factors provides an important technical and psychological opportunity to link a neutral model of the way in which a business works to those highly powerful and persuasive accounting techniques which are used to evaluate line managers. Thus, in the automobile business (to return once more to this example), the measurement system must integrate two streams of knowledge; first, those key operational tasks which need to be performed if the automobile is to be designed, manufactured, and sold at an acceptable profit, and second, those key engineering, manufacturing, purchasing, and marketing line managers whose judgments will be incorporated into the goal-setting process, whose influence will guide others, and whose performance must therefore be measured.

Finally, those choices made concerning factors and people to be measured provide a rational framework for using the power of a reward system to secure organizational objectives. The presence of detailed formulas to govern reward distributions is less important to the theme of this chapter, however, than the idea that there should be a visible scheme which says that funds will be set aside for reward payments, that known procedures will be adopted for formal managerial review, and that certain steps will define in advance the general routes toward individual recognition. For example, a consulting firm recently built its reward system on the basis of a very exact predefinition of the percentage of profits to be set aside for employee bonuses. In addition, each employee knew that once a year he would be formally reviewed by a committee which would assess his progress on the basis of a variety of factors such as the ratio of sold hours to paid hours, the amount of new business created, the time written off on jobs supervised, and the extent of professional expertise developed as indicated by published articles and the like. As a result of this reward system, each employee is now in a position to get excited about the monthly growth of the bonus pool, while top management can simultaneously avoid entrapping itself into a single measure of organizational performance which might otherwise motivate employees to allocate all their attention to a single reward factor at the expense of other elements in the situation.

This last example leads to the theme that unidimensional summary measures are not of themselves the solution to measurement and reward systems. Or put another way, that overemphasis of the quantifiable and the partial is an inappropriate use of power because most of the time management is still confronted with the problem of having to measure situationally—that is, of having to measure what a man is doing versus what he could be doing versus what he should be doing versus what is being done to him by the environment. Clearly, in these circumstances a prerequisite to power must be that measurement and reward systems are placed in the hands of imaginative and far-sighted people who have the capacity to create a climate in which cooperation can be balanced against competition, in which short-term profits can be balanced against the need to invest in long-term objectives, and in which measured elements can be balanced against unmeasured aspects of performance.

Summary

Strategy implementation is concerned with converting purpose into action. To do this, it focuses on the design of those key managerial tasks and sources of influence which are identified by a company's strategy, its structure, its internal communications, and its systems of measurement and rewards. The task of the manager is to keep these sources of influence interrelated and in harmony with corporate strategy and to take great care to understand the limitations of these sources of influence and the possible reaction of individuals to their application.

Leadership

At the beginning of this chapter the idea was expressed that new managerial skills must be acquired as a manager moves from lower to higher management positions. Although there are those who maintain that there are increasingly less and less interesting things to say about leadership, it may now be worthwhile to return to this idea as a brief way to summarize some of the principal arguments of this chapter.

Thus, the senior executive is more than a floral centerpiece. Rather, the path to leadership is paved by the acquisition of multiple abilities: the ability to understand the organization as a whole and to relate its skills to the emerging environment; the capacity to work with wide time dimensions and to assign resources over extended periods; the capacity to integrate the many different themes that connect the slippery logic of strategic planning; the ability to discipline and to set standards of performance; and last, and perhaps most important, the ability to create a social organization which can relate to formal structure and which can demonstrate a continuing faith in the validity of the company's purpose.

The requirement of leadership is therefore to develop an attitudinal as well as an analytical approach to problems: to develop commitment and initiative; to bring together good people in a good atmosphere; and finally to stress attention to intangibles, since intangibles cannot be measured and since intangibles become increasingly important as built-in tensions mount in the roles played by management.

Concluding comments

The purpose of this chapter has not been to say anything new; rather, it has been an attempt to share the personal excitement that this author has found in a brief academic and industrial exposure to the ideas of business strategy. The main weakness of this approach may lie in its pictorial quality, but as Alice thought in *Alice in Wonderland* ". . . what is the use of a book without pictures or conversations?" Besides, most of the subjects which have been touched on here are covered in much greater depth by the sources quoted as well as by many of the other chapters in this volume.

In conclusion, strategy is in essence a feat of association. Managers engaged in this feat must seek to illuminate choices while there is still an opportunity to choose, must seek to locate those sources of managerial influence which will accomplish key tasks, and finally must seek to bring together the organization so that it can recognize the total corporate purpose. For, to borrow a phrase from Erich Fromm, a corporation must respond "to life not just with [its] brain but with [its] whole personality."

Corporate organization

Robert Jerrett, Jr.*

At first glance a concern with corporate organization might seem to fall somewhat outside the financial executive's normal range of responsibilties. It is entirely natural to think of this subject, at least in terms of principles, structure, and description, as the realm of the personnel or administrative executive. It is not unusual to find the responsibility for constructing organization charts, writing position descriptions, and producing policy manuals assigned to such departments. This can lead the financial executive to consider himself merely as user of these devices and services, and therefore not involved in them directly in any major way. In truth, however, the financial executive, as a member of top management, is an advisor to the chief executive on major policy matters and has an important point of view to present in matters involving company organization.

The financial executive's concern with organization

As the head of a major management activity, the financial executive has much at stake personally in the way his company is organized. It can have an important bearing on how well he performs his primary tasks and discharges his overall responsibilities. In fact, his stake may be even greater than that of his top management colleagues because of the across-the-board involvement and impact of financial policies and practices.

---

* President, Venture Resources, Inc., Marblehead, Massachusetts.

Organization is a basic management process which provides a tool of utmost importance to the successful execution of managerial tasks. It is the vehicle through which action is taken, and determines in large measure the effectiveness with which major decisions are implemented and policies and practices are followed. The best conceived strategy and plans can be made ineffective by poor or haphazard organization.

In a more specific sense, the manner in which a company is organized has a direct effect on the primary responsibilities of the financial executive. It bears on his responsibility for the company's resources; financial statements and reports; management control information for internal use; the external image of the company in the eyes of stockholders, the financial community, and regulatory bodies; and the determination of costs and profits in the various segments of the company's business.

Bearing on responsibility for resources

In a well managed company a broad responsibility for total resources —human, physical, and financial—rests with the financial executive. While the ultimate responsibility is that of the chief executive, and while various operating executives manage these resources, the financial executive measures them, evaluates the effectiveness with which they are employed, and renders an independent accounting of them. In the case of financial resources, he also performs a direct managerial function.

How does the organization structure affect his performance of this responsibility? First, it *delineates responsibility and accountability*. It identifies where responsibility for the employment of various resources lies and where to look for accountability. If there is vagueness, overlap, or a random arrangement of people and/or functions, it is difficult to establish this identity with any degree of confidence. In such an environment inconsistencies and inaccuracies in the inputs to the financial reporting system are bound to develop, leading to uncertain measurement and obscurity of stewardship. This can severely compromise the financial executive's ability to perform his reporting functions and to advise the chief executive as to the financial health of the company.

Organization also plays an important part in the *allocation of resources* to the various parts of a business. It provides the base upon which given resources can be distributed so as to achieve optimum utilization. Even in a small company, or in a relatively simple single product, single location type of business, manpower, physical facilities, machinery and equipment, and working capital applied in random fashion can lead to waste, low utility, and a poor return on the capital employed. Only in a properly organized environment can resources be applied with any degree of confidence, because only in such an environment can they be tracked and accounted for, or can productivity be measured. Here again, the financial executive has a primary role to play.

Finally, good *performance measurement and control* are dependent upon good organization. Again, the clear identification of responsibilities and authority through organization structure will reveal where decisions and commitments are made and where accountability for results lies. Thus, the evaluation of managerial people in terms of their contribution to the company's success is heavily dependent upon the soundness of its organization. Controls, or the devices, procedures, and methods by which improper or unproductive use of resources can be detected and remedied, and through which red flags and danger signals can be raised, are equally dependent upon sound organization. The financial executive is expected to furnish the rest of the top management team such accurate, objective and timely measurements and controls.

Bearing on financial statements and reports

It follows that the very *validity of financial statements* and reports is also affected by the way in which the company—and the financial function within the company—is organized. This, of course, is of prime concern to the financial executive. He is expected to prepare such statements and reports in a manner that will meet all of the requirements of public accountants and the various regulatory agencies as to format, content, consistency and timeliness. In this day of increasing emphasis on full disclosure and the detailed breakdown of financial statements, the organization structure becomes more important if such information is to be both proper and meaningful. Unless that structure makes sense and yields consistent and accurate data, financial statements and reports will fall short of these increasingly exacting requirements.

The *internal reporting structure* is also affected by organization. Accounting systems, policies, and practices are one thing, but they cannot produce timely, accurate, and meaningful information for operating use unless they relate to and serve the special needs of operating executives. If areas of responsibility are not clearly defined and structured to fit logical segments of the company's business and management functions, an effective reporting structure cannot be established.

A final, and most important, bearing of organization on financial statements and reports is the *integrity of the accounting system* itself. Independent surveillance and measurement is essential to ensure the reliability of both internal and external financial information. Therefore, the relationship of the financial executive to the various parts of the financial organization vis-à-vis that of various operating executives is most important. The eternal question of line versus functional authority is deeply rooted here. Whatever relationship is established, the organizational arrangement must be such as to induce operating management to embrace the financial function easily and naturally to make full use of financial data. At the same time the independence and reliability of financial statements must be immune to capricious or opportunistic tampering. If reporting relationships are such that accounting practices are loose, or discretionary, and subject to undue pressure by operating managers, the very integrity of the system can be seriously compromised.

Management control information

The flow of information to decision-making and commitment-making points in any company is affected in a major way by the organization structure. Such information must be accurate and consistent in content. It must be pertinent and expressed in terms which are meaningful to the decision maker. And above all, it must be timely. To devise a good management information and control system, responsibilities at all key levels of authority must be clearly defined and commitment limits must be established. Interrelationships within given functions and among various organizational units are basic to a system which will permit people to make decisions with confidence and recognize the need for action quickly and clearly.

The external image of the company

The organization structure and philosophy of a company has an important bearing on its reputation in the outside world. Of particular concern to the financial executive is the image of his company in the eyes of the financial community, stockholders, and regulatory bodies. In today's world a business is analyzed in depth. Balance sheets and earnings statements are only part of the representation it makes to outsiders. Its organization gives important clues to management strength and ability to control its activities. Good financial management is characterized by clear lines of responsibility, appropriate limitations of authority, and such separation of authority as will guarantee checks and balances and reliable accountability. In his dealings with the outside world the financial executive must be in a position to appraise his company's management and its ability to meet significant changes in business and economic climate, the challenge of growth, and the demands of competition. If he can point with confidence to his company's organization structure and identify its key management strengths, he can be assured of a more favorable evaluation by investors, bankers, and regulatory agencies than he might receive with poor organization.

Determination of costs and profits

Surprisingly, perhaps, the way a company is organized has an important effect on the determination of costs and profits in various segments of the business. Very few companies can operate efficiently without reliable and detailed costs and profit data by product or type of business. Organization structure plays a part here, too, because it forms the basis for identifying costs and profit centers and the responsibilities associated with them. It is particularly important to the proper allocation of common costs among a number of products or activities. Unless costs and profits are tied to responsibilities, they have little or no value either as a measurement of performance or as a means of control.

Because of the impact of organization structure on these numerous aspects of the financial manager's direct interests and responsibilities, he must involve himself in any major organizational change. It is not enough for him merely to be aware of its importance to him. He must also play a direct part as a member of top management in determining how his company is organized and in reviewing organization periodically to be sure it is effective and adequate to the company's needs. Therefore, he must be familiar with *organization principles,* know how to *approach an organization problem,* and be aware of the *need for reassessment* as the company grows and its business changes.

Organization principles

All too often organization is thought of solely in terms of charts, or an arrangement of boxes and lines with names or titles neatly inscribed. It is, of course, far more than this. Charts are only a convenient means of depicting an organizational structure in graphic form. The less obvious, but most important, aspect of organization is the process itself, which entails a recognition of the functions to be performed, the relationships among those functions, the flow of authority and responsibility throughout the structure, and the designation of people to carry out the tasks involved.

Organization is frequently not a popular subject at the top level of management, an attitude that may indicate a lack of understanding or appreciation of the value of sound organization to the successful management of a business enterprise. The result is likely to be confusion among decision-making executives, overlap or omission of important tasks, and a waste of manpower and executive talent. Lack of serious attention to organization from the top level of management down is a mark of management weakness or immaturity.

Formal organization is often downgraded, particularly in young companies where changes occur rapidly and management is inexperienced. The mistake made in such cases is to regard organization thinking and principles as being applicable only to long-established, relatively stable businesses where changes are more gradual and less frequent. Even where some attention has been given to the subject and charts have been drawn, there is a tendency not to take the matter seriously. One often hears remarks such as, "Well this is how it looks on the charts, but it is the informal organization that really works." Informal organization is dangerous, because it is based mainly on sentiments, emotions, and intuitive ties which can lead to confusion and inconsistency.

Sound organization development and administration starts with the recognition of certain basic principles. These are neither complex nor profound, but rather are truths which have come forth from the experiences of the years, going back almost to the beginning of time. Wherever groups of people have banded together to accomplish a given objective these principles have been applicable.

An orderly array of functions and people

Broadly stated, the organization process should identify, classify, and place in orderly relationship to each other the functions necessary to the running of a business and the assignment of people to carry out these functions. The result should be an arrangement of these functions and people in a manner that will assure performance of the functions and the effective employment of the skills and efforts of the people. To do this the following major principles must be observed:

1. Responsibility must be clearly stated and must be accompanied by the requisite authority.
2. The span of control of individuals at all levels must be kept within practical limits.
3. Line and staff functions must be clearly identified and fully described as to responsibility and authority.
4. The capabilities and characters of key people must be taken into consideration in the assignment of responsibilities. Here it is important to assess *management* capabilities where supervision is involved.
5. The structure should contemplate and provide for advancement and development of people both vertically and horizontally within the company.
6. The lines of communication and the procedures governing the flow of information must be clearly established.
7. The important decision-making points must be recognized and placed in the structure where they can be fully served in the flow of information, and appropriately monitored and evaluated.
8. Organization must be as dynamic as the business and its environment. It should not be thought of as fixed or static.

These are not all of the principles involved, nor are they particularly profound. However, they are basic to the process of organization design.

The approach to organization design

It is important to recognize that the organization structure of a company must be tailor made to fit the particular character of the business and its people. There is no standard package or fixed pattern which can be universally applied with effective results. Of course, there are some general concepts, such as a centralized, or de-centralized, organization, which are discussed in some detail later; but even these come in a wide range of shapes and sizes and must be specially fashioned to fit each individual case. It becomes necessary, therefore, to study a number of important facts about the company, its people, its management philosophy and objectives, and the forces that will bring about changes in the foreseeable future.

Analyze the business and industry

The very base of a sound approach to organization is the identification and understanding of the kind or kinds of business a company is engaged in, and some of the principal characteristics of its industry. In this day of diversification, conglomerates, and overlapping technologies, this is not always an easy thing to do. It is important, however, to *identify the chief orientation or orientations of the company.* This can be accomplished best by considering what the company is in functional terms. If skill in production or manufacturing is the prime requirement for success, the company can be described as manufacturing oriented. If, on the other hand, success is dependent principally on marketing or merchandizing skill, then this is the company's orientation. By the same token a company can be engineering oriented, or financially oriented—or it may be in a business where purchasing skill is essential.

In a more obvious way, there is a wide difference among industries. The important functions and disciplines in the transportation industry are quite different from the drug business, or the banking business, or the mining industry.

Each one of these areas of emphasis has its own organizational requirements and relationships with other functional areas. It is important to build organization around the area of greatest importance and company goals, bearing in mind that there must be an appropriate and workable balance among all basic management functions. For example, if the principal orientation of a company is in marketing or distribution —if its skill in these fields is the key to profitability—the organization of these functions becomes the core around which all other functions are arranged. However, the domination of the marketing function should not be so great as to isolate it from the support it needs from the other functions or to result in an obvious downgrading or second-class status for them. Study will reveal those places in the organization where the most sensitive and important decisions are made. This will indicate the type of information flow and other support required, and will help identify the proper points for control and monitoring. It will also suggest the logical grouping of the various functions and the people who perform them to assure coordination, the appropriate spread of individual responsibility, and the level of managerial skill and experience required to exercise independent authority.

Where there is a single major orientation, the organization structure is relatively simple to develop. But where there is more than one orientation, organization becomes more complex. Here again, it is important to guard against domination which will place a limitation or undue restrictions on any important segment of the business.

Develop a financial profile

Every business and every company has a financial profile. What is meant by a financial profile? In many ways it is similar to a model which demonstrates the financial interactions and relationships which occur in the normal course of conducting the business. In its basic form it shows the normal distribution of assets, fixed and current, which are required to carry on the business, and the changes that can occur in this distribution over a range of probable conditions. It provides a means of projecting the impact of changes in the level of activity of the business, outside forces, and major long-term commitments on profit, cash flow, inventory accumulation, and receivables build-up.

Some companies have developed quite detailed and sophisticated models which have been programmed for computer processing. While it is desirable to have as much precision as possible, the absence of an elaborate and mathematically tested model does not mean that a profile cannot be made. A relatively simple hand-made model will serve a useful purpose. The "long-range planning" done in many companies is really a simple model of sorts, and helps in identifying the organizational implications of future developments.

What has a financial profile to do with organization? It is a well recognized fact that profiles or models are useful in developing control systems and making long- and short-term projections. But the use of such a device in organization planning is not so readily seen.

The financial profile identifies the points of greatest sensitivity of a company's business to outside factors and internal decisions. It underscores the types of management action that have the greatest and most immediate impact on the company's operations and financial condition. This, therefore, provides a clue to where the most important decision-making points are, and meets one of the basic organization principles discussed earlier, namely the identification of these decision-making points and their proper place in the organization structure. Formal models, one type of financial profile, are discussed in Chapter 14, "Systems analysis and simulation."

Consider the appropriate organizational concept

It was mentioned above that there are some general organizational concepts around which structure can be designed. Some of these concepts are established as the management philosophy of the company. Others depend on factors that are far less discriminatory.

Let us first consider the *management* or *operating company*. This type of company is one in which the management from top to bottom is closely and almost exclusively involved in the operating functions of the business. Its business is usually homogeneous and closely related to a single and well defined industry, although it is possible for a diversified company to employ the "operating company" concept. In any case the major management job in such a company is the day-to-day running of the business. Operating decisions are the dominant ones at all levels of management.

In contrast to this is the *holding company*, where the major concern of top management is heavily financial and little involved in operating decisions. The various operating elements in this case are often quite unrelated to one another and are fully integrated, independent businesses in their own right.

The appropriate organization structures for these contrasting situations are quite different. In the instance of the operating company line authority usually extends right to the topmost level of management. The chief executive is likely to be the chief operating officer, and there will be top level responsibility on a functional basis, such as manufacturing, marketing, and engineering. Staff functions also tend to be vertical, but may not extend downward as far as the line functions. In this type of organization, there is frequently a narrower range of delegated authority, and more limited responsibility for major decisions. Real authority may not exist below the top management level. Of course, decentralization can be introduced into such an organization to achieve a greater degree of delegation and some autonomy, but there is usually a high degree of uniformity in policy matters established at the top level. *Operating* skills and experience are prime requisites at all management levels.

In contrast, the holding company concept places operating authority *below* the top management level. Top management is rarely concerned with operating decisions and policies. Organization is multiple and can include as many different structures as there are operating units. In such a company there is likely to be very little horizontal movement of people from one operating unit to another. The interrelationship of functions, the flow of information, scope of responsibility and authority, and need for coordination is contained within each unit. The job of managing this type of business at the top level is quite different from that of the operating company. From the financial executive's point of view, it presents a completely different range of concern and involvement with controls, resources allocation, and evaluation. He must deal with more complex financial statements, and his ability to assure himself of the integrity of the accounting system employed is somewhat limited.

Falling between these two extremes, the operating company and the holding company, is the so-called *conglomerate*. This comes closer to the holding company in organizational form, but there are some differences. Very frequently the relatively autonomous operating entities in the conglomerate can be formed into closely related groups in terms of a commonality of market, product, or technology. Yet they retain their autonomy to a large extent. However, an additional management level is usually created. While the top management interest in a holding company is essentially that of an investor, the conglomerate top management has a somewhat deeper concern with operational matters, although on a broad basis. It is, however, concerned with the activities of the various operating units. Both the holding company and the conglomerate, however, necessarily involve a high degree of delegated authority and require that the spheres of interest and scope of each operating group making up the whole be clearly defined.

To some extent the choice among these three organization concepts is a function of corporate strategy as reflected in the range of different industries in which the corporation is involved. If a management company policy is decided upon, it means that the company management desires to concern itself from top to bottom primarily with "running the business." In making this choice management must recognize that it calls for an organization which will permit only limited delegation of authority and only partial autonomy at the lower levels of management. It will retain at the top level the responsibility for making major operating decisions. It will also require a relatively large headquarters staff. Precise identification of responsibilities and relationships at all levels must be made, and a comprehensive means of measuring individual performance must be developed. Where full profit-making responsibility is not delegated, individual contribution and accountability are difficult to pinpoint. This type of organization in a growth environment presents some dangers. Flexibility and timeliness in operating decision making can be unfavorably affected. One remedy here is to introduce some degree of decentralization, which involves substantial organizational adjustment. The management company organization also involves some delicate problems with respect to relationships between line and staff functions and authority.

By contrast, the holding company organization involves a relatively small and simple headquarters function. The main concern is financial. Often there are virtually no other staff functions—and no operating functions at all. Provision must be made for performance evaluation and measurement, the setting of goals, and long-term corporate planning. However, these are usually expressed mainly in financial terms and can usually be accomplished by the financial staff. Organization below the corporate or headquarters level is a multiple concern, with each operating entity developing its own concept and structure without reference to any other, and with only broad review at the top.

Where a company starts life as a holding company its organization problems are relatively simple and reorganization and modification are infrequently needed. However, when a company makes a conscious change to holding company from management company, reorganization is essential, and can be complicated. The removal of operating responsibility and involvement from the top level creates potentially delicate personnel and morale problems. The establishment of clear statements and understandings of the responsibilities and accountability of the top management of each operating unit is mandatory. There is also the possibility that there may not be executives available who are capable of assuming chief executive roles, for many management companies do not offer exposure or training in general management at lower and middle levels.

Centralized and *decentralized* are two widely used words in organization jargon. In a sense they are more often misused or abused than used properly. The impression is often created that they adequately describe discrete and precise organization forms. In correct usage they should be accompanied by some sort of modifier, such as *highly* or *partially*, or should describe what functions or parts of the business are directed from a central point as against those in which direction is dispersed to points other than the headquarters office of the company. Centralization and decentralization are really a matter of degree.

In general terms, central direction offers the best control over major decision and commitment making. It sometimes offers efficiency by providing support and service functions through a single organizational unit. On the other hand, multiple direction, decentralized from the headquarters organization, can provide flexibility, quick response and decision making, and a means of developing executive capability over a broad front. It also can provide the basis for the development of detailed and meaningful cost and profit data and the resultant performance measurement of people and segments of the business. In a rapidly growing business, or one with considerable diversification in products, markets, or business character, the decentralization of direction and major executive responsibility seems to be the path chosen most often. The advantages mentioned above tend to offset the probable higher costs and weakening of control.

While it is not really a matter of concept, the clear definition and application of *line and staff responsibility and authority* in any type of organization is of basic importance. Staff responsibility is principally aimed at *ascertaining* what actions should be taken in the management of the business or one of its parts and *indicating* how these actions should be executed, with authority only to recommend. Line responsibility embraces the *execution* and *direction* of these actions, with authority to order and direct the activities of others. All too often this major distinction is not recognized, and relationships between line and staff executives become strained, with a harmful effect on the performance of both.

Geography is a factor

Because good organization calls for the orderly alignment of functions and people, and must recognize the interrelationships among them, the physical location of these functions and people becomes an important consideration. As the number of separately located parts of a business increases, and the distance between these parts becomes greater, a more complex organization structure is needed for good direction and control. Despite modern communication and transportation, physical separation lessens the degree of control and effectiveness of direction that a single person can exercise. The simplest situation, of course, is a business operated in its entirety at one location. But in a majority of businesses this is neither possible nor desirable. There are a number of compelling reasons why multiple locations must be used.

To assess the appropriate impact of geography on organization requires first that the reasons for multiple locations be examined and verified as to current and future validity. In some cases, the location of a company unit is entirely historical, or due to circumstances that no longer exsit. It might even be attributable to the personal preference of some key person or persons. In such instances, consolidation may be possible and quite desirable. In other cases, the location of facilities may be dictated by such things as sources of supply, labor markets, marketing areas, industry centers, or tax and legal considerations. In still others, multiple locations may have resulted from the acquisition of other companies. Whatever the reason for separation, it should be examined and reassessed before organization is developed to accommodate it and perpetuate it.

Where geographic separation is necessary or desirable there are certain mandatory organizational requirements. First and foremost, there must be someone placed in charge of each location with decision making authority and responsibility commensurate with the function or functions performed. Whether the unit involved is a warehouse, sales office, factory, or foreign subsidiary, on-the-site supervision and direction is necessary. This may produce a supervisory level in the company organization that would not exist if the unit were combined with others. Thus it usually involves higher costs. Multiple locations also need some form of coordinating vehicle, particularly if the unit has a dependency, or significant impact, on other units.

One further word on geography: Separate physical locations do not automatically dictate a high or low degree of centralization in major decision making. Neither does a multiple-site situation require that each location be given the same status or organizational nomenclature, i.e., division, department, plant, etc. This is determined by quite different factors, as discussed below. However, each location does have to be set up so that its part in the total business can be properly measured and controlled.

Ownership and control

While organization is primarily a tool for *managing* a business, the type of organization structure and reporting relationships, the flow of information, and the placement of major decision making responsibility and authority can be influenced by the attitude and degree of direct involvement of its owners. This influence is felt mainly at the top level of management and in the determination of the basic organizational concept embraced.

In a closely held owner-managed business there is likely to be far less delegation and decentralization of major responsibility and decision making authority. Information flowing to the top usually proceeds quite directly from its source and employs a highly individualistic and often unconventional format. Many of the relationships among key people tend to be very informal, and the organization structure usually reflects strong subjective overtones dominated by personal rather than functional relationships. In this environment serious attention to organization is frequently neglected, and the values of good organization lost to the management.

At the other end of the spectrum is the publicly-owned, widely held corporation employing "professional management" from top to bottom. Here, attention to the organization structure and a formalized, objective approach to the functional requirements of the business are likely to prevail. The board of directors becomes a more important and meaningful body. Clear delineation of responsibilities and authorities, and the delegation of decision making below the top level is a must. Unfortunately, organization as such is not always recognized for the valuable tool it is even in this type of company, and responsibility for it may be relegated to some obscure, low-level staff function where little impact can be generated.

Other instances in which ownership and/or control have a bearing on organization are those where they are vested in a small group outside of the management, either on the board of directors or in some entirely different company or business environment. Similarly, in the case of a bankrupt company, or one that is under the supervision of trustees, organization must reflect the authority, special requirements, and interests outside the management. Obviously, a company in the process of liquidation has special organizational requirements, even if only to bring about an orderly and effective liquidation. In the case of a bankrupt or near-bankrupt company major organization change is usually mandatory, for all too often such a company's troubles are due in some measure to poor organization.

Division or subsidiary?

The matter of legal form is only one consideration in the determination of the nomenclature used to describe organizational subunits. Hence, there is not much consistency or comparability among such organizational units from company to company. The same can be said for other designations, such as department, section, group, branch, office, plant, works and so on. Aside from tax and legal considerations there is a wide range of possibilities in most companies. The important thing is to treat subunits in a consistent manner within the total organization so that nomenclature has meaning beyond mere identification. This has an important impact on people and their relationships with one another. When an executive bears the title of "Division Manager" this should carry with it the same personal stature and range of responsibility and authority as all other executives with the same title.

In determining the nomenclature to be used, the nature, size, and relative importance of each separate unit should be taken into account. If it is self sufficient, or highly autonomous, it will be necessary to select appropriate descriptive terms to describe its subunits. If it represents a segment of the company's business of sufficient importance to be placed under the direction of a corporate officer, the designation given to it should be appropriately high in the list of terms employed.

The subsidiary organization having its own corporate status is a special case. There are always tax and legal considerations to be taken into account when using this type of subunit designation. It is most useful where there is reason to limit certain liabilities to a part of the company's business, such as in foreign operations. Sometimes the separate tax status of a subsidiary is important. There is also often good reason to maintain a corporate separateness because of the nature of the business, or its relationships with other companies or other parts of the parent company's business, or to measure the performance of its management on an independent basis. Where the subsidiary is used, however, there are certain arbitrary or statutory organizational requirements such as its officers, directors, capitalization, and financial reporting status which are not involved in the use of other organizational forms. This also requires that the functions of these officers and directors with respect to the parent company organization be determined and described. The subsidiary most often appears as an organizational unit in holding companies or conglomerates, where the unit has been acquired, or in some cases, where it may be a prospective spin-off.

While they are not necessarily a part of a consideration of nomenclature, or type of organizational unit, *joint ventures* and *minority* interests do come into the total organizational picture. The main question is one of relationship and company interest. In the joint venture there is usually an operating interest related closely to some specific part of the business. It is here that the authority to make decisions and the responsibility to represent the company's interests are usually lodged, so this is where the reporting relationship should be established. The minority interest sometimes is almost entirely financial, in which case the reporting relationship should be with the company's chief financial officer. In both cases, however, the financial executive has a concern with matters of performance and the value and safety of the company's financial state. Therefore, he must be a part of the formal organizational tie-in.

Fitting the structure to the people

While the ideal organization structure is built around the functions to be performed, it must be remembered that it is the people, the human resources of a company, that make it work. Therefore, the organization structure cannot align or group functions without appropriate regard to the capabilities, interests, and even the temperament of the people who will assume the key responsibilities. This is not to say that such regard should go to such an extreme that it results in a hodgepodge. Remember, good organization is an *orderly* array of functions *and* people, and there are distinct limits in the span of control a single person can embrace efficiently. There are also certain functions which ought not to be combined under common direction where conflicts of interest or attention would result.

Another thing to remember about people is that they do and should move and embrace new responsibilities as they gain in skill, experience, and maturity. The organization structure should not be formed so rigidly around the peculiar attributes of specific people that it will not be able to function without those people. If it were necessary to undergo significant reorganization with every promotion, retirement, resignation, or other change, the basic stability of the total organization would be seriously threatened.

A further consideration is the need every company has for developing and extending the capability of its people, and for providing for advancement in a logical manner in the organization structure. The best arrangement of functions will anticipate the movement of people, both vertically and horizontally, through careful attention to the relative scope and skill requirements of each position in the structure. The objective should be to consider that each supervisory position can be filled from within the organization, preferably from the position next below. Of course, where new or highly specialized functions come into being, this may not always be possible. However, the organization structure and the assignment of people should place emphasis on the need to attract, develop, and retain capable people.

What about tradition?

In most companies, particularly the older ones, tradition in organizational matters has to be taken into account. Many traditional concepts, policies, and practices are quite admirable and should be preserved. However, all too often tradition is used to cover up resistance to change. Unless circumstances are pressing, or a crisis has developed in the management, the inclination to go along in the same old comfortable way is very strong. It is easier not to change or upset relationships and practices of long standing, even though the nature of the company's business or its size may be changing rapidly. The inadequacy of an outmoded organization may not become apparent until it is too late to effect changes in an orderly transitional manner. Because of this, it is easy for those who regard change with suspicion, or just plain dislike, to declare "You can't argue with success," or, "Why change a winning team?" At best, this attitude leads to a complacency which can be unfortunate in today's fast-changing environment.

It is important to examine carefully the validity and value of these tradition-protected interests. Sacred cows sometimes have to be respected where they are vested in the active management or directorate of a company. But where they are relics of the past, or supported only on an emotional basis, the courage to challenge them is essential if management is to keep pace with the business environment and its increasingly exacting demands.

The organization chart

The organization chart is the most familiar and easily recognized product of the organization process. But it must be accepted for what it is—and what it is not. It is not an organization in and of itself, or even a complete graphic description of an organization. It is a visual representation of certain aspects of a company's organization, but is very limited as to the details of organization it can present. After all, it is only two-dimensional, and in no way can it show qualitative information. In fact, it is quite limited in the amount of qualitative data it can depict. Basically, the organization chart is a visual description of the important segments of the work performed by the organization, the nomenclature employed to describe them, and *major* responsibility relationships (superior-subordinate), or lines of authority.

Many efforts have been made to make organization charts do more than this—and it is tempting to read more into them then they are designed to present. For example, the relative level on the chart of the various boxes tends to be translated into relative importance in the organization, or salary level. It is not the function of an organization chart to do this.

Despite its limitations, the organization chart is an essential part of the organization process. Charts are produced in a number of ways and formats, and there really is no one best form. Perhaps the best rule to follow is to keep it simple and not try to show too many things on a single chart.

Organization is not static

Organization must be an on-going daily concern in a well managed company. It must move with the company's business and with the environment in which it operates. Economic growth, technological advances, broadening markets, and the tide of mergers, acquisitions, joint ventures, and other major changes are all elements of a dynamic society and increasing complexity in the management job. The advent and increasing impact of mechanical and electronic means of collection, processing, storing, and applying information are having significant bearing on management tasks, and therefore on the manner in which they are organized.

There is still a strong tendency in management to look upon organization as a one-time, or only occasional, matter for attention and action. This attitude, in the extreme, leads to vast reorganizations from time to time, which have an unsettling and disruptive effect on the operation of the business. Much of this effect can be avoided if the organization process is appraised and reappraised frequently. It has an important place in the long-range planning process, as well as in the shorter-range planning and strategy of any business. Any significant change will have an impact on organization, and anticipation permits organizational adjustment and change on a progressive, unrevolutionary basis.

All this does not mean that major reorganization can be avoided entirely. Sometimes developments of large magnitude occur without much advance warning. This is particularly likely in connection with mergers and acquisitions. However, if a company's organization process is constantly geared to its current needs, even these changes can be affected with relatively little disruption.

The financial executive's role in organization

In most companies direct responsibility for organization matters is not a part of the job of the financial executive. The responsibility for spelling out concepts, identifying responsibilities and job content, producing charts, guides, descriptions, specifications, etc. is usually assigned to some other function or to a specialist. However, the stake of the financial executive in organization is large, and his own performance of those primary tasks for which he is responsible—those tasks which are treated in detail in the rest of this handbook—can be greatly influenced by the adequacy of the corporate organization of the company and of its various organizational subordinate parts. Furthermore, in his role as scorekeeper and objective measurer of performance, he must understand what he is measuring, how it should be measured, and what its impact is on the financial health of the company.

One final point: The organization process is that function which mates the human and financial resources of the company. The financial executive's responsibility for accountability of resources requires that he be continually aware of the effectiveness with which these resources are being used.

Operating in the foreign environment

Herbert C. Knortz*

The financial executive of a company operating in the foreign environment is faced with all of the professional challenges of his domestic counterpart but, in addition, he must contend with the economic trends and political developments of the international world. In general, his operations must be highly sophisticated and creative since they are affected by a wider range of business influences than prevails in the domestic economy.

The subsequent paragraphs of this chapter will identify some of the economic factors which are characteristic of the international environment in developed and underdeveloped countries, and the importance of U.S. participation in the international scene is explored. In addition, the various corporate approaches to participating in foreign business are evaluated and these organizational forms are related to the various aspects of risk which govern international investment. The various controls and incentives which are applied by the United States and by foreign governments in the field of foreign operation are indicated.

Finally, the organization of the corporate treasurership and comptrollership function is discussed. The significance of adjusted reporting practices[1] and the use of specific economic indicators is related to the effectiveness of operations in the international world. It is evident from all of these discussions that the financial executive is often the key officer

---

* Senior Vice President and Comptroller, International Telephone & Telegraph Corporation, New York.

[1] American Institute of CPAs, *Professional Accounting in 25 Countries,* 1964.

in establishing the strategy and organization for his company's activity abroad.

Environment of international operations

Trends in international activity

In the last fifteen years international activity has increased to an extent which far outreaches the forecasts and parameters laid down by the economists who predicted the economic world that would follow World War II. With this unexpected expansion, business and political life has assumed new dimensions of complexity and involvement. Moreover, the recurrent problems in money, employment, flow of funds, and national budgets which vex us daily suggest that the present environment is only a transitional phase of development—merely a part of the gradual expansion of economic interests which began in the days of the Egyptian trading caravans. In any event, it seems urgently necessary for financial executives to become more aware of the international scene and the problems inherent in financing those foreign operations.

The present scope of American internationalism is worthy of consideration since its size crystalizes the significance of the financing problems incident to foreign operations. It has been estimated[2] that nearly 3,000 American firms have foreign subsidiaries and that their sales abroad are double what the United States exports. Private foreign investment now approximates $17 billion a year[3] and "with private foreign investments having a book value in excess of $86 billion, the United States has become the largest offshore investor in world history."[4]

The sales and assets of U.S. manufacturing firms abroad amounted to $42 billion and $36 billion, respectively, in 1965. Each figure has increased by 50 percent from the data reported for 1962.[5] Therefore, the nation must not only concern itself with the magnitude of the international operation but also with the rapidity of its expansion. Fortunately, the earnings from these foreign activities have increased at an even better rate and exceeded $2 billion in 1965.[6]

The tremendous size of these activities cannot be ignored. Observers in other countries are aware that it would take 13 of the largest European companies to equal the sales of General Motors, and they find it

[2] Howe Martyn, *International Business* (London: Collier-Macmillan Ltd., 1964), p. 1.

[3] Hufbauer and Adler, *Overseas Manufacturing Investment and The Balance of Payments* Washington, D.C.: Tax Policy Research Study No. 1 US. Treasury Department, p. 11 and p. 20.

[4] Thomas J. Watson, Jr., "Atlantic Trade Gap Widening" *Management Review,* American Management Assn., Jan. 1968, p. 52.

[5] Hufbauer and Adler, op. cit.

[6] Ibid.

difficult to live with that fact. Nevertheless, the investment of the United States in Europe still only represents one percent of the total investment there.[7] Nor should it be forgotten that there are significant investments made by Europeans in American companies. Thus, in balance, the great concern about the industrial "invasion" would appear to be more of an emotional problem than an economic one.

Vital need for U.S. participation

The leading companies in American industrial life have developed a great capacity for growth and this capacity buttresses their basic urge to protect the long-term interests of their shareholders by continuing to expand. In earlier days, companies grew by vertical and horizontal mergers and expansions. This time was short-lived, however, because political administrators became more concerned about the potential of large firms to do evil than they were gratified by the accomplishments of large scale business. Thus, some firms were induced by government practices to expand into new product lines where they could not be accused of monopolistic abilities.[8] Other firms decided to stay with their proven operating skills but to take them into new areas of the world.

It should not be assumed, however, that all international growth stems from constraints established by government. Many firms have gone abroad as a form of economic protection. They look upon their dispersion to foreign areas as a form of profit averaging—an insulation from the problems of local economic contraction. Others have gone to the foreign world in search of the high profit margins which were reported in the early 1960's and which still persist to a limited degree. In almost all cases international activity was caused by the need to put skills and assets to work—the only alternate course open to a successful management is that of an uneconomic divestment to the shareholders.[9]

The participation of American firms in foreign environments is extremely important to the continued status and capacity of our nation. Insularity of action can lead only to a weakening of industrial skills and a reduction of American influence in the capitals of the world. On the other hand, by remaining in the forefront of international activity, the American firm is able to expand the sphere of American products and to continuously induce the selection of those products. By licensing product developments and by supplying management skills, the international firm can bring various fees into the United States. Obviously, increased

---

[7] John H. Hickman, "International Financing: An Overview of the Entrepot Capital Market," *Management Bulletin No. 95* (American Management Assn., 1967), p. 2.

[8] Martyn, *International Business,* p. 35.

[9] Donald Kircher, "Now The Transitional Enterprise," *Harvard Business Review,* March-April 1964, p. 7.

dividends, along with export receipts and fees, play an important role in the balance of international payments which, in turn, constitute an important factor in the support of U.S. currency.

It is important to note, however, that American firms cannot expect to exploit the territories in which they operate. They must act as responsible corporate citizens, and through their specialized know-how must contribute to the improved productivity of the local environments. No firm should "go international" simply because that is the fashion of the times; nor should it go for a short-term objective. Instead, it should expand its operating area only if it sees a need for its participation in a country, and only if it can compete fairly over a long period of time.[10] It must be remembered that short-sighted and unsupported entries into the international scene can do irreparable damage to the commercial diplomacy of the United States, while exposing the shareholders to unwarranted financial risks.

It is a basic philosophy of American policy that the less fortunate shall share in the benefits of industrial advances. It is not surprising, therefore, that when American firms go abroad, they bring with them vital improvements in employment conditions, fiscal practices, operating methods, and living conditions. These changes are sometimes disturbing to the local environments during the initial stages, but gradually they become a welcome part of the local life. Evidence indicates that the persistent influence of the international firm appears to be more effective than political subsidies and assistance projects in raising the standard of living around the world.

Developed versus developing nations

The ten most highly industrialized countries in the world have 18 percent of the world's population and a per capita income per year of $1,250. The other 82 percent have a per capita income of only $125.[11] One of the challenges of modern civilization is that of minimizing this gap. The international firm operating in the underdeveloped world can facilitate progress.

For the most part, the developing nations must place their dependence on natural products and extractive materials. Unless these can be produced at low cost and sold internationally at high prices, the consumption level of the nation must be kept low. To adopt any other course will inevitably drain off all foreign exchange and impair the credit of the nation.

---

[10] "Obstacles and Incentives to Private Foreign Investment 1962–1964," *Studies in Business Policy No. 115* (New York: National Industrial Conference Board, 1965), p. 194.

[11] John G. McLean, "Financing Overseas Expansion" *Harvard Business Review,* Mar.-Apr. 1963, p. 54.

The obvious needs in the developing nation are for the creation of multiple centers of industrial activity, the development of a stable currency and a reliable banking system, and the evolution of a middle class. These objectives will be enhanced by the participation of the substantial international firm which is prepared to remain a long-term part of the local environment. From the viewpoint of maximum local benefit, such firms, when well managed, should get the first participation in investment grants and should be supported by host-country officials who have learned to understand and appreciate the mutually beneficial aims of private capital.

International firms are willing to risk their funds in developing countries—Americans have over $1 billion in assets in Brazil.[12] Furthermore, they are anxious to keep those funds in activities which can contribute to the industrialization and capitalization of the country. Their rights of ownership must be protected, however, and this protection must include protection of the value of the currency, of the right to remit, of fair treatment under the tax law, and of reasonable treatment in government quarters. A government cannot properly induce an international firm to begin operations in its country and then, by open or covert means, force it to surrender its position to local interests without appropriate compensation.

In Latin America the gap between the rich and poor is very great. In many of the Latin American countries the top five percent of the population has in excess of 30 percent of the income. In developed countries, such as the United States, the top five percent has less than 20 percent of the income.[13] The gap must be narrowed, and business and government must each participate in carrying out the burdens of development. As D. C. Burnham of Westinghouse has said, "Only private enterprise in pursuit of fair profits can provide the basic economic leadership to raise the productive levels in underdeveloped countries."[14]

Since the social pressures indicated in the foregoing paragraph will affect market and political arrangements for many years in the future, the financial manager will find it expedient to channel corporate resources to these areas. By the same token, the governments of underdeveloped nations will continue to welcome international participation.

Currency and trading areas

Until 1967 the literature of international operations made regular references to the "sterling area," the "dollar area," and hard or soft currencies. With the recent weakening of the English pound and the

---

[12] "Brazil: Costa e Silva Begins to Build," *Business Abroad*, May 7, 1967, p. 12.

[13] "Indicators," *Business Abroad*, Oct. 2, 1967, p. 2.

[14] "How Profits Set the Pace for Investment Abroad at Westinghouse," *Business Abroad*, Oct. 30, 1967, p. 9.

recent attacks on the U.S. dollar, the use of these terms takes on a modified meaning.

The terms sterling area and dollar area have no official significance but merely show that the indicated currencies are the principal exchange medium in particular trading groups. At one time the stability of the two currencies had made them the "reserve currencies"—those that were used on an extensive basis in settling international balances—but this is now true in a much lesser degree. Currencies like the German Deutsche Mark are finding new popularity.

The terms "hard currency" and "soft currency" are the customary ways of expressing the probability of devaluation within the near term. A currency which is hard has the least susceptibility to being devalued in its relation to other currencies. Since the complex activities of modern business are so dependent on a predictable monetary value, it is important that the international financial executive have a strong awareness of currency matters and the devaluation potential existing in a given situation.

The "trading area" is an international development which became important after World War II. In general, it represents an association of countries for the purpose of improving trading conditions between the members and with countries outside the group. Although there have been many collateral activities, the principal technique of the trading group is the regulation of tariffs, usually with the objective of removing the various barriers separating the members while maintaining a protective preference in respect to outside influences. This internal preference induces foreign companies to establish activities within the trading group rather than relying on export operations from their homeland. Unless other controls are implemented, some of the protected profits get to outside owners in the form of dividends.

In one sense the states of the United States constituted one of the older trading blocks, but in the postwar world the EEC (European Economic Community) is acknowledged to be the most successful development. This group (which includes France, West Germany, Belgium, the Netherlands, Luxembourg and Italy) has steadily improved its economic position and moved along the road toward the achievement of its many objectives. In the middle of 1968 the common market countries, after ten years of gradual reduction of tariffs, finally eliminated all tariffs within the group and established a common external tariff, thus vastly facilitating trade within the group.[15]

In Europe the principal competitor to the EEC has been EFTA (European Free Trade Association). This trading group is the economic rejoinder of those major countries that were not a part of the EEC.

---

[15] "Europe and the U.S.: What Business Planners Can Expect," *Business International,* Mar. 29, 1968, p. 97.

Known as "the outer seven," the EFTA group includes Austria, Denmark, Norway, Portugal, Sweden, Switzerland and the United Kingdom.

In Latin America trading groups include the Latin American Free Trade Association (Mexico, Argentina, Chile, Ecuador, Bolivia, Paraguay, Uruguay, Brazil, Colombia, Peru and Venezuela) and the Central American Common Market (Costa Rica, El Salvador, Guatemala, Honduras, and Nicaragua). The progress of these groups is slow, but it can be expected that some of the nationalistic tendencies will be minimized in due course. Certainly the new economic structures which have been developed can be more appropriately dealt with by the international operator than was possible under the confused and unstructured environment of earlier years.

Sources of international intelligence

The international business arena is characterized by swift changes in political and economic trends. It is essential that the financial executive be firmly grounded in the business influences which affect his area of operation but, in addition, he must have constant awareness of the financial, legal and political changes. Obviously, it is more difficult to keep informed on these international developments than on domestic changes, but the task must be undertaken.

It is not feasible to present a comprehensive list of reading materials for the international financial executive, but the following list of materials will serve as a brief but useful starting point:

Business Abroad (Dun & Bradstreet)
Business International (Business International)
Foreign Commerce Weekly (U.S. Dept. of Commerce)
Foreign Information Service (First National City Bank)
World Business Reports (Chase Manhattan Bank, N.Y.)
Rundt's Weekly Intelligence (S. J. Rundt & Associates, N.Y.)
Pick's World Currency Report (Franz Pick, Publisher, N.Y.)
Gallatin Letter (Copley International Corporation, N.Y.)
Overseas Business Reports (U.S. Dept. of Commerce)
World Trade Information Service (U.S. Dept. of Commerce)
Investing, Licensing and Trading Condition Abroad (Business International)
Arthur Andersen Tax & Trade Guides
Price Waterhouse Information Guides
Lawyers Guide to International Business Transactions (Surrey & Shaw, American Law Institute and American Bar Assoc., 1963)
European Taxation (International Bureau of Fiscal Documentation, Amsterdam)
AMA Reports (American Management Association)
Professional Accounting in 25 Countries (American Institute of CPAs, 1964)

However, although the well-informed financial man will wish to be acquainted with the above material, no amount of reference material will serve as an adequate substitute for good counsel. The effective internationalist will, therefore, consult frequently with international bankers and lawyers, with tax experts and independent accountants, and with economists and politicians. He will use his trade and professional associations at home and abroad. In addition, he will take full advantage of the informational service units of various government agencies in the United States and in foreign countries. All of these sources will be anxious to provide assistance, but each source serves its own specialized interest and a certain amount of independent cross-checking is prudent.

Where a company has significant local activities in existence, its local personnel should serve as a useful means of keeping the home-office executives informed. It is recommended in these cases that the financial executive include in his formal system of reporting an appropriate provision for the disclosure of the major activities of foreign competitors, of developments on the political scene, and of changes in the legal environment of doing business.

Organizational approaches to foreign business

The financing of foreign business is dependent in its form upon the organizational approach taken to obtaining participation in the foreign area. In the following paragraphs consideration is given to several of the more important types of international activity.

Exporting

The initial stages of a firm's foreign activity usually emphasize the export to foreign lands of goods manufactured in U.S. facilities. The principal incentive for entering the export market typically results from a need to use excess domestic manufacturing capacity as a means of absorbing fixed costs. The export supervision generally rests in the hands of the marketing executive who operates either through domestic agents or agents located abroad, or through sales made to foreign buyers by company employees at home or abroad, or to subsidiaries located in foreign lands.

Where business is carried on through the use of the professional trading specialists, the manufacturer escapes most of the financial responsibility and operational complexity of foreign operations. However, he also surrenders a large share of his control over the expansion of his market volume. Where agents are appointed, it is essential that the agency agreement make provision for duration and cancellation of the contract; for agency rights and territory; for use of names and trademarks; for warranty and returns; for promotion and collection; for pricing and commissions; for quotas, procedures and reports.

As indicated, there is relatively little need for special financing arrangements for export shipment. However, the trader should be fully versed in the documents of trade and their applicability to the territory concerned. The various forms of letters of credit (revocable, irrevocable, confirmed), export drafts (sight, time), consignment sales, and cash payment requirements should be investigated. The foreign department of any large commercial bank can illustrate the potentials and advise on the use of the various techniques.

It should be noted that companies organized in the United States but doing business in U.S. possessions, in the western hemisphere, or in China can obtain special advantages under the Internal Revenue Code. All other U.S. companies trading in foreign countries are taxed as though they were doing business domestically. More will be said about the respective tax differences in a later section.

When studying the nature of export operations, it is important to acknowledge that a large share of export activity is stimulated by the existence of foreign subsidiaries. In addition, exports are supported by the aid-tying policies which have characterized project loans in recent years. It has been estimated[16] that 60 percent of the total increase of $2,160 million in commodity exports between 1960 and 1965 was directly or indirectly the outcome of U.S. economic assistance.

Licensing

The importing of goods into a foreign country is frowned upon by the local governments since it represents a drain on the balance of payments, and since it fails to give employment to local residents. As a result various trade barriers in terms of quotas and tariffs have been used to inhibit many types of importing. Nevertheless, despite the undesirable nature of foreign imports, local residents have wished to share in new products and have constituted a demand for goods that could not be denied. One approach used in overcoming the disadvantages of importing while satisfying the needs of the consumer has been that of licensing.

Under this technique of foreign operations, the manufacturing capacity of the domestic inventor is retained for profitable local purposes but the right to employ blueprints and technical "know-how" used in manufacturing the product is made available to a foreign manufacturer. The foreign operator pays for this right under the terms of a "licensing agreement" and usually pays a fee based on the units or values manufac-

---

[16] Hyson and Strout, "Impact of Foreign Aid on U.S. Exports" *Harvard Business Review*, Jan.-Feb. 1968, p. 67.

tured or sold. The owner of the patent thus participates indirectly in the market while restricting his exposure to expropriation and his need to provide financing.

Most managements look upon licensing fees as "plus" income[17] and in many cases consider it to be an offset to the cost of the research and development program. It is important, however, to remember that to-day's licensee may be tomorrow's competitor. Discretion should be used in offering licenses on new patents or on processes which are fundamental to the long-term success of the U.S. business.

On the other hand, the sharing of patents with other nations tends to widen the scope of product promotion and may thus serve to stimulate a latent demand which can be subsequently exploited because the license has a limited time duration or is of a non-exclusive nature. As a rule license fees are a good tax deduction in the country paying the charges and often are remitted without withholding taxes.

It must be recognized that patents have varying legal protections in the several national areas of the world. The interpretation of these protections and the related obligations for filing require the services of lawyers specializing in the field of international patent law. Even with expert legal assistance, it will probably be impossible to uphold a patent in an "unfriendly" nation[18] and in many areas it will be difficult for a foreign company to win adequate compensatory awards in the event of patent invasion. Nevertheless, companies having extensive research and development budgets may find licensing to be a necessary and very profitable form of foreign operation.

Investment

The avoidance of trade barriers, exchange controls, and freight costs while maintaining control of foreign activities can be achieved by means of direct investment in foreign countries. This investment may take over the operation of existing activities, or it may be used to establish new operations. In the first case, there is a great saving in time, risk, and manpower.[19] In the second, there is an assurance that the foreign practices will be compatible with existing domestic policies and that there will be no need to write off the unabsorbed errors of a prior management.

The foreign investment may take the route of the "foreign branch." In such a situation the income is taxed to the parent on a current basis as though it had been earned domestically. Thus, for tax reasons, it may be

---

[17] J. K. Lasser, "How To Do Business Abroad," *Business Management Handbook*, McGraw Hill, 1954, p. 787.

[18] Raymond L. Brittenham, "Expropriation of Foreign Investment," *International Handbook of Management* (New York: McGraw Hill, 1965), p. 273.

[19] K. K. White, *Financing Company Expansion*, AMA Research Study 64, American Management Association, 1964, p. 100.

particularly useful to operate "branches" when losses are anticipated in the early years of life. In addition, companies like Singer Manufacturing Company have found the branch format to have operating advantages of considerable importance.

In recent years, however, most corporations who have gone international have preferred to establish subsidiary corporations. This format permits the deferral of U.S. taxation on income until such income is remitted in the form of dividends and thus, if applied in countries having low tax rates or special tax privileges, may significantly reduce the need of providing dollars for the payment of taxes on the foreign earnings. In addition, the corporate format lends itself to large local borrowing more readily than the branch format, and may also be more satisfactory for recruitment and government relations.

Where the corporate technique is employed, it is often suggested or required that local interests be permitted to share in the equity as equal or minority interests. It is generally suggested that such participation will make available a valuable knowledge of local conditions, improve relations with banks and government people, and reduce the amount of the initial capital investment.[20] The local interests generally wish to be a part of the success that the new venture is expected to achieve, and the government is receptive to the reduction in cash drains through the dividend route which results from a local participation in the ownership.

In many cases, the joint venture is the only feasible way to enter a particular national market and in some instances it may obtain special marketing advantages from being associated with local people and lower acquisition costs. However, to operate successfully, a joint venture must very clearly identify the executives who are responsible for daily operations and those points of policy that are to be dealt with by a vote of the equity interests. In the past, many American firms have found it necessary to buy out the equity interests of their foreign or American colleagues so as to control the basic financial and management policies within one compatible framework. Since the economic circumstances of the joint venturers are not identical, the corporate policies are potentially unsatisfactory to one element or the other—each of the joint venturers will claim credit for the successful operations, but unsuccessful operations will be claimed by neither.

Despite the desire on the part of foreign nationals to avoid ownership by outsiders of major segments of industry, the corporate approach to foreign investment is likely to be the format used for major penetrations into international activity. It is important therefore that a reasonable and long-term program of growth and dividend payment be developed for each subsidiary operation. The varied interests of the investor, the consumer, and the nations involved in the arrangement must be protected.

---

[20] Myles L. Mace, "The President and International Operations," *Harvard Business Review*, Nov.-Dec. 1966, p. 77.

Supervising the foreign entity

In an organizational sense, it is necessary to identify the appropriate line of command for the execution of corporate decisions bearing on the international operations. It is particularly important to identify this channel since it does not necessarily match the legal structure of the related interests.

Under many conditions the ownership of the stock of related subsidiaries has been placed with holding companies. Through the holding companies, securities are owned, public offerings are made, and tax status is derived. The holding corporation may also be the management corporation, but this need not be the case. However, where differences occur, the nature of operations must be carefully monitored to be certain that activities are so arranged as to maintain optimum tax advantages over the long term without impeding the fundamental direction of the international activities.

The management group may operate as a department of the domestic headquarters, or it may be located abroad as an area management. If the management group is incorporated, it will generally be established as an American corporation so as to minimize the taxation of service fees while utilizing the operating expenses as allowable deductions in the consolidated tax returns of the U.S. operations.

It is important for significant technical reasons that appropriate organizational steps be taken insofar as the supervising entities are concerned. Furthermore, where important international operations are intended, the responsibility for optimum organizational approaches should be assigned as a continuing managerial function in order to accommodate the continuous regulatory changes which are legislated either in the United States or in the foreign country.

Qualitative nature of risk

The operation of an international business necessarily involves a degree of risk that is far greater than similar activities in the domestic environment. These risks are of varying quality, and are dependent upon the stage of development, the economic cycle, military considerations and many national factors. In the subsequent paragraphs consideration is given to the qualitative nature of risk insofar as it concerns the protection of capital, the adequacy of a fair return, and the assurance of investment repatriation.

Protection of capital

The minimum proper expectation of an investor is that he shall maintain the value of his investment. This maintenance of value must exist in terms of the translated currency of the investor. Although investment capital should be committed on a relatively permanent basis, it should not be so restricted that it cannot be recovered by the investor in a reasonable period of time for alternative purposes. Whenever the free choice of the investor becomes inhibited, the supply of capital will decrease if all other factors are equal.

Foreign capital is held to be "suspect" in most of the underdeveloped areas of the world. The long history of economic exploitation in these areas is a constant warning to local politicians who are honestly seeking to protect the interests of the local citizens, and it establishes a convenient "whipping boy" for those who wish to gain local support at any cost. Nevertheless, an adequate supply of capital is the best assurance which the underdeveloped nations have for the development of their natural resources and the creation of a competitive industrial economy. Since such capital is not available locally, it must be brought in from other nations.

Where capital is invested in a foreign environment it becomes involved in the economic fortunes of that area. In order to support the local economy in certain situations, the foreign investor will have to forego business moves that appear to be financially desirable. Raytheon found that it could not act freely in closing its Sicilian plant in 1968, and Sperry-Rand received unfavorable publicity when it sought to curtail a portion of its French activity. The international investor must employ his foreign capital in a manner which supports—rather than exploits—the economy in which he is a guest.

Certain foreign investments will attract special attention because of their particular characteristics. Thus, extractive natural resources are felt to belong to the people; utility services are given quasi-government constraints; sophisticated products in the electronic and computer fields are felt to be essential to national economic development; and defense items are, of course, viewed from the viewpoint of military logistics. Each of the above considerations leads the local people and their political leaders to question the foreign ownership of the related enterprises.

In a number of cases the local governments have sought to counteract or remove the influence of foreign capital. For instance, in France the "plan calcul" represented a subsidization of local computer development. In England, government support of the merger of General Electric Company and Associated Electrical Industries was intended to combat positions established by Swedish and American equipment manufacturers. In Brazil, expropriation (whether achieved by the regulation of utility rates or by outright decree) attempted to remove foreign interests from various utilities. The nationalistic views which lead to these approaches are clearly understood by the foreign investor, and he will introduce or maintain his capital in a country only where there is a reasonable assurance that it will not be unfairly treated.

Requirement for a fair return

It has been shown that international investment is essential to social development in some foreign environments. Investors, however, are not usually motivated by purely social considerations and must be induced by other means to move their capital from the security of its home area. In this connection, it must be understood that profit is the reward for risk. Consequently, any judgment concerning the propriety of a given rate of profit must give consideration to the risks involved. If, in a given situation, an operation is entitled to a return of 10 percent on shareholders' investment in the domestic environment, then the rate of return must be higher when the operation occurs in a foreign world where the special interests of the local community may not be in complete agreement with those of the investor. Similarly, if a high rate of devaluation or a possibility of expropriation must be contemplated, then an additional rate of return is needed to compensate for that added risk. If the enterprise is subject to the exigencies of war, an even greater premium is appropriate. The rate of return can be properly assessed only after a consideration of the foregoing risks, but offsetting allowance should also be made for the reduced profitability resulting from time delays, management weakness and similar operating impediments of foreign activity.

It is also important to note that the rate of return should be measured after the inclusion of interest costs—even when those costs are material and develop because of the basic undercapitalization of the enterprise. Interest cost is partially an offset to the gains which a debtor enjoys in an inflating economy. Since these gains become a part of the operating return, the full cost of the borrowed capital must also be reflected therein.

Some managements seek to measure the rate of return before income taxes on the theory that such taxation is not controllable by the enterprise. Such a practice is particularly disturbing when used in international operations because the tax structures of the various countries are not uniform. Costs of government services which are covered by turnover taxes in one nation may be supported by income taxes in a different country. If comparative judgments on the rate of profit are to be drawn, the full costs of operation and taxation must be included.

Repatriation of funds

As was stated earlier, the investor must at least be assured of the maintenance of the value of his investment, but also he should be assured that the values can be brought back into his domestic area at some time. Although many nations have exchange controls and rules on remittance, these devices should be employed as a means of regularizing transactions and preventing unwarranted monetary strains on the money system. They should not be used as a means of depriving investors of their right of repatriating investments in a reasonable period of time.

For some years Brazil maintained a prohibition on the repatriation of profits earned therein. The monetary problems of that country justified special procedures, but the program could not continue for long without shutting off the entry of new capital. Earnings are truly the reward for bearing risk, but such earnings must be heavily discounted if they cannot be readily remitted to the shareholders in the form of dividends.

Investment in foreign activities must not be confused with short-term exploitations. In too many cases Americans have aimed at a full repatriation of investment within five years while expecting to obtain an unrealistic 15 percent return on the original investment.[21] Where the recovery of invested funds can be confidently expected in the near term, the required rate of return can be decreased.

U.S. aids and restraints

International operations involve important questions of national interest. Problems associated with the flow of funds, with the taxation of foreign income, and with the unreasonable restraint of trade must be appropriately dealt with by the national government. Consequently, the legislation of the United States imposes certain restraints and grants certain privileges which bear specifically on foreign activities. These regulations must be fully understood before any financing or any international operation is undertaken. In addition, the primary purpose of certain agencies of the State Department and of the Commerce Department is to help American business abroad. These are more fully discussed in Chapter 63, "Relations with Government Agencies."

Flow of funds

The value of the U.S. dollar in relation to the other currencies of the world is dependent in part on the flow of funds. If, over an extended period of time, U.S. interests—whether in the public or private sector of the economy—pay out more cash or credits to foreigners than they bring in to the country, then the dollar will weaken since gold will be transferred to settle the negative balance. In this connection, it must be noted that "with the exception of 1957, a year of surplus, the United States has been running an annual deficit of about $2 billion in its international payments. In 1967, according to Government figures, the United States spent $3.6 billion more abroad than it returned to the U.S.—more than

---

[21] John H. Hickman *International Financing: Tapping the Entrepot Capital Market*, Management Bulletin 95, American Management Assn., 1967, p. 27.

double the 1966 level."[22] Although a small favorable flow occurred in 1968, this resulted from certain special capital movements which are generally viewed as being non-recurring. The continued pressure on the flow of funds represents a major economic challenge to the nation—a challenge which is neither temporary nor the result of direct investments in foreign countries.

The outflow of long-term capital is one element of the adverse balance of payments. In July of 1963, President Kennedy proposed an Interest Equalization Tax which provided for a tax of one percent per year on the acquisition by U.S. investors of foreign securities with maturities of over three years.[23] In a later move the tax was also applied to bank loans of one year or more. The intent of the taxation was that of making it less attractive to sell foreign securities in the United States since the interest rate would have to be increased to a level which would compensate the investor for his added tax. The program was largely aimed at curtailing portfolio investment by Americans, and it worked for a while as investors liquidated their holdings, but by 1968 the annual purchases were again setting new records. In any case, the Interest Equalization Tax aimed at discouraging rather than preventing the continued expansion of investment into foreign business, and, as was demonstrated in early 1969, the rates are subject to adjustment in accordance with changes in international interest rates.

Military expenditures and subsidies to developing nations, together with a weakening of the U.S. trade balances, brought about a crisis which resulted in the voluntary program for the balance of payments as announced by President Johnson in February, 1965. The program urged borrowing from foreign rather than the U.S. banks, an increase in exports, and a repatriation of all possible funds. The so-called "voluntary" program was accompanied by a requirement for voluminous reporting and a high degree of "moral suasion." Even when announced, it was generally acknowledged to be the forerunner of a regulatory program. Its immediate effects were the dampening of fund exports to foreign areas and a gradual increase of foreign interest rates. Investment abroad was still freely possible, but involved a higher financing cost.

The voluntary program produced certain improvements in the flow of funds, but these were partly offset by the liquidation of U.S. securities by non-residents.[24] Since the problem was not eliminated by the voluntary approach, President Johnson found it necessary in January, 1968, to initiate the mandatory program. By regulation, the government sought to

[22] Neil A. Martin, "Foreign Investment Curbs: A Nightmare," *Wall Street Journal,* July 18, 1968.

[23] Garrett and Harris, "Opportunity in Foreign Bonds," *Harvard Business Review,* Nov.-Dec. 1965, p. 74.

[24] Bruck and Lees, *Foreign Investment, Capital Controls and the Balance of Payments,* New York University (GBA), 1968.

cure a condition that had not been eliminated by the goodwill and cooperative effort of the major international firms.

The new regulations based allowable investment on the experience of the respondent in a base period of 1965–66 and listed countries under one of three groups, with each group having a different rate of allowability. Thus, the underdeveloped countries were given particular support; the capital-requiring countries were separately considered; and the remainder of the world had the lowest allowable rate. Direct investments from the U.S., together with retained earnings, were then related to this allowable base and all excess amounts were required to be repatriated— even if money had to be borrowed to accomplish this. Early in 1969 the Nixon administration took steps to reduce the economic burden of compliance. In addition to changing some banking regulations, the new rules freed many smaller companies from the need to report, and offered an alternative to the base-period calculation which would permit 30 percent of the 1968 earnings of foreign subsidiaries to be invested abroad. Despite the changes, the regulations as they exist in mid-1969 contain many inequities and unworkable concepts and seem certain to require additional relief from appeals boards or the courts. As F. Michael Adler of the Wharton School has said, "In the longer run the mandatory controls seem likely to do more harm than good to the U.S. balance of payments."[25] To date, the principal result has been a great increase in overseas internal financing. The resultant higher interest costs will bring pressure to bear on profits, and it is quite possible "that cumulative losses in the current-account sector could be substantial after eight or ten years."[26] In any event, the regulations currently inhibit the investment of U.S. funds and the use of capital stock for investment purposes, and require the repatriation of an unusual level of dividends. Investors who wish to acquire foreign enterprises are being forced to count upon borrowed funds both to obtain and to maintain the new activity, since 100 percent of every dollar earned by a new company must be repatriated (unless excess allowable base is available from other operations).

Concurrent with the restraints on investment and repatriation is a program to increase net U.S. exports, including the 25 percent of exports which go to foreign subsidiaries of U.S. corporations. This program is under stiff pressure because of the continuing increase in U.S. prices. The trade surplus which amounted to $7 billion in 1964 had dropped to $4 billion in 1967.[27] It decreased even further to $500 million in 1968. Attempts are being made to stimulate exports by various forms of protection (e.g.-AID-tying, Webb-Pomerene arrangements), but it is quite

[25] F. Michael Adler, "The High Cost of Foreign Investment Restraints," *Columbia Journal of World Business,* May-June 1968, p. 74.

[26] Bruck and Lees, *Foreign Investment, Capital Controls and the Balance of Payments,* New York University (GBA), 1968.

[27] "The Threat to U.S. Trade," *Business Week,* Feb. 24, 1968, p. 33.

obvious that the trade balance will not improve significantly unless U.S. companies can market competitively, and that requires either an increase in U.S. productivity and a lowering of wage, tax, and materials costs or comparatively smaller improvements on the part of foreign competitors.

Income tax considerations

The financial requirements of foreign investments are likely to hinge very heavily on the organizational format and location of the new operations and their resultant tax status. Since taxes represent the greatest single cost in today's business, the minimization of such charges will have a high impact on the profitability and cash needs of any venture.

A corporation which is doing business abroad may be organized as a domestic corporation (i.e. organized under the laws of any one of the states or the District of Columbia), or as a foreign corporation. Associations, partnerships, and joint ventures are not taxed as entities, but each related individual owner becomes proportionately responsible for reported gains and losses.

In the case of domestic corporations, all income is taxed at regular U.S. income-tax rates regardless of where it is earned. However, it should be noted that, if a domestic corporation can qualify as a Western Hemisphere Corporation or if it operates principally in a U.S. possession, it is entitled to special advantageous tax treatment.

In the case of foreign corporations, a corporation is not subjected to tax on income from any source outside of the United States. Although the U.S. shareholders of Controlled Foreign Corporations may be subjected to U.S. tax on undistributed income of a certain type, their income is generally taxable only upon its remittance to the United States or when it is realized through the profitable sale of equity. Additional tax advantages may be gained if a foreign corporation meets the definition of a Less Developed Country Corporation. On the other hand, closely held foreign corporations dealing in investments may become taxable on both distributed and undistributed income if they are classed as Foreign Personal Holding Companies.

U.S. income-tax procedure determines the nature of tax incidence according to the place of citizenship and the source of the related income.[28] Almost all other industrialized countries use the country of residence as the primary determinant. Obviously, in view of differing rates and regulations, it is sometimes better in doing business abroad to qualify as a U.S. incorporated entity instead of one which is incorporated in a foreign country. However, since the two legal approaches may

---

[28] Walter F. O'Connor, "Tax Considerations in International Operations," *Financial Executive*, June 1967, p. 56.

encompass an operation in the rules of both nations at a single time, it is necessary to provide special protection to avoid double taxation. Consequently, the United States has entered into tax treaties with about two dozen foreign countries which chiefly provide for the prevention of "taxation by one country of certain types of income derived in that country by a business enterprise located in another country if it does not have a place of business or general agency arrangement in the country where the income is earned."[29] The related stipulations apply principally to royalty and interest income, but they may also affect the withholding tax on dividends.

For the most part, the income of foreign corporations is not subjected to U.S. income tax until it is remitted to U.S. taxpayers. Similarly, expenses and losses incurred by foreign corporations may not be deducted in calculating consolidated taxable income. Consequently, it may sometimes be desirable to operate an activity as a "branch" of a U.S. corporation until its profitability is established. After profitable operation is assured, the activity can be converted to a "foreign subsidiary" so that earnings may reman free of U.S. tax on earnings until they are remitted.

In 1960 and 1961 there was considerable agitation in government circles for the U.S. taxation of all income earned by foreign subsidiaries. It was argued that corporations were unreasonably accumulating funds abroad to avoid tax and thus were acting to the detriment of other taxpayers while misstating income for the consolidated financial statements. After a great amount of testimony, the proposals for taxing subsidiaries as though they were branches was defeated. However, in the Revenue Act of 1962, certain provisions were written into Subpart F of Section 951 to prevent the build-up of passive-type income abroad, and to prevent companies from establishing arrangements with related entities whereby income from sales and service could be funneled into low-tax countries, even though sales and manufacture did not occur therein.[30]

The allocation of income and deductions among organizations controlled directly or indirectly by the same interests is governed by Section 482 of the Internal Revenue Code. This section establishes an "arm's length" criterion for transfer pricing and identifies in great detail the three methods that are allowable in setting such price (i.e. comparable uncontrolled price, resale price, cost-plus price).[31] It also makes provision with respect to interest-free loans to foreign subsidiaries, the royalty-free use by foreign corporations of the intangible assets of a U.S.

---

[29] Jesse M. Miles, "Foreign Taxes and U.S. Tax Implications," *Journal of Accountancy,* May 1966, p. 47.

[30] *Ibid.,* p. 49.

[31] Abraham J. Briloff, *"The Mad, Mad, Mad, Mad World of 482,"* *Journal of Accountancy,* August 1967, p. 51.

corporation, and the allocation of overhead-type headquarters expenses. Audit enforcement of Section 482 is currently being emphasized by Internal Revenue agents.

U.S. taxpayers who have earned income abroad and who have paid an income tax (or a tax levied in lieu of such tax) to a foreign government are given relief from U.S. taxation under the "foreign-tax credit" provisions of the Internal Revenue Code. Election to take the credit against taxes due on foreign-source income may be made each year and may be computed on a "country basis" or an "overall basis."[32] The provisions surrounding the foreign-tax credit are extremely involved, but it is sufficient to say for the present purpose that in the main they are aimed at avoiding the double taxation of foreign-source earnings.

Western Hemisphere Corporations are defined as domestic U.S. corporations which do all of their business, other than incidental purchases, in the western hemisphere. To qualify, a corporation must derive for a three-year test period 95 percent of its gross income from sources outside the United States, and 90 percent of its gross income must be derived from the active conduct of a trade or business.[33] If an organization qualifies, it can then pay a tax of only 34 percent, or 14 points below the ordinary tax rate. When dividends are distributed, the corporate dividend tax will increase the tax costs on such profits to some extent, but they will still be less than the regular rates.

The tax exemption given to the undistributed profits of domestic corporations operating principally within possessions of the United States represents a significant advantage. Of course, when the earnings are distributed as dividends, they become subjected to full tax. Thus, unless the subsidiary can be liquidated by some form of tax-free transaction, the exemption should be viewed only as a useful deferral rather than a complete escape from taxation.

The use of the tax-sanctuary device must be approached with some caution. Those countries which have been publicized as "sanctuary areas" (e.g. Liberia, Bahamas, Bermuda, Panama, Liechtenstein, and Hong Kong) invite the scrutiny of the Internal Revenue people and must be defended periodically.[34] Nevertheless, where sound counsel justifies the use of these tax devices, they can be very beneficial in that they generate low-taxed foreign-source income, which serves to use up excess foreign-tax credits developed in other operations, and because the undistributed low-taxed income can be retained for corporate investment purposes.

---

[32] Paul D. Seghers, *Tax Considerations in Organizing Foreign Operations* (Management Bulletin 108, American Management Assn., 1967), p. 9.

[33] Richard C. Munsche, *Tax Management Problems of Foreign Income,* International Management Series No. 1, International Management Assn. (1956) p. 48.

[34] Walter F. O'Connor, "Tax Considerations in International Operations," *Financial Executive,* June 1967, p. 49.

The influence of the U.S. tax system on the organizational format and location of foreign operations is necessarily material. Before taking any final steps toward the establishment of operations, a corporation should make a realistic forecast of its financial expectations in the near term and for some extended future period, and it must then seek expert guidance both in the United States and in the country of operation before selecting a course of action. It must not assume that its intercompany pricing will be free of examination and it must take steps to avoid "Subpart F" income. Sidewise loans between sister operations should be set up so as to avoid any danger of their unexpectedly being declared as "constructive dividends."[35] The value of tax holidays, investment grants and Western Hemisphere status must be made a part of the operational plan.

Anti-trust legislation

The attitude of the American Government is quite ambivalent in respect to its anti-trust legislation. In domestic affairs there is a vigorous and long tradition aimed at maintaining competition in the market place. Tendencies toward monopoly are subjected to restraint by court action and other more subtle pressures. On the other hand, in foreign affairs American producers are enjoined by the U.S. agencies from making any agreement which might inhibit their ability to gain a complete monopoly and saturation of a given market.

Indicative of the willingness of the U.S. government to allow non-competitive arrangements in respect to foreign business is the whole class of activities known as the "Webb-Pomerene" Associations. Since 1917 these groups have been urged to combine to fix prices and arrange selling terms as an aid in opposing foreign cartels. In general, they have only appealed to smaller manufacturers who find it useful to work through an associated export corporation, a central selling agency, or with an existing foreign agent of the manufacturer. Recurrently, the U.S. agencies seek to stimulate exports by encouraging these associations, but no great success is currently evident.

The foreign and domestic anti-trust approaches are logically opposed to each other and, unfortunately, the interpretive rulings become increasingly narrow. As a result, American firms may not join the clubs, associations, syndicates and cartels which are so prevalent abroad. In addition, when entering into joint ventures, they must be very careful to consider the relationships of the partners in respect to the laws of the host country and the position of their own officers and directors in relationship to the U.S. law. The anti-trust interpretations of executive responsibility are extremely restrictive.

Although AID has consistently refused to grant loans to U.S. compa-

---

[35] *Ibid.,* p. 50.

nies seeking the quasi-monopolistic status of "integrated industries" in the Central American Common Market (CACM),[36] there has been little legal interpretation of joint-venture relationships as they apply to under-developed countries. It appears unlikely that any strong anti-trust action will take place in these areas at this time. Nevertheless, the uncertainty of the U.S. legal position in respect to foreign anti-trust matters is causing many U.S. corporations to forego the use of the joint-venture technique and even, in some cases, to remain out of attractive foreign markets altogether.

There is an obvious need for clarification of the government's position, but in addition it must be recognized that many of the principles contained in the U.S. anti-trust approach are being rejected by those nations which are currently reviewing anti-trust regulations. In both England and Australia the concepts of violation "per se" and "prospective restrictive influence" have been discarded in favor of a balance of desirable and undesirable features, and of immediately provable effects.[37]

Not only is there an international dissatisfaction with the U.S. anti-trust concept, but also it is evident that the ability of the United States to win compliance to its viewpoints in foreign countries is greatly restricted. Although in 1927, in the Sisal Sales matter, it was feasible for our Supreme Court to discount and ignore a Mexican law because it had been passed through the influence of American business interests having monopolistic intent, such an attitude would not be acceptable today. Anti-trust colonialism is more likely to meet with opposition and to draw reactions such as the Watkins Report to the Canadian Privy Council in which it recommended legislation that would prohibit both enforcement and compliance with foreign anti-trust decrees. Indeed, as reflected in the Lauritzer decision (*Lauritzer* v. *Larsen,* 345 U.S. 571, 582 [1953]), the recommendation for "mutual forebearance if retaliation is to be avoided" suggests that a softer enforcement attitude may prevail when U.S. anti-trust goes international.

Foreign incentives and controls

The expansion of American firms into the international business arena has been of material value to the economy of the United States and to those individual firms which have moved into the foreign fields. However, this expansion has also been of great benefit to the economies of the foreign countries and this has been acknowledged by their development policies. Although the related national attitudes change from year to year, there has been a basic encouragement of such investment by the

---

[36] Leo M. Drechsler, "Risky Joint Ventures: How the Long Arm of U.S. Anti-Trust Law Can Reach Overseas," *Business Abroad,* Oct. 30, 1967, p. 32.

[37] Ivan C. MacDougall, "Anti-Trust Abroad—Room for Compromise," *Conference Board Record,* June 1968, p. 3.

potential host countries, and many incentives have been used to induce increased international participation.

Economic objectives of the host country

A foreign country which enters into a development program that encourages the participation of international interests is pursuing specific local objectives. These objectives must be understood before the propriety of any financial commitment can be evaluated. Experience has indicated that particular projects and enthusiasms of nations can be changed frequently, but that the basic needs of countries have a long and unchanging continuity. It is prudent, therefore, to place one's major investment reliance upon this latter necessity when planning new operations.

The velocity of business affairs has increased in great geometric bounds. This expansion of velocity has not been matched by an equal increase in currency reserves.[38] As a result, there is a basic shortage of foreign exchange throughout the world and, in varying degrees, all nations must be concerned with their balance of international payments. Since the importing of foreign goods is the most immediate cause of the loss of exchange, most host countries are anxious to induce investors to enter their countries for the purpose of stimulating local manufacture. If in addition to curtailing imports, the new enterprise can develop added exports, it is particularly welcome in most areas of the world.

Investment within a country can employ a great amount of capital goods or it can utilize a proportionately greater amount of local labor. To a significant degree, the less developed countries such as Chile are anxious to provide employment for their populace.[39] They see such activity to be a stage in training their people for a more qualified participation in industrial life. On the other hand, the more industrialized countries view the need for large amounts of labor as an undesirable inflationary pressure and only seek to stimulate such investment in special underemployed areas (e.g. Italy's Mezzogiorno, Brazil's Northeast, Belgium's Borinage.)

The importation of capital goods is equated with an improvement in the technological resources of the country. Where such importation is reasonably consistent with the balance of payments and employment objectives, it will be encouraged. Probably, in the long run, the host country will benefit even more than the investor from this aspect of investment since it tends to lower the competitive costs within the area and makes the host country a more stable trading partner with other

---

[38] "Annual Forecast Part III," *Business International,* Oct. 27, 1967, p. 339.

[39] Henry Lee, "Guerrillas, Joint Ventures, and Oil," *Business Abroad,* Oct. 2, 1967, p. 18.

nations of the world. However, without full employment the production of product for the local market can be socially and politically unwise.

In some cases the major nations of the world have stimulated investment as a means to military self-sufficiency. Thus, England and France have urged the development of activities in computers, rocketry, aircraft, and lasers. Obviously, these activities have certain commercial values, but for military reasons they are maintained on a national basis even when the related products can be more profitably imported from abroad.

For the above specific reasons and perhaps also for the more intangible one of national pride, nations invite their international colleagues to invest in their country so as to increase productive facilities. For the most part, the experiences have been satisfactory, but it should be noted that investments which are not directly related to the basic needs of the host country have a great potential for eventual embarrassment.

Incentives for investment and expansion

The establishment of a significant foreign activity usually requires a material amount of capital investment and an extended period of reduced income. Most foreign investment incentives aim at cushioning the shock of this initial period of liquidity pressures.[40] Since it is impossible to present a comprehensive list of the incentives offered by the various host countries, the following illustrative items are tabulated as an indication of the type of advantage which has been offered.

1. Investment grants. In various forms these grants rebate to the investor a portion of his cost for investments in plant and machinery. In some countries the subsidy is handled as a reduction of taxes due, while in others a direct reimbursement is made.

2. Training allowances. Since it is recognized that the improvement of the skills of the local work force is nationally advantageous, allowances are granted for each worker of a given class who is employed during a given period. Both classes and on-the-job activity may be involved in the related training.

3. Fast and redundant depreciation. Where a large part of the investment involves capital goods, it is important to recover untaxed income to permit timely payment of the suppliers. This is accomplished by various forms of quick depreciation which lower the reported taxable profit in the early years of the asset life. In some cases depreciation has been authorized which exceeded cost or its price-adjusted equivalent.

4. Treatment of special reserves. Expansion is encouraged by the use of special reserves which defer the taxation of profits until the reserves

---

[40] Studies in Business Policy No. 115, *Obstacles and Incentives to Private Foreign Investment 1962–1964*, National Industrial Conference Board (1965), p. 33.

are reversed. These reserves give substantial flexibility to the reporting of income and its related taxation.

5. Export bonuses. In some countries a bonus is paid by the government on all goods exported. In a few cases this is related to a rebate of amounts paid for import duties.
6. Preferential duties. To stimulate local production, many countries offer major tariff walls to investors. This protection subsidizes the local operation during its dangerous years of initial operation by eliminating effective international competition.
7. Duty exemptions. Permission is sometimes granted for the duty-free import of capital goods or raw materials.
8. Tax holidays. Freedom from income tax or local property tax for a stipulated period of years is often offered as an inducement for investment, particularly when it is to the original investor in the particular industry.[41]
9. Low-cost loans. Some governments have arranged for supplies of initial credit and in some cases have subsidized the interest costs.

The above incentives are typical of the concessions made available by various foreign agencies. They are of particular importance to Americans now that the mandatory program on the balance of payments of the United States has sharply limited the ability of international companies to use their domestic financial resources for foreign development. Reference to the various guides on trade and taxes will provide a more particular insight into the programs used by each country.

Economic restrictions

The financial requirement involved in starting a new or expanded foreign operation is dependent to a large extent on the available investment incentives, but the continued safety and profitable operation of the enterprise is more likely to depend on the various economic restrictions affecting business within the host nation and in respect to international relationships.

The U.S. financial executive operating internationally usually finds himself frustrated by the practices of tax administration. In general, the written regulations will appear adequate; but the disbelief in reported data, the continuous negotiation, the harassment of the foreigner, and the general instability of rates seriously undermine managerial confidence and interfere with effective planning. In countries such as Brazil and Italy, there is great room for continued improvement but, fortunately, as countries mature in international practice their tax administrations usually become more reliable. It is obvious that the enforcement of tax law is more important than the form of the law itself.

---

[41] "Brazil: Costa e Silva Begins to Build," *Business Abroad*, Aug. 7, 1967, p. 13.

Private industry in some countries is obstructed in its expansion programs because the state-owned industries have been given monopoly or preferential situations (e.g. utilities, railroads, tobacco). Needless to say, when there has been a recent history of the extension of such government interests, the private investor must recognize the possibility of further intervention and, in any case, he must be prepared to overcome any special advantage affecting his own activities.

In some countries the government has found it desirable to protect the interest of its local investors by requiring certain guarantees from the international owners. Thus, in Germany, "control agreements" identified the nature of foreign interest and protected the equity interests of the minority shareholders in foreign subsidiaries. But even where no formal document exists, the foreign investor must always be most circumspect in his actions.

Legislation of a socialistic nature often creates unrealistic working arrangements in foreign subsidiaries. Thus, in Spain, the inability to discharge workers places an intolerable strain on profits when the business cycle slows down. Similarly, in Brazil, the extremely high employment severance payments make it difficult to achieve qualitative improvements in the work force. In general, the high level of traditional or mandatory fringe benefits adds significantly to the cost of investing abroad and may even inhibit investment unless exceptional profits are available.

American managers are largely accustomed to operating in a relatively free financial environment and under conditions of mild—though persistent—inflation. It is essential that they learn new approaches when they must contend with the multiple exchange rates, currency controls, and highly spasmodic inflationary tendencies of the foreign world. The granting of premium rates to exporters while offering unfavorable rates to importers; the use of barter, swaps, and hedges; the requirement for getting permission from exchange authorities to pay bills and remit profits; the strict controls and delayed clearance of goods in customs;—all of these are characteristic of international operation. They add materially to the complexity of operation and give added opportunity for the creative activity of the good financial executive.

The requirements for local participation in equity and the restriction on the employment of foreign managers and personnel often establish uneconomic operating conditions. The desire of local nationals to participate in the local activities can be readily understood, but from the viewpoint of the principal investor it is essential that the viability of the enterprise not be destroyed in the pursuit of nationalistic objectives.

The typical American executive is likely to be shocked by basic weaknesses in the international infrastructure. Inadequacy in the banking facilities, lack of appropriate independent auditing, poor codes of commercial practice, weak transportation and communication will cause delays and irritations. Inevitably an allowance must be made for these deficiencies if realistic targets are to be formulated.

Behind all international operation is the ever-present threat of intervention, nationalization, or expropriation. Such action need not take place by decree or legal action; it can in some cases be the inevitable result of rate regulation, biased administration, economic pressures, or enforced sellouts. In any case, the threat lies in the potential loss of assets, and it is wise where such an atmosphere exists to consider the minimization of assets and the maximization of liabilities.[42] It should be noted, however, that nationalization seldom occurs without some form of compensation. The adequacy of such compensation and the loss of developing opportunities is generally more at issue than is the right to repayment. In any event, an increase in local participation and a sharing of patents and licenses will tend to reduce the likelihood of intervention.

Administration of international finance

The identification of the corporate approach to international business and the subsequent consideration of programs for the financing of such operations is of paramount importance. However, it is also necessary to consider the nature of the administrative organization, the reporting practices, and the points of measurement which provide for the subsequent effectiveness of the financial operations.

Organizational expertise

In the international environment there is an inexhaustible need for information, for contacts, and for creative conceptual approaches. Consequently, the usual American patterns of "line and staff" responsibility are subject to alteration. At least, in the larger international operations, the chief local executive becomes more of a contact specialist with government agencies, banks, and major customers than a production or marketing expert. To insure that his approaches are both informed and consistent with the plans of the consolidated group, he is generally supervised by a knowledgeable regional or international headquarters, and he is sometimes given the benefit of advice from foreign directors or from an advisory council of senior foreign business statesmen.[43] The local financial specialists, on the other hand, tend to become more strongly linked to the corporation headquarters and to aim at providing perceptive factual data and at executing the integrated corporate financial programs which derive from such data.

---

[42] Raymond L. Brittenham, "Expropriation of Foreign Investment," *International Handbook of Management*, McGraw-Hill (1965), p. 274.

[43] "What a European Advisory Board Can Do For You," *Business Abroad*, Oct. 30, 1967, p. 10.

The treasurership activity takes on many of the aspects of a government financial department. It must be totally knowledgeable about money movements, availability of funds, and changes in the legal or economic environments. The functional integration of programs for money management are usually directed from a central headquarters point so as to be sure that the programs are consistent and of optimum effectiveness. The central direction is particularly essential when the management organization deviates from the legal structure, because the basic flow of funds and government regulation will follow the legal organization.[44]

The controllership function must be sufficiently independent to be certain that unbiased and realistic financial data will reach the senior executives. Some companies have found it desirable to have all field controllers report directly to the Corporate Controller as a means of heightening the professional standards of reporting. Although this arrangement is conceptually troublesome to foreign executives, it has been found to be both workable and beneficial to all concerned.

Reporting practices

In most foreign countries, finance as an action-oriented influence is a new concept. More customarily, the chief financial executive was the protective confidant of the chief executive and was principally counted upon to deal with government agencies, banks, auditors, and tax people. Only secondarily were his official books of account intended to serve as a dynamic challenge to the operational activities. Moreover, since the "official books" were subject to examination by outsiders, they did not always include all of the data shown in the "private ledgers." From the American viewpoint, the maintenance of the several sets of accounts is felt to have a tendency to destroy the impact of the control system, and is consequently viewed by most Americans as an undesirable tradition. It is certainly true that the multiple sets of accounts has introduced suspicion and confusion into the relationships between corporate management and its local counterparts.

There is a general opinion that the rules of accounting are materially different in foreign countries from those known as "generally accepted accounting principles" in the United States. This subject is reviewed more fully in Chapter 60, "International Accounting," but it is appropriate to say that there are more similarities than differences. However, in accepting financial statements for inclusion in the consolidated corporate reports, it is essential that adjustments be made to conform to commonly understood practices before managerial conclusions are drawn. This is customarily carried out at the headquarters level and is facilitated in

---

[44] B. H. Witham, Jr., *Some Basic Questions, Financing International Operations*, American Management Association, 1965, p. 12.

most international companies by establishing standard practices and formats.

Furthermore, to insure the propriety of all financial reporting—both for internal and external consumption—major companies have emphasized the need for competent audit. In some cases complete reliance is placed on the report of the independent accountant; in others the outside audit is supplemented by internal audits directed from the corporate headquarters. Most of the large independent accounting firms in America have extensive international relationships which permit them to serve the reporting needs of the parent corporation while bridging the gap to local practice and understanding.[45]

The international corporation relies greatly on the professional abilities and objectivity of the large-scale independent accounting firms, and this reliance is a trust that the accounting firms must guard with care.

Profitability measurement

The evaluation of the effective use of corporate resources requires a consistent and realistic statement of financial facts. In this connection it is important that local rules be adjusted to a common standard so that comparative judgments can be drawn more effectively. Although specific local objectives may lead a corporation to adopt practices which take proper advantage of local tax-law reporting practices, or contractual relationships, it is important that these deviations be understood and that they be given recognition when making corporate decisions.

The allocation of capital costs, the sharing of various corporate expenses, and the establishment of reasonable inter-divisional transfer prices are obvious requirements to the improvement of corporate profitability tests. The use of deferred tax accounting, the protection of the accounts from inflationary or currency aberrations, and a consistent approach to depreciation, to inventory costing, and to reserves are also essential steps in sound financial control. The control and accounting procedures of the corporation should contain a formal approach to identifying desired policies and to remaining continuously aware of significant differences. Only through reasonable and uniform practices will the financial reports become usable tools for the evaluation of foreign activities.

Economic indicators

International operations are necessarily associated with the environments in which they exist. The economic and political conditions of those environments will have a material influence on the subsequent corporate

---

[45] Myles L. Mace, "The President and International Operations," *Harvard Business Review*, Nov.-Dec. 1966, p. 78.

operations, and they should therefore be a factor in the related policy decisions.

A knowledge of the actions of competitors and of changes in the specific markets in which a firm is active in highly desirable. In addition, an awareness of certain basic economic indicators will be invaluable. Some of the more commonly quoted indices of macro-economics are as follows:

1. Trade balances
2. National budget totals
3. Wage and employment trends
4. Raw material price indices
5. Population curves
6. Productivity expectations
7. Currency reserves
8. Cost-of-living indices
9. Balance of payments
10. Money in circulation
11. Interest rates
12. Foreign exchange rates

This type of data, when maintained on an historic basis and when reviewed comparatively, can provide an added insight into the probable future profitability of certain operations. With such insight, the financial executive and his colleagues can more effectively channel resources to areas of maximum advantage, while avoiding dangerous locales to the greatest possible extent. Both the initial financing program and its subsequent evolutions can be guided by an awareness of the principal economic trends.

Executive compensation

John J. Grela*

One of the most important accountabilities the chief executive of an organization carries is to develop an executive group which in quality and depth assures effective managerial performance and management continuity. Interwoven with this accountability is a demand upon the chief executive to achieve profitable results as measured by *return on investment* and also by the company's earnings in relation to general and specific trends in the industry and the economy.

Probably the single most important tool the chief executive uses to carry out these and his other accountabilities is the administration of an executive compensation plan, for it is the executive group upon whose shoulders rest the direction and success of the enterprise. The need to attract, retain, and motivate a competent executive group is of prime importance. Whether or not there is success in achieving these aims can turn on how carefully the executive compensation policy is determined, how realistically the compensation plan is constructed, and how skillfully the plan is carried out. The financial executive plays a key role in developing the makeup of the compensation plan, and its administration and control.

Executive compensation policy

To be effective, a company's executive compensation policy must clearly reflect what is to be achieved, and the program which results

---

* Vice President, Organization and Management Development, Sperry Rand Corporation, New York.

from it must provide the means of accomplishing that end. There is need, therefore, for an integrated total plan. The parts must have appropriate relationship to each other and to the whole. Too often, the executive compensation plan is composed of subparts, each designed separately to achieve some subobjective, rather than designed in connection with each other. It should all start with a policy that takes into account the various interests—those of the individual executive, the company, and the stockholders.

The executive compensation policy, then, is aimed at providing executives with fair, competitive compensation commensurate with their contributions to the achievement of company objectives and in a manner which will motivate them to top performance, so that the company receives a maximum *return on its investment* in executive compensation and benefits. Implicit is the need to attract, retain, and motivate competent people. With the increasing shortage of top-talent manpower, the "holding" ability of a plan which resists executive raiding becomes especially important. Thus, a responsive executive compensation plan reflecting these important policy elements would give recognition to the most critical element—the executive himself, and the various factors that motivate him.

The executive at the top of a business organization is to one degree or another interested in a number of things which will influence the compensation and benefits arrangement most meaningful to him. He's interested in a competitive basic salary that will meet his current needs. Additionally, he is interested in some return reflective of his performance—either bonus, deferred compensation, or higher current compensation. To motivate him as a member of the top team and also as one who affects profits, some form of stock option arrangement would have its appeal. Additionally, the matter of income taxes needs to be considered. Finally, consideration should be given to the executive's potential total career earnings and to his final estate possibilities, with a particular tie-in relationship to stock options. An appropriate balance of these factors, and others as well, will produce a plan which carries these main parts: base salary, incentive payments, and stock options.

Base salary

An executive expects to receive a base salary which is fair and competitive, and which will motivate him to top performance. The method by which his salary is determined should make sense to him. He should be able to see logic in two comparisons—one, between his job and those of his colleagues; the other, between his job and similar jobs in other companies. To achieve these ends certain practices should be followed.

Position descriptions

Well written, up-to-date position descriptions for all executive positions are essential to a sound executive compensation plan. They are not only important in the job-evaluation process, but also in selection, development, performance appraisal, clarification of assignments, and other activities. Descriptions should be job-oriented and directed toward the results to be achieved by the position, rather than toward the "duties" or activities which are carried on to achieve these results.

Job evaluation

Some means of measuring the elements of the job is necessary. It ought to provide the basis for fair and rational internal comparisons with the outside market place. It is essential that the evaluation process make sense to the executive.

To be meaningful, the evaluation plan should be oriented toward the job and not the man. It should be one that describes and evaluates the common characteristics of executive jobs no matter how high in the organization—including the president's job. Not every job-evaluation process can be used for executive jobs. Plans that have been developed for lower-level salaried jobs or shop jobs do not apply to the core characteristics of executive jobs.

There are various ways to evaluate executive jobs, but no matter which method is used it will need to take into account these characteristics: the *know-how* that is involved in the position, the *problem solving* or mental contribution required, and finally the *accountability* or the measured effect of the job on end results for which it exists.

Know-how is the sum total of every kind of skill, however acquired, that is needed for acceptable executive performance. There are several kinds of know-how. There is know-how pertaining to procedures, to specialized techniques, and to scientific disciplines. Additionally, there is know-how in the area of human relations. And, from the standpoint of managing, there is the know-how involved in coordinating the functions of the organization: organizing, planning, leading, and controlling.

Problem solving takes into account the original, logical thinking required for making decisions. There are two aspects of problem solving which need to be examined. There is the scope or environment within which the thinking takes place, ranging from a fairly tightly controlled context to one whose limits are only the broadest of principles. The other aspect of problem solving is the challenge presented by the thinking to be done—that is, the range of difficulty of problems to be solved and creativity required.

Accountability is the factor which is concerned with end results. It is the answerability for action and for the consequences of that action. There are several areas to look at in accountability: *freedom to act,* the presence or absence of procedural control and guidance; *job impact on end results,* whether direct or indirect; and *magnitude,* shown by the dollar size of the area affected by the job.

EXHIBIT 1

When the evaluation of executive jobs is carried out in terms of the central, key characteristics of the job, there is opportunity to achieve one of the important needs of an effective executive compensation plan—internal consistency between positions. A scale of point values can be worked out for each of the individual elements of the key job characteristics and these can be totaled to provide point values for the characteristics themselves and thus for the total job. The factor-point method and the guide-chart method are two approaches that are available to the personnel executive who is responsible for job evaluation. The American Management Association describes these methods in its Executive Compensation Service reports. Exhibits 1, 2, and 3 show charts from the guide-chart system developed by Edward N. Hay & Associates. The numbering pattern and text are illustrative only. Sample evaluations of two executive positions are shown in Exhibit 4 using the illustrative charts in Exhibits 1, 2, and 3.

In smaller companies or where the guide-chart evaluation method is not used, some sort of position-ranking method should be followed in

EXHIBIT 2

HAY GUIDE CHART

PROBLEM-SOLVING

Hay Guide Charts are custom designed for each installation.
The numbering pattern and text shown here are illustrative only.

ILLUSTRATIVE E40

Problem Solving is the original, "self-starting" thinking required by the job to: (1) identify, (2) resolve a problem. Ideas are put together from something already there. Therefore, Problem Solving is treated as a percentage utilization of Know-How.

Thinking Within:

		THINKING CHALLENGE				
		1. REPETITIVE Identical situations requiring solution by simple choice of learned things.	2. PATTERNED Similar situations requiring solution by discriminating choice of learned things.	3. INTERPOLATIVE Differing situations requiring search for solutions within area of learned things.	4. ADAPTIVE Variable situations requiring analytical, interpretative, evaluative, and/or constructive thinking.	5. CREATIVE Novel or nonrecurring pathfinding situations requiring the development of new concepts and imaginative approaches.	
T H I N K I N G E N V I R O N M E N T	**A. STRICT ROUTINE:** Simple rules and detailed instructions.	10%	15%	20%	25%	30%	A
	B. ROUTINE: Established routines and standing instructions.	12%	18%	24%	30%	40%	B
	C. SEMI-ROUTINE: Somewhat diversified procedures and precedents.	14%	21%	28%	36%	50%	C
	D. STANDARDIZED: Substantially diversified procedures and specialized standards.	16%	24%	33%	44%	60%	D
	E. CLEARLY DEFINED: Clearly defined policies and principles.	18%	28%	38%	52%	70%	E
	F. BROADLY DEFINED: Broad policies and specific objectives.	21%	32%	44%	60%	80%	F
	G. GENERALLY DEFINED: General policies and ultimate goals.	24%	36%	50%	70%	90%	G

EDWARD N. HAY & ASSOCIATES
COPYRIGHT 1968

order to develop the internal relationships of executive jobs to each other. A simple way is to develop a series of salary ranges or grades sufficient to cover all positions to be evaluated and then employ a committee composed of the general manager, the personnel head, and the financial head to analyze position descriptions, organization charts, and job scope and then classify the jobs within the various salary ranges. If a point system of evaluation is used, a determination can be made as to what spread of point values apply to each pay range or grade. Whatever the method of evaluation or ranking used, once the relative relationships are worked out there is then a basis for comparison with salaries paid for similar jobs in other companies.

EXHIBIT 3

HAY GUIDE CHART

ACCOUNTABILITY

Hay Guide Charts are custom designed for each installation.
The numbering pattern and text shown here are illustrative only.   ILLUSTRATIVE E40

Accountability is the answerability for action and for its consequences. It is the measured effect of the job on end results. It comprises:
• Freedom to Act.
•• Job Impact on End Results — as defined below.
••• Magnitude of area most clearly affected by the job.

••• MAGNITUDE (ANNUAL DOLLARS)

•• IMPACT

	1. VERY SMALL OR INDETERMINATE				2. SMALL				3. MEDIUM				4. LARGE				
	Under $				$ to $				$ to $				$ to $				
	Remote	Contrib	Shared	Primary	Remote	Contrib	Shared	Primary	Remote	Contrib	Shared	Primary	Remote	Contrib	Shared	Primary	
A. PRESCRIBED: Detailed instructions under close supervision.	10	15	20	25	14	19	22	29	20	27	33	44	25	38	52	66	A
B. CONTROLLED: Established work routines. Close supervision.	15	20	25	30	22	33	44	55	30	40	50	66	50	68	77	99	B
C. STANDARDIZED: Standardized practices and procedures. Supervision of progress and results.	22	33	44	55	30	44	66	88	40	55	75	100	75	90	110	140	C
D. GENERALLY REGULATED: Practices covered by well defined policy. Supervisory review.	40	50	66	80	40	66	90	120	60	88	130	190	100	120	145	220	D
E. DIRECTED: Broad practice covered by functional precedents and policies.	50	70	100	130	66	99	133	200	100	125	200	300	150	180	230	330	E
F. ORIENTED DIRECTION: Functional policies and goals.	80	120	160	200	110	144	200	300	150	185	300	400	210	260	360	440	F
G. GUIDANCE:	120	170	220	300	160	200	300	400	220	330	440	550	310	420	540	700	G

(left vertical label) FREEDOM TO ACT

•• IMPACT OF JOB ON END RESULTS

EDWARD N. HAY & ASSOCIATES
COPYRIGHT 1968

1. REMOTE: Recording or incidental services for use by others.
2. CONTRIBUTORY: Advisory or facilitating services for use by others.
3. SHARED: Participating with others in taking action.
4. PRIMARY: Controlling impact on end results.

External comparisons

Just as important as internal consistency is the ability of the executive compensation plan to have external consistency—that is, the ability to make meaningful comparisons of jobs between related companies. (The uselessness of comparisons simply by job title is evident.) Of course, the end purpose of such comparison is the determination of the market price of executive jobs. An evaluation system based on the central characteristics of the executive job—know-how, problem-solving, and accountability factors—will provide the basis for meaningful external comparisons

EXHIBIT 4

Title	Know-How	Problem Solving	Accountability	Total
General Manager....................	G IV 3 109	F 5 (80%) 87	F 3 Prime 400	596
Marketing Manager.................	F III 3 95	F 4 (60%) 57	E 3 Prime 300	452

EXHIBIT 5

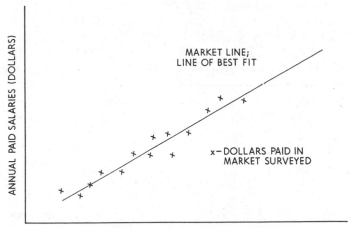

MARKET LINE;
LINE OF BEST FIT

x – DOLLARS PAID IN
MARKET SURVEYED

ANNUAL PAID SALARIES (DOLLARS)

EVALUATION POINTS OR JOB RANK – AS ASSIGNED TO PAY GRADES

and assessments of the market price. Comparisons are made through the conduct of a salary survey of jobs, which have been or can be identified in terms of evaluations applied to jobs internally. In a sense, all surveyed jobs, regardless of company affiliation, are identified and related to each other as though they existed in one company. With the relationships so derived, a "market line" can be established by plotting evaluation points or the pay grades of surveyed jobs versus dollars actually paid, as illustrated in Exhibit 5. Once the market values are known the company is then able to make a business decision. It can set the pay rates it feels are needed to attract and retain its key executives and at costs the

EXHIBIT 6

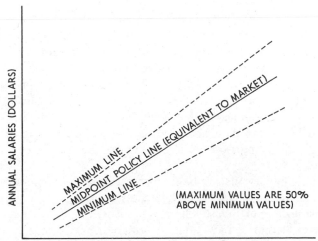

MAXIMUM LINE
MIDPOINT POLICY LINE (EQUIVALENT TO MARKET)
MINIMUM LINE

(MAXIMUM VALUES ARE 50%
ABOVE MINIMUM VALUES)

ANNUAL SALARIES (DOLLARS)

EVALUATION POINTS OR JOB RANK – AS ASSIGNED TO PAY GRADES

company is prepared to pay. Exhibit 6 shows what a company's pay policy line might look like if it decided to meet the market. The maximum and minimum lines are derived from the midpoint of prevailing salary line. The percentage spread between the minimum and maximum values generally is smaller at the low end of the line and greater at the high end. Many companies use a point spread of 35 percent at the low end and 50 percent at the upper end.

Exhibit 7 shows what a company using pay grades might do in making comparisons of their paid salaries with those reported in a survey.

EXHIBIT 7

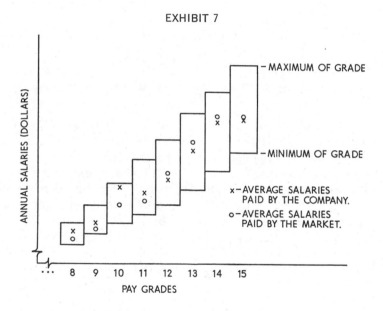

Conducting salary comparisons with other companies calls for a high degree of realism and objectivity. The jobs being compared must be broken down into their core elements so that there is assurance that the jobs are indeed comparable. Additionally, similar companies in similar industries should be compared. Yet there must be a sufficiently broad cross section of companies so that there is adequate perspective in the comparison. Then, the data analyzed and presented should permit understanding and comparison without being buried in a sea of meaningless averages.

The actual comparisons can be made by having the responsible official sit face-to-face with his counterpart in the surveyed company and determine comparability of jobs by breaking them into their elements. The subsequent exchange of pay range information and actual paid rates is thus more meaningful.

It is not necessary to survey or compare every single job. A representative sampling of jobs is sufficient as long as the internal relationships between the various jobs are consistent. Appropriate salary lines and grades can be constructed from the sampling of bench-mark jobs.

Salary survey information is available from a number of sources so that it is not necessary for a company to conduct its own survey. The A.M.A. Executive Compensation Service produces annual survey reports of executive compensation in small, medium, and large organizations. Referral to this service will provide helpful comparative information. McKinsey & Company, the National Industrial Conference Board, the U.S. Department of Labor, and others report salary information. Edward N. Hay and Associates prepare salary information related to the guide chart evaluation system.

In summary, the procedures used to obtain salary survey information should withstand the scrutiny and test of the executive heads and boards of directors who are asked to approve the recommendations which are based on the survey results.

Incentive compensation

An increasing number of companies are including incentive compensation—bonus payments—in their total executive compensation program. In a survey conducted by the A.M.A. almost half the companies covered reported making bonus payments.

A general approach is to pay a competitive base salary plus some amount as bonus. The competitive nature of the base pay is determined by surveying the base pay in comparable bonus-paying companies. A somewhat different approach is to establish the base pay (or base-pay line) at some discount (10 percent, 15 percent, etc.) below the competitive base line, but then pay a larger bonus and with stimulated performance have the "new" total compensation be even greater than under the first approach. This second approach is more appropriately applicable only to the very top positions in an organization. With both approaches the total compensation is surveyed in bonus-paying companies to be sure that base and total pay are competitive.

Incentive compensation is designed to encourage and reward the extra performance of those executives whose positions have substantial impact on profits—the end result of the corporate effort. But like the other elements of an executive compensation program, the procedure for providing incentive payments should be rationally integrated into the whole executive compensation plan. Stated another way, bonus payments are not substitutes for an inadequate base-salary plan. Bonus payments are most effectively used as annual motivators measured against a year's performance and not as a last-minute supplement to base salary. The base salary should stand by itself so as to permit the bonus to do what it is supposed to do—stimulate and reward extra performance. The actual bonus payments can be in the form of cash, stock, or a combination of the two. Some plans permit the election of receiving stock options rather than cash at the time the bonus is awarded.

A bonus plan that meets the tests of fundamental soundness and effectiveness must deal adequately with several critical areas: the source of the bonus money; the amount of bonus money available; who should participate; and the method of bonus distribution.

The *source of bonus money* is profits. Bonus payments are paid for "extra" performance which should result in "extra" profits. If ordinary good performance results in anticipated regular profits, then the base-compensation plan should be adequate. In some situations extra performance may not result in extra profits—or even in profits—but the outstanding performance should be rewarded if the executive's performance minimized losses, possibly in the face of an overwhelming industry-wide condition. This may be a necessary "investment" in order to gain future profits. Ultimately, however, bonus payments must be generated by the extra profits that the stimulated performance of the executive produces.

The amount of *bonus money available* is normally a percentage of profits attained. Whatever the percentage is, the formula should anticipate first a fair return to the owners of the business. The profit goals should be realistic and attainable. Profits are, of course, relative and they vary from industry to industry and company to company. What proportion of the profits under a particular incentive plan should go to the owners and what proportion should be allocated for bonus purposes is one of the more difficult decisions to be made. The formula used to determine the bonus fund should take into account the number of participants and the size of individual bonus award that will have motivating impact. It should provide an amount of money directly related in size to the level of overall business performance during the year under consideration, and should swing up or down from year to year as a function of business performance. Certainly there is no automatic formula, nor should someone else's formula be copied. The formula which is finally developed should be one that is cut to fit a particular company situation. Companies which set aside profits for the owners before distribution of profits in the form of bonuses generally do so by designating a percent of capital representing the amount set aside as a return on the capital investment. When this method is used, this percentage of capital ranges from about 5 to 10 percent. Some companies set even higher percentages. The percent of profits set aside for bonus payments varies to a considerable degree but 10 percent appears to be the rate used by a number of companies with a range of 5 to 15 percent covering the bulk of companies. The financial executive should be directly involved in the establishment of the bonus formula. A review by the financial executive of proxy statements of other companies in the industry will give an indication of prevailing practice. Direct contact with the financial executives in these companies should reveal how the bonus formulas have worked out.

Who should participate in the bonus plan is a question which turns on the basic purpose of the plan. Since the plan should be designed to increase profits, only those positions which have direct or substantial impact on the profitability of the enterprise should participate. There are degrees of impact on profit insofar as bonus participation is concerned. The executives with direct profit-center responsibility of course have impact, but key managers and staff people also have significant impact, although perhaps to a different degree, and are included in the plan. If people are included who do not have real profit impact, then the plan is something other than an incentive plan—it is a "goodwill" type of profit distribution. Too often what has started out as an executive incentive plan has turned into a general profit-sharing arrangement without meaningful motivating ability and which eventually becomes open to most or all management or salaried employees. When a plan is used in this manner, the size of the awards becomes smaller, the motivating power of the money diminishes, and the original purpose of the plan disappears. Again, there is need not only to develop an integrated executive compensation plan with interrelated elements, but there is just as much need to maintain the integrity of the elements and their basic purposes.

The appropriate definition of who should participate can make the difference between getting full measure for the money expended or being worse off than if no bonus were given. If the rules on participation are relaxed and noncontributors to profit are allowed to slip in or are kept in after some change justifies their removal, the program starts to crumble. The motivational value is not only lost, but it becomes negative. When an executive whose performance has been outstanding realizes that politics, favoritism, or indecisiveness has resulted in payment to someone who has either not worked as hard or achieved as much or is not truly in a position to influence profits, the executive thus sees his own share, regardless of size, as less than it should be and meaning less than it should.

Job descriptions which define accountabilities and end results to be achieved will help identify those positions which should participate in bonus distribution. Jobs which have a greater impact upon the organization's total profit performance should have a greater bonus involvement. Jobs which have an impact upon a smaller portion of the profit, or which have less profit-generating possibility should thus have less bonus-generating capability.

Affecting the situation is the degree to which the job permits *freedom to act*. Those jobs with greater freedom to act—and therefore greater freedom to fail—have greater bonus possibilities. Relative freedom to act is a matter of the presence or absence of guides and controls. Thus, jobs eligible for bonus can be separated out in accordance with the degree of freedom to act. Exactly where the line should fall between bonus and nonbonus jobs should be the result of assessment of various organizational factors. With the guide-chart method of evaluation, the *accountability* points provide a measure of impact on end results and thus give an indication of the opportunity to affect profits. Points need not be used, however. More important is the judgment of profit impact on the basis of relative accountability for end results.

Another factor that is looked at in determining eligibility for participation is salary level. A problem with this, however, is that actual salaries have a way of moving up faster than the eligibility salary and soon more people than intended become "eligible." Thus, there can be a tendency to put too much emphasis on salary and not enough on the relationship to profits.

An allocation of bonus money should be based on the executive team's performance relative to its goals. These performance goals are the targets made at the beginning of the year in terms of profits to be gained.

Those individuals who share in the bonus fund should share in accordance with their contributions. More specifically, the amount of bonus an executive should receive depends on how effectively he achieved the results demanded by his job. Decisions affecting bonus awards frequently are made by bonus committees with the president, the financial executive, and the personnel executive as key members.

Investigations indicate that incentive bonuses in American industry run about 30 percent of the pay of those receiving them. This figure varies from industry to industry with a low average of about 10 percent and a high of 50 percent. In addition, within these industries the size of the award varies with the organization level and the function in the company. Consequently, there is considerable variation in the size of individual awards.

Stock options

Too often, stock-option arrangements are developed with no relationship to the other elements of the executive compensation plan. Actually, they can play a key role in shaping an executives total compensation program properly integrated with his estate planning. Stock-option plans are used most effectively where profits and thereby stock prices can be realistically affected by the executive who receives stock options. Though many things may affect the market value or price of a company's stock, the real impact comes from earnings. When the motivating effects of stock options serve to increase earnings, this earnings growth through its effect on the price/earnings ratio serves to enhance the price of the stock and thus brings greater reward potential to option holders. Of course, there are some stocks with unusually high P/E ratios which have been created by factors very little related to current earnings. While there may be some gain to the option holder it can be expected that unusually high P/E ratios cannot be sustained unless they are supported by growth in earnings. An important factor is the executive's influence in growth and earnings which in turn provides improved stock prices and greater stock option values.

Purpose

Like bonus payments, stock options are used as performance motivators. Unlike bonus payments, stock options are generally not short-term motivators, but rather are intended to be long-term motivators. The basic purpose of the stock option is to provide a long-term incentive to the executive to improve profits by offering him an opportunity to share in the profits. In today's atmosphere of high individual taxes and rising stock prices, stock options become attractive to executives.

There are other purposes for incorporating stock options in the total executive compensation plan. Stock options create a proprietary interest on the part of the executive. If he can see the relationship between his ownership of stock and the return to him and to the company as the stock grows in value and income-producing ability, the worthiness of excellent performance on his part is apparent.

Stock options are effective as an inducement in attracting new executives. Base salary and bonus payments alone may not provide the reward and challenge to induce high-talent executives to join the company. Stock options serve to attract the executive who has the ability to affect profits favorably.

Stock options are useful not only in attracting executives, but also in retaining them. They provide the stake in the company that keeps the top executive producing and satisfied. Of course, the important by-product is the continuity of the top management group.

From a personal viewpoint, stock options enable the individual executive to enhance his own situation. They provide a hedge against inflationary forces. At the same time, if the company is doing well, they are adding to the executive's personal capital resources and, of course, there are the advantages of potential long-term capital gains treatment. All this can be a planned part of the executive's retirement income and his personal estate.

"Qualified" plans

Under Internal Revenue regulations a "qualified" stock option is one which is granted after December 31, 1963 and meets specified requirements. The advantage of a plan which complies with the Internal Revenue Code and which provides "qualified" stock options lies in its beneficial tax treatment. It is indeed important to have competent tax advice in developing the stock option arrangement in order to obtain desirable tax features. In general, while there are a number of features to consider in connection with a "qualified" stock option, one of the main features is that the option is not exercisable after the expiration of five years from the date the option is granted. Another key requirement is that no disposition of shares be made within the three-year period beginning on the day after the day of transfer of shares if long-term capital gains treatment is desired. If the 1954 Internal Revenue Code requirements are met, the executive exercising an option is entitled to long-term capital gains benefits on profits obtained from selling stock acquired under a "qualified" stock option plan. Also he does not realize income at the time of the granting of the option or upon receiving the stock by exercising his option.

"Nonqualified" stock option

So-called "nonqualified" stock-option plans can be used. The terms and conditions for eligibility, participation, and duration can be varied but the essential characteristic is simply that either the granting or the exercise of such an option results in fully taxable ordinary income. The granting of the option is the taxable event if the option has a readily ascertainable fair market value under specific IRS tests; otherwise the exercise of the option is the taxable event. However, appreciation occurring after the taxable event is subject to potential long-term capital gains treatment. Since the nonqualified stock option has unusual features, careful tax planning is necessary to prevent unexpected tax hardships on the employee. A different kind of plan is the phantom stock plan where stock is not actually issued, but the appreciation of the stock and accumulated dividends are granted from the date of the award until termination of the arrangement. Here, there is no favorable long-term capital gains benefit.

Restricted stock plans

A number of companies have found it worthwhile to use a restricted stock plan because of the favorable tax treatment that has been possible for the executive. Under the restricted stock arrangement the executive is given a bonus in the form of stock but with restrictions as to disposition. Usually he is prohibited from selling or otherwise disposing of the stock during his employment or for some duration of time. From a tax standpoint, the restrictions on disposition are designed to eliminate taxable income to the employee at the time he receives the stock. When the restrictions end, the executive is subject to ordinary income tax on either the value of the stock at the time the restrictions end or at the time the stock was transferred, whichever is less. If at the time the stock is sold it has appreciated in value, he receives capital gains treatment for the appreciated amount.

The Treasury Department recently proposed to remove the tax advantage for restricted stock, and legislative proposals intended to accomplish that purpose were pending before Congress in mid-1969.

Participants

The number of participants in a stock-option plan and the eligibility of the participants are matters of not just passing importance, but of basic significance. Again, the answer turns on an understanding of the objectives to be accomplished by the executive compensation plan and more specifically the stock-option plan. The main purpose of the plan is to provide a longer-term incentive to top performance on the part of those who have impact on the profit results of the organization. Consequently, the number of participants should be restricted to those who have significant profit impact. To increase the number for goodwill purposes turns it into a goodwill plan, cuts down the amount of stock available to top officers and key employees, and dilutes the impact of a stock-option program.

By and large the actual declarations of persons eligible to receive options is left to the discretion of the president and an option committee, but those named usually fall within the broader category of officers and key executives. Generally these are positions with influence on the long-term results of the company. There are relatively few positions of this nature as contrasted with jobs having short-term influence. Occasionally, minimum screening requirements are set such as amount of base salary and length of service. For example, in some companies an executive must earn $20,000 per year to be eligible, but in many companies the amount is higher. In some companies executives above age 65 are ineligible to take part. Under some arrangements executives must have a certain amount of minimum service, such as two or three years, to be eligible. Though there is a correlation between salary and profit impact, just using a specified salary as a floor for eligibility purposes can cause inequities. Eligibility based on an evaluation of a combination of salary floor and a recognition of the inherent impact of the job in long-term growth and profitability of the company is a much sounder approach.

Individual allotments

Since the purpose of a stock option is to provide an incentive, the size of the individual allotment ought to be large enough to provide the incentive to give top performance. Most plans do not specify precise amounts of stock to be granted, except that the maximum amount an individual may receive is frequently specified. How much to grant, then, must be rather carefully assessed. One of the dangers in allotting too much is that it might become more of an inducement to leave than an incentive to perform. On the other hand, granting too little can also be discouraging and result in departure. For example, if a $25,000 per year executive is given an option for 5,000 shares of a stock selling at 50 in a company with even a moderate growth rate, it won't be long before he has a substantial equity position that tends to give him an "independent" feeling. Complicating it, of course, is the problem of raising a quarter of a million dollars. It typically means that much of the stock gets sold to pay for what can be retained. On the other hand, if the same $25,000 per year executive is given an option for 200 shares selling at 50, it can produce the feeling that he ought to look to some other employer for a more adequate portion of options. A more realistic thing to do is to grant perhaps a 500 or 1,000 share option to the $25,000 per year executive. If, say, he is receiving a 20 percent bonus, on the average, there is good likelihood he will be able to pay for the option without selling any or much of the stock.

Thus, a way to deal with the matter of individual allotments is to plan on granting smaller allotments, but more frequently and over a longer period of time. Thus, there can be a long-term tie-in to what the executive's estate can be, progression toward achieving this goal, and reasonable balance with the speed with which the benefits should be obtained. Yet there is sufficient flexibility in the plan to deal with someone whose performance falls off and who might otherwise be left sitting with large options. The string of smaller options can be interrupted or completely discontinued. Also, there is less chance of a top executive cashing in on a large allotment of options and leaving the company for another company where he picks up a large batch of new options. Further, if there is an understanding that there can be additional grants, the individual is likely to accept a smaller grant.

A balancing factor in determining the size of the individual allotment is that an extra-large grant may create financial burdens that the executive can manage only by wholesale cashing in or may result in his inability to raise all the cash required. If the number of shares granted has some relationship to the executive's current financial situation and his ability to pay, there is a better chance that he will retain the shares and thus achieve one of the objectives of a stock-option plan—the promotion of equity interest in the company.

Exercise of options

In planning an option program attention will have to be given to the administrative matters involved in the exercise of options. Most plans require a *waiting period* following the grant of the option before it can be exercised. The usual waiting period is one year. A number of plans permit the exercise of the option only on an *installment basis.*

Under the current Internal Revenue provisions the maximum option period is limited to five years. Most option plans now allow this maximum period. Those plans that provide installment exercising, frequently call for 25 percent of the option to be eligible for exercise for each of four years after a waiting period of one year.

In view of the objective of using the stock-option plan as a means of retaining executives, most plans call for the *cancellation of future exercise rights* if the executive terminates. Many plans provide for the transfer of options by will or by inheritance.

In view of the fact that tax laws are constantly changing, the foregoing must be viewed only as ideas to be considered in developing a comprehensive compensation plan, the details of which must be thoroughly tax tested not only at the design stage but with every change in tax laws or regulations.

Deferred compensation plans

The need for an integrated executive compensation plan which carefully relates the various elements to each other becomes increasingly clear as the compensation of particular executives reaches relatively high levels. Valued top executives whose services the organization needs to retain will find less and less meaning to a salary increase when their salaries are in the top brackets. Rising personal income taxes will take their toll. When executives are at high compensation levels and are approaching retirement, some form of deferred compensation tends to have increasing significance when contrasted with current income. Moreover, such deferred arrangements help keep top executives from moving to other companies.

It doesn't automatically follow that a deferred compensation plan is desirable for all executives. It can well be that an executive will be better off taking the money currently and paying the added tax because he will be able to invest or otherwise use the money to better advantage. Thus, to some executives, a deferred plan would cost them money by depriving them of the use of the money and the income it would generate. Consequently, in developing a deferred compensation plan it is important to make its application on an individual basis and responsive to the particular executive's personal situation.

The *income tax* aspects of deferred compensation plans require careful review. Basically, the deferred compensation arrangements currently possible and applicable to the needs of top executives are "nonqualified" in that they do not comply with certain provisions of the Internal Revenue Code. The general aim is to provide "reasonable" compensation that can be declared a deductible business expense. Deductions are taken when the deferred compensation is paid and not when it is earned. From the standpoint of the employee, however, it becomes important that he doesn't find that the compensation was constructively received at the time the awards were made. Consequently, to avoid this possible pitfall, tax counsel should be used in the formative stages of the plan.

The *establishment of funds* and the *amount of awards* are generally worked out in the same way as for current incentive payments, or bonus payments, because in many instances what is being deferred is the incentive compensation. A whole variety of ways of *timing deferred payments* can be developed. A way which takes into consideration the purposes of deferred compensation is to grant a portion of the award the first year, say 20 percent, and stretch out the balance over the following five years. The form of award does not necessarily have to be cash. The particular circumstances can be benefited by an award of a combination of cash and stock.

Sometimes, because of the particular situation facing a company, it is desirable to work out some deferral arrangement for bonus payments. A deferred profit-sharing plan can be used where a percentage of profits is transferred to individual accounts and actual payment is deferred until retirement.

As with the other features of an executive compensation plan, it is important to look carefully at executive needs before deciding what must be done in the area of deferred compensation.

Employment contracts

For special individual situations it may be desirable to use employment contracts. They are used primarily to induce the continued employment of a particularly valuable employee or to secure the employment of a highly-talented individual.

Contracts which cover current compensation arrangements simply state as key features the amount of compensation and the duration of the contract period.

Contracts which have deferred compensation arrangements are designed to provide some degree of security and continuity of compensation over a period of years. The provisions of deferred compensation employment contracts are fairly basic. They cover an annual salary for a period during which the executive holds and performs his job satisfactorily. The period is of either a stated duration or until retirement or termination. The other main provision covers the size and duration of deferred payments beginning at termination.

Many employment contracts have contingencies with regard to future services of the executives. The most common contingencies call for the executive to act as consultant to the company after he ceases employment, and to agree not to enter into any competitive activity during the life of the contract.

Care must be taken when deciding to use an employment contract for some special individual, since it can be construed by other key executives as favored treatment and it might generate dissatisfaction. Too often an employment contract is used to "contain" an executive who is no longer useful. When there is no other suitable course of action available this has been done, but it is probably a case of taking the easy way rather than dealing with the personnel problem at hand—of reassigning or retiring or terminating an executive who is no longer carrying his weight. The endless possibilities of contract terms make the employment contract a really individual part of the total executive compensation plan.

Executive compensation administration

The chief executive needs at some point to look at the various elements of the executive compensation plan and decide whether the plan is operating the way it should. He will turn to the financial executive and the personnel executive and want to examine with them the performance and turnover of the executive group, the costs to the company of the plan, and the measures that determine whether company objectives are being met. Plan administration and control require sensitive attention.

Communications

If a key objective of the executive compensation plan is to attract, retain, and motivate competent executives, then the executives need to understand how the plan works. They also need to know that the plan does achieve its objectives. Therefore, there ought to be clear communications with each executive as to how each element fits into the whole and how each affects him personally. It is especially important that the executive understand the workings of the incentive arrangement so that he knows how his performance relates to the return he receives.

Cost

When all the elements of the executive compensation plan are fully integrated in terms of central purpose and goals, and when the elements are carefully designed to meet the problems of the particular company situation, the top executives charged with the administration of the plan have a management tool of considerable usefulness. For the first time the top management of the company may be in a truly realistic position to know what executive compensation costs and whether these costs are high or low, reasonable or unreasonable. It's another way of saying that the top management team is in a position to make sound business

EXHIBIT 8.   Bonus Plan 19__

(relationships: division characteristics versus accountability points)

Division	Total Accountability Points	Revenue v. Accountability Points	Assets v. Accountability Points	Total Employees v. Accountability Points	Payroll v. Accountability Points	Bonus $ v. Accountability Points	No. of Bonus Employees v. Accountability Points
A. This year........							
Last year........							
B. 19___........							
19___........							
C. 19___........							
19___........							
Etc.							
Division total........							
Executive offices 19___.....							
19___.....							
Total 19___.....							
19___.....							

EXHIBIT 9.   Bonus Plan 19__

(relationships: bonus dollars versus divison characteristics)

Division	Bonus Dollars	Bonus $ v. Revenue	Bonus $ v. Assets	Average Bonus per Division Employees	Average Bonus v. Bonus Employees	Bonus $ v. Payroll
A. This year........						
Last year........						
B. 19___........						
19___........						
C. 19___........						
19___........						
Etc.						
Division total........						
Executive offices 19___.....						
19___.....						
Total 19___.....						
19___.....						

decisions. For example, studies can be made as to the cost of managing one division as compared to another. Studies can be made as to the executive costs per revenue dollar or per profit dollar or on some other basis. The cost of levels of management can be determined and related to standards for acceptable performance. Exhibit 8 shows how accountability points can be related to various operating unit characteristics such as revenue, assets, and so on. Bonus costs both on an individual basis and on a group basis will reveal costs of short-term incentives so that profit results can be assessed with respect to this. Exhibit 9 reveals a way of relating bonus dollars to assets, payroll, and so on.

Unit performance

Exhibit 10 shows a form which can be used to review division or unit performance. Based on the relative performance of each of the units, the total bonus fund can be allocated. The following scale should be used by the division president to rate the performance of his operating units:

> 150—Readily recognized superior
> 125—Above expectancy
> 100—Fully satisfactory
> 75—Not satisfactory, corrective action in process
> 50—Not satisfactory, basic action in process

The Summary Performance Rating should reflect the overall impression of the division president, not the sum of individual item ratings. Columns 1, 2, and 3 provide the basic measurement of division performance which is summarized in Rating Column A. Columns 4 through 10 provide a rating of management factors, which are summarized in Rating Column B. In the determination of the Final Summary Rating, the overall divisional performance rating (Column A) may be modified by the rating of management factors (Column B). This modified rating is the Final Summary Rating, which is recorded in Column C. In all cases, not only performance but the degree of difficulty on specific assignments should be considered.

Items 1–4   Do not use Rating Scale, but report Actual Performance as percentage to Plan.

Item 5   Asset Management. Consider the adequacy of handling specific programs agreed upon regarding turnover, the aging of receivables, the handling of inventories, rental machines, etc.

Item 6   Consider the concern for and quality of planning beyond operational fiscal year plans.

Item 7   Give an overall rating to the quality and potential of the management group in each organizational unit.

Item 8   Evaluate the organizational unit's replacement charts, considering the overall quality and current availability of candidates.

EXHIBIT 10

Executive Bonus Plan Performance Measurement

ACTUAL PERFORMANCE TO PLANS			EFFECTIVENESS OF STRATEGIC PROGRAMS					DIVISION ORGANIZATION UNIT	QUALITY AND POTENTIAL OF MANAGERIAL CAPABILITY				A	B	C	COMMENTS
(1)	(2)	(3)	(4) GROWTH			(5)	(6)		(7)	(8)	(9)	(10)	Summary Rating	Summary Rating	Final Summary Rating	
Revenue	Profit Before Taxes	R O A Before Taxes	% Increase Revenue	% Increase Profit	5-Year Average	Asset Management	Planning		Incumbents	Replacements	Corporate Cooperation	Personnel	Columns 1,2,3.	Columns 4-10		
			5-Year Average	5-Year Average												

REVIEWS

Div. Pres. Signature _____ Date

Corporate Signature _____ Date

EXHIBIT 11

Executive Bonus Plan

(1) Organization Unit/Fund Bonus .... $ _____

(2) Total Adjusted Accountability Points (Total All Column 9) _____

(3) Value Per Point (1 divided by 2) . . . . $ _____

(13) Division Organization Unit _____

Page _____ of _____

(4) Fiscal Year Ending March 31, 1968

PARTICIPANTS' NAME AND TITLE		Bonus Paid			(5) Salary to be Paid Year Ending 3/31/69	(6) Performance Rating %	(7) Total Evaluation Points	(8) Accountability Points	(9) Adjusted Points (6) x (8)	Bonus Recommended (10)		(11) Total Compensation (5) + (10a)	(12) Bonus Approved if Different From Col. (10a)	COMMENTS
Name	Title	(a) Actual Salary Paid $	(b) Amount $	(c) Percent of Salary	(d) Total Compensation $						(a) Amount (9) x (3)	(b) Percent of Salary (5)			
Total		Total	Average	Total		Total			Total = (2)	Total = (1)	Average	Total	Total	

CORPORATE APPROVAL

_____ (Participants This Page)

$ _____ (Total Approved Bonus)

PLEASE COMPLETE TOTALS, EACH PAGE.

Item 9   Rate the unit's overall response to others. Consider the unit's response to corporate needs, task force services, and intra-divisional assignments.

Item 10   Consider the quality of the personnel function as well as any key programs in recruitment, selection, wage and salary administration, and labor relations training. Also consider the image the division conveys to prospective employees, the morale of present employees, and the turnover rate compared to others.

Individual bonus awards

Once the bonus fund has been allocated to the individual units, a form similar to Exhibit 11 can be used to arrive at bonus allocations for individual employees. The references to accountability points are applicable to organizations using the guide-chart evaluation method. Ac-

EXHIBIT 12
Performance Rating on Present Job

150—Exceptional promise.
125—Above expectancy in present job, a developmental potential.
100—Fully competent.
 75—Needs improvement, has potential to grow to satisfactory level in this or other job (should be rated 50 if subsequent experience does not show expected promise).
 50—Inadequate, some action is planned.

countability points need not be used, however, and judgments based on performance can be made to arrive at the amounts of the bonus awards. The performance rating scale in Exhibit 12 should be used to evaluate the individual's performance in his job.

Controls

Budgeting is the basic way to plan and control compensation expenditures. Each unit anticipates over the fiscal year what additions and deletions will be made to the executive force and in its dollar net change. Anticipated salary changes are also considered. Standard budgetary forms and procedures are more than adequate to determine what the changes are to be and to keep track of them as they occur.

The use of compa-ratios is helpful in reviewing the status of both individuals and departments and comparing them with other individuals and departments. The compa-ratio is obtained by comparing an actual salary to some comparison point, i.e., the ratio of the actual salary to the midpoint or the ratio of the average of the actuals to the average midpoint of the department or pay group being compared. Exhibit 13

EXHIBIT 13

Pay versus Performance

Salary Ranges: Mid = $20.00 P + $2500.00

Job No.	Position and Name	Total Points	Annual Salary "A"	x .80% = min.	Midpoint "M"	x 120% = max.	Position in Range (A/M) %
	GROUP 1						
1	Jones	1450	$ 32,000	$25,200	$ 31,500	$37,800	102
2	Smith	1150	28,000	20,400	25,500	30,600	110
3	White	1100	23,000	20,300	24,500	30,500	94
4	Adams	800	17,000	14,800	18,500	22,000	92
	CR = 100	4500	$100,000		$100,000		
	GROUP 2						
5	Hunt	700	$ 16,000	13,200	$ 16,500	19,800	97
6	Pilgrim	680	13,500	12,900	16,100	19,300	84
7	Flynn	640	12,100	12,200	15,300	18,400	*79
8	Lynch	600	12,500	11,600	14,500	17,400	86
9	Black	580	14,900	11,300	14,100	16,900	105
10	Edwards	500	11,000	10,000	12,500	15,000	87
11	Hilton	425	10,000	8,800	11,000	13,200	91
	CR = 90	4125	$ 90,000		$100,000		
	GROUP 3						
12	Conrad	400	11,000	8,400	10,500	12,600	104
13	Franks	375	9,000	8,000	10,000	12,000	90
14	Johnson	325	12,000	7,200	9,000	10,800	133#
15	Bailey	325	11,000	7,200	9,000	10,800	122#
16	Rooney	325	10,000	7,200	9,000	10,800	111
17	Waters	325	10,000	7,200	9,000	10,800	111
18	Gould	325	9,000	7,200	9,000	10,800	100
19	Hill	325	8,000	7,200	9,000	10,800	89
20	Rivers	300	10,000	6,800	8,500	10,200	118
21	Carroll	300	10,000	6,800	8,500	10,200	118
22	Henry	300	10,000	6,800	8,500	10,200	118
	CR = 110	3625	$110,000		$100,000		
	Grand Total	12,250	$300,000		$300,000		

Position in Range $(\frac{A}{M})$ %: columns 1 = 80%, 2 = 88%, 3 = 96%, 4 = 104%, 5 = 112%, 120%

* = Below Min.   Above Max. = #

PERFORMANCE: 1 Marginal, 2 Fair, 3 Acceptable, 4 Commendable, 5 Distinguished

Legend: ⊗ Performance Higher   ✕ Pay Higher

shows the use of the compa-ratio (CR) in the comparison of several jobs.

Exhibit 13 is a convenient and oftentimes revealing way to relate pay to performance as well as cost.

The company which does not have a sound executive compensation plan faces serious administrative problems. High-level managers and professionals are increasingly mobile, and with the increase in early-vesting pension plans, this trend may grow. Companies will be subject to bargaining by applicants and if, because of a poor plan, companies are without a true understanding of job worth, they will not attract needed personnel or will overpay and disrupt internal relationships.

All in all, when plan objectives are clear and all elements are designed with these objectives in mind, the administration becomes one of management's most important tools rather than merely a housekeeping task to be performed.

Conclusion

There are indeed complexities of many varieties involved in developing an executive compensation plan. The many tax and legal ramifications make it imperative that competent legal and tax counsel be used in the development of the plan.

The detail of the individual provisions and features of the various elements of the plan can be worked out once the plan principles have been determined. There are a number of sources of detailed information on the wording and description of various executive compensation plan provisions. Notable among these are the National Industrial Conference Board and the American Management Association.

To be effective, an executive compensation plan must be carefully and individually tailored to the needs of the executives and the company. It should provide the means to attract, retain, and motivate top-talent personnel within reasonable cost limits. A competitive base salary, a bonus plan that motivates in the short run, and a stock option plan that promotes top performance in the long run are the crucial activators of the program.

Bibliography

There is extensive variation and detail in the approach to the application of executive compensation features. The following references can be used for those who would like to do more reading:

CARPENTER, RUSSELL B. "High Cost of Restricted Stock Incentives," *Harvard Business Review* (November–December, 1968), p. 139.

"Executive Compensation," *Business Management,* (January, 1968), p. 25.

PURVES, DALE, AND ROCK, MILTON L. "How to Evaluate Executive Jobs," *Business Management* (July, 1962), pp. 60–62.

SIBSON, ROBERT E. "Plan for Management Salary Administration," *Harvard Business Review* (November–December, 1956), p. 102.

AMERICAN MANAGEMENT ASSOCIATION. Executive Compensation Service. New York, 1968.

THE DARTNELL CORPORATION. "Executive Compensation," Chicago, 1966.

NATIONAL INDUSTRIAL CONFERENCE BOARD. Top Executive Compensation. New York, 1968.

EDWARD N. HAY & ASSOCIATES. "The Guide Chart-Profile Method of Job Evaluation." Philadelphia, 1968.

Reports to top management

O. D. Center*

Reports designed for delivery to Top Management represent the culmination and final abbreviation of a management information system.
However, determination of intent and content during the report creation
phase requires understanding of the functional characteristics of reports.
Just as a master craftsman or surgeon is proficient in the selection of tools
which have been carefully designed for each task, and he is equally
knowledgeable in the use of that tool; the report is also a tool and the
skills of usage must be understood in order effectively to design the
report tool.

Three broad functional characteristics of reports are readily identifiable.

1. *Action-Oriented Reports* will most often not be reports of routine
   nature, but will deal with a specific subject. Action-oriented reports
   are designed to be used as tools to obtain action or decisions. Some
   examples are: reports embracing a series of models to show alternate
   results, such as the variety of financing options available to an acquisition; time and expenditure phasing alternates on a production-expan-
   sion or product-diversification program. They furnish the opportunity
   to present facts coupled with pro and con arguments embracing the
   related intangibles and judgmental factors which must be highlighted
   in this type of report. Therefore, both the compiler and the user of all
   reports must be attentive to the action function, whether it be by
   footnote, interpretive comments or questioning by the user.

* Vice President-Administration and Finance, Stromberg-Carlson Corporation,
Rochester, New York.

2. *Results Reports* convey passive historical happenings, usually with comparisons to other periods of time and/or a plan of what was projected to happen. Results reports which portray history are used for evaluation of performance of management and the general health and well being of the business. These reports typically must include comparatives such as actual, budget, prior period, etc: Some examples are: profit and loss detail; gross margin or operating profit by product line; balance sheet; cash flow; share of market. On such reports we can say that they convey values of information, but the creator must also ask if they convey information of value.

3. *Trend Reports* project the future either through trend extrapolation or judgmental projection of what management believes can be made to happen. Trend reports may very well establish bench marks for future performance. Properly presented, they will express projections and forecasts; they portray a picture of that which is expected to happen in the future hopefully superimposed on past experience. An increasingly meaningful variation of reports on the future is the trend-analysis type which extrapolates experience into a future potential. Some examples are: budgets; long range plans; market research projections.

All management levels require reports of the three types defined above. However, top management embraces that level of senior management charged with total overall responsibility for the business enterprise, and consequently has need for a broader, more condensed spectrum of reports. Top management may be classified in a range from the board of directors to a corporate officer group to the executive staff of a divisional profit center. The board of directors, as overseers of ownership interests, can neither be classed outside nor above top management for report-structuring purposes, although their role may vary substantially from passive to active management.

Scope of top management's need for reports

Management classifications

BOARD OF DIRECTORS. The board of directors' role is primarily that of ownership representation for overall guidance of the business direction, for policy setting and for control of management within these prescribed policies, for selection of the management, and monitoring this management's performance and proof of capability. Boards may be composed of various ratios of insiders and outsiders, but in no instance should this influence the report content to the board members unless report omissions are directed by the board. It is highly desirable that the chief financial executive be a member of the board, or, in lieu of membership should attend board meetings. He is there to present reports, but also to interpret reports and to sense board reaction for subsequent changes in reports which can improve the communication process between management and the board members.

CHIEF EXECUTIVE OFFICER.   Since the chief executive officer is a full-time manager and also typically an individualist, three considerations are important in the preparation of reports for his use. First, his full-time presence in the business environment results in a substantially more intimate knowledge of the daily business activities, probable trends and desirable practices than outside board members enjoy. Reports with passive background information for the chief executive officer have minimal value compared to dynamic action-oriented reports, results reports and trend reports. Second, because he is an individual with a certain amount of human bias through nature and experience, reports may advisable be tailored to complement or supplement this bias. Considering his highly active itinerary, strenuous efforts must be made to tailor reports to optimize the efficiency of communicating vital data to him. Third, he has a continuous exposure to both outsiders and insiders who may frequently be selling him (which is essentially an effort to obtain a bias) on their community of interests. The structuring of reports should be carefully designed to avoid enhancement to any of these biases.

CHIEF ADMINISTRATIVE OFFICER.   In those organizations where this management position exists, usually a unique operational relationship will exist between this officer and the chief executive officer. The report criteria for the latter are equally pertinent to this office; however, a greater depth of information detail will frequently be called for by this office.

EXECUTIVE COMMITTEE.   Recent studies have shown that executive committees are found in only 20 percent of companies with $10 million or less in assets, but in nearly 90 percent of those companies with more than $1,000 million in assets. The assignment of responsibilities, the frequency of meetings, and the nature of actions are so diverse that broad generalizations on report requirements are of questionable value. In some companies the executive committee acts as a *de facto* board of directors; in others the powers of the executive committee are so restricted that it is difficult to identify any useful function other than perhaps exploratory and recommendation activities. However, if the executive committee is established by the board, and membership is, essentially, board members, the reports prescribed for an active board will usually furnish the executive committee with the tools required to fulfill its responsibilities.

If the committee is established by the chief executive officer and composed of insiders, a selection of reports supplied to the chief executive officer, the chief administrative officer, or the operating staff will approach the needs of this committee.

OPERATING STAFF. An operating staff typically will be composed of all or most of those in the first tier of the chain of command reporting directly to the chief executive officer. In this framework of definition, each member of the staff has assignments consisting of specific functional responsibilities, and therefore will have a specialized interest for more depth of information within the framework of his specialized responsibility. In addition, he will have the obligation, but sometimes not the desire, for exposure to the trends and projections of the overall business performance. This is the highest level to which results reports in detail are strongly recommended. The head of a function must be in constant touch with current and past results in his area of responsibility, to such a degree that his experience and judgment will produce effective direction to cope with these trends and to control performance where there is a variance from expectations and plans. In addition, each individual at the operating staff level has a substantial need for action-urging reports, as well as trend reports, which will originate both from within his organization and from the financial organization. The chief financial officer, or his chief lieutenant, must be a member of this staff in order to interpret, clarify and otherwise provide the education and understanding that others of the staff who are in various stages of their career development may require, so that they may obtain a thoroughly broadened understanding of the overall business environment.

Objectives in reports design

Reports should have eye appeal; by this we mean that their appearance must solicit attentive readership. The reader's attention must be focused immediately on the subject of the report, so usually an accepted and recognizable format is suggested; if a new report style is introduced, then a screaming headline is suggested for attention purposes. The reader's time is too valuable for him to be confronted with a report that requires excessive time to determine the subject matter, the reason for, or the message of a report. Standardized-format reports are usually accepted by experienced identification of subject matter, and through prior exposure the reader will have established a pattern of immediately searching for those portions of the report which convey the information values which he has previously determined are relevant. New or special reports are a challenge to the communication process. The subject matter of such reports must be introduced to the reader promptly, there must be a clear alert with reasons for making this demand on his time and attention. Then his attention must be focused on the action demanded or the compelling circumstances that justify his readership attention. Unless this is handled with personal confrontation, it is a most challenging communication problem.

The question will be raised as to where top management will find the essentials for use in policy guidance. Seldom can a specific report carry the thrust that will be highly significant to policy guidance. But a "collection" of facts and trends coupled with intelligent or inspired interpretation will typically be the tools that have an impact upon policy guidance.

Regardless of report category, each report should be preceded by a succinct summary or interpretation. There can be no question but that there are those in management who comprehend a picture or graphic portrayal more readily than a numeric display. Conversely, a narrative description of the picture is adequate for others. So, we have the diversity of human nature, even in top management, that suggests two fundamental rules:

1. Wherever possible, portray reported information in both numerical values and in graphic format.
2. Summarize appropriate interpretations either preceding or following on a facing page, to preclude such buck-slip responses as: "Interesting!", "What else do you have?", "Keep your eye on this and bring it back when there is something significant!"

Audience tailored reports

Tailoring of reports to the audience is essential to improving the communication value of reports. However, undesirable bias towards the audience area of interest may distort the value of the report content if it is not carefully appraised in an objective manner.

Therefore, the reader's interests must be recognized as a meaningful determinant of report content. As we have seen under the Management Classification section, the reader's breadth of responsibility and the limited time available for assimilation of reported data, are essential determinants for report preparation. If top management wants only the "big picture," then action-oriented reports must be used more frequently than routine fact and trend reports with great detail. Essential facts must be reported; however, the buildup and relevance of such facts can be deleted if the audience has the background of understanding to effectively use the facts in brief.

Preconceptions of the reader's interests and his ability to assimilate and digest must be avoided. In other words, overshooting the audience can occur when background understanding is assumed in the reader but is either inadequate or not coordinated to the report content. All report structuring must assume the reader's ability to understand. Report expansion, consolidation, supplementing and other tactics can be used with reasonable frequency to test audience reaction as well as the degree of utilization of reported information. The report author should think in terms of audience reaction rather than only the typical cold reproduction of facts.

Reporting techniques and presentation modes

FREQUENCY OF REPORTS. This is typically predetermined by calendar periods or accounting periods or board meeting dates. Although this is the normal practice, it should never be permitted to preclude intermittent issuance of action-type reports either when action is indicated or when the subject matter is perishable.

TIMELINESS OF REPORTS. This probably needs more dynamic attention in more companies than any other element of reporting. Timely reporting requires a constant struggle to produce a perishable product before it loses its freshness, flavor and value to management's control responsibilities. Results reporting is frequently allowed to bog down in the accounting department because of the audit discipline in the accounting manager's training. Timeliness in results reporting far outweighs the immediate need for audit trails. A reasonable rule of thumb for the timeliness of results reports is issuance within the first third of the subsequent period. In partial satisfaction of this demanding schedule, "flash reports" may be used quite properly. With the use of flash reports, it is easier to deal with preliminary indication of results and to follow later with auditable and accurate detail reports. However, top management will frequently not relish the time-divided preview and full-disclosure reporting technique. Extensive opportunities exist in most industrial accounting functions to rely more on high-integrity forecasting to produce interim reports more expeditiously. The financial executive can substantially increase the value of accounting reports by accelerating the timeliness even to the extent of deterioration in finite detail and some reduction in accuracy.

HIGHLIGHTING. Red-flagging significant items in reports improves report utility. The "better" or "worse" technique is a derivation of highlighting. A plan or a prior period are the typical reference points for better-or-worse judging; thus the highlighting technique will become a routine mechanical activity. Is the reader expected to determine that which is significant in the report? Highlighting within reports may use color, arrows, shaded areas and bold face type. Highlight extracts from reports can use a summary format for display of noteworthy content with comments, explanations and recommendations.

FORMAT STANDARDIZATION. This is a well-justified report technique and is essentially followed to improve readership understanding and acceptance of the information presented. It also facilitates comparison which, once again, is a reader benefit. Although the technique of varying the content is suggested as a means of testing audience interest, too much variation from standardized formats can lead to readership distrust, confusion, misinterpretation, and, sometimes, to making inappropriate comparisons.

ACCOUNTING MECHANICS REDUNDANCY.   This is a common failing in many top management reports. Subtotals often have no value except to the preparing accountant. Merging of organizational responsibility values is frequently appropriate accounting, but deteriorates the information value to top management. The breakout of values following generic accounting treatment must be "common sensed" for value to top management, as opposed to responsibility reporting.

SECURITY OF REPORTS TO TOP MANAGEMENT.   The security factor is given substantially more attention by many than logic would suggest is required. Certainly there is confidential and private company information. If any top manager in the group defined previously cannot be entrusted with significant events, forecasts, and results information about the business, it is highly questionable that he can contribute materially to managing or guiding the destiny of the business. On the other hand, the financial executive should adopt a mechanism permitting the recipients of top management reports to return them to the point of origin either at their option or on a prescribed return schedule basis. This practice not only provides some security for the data but avoids file buildup as well. Top management mobility, retirements, and changes are such that a practice of surrendering reports after a reasonable time, such as three to six months, is recommended.

WALK THROUGH-TALK THROUGH REPORTS.   These are a vital communication technique of the financial executive. The Report Center or Chart Room is an increasingly effective device whereby the information to be reported can be displayed effectively in both numeric and graphic values. Additionally, color is readily available, and updating can be as rapid as the alternate cycle of typing, reproduction and distribution. Although these features are practical advantages, the really significant value lies in the practicalities of presentation: a presentation "talk through" of the report data; interpretations of actuals to budget, to forecast, to prior period are self-evidently required in a presentation to a vitally interested audience. An oral presentation of report data can use the entire scope of reporting techniques: it permits graphics to supplement the numeric values; it forces interpretive comments; and it automatically highlights and red flags special items.

Preparation for such presentations cannot be taken too lightly. Prior to presentation, dress rehearsals offer presentation improvements. An anomaly seems to exist in this type of presentation in that the audience thirty feet from the charts will see something—sometimes more profound than what is seen by the executive making the presentation only three feet from the charts.

Should financial data as prepared and used in this presentation mode be made available for continuous access? If equivalent information is or would otherwise be distributed in printed form, the continuous access question is quickly answered. This, of course, implies continuous access available to the management group normally exposed to this level of information. Photographic and projection media in the Chart Room obviously preclude the philosophy of continuous access data.

Construction of the Report Center or Chart Room need not represent an extensive investment. No more than a three-foot depth on one wall of a board room will permit installation of side-hinged chart boards, allowing about 25 charts for each 10 linear feet of wall space—using both sides of the hinged boards. Partitioning and security of the chart material can be accomplished with sliding doors with locks or similar devices.

Check list of information considered for reporting

In some organizations, the financial executive will be a total information source and in others he will be restricted to pure financial data, due to the existence of other functional specialists such as Vice President–Industrial Relations, Vice President–Corporate Development, Vice President–Economic Outlook, or others. These functional heads may or may not render reports in separate functional formats.

Following is a check list of many of the significant items to be considered for inclusion in top-management reporting. Those items marked with an asterisk (*) are critical if subject to public press announcements.

Data	Source	
Profit & Loss—top summary	Financial	
Profit & Loss—profit center	"	
Operating Profit or Gross Margin (by major product families)	"	
Balance Sheet	"	
Source & Use of Funds	"	
Capital Appropriation	"	
Capital Spending	"	
Major Accounting Policy Changes	"	
* Financing Plans	"	
Stock Trading Activity	"	
Changes in Significant Share Holdings	"	
Employee Census	Industrial Relations	
Employee Turnover	"	"
Industrial Safety Record	"	"
Pension Funding—Appreciation	"	"
Stock Purchase Plan Activity	"	"
Employment Contracts (New, Lapsed, Renewed)	"	"
* Union Contracts	"	"
Union Relations	"	"
Product Pricing	Marketing	
Competitive Price Trends	"	
* Trade Shows	"	

Data	Source
* New Products	Marketing
(Announcements, Planning)	
Distribution Method Changes	"
Advertising	"
(Programs, Strategy)	
Market Changes	"
(Size, Trend)	
Market Penetration	"
(Accomplished, Planned—Strategy)	
Manufacturing Plants	Manufacturing
(Location, Size, Expansion,	
Retrenchment, Environmental Changes)	
Manufacturing Facilities	"
Cost Reduction	"
(Plans, Accomplishments)	
Employee Census	Engineering
(Research, Development, Technician,	
Administrative, etc.)	
Patent Position	"
(Patents held, Docketed, Applied for)	
Utilization of Funds	"
(New Products, Sustaining, Research,	
Advanced Development)	
Technical Agreements	"
(Given to others, taken from others)	
Acquisitions	Corporate Development
Divestments	" "
New Business Opportunities	" "
Litigation	Legal
Legislation Effects	"

Training value of reports

The tool maker must constantly keep abreast of the materials available as well as the developing techniques in the use of the tools that he creates. In the environment of reports, this continual update process can be called feedback. Both the user and the producer of reports must keep in touch with the kind of information required as well as that which is available in the area of facts and trends to more valuably enlighten management which will permit more significant business results.

A report structure which results in negligible feedback from the audience is probably not reaching this audience because of faults in either content, format, significant highlighting, meaningful interpretation or presentation techniques. Therefore, requests for interpretation and elaboration on reported data should be both expected and encouraged. Elaboration on a specific item, explanation or discussion of interrelated values, and critical evaluation of timeliness, intent, and report mechanics will sometimes be necessary. The financial executive and key subordinates should be solicitous of such feedback as it offers the opportunity for improvements as well as training value. The training of reporters in what to report and how to report it, is equally a problem in human relations and a problem in soliciting improvements in management control of the enterprise. Report format and content can as readily lend themselves to the "give and take" of compromise as any other part of the business. In this, however, the financial executive must both make his subordinates recognize that they are learning while revising or modifying content, and also maintain a firm posture in reporting essential information to top management for their awareness of the direction and speed at which the business enterprise is moving.

Can it be said that the report audience finds an educational value in report content? Top management must be given facts, trends and the tools to permit increasingly meaningful management actions and policy determinations. And then, the functional or specialty manager member of top management has the continuing opportunity to expand his understanding of the total business environment as a training prelude to his potential advancement into general management. The financial executive has a greater responsibility than is typically set forth in his formal job description. This is to be constantly alert and active in interpreting and correlating report information with his peers as a training device to aid in their career development and preparation for broader responsibilities.

PART II

The financial
executive as the
administrator of a
major corporate
function

Organization of the financial executive's functions

W. Joseph Littlefield*

Profits for the owners of a business, the primary purpose of an enterprise, are attained through the endeavor of the members of the enterprise. Effective administration of these members is one of the most important means to the attainment of corporate objectives. Organization is a means to such effective administration. The organization of an enterprise is discussed in Chapter 3, "Corporate organization." This chapter deals with the organization of the financial executive's functions.

Organization of financial functions

A financial executive has two types of responsibilities. One is the traditional responsibility of administering the financial people who are under his jurisdiction. The other is to act as adviser to the operating manager he serves with respect to financial questions. The latter is by far the more important responsibility, requiring the greater skill and contributing far more to improved profits if effectively performed.

Accordingly, the chief financial officer should be the assistant and adviser to the chief executive officer with respect to broad policy issues, particularly as they involve financial questions. He also administers the financial people under his leadership within the corporation. In addition, he prescribes the principles, policies, and methods which govern the performance of financial functions throughout the enterprise,[1] to the

---

* Controller for Financial Analysis (Retired), Johns-Manville Corporation.

[1] Enterprise as used herein means the firm, or the corporation and its divisions and subsidiaries.

extent to which he has jurisdiction. This last responsibility may extend to subsidiaries in which the corporation has a controlling interest, but perhaps not to subsidiaries in which the corporation has only a minority investment. He is also responsible for carrying out agreed policies and actions. The chief financial officer and his deputies provide the information and service required by operating managers in the performance of their responsibilities. Briefly stated, the chief financial officer and his principal deputies are consultants to management in the field of finance.

In this chapter the organization of financial functions in the parent corporation will be dealt with first, and then some of the problems of a multidivisional enterprise will be discussed.

Planning the organization

In his analysis of organization, Alvin Brown, Vice President, Johns-Manville Corporation, stated: "Organization defines the part which each member of an enterprise is expected to perform and the relations between such members, to the end that their concerted endeavor shall be most effective for the purpose of the enterprise."[2]

Accordingly, the organization of financial functions is planned to bring together the duties which require financial people with similar qualifications so that they can work more effectively together. For this reason financial functions are usually divided into several groups: (1) planning and control functions, sometimes called controllership functions; (2) the handling, custody, and protection of cash and other assets, usually referred to as treasurership functions; (3) other financial functions which may not be included in the first two groups; and (4) certain auxiliary services which may be delegated to the chief financial officer.

Usually the chief financial officer will retain for his personal attention part of the responsibility which has been delegated to him, depending on the situation in the company. Similarly, the chief executive may retain as his own responsibility certain matters which in other companies are delegated to the chief financial officer. The selection of such personal responsibilities usually reflects the background of the chief executive, and his successor might well decide that the chief financial officer should handle them.

THE PLAN OF ORGANIZATION. The organization plan consists of a detailed description of the responsibilities assigned to each position, and usually a group of charts depicting the lines of authority and responsibility. A chart describing the first stage of redelegation of financial responsibilities by the chief financial executive is shown in Exhibit 1. While titles are not important, for ease of description titles in general use are em-

---

[2] Alvin Brown, *Organization, a Formulation of Principle* (New York: Hibbert Printing Company, 1945), Chap. 1.

EXHIBIT 1

Lines of Responsibility to and from Chief Financial Executive

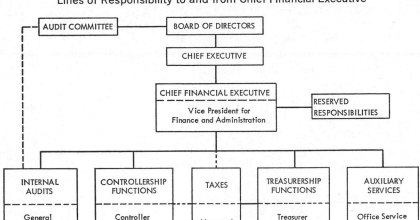

* Tax Manager may be supervised by either chief financial executive, treasurer, or controller, depending on situation in company.

Source: Exhibit 1, and other exhibits in Chapter 7, are based on similar Exhibits in *Developments In Financial Organization 1915–1965*, a special supplement to *Financial Executive*, September, 1965; Financial Executives Institute, 50 West 44 Street, New York, N.Y. 10036.

ployed. Thus in this chart the chief financial officer is listed as Vice President for Finance and Administration.

INFORMAL ORGANIZATION. Every company develops an informal organization over the years; people in different parts of the organization, but at the same location, work together to accomplish their respective tasks. For instance, credit men in the field will provide credit information directly to the local sales force. In a plant a financial analyst might work with an industrial engineer who is preparing a proposal to purchase certain equipment. Both will use the same data, and the engineering report would include a financial section prepared by the financial man regarding the financial desirability of the proposal. Such an informal organization saves time, reduces the load on supervisors, and is valuable provided the personnel concerned have been carefully trained and do not presume to make decisions jointly which should be made by higher authority.

In discussing "what is organization," Louis A. Allen stated: "In the informal organization, people work together because of their personal likes and dislikes."[3] The informal organization can be an effective force

[3] Louis A. Allen, *Management and Organization* (New York: McGraw-Hill Book Company, Inc., 1958) Chapter 3.

in enabling executives to accomplish things with a minimum expenditure of time.

Controllership functions

Controllership functions under the responsibility of a finance executive usually called the controller fall naturally into four groups, both for ease of administration and to facilitate the assignment of personnel with the specific training and experience required. These groups are: (1) financial and economic analysis, (2) planning and budgeting, (3) accounting, and (4) data processing.

It is significant that the first two functions deal almost entirely with the future; accounting deals with the present and immediate past, while

EXHIBIT 2

Delegation of Controllership Functions

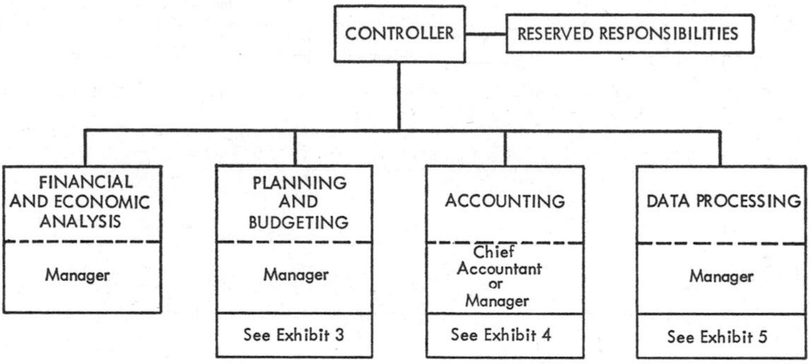

Source: See Exhibit 1.

data processing serves the other three functions as well as operating executives. One plan for redelegating these controllership functions is charted in Exhibit 2.

Financial and economic analysis

Financial and economic analysis is not new, because successful businessmen practiced it to some degree long before it was recognized as a separate function in the early 1930's. Its development was a natural consequence of the growing use of budgeting during the 1920's. In the early 1940's many companies used this function extensively to determine the most desirable capital expenditures being considered for the post-war period. Its use spread to examination of every part of the business to see where profits could be improved. Operations research which developed in the early 1940's is so closely related to financial and economic analysis that it is difficult to identify any difference between them.

It was natural that this function should expand to the study of alternate plans for future operations in order to select the most desirable. This was first done with respect to capital expenditures, but soon spread to examination of various plans for marketing, manufacturing, and financing. One of the essential characteristics of financial and economic analysis is the establishment of criteria for decisions, such as return on investment. All managers should use economic analysis; where the problem is complicated they will naturally use specialists trained in this function to help them.

The use of financial and economic analysis in the examination of proposed mergers or acquisitions is imperative. In some companies, selected chief analysts devote all of their time and effort to this aspect of the corporation's growth policy.

The number of persons performing financial and economic analysis varies with the needs of the company. In a small company this function might be performed by the controller as his main reserved responsibility. In larger corporations a section would be organized to perform this service for the benefit of all parts of the enterprise. In such cases the function would be supervised by a manager for financial and economic analysis, and he might have a score or more people in his section. Senior analysts would head units of about five or six, and each would be required to become familiar with a specific part of the business to provide more effective service. In each analytical unit the senior analyst would have two analysts, one or two senior technicians (about the same grade as senior cost accountant), and one or two technicians. A service unit would provide clerical and computation service.

The organization of this function in operating divisions is discussed later. The use of this function in training and development of financial executives is discussed in Chapter 8, "Training and development of financial executives." More detailed information about methods of financial and economic analysis will be found in Part III, "Financial and economic analysis."

Planning and budgeting

The main responsibility of financial people in the planning and budgeting function is to assist operations people as they prepare their detailed plans and budgets, and to analyze the plans so prepared for the benefit of the chief executive. In a small company the controller could reserve this as one of his own responsibilities, or an assistant, acting as planning and budget manager, could closely scrutinize the reports on budgets. In larger companies, organized functionally with the chief manufacturing and marketing executives both responsible directly to the chief executive, a number of people will be needed in the budget section to assist various top executives in the preparation of their budgets. In this type of organization the manager of planning and budgeting is responsible for examining budgets to see that they conform to the budget directive issued by the chief executive at the start of the budget period.

In a divisionalized enterprise, where division controllers perform the planning and budgeting function for division general managers, the size of the budget and planning section at general headquarters of the corporation would be reduced accordingly, although the degree of responsibility of the manager of planning and budgeting would be greater. This is explained below under earnings forecasts.

BUDGET DIRECTIVE. A budget directive is usually distributed at the beginning of the budget preparation period (four to six months before the start of the budget year) indicating, among other things, the economic conditions expected for the coming budget year, which should be used as a basis for preparing budgets. Such an economic forecast has much greater authority if issued over the signature of the chief executive, and especially if he is directly concerned with its preparation. For this purpose he would draw on all the talent at his disposal, including top advisers in the fields of marketing, research, manufacturing, finance, and economics. Such a directive would also include instructions from the budget manager which have not previously been issued.

EARNINGS FORECASTS. Most companies find it desirable to have a separate forecast of earnings for the entire enterprise for comparison with the budgets prepared by operating people. The preparation of such a forecast may be directed personally by the chief financial executive or the controller, although it is prepared by the manager for planning and budgeting. Such a forecast may be revised as a result of attempted reconciliation with operating budgets, but it would still be considered a better forecast of earnings for presentation to the Board of Directors than a mere consolidation of budgets. This forecast is prepared while operating people are preparing their budgets. In a divisionalized enterprise, separate forecasts would be prepared for each operating division or subsidiary for comparison with their respective operating budgets.

Sales forecasts. The basis for any forecast of earnings is the forecast of sales. Many companies now require that sales budgets be prepared first, and submitted to the manager for planning and budgeting. These forecasts are scrutinized by specialists in marketing, manufacturing, and research, as well as by members of the planning and budgeting function, to determine whether they properly reflect the volume attainable under economic conditions expected in the budget year according to the budget directive. The marketing function usually has a group specializing in economic and marketing analysis, whose sales forecasts may be considered more reliable than the sales budgets of operating people, which may be tinged with either wishful thinking or even unrealistic pessimism. Comparison of sales budgets with sales forecasts prepared by this group of specialists will indicate where differences should be reconciled before operating budgets are prepared.

OTHER RESPONSIBILITIES.   The planning and budgeting function includes numerous responsibilities. Most of these are listed in Exhibit 3.

EXHIBIT 3

Principal Responsibilities of Manager—Planning and Budgeting

1. Prescribes the methods and procedures to be followed in preparation of profit plans and budgets.
2. After consultation with divisional and functional controllers, designs the forms for accounting statements of the transactions of the various divisions and departments of the enterprise to compare actual results with planned operations.
3. Appraises proposed profit plans or budgets for the chief executive and consolidates such plans to show resulting earnings.
4. Receives proposals for capital expenditures requiring decision by the chief executive or board of directors and submits them to the appropriate responsibility with required financial analysis.
5. Prepares forecasts of earnings, cash, and investment for the enterprise.
6. Recommends the basis for allocation of general expense among operating divisions.
7. Determines annually the amount of general expense to be charged to each division during the year, based on the approved basis for allocation of such expense.
8. Follows up and reports on significant deviations of actual results from planned profit plans, budgets, and capital expenditure proposals.
9. Continuously appraises economic and social forces and government influences, and interprets their effect on the sales costs and earnings of the enterprise.
10. Appraises plans for attainment of long-term objectives, profit plans, and budgets.
11. Periodically follows up and reports on the status of plans for attaining objectives.
12. Develops plans for an information system which will provide information needed by each responsibility head in carrying out his responsibilities. The plans will be turned over to the manager—data processing.
13. Recommends changes in organization of the enterprise to enable it to achieve its long-term objectives. Maintains a manual of organization as approved by the chief executive officer, and incorporates such changes as are approved by the chief executive officer of the enterprise.

Source: See Exhibit 1.

More detailed information about methods will be found in Part IV, "Planning and budgeting."

Accounting

The accounting which provides data for company reports must, of course, be uniform throughout the enterprise. Accounting done for control purposes within a division or department should be tailored to fit the situation. Among different operations the detailed accounting and cost accounting can vary greatly, as long as the basic summaries needed for consolidation into the figures for the entire enterprise are uniformly derived.

CHIEF ACCOUNTANT (manager of accounting). Usually the chief accountant is charged with the responsibility for establishing the accounting principles and system of accounts for the enterprise as a whole. He may also have review power over the accounting and cost accounting systems established for various subsidiaries and divisions. The accounting in divisions, plants, or subsidiaries may or may not be done by people responsible to the chief accountant, but he retains functional control in any case. Therefore, the chief accountant retains for his personal atten-

EXHIBIT 4

Principal Functions of Chief Accountant (manager of accounting)

Reserved Responsibilities

1. Recommends principles to govern accounting throughout the enterprise.
2. Prepares the accounts of the corporation, except such as are entrusted to other responsibilities.
3. Provides accounting advice in situations concerning government contracts, tax liabilities, mergers and acquisitions, research or know-how contracts, lease-back arrangements, pension or trust funds, and others.
4. Consults with manager—data processing in order to achieve maximum use of computer-communication systems in the handling of accounting data throughout the enterprise.
5. Supervises deputies performing following responsibilities:
   a. Prescribes accounting methods to provide accounting data required for corporate statements, statements to be issued to stockholders and the public, and for state and federal tax returns.
   b. Prepares such corporate statements as are required.
   c. Cooperates in designing forms for such statements or annual reports to stockholders, etc.
   d. Prescribes methods of accounting to provide accounting data required for reports of performance of operating divisions, and of functional departments throughout the enterprise.
   e. Using forms designed by the manager—planning and budgeting, prescribes the content of reports of performance of the various responsibilities for which such reports are required.
   f. Recommends principles and prescribes methods for determination of cost of product.
   g. Assists divisional finance people in the installation of cost systems.
   h. Prepares such statements of operations as are prescribed by the controller.

Source: See Exhibit 1.

tion certain of his responsibilities, and delegates others, as illustrated in Exhibit 4. Accounting within operating divisions is discussed later in this chapter. For further details on accounting see Part IX, "Financial accounting policies."

Data processing

The facilities used in data processing include the computer(s) and peripheral equipment and also the communications (telephone, telegraph, teletype, or radio) which receive and transmit data and questions.

Because of the advantage of large high speed units, the trend is to centralize their location, placing in outlying parts of the country only such equipment as is necessary for effective operation of the entire complex. Because of the speed of the computer, an operation in California, for example, can obtain almost immediate response to a question asked on the computer located in New York.

The computer is usually located in the finance organization both because finance serves all parts of the enterprise and because much of the data being handled by the computer are financial. But the chief financial officer must make certain that financial people do not get the idea that the computer is operated primarily for their financial work. Priority in use of the equipment should go to producing the information needed for improving profits, which makes it likely that the needs of operating executives in marketing or production will frequently have priority.

Usually the manager of data processing will be responsible directly to the controller, because of the need for close coordination of information handling with other controllership functions. When this function was first developed in a few companies the chief financial officer directly supervised the head of data processing. However, he soon found that the task of coordinating this with other functions took up too much of his time, and transferred the task to the controller.

The manager for data processing now usually has four assistants who carry out his responsibilities. They are in charge of Systems Planning, Computer Programming, Computer Operations, and Communications. A chart showing lines of responsibility to these assistants is shown in Exhibit 5. More detailed information about these functions may be found in Part V, "Information technology."

SYSTEMS PLANNING. Systems planning responsibilities are a consolidation of various old methods and procedures which with centralized data processing must be adapted to computer operations. In most companies office methods and procedures are compiled to indicate the approved methods of handling paper work. When computers do this same work changes in procedures are necessary. However, a company must have all work done according to a single systems pattern, whether it is done by machine or by hand. In as much as work done by computer in one part of the company might be done by hand in another location, there would be utter confusion unless all work were performed according to a uniform plan. In some companies these methods and procedures are known as "systems," which is the term used herein. Such systems may prescribe, among other things, the design of many forms (purchase orders, customer orders, etc.) and their distribution, methods of pricing orders received from customers, the systems of inventory control in plants and warehouses, and determination of when an office should use electric calculators rather than hand calculators. The budget manager prescribes the forms and methods to be used in preparing budgets through a set in systems. The employee relations department will prescribe the forms to be filled out and data secured when a new employee is hired, or when one leaves the company, through another set of systems. The chief accountant may prescribe accounting methods in another set of systems. Systems will indicate what questions the computer has been pro-

EXHIBIT 5

Principal Deputies of Manager—Data Processing

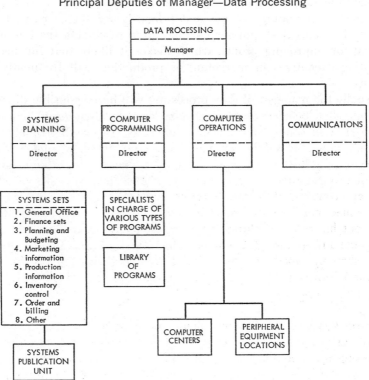

Source: See Exhibit 1.

grammed to answer, and how the question should be put to the computer.

In general, the various systems under the supervision of the director for systems planning include systems for (1) general office work, (2) finance, (3) planning and budgeting, (4) marketing information, (5) production information (manufacturing or mining), (6) inventory control, (7) order and billing, (8) the treasurer's operations, and (9) special projects.

Systems publication unit. The work of editing systems is done by a systems publication unit under the responsibility of the director for systems planning. Thus instructions for individuals or computers are coordinated. Those who prepare instructions for issuance in systems receive back an edited version to be sure the editing has not inadvertently changed the instructions as intended by the originator.

COMPUTER PROGRAMMING. The director of computer programming designs and writes all programs for use of computers. He reviews various systems and recommends which work should be done on computers. He recommends improvement in methods or equipment for reporting, recording, computing, and communicating data. He maintains liaison with those in other responsibilities who are installing or maintaining their own computers in order to assure optimum utilization and compatibility of all facilities in the enterprise. He confers with various responsibilities regarding programming computers for various types of special, nonroutine work, such as correlation analysis for development of a sales forecast, special computations for engineers and researchers, and use of computers in automation of operations.

COMPUTER OPERATIONS. The director for computer operations is responsible for computer operations throughout the enterprise, with the chiefs of operation at each computer center responsible directly to him. As the computer is still in its infancy, and growing fast, little is gained by trying to enumerate here the infinite variety of things that the computer can do. It is the responsibility of the director for computer operations to keep up to date on the latest developments regarding hardware and software which might be used to advantage in his operations.

COMMUNICATIONS. The opportunity for better coordination of communications throughout the enterprise, including the transmission of data for use on computers, became evident as soon as computers were used in an enterprise with scattered operations. The director for communications supervises the operation of telephone, telegraph, teletype, and other communications by wire and radio throughout the enterprise. Some of the data formerly transmitted by a teletype operator to another teletype machine may now be transmitted to a computer directly, or may be transmitted by a teletype operated by a piece of computer hardware. Therefore it seems logical that the director of communications should be supervised by the manager for data processing, with whose people he must work so closely. He will still study the use of communication facilities to appraise their adequacy and to improve efficiency, but always with the computer in mind. He will install, repair, move, or replace communication facilities throughout the enterprise, bearing in mind the part these facilities now play or will play in the computer communication complex.

Treasurership functions

The title treasurer as used in this chapter, refers to the financial executive who has charge of the functions dealing largely with receipt, disbursement, or protection of cash; the preservation of company assets; and the investment of surplus funds, or pension or trust funds. In some companies the title treasurer is given to the chief financial executive, in which case the executive who performs some or all of the duties of treasurer described herein may be called the assistant treasurer. If the chief financial officer is called vice president and treasurer, he too will supervise the entire finance organization, but is likely to retain for his own personal attention some of the treasurership functions which may have a significant effect on earnings.

EXHIBIT 6

Organization of Treasurership Functions

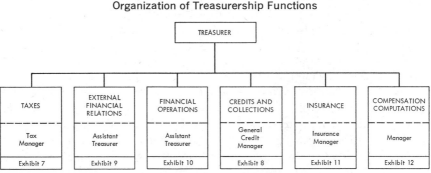

Source: See Exhibit 1.

The six areas over which the treasurer usually has jurisdiction include (1) credits and collections, (2) relations with external financial houses, (3) financial operations including handling of cash, (4) insurance, (5) payment of compensation to employees, and usually (6) taxes. This organization is pictured in Exhibit 6. Several of these functions are discussed in more detail in Part VII, "Asset management and control."

Tax administration

Tax administration is usually under the supervision of a tax manager. A rare exception would be a small company in which the opportunity for saving money by attention to taxes is so great, compared to other functions of the treasurer, that the latter supervises this activity himself. Usually, however, the complexity of tax problems requires virtually all the time of an individual to deal with the function effectively, warranting the employment of a tax manager.

Tax administration involves not only a continuous study of tax laws, but frequent dealings with tax officials at federal, state, and city levels concerning tax problems of the various parts of the enterprise. The treasurer naturally has many more outside dealings than the controller because of his other responsibilities. He must provide the cash with which to pay taxes. However the controller also has a keen interest in taxes, as profit planning and budgeting require adequate tax information. The people in controllership can frequently point out ways to save money in taxes. We have heard a great deal about "tax accounting," meaning the decisions regarding depreciation policies, when to charge sales taxes to the customer, how to minimize local and state taxes, and what to do about foreign taxation or U.S. taxes on foreign operations.

Most companies consider that this interest on the part of the controller does not outweigh the advantages of having the tax administration under the treasurer. But it does point up the necessity of close organizational relationships between those in controllership and treasurership functions. This applies not only to taxes but also to other fields of common interest.

The responsibilities of the tax manager are shown in Exhibit 7, and details of the operation are discussed in Chapter 9, "Tax planning and management."

EXHIBIT 7

Responsibilities Delegated to the Tax Manager
(assisted by chief tax accountant and other appropriate assistants)

1. Determines the tax liabilities of the corporation and its subsidiaries.
2. Prepares and files tax returns.
3. Studies and becomes familiar with tax laws and regulations, or proposed laws and regulations, to recommend, as authorized, action to protect the interests of the enterprises.
4. As authorized, deals with the appropriate agencies of governments—federal, state and local—regarding any problems that arise in respect of the determination of taxes.
5. Interprets the laws and regulations that govern sales or use taxes and supplies information regarding the invoicing of such taxes to all whose responsibility requires such information.
6. Ascertains the amounts of sales and use taxes billed customers and pays such amounts to the appropriate government authority.
7. Arranges for use of computer-communication facilities for any of the above responsibilities.

Source: See Exhibit 1.

Credits and collections

Occasionally the general credit manager has so conducted his responsibility as to be referred to as one of the company's best salesmen. Credit information must be furnished to the sales force quickly on demand. For this reason, before computers the function was highly decentralized. As credit information has been computerized, the data become highly centralized, yet still immediately available in the field. Of course visits to delinquent accounts are still desirable from time to time. The responsibilities of the general credit manager are shown in Exhibit 8.

EXHIBIT 8
Responsibilities Delegated to General Credit Manager

1. Proposes policies for extension of credit to customers and special arrangements for financing sales.
2. Authorizes extension of credit to and collects money due from customers.
3. Prescribes the form of evidence and manner of collection of loans to employees.

   Source: See Exhibit 1.

External financial relations

Because of the importance of relations with banks and financial institutions, the chief financial officer, and perhaps even the chief executive of the company, may help the treasurer in establishing such relationships. However, the day to day dealings are performed by the treasurer in smaller companies or by an assistant treasurer in larger companies. Details of this responsibility are shown in Exhibit 9. They are discussed at greater length in Chapter 47, "Relations with capital suppliers."

EXHIBIT 9
Responsibilities Delegated to
Assistant Treasurer for
External Financial Relations

1. Prepares forecasts of the requirements for capital in the enterprise, and proposes plans for provision of such funds.
2. Maintains adequate sources for current borrowings.
3. Proposes principles and establishes practices to govern the receipt, banking, custody, and disbursement of money and securities.
4. Receives and has custody of money and securities, except at locations at which, by authorization of the treasurer, such duties may be entrusted to others.
5. Proposes what banking depositories shall be employed, and the policies to govern such employment, and conducts relations with such depositories.

   Source: See Exhibit 1.

Financial operations

Besides the funds needed for day to day operations, an enterprise may have surplus funds, self-insurance and trust funds (for retirement of employees or deferred payment of compensation). In recent years the amount invested in pension and profit sharing funds has grown so large that it often exceeds the company's net worth. For this reason pension and profit sharing funds command the close attention of the treasurer.

In some companies the investment of these funds and the custody of securities is placed in the hands of trustees (banks or trust companies), while in others the decisions regarding investments are made by an assistant treasurer (designated as investment manager) working under the general direction of the treasurer. Either method—the use of trustees or the use of the company's own investment staff—has proven to be effective.

The return on investment in these funds will affect the size of the contribution to retirement funds to be made by the company or the benefits received by employees or both. Hence the treasurer is giving more and more attention to administration of such funds. The responsibilities of the assistant treasurer in charge of financial operations are shown in Exhibit 10.

EXHIBIT 10

Responsibilities Delegated to
Assistant Treasurer—Financial Operations

1. Invests funds of the corporation.*
2. Recommends where the receipt and disbursement of money can best be performed by the financial department, and where best by others.
3. Prescribes methods governing the receipt and disbursement of money.
4. Receives money.
5. Disburses money, except at locations at which, by authorization of the treasurer, this duty may be entrusted to others.
6. Provides for loans from one affiliated corporation to another, and for the payment of intercompany accounts.
7. Observes and reports the manner of performance of fiscal policies and methods by other departments and the divisions.

* Note: The funds of the corporation include, among others, surplus funds, self-insurance funds, trust funds under plans for deferred payment of profit sharing, and for retirement. In some companies trustees are selected to manage the investment of funds and custody of securities. In a few companies a separate assistant treasurer is designated as investment manager to perform the actual investing, under the general direction of the treasurer.
Source: See Exhibit 1.

Insurance

Various forms of property and liability insurance are intended to prevent a disaster from doing irreparable damage to the financial condition of the company. Many companies with widespread operations will self insure, because the chance of disasters hitting all these operations is very unlikely. If one of the operations is very large compared to the others, some sort of disaster insurance might be carried, protecting against very large losses, but not against small losses which would be self insured. Other companies insure with a group of companies whose requirements for preventive equipment are very strict, and initially costly, but which have on occasion paid a "dividend" (return premium) greater than the premium, reducing the insurance cost to the expense of compliance with regulations of the insurance companies. Because of his responsibility for preserving the assets of the company, the insurance function is usually placed under the treasurer, with an insurance expert

EXHIBIT 11

Responsibilities Delegated to
Insurance Manager

1. To keep informed of the company's exposure to loss in all areas where insurance protection is customarily available, and recommend timely changes in company policy as to what losses it is desirable to insure.
2. To purchase insurance against loss where company policy indicates that insurance is desirable, using approved criteria to choose among alternatives.
3. To keep records of significant losses and exposure to loss where company policy indicates that risk assumption is more desirable than insurance.
4. To consult with the manager of employee benefits on group life and health insurance, assist him in preparing specifications for such insurance, and negotiate for and purchase such insurance at minimum cost or recommend self insurance where desirable.
5. To receive group life insurance applications from salaried employees and to keep records of such insurance.
6. To file claims for losses and to negotiate settlement of claims.
7. To observe and report upon adherence, throughout the company, to approved policy respecting insurance and to give timely warning of any circumstance or course of action that appears contrary thereto.
8. To make a continuing study of means of reducing the cost of insurance, and to propose to the treasurer any change in practice which would contribute to this objective.

Source: See Exhibit 1.

in charge of its operation who is sometimes called the insurance manager. Some of the insurance manager's responsibilities are listed in Exhibit 11.

Compensation and employee benefits

Incentive compensation has grown in popularity at all levels of employment. Sometimes the compensation to be paid requires intricate calculations. There is need, therefore, for a single office to see that compensation is paid only in accordance with approved plans. The payment of compensation is further complicated by withholding both taxes and payments due the company by employees for various reasons. However computers have helped this operation greatly, especially where statements must be rendered to employees periodically regarding the

EXHIBIT 12

Responsibilities Delegated to Manager—Compensation Computations

1. Prepares payrolls not prepared at other locations and withholds designated amounts that apply to income taxes, etc., and pays such amounts to the appropriate government agency.
2. Prescribes methods for those entrusted with payment of employees at other locations regarding withholding and method of payment of income taxes withheld.
3. Computes incentive compensation payable to employees, except where such incentive compensation is computed at other paying locations.
4. Maintains the records of the retirement plan.
5. Administers stock purchase and stock option plans for employees.
6. Arranges for use of computer-communication systems for any of above responsibilities.

Source: See Exhibit 1.

status of their funds for retirement or for purchase of stock in the company. The responsibilities assigned to the manager of the compensation section are shown in Exhibit 12.

Internal auditing

The auditing function in most companies is a neglected opportunity for improving performance and earnings. An internal audit may be accurate and yet contribute nothing of great value to earnings; on the other hand, some imaginative thinking and intuitive analysis by the auditor may make a real contribution to higher earnings. In some companies the auditing function is considered one of the best training grounds for executive development because the general auditor has encouraged the members of his department to do more than a perfunctory audit when they visit various locations.

An auditor may discover that procedures are being followed to the letter, but that a change in procedures would improve efficiency and lower costs. Another may discover that two employees who should be working closely together have a personality conflict that prevents smooth operation and that one should be moved to another operation. If the auditor discovers a situation that he believes should be investigated as a project which might add to earnings, but either does not have the time to do so himself, or believes that the situation would require a lengthy study, he should report the situation to the general auditor. The latter would usually send the auditor to discuss the situation with the manager of financial and economic analysis. The latter might decide to have a thorough analysis made, and of course would give the auditor credit for having brought the project to his attention. Increasingly, the general auditor is asked by the chief executive to perform management audits, seeking specific data or information.

Of course the routine work of internal auditing complements the work of external auditors and is also important for this reason. There is usually close contact between the general auditor and the audit committee of the board of directors. While the general auditor is usually supervised by the chief financial executive, in a few companies he reports directly to the chief executive. In either case the appointment of a general auditor is usually subject to approval by the audit committee of the board of directors, and the latter may also specify the size of the internal audit department to be sure the function is not neglected. For further information about internal auditing see Chapter 12, "Internal auditing."

Auxiliary services

The auxiliary services under the responsibility of the chief financial officer vary greatly among companies, and depend largely on the type of corporate organization. One usually found in the financial organization is office services, which will be discussed first.

Office services

Office services became part of the financial organization in the early 1900's and has been there ever since. Some of the services are routine, but many are important and require some attention from a top executive. Hence the manager of office services is responsible to either the chief financial officer, or to his deputy if other services are also in the financial organization.

The members of the office services unit have a variety of duties. They may handle customers orders, price them according to systems, and transmit them to the proper plant or warehouse for shipment. They may operate the intracompany communications systems, and also operate some of the peripheral equipment of the computer.

A great change occurred in the work of office services units with development of the computer communication complex. Office people now operate with information secured not from files but from computers, and they transmit data to computers rather than send papers to other people.

The manager of office services has many responsibilities in addition to administration of people in office services units. His reserved responsibilities may be described as follows:

The office services manager appraises the requirements for office space at all locations, and approves leases and renewals thereof. He provides accommodations for company headquarters, if not owned by the company; in either case he administers the space used, providing decoration, maintenance, cleaning, light, heat, water, air conditioning, sanitary facilities, and mail dispatch. He prescribes the type of furniture to be used and administers its use. He arranges for and administers restaurant and cafeteria services for employees at various locations. He arranges for communication services through the director of communications. He may also administer leased car plans for salesmen and others, and review automobile allowance plans periodically in order to recommend improvements when needed.

He prescribes the types of office equipment to be used, being guided by the advice of the manager—computer services where the equipment in question may become an integral part of the computer communication systems. He secures the help of the manager—financial analysis in setting criteria for the most economical use of certain types of office equipment. In other words he is the housekeeper for the operating and staff executives at all locations in which he has jurisdiction.[4]

---

[4] *Developments in Financial Organization 1915–1965,* Supplement to *Financial Executive,* September, 1965.

Other auxiliary services

In multidivisional companies there are, occasionally, other auxiliary services under the direction of the chief financial officer. These might include the headquarters organizations for purchasing, traffic, engineering, sales promotion and advertising, economic and marketing analysis, and similar services which normally are the responsibility of vice presidents for marketing or manufacturing in a functionally organized company. If more than two such services were placed under the general direction of the chief financial officer he would administer them through a deputy for auxiliary services. In some very large companies where this is done, the chief financial officer has the title of Executive Vice President, and he would not necessarily have come up through the financial organization.

So far in this chapter we have discussed functions of the financial executive as organized at the headquarters of the parent corporation of an enterprise. Very little reference has been made to the operation of these functions in operating divisions or in subsidiaries, either domestic or foreign. Many of these functions at the corporate level, such as financial and economic analysis, serve two purposes: (1) they provide assistance to top operating executives, and (2) they formulate policies and methods as guides to those performing the function in outlying areas, in divisions or in subsidiaries. In the next few sections some of the problems which arise in a divisional organization will be discussed.

Responsibilities of division controllers

Divisionalization of enterprises spread rapidly during the 1940's, partly as a result of diversification during and following the second world war, and partly to secure improved headquarters control but greater decentralization of operations. The organization of finance in outlying areas (such as a plant) seems to have made a complete cycle during the past fifty years, and today we find some evidence of reversion to the pattern of organization of the 1920's, mainly as a result of computers, as will be discussed below.

With the spread of divisionalization there immediately developed a conflict between the points of view of corporate directors and top executives, and those of division general managers. The latter wanted their division controllers to be responsible directly to them, while the former group felt that the new division managers were not yet competent to supervise finance since they had no experience in this field and were not yet experienced in their primary responsibility of coordinating marketing and manufacturing. This was a question as to whether the division controller should "be responsible directly to" the chief financial officer and "work for" the division general manager, or should "be responsible directly to" the division general manager with the chief financial officer exercising "functional control." In many newly divisionalized companies the division controller was made responsible directly to the chief corporate financial officer, and the plant accountant, who performed most of the accounting work within the division, was responsible directly to the division controller.

Today the preference is to have the division controller responsible directly to the division general manager who has now developed in his responsibility and has been trained in the use of financial functions. (Some division general managers have come up through the finance organization.) However the division controller adheres to the financial policies and methods prescribed by the corporate financial officer. One of the big advantages of this is that the division controller is now a true member of the division team, on the same footing with other executives who are responsible to the general manager. Moreover, he is now a "line" officer and no longer a "staff" officer, which broadens his promotion opportunities.

The division controller has two main responsibilities: (a) as administrator of financial functions within the division, and (b) as adviser to the division general manager with respect to financial questions. Many of the controllership functions are practiced within a division. The division controller has little, if anything, to do with treasurership functions and auditing, and is concerned with few, if any, auxiliary services.

Controllership functions

The most important finance function in a division is financial and economic analysis, which is the division controller's prime responsibility as financial adviser of the division general manager and his principal deputies. Many more decisions are made within a division than at corporate headquarters. While the decisions made at corporate headquarters are of greater importance on the average, most of them are based on proposals and recommendations (decisions) made by division general managers.

The division controller is responsible for preparing a financial and economic analysis of each capital expenditure being considered by the division general manager. Such an analysis shows, of course, the additional earnings expected from the investment, and of course the projected earnings are based in large part on the projected sales and costs.

PLANNING AND BUDGETING.   The division operating executives making plans or budgets are assisted by finance personnel in the office of the division controller. The division controller is responsible for consolidating the various budgets into an earnings budget for the benefit of the division general manager. The division controller also recommends the type of statements which he believes will best indicate the performance of the division compared to plan.

DATA PROCESSING. Of course the operation of the computer communication systems is of great interest to divisions. Some divisions or groups of divisions may have their own computers, but in many cases a single large computer communication system serves all divisions. At the moment most of the use of computers at a division headquarters is through the division controller's office. However, operating executives are learning little by little the advantage of communicating directly with the computer system, asking their questions and receiving the answers directly, without going through the division controller.

Treasurership functions

Most of the functions supervised by the treasurer are centralized for the entire enterprise. Credit information for all divisions is furnished by corporate headquarters; divisions pay bills or collect receivables under the regulations prescribed by the treasurer. Usually all salary checks are prepared in the treasurer's office. The paying of employees in plants is conducted by financial men in the plant, but following procedures prescribed by the treasurer. Some companies arrange to have a local bank receive a copy of the payroll. The bank then pays employees, deducting at that time amounts for purchase of U.S. bonds, mortgage payments, and transfers to savings accounts, etc. Usually, funds in local banks at the disposal of the local finance manager are strictly controlled by the treasurer's office.

Financial functions in the plant or sales office

The division controller has little to do with accounting at division headquarters or in the plants or sales offices, unless the division has a computer in the controller's office. Until a few years ago the finance manager at a plant or sales office was responsible for all the financial functions performed at his location.

At plants the greater part of the work was plant accounting and cost accounting, much of which has now been converted to computers. Now people in plants and sales offices merely transmit data to computers from original source papers. The main responsibility left for the finance manager at a plant is as adviser to the plant manager concerning financial matters. This means his most important functions are now financial and economic analysis and planning and budgeting.

Hence in the plant organization we find the tendency to return to the type of organization which prevailed in the early part of this century where a staff executive supervised many functions besides accounting. In some companies they have a "manager of services" at a plant location with responsibility for finance, traffic, purchasing, production scheduling, and customer service. Finance is the responsibility of a "finance supervisor" who may have an accountant under him, but whose main responsibility as mentioned above is as financial adviser to the plant manager. The most important staff function now responsible directly to the plant manager is employee relations, which about fifty years ago was usually not even a separate function.

Finance responsibilities in subsidiaries

A subsidiary, being a separate corporate organization, may have all the finance functions of the parent organization, but somewhat reduced in scope. A subsidiary corporation whose main purpose is simply to own facilities in a particular state is treated like any plant within the parent corporation as far as operations are concerned. The separate corporate accounting is performed only for tax purposes at corporate headquarters. A subsidiary which has marketing and manufacturing functions under a chief operating executive is usually treated like any operating division for operations purposes. But it might have some treasurership functions and some corporate accounting for corporate purposes. These functions might be carried out at the headquarters of the parent corporation. If the subsidiary is not wholly owned, greater care is exercised to have accounting done within the legal entity to keep an accurate record of earnings. In subsidiaries in which the corporation owns only a minority interest, and in many foreign subsidiaries, the policies prescribed by the parent corporation are subject to approval of the directors in the subsidiary. Thus the degree of control will vary greatly among them.

A forecast of change

A good finance executive has a broad knowledge of all operations of the enterprise. For instance he may not know as much about marketing as a marketing executive, but he probably knows more than most manufacturing or research executives. Operating executives thirty years ago were woefully lacking in knowledge of finance—most did not even understand the basic rudiments of accounting. Yet they made financial decisions, because practically all decisions in a company have an effect on earnings. Today they are becoming pretty good financial people, understanding financial statements and the fundamentals of accounting, financial and economic analysis, and financial planning and budgeting.

Thirty years from now, perhaps, financial and economic analysis and the techniques of sales forecasting, planning, and budgeting will be the normal skills of any operating executive. All executives will communicate directly with computers and use them for planning and decision making. The controller and treasurer will have more complex problems to solve, and the chief accountant will still prescribe how data should be manipulated by the computer to produce reports showing operations compared to plans, and to prepare reports for stockholders. Will each top executive have a television screen on his desk on which the computer will show a curve of sales and earnings and the changes therein that might result from a reduction in price? Will the computer be programmed to show the executive the financial results of placing a plant on some planet? We will see these things, and perhaps within thirty years.

Selected bibliography

Books

Brown, Alvin.   *Organization: A Formulation of Principle,* Hibbert Printing Co., 1945.

McNulty, James E.   *Some Aspects of Business Organization,* University of Pennsylvania Press, 1964.

Rubenstein, Albert H. and Chadwick J. Haberstroh.   *Some Theories of Organization,* Richard D. Irwin, Inc. 1960.

Sampson, Robert C.   *The Staff Role in Management,* Harper & Brothers, 1955.

Solomons, David.   *Divisional Performance: Measurement and Control,* Financial Executives Research Foundation, 1965.

Monographs

Littlefield, W. Joseph and James P. Thompson.   *Developments in Financial Organization 1915–1965,* Financial Executive, Supplement to September 1965 issue.

Simon, Herbert A. et al.   *Centralization vs. Decentralization in Organizing the Controller's Department,* Financial Executives Research Foundation, 1954.

Periodicals

Cleland, David I. and Wallace Munsey.   *Who Works With Whom?* Harvard Business Review, September–October 1967.

Greiner, Larry E.   *Patterns of Organizational Change,* Harvard Business Review, May–June 1967.

Lippitt, Gordon L. and Warren H. Schmidt.   *Crises in a Developing Organization,* Harvard Business Review, November–December 1967.

Training and development of financial executives

W. Joseph Littlefield*

The better qualified its people are, the closer a company will come to achieving its objectives. The more competent its executives, the more likely they are to train and develop the people in the company. This chapter deals with the problems of training and developing financial executives.

Why train and develop financial executives?

An effective program for training and developing financial executives has three major objectives. First, it will reduce the number of occasions on which an executive becomes an "executive dropout" by being passed over for promotion in preference to a man brought in from outside the company. An executive who has grown up in the company has a wealth of knowledge about the company's business and the informal organization.[1] He knows the personalities, attitudes, and idiosyncrasies of his associates. No executive brought in from outside the company is so well equipped in these ways, and it will take a long time for him to catch up. If an executive in the company has been given and has taken every opportunity to develop, and has succeeded in this development, he should be preferred over any outsider.[2]

---

* Controller for Financial Analysis (Retired), Johns-Manville Corporation.

[1] For a description of "informal organization" see Chapter 7, "Organization of the financial executive's functions."

[2] There are, of course, cases in which the knowledge required for a particular position cannot be found among executives in the company, and it is not possible to wait for a company executive to be trained for the position.

Second, an effective program will help to retain in the company those who appear to be most likely to qualify for higher responsibility. This means that the best will be available when needed to fill top management positions.

Third, it will be a means of training all employees in the company so that they will be better qualified to carry out their tasks.

Qualities needed in financial executives

Successful financial executives have certain qualities, and those selected for development should show signs of being able to develop these qualities. One of the purposes of a program to train and develop employees is to help them improve in these qualities.

For financial executives the following qualities have been found most useful: (1) aptitude for mathematics; (2) ability to think straight (reason logically); (3) ability to express thoughts clearly and concisely (verbally and in writing); (4) ability to visualize; (5) ability and willingness to absorb new ideas; (6) ability to deal with people and get results through people; and (7) inner drive. A brief description of these seven qualities will be helpful in understanding the direction which training and development should take.

APTITUDE FOR ARITHMETIC. A financial executive uses numbers, and should have the skill to handle them in many ways. He should be competent in arithmetic, and other forms of mathematics, including the so-called "new math." (He need not know how to use calculus or higher mathematics.) This mathematical ability enables the higher financial executive to read and understand a report quickly, and catch errors in data or calculations.

ABILITY TO THINK STRAIGHT. This includes the ability to reason logically, and to exercise good judgment. This skill also enables a financial analyst to identify the problem in any situation, to decide what facts are relevant, and to reason from these facts to a conclusion. Financial and economic analysis may provide a financial conclusion, but the executive who has these qualities may also find that the financial conclusion is not the whole story.

ABILITY TO EXPRESS THOUGHTS CLEARLY AND CONCISELY. Many an ambitious executive has reached an impasse because he lacks the verbal skills (oral or written) to convey his ideas, proposals, or thoughts to others so they could understand and accept them. Most financial and economic analyses are made in writing; the length of the report depends in large part on the ability of the author to express himself clearly and concisely; one analyst might use a five-page report to cover the same significant thoughts that another will convey in two pages.

A corollary of the ability to write clearly is skill in talking before a group; a person need not be an orator to talk effectively on a subject he understands. Some people can explain something in a speech more effectively than in writing, and the reverse is also true. An executive who has both skills is fortunate. He can acquire both to a reasonable degree by practice.

ABILITY TO VISUALIZE.   This attribute has several facets. It helps some to develop foresight; in others it takes the form of creativeness. Certainly a top financial executive should have both these qualities. All of these skills play an important part in his success in proposing changes, suggesting amendments to proposals, and having the vision to see the ultimate result of any proposal.

The ability to visualize enables a financial executive to understand a capital expenditure proposal, to envisage the machine or plant for which blueprints are provided, and to comprehend the essential details of the proposal. He can "see" if the objective of the proposal is attainable, or if some other method might accomplish the objective better.

ABILITY AND WILLINGNESS TO ABSORB NEW IDEAS.   Every executive will have smart young people who will propose ideas which are new to them. The executive who will not listen, who responds with the discouraging retort, "That's been tried before and doesn't work," will soon find himself with a group of frustrated employees. It is better to be an enthusiastic listener and let the proposer investigate it further. He will learn much from his study, even if the idea is no good.

The other side of this coin is willingness to adopt a new idea, even though it means a lot of initial bother and trouble. The words, "We have always done it this way," should be a challenge to any financial executive; he should be the first to admit that the way he is doing something may not be the best way. Unless he is flexible and adaptable he cannot generate enthusiasm among his own people when something new is to be tried.

ABILITY TO DEAL WITH PEOPLE AND GET RESULTS THROUGH PEOPLE.   This is a fundamental quality which helps an executive be successful. He accomplishes his tasks through, and with, people. To do this effectively he must sincerely like people and be liked and respected by them; he must gain their confidence by always being fair and living up to his word; he must be calm and not lose his self control under pressure; and he must be quick to give credit to a subordinate for a good job, regardless of how much he himself may have contributed to the task. He should train his subordinates and coach them so that they can learn their tasks more quickly. He must always be considerate of others, both outside and inside his own group.

INNER DRIVE. Inner drive is a force developed within a person which pushes him to accomplish things through persistent effort. It includes the initiative of reaching out for more things to do—of going beyond strict organizational limits and tackling a messy situation which no one wanted to deal with. It is the state of mind which welcomes the tough jobs as an opportunity. Carried to an extreme, it might develop an ambition which makes a man willing to accept great personal sacrifice in order to be president of the company.

Educational background

Much thought has been given to determining the educational background considered desirable for financial executives, which might also help him to develop the qualities mentioned above. Such an education can be acquired partly before and partly after joining a company. People who have developed into good financial executives and who appear to have the qualities mentioned above have majored in one or more of the following: accounting, industrial engineering, science, mathematics, law, English, and philosophy. Among the subjects whose study has helped develop the desirable qualities are logic, history, psychology, navigation, civil engineering, mechanical drawing, advanced mechanics, and behavioral science. The study of Latin and Greek not only helps train the mind, but provides fundamental background for English and other subjects.

Most companies would like to depend on employees rising through the ranks to fill executive jobs throughout the enterprise. However many of the employees in a financial organization are performing tasks which do not require a college education. Even the increasing use of electronic data processing has not changed this situation significantly.[3] A company would not find it feasible to hire only college graduates for such jobs. The turnover would be prohibitive.

Yet a college education is considered desirable for a financial executive. Usually a financial organization cannot depend on enough employees coming up through the ranks who have the qualifications required to fill higher executive positions as they become vacant. To fill the gap they take on some people who have already secured an education in college or graduate school.

Preparing employees for executive development

A company should give every opportunity to all employees to participate in the executive training and development program. Of course in

---

[3] Many companies have successfully taught sixth grade students to program for the computer.

the beginning this takes the form of preparing for broader responsibility, and it is later in the career of the employee that he is made aware of opportunities for higher executive positions.

Training new employees

All new employees, regardless of the position for which they are hired, should receive early indoctrination, as well as specific training, for the jobs they are to fill. It is the responsibility of a man's immediate supervisor to see that he is properly trained for the work he is doing. It is also the supervisor's duty to see that he receives general indoctrination to the company, even though that indoctrination may be handled by industrial relations people.

INDOCTRINATION OF NEW EMPLOYEES.   There is something very embarrassing about a new employee who must admit to a friend outside the company that he does not know the name of the president of the company he has recently joined, nor the names of the local manager or the head of his own department. It is even more embarrassing if he does not know his own supervisor's name. A new employee's first impressions are important, and the supervisor should take the time to give him this kind of information on the first day, to make him feel that he is joining a team. In some companies, industrial relations people give the new employee this and other information before he is taken to the department in which he will work.

Employee benefits.   The industrial relations department usually gives new employees a document which tells a great deal about the company and also outlines the employee benefits for which he will become eligible as time passes. They make certain that he understands these and takes full advantage of them when he becomes eligible.

Aids for further education.   Among the employee benefits of most companies are aids for further education. The new employee will be told by his supervisor about the training courses which he can take to improve his skill in his job. He will also be told, if this is the case, that the company encourages employees to take courses which will prepare them for higher responsibility.

HIRING PEOPLE WITH A COLLEGE EDUCATION.   A company has to hire some employees with a college education, and even a master's degree, to assure that enough competent financial people will be available for the top management positions in finance. Generally they will be given the same indoctrination as any new employee, but probably a good deal of the information is given them during the hiring interview as an inducement to join the organization. Most employees hired into the financial organization with this type of education are given as much responsibility as they are able to handle or can be trained for quickly. If the executive who does the hiring believes such a college trained individual is likely to qualify for executive training, as described later in this chapter, the new employee may be moved several times during his first year of employment to give him a broader knowledge of the company's operations.

Some firms find it desirable to hire graduates of college or graduate school after they have had one or two years experience with another company, rather than to take them on directly from the college or graduate school. They believe that someone else will then have finished the task of breaking them in. Moreover, at this later date the prospective employee will have a better idea of business and the part he wants to take in it. His experience in another company will have broadened him.

The variety of education and training

The education and training of employees may be accomplished in a variety of ways. One thing is certain: it cannot be forced upon them! The individual has to have the desire to prepare for higher responsibility. But the company and its executives can provide the atmosphere, opportunity, and financial support which will help the individual to carry out his own purpose.

TRAINING WITHIN THE COMPANY. Training by supervisors or others in the department in which the employee works is usual. Not only will he be trained in the work he is to do, but he will be given courses, during business hours, in subjects with which he should be familiar. Thus all new employees in the financial organization should be given a short course in accounting and cost accounting as practiced in the company, or a more comprehensive course if they have never studied accounting. Before being given a supervisor's job the employee should be given a course in organization principles and an elementary course in administration in which he will learn how to deal with subordinates. One of the benefits from training supervisors is that they in turn will train the people under them.

Those members of the financial organization who show promise of advancing to somewhat higher positions should be made familiar with a number of subjects as practiced in the business. One of the most important is an introduction to electronic data processing, unless the employee is already working in this area, in which case he would be given more advanced courses in the subject.

Of equal importance are seminars in financial and economic analysis as practiced in the company, to be given to all finance people at the grade of accountant or higher. Financial and economic analysis is probably the most useful skill that any financial person can have. These seminars are usually conducted by top financial executives with wide experience in the subject. This enables such executives to get acquainted with financial employees in the lower echelons.

FURTHER STUDIES IN COLLEGE OR UNIVERSITY. A large number of employees in the lower levels of a financial organization will lack a college or graduate education. Some of these will wish to secure a bachelor's degree or an MBA, and others will prefer to pursue selected studies. The company should provide encouragement and assistance. The latter is usually in the form of a rebate for a substantial part of the tuition fee and other expenses (textbooks and sometimes travel) upon successful completion of a course. The encouragement is provided by making it clear that the chances for promotion will be greater if the individual is better qualified. This means that promotion should be on the basis of merit and qualifications only.

Some of the people hired who have already received a bachelor's degree or an MBA may still want to pursue other studies at a local university. Occasionally such new employees believe they are already prepared to take over the supervisor's job (or even the president's) and must be disillusioned. Many have no desire to do more studying, after six years spent in college and business school. They have the feeling that they have done all they need to in this direction. One employee who had an MBA from a prominent graduate school of business administration expressed this feeling, and asked when he would be able to stop studying. The answer was, "When you retire!"

OTHER TYPES OF EDUCATION AND TRAINING. Other types of education and training include seminars both within and outside the company, and courses given by other institutions which take the full time of employees during participation. Occasionally an employee is disinclined to study in classes where progress is restricted by the class, but prefers instead to study alone. Some take correspondence courses, and others do a great deal of reading in subjects which will broaden their intelligence. Usually this type of self development is confined to those who already have one or more degrees and are not interested in securing other advanced degrees. Good supervisors should be aware of this type of self development, and endeavor to understand what the subordinate is trying to accomplish. He should also give encouragement by suggestions for books to be read, by sometimes providing such books by buying them first for the department library, and by keeping abreast of the progress of the individual.

First stage of executive development

A few years ago, in a talk before the Financial Executives Institute, Mr. L. C. Guest, Jr., senior vice president of Sylvania Electric Products, Inc., stated:

I believe that the successful manager, in the years ahead of us, will be spending more and more time educating himself. As the business problems he is called upon to face—and the means of solving those problems—become more technical and more complex, I predict that the manager will find that a large part of his time is spent on one form or another of education. This trend is becoming obvious in my own company. Virtually all our financial, marketing and production managers have spent a month or more sitting in classrooms during the past year—and I am talking about normal business hours. I am not even considering the additional time they must have spent at evening seminars—or in personal reading. Nor am I talking about education in their own areas of interest.

This describes what is happening in all companies which want to have executives capable of dealing with the competitive situation.

Selecting employees for executive development

Many supervisory positions are the first step up the ladder for ambitious employees. In other types of financial endeavor those who demonstrate ability are selected for more responsible jobs, but not necessarily jobs involving supervision. Usually men with degrees from college or graduate school will be hired into these positions in the controller's or treasurer's departments. They will all receive intensive on-the-job training, and can continue whatever education plans are suitable to them and to the company.

The progress of all of these employees, whether having been promoted from the ranks or hired into these positions, is measured through the periodic review of progress which is discussed later in this chapter. These employees are watched a little more closely than they were before attaining their first promotion, and the ones who show the desired qualities and progress are considered for executive development. This is so whether the employee is located at a plant, a sales office, or at the headquarters of a division or the company.

Development of financial executives, and perhaps those in other fields of endeavor, may be said to take place in two stages. Those selected for the first stage of executive development will already have received certain training, experience, and education. Each will have demonstrated that he has the qualities mentioned earlier as required for successful executives, at least to a reasonable degree. He will have attained the educational background considered desirable for a financial executive. In some companies no one is selected for this first stage of executive development who is not considered by those making the selection to be capable of reaching top management level in the company. Inasmuch as the company will spend quite a little money in developing those in this group, a very high standard for selection is warranted.

No matter how careful a company is in selecting people for the first stage of development, some will be lost to the company. Some will leave because their high level of competence attracts offers from other companies. Others, having attained a high degree of analytical ability, will analyze their own situations and decide that they can progress further or faster elsewhere. Every effort within reason should be made by the company to retain the best of those in this first stage of development; supervisors several levels above should get to know the employee and determine his aspirations and ambitions, as well as his family and financial situation. If this is done effectively, so that the employee feels he is part of the management team, he will usually go to his supervisor to discuss matters before accepting an offer from another company.

Types of development in first stage

There has been a good deal of discussion during the past few years about the manner in which executives can be trained to make the right decision; many point out that this cannot be done through the use of case studies and hypothetical situations. It seems obvious to many in business that if an employee could serve in every level of every department of the company, having made the decisions required at each level, he would be admirably trained to assume high responsibilities. The training and development of employees for executive levels should come as close to this concept as possible, and therefore should not be a fixed program, but one which is flexible so each employee will receive the type of training and experience he needs and wants.

Those selected for the first stage of executive development should receive an opportunity to broaden their knowledge of the company, and to gain a variety of experiences. Some might be sent from headquarters to a plant for from three to six months or more, and while there handle a cost system and have an opportunity to supervise those in the cost accounting unit. One employee at a plant might be given a tour of duty in planning and budgeting, either under a division controller or at headquarters. Another might have a tour of duty as an auditor under the general auditor, where he will gain a broad view of the company. Those who have not already been engaged in financial and economic analysis will be given broad experience in this technique.

Those in the first stage of development will attend seminars in subjects of the company's and their own choosing, and will take courses given either within or outside the company in such subjects as public speaking, advanced organization, and advanced administration and management. The company will be more liberal in approving courses for study in universities. Each will be given a more advanced course in the use of electronic data processing, and all should have a basic course in making flow charts for programming and in programming for computers used by the company.

Those who show good progress during the first two years in this first stage will be considered for promotion into positions in which they will gain valuable experience in advanced problems of finance. Each should have the opportunity to perform financial and economic analysis with responsibility for the analysis from start to the finished report. Various positions in the controller's or treasurer's departments provide opportunity for gaining good experience.

One of the best positions in which a member of the development group can demonstrate his ability to handle a finance executive's job is as division controller. The division controller has all of the controllership functions to perform, except handling the computer, if this is centralized for the company. He has, however, much to do with the use of the computer. He will have to demonstrate his ability to get along with the other division executives and yet make them respect the financial function and what it can do for them. He has to exhibit all of the fine qualities which make a division controller a participating member of the division team. This is so whether he is responsible to the division general manager or to the chief financial executive. In the latter case he has to try just a little harder.

Second stage of executive training and development

The purpose of the second stage of executive training and development is to prepare executives for appointment to the top financial positions as they become vacant through retirement or for other reasons. Hence the number of executives in this program will vary from time to time, depending on the expected demand.

Inventory of financial executives

The problem before top management is how to match the expected demand for top management executives with a supply sufficient to fill that demand on time.

DEMAND.   One method of measuring expected demand is to list all the top financial positions which will require special training and development to fill. These would include the chief financial executive and probably the first two levels of financial executives under him: the controller, treasurer, general auditor, and any others responsible directly to the chief financial executive; the managers of financial and economic analysis, of planning and budgeting, and of electronic data processing; and also the chief accountant and the half dozen managers under the treasurer. In addition would be added the particularly important positions of group or division controllers, and any chief financial officer of a subsidiary. This will total about 15 or 20 who are primarily responsible for the financial functions.[4] These are the positions that it is desirable to

---

[4] See Chapter 7, "Organization of the financial executive's functions," Exhibits 1, 2, and 6.

EXHIBIT 1. Demand (list A—vice president, financial and levels below—prepared 15 Feb 1955)

1 Organization number	2 Job level	3 Title	4 Name	5 Joined company	6 Appointed present job	7 Birth date	8 Retires first of	9 Develop program stg. date	10 Notes
1	30	Vice President, Finance	B. Crowell	Jan 42	Oct 46	12-15-93	Jan 59	2 44	Q VP F #1
11	26	Controller	L. Walters	Nov 34	Oct 46	8-23-94	Sept 59	2 45	Q VP F #1
12	26	Treasurer	H. Rogers	July 43	Oct 46	2-08-01	Mar 66	2 47	TQ #12
13	23	General Auditor	C. Sparks	Jan 30	Jan 40	9-18-94	Oct 59	1 44	TQ #13
14	22	General Office Manager	F. Johnson	Sept 27	Apr 46	3-15-07	Apr 72	2 50	Q #11
15	23	General Division Controller	I. Watch	Jan 22	Oct 54	10-07-95	Nov 60		
111	23	Manager, Financial and Economic Analysis	J. Lake	July 31	Jan 51	4-17-12	May 77	2 Apr 53	TQ #11 or #12
112	22	Manager, Planning and Budgeting	S. James	July 37	Jan 51	4-01-07	May 72	2 Jan 54	TQ #12 or #11
113	22	Chief Accountant	G. Jones	July 23	Oct 46	3-17-00	Apr 65	2 50	TQ #13
114	23	Manager, Information Technology	B. Henry	July 45	Jan 53	7-04-18	Aug 83	2 54	
121	22	General Credit Manager	W. Josephs	July 21	Jan 40	12-07-94	Jan 60	2 46	TQ #12
122	21	Assistant Treasurer	R. Johnson	Jan 35	Oct 46	7-14-99	Aug 64	2 Jan 54	Q #121 & #13
123	21	Assistant Treasurer	M. Richman	July 33	Jan 41	8-30-98	Sept 63	2 Jan 55	TQ #121 & #14
124	20	Manager Taxes	B. Agar	Oct 41	Jan 54	6-19-07	July 72	1 50	TQ #13
125	20	Manager Insurance	S. Beers	Sept 30	Apr 45	9-06-97	Oct 62	1 47	TQ #14
126	19	Compensation Manager	C. Calcos	Sept 30	July 54	1-16-04	Feb 69	1 50	TQ #124 & #125
131	19	Manager, Corporate Auditing	A. Bradley	July 51	July 53	6-07-28	July 93	1 Jan 54	TQ #113
132	19	Manager, Divisional Auditing	C. Vreeland	Sept 52	July 54	5-04-29	June 94	1 Jan 55	
141	19	Manager, Plant Office	P. Martin	Aug 37	Oct 46	9-04-15	Oct 80	1 Apr 53	Q #14
142	19	Manager, Sales Office	J. Benton	Sept 38	Oct 46	8-07-16	Sept 81	1 Jan 54	TQ #14
142	18	Headquarters Services	M. Parker	July 42	Oct 48	4-30-19	May 84	1 Jan 55	
414	22	Controller A Group	R. Townsend	July 43	Jan 53	3-13-07	Apr 72	2 Apr 53	Q #15
424	22	Controller B Group	W. Williams	July 43	Jan 53	3-17-13	Apr 78	2 Apr 55	TQ #13
434	22	Controller C Group	M. Oscar	July 43	Oct 54	7-02-11	Aug 76	2 Jan 54	TQ #13

First digit of all organization numbers has been omitted (president's digit).
In column 10: Q means qualified, TQ means tentatively qualified (could handle job on acting basis in an emergency), first organization number given for any-one is one for which best qualified or TQ.
All names used herein are entirely imaginary and have no relation to any persons, living or dead.

fill with well qualified executives. This is particularly so because the chief financial executive should be able to depend on these executives performing their tasks with a minimum of supervision.

The inventory listing shown in Exhibit 1 is arranged in the same manner as responsibilities are listed in the organization manual, but including only the first three levels of responsibility, with the chief financial officer at the top. The organization number of the job, its job level (salary standard level), and its title with the name of present incumbent are shown. The list includes pertinent dates for each individual: date of joining the company, date moved into present position, year of birth, month and year of retirement, and date brought into the first or second stage of executive development. (All retirements are on the first of the month following an employee's 65th birthday.) The organization numbers of each job are useful in indicating the positions for which the man is being considered. Space to the right of the data is provided for notes of this kind. The list would be prepared by the industrial relations department for the chief financial officer, and usually would be run by the computer.

SUPPLY.   Each responsible executive at the third level (those with three digits in the organization number shown in Exhibit 1) would have a similar list prepared showing the people under his supervision down to and including the level of accountant or technician. (This is the lowest level for which an employee would be selected for the first stage of development.) Thus, in the example illustrated in Exhibit 1, there would be a total of 18 such lists prepared. (An example of one of these is shown in Exhibit 2.) It will be noted that the three group controllers in the third level of responsibilities have organization numbers starting with 4, while others have numbers starting with 1, which is the digit of the chief financial officer. This is because the group controllers are responsible directly to their group vice presidents. (Similarly, a division controller is responsible directly to the manager of his division.) The general division controller has been delegated responsibility by the chief financial officer to exercise functional control over the group controllers.[5] (The group controllers exercise functional control over division controllers.) Financial people in divisions are included in these lists so they may be considered for training and development as financial executives. Of course some may decide to accept a position in their division outside of finance; on the other hand, some men in manufacturing, sales, or research may want to shift to finance. Such flexibility is desirable.

With more than about fifty persons in the finance organization, a single list of all financial people would be too cumbersome to use. Moreover, the lists for the third level of responsibilities are useful for

---

[5] In this illustration the company is organized with three groups of four divisions in each. There are no subsidiaries.

EXHIBIT 2

List A111—Mgr Fin & Ec Anal & All Levels Down to Incl 16—Prep 15 Feb 1955

1 Organization number	2 Job level	3 Title	4 Name	5 Joined company	6 Appointed present job	7 Birth date	8 Retires first of	9 Development program stg date	10 Notes
111	23	Manager, financial and economic analysis	J. Lake	July 32	Jan 51	4-17-12	May 77	2 Apr 53	TQ #11 or #12
1111	21	Senior analyst	G. Stearns	July 47	July 47	3-20-10	Apr 75	2 Apr 53	Q #111, #112, #414
1112	21	Senior analyst	W. Harris	July 46	July 49	5-17-15	June 80	2 Apr 53	Q #112, #111, #414
1113	21	Senior analyst	C. David	July 49	July 52	6-07-16	July 81	2 Apr 53	TQ #112, #111, #414
11111	20	Analyst	L. Thomas	July 42	Oct 46	3-12-18	Apr 83	2 Jan 54	Q sr analyst
11121	20	Analyst	B. Lyon	Oct 44	July 48	6-10-20	July 85	2 Jan 54	Q sr analyst
11112	20	Analyst	P. Frederick	July 45	May 50	2-20-22	Mar 87	1 Jan 47	TQ sr analyst
11122	20	Analyst	F. Arthur	July 47	Oct 50	9-08-24	Oct 89	1 Jan 49	
11131	20	Analyst	G. Goldman	July 50	July 53	2-12-26	Mar 91	1 Apr 51	
11132	20	Analyst	Vacant						
11114	18	Senior technician	M. Michaels	July 52	July 53	12-07-27	Jan 93	1 Jan 53	Q job level 19
11124	18	Senior technician	B. Edwards	July 52	July 53	6-19-28	July 93	1 Jan 53	Q job level 19
11134	18	Senior technician	A. Carl	July 52	Oct 53	3-22-29	Apr 94	1 July 53	
11135	18	Senior technician	S. Stewart	July 53	Oct 54	9-07-30	Oct 95	1 Jan 54	
11116	16	Technician	W. Warren	July 53	July 53	5-29-31	June 96	1 Jan 54	Q job level 18
11126	16	Technician	W. Eric	July 54	July 54	9-22-31	Oct 96	1 Jan 55	Q job level 17
11136	16	Technician	V. Anthony	Aug 54	Aug 54	3-18-32	Apr 97	1 Jan 55	
11137	16	Technician	V. Johns	July 51	Aug 54	7-16-32	Apr 97	1 Jan 55	
11117	16	Technician	W. Struble	July 52	Sept 54	8-10-32	Sept 97		
11127	16	Technician	S. Clark	June 50	Sept 54	6-04-31	July 96		

First digit of all organization numbers has been omitted (president's digit).

In column 10: Q means qualified, TQ means tentatively qualified (could handle job on acting basis in an emergency), first organization number given for any-one is one for which best qualified or TQ.

All names used herein are entirely imaginary and have no relation to any persons, living or dead.

considering recommendations by various supervisors for salary increases, promotion, and for bringing an individual into the first stage of development. They are also used to consider candidates for the second stage of development.

Selecting candidates for the second stage

One criterion for selecting anyone for the second stage of executive development is that he probably would be qualified, after such training and development, to be considered for appointment as chief financial executive. Another is that his performance is likely to be much improved in his present position by such training, and he can do a better job of training subordinates even though he might not be promoted beyond that job. Exhibits 1 and 2 will be used to illustrate the process of selecting employees for the second stage of training and development as used in Gismo Manufacturing Company.

SITUATION ON FEBRUARY 15, 1955. In the Gismo Manufacturing Company, reviews of progress of personnel were made annually. On each occasion some supervisors were selected for inclusion in either the first or second stage of executive development. Early in 1953 some important decisions were made by the company's president upon the recommendation of the vice president for finance.

1. Either the controller or the treasurer were then qualified to assume the duties of vice president for finance.

2. The situation should be reviewed early in 1955 as the vice president and three of his deputies would retire during 1959 and 1960. Because of this, certain executives were selected to join the second stage of development as shown by the dates opposite their names in Exhibits 1 and 2. Others were selected for the first stage of development.

3. The general office manager would probably remain in his present position until retirement. Before that time contemplated changes in organization might eliminate his job.

4. Those selected for the second stage of development fell into three general groups. (a) Some had an MBA received after two years of graduate study. These would be sent to take comparatively short courses (two to four weeks) in areas where they needed study most, particularly seminars or courses involving use of the computer. (b) Some had an MBA based on only one year of graduate study. These would be given somewhat more comprehensive courses. (c) Others had only a bachelor's degree, and would be sent to take a thirteen week course in advanced management such as that given by the Harvard Business School, but not all would be sent to the same university. Early in 1955, tentative selections would be made for vacancies that would appear, and job rotation would be considered for those candidates.

EXHIBIT 3

Some Decisions Made in Gismo Manufacturing Company in February 1955

Original Job					Preference in Consideration for jobs			Date of Decision
Number	Level	Title	Name	Moves to be made	(First)	(Second)	(Third)	
14	22	General Office Manager	F. Johnson	Spec. develop for job #13	#13 (23)			Sept 56
111	23	Manager, Financial and Economic Analysis	J. Lake	Move to #414 (22)—raise temp to level 23 if necessary)	#15	#11	#11	Sept 56
112	22	Manager, Planning and Budgeting	S. James	Move to #424 (22)	#12	#13	#11	Sept 56
113	22	Chief Accountant	G. Jones	Promote to #111 (23)	#13			Sept 56
414	22	A Group Controller	R. Townsend	Move to #112 (22)	#11	#13	#15	Sept 56
424	22	B Group Controller	W. Williams	Move to president's office on special duty under president	#12	#11	#15	Sept 56
1111	21	Senior Analyst	G. Stearns		#111	#11	#12	Sept 56
122	21	Assistant Treasurer	R. Johnson	Move to #1111 (21)	#121	#13	#12	Oct 58
123	21	Assistant Treasurer	M. Richman	Move to #122 (21)	#121	#13	#12	Oct 58
124	20	Manager, Taxes	B. Agar	To 2d stage development	#113	#13		Sept 56
1131	20	Manager, Corporate Accounting	D. Jameson	Move to #11131 (vacant)	#113	#13		Sept 56
11111	20	Analyst	L. Thomas	Move to #1131 (20)	Sr analyst	Group contr		?
11121	20	Analyst	B. Lyon	Move to #123 (21) (acting—not promoted now)	#123	Sr analyst		?

All moves to be made 4-1-55.

EXHIBIT 4

Memorandum Prepared by Vice President for Finance Listing Candidates for Promotion to Various Positions

Controller #11 level 26 retires Sept 59	Treasurer #12 level 26 vacant Jan 1958	General division controller #15 level 23 retires Nov 1960	General auditor #13 level 23 retires Oct 1959	General credit manager #121 level 22 retires Jan 1960
R. Townsend	S. James	J. Lake	F. Johnson	R. Johnson
S. James	R. Townsend	R. Townsend	G. Jones	M. Richman
W. Williams	J. Lake	W. Williams	B. Agar	S. Burpee (Credit manager, eastern area)
J. Lake	W. Williams	M. Oscar		

Positions that may become vacant due to promotion—starting about July 1957

Manager financial and economic analysis #111 level 23	Manager planning and budgets #112 level 22	Group controllers #414,424,434 level 22	Chief accountant #113 level 22
W. Williams	G. Stearns	G. Stearns	D. Jameson
S. James	W. Harris	W. Harris	L. Thomas
J. Lake	C. David	P. Martin (div contr)	B. Agar
G. Stearns	M. Oscar (for exp) same job level	H. Brown (div contr)	

Copies to: LW, HR, CS, IW, and WJ.

DECISIONS MADE IN FEBRUARY, 1955.   After studying individual records of the people in finance, and the data on the lists such as those shown in Exhibits 1 and 2, B. Crowell, the vice president for finance, conferred with his five deputies and then made the following recommendations which were agreed to by the president of the company.

When Mr. Crowell retired, H. Rogers, the treasurer, would succeed him. The latter would be made assistant vice president for finance one year ahead on January 1, 1958, and spend the first six months of 1958 being trained personally by Mr. Crowell, and the second six months handling the job alone. Mr. Crowell would move to another office to work on a special project, but would be available for consultation.

The other decisions are illustrated by notations made on the lists as shown in Exhibit 3. It should be noted that only recommendations affecting appointments to the first three stages of responsibility were placed before the president for decision. The others were within the authority of the vice president for finance, with the concurrence of the group or division general manager where group or division controllers were concerned.

After the decisions were made the vice president for finance prepared a memorandum (Exhibit 4) in which he listed the positions that would become vacant in 1959 and 1960, and also the important ones that might become vacant because of promotions into these positions. For each job, he listed the candidates under consideration roughly in the order of preference at the time. Copies of the list were sent to the three deputies who would retire and to the treasurer who would be promoted to the top position.

During the years that followed these decisions, most of the planned promotions and transfers were implemented. Of course, numerous other changes were made from time to time bringing new people into either stage one or stage two of the development program, and having executives exchange jobs to get a variety of experience. The task of annual review of the inventory of demand and supply of financial executives continued.

It appears desirable to identify qualified candidates for the chief financial officer's position at least five years before he retires, and sooner, if there is any chance that he might move out of the position at an earlier date. Hence it seems desirable to appoint as deputies of the chief financial officer only executives who are likely to qualify for that position.

Manner of training in the second stage

Those selected for grooming for top positions should be given the type of development which will broaden their background and properly prepare them for the position. Technical knowledge at higher levels is not as important as the qualities previously mentioned as desirable for executives, but an intimate knowledge of the capabilities of the computer and how it is used throughout the company is important. Probably those selected to prepare for the first three executive levels (the positions of chief financial officer, general auditor, controller, treasurer, etc. and their principal deputies) would be sent on company time and at company expense, to attend one of the one- to thirteen-week advanced management courses given by graduate schools of business or by one of the management associations. The particular schooling selected would depend on the state of education and development of the individual.

Besides the education described above, those in the second stage would be given the experience which they may have missed on the way up. This was illustrated in the discussion of Exhibits 1, 2, and 3 above. To give executives the advanced training they should have in financial and economic analysis, the positions of senior analysts in the financial and economic section of the controller's department are ideal. They should be reserved for occupancy only by those in the second stage of training and development. The work in this section is in the form of project assignments lasting anywhere from one day to a number of months. The senior analyst performs many analyses personally. Hence a new man taking over the unit can easily pick up the work with a minimum of briefing. Moreover, men of unusual ability are required in these positions. It would not do to fill them with people who would not qualify for further advancement, thus blocking the use of these positions for executive development. There are other positions at the same salary level in which good men who qualify can be placed. Such positions should be used for men who are not likely to qualify for further advancement in the near future, and when it is desirable to have each incumbent in the position for several years.

Periodic review of progress of financial executives

A supervisor should review progress with each of his subordinates at least once a year. Many companies require an annual rating of all employees, and this is an appropriate time for a review.

Rating of employees

Some companies have an elaborate form on which to rate employees as to personal characteristics, proficiency in present job, aptitude for the next higher position, extent of education, desire for self development, and a number of other criteria. One of the problems with such ratings is that different supervisors rate in different ways, and hence the employee ratings by one supervisor are not comparable with those of another.

Consistency and continuity in such ratings from year to year is desirable, and for this reason arrangements are sometimes made for the supervisor and his immediate superior to rate each of his employees; sometimes two supervisors in neighboring offices are in a position to rate the employees of both.

Discussing progress with employees

There is some difference of opinion as to whether the rating given an employee should be discussed with him.[6] Much of the criticism of this practice stems from the lack of expertise used both in preparing the rating and in the interview between supervisor and employee. The characteristics being rated usually require judgment with few, if any, facts to support the judgment. This is especially so the higher up the ladder the subordinate is. Despite this, a reasonably good rating can be made if the rater is properly trained and if he is aided by a second person, usually his own supervisor, who also knows the person being rated.

Using an interview between supervisor and subordinate to discuss his rating is also criticized because of the lack of training of the supervisor for such a confrontation. But this situation can also be improved. The writer's own experience is that discussing the rating with an employee is a valuable tool of development. The employee should have the opportunity of discussing his rating not only with his supervisor, but also with the latter's superior. The rating then becomes a means of discussing progress with an employee in a manner more satisfactory to the employee.

OCCASIONS FOR REVIEW OF PROGRESS.   A salary increase or a promotion is a fine opportunity to discuss progress with an employee. At that time, some form of rating should probably have been made by the supervisor before recommending the salary increase, and it can form the basis of the review of progress.

Some executives believe that the completion of a major assignment, whether well done or poorly done, is an appropriate time for review of progress. Another good time is when the employee returns from his annual vacation or when he is selected for either stage one or two of development. An outline for the discussion would be made by the supervisor listing the strengths and weaknesses of the employee, and after consultation with his superior these would be discussed with the subordinate. This discussion would cover the type of training or education the supervisor recommends or the employee requests. A summary of

---

[6] See McGregor, Douglas, "An Uneasy Look at Performance Appraisal," *Harvard Business Review*, May–June 1957, p. 89; Kelly, Philip R., "Reappraisal of Appraisals," *Harvard Business Review*, May–June 1958, p. 59; Patton, Arch, "How to Appraise Executive Performance," *Harvard Business Review*, January–February, 1960, p. 63; and Mayfield, Harold, "In Defense of Performance Appraisal," *Harvard Business Review*, March–April, 1960, p. 81.

the discussion would be prepared by the supervisor with copies for all present at the interview. The employee then has an opportunity to object to anything in the memorandum, which becomes part of his record.

Whenever a supervisor discusses progress with an employee, the occasion assumes greater importance if one or two higher levels of supervision are present. Some controllers and treasurers sit in on the review of progress of all employees who are being considered for selection for the first stage of executive development, and of course for all levels of responsibility above that.

Other means of measuring qualifications of employees

High-level financial executives frequently visit various offices of the financial organization to inspect methods being used and also to give seminars on certain special subjects. Thus they become acquainted with financial employees with whom they would otherwise not have contact. Over a period of time they should get a pretty good idea of the abilities of many such employees, and be in a position to name some who appear to be outstanding. This appraisal, when added to other appraisals by those who have close contact with the employee, will add up to a more comprehensive total appraisal of a candidate being considered for greater responsibility or for selection into the first stage of executive development.

One benefit from having top financial executives give courses to others in the financial organization, and of using the complete lists when considering people for selection to training programs, is that it makes it almost impossible for a supervisor to hoard a promising financial employee who is really doing most of his work and whom he is therefore loath to lose.

Salary administration of financial personnel

Finally, it seems appropriate here to discuss the use of salary administration as a tool in development of financial personnel.

Job levels

Most large business firms have established a number of job levels, each level having the same salary standards including a hiring or starting salary, and a maximum salary with from two to five steps in between, depending on the company and the job level. The salaries at various steps within the job level are usually about 4 to 8 percent apart, again depending on the company and the job level. The theory behind this is that people who remain at the same task become more proficient as time passes, and should therefore have a higher salary, without involving a promotion to a higher job level. Frequently, within the job level some greater responsibility might be given the individual with each step increase in salary, without involving a major change in his responsibility.

Salary increase

When a salary increase is given to an employee it should be for merit. If a supervisor makes it a practice to give salary increases at regular intervals without regard for comparative advancement and proficiency of individuals, he will have lost one of the most effective tools for encouraging self improvement by the employee. But when an increase in salary is given for proficiency or some major achievement, and the reason is discussed with the employee at the time he is notified of the increase, maximum benefit will accrue. The informal organization has a grapevine through which such news travels fast. Most salary increases are given at about 9- to 15-month intervals. An exception might be the case of a new employee, where a salary increase might be given after 6 to 9 months to encourage further progress, if any progress has been shown.

INCREASE FOR SPECIAL ACHIEVEMENT. Special achievement by an employee can be recognized by an increase at a much shorter interval, or by a double increase if one is due at about that time. This might be done for an outstanding financial employee who is due for a promotion that must be delayed for lack of a vacancy in the organization.

PROMOTION. A promotion to a higher responsibility is a recognition of progress welcomed by any executive. Usually such promotions are planned so that a salary increase is given at the same time. Sometimes no salary increase is given at the time, if one was recently given, and the individual is told that a salary increase will depend on his progress in the job as usual. Similarly, when executives exchange jobs to further their training, salary increases are not necessarily given at that time.

Promotion of a person into a job, just because a vacancy exists and not because the person is qualified for the job, is a mistake. If someone must handle the position and he is the one best qualified who is available, it is better to make him "acting" chief or manager. He should be told that he does not have a stranglehold on the position; but he should be able to figure out for himself that he is in a better position than anyone else to demonstrate his qualifications by doing the job well. By making it a temporary appointment, much embarrassment is saved if he cannot qualify for the job.

How do you motivate executives?

Much has been written, and much more will be written, on the subject of motivating employees to high performance. Many of the first incentive plans for salesmen, production people, and executives were based on the theory that the best incentive was to let the individual have his reward immediately, in his weekly or monthly pay check. At some point in his career an executive begins to think of the advantages of having his bonus deferred to retirement: his income tax on it will be lower, and he will need the money more then.

It seems apparent, too, that recognition of high performance is very desirable, if not necessary, in motivating executives. For instance one vice president for finance seldom issued a report over his own name; after completing the analysis and the report he would send it to the controller and ask him to read it, and if he agreed with it, to issue it as a controller's report (without showing who had prepared it). Similarly, the controller issued only one report monthly over his name—the one-page summary of the current situation for the president. No matter how much he had worked on another report, he brought in one of the senior analysts to help him and then asked him to review it and suggest changes. Then it was issued as a report of that senior analyst, with names of others who had worked on the report also listed. It was clear to all members of that financial organization that the top executives were not trying to claim all the credit, but were going out of their way to give credit to their subordinates. The result was a high degree of harmony and enthusiasm among the members of the organization.

To cover everything that has been said about motivating executives would take a large book, and then the reader would still have to decide for himself what is best for his own people. The pursuit of this subject is recommended highly. Success in motivating an executive will bring about an enthusiasm about being trained and developed for higher responsibility. It will also make him see the need for training and developing those under him so that they will help him to show better progress, and perhaps push him upstairs. Thus the company will come closer to achieving its objectives because its people will be better qualified.

Bibliography

ARGYRIS, CHRIS, *Interpersonal Competence and Organizational Effectiveness,* Homewood, Illinois, Richard D. Irwin, Inc. and the Dorsey Press, 1962.

BRADSHAW, T. F., *Developing Men for Controllership,* Boston, Harvard University Press, 1950.

CROOKS, LOIS, editor, *Issues and Problems in Managerial Manpower Planning,* Princeton, Educational Testing Service, 1967.

MCGREGOR, DOUGLAS, *The Human Side of Enterprise,* New York, McGraw-Hill Book, Co., 1960.

ALBROOK, ROBERT C., "Those Boxed-In, Left-Out Vice Presidents," *Fortune,* May, 1969.

HERZBERG, FREDERICK, PAUL, WILLIAM J., JR., and ROBERTSON, KEITH B., "Job Enrichment Pays Off," *Harvard Business Review,* March–April, 1969.

LAWRENCE, PAUL R., "How to Deal with Resistance to Change," *Harvard Business Review*, May–June, 1954, also January–February, 1969, p. 4.

MINER, JOHN B., "Bridging the Gulf in Organizational Performance," *Harvard Business Review*, July–August, 1968.

WALKER, JAMES J., "Trends in Manpower Management Research," *Business Horizons*, August, 1968, p. 37.

WALKER, JAMES J., "Forecasting Manpower Needs," *Harvard Business Review*, March–April, 1969, p. 152.

Tax planning and management

William M. Horne, Jr.*

One of the key functions of the corporate financial executive is that of tax planning and management. Although tax planning is essentially a staff function while tax management is a line-oriented one, their interrelationship makes it desirable to combine them in an integrated tax activity.

The knowledgeable financial executive is well aware of the importance of the tax activity to the corporation's economic health and growth. He recognizes that the federal government, as a mandatory and not-too-silent partner, has a priority claim on approximately one half of the total profits earned by the business. State and local governments, demanding ever-increasing shares of the corporation's earnings, are frequently no longer content with the non–profit-related tax sources, such as property taxes, and sales and use taxes.

The knowledgeable financial executive is also well aware that tax laws are replete with inconsistencies and overlapping claims by different tax jurisdictions. Unless the corporation's financial plans are carefully charted with these tax shoals in mind, the corporation's profit plan may run aground or be thrown off course.

This point is emphasized when the financial executive relates a dollar of tax savings to the quantum of additional sales required to produce the equivalent of a dollar of tax savings. Assume that the corporation's pre-tax profit return on sales is 15 percent. At a 52 percent tax rate, the after-tax return on sales is 7.2 percent. Approximately $14 of sales are required to produce $1 of after-tax profit. By contrast, $1 of tax savings produces $1 of after-tax profits.

---

* Vice President, Commercial Credit Company, Baltimore.

While the effect of tax savings on the corporation's earnings per share is dramatic, the role of taxes in the corporation's cash flow projections is equally compelling. By careful analysis of the tax deductions or credits available through accelerated depreciation, percentage depletion, and the investment tax credit, the financial executive can improve the corporation's cash flow and lessen its dependence on external borrowing to finance replacements or expansion of facilities.

Importance of the tax function

The place of the tax function in the corporation's organization chart appears to relate primarily to the size of the corporation. In major U.S. companies there is an acute awareness of the importance of their relationships with government, particularly the federal government. Since the field of taxes is one of the key areas in which this relationship is most visibly demonstrated in financial terms, there is a growing trend on the part of major U.S. companies to stress the tax function and to elevate the tax executive to membership in the top-management team. An increasing number of major companies (over $500 million in sales) are making the financial executive who specializes in taxes a corporate vice president who is brought in at an early stage to advise on important policy decisions. The need is obvious in the case of corporate acquisitions. or disposition of subsidiaries or facilities. The need may equally exist, but be less apparent, in decisions relating to new plant location, changes in employee benefit programs, new financing or distribution techniques, etc.

In the case of large corporations (generally $100 million to $500 million in sales), the tax function is usually the responsibility of a director of taxes[1] who is a key member of the financial vice president's staff. With the many other competing demands on his time, the financial vice president must rely heavily upon the director of taxes in questions of tax policy.

For the medium-sized corporation (generally $10 million to $100 million in sales), the tax function is usually handled by a tax manager who reports to the controller or treasurer.

In the small corporation (sales of $10 million and under), the controller or treasurer will usually be directly responsible for tax matters in addition to his other duties.

These classifications are based on what appear to be emerging patterns. They will vary, of course, reflecting such factors as the nature of the industry and the complexity of its tax problems, the corporate struc-

---

[1] The title of director of taxes appears the more prevalent one today. Certain major corporations, however, still employ the title of tax manager, or its equivalent, for the head of the corporation's tax function.

ture, the corporation's involvement in foreign operations, and the factor which usually affects any organizational chart—the strength of the individual executives for whom the chart is designed.

Organizing the tax function

The organization of the tax function is also generally related to the size of the corporation. Obviously, for the small corporation there is no problem. The controller or treasurer may have the tax returns prepared by an accountant or clerk under his supervision or, as is more likely to be the case, will have the returns prepared by the corporation's public accounting firm.

In the case of medium-sized corporations, the tax manager will generally have from one to four technical or clerical employees who will assist him in preparing the tax returns.

For the large corporations, particularly major corporations, the organization of the tax function becomes a matter of concern, since an effective organizational pattern is essential to developing maximum utilization of highly trained and highly paid personnel.

In major corporations, there may be over a hundred employees devoting full time to tax planning and tax compliance.[2] These may include individuals with specialized educational and professional backgrounds, such as lawyers, accountants, economists, and engineers. Substantially all of the professional employees and many of the clerical employees will have college degrees. The professional employees will frequently also have graduate degrees in law or business administration and may have had extensive professional experience with public accounting firms, law firms, or with the government.

To channel the skills of these highly trained professional personnel into a smoothly functioning tax department requires that careful consideration be given to the organizational structure. Obviously, no one form of organization is best suited for all companies. Adaptations must be made to accomodate their particular needs as well as the range of their managerial and professional talent. For example, a corporation that is well advanced in the art of reflecting its operations and maintaining its records by electronic data processing may place a different emphasis on organizing the tax compliance function than will a corporation which is not so well advanced.

In broad general terms, there are three types of organizational pat-

---

[2] For example, Corporation "X" has 120 employees in its tax department in the U.S. and 75 employees in a number of foreign subsidiaries. Corporation "Y" has 88 employees in the tax departments of its U.S. holding company and domestic subsidiaries and an additional 100 employees engaged in tax work for its foreign subsidiaries and affiliates.

terns which tax departments of major corporations appear to follow today: (1) organization by function, (2) organization by type of tax, (3) composite organization.

Functional organization

The functional organization will recognize two or three principal functional areas—generally planning, legal, and compliance.

The planning function takes into account the needs of the corporation for skilled tax advice in making corporate reorganizations and acquisitions, in selecting between alternative methods of new debt or equity financing, in establishing new foreign ventures, and in meeting a host of other questions of major corporate policy. Personnel assigned to the planning function must have a detailed knowledge of the intricacies of federal, foreign, and state tax laws. They should also possess a comprehensive knowledge of the corporation's operations, including a familiarity with its products, subsidiaries or divisions, and accounting procedures.

To be effective, tax planning personnel must have the confidence and respect of top management, heads of operating units, and the heads of other staff departments, particularly legal and accounting. They must be able to coordinate tax objectives with the long-range plans of the corporation's planning department. They must keep abreast of changes in governmental statutes and regulations outside the tax field which will decidedly affect tax planning: for example, the restrictions which might be imposed by a foreign government on the repatriation of earnings from a foreign subsidiary. In addition, tax planning personnel must keep in touch with developments in the area of tax compliance so that future plans can be shaped to avoid the problems created in current tax audits.

The legal function will, in the case of some corporations, be centered in the legal department rather than in the tax department. It appears preferable, however, to include the tax lawyers in the tax department where they can be available on a day-to-day basis for consultations on the legal aspects of current tax problems. The tax lawyer who becomes familiar with the ramifications of the corporation's domestic and foreign operations frequently becomes the logical choice to head the planning function.

In addition to researching and advising on current tax questions, tax lawyers in the legal function will frequently prepare protests or briefs and argue the corporation's position before the Appellate Division of the Internal Revenue Service and before state revenue department heads or state tax commissions. Generally, they will also prepare requests for tax rulings or determination letters on such matters as corporate reorganizations, changes in pension or profit-sharing plans, changes in accounting methods, and similar matters in which prior governmental clearance is required or desired.

The compliance function is the largest function of the tax department, both in terms of scope and in number of personnel. The compliance function is responsible for timely filing of the myriad tax returns required of a major corporation. These include income, franchise, property, sales and use, payroll, and miscellaneous returns. In addition, the compliance function is responsible for all tax payments and for filing all the information returns that are required by federal, state, and local governments.

Generally, personnel in the compliance function will handle the audits of the corporation's tax returns. They must locate and supply to the examining agent voluminous records on prior years' transactions in order to satisfy his requests. Compliance personnel have the burden of persuading the agent not to assert deficiencies, by convincing him that the transaction was properly reported by the corporation on its tax return.

Organization by type of tax

The second major type of tax department organization is organization by type of tax. Here, the planning and compliance functions are combined, and the department is subdivided according to the type of tax which is handled. Depending upon the scope of the corporation's operations, there may be (1) a federal tax section, (2) a foreign tax section and (3) a state and local tax section. The state and local tax section may be further subdivided into two or more of the following: income and franchise taxes, property taxes, sales and use taxes.

Payroll taxes, both federal and state and local, are usually administered in a separate section. In some corporations, the payroll tax function is located outside the tax department, usually along with the payroll department which may report to the treasurer or to the director of personnel.

Composite organization

The third principal type of tax department organization is the composite organization. In these cases, the tax department may be organized along both functional lines and by type of tax. In most instances, the compliance function is broken down by type of tax, while the planning and legal functions generally are not subdivided but instead have one or more assistants reporting to the individual heading the function.

The composite organization may include specialized sections, depending upon the corporation's principal industry. For example, a major oil company might include an engineering and valuation unit as an important element in its organizational structure.

Training of tax personnel

As tax laws grow increasingly complex the need for qualified and trained tax personnel grows apace. The experienced corporate tax executive must combine a solid technical background with administrative ability. He must also combine meticulous attention to detail with insight and imagination in dealing with complex corporate tax problems. Today's corporate tax executive may have been trained as an accountant, as a lawyer, or may have received a general business education. In many instances, he combines these professional skills with a graduate business degree. Whatever his educational background or experience, the tax executive must be able to communicate his knowledge; to deal effectively with other management personnel within the company; and, on the outside, with government tax administrators and legislators.

Because the experienced tax man is much sought after today, not only by corporations but also by the legal and accounting professions and by the government, the corporate tax executive must look to a number of recruiting sources to build an effective tax department. Frequently, the tax executive will look to other departments of his company for tax trainees. Particularly in the accounting and auditing departments, he may find young men who are capable of being trained as tax men. If he needs more experienced personnel, he will frequently turn to the public accounting firms or to the law firms to find an individual who has already received his basic tax training in private practice. Other important recruiting sources are government tax men, particularly those who have been trained by the Internal Revenue Service. Since there is a growing tendency on the part of the professions to pay salaries to their younger men at levels which the corporate tax executive finds difficult to meet,[3] he frequently finds it necessary to go to the colleges, the graduate business schools, and the law schools to find young trainees who have the necessary educational background to qualify for more tax training.

Because of the scarcity of trained tax personnel, it is increasingly important that the corporate tax executive develop a training program for individuals within his department. Probably the most effective training is on-the-job training. The young tax accountant or trainee can be assigned to various jobs within the compliance section. As he develops more experience, he can be given increasingly difficult assignments. As he enlarges his technical background, he will also gain more insight into his company's operations.

To supplement this on-the-job training, several specialized training programs have recently been developed by the Tax Executives Institute,

---

[3] See e.g. article "Wall Street Firm Raises Starting Pay by $5,000 to $15,000," appearing in February 8, 1968 edition of *The Wall Street Journal.*

an international organization composed of tax executives from leading U.S. and Canadian companies. One such course is the Summer Tax Course, recently instituted at Georgetown University. The Tax Executives Institute has also conducted an introductory course in automatic data processing for tax personnel. This course has been conducted in several sessions at Georgia Tech Graduate Business School.

A number of universities throughout the country hold various tax institutes and tax seminars. While these are valuable in up-dating the technical skills of the experienced tax man, they tend to be slanted towards the private practitioner rather than the corporate tax man.

Another important aspect in the training of tax department personnel is found in the various management training programs that most progressive companies today offer to middle management. These training programs are usually well designed to instill in the potential executive the basic management skills which he will require for administering a large department, such as a tax department.

Federal tax planning and reporting

Planning for effective minimization of the federal income tax burden is the most important responsibility of the corporate tax executive. It is here that he can make his most significant contribution to his company's progress.

The experienced tax executive is well aware, however, that tax planning is only an element in overall corporate strategies. The tax planning must be adapted to operational goals and objectives. A corporate plan that is primarily based on tax considerations rather than on general business objectives will usually come to grief.

On the other hand, corporate strategies which are formulated without reference to tax consequences may result in unexpected and disastrous tax penalties. There is an obvious need for proper communications to avoid these results. The tax executive should be apprised at an early stage of the intended plans and objectives. Then he can properly assess the tax consequences and suggest alternative and less costly means of achieving the objectives, if he determines that the original plans contain tax pitfalls.

The areas in which proper tax planning can prove of critical importance are nearly as broad as the scope of the corporation's activities. A few specific examples can probably best illustrate the point.

Case A. Corporation X, in acquiring Corporation S, represented to S's stockholders that the transaction would be a tax-free exchange of stock. To insure this result, X's outside tax counsel obtained from the Internal Revenue Service a favorable tax ruling. The ruling contained as one of its conditions the representation by X that S would be continued as a subsidiary. X's top management relied on the fact that a favorable ruling had been obtained, but did not bother to check its details. Shortly thereafter, *X's* management decided to liquidate S and operate it as a division. As a result of this action, the tax ruling was vitiated. *S's* stockholders were taxed on the transaction and sued *X* for damages.

Case B.   Corporation *Y's* top executives had pre–1964 restricted stock options with option prices of $75 to $90. These options had 6–8 years remaining in which they could be exercised. Since *Y's* stock was currently selling at $45, *Y's* management, without benefit of tax advice, asked its executives to surrender their restricted options and receive instead an equivalent number of new qualified options exercisable at $45 within a 5-year period. The net tax result was to nullify the new options.

Case C.   Corporation Z had owned its computer installation for 46 months when it sold the computer and replaced it with a new model. If *Z's* computer department had obtained tax advice before acting, it probably would have delayed the replacement for at least two months, thereby saving a substantial amount of investment tax credit. The tax credit was lost because the property was not held for the minimum 4-year period.

Case D.   A corporation was engaged in highly seasonal business with losses during the winter months being a regular occurrence. In prior years, a fiscal year ending September 30th had been established. By shifting to a calendar year for income tax purposes, the company was able to defer substantially all of its estimated tax liability until the last two estimated tax payment dates.

While these examples illustrate both dangers involved in decisions taken without regard to tax consequences or possible savings that come from review of operating conditions by an informed tax executive, they also bear on another problem—the necessity for the corporate tax executive to keep abreast of current tax developments. There is a constant stream of new tax legislation, regulations, rulings, and court decisions with which the tax executive must be familiar. The tools which the tax executive must employ to keep abreast of current developments include daily reading of tax publications; intensive study of new laws, regulations, rulings, and court decisions that may directly affect his company's operations; participation in the deliberations of tax committees of various industry and trade associations; and attendance at advance tax institutes and seminars. Unless the tax executive is well informed on recent developments, he may cause his company to incur needless expense based on improper tax advice.

Federal tax compliance

The need for keeping up with current developments is as equally applicable to the area of tax compliance as it is to planning. In preparing tax returns, discussing issues with government agents on audits, or in settling tax disputes at the appellate level, tax department personnel must be knowledgeable on the latest laws, rulings, or decisions which could affect the tax issues with which they are dealing.

In the compliance function, the preparation of returns plays the most important role, not only because of time deadlines but also because the manner in which the returns are prepared may determine the issues which will be raised by the revenue agent and which may ultimately have to be appealed to the appellate division or to the courts.

There are a number of techniques which the well-organized tax department will employ to facilitate its job of preparing tax returns. One of these is a Tax Department Manual which prescribes general instructions and assigns responsibility for the preparation and review of the returns. The department will normally also maintain a tax calendar to insure that returns are prepared and reviewed within the proper lead time in advance of filing. The calendar will also contain the tax payment dates, as well as filing dates and dates on which statutes of limitations will run out.

Estimated tax payments present a special problem since the tax department should keep the estimated payments to the allowable minimum in order to reduce the drag on cash flow. However, if the estimates fall below the allowable minimum, the corporation will be subjected to a non-deductible 6 percent penalty. Since the permissible margin of error was reduced in 1968 from 30 percent to 20 percent, the need to obtain accurate and up-to-date financial reports is apparent.

Where the corporation has a number of divisions or subsidiaries, the tax department will generally devise work papers for tax returns and tax estimates. These work papers are distributed to the financial reporting centers where the data from the financial statements can be translated into the appropriate tax-work paper categories. The completed tax-work papers are returned to the tax department which uses them to prepare the tax returns and to determine estimated tax liability.

Tax files are generally maintained for each tax reporting unit and jurisdiction by taxable year. The tax files will contain the tax-work papers and any special instructions or comments noted in the preparation or review of the return. If there is a recurring adjustment, as a result of a prior tax audit, this is noted in the tax file, along with any special exemption or ruling that might be otherwise overlooked. The tax files for the immediately prior years should always be checked before the return is prepared for the current return year.

Tax audits

The manner in which the Internal Revenue Service will conduct its audit of the taxpayer's federal income tax returns is influenced by the size of the corporate taxpayer and by any special complexities of its industry.

In 1966, the IRS inaugurated its Coordinated Examination Program to deal more effectively with the tax audits of large corporate taxpayers.[4] In applying this program, the IRS has used a cut-off point of $250 million of assets. The principal feature of the program is its emphasis upon the "team audit." This involves two or more revenue agents working on the examination under the direction of a managing auditor. The managing auditor analyzes the returns, the government's files on the taxpayer, and the results of prior audits to determine what issues are likely to be raised and what specialists may be required on the audit—an engineer agent, an international agent, a pension trust specialist. The managing auditor also develops an audit plan and sets a timetable for progress on the audit.

The institution of the Coordinated Examination Program by the IRS was undoubtedly influenced by the recent increase in number of large conglomerate enterprises whose subsidiaries or divisions cut across a number of widely disparate industries.

The experiences of large corporate taxpayers with the Coordinated Examination Program in its early stages were surveyed by the Tax Executives Institute, and a report was published indicating both the successes and the deficiencies in the program from the taxpayer's point of view.[5] The principal criticism raised by taxpayers related to the need for the managing auditor to exercise more control over the other revenue agents on his team in order to avoid excessive detail work and the raising of inconsequential issues.

An important area in which the structure of the Coordinated Examination Program is still developing is the question of shifting jurisdiction for the examination among different Internal Revenue districts. Generally, the district in which the parent company files its tax returns will control the audit and will determine the extent of the audits made of the parent's subsidiary or affiliated companies in other districts. The so-called "support district," however, may prove unwilling to completely turn over its responsibility for the audit of the subsidiary or affiliated company. It may be less than enthusiastic over the prospect of having its agents working under the control of a managing auditor from another district. To avoid these jurisdictional problems, the managing auditor may send agents from his own team to the outlying district to examine the books and records of the subsidiary.

Another important development in the audit practices of the Internal Revenue Service is the identification on a nationwide basis of so-called

---

[4] See article by Assistant Commissioner Donald W. Bacon. "Progress Report on The Coordinated Examination Program," 19 *The Tax Executive* 165 (April, 1967).

[5] "A Report of TEI Member Experiences with the Coordinated Examination Program of the Internal Revenue Service," *Tax Executives Institute,* February, 1968.

"industry issues." The national office of the IRS has held a number of industry meetings to which it calls in audit representatives throughout the country from various regions and districts in which a particular industry is located. These meetings seek to identify special tax problems peculiar to the particular industry and to insure that a uniform audit approach is taken to these special industry problems.[6]

In the case of the smaller company, the Revenue Service has tended to continue its more traditional "one-man, one-case" approach. Even in these audits of smaller corporate taxpayers, however, there is a growing tendency on the part of the examining agent to call in a specialist for assistance on some particular phase of the audit, usually in the depreciation area where the assistance of an engineering agent is obtained.

Relations with the agent

Taxpayers' methods of dealing with the revenue agent differ widely. Some corporate tax executives have found it expedient to insist that all requests for information made by the revenue agent (or by the managing auditor in the case of a team audit) be made in writing and numbered to facilitate handling. The taxpayer will then identify on the agent's written request the type of documents which were supplied to the agent, the date the information was furnished, and the date the documents were returned by the agent. If the agent's request involves a summary of procedures followed by the company, this information will be given to the agent in a written response with a copy retained in the taxpayer's audit files.

Other taxpayers tend to be more informal in their relations with the revenue agent. They attempt to supply information orally wherever possible, and keep a record of any documents which have to be furnished to the agent only after a tax issue has been clearly joined.

Another area in which practices differ widely is with respect to the degree of control exercised over the agent's contacts with other employees of the taxpayer. Some corporate tax executives insist that the revenue agent's contacts should generally be limited to representatives of the tax department. If it becomes necessary for the agent to speak directly to another officer or employee of the company, this is always done with a tax department employee present. Most revenue agents or managing auditors will abide by these constraints, recognizing that in the long run they are timesaving and more effective in closing out the audit. When the agent deals directly with non-tax personnel, he frequently wastes time because he is supplied with irrelevant information which he culls through before he recognizes that it is not responsive to his question.

Both the tax executive and the revenue agent will recognize the

---

[6] See Footnote 4, *supra.*

advantages inherent in an early disposition of the audit. A major emphasis of the Coordinated Examination Program is directed to putting the audits of major corporations on a more current basis. When tax audits are conducted for taxable years dating back ten or more years prior to the year in which the examination is made, there are obvious problems in obtaining documentation and in locating personnel who had direct personal knowledge of the transactions in question. Several major corporations have found it advantageous to push for a closing of the audit gap to the point where the earliest year under audit is never more than two years prior to the current year. To accomplish this closing of the audit gap may require a firm policy on waivers of the statute of limitations. Waivers are granted only for the absolute minimum period the IRS requires to complete its audit. By restricting the waiver to 10–30 days at a time, the objective of expediting the audit is met. The Internal Revenue Service is usually most cooperative, since it has a similar objective of putting its audits on a more current basis. This is contrary to the widely held belief that the IRS will make arbitrary and unreasonable assessments if the taxpayer refuses to execute extended waivers.

Problems raised by EDP

The increasing use of electronic data processing by corporate taxpayers raises special auditing problems. The tax department must be familiar with data processing procedures and must be prepared to answer the difficult questions of what print outs must be made and retained to insure an audit trail that will meet IRS requirements.[7] As direct entry of original input data into the computer becomes more commonplace, it will become increasingly difficult, if not impossible, to satisfy the IRS audit requirements. It appears likely that the IRS must ultimately be prepared to make current on-the-spot checks of the computer operations to determine that the corporation's prescribed data processing procedures are, in fact, being followed. The IRS is currently reviewing EDP testing procedures which it may adopt in an effort to resolve these auditing problems.

A related problem is the degree of acceptance by the IRS of records maintained on microfilm. The IRS will not accept the use of microfilming for general ledgers, cash receipts and disbursement journals, and similar books of original entry.[8] On the other hand, all subsidiary records and documents can be microfilmed. With good referencing, the use of microfilming generally expedites the production of data required by the agent and thus helps to shorten the audit time.

---

[7] The Internal Revenue Service has published guidelines for record requirements to be followed where accounting records are maintained within EDP systems; see *Rev. Proc.* 64–12, 1964–1 (part 1) C.B. 672.

[8] See *I.T.* 3866, 1947–2 C.B. 68.

From the tax department's standpoint, there are definite benefits derived from the use of data processing in keeping the corporation's accounting records and statistics. Programs can be devised to quickly calculate the tax depreciation allowable under different methods, such as sum-of-the-years digits and double declining balance, as well as the depreciation deduction available under the different allowable methods of grouping assets. Not only can taxes, such as sales and use taxes and payroll taxes, be quickly calculated on individual transactions, but total taxes due can be determined by the computer and returns printed out on a quarterly or annual basis. The computer can also be utilized in tax planning by rapidly calculating the tax results of available alternatives.

The revenue agent's report

Eventually, the audit examination reaches the stage where the corporate tax executive and the revenue agent determine that there are unresolved issues upon which they cannot reach agreement. In the usual course of events, these disagreements arise from differences in interpreting statutes or regulations or in the construction to be given to an agreed set of facts. In a few instances, the facts themselves may be in dispute or the agent may claim that the taxpayer has failed to obtain the necessary facts to support its claimed deduction. Wherever possible, it is well to produce all relevant facts during the course of the agent's examination.

Where the taxpayer and the revenue agent have reached an impasse upon a group of issues, the agent writes up his audit examination in a report referred to generally as the R.A.R. (Revenue Agent's Report). The report sets forth all of the proposed adjustments with the agent's reasons for making them, and calculates the deficiency proposed to be assessed.[9] The agent then sends in his report through his group supervisor to the district review staff for review. After the review staff has checked the agent's calculations and determined that the adjustments appear warranted under present IRS policy, a copy of the agent's report is sent to the taxpayer with a "30-day letter" advising the taxpayer of its right to request an informal conference at the district level or a hearing before the appellate division.

Increasing use is being made of the conference at the district level, particularly where the amount in dispute is small[10] or the issues turn upon an interpretation of an agreed set of facts. Where the issue involves

---

[9] Under certain circumstances the report may determine an overpayment of tax and propose a refund to taxpayer.

[10] Where the total amount of proposed additional tax, proposed over-assessment or claimed refund does not exceed $2,500 for any taxable year, a district audit division conference will be granted upon request without the prior filing of a written protest, and, further, the settlement authority of the chief, conference staff, may be extended to include evaluation of litigation hazards under certain conditions. See *Proced. Rules,* Sec. 601.105(c)(2)(ii) and (c)(5).

an interpretation of a statute, treasury regulation or ruling, the IRS will usually urge the taxpayer to waive the district conference and take the dispute to the appellate division.

Appellate procedures

A prerequisite to a conference with an appellate division conferee is the filing of a written protest with the district director.[11] No particular form is requird for the protest, but certain information is essential to filing a clear and precise statement of the taxpayer's argument.[12] The protest must be signed under penalties of perjury by an authorized officer of the taxpayer.[13] It is obviously important that the facts be fully and accurately developed for inclusion in the protest.

Where the protest involves a number of complicated issues, the district director will generally grant the taxpayer an extension of time from the normal 30-day period for filing it. If a protest was previously filed prior to a conference at the district level, a new one is not required for those issues on which the district conference failed to produce an agreement.[14]

There are definite advantages to settling the case at the agent or district conference levels. By executing Form 870, in which taxpayer agrees to pay the tax deficiency resulting from the settlement, the taxpayer is not precluded from later filing a claim for refund within the statutory period and, upon disallowance of the refund claim, filing suit for refund in its local district court or in the Court of Claims. The taxpayer should also be aware of the partial settlement procedures which are available, permitting the taxpayer to execute a Form 870 as to certain issues resolved at the agent or district level while continuing its appeal of other issues to the appellate division.[15]

Where issues remained unresolved and a written protest has been filed, the appellate conferee in the appellate division, after appropriate review of the file, will invite the taxpayer to a settlement conference. While the conference is informal, the taxpayer should be careful to thoroughly prepare its case and to brief any applicable Treasury regulations and rulings or court decisions. The appellate division has authority to settle disputes by taking into account the hazards of litigation.[16]

---

[11] See *Proced. Rules,* Sec. 601.105(d)(2) and 601.106(b). A written protest is not a prerequisite to appellate consideration and hearing where the case does not exceed $2,500 for any year and a district conference previously had been held with respect thereto.

[12] These requirements are set out in Form No. 5 (Rev. 8–64), which accompanies the 30-day letter.

[13] See *Proced. Rules,* Sec. 601.106(f)(5); *Rev. Proc.* 61–36, 1961–2 Cum. Bul. 575 and TIR 343 (10/31/61).

[14] See *Proced. Rules,* Sec. 601.106(b).

[15] See *Proced. Rules,* Sec. 601.105(b)(4), 601.105(c)(4) and 601.106.

[16] See *Proced. Rules,* Sec. 601.106(f)(2).

Where settlement is achieved at the appellate division level, the taxpayer is requested to execute a Form 870–AD. Its execution by the taxpayer and the government is generally regarded as binding in the absence of fraud or misrepresentation.[17]

If agreement is not reached with the appellate division, the taxpayer is then issued a 90-day letter. This is the deficiency notice which gives the taxpayer 90 days within which to file a petition in the Tax Court, and have its case heard without necessity of first paying the tax in advance. Alternatively, the taxpayer may let the tax be assessed, pay the tax, and file a claim for refund. After the refund claim is denied by the IRS or, if the IRS fails to act on the claim in the prescribed statutory period, the taxpayer may maintain suit for refund in the appropriate federal district court or may bring its action in the Court of Claims.

The decision as to whether taxpayer should pursue its remedies in the Tax Court or should pay the tax and bring suit in the district court or Court of Claims is an important one. Among the factors to consider are whether the issues involved have been previously decided by the respective courts. Not infrequently the same issue may have been decided one way by the Tax Court and in a different manner by the Court of Claims or by one or more district courts. Also, the type of issue may be determinative. A complex, technical issue may be more readily understood by the Tax Court with its specialized jurisdiction than by the Court of Claims or district courts which hear issues in a number of other fields. Another factor is the cash consideration. If the taxpayer is faced with substantial deficiencies, which it is confident will be ultimately disposed of for a fraction of the amount assessed, it may be reluctant to pay the deficiencies and rely for recovery of the tax on a suit for refund.

Whether the taxpayer decides to pursue its remedies in the Tax Court or via a suit for refund, there still exist settlement possibilities at any stage up to final judgment.

Foreign tax planning and reporting

For the corporation engaged in extensive foreign operations, proper tax planning is essential. Without proper planning, it is possible for the aggregate of U.S. and foreign tax liabilities to exceed 100% of the profits earned. A close coordination of federal and foreign tax planning must be maintained.

Tax department personnel assigned to foreign tax planning should be well grounded in U.S. income taxes, particularly the corporate reorgani-

---

[17] Although there is judicial conflict as to whether a taxpayer is estopped from maintaining a refund suit filed subsequent to the running of the statute of limitations on further assessments with respect to a period for which an 870–AD was executed (compare, e.g., *Daugette* v. *Patterson*, 250 f.2d 753 (C.A. 5th), cert. denied, 356 U.S. 902 and *Uinta Livestock Corp.* v. *United States*, 355 f.2d 761 (C.A. 10th), the execution of Form 870–AD is practically regarded by most tax practitioners as a binding commitment not to reopen the case.

zation provisions, foreign income, and foreign tax credit provisions. In addition, the foreign tax specialist should have a basic knowledge of the tax structure of the principal foreign countries in which the corporation operates. If the corporation's foreign activities are widespread, he will undoubtedly have to rely upon tax advisors in a particular country for the detailed application of the foreign law to a proposed transaction. Unless the tax department is large enough to maintain its own tax specialists abroad for a given country or region, it will normally maintain a close liaison with outside tax practitioners in the foreign country, usually those associated with branches of U.S. accounting or law firms.

When the corporation first decides to extend its operations to a particular foreign country, it has alternative methods of operation available to it, each of which involves important differences in tax consequences. The corporation may prefer to gradually build a market for its product by exporting from the U.S. and selling through local distribution of its products in the foreign market. In either case, a question is raised as to whether the product needs to be warehoused locally to facilitate distribution. Also, a decision must be made on whether to form a local sales subsidiary or to operate through a branch of the parent U.S. company, through a branch of a U.S. subsidiary, or through a branch of a foreign subsidiary.

The foreign tax specialist must take into account not only the U.S. and foreign tax effects of the alternative methods of operation, but he must also consider tariff and import quotas, restrictions on foreign exchange and on repatriation of earnings, and the application of the U.S. limitations on foreign direct investment.

If the corporation sells its finished products, components of its products, or raw materials to its foreign subsidiary for further manufacture, assembly, or sale, the foreign tax specialist must consider the application of the Treasury Regulations under Section 482 of the Internal Revenue Code. The thrust of these regulations is to insure that the price charged by the U.S. company to the foreign subsidiary is equivalent to an arms-length price. The practical application of these regulations, in situations where an arms-length price does not exist or where foreign governmental restrictions influence market policy, can lead to costly tax traps for the unwary. Also, the thrust of the Section 482 regulations extends not only to sales but to other transactions between the U.S. corporation and its foreign subsidiary, including licensing of patents, trademarks, or know-how; interest charged on loans; rent charged for the use of property; charges for engineering or similar services; and other intercompany transactions.

The foreign tax specialist must be fully conversant with the detailed rules and exceptions under Subpart F of the Internal Revenue Code. These rules determine whether the income earned by a foreign subsidiary will be currently subject to U.S. income tax, or whether taxation is postponed until the earnings are repatriated in the form of dividends, or the investment in the subsidiary is disposed of by sale or otherwise.

The foreign tax specialist should also keep abreast of developments in the field of tax treaties. By individually negotiated tax treaties with major foreign countries, the United States has reduced the instances in which differences in the tax laws of the signatory countries can result in an inequitable burden of double taxation. There remain, however, many potential problems of double taxation, arising in no small part because of the lack of acceptance by foreign governments of the relatively rigid allocation rules adopted by the U.S. Treasury in its Section 482 regulations.

Foreign tax compliance

The foreign tax compliance function, as well as the reporting function, has been complicated by the increasing assertion of U.S. tax jurisdiction over the current operations of foreign subsidiaries. Even where no U.S. tax liability exists because of exceptions under the Subpart F rules, detailed information returns must be submitted on an annual basis.[18] The expanding U.S. tax jurisdiction has also greatly increased the problem of tax audits where the U.S. taxpayer has a number of foreign subsidiaries. Foreign tax specialists of the Internal Revenue Service, usually referred to as OIO[19] agents, conduct extensive examinations into all intercompany transactions between the U.S. corporation and its foreign subsidiaries. Special emphasis is placed on intercompany pricing, with the taxpayer being under a heavy burden to defend its pricing policies.

While the tax department is generally responsible for foreign as well as U.S. tax returns, the normal procedure is to have the foreign returns prepared locally, usually by the outside auditors for the foreign subsidiary. Where time permits, the tax department will review the returns before filing, since the foreign returns will affect the U.S. returns both directly and indirectly. The tax liability determined for the foreign return may have a direct impact on the Subpart F liability of the U.S. taxpayer. Also, it will affect the U.S. company's computation of foreign tax credit if dividends are paid by the foreign subsidiary. Indirectly, some of the decisions made in preparing the foreign return may also affect the taxpayer's subsequent dealings on audit with the OIO agent.

---

[18] See, e.g., Forms 959 and 2952 and 3646.

[19] OIO—Office of International Operations. When the IRS expanded its audits of the foreign operations of U.S. companies, it initially had this phase of the audit examination conducted by specialists from its Office of International Operations who reported their audit results to the OIO national or area officer. Later, the IRS changed its approach and treated the OIO specialists as a member of the audit team. See *Rev. Proc.* 62–37, 1962–2 C.B. 537, as modified by *Rev. Proc.* 65–11, 1965–1 C.B. 751. Also see Bacon, "The New Changes Taking Place in the Office of International Operations," 22 *Journal of Taxation* 361 (June 1965).

As U.S. business grows increasingly international in scope, the conflicts between U.S. and foreign tax laws and their application will become a matter of growing concern. The taxpayer is caught in the middle. The present mechanisms for resolving these conflicts by discussions at top governmental levels appear unduly cumbersome and inadequate.

State and local tax problems

For some corporations, state and local tax problems overshadow federal income taxes in their effect on corporate earnings. For most corporations, state and local taxes are a matter of increasing concern.[20]

The needs of the populace for better schools, better roads, better housing, and better services in general have strained state and local budgets, caused property taxes to reach levels that drive industry from the community, and have forced the state and local governments to look to new sources of taxation.

The tax department of the multistate corporation must not only keep abreast of the frequent changes in state and local tax laws, but must also seek to resolve the problems that arise because the states apply differing jurisdictional standards to the same transaction. These different standards can result in overlapping taxes by two or more states, unless solutions can be worked out with the state tax administrators.

Congress has evinced an interest in this problem. A congressional joint committee made a thoroughgoing analysis of the burden of state and local taxation on interstate commerce.[21] As a result of that study, bills have been introduced in Congress to prescribe limitations on the jurisdiction of the states to tax interstate transactions.[22]

State tax departments have been concerned by the limitations that Congress would propose on their taxing powers. As a countermeasure, a number of states have entered into a multistate compact under which they would outline a general agreement for determining income allocation methods for multistate taxpayers, uniform tax regulations and forms,

---

[20] In recent years state and local taxes have increased more rapidly than federal taxes. From fiscal year 1960 to fiscal year 1968, federal taxes, according to Tax Foundation statistics, increased about 67%. By contrast, state taxes in the same period rose 88%, local taxes 77% or a combined increase of 83%. In 1960, state and local taxes represented 29.7% of the total U.S. tax burden. For 1968, the percentage represented by state and local taxes had increased to an estimated 32.1%.

[21] See *Report of the Special Subcommittee on State Taxation of Interstate Commerce of the Committee on the Judiciary House of Representatives* (June 15, 1964), House Report No. 1480, 88th Congress, Second Session.

[22] These bills have usually been referred to by the name of their former principal sponsor, Congressman Willis of Louisiana. In the 90th Congress, the House of Representatives approved the so-called Willis Bill (H.R. 2158) but the Senate did not take action on the bill. In the 91st Congress, a new version of the bill (H.R. 7906) was reported favorably without amendment by the House Judiciary Subcommittee on 5/7/69.

and arbitration procedures for settling disputes over income allocation and apportionment.[23]

In addition to these national or multistate developments, the corporation's tax department must keep informed of legislative developments within each of the states in which the corporation has significant operations. In the course of legislative hearings, the tax department must be alert to present to the legislators, either through trade associations or by direct testimony, the impact of proposed tax changes on the corporation's present or proposed activities within the state.

In the field of property taxation, tax rates and methods of assessment may determine whether an operation can be successfully continued at its present location. The desirability of close liaison with local assessing officials cannot be overemphasized. Frequently, this contact is best maintained by local plant managers who are aware of the community's needs for revenue and who are readily available for consultation with assessing officials. The tax department, however, should brief the plant managers as to latest developments in assessing techniques that will help them to present fairly the values to be placed on machinery and equipment and inventory, where applicable, as well as on real property. In most instances, it will prove helpful to have a tax department representative present at the meeting with the local assessor. Where the corporate taxpayer's assessment represents a significant percentage of the total assessments for the taxing jurisdiction, it is usually desirable for the corporation to involve itself in budget hearings, so that it can be assured that the proposed expenditures are genuinely needed and that proper expenditure controls are maintained.

In the planning area, state tax considerations may be one of the more important factors influencing management's decision in choosing between several alternative plant sites. The tax department will usually be called upon to assess the relative tax burdens as between two or more potential locations. In this connection, the tax department must determine whether the state offers any special tax exemption to attract new industry, and whether the methods of property valuation by local assessing officials tend to value all property uniformly, or whether industrial property bears a disproportionate burden where the assessor is an elected official who believes he must curry favor with the voters in his district.

State and local tax compliance

For the large, multistate taxpayer, state and local tax compliance becomes a voluminous operation of hundreds of separate returns and tax

[23] See, e.g., Hogan, "H.R. 2158 vs. The Multistate Tax Compact: Are They Mutually Exclusive?" 20 *The Tax Executive,* January, 1968, p. 93. See also, *First Annual Report of the Multistate Tax Commission.* As of February 1, 1969, the Multistate Compact had been enacted as a uniform law by the 15 following states: Kansas, Washington, Texas, New Mexico, Illinois, Florida, Nevada, Oregon, Missouri, Nebraska, Arkansas, Idaho, Hawaii, Colorado, and Wyoming.

payments that must be processed annually, quarterly, or even monthly. The organizational structure of the tax department must be designed to make the most effective use of personnel at the peak filing periods, while at the same time realizing the benefits of specialized knowledge in areas such as income and franchise taxes, sales and use taxes, property taxes, and payroll taxes.

Effective use of tax manuals, tax calendars for returns and payments, and proper review procedures are necessary techniques to insure that volume operations will proceed on schedule while maintaining the corporation's tax liabilities at the lowest allowable levels.

To help alleviate the problems caused by the volume of state and local returns, a number of corporate tax departments are already effectively employing electronic data processing in obtaining relevant information and, where feasible, in the actual preparation of the returns.

Tax audits of state and local returns present a special problem to the large multistate taxpayer because of their multiplicity. The same basic information may be audited by representatives from several states, each employing different regulations and auditing techniques. The states that have entered into the multistate compact have recognized this problem and are exploring the uses of a single audit by one state tax department to determine liability for operations in all states subject to the compact.

Many states tend to rely upon a so-called "office audit"—an audit of the taxpayer's return in the state tax department's own offices. This helps to reduce the need for a large and expensive staff of traveling auditors, and has the merit of insuring more uniformity in the treatment of taxpayers similarly situated.

Where the state and local audits result in unresolved issues, the review procedures for handling the disputes differ widely among the states. Generally, however, the review procedures tend to be more flexible and adptable to practicable and workable solutions of the issues than is the case with federal income tax disputes. Where the issues remain unresolved at departmental levels, the corporate tax department may argue its case before the state's tax commission or similar administrative appellate agency. If further appeal is required, the tax department will usually bring in outside counsel to present its case in the local courts.

Conclusion

The best conclusion for this truncated review of the corporate tax department function is a restatement of the opening sentence—Effective tax planning and tax management is a key function of the corporate financial executive.

Legal aspects of corporate affairs

Charles H. Resnick*

Even the financial executive who is a devoted fan of Perry Mason is well aware that the lawyers with whom he will have the most frequent contact are rarely to be found in the courtroom cross-examining witnesses in a murder case. The nature of the financial executive's position will, however, involve him with lawyers on a frequent basis as he deals with problems of corporate organization and reorganization, financial instruments and agreements, government regulation, fringe benefits and other matters with important legal implications. The purpose of this chapter is to create a better understanding on the part of the financial executive of the nature of the legal function so that he can use the lawyer's professional services most effectively in order to do his own job.

Organization, allocation of authority, and professional status

ORGANIZATION. On nearly all senior-management organization charts, a box will appear for the principal corporate lawyer. Whether his title be General Counsel, General Attorney, Corporation Counsel or Vice President–Legal, the function is quite uniformly to guide the legal affairs of the corporation. In many of the areas in which counsel operates, the financial executive is either the "client" or is one of the business executives who has responsibility for the financial outcome of the transaction being guided by and advised upon by the lawyer.

There is no magic formula which dictates the precise relationship

* Vice President, Secretary and General Counsel, Raytheon Company, Lexington, Massachusetts.

between the General Counsel and other officers of the corporation. Typically, the principal corporate lawyer reports to the chief executive officer of the corporation, although in some cases he reports organizationally to an Executive Vice President, a Senior Vice President or the Vice President–Finance.[1] Whatever the organizational reporting relationship, the lawyer represents the corporation which employs him, as distinguished from the officers, directors or stockholders of that corporation. No problem should arise out of this fact since, of course, the financial executive is also employed to promote and protect the interests of the corporation.

The best organization will vary from one company to another since a principal aspect of the reporting relationship is the determination of priorities in work assignments. If the President or Board Chairman is the heaviest user of legal services, it may be well to have the General Counsel report to him. If problems with legal content are normally handled by another executive, a reporting relationship which recognizes this fact may be desirable.

LAW OFFICE ORGANIZATION.   In most companies the principal lawyer in turn requires a staff in order to handle the work load imposed upon his department. The organization of the law department (as it is frequently called) must be responsive to the needs of the individual company. In some cases a centralized group which includes the principal legal specialties required to serve the needs of the company will be best. In others, geographic or product-line diversity dictates a need for division counsel who are located at the divisions which they serve rather than at corporate headquarters. In many larger companies a combination of the two organizational concepts is used with optimum effect, i.e., a group of legal specialists are maintained at the corporate headquarters while division or area counsel handle the day-to-day work which arises in their divisions or geographic areas. Most lawyers prefer in either case to maintain a relationship which has them reporting to the General Counsel. The principal reason for this is that professional independence, which is required in order to perform the duties properly for the corporation, is best maintained through a purely professional organizational relationship. In a number of large companies, however, division counsel report administratively and for salary purposes to the Division Manager, while reporting functionally to the General Counsel. In practice both systems seem to have worked well, probably because there is close consultation between the "client" Division Manager and the General Counsel with regard to the performance of the individual lawyer.

ASSIGNMENTS.   While lawyers employed by the corporation are typically assigned to specific functional areas or to specific operating seg-

[1] See *Top Management Organization in Divisionalized Companies,* Studies in Personnel Policy, No. 195, National Industrial Conference Board, 1965, pp. 63–67.

ments of the company, their doors are generally open to any employee of the corporation who has a legal problem involving the corporate interest, since in the larger sense their true client is the corporate entity. Priority of assignments must be one of judgment just as it is in any job. Sometimes the more urgent matter must be handled before the more important matter. On a day-to-day basis lawyers can determine these priorities for themselves. The law department head will invoke priorities where necessary and, of course, the executive to whom the lawyer reports will in turn determine priorities where necessary.

The education and skill of the lawyer can often be brought to bear on matters which are not strictly legal in nature. Whether he is asked to undertake assignments beyond the normal scope of purely legal matters is frequently a function of the personality and capabilities of the individual. One would scarcely assign an introverted lawyer to a problem needing skills primarily of advocacy and persuasion. Neither will a sensible businessman use a lawyer (whose starting pay out of school may be more than $15,000 annually) for a job which could be done, albeit not quite so well, by a far lower paid clerk. Many lawyers, however, demonstrate a high level of skill as business negotiators. In these cases, a financial executive may achieve gains for the corporation by expanding the negotiating role of the lawyer beyond the strictly legal aspects of a transaction.

WORKING AS A TEAM. While there is often a clear demarcation between the strictly legal matter and the business matter, equally often there is not. There is little difficulty in determining who has responsibility for the outcome of an appeal to the Supreme Court or a title examination to real estate. On the other hand, many corporate problems require the combined efforts of a number of skills including those of lawyers. In those situations, never view your counsel as a necessary hurdle or obstacle to be overcome or put behind you. The lawyer is a necessary member of the management team, and in many companies works most closely with the financial executive. Early consultation will avoid wasted time in the pursuit of avenues which are blocked by legal obstancles and, in the give and take of discussions of objectives, may produce new methods of accomplishing corporate objectives.

No lawyer can function if his client supplies him with incomplete information. Neither will the lawyer be making a maximum contribution if the financial executive attempts to limit him to counseling on abstract questions of law. Both the financial executive and the lawyer need to study all the facts in any transaction, the applicable law, and the possible avenues of approach. Lawyers have both a legal and ethical standard which imposes upon them a duty to respect information imparted to them in confidence by their clients. They may not be required to divulge such information against the client's wishes even on the witness stand. Your lawyer should be trusted with all of the information pertinent to giving sound advice. The financial executive cannot always judge which facts may be relevant to a sound legal judgment on the issue, and hence, should rely upon the lawyer's judgment as to what he must see and know about a problem.

HOUSE COUNSEL V. OUTSIDE COUNSEL.   Statistics developed by the American Bar Association over recent years indicate a growing trend toward the use of lawyers employed full time by the corporation. Their activities may be in addition to the services of outside counsel, in substitution for them, or a little of each. Inside counsel are often more available and can function at lower cost to the corporation than the outside lawyers. As one company President put it, "House counsel are there when you need them. Outside lawyers have other demands for their time and naturally can't be as close to the day-to-day operations of a company."[2]

On the other hand, the outside law firm can frequently marshal higher degrees of specialization in such fields as tax, securities regulation, and antitrust, and more manpower to cope with the demands of litigation. Whether a given company should consider hiring house counsel will depend upon its individual situation.[3] Is it in a highly regulated industry? Does the nature of the business give rise to frequent litigation? Is the need for legal service likely to arise with little advance notice and a need for prior background information? Does the corporation need counsel the allocation of whose time it can control? Are contracts uniformly entered into on standard forms? What has been the historical cost of outside counsel fees? Is there a clear need for an active preventative law program?

The financial executive will often be in the position of making or participating in the making of the decision as to what combination of house counsel and outside counsel best suits the needs of his individual company. If the choice is the one followed by most major corporations toward a strong inside General Counsel, then the General Counsel must be permitted to make the decision as to when, and under what circumstances to use outside counsel and whom he wishes for that function. If the General Counsel is bypassed on this question, he cannot accept full responsibility for the legal affairs of the corporation nor can he adequately maintain his professional stature with other lawyers. It is quite in order for the financial executive to suggest, on suitable occasion, the use of outside counsel where an inside law department exists, but the final decision on this question should be made by the General Counsel.

Where, on the other hand, the corporation has opted to have outside

---

[2] "How Companies Are Using the Corporate Counsel," *The Wall Street Journal* (July 16, 1965).

[3] *Organization for Legal Work*, The Conference Board Business Record, October 1959, pp. 463–468.

counsel act as its General Counsel, it should similarly be responsive to their recommendations with regard to the need for additional inside staff, the engagement of counsel in other cities, states or countries, and the use of specialized co-counsel.

PROFESSIONAL QUALIFICATIONS.   The chairman of the board of a large diversified corporation, when asked by a group of lawyers to speak about what was expected of them, replied:

. . . the chief executive expects the law department to do everything super-latively well. He expects it to be courageous but not rash; vigilant in the pro-tection of the company's assets and property, but not inhumane; firm in representing us but tactful. He expects its members to have opinions but not to be opinionated; he expects the lawyers to be learned but not pedantic; expects them to be self-confident but not arrogant; he expects the law department to have pride in the law as a profession, but not to deprecate or belittle the pro-fessions of others.

In short, the chief executive expects that his law department will have all of the virtues—and none of the vices—of mankind in general.[4]

In this chapter it is assumed that the financial executive has corporate counsel who meet fully the expectations described above. To be of value, the lawyer must not only have recognized competence, but also common sense and an ability to work within realistic timetables. The financial executive who does not have such a lawyer should find one.

RECRUITING.   As is so often the case in other professional fields, lawyers are best judged by their peers. If the financial executive is starting from zero and seeking to engage counsel initially for the corpo-ration, he will do well to turn to other lawyers for advice. For example, the General Counsel for Company A and Company B may well be able to suggest well-qualified outside counsel or candidates for the position of house counsel to the financial executive of Company C who has none. If the corporation has pre-existing and satisfactory relationships with either inside or outside counsel, they may often be relied upon to do the recruiting for the corporation. Normal channels of recruiting include bar associations, law school placement offices and law firms themselves.

INDEPENDENT PROFESSIONAL STATUS.   Tradition has clothed the law with the status of an independent profession. Members of the bar in the United States carry their independent professional status with pride. Whether your counsel is an employee of the corporation or a member of an outside law firm, he should be expected to maintain this status and to give you the objective opinion he believes to be correct rather than the

---

[4] Ben Heineman, Chairman of the Board, Chicago and Northwestern Railway, "What the Chief Executive Expects of the Law Department," address before Annual Corporate Counsel Institute, October 16, 1964.

opinion you might like to hear. Where advocacy is required, the financial executive has every right to expect that his lawyer will espouse the company's cause articulately and eloquently. However, most situations in which the executive is dealing with his lawyer involve counsel and advice. In these situations, the lawyer who will not stand his ground because his opinion is unpopular is more of a liability than an asset. Much of the time, unpopular advice involves a business risk which the manager may reasonably decide to take notwithstanding the advice. This is perfectly in order, but the lawyer who gives you advice which you may not wish to hear should be entitled to your respect rather than your neglect. On the other hand, if the lawyer's advice pertains to a violation of criminal laws by the corporation, he has an obligation to bring to the attention of the highest levels of management any decision to pursue the criminal course.

PREVENTIVE LAW.　Probably the most valuable function which the corporate lawyer can serve is in helping the corporation steer a course which avoids the necessity for litigation, whether as plaintiff or defendant. For the most part, litigation is costly, time consuming, and seldom productive of as satisfactory a result for either party as a good-faith negotiation would have produced. This is not to say that you must not at times litigate with the stubborn or stupid business adversary, but rather to say that a lawyer who is worth his salt will have helped you to avoid most of the situations which might give rise to such a confrontation.

RECOGNIZING THE PROBLEMS.　The first ingredient of a sound preventative law program is to create an awareness among operating personnel of legal pitfalls to be considered in their day-to-day operations. They must know enough to recognize that an antitrust, contract, or securities problem exists on which advice is needed and to bring it to the lawyer. The creation of such awareness often requires education, the nature and extent of which will vary depending upon the size and organization of the corporate client. One well-established method of launching a preventative law program is through lectures by lawyers to management trainees, management clubs, sales meetings, meetings of purchasing agents, and similar forums. In some companies legal bulletins are a useful method of spreading a message concerning new developments in the law, quickly to a large number of people. In other organizations, formal legal procedures exist which require anyone taking certain types of action on behalf of the corporation to first consult with counsel. Any combination of one or more of these techniques can be effective; they will depend to a great degree on the attitude of top management for their success. If the financial executive regards the lawyer as an impediment in the path of progress, the message will soon filter through the organization that the lawyer is to be bypassed whenever possible. If, on the other hand, the executives in the organization make it a point to assure themselves that satisfactory legal participation has been afforded each transaction, others will cooperate in the same way.

Specific legal problems

INCORPORATION AND CAPITALIZATION.   One of the most common transactions turned over to counsel is that of incorporation of a new business enterprise or subsidiary. Too frequently this is done without adequate thought as to the choices and decisions which may affect the future operation of the corporation. Is it desirable to incorporate in the state where the business will be conducted? Is there some advantage to incorporating instead under the laws of a state with more liberal statutes regarding changes in charter, bylaws, merger or capitalization? What should be the capital structure of the organization? Will it be a simple one with common stock only? How many shares is it desirable to authorize? Should the authorization be greater than the amount of stock actually issued? Will there be a need for preferred stocks or for more than one class of common stock? Any of these questions can be answered for the financial executive by the lawyer who has been adequately familiarized with the transaction involved. Extra money spent at the outset will often save considerable amounts later on. None of these questions ought to be passed over with a "do it the usual way," since there is *no* usual way. There is a *right* way which depends upon all of the plans and circumstances.

Once the corporation is engaged in doing business, its efforts and endeavors in the various states of the United States and in foreign countries should be examined periodically to determine whether it is necessary or desirable to qualify the corporation in states other than its state of incorporation or its state of principal business. Serious penalties can be involved for the corporation which fails to qualify itself in a state where it is transacting business. Not the least of these penalties can be the inability to enforce contracts which were entered into within the state while unqualified. On this basis, failure to qualify could prevent you from collecting a substantial debt owed to your company.

For some enterprises, it may be desirable to use a corporation formed under the laws of a foreign country. Typically this should be considered only where the business to be conducted will be carried on in the country of incorporation. Even then there can be advantages to using a corporation formed under one of the United States and qualifying it to do business in the foreign country. Incorporation statutes in many foreign lands are far more cumbersome than those in the United States with the result that many formalities must be observed and corporate changes which are routine here become a major issue abroad. Winding up a corporation which has discontinued its business is also far more difficult abroad than it is in the United States. If the nature of the enterprise is one which will probably entail such a windup, it would be worthwhile to have your lawyer examine the statutes of the several states to determine where dissolution can be accomplished with the least inconvenience.

FINANCIAL INSTRUMENTS AND AGREEMENTS.   In most corporations the financial executive, whether he be Vice President–Finance, Treasurer, or Controller, will have the responsibility for the basic agreements under which the corporation borrows. He normally should and does work out with lenders the term, schedule of payments of principle, rate of interest to be charged, right of prepayments, and other basic terms. He should not then assume that the rest of the boiler plate which the banker requests be signed is "routine" or "standard." Here is an area where your lawyer's advice may enable you to secure provisions which turn out to be literally worth their weight in gold. All of the terms of the loan agreement are negotiable. Think about such questions as these: Does your loan agreement require the lender to notify you of a condition of default? Does your agreement provide a period of time during which any default can be cured before the loan is accelerated? What negative covenants are you required to adhere to? To what extent do they permit you to conduct the business in its normal fashion without constantly requiring the bank's consent? Are you free to borrow money from other sources while the loan is outstanding? You want and should negotiate for as much latitude as possible in the operation of your business, and as little likelihood as possible of having the loan accelerated through default.

Similarly a decision to issue debentures or convertible debentures to the public entails more than the coupon rate and maturity. Consider with your lawyer all of the other detailed provisions in the debenture itself and in the trust indenture. Should your corporation get into financial hot water at some future time, the provisions governing trustees' rights may influence the company's ability to survive.

A simple form of short-term borrowing which has become common with high-credit–rated corporations is the issuance of commercial paper. Its simplicity is real and appealing, since the corporation merely issues and sells a basic form of promissory note. However, the lawyer should review the respective obligations of the issuing bank (if there is one), the issuing corporation, and the underwriter, to be sure that there are no misunderstandings or unnecessary risks.

REORGANIZATION AND BANKRUPTCY.   While few financial executives like to contemplate the possibility of either reorganization or bankruptcy, these are situations with which every business executive requires some familiarity. Your company may never be a party to such a transaction, but some of your customers or vendors may. Under these circumstances you will need to know, and quickly, the answers to such questions as:

Can I do business with the trustee in bankruptcy and be sure of being paid? What is the effect of my filing a claim on a secured debt? If I had contracts to buy from the bankrupt organization, must the trustee in bankruptcy sell? Your lawyer should act as a focal point in any dealings with a trustee in bankruptcy or assignee for the benefit of creditors. If your relationships with the bankrupt corporation go beyond the simple filing of a claim, be sure that your lawyer is a participant. This is no field for the uninitiated.

SEC REGULATION.   If your corporation is wholly owned by one or two private investors, you may still need counsel on SEC matters because the SEC's power extends to debt securities as well as equities. If stock in your company is publicly held, or if you contemplate a public offering at some time in the future, then you probably are already concerned with the regulation of securities by federal and state governments.

Most important of the regulatory agencies is, of course, the Securities and Exchange Commission. It administers both the Securities Act of 1933 and the Securities Exchange Act of 1934. In the administration of both statutes, the name of the game is "Disclosure." The whole objective of the legal scheme is to create an investing public which is completely informed when making its initial investment and when considering any change in investment status.

Your company may desire to issue stock under a variety of circumstances. These could include mergers and acquisitions, employee stock plans of various sorts, and outright sale. Some of these transactions will entail exemptions from the registration requirements of the Securities Law, but your eligibility for exemption should be checked carefully with your counsel. Such exemptions as those entailing a private offering or the "no sale" theory of a merger carry many limitations and no presumption of their availability may be made.

Registration statements.   If registration is required, the financial executive is one of the most important participants. The figures which he furnishes for publication in the prospectus are of primary interest to the investor. They must be neither misleading of themselves nor omit to state any material fact required to prevent what is included from being misleading. This is a field where the responsibilities are great. Everyone who signs the registration statement (and this always includes the chief financial officer and a majority of the board of directors) has personal liability for any material misstatement of fact or omission of a material fact in the prospectus. This is not a job to be delegated to others. *You* must read, understand, and satisfy yourself as to the accuracy of everything in the prospectus before it can be distributed publicly.

The registration statement, to put it simply, is a trap for the unwary. The investor to whom the prospectus is sent may never read the prospectus until after the stock he bought declines in value by 50 percent. It is then that he and his lawyer will go over your prospectus with a fine-tooth comb and the benefit of hindsight, to see whether you have omitted some bad news which ought to have been included, or whether you have misstated some piece of information which he can claim to have been false. Only if you and your counsel have done the same thing in advance can you feel confident that you and your business colleagues will not be caught in the trap.

State regulation.   State authorities may not be ignored completely. While most states offer exemption for listed securities, and many for those registered with the SEC, some may still require registration with their offices. The so-called "Blue Sky" laws of each state in which the offering will be made should be examined.

Insider trading.   After your stock is outstanding in the hands of the public, you still have obligations not to take unfair advantage of your position as an insider. Sound advice on this subject is indispensable. Some of it will have to do with Section 16(b) of the Securities Exchange Act which, in effect, imposes a six months' time interval between any purchase and any sale by an officer or director, of the stock of his corporation. One who cheats on the six months runs the risk of losing whatever profit, real or paper, was made on the purchase and sale or sale and purchase. Even if the six months' insulation is taken care of, another provision, made famous by officers of the Texas Gulf Sulphur Company (Rule 10(b)(5) under the Securities Exchange Act), requires that you not trade in the stock of your company when you have available to you any material information likely to have an impact on the price of the stock which has not been made generally available to the investing public.

These rules have teeth in them and you, as the financial executive in your corporation, should be certain that information flows as rapidly and as accurately as possible to the financial press and the investment community at large. Play no favorites; make your distribution of financial releases general and broad. Your lawyer should be a participant in the preparation of all materials for stockholders and all press releases regarding financial performance of the company.

In addition to the materials required when your company issues stock publicly, those companies whose stock is listed on exchanges, or who have more than certain minimal numbers of stockholders, required to make periodic filings with the Securities and Exchange Commission reflecting any changes in their financial or management status. Similarly, the New York Stock Exchange and other major stock exchanges require reports on a timely basis, to them and to the public at large, of major developments within the corporation.

THE CORPORATE SECRETARY.   Every corporation is required by statute to have an officer who is in charge of its records. Normally called the

Secretary or Clerk of the corporation, he has duties which include: preparation of agenda for board and shareholder meetings; drafting of votes for such meetings; maintaining lists of shareholders; maintaining facilities for the ready transfer of corporate securities; preparation of minutes of meetings in which corporate action has been taken; and the maintenance of the corporate seal. A poll by the American Society of Corporate Secretaries[5] discloses that about half its members are lawyers. The rather extensive need by the corporate secretary for legal advice makes it understandable that many corporations have facilitated the giving of such advice by electing either the principal legal officer of the corporation, or one of his staff, as Secretary. Combining the two functions in this way eliminates a certain amount of unnecessary effort and, in some cases, unnecessary staff.

TAXES. Every business transaction generates tax consequences. In an era when more than half of every profit dollar goes to the tax collector, the financial executive must be alert to every opportunity to avoid unnecessary tax burdens. There is nothing unethical or immoral in a policy designed to keep the tax burden on your company at a minimum. As the late Judge Learned Hand stated:

Over and over again courts have said that there is nothing sinister in so arranging one's affairs as to keep taxes as low as possible. Everybody does so, rich or poor; and all do right, for nobody owes any public duty to pay more than the law demands: taxes are enforced exactions, not voluntary contributions. To demand more in the name of morals is mere cant. (*Commissioner* v. *Newman*, 159 F.2d 848 (2d Cir. 1947))

Tax organization. One finds the tax function organized in many ways in U.S. companies. In some, a tax director reports to the Treasurer or Controller. In some, a Vice President in charge of taxes reports to the President or another senior officer. In some, accountants play the lead role in tax planning as well as tax administration. In others, lawyers dominate the tax planning function and review all major administrative decisions in that field. The organization best suited to the individual concern will be dependent upon individual circumstances. Whatever the organization, the tax lawyer should be a major contributor who can foresee new developments in time to plan for them, find imaginative solutions to existing problems, and act as the company's advocate in disputes with tax authorities.

INTERNATIONAL TRANSACTIONS. When buying, selling, or engaging in production outside the United States, it is natural that most executives will turn to their lawyers rather readily for advice on the laws of the

---

[5] *Responsibilities of a Corporate Secretary*, American Society of Corporate Secretaries, Inc., June 1965, p. 40.

foreign country. Do not expect the American lawyer to know all about the local laws of Italy, Japan, or Liberia. He will, however, have sources for determining who is a sound lawyer in the country in which you are dealing. At the early stages, your U.S. lawyer will normally be able to frame the transaction in a manner meeting your business objectives. He may then wish to consult with local counsel to ascertain what pitfalls should be avoided arising out of peculiarities of local law. For example, systems of taxation vary greatly from country to country; the obligations of employers with regard to employees are considerably different in Latin countries than in the United States; rights and obligations between stockholders of the same company are normally different in other countries than they are in the United States.

After you have made your deal, you normally expect it to be performed. However, now and then there is a breach of contract, and you will wish to have the benefit of your bargain. Typically, Americans are well advised to avoid litigation in a foreign country. The normal solution which your counsel will recommend is to arbitrate any dispute, in the United States if possible, but at least in a neutral country. This is typically faster, cheaper, and less acrimonious than litigation in the country of which the other party is a national, but it also tends to assure a fairer hearing of your case. Here again, however, the drafting of the arbitration agreement is no job for amateurs.

REAL ESTATE TRANSACTIONS.   In the United States, few transactions are as replete with legal niceties as the purchase, sale, or lease of real estate. None of these transactions should ever be entered into without the benefit of counsel's advice.

Buying. If you are buying real estate, you must know: Whether the property you have seen is the one described in the contract; what encumbrances a seller will wish you to accept when he tenders title; what your remedies are in case the property is damaged by fire or other casualties prior to your closing; what arrangements can be made for financing the transaction. These and a myriad of other terms should be resolved by your counsel at the time of the contract, and you should be advised of any problems which he considers to be unusual. Spending the effort required at the negotiation stage often avoids costly wrangles when the closing is reached.

Leasing.   In leasing real estate, it has become common for the owner to present the lessee with five to ten pages of fine print, all of it designed to deprive the lessee of all the rights he might otherwise have. This is probably very satisfactory if you are the lessor and your lawyer has prepared the document. However, if you are the lessee, never accept anyone's statement that this is the "standard form." Be sure that your lawyer reads it and requests whatever changes are necessary for your protection. For example, what is your right to terminate if the premises become unfit for use? What are your rights if the property is taken by eminent domain? To what extent does the landlord agree to maintain the building? What are your obligations with respect to the condition of the premises when the lease terminates? If a fire starts through negligence of your employees, are you liable?

ANTITRUST. The financial executive is nearly always influential in his company's decisions on product pricing, new product decisions, and marketing efforts. In such decisions, he can and should be conscious of the risks of antitrust violations. Though there is much which is uncertain regarding the meaning of the antitrust laws, there is also a good deal which is crystal clear.

Hard core violations. What constitutes a hard-core violation is seldom in doubt. These are areas where there is no room for a decision to take business risks. The problems and expenses of treble damages, fines, and jail sentences, coupled with the bad publicity, can never be justified.

Like the Ten Commandments, engrave upon your conscience the following prohibitions: Do not discuss with competitors your pricing practices or theirs. Do not discuss with your competitors the territories in which you or they market. Do not discuss with your competitors decisions to enter or refrain from entering a new product field.

Any one of these can involve criminal violation of the Sherman Act's prohibitions against agreements, combinations, and conspiracies in restraint of trade. The jail sentences meted out in the now-famous electrical-equipment conspiracies were well publicized. Less publicity was afforded the impact on profits of the defendant corporations. Plaintiff's lawyers had a field day. General Electric alone admitted to an after-tax profit degradation, as a result of the actions brought against it, of $43,000,000 in 1964 alone, plus over $1,000,000 in counsel fees.

Acquisitions. Acquisitions are a much different problem. Lawyers enjoy enormous intellectual exercise discussing endlessly the ramifications of decisions of the Supreme Court in the acquisition field. They may study along with you the economic ramifications of a proposed acquisition and its impact on competition; whether it is a conglomerate, product extension, horizontal or vertical acquisition; and a host of other considerations thought to be relevant to a decision on whether a given acquisition will survive scrutiny under antitrust laws.

This is all quite unnecessary. The law is really very simple. What the Supreme Court has been saying for the past ten years is that if the Government chooses to challenge an acquisition, then the Government wins. The decision you and your counsel must make, therefore, is not whether the acquisition can survive a challenge by the Government, but whether it is likely that the acquisition will be of such a nature that the Government will challenge it. Your counsel can supply you with the guidelines recently issued by the Department of Justice Antitrust Division, which set forth in terms of market share those situations where it is the normal policy for the Department of Justice to challenge, or not to challenge, a given acquisition. The Federal Trade Commission has no similarly preannounced policy except for specified industries, but they might be expected generally to follow those of the Antitrust Division. Studies of conglomerate mergers undertaken by Congress and several agencies indicate a real likelihood of new legislation in this field in years to come.

Similarly some unpublished conclusions can also be given you by your counsel. Acquisitions will be less likely to be challenged in developing industries than in mature ones. Ease of entry by new competitors, as demonstrated by market conditions, may often be a factor in determining whether a given acquisition will be challenged. As the law presently stands, this is an area where you may choose to take the business risk of challenge, since the penalty which is paid for the wrong decision is an ultimate order to divest yourself of the acquisition once made. While nothing to look forward to, such an order is a great deal less horrendous than the consequences of a hard-core violation.

Robinson–Patman Act.   The financial executive is likely to hear a great deal of the Robinson–Patman Act. In its purest form, this statute requires that you sell to all customers at the same price f.o.b. your plant. The law has, however, a good many exceptions which may apply to your business. The exceptions are inexact in their nature, tending to create significant problems of interpretation. To the extent that your company departs from uniform f.o.b. pricing, or institutes promotional programs among customers, the programs for doing so should have careful legal review. It may be impractical and unduly cumbersome for your counsel to review each individual pricing decision to determine whether the exception which may be proposed by your marketing man is applicable to the given case. Often more valuable will be an educational process which helps the marketing man to judge for himself, initially, whether the situation is such that he can reasonably grant a lower price because of the availability of such exceptions as the lower cost of manufacturing, selling, or delivering; differences in kind and quality of the product being sold; or other exceptions. Never accept blithely the assumption that because one buyer is purchasing a larger quantity than another, he automatically becomes entitled to a lower unit price. It is essential that the lower price be established to fit within one of the exceptions provided by the law; otherwise to grant it will be unlawful.

CONTRACTS.   One of the most commonly misunderstood areas of law is that of the contract. Contracts are by no means limited to the formal document in a blue backer, replete with ribbons and fancy seals. Sales orders are contracts. Purchase orders are contracts. Letters are frequently contracts. Any of these instruments may bind your company to the terms stated in those documents. If the terms are incomplete, the law will frequently supply the missing terms—often on a basis contrary to what you would have wished.

The instruments which your company uses on a repetitive basis, its contract forms, should be complete both on their face and also with respect to any terms which are printed on the reverse side or on an attachment. Terms which are thus incorporated by reference must be referred to plainly and conspicuously; otherwise they may be held inapplicable. Before using a purchase order adapted from a form supplied by a trade association or similar source, have your lawyer review it. Are all warranties plainly stated? Do you benefit from implied warranties? Does it provide the manner and terms on which goods are to be shipped? Does it provide the alternative right of rejection or the right of repair in the event that the goods do not meet the specifications? Does it provide a measure of damages in the event that the goods are inadequate? Does it protect your rights in the event of the bankruptcy of your supplier? You must consider and answer these questions for yourself. Otherwise the law will supply the answer, but not necessarily in the way you would have wished.

Similarly in the case of sales orders, it is essential that any limitations on warranty be spelled out carefully. If you do not wish to be responsible for the profit which a customer loses when product is delayed in shipment or does not meet specifications, it is important that the contract say so in unequivocal language and in large print.

Every company periodically enters into unique transactions not suitable for a sales-order or purchase-order form. If the amount involved will justify it, these contracts should be prepared by counsel. His training and experience are needed to consider and anticipate the variety of events which may occur, but which the businessmen who consider only the business motivation for the transaction normally do not take up. Too often the parties think they have reached agreement, but upon questioning find that they ascribe different meanings to the same words. Future problems, disputes, and rancor are avoided if such misunderstandings are resolved at the negotiation stage.

Uniform Commercial Code. An important factor to be considered in drawing any contract is the Uniform Commercial Code which has been widely adopted in the United States. Only one jurisdiction, Louisiana, has failed as of this writing to adopt it. It may, therefore, be assumed that in all of the more populous states where business is done, the Uniform Commercial Code, or some variation of it, is in effect. For the most part it will tend to expedite business and banking transactions, although its provisions tend to be more favorable to bankers than to their customers, and more favorable to buyers than to sellers. In the sale of goods, for example, warranties of merchantability, fitness for use, freedom from patent infringement, and of title, are implied unless conspicuously excluded.

PATENTS AND LICENSING.   The financial executive is generally charged with the responsibility for protecting the company's assets. He is vigilant in his efforts to assure himself that machinery, equipment, and inventory are both adequately insured and otherwise protected from theft. He takes measures to be sure that financial controls prevent embezzlement of corporate funds. In some cases, however, he is very loose with the company's intellectual property. By intellectual property is meant the patents and proprietary information owned by the company. These are the fruits of investment, research and development. A planned program is essential to protect this property as fully as physical property is protected. Such a program will entail appropriate legends on proprietary information; establishment of procedures which limit access to proprietary information and processes to those having a need to know; execution of suitable contracts by employees who will have access to corporate proprietary information; occasional institution of litigation against those who have misappropriated intellectual property; and the development of patent protection covering new inventions evolved by the corporation's employees.

If efforts to protect the company's intellectual property have been successful, it will probably be found that a number of concerns are willing to pay a royalty in exchange for the right to use the company's intellectual property. While a suitable price or rate for the royalty is normally determined through negotiation and experience, a ready measure of the value of know-how is what it would cost the licensee to develop the same information at its own expense through a program of research and development. Patent royalties should normally bear a reasonable relationship to the percentage profit to be enjoyed on the patented device.

Auditing licensees.   The usual vehicle for permitting others to use intellectual property is a license agreement. Typically, the license requires that the licensee report at stated intervals in the extent of his use of the owner's intellectual property, and make payments at the same time. Where there is a question of whether a given product line is or is not covered by the license agreement, the licensee may well decide the issue most favorably to himself and pay royalty only on the most exclusionary basis. To guard against the loss of income which would occur in this case, the financial executive should arrange for periodic audits of the accounts of the licensee. Agreements typically make provision for such audit. Any audit of the license should be conducted not only by an accountant, but with the benefit of product-line analysis by a patent lawyer familiar with the product line covered.

Defensive values. Intellectual property has defensive as well as offensive values. If others assert that your company is using their patents or other intellectual property, it is often fruitful to determine whether the claimant is an unlicensed user of your patents or proprietary information as well. The ability to point to an unauthorized use by the claimant, or to offer the use of property owned by the alleged infringer can result in a lower royalty rate in the resultant cross-license; sometimes in a royalty-free exchange; in a *de facto* standoff with neither side pushing the issue to litigation; or in other values which minimize the requirement that the claimed infringer pay royalties to others.

EMPLOYEE BENEFITS. The financial executive is customarily charged with many responsibilities in connection with stock-option plans, stock-purchase plans, and retirement benefits. Such plans always entail a number of legal problems which require the benefit of adequate advice to be sure that the tax objectives are achieved, and that the corporation meets its responsibilities under the Securities Law. Some of the problems which can arise are as follows:

Stock plans. The corporation grants stock options but does not desire to file a registration statement under the Securities Act. Optionees who exercise are required to agree with the corporation that they are taking for investment only, and not with a view to redistribution or resale. The optionees later desire to resell some of their stock. Is the offering exempt at that time? Can a no-action letter be obtained from the Securities and Exchange Commission? If a no-action letter is obtained, is this insurance against possible suit? Only your counsel can answer these questions in view of the peculiar facts and circumstances involved in your case.

Stock-purchase plans are another popular method of increasing equity participation by employees of a corporation. A number of variations of stock-purchase plans are available, depending upon the objective to be achieved. These can range from a program for rewarding top management to a general plan available to all employees. Some plans offer tax benefits to the employer; some plans offer tax benefits to the employees; some offer partial tax benefits to both. In considering a stock-purchase plan, evaluate the purpose for establishing it, and adopt a plan which is suited to the company's specific objectives rather than a copy of one which happens to have been adopted by others in your industry.

Pension plans. Pension plans have a way of growing like topsy. In a growing company, new employees are added; acquisitions are made of companies with existing pension plans; it is desired to change benefits from time to time; plans are affected by changes in the Social Security Law and by questions of interpretation of language once thought to be clear. In deciding to adopt or amend a pension plan, do not limit consideration to advice of actuaries or pension counselors, helpful though they may be. Evolve a plan which takes into account the possible changes which will occur in the future, and the possible need to merge with it other plans drawn by other people.

Disputes and litigation

LITIGATION VS. NEGOTIATION.   A decision to sue or not to sue to enforce the corporation's rights is not to be taken lightly. Never adopt the attitude of "Sue first and ask questions later." Evaluate both sides of the case. Rarely are results of litigation nearly as satisfactory to either party as a negotiated settlement would have been. While you cannot afford to have your corporation's rights trampled upon without fighting back, always consider the alternatives before embarking on litigation. Lawsuits have a way of engendering bitterness in positions which make it more difficult to negotiate a settlement after suit than before. If, after due consideration, you decide that your company must sue, be prepared to go all the way. The company which sues thinking that it will make settlement possible is often fooled, and winds up on the receiving end of a vigorous counterclaim. Discuss fully and in detail with your counsel all of the ramifications of suit, including the time which will be involved by management, and the likely outcome.

If you are sued by others, you have no choice but to defend. On the other hand, you should want to know why you are being sued. As was stated in the opening section, the corporation which receives good legal advice should seldom have to sue as a plaintiff or be sued as a defendant. On the other hand, if the claim against your company is unreasonable, you have no choice but to defend aggressively. If the claim has merit, you should consider the possibility of settlement early in the game, before expenses and built-in positions make settlement more difficult or impossible.

Preparation.   Remember, in litigation your counsel can do only a certain amount. He will perform the role of the advocate, but the adequacy of his preparation depends upon the information which you are able to impart to him. At the outset you know the case, and he does not. Be sure that he receives all of the documents and all of the background information you can possibly think of which could have any relevancy to the suit.

Witnesses.   When depositions are called for, or the case comes to trial, and it is necessary for members of management to be witnesses, don't moan and roan. It is *your* case, not your lawyer's case. He is defending *your* position. If you do not want to testify, then you must take the consequences. When appearing as a witness, testify with conviction and sincerity, and your chances of prevailing in the ultimate disposition of the case will be greatly enhanced.

One further bit of advice cannot be resisted. A lawyer's time and advice are his stock in trade. As is true in other matters, you receive what you pay for. If you are willing to pay, either in time or in dollars, only for a quick off-the-top-of-the-head opinion, that is what you will receive. Do not expect sound, mature, experienced advice without being prepared to make the necessary investment of your own time and the company's money to warrant it.

Government contracting

R. E. Carroll*

The operating requirements of the United States government cover a broad spectrum. They range from the need to procure office and maintenance supplies to the design, development, fabrication, and operation of complex weapon systems and space boosters and vehicles.

The biggest segment of this market, from the procurement budget point of view, is in the aerospace-defense area. In the government fiscal year of 1968, approximately $81.3 billion were expended for these activities.

Statutory and regulatory basis

Dual personality

The United States Supreme Court gave early recognition to the principle that the government has the inherent power to enter into contracts. The Court has also distinguished the dual personality of the government, that is, its role as a party to a contract and its role as a sovereign.

Although it submits itself to the same basic tenets of contract law as apply to individuals when it acts as a party to a contract, the government cannot be held liable for any adverse impact on the performance of that contract arising out of its acts, legislative or executive, which result from the exercise of its power as a sovereign.

* Vice President, Business Operations, Space Division, North American Rockwell Corporation, Downey, California.

Authority of government agents

There is a basic distinction between the liability of individuals, or groups of individuals, and the liability of the government with regard to the power and authority of those acting as their respective agents. The former are liable to the extent of the authority that they have *apparently* granted to their agents. The government, however, is liable only to the extent of that power *actually* and specifically granted to its agents to act on its behalf.

It is extremely important, therefore, for a person contracting with the government to determine at the outset the specific extent of the government's agent's *actual* authority. Such an agent is normally referred to as a contracting officer. The risk of the contracting officer's lack of authority falls on the party contracting with the government through an agency of this kind.

The Armed Services Procurement Act

This act, approved by the President in February 1948 as Public Law 413, 80th Congress, pulled together in one statute all Department of Defense procurement authority and replaced all former laws on that subject. In 1956, Public Law 1928, 84th Congress, revised and codified existing law affecting such procurement under Title 10, United States Code. Similar acts of Congress establish the authority of other governmental agencies to contract for their respective requirements.

The Armed Services Procurement Regulations

The Department of Defense has implemented the basic authority granted it by the publication of the *Armed Services Procurement Regulations* (ASPR). These regulations and the supplementary Army Procurement Procedures (APP), *Air Force Procurement Instructions* (AFPI), *Navy Procurement Circulars* (NPC), and *Defense Supply Procurement Regulations* (DSPR) cover the general policies and procedures for practically all procurements of supplies and services which obligate appropriated funds. The ASPR and the supplementary Service implementing regulations constitute the "bible" of the defense business.

Other regulations

The Federal Procurement Regulations System generally covers the civilian federal executive agencies. As a part of this system, the Federal Procurement Regulations (FPR) are published by the administrator of the General Services Administration (GSA) under the authority of the Federal Property and Administrative Services Act of 1949, and other laws. FPR applies to procurement of personal property, nonpersonal services (including construction), and real property by lease.

The National Aeronautics and Space Administration (NASA) has issued detailed implementing regulations (NASA-PR). It is NASA policy to follow, to the maximum extent practical, procurement policies and procedures consistent with those set forth in the ASPR. The statutory basis of the NASA-PR is the National Aeronautics and Space Act of 1958.

Contract acquisition activities

The Armed Services Procurement Act states that the "formal advertising" technique is the preferred method of procurement. In advertised procurements, the award is made to the lowest, responsive, responsible bidder. If the bidder is financially responsible, responsive to the terms of the Invitation for Bid (IFB) and submits the lowest price, he wins the award. The act authorizes, however, the use of the "negotiated" technique as an approved method, when it is determined by the procuring agency that the procurement falls within a specified exception to the requirement for use of the formal advertising method. The act sets forth 17 exceptions, ranging in scope from national emergency to perishable supplies.

The major portion of funds appropriated for procurement purposes are utilized on contracts let by the negotiated method. The close scrutiny of these negotiated procurements by the Comptroller General of the United States, the members of various committees of the Congress, and members of the industrial community has resulted in the development of extremely refined and detailed "competitive negotiated" procurement policies and procedures.

The contracting officer must make a decision on each proposed procurement as to whether the procurement will be made by advertising or by negotiation.

Advertised procurements

The criteria for the use of formal advertising require that, (1) the procurement is described by full and complete specifications; (2) there is an adequate number of suppliers that would bid, thereby assuring effective competition; and (3) time is available to follow the detailed sequential steps of the formal advertising method. The buyer prepares an IFB, listing all pertinent procurement information, and sends it out to a representative number of potential suppliers. It is then announced in the Department of Commerce publication, "Synopsis of U.S. Government Proposed Procurement Sales and Contracts Awards." When the bid opening date specified in the IFB arrives, the bids are opened and the award made to the lowest, responsive, responsible bidder.

Negotiated procurements

If it is determined that the procurements fall within one of the 17 exceptions to the use of the formal advertising method, then the contracting officer must document the specific reason for determining that the facts sustain a decision to use the negotiated method. This formal Determination and Findings (D&F) must, in the case of some major procurements, be approved by the head of the procuring activity. After approval of the D&F, a Request for Proposal (RFP) is prepared by the contracting officer. It should contain as complete as possible, specific description of the items to be procured, together with all applicable specifications, quantities, time and place of delivery, method of shipment, etc.

The RFP may request a proposal based on a particular type of contract. A contractor should respond to all of its terms and conditions, but he may also submit alternates to those terms and conditions.

Types of contracts

On the basis of classification by method of payment, there are two basic types of contracts: fixed price and cost reimbursement. There are many variations within each type; however, the general distinction between the two remains the same.

Fixed price

In a fixed-price type contract, the contractor must produce and deliver the prescribed product or service at the price and time(s) set forth in the contract schedule, regardless of what it actually costs to perform the contract. There are various forms of fixed-price contracts; firm fixed price (FFP), fixed price with escalation (FPE), fixed price redetermination (FPR), fixed price incentive (FPI), and fixed price performance incentive (FPPI).

Cost reimbursement

In a cost-reimbursement type contract, the product or service is paid for on the basis of the contractually specified portion (up to 100 percent) of the actual allowable costs of performance. It may also specify a fee to be paid in addition to the actual costs. This fee cannot, by statutory prohibition, be determined-based upon a percentage of the actual costs incurred in performance of the contract. This prohibited contracting technique is known as Cost Plus Percentage of Cost (CPPC).

Under the cost-reimbursement type contract, the contractor agrees to use its best efforts to complete the contract within the estimated costs set forth in the contract schedule, *BUT* has no obligation to continue performance when, despite his best efforts, the contract is not fully performed at the time he has expended the total estimated cost set forth in the schedule. There are various kinds of cost-reimbursement type contracts: cost, cost sharing, cost plus fixed fee (CPFF), cost plus incentive fee (CPIF), cost plus performance incentive (CPPI), and cost plus award fee (CPAF).

There is also a hybrid type known as Time and Material (T&M). Under this type of contract, the contractor is paid a fixed price for each labor hour utilized, plus the actual cost of materials employed. The fixed price per labor hour includes labor costs, indirect expenses, and profit.

The importance of the type of contract cannot be overemphasized. In negotiated procurements, the contractor, when some doubt may exist as to which type of contract will best serve the interests of both parties, should consider preparing his proposal on more than one type. The contractor should always consider what the impact of the type of contract will be on both the specific procurement and the interrelationship of that contract with his other business.

Basis of selection of contract type

Section 3-402 of ASPR sets forth the "Basic Principles for Use of Contract Types." It emphasizes that the type selected should provide the contractor with an incentive to perform efficiently. The amount of profit negotiated should be consistent with the degree of responsibility and risk which the contractor assumes under the type of contract utilized.

The major consideration in contract type selection should be the degree of certainty as to the contractor's ability to produce the item or provide the services specified in the statement of work and as to the delivery schedule set forth in the proposed contract. If the contractor is reasonably certain of his capability to perform, and if the price is reasonable (including adequate coverage for contingencies and risks involved in the performance), then a firm fixed-price contract is the best from the contractor's viewpoint.

On the other hand, the contracting officer must determine whether the fixed price proposed is reasonably commensurate with the government's analysis of the costs of performance and the risks involved in such performance. If there are unusual contingencies which have caused the contractor to substantially increase the proposed fixed price, then the contracting officer must either, (1) negotiate a price whereby both parties share in such risks or (2) use contract provisions for price adjustments, dependent upon the actual occurrence of those contingencies. This would be done by selecting one of the appropriate fixed-price contract forms previously mentioned.

In those procurements where there is doubt that the contractor can perform the contract due to uncertainties in the definition of the product, the developmental nature of the materials or production techniques required, or in any other of the contract requirements, then it is questionable that the contractor can develop a reasonable estimate of the costs of performance. These procurements must include protection for the possible occurrence of many contingencies and, in these circumstances, a cost-reimbursement type contract should be utilized. Here again, the form of cost-reimbursement type contract should be tailored to the specific conditions and contingencies involved.

Negotiated proposal process

Purpose

The purpose of a proposal is, not only to respond to the terms and conditions set forth by the government buyer in his RFP, but also to sell the managerial and technical capabilities of the contractor in carrying out the required tasks at a reasonable cost and schedule. It should contain material which will convince the prospective customer that the contractor's solutions to the provisions of the RFP are the best available, and that the contractor has adequate organization, management, personnel, and facilities to carry out the statement of work within the specified price and schedule.

Most proposals consist of three basic sections: technical, management, and cost.

The technical section

In procurements of complex systems or those of a developmental nature, this section is the most important part of the proposal, since it illustrates the contractor's understanding of the technical requirements of the procurement and presents proposed solutions. It should be so organized as to be compatible with the statement of work set forth in the RFP. It should also provide an analysis of the technical problems, a discussion of the operational environment, and, consistent with the type of contract proposed, an accurate and clear description of the proposed hardware or system.

The customer is primarily concerned with what the item or service will do for him. The proposal should explain how the item will accomplish the results required. If at all possible, exceptions to the requirements of the RFP should not be taken; rather, performance "trade-offs" should be proposed. Such a trade-off should be an approach which shortens development lead-time and reduces development costs, without affecting minimum performance requirements set forth in the RFP.

In major systems procurements especially, the "cost effectiveness" of the proposed technical approach should be analyzed and emphasized.

The technical section also includes the proposed delivery or completion schedule and, as appropriate to the size of the procurement involved, a program plan, engineering plan, manufacturing plan, etc.

The management section

In proposals for significant development effort, complex weapons or aerospace systems, or high-dollar-value procurements with difficult delivery or completion schedules, it is important that the government contracting agency be informed as to the precise manner by which the contractor intends to manage the proposed contract. This elaboration on the history, organization, management experience, and management policies and procedures of the contractor may well be the key factor in the selection of the successful bidder. This is especially true in procurements where the technical capabilities of the various bidding contractors are relatively equal and the estimated costs are within a close range.

The type of management proposed should demonstrate the contractor's analysis of the size, complexity and definition of contract tasks, and the relative importance of such management to the overall needs of the procuring agency. The term "project, or program, management" has been applied as a generic label to many different approaches to the problem of identifying a specific management element within the contractor's organization, as well as to the application of planning and controlling techniques to the performance of requirements set forth in the terms of an RFP.

The proposed type and extent of project management should be specified, and the kinds and types of planning and control techniques should be described and illustrated. The project manager may vary from a mere staff coordinator and progress reporter, to a full-scale manager of all those personnel within the contractor organization who are devoting their efforts to the performance of the contract. Whatever degree of authority to be given to the project manager should be reflected in the management system by which he will attempt to manage the project. Past successful utilization of any proposed management system should be highlighted, and actual results described if at all possible. Frequently, "intelligence" as to the method of project management favored by the procuring agency can be of significant value in the proposal preparation process.

What is known as "matrix management" has become very popular in trying to bridge the special interests of individual projects and the organizational simplicity of total functional management. Under matrix management, the personnel in each of the functional operating organizations receive project task definitions, schedules, and budgets from the respective project managers and, at the same time, receive functional policy guidance (operating techniques and procedures) from the respective functional managers.

The cost section

When the procuring activity intends to use an FFP type contract, the price set forth in the cost section of the proposal is normally the decisive factor in the competitive evaluation. In cost-type contract situations, the cost breakdown and its relationship to the proposed method of performance contained in the technical and management sections are utilized to determine the contractor's real understanding of the total effort required.

The cost proposal should be presented in such a manner, and to such depth of detail, that the contracting officer and his supporting proposal analysis team are convinced of the reasonableness of the proposed cost estimate for the work required by the statement of work. Frequently, not recognizing that the cost proposal is a communication device, contractors approach the preparation of this section as if it were simply an accounting exercise. It is extremely important that the cost breakdown be capable of analysis which demonstrates the interaction of technical and management solutions on the estimated and proposed costs.

There is considerable debate as to the best method of cost estimating. The "grass roots" technique is to have each department involved in the performance of the proposed effort submit individual estimates of the direct labor, materials, and other cost factors required for its part in the overall performance. Individuals favoring this approach point out that those who are going to perform should be best qualified to determine what's required for that performance. Those opposing the approach claim that there is not only a potential conflict between performance requirements versus department budget problems, but that this adding up of a series of individual estimates ignores the impact of departmental interactions on the total cost of performance.

The other extreme in cost estimate preparation is a centralized estimating method. In this case, the estimates for all required activities are generated by professional estimators. Its opponents believe that this method may be appropriate if there is much historical or performance trend data available from previous equivalent performances, but not when the procurement is for a complex development or the attainment of technical or production techniques beyond the then current "state of the art."

The pros and cons of both techniques should be weighed in each proposal situation and tailored to its individual situation. A combination of the two provides a reasonably effective check and balance system.

Most companies consider the method of estimating, the cost history data, and the specifics of the cost estimate on an individual proposal as proprietary. The Congress, through enactment of the various procurement system authorizing statutes, has deemed otherwise. The policy thus established provides for submission of cost details and for access to cost records for all negotiated procurements. This is required, in negotiated procurements, so that the reasonableness of the proposed price (or cost plus fee) can be ascertained prior to contract award. The next section of

EXHIBIT 1

Typical Program Work Breakdown Structure

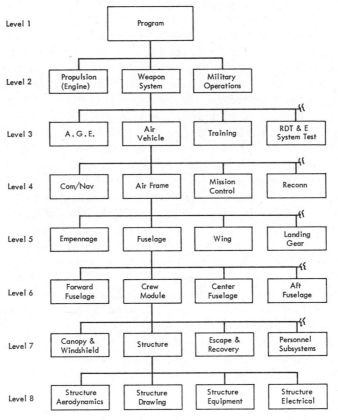

Level 1	Program			
Level 2	Propulsion (Engine)	Weapon System	Military Operations	
Level 3	A.G.E.	Air Vehicle	Training	RDT & E System Test
Level 4	Com/Nav	Air Frame	Mission Control	Reconn
Level 5	Empennage	Fuselage	Wing	Landing Gear
Level 6	Forward Fuselage	Crew Module	Center Fuselage	Aft Fuselage
Level 7	Canopy & Windshield	Structure	Escape & Recovery	Personnel Subsystems
Level 8	Structure Aerodynamics	Structure Drawing	Structure Equipment	Structure Electrical

this chapter contains reference to, and comments on, those contract cost principles which have been adopted by the government in compliance with congressional policy.

Any organization engaging in substantial government contracting must not only understand those cost principles, but should also familiarize itself with the different techniques of cost/price analysis utilized by the procuring agencies. In major procurements, there may be a requirement for the total task to be broken down into sub-tasks and sub-subtasks. This is called a "work breakdown structure" and the various elements of the structure are called "work packages." Exhibit 1 depicts a typical work breakdown structure.

The relationship of cost, profit and price is discussed in the ASPR, section 3-806. This relationship is frequently misunderstood and misapplied by many personnel on both sides of the contracting table. ASPR 3-402 points out that the type of contract is of primary importance in the government obtaining fair and reasonable prices under all the circumstances. The contract type and pricing are interrelated and should be so considered in negotiation.

Contract cost principles

Section XV of ASPR sets forth the general cost principles and procedures for the determination and allowance of costs in connection with the negotiation and administration of cost-reimbursement type contracts. It contains guidelines for use, where appropriate, in the evaluation of costs of certain negotiated fixed-price type contracts, as well as contracts which have been terminated for the convenience of the government.

During government fiscal years 1965–1967, approximately 30 percent of the aerospace-defense renegotiable sales were under cost type contracts and another 15 percent were expended on fixed-price types which require cost determination at some stage of their performance. The ASPR XV cost principles thus applied to this 45 percent of the aerospace-defense contract dollars.

The cost principles apply to both direct and indirect costs. In addition to setting forth definitions of both reasonableness and allocability, there are definitions of those costs which will be considered to be direct and indirect.

These cost principles were not developed overnight, but are the result of many years of evolutionary development. They represent the latest definition of those costs which the government believes it should recognize in paying for products delivered or services rendered under the various types of contracts. Based on Hoover Commission recommendations made in 1955, action was initiated by the Department of Defense to update and integrate all previous cost principles which were then set forth in many different documents and regulations. The present cost principles, after much preliminary discussion between defense industry and government representatives, were issued in 1959 with a mandatory application as of July 1960.

The general industry position has been that all reasonable costs incurred, which are allocated to the various contracts in accordance with the contractor's regular system of accounting, should be allowable, provided that the contractor's system of allocation is consistent with generally accepted accounting principles. The cost principles do not accept this criterion. They set forth specific criteria to be used by the government personnel in evaluating the allowability, allocability, and reasonableness of the various kinds and types of costs.

Many contractors spend so much time debating the question of unallowable costs that they fail to take the necessary action to secure reimbursement for the allowable costs. If a contractor intends to do a significant portion of its total business with the government, it is only common sense that it acquaint itself with the rules of the game and take those actions necessary to establish an accounting system designed to maximize the recognition of reimbursement of costs in accordance with the provisions of the cost principles.

Contract clauses with special financial implications

There are numerous terms and conditions of government contracts which have special financial implications. The specific clauses are set forth in the ASPR, NASA-PR, FPR and other departmental regulations referred to at the beginning of this chapter.

Any company planning to engage in a significant amount of government contracting should become familiar with these clauses, and the interpretations of them which have been made by the various courts and appeal boards of the government. It is not possible to treat the subject exhaustively in this chapter, but it is important that the following contract clauses be understood by those entering the government contracting marketplace.

Inspection and correction of defects and warranties

These clauses should be considered together. All government contracts contain some form of inspection and correction of defects clause. The standard inspection clause in fixed-price contracts, as set forth in ASPR 7-103.5, provides that all supplies shall be subject to inspection and test by the government to the extent practicable at all times and places, including the period of manufacture and, in any event, prior to acceptance. The clause further provides that inspection and test by the government does not relieve the supplier from any responsibility regarding defects or other failures which may be discovered prior to acceptance. Acceptance is, however, generally considered conclusive except as regards latent defects, fraud, or such gross mistakes as amount to fraud.

"Inspection" is defined as the examination and testing of supplies or services to determine conformance to contractual requirements. "Acceptance" is defined as the action of an authorized agent of the government by which the government assumes ownership of supplies tendered for acceptance, or as the approval of specific services rendered as partial or complete performance of the contract requirements. "Latent defects" are defined as those defects existing at the time of acceptance which would not have been discoverable by reasonable inspection processes. There is no time limit on the assertion of claims based on latent defects.

The standard inspection clause for cost-reimbursement type supply contracts, ASPR 7-203.5, provides for similar availability to inspection and testing at all times, *BUT* differs with regard to the correction of defects provisions. The clause provides that at any time within six months after acceptance of supplies delivered in accordance with contractual requirements (or such other periods as provided in the contract schedule), the government may require the contractor to correct or replace any supplies which, at the time of delivery, were defective in material or workmanship or otherwise did not meet contractual requirements.

The cost of the correction or replacement may be borne by the government, but the contractor shall receive no additional fee. Also, if the contractor fails to act with reasonable promptness, the government may contract the work done and charge the contractor the additional costs or reduce the original fixed fee. Thus, the finality of acceptance by the government is substantially different under cost type contracting than under fixed-price arrangements.

Warranty clauses grant the government an additional period of time after acceptance to assert claims regarding defects which were not discovered during the original inspection and acceptance. These are known as "patent defects." Contractors should consider the inclusion of an additional cost in proposals containing a warranty clause, as insurance against potential claims. The contracting officer should conduct an evaluation of the probability of items being accepted with patent defects as compared to such added costs, as well as the potential alternate of the costs of tighter inspection and more stringent testing prior to acceptance.

Warranty clauses have been utilized in different ways by the various government procuring agencies. The Navy Department has advocated their use, while the Army Department has generally avoided them. The Air Force has applied them in specific instances when it was believed appropriate for protection against special problems.

The United States Comptroller General has consistently objected to the use of warranty provisions, unless it was clearly demonstrable that their use in each specific instance was in the best interests of the government. The cost of a warranty often may exceed the benefit from it.

Patents and rights in data

In the performance of government contracts, many problems have arisen as regards both patent rights and proprietary data. The President of the United States, on October 10, 1963, promulgated a statement of the patent policy applicable to all executive departments and agencies of the federal government. This statement is set forth in ASPR 9-107.2 and 107.3. The early commercial use of inventions, which have been developed as the result of expenditures for federally sponsored research activities, underlies the basic intent of the policy.

The policy statement provides that this intent can be achieved in three ways. First, the government can acquire title to such inventions. Second, if the contractor has demonstrated its ability to commercialize its inventions, then the contractor can take title, with the government receiving the license rights. This means that the government can use the invention without payment of royalties to the patent holder. Third, the determination of title to the patent rights may be deferred until the time of disclosure of the invention.

As a general rule, the government will require or seek to obtain patent rights to inventions only in those instances where they evolve from the performance of research and development contracts, not from contracts for the manufacture and delivery of supplies.

Data, as defined in ASPR 9-201, means writings, sound recordings, pictorial reproductions, drawings, or other graphic representations and works of similar nature, whether or not copyrighted. It does not include financial reports, cost analyses, and other information incidental to contract administration. The definition set forth in the ASPR is narrower than the one stated in Department of Defense Instruction 5010.12., "Procurement of Technical Data and Information." The term "data" is stated therein to include all technical data and information, regardless of functional application, which has been generated during any phase of development.

The ASPR section is applicable only to rights in data which are required to be delivered in accordance with the terms of a contract. The Instruction is a policy statement to the effect that only such data as are specifically needed should be bought, and it provides procedures for determination of the requirements for "technical data." This technical data concept disregards the previously utilized terminology of "proprietary data." It provides for the listing of the technical data which must be furnished with either unlimited or limited rights to the use, reproduction, or disclosure of that data by the government.

Under the provisions of the Rights in Data clauses, unless there is timely delivery of the required data, 10 percent of the contract price (if fixed-price type) or the allowable costs and fee (if cost type) can be withheld.

Data which is provided to the government as a part of the proposal activity should be identified as being restricted data, unless its development fell within the provisions of previous contracts containing clauses such as those described above.

Financing

While it is the policy of government procuring agencies to expect contractors to depend upon private financing, it is recognized that there are many valid instances where performance of government contracts may strain the financial capability of contractors. Appendix E, ASPR contains the basic policies and procedures whereby the government will provide financial assistance.

Under cost type contracts, contractors are reimbursed for expenses incurred on a weekly or monthly basis, so that need for other types of financial assistance is normally limited. Such a need is far more prevalent in the performance of fixed-price type contracts.

The order of preference for a contractor to obtain working capital, as set forth in the ASPR is (1) private financing, (2) normal progress payments, (3) guaranteed loans, (4) unusual progress payments, and (5) advance payments. What is known as partial payments is not really a method of financing, in that these are payments made for delivery of part of the total number of completed items called for in a contract.

Normal progress payments are made on the basis of the progressive performance by the contractor toward the completion of a contract. Such payments do not require the delivery of completed items. They would apply to the recoupment of costs during long and extensive preproduction or development activities. ASPR Appendix E established limitations as to preproduction period, size of contract, and percentage of payment. Progress payments beyond those limitations are called unusual progress payments.

A guaranteed loan is one made by a bank to a government contractor or subcontractor, a percentage of which is guaranteed by the government. Such a loan may be based on one or more defense production contracts. Normally, the government will only act as guarantor when a contractor possesses some unique capability or capacity.

An advance payment is a payment made by the government in advance of, and in anticipation of, complete performance under a contract. Advance payments are distinguished from partial or progress payments in that deliveries are not required, nor even is progress toward completion of the work called for by the contract. This technique is to be used only when no other method of financing will meet the financial assistance requirements.

Taxes

Federal, state and local taxes are frequently significant factors in estimating a contract price. Section XI of the ASPR contains both general policy relative to taxes and specific information on their applicability to both advertised and negotiated contracts.

Many articles which the government buys are not subject to any federal excise tax. When federal excise taxes are applicable, the overall financial interests of the government are not adversely affected, because what is paid out under the terms of the contract is recouped by the collection of such taxes.

This is not true, however, in the case of state and local taxes. The imposition of these taxes results in higher net costs to the federal government. Therefore, contracts will generally be drafted with the aim of minimizing the imposition of such taxes. The basic principle relied upon is that a state has no constitutional authority to levy taxes which would impede or burden the operations of the federal government. This principle is not applicable in all cases, however, and care must be exercised in individual tax situations. Generally, a contractor must pay all state and local taxes and should consider them in his proposal preparation.

Insurance

Upon entering the field of government contracting, a firm is immediately faced with financial implications concerning the risks of loss or damage to its own or government property, and liabilities for damages to persons or property of other persons arising out of contract performance.

Generally, the federal government acts as a self-insurer, since it is more economical to do so, particularly with respect to government-owned property. Thus, contractors are not held responsible for loss or damage to such property caused by certain perils, when it is furnished under: (1) a facility contract or (2) a procurement contract for which cost or pricing data are required.

ASPR Section X, Part 3, delineates the general principles and policies applicable to insurance under contracts of the military departments for supplies and services.

Usually, the amounts and kinds of insurance carried by contractors under a fixed-price contract is of little concern to the government. Here, the contracting officer's responsibility is limited to obtaining evidence that firms have complied with applicable state and federal statutes regulating workmen's compensation and employer's liability, etc. In reality, the contractor is responsible for all risks, except those expressly assumed by the government under a fixed-price contract arrangement.

Under cost type contracts, however, it is the general policy of the government to require contractors to carry workmen's compensation and employer's liability insurance, automobile and aircraft liability insurance, and general liability insurance which provide protection for injuries to third persons arising from the performance of the contract. That portion of premiums allocable to his contracts for such required liability insurance is reimbursed to the contractor.

Under Title 10, U.S. Code, Section 2354, the government may assume other risks normally covered by insurance, specifically in research and development contracts where contractors perform unusually hazardous work. In such cases, the government may indemnify contractors against claims of third persons and/or loss or damage to property of the contractor.

Labor

There are a variety of regulations, administrative rulings and general laws governing the use of labor under Government contracts. Penalties for non-compliance are rigorous, and the administration of their provisions is strict.

It is the policy of procurement agencies to refrain from taking a position in any dispute between labor and management. Quite often, a clause, Notice to the Government of Labor Disputes (ASPR 7-104.4), must be inserted in supply contracts for items of special or urgent concern to the agency, so that the Government is alerted at once to potential interruptions in deliveries.

Walsh Healey Public Contracts (1936)

The Secretary of Labor administers this act (for labor engaged in government supply contracts exceeding $10,000) through regulations entitled "Walsh Healey Public Contracts Act, Rulings and Interpretations." ASPR 12-605 incorporates by reference these rulings as well as stipulations of the act itself. The general subjects covered relate to minimum wages, maximum hours, child and convict labor, working conditions, overtime, etc. Excluded from the act are contracts for construction of public works, and ships other than naval vessels, personal services contracts, public utility services, and for rental of real or personal property. It does not apply to subcontracts.

Davis Bacon Act (1931)

This statute provides protection solely for laborers and mechanics employed in the construction, alteration, or repair of public buildings and works exceeding $2,000, insuring they obtain certain minimum predetermined wage rates. Minimum wage rates are advertised in the contract specifications and contained in the contract. The ASPR clause used (*18-703.1(a)*) provides that contractors must pay such labor, not less than once a week, the full amount accrued, computed at not less than rates stated in the wage determination of the Secretary of Labor which is attached. Another statute, the Copeland Act, insures there will be no kickbacks or wage rebates.

Other labor regulations, such as those pertaining to equal opportunity and nondiscrimination in employment, and the Service Contract Act of 1965 (Public Law 89-286), which extended benefits to contracts for housekeeping functions, contain important details of immediate concern to government contractors.

Contract performance activities

A contract is an exchange of mutual promises. The government promises to pay the contractor in accordance with the terms of the contract in exchange for the contractor's promise to perform in accordance with the terms of the contract. The government may also have promised other things, such as the furnishing of certain facilities, equipment, or materials for the contractor to use in his performance.

The various government contracting activities have established detailed contract performance surveillance and administration procedures to protect and exercise its rights and obligations under the terms of the contract. Many contractors fail to organize in such a manner as to protect their rights and monitor their compliance with the complex obligations they assumed upon execution of a government contract.

It has been said, "If the contractor has correctly analyzed the Request for Proposal, if he has prepared his proposal fully responsive to that RFP, if he has properly costed and negotiated the contract, if he insures that the contract is truly responsive to the agreements reached in the negotiation, and if his administrative procedures are geared to the peculiar problems of government contracts, his administration problems will be minimized." That's a lot of ifs. It does illustrate, however, that good contract performance starts with good RFP analysis.

Many companies spend more time complaining about government red tape than they do in analyzing government contract requirements and developing good management procedures to maximize their return from those contracts. If a company is going to participate in the government market then it should properly prepare itself.

As stated previously, good contract performance management starts with the receipt of a proposal request. It ends only after receipt of final payment and disposition of all rights and obligations of both parties. Since so many different organizational elements of a government procuring agency participate in proposal analysis, negotiation, review, and contract preparation, it is especially important that when the contract is received for execution by the contractor, the entire document and all its attachments and references be examined to make certain that it truly represents the results of the negotiation.

Organization and performance planning

The contractor's organizational element which is assigned the task of contract management must be operationally free of internal conflicts. Such freedom is necessary to provide internal stature and authority, and to insure that company obligations under the contract are made known to top management, even when compliance therewith may be repugnant to one or more of the operating departments.

During the course of proposal preparation, a plan should be prepared of those actions required to meet the proposed time schedule and esti- mated costs. This plan, as necessarily modified by changes resulting from the negotiation, should be established as the master document for the tracking of those activities which must be performed to carry out the contractual obligations.

Management systems and procedures should provide for the issuance of internal work authorizations and budgets which are in compliance with such a plan. Control techniques and reporting requirements on the three major performance areas (technical, schedule, and cost) should be established and monitored.

There are numerous techniques for laying out such plans. Networks, consisting of the interrelated actions of the various performing organiza- tions, should be constructed. These activities could be time-phased so as to assure progress to completion per the contract schedule. Chapter 24, "Project Scheduling and Management," discusses in depth the various methods of project scheduling, including PERT and CPM.

Performance evaluation

It is extremely important that actual performance be continuously evaluated against the plans. This monitoring should present information

EXHIBIT 2

Typical Input-Output Chart

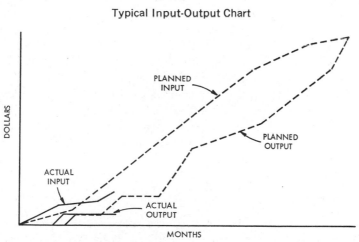

to contractor management of *those activities needing special attention* if ultimate contract performance requirements are to be met.

Progress and completion types of schedule milestones can be assigned cost accomplishment values and tracked in comparison to actual costs. This technique is known as "Input-Output." Exhibit 2 illustrates this.

The ultimate profitability of any given contract is determined by management knowing at the right time that some corrective action is required, and then monitoring to assure that the action taken does, in fact, solve the problem. The project, or program, management systems described in Chapter 25 are designed to meet these requirements on complex or high risk contracts.

Contract change activities

Government contracts contain "changes articles" which provide the contracting officer the right to direct changes in various elements of the contract terms and conditions. The clause for use in fixed-price type supply contracts is contained in ASPR 7-103.2. It states that the contracting officer may by written order make changes in:
1. Drawings, designs or specifications where supplies are being specially manufactured for the government.
2. Method of shipment or packing.
3. Place of delivery.

The clause for cost type supply contracts, ASPR 7-203.2, is the same but it also provides that the contracting officer may make changes in the amount of government furnished property. Special language may also be added, granting the contracting officer the right to change quantities and delivery rates within specified ranges.

The clauses provide that if any directed change causes an increase or decrease in the cost of or time required for performance, an equitable adjustment shall be made to the price (or cost plus fee) and/or the delivery schedule. Failure to agree to any claimed adjustment can be treated by the contractor in accordance with the provisions of the "disputes" clause of the contract, *but* he must proceed with the work as changed by the contracting officer's direction.

Adequate recognition of directed changes and the proper interpretation of their impact on the contractor's performance requirements is often the difference between a profit and a loss on the contract. This requires diligence in analyzing directions received and skillful negotiation of the estimated impacts.

Disputes and appeals

Because of the complex and, in many instances, peculiar nature of government contracts and related procedures, there arise many instances when the contractor and the contracting officer cannot agree on interpretation and compliance with various terms and conditions of the contract. ASPR 7-103.12 contains the standard Disputes Clause for inclusion in all Department of Defense contracts.

The clause states that, unless otherwise specifically provided for in the contract, any dispute concerning a question of fact shall be decided by the contracting officer, and the contractor informed in writing. That decision shall then be considered final, unless the contractor files an appeal within 30 days of receipt of the decision. The appeal, although delivered to the contracting officer, is to be addressed to the secretary of the military department involved. The subsequent decision of the secretary in the determination of such appeals shall be final and conclusive to the extent permitted by U.S. law.

There may frequently be disagreement as to whether a dispute is over a question of fact rather than a question of law. In view of the confusion in this area, a contractor would be wise to first process any dispute under the provisions of the Disputes Clause and, if either the contracting officer or the Armed Services Board of Contract Appeals finds it to be a question of law, or if the contractor believes it to be such, then file an appeal with the Comptroller General or the U.S. Court of Claims, as appropriate.

Contract termination

The government may terminate a contract for default or for its convenience. The rights and liabilities in termination for default are set forth in the Default and Termination Clauses (ASPR 8-707 and ASPR 8-702). These provide that the government may terminate the contract for default when there is failure or refusal of the contractor to deliver the required supplies, perform the required services or otherwise perform the contract, or so fails to make progress as to endanger performance of the contract. This right of termination can only be exercised after notice to the contractor and opportunity to cure the alleged default have been given. Failure to make timely delivery is exempted from this notice and opportunity proviso.

In fixed-price contracts, the government acquires the right to repurchase the terminated items from another firm and hold the contractor liable for costs in excess of the original contract price. In cost-type contracts, because of their "best efforts" nature, the procedures of a default termination are generally the same as a termination for convenience. Implicit in this best efforts provision is the assumption that, until he stops work, the contractor is entitled to recover all allowable costs. If a contractor were faced with a disallowance of cost upon default, the entire concept of cost-type contracting would be negated.

Section VIII of the ASPR also contains respective Termination Clauses to be used in the different type contracts. These clauses set forth the right of the government to terminate for its convenience, in whole or in part, the remaining work under a contract. In addition to Section VIII, Sections XV, Cost Principles, and XXIV, Disposition of Government Property in Possession of Subcontractors, are applicable.

When a fixed-price contract is terminated for convenience, a contractor can select one of three methods of preparing the Termination Claim. These are: (1) the inventory basis, (2) the total cost basis, and (3) the percentage of completion basis. The inventory basis is generally preferred by the government. This method is preferred because it deals only with the costs directly related to the terminated portion of the contract. Using the total cost basis, the total costs of performance on the contract up to the point of termination are recognized.

The total cost method is not advantageous to the contractor if he is earning, as of that point in performance, a higher rate of profit than he would earn over the total performance of the contract. On the other hand, it would be more advantageous to use this method if he is earning less than his anticipated rate of profit, or operating at a loss.

The government prefers the inventory method, because it is simpler to audit only the costs connected with the termination inventory rather than to review them over the entire life of the contract.

The fact that a contract may have been negotiated with a certain profit percentage projected at completion does not mean that the same percentage is applicable to the terminated portion of the contract. The profit should be based on the difficulty of the completed work at the point of termination. ASPR 8-303 sets forth the policy and factors to be considered in determining profit in the settlement of termination claims.

Many contractors make the mistake of always negotiating profit as a percentage of costs to be incurred. Not only is this contrary to the intent of the procurement regulations, but, especially in terminations, does not give recognition to the fact that there is greater management and technical skill required in the development and initial production phases of a contract. It is this factor which logically should be the basis for the profit portion of the termination claim.

ASPR Section VIII, Part 4, covers the settlement of terminations for cost-type contracts. A contractor may submit vouchers and propose a negotiated settlement. The negotiated settlement method is advantageous when, under the contractor's normal accounting procedures, not all of the costs related to performance to the point of termination have been booked. The same principles apply to fee determination, as stated earlier, relevant to profit.

Audits

The Budget and Accounting Act of 1921, which established the Bureau of the Budget, also created the General Accounting Office (GAO), headed by a Comptroller General. The GAO is an agency in the legislative branch, completely independent of the executive branch. The prime responsibility of the agency is to investigate all matters relating to the receipt, disbursement and management of the government's financial affairs. One of its major functions is to make independent audits of the activities of government departments, including certain contract activities.

The Armed Services Procurement Act, Federal Property and Administrative Services Act, and Atomic Energy Act require that contracts negotiated without formal advertising include clauses permitting an examination of records by the Comptroller General. This clause permits examination of a contractor's (or subcontractor's) books, documents, papers, and records that directly pertain to, and involve, transactions relating to the contracts or subcontracts.

Of particular interest here to the financial executive is the fact that the GAO's access to books, documents, records, etc. is *not* limited to the formal cost accounting records and supporting data, but also includes *all* underlying data concerning contract activities and operations which afford the basis for pricing and incurrence of costs by the contractor.

Not all contracts are examined—consideration is given to the size or type of contract, basis for award, nature of cost or pricing data furnished, and a variety of other factors affecting the government's interest. Some audits stem from congressional committees or individual members of Congress. Recent years have seen a change in emphasis in GAO audits, from that of focusing on accounting matters and whether expenditures were made in accord with the intent of Congress, to that of how effectively and economically government business is being conducted. It is this latter type of GAO audit that has created adverse publicity and problems between federal agencies and their contractors and the Comptroller General.

Contract audit is also the responsibility of the Defense Contract Audit Agency (DCAA), which began operations in 1965, and took over audit functions formerly performed by the separate military departments. Department of Defense Directive 5105.36 grants a broad range of functions to the DCAA, in addition to its basic audit functions—including reviews of a contractor's general business practices, purchasing, property administration, and cost estimating incident to award, negotiation, modification, change administration, termination or settlement of contracts.

It is NASA policy to use the services and related field support capabilities of the Department of Defense, including the use of DCAA, to perform surveys of contractors' accounting systems, audits of proposed prices, and financial management operations. Such evaluations are often made prior to contract award, to ascertain whether a prospective contractor has the necessary business management capability to control the application of resources in accordance with a proposed plan. Factors considered are whether the contractor's organization structure reflects those functions which are essential to "project cost control," and whether the accounting system is adequate to permit administration of the type of contract proposed.

Renegotiation

The Renegotiation Act of 1951, as amended and extended, applies to contracts and subcontracts of the following government procurement activities: Departments of Defense, Army, Navy, Air Force; General

Services Administration; Atomic Energy Commission; Maritime Commission (Commerce Department); Federal Maritime Board; Federal Aviation Agency; and the National Aeronautics and Space Administration.

Almost all contracts awarded by these procuring activities contain a clause making them subject to the provisions of the Renegotiation Act. Some contracts and subcontracts are mandatorily exempt under the act, such as those with other governmental agencies; for certain agricultural commodities; with common carriers or public utilities; with tax-exempt charitable, religious, and educational institutions; for standard commercial articles; etc. Prime contractors and subcontractors are subject to renegotiation if the aggregate amount of business from those contracts in any one company fiscal year is greater than $1,000,000.

The act provides for the establishment of a Renegotiation Board. It is composed of five members, appointed by the President, by and with the advice of the Senate. The members are not allowed to engage actively in any business, vocation, or employment while serving as members. Regional boards have been established in Washington, D.C. and Los Angeles for reviewing cases and submitting recommendations to the Board.

Each contractor or subcontractor subject to renegotiation must file a report with the Board on or before the first day of the fifth month following the close of the company fiscal year. These reports are reviewed to determine the potential existence of renegotiable profits. The criteria used are preestablished profit to sales ratios based on industry averages. This criteria is only a guide, and even those profits below the industry average may be subject to Board action.

The Board has one year after a company files its report to give notice to the contractor of its intention to initiate renegotiation proceedings. The proceedings must be completed within two years after commencement.

The essence of the renegotiation process is an attempt to determine how much, if any, of a company's profits, derived from contracts subject to the act, are considered to be excessive. This is not done on a contract-by-contract basis, but rather on the total profitability of all such contracts performed in that fiscal period.

The act provides six statutory profit factors:
1. The contractor's efficiency as regards quantity and quality of production, reduction of costs, economy in use of materials, facilities, and manpower.
2. Reasonableness of costs and profits, with particular regard to volume of production, normal earnings, and comparison of war and peacetime profits.
3. The net worth, with particular regard to the amount and source of public and private capital employed.
4. The extent of risk assumed, including the risk incident to reasonable pricing policies.

5. Nature and extent of the contribution to the defense effort, including inventive and developmental contributions and cooperation with the government and other contractors in supplying technical assistance.
6. Character of the business, including source and nature of materials, complexity of manufacturing technique, character and extent of subcontracting, and rate of turnover.

Industry has frequently criticized the Board as having ignored the application of those factors and having based its determination solely on industry averages. This pushes the eventual net profit of an outstanding, efficient performer down to the profit level of an inefficient one.

Renegotiation Board Regulations (together with *Renegotiation Rulings and Bulletins*) may be obtained from the Superintendent of Documents, U.S. Government Printing Office, Washington, D.C. 20402, at a subscription price of $6.50.

Contractors can take steps to reduce the probability of an adverse determination by the Renegotiation Board and to stand in a better position in the event such a determination is ever made. Contracting officers are required by ASPR 1-319 to maintain a contract file on performance, including the extent and effectiveness of competition experienced in the negotiation and award of the contract, extent of risk assumed by the contractor, his efficiency, reasonableness of profits, basis of target and incentive formulae built into the contract, and other pertinent facts. These data are used to compile contract performance records which are furnished to the Board.

To support their position in the renegotiation process, contractors should maintain detailed records of contract performance, highlighting favorable aspects of their operations. Supportable management assertions and statements of fact may be structured into a periodic analysis of performance and provided to contracting officers and plant representatives, either on an individual contract basis, or from a companywide government business standpoint. Such a document is extremely valuable, since government contract files are usually filled with data on problems and seldom emphasize favorable aspects of the firm's performance.

Responsibility for assuring that such performance data are accumulated, analyzed, and maintained should be assigned within the firm to an executive who is intimately familiar with the renegotiation process and the financial structure of the company itself. One of his primary tasks is then to implement a system of identifying, gathering, analyzing, and filing favorable performance data from *all* functions within the company; another task is to convince the management of these functional organizations that such a system is important to the financial well-being of the firm, and not to be overlooked in the day-to-day rush of getting the contract job done.

This kind of documented performance data can be advantageously used by contractors for purposes other than renegotiation. It is useful in the Contractor Performance Evaluation (CPE) system, which the Department of Defense instituted in 1965. This system provides for a government evaluation of a contractor's cost, schedule, and technical performance every six months and upon contract completion. The NASA participated in the development of the CPE system, and applies it to selective procurements. As a part of the CPE process, contractors may make narrative responses to government evaluations of their performance, and it is here that documented, supportable performance data may be used in much the same manner as in renegotiation. CPE ratings have far-reaching effects, since the program is designed to create a memory bank of each contractor's performance, and various government agencies are to take this record into account in future source selection actions, profit and fee negotiations, as well as renegotiation actions.

Thus, there are ways that contractors can plan and organize to mitigate the adverse effects of government evaluations of their contract performance. In addition, firms should insure that contract Statements of Work are definite and unambiguous, and that the government's rights and responsibilities are carefully defined therein. Contract administration procedures within the company should be constantly refined to assure that, when changes in the contract occur, the contract document itself is adjusted to reflect the overall impact of changes on the firm's commitments. Indeed, the management of changes is becoming an increasingly crucial feature of profitable government contracting.

Make-or-buy and subcontracting

A contractor's make-or-buy program, his purchasing system, and subcontracting techniques have resultant effects on the negotiation of contract prices and contract performance, as well as government programs for small business and labor surplus areas. Within the firm, these systems have important management and financial implications, for they go to the heart of profitability on any given contract.

Generally stated, a firm's make-or-buy program is a written plan delineating the major subsystems, assemblies, sub-assemblies, and components to be manufactured, developed, or assembled in its own facilities versus those which will be procured elsewhere by subcontract. The government has become increasingly interested in make-or-buy decisions and has developed detailed techniques for their evaluation and approval. Once approved, the program cannot be altered without prior approval of the contracting officer. Approval of the contractor's purchasing system does not constitute approval of his make-or-buy program.

Due to the increasing complexity and costs of modern weapon systems, the government's role in reviewing and approving purchasing practices of prime contractors has grown. ASPR Section XXIII contains the procedures for this approval. They come into play only where the work is complex, where there is no adequate price competition, and where the dollar value involved is significant.

For the financial executive, establishing his firm's proper relationship with perhaps hundreds of subcontractors is a critical prerequisite to success in government contracting. Except for certain statutory requirements and executive orders and the requirements of the prime contract, the terms and conditions of any subcontract are subject to negotiation. The final relationship depends on the bargaining positions of both parties.

Bibliography

COMMERCE CLEARING HOUSE, INC. *Government Contracts Reporter.* New York, 1968.

McDONALD, PAUL R. Government Prime Contracts and Subcontracts Service. Covina, California, 1968.

Internal auditing

Frederic E. Mints and Herbert Witt*

This chapter is intended to aid those executives who wish to obtain a better understanding of modern internal audit concepts by providing, first, illustrations of the services which management can obtain from an effective internal audit organization, and second, suggestions for the organization and manning of such a staff. Statements of the benefits obtained from internal audit programs have been publicly voiced by top executives of business concerns and governmental agencies. The following statements are illustrative of internal auditing services which are explored in this chapter.

"The auditor is . . . a manager who assures a flow of reliable, objective information throughout the organization; one who sees to it that the information flow is complete, and that information is current, accurate, proper, and timely."[1]

"Dollar for dollar, operational auditing has been one of our soundest investments."[2]

"I do not look upon auditors as people who report conditions which are embarrassing but, rather, as associates in achieving our objective . . . members of sales management's team."[3]

---

* Manager of Internal Auditing (Retired), Lockheed-California Company, La Cresenta, California, and Regional Audit Director, Department of Health, Education, and Welfare, San Francisco Region, respectively.

[1] W. G. Phillips, President, The Glidden Co., *The Internal Auditor*, March/April 1968, p. 38.

[2] D. J. Haughton, Chairman of the Board, Lockheed Aircraft Corp., *The Manager's Letter*, AMA, December 20, 1960.

[3] D. A. Challis, Jr., Vice President–Sales, U.S. Steel Corp., *The Internal Auditor*, Winter 1965, p. 47.

"A good many of our management and fiscal problems could be avoided if we had available, and used, the expert services of internal auditors before we made some of our moves . . ."[4]

Nature of internal auditing

Definition

The Institute of Internal Auditors promulgated the following widely-accepted definition of the internal audit function in 1957:

Internal auditing is an independent appraisal activity within an organization for the review of accounting, financial and other operations as a basis for service to management. It is a managerial control, which functions by measuring and evaluating the effectiveness of other controls.[5]

Objectives

In a very small organization the manager can personally inspect and control all of the activities; in larger organizations he must delegate responsibility and rely on reports. The internal auditor, independent in approach, can extend the manager's reach by providing some of the assurance the manager, or owner, of a small organization can obtain through personal observation.

A 1963 survey of 177 companies by the National Industrial Conference Board disclosed the following five principal objectives of the internal auditing programs in most of these companies:[6]

Determine the adequacy of the system of control.

Investigate compliance with company policies and procedures.

Verify the existence of assets, see that proper safeguards for assets are maintained, and prevent or discover fraud.

Check on the reliability of the accounting and reporting system.

Report findings to management and recommend corrective action where necessary.

Some of the secondary objectives revealed by the N.I.C.B. survey are to:

Provide a training ground for personnel.

Appraise personnel performance.

---

[4] Glen Lipscomb (Cal., R.), Member, U.S. House of Representatives, *The Internal Auditor,* Spring 1967, p. 11.

[5] *Statement of Responsibillities of the Internal Auditor,* The Institute of Internal Auditors, 1957.

[6] F. J. Walsh, Jr., *Internal Auditing,* Studies in Business Policy No. 111, (New York: National Industrial Conference Board, Inc., 1963), p. 5.

Assist in profit-improvement activities.

Investigate compliance with the rules of regulatory agencies.

Provide general assistance to management through objective analyses, appraisals, recommendations and pertinent comments regarding the effectiveness of the activities reviewed.

The N.I.C.B. study pointed out that there had been a decided shift in emphasis from the earlier primary objectives (protection of assets and fraud detection) to the evaluation of operating data, reports and other elements of administrative control systems, and the provision of objective information on weaknesses and potential hazards. This trend in both industry and government seems to be toward even greater utilization of the internal auditors' ability to analyze operating problems from a managerial point of view. Executives of many major companies have endorsed the substantial benefits achieved through this expansion of their internal audit program.

Types of audits

Several terms have been used to categorize different audit approaches, or types of examinations, those most commonly used today being: financial; operational; organizational; functional; and managerial. These are briefly described and distinguished as follows:

Financial audits. These include those evolved from the traditional, largely protective, functions of the early internal auditors—primarily directed toward preventing misuse of the cash and other readily-convertible assets—and so involve appraisals of the related systems of internal control. The term is also used to describe examinations covering the reliability of the accounting records and the financial reporting system.

Operational audit. This is the term generally used to describe reviews of the adequacy and effectiveness of the managerial control systems covering all business activities, such as production, marketing, engineering, personnel, traffic, procurement, and research, as well as the activities of accounting and financial organizations. This development expanded the usefulness of the internal audit function to provide assistance to the managers of other functional areas.

Organizational audits. These audits are confined to the activities of a particular organizational unit, whether it be engaged in financial or other activities. The purpose is to form an opinion on the effectiveness of that particular organization in carrying out its assigned responsibilities. While the auditor may note that certain of the activities are affected by related matters in other organizations, he does not usually pursue these at the time. Instead, he brings the facts to the attention of those responsible, so that they may make a further investigation.

Functional audits. These commonly cross over organizational lines in pursuing all of the factors relevant to the successful attainment of a functional objective; for instance, a functional examination of materials management might include work done in connection with purchasing, receiving, inspection, handling, storing and requisitioning.

Managerial (or management) audits. This type is generally considered to be synonymous with operational audits. However, some internal auditors have extended their coverage to include the evaluation of management results in terms of achievement of objectives, as well as to the systems of internal controls. Also, internal auditors in a few of the larger firms have begun to experiment with extensions of their internal control appraisals into areas beyond those generally covered in the so-called operational audit. They believe that the same techniques successfully applied to the control problems of operating, or middle management, might be applied to some of the control problems of higher level management, such as: the evaluation of organizational structure, long-range programs, policy, profit planning, and similar matters.

In some concerns special reviews are made by internal auditors of construction contracts, vendor pricing proposals, and proposed acquisitions, and a number of other special studies are conducted for management.

The view held by many internal audit leaders is that there is, or should be, no basic distinction between financial and operational audits —that operational auditing is largely a state of mind, or a viewpoint used to approach the audit, which can and should be applied to financial audits as well as to audits of other activities. A traditional financial audit can be broadened to include the administrative controls over the functions involved, measuring their overall effectiveness instead of clinging to the narrower concept of determining the reliability of the accounting records. These auditors advocate that the principles and techniques developed for the so-called operational audit be applied to all internal audits. Many of the larger business concerns and governmental agencies have given increased emphasis to the performance of operational audits rather than strictly financial audits.

In practice, some internal audit staffs may not be capable of performing more than the traditional financial audit. This may be reflected in management attitudes as to the role of internal auditing in the company. As the internal audit staff improves in capability, management becomes more aware of the benefits of a broadened scope of audit.

Relationship to other control activities

Internal auditors have, by the very nature of their work, a close relationship with both the independent verification of financial statements by public accountants and the development and installation of various procedures and methods by internal systems experts. A somewhat lesser relationship also exists with such other managerial control activities as: budget and forecast, long-range planning, standards development, time studies, data processing systems, and cost-reduction analysis.

Public accountants

The current tendency seems to be for close cooperation between internal auditors and public accountants to avoid duplication of effort. In the past, internal auditors frequently did much detailed work to assist the public accountants, such as preparing account analyses, assisting in inventory counts, and verifying assets in outlying locations. Although the scope and objectives of internal and external audits differ, there are many points of common interest, and costs can be reduced by coordinating examinations of these matters, with the internal auditor augmenting and supplementing the services of the external auditor. For example, public accountants frequently use the internal auditors' reports to provide assistance in their evaluations of internal controls. On the other hand, it is recognized that the internal auditor's value can be considerably diminished if he acts as a clerical assistant to the public accountant, and this is becoming less prevalent.

As the scope of internal auditing has broadened to include many non-financial reviews, there has been a separation of the responsibilities and work coverage of the two functions in many companies. Thus, modern internal auditing is providing management with reviews of administrative and operating areas, as distinct from financial audits performed by public accountants.

Systems and procedures staffs

Since the internal auditor is concerned with the adequacy of the various systems of internal control, it is natural that he should work closely with systems and procedures staffs. Frequently, audit findings disclose the need for studies by systems analysts, and the auditor must provide them with necessary information. It is generally agreed that the auditor must avoid getting involved in the details of design and installation, since he must eventually perform an independent evaluation of the adequacy of the system. However, this does not prevent his early review of proposed procedures to point out potential risks and the need for control points around which the systems expert can then construct a series of protective devices. The auditor's ability to contribute to the effectiveness of complicated control systems in the early stages of their development has recently been substantiated in many companies in connection with EDP installations.

Services to management

A well-organized and properly trained internal audit organization can provide many different types of service to assist management in carrying out its responsibilities. Objective analyses, appraisals, and studies of many kinds can supply reliable information for managerial decisions affecting all phases of the business activity. Some of the principal services performed by many internal audit staffs are described in the following sections.

The appraisal of internal control systems

The management of a large organization relies heavily on the proper functioning of its many and varied systems of control. It is therefore essential that some means be provided to ensure the effective operation of these systems. This responsibility is now generally assigned to the internal audit staff, and the internal auditor has come to be recognized as an expert in the review and appraisal of internal control systems. In many organizations the internal audit staffs direct much of their effort toward continuing reviews of the controls over all phases of the business activity.

The appraisal of internal control systems usually is considered to have two phases: (1) The adequacy of the system—does it include all of the provisions necessary to ensure achievement of the objectives, considering the current environment and reasonably anticipated changes; and, conversely, does it call for unnecessary or excessively severe restrictions, which may increase the costs of operation more than the benefits to be obtained? (2) The effectiveness of the system—are employees actually doing what the system calls for; and how well does it work in practice? By answering these questions internal auditors frequently prevent substantial losses, calling attention to conditions which might prevent the orderly accomplishment of objectives or result in the waste of scarce resources.

For example, an internal audit disclosed that excess purchases were being made of production materials, resulting in additional investment of funds and storage costs. Further review indicated that additional coordination was needed between production and purchasing departments to assure that need-to-buy decisions reflected current changes in production requirements. In another case, it was found that controls over the company's lease procedures needed strengthening to prevent excess costs. Examination of equipment leases indicated that the company was not exercising options to buy when equipment was leased for longer periods than intended. Savings were obtained by following the internal auditor's recommendation to take advantage of the purchase options when there was a continued need for the equipment.

Evaluation of performance

While most internal auditors agree that they do not, and should not, attempt to report on the performance of individual employees (except in unusual situations involving fraud or other malfeasance), some auditors attempt to determine whether or not a particular organization has achieved its objectives by measuring actual results against performance standards.

This measurement of results against performance standards may be regularly provided to management through operating reports. In such cases, the auditor need only make sure that the reports are accurate, timely, and meaningful, and are being used effectively. On the other hand, the auditor may be called on to take an active part in such appraisals of performance. This involves the determination of (1) the objectives, (2) the applicable standards for measurement, (3) the actual results, and (4) the comparison of the actual results with the standards and justification for significant differences. Where standards have been previously established for the particular operation, this poses no problem. But where no suitable standards have been predetermined, the auditor must exercise great care in selecting his criteria for measurement, and should consult with the affected line management to obtain general agreement on what reasonable expectations might be.

There are numerous areas where such appraisals may be made. A few of them are as follows:

Determination that payments to trade creditors are made on time, particularly when discounts are available.

Determination that quality standards are met, both at various process stages and in the final product or service.

Measurement of waste materials to determine whether factory performance meets expectations and whether proper revenue is obtained from salvage.

Determination that production schedules are met.

Comparison of absentee rates with industry norms.

Training for future executives

The modern concept of comprehensive internal auditing requires an understanding of human relationships, as well as such managerial principles and techniques as methods of quantitative analysis and scientific decision-making. In addition, the internal auditor's day-to-day assignments provide ample opportunity to acquire and practice managerial viewpoints in meeting common objectives. Not the least of many skills which may be developed during an internal audit training assignment is the improvement in writing and speaking skills, which are an integral part of the auditor's normal activities. Development of the capacity to communicate in clear-cut, positive terms is rated by many top managers as one of the more important results of internal audit training. In addition, the internal auditor obtains useful experience in reviewing the control aspects of a business.

Many internal auditing departments have planned programs for developing the executive abilities of their employees. As the staff member progresses, he is given opportunity to improve his supervisory and managerial skills. Diversified assignments are provided, to extend his capabilities in various operations of the company.

A number of major concerns have made a tour of duty in internal auditing a regular part of their executive training program. These tours, which vary from two months to two years in length, serve to acquaint the future executive not only with the analytical techniques and objective viewpoint characteristic of modern internal auditing, but may also provide an excellent insight into both the individual problems of various parts of the operating functions and their relationship to other activities.

Where the internal auditing training assignment is not part of a regular, planned program for all executive trainees, occasional assignments are sometimes made to fit the needs of particular individuals. In numerous cases, young men who started their careers as internal auditors have profited from the opportunity to gain a first-hand knowledge of managerial problems, and have later been promoted to fill supervisory and managerial openings as a result of demonstrating their abilities on the job.

Evaluation of EDP systems

The impact of EDP on business operations and record keeping has raised many problems for management. The complexities of the systems make it difficult for the layman to understand the problems involved in the acquisition and application of equipment, and even more difficult to later measure the effectiveness of the completed systems. Managers must therefore often rely on reports and appraisals made by others.

The well-trained internal auditor will have acquired a sufficient working acquaintance with EDP equipment and techniques to know the capabilities of the various principal items of equipment, and to understand the logic charts used to describe the systems. With these tools, and his knowledge of internal control principles, plus his analytical ability, he is well equipped to participate in evaluations of rent-or-buy proposals, and system-feasibility studies. He can also review and appraise the proposed system provisions to determine whether all required controls have been provided, determine that adequate tests have been made to debug the system before conversion, and, after the installation has been completed, review its effectiveness in accomplishing its objectives.

In some organizations, the internal audit staff not only performs these services, but also carries on continuing reviews to ensure that the built-in controls are effectively maintained, particularly those that require human participation. Periodically, after numerous changes have been "patched in" to the system, the auditors may again make a comprehensive review to assure that none of the essential controls has been lost.

In organizations where there are fewer trained personnel available, the internal auditor is sometimes called on to participate in actual system design and installation, as a working member of the task force. Some problems exist in such assignments, particularly if they result in the loss of the auditor's basic responsibility for independent review and appraisal. This dilemma is sometimes met by assigning one or more members of the audit staff as EDP experts to participate in the systems work, while other auditors later review and test the effectiveness of the controls.

Cost-reduction suggestions

The continuing squeeze on corporate profits has led many internal auditors to emphasize the detection and reporting of cost-reduction opportunities. As a result of his assignment to various parts of the operations, frequently covering different geographical locations, the internal auditor has an unrivaled opportunity to compare the practices followed by different organizational units. Such comparisons sometimes reveal more efficient methods, which he can then suggest to other local managers. Duplication of effort among several related organizations, the continued preparation of unnecessary reports, and other similar costly practices are frequently brought to light through his analyses of operating practices and control systems. Alertness in helping to shut off wasteful practices is an essential part of the modern internal auditor's training.

In one case, the internal auditor found that reports were being prepared which were in excess of operating requirements, resulting in unnecessary costs. In another case, production standards for manufacture of parts were found to be more rigorous in one plant than in others; cost savings were achieved by reducing the specifications to actual requirements.

Improved communications

One of the important benefits from internal audits is the improved communications established, especially in companies with widely dispersed operations. The auditor is frequently able to explain and interpret home-office policy to branch employees, and thus help achieve greater uniformity of operations and records. He is also sometimes able to suggest more efficient practices, based on his observations of methods used in other branches or on his knowledge of home-office procedures. In addition, the audit report usually provides information as to areas requiring management attention.

The financial vice-president of a large steel producer recently said, in this respect:

"One of the greatest problems in multi-plant operations is communications. It is impossible to fully convey policy by letter. The internal auditor often represents the best contact plant personnel have with the home offices. By being conversant with current management thinking, he can help the outlying managers recognize over-all company problems and perhaps help them to think more broadly."[7]

Conflicts of interest

A number of company managements have assigned to their internal audit staffs the responsibility for searching out possible conflicts of interest and bringing them to the attention of the top executive or the board of directors. This work usually takes the form of reviewing the adequacy and effectiveness of the procedures which call for disclosures of interests by employees in a position to influence dealings with suppliers and customers, particularly the placement of purchase orders. For example, in one large manufacturing company the auditing unit is responsible for checking the information supplied in questionnaires on employees' financial affairs that fall within the area covered by the company's conflict-of-interest policy statement, and for reporting its findings to a special committee of the board.

Compliance with laws and regulations

The growing demands made on business by a multitude of governmental regulations, both local and national, require increasing vigilance to avoid unintentional violations. In such areas as income, sales, employment and property taxes; wage and hours regulations; S.E.C. reports; and pricing restrictions and similar matters, the auditor performs reviews for compliance with requirements. Parts of the financial audit program are usually directed toward assuring adequate coverage of these matters. In other areas, such as safety codes, building restrictions, and import and export regulations, a general awareness of potential problems and a knowledge of where to obtain advice when specific questions arise are all

---

[7] H. J. Haughton, Vice President-Finance; Treasurer, Jones & Laughlin Steel Corp., *The Internal Auditor*, Winter, 1964, p. 20.

that is generally expected, unless the employer is regularly involved in activities requiring a more detailed knowledge.

Outside audits

Some companies use their internal audit staffs to make audits at outside organizations with whom they deal, including, for example, suppliers with whom contracts are on a cost-plus or time-and-materials basis, licensees, joint ventures, and companies being considered for possible acquisition. Such audits vary, of course, with the circumstances and may be concerned solely with verification of financial statements, cost analyses, sales records, or other financial records. They may, as in the case of a potential acquisition, go deeply into the operations to evaluate relative efficiency, the adequacy of controls, opportunities for cost reduction and profit improvement, and manpower and facility utilization. In some acquisition cases, regular audit personnel may work with staff experts in the various functional fields of the business to provide the technical knowledge necessary to make an evaluation.

Conducting the audit

Because of the many specialized and technical considerations involved in accounting examinations, which are adequately described elsewhere, this will be confined to a description of the factors affecting and the processes followed in a so-called operational audit (an examination of the controls over the activities of an operating unit or function) to illustrate the audit process.

An operational audit usually has four basic steps:

Familiarization with basic objectives and physical operations of the activities to be audited.

Examination of the mechanisms used to control the operations and achieve the objectives.

Appraisal and evaluation of the adequacy and effectiveness of the control mechanisms.

Reporting of findings and constructive recommendations.[8]

The first three of these basic steps are briefly discussed in the following paragraphs. Audit reports are covered in the next section.

Familiarization

This is a vital first step. The auditor must understand and see the operations through the eyes of those responsible for them. The objectives to be achieved, the control methods used to ensure that pertinent matters

---

[8] Bradford Cadmus, *Operational Auditing Handbook,* New York: The Institute of Internal Auditors, 1964, p. 459.

are brought to attention, the problems seen by those in the operating organization; the way the work is organized, and the standards of performance used in judging the quality of the work, must all be understood before he has the necessary grasp of the situation. While acquiring this understanding, the auditor must also learn the specialized language employed so that he can talk with the employees in their own terms.

A walk through the areas in which the functions are physically performed is helpful in visualizing the flow of work and the form of the end products. The auditor cannot fulfill his assignment of appraising results and controls unless he becomes familiar with the operations.

The auditor will be particularly anxious to gain an understanding of the organization structure, the policies, procedures and written job instructions, the interrelationships with other organizational units, the reports prepared to show operating performance, and how the department heads supervise the operations and evaluate the results achieved.

Examination

After familiarizing himself with the objectives and responsibilities of the organization, the auditor must then prepare a program for the analysis and verification phase. This is frequently done in the form of a series of questions, with corresponding audit tests to get the answers. In making these tests, the auditor uses the basic audit techniques of verification—direct observation, inquiry, confirmation by third parties, and substantiation by documentary evidence—to assure himself that the approved procedures are actually followed in practice.

Since the sampling of actual transactions plays such a large part in the determination of the effectiveness of the controls, progressive auditors are using modern statistical techniques to provide assurance that their samples are representative and that conclusions drawn from the sample can be applied to the whole population. Some auditors are also using the techniques of quantitative analysis, such as linear programming, to provide even deeper studies of the affected operations.

The auditor is primarily concerned with establishing facts, to determine whether or not the control systems are being followed in actual practice; whether the prescribed check points are enforced; whether the operating reports are complete, factual, timely, and meaningful; and whether the standards of performance provide an effective basis for the appraisal of operating results.

Appraisal and evaluation

There is no definite dividing line between examination and evaluation. Rather, the evaluation process continues during the entire period of the audit, from the first familiarization conference, through completion of the last test in the examination phase and into subsequent discussions of the findings with various levels of management. As his work progresses, the auditor will make tentative evaluations at each stage, correcting and adjusting them as additional information is obtained.

Forming opinions on the adequacy of the control systems employed requires comparison with some accepted criteria of minimum requirements. The internal auditor must determine the criteria to be used in the particular circumstances as a basis for measuring the adequacy of the system. Obviously, this requires a sound background in the theory and practice of internal control.

In contrast, the determination of whether or not the system is followed would seem to be an easier task, since it requires only a comparison between practice and procedures. But the auditor must go considerably beyond the determination of conformance. If there are deviations, he must consider the reasons for them. Sometimes the fault lies with the controls themselves; while in other cases it may be poor instructions, inadequate training, environmental factors, poor supervision, or deliberate sabotage.

Additionally, the auditor should, wherever possible, attempt to make constructive suggestions for improvement, although he will encounter many situations where no definite recommendation is possible—either because his experience does not qualify him, or the available facts do not permit it. Here, he will simply refer the apparent problem to the affected management.

An important part of the evaluation process is the testing of conclusions in discussions with the affected employees, both those engaged in the actual performance of the work and those in various levels of supervision. The auditor never works in a vacuum or ivory tower, but must continually justify and test his conclusions in the practical world of actual working conditions.

Reporting audit results

Audit reports fall into two classes: (1) reports on the findings and recommendations on individual audit projects; and (2) periodic reports of overall audit accomplishments and evaluations.

Individual audit projects

The final audit product, by which the value of the auditor's work is generally judged, is the audit report, in which the audit findings, conclusions, opinions and recommendations are set forth. The value of the auditor's work is increased if the report is prepared in such a way as to make it easy for the readers to grasp the ideas presented.

Some auditing organizations have developed a dual system of reporting, involving a condensed report summary of the essential facts for top management, and a more detailed discussion for lower levels of operating management, who need supporting information to implement any necessary corrective action. Some internal auditors attempt to reduce the length of reports by describing only exceptions to approved practices, while others believe that a true appraisal requires the reporting of satisfactory as well as unsatisfactory matters. Whichever policy is adopted, the audit reports can be made brief and to the point without the long, rambling discussions and emphasis on minor matters that, too often, have characterized reports of both types. Progress reports issued during the course of the work are sometimes used to achieve prompt consideration of important matters.

Many auditors recommend the practice of reviewing a draft of the report with those responsible for the operations covered, before the report is finally issued to higher level personnel. Some companies follow a pattern of review "up the ladder," discussing the report with each tier of supervision before proceeding to the next level, and this is stated to be a strong factor in obtaining acceptance.

An effective checklist for improving audit report content is suggested in the "Operational Auditing Handbook."[9] Some of the items suggested there are:

> Stress items that will improve business operations; operating managers are more interested in changes that will reduce costs than those that will improve protective control.
>
> Do not expect the operating manager to think in auditing terms; write the report in language which he is accustomed to.
>
> Make no criticism without a constructive recommendation and supporting factual data.
>
> As far as possible, secure prior agreement on recommendations from operating managers and present them as joint recommendations.
>
> Where agreement on recommendations cannot be reached, be sure there is agreement on factual background material. Write the counter opinions into the report along with those of the auditor.
>
> Send copies of the report to all operating managers affected by it, and publish no material not in the report. (The latter point is subject to modification when matters of fraud or malfeasance are discussed.)

Audit progress and results

Many internal audit managers submit regular periodic reports to the executive to whom they report, summarizing their work, and in some cases these are routed as high as to the board of directors for review. In most cases these reports are prepared on an annual basis, although

---

[9] Cadmus, p. 32.

sometimes they are made as frequently as each quarter. Typically, such reports cover two areas, the first relating to the performance of the audit department, and the second to the overall impressions of the effectiveness of operations gained from the individual audit reports.

Typical items of audit accomplishments are: comparison of actual audit costs with budgets, progress toward audit objectives, significant findings reported, projected audit operations in the future, and, sometimes, savings resulting from audit recommendations. In some cases it may not be possible to put dollar evaluations on the benefits obtained from internal auditing since many of them are intangible (how much value can be placed on a recommendation for an improved control system which may prevent a future loss?).

The reporting of combined statistics on audit opinions and findings is practiced in relatively few audit organizations, but seems to be gaining favor. Those audit managers who have regularly reported to top management on audit results claim that it provides a good basis for directing managerial attention to potential trouble areas, and reemphasizes to operating management the higher level support for the audit activity. Among the matters included in such reports are: overall ratings of the adequacy and effectiveness of control systems; trends of improvement or deterioration over a period of time as measured by the type and seriousness of audit findings; the timeliness of corrective action after the reporting of audit findings; the extent to which major problems recur; and basic causes of control problems.

Establishing an effective internal auditing department

Place in the organization

Much has been written about the internal auditor's need for independence from anyone whose work or responsibility he is to review and appraise objectively. It has been argued that the chief internal auditor should report directly to the board of directors, to an audit committee of the board, or at least to the president; this is done in some cases. In many concerns, the internal audit function is under the financial or administrative vice president or the controller, a relationship derived from the origins of the function in the review of financial records.

Despite the variances existing in different organizations, most executives agree with the statement by The Institute of Internal Auditors that:

"The head of the internal auditing department . . . should be responsible to an officer of sufficient rank in the organization as will assure a broad scope of activities, and adequate consideration of and effective action on the findings or recommendations made by him."[10]

[10] *Statement of Responsibilities of the Internal Auditor,* The Institute of Internal Auditors, 1957.

Size

The size of internal auditing staffs, which varies greatly among different concerns, depends on many factors. Company size and organization are important determinants. The nature of the company's activities should be considered, e.g., the auditing staffs of banks may be large because of the type of activities involved.

The objectives of the company's internal audit program also represent an important factor. Extensive use of auditors in testing financial transactions may require additional staff. In performing operational audits, a smaller staff of senior auditors may suffice in some companies. On the other hand, if comprehensive coverage is given major operating segments, larger staffs may be required.

The size of the internal auditing staff must also be weighed in terms of costs versus benefits. Although the benefits may not be completely measurable, budgets prepared for the internal auditing department should be adequately supported to justify the number of staff requested.

In general, the size of the internal auditing staff cannot be prescribed from outside, since it is a question of what management wants to accomplish and how much it is willing to spend. As a result, there are significant differences in numbers of internal auditors in companies with relatively the same type and size of operations.

Internal structure

The complexity of the internal auditing organization's structure varies with the size of the staff and the nature of the operations. The chief internal auditor (variously titled as General Auditor, or as Director, Manager, Superintendent or Supervisor of Internal Auditing) may have one or more assistants in charge of different phases of the activity. Below the assistant level, the job titles are usually similar to those of public accounting firms—supervisor, seniors, semi-seniors or senior assistants, juniors, and special assistants or associates.

Sometimes the organization is decentralized geographically into regional offices to reduce the amount of travel required. In such cases a regional auditor, or audit manager, may, in turn, supervise a staff of some size with the same arrangement of subordinates at junior, semi-senior and senior levels. Sometimes the staff is divided into home-office and traveling or field audit personnel, or into functional-specialist groupings, such as: marketing, production, vendor, and international units.

Regardless of the job titles used, the fundamental principle involved is the provision for close, personal supervision and review of each phase of the work by a more experienced auditor, so as to ensure adequate coverage in the examination, and the complete reliability of the final report. This chain relationship, with the work of the junior reviewed by the senior assistant, that of the assistant by the senior, and the complete package by the supervisor and manager, in turn, provides a system of "defense in depth" which has done much to build the reputation for reliability which is an essential attribute of the internal auditor.

Planning and controlling audit assignments

Effective planning of audit assignments requires periodic analysis of management's current as well as long-range audit needs. Most audit managers prepare their audit schedules on an annual basis to assure responsiveness to changing conditions and to get authorization for adequate staff assistance. Some managers advocate annual preparation of longer range (3-year to 5-year) schedules to maintain a more stable staff level, where it is practical to do so.

The principal scheduling problem comes in providing adequate coverage for regular, repetitive reviews of "sensitive" areas, while still providing sufficient flexibility to handle the special "fire-fighting" assignments which inevitably are requested by management. Some managers suggest doing this by providing for a pool of unassigned audit time, based on past experience, to cover emergency requests.

Audit assignments are generally controlled by providing time budgets for each project. These budgets are usually based on past experience for similar work. The manager must also consider the risks involved in the activities under review, in comparison with the overall risks in all the activities to be covered by his examinations, as a limiting factor on the total amount of time which can be devoted to any particular phase of the work. The original budget estimate is usually made as a part of the annual or longer term schedule preparation. When the actual work is started, the senior in charge and his supervisor prepare a more detailed breakdown of the total budget, allocating estimated time requirements to various segments of the job. Then actual time spent is reported weekly against the budget allowance for each segment, to provide a basis for administrative control by the supervisor and audit manager. A provision for amending or changing the original budget estimates is recommended to cover unexpected developments during the course of the work.

In addition to the cost and schedule control provided through the audit time budgets, it is generally desirable to provide for the establishment of specific dates for the completion of the audit report and its review with the affected management personnel, so as to avoid long delays between completion of the field work and issuance of the final report. The early detection and reporting of deficiencies is important in order to enable management to take prompt corrective action. Various mechanical devices are available for audit managers to keep track of progress on individual projects, depending on the size of the organization. Development of a reputation for prompt reporting of results is an important factor in the acceptance of the internal audit service by management.

Written instructions

Written instructions to guide auditors in the conduct of their work take several forms, including audit manuals, standard programs or checklists, staff bulletins, and statements of audit procedures. The audit manual is commonly used in all but the smallest staffs.

These instructions may be general in nature or include specific audit procedures to be followed. They are generally used as guidelines only, with audit programs developed to fit the needs of specific assignments. Good written instructions are important in setting standards and serving as a basis for training staff members.

Selection and training of personnel

Qualifications and attributes

The modern internal auditor must play many roles. First of all, he must be a *business analyst,* with particular expertise in the field of internal control. But the value of his services may be diminished if he is not also a *communications expert,* skilled in conveying precise information both orally and in writing. Because his work necessarily deals with fundamental human failings which provoke deep-seated reactions, he must also have some training in *human relations.* His continuing need to keep abreast of the rapid developments in business practices, as well as in the latest tools for better analysis, make him a perpetual *student.* Finally, he plays an important role as a *teacher,* not only in training his own assistants, but also in explaining and selling company policy to operating employees who do not always understand or appreciate the needs of higher levels of management for effective controls.

Many of the skills mentioned are, of course, found in only rudimentary form in the beginning auditor, and must be developed through actual experience on the job. But there must first be a sound foundation of basic education and native ability. The following sections offer some specific guidance toward these requirements.

Education

A college degree with a business administration major seems to be a fundamental requirement. Many audit managers prefer to hire accounting majors because of the direct relationship to much of the internal audit work, particularly the analysis of accounting records. However, in a few cases, managers have expressed the opinion that, with the extension of the internal auditor's responsibility into a broader range of activities, a thorough grounding in the principles of business administration is becoming even more important than the basic accounting training. An ideal combination might well be a bachelor's degree in accounting, with graduate work in management, or vice versa.

Few courses in internal auditing have been offered by the colleges. Courses that are offered are generally sponsored by a local chapter of The Institute of Internal Auditors, the professional society, and are usually considered to be supplementary training for those already employed in the field, rather than undergraduate preparation for entrance into it.

Experience

Although there is always some movement of auditors, like other employees, from one company to another, the rapid growth of the field in recent years has created a demand far exceeding the supply. Aside from a basic cadre, most companies must develop and train new audit personnel. Many people who have entered internal auditing have first had some experience in public accounting, and in some instances possessed a CPA certificate. This background was perhaps more sought after in earlier days when accounting audits made up the bulk of the work, but the experience acquired in public accounting is still considered helpful because of the basic grounding it contributes in the principles of audit verification, still a fundamental part of the internal auditor's job.

Although some companies take on young men directly from college, most regard some type of basic business experience as essential. As a result, candidates are frequently drawn from the company's accounting or other departments. A preliminary acquaintance with the company's policies and practices is one of the requirements satisfied by this practice of selection from within the company, and this is considered particularly important for operational auditing. In fact, at least one company traditionally assigns only experienced managers to a tour of duty as internal auditors.

Training methods

Staff training is generally informal with smaller staffs, being limited to direct instruction by the chief auditor and normal interplay on the job with other auditors. In larger organizations the training plans may be more formal, including planned courses of study as well as on-the-job training.

New recruits are usually given a basic indoctrination to acquaint them with the employer's policies and practices. This may take from several days to a week or more. After completing the indoctrination, the new auditor is usually assigned to an audit team where he will work under an in-charge auditor and perhaps other, more experienced, assistants. At first the new man is given fairly routine duties, with explicit preliminary instructions and close supervision. Gradually, he progresses to more complex assignments, but still with close supervision until his ability to proceed on his own is established. This process of "learning by doing" continues as he moves up from junior to senior status usually taking from 3 to 5 years, depending on his prior experience, training, and native ability.

This on-the-job training is supplemented in various ways to provide for more theoretical background. Methods used include reading assignments in professional publications and standard texts, attendance at staff meetings where auditing problems and new developments are discussed, sponsored attendance at seminars and workshops presented by professional associations, and other special training courses in data processing techniques and other fields.

Where travel assignments do not interfere, auditors are usually encouraged to enroll in graduate courses in business administration at local colleges. Some concerns also arrange correspondence courses for traveling auditors.

Problems in improving audit service

The ability of internal audit organizations to reach their full potential as contributing members of the management team is dependent on many factors. Some of these are capability of staff, management acceptance and support, and resources available.

The chief internal auditor must have the capacity to perceive the many possibilities for furnishing the extended services which are possible, and the ability to train and lead his staff to make them effective. In addition, his staff must possess the flexibility to adjust to new ideas and the capacity to carry out a progressive program based on sound, management-oriented thinking. Effective recruitment, training, and performance-appraisal procedures are important in increasing staff capability.

Management acceptance and backing are essential for the internal auditing function. Regardless of the ability of the audit staff, progress will be slowed unless active support of the audit objectives is given at the highest level of management. If management has positive desires to extend the audit function to its full range and is willing to make this clear to lower level management and supervision, the contribution of the internal auditing organization can be significantly increased.

The provision of an adequate budget and other resources to handle all the desired coverage is important. The competent auditor is a scarce commodity, with many employers bidding for his services. Providing a salary scale which will offer competitive attractions, plus the usual fringe benefits, is essential. Similarly, appropriate provision for facilities and adequate secretarial and clerical assistance is necessary. Finally, adequate compensation for extended travel requirements, with provision for family men to return home at reasonable intervals, is also needed.

In some cases, the auditors never manage to accomplish all the hoped-for things because their services are constantly demanded for assignments to special task forces, fire-fighting in emergencies, and sometimes clerical duties to relieve overloaded line organizations. While the audit staff may be the only available source of help in some cases, it should never be permitted to engage in such special assignments for any long period of time at the expense of regular audit duties. Time for such special services may be obtained by providing for additional audit-staff time, over and above the needs of the regular program, based on an annual estimate of what is feasible, and then carefully screening requests for special services to stay within the allotted budget.

Long-run considerations in the kind of services provided by the internal auditing function are business needs and the professional abilities of staff. Internal auditors have demonstrated the ability to shift from conventional auditing to operational auditing in response to managerial needs. As business conditions change and become more complex they will be faced with additional challenges in providing assistance to management. Through increasing their professionalism and furthering research and training in advanced audit techniques, internal auditors have indicated strong interest in meeting the challenges.

Use of professional services*

Wilson Seney†

The financial executive may retain professional services in areas of his own major responsibilities, and he may also work with professionals in situations for which he is not directly responsible. In addition, his relationships may be with professionals on his own company's payroll or with independent professionals who are retained on a fee basis. The term "professional" refers to both licensed and unlicensed practitioners, such as attorneys, certified public accountants, management consultants, actuaries, and financial public relations counsellors. This chapter is written in terms of dealing with outside professionals, but the comments also are largely applicable to dealing with inside services.

Effective use of professional services begins with an awareness of the values obtainable from such services and an acquaintance with those who offer such services. It is achieved by developing and practicing productive working relationships, both with the professional and with one's associates in management.

Basic values offered by professionals

Professional services are used for two basic reasons: (1) to stimulate, create, or implement change to improve company performance; and

* Substantial parts of this chapter are adapted from *Effective Use of Business Consultants*, by Wilson Seney, published by Financial Executives Research Foundation, New York, 1963; and from "The Use of Consulting Specialists," a chapter in the *Handbook of Business Administration*, published by McGraw-Hill Book Company, Inc., New York, 1967. Grateful acknowledgment is also made to the other sources listed in the Bibliography.

† President, Wilson Seney, Inc., and Management Consultant, New York.

(2) to insure that the necessary diligence is exercised in protecting and promoting the stockholders' interests in the conduct of company affairs. All specific services are means to achieving these ends. In varying degrees, professionals can provide the following services:

1. Helping the client to bring a problem into focus.
2. Helping the client to get results.
3. Rendering an independent opinion.
4. Helping the client to improve intra-company communications.
5. Helping the client in the conduct of the company's external affairs.
6. Supplementing client efforts with specialized skills and know-how.
7. Training client personnel.
8. Providing a confidential service in which the identity of the client is concealed.
9. Providing temporary personnel for client purposes.

Bringing problems into focus

The basic responsibility for defining problems lies with management itself. The professional is acting in an advisory and consulting capacity. He should, however, bring to problem definition some characteristics that may be difficult for client management to duplicate. He has time to concentrate on the definition of problems and alternative solutions, because he is free from day-to-day operating pressures. His independent position also helps to resolve differences of opinion, if it is recognized that he is retained to arrive at the best objective solution rather than to promote any special interest. Also, the professional's position as an objective outsider makes it easier for him to maintain the perspective to see the forest instead of the trees. Finally, as a relative matter, depending on the experience and ability of the client's own staff, the professional may have superior competence in analyzing and synthesizing complex situations.

Getting results

A fundamental value offered by professionals is in helping managers to get results. Here again, the responsibility lies with management itself, and the professional acts only as another resource in accomplishing the task. He may contribute by helping the client to achieve better end results, to achieve them faster and more economically, or to reduce the risks in moving toward these ends.

Achieving the best results depends, in part, on the professional's making available to the client choices among sound practices and techniques developed by other companies that have faced similar problems.

The professional may also help to reduce the risks of change, because he is experienced in handling change as such. The average executive deals infrequently with the detailed programming of major changes. A professional spends most of his time in such activities.

Also, the mere presence of outsiders may help to get results by overcoming inertia. The fact that time and money are being spent on professional services indicates that management is directly interested in the situation and is looking for decisions or results.

Independent opinion

An independent opinion is a formal statement by an expert or professional man of what he thinks, judges, or advises on a matter submitted to him. Implicit in this definition are assumptions of competence, objectivity, and integrity.

The professional is familiar with the field involved, and should have the perspective and skills necessary to interpret and evaluate findings. He should know how things are done in the area of his competence. He should display objectivity in working for the long-term interests of the client. His integrity should guarantee that he performs conscientious work, and does not trade on his reputation to rush into ill-considered judgments.

Improving intra-company communications

The professional may help to solve communications problems in a way that is often not within the grasp of the financial executive, especially in larger companies. First, and this is closely related to the value of objectivity, he may lift communications above the competitive level. Second, because he is not tied down on an organization chart, he may cut across functional lines and supervisory levels to accomplish relatively unfiltered communications.

Achievement of consensus is often required before an independent opinion is translated into practical results. Therefore, the professional serves by helping the client to develop a common acceptance and interpretation of facts throughout the organization. He also contributes simply by acting as an audience. When executives are required to explain to an objective and critical outsider the causes they are promoting, the very act of explaining the situation may give them new perspectives.

Conducting external affairs

Apart from the licensed status of attorneys and certified public accountants and their often legally required services to insure that companies conform with legal and tax requirements, other professionals may provide specialized know-how about situations external to the company.

For example they can help in such areas as: counsel in connection with entering foreign markets, labor relations, governmental relations, and financial public relations.

Specialized skills and know-how

Providing specialized industry and market know-how and helping companies to keep up with changing technological trends and techniques are probably the most widely recognized professional service values. Accepting the validity of such recognition, it is also valid that a professional should possess not only technical competence, but also the perspective to know how his specialty fits into the general scheme of things. If he thinks that his specialty takes precedence over all other considerations, he is not the most effective professional.

Training client personnel

Almost all professional services involve some responsibilities for training client personnel, depending on the nature of the problem and the field of professional specialization.

Sometimes the financial executive may be looking for information to use as raw material in planning. Such information is provided by a wide range of services, beginning with the business press. With this approach, the executive is exposed to the information, but there is no obligation, real or implied, to advise him what to do or to evaluate what he is capable of doing.

If the executive is asking specifically, what shall we do and how shall we do it?, the professional may respond by discussing how other managements have approached and solved similar problems, by interpreting legal and tax requirements, or by undertaking a design and installation program with the client. If internal program accomplishment depends on attitudes or skills new to the company, training on a fairly large scale is of the essence. On the other hand, if accomplishment consists of administering external legal or financial relationships, training may be limited to the financial executive and his immediate associates as they work their way through the specific problem with the professional.

Confidential service

Professionals are sometimes retained because the client wants to conceal his identity. A company may want to conduct a market survey, search for a new product, look for an acquisition, or seek out executive talent, without showing its hand.

The professional who serves in the above areas may also be providing specialized skills not available within the company. The executive who retains a professional to search for personnel may also obtain advice on matters of executive compensation and the talent market.

Providing temporary personnel

Many engagements create a workload that the client is not prepared to handle. For example, in the installation of an automatic data processing system, the professional may provide a number of his own programmers who both do the actual programming and train client personnel to carry on the activities. Many budgetary control, industrial engineering, and wage and salary administration installations are accomplished on the same basis.

Staffing for professional services

The need for professional services of one sort or another exists to some degree in all companies. Even the individual businessman is well-advised to have the help of an attorney, a certified public account-ant, an insurance advisor, and a banker. A corporation can do with no less, and ordinarily requires other services, too.

The company's plan of organization should define what services are maintained on the payroll and what services are maintained by ongoing retainer arrangements. Then, if the need for any other service arises or if new tasks and workloads occur in existing services, management faces this decision: Should the plan of organization and staffing be revised or should the need be met by retaining independent practitioners working on a project basis?

Some outside services are required by external regulation as, for example, in certification of shareholders' reports. Such cases aside, deter-mination of the use of inside or outside services depends primarily on considerations of (1) costs, and (2) the importance of evaluating needs for changes in goals and practices and the accomplishment of these changes.

Considerations of costs

A small businessman may call on his CPA, not only for filing tax returns, but also for performing detailed accounting work. Even though the operations are repetitive, the volume is so small that it is more economic to pay professional fees than to employ an accountant. At the other extreme, a large company employs many professionals to manage essentially all corporate accounting operations and to recommend and/or decide basic accounting policies affecting tax returns.

When operations are not routinely repetitive, but do present recurring workloads, volume may justify inside services. Fairly wide-spread examples of this situation include market research, industrial engineering, and product design departments. To a lesser degree, some large companies maintain management consulting departments.

Other considerations are the importance of specialized know-how and the amount of time it takes to acquire it. A company patent department may keep up to date on all developments in an industry, in addition to pursuing specific patent applications. This is, however, a relative matter. In any given case, a firm of patent attorneys may have more industry background than the company's patent department.

Considerations of achieving change

The truism of a changing world poses continuing needs for changes in corporate goals, policies, and practices. Achieving the right changes at the right times is not easy. "All institutions . . . find it hard to abandon yesterday's tasks and to stop doing the unproductive."[1] Three basic factors underlie this problem, and the existence of any one of them may call for the services of an independent outsider.

First, the decision-making process has always been "a field of personal ambition and sharp competition in all practical situations," both with respect to basic policy decisions and to the subordinate decisions involved in executing policies.[2] Even in well-run companies, stalemates may occur and vital decisions may be postponed.

Second, the growing number of "knowledge workers" has introduced new elements of frustration and inertia into the decision-making process. ". . . a generic problem grounded in the ambivalence of the knowledge worker's status (is) . . . the hidden conflict between the knowledge worker's view of himself as a "professional" and the fact that he is within organization and a successor to yesterday's craftsman rather than to yesterday's professional."[3] If decision-makers look at the professional staff as craftsmen instead of counsellors, even the best recommendations may not be well-received. It is difficult to accept an independent opinion from one who is regarded as not independent, as not having full access to information because of the restrictions of his job description, and as not, therefore, possessing full perspective on the situation.

Third, management of change calls for different skills than management of continuity. As a matter of course, an able manager plans and controls personal competition, line-staff relationships, and other key aspects of the business in a stable situation. The same manager, when faced with needs to adjust the company to new circumstances and to weave new functions into the organization, may find that his personal

---

[1] Peter Drucker, *The Age of Discontinuity* (New York: Harper & Row, 1969), p. 226.

[2] Lyman Bryson, "Notes on a Theory of Advice," *Political Science Quarterly,* September, 1951.

[3] Drucker, *op. cit.,* pp. 291–2.

convictions and decisiveness are diminished and that there is no one within the company who can help him to regain those necessary qualities.

Again, the above considerations are relative. In theory, any company may organize to achieve change rather than to prevent it. The fact remains, however, that a substantial portion of professional income is derived from serving large organizations that have highly developed staff departments.[4]

Working with the professional

Constructive results from the use of professional services depend on: (1) adequate definition of the purpose, scope, and nature of the project for which professional help is retained; (2) selection of a qualified practitioner; (3) maintenance of productive working relationships with him; and (4) client willingness to take action on recommendations.

Problem definition

Proper use of professional services begins with practical definition of the purpose, scope, and limits of the problem or problems on which the professional is to work.

Problem definition is usually accomplished in steps and usually extends over some period of time. It is an ongoing process. The financial executive defines and solves problems as a matter of course in the discharge of his normal duties.

However, in coping with any particular problem, the executive may explore the desirability of professional assistance. It is at this point that the search for a professional properly begins. From here on, negotiations with professionals may be helpful in refining or changing the definition of the problem. Even after a professional is retained, further changes in the purpose, scope, and limits of the project may occur. This is, of course, a relative matter depending on many factors, such as the complexity of the situation, the ease of communication between client and professional, the experience of the client in working with professionals, and the background that the professional brings to the situation.

Both before and after contact with a professional, and regardless of whether he is finally retained, the executive should try to answer the following questions about most problems with which he is faced:

What is the real purpose of the project? For example, is it really to install inventory controls, or is it really to review and revise product lines?

Does the project promote or conflict with long-range plans? Under ordinary circumstances, there is little use in developing refined manage-

---

[4] For example, see Wilson Seney, *Effective Use of Business Consultants*, p. 6.

ment techniques to plan and control an operation that the company plans to discontinue.

What benefits are likely to occur if the project is accomplished? Are the expected benefits sufficient reward for undertaking the work? And, in view of the demands on management's time, is the project in an area of potentially greater return rather than in an area of less important return?

What is the receptivity of company executives to change? Retaining a professional to help accomplish change may not work, if managers take the attitude that they want change without any changes being made.

Will successful accomplishment of the project affect other areas of the enterprise? If a new accounting system uncovers excess costs, is management prepared to do something about them? If a computer is installed, will it call for redefining management responsibilities for information systems?

Is the organization able to carry the workload of the proposed project in light of other ongoing work? Most companies are equipped to handle a limited number of special projects, at any one time, and selection of projects becomes a matter of priority.

How have other financial executives solved similar problems? Discussions with experienced executives of other companies may aid in defining the dimensions of a contemplated program, the advantages which may be anticipated, and the hazards and workloads involved in achieving results.

Who can or should do the job? Executives define and solve problems, as a matter of course, from day to day and year to year. Therefore, there should be specific reasons for deciding to use outside services in any given situation. These reasons may refer to any one or more of the basic values offered by professionals as listed earlier in this chapter. In any case, however, the reasons should be clear before the professional is retained.

Selection of the professional

Sound selection of a professional requires: (1) obtaining general information about him, and especially obtaining specific recommendations of his services; (2) developing confidence in him and in the validity of the project for which he is to be retained, by careful review of the problem with him, which on occasion may call for a preliminary survey; and (3) following the general principles of negotiating a useful basis for working together.

INFORMATION AND REFERENCES. Information about professionals is available from a variety of sources. Publications of professional societies and associations describe the scope and nature of services performed and provide statements of ethics. Representative groups include:

The American Bar Association (Chicago) and related societies organized along state, county, and city lines

The American Institute of Certified Public Accountants (New York and related state and local organizations

The Society of Actuaries (Chicago) and The Conference of Actuaries in Public Practice (Chicago)

The Association of Consulting Management Engineers, Inc. (New York)

The Society of Professional Management Consultants (New York)

The Association of Management Consultants (Milwaukee)

The New England Society of Management Consultants (Boston)

The Institute of Management Consultants, Inc. (New York)

The Public Relations Society of America (New York) and about 60 local chapters

The Association of Executive Recruiting Consultants (New York)

In any field of endeavor, licensed or unlicensed, not all qualified practitioners are members of the organizations representing the field. Often, however, these organizations can provide information about nonmembers as well as members.

Personal contacts may be valuable sources of information. These include executives of other companies who have retained professionals; company directors affiliated with other companies that may have used professionals in the field under consideration; and the company's normal banking, legal, and CPA contacts.

A sort of round robin situation obtains in the area of general information about professional firms and individuals, in no small part because the conduct of corporate programs so often involves the concerted efforts of several different outside services. Under these circumstances, the various professionals come to know one another directly or indirectly. Bankers and attorneys have opinions about actuaries and management consultants. CPA's have opinions about attorneys, actuaries, and management consultants. Management consultants have opinions about other practitioners.

General information of the above sort is useful in finding out who specializes in some particular area of any practice. It is also useful in a defensive sense—to help the financial executive avoid becoming involved with someone so unqualified that other people don't mind saying how unqualified he is.

In a more constructive sense, it is more useful to investigate pertinent references obtained from the professional himself. Two or three references checked in depth may be more revealing than many references checked superficially. Some professionals do not provide references. But in these cases, it is usually possible to identify some clients served by the professional simply by asking other sources.

References should be contacted by a qualified executive. Any number of people can check a professional's credit rating and find out how long he has practiced. It takes an experienced executive to evaluate the quality of work done by him in previous situations and to assess the transferability of his skills to the existing situation.

A personal visit to these references is the most effective check. Questions should be directed to more than one executive, in order to find out how the professional gets along with different levels of management and how he performs both in technical and working relationship areas. This again is a relative matter, because some professional relationships, such as those with attorneys or actuaries, may involve very few client personnel.

Basic questions to ask in reference checks include: What was the nature of the work done by the professional? Were his findings accepted? Were his recommendations carried out? If he helped to implement the recommendations, how effective was he? Were his working relationships with client personnel pleasant or otherwise? Were real benefits obtained? If the client had to face the problem over again, would he be willing to engage the professional again?

Avoiding potential conflict-of-interest situations is a consideration in selection. Some conflicts of interest have been defined by statute or regulation (such as SEC rulings defining "lack of independence" of attorneys and CPA's under given conditions). However, many questions in this area remain unresolved, and this places the burden to assess the situation on the client.

Any reputable professional will candidly discuss the policies governing his practice on such matters as his directorships of companies; whether he serves competing clients; whether the combination of services he offers may conflict (for example, providing actuarial or management consulting services and also certifying the client's financial statements); whether he takes an investment position in either client or competing companies; and whether he accepts fees or commissions from those whose equipment, supplies, or services he recommends.

CONDUCTING NEGOTIATIONS.   Negotiation, in a broad sense, is preliminary to the use of any professional service. The degree and kind of negotiation may vary greatly. Negotiation is generally uncalled for if an attorney, CPA, or other professional is on a retainer basis and if the service sought is an independent opinion on the advisability of some specific action, the interpretation of some regulation, or the provision of some specific information. In other situations, particularly those involving extended programs, the comments in this section apply.

The objective of negotiation is to arrive at a common understanding as a basis for working together. Since, however, negotiating begins with the first contact with one or more parties and continues until final acceptance or rejection of proposals, it plays an important part in selecting the professional.

An important value of negotiation is that it gives the client executive the opportunity to review the aspects of problem definition previously discussed, and thus to reassess the desirability of proceeding with the project before making a final decision to do so. In complex situations, such review may include a preliminary survey to spell out agreements about the purpose, scope, and limits of the project. Such surveys are conducted on a regular fee basis. The practice in this respect is summarized as follows:

If the problem is so complex that the method of solving it or the time required for potential results cannot be determined without gathering additional information, the consultant should recommend a preliminary survey. This preliminary survey will usually produce something of value to the client. It may be a clearer definition of the problem, the development of a method of solving the problem which the client may use himself without further assistance if he desires, or it may take the client part of the way toward the solution of his problem. In such cases, it is entirely proper to charge normal fees for the time spent in making the survey and developing a report of the findings. Surveys made for a reduced fee for the purpose of gaining more opportunity for the selling of an assignment are unprofessional and are not used by ethical practitioners.[5]

With or without a preliminary survey, the professional submits a letter of proposal, agreement, or confirmation, before proceeding with the task. The amount of detail and precision varies widely from one situation to another. In complex situations, the letter covers, to some degree, each of the following subjects: definition of the problem; objectives, scope, and nature of the engagement; areas of the business to be covered by the study; recommended program for accomplishing the work; general methods to be used; who is to do the work (especially if time and effort of the client's personnel will be required to a large extent); estimate of the elapsed time necessary to accomplish the work; and estimate of fees. In addition, the letter sometimes includes a statement of approximately when the professional would be available to begin work, and may also include a description of the method of billing—monthly, weekly, etc. If the program involves several phases, the letter may outline in some detail the first phase and deal in more generalized terms with future steps.

At this point, the executive should be able to decide whether or not to retain outside assistance. In fairness to those who were interviewed, the decision should be reached promptly, especially if a staff is being held in readiness. If the decision is to proceed, the professional should be notified (a formal contract is generally not required). If the decision is against retaining outside help, the professional should be so informed.

---

[5] Association of Consulting Management Engineers, Inc., *Professional Practices in Management Consulting* (New York, 1959), p. 32.

PRINCIPLES OF NEGOTIATION.   Experienced executives and professionals emphasize the following guidelines for conducting negotiations:

The client should begin in control of the situation.   The executive who establishes a preliminary definition of the problem before meeting with professionals and who looks on negotiations as a way of evaluating that definition is in a position of control. The executive who begins negotiations at the same time that he begins serious definition of his problem is starting with a handicap.

Negotiating with too many professionals is time-consuming and self-defeating.   Negotiating time increases rapidly as more competitors are considered. If the executive talks with A and B, he has one cross comparison to make. If he talks with A, B, and C, he has three cross comparisons to make; and if he talks with A, B, C, and D, he has six cross comparisons to make. And the validity of comparisons decreases as the number of practitioners increases. Exploratory discussions with A and B are likely to influence the executive so that he is talking differently by the time he gets to C and D. It is difficult to describe the problem in exactly the same terms to the last professional as to the first.

It pays to be candid with the professional.   At best, withholding information or glossing over problems can only hinder arriving at a sound understanding of the work to be done and the possible benefits to be achieved. At worst, lack of honesty in dealing with professionals may lead to distressing results, ranging from the frustration of time and money wasted to the tragedy of jail sentences.

There should be clear understanding of the proposal and its implications before final commitment to the program is made.   Especially when the problem is unfamiliar to the executive, achieving such understanding is very important. Professionals are supposed to be knowledgeable, articulate, and candid. Therefore, even when dealing with abstruse matters, they should be able to communicate with and educate the client. But this sort of communication is a two-way street. Client executives should expend the effort and time required to obtain a real grasp of the proposal.

A professional should not be selected on the basis of fee alone.   In the first place, different estimates of fees may mean different definitions of the problem. It is one thing to design and install a standard cost accounting system that accepts existing operating standards, and it is another thing to include review and revision of operating standards in the program. Even when it is proved that estimates are based on the same proposal, the executive should still consider which professional he thinks will do the better job and whether the low quoter is reacting unwisely to competitive pressures.

Negotiations should result in understandable estimates of time and fees.   There are, of course, exceptions to this rule. If one embarks upon litigation, both he and his counsellors may be at the mercy of circumstances. And even in more controllable situations, estimates may be subject to unexpected complications, But, in general, in normal situations when negotiations have been properly conducted, the professional should be able to quote estimates of elapsed time and fees to accomplish the task. In such cases, estimated time is generally quoted in minimum to maximum number of weeks or months, and fees are quoted on a bracket basis (minimum to maximum).

The personal aspects of working with the professional should be considered. Anticipation of friendly and productive relationships based on mutual respect is an important factor in selection. This does not mean that the executive should select a counsellor simply because he likes him or shares similar views with him. It does mean that evaluating advice, particularly advice contrary to one's own wishes, is a difficult job on occasion, and that the job is more likely to be constructively performed in an atmosphere of mutual trust and respect.

Program accomplishment

The purpose, scope, and content of programs vary widely among the areas in which the financial executive may seek professional help. In many cases, there may be no program in the common sense of the word. For example, the executive may ask for an opinion on the acceptability of some statement or presentation or he may ask for suggestions about alternative ways of accomplishing some corporate action and the professional may respond by providing an opinion orally or in writing. In such cases, rendering the opinion is an end to the matter as far as the professional is concerned, unless he is invited to participate in some further activity.

In other cases, the program may be relatively lengthy and formalized. Then, even though detailed events may change from case to case, the following generalized comments may be made about (1) the importance of an engagement plan, (2) the role of the liaison executive, (3) introducing the professional to the organization, and (4) exercising supervision of the project.

THE ENGAGEMENT PLAN. The engagement plan is a double check on mutual understanding of the objectives, scope, and nature of the project. It may be developed by the professional and reviewed by client personnel, or it may be developed jointly by client and professional. Sometimes, detailing the plan uncovers points on which more information may be needed in order to estimate workloads or to determine the sequence of steps.

The engagement plan is like any other plan—subject to revision to meet changing circumstances or new understandings, but a very necessary yardstick for measuring accomplishment of action steps.

THE LIAISON EXECUTIVE.   Formal designation of a liaison executive to work with the professional is important. His responsibilities are to see that the work conforms with the defined objectives and scope of the project or that modifications are reviewed and approved, that matters of policy are reviewed and confirmed or changed as required as the study progresses, that client responsibilities for scheduling and accomplishing work are fulfilled, that roadblocks to the program are removed, and that understanding on the part of top executives is facilitated.

In many cases, the financial executive may work with several advisors on a single project. For example, the introduction or review of deferred compensation plans may involve the services of actuary, legal counsel, CPA, and management consultant. Changes in a company's internal planning and control methods recommended by a management consultant may require review by the CPA. The consideration and accomplishment of an acquisition may involve the efforts of attorneys, CPA's, actuaries, consultants, and public relations counsellors. Under these circumstances, the liaison executive's planning, coordination, and control of the project are critical for economic and effective results.

For projects directly related to the financial and accounting areas, the chief financial executive is, of course, the logical choice for the liaison job. In other cases, he may be involved in assignments for which he is not the prime mover. For example, acquisition programs may be the responsibility of another corporate officer. Programs in marketing, manufacturing, and other functional areas may call for provision of facts and figures from the financial function. Under these circumstances, the financial executive should make his contributions on the basis of understandings with whichever one of his associates has been designated as the company's liaison executive.

The liaison executive provides for availability of other company personnel, as may be required. This may involve some transfers of duties, temporary staffing, review of travel and vacation schedules, and the like. On occasion, the client may provide for access to people outside the company, such as customers or suppliers. Other resources to be provided may include such items as rented or purchased equipment and outside services, such as computer service centers, credit rating agencies, and market research firms. If the professional is to work on the premises, he is provided with office space, equipment, and secretarial services.

INTRODUCING THE PROFESSIONAL.   The professional should be introduced to the client organization before he begins contacting personnel other than those he met during negotiations. In some cases, of course, the professional's contacts may be limited to the handful of people he has already met. The following comments apply to situations in which the programs involve substantial numbers of company personnel.

Sensitivity to personnel problems in this area is important. First, the mere presence of an outsider may be taken as an implied criticism of the company's executives and supervisors, particularly where specialties overlap. Second, especially in companies that are not accustomed to using professional services, the presence of an outsider may be interpreted as a threat to freedom of executive decision or even to job security. Therefore, executives and supervisors should be informed about the objectives of the project, why these objectives are in the interest of the company, and why a professional has been retained to work with the organization.

The introduction, beyond personal introductions to those with whom the professional will be working closely, generally takes two forms: first, a written announcement given general circulation; and second, a meeting or series of meetings.

The announcement is prepared jointly with the professional. It covers the purpose of the project, and states that the professional has been retained and that a designated executive has been assigned liaison responsibility. It indicates that the professional will be making requests for company time and effort, and urges that he receive full cooperation.

If meetings are held following the announcement, they generally correspond with organizational lines. Each meeting is presided over by the appropriate executive, who describes his understanding of the study, introduces the professional, and chairs any discussion in which questions may be asked and answered.

SUPERVISING THE PROJECT.   When the work begins, the financial executive is both supervising the project from the company point of view and cooperating with an outsider on a teamwork basis. Thus, his relationship with the professional is fundamentally different from his relationships with other corporate employees. First, the professional is not subject to the normal command exercised over subordinates by a superior officer. Second, as an outsider, he needs management backing because he cannot exercise any authority in the client organization. The financial executive, assuming that he is the executive responsible for the project, should act on the principle that overall supervision of the project is part of his management job. The professional is a resource that has been added to the company's other resources.

Some principles to follow in accomplishing the project are outlined in the following paragraphs.

Management backing of the project should be genuine.   Actions speak louder than words. A formal announcement that management has approved a project is just a piece of paper. Appointment of a top-level executive as liaison with the professional is tangible evidence of management interest. Assigning competent company personnel to the project team is also constructive action. Direct intervention by top management in a project may be called for on occasion. To be avoided at all costs is the posture that the professional should sink or swim, while responsible executives stand by not participating in the solution of practical problems.

Client personnel assigned to work with the professional should be relieved of their regular duties as required. It is not reasonable to expect people to work extensively on a special project and, at the same time, to perform their regular jobs. This can lead to scheduling problems and excess costs. More importantly, it demonstrates that the project is not very highly valued by management.

Client management can properly discharge its responsibilities in a professional relationship, only if it keeps informed about what is going on. Much of this information will naturally come from the professional and the liaison executive. However, company personnel should also be reporting progress and status through normal channels.

The progress meeting is a major tool for keeping informed. The liaison executive and the professional, using the engagement plan as a base, should work out meetings with appropriate personnel to keep them informed of progress, to get the benefit of their reactions, and to be aware of problems in any area of the project as they arise. When client and professional meet periodically to discuss the project, items on the agenda should include: Is the last definition of the problem still valid? If so, is the work still on the track toward the goals agreed on and is it within the boundaries agreed on? Do anticipated benefits still seem reasonable and attainable? Is the work being accomplished on time? Do involved company personnel understand the program?

The client should participate in thinking through the alternatives before formal recommendations are made. The client's advice and criticism are more useful at this stage than later on. In addition, it is just as worthwhile for the client to understand what alternatives were eliminated and why, as for him to understand the recommended solution. For one thing, such understanding assures the client that his decision was reached only after review of all reasonable alternatives. For another, it equips him with well-considered answers for those who may subsequently question the decision by wondering if something else might have been done instead.

Client participation should extend through each phase of an engagement. At the beginning, the client shares responsibility with the professional for definition of the problem. Follow-through from this point is equally important. Findings and conclusions developed during a study have practical applications only to the extent that the client reviews them, challenges them, understands them, and accepts them.

All company personnel should be kept informed about the project in degrees appropriate to their involvement. One hazard in the use of professional services is that the responsible client executive and the professional may develop channels of communication that exclude other company executives and subordinates. This may happen in the beginning because there is need for considerable contact with the professional, and this takes time away from the executive's normal contacts with his associates. Second, the professional is usually in a position to see the whole picture of the project better than many of the executive's associates, so the executive comes to depend on the professional more. This may develop to the point where the executive is making decisions or taking actions based almost entirely on the professional's recommendations. If this point is reached, the responsible executive is short-circuiting his own associates. He is also exposing himself to the risk of accepting recommendations that have not been submitted for review by other personnel who will have to make them work.

TAKING CONSTRUCTIVE ACTION.   In most cases, the final value of professional services is reflected in constructive action. This may be the accomplishment of a single transaction undertaken with the assurance that legal requirements are satisfied, or it may be the achievement of productive change in company direction and practices.

The problem of failure to take action on recommendations occurs more frequently in the study-type project that necessarily precedes action in a complicated situation. In action-type projects, the problem tends to be minimized by the structure and programming of the project itself.

A frequent pitfall to be avoided is the feeling that a problem is solved because a professional has stated an opinion or submitted a report. Opinions and reports do not solve problems. People solve problems. These truisms may be over looked, especially if client executives are not experienced in the use of professional services. There is often the desire to relax at the end of a lengthy project, and there is always the pressure of other business to justify delaying action.

A realistic attitude helps to provide the staying power to accomplish recommendations.   In many cases, putting recommendations into effect will take the dedicated effort of many people. The gap between acceptance of recommendations in theory and application of them in practice is not closed overnight.

The report or written opinion should be reviewed on a formal basis by all appropriate company executives.   There should be a consensus on each recommendation submitted, even if it is the consensus not to take action now. And sound concensus is best achieved when appraisal of the recommendations and full consideration of their implications are based on review and discussion of the report by those who will have to accomplish the recommended actions.

Accepting some recommendations and rejecting others on an unilateral basis is hazardous.   Programs are usually developed to include those recommendations that, taken together, make for success. Elimination of some of them might endanger the whole program. Therefore, each point of the report should be reviewed with the professional before management decides to accept or reject the recommendations, either in whole or in part.

Evaluating results

As a means of achieving effective use of professional services, evaluation should be inherent in the whole project from beginning to end. Results should be checked as the work proceeds. This is the time to evaluate, because judgment may influence coming events favorably. In contrast, the post-mortem judgment may praise or blame, but it cannot change what has already happened.

In terms of follow-up after completion of the work, some projects may be measured quantitatively—for instance, cost reduction projects. Other projects defy quantitative measurement. If they have long-range implications, measurement immediately at the end of the project depends on a nonexistent ability to predict the future. And if the project is reviewed after the passage of some years, it may have become merged with the total business as a going concern, and precise yardsticks are hard to apply. At this point, evaluation becomes primarily a matter of judgment and is stated in general terms. For this kind of review, the following criteria (which are expanded in *Professional Practices in Management Consulting* and in *Effective Use of Business Consultants*) may be used to assess results:

1. Has the work achieved the objectives as set forth in the initial proposal or as modified by agreement during the course of the work?

2. Was the work accomplished within reasonable time and fee limits? Did the original estimates hold up? If not, did revisions come as a surprise, or were they identified well in advance?

3. Have the over-all, long-term interests of the company been protected? Has it moved into its new position without losing image, customers, sources of supply, trade relationships, employees, or anything else of value that it really wanted to keep?

4. Were all reasonable alternatives explored before the company was committed to the final course of action?

5. Is the organization trained to carry on the new activities?

6. Is there improvement in the teamwork of client executives? Is there actual or potential profit improvement? Do executives agree that the new ways are better than the old ways of doing things?

7. Was the professional professional? Was he objective? Did he promote the company's interests? Did he make a valid contribution in helping to achieve results?

8. Did the professional conduct the work in an economic manner? Did he utilize the services of client staff when available? Was the project accomplished without undue disruption of normal operations?

9. Is the financial executive satisfied with the performance of his own organization in working with the professional?

10. Has there been discussion with the professional, so that project performance is evaluated on a mutual basis?

11. Is company management better equipped to handle similar problems in the future as a result of working with the professional?

12. Under appropriate circumstances, would the professional be retained again?

Conclusion

The financial executive is not relieved of responsibility when he retains professional services. The problem is his before the professional arrives, and remains his after the professional leaves. Therefore, the financial executive obtains best results when he is convinced that the project is worthwhile. And that conviction in turn is best developed when the executive practices sound problem definition, exercises care in selection of professional services, works on a practical basis with the professional, conscientiously evaluates project progress, and acts decisively on recommendations.

Bibliography

American Institute of Certified Public Accountants, Inc., *Code of Professional Ethics,* New York, 1967.

Association of Consulting Management Engineers, Inc., *Professional Practices in Management Consulting,* New York, 1968.

Axelson, Kenneth S. "Are Consulting and Auditing Compatible?" *The Journal of Accountancy,* April 1963.

Bower, Marvin. *The Will to Manage.* Chap. 8, New York: McGraw-Hill, 1966, Chap. 8.

Bryson, Lyman. "Notes on a Theory of Advice," *Political Science Quarterly,* September 1951.

Drucker, Peter. *The Age of Discontinuity,* New York: Harper & Row, 1969.

Public Relations Society of America, Inc., *Public Relations and Public Relations Counseling,* New York, 1966.

Seney, Wilson. *Effective Use of Business Consultants,* New York: Financial Executives Research Foundation, 1963.

———— "The Use of Consulting Specialists," *Handbook of Business Administration,* New York: McGraw-Hill, 1967.

Trueblood, Robert M. "The Management Service Function in Public Accounting," *Journal of Accountancy,* July 1961.

PART III

Financial and
economic analysis

Systems analysis and simulation

Robert D. Dahle and S. M. Zivan*

Systems analysis is the study of a system for the purpose of identifying its overall objectives, defining its scope, and improving its performance. In general, the system under study is a group of interdependent functions or subsystems organized to accomplish a common objective.

The systems analysis function is commonly identified with the study of administrative and accounting systems. Standard procedures and practices are developed through the use of systems analysis, allowing for improved system effectiveness. Errors in invoicing systems are minimized. More timely reporting is achieved from ledger systems. Greater flexibility is built into commission systems.

Computerization of large segments of many administrative and accounting systems has allowed for greater efficiency in the operation of these systems, as well as developing new challenges in their analysis. More important to the financial executive is the change in scope of systems analysis brought about by the realization that the business process itself is a system amenable to analysis. Systems analysis continues to connote the development of efficient methods for carrying on the administrative functions necessary for the operation of a business enterprise. Now, however, systems analysis also includes the study of the business process and the various major functions within this process: marketing, manufacturing, distribution, and research. In addition to the procedures for billing customers, the process creating these billings is also considered a system subject to analysis.

This change in scope for systems analysis represents a major modern

---

* Manager, Analytical Support, Advanced Development Dept., and Regional Controller, respectively, of Xerox Corporation, Rochester, New York.

day management advance. The importance of analysis turned toward improving administrative business procedures cannot be denied. There is, however, no comparison between what can accrue to the enterprise from such efforts and what one may expect from careful analysis of the firm itself, considered as a system organized to generate economic profit.

Systems analysis has now become a major decision-making aid to top management and is being applied for the first time to top management's problems. Its use will grow as top management comes to understand it better, and to fear the advantages that competitors will gain if their use of it is not matched.

The analysis of an entire business firm as a system will become commonplace. This chapter will be devoted to this new role for systems analysis. The older, somewhat less formal, uses of such analysis for specific types of decisions such as pricing and capital expenditures are discussed in the next few chapters.

What to expect from systems analysis

The executive must be aware of certain gains to be achieved through the use of systems analysis before adaptation of this discipline can be assured. Merely stating that systems analysis will make a business more effective is not sufficient. Every business executive considers the enterprise he manages as a system, even though he may never have called it one. Every business executive believes he is managing his enterprise in a manner that will achieve maximum effectiveness. Why then should systems analysis of a business firm be used? What is to be achieved from it? In short, how should systems analysis be expected to improve the effectiveness of the firm?

First, the systems analysis effort will precipitate a clear statement of the objective or objectives of the business firm subjected to analysis. Analysis directed at improving systems effectiveness must start by defining what the measures of effectiveness are. Evidence exists that many enterprises operate without clearly stated goals, or with goals that are so poorly expressed that they hinder rather than help. A system is not amenable to analysis if it does not have clearly stated objectives. Without objectives, the scope of the system cannot be defined, and no framework for decision-making in planning and operating can exist. An example of one set of objectives is to achieve a 10 percent growth in after-tax income over the next ten years while maintaining nondecreasing employment levels.

Systems definition is the next benefit received from the analysis effort after objectives have been outlined. The extent or scope of the system is determined. The various functional or environmental subsystems that are contained within the firm's scope are defined, and their interrelationships and interdependencies in planning and operating are determined.

Briefly, the various key pieces of the firm, now considered a system, are enumerated in a manner that clearly displays the influence of each on the effectiveness of the total system.

Once the system is thus described, its operations may be simulated by varying the operations of the functions included within the scope of the defined system and measuring the effectiveness of the total system in meeting objectives. One may seek direct answers to certain operating decisions through this simulation phase. Usually, however, system simulation will be most useful in educating involved executives in the nature of the business enterprise under various operating assumptions, a luxury not permitted through experiences with the real firm. The "feel" of the firm is realized through simulation because the total effect of specific decisions may be quickly obtained.

Redesign and operational control of the business system may then be sought as the last step in utilizing systems analysis to guide the firm to its prescribed objectives. Here the analytic effort becomes a working tool of the executive in planning the firm's future. Product characteristics, budgetary allocations, and pricing decisions are among the managerial actions which may be directly influenced by systems analysis.

To summarize, the executive should expect systems analysis to identify opportunities for improving the effectiveness of his business enterprise. This greater effectiveness is realized first by demanding definitive objectives for the firm. Next, the analysis effort will define the various elements or subsystems that make up the business enterprise. With the system designed, it may now be simulated, showing the executive how the firm's performance would respond to different decisions. Finally, the analytic effort could be used directly in the management of the firm. It should be realized that the accomplishment of any one of these steps through the implementation of a systems analysis program would probably be justification enough for the program. As an example, use of systems analysis to assure the existence of established objectives and to define the scope of the firm to executives may be the most an organization could hope to achieve from an analysis program. In turn, these two accomplishments are essential steps in permitting increased effectiveness of a business firm.

Organizing for systems analysis

Placing responsibility

No universal answer exists for the question, "Where should the systems analysis group report?" Virtually all systems analysts would prefer a direct reporting relationship to the firm's chief executive officer. Such preferences are not limited to systems analysis, however, and are unrealistic. Actually, it may be more advantageous to place the analysis activity elsewhere to assure close and continuous guidance from an executive who could devote more time to it than the chief executive could. Executives responsible for managing planning, finance, or research functions would be appropriate. It is essential that the scope of the function chosen to include systems analysis involve the entire enterprise.

The entire subject of organizational placement may be academic. Rarely should one expect a systems analysis effort to be formed without some other embryonic beginnings. An enlightened executive may initiate an analysis group within his function, and the successes of this group may then allow it to broaden the scope of its work. The responsibility for systems analysis will usually continue under the executive function where it first began to bear fruit.

One important caution should be mentioned. No benefit is seen through the placement of systems analysis within a data processing organization, as is frequently done simply because the systems analyst uses computers, or because both functions are technologically based. Usually, the data processing function is far from the center of decision-making gravity and is, therefore, a poor location for the type of systems analysis discussed here.

Forming the group

The systems analysis group must include people aware of the total business process, the economics of the firm, business finance, statistics, operations research, and computing, as well as people who possess sales ability. Such an organization may be enlisted by recruiting from the ranks of those interested and experienced in the fields of corporate planning, business economics, financial planning, management science, and scientific computing. An in-house computation capability is recommended because of the eventual use of computers for this work and the difficulty most organizations of this type have in securing needed data processing support from existing programming activities. A scientific computational capability is thought to be appropriate since the work of the systems analysis group will involve problem formulation and solution as opposed to repeated calculation and processing.

Staffing of the systems analysis group should result, for the most part, from recruitment outside the firm. Two reasons exist for this. First, the analysis group will be responsible for uncovering deficiencies in present techniques and designing new methodologies. Use of present employees for the purpose of changing things they are accustomed to is not ideal, and is not recommended as a common practice. Second, there is a continuous need within most firms to fill management positions with people aware of the total business process. This makes the systems analysis group a unique training ground for the new employee with potential for greater decision-making responsibility.

The group should possess a nonstructured organization for as long as possible because this method of operating fosters professional communication, and there is little benefit in creating unneeded hierarchies. A submanager position may be necessary for supervising programmer personnel if as many as three such employees are needed. The systems analysis manager should not be expected to have the professional background needed to manage programmers or to devote much of his time to this. A sample organization chart is shown in Exhibit 1.

EXHIBIT 1

Organization of a Systems Analysis Group

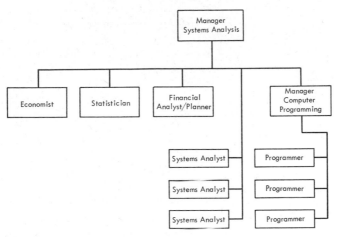

Planning the systems analysis program

It is essential to develop a plan for the work of the systems analysis group before major programs are begun. When completed, the plan should be reviewed with all involved executives to assure overall awareness of the effort, a cooperative working environment, and redirection where required. In addition, this plan will serve to demonstrate that the systems analysis group intends to practice what it attempts to encourage in others: effective management practices. Too often, systems analysis is performed in a nonsystematized, uncontrolled manner. Where this is true, programs often flounder, executives are left with no yardstick with which to measure performance, and the potential benefits of systems analysis are lost to the firm.

Elements suggested for inclusion in the systems analysis plan, in order of their performance, are (1) analysis seeking improvement of the firm's decision-making system, (2) analysis aimed at increasing the reliability of data and assumptions used in planning, (3) application of techniques capable of increasing the effectiveness of critical functional subsystems of the firm, and (4) analysis that can aid in determining budgetary allocations.

Adherence to this long-range program for performing systems analysis will provide greater assurance that this effort will be both lasting and used by management. The remainder of this chapter will examine specific examples of systems analysis efforts linked through an adherence to the above-described program. Examples are given to illustrate the use of systems analysis initially in the study of management's decision process. Next, application of the analytic approach in improving the quality of information used in the decision process is surveyed. Finally, an example of the use of systems analysis in improving the performance of a function of the total system is surveyed, and use of systems analysis in budgetary planning is illustrated.

The decision process

Any decision process involves selection of a course of action from two or more alternatives. Business firms establish formal planning processes to assure, among other things, that alternative courses are developed purposefully, that they are evaluated with respect to objectives, and that the chosen action steps are implemented. Time and effort is allocated to projecting the firm's future performance under its present course. Problem areas, where it appears that objectives will not be met, are identified. Alternatives aimed at closing planning gaps are developed and evaluated. New plans are adopted by choosing from considered alternatives. Operating plans and budgets are then developed, specifying the resources needed to implement the plans.

The establishment of policies to guide the firm's decision or planning process is clearly the responsibility of the chief executive. In many instances, he may delegate this responsibility to a planning officer who is responsible for first developing and then monitoring the planning process. Chapter 26, "Corporate long range planning," discusses this and other aspects of the process in more detail; here, we will focus on the role of systems analysis in the economic evaluation of alternative plans.

The systems analysis group should have the clear responsibility for development of the procedure used in the evaluation of proposed plans. This procedure must accurately predict the plan's effect upon the operation of the firm, and it must be responsive to management, allowing for the evaluation of several different courses of action within short periods of time. This procedure will be the backbone of the planning process, and its successful development will work to establish other meaningful contributions for systems analysis. Thus, this task is of highest priority for a newly-established systems analysis group.

The plans evaluation procedure

The plans evaluation procedure developed by the systems analysis group will formalize and document the methodology used in evaluating proposed plans. Lacking formalism, a methodology may not be systematically repeated. In the case of business planning, lack of formal procedures will mean subjecting each proposed plan to a different test, negating the value of comparison.

The development of financial projections showing cash flow and net income for the firm for each plan under study is common to most plans

EXHIBIT 2

Simple Information Network for Calculating Net Income

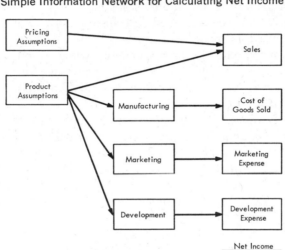

evaluation procedures. The procedures used in developing sets of financial projections should, therefore, be made the subject of study by the systems analysis group.

Normally, the development of procedures of this kind would be thought of as a financial function with accounting definitions for each line of the income statement being all that is required. In the case of procedures for plans evaluation, however, detailed logic networks must be built which have the ability to transform the salient descriptors of a business plan into resource requirements, costs, revenues, and profits, all time-phased as to when their impact will occur. For this, a systems analysis capability is needed. The systems analysis group must develop an information network showing the flow of data required by each subsystem, i.e., marketing and manufacturing, to develop its contribution to the income statement for each plan analyzed. A simple schematic of such a network is illustrated in Exhibit 2. When extended into more detail, such a network is called a model of the firm. The comprehensive model in Exhibit 2 is composed of a set of smaller subsystem models.

Model building

The data required for each subsystem model can only be determined after each such model has been created. The subsystem models are built to depict each of the various functions of the firm. The models develop resource requirements within each function for various business activity levels. Determining the input and output data for each subsystem model establishes the logic network for the total system.

Subsystem models of marketing or manufacturing are not new concepts. There is little new involved in transforming a sales forecast into resources required by manufacturing to fill forecasted sales. The manufacturing planner does this for his general manager constantly. Therefore, the logic used by the planner within each functional organization must be obtained by the systems analyst and incorporated into the subsystem model.

Using the "bottoms up" approach in model building, documenting the presently-used planning logic, will result in models that are used. This approach is not without problems. To build a formal model based on the present planning logic, the systems analyst must first find out what it is. Functional planners may not be overly anxious to present this logic to the systems analyst. Fear that such disclosure would provide an audit instrument for evaluating subsequent budget submissions, and lack of confidence in present decision-making methodology are strong reasons for the functional planner to respond cautiously to an inquiring systems analyst.

Two arguments should aid the systems analyst in gaining cooperation from the functional planners. First, the systems analysis effort usually will have been built from an organization that has proved its value on other problems. Knowledge of this, plus evidence of professional execution of past tasks, will serve to inspire confidence in the systems analysis activity. Second, the mission at hand should be presented as benefiting the subsystem as much as the firm or total system. These two points should serve to gain the needed acceptance for the systems analyst, and to foster the communication needed between the functional planner and the analyst.

At this point, an additional problem may arise. The systems analyst may find that the existing planning logic is unacceptable for use in the model of the firm. Suppose, for instance, that a sales department planner develops his estimates of the resource requirements for the selling function by first calculating selling expense as some percent of revenue and then determining the number of salesmen required by dividing selling expense by some average compensation per salesman. This type of model is not descriptive of the effects of changes in the form of the firm's business and cannot be accepted. The diplomatic disclosure of this inadequacy and the subsequent development of more usable logic is then the challenge to the systems analyst.

An example of model logic

The logic that a firm involved in servicing field equipment might use to determine the total cost of service associated with a given plan is illustrated in Exhibit 3. Service expense, as computed here, includes the cost of salaries, parts, and facilities. Each of these cost elements is, in

EXHIBIT 3

Partial Diagram of Model Logic for "Service Expense"

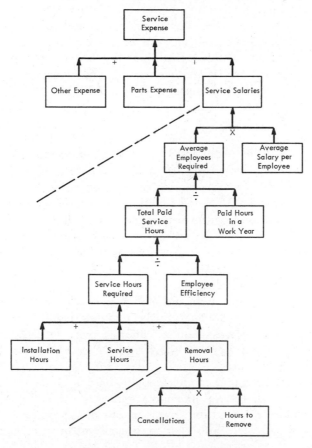

turn, the result of a series of logical computations, some of which are shown in the Exhibit. The average number of service employees required, for example, is developed by dividing total paid service hours by the paid hours in a work year. Total paid service hours is developed by dividing projected manpower efficiency into service hours required. Service hours required is developed by adding total hours required for field maintenance to total equipment installation hours and hours required to remove cancelled units. The latter quantity is developed by multiplying the number of cancellations (a "product-associated variable") by the number of standard hours required to remove the piece of equipment (a "functional-associated variable").

This logic represents a simple model of a service function. Given estimates of both product-associated and functional-associated variables, the model can be used to calculate the amount of operating expense required for the service function. When logic similar to this is developed for marketing expense, development expense, and the other functional elements of the firm, the result is a model of the entire business system. Various mixtures of product programs, each specifying forecasts of sales and other product-associated variables, may be fed into this model, and resultant activity in each function is calculated and summarized into an income statement for measuring the effectiveness of the plan being studied. Construction of this logical model will represent a major contribution of systems analysis in determining and documenting the way plans can be evaluated in a consistent fashion.

Computerization of models

Assurance that the model will bring about both timely and consistent plans evaluation can only result from the computerization of the system model outlined above. Programming the model's logic for computer execution assures that this logic will repeatedly be employed in an identical way in projecting the firm's performance under various assumed conditions. The computer's speed will allow the execution of this logic in minutes as opposed to weeks, permitting both a quick response in evaluating any particular plan and the ability to examine numerous alternative courses of action.

Providing file organization and data access routines is one of the greatest problems in computerizing the planning logic. Thorough documentation of the systems analyst's findings will present the various modules or functional parts of the system in computer programmable form. Organizing a firm's planning data for use in a multi-product, multi-functional computer model is both difficult, and essential to the project's success. In general, the file organization should (1) allow for the easy addition of operating divisions and new products, (2) permit product-associated variables either to be constant or to change for each time period, and (3) permit similar flexibility in the values assigned to functional-associated variables.

Most importantly, the computerized system should not be used for anything until its results have been carefully checked out by all involved planners.

Data base

Continuous and meaningful use of models for decision analysis requires the maintenance of a data base of updated information for the business system under study. The data base contains the system's parameters (values for the basic variables) which amount to the total model input. Acceptable model logic must be complemented by a planned, systematic approach toward the establishment of a representative and current data base.

The mere construction of the model establishes the nature of its data base by identifying needed input. Quantifying the input must be accomplished through the analysis of current operations and forecasting. Assuring the validity of the data base is the most difficult and costly part of the systems analysis effort. Because of this, in cases where large data bases are employed, analysis should first be directed at the validation of those parameters for which the output of the model (the projected performance of the system) is most sensitive. The model itself should be used for "sensitivity analysis" to identify these crucial variables.

In most instances, it will be found that market assumptions, sales quantities, and pricing policies are the most crucial assumptions in planning. Utilization of a systems analysis approach in deriving these assumptions will now be discussed as the second task in the systems analysis program plan.

Market analysis and research

The simulation model outlined in the preceeding section is, in a sense, a "reactive" model. That is, the model transforms a given level of market activity into the resources required to support that activity. This type of model leaves the question of how to determine the level of market activity completely unanswered. Obviously there is a need to embellish the reactive model with a more definitive means of predicting market activity. This section will describe the steps involved in developing and integrating market analysis into the system simulation concept.

Determining present market position

The first question which needs to be answered pertains to the present market position. How many customers do we have, where are they, and what do they buy? A second question concerns how many customers make up our market and what the total industry's penetration of the *potential* market is. A third question relates to our firm's share of the currently-penetrated market, recognizing the kind, quality, and amount of competition which the firm faces. Finally we must study the market to determine how well the customers' needs are being met, and what new products or services can be added to enhance our competitive position and profits.

Perhaps the most logical place to start with market analysis is to look at the current position of the company. A large amount of information on the customers, how much and what they purchase from the firm, and where they are located is usually available in the records of the firm. The analyst should be able to cross-classify these customers by region, product, and/or volume. For some businesses this type of analysis is a relatively easy task; for others it is an extremely costly, time consuming, and difficult task. Completion of this should, in itself, provide the firm with an increased understanding of their customers and their customers' purchasing habits. Many companies have built this kind of information into their market analysis system, but have failed to use it in the planning process.

Clearly this type of analysis is not limited to manufacturing firms. Service organizations such as banks and retail distribution companies can also benefit from this basic classification of their present customers. Patterns of customer–product relationships may develop as a result of this analysis which will suggest a multitude of questions to which answers will have to be found. Only after classification and study of present patterns can definitive ideas be developed about how to estimate the total market potential.

Market potential and projected penetration

Analysis of market potential raises questions regarding (1) what sources of information should be used, and (2) how present market activity should be projected to estimate the total market potential. For instance, a service company may examine the number of dwellings or households in its service area. Then, by using a subclassification based upon assessed value, an estimate of the potential market could be made. This would assume that market potential was related to disposable income, which in turn was related to assessed valuation of homes in the market area. A manufacturing company may wish to examine the number of companies by geographic area and employee size in order to determine its market potential. It may assume that its potential sales are related to the number of blue collar employees in a given firm, with specified differences between regions. Common sense and knowledge of a specific industry should provide an adequate classification scheme for the initial estimate of market potential. In time, refinements can be made to the system to increase the amount of information yielded per dollar of analytic investment.

The present penetration of our firm in the total potential market may be computed by dividing our present volume by the estimated market potential. This gives an estimate of our market position as if there were no one else in the market place.

Up to this point the initial ingredients for determining total market potential have been discussed, and the calculation of present market penetration at a given point in time has been defined. Historically,

EXHIBIT 4

Schematic Diagram of Interrelationships in Market Information

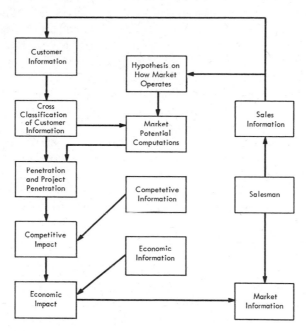

market data about one firm's penetration percentage can be likened to a series of snapshots of the marketplace. The question of where the firm is can be adequately answered, but the question of how the firm got to that position remains somewhat of an analytic mystery. With the introduction of computers into market analysis, constant updates of the information base can be made. This permits the questions, "Where are we?" and, "How did we get here?" to be answered in a dynamic manner. That is, it enables the firm to use its information base to direct and measure sales effort. If we liken information updates to frames on a movie film, we now have what appears to be a movie rather than a series of snapshots—a more dynamic system. In Exhibit 4, a schematic diagram is used to summarize these concepts.

Competitive impact

Having laid the basis of our market analysis system by classifying present customers and developing estimates of total market potential, external factors can be introduced to modify the market estimates. Obviously, a company does not control the market in total; competition exists in the form of other companies who compete either directly or by offering a substitute product or service. Also, the total market potential may be influenced by direct or indirect government regulation. How the effects of competitive and environmental factors are handled with respect to penetration and market potential is very dependent upon the nature of the competition and the competitor's relative strength in the firm's market area. Many times the most direct competition, as between two breakfast cereals on a supermarket shelf, is the most difficult type of competitive activity to analyze, while the effects of the Federal Reserve rediscount rates on two banks in the same market area may be relatively straightforward. Regardless of estimation difficulties, we are forced to temper our estimates of our penetration of a potential market by recognizing competitive market conditions and external events.

It is at this point that traditional market research techniques can be applied with great benefit. Segmenting the market place into four broad groups—customers who buy exclusively from us; customers who buy from us and our competitors; customers who buy exclusively from our competitors; and customers who may have needs but don't now use our products to fill those needs—can be useful in gaining an overall perspective on competitive position. Based upon market research information from these four areas, models can be developed to estimate the competitive interactions which may be experienced.

The type of models which are required depend upon the nature of the business of the firm. If the company sells through retailers, then a model to represent the behavior of the retailer must be developed; if salesmen sell the products then the behavior of the salesman must be modeled; and so forth. The important point is not what should be modeled to gain a perspective upon the competitive effects, but that the phenomena of the market can be modeled. Acceptance of the model-building approach to competitive analysis requires a commitment to testing and model validation and to participation, and not to abdication, buy top management.

Since the marketplace is dynamic and the firm is engaged in counter strategies with its competitor, market research must be a continuing effort. It is as important to know that nothing has changed as it is to know that important changes have taken place or are taking place in a given market segment.

Economic conditions

Information on market size, market potential, and competitive share must be projected over some time horizon if we are to make useful calculations of our profits in successive time periods. After projections have been tempered by considering competitive activity, the impact of changing economic conditions must be taken into account. Such studies may be as simple as trend analysis under status quo economic assumptions, or may be based upon complex econometric models with varying assumptions. In some cases, future technologies may have to be forecast and their adoption rate and impact estimated. Even if some of these complexities are dealt with only informally, their effects must be integrated into the market analysis in order to derive a useful sales forecast.

Summary

At this point in the market analysis system development, a huge amount of data have been gathered and analyzed. If the business is fairly complex, the only way that this sort of market analysis can possibly be done is by the use of advanced data handling technology—the computer. Computers and their peripheral equipment and manpower, both operating and programming, are expensive. Thus, the question becomes: How can the market be known, that is, how can a sophisticated market analysis system be developed, and the expenditure for computers, manpower, market research, and data storage be justified? One way is by integrating the market analysis and research system into the sales program of the company.

Knowing where the market is, how much business is there, and what kind and how much competition the firm faces is of little use unless the information reaches the sales point, be it a salesman, distributor, or route delivery-salesman. Additionally, supplying the sales point with information does not assure a payoff unless measurements are made of the degree of effectiveness in utilization of this information. Measurements of effectiveness can be made through rather simple follow-up procedures. If a salesman is furnished with a set of prospect cards, the system should contain a procedure whereby new orders are checked against the list furnished to the salesman. In a computerized file, the new order file and the original prospect file are compared to yield this measurement of effectiveness. Thus, a viable market analysis and research system contains a complete feedback loop involving the sales program as well as the measurement and projection of the market. In short, the market analysis and research system is an integral part of the operation of the firm and not separate from or extraneous to the day-to-day operations.

Up to this point, the assumption has been made that we were dealing with viable products. Obviously, this vast pool of market information can also be brought to bear upon the development and introduction of new products. In the next section, new product definition and development will be discussed in detail.

Analysis for program definition

Program definition, the development of new products or new uses for old products, is, in a way, just an extension of market analysis and research. Some firms view it as an integral part of market analysis and research. The important thing in program definition is not the label applied to it; it is a recognition that it is a separate area for systems analysis. We must give proper emphasis to program definition prior to intergrating it into the market analysis system.

The environment

Suppose that a firm has examined the information from its market analysis and research system and has found a specific market segment in which it thinks there might be an opportunity for internal diversification. How can a new product concept for entry into this market be developed? First, an understanding of the detailed operation of the customer unit in the market—a household, a repair shop, a bank, a laboratory, a classroom, or some specific definable environment—must be gained. After defining the new market, the next step is to ask whether there are different-sized units, that is, to pick a relevant measure of throughput that is related to the objective of the environmental unit. If the analysis indicates that the market should be segmented on the basis of throughput, then the analytic system must be constructed so that the market penetration estimates can be easily changed to accommodate various throughput configurations.

Based upon this knowledge about the market environment, it is then possible to construct a model of the customer unit, as it exists at the time, and to test that model to see if it is a valid representation of the environment. Testing is an iterative procedure, and requires attention to detail.

Use of an expert from the market being studied can provide some assurance that the model is a fair representation of the market environment. The expert will also provide some idea of the thought processes of people who earn their living by operating in the environment, and these insights into behavioral patterns will have to be taken into account in product design. In the process, the analyst will learn a great deal about the new market—tricks of the trade, ethical considerations, market perceptions, competitive information, and so forth.

Introducing the new product

Many times the analysis required to develop this "environmental simulator" leads to a modification of the original product concept. Sometimes totally new concepts appear as a result of the analysis. Once the new market has been successfully represented, the product concept can be tested in this simulated environment. Comparisons can then be made between the sales volume with the existing product line and the results if the new product is introduced. Again the process may be iterative, in that the company analyst may wish to try out different product concepts with different capabilities to judge the relative merits of each. If sufficient information is available, analysis of the possible competitive response to your product can be made. A schematic representation is presented in Exhibit 5.

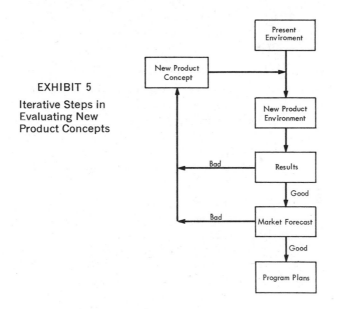

EXHIBIT 5

Iterative Steps in
Evaluating New
Product Concepts

If the new product concept proves to be viable, then the next step is to examine the market potential for the product. At this point, the market analysis and research system is used to provide data on market potential and growth factors. Subsequent analysis then leads to the development of sales forecasts and other product-associated variables, as described earlier for old products. Once all the parameters are estimated, the model is then used to estimate the profitability of the new product over the first several years of its life.

In the concluding section, the means of making the analytic systems developed in the preceding discussion fit into the accounting framework of the organization will be developed.

Analysis for budgetary control

The budget should be the end product of the planning process. The budgeting process is a system through which the business unit internalizes information about the market and activities in the market to develop detailed short-range plans and evaluate their financial effect. Chapter 23, "Profit planning and budgeting," discusses this process in more detail. Once a plan has been selected, the budgeting process translates that plan into the accounting language of the firm for subsequent comparison of actuality to plan. There is no reason why this translation cannot be handled using a model which, although considerably more detailed, has the same essential characteristics as the planning model discussed previously.

Budget simulation

Budgeting simulators have been in use by many companies for a long period of time; in fact, the process is exactly equal to the manual process. Automation of the budgeting process can assure that several things will happen: (1) consistent definitions and policies will be utilized; (2) computational errors will be minimized; (3) the budgeting system will be integrated into the planning system, to assure consistency for all areas of activity, and (4) changes in the market place can be rapidly evaluated by preparing revised budgets.

Perhaps the most important benefit of doing the budgeting process as the last step in the planning process is that of integration and consistency. Experience has indicated that unless the budgeting process is highly formalized, the translation of an operational plan into a budget may not be consistent with plan requirements, and/or budgets for the various functional activities may be internally inconsistent. Maintenance of internal consistency requires a formalized approach which is gained through systemization.

Many of the specific figures in a budget are, in turn, based on estimates of an activity rate multiplied by a monetary measure. Both the activity rate (the number of items sold) and the monetary measure (price per item) may change over the life of the budget. For budgetary control, both pieces of information are required in order to analyze subsequent variances from budget. With slight modifications, most budgetary systems can produce an analysis of the effect of changes in either or both parameters; thus, the manager not only receives information that there has been a deviation, but some explanation as to what caused the deviation. This approach can, when carried to the lowest level of the organization, provide each level of management with trackable information on performance deviations.

Some automated production reporting systems already do this type of reporting; however, there has been no strong movement to extend this system concept into other parts of the organization in order to enhance management's ability to control activities. Also, the concept of responsibility accounting based upon variable budgeting concepts is fully complementary to the use of simulation approaches to financial systems analysis.

Summary

Exhibit 6 is intended to place the material covered in this chapter into perspective with respect to the earlier definition of systems analysis. The goal of systems analysis is to identify objectives and to evaluate alterna-

EXHIBIT 6

Logic Steps in
the Application of
Systems Analysis

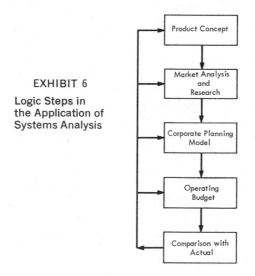

tive ways of meeting those objectives effectively. Logically we start with a product concept, examine its implications in the marketplace, develop a business organization to design, manufacture, distribute, and sell the product, and prepare financial controls to monitor our performance. If our expectations are not met, we make changes in one or more of these segments to bring the organization into "proper" balance.

Thus, we have developed a system which meets the objectives in an efficient and effective manner. In most cases, the systems analysis will proceed in reverse order from our logic chart because of the fact that most systems work is undertaken in firms already in business and the existing control system is a good base from which to build toward planning-analysis systems.

Make or buy decisions

Myron J. Hubler, Jr.*

Make or buy analysis for decision-making is an area of management theory and practice with which every financial executive should be familiar. Make or buy decisions must be made periodically by nearly every manufacturing company and often these decisions are major determinants of enterprise profitability.

Chapter 19 of the Handbook includes a discussion of asset purchase feasibility and Chapter 20 discusses lease-buy analysis. Such topics are ordinarily proposed studies which extend over a span of several years and would not be included in make or buy studies.

The information in this chapter should be used only as a suggested tool for the evaluation of make or buy decisions. These decisions are concerned with virtually an infinite number of variables. The constraints on make or buy decisions are limited only by the ingenuity and rational logic for decision-making of the financial executive.

An important application for the principles of make or buy analysis is in establishing a standard policy for interdivision purchases of products or parts as compared to decisions to purchase from outside vendors. The subject of interdivision transfer pricing, however, is a separate topic and will include factors other than those discussed in this chapter. (See Chapter 36, "Measuring divisional performance.") Joint ventures also may offer limited possibilities for cost-sharing by the participating enterprises to achieve the semiadvantages of make or buy analysis.

The procedures for make or buy analysis can be applied to a wide

---

* Controller, Instrument Division, Reliance Electric Company, Columbus, Ohio.

range of decisions—new buildings, new equipment, tooling, parts needed for the production of goods for sale, mergers and acquisitions, etc. For the sake of simplicity, the subject matter of this chapter is limited to consideration of make or buy decisions for component parts of products manufactured for sale in the normal course of business. The basic objective of these decisions is to provide the right part at the right time in the right quantity at the lowest cost.

This discussion will be confined to major factors ordinarily considered in evaluating a proposed purchase of parts from outside vendors or other sources of supply, even though existing internal manufacturing facilities are adequate for the manufacture of these parts.

By limiting the scope of the chapter, it is possible to use the various levels of productive capacity available from existing capital equipment facilities for cost analysis and avoid such factors as the impact of vertical integration; discounted cash value of funds invested in new capital facilities; anticipated useful economic life of these facilities, and similar matters.

Even with the above limitations, the make or buy decision is frequently complex. There are usually many ways of designing the same product and there may be a wide variety of alternative materials that might be suitable for product manufacture. The selection of any of these alternative choices may require a revision in manufacturing method or scheduling, either inside or outside the company.

Management responsibility

It is important that the chief executive officer of the company outline the basic policies governing make or buy decisions, and specify the division of responsibilities among the members of the management team.

The composition of the management team will depend on the organization structure and capabilities of the individuals of the particular company.

It is suggested the major functions of the enterprise be made aware of the significance of make or buy analysis through meetings or written policy.

The financial function is frequently one of the major participants in this analysis. Engineering, sales, purchasing, and manufacturing functions are also vitally concerned with the completeness of make or buy analysis. Other functions which may contribute to broaden the analysis should be included in the management team depending on the particular company organization.

The management team should be utilized whenever possible for decisions involving more than a minimum commitment of funds. It may be helpful to suggest staff meetings of accountants, industrial engineers, production, purchasing, and sales management to discuss the procedure to be followed to determine the feasibility for a particular make or buy analysis.

In operation, it may be desirable to delegate the make or buy responsibility to a specific department or function, with provisions for periodic group re-evaluation by the team to measure the effect of the make or buy program.

The cost accounting function often is a logical area to determine whether a product should be produced or purchased. Frequently the purchasing department is the one to initiate make or buy studies, and the production and industrial engineering departments often take part. For an established product line, many of the production details (including make or buy) may be left up to the particular cost centers most closely concerned.

Whatever the exact form of organization, all the specialized knowledge and skills of the management team should be applied to these decisions, and an effort should be made to ensure that the basic policies become ingrained in management thinking.

Features of basic policy

One of the principal features of a make or buy decision is that it is possible to exert an immediate influence on profit performance.

Encouraging management awareness of the profit improvement possibilities of such decisions should become an established segment of the corporate management development program.

Significant formulas, ratios, and factors to be considered in make or buy decisions might well be included in a management procedures manual as a guideline for comprehensive coverage of the topic.

Every decision will require a logical analysis and then a judgment determination based on the known factors at a given point in time. Of course, the longer the term for the commitment of funds, the more important becomes the need for expanding the coverage of the make or buy study.

The management program for review of the basic corporate policy for make or buy decisions should include features such as the following:

1. Describe the extent of unusual product design requirements.
2. Determine specialized labor skills and equipment required.
3. Evaluate the price and volume differentials.
4. Special materials handling should be specified.
5. Adequate warehouse storage and protective facilities may be needed.
6. Guarantee and warranty responsibilities may be of significant importance.
7. The relative importance of having multiple suppliers available versus a single source may be significant.

8. The possibility of outside sales if the product is made rather than bought.
9. The risk or inherent danger of loss of proprietary rights or captive replacement business.
10. Convenience of manufacture may be a matter for consideration.
11. Determine the effect of international transactions (where applicable) especially import-export duties and government tariff policies. As international activity increases within the company, the effect of government influence through tariffs, artificial barriers, and closed borders may be factors of increasing importance. The "in-country" pride of product origin may also require consideration—Made in U.S.A., Canada, Japan or other countries may be of significant importance.

A helpful check list for a preliminary review of a proposed make or buy analysis might be structured somewhat as shown in Exhibit 1.

EXHIBIT 1
Make or Buy Analysis
(Check applicable items)

Reasons for Making

1. Cost studies indicate it is cheaper for you to make than to buy. _____
2. Making fits your knowhow, your equipment, and your tradition. _____
3. Idle capacity is available to absorb overhead. _____
4. What you are considering is unusual or complex; direct supervision is needed to assure control. _____
5. Making will facilitate your control of parts changes, inventories, and deliveries. _____
6. The part is hard to transport. _____
7. The design of the part or its processing is confidential. _____
8. You do not wish to depend on a single outside source of supply. _____

Reasons for Buying

1. Cost studies indicate it is cheaper for you to buy than to make. _____
2. Space, equipment, time, and/or skill are not available for you to develop the necessary production operations. _____
3. Because of small volume, or other capital needs, the investment in making is not attractive. _____
4. You wish someone else to face seasonal, cyclical, or risky market demands. _____
5. The need for special techniques, or equipment, makes buying more logical. _____
6. You think it is best for your executives to concentrate on your specialty. _____
7. You want a check on your own operations. _____
8. Patents or customer-supplier relationships favor going outside. _____

Other policy considerations

One of the difficult aspects of make or buy analysis is developing a program to assure an adequate reporting procedure for review and evaluation of product lines to improve profitability. Since the subject of make or buy is concerned with so many variables, the program is really never finalized. Thus, the program for submission of parts or products for make or buy consideration becomes of significant interest. The program offers unique opportunities for development of creativity throughout the organization. Whether the program for make or buy should include a formal written form to initiate such studies will be a matter for the particular company to decide.

There are frequent misunderstandings among various levels of management as to what factors should be included for make or buy analysis. Ordinarily, return on investment would not affect these analyses. Imputed interest or financing costs should also be excluded on the theory that the initial decision to enter the industry as a competitor for profit has already assumed the necessary risk-bearing rate of interest in the product-pricing structure.

Often the typical make or buy decision will be concerned only with a recovery of variable costs. To the extent that additional space, equipment, tooling, or manpower are required, then the make or buy decision must be held in abeyance until feasibility studies have been completed. It is suggested that such studies be conducted outside the scope of the make or buy analysis. As the results of these studies become known, such data as are pertinent may be included in the make or buy analysis, minimizing the overlapping of concurrent analysis.

Higher levels of management must be aware of the responsibilities associated with make or buy analysis and the seriousness of incomplete corporate policy which would neglect to recognize total cost recovery plus profit as their primary responsibility to the board of directors and shareholders.

The make or buy decision may be one of the most evasive the financial executive has to evaluate. The variable factors to be considered in each decision are virtually unlimited. One of the difficulties frequently encountered in efforts to research information from business associates in support of a particular make or buy decision is that the *right* decision will be profitable and therefore not readily disclosed for fear of loss of competitive advantage; the *wrong* decisions are not often voluntarily disclosed because these are usually unprofitable, and tend to reflect on executive performance.

Make or buy analysis should be designed to emphasize the importance of careful and intelligent appraisal of make or buy factors. All make or buy decisions should be completely re-evaluated on a periodic basis to avoid manufacturing stagnation and the effect of "creeping overhead." Regular and systematic make or buy analysis should be an established part of corporate management procedure.

Noncost factors which may affect decisions

Normally the make or buy decision depends upon an analysis of comparative costs. There are, however, a number of factors other than product costs that may be of significant—in some cases overriding—influence in the make or buy analysis. Among these factors are the following:

1. *Manufacturing capacity.*   Any decision to make or buy must be preceded by an analysis of the capacity of existing facilities. Issues to be considered include the number of shifts the facilities will be in operation; when overtime should be included (for example, if three shifts are already working); and, possibly, the types of work to be subcontracted as the plant approaches capacity.

2. *Product quality.*   In most cases it is assumed that comparable quality is available from internal and external sources of supply. This is not necessarily so. When special tolerances or special skills are required in the manufacture of a part, the advantages of specialization may favor the buy decision. To some extent, however, product quality is an intangible value. Appearance may affect subjective "quality," as in the use of chrome vs. aluminum boat fittings, without necessarily relating to "quality" as expressed in terms of product performance. Whether the part is to be an internal or external component may be an influencing factor in practical quality requirements.

Product value analysis is often a separate company program in conjunction with make or buy review. Value analysis is concerned with the functional aspects of the product reviewed. For example, purchases of pencils may be considered as a means to transcribe, to record data, or to make a legible mark, etc. This interesting method for analysis is intended to identify the best functional solution for achieving the objectives of the analysis. The purchasing department frequently assumes responsibility for value analysis.

3. *Fluctuations.*   In some industries the existence of seasonal and cyclical sales and production fluctuations may make internal manufacture of a part more desirable than it would be otherwise. Items that would normally be purchased on the outside can be produced on existing facilities to level out production.

4. *Trade secrets.*   Companies in defense production or those enjoying a definite market advantage from design patients or process secrets may prefer to do their own manufacturing in order to retain this advantage.

5. *Employee welfare and good will.*   Even when a buy decision seems fairly obvious, management may, for reasons of community stability and retention of skilled labor, wish to continue to manufacture products that might be purchased more economically. The continued availability of a dependable, trained manufacturing labor force is an intangible asset whose value defies quantification for make or buy analysis. Such decisions should be re-evaluated periodically by top management to minimize technological stagnation of the labor force.

6. *Technological innovation.*   In industries that characteristically have a substantial amount of change in product from one year to the next, there is a tendency to favor outside sources of supply. The greater

potential for technological obsolescence creates the risk of a much shorter period of cost recovery for manufacturing facilities and equipment. Particularly when exotic materials, highly specialized labor, and special tooling must be used, manufacturers often prefer to shift the risk to suppliers if they can until training and other internal adjustments are accomplished to justify manufacture.

7. *Other factors.* There are other factors that may favor either a make or buy decision.

a) If the prices charged by vendors appear unreasonably high in comparison with estimated costs of manufacturing.

b) If special product guarantee or liability responsibilities are involved, the company may consider manufacturing the parts.

c) Trade practices of competitors.

d) The estimated future demand and continuity of design of the product.

e) The value of the component as compared to the total volume of business of the product (usually based on one year's usage) may influence the decision either way, depending on the outcome of the analysis.

These and other pertinent considerations that may be known to the management should be included in the list of factors to be evaluated in making an informed decision.

Product costs applicable to decisions

There is a wide range of opinion as to the costs that should be included in make or buy analysis. As a general rule out-of-pocket, incremental, and total costs may be pertinent and should be included when appropriate.

Generally, an analysis of make or buy comparative costs should be done on a worksheet that provides for comparison of vendor quoted (or known) prices and company manufacturing costs. A worksheet form such as that shown in Exhibits 2 and 3 is suggested for use in formal make or buy analysis.

The purpose of the worksheet illustrated in Exhibit 2 is to mention such matters as may have an important bearing on the outcome of a make or buy decision but are outside the scope of such decisions. These matters would ordinarily be resolved before proceeding with the cost analysis.

Exhibit 3 is a worksheet used to summarize the direct variable costs of material, labor and overhead in accordance with a standard program. Such a form provides an uniform approach to make or buy review. (The use of such a form is assumed in the following comments about selected costs; it should be referred to for a clearer understanding of this discussion.)

Direct variable costs.   It is generally agreed that the direct variable costs should be included in the accumulated manufacturing cost. Among the direct variable costs are all direct material and direct labor and any other specific out-of-pocket costs. Under unusual circumstances (such as tight production capacity) any subcontract work costs incurred should be included as direct variable costs.

Some make or buy analyses will assume that direct material and labor costs are comparable between the vendor and the manufacturer, that the "other costs" of the vendor, plus the vendor's profit will be realized by the decision to manufacture and thereby absorb all other costs with the existing organization.

Thus, the recovery of only direct variable costs is the basis for the theory that it is always cheaper to manufacture than to buy. The use of such theory as company policy can lead to costly errors. In instances where plant capacity is exceeded as a result of such decisions, overcrowding and rerouting of material through the production process will disrupt the load and schedules for machines. Long, efficient equipment runs may be replaced by shorter, less continuous cycles, greatly increasing set-up, overtime premiums and similar costs as a result of operating inefficiencies.

Direct material costs.   These will occasionally not be the same for the outside vendor and the company proposing to manufacture. This difference in purchase price may be due to the vendor's history, regularity, or quantity of purchase which may provide a lower price schedule to the vendor than to the company proposing manufacture of this part. In addition, the vendor's knowledge of alternative sources of supply may be superior to that of the manufacturer. Also, the vendor may be able to purchase from different levels of supply such as from the processor while the company proposing to make its own parts may have to buy from distributors.

Economic order quantities (EOQ).   These will be determined by the purchasing department from established formulas and should be recognized in estimating material costs.

The extent of inventory commitment in accordance with maximum-minimum quantity or dollar limitations for the make or buy decisions may be determined by the materials planning department.

Direct labor.   Labor cost comparisons between the vendor and the manufacturer should be realistically evaluated to avoid costly errors. By way of example, the company proposing to manufacture may have established labor rate scales substantially in excess of vendors who may use semi-skilled labor, part-time skilled labor, students, etc., which oftentimes do not reflect full rate or fringe costs.

Variable overhead.   This is more difficult to define as an out-of-pocket

EXHIBIT 2
Make or Buy Worksheet

CABINET

Part No. *XP 250469*

Date *Sept 29, 1969*

The following items are suggested additional areas of cost consideration for evaluating the proposed make or buy decision:

	Estimated Additional Cost	Make	Buy
TOOLING:			
None Required		—	—
Available	375 ᵘᵘ	*No*	*No*
Required *Welding Fixtures*		*Yes*	*Yes*
EQUIPMENT:			
A. Production			
Available		*Yes*	*Yes*
Required		*None*	*None*
B. Material Handling			
Available		*Yes*	*Yes*
Required		*None*	*None*
SPACE			
Available		*Yes*	*Yes*
Required *If volume*			
Rearrangement required *exceeds 2,000 units*			
Sq. ft. *1,000* Cost			
MANPOWER – AFFECTING OTHER DEPTS.			
A. Direct:			
Available		*None*	*None*
Required			
Premium required			
B. Indirect:			
Available		*Yes*	*Yes*
Required *For storage of finished*			
Premium required *Cabinets if volume*			

COMMENTS. *exceeds 2,000 units*

EXHIBIT 3

Make or Buy Cost Worksheet

Part No. _XP-250469_

Date. ___10/10/63___

1. MATERIAL REQUIRED

Source	Material	Qty.	Unit Cost	Total Mat'l Cost
Standard	36"x 96"-16 ga. C.R.S.	2	3.60	7.20
Purchased	36"x 10"-16 ga. C.R.S.	1	.40	.40
Material	Paint	1 pint	.30	.30
	Grommets + Fittings	12	Various	1.80
				9.70

2. LABOR REQUIRED

Operation	Dept.	Hours	Rate/Hour Dept.	Rate/Hour Composite	Total Labor Cost
Shearing + Punching	426	.15	2.70	2.65	.41
Forming	426	.02	2.70		.05
Welding	432	.30	2.80		.84
Finishing	436	.05	2.60		.13
		.52			1.43

3. OVERHEAD APPLIED

Operation	Dept.	Hours	Rate/Hour Dept.	Rate/Hour Composite	Total Overhead Cost
Use standard variable overhead rate (Note A)				3.00	1.56

4. NOTES: Note A. Plant capacity is presently available. In the event production exceeds 5,000 units, the overhead rate should be revised to include additional floor space requirements for storage and welding.

or incremental cost. Among the overhead cost items that may be pertinent are the following:

1. Additional material handling costs.
2. Indirect labor.
3. Additional hourly supervision.
4. Special skills or training required of employees.
5. Overtime premiums (as capacity costs begin to creep in).
6. Fringe-benefit costs and other variable overhead costs peculiar to a particular industry.
7. Setup and tear-down time required for equipment conversion. (Conceivably there could be down-time initially to halt an operation already on the machines, setup time for the next part, tear-down time upon completion of manufacture of the new part, and new setup time required to resume production.)

Any unusual capacity costs incurred as a result of exceeding the normal capacity of the existing plant facilities should be included under variable overhead costs. For some products there also may be special tooling charges of substantial size.

Semivariable and fixed costs.   The question of whether to include semivariable and fixed costs in the analysis is one of the most controversial in the discussion of make or buy. Most production supervisors will insist that only direct variable (out-of-pocket) costs should be considered in any make or buy decision. Conversely, almost all the technical literature on the subject contains warnings that it may well be disastrous to ignore the fixed and semivariable costs.

The answer probably lies in the length of the time period to be covered by the make or buy analysis. A short-run make or buy decision —for example, temporary internal manufacture of the component—may very well be based on only direct variable costs. However, since semivariable and fixed overhead costs will inevitably change over the long run, they should always be included in any analysis involving the long-range manufacturing program.

For purposes of make or buy analysis, an adequate definition of short-run production may be devised on the basis of a representative allocation of direct labor standard hours. Production hours in excess of this would be considered long-run. The duration of manufacturing facilities commitment to the proposed decision may also be measured in terms of days or months of utilization. Exhibits 4 and 5 are examples of work sheets used for short and long-term analyses.

Exhibit 4 is intended for use with short-term make or buy decisions which do not require changes in basic operating policy. The direct variable costs and specific incremental costs are usually adequate for this purpose.

Exhibit 5 is for long-term make or buy decisions which require

EXHIBIT 4

Make or Buy Analysis
Short Term

Department# _____472_____
Project or Part #XP 250469
Usage Forecast _____100_____
Est. Std. Cost/Unit _____12.69_____
Date Needed _____12-1-69_____
Lot Quantity _____10_____

☐ Make   ☒ Buy
Date _____10-15-69_____
Prepared By _____C. Rai_____
Approved By _____R. Filter_____
Estimated Savings _____N/A_____
Total DLSH _____N/A_____

MAKE

Reliance
Manufactured
Unit Cost

A. DIRECT VARIABLE COSTS: Note A
    1. Material - Include Variations $ 9.70
    2. Labor - Include Variations as Needed   1.43
        a) Set-up
        b) Fringe Costs
        _____DLSH @ Rate_____
    3. Subcontract
B. OVERHEAD (INCLUDE SPECIFIC INCREMENTAL COSTS AS NEEDED)
    1. Material Handling $
    2. Indirect Labor
    3. Hourly Supervision
    4. Training (Include special skills)
    5. Overtime Premium
    6. Tooling
    7. Supplies
    8. Other Variable Costs:

        _____
        _____   1.56
        _____

                    Total Reliance Costs $ 12.69

BUY

A. VENDOR INVOICE OR QUOTATION

	Vendor	Delivery Time	Unit Cost
1.	XYZ Co.	3 weeks from order	40.00
2.			
3.			

OTHER

A. CHECK STATUS FROM ONE OF THE FOLLOWING:
    1. ☐ New Part
    2. ☐ New Part which Replaces an Existing Part
    3. ☒ Purchased Part
    4. ☐ Reliance Manufactured Part

B. WORKSHEET ATTACHED:
    ☒ Exhibit I
    ☒ Exhibit II
C. SPECIAL OR EXTRAORDINARY TOOLING
    CHARGES SHOULD BE INCLUDED
    ☒ YES   ☐ NO

COMMENTS
*Welding fixtures required will be unavailable
for 6-8 weeks. Part should be re-evaluated if
there is a larger usage forecast.*

NOTE A: Separate departmental labor hour overhead rates may be preferable to the
         use of composite rates.

EXHIBIT 5

Make or Buy Analysis
Long Term

Department# _472_
Project or Part # _XP250469_
Usage Forecast _10,000_
Est. Std. Cost/Unit _14.54_
Date Needed _12-1-69_
Lot Quantity _1000_

☒ Make   ☐ Buy
Date _10-15-69_ _Sutherland_
Prepared By _C. Roxy_
Approved By _C. Hughes_
Estimated Savings _10.46/unit_
Total DLSH _5.200_

Worksheet Attached
  Exhibit I   ☒
  Exhibit II   ☒

	Outside Purchased Unit Cost	Reliance Manufactured Unit Cost
A. DIRECT VARIABLE COSTS - NOTE A:		
1. Material - Include Variations	$ 8.00	$ 9.70
2. Labor - Include Variations		1.48
Reroute		
Shift Premium		
Set-up _3 hours / 1,000 units_	1.50	.01
Fringe Costs		
Incentive Pay		
Etc.		
3. Subcontract - _Uncertain at this time_		
B. OVERHEAD (INCLUDE SPECIFIC INCREMENTAL COSTS AS NEEDED)		
1. Material Handling		.10
2. Indirect Labor		
3. Hourly Supervision		.05
4. Training - Include Special Skills		
5. Overtime Premium		
6. Vacation and Holiday Pay		
7. Tooling _$375.00 estimated ÷ 10,000 units_		.04
8. Supplies		
9. Other variable costs:		
Overhead Rate	1.50	2.11
C. SEMI-VARIABLE AND FIXED COSTS - NOTE B:		
Storage Facilities, 1,000 ft.²	1.50	.50
@ $10.00/ft.² - 2 yrs. (Reliance only)		
Profit to Vendor	7.50	
D. OTHER COSTS AND EXPENSES - NOTE C:		
1. _Procurement, Storage, Shipping & Testing_	2.00	.20
2. Division Administration	1.00	.20
3. Division Engineering	2.00	.20
TOTALS	$ 25.00	$ 14.54
	(Note D)	

COMMENTS
1 extra person will be required - will be split
between PSST, Admin. & Engrlg.

Check Part Status From One of the Following:

1. New Part ☐   2. New Part which replaces an existing part ☐

3. Purchased Part ☒   4. Reliance Manufactured Part ☐

A. Separate departmental labor hour and overhead rates may be preferable to the use of composite rates. The divisional rate for overhead applied should be redetermined as substantial amounts of direct labor hours are absorbed in the make or buy products.
B. Semi-variable and fixed costs such as tooling, depreciation, etc. may be included for specific items.

C. These incremental and out-of-pocket costs are included only when quantities being considered are very high, e.g., 5% of total labor is eliminated by use of the purchased part.
D. Includes vendor's invoice price and adjustments for out-of-pocket non-compensating costs included in the manufactured column.

changes in operating policy. Total cost recovery should be anticipated for such an analysis.

Note: DLSH means Direct Labor Standard Hours.

Management often assumes that if there are direct labor hours available because of idle capacity, then this labor should be put to work on manufactured products. It is important to remember, however, that as substantial amounts of direct labor hours are applied to the manufacture of a product, any distribution of overhead based on such direct labor hours should be revised accordingly.

Even in short-run make or buy analysis, it is frequently desirable to determine separate departmental labor hour and overhead rates instead of using a composite rate for the company. Thus, the manufacturing costs that are calculated will correspond more closely to the costs quoted by outside vendors, and departmental overhead responsibility will be more closely defined as a result.

For the long-run make or buy decision, such additional semivariable costs as shift premiums and incentive pay should be considered as incremental costs. Other examples of incremental semivariable costs which may be incurred outside the direct production areas include:

1. The purchasing department may be more costly to operate when it has the added responsibility to buy the raw materials necessary to manufacture the new component.
2. Storage facilities required for these purchases may also be an incremental cost.
3. The engineering department is likely to incur substantial out-of-pocket costs for design changes, preparation of working drawings, and consultation and coordination with the production control department on the best methods of machine loading, routing, etc.
4. The sales department may increase its costs if the newly manufactured component is added to the product line.
5. Other administrative, cost accounting, clerical and similar incremental costs may be incurred under particular circumstances and should be evaluated for possible inclusion in the long-run analysis of comparative advantages and disadvantages.

Effect of incremental costs. Exhibit 6 indicates the effect of incremental costs on total costs at various levels of production. The fixed overhead section of costs is shown directly above the direct variable costs. In many short-run make or buy studies no attempt would be made to recover these fixed costs; only direct variable costs would be included. The problem for management is to evaluate the significance of these costs for the make or buy decision.

Total range of capacity. Exhibit 6 covers the total range of capacity for a plant facility. At the extreme lefthand side of the exhibit are the start-up costs incurred as the result of opening the doors of the new plant.

As capacity utilization approaches the normal level, the unit product costs should decline. At the extreme right hand side of the exhibit total costs begin to increase, adding substantially to the cost of producing the additional or incremental units.

The right-hand vertical margin of this exhibit represents the ultimate capacity of the existing facilities. The dotted line above and to the right of total capacity represents a shift in capacity—for example, if additional

EXHIBIT 6

Effect of Incremental Costs at All Levels of Capacity

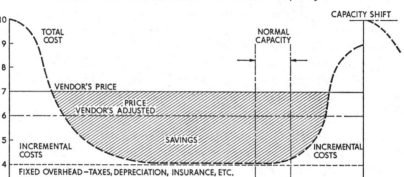

facilities were provided through renting or constructing space and adding to equipment.

The horizontal line representing the vendor's selling price (the buy option) partly outlines the cross-hatched portion of the exhibit. The cross-hatching represents the potential recovery of costs as a result of the decision to manufacture the part.

Two areas on Exhibit 6 have special significance in the make or buy evaluation. The areas from 10 to 40 percent of capacity and from 70 to 95 percent of capacity (as shown) may offer possibilities for price concessions to be negotiated from vendors as an added incentive to buy. The reason for this is that it is at these approximate points of capacity that the total management organization is especially aware of semivariable and fixed-cost budget adjustments due to volume shifts and is usually more receptive to review and revision of cost alternatives. In some instances the vendor's price will always be lower than the manufactured cost, but at these two particular levels of capacity, the purchasing department may be able to negotiate price concessions from vendors, special delivery terms, warehousing arrangements, etc. which may encourage outside purchase.

As production increases within the capabilities of the existing facilities, all variable and fixed costs must eventually be recovered through adequate pricing of the final product by the marketing department.

If short-run manufacturing cycles consume a large part of the production schedule for the manufacturing facilities, the costs incurred should probably be analyzed on a job-shop basis for total cost recovery. This type of analysis is also appropriate for a series of long production runs on manufactured parts that use a substantial portion of the direct labor hours within the limitations of the facilities.

The final point of this discussion—and one of great importance—is that an analysis prepared for a make or buy decision should never be used as the basis for the cost computations needed to increase the gross profit percentages on sales product lines, and should not be used in such a manner as to obscure the analysis of other, more complicated problems confronting management.

There is always some way to reduce product costs. The problem for those responsible for the make or buy decision is to determine which choice will save money, how much it will save, and whether the time required for the analysis is justified by the saving eventually achieved.

Bibliography

Books

CULLITON, JAMES W. *Make or Buy*, Boston: Harvard University Division of Business Research, 1961.

GROSS, HARRY. *Make or Buy*, Englewood Cliffs, N.J.: Prentice Hall, Inc., 1961.

OXENFELDT, A. R. and WATKINS, M. W. *Make or Buy*, New York: McGraw-Hill Book Co., 1956.

Periodicals

CADIZ, C. C. "Stampings—Should You Make Them or Buy Them?" *Iron Age*, (September 23, 1954), pp. 107–111.

HIGGINS, CARTER C. "Make or Buy Re-Examined," Boston: *Harvard Business Review* (March–April, 1955).

HUBLER, MYRON J., JR. "The Make or Buy Decision," *Management Services*, (AICPA-New York), Vol. 3, No. 6 (November–December, 1966), pp. 45–51.

PATON, WILLIAM A. "Make or Buy Decisions—Factors and Measurements," *Michigan Business Review*, Vol. XVIII (March, 1966), pp. 7–13.

Pricing decisions

David C. Skinner*

Pricing is the expression of the economic rationale which exists between the firm and the marketplace. This chapter will not deal with the broad philosophical and economic issues implicit in that statement. Rather it will discuss the firm's activities in establishing pricing policy, evaluating specific pricing decisions, and administering pricing policy within the firm.

Establishing pricing policy

Basic considerations

Pricing policy must be rooted in the financial objectives of a business. Price determines the revenue to be realized from the sale of a unit, and such revenue must be sufficient to compensate the firm for the resources required to produce, market, distribute, and service that unit. The pricing policy issue facing each business firm is how to determine the magnitude of that compensation. Prices may be established without regard to this basic issue (and very often are), but a price places a value on the use of company resources whether or not that price is the result of a well-considered policy.

Financial objectives

The utility of financial objectives is dependent upon the degree to which they are stated in terms which are measurable and controllable.

---

* President—Logic Resources, Inc., Los Angeles, California.

Otherwise, the company will find it difficult to apply policy to specific decisions, and to establish financial controls which embody its objectives.

The financial results of a firm's activities may be measured in a variety of ways, and so, accordingly, the firm's objectives may be stated in many forms. The single most meaningful *long term* measure is return on capital employed, or return on investment (ROI). There has been much debate on this subject, not only as to whether or not ROI is the most effective measure of financial performance, but also about the most appropriate method for calculating return on investment. It is beyond the scope of this chapter to enter such debates. (See Chapter 19, "Analysis of capital expenditures," for a discussion of ROI methodologies.) Of more significance than the debate itself is the common agreement by most participants on the importance of measures of performance.

In grossly oversimplified terms, ROI is considered to be the most effective measure of financial performance for two major reasons: First, by whatever method may be used in its calculation, ROI encompasses both the company's ability to earn a profit and its stewardship of the assets used for this purpose. These two aspects of management are inseparable in any comprehensive view of performance. Second, a business firm of any size cannot long endure without adequate capital. Without the prospect of adequate financial return for its use, capital will not be attracted to the enterprise. And where expected returns are less than can be found elsewhere under similar conditions of risk, capital will seek alternative employment.

Because price establishes the income of the firm, and income is one of the two determinants of ROI, pricing policy must be a function of the company's objective for ROI. Later it will be seen that an ROI objective will lead to the establishment of other financial objectives related to asset management.

RETURN ON INVESTMENT. The statement of an objective for ROI requires an understanding of how ROI is determined. Return on investment may be viewed in two general ways: first, the classical financial statement approach, and second, the cash flow approach. Over a period of time the two approaches are equivalent in absolute dollar terms, but the second is more amenable to decision-making for specific investments. However, both approaches are needed to determine financial objectives and policies.

Under the classical approach, ROI is calculated as follows:

1. Current assets − current liabilities = net working capital.
2. Net working capital + fixed and other assets = invested capital.
3. Invested capital ÷ net profit after tax = ROI.[1]

---

[1] Many firms prefer to calculate ROI on the basis of average invested capital. Various techniques are employed to estimate the average amount of capital invested in the business during the period in which the net profit was realized. Some firms

The financial statement approach is highly important because financial statements are a primary means of communication between those who manage the firm and those who supply capital to it; a statement of policy must ultimately be reflected in this form. The classical approach is important also because it focuses attention on the need to establish financial policies for effective asset management. Clearly, if net working capital or fixed assets can be reduced while profits are held constant, ROI will increase. This means that any ROI objective requires further explicit objectives for asset management, and these objectives may be reduced to specific financial policies which can be applied and controlled. For example, in the management of current assets:

1. Cash levels can be related to revenue levels.

2. Accounts receivable turnover can be related to revenue levels or the number of days sales outstanding.

3. Inventory turnover can be related to shipment volume.

The critical relationship between financial management policies and ROI and, therefore, pricing policy is often overlooked. Asset management can be as significant a factor in pricing policy as is profit and loss.

A brief description of return on investment under the cash flow method follows.

1. Annual cash inflows and outflows are developed for the foreseeable life of an investment.

2. The discounted cash flow rate of return, often called internal rate of return, is calculated by determining that discount factor which, when applied to the period cash flows, results in the sum of all discounted flows equal to zero. The purpose of this calculation is to determine what annual rate of return is earned by the use of funds.

3. The present value of an investment is calculated by applying a given interest factor (usually corporate ROI goals) to the cash flows and summing the adjusted flows to determine the present worth of the investment.

The internal rate of return is used to evaluate an individual investment as to whether or not it meets corporate ROI goals. The present worth approach is used to compare investment alternatives. Analysis of pricing decisions utilizes both methods.[2]

The cash flow approach to ROI has evolved in recognition of limitations inherent in the financial statement approach. The principal limitations are found in the area of evaluating investment decisions. For example, note the following.

---

calculate returns on a before tax basis. Variations such as these illustrate the point that the reduction of objectives to measurable terms may be of greater import to financial management than the specific measure used.

[2] Considerable literature describing these techniques in more detail is readily available. The *Harvard Business Review* report series entitled "Capital Investment" is particularly useful as an introduction to the subject.

1. Where a proposed new product has a long life, and where substantial investment is required in earlier years in order to produce profits in later years, a traditional statement of financial results at a given point in time during the product's life may be very misleading. The cash flow approach permits a view of the financial impact and ROI of the investment over its foreseeable life rather than at a point in time during its life.

2. The traditional financial statement approach ascribes no time value to the use and return of funds. In attempting to compare alternative uses of capital, where timing and magnitude of funds flow differ, the application of time-related interest rate factors to the flows to determine the present worth of each alternative permits comparison on equivalent economic grounds.

3. Accounting practices which underly financial statements, particularly with respect to allocations of costs and assets to products, are extremely cumbersome to apply to specific investment decisions. The cash flow approach identifies, quantifies, and evaluates the projected incremental impact of economic decisions on sources and uses of capital. The incremental aspect of the approach, when combined with the simplifications necessary in forecasting procedures, produces a logic system which is readily adaptable to computerized simulation techniques, and, hence, to decision-making. Three observations are worthy of note here. (a) The incremental aspect of the cash flow approach can lead to the dangerous conclusion that all decisions are incremental to the present size and character of the firm, with the result that no decision bears the responsibility for expanding corporate overhead. (b) Some of the major assumptions which are used in cash flow forecasts involve financial policies which may or may not apply to the specific decision under consideration. Very often, in fact, these assumptions are taken as constants rather than as variables. This observation highlights the importance of financial policy in relation to its impact on ROI and, therefore, its relevance to pricing which is a primary economic decision. (c) The pressures for rapid decision-making have, in some firms, resulted in efforts to accelerate bookkeeping practices. Such efforts, which can be enormously expensive, may provide earlier day-to-day operating information, but they should not be viewed as contributing to corporate decision-making capabilities. Corporate decisions should reflect an evaluation of the major economic and other factors which affect the future of the firm.

THE RETURN ON INVESTMENT OBJECTIVE. There is no formula by which an ROI objective may be determined. The objective can only reflect a composite of factors, chief among them being:
1. The economic characteristics and performance of the industry in which the firm competes.
2. The aspirations and goals established by top management.

3. The applicable past experience of the firm.

4. The state of the firm's financial management practices and policies.

Within this context, any ROI objective will necessarily be arbitrary. Two comments may be useful as an aid to establishing an ROI goal. One is that for long established firms the goal should exceed the past average performance of the firm. Otherwise, future performance will fall below past performance. This is so because specific investment decisions will either exceed or fall short of the goal, but the average performance should approximate the goal. Companies which have experienced rapid profit growth may not be able to adopt this rule. Their average past performance may have produced such a high ROI that it is unreasonable to expect to maintain the average, let alone raise it. Such firms must use more arbitrary guidelines for setting ROI goals for future investment decisions.

A second comment is that the ROI goal should be demanding but realistic, a criterion which applies to any worthwhile goal. It is acutely important in economic decision-making. An unrealistically high goal may cause the firm to reject investment opportunities which it should undertake to achieve long term improvement in ROI results.

OTHER FINANCIAL OBJECTIVES. During the discussion of ROI, the point was made that from an ROI objective flows considerations of other financial objectives. These further objectives may be classified as follows: asset management, financial structure, profit management, and financial growth. All of these areas are dealt with in other sections of this handbook. They are noted here, however, to reemphasize the importance of the impact of these areas upon ROI, itself the basic measure to which pricing policy must be related.

Evaluating pricing decisions

Pricing decisions are at best imperfect. Quantitative analyses can provide necessary guidelines in clarifying management options and comparing alternatives with financial objectives, but management judgment is perhaps the most essential ingredient in pricing decisions. Three areas of judgment are of principal concern in reaching pricing decisions: (1) Products competing for the same market typically have dissimilarities with respect to quality, product features, service, marketing support, advertising effectiveness, and so on. Because these product differences cannot be reduced to absolute economic values in customer terms, a specific price can only approximately incorporate such differences. This approximation requires management judgment. (2) In a competitive industry, change and technological innovations are constant threats to the economic axioms of that industry. Not only is change external to the firm of paramount importance, but changes internal to the firm may be of equal importance. A firm's own technological advances can be a major factor in pricing its present products. Management judgment in estimating the impact and timing of change is crucial to the determination of pricing. (3) Forecasting techniques can at best establish ranges of potential demand. Management must make the basic assumption as to likely demand for purposes of forecasting volume.

Pricing poses special management problems in industries, such as steel and oil, which are characterized by huge capital investment, high volume of production, and product similarity. Share of market is of prime concern to management. Companies in such industries must preserve a certain volume of production if they are to pay for their past investments and retain or attract sufficient capital for future investments. In an industrial context where production facilities, products, and methods of distribution are similar because of economic determinants, prices tend to be similar as well. Here management must apply its judgment to delicate pricing considerations, not the least of which is the Robinson-Patman Act which precludes price fixing and its varied guises. Typically, in each of these industries there are firms whose market share is larger than that of other firms in its industry. These firms tend to establish price levels and the other firms decline to follow suit at their peril, as the so-called "gasoline wars" demonstrate. Price leading firms may be hesitant to reduce prices for fear that they will be accused of using their economic power to force smaller firms to the wall. And they may be reluctant to raise prices and suffer the consequent contentions of price fixing. Under these hazardous conditions, elaborate methods of "economic temperature taking" have evolved so that these industries may respond to market dicta without running afoul of statutes. The fact that basic industries are often fair game for political pressures adds new dimensions to the difficulties their managements face in establishing economically rational prices.

The financial executive plays a major role in the preparation of quantitative analyses. He should assure his company's management that the necessary analyses are properly prepared and presented, and that issues in those areas requiring management judgment are clearly drawn. This section of the chapter will outline the conceptual approach to quantitative analyses, and discuss evaluation techniques which can be derived from that approach.

Approach to quantitative analyses

As stated earlier, pricing reflects the economic rationale which exists between the firm (or a product) and the marketplace. Quantitative analyses for pricing decisions center upon an attempt to describe this rationale in measurable financial terms. Exhibit 1 illustrates a simplified logic system which represents the interactions between the firm and the market and the linkages between that logic system and the "financial statement" and "cash flow" ROI approaches described earlier. (See Chapter 14, "Systems analysis and simulation," for a more detailed discussion of logic models and their use in simulating financial performance.)

EXHIBIT I

Framework of Quantitative Analyses

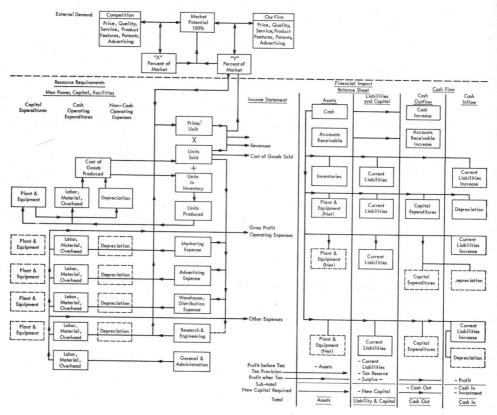

EXTERNAL DEMAND. The upper portion of Exhibit 1 diagrams external demand for a firm's product. Market research studies are used to develop an estimate of total market potential in future time periods. These estimates are imprecise and are typically expressed in ranges. Estimates of the firm's share of total market are made by comparing values of the firm's product against those of competitive products in relation to market needs. These estimates, too, are usually expressed in ranges. From these estimates a base forecast is developed under a given set of assumptions. (In many industries the forecast will be determined as much by assumed marketing and advertising expenditures as by a comparison of values.) Referring to Exhibit 1, this forecast would assume (for a particular time period) Y percent of the market, or so many units sold at some price. The resulting revenues represent a share of the total external demand and the consequent use of the firm's resources to, in fact, sell and deliver forecast units. (Share of market may not be constant for all future time periods.)

RESOURCE REQUIREMENTS. The resource requirements related to a forecast of revenues are translated into needs for manpower, facilities, and capital which can, in turn, be expressed in financial terms. The lower portion of Exhibit 1 shows the nature of resources required and their impact on the income statement, balance sheet, and cash flow. The exhibit does not show the timing relationship among these various elements. For example, perhaps a plant must be constructed and equipped before the product can be manufactured and shipped. The logic format provides a means for structuring such relationships over several time periods.

RESOURCE INTERACTIONS. The lower part of the diagram in Exhibit 1 suggests the interplay of demand among functional areas. For example, the number of units to be sold in a given time period has a direct relation to units to be produced, marketing and advertising expenses, and so on. Thus, units to be sold has a direct relation to costs and investment for a given level of production. On the other hand, while production capacity may be able to support a unit sales forecast which is based upon market potential, the marketing organization may not be able to hire and train sufficient sales and service personnel to meet that sales forecast. In this case, it may be necessary to reduce assumed production, with concurrent temporary increases in selling prices and unit costs (and reduction in market shares). This kind of dynamic interplay between functional areas in response to the resource requirements of a given forecast is clearly of utmost importance in establishing prices. The diagram in Exhibit 1 barely suggests the nature and complexity of such interplays.[3]

The major point is that the financial results of any specific price can be determined only through the development of a sales forecast, and the subsequent derivation of the costs and investment which relate to that forecast. In the determination of the cost and investment implications of a sales forecast, the impact on financial management is illustrated by the diagram. For example, units produced differs from units sold by the units required for inventory. Thus, inventory policies and management (themselves dependent upon the efficiency of warehousing and distribution systems) can significantly affect unit costs as well as investment in

---

[3] Jay Forrester's book, *Industrial Dynamics* (Cambridge, Mass.: M.I.T. Press, 1961), deals in depth with resource interactions as a function of demand levels.

inventory. Similarly, company policies with respect to collection of accounts receivable and payment of invoices (current liabilities) will affect the investment required to finance a given level of sales.

Evaluation techniques

The financial executive should address three aspects of quantitative analyses of pricing proposals in meeting his responsibilities to management: (1) the forecast itself should be thoroughly documented so that management can understand the reliability of the basic forecast; (2) the resource requirements and interactions should be a realistic reflection of the forecast, both as to amount and timing; and (3) the financial results of the analyses should be presented in a manner which permits management to understand them readily, as well as to examine possible alternatives.

The first aspect is primarily a matter of reviewing market research logic, the methods of calculation used, and the applicability of conclusions. The second aspect is concerned with determining that all necessary elements related to the product forecast are present and properly accounted for. The third aspect will be the subject of further scrutiny and discussion below.

BASIC FINANCIAL RESULTS. Every company's management has its particular requirements in the format it uses for presentation of financial results. While formats may vary, the essential information requirements are detailed in Exhibit 2. Those items shown under "Basic financial results" will give management a quick picture of whether or not the ROI objective is met, what the impact on earnings will be, what capital requirements and exposure is implied, and what are the major underlying financial assumptions. The use of high and low forecasts can also be helpful in establishing limits of risk and performance. But even these forecasts represent only three possible sets of conditions. Management will want to know what factors have the greatest impact on financial results, and what might happen if one or more of these factors could be altered in some way.

ANALYTICAL PRESENTATIONS. Exhibit 2 lists two types of analyses which should be presented to management for their review of pricing decisions. Many others could be added, but these are the analyses which permit examination of management options. It should be noted that the presentations suggested here have applications beyond pricing decisions alone, such as evaluations of new product proposals.

1. *Sensitivity Analysis.* In their evaluation of a pricing proposal, management will want to know what happens to the financial outlook if prices are raised or lowered from the assumption used in the base

EXHIBIT 2

Presentation of Analyses

I. Basic financial results

ITEMS TO BE PRESENTED

a. Summary *(total forecast life)*		*b. Details by Period* *(total forecast life)*
Total revenues	$26,000	Income statement (Exhibit 4)
Total profits	$ 1,375	—Earnings per share
ROI *(DCF)*	14.5%	Cash flow (Exhibit 5)
Maximum cash outflow		Summary of Major Assumptions
—Amount	$ 1,730	(Exhibit 6)
—Year	Year 3	—Price/unit
Cash flow breakeven year	Year 6	—Units sold
Present value @		—Unit cost
10%	$ 275	—Expense items
20%	$ (283)	—Working capital
		—Working capital

a. All items to be shown for base forecast and for high and low forecast.
   (Data used are from base case, Exhibits 4 and 5.)
b. All items to be shown for base forecast. Optional for other forecasts.

II. Analytical presentations
   a. Sensitivity analysis—Show impact on ROI of changes in major vari-
      ables.
   b. Trade-off analysis—Determine alternative combinations of two non-
      interacting variables yielding equivalent results.

forecast. They will also want to know the relative significance of price
and other major variables to overall profitability. Through sensitivity
analyses, management can gain some additional insights not provided by
more traditional presentations.

Exhibit 3 contains a table illustrating the results of a sensitivity
analysis. The table is based upon a hypothetical financial forecast, the
essentials of which are found in Exhibits 4–6. Sensitivity analyses are
prepared by changing the value of a major variable plus or minus the
assumed value in the base forecast, and recalculating the ROI using the
new value. For example, if price per unit increased 10 percent over the
base case assumption (from $10 to $11) the ROI for the program would
be 24.5 percent. From Exhibit 3 it can be seen that ROI is relatively
insensitive to changes in some variables (marketing, engineering), and
very sensitive to changes in others (price/unit, cost/unit). These results
are displayed also in graphic form, and the slope of the curves for each
variable visually indicates sensitivity.

For the sake of simplicity, the calculations assume that values for one
variable are changed without affecting other assumptions, that is, variables are taken to be independent. Clearly, such would not be the case in
real life, e.g., changes in unit price would have an effect on the number
of units sold, and upon cost per unit. Through use of computerized logic
models, which utilize detailed interdependent values, a complete simula-

EXHIBIT 3

Sensitivity Analysis

(return on investment @
percentage change in variable)

Major Variable	−20%	−10%	Base Case -0-%	+10%	+20%
Price/unit	Neg.	3.3	14.5	24.5	34.5
Units sold	5.7	10.0	14.5	18.1	22.0
Unit cost	27.1	20.6	14.5	7.6	0.9
Marketing expense	19.2	16.7	14.5	11.6	9.2
Engineering expense	16.9	15.5	14.5	12.9	11.6

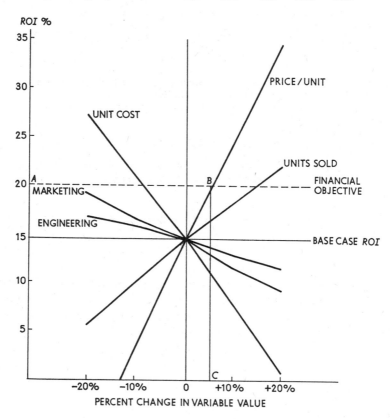

tion of the effect of changed variables can be made. The development of such detailed models and values requires enormous effort, both to establish and to maintain the logic system and the necessary data bank. In the absence of such a powerful (and expensive) tool, the more simplified approach used here can still be of great value.

Assuming an objective of 20 percent ROI, management could draw the following preliminary conclusions from the sensitivity analysis:

a) A minor change in price would have a dramatic effect on profitability,

EXHIBIT 4

Hypothetical Financial Projection
(income statement—base case)

$(000)

	YEAR IN PROJECT LIFE							Total Project
	1	2	3	4	5	6	7	
Revenues	-	2000	4000	6000	6000	5000	3000	26000
Cost of Sales	-	800	1600	2400	2400	2000	1200	10400
Gross Profit	-	1200	2400	3600	3600	3000	1800	15600
Operating Expenses:								
Marketing	100	500	800	1100	1000	750	500	4750
Advertising	250	500	500	500	500	500	300	3050
Warehouse & Distribution	50	250	400	550	550	450	300	2550
Total Operating Expenses	400	1250	1700	2150	2050	1700	1100	10350
Operating Profit (Loss)	(400)	(50)	700	1450	1550	1300	700	5250
Other Expenses:								
Engineering	1000	300	200	200	100	50	-0-	1850
Other	50	100	100	100	100	100	100	650
Total Other	1050	400	300	300	200	150	100	2500
Profit before Tax	(1450)	(450)	400	1150	1350	1150	600	2750
Tax @ 50%	(725)	(225)	200	575	675	575	300	1375
Profit after Tax	(725)	(225)	200	575	675	575	300	1375
# Shares Outstanding (000)	10000	10000	10000	10000	10000	10000	10000	10000
Earnings/Share	$(0.073)	$(0.023)	$0.020	$0.058	$0.068	$0.058	$0.030	$0.138

EXHIBIT 5

Hypothetical Financial Projection
(cash flow statement—base case)

$(000)

	YEAR IN PROJECT LIFE								Total
	1	2	3	4	5	6	7	8	
Cash Outflows:									
Capital Expenditures	200	300	60	60	-	-	-	-	620
Increase in Working Capital:									
Inventory	80	80	80	-0-	(40)	(80)	(120)	-0-	-0-
Other	-0-	200	200	200	-0-	(100)	(200)	(300)	-0-
Total Cash Outflows	280	580	340	260	(40)	(180)	(320)	(300)	620
Cash Inflows:									
Profit after Tax	(725)	(225)	200	575	675	575	300	-0-	1375
Depreciation	-	100	120	140	140	120	-0-	-0-	620
Total Cash Inflows	(725)	(125)	320	715	815	695	300	-0-	1995
Net Cash Flows:									
Annual	(1005)	(705)	(20)	455	855	875	620	300	
Cumulative	(1005)	(1710)	(1730)	(1275)	(420)	455	1075	1375	1375
ROI = 14.5%									
Present value at									
10%	275								
20%	-283								

e.g., a 5 percent increase in price/unit would increase ROI from 14.5 percent to 20.0 percent (*A, B, C*).

b) Profitability is sensitive also to unit costs and to units sold.

c) Profitability is relatively insensitive to engineering expense.

2. *Trade-off analysis.* The sensitivity analysis focuses management attention on price/unit, unit cost, and units sold as the key variables which affect program profitability. That conclusion suggests other questions, such as: If prices were raised (lowered), how many fewer (more) units would have to be sold to result in the same (higher, lower) program economic value? Because profitability is sensitive to unit costs

EXHIBIT 6

Hypothetical Financial Projection
(summary of major assumptions—base case)

	YEAR IN PROJECT LIFE						
	1	2	3	4	5	6	7
Revenue							
Price/Unit	–	$10	$10	$10	$10	$10	$10
Units Sold (000)	–	200	400	600	600	500	300
Cost and Expense							
Cost/Unit	–	$4	$4	$4	$4	$4	$4
Marketing – % of Rev.		25%	20%	17%	17%	15%	17%
Advertising – % of Rev.		25%	13%	8%	8%	10%	10%
Warehousing & Dist. – % of Rev.		13%	10%	9%	9%	11%	10%
Engineering – $(000)	1000	300	200	200	100	50	–
Working Capital							
Inventory	10% of succeeding year's cost of sales						
Other	10% of present year's revenue						
Capital Expenditures (000)							
Assembly Line #1	$200	$50	$30	$30			
Assembly Line #2	–	$250	$30	$30			

Note: All assumptions shown are for illustration only. They would all require documented substantiation. Price/unit and cost/unit assumptions would normally vary from period to period, reflecting competition, learning curves, etc. Some expenses are shown as "% of revenue"—there may be more meaningful ways of summarizing these assumptions. In large scale programs other assumptions, such as space and personnel, would be summarized.

and insensitive to engineering expenses, would it make sense to invest more in engineering to reduce unit costs—and if so, how much more? These questions are typical subjects for trade-off analysis.

Trade-off analysis differs from sensitivity analysis in that it simulates the economic effect of several combinations of two variables. For example, the first question above is one of exploring the possible consequences of changes in price. The sensitivity analysis showed that ROI could be increased very significantly by raising prices, or increased significantly by selling more units at the assumed price. In trade-off analysis, profitability under various combinations of price/unit and units sold is deter-

EXHIBIT 7

Trade-Off Analysis
(constant present value dollars at various discount rates)
(price/unit vs. units sold)

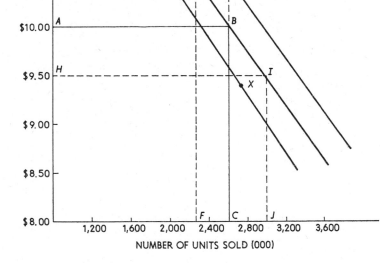

mined. These combinations can then be compared with market research elasticity of demand studies to see whether prices should be raised or lowered.

Exhibit 7 contains an example of a trade-off analysis between price-/unit and units sold. The example is based upon the hypothetical financial projection used previously. The exhibit's three diagonal lines represent constant present value dollars at the indicated discount rate. Any combination of price/unit and units sold which falls on a line will result in the return indicated by the line. The base case combination of $10 per unit selling price and 2,600,000 units (A, B, C) falls on the 14.5 percent return line. The 10.0 percent and 20.0 percent lines are constructed to aid in the evaluation of other combinations.

With this tool, management can begin to review alternatives. For example, *D, E, F* represents a combination of selling price ($10.50) and units sold (2,260,000) which would result in a 14.5 percent ROI, the same as the base case. The conclusion to be drawn is that if selling price can be raised from $10.00/unit to $10.50/unit (a 5 percent increase), units sold would have to fall below 2,260,000 (a 13 percent decrease)

EXHIBIT 8

Trade-Off Analysis

(present values under various discounts)

Discounts Assumptions	Present Values—$(000) 10.0%	14.5%	20.0%
Base case	275	−20*	−283
Unit prices			
$9.00 (−10%)	−432	−624	−788
$9.50 (−5%)	−78	−322	−535
$10.00 (base case)	275	−20*	−283
$10.50 (+5%)	628	282	−31
$11.00 (+10%)	982	584	222
$11.50 (+15%)	1,335	886	474
$12.00 (+20%)	1,688	1,188	727
Units sold (000)			
2,080 (−20%)	−276	−486	−667
2,210 (−15%)	−138	−369	−571
2,340 (−10%)	–0–	−253	−475
2,470 (−5%)	137	−137	−379
2,600 (base case)	275	−20*	−283
2,730 (+5%)	413	96	−187
2,860 (+10%)	551	213	−91
2,990 (+15%)	688	329	5
3,120 (+20%)	826	446	101

* Theoretically should be 0; rounding error.

before program profitability was reduced from the base case. Market research and management judgment can be applied to estimate the likelihood of a 13 percent decline in units sold at a 5 percent price increase. Clearly, if it is probable that units sold would decline by less than 13 percent, program profitability would be improved. (This statement is not absolutely true, because unit cost would increase slightly as units sold declined. There could, however, be offsetting reductions in marketing and warehousing expenses. Trade-off analyses are not designed for that precise a level of analysis; rather they point to tentative conclusions which can be confirmed by more detailed analysis.)

Returning to Exhibit 7, if at a price of $10.50 units sold were to remain the same as assumed in the base case (*D, G, C*), program ROI would rise to 20.0 percent. (Note that this is the same result that was derived in Exhibit 3.) If, to take another example (*H, I, J*), unit price were to be reduced by 5 percent to $9.50/unit, units sold would have to increase by 15 percent to 3,000,000 units in order to achieve a 14.5 percent ROI. Again, market research can assist by estimating the elasticity of demand in order to determine the likelihood of achieving a 15 percent increase in volume at a $9.50 price.

These examples demonstrate the use of trade-off analysis by manage-

EXHIBIT 9

Trade-Off Analysis
(unit price @ various discount rates vs. $ present value)

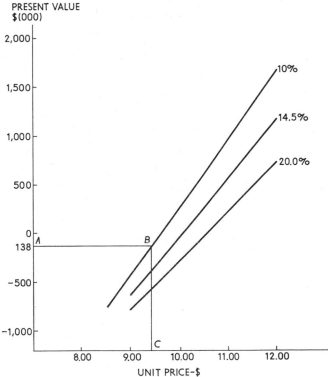

ment to explore potentials for improving program profitability (as well as potential risks). The same approach would apply to other trade-offs, such as the engineering vs. unit cost question raised earlier. A graph developed for that particular analysis would show management the reduction in unit cost required to offset a given increase in engineering expense. The engineering people could then estimate the likelihood of achieving that cost reduction within the required spending limits.

Exhibit 7 was developed from Exhibits 8, 9, and 10. In Exhibit 8, present value dollars are developed under various assumptions. In Exhibit 9, one of the two variables (in this case, unit price) is charted to develop a curve of present value dollars for any assumed value of unit price. In

Exhibit 10, present value equivalents are determined and the applicable combinations of price/unit and units sold are derived (see example in Exhibit 10). The values from Exhibit 10 are then charted in Exhibit 7 (point X represents the plot for the example used in Exhibit 10).

There are many refinements to trade-off analyses which are possible, and quite practical, given the proper logic models and data. One obvious refinement is the extension of trade-offs to more than two variables. A second useful refinement is the development of minimum revenue curves

EXHIBIT 10

Trade-Off Analysis
(present value equivalents)
Derived price/unit

Discounts	10.0%		14.5%		20.0%	
Assumptions Units sold (000)	$PV	Price	$PV	Price	$PV	Price
2,080	551	10.40	466	10.80	384	11.30
2,210	413	10.20	349	10.60	288	11.10
2,340	275	10.00	233	10.45	192	10.90
2,470	138	9.80	117	10.25	96	10.75
2,600 (base case)	–0–	9.60	–0–	10.00	–0–	10.50
2,730*	−138	9.40*	−116	9.85	−96	10.35
2,860	−276	9.20	−233	9.70	−192	10.15
2,990	−413	9.00	−359	9.50	−288	10.00
3,120	−551	8.80	−466	9.30	−384	9.80

```
   * Example:
    1. Base case $PV @ 10.0% (Exhibit 8)             $ 275,000
   2,730,000 units sold $PV @ 10.0% (Exhibit 8)        413,000
   Price/unit $PV @ 10.0%                            $(138,000)
      2. Price/unit @ $(138,000)—A,B,C in Exhibit 9    $  9.40
```

for a given volume of units sold. Examples will not be given here, but their existence is noted for the benefit of those to whom such analyses appeal.

CONCLUSION. The two examples of special analyses given here are intended to be illustrative of the techniques which can be developed as part of a company's approach to quantitative analyses. As observed earlier, pricing decisions require a large injection of management judgments. Analytical techniques such as these can assist management by providing better means for the application of those judgments.

Administering pricing policy

The importance of pricing policies and decisions to the economic success of a company cannot be overstated. The importance of pricing should accord it the necessary organizational stature it deserves. Many companies have top level pricing committees which review all present or proposed prices. It is not unusual for the chief executive officer to reserve to himself all pricing decisions.

The financial executive bears a major responsibility in the administration of pricing. Not only does he prepare quantitative analyses and, usually, participate in pricing decisions; he bears also the responsibility for monitoring and updating the financial assumptions used, for assuring proper methodology in preparing financial analyses, and for continually reviewing the financial objectives of the firm.

Whatever measures may be used for fulfilling these responsibilities, their success will be ultimately dependent upon the ability of the financial executive to make certain that corporate financial objectives are expressed in measurable terms, and that assumptions used in quantitative analyses are explicit and translated into financial terms which can be reviewed in the light of operating experience.

Analyzing product-line profitability

John E. Crossen*

One of the strengths of American businessmen is their presumption that no matter how large or profitable their present enterprise may be it can always be larger and more profitable in the future. The manager is constantly seeking to discover actions which he may take to bring improvements designed to ensure the growth and vitality of the organization. Sometimes he is motivated by his knowledge of the achievements of his competitors, sometimes he becomes explicitly aware of deficiencies in the performance of his organization or products, and sometimes he simply has a compulsion to lead his organization to greater heights of performance. But no matter how he is motivated he will need to consider alternative approaches to achieving his objectives. In considering his possible courses of action he will, among other things, wish to analyze product-line profitability.

Defining the line

Since it is possible to group items into product lines in different combinations, the manager will need to decide which grouping will suit his purposes best. In a consumer business the nature of the delegation of profit responsibility may well determine the grouping of products into product lines for profit and loss statement purposes. A product-marketing manager often has some degree of indirect profit responsibility for a group of related items which can be grouped into a product line for the preparation of profit and loss statements.

* Senior Vice President-Latin America and Pacific, H. J. Heinz Company, Pittsburgh.

There are other bases for grouping items into product lines. Items which compete rather directly with one another for the consumer dollar may be grouped into product lines. Items which largely utilize the same production facilities may also be grouped into product lines for profitability statement purposes.

The common thread in these groupings is usually a desire on the part of top management to have some basis for planning and controlling the activities of their subordinates by measuring profit performance.

Preparation of profit and loss statements

Accounting conventions

Profit and loss statements for the line will normally be prepared by accountants who have been trained in certain accounting conventions which affect the compilation of the data and its usefulness to the manager.

For example, it is common practice to prepare product-line statements for specific time periods, i.e., months, quarters, or years. The beginning and ending dates which determine these periods have been chosen in accordance with accounting conventions. However, a business ordinarily does not start and stop with the calendar. Rather it is a continuing stream of events. Sales, shipments, and costs go on more or less continuously although this is not always the case. Most accountants are familiar with last minute rushes of orders and shipments to achieve budgets which cover artificially established accounting periods.

Organizational structures and accounting practices are changing over more extended time periods. The "sales accounting" department is an example of an organizational component which could be called selling expense at one point in time and financial or general and administrative expense at another time. Since these two types of expense may be allocated to product lines on different bases, a product line's profitability might be altered by the change in organizational structure without any change in the quantity or quality of the service performed for the product.

A change in depreciation policy from an accelerated basis to a straight line basis may materially affect trends in product-line profitability even though there has been no change in the product or its manufacturing facilities.

Variable and fixed elements

It is highly desirable that product-line profit statements contain a breakdown of those costs that vary most directly with volume, those expenses which can be most accurately assigned to the line, and those costs and expenses which are generally allocated on some indirect basis.

Such a statement might have the following captions:

Unit Volume
Net Sales
Less: Variable Manufacturing Costs
   (accurately assigned costs)
    Variable Gross Profit
Less: Direct Marketing Expenses
   (accurately assigned expenses)
    Contribution Margin
Less: Manufacturing Overhead (allocated)
   Indirect Marketing Expense (allocated)
   General and Administrative Expense (allocated)
    Profit Before Taxes

Thoughtful use of profit and loss statements

Caution should be exercised in the use of such statements. Captions such as Variable Manufacturing Costs and Manufacturing Overhead do not necessarily contain completely homogeneous costs. There are also overlaps and gray areas surrounding these classifications of costs and expenses. For example, electricity may be a variable manufacturing cost in an electrolytic plating process and a manufacturing overhead cost when it furnishes illumination in the same factory.

Thoughtful accountants are well aware of the limitations of their systems for recording accounting data and allocating costs among functions of the business or among products. However, many managers are misled by the apparent precision and definiteness of nicely arrayed numerical series. It is up to the accountants to educate their managements in the proper use of accounting statements however difficult a task this may be.

When approaching the analysis of profit and loss statements for product lines it is almost self-evident that the analyst must be aware of the accounting conventions which guided the preparation of the statements. Indeed, from time to time he may wish to adjust the published figures to avoid inconsistencies and resulting erroneous inferences. In the example of the change in depreciation policy cited above, the analyst may adjust published profit data so that depreciation is recorded on a common basis across several historical periods. The amount of this adjustment and other similar adjustments will be clearly stated.

Understanding management thinking

Good financial analysis involves the knowledge of managerial approaches to improving business profitability over an extended time period. This may involve short-term reductions in profitability because this action is expected to produce longer term profit improvements not thought to be available in other ways. Managements are always under pressure to produce immediate profits and at the same time make a large enough investment in the business to assure future growth. The best managers achieve an optimum balance between these two pressures.

But equally important, the best managers are prepared to evaluate their proposed actions as they affect the profitability of the whole line or enterprise. For example, the addition of a larger size package of a consumer item which is priced for economy to the consumer may result in a lower gross margin per unit of product to the manufacturer than the smaller size he presently markets. It is highly likely that some of the volume sold in the new large size will come from present consumers of the smaller size because of the economics involved. The critical question then becomes a judgment of how much volume results from the introduction of the new larger size and how much of that volume will come from former users of the smaller size. The capable manager will consider this proposed action in the light of its overall profit impact and ideally will seek to quantify the incremental volume he expects to attain by the introduction of the new size. A financial analyst may participate in this financial analysis of product-line profitability, but the judgment as to the amount of incremental volume is the responsibility of line management. At some point in time the line management will be accountable for the attainment of the new volume objective.

Profitability analysis

How to begin

The analysis may begin in a number of ways. For example, variations from a previous financial plan may suggest specific areas for inquiry. Similarly, trends in financial data over some historical period may also suggest the need to investigate particular aspects of the business.

The analysis of product-line profitability may also begin with the consideration of job performance by an employee. One salesman may be making more sales than another, there may be evidence that raw-material shrinkages in the factory are too high, or maybe the buyer appears to be paying too much for the material content of the products. A difficult judgment may be involved here because of the lack of truly dependable standards of performance and because of the intricate and complex relationships among the functions of a modern business organization. An engineer may design a product and its specifications in such a way as to affect adversely the performance of salesmen, factory managers, and buyers.

The heart of the matter

It is the job of the analyst to attempt to discern some pattern or order or some cause- and effect-relationships among a large number of variables on which he may have more or less reliable data. Not only is some of the data often of doubtful reliability, but it frequently does not fit together geographically, in exact time periods, or even in agreement of what quantity has or has not been moved through distribution channels to the consumer. In spite of these difficulties, the analyst will need to consider the impact of a number of these variables on the product-line profitability.

For example, the analyst will evaluate trends in the total market for his product line, i.e., the sum of his own and competitive volume trends. The performance of the total market will be particularly important if his own company's product line dominates the market and is following a marketing strategy designed primarily to increase total market growth. In short, the analyst may be seeking to discover whether the marketing strategy which has been adopted by the management is accomplishing its objectives. Ideally these objectives will have been quantified as carefully as possible.

It is highly unlikely that the first analysis will discover a simple cause-and-effect relationship between the company's marketing strategy and its volume or profit results. Thus, the analyst will need to consider the impact of a number of other variables and their relationships to one another. Among these are the observable—and hopefully measurable—actions taken by competitors; the competence with which the marketing strategy adopted has been implemented; the quality and performance of the product itself; the performance of various components of the distribution network; changes in consumer using habits; and the impact of indirect competitors operating in peripheral product lines. Indeed, the number of variables considered is limited only by the ingenuity and creativeness of the analyst. Not only must the analyst attempt to discover the interrelationships among these variables in the past, but he must also attempt to predict which of them will be important factors in planning for future actions to achieve improved product-line profitability.

Usually the analyst will be able to formulate some hypothesis to connect physical volume and the various events which had any influence in bringing about that volume.

Volume effects on profitability

As a matter of interest, in a consumer business invoiced factory shipment data is likely to be the most reliable data available to the analyst. This information is usually available in a wide variety of classifications systems—such as by item, by sizes, by method of shipment, by geographical segments, and the like. However, it might be worthwhile to note that the matter of physical volume is not necessarily as simple a subject as may appear on the surface. For example, what should be the unit of physical volume common to a line of items? A line of six different cold cereals might be marketed in packages of varying net weights for the same item, and another range of net weights for another item of the line, and so on across the line. For various reasons, such as retail pricing practices and serving sizes, these package weights probably will not be related to one another in any systematic way. Yet all of them probably compete with one another for consumer attention and it is important for the marketer to be able to know how much of his line is being consumed. In the cereal industry the common unit is ten pounds of cereal. This unit of cereal volume has been used for many years although the number of consumer servings from ten pounds of cereal has changed materially over the years as changes have occurred in such things as the density of breakfast cereals. There have also been significant changes in the retail price paid per pound of cereal. It may be seen that there are problems in the establishment and maintenance of common units of physical volume, even for a product seemingly as uniform as cold breakfast cereal.

In the previous paragraph the point was made that there are difficulties in establishing a common unit of volume for the items of a line of products. One approach to this problem is to use dollar sales as the common unit. Unfortunately, because the different items of the line frequently have different per unit selling prices, this does not give a wholly satisfactory answer to the need to know what quantity of product has been sold.

The "mix" problem

The cost of an item in a line is not necessarily the same percentage of the selling price as the cost of another item in the same line is to its selling price. To analyze this factor the sales can be classified by item, in dollars. Then the costs associated with each item may be deducted from the sales figures. The resulting profit, by item, then becomes an analytical tool for comparison with history, financial budgets, or desired future results. It will be readily apparent when the profitability of the line has been affected by changes in proportion of sales achieved by each item of the line. This variation is frequently called a "mix" variation.

A similar approach may be taken for varying sizes or models of the same item. It should be borne in mind, however, that the more refined the analysis, the more likely that the spread of costs among the components contains questionable assignments of costs.

Variable costs

The disclosure of variable manufacturing costs and associated unit volume under most conditions will make it possible to calculate the variable gross profit effect of volume changes. A safe close approximation may be made when the volume variations are a small proportion of the total. But variable gross profit calculations resulting from halving or doubling volumes can be misleading. This situation arises in some industries because so-called direct labor costs may not vary in direct proportion to changes in the volume of production when large volume changes are involved. Small volume changes may not be significant, but when the volume changes are large it may very well be a different matter. It may not be possible to reduce crew sizes on a packing line by half even though volume is cut in half, because there must always be a certain minimum number of operators on the line. There are other manufacturing costs commonly classified as variable which behave in a similar fashion to that described for labor. For example, raw material costs may contain some wastage resulting from startup and shutdown procedures, and these are not likely to vary with volume. When volume changes are small this fact is not significant, but when volume changes are large raw material costs may be significantly misstated if treated as strictly variable.

Moreover, there are occasions when even a small variation in volume may not give rise to an exactly proportionate increase in variable gross profit. If the base volume is close to the maximum capability of the labor force, a small increment of volume may require a whole new crew of employees, thereby altering the volume-profit relationship shown in the statement.

Up-to-date cost accounting practices recognize the existence of step-costs or semivariable costs such as those described in the previous paragraph. These costs may not be disclosed formally on profit and loss statements, but the financial analyst will be aware of them and make allowance for them in his analyses.

Nonvariable costs and expenses

The class of costs commonly called nonvariable frequently does, in fact, vary with volume in absolute terms even though by definition it should not. As in the case of the variable costs, the determination must be made in view of the size of the volume change and the portion of the volume spectrum where the change occurs. Factory supervision might be an example of this kind of variability. A change in volume may require another operating shift with the need for a whole new supervisory staff and possibly additional clerical personnel as well. Once again the analyst will be aware of this possibility and adjust his calculations to the purpose of the analysis.

General Administrative Expenses, as well as Indirect Marketing Expenses—such as those for a sales force handling several lines—are often considered to be nonvariable expenses. Up to a point there is validity to this approach, but there will come a time when additional volume causes added expenses in these categories. Another payroll clerk may be needed or additional salesmen may be required. Cost changes in these categories of expenses are difficult to tie down to specific volume changes unless there are dramatic variations in the volume. In analyzing product-line profitability, these types of expense variations tend to become visible over longer time periods. The analyst should look for them and attempt to estimate their impact on future periods.

In summary, whether an analyst is examining past product-line profitability or assisting in evaluating future plans, he will be aware that variable costs per unit sometimes do change and that nonvariable costs or expenses per unit may not behave in accordance with theoretical definitions. He will then make due allowances in his profit analyses.

Selling price analysis

In many businesses, selling prices are related to the method of shipment of the merchandise or to the size of the order or to both. Thus a shipment by rail may be priced lower than the same size shipment by truck, or the unit prices in a large order may be lower than those for a smaller order. It is common for the price differential to be of a different magnitude than the cost differential for the same shipment. When this is true, a shift in the distribution pattern or mode of shipment may affect profits materially. This may be discovered by analysis, but the accuracy of the evaluation may be impaired by the difficulty of coping with the many details involved and the lack of precise cost variations relating to the variations in the handling of the product. This is a particularly difficult problem where transportation rates are a compound of in-transit rates extending from a raw-material origin point through to finished goods delivered to a consuming point. It is also difficult where the transportation rate involves both cubic utilization of the transportation vehicle and weights of product shipped. For example, the freight cost for a rail car of product may be determined by the combined freight classifications of a high-density-per-cubic-foot low unit volume product and a low-density-per-cubic-foot high unit volume product. This type of rate structure may occur in many combinations. But even if it is difficult to sort out these problems, it may be financially rewarding to do so.

Setting selling prices is essentially a matter of competitive strategy. One seller may elect to maintain list selling prices as high as possible on an overall basis and compete on a geographically selective basis through deals and allowances. Another seller may elect to set selling prices at a somewhat lower level and compete by product design, product differentiation, or merchandising activities. In either case, alterations may be made to selling prices from time to time in order to optimize the volume/selling price/marketing expense/profit combination. The analyst should be aware of the nature of the strategy adopted by the management in order to predict its effect and analyze the results.

Analyzing terms of sale

Occasionally changes in such things as cash discount terms are used competitively. In these cases the analyst will attempt to estimate the less obvious costs resulting from these tactics. As an example, a lengthening of the period in which the buyer is permitted to pay for his purchases and still take a cash discount will probably require more cash and result in an interest expense penalty. This may be set alongside the profit impact of incremental volume expected from the change in selling terms.

Changing the number of items in the line

Changing the line by the addition or deletion of an item creates additional problems for the financial analyst. The volume effect of the addition of an item or the deletion of an item may well be more noticeable and important to the business than a similar change in volume for a continuing line of items. Moreover, predicting the impact of such a change on the competitive or consumer climate is likely to be more difficult. Yet the potential rewards for taking these actions are often great enough to stimulate managements to add or drop items.

Managements may elect to add an item to a line for offensive or defensive reasons. Each of these reasons involves its own set of profitability analysis problems.

On the offensive side, the management will be seeking by its action to produce incremental revenues greater than incremental costs. This may mean that an item would be added to the line of one marketer and not to the line of his competitor. This might happen even though both the lines of products were otherwise quite similar.

As an example, the following management considerations might occur to a marketer of a line of cold breakfast cereals. First, he might examine his own line and those of his competitors in comparison to his assessment of the consumer needs which already exist for cereals, or in comparison to his judgment as to whether he could create a consumer need by a product development and/or a marketing program. In doing this he might conclude, through the use of research techniques or out of his own judgment or both, that there is a market segment whose needs are not being served with the cereals presently available and that this market segment is large enough or can be made large enough to justify the product development, marketing costs, and risks involved. Since there is presumably a limit to the total quantity of cold cereals which will be consumed in a given period, the marketer faces one crucial question. That question is—Where will the volume of his new cereal item come from? What combination of total market growth, loss of volume from his own present cereal line, or loss of volume from competitive cereal lines, will add up to the volume achieved by his new item? The origin of "stolen" volume may well be related to the degree of similarity between the new item and his own present line, or the new item and the competitive lines. The best management will insist that these matters be examined even if only with hypothetical figures. A thorough discussion of this marketing and profit question is beyond the scope of this section, but from this discussion it will be apparent that an identical new cereal item might be judged to be a worthwhile addition to the line of one competitor and not to that of another.

The selling price/cost of manufacturing/marketing expense relationships for the new item versus the rest of the line may also be a factor. The marketer of the cold cereals in the example above might be willing to take the same or even lower volume for his whole line after the addition of the item as compared to a line without the new item. This strategy might be adopted if the resulting profits were predicted to grow more rapidly in the short term by the addition of the item than otherwise. This strategy is not likely to be a desirable one over extended time periods in a consumer goods business because erosion of share of market may well lead in the long run to loss of strength with the consumer and a steady long-term volume decline. It might be a more viable strategy for a manufacturer of scientific laboratory equipment, for example, where there is less opportunity for repeat business with the same customer or at least where purchases are more widely spaced in time.

If one's competitor chooses to add a new item to his line, a marketing judgment similar to that required in an offensive maneuver might be required. That is, where will the volume of the new item come from and what will be the profit consequences over an extended time period? In this instance, however, the defending competitor may be compelled to add an item to his own line as quickly as possible in order to minimize the volume and profit loss on his own line. In this case he is seeking to maintain his profits rather than increase them, especially in the short term. In the longer term, this strategy may even increase his profits. For example, the vigorous product and marketing competition induced by the addition of similar items in the lines of different competitors may accelerate the growth of the total market to the benefit of all competitors in that category.

Obviously there are some special costs involved in the development of the new items to be added to the line. These might arise from such activities as product design, market research, technical research, and start-up costs. Sometimes these development costs may be capitalized and written off over a period of years, thus minimizing their profit impact in any given year. More conservative accounting treatment would result in taking the expense when it is incurred, and this might result in larger amounts being charged to profits before the new item made any significant profit contribution.

Either accounting treatment results in some charges against current profitability and automatically raises the question as to method of charging against current product lines. It could be argued that, since the new items will be added to a line, any costs incurred should be borne by that line. It could also be argued that, if the development group is organizationally outside the line management structure of the current line, the costs should not be charged to the current line. It would seem that this decision should be based more on facilitating management planning and control activities than on purely accounting considerations.

When an item is dropped from a line, the business loses the variable gross profit earned by the item with the result that the remaining items will have to absorb any overhead formerly carried by the dropped item. As a matter of fact, one of the principal criteria for dropping an item might be stated in terms of the overhead absorbed. That is, the item should be dropped if its contribution to overhead absorption is low. On occasion, dropping an item from a line may present opportunities for a reduction of overhead expense. It takes persistent effort to ferret out these opportunities and capitalize on them.

Adding a new line

The addition of wholly new product lines to a business may also present opportunities for business growth. This may come about through acquisition or through internal development. The analysis of the potential profitability of an acquisition is a specialized subject which is discussed in Chapter 18. A new line may be built up internally by developing and adding a few items at a time. The considerations outlined in the previous sections would apply in this program. There are also some additional aspects to analyzing the profitability of such a program.

In the first place, the profit impact on the current lines is likely to be minimal unless it involves the diversion of management attention to the new program, or the establishment of a development group for the specific purpose of creating a new product line. In the final analysis the costs of these development activities will have to be borne by the current businesses, but for internal management planning and control purposes, it probably would be more helpful for them to be recorded separately rather than being charged to the current lines.

Internal development of a new line presents certain special forecasting problems. The fact that the proposed line is new obviously means that there is likely to be a fairly low level of knowledge in the organization about the critical factors involved. Because of this, the forecasting of volumes, selling prices, marketing expenses, capital investment, and manufacturing costs is likely to be more difficult than it would be for current lines. Precision forecasting under these circumstances is not likely to be very helpful in making management decisions. The analysis of product-line profitability under such uncertain conditions is probably best expressed in terms of upper and lower limits for the key factors together with a probability distribution describing the most likely outcome in the aggregate.

New line development is usually carried on over extended time periods. Moreover, the development effort becomes more and more costly as the items are carried from the idea stage, to the prototype product, to market testing of more extensive kinds. Over this time period it is also probable that more refined estimates of the critical factors can be developed. To cope with these events, a mathematical model of a profit and loss statement (or other financial evaluation techniques) may be devised by the financial analyst and an operations research technician. Periodically new data and new probability estimates can be fed to a computer and new limits and a new probable outcome calculated. In this way decisions may be taken either to avoid the more costly next steps in the development process or to accelerate development activities to take advantage of profit-improvement opportunities.

It is not so important that a mathematical technique be used as it is that product-line profitability analysis be carried out on a continuing basis over the life of a development program. This is most important, not only to minimize cost and risk, but also to assist in seizing opportunity as quickly as possible.

This last section was only one illustration of the creative aspects of product profitability analysis. The product-line analyst finds himself involved in almost every part of a business. He has an opportunity to synthesize as well as analyze, and to grow as well as act. The problems are many and the interrelationships of business events are complex. Product-line profitability analysis is a stimulating and challenging activity.

Analysis of potential acquisitions

Benjamin R. Makela*

Most corporate managements have been or will be involved, sooner or later, with a question of mergers or acquisitions, either as a purchaser or as a seller. Because of the importance of acquisitions as a corporate concept, all should appreciate the problems and techniques involved in the acquisition process.

The first step should be a most exacting definition of corporate objectives. Not all objectives can be met by merger or acquisition. Some can only be attained through internal development.

The objectives which may be attained by acquisition include a broader product line and/or modified or expanded techniques of distribution. For example, a company having only wholesale distribution may acquire another that specializes in selling direct to retailers or door-to-door to consumers; another, which has been deficient in research and development, may acquire a company which is more research oriented in order to obtain their skilled personnel, patents, facilities, and know-how.

Many smaller companies are interested in the subject of acquisitions, but more as a potential seller than as a prospective buyer. The objectives of the smaller companies are different than those of larger, publicly-owned companies. For purposes of definition, in this chapter, a small company is one that has closely held ownership and/or does not enjoy a dominant market position in its selected field. The reasons that motivate a potential seller to consider a prospective buyer are very often personal ones. When acquiring a company, it is important that the purchaser

---

* Editor *Financial Executive Magazine*, New York.

know the "real" reasons for the seller's willingness to sell. Knowing the real reason very often affects the purchase price and most certainly makes the transaction easier to accomplish for both purchaser and seller.

Some of the reasons for considering a sale are: the owner's desire for diversification of investment, improved liquidity to soften the potential impact of estate taxes, the opportunity to realize the profits of years of endeavor through capital gains rather than dividend income, and the opportunity to take advantage of the acquiring company's greater financial resources and advanced technology.

Initial steps

The initial decision to buy another business, or to sell part or all of an existing business, is a matter of highest corporate strategy. The financial executive's role in that decision-making process is discussed in Chapter 2, "Strategy formulation and implementation." This chapter begins with the presumption that such a decision has been made, at least tentatively, and the discussion here focuses on (1) the initial steps to implement the decision, (2) obtaining and analyzing the data necessary for the evaluation of the buyer or seller, and (3) determination of the price. Subsequent chapters in this handbook are devoted to "Financial aspects of acquisitions and mergers" (Chapter 51) and "Accounting for business combinations and goodwill" (Chapter 57).

Organizing for acquisitions

Assuming that the corporate objective includes acquisitions as a definite program for growth, how can this best be accomplished? It is not uncommon for the president of the company to serve as his own acquisition committee. He may handle the acquisition from concept to final negotiation.

Other companies may have a vice president for corporate development, an acquisition committee, or both. Experience seems to indicate that the most effective method is the establishment of an acquisition committee. This committee generally consists of the president, a nonmanagement director, and a second high level officer who is often designated as Vice President for Corporate Development. If a company is dedicated to an acquisition program, the president must be committed to the concept and be prepared to put a fair share of his time in the effort. A second high level officer is needed in order to provide full time effort on the program; such an officer also conveys to prospective purchasers and others the sincerity and continuity of the program. The presence of the nonmanagement director can give objectivity to temper the individual and collective enthusiasm of the two management officers.

Selection of the vice president for corporate development should be made with care. This man must be both mature and imaginative; he must have an analytical nature, yet be highly articulate; he must be able to get along with people, but have an inherent shrewdness in negotiating. The success of the program will depend largely on the dedication, drive, and competence of the officer assigned to direct and coordinate the acqusition activity.

Beginning the search

For each industry of interest identified by the prospective buyer in his overall corporate strategy, the first action is a careful study to identify the most likely acquisition prospects. After the list is prepared, a priority should be assigned to each prospect and the method of approaching the seller should be given careful consideration. The advantage of going "direct" is the saving of time, but many sellers are reluctant to be specific with a proposed buyer, believing that he might only be on a "fishing expedition" or might obtain information which could impair their competitive position. When approached directly, it always seems easier to say no. The third party approach has the advantage of getting the seller to accept the concept of sale before getting involved in specifics. Third parties who are particularly helpful, both as to sources of ideas and as "door openers" are commerical bankers, trust officers, trade associations, CPA firms, and consultants. Business brokers are frequently used. When engaging a broker or "finder," both the buyer and prospective seller should make certain they have a definitive contract outlining (1) his responsibilities (and particularly his role, if any, in the negotiations), and (2) the fees which will be paid. Law suits are not unusual when such agreements are loosely drawn or nonexistent.

The initial contact

When an acquisition-minded company identifies, by whatever means, a prospective seller that appears to be attractive, there are many ways in which the initial contact may be made. The important thing is that the buyer must have done his homework, and he must remember that the first meeting is purely exploratory.

Conscious attention should be devoted to the critical question of *when* the first telephone call should be made to the prospective seller. The strategy for the successful acquisition really begins at this stage. A hurried, unprepared call can create a feeling of anxiety with the seller and he could play hard to get. Conversely, a delayed call could indicate indifference, and the prospective seller might begin negotiations with other potential purchasers. The experienced companies know the value of timing which becomes most important at this early stage.

The call should only be made after the buyer has made some preliminary investigations, has determined the nature of the prospective seller's business, his status in the industry, and has made a quick canvas within his own organization to determine who may be familiar with the situation. Secrecy is also critical; the buyer does not want to broadcast his interest in, or the possible availability of, the prospective seller at this early stage.

The purpose of the first telephone call is to establish a mutuality of interest and to arrange a convenient meeting time and place. It is not uncommon to request the prospective seller to send a condensed balance sheet, a five-year summary statement of sales and profits, a product catalog, and other preliminary data to the "personal and confidential" attention of the purchaser's designated officer.

It is important that a specific date be established within a few days after the preliminary financial information has been reviewed. Again, timing is most important.

The first meeting should include the vice president—corporate development and possibly another member of the acquisition committee, and whomever the seller chooses to bring along. This meeting is of vital importance as many of the subtleties affecting future negotiations can be identified at this early stage. The meeting should be purely exploratory and only the most pertinent aspects should be discussed, such as the basic reasons for a sale, alternative methods of payment, and the parameters of the asking price. It is at this meeting that the alert buyer will fill in many of the information gaps that he and his associates might have about the seller.

If the seller has several of his key personnel available it may indicate that they have discussed a potential sale in detail and are most eager to move. This should be an "alert" to the buyer. Conversely, if only one or two of the seller's key personnel are at the meeting it might signal a division of opinion within the seller's organization, thereby lessening the chances of consummating the transaction. On the other hand, experience has dictated that neither party should bring in its full financial and legal personnel into the first meeting. This is not the time to talk about a contract.

After the meeting, those in attendance from the buyer's side prepare independent reports for the corporate president. The purpose of the independent reports is to pick up any pertinent observations which generally are made singly and can be lost by writing a combined report.

After the president has reviewed these data it should be quickly determined whether or not negotiations should proceed. If it is decided that the potential seller is of little interest, he should be advised promptly. Very often, the seller may indicate to others that he is in negotiation with a particular buyer; if too many situations are reviewed and none consummated, the buyer may find that the more attractive prospects will not come readily to his attention. If the decision is made to proceed with the acquisition, time again is of the essence. When a company decides to sell, the old adage of striking while the iron is hot applies.

The acquisition committee should quickly formulate a program for the second meeting. Prior to this meeting, they should confirm or establish the parameters on price, the legal form of the transaction, and the method of payment. They should also determine what further data are required to formulate a definitive report for the executive committee and/or board of directors.

It is imperative that those who are to attend the second meeting be given permission to negotiate within well-defined parameters such as price, method of payment, broad concepts of implementation, time of closing, etc. The successful acquisitions are made by those who have a definitive program and proposal at the earliest possible time.

The second meeting

The second meeting should be held to the minimum number of attendants, but should include legal counsel. The purpose is to establish jointly the extent of detailed information required and further methods of investigation. A mutually acceptable timetable should be formulated as to the time of the plant visits, if any, and meetings between counterpart personnel in the two organizations. Also, the extent of the warranties to be asked by the purchaser and to be given by the seller should be fairly well defined in the interest of saving time in future negotiations. Finally, the role of the respective public accounting firms, if they are to be involved, must be established covering the need for and extent of an interim audit, acceptance of previous work papers, etc.

It is at this meeting, or certainly no later than the next, that the purchaser should ask for a "letter of intent." The basic purpose of this letter is to obtain an agreement from the seller that he will not conduct negotiations with another until it is mutually agreed that further negotiation is impractical. This letter of intent states the general purpose of the negotiations and indicates a specific timetable. One must be careful that the letter of intent is not too detailed, for it is not a substitute for a finalized contract, and it is not generally legally enforceable.

Data requirements and analysis

As the buyer and seller begin the process of learning more about each other, both must be aware of the importance of time and availability of data and recognize that too much analysis and too much data can lead to mental paralysis and neither party will be able to make a decision.

Other than total price, terms, and method of payment, the seller frequently needs to know only a few facts about the buyer. He will want to know about protection of employees, management employment and salary contracts, and the transfer of stock options and pension rights. The seller will want to know something about the buyer's managerial philosophy, how he has treated previous acquisitions, and the general nature of his future plans. But, particularly if the transaction is for cash or for the securities of a major publicly-held corporation, he will not need all the detailed information that the buyer will require from the seller.

Theoretically, there is no limit to the amount of information that the buyer would want, but practical considerations put obvious constraints on the amount of information that can be obtained and usefully evaluated. An experienced buyer will, in time, develop a very detailed checklist recognizing, however, that the information he actually asks for, and obtains, will vary with each acquisition.

Financial data

Broadly speaking, the general classes of useful financial information about the seller are those given below.

1. *History of the business and its general description.* A history would include a ten-year comparison of sales and profits by divisions and major product lines, and description of products and their relative importance within both the company and the industry.
2. *Equity structure of the company.* This would cover the number and types of shares, and their market performance for the past five years.
3. *Current financial information.* This includes audited financial statements for the past five years and the most recent unaudited statement. The statements should show cost of sales, selling, general and administrative expenses, and research and development expenses. The latest chart of accounts and manual of descriptive accounting practices is needed to interpret the statements.

In analyzing the balance sheet data it is often necessary to "get behind" the figures given in order to determine their significance. For example, Accounts Receivable should be aged and previous loss experience examined to determine the proportion of the receivables that will actually be collectible. Inventories can also have values quite different from those presented on the balance sheet. The market or replacement value of fixed assets can be significantly different from those shown, so additional breakdowns of fixed assets are useful. The terms and covenants of outstanding liabilities should be obtained.

Contingent losses or liabilities should be investigated thoroughly in order to avoid delays in their definition and resolution during final negotiations. Often, they are dealt with by putting an agreed fund in escrow, either until a specific date or until the statute of limitations has expired. Some of the contingencies for which such funds may be escrowed include unfunded pension costs, possible losses on sale of obsolete assets, payments required under performance contracts or royalty agreements, and reserves under compensation claims when the seller is self insured.

4. *Projected financial data.* Most sellers attempt to justify their asking price by pointing out the value of future earnings. They emphasize that many of the expenditures of the past have been made in order to ensure increased earnings for the future and they wish to recoup the value of these expenditures if the business is to be sold. It is not uncommon for the purchaser to acknowledge this claim by agreeing to a contingent payment, an increase in the purchase price, to be made if the earnings exceed an agreed-upon level. The potential problem is in the subsequent measurement of earnings after acquisition; future earnings are influenced by past efforts of the seller, future management of the buyer, and economic conditions beyond the control of either the buyer or seller. Contingent payment contracts are rarely feasible except when the buyer really intends to maintain the seller as an autonomous subsidiary with continuity of the seller's management.

Even though the final price is not contingent upon future earnings, the value of the acquisition must by necessity be evaluated in the light of the future. Therefore, the seller's projections of sales, costs, and profits must be painstakingly analyzed against past performance and industry norms.

5. *Tax status of the seller.* Taxes are an increasingly important segment of all business costs. Legal counsel will want to insure that, if a tax-free exchange of securities is intended, it will be allowed by the Treasury Department. For federal and state income taxes, attention should be given to loss carry forwards, the latest year of tax audit, and outstanding deficiency claims. The tax status of the proposed acquisition must be supported by joint recommendations of the attorneys and the public accountants and the plan must have mutually acceptable tax benefits for both buyer and seller.

Marketing data

The financial data are obviously important in establishing a purchase price and learning the details of the operation, but marketing information can often be more definitive in both respects. Does the potential acquisition enjoy a unique position in its industry, or is it a "me too" company? Are the company's strengths dependent upon patents, processing skills, or just being there first? The "me too" company supplies products readily available in the market place from one or several competitors, and the seller's success may be dependent upon marketing savvy, plant location, or product styling, all of which can or may eventually be eroded by an aggressive competitor.

To fully appreciate the problems and potentials of the acquisition, detailed marketing information must be obtained and evaluated. Again, like the financial data, it may not all be readily available within the desired time limits. For each acquisition, certain facts are more important than others.

Information on products should include sales and gross profit by product and product line, anticipated growth, and share of the market. The distribution channels should be analyzed in terms of the pattern of regional strengths and weaknesses in the light of the use of full-time salesmen or manufacturers' representatives, and the geographical location of the seller's plants. The sales department must be evaluated in terms of its personnel, compensation plans, and sales policies. Sales information gathered should be divided between foreign and domestic sales. Many sellers emphasize the future importance of the foreign market even though their own experience may be limited.

In order to evaluate the seller's past performance, its market share should be reviewed against the performance of the entire industry. Some of the factors to be reviewed are: size and growth potential, technologies used, seasonal and cyclical stability, present and past pricing patterns, capacity, and cost and profit margins. This approach leads to specific reviews of the seller's leading competitors. The proposed price should most certainly reflect the company's competitive status. If it is weak, the buyer can't overlook the future costs of strengthening its position. Conversely, if it is strong, the acquiring company must review its own capability to sustain that strength by the various management tools and personnel at its disposal.

Considerable emphasis should be given to analyzing sales expenses. This is the area where savings by consolidation are most likely to result—where the synergy of $2 + 2 = 5$ is most likely to be realized. Potential savings should be given the most careful review and consideration before determining the final price.

Finally, in evaluating the entire sales activity, the buyer must reconsider the sales potential of the combined companies. Will there be a sales increase if the products are redesigned, the product lines integrated, the sales organization revitalized, and more funds devoted to advertising?

Engineering and research

The success of most manufacturing enterprises depends on the introduction of new products as well as improvement of existing products. The extent of the seller's engineering and research facilities and expenditures will give some indication of the company's future ability to meet increasing and changing competitive conditions. A seller will sometimes claim that future earnings will dramatically increase with the introduction of new products from its lab, and will want the buyer to include these prospects as an important factor in the purchase price. This claim is one of the most difficult to evaluate because the seller is usually reluctant to disclose detailed information, fearful that if the deal is not consummated, competitive strength will be revealed to another.

It must be recognized that the profitability of a new product cannot be evaluated realistically until it has been tested in the market for some period of time. However, if the seller has a long history of successful product innovation, this increases the credibility of his projections for the future.

Organization of the research and development section and its stature within the company will give a clue to whether the company actually does pure or applied research as differentiated from product improvement. The organizational status of the head of the research and development group generally gives an indication as to whether the seller's management is research-oriented. If the research group operates at the divisional level and its costs are absorbed by divisional profit centers, research efforts will tend to be low-risk, fast-payback product modifications. If the research group reports directly to top management and its survival depends on major new products, the research will tend to be more fundamental—and perhaps more profitable in the long run. Many large corporations have both corporate and divisional research groups in order to achieve both results.

It is not uncommon for a new management to try to change the organizational status of the seller's research and development group. Some managements are intent on having a centralized research group, hoping to attain cross-fertilization of ideas, increased objectivity, and increased efficiency through detachment from operations. Other managements believe the most effective research is done at the divisional level, where the group is in close contact with the operating personnel and related commercial problems. If the seller's research group has been operating at the divisional level, it may not be able to provide a useful addition to the buyer's central research group. Conversely, a group which has been involved in the longer view may resent being effectively demoted to the status of a product development group when the seller becomes another of the buyer's divisions. When a group of research personnel become unhappy, they often depart en masse, taking valuable information either to a competitor or to another field. The impact of their departure can seriously impair the expected future operating results, although the impact on profits may not be felt immediately.

Other factors to consider are the short and long range research objectives, the extent, nature, and responsibility for research budgets, the coordination of plant, production, engineering, and research functions, and the condition of the labs and other physical facilities. In sum, ascertaining a dollar value for a research and development activity is most difficult. It can be a source of hidden assets. Proprietary techniques cannot be readily replaced. Tools, dies, and molds may have been charged off in the past, but have a substantial replacement cost, to say nothing of the time advantage of having a "going shop." Conversely, the seller's management may have capitalized its research and development expenses, hoping to charge it off against the sale of new products. Recovery of the value of this capitalized expense must be seriously questioned, particularly in view of the short life of new products, accelerated by rapidly advancing technology. Again, the final evaluation depends on the appraisal of the facts and on human judgment.

Organization

A review of the financial, marketing, and research data should disclose many hidden assets and liabilities of the seller that will affect the buyer's ultimate willingness to consummate the transaction. However, the most important factor in most acquisitions is the buyer's appraisal of the quality and depth of the seller's management personnel. The success, in the final analysis, depends on the people. Many of the judgments in this area will be subjective; the organization charts will indicate responsibilities, but not necessarily reflect the competence of the individuals. Financial and marketing data can be evaluated with a fair degree of accuracy. The same precision is more difficult to achieve in the evaluation of people.

An overall organization chart of the seller, supported by detailed organization charts in the major functional areas, such as marketing, engineering, manufacturing, and finance, can provide much information. If the seller's predominant strength lies in its complex manufacturing processes, perhaps more information would be required on this segment, than on marketing. Conversely, if it is a consumer products company, greater emphasis would be given to the marketing organization.

Careful study should be given to a list of key operating personnel in terms of job descriptions, dates of hiring, and salaries and bonuses for the past five years. A list of directors should also be analyzed in terms of numbers of shares owned, dates of election, and other business affiliations.

It is well to obtain the names of directors who have severed their connections within the past five years to determine whether their resignations were due to the normal course of events, such as age or other interests, or whether they were a result of a basic conflict with the operating management. A departed director, officer, or employee, if not basically malicious, can often give insights into the company which cannot be obtained as effectively elsewhere.

The above suggestion relates to management personnel, but equal thought must be given to the factory and office personnel. An evaluation of this group can be more objective, and better lends itself to statistical analysis. Factors to consider are: number of employees by location divided between plant and office, labor turnover and absenteeism, types and cost of fringe benefits, ratio of total direct and indirect labor costs to sales, appraisal of working conditions by plant, and management's general philosophy toward its employees.

There should be detailed information on labor unions by location, date of management recognition, record of strikes by plant and office, and record of strikes in neighboring plants and offices. If the union situation is particularly critical, there must be information on the latest union demands which were not granted by previous negotiation. These undoubtedly will be the focal points in the next negotiations and could result in increased costs or unanticipated work stoppages. Union negotiators are often tougher with a new management. Old loyalties are easily forgotten and the union may want to show its strength to its members as well as the new management. It is not uncommon for the new owners to be confronted early after the takeover with new demands from the unions and employees, who emphasize that these demands must be filled in order to meet "local conditions." Unless one is knowledgeable about the local area, costly and unnecessary concessions can be made with the obvious effect on the future operations.

The final evaluation of personnel and personnel policies has a large element of judgment. Will the employees be motivated to the same extent under new leadership as previously? Will the employees be content to be employed as a division of a large entity and by a different employer, or will they first fear and later feel the loss of their previous identity when they become part of another operation? Will the employee who may have enjoyed some degree of security under his previous employer become concerned with insecurity and start looking elsewhere for other opportunities? These questions must be anticipated and quickly answered at the time of implementing the acquisition. Any undue anxiety may put the entire organization off balance, and the new management may have obvious or subtle problems in the first few months of operation which will take years to resolve satisfactorily. Much has been written on human motivation; its importance, for all personnel, cannot be underestimated in determining the success of a proposed acquisition.

Determining the purchase or selling price

Early in the negotiation, and during the various stages of evaluation, both the buyer and the seller will have determined the parameters of a price which they believe will be equitable to their respective interests. Seldom will they be in agreement. As price cannot be determined with mathematical precision, it will be the result of several meetings and several opinions and will ultimately be determined by the respective trading skills of the buyer and seller. The comments below assume that the buyer is an industrial concern seeking to acquire a similar, usually smaller, company. Public utilities, insurance companies, personal service companies, etc. have many variables which are beyond the scope of this chapter.

Basically, the value of any acquisition is dependent upon the opportunities it offers in increasing and/or sustaining the earnings growth of the buyer. In an exchange of common shares, the added earnings of the seller must permit a long term increase in the earnings per share of the buyer, a ratio dependent on both the seller's future earnings and on the number of shares which must be given the seller. The buyer hopes that these increased total earnings and earnings per share will be reflected favorably in his current price/earnings ratio, mirroring the expected growth potential. Both added earnings and added earnings growth are needed to enhance the purchaser's image to present and potential investors.

The price will also reflect current economic conditions. Higher prices are usually paid during periods of increasing gross national product, high employment, increased capital investment, and rising consumer purchases. During periods of declining economic activity the price could be less than during a period of economic expansion. The conditions of the capital markets are also a factor in the price. A period of easy money and low interest rates frequently makes it possible for a seller to get a better price than when capital is tight and interest rates are higher.

Aside from the national and global economy, the conditions of a specific industry have an influence on the price. The merger movement in the late 1960's was dominated by the drug, chemical, food, paper, and electronics industries. Purchasers in these industries were willing to pay more for the projected earnings of prospective sellers than for companies in the so-called mature industries.

From the buyer's viewpoint, any acquisition that doesn't permit increased earnings per share of the combined companies should be most carefully evaluated. In addition to increased earnings per share, the price earnings multiple cannot be overlooked. Equal attention should be given to the price earnings multiples as well as the increased earnings per share. The price earnings multiple is based on a number of factors such as the general climate of the market, the nature of the industry, and the future earnings per share. If future earnings are based on heavy research and development expenditures the price earnings multiple will be higher than otherwise. The higher multiples for drugs and electronics as opposed to mining and railroads are obvious examples. Earnings for recognized growth industries are given higher multiples than the so-called investor or blue chip industries.

It is well known that a high price earnings multiple has incontrovertible advantages such as:

a) Makes debt and equity financing easier.

b) Gives the combined company a favorable investor and public image.

c) Puts pressure on the combined managements to sustain earnings and the market values of the present and newly issued securities.

d) Gives additional value to stock options, thereby making it attractive for present management to remain and combine their efforts.

e) Makes stock dividends attractive, thereby making it possible to retain cash for further growth or debt retirement.

f) Generates the possibility of capital gains for present and future shareholders, thereby making the acquisition easier.

If the buyer must offer a premium to make the acquisition, careful consideration should be given to the time it will take to offset any short term earnings dilution. Even a reversal in earnings for a year or two, although fully explained and justified, can have an adverse effect on the market value of the buyer's stock. This can bring disenchantment to present and prospective shareholders which is often disproportionate to the monetary effect.

The seller should attempt to understand the financial objectives of the buyer. The seller may find that the buyer may be willing to pay a higher price if the seller will take cash or debt securities instead of common shares or convertible securities that will ultimately reduce the buyer's earnings per share. Conversely, in other situations, the buyer may be willing to pay a premium if the seller will (1) agree to hold the buyer's newly issued common stock for the long term by giving an investment letter, and/or (2) agree to a special class of common stock with dividend restrictions. Very often the buyer will attempt to negotiate a price dependent in part on a contingent payment based on the attainment of predetermined objectives. If the seller has confidence in his operation he can very often obtain a substantially higher price because he provides the buyer with some protection for unforeseen contingencies.

The buyer, on the other hand, should recognize that the seller may accept a lower price if he has a tax-free exchange of securities, is unrestricted in the sale of the stock, and is given certain emoluments in the form of salary contracts, stock options, deferred compensation, or increased salaries. Also, he may accept a lower price if the buyer assumes all present and contingent liabilities.

The ideal method of establishing a selling price would be for the buyer to pay a predetermined fixed amount and an additional amount based on the seller's projected earnings. This is known as the contingency "earn out," and has several advantages to the buyer such as:

1. It increases the earnings per share because of the lower initial purchase price.

2. The buyer has protection should the projected earnings not meet expectations.

3. The seller's continued management efforts are assured because he must earn the additional purchase price.

4. The guesswork on the fairness of the purchase price, and the potential criticism of dissident stockholders, is minimized.

However, the seller must have complete autonomy over the factors affecting future profit and loss, and all parties must be willing and able to cooperate; experience has indicated that not all the contingencies of the combined operations can be anticipated.

In the final analysis, there is no precise formula for establishing an equitable purchase price. Only the future can determine whether both parties made a good deal.

Barriers to completing the transaction

The officers of the buyer and seller have agreed in principal as to the price, method of payment, and basis of operating the combined companies. Respective boards of directors have been consulted and everyone appears to be in complete agreement that the proposed acquisition is for the mutual advantage and profit of all concerned. Rumors of the impending merger are now confirmed, and only the details have to be resolved before the directors and/or stockholders can vote and final contracts are drawn.

However, experience has indicated that many of the proposed transactions are never consummated. Why does this happen after all the information has been prepared, evaluated, and confidences exchanged? There are several reasons, and if the parties involved are aware of these, steps can be taken throughout the negotiations to minimize their occurrence. Some of the principal reasons given for failure to consummate the transaction are listed below.

1. *Price.* Price is generally the major point of departure. Initially, the buyer may agree that the proposed seller's price may not be unreasonable. The subsequent investigation of past operating statements and projected earnings confirm that the seller is more optimistic about his prospects than an objective, detailed study justifies. Other principal reasons include actions of the securities markets and external pressures from sources with vested interests.

2. *Methods of payment.* The methods of payment often prove unworkable from the standpoint of the seller. He finds that some of his stockholders prefer cash, another group may want a fixed return on a new security, while others wish to retain their equity interest so that they may share in the future of the combined operations. Without unanimity it is often impossible for the seller to get the required support to consummate the proposed transaction.

3. *Loss of identity.* In the early stages, the management of the seller is enthusiastic about the prospects. As investigations proceed, the officers of the seller begin to realize that they may lose their individual

identity, their salaries might be reduced, or contracts of employment may not be renewed. Their loss of enthusiasm has its impact on their associates and the buyer then begins to question whether he can profitably operate the proposed acquisition if the key personnel are not fully enthusiastic and cooperative. He has the alternative of replacing a large segment of the acquired company's staff, but this can only be done at the risk of lower earnings. This prospect, in turn, would require a reduction in the selling price which may not be acceptable to the seller.

4. *Management compatibility.* During the periods of investigation, the personnel of both companies get to know one another better. Both companies often discover that the other organization is really not "their kind of people." The one group may be interested in scientific management, whereas the other prefers informality. One may be an exponent of fully autonomous operations and the other a more centralized operation. As time passes, it may become apparent that their basic organizations are incompatible and negotiations are often terminated without comment from either party.

5. *Operating problems.* The early concept of the proposed acquisition was based on the eternal hope that the profits of both companies would be improved by operating as a single entity. Initially, these premises are, at best, conceptual and conjectural. As time passes and detailed analyses are made by the prospective buyer, he finds many problems which he was not aware of and which have gone either unnoticed or ignored by the seller. As the facts emerge from the investigation, the purchaser concludes that the required time and money are hardly justifiable in the best interests of the shareholders. As reality is substituted for hope, the prospects are diminished and, most generally, negotiations terminated.

To summarize, when a proposed merger is called off it is either because of the people involved, or because the facts fail to justify the initial promise.

Bibliography

DRAYTON, C. I., EMERSON, CRAIG, GRISWOLD, J. D., and YOUNG, C. RICHARD. *Mergers and Acquisitions: Planning and Action* (New York: Financial Executives Research Foundation, 1963).

HUTCHINSON, G. SCOTT (Ed.). *The Business of Acquisitions and Mergers* (New York: President's Publishing House, Inc., 1968).

McCARTHY, GEORGE D. *Acquisitions and Mergers* (New York: The Ronald Press, 1963).

MACE, MYLES L., and MONTGOMERY, GEORGE G., JR. *Management Problems of Corporate Acquisitions* (Boston: Harvard University Graduate School of Business Administration, 1962).

Analysis of capital expenditures

Joseph F. Abely, Jr. and C. Ronald Hummel*

This chapter deals with the analysis of individual capital expenditure decisions in the context of business strategy formulation and long-range planning.

Strategy formulation and planning

Corporate strategy is a starting point for evaluating a capital expenditure decision. Strategy formulation can be defined as a top management activity concerning the development of (1) broad business objectives and (2) policies which govern the way resources will be utilized in order to meet these objectives. Business objectives provide a basis for allocating all the resources of the firm, including capital resources, by identifying the most productive outlets. (Chapter 2 of this handbook is devoted to "Strategy formulation and implementation.")

To illustrate, top management might establish a corporate sales and profit growth objective of 10 percent per year while maintaining the existing return on equity. It might further establish strategies for meeting these objectives, such as expanding into consumer rather than defense-related products using an existing base of aerospace knowhow. This strategy then forms a basis for deploying the resources of the firm and, in particular, for assessing the merits of an individual capital project. In the absence of an explicit corporate strategy, the evaluation of a major capital project is almost impossible.

---

* Vice President and Controller, and Director, Financial Planning and Analysis, respectively, General Foods Corporation, White Plains, New York.

Long-range planning

As a more detailed expression of strategy, the corporate long-range plan provides for the identification of specific programs for employing resources (see Chapter 26 for a discussion of "Corporate long range planning"). The plan, which is normally prepared annually for the next two to five years, includes a number of segments such as the capital budget, the operating budget, a financing plan, and so on. The capital budget provides an identification of capital expenditures necessary to support the plan, the impact of these capital expenditures on other segments of the plan, as well as a preliminary evaluation of individual expenditure proposals included in the first year.

The development of the long-range plan requires an analysis of (1) the ability of the firm to undertake capital expenditure programs and (2) a number of trade-offs central to the management of the business, both of which effect the size and composition of the capital budget. Financial and manpower resources in particular must be analyzed in terms of the capital expenditure budgets. Trade-offs relating to the capital budget concern balancing short-term profit and return requirements with long-term objectives, as well as weighing the competing needs of the business. For example, the size of the cost reduction program which may provide immediate profits must be assessed against capital expenditures which exploit growth opportunities, but which depress short-term profits. (For a discussion of the capital budgeting system, see Chapter 27, "Capital budgeting procedures.")

Evaluating the individual proposal

Given this perspective of how capital investments relate to the firm's strategy and long-range plan, this chapter will focus more narrowly on individual capital expenditures,[1] especially the framework and techniques for evaluation of a specific proposal.

Evaluation systems

Because a capital expenditure usually represents long-term commitments by the company, the evaluation of individual capital expenditure proposals is normally a key feature of the total planning and control system.

As previously discussed, capital expenditure requirements rarely have

---

[1] Individual capital expenditures involve the purchase and development, installation, or construction of new land and/or facilities to support an existing business. Acquisitions of new businesses are not included. In accounting terms, a capital expenditure is recognized by an increase in long-term fixed assets.

been subjected to a thorough evaluation at the time the annual or long-range plan is prepared and agreed upon, which is accomplished normally just prior to the commitment of funds. Evaluation can be delegated to lower levels of management, leaving only the most important projects for top management review. There are three ways of describing capital expenditures for purposes of delegation of approval. Often a careful blending of the three is the most workable. First is the dollar amount of the investment; second, whether or not the project has been included in the capital budget; and third, the importance of a project to corporate strategy and/or the degree of business risk. The first method assumes that the importance of a project is related to the size of the capital investment required. The second method recognizes that if a capital expenditure, regardless of size, is necessary to support an approved plan, the plan may be carried out without further review of decisions to go ahead with individual programs. The third method recognizes that many capital expenditure decisions are routine enough not to require top management time. For example, routine cost reduction expenditures can be delegated to lower levels of management so long as they meet a minimum set of criteria usually expressed in terms of payback and return on investment. On the other hand, top management may correctly require that all investments supporting new products, irrespective of size or whether or not they were an element of an approved capital budget, receive individual approval because of their strategic importance and relatively high risk.

Elements of evaluation

There are four essential elements of a capital expenditure evaluation, as discussed below.

1. RELATIONSHIP TO PLANS. Any major capital expenditure should be related to the long-range plan in terms of (1) whether it was included in the capital budget and therefore whether it is consistent with business strategy, and (2) how it compares to the plan's original projections for profits, working and fixed capital requirements, manpower needs, and so on.

2. SUPPORTING ASSUMPTIONS. Key assumptions supporting the proposal, and in turn the facts and analyses supporting the assumptions, must be clearly identified. For example, key assumptions might be based upon pilot plant tests, market tests, or experience with similar facilities and products.

3. PROJECT BENEFITS. The enumeration of the specific benefits of a capital expenditure proposal is the most difficult part of the evaluation

process. In some cases, the benefits are purely financial, as in the cost reduction project which upgrades packaging machinery in order to improve operating efficiency. In other cases, such as an investment in a building to create needed office space the benefits are not so easily quantified. Usually, projects have both financial and nonfinancial benefits. Where multiple benefits are anticipated, these benefits should be ranked in order of importance.

4. ALTERNATIVES.   Finally, a capital project evaluation should thoroughly explore other alternatives or the consequences of "doing nothing." Obvious alternatives to a capital expenditure are lease vs. buy (see Chapter 20, "Lease, rent or buy decisions"), make vs. buy (see Chapter 15, "Make or buy decisions"), repair rather than replace, etc.

Both the broad elements of evaluation noted above and any specific areas peculiar to certain types of projects are often best incorporated into the formal capital budgeting system in the form of guidelines or a checklist for evaluation.

Financial evaluation techniques

The most common techniques for determining the value of a capital expenditure are financial techniques which quantify project benefits when they are in fact measurable. Although a great variety of financial techniques exist, they can be grouped into three categories for discussion: (1) payback, (2) accounting return measurements, and (3) discounted cash flow measurements.

1. PAYBACK.   Payback is a simple measure of liquidity or risk which is best used along with a return on investment measure. It may be defined as the period of time required for the cash flows related to a capital expenditure to break even. As detailed in Exhibit 1, consider an expenditure proposal to purchase new equipment in order to effect raw material savings. As shown, an initial investment in the new equipment and in the inventory which is also required to generate the material savings is "paid back" in almost exactly two and one-half years. Note that depreciation adds to cash flow by reducing taxes.

The payback measure, using this illustration, can be refined further to sharpen the definition of project liquidity or risk. Assuming that the $50,000 inventory investment is fully recoverable, and the equipment has a salvage value equal to half the $100,000 purchase price at any point in time, payback on the nonrecoverable portion of the investment (or the funds "at risk") occurs in just under one year.

While simple and useful, particularly as a screening tool in the initial stages of evaluation, the payback measurement has severe limitations. If, for example, a series of investments is required over a period of time, let us say to accomplish a gradual expansion of factory capacity, the payback may be an inordinately long period of time. Businesses which are expanding and therefore require a net use of funds, do not "pay back"; neither do certain capital expenditures with the same characteristics. Under these circumstances, how can a "maximum" payback period be established? Another limitation is that the payback measure does not

EXHIBIT 1

Expenditure Proposal—New Machine Cash Source (Use)
in $000's

		End of Year			
	0	1	2	2½	3
Investment in					
Equipment................	$(100)				
Inventory.................	$ (50)				
Material savings............		$107	$107	$ 54	$107
Taxes[1] related to					
Material savings..........		(54)	(54)	(27)	(54)
Depreciation[2].............		6	6	3	5
Net cash flow					
Each period...............	$(150)	$ 59	$ 59	$ 30	$ 58
Cumulative...............		(91)	(32)	(2)	56

[1] Assumed to equal 50 percent.
[2] Figured on 15-year sum-of-digits basis.

provide any expression of the value of cash flows after the payback period. In fact, only after payback has been attained can a return on investment be realized. This means that return on investment must also be developed to measure project worth.

2. ACCOUNTING RETURN MEASUREMENTS. A traditional means of measuring the financial benefits of a capital expenditure is the use of accounting records, including the profit and loss statement and the balance sheet. "Accounting" return, for example, can be projected by simply relating book profits to the average balance sheet investment over the life of a project, or on a year-by-year basis. Consider the earlier illustration of a proposal to purchase new equipment to effect raw material savings. The financial characteristics of this proposal are shown in Exhibit 2 as they would be reflected in the company's financial statements.

Referring to Exhibit 2, the average accounting return over the assumed life (15 years) of the project is 52 percent. The year-by-year return, of course, varies according to the depreciated value of the machinery. The annual return could be held constant in this example by calculating the return on *gross* investment (a practice followed by some firms using this technique), but in reality projects normally have irregular cash flow patterns and thus irregular annual accounting returns.

Advocates of accounting return point out that business objectives have to be expressed in terms of accounted profit and investment. A capital expenditure, therefore, must be measured in terms of its impact on these objectives. While this is true, accounting return is a very approximate measurement. It lacks precision because it is not sensitive to the duration and timing of cash flows. It cannot, for example, distinguish between two alternatives with different cash flow patterns. It cannot be used to distinguish between an investment proposal and an alternative which requires no investment, e.g., make vs. buy. Finally, it bears no relation-

EXHIBIT 2

Expenditure Proposal—New Machine in $000's

	Year			Average 15 Years
	1	2	3	
Profit after taxes[1]	50	50	50	50
Net investment in				
Equipment	93	86	79	47
Inventory	50	50	50	50
Total	143	136	129	97
Accounting return	35%	37%	39%	52%

[1] Depreciation figured on 15-year straight line basis for book purposes even though accelerated basis taken for tax purposes.

ship to a "true" rate of return. Thus, an annual accounting return of 10 percent cannot be considered the same as earning interest of 10 percent per annum in a bank.

3. DISCOUNTED CASH FLOW MEASUREMENTS.   Several variants of discounted cash flow applicable to the evaluation of capital expenditures will now be discussed. The discounting of cash flows recognizes that it is better to receive a dollar today than next year because the dollar received today can be invested to yield an immediate return. Thus, the discounted cash flow technique gives greater weight to cash flows early in the life of the project.

Perhaps the most widely used discounted cash flow measurement is internal rate of return. Internal rate of return is simply that interest rate which equalizes both negative and positive cash flows over the life of the project by weighting them according to when they occur. Cash flows are weighted using the principle of compound interest. Consider, for example, a compound interest rate of 39 percent (this rate is chosen because it ties in with the illustration below). A dollar invested today will equal $1.39 at year end, assuming the interest is received at the end of the year. Conversely, a dollar received at the end of the year is worth $\dfrac{\$1.00/}{\$/1.39}$ or $\dfrac{72/}{/100}$ as much as a dollar received today. The discount factor 0.72 can be used to express the value of a dollar received at year end versus the value of one received today.

Discount factors can be applied to the stream of cash flows resulting from a capital expenditure decision in order to determine the internal rate of return. Using again the expenditure proposal for a new machine, cash flows can be discounted to arrive at an internal rate of return which equalizes cash flows over the life of the project. As illustrated in Exhibit 3, it is assumed that the proposal has a life of 15 years, that the

EXHIBIT 3

Expenditure Proposal—New Machine Cash Source (Use) in $000's

		End of Year			
	0	1	2	3	15
Investment in					
Equipment............$(100)					
Inventory.............. (50)					$ 50
Material savings.........		$107	$107	$107	$107
Taxes related to					
Material savings........		(54)	(54)	(54)	(54)
Depreciation...........		6	6	5	1
Total annual cash flow....$(150)		60	59	59	104
Discount factor........... 1.00		0.72	0.52	0.37	0.01
Present value cash flow					
Each period............$(150)		42	31	22	1
Cumulative............ (150)		(108)	(77)	(55)	0

equipment has no salvage value, and that the inventory investment of $50,000 can be recovered after the end of the project life or at the end of year 15.

As shown, if the cash flows for each period are discounted at a 39 percent interest rate, the total discounted cash flow is approximately equal to zero. In other words, an investor would presumably be indifferent to investing $150,000 in this proposal or putting the same amount in a bank at 39 percent interest, ignoring, of course, liquidity and risk factors.

The internal rate of return implicitly assumes reinvestment of cash throw-off at the internal return rate. Some students of capital budgeting believe this gives an undue advantage to certain kinds of capital projects, particularly those with heavy initial cash flows and a high internal rate of return. In order to avoid this problem, increasing use is being made of the present value variant of the discounted cash flow technique. Present value of cash flows is simply calculated by discounting absolute cash flows at a specified hurdle rate representing, for example, the *opportunity cost of capital for investments in a given risk category*. The present value of the illustration in Exhibit 3 using a 10 percent discount rate is $297,000; using a 20 percent discount rate, it amounts to $122,000. The higher the present value of cash flows at a given hurdle rate, presumably the more attractive the project.

Others argue that present value of cash flows can be misleading because this technique may lead to an erroneous *ranking* of projects. For example, two projects having a present value of $50,000 each, or a total of $100,000, might be rejected in favor of the example in Exhibit 3 discounted at 20 percent. This decision might be made even though the investment required for the two projects might be less than the present value of $122,000 for the project illustrated. This has led to the use of a profitability index, for purposes of ranking projects, which is simply the ratio of the present value of cash flows other than the investment to the present value of the investment.

Financial evaluation techniques—summary

No single evaluation technique completely describes the financial consequences of a capital expenditure decision. Normally, discounted cash flow financial measurements are adequate tests of the financial value of a capital investment. When the internal rate of return for two alternative projects is close, or when projects must be ranked, however, present value of cash flows and a profitability index are additional and often very necessary guides for decision making. Management may correctly choose a project which is ranked higher than a mutually exclusive alternative on the basis of present value, even though it ranks lower than the alternative on the basis of internal rate of return.

The accounting return is often a strong ally of the internal rate of return. However, the accounting return is best used together with discounted cash flow techniques to explore more fully the financial consequences of a capital expenditure decision. A capital project with a high internal rate of return, for example, might be unacceptable to management because of the near term impact on the accounted return for the total business.

Nonfinancial techniques

Based upon an assessment of the needs of the business in the context of strategy, some firms have attempted to quantify the importance of *qualitative* aspects of a capital expenditure to develop a project rating. Nonfinancial techniques recognize that the merits of certain capital projects are not measurable in purely financial terms and, even when they are, financial benefits are rarely the sole criterion of acceptability.

Largely depending upon the business, a theoretical nonfinancial rating system can be built by identifying the importance of certain qualities of capital expenditures. For example, a firm could decide that strengthening the distribution system is worth 10 points in a scale of 100, improving product quality is worth 20 points, and so on. To the extent that a capital project did contribute to strengthening the distribution system, it would receive a portion of the available 10 points. In a similar fashion, points could be given for each other quality to come to an overall rating.

Risk analysis

In order to make a capital expenditure decision, ideally the manager should know what the chances are of the various possible outcomes, and therefore what his risks are. Every capital expenditure involves assumptions, thus, uncertainty and risk. The best estimate of each assumption along with the best estimate of payback and return is not appropriate to assess risk. Often "high—best guess—low" estimates of payback and return are calculated for a capital expenditure; these are useful, but again insufficient to appropriately assess risk. For example, if the high—best guess—low return for a project is 20%—15%—7%, a manager cannot determine what the odds are of achieving each of these values. He cannot assess the chances of achieving the firm's hurdle rate of 10 percent, and because of the foregoing, he cannot compare the risks inherent in this project with other projects. In comparing two projects, a manager must weigh the odds of achieving certain results against the stakes necessary to achieve these. A manager may accept very low odds of achieving a high return if the stakes are small, but forego this decision if the stakes are so high that failure would bankrupt the firm. Often the key assumptions supporting a project such as market size, market growth, and share position, can be considered individually to estimate the odds of each occurrence. These individual estimates, however, must be combined to understand the risk inherent in the total project.

Risk analysis systems

A growing number of firms have developed "risk analysis" systems to assist the manager in understanding capital expenditure risks. (For a technical review of developing systems, see Chapter 14, "Systems analysis and simulation.") These systems have in common the ability to combine the variabilities related to all key estimates supporting a capital expenditure decision. This is done through computer-assisted simulation of outcomes in accordance with their estimated probabilities of occurrence. Two basic steps are required to make such a system work.[2] First,

---

[2] See Hertz, David B., "Risk Analysis in Capital Investment," *Harvard Business Review*, Reprint, January–February, 1964. Copyrighted by the President and Fellows of Harvard College.

estimates of the range of values for each key assumption supporting a project, along with the likelihood that each value will occur, must be prepared. Normally, functional experts are called upon to make these estimates. The marketing manager may prepare market forecasts, and so on. Firms using risk analysis have found estimates of this type relatively easy to prepare. A marketing manager, for example, may be much more willing to forecast a range of possible share of market positions if it relieves him of the almost impossible task of "going on the line" with a single budget estimate. Each forecast must, of course, be related to others where the variables are interdependent. Forecasts for market share must, for example, be related to selling prices.

Second, the estimates generally must be run through a computer-assisted simulation due to complexity. This involves the selection and combination of all of the variables at random, and the computation of financial data for each random combination. This is done literally hundreds of times to arrive at the odds of the occurrence of each possible return rate. In addition, the expected outcome of the capital expenditure decision is arrived at by figuring the average of the values of all outcomes weighted by the chances of each occurring.

Uncertainties, or risk, are clearly shown in the output. For example, the odds of achieving various rates of return can now be shown, as follows:

Percent Return	Probability of Achieving at Least Return Shown
0%	95%
5%	82%
10%	70%
15%	40%
20%	14%
25%	9%

Thus the odds are 82 out of 100 that the return will be at least 5 percent. Other questions can also be asked, such as, "What are the chances of showing at least a net profit breakeven by the third year?" or, "What are the odds that plant capacity will be more than 10 percent idle?"

The system can be "rerun" to test changes in assumptions on the possible outcomes. New data on market shares, for example, might be input to determine the sensitivity of this new set of assumptions on the financial consequences of the capital expenditure evaluation.

One caveat regarding risk analysis is worth noting. While this approach forces a more rational segmentation of the elements of the capital decision, the basic input remains the subjective judgment of the business managers involved. Although these judgments are no doubt the best available, they are also subject to error. For this reason, a usual final step in the use of risk analysis is a review of the elements of the decision in order to determine which individual judgments were the most important in terms of producing the final result. Armed with this information as to sensitivity, the wise manager will then review these critical assumptions and the basic factual support. This review may point up the need for further research into critical aspects of the project.

Simple tools

Risk analysis systems described above are both time consuming and relatively expensive to use, and therefore are normally applied to a firm's larger or more complex investment decisions. Other simple tools can be applied to lesser projects to give management more limited but adequate information on risk. For example, each assumption can be changed ± 10 percent to determine its impact on payback and return for a capital expenditure. Simple computer programs have been developed to quickly perform the mathematics required to compute a new payback and return, given new assumptions. These programs have proven to be valuable working tools to help with the infinite number of "What if . . . ?" questions which arise in the early stages of project evaluation.

Measuring incremental cash flows

Typically, capital budgeting policies require that incremental cash flows be used to evaluate a capital expenditure. One representative capital budgeting manual reads: "Costs and revenues should be incremental. The incremental concept requires that capital investments and cash flow projections include only items which will be realized, incurred or made directly as a result of or attributable to the capital expenditure." The translation of such policies into practice presents a most difficult phase of capital expenditure analysis for the capital budget analyst and financial executive alike.

The problem of identifying cash flows will be explored below using as an example a capital expenditure decision to acquire new packaging machinery to produce a new soap product for sale in grocery stores. Production of the product involves the use of existing processing equipment and factory space. The firm introducing the product has a competing line of soap products already in the market.

Incremental investment

This capital expenditure for a soap product relates to an existing business in which capital is already invested. An "incremental" analysis of the soap project would normally *exclude* a charge for the use of existing capital investments, e.g., a portion of the processing equipment and factory space, yet the depletion of these resources is usually a real "cost" of doing business. Assuming the total business is expanding, profitable activities may create the need for the construction of new supporting facilities. The firm considering the soap project has in its annual and long-range capital budget separate projects which are required to support the soap and other new product projects. These separate projects include new utilities, additional warehouse space, and other needed capital expenditures which may not be justified on the basis of "profitability."

The problem of accounting for the inevitable utilization of existing capital investments can be handled in a number of ways. No single method, however, provides an "answer" that can be routinely applied to all situations. First, the project can be charged for identified increases in costs associated with the use of existing assets. For example, the soap equipment will overcrowd existing storage space, resulting in outside storage costs. These outside storage costs should be identified and charged to the project.

Secondly, the capital expenditure can be increased to include the book value or replacement cost of that portion of existing investments utilized by the project. This technique assumes that the existing assets utilized have a future profitable use. In practice, allocating assets must be somewhat arbitrary; nevertheless, the result indicates whether the soap product profits are sufficient to earn a return on all the assets employed to produce the product. Initial evaluations of this soap product, for example, indicated a high return on the incremental capital expenditure or machinery but a low return on total assets employed. Comparisons to the return earned by other soap products on total assets employed resulted in a further analysis of pricing and product formula to improve profit margins.

Finally, the problem of making sure a business earns a return on all assets can be at least partially resolved during long-range planning. At this time a balance must be achieved between "profit increasing" capital programs and support facilities such as utilities.

Incremental costs

Unlike a simple cost reduction project where rather precise estimates of costs can be made, the soap project illustrates the problems of identifying so called incremental costs. Expansion into this new soap product was projected to double the firm's market share with a corresponding doubling of soap production. The impact of the program on the firm's cost structure was difficult to measure. In addition to "directly variable" costs, such as raw material which can be estimated on a volume basis, some increases in "period" costs, such as an addition to the quality control and maintenance staff, might be directly related to the capital expenditure decision. Other period costs such as the controller's budget might increase over time, but are difficult to tie to any specific action. Thus, depending upon the size and complexity of the project, period costs can be added to incremental costs to provide for such gradual increases in indirect overheads.

An initial evaluation of the soap project, for example, indicated incremental profit margins were forecast to be twice those earned on the company's existing soap business. Overhead cost factors were added, knowing that the profitability of the firm's total stake in the soap business was unlikely to increase significantly over the long term. A study of the margins earned by other soap manufacturers of comparable size supported this decision.

Incremental revenues

The soap project also illustrates some of the problems of identifying incremental revenues. First, the soap manufacturer predicted that the existing soap business would decline if the new soap product was not introduced. The profit impact of the decline was added to incremental revenues for purposes of evaluating the capital expenditure. Note that these so-called incremental revenues never will contribute to an increase in the existing profit level of the firm. In addition, the firm figured the entry of the new soap product would replace some sales of its existing soap products. The profit contribution of existing sales projected to be "cannibalized" by the new entry was subtracted from incremental revenues for purposes of evaluating the capital expenditure. Whether a competitor would have cannibalized existing sales anyway, or whether cannibalization actually occurred, can be argued. The point is that judgments in these difficult areas related to determining incremental investment may materially effect the outcome of the financial evaluation.

Problems summary

The problems of measurement discussed above indicate clearly that the process of defining and understanding incremental investment, costs, and revenues is the essential part of the evaluation process regardless of the techniques used for measuring project worth.

The financial executive must insure that individual capital project evaluations, while technically correct, are related to and are fully consistent with the characteristics of the business as a whole. Some students of capital budgeting contend that the value of capital investments in a business is largely determined by the characteristics of the total business and not by the specific elements of the incremental evaluation for each individual proposal.

Criteria for acceptability

Both nonfinancial and financial criteria can be employed to determine acceptability of a capital expenditure. Nonfinancial criteria should relate to the strategy and long-range plans for the firm. These plans determine the "business need" for the capital expenditure, as well as its impact on the business results. If a capital expenditure to enter a new business is inconsistent with strategic growth objectives, it should be rejected despite an apparently high rate of return.

General financial standards

In theory, the rate of return for an individual capital expenditure can be measured against either the firm's cost of capital or an opportunity rate to determine whether it is an acceptable financial proposition. "Cost of capital" can be variously calculated on the combined base of debt and/or equity capital supporting the business. One approach is to take an expected or ideal debt/equity structure and develop a weighted average cost of capital for both the debt and equity component. Cost of capital is difficult to calculate in practice, and is not an entirely acceptable guideline because a firm presumably sets out to earn a business return over and above the cost of funds in the business.

In addition, rate of return for a capital expenditure can also be compared to an opportunity rate. An opportunity rate is simply the return which can be earned through available alternative investments. A conglomerate business, for example, could decide on the basis of opportunity rates among industries to redeploy assets from one industry to another. To further illustrate, a proposal to purchase rather than lease a fleet of automobiles could be rejected because the return on purchase is lower than returns which can be earned on alternative uses of capital resources.

Acceptability and business management

Financial criteria recognize that business growth is achieved with a mix of capital investments with inherent differences in return on investment, depending upon their purpose. Thus, criteria must be keyed to type of investment as well as to acceptability across the board.

The return on investment which can be earned on various types of capital projects usually depends on several variables: risk, the characteristics of the business benefiting by the capital expenditure, and the state of the firm's development in that business. Financial criteria should recognize these key variables.

Bibliography

The financial executive will find that the following references give further and more detailed insight into the analysis of capital expenditures.

Capital Investment Decisions. Reprints from *Harvard Business Review,* Boston, Mass., various dates 1954 through 1964. Collection of thoughtful articles on capital investment decisions, ranging from the administration of capital spending to risk analysis.

National Association of Accountants, *Financial Analysis to Guide Capital Expenditure Decisions.* Research Report 43, New York, July, 1967. A thoroughly researched study of the application of financial analysis to capital expenditure decisions.

National Industrial Conference Board, *Managing Capital Expenditures.* Business Policy Study 107, New York, 1963. Excellent practical working guide on procedures used by other companies to manage capital expenditures.

QUIRIN, DAVID G. *The Capital Expenditure Decision.* Richard D. Irwin, Inc., Homewood, Illinois, 1967. Theoretically oriented discussion of techniques for evaluating capital expenditures.

USRY, MILTON F. *Capital Expenditure Planning and Control.* University of Texas Studies in Accounting No. 1. The University, Austin, Texas, 1966. Defines and evaluates the requirements of an effective capital budgeting program through a depth field study of the Continental Oil Company.

Lease, rent, or buy decisions

W. S. Swayze*

A firm can obtain the use of property, plant, or equipment by buying, renting, or leasing. Each alternative has somewhat different benefits and costs, most of which can be evaluated in economic terms. This chapter describes how to make that economic evaluation, but, because non-economic factors may bear heavily on the decision, the discussion begins with some comments on intangible considerations. This chapter is related to chapter 19, "Analysis of Capital Expenditures," which discusses that topic in greater detail.

Intangible considerations

Sometimes there is no alternative to leasing. Some foreign governments will lease land for long periods of time, under terms that have all the characteristics of ownership, but will refuse to transfer title. The lessee may clear the land, erect buildings, sublease, and do other things that make the lease substantially equivalent to ownership. Private parties may elect to do the same; for example, property is sometimes bequeathed to a trust under terms that require the trustees only to lease the property. Some users want convenience in arranging for acquisitions and disposals, and are willing to pay a premium to the owner for these services. Further, a rental agreement offers a flexibility in planning for the time and size of replacements and additions that is less true of purchases. Some firms prefer to lease because the balance sheet will not list assets

---

* Controller, Mobil Oil Corporation, New York.

or liabilities but the income statement will show earnings. This looks better to an unsophisticated investor who measures management performance by calculating the amount of earnings generated by each dollar of assets; if management lists less assets, the return-on-assets measurement is higher. Professional analysts, who are more likely to read footnoted information about leases, may still not have enough information about the leases to prepare precise appraisals. Further, even if there were full disclosure, analysts may not appraise capital structure as if there were dollar-for-dollar financial equivalence between a lease and a debt. In this way lease financing may act to increase debt capacity. (A firm can recognize this intangible financial advantage of a lease by being willing to pay a small—say ½ percent—premium in interest cost for the lease compared with debt.)

Economic considerations

The lease or rental fee represents, in part, the profit and financing cost of the lessor. Unless the lessor's financing costs and profitability demands are lower than the lessee's, it will be unusual for a lease to demonstrate an economic advantage. Some situations, however, consistently favor a lease.

A lease is useful if the user needs only a part of a property (for example, office space in a building or such rights as mineral or air space), or needs an asset for only part of its total useful life.

The lessor may have a buying advantage or may make the property himself, so that, to the lessee, the payments are cheaper than ownership despite the interest cost.

A user can "borrow" in smaller units with a lease than in a direct debt financing. The borrowing is obtained when needed for the acquisition of specific assets, so that there is no lead time when direct debt proceeds would be invested in short-term securities yielding less than the interest cost. Generally there are no underwriting fees, but usually there are considerable legal and other fees.

The entire lease payment is generally deductible for tax purposes. If, alternatively, the user borrowed the funds directly to finance a project, only the interest portion would be tax deductible and the principal payment would not be tax deductible. This suggests that leasing has a real advantage over ownership, but this is largely illusionary in cases where the full asset is depreciable. Since companies now normally take accelerated depreciation, ownership usually has distinct tax advantages over the normal lease.

The tax deductibility of lease payments can be important where the lease is for land and other non-depreciable assets. This benefit is offset by the fact that the user will lose title to the asset at the end of the lease period, although minimal lease terms can be maintained for long periods.

Recent revenue acts have made available to purchasers of certain types of depreciable property a credit of 7 percent of the amount of new investment against the purchaser's income tax. Congress added a specific sub-section allowing this credit to be passed through by an owner-lessor to the user-lessee, provided that an appropriate election of such treatment is made. This election may be made only where the lessor purchases new property that he subsequently leases, and is not available where the lessor acquires used property in a sale and leaseback transaction.

Finally, the lessor may be in a better position to assume ownership risks because he "pools" them. A single computer user who must have the latest in computer technology, for example, would have to assume the risk of obsolescence if he bought. He would have to assign a low residual value to the computer because he would have no alternative use when a new model came out, and he would not be likely to know of opportunities for sale to subsequent users. The lessor, however, through a knowledge of the market for computer capability, can "pool" the risks and increase the probability of finding another user. The lessor can assign a higher residual value.

When a lease is suspected of having an economic advantage, an evaluation should be made to measure the advantage. When a lease is chosen regardless of the economics (for example, for convenience), an analysis is still useful because it measures the effect on the company of selecting a more costly alternative. Further, if the leased asset is to be used in a project that must compete with other projects for investment funds, it will be necessary to compute the profitability of the leased-asset project in a way that makes it comparable to owned-asset projects.

The difference between renting and leasing

This chapter will make the same distinction between the terms "renting" and "leasing" that is used frequently by other authors, although many people continue to use the terms interchangeably.

When a user buys an asset he makes a long-term investment decision: he makes an initial outlay in the expectation that the asset will provide a stream of earnings in the form of either increased profits or reduced costs. By buying, the user assumes all the risks of ownership, including the risk that the asset will gain or lose its value more quickly than expected. A user may shift that risk to someone else, however, by renting.

In a *rental* agreement, the user pays rent only as long as he wants to use the property, but is not obligated to make payments beyond some nominal period, say 90 days. Fluctuations in value are realized by the lessor. In consideration for assuming the risk of ownership, of course, the lessor is entitled to a return, and if the user keeps the property for its entire useful life the user would have paid more than if he had bought.

A *lease* looks like a rental agreement but it lasts longer: it lasts long enough for the owner to recover his purchase price and financing costs, which generally means for a significant part of the life of the asset. The user thus really assumes the ownership risk. In effect, the user who leases is making the same kind of decision that he would have made if he had bought the property and borrowed the money to do so.

A user who buys, then, makes an investment decision; he assumes ownership risks and makes an initial capital outlay in order to increase profits or reduce costs. A user who rents makes an expense decision; he avoids ownership risks and incurs a series of expenses in order to increase profits or reduce costs. A user who leases makes a combination investment and financing decision; he is obligated to a series of payments that is the same as a combination of buy-and-borrow.

In some applications it is difficult to classify a particular arrangement as either a rental agreement or a lease. It may have elements of both, so that the terms shift part—but not all—of the risks of ownership to the user. These complications will be discussed in a later section.

Method of evaluation

The method of evaluation to be used here was selected because it can be used for either of the two usual classes of business decisions.

One class asks which is the *more profitable* of two competing and mutually exclusive proposals. One proposal, for example, might involve purchased assets and the other leased or rented assets, but each proposal requires separate assessment of prices, volumes, and operating costs and expenses to see which is more profitable.

Another class asks which is the *less costly* of two competing and mutually exclusive proposals. For example, should the firm buy one big pump or two little pumps? Should the firm buy a good pump that will last ten years or two lesser pumps that will each last five years? Should the firm buy the pump or rent it?

Sometimes the analysis for least cost stands alone and a capital expenditure is presented as a "cost reduction" proposal. Other times the least-cost analysis is preliminary and supplementary to a profitability analysis, and the resulting capital expenditure is a component of a "new business" proposal. In either case the analytical requirements are, or should be, identical.

The method is this: (1) estimate the amount and timing of the cash flow separately for each alternative, where the cash flow may be either net cash income or net cash cost; (2) find the present value of the cash flow, where the discount rate measures the opportunity cost of the funds employed; (3) if choosing among alternative net cash incomes, choose the largest positive present value as the most profitable; or (4) if choosing among alternative net cash costs, choose the smallest negative present value as the least costly.

The principles and procedures will be developed by means of a series of exhibits. These exhibits show both the form and content of the evaluation required for the lease, rent, or buy decision.

Investment decision

The first illustration applies this method to profitability analysis.

Profitability analysis. Exhibit 1 illustrates the method for a proposal using owned assets. For simplicity the example uses an 8-year life and omits details on the derivation of revenues; for illustration the example uses 10 percent as the after-tax opportunity cost of the funds employed.

EXHIBIT 1
Profitability Analysis of Owned Asset*

Item	Total	Annual cash flow to end of period								
		0	1	2	3	4	5	6	7	8
Cash flow from operations:										
1 Revenues.............	1 870.0	...	250.0	300.0	300.0	250.0	225.0	185.0	180.0	180.0
2 Operating costs.......	(750.0)	...	(75.0)	(100.0)	(100.0)	(100.0)	(100.0)	(95.0)	(90.0)	(90.0)
3 Operations...........	1 120.0	...	175.0	200.0	200.0	150.0	125.0	90.0	90.0	90.0
Cash flow from ownership:										
4 Capital outlay.........	(700.0)	(700.0)	...	...	...	...	...	...	...	...
5 Depreciation tax shield...............	336.0	...	74.6	65.3	56.0	46.7	37.3	28.0	18.7	9.4
6 Investment credit.....	49.0	49.0	...	...	...	...	...	...	...	...
7 Ownership...........	(315.0)	(651.0)	74.6	65.3	56.0	46.7	37.3	28.0	18.7	9.4
Net cash flow:										
8 Undiscounted........	805.0	(651.0)	249.6	265.3	256.0	196.7	162.3	118.0	108.7	99.4
9 Present value of $1 @ 10%.................	...	1.000	0.909	0.826	0.751	0.683	0.621	0.565	0.513	0.467
10 Discounted cash flow..	391.4	(651.0)	226.9	219.1	192.3	134.3	100.8	66.7	55.8	46.5

*Thousands of dollars after tax; ( ) denotes outflow.

The example first shows the cash flow expected from operations (lines 1–3) and then displays the cash flow from ownership (lines 4–7). The net cash flow (line 8) is discounted at 10 percent to derive a net present value of $391,400 (line 10). This figure means that, if there are no other alternatives, the proposal's income pays for all costs, including the opportunity cost of the funds employed, and the proposal is acceptable.

If the same proposal could be effected with rented assets, say at the annual rate of $164,000, a profitability analysis could be prepared as displayed in Exhibit 2.

The rented asset will have the same cash flow from operations (lines 1–3), but instead of the costs of ownership the project will incur the costs of rental (lines 8–10). Because rental is more costly than ownership the net present value is $338,500, $52,900 less than in the case of ownership. Note that the project is still acceptable, even though less profitable.

Least-cost analysis. In cases where revenue and operating costs are

EXHIBIT 2

Profitability Analysis of Rented Asset*

| Item | Total | Annual cash flow to end of period | | | | | | | | |
		0	1	2	3	4	5	6	7	8
Cash flow from operations:										
1 Revenues..........	1 870.0	...	250.0	300.0	300.0	250.0	225.0	185.0	180.0	180.0
2 Operating costs.....	(750.0)	...	(75.0)	(100.0)	(100.0)	(100.0)	(100.0)	(95.0)	(90.0)	(90.0)
3 Operations.........	1 120.0	...	175.0	200.0	200.0	150.0	125.0	90.0	90.0	90.0
Rent:										
8 Payments before tax...............	(1 312.0)	...	(164.0)	(164.0)	(164.0)	(164.0)	(164.0)	(164.0)	(164.0)	(164.0)
9 Tax shield..........	629.6	...	78.7	78.7	78.7	78.7	78.7	78.7	78.7	78.7
10 Payments after tax..	(682.4)	...	(85.3)	(85.3)	(85.3)	(85.3)	(85.3)	(85.3)	(85.3)	(85.3)
Net cash flow:										
11 Undiscounted......	437.6	...	89.7	114.7	114.7	64.7	39.7	4.7	4.7	4.7
12 Present value of $1 @ 10%...........	...	1.000	0.909	0.826	0.751	0.683	0.621	0.565	0.513	0.467
13 Discounted cash flow.............	338.5	...	81.5	94.7	86.1	44.2	24.7	2.7	2.4	2.2

* Thousands of dollars after tax; ( ) denotes outflow.

EXHIBIT 3

Least-cost Analysis*

| Item | Total | Annual cash flow to end of period | | | | | | | | |
		0	1	2	3	4	5	6	7	8
Memo:										
1 Present value of $1 @ 10%........	...	1.000	0.909	0.826	0.751	0.683	0.621	0.565	0.513	0.467
Owned asset:										
2 Capital outlay.....	(700.0)	(700.0)	...	...	...	...	...	...	...	...
3 Depreciation tax shield..........	336.0	...	74.6	65.3	56.0	46.7	37.3	28.0	18.7	9.4
4 Investment credit.	49.0	49.0	...	...	...	...	...	...	...	...
5 Undiscounted cash flow........	(315.0)	(651.0)	74.6	65.3	56.0	46.7	37.3	28.0	18.7	9.4
6 Discounted cash flow (line 1 x line 5).........	(402.3)	(651.0)	67.8	53.9	42.1	31.9	23.2	15.8	9.6	4.4
Rented asset:										
7 Payments before tax.............	(1 312.0)	...	(164.0)	(164.0)	(164.0)	(164.0)	(164.0)	(164.0)	(164.0)	(164.0)
8 Tax shield.........	629.6	...	78.7	78.7	78.7	78.7	78.7	78.7	78.7	78.7
9 Undiscounted cash flow........	(682.4)	...	(85.3)	(85.3)	(85.3)	(85.3)	(85.3)	(85.3)	(85.3)	(85.3)
10 Discounted cash flow (line 1 x line 9).........	(455.2)	...	(77.5)	(70.5)	(64.1)	(58.3)	(53.0)	(48.2)	(43.8)	(39.8)

* Thousands of dollars after tax; ( ) denotes outflow.

unaffected by the rent-or-buy choice, of course, it is unnecessary to make them part of the cash flow. If the decision aims solely to choose the least costly alternative, either as a "cost reduction" proposal or as a preliminary part of a "new business" analysis, the cash flow need state only the costs of each alternative.

Exhibit 3 isolates the cash flows associated with ownership (lines 2–6) and with a rented asset (lines 7–10).

Undiscounted, the total cost of owning for 8 years ($315,000 on line 5) appears $367,400 less costly than renting ($682,400 on line 9).

An earlier section explained that although the risks of ownership are avoided by renting, renting incurs added costs over the life of the asset. The rent-or-buy decision turns on whether saving these added costs by owning will adequately compensate for the ownership risks assumed. This requires a very subjective judgment, most of which, however, is best directed toward and expressed in the selection of an appropriate rate of discount. The funds employed in either renting or buying could be employed elsewhere, and the discount rate—here assumed at 10 percent —is by definition a measure of the foregone opportunity to use the funds elsewhere at equivalent risk.

The discounting operation makes the riskier ownership alternative with its large initial outlays relatively more costly (the present value of its cost becomes $402,300 on line 6), and the less risky renting alternative with its deferred payments relatively less costly (the present value of its costs becomes $455,200 on line 10). Even after this adjustment for the opportunity to use funds elsewhere at equivalent risk, however, the rental alternative remains $52,900 more costly (the same amount by which the owned-asset proposal was preferred in the profitability analysis).

It is evident that the assessment of the economic consequences of the decision is heavily influenced by the selection of the appropriate rate of discount. A higher rate of discount would further narrow the gap between the cost of renting and owning, and at a sufficiently high rate of discount we would even expect renting to appear less costly. The subjective judgment about the amount of savings necessary to compensate for the risk of ownership is not avoided by discounting—it is expressed by it. The considerations required in selecting the appropriate rate are discussed in chapter 19.

An investment decision—rent or buy—may thus proceed by comparing the present values of the alternatives, discounted at the opportunity cost of funds employed.

Leasing decision

A leasing decision, however, is not a pure investment decision. It is partly a financing decision. Unlike rental, the lease, as defined, is a commitment of the credit of the firm to a series of payments that, in total, will repay purchase price and financing costs. The lease is a combination of investment and financing alternatives. To the extent that the alternative to the lease would require a capital expenditure, the lease is an investment decision. To the extent that the alternative to the lease would require a long-term borrowing, the lease is a financing decision.

A lease, then, is equivalent to a combination buy-and-borrow alternative. One way to proceed would be to add to the investment decision—the "buy" alternative—a borrowing that represents the same amount of financing that the lease commits. The present value of the combined buy-and-borrow alternative could then be compared with the present value of the lease alternative and the less costly alternative chosen; they are comparable because each alternative has the same amount of financing. The cash flow of the foregone borrowing opportunity—the equivalent cash proceeds and the amortization stream—must be developed from the terms of the lease itself, rather than from the amount required to purchase the asset, otherwise each alternative will not have the same amount of financing.[1]

Another way that gives the same answer is to *subtract* from the lease the foregone borrowing opportunity. The remainder is an "investment equivalent" whose present value may be compared with the present value of the buy alternative to determine the less costly alternative; they are comparable because neither includes costs of financing.

Both give the same answer and we will show the arithmetic for both. The first way, however, is less versatile. Neither the cash flow of the lease nor the cash flow of the buy-and-borrow alternative can become part of a normal profitability analysis,[2] and neither present value is comparable to the present value of a rental in a least-cost analysis. The second way can be used for either subsequent analysis.

Debt equivalent. The debt equivalent of the lease is the cash flow that would occur if the lease's payment plan were committed to a general creditor by the firm—say, to a bank—instead of to the lessor. The creditor would give the firm cash proceeds in return for a promise to make the same installments as are made in the lease-payment plan. The amount of the cash proceeds is the present value of the installments at the firm's borrowing rate. The interest portion of the installment payment is deductible for tax purposes, so the cash flow of the debt equivalent has three parts:

1. Equivalent cash proceeds (equal to the present value of the lease payments at the firm's borrowing rate, or "capitalization"),
2. Series of installment payments (equal to the series of lease payments), and
3. Series of tax reductions resulting from deduction of interest portion of the installment payments.

Because the deductible interest portion of the payments is computed on the unpaid balance of the cash proceeds, which changes as the proceeds are repaid, the tax reductions are different in each period.

---

[1] See R. F. Vancil, *Leasing of Industrial Equipment* (New York: McGraw-Hill, 1963), chap. 5, for a discussion of the amount of financing that a lease commits.

[2] See W. D. McEachron, "Leasing, A Discounted Cash Flow Approach," *The Controller* (May, 1961), for a discussion of leasing in profitability analysis.

Exhibit 4 shows how the cash flow of the debt equivalent is derived for an 8-year lease calling for annual payments of $110,000 when the firm's cost of borrowing is 6 percent before tax, and the tax rate is 48 percent.

The equivalent cash proceeds of the lease are $683,000 (total line 3), and were computed by discounting the before-tax lease payments (line 1) at the firm's before-tax cost of borrowing (line 2).

EXHIBIT 4

The Debt Equivalent of a Lease*

Item	Total	Annual cash flow to end of period								
		0	1	2	3	4	5	6	7	8
Capitalization:										
1 Lease payments......(880.0)		...	(110.0)	(110.0)	(110.0)	(110.0)	(110.0)	(110.0)	(110.0)	(110.0)
2 Present value of $1 @										
6%................	...	1.000	0.943	0.890	0.840	0.792	0.747	0.705	0.665	0.627
3 Discounted cash flow.(683.0)		...	(103.7)	(97.9)	(92.4)	(87.1)	(82.2)	(77.6)	(73.1)	(69.0)
Amortization:										
4 Opening unpaid balance...........	...	...	683.0	614.1	540.9	463.4	381.2	294.1	201.7	103.8
5 Payments (line 1).....(880.0)		...	(110.0)	(110.0)	(110.0)	(110.0)	(110.0)	(110.0)	(110.0)	(110.0)
6 Interest (6% × line 4).......(197.0)		...	(41.1)	(36.8)	(32.5)	(27.8)	(22.9)	(17.6)	(12.1)	(6.2)
7 Principal (line 5 less line 6)..............(683.0)		...	(68.9)	(73.2)	(77.5)	(82.2)	(87.1)	(92.4)	(97.9)	(103.8)
8 Closing unpaid balance (line 4 less line 7).............	...	...	614.1	540.9	463.4	381.2	294.1	201.7	103.8	...
Debt equivalent:										
9 Cash proceeds (total line 3)........ 683.0		683.0	...	...	...	...	...	...	...	...
10 Payments (line 1).....(880.0)		...	(110.0)	(110.0)	(110.0)	(110.0)	(110.0)	(110.0)	(110.0)	(110.0)
11 Tax reduction on interest equivalent (48% × line 6)...... 94.5		...	19.7	17.7	15.6	13.3	11.0	8.4	5.8	3.0
12 Net cash flow after tax................(102.5)		683.0	(90.3)	(92.3)	(94.4)	(96.7)	(99.0)	(101.6)	(104.2)	(107.0)

*Thousands of dollars; ( ) denotes outflow.

The interest portion of each payment (line 6) is computed by taking 6 percent of the opening balance (line 4). The initial opening unpaid balance is the equivalent cash proceeds of the lease. Subsequent opening unpaid balances are the closing balances of the prior period (line 8). These closing balances are computed by deducting from the opening balance the portion of the total payment that is not allocated to interest —the "principal" payment (line 7).

The cash flow of the debt equivalent (line 12) is, then, the net of three items: (1) cash proceeds, (2) series of payments, and (3) series of tax reductions on the interest equivalent.

Buy-and-borrow. One way of using the cash flow of the lease's after-tax debt equivalent is to add it to the after-tax cash flow of the ownership flow and compare the present value of this combined buy-and-borrow decision with the present value of the equivalent decision, the lease. Exhibit 5 shows this comparison.

EXHIBIT 5

Comparison of Lease with Buy-and-Borrow*

Item	Total	Annual cash flow to end of period								
		0	1	2	3	4	5	6	7	8
Memo:											
1 Present value of $1 @ 10%..	...	1.000	0.909	0.826	0.751	0.683	0.621	0.565	0.513	0.467
Lease:											
2 Payments after tax (52% × $110.0/year before tax)...	(457.6)	...	(57.2)	(57.2)	(57.2)	(57.2)	(57.2)	(57.2)	(57.2)	(57.2)
3 Discounted cash flow (line 1 × line 2)..........	(305.1)	...	(52.0)	(47.2)	(43.0)	(39.1)	(35.5)	(32.3)	(29.3)	(26.7)
Buy and borrow:											
4 Buy (table 3, line 5).........	(315.0)	(651.0)	74.6	65.3	56.0	46.7	37.3	28.0	18.7	9.4
5 Borrow debt equivalent (table 4, line 12).........	(102.5)	683.0	(90.3)	(92.3)	(94.4)	(96.7)	(99.0)	(101.6)	(104.2)	(107.0)
6 Undiscounted cash flow....	(417.5)	32.0	(15.7)	(27.0)	(38.4)	(50.0)	(61.7)	(73.6)	(85.5)	(97.6)
7 Discounted cash flow (line 1 × line 6)...........	(236.9)	32.0	(14.3)	(22.3)	(28.8)	(34.2)	(38.3)	(41.6)	(43.9)	(45.5)

*Thousands of dollars after tax; ( ) denotes outflow.

The present value of the after-tax lease payments, discounted at 10 percent, is $305,100 (line 3). The present value of a combination of the cash flows of buying (line 4) and of committing the same amount of financing that the lease represents (line 5) is $236,900 (line 7).

This method shows the lease is $68,200 more costly.

Purchase equivalent. Another way of using the cash flow of the lease's debt equivalent is to subtract the debt equivalent from the cash flow of the lease. In effect this removes the financing from the lease and the remaining cash flow is a "purchase equivalent" that is comparable to the cash flow from ownership (which also has no financing). Exhibit 6 shows the comparison.

The present value of the cost of the purchase equivalent of the lease is $470,500 (line 5), and of ownership, $402,300 (line 7), so again ownership is shown to be $68,200 less costly. That the answer is the same as the buy-and-borrow solution is not a coincidence, of course, and simply demonstrates that the two methods are interchangeable.

The purchase equivalent method is more versatile, however, because its cash flow can be entered into a profitability analysis—that is, an analysis that includes revenues—to yield a profitability index (net present value, discounted cash flow rate of return, etc.) that is comparable to other unlevered, owned-asset projects in a whole portfolio of alternatives. Exhibit 7 illustrates this.

The proposal using a leased asset has a net present value of $323,000 which means that it is acceptable. Because the cash flows use the purchase equivalent of the lease—and thus exclude the financing elements of the lease decision—the net present value is comparable with the net present values of ownership ($391,400) and rental ($338,500), and leasing is therefore less profitable than either of these.

EXHIBIT 6

Comparison of Purchase Equivalent with Ownership*

		Annual cash flow to end of period								
Item	Total	0	1	2	3	4	5	6	7	8
Memo:										
1 Present value of $1 @ 10%............. ...		1.000	0.909	0.826	0.751	0.683	0.621	0.565	0.513	0.467
Purchase equivalent:										
2 Lease payments after tax (52% × $110.0/year before tax)............(457.6)		...	(57.2)	(57.2)	(57.2)	(57.2)	(57.2)	(57.2)	(57.2)	(57.2)
3 Less: debt equivalent (table 4, line 12).......(102.5)		683.0	(90.3)	(92.3)	(94.4)	(96.7)	(99.0)	(101.6)	(104.2)	(107.0)
4 Purchase equivalent (line 2 less line 3).......(355.1)		(683.0)	33.1	35.1	37.2	39.5	41.8	44.4	47.0	49.8
5 Discounted cash flow (line 1 × line 4).........(470.5)		(683.0)	30.1	29.0	27.9	27.0	26.0	25.1	24.1	23.3
Ownership:										
6 Cash flow (table 3, line 5).................(315.0)		(651.0)	74.6	65.3	56.0	46.7	37.3	28.0	18.7	9.4
7 Discounted cash flow.....(402.3)		(651.0)	67.8	53.9	42.1	31.9	23.2	15.8	9.6	4.4

* Thousands of dollars; ( ) denotes outflow.

EXHIBIT 7

Profitability Analysis of Leased Asset*

		Annual cash flow to end of period								
Item	Total	0	1	2	3	4	5	6	7	8
1 Cash flow from operations (table 1, line 3)...............	1 120.0	...	175.0	200.0	200.0	150.0	125.0	90.0	90.0	90.0
2 Cash flow of purchase equiva- lent (table 6, line 4)...........	(355.1)	(683.0)	33.1	35.1	37.2	39.5	41.8	44.4	47.0	49.8
3 Net cash flow....................	764.9	(683.0)	208.1	235.1	237.2	189.5	166.8	134.4	137.0	139.8
4 Present value of $1 @ 10%......	...	1.000	0.909	0.826	0.751	0.683	0.621	0.565	0.513	0.467
5 Discounted cash flow..........	323.0	(683.0)	189.2	194.2	178.1	129.4	103.6	75.9	70.3	65.3

* Thousands of dollars after tax; ( ) denotes outflow.

If, for one of the reasons cited earlier, the lease must be or will be selected, the purchase equivalent method has both measured the extra cost involved and provided a profitability measurement that can be compared with other proposals in the portfolio of alternatives to be budgeted.

For purposes of explanation, the purchase equivalent has been derived as the residual cash flow when the debt equivalent was subtracted from the after-tax lease payments. When using the technique, however, it is more efficient to compute the purchase equivalent more directly. Exhibit 8 (next section) shows how this may be done; the calculations in effect factor the lease into two parts, a purchase equivalent and a debt equivalent. The sum of the after-tax net cash flows of the purchase equivalent and the debt equivalent "prove" to the after-tax cash flow of the lease payments, demonstrating that the computations have indeed factored the lease into these two parts.

Summary guidelines

Exhibit 8 recapitulates the least-cost analysis of a lease, rent, or buy decision as displayed for decision by one firm.

EXHIBIT 8

Recapitulation of Lease, Rent, or Buy Decision

PROJECT EVALUATION: BUY, RENT OR LEASE ANALYSIS   CO-2528C (9-60)

COMPANY UNIT: Research Laboratory		PROJECT: Purchase, Rent, or Lease #1342 Computer System		EXHIBIT	
PREPARED BY: A. N. Alyst	DATE: 1/2/69	CASE: Most Probable			

L I N E NO.		ITEMS & UNITS	TOTAL	ANNUAL CASH FLOW ($ THOUSAND)										
				0	1	2	3	4	5	6	7	8	9	10
1		DEPRECIATION	(700.0)		(155.5)	(136.1)	(116.7)	(97.2)	(77.8)	(58.3)	(38.9)	(19.5)		
2	BEFORE TAX	MAINTENANCE												
3														
4														
5		CAPITAL OUTLAY	(700.0)	(700.0)										
6		DEPRECIATION TAX SAVING (-T × LINE 1)	336.0		74.6	65.3	56.0	46.7	37.3	28.0	18.7	9.4		
7		MAINTENANCE = (1 -T) × LINE 2												
8	AFTER TAX (T= 48%)	Investment Credit	49.0	49.0										
9														
10														
11														
12														
13		CASH FLOW (TOTAL LINES 5 TO 12)	(315.0)	(651.0)	74.6	65.3	56.0	46.7	37.3	28.0	18.7	9.4		
14	PRESENT VALUE	PV OF $1 @ 10%		1.0000	0.909	0.826	0.751	0.683	0.621	0.565	0.513	0.467		
15		DISCOUNTED CASH FLOW (LINE 13 × LINE 14)	(402.3)	(651.0)	67.8	53.9	42.1	31.9	23.2	15.8	9.6	4.4		
16		RENTALS	(1312.0)		(164.0)	(164.0)	(164.0)	(164.0)	(164.0)	(164.0)	(164.0)	(164.0)		
17														
18	BEFORE TAX													
19														
20														
21														
22		TOTAL (LINES 16 TO 21)	(1312.0)		(164.0)	(164.0)	(164.0)	(164.0)	(164.0)	(164.0)	(164.0)	(164.0)		
23	AFTER TAX	CASH FLOW (1-T) × LINE 22	(682.4)		(85.3)	(85.3)	(85.3)	(85.3)	(85.3)	(85.3)	(85.3)	(85.3)		
24	PRESENT VALUE	PV OF $1 @ 10%		1.0000	0.909	0.826	0.751	0.683	0.621	0.565	0.513	0.467		
25		DISCOUNTED CASH FLOW (LINE 23 × LINE 24)	(455.2)		(77.5)	(70.5)	(64.1)	(58.3)	(53.0)	(48.2)	(43.8)	(39.8)		
26	AMORTIZATION EQUIVALENT	LEASE PAYMENTS (For Unequal Payments use Line 38)			Lines 38 to 45 used for illustrative purposes.										
27		PV OF $1 @ 6 %, INVERTED												
28		AMORTIZATION EQUIV. (LINE 26 × LINE 27) OR LINE 44	(683.0)		(68.9)	(73.2)	(77.5)	(82.2)	(87.1)	(92.4)	(97.9)	(103.8)		
29		INVESTMENT EQUIV. (LINE 28 "TOTAL" COLUMN)	(683.0)	(683.0)										
30		AMORTIZATION TAX SAVING (-T × LINE 28)	327.9		33.1	35.1	37.2	39.5	41.8	44.4	47.0	49.8		
31	AFTER TAX (T= 48%)													
32														
33														
34														
35		CASH FLOW (LINES 29 TO 34)	(355.1)	(683.0)	33.1	35.1	37.2	39.5	41.8	44.4	47.0	49.8		
36	PRESENT VALUE	PV OF $1 @ 10%		1.0000	0.909	0.826	0.751	0.683	0.621	0.565	0.513	0.467		
37		DISCOUNTED CASH FLOW (LINE 35 × LINE 36)	(470.5)	(683.0)	30.1	29.0	27.9	27.0	26.0	25.1	24.1	23.3		
38		LEASE PAYMENTS	(880.0)		(110.0)	(110.0)	(110.0)	(110.0)	(110.0)	(110.0)	(110.0)	(110.0)		
39		PV OF $1 @ 6%			0.943	0.890	0.840	0.792	0.747	0.705	0.665	0.627		
40		DISCOUNTED PAYMENTS (LINE 38 × LINE 39)	(683.0)		(103.7)	(97.9)	(92.4)	(87.1)	(82.2)	(77.6)	(73.1)	(69.0)		
41		OPENING UNPAID BALANCE (Enter Total Line 40 in yr. 1)			683.0	614.1	540.9	463.4	381.2	294.1	201.7	103.8		
42		LEASE PAYMENTS (LINE 38)	(880.0)		(110.0)	(110.0)	(110.0)	(110.0)	(110.0)	(110.0)	(110.0)	(110.0)		
43		INTEREST (6% OF LINE 41)	(197.0)		(41.1)	(36.8)	(32.5)	(27.8)	(22.9)	(17.6)	(12.1)	(6.2)		
44		AMORTIZATION EQUIVALENT (Line 42-Line 43; Enter on Line 28)	(683.0)		(68.9)	(73.2)	(77.5)	(82.2)	(87.1)	(92.4)	(97.9)	(103.8)		
45		CLOSING UNPAID BALANCE (LINE 41 – LINE 44)			614.1	540.9	463.4	381.2	294.1	201.7	103.8			

The purchase and rental alternatives are similar to those previously displayed here. For the lease, similar capitalization and amortization items are shown that were used to isolate the debt equivalent (see table 4).

The after-tax cash flow of the purchase equivalent (line 35) has two parts: (1) the equivalent purchase price (line 29), which is the same as the capitalized value of the before-tax lease payments (total line 44), and (2) the equivalent tax reduction traceable to deduction of amortization of principal (line 44), which is analogous to the deduction of depreciation charges in an owned asset.

The analysis yields the present value of the costs of each alternative, from which the least costly may be selected:

	Present Value of Costs
Buy	$402,300
Rent	455,200
Lease	470,500

Supplementary measures

The foregoing presents a complete and consistent method of lease evaluation. It is complete in that it explicitly values both the investing and borrowing components of the lease in terms of the appropriate opportunity rate of return. It is consistent in that the "least-cost" solution —whether lease, rent, or buy—is expressed in terms that can be inserted in a study of total project profitability.

Other measures, while less complete or consistent, may still be useful in describing selected economic facets of the decision. To the extent that these supplementary measures give the decision-maker a better "feel" for the alternatives, it is worthwhile to compute and present them. Because they are incomplete, however, they may give solutions that in marginal cases are in conflict with the solutions we have advocated. It must be remembered, therefore, that these supplementary solutions do not yield criteria for decision, but simply focus on a particular dimension of a decision and gauge its size.

Borrowing rate. One supplementary measure focuses on the financing dimension of the lease, and measures the implied before-tax borrowing rate. The net amount required to buy the asset (purchase price less investment tax credit) is defined as the amount of the borrowing, and the lease payments as the amortization; the implied borrowing rate is the rate of discount that makes the present value of the lease payments equal to the purchase price.

The rate is found by trial and error. Exhibit 9 illustrates the process. The lease payments were first discounted at a rate of 6 percent and the present value of the cost was $683,100, $32,100 more than the purchase price of $651,000. This means the future payments should be discounted at a higher rate to reduce further their present value; at 8 percent the present value is $632,200, $18,800 less than the purchase price. By interpolation, a rate of 7 percent will equate the present value of the before-tax payment with the purchase price, and is the implied before-tax cost of borrowing.

This before-tax borrowing rate is comparable with the firm's before-tax borrowing rate and, in our illustrative case, indicates that the lease has a higher implied interest rate than the firm's normal borrowing rate of 6 percent.

EXHIBIT 9

The Borrowing Rate of a Lease*

Item	Total	Annual cash flow to end of period								
		0	1	2	3	4	5	6	7	8
1 Net purchase price....	651.0	651.0	...	...	...	...	...	...	...	...
2 Lease payments before tax.................(880.0)		...	(110.0)	(110.0)	(110.0)	(110.0)	(110.0)	(110.0)	(110.0)	(110.0)
Trial @ 6%:										
3 PV of $1.............. ...		1.000	0.943	0.890	0.840	0.792	0.747	0.705	0.665	0.627
4 Discounted cash flow..(683.1)		...	(103.7)	(97.9)	(92.4)	(87.1)	(82.2)	(77.6)	(73.2)	(69.0)
Trial @ 8%:										
5 PV of $1.............. ...		1.000	0.926	0.857	0.794	0.735	0.681	0.630	0.584	0.540
6 Discounted cash flow..(632.2)		...	(101.9)	(94.3)	(87.3)	(80.9)	(74.9)	(69.3)	(64.2)	(59.4)
Proof @ 7%:										
7 PV of $1.............. ...		1.000	0.935	0.873	0.816	0.763	0.713	0.666	0.623	0.582
8 Discounted cash flow..(656.8)		...	(102.9)	(96.0)	(89.8)	(83.9)	(78.4)	(73.3)	(68.5)	(64.0)

* Thousands of dollars; ( ) denotes outflow.

Lessor's return. Another supplementary measurement is the implied after-tax rate of return that would be earned by the lessor. The lease payments represent income to the lessor, and his ownership costs are likely to be the same as the user's would be if the user had purchased. Exhibit 10 illustrates the calculation, which again requires trial-and-error determination of the rate.

EXHIBIT 10

Calculation of Lessor's Return*

Item	Total	Annual cash flow to end of year								
		0	1	2	3	4	5	6	7	8
1 Income: Lease payments after tax............................	457.6	...	57.2	57.2	57.2	57.2	57.2	57.2	57.2	57.2
2 Costs: Ownership after tax (table 3, line 5)........................(315.0)		(651.0)	74.6	65.3	56.0	46.7	37.3	28.0	18.7	9.4
3 Net cash flow....................	142.6	(651.0)	131.8	122.5	113.2	103.9	94.5	85.2	75.9	66.6
Trial @ 4%:										
4 PV of $1......................... ...		1.000	0.962	0.925	0.889	0.855	0.822	0.790	0.760	0.731
5 Discounted cash flow............	29.9	(651.0)	126.8	113.3	100.6	88.8	77.7	67.3	57.7	48.7
Trial @ 6%:										
6 PV of $1......................... ...		1.000	0.943	0.890	0.840	0.792	0.747	0.705	0.665	0.627
7 Discounted cash flow............	(17.3)	(651.0)	124.3	109.0	95.1	82.3	70.6	60.1	50.5	41.8
Proof @ 5%:										
8 PV of $1......................... ...		1.000	0.952	0.907	0.864	0.823	0.784	0.746	0.711	0.677
9 Discounted cash flow............	5.7	(651.0)	125.5	111.1	97.8	85.5	74.1	63.6	54.0	45.1

* Thousands of dollars; ( ) denotes outflow.

The rate of return earned by the lessor in the illustrative case (which assumes no residual value is to be received by the lessor) is 5 percent after tax. In some cases it may be useful to refine the calculation by making more precise assumptions about the lessor's net cash flow. A lessor may be known to have a different effective income tax rate, or use a different depreciation schedule, or have a different purchase price or construction cost, or have a different residual-value assumption, for example, and these more precise assumptions can be made part of the calculation. As an additional refinement, the lessor may be assumed to finance his ownership costs by assigning the lease payments to a creditor (in effect, using the user's credit to finance ownership), and a calculation can be made of the lessor's return on his equity alone.

Break-even residual. Most lease, rent, or buy decisions hinge on the assumption made about residual value. As mentioned above, it is even conceivable that the lessor and user knowingly and with good reason make different assumptions about residual value. Because of the sensitivity of the decision to this factor, it is frequently useful to compute the break-even residual: the value that makes the user indifferent between buying and leasing. The prospective user can compare this value with his own guess about future value and determine how far off his guess would have to be before he regretted his choice.

The technique is simple. Compute the present value of the cost of buying with a zero residual. Compute the present value of the cost of leasing. If buying is more costly with a zero residual, compute the future value—at the time of salvage—of the additional cost. This is the after-tax value that must accrue to the owner to make him indifferent. If the user expects the after-tax value to be more, he should buy so that the extra value will accrue to him. If he expects it to be less, he should rent to avoid the loss.

Complications

The foregoing discussion has avoided certain complications in lease evaluation in order to develop first an understanding of the underlying principles. These principles, however, have to be adapted to specific cases, and the following discussion identifies some complications that may arise and suggests ways for handling them.

Near-payout leases. The techniques presented here make a distinction between a lease agreement (debt-like) and a rental agreement (expense). In most cases the difference is readily identified. A 10-year tanker charter that obliges the user to make payments enabling the lessor to recover fully his investment and financing costs is clearly a full-payout debt-like obligation; a spot charter that expires at the end of a single voyage is clearly not. In the first case the user assumes the risks of ownership; in the second, the lessor.

Not all equipment markets offer such clear-cut alternatives, especially those with shorter useful lives, such as computers. Computer manufacturers typically offer rental terms that can be canceled in, say, 90 days, and are clearly non-payout expenses. So-called "third-party" lessors, however, will buy the equipment and require significantly lower payments than the manufacturer's rentals in return for a significantly longer period of commitment. Originally such third-party lessors dealt exclusively in full-payout leases, but as the computer-leasing market became more competitive the lessors began to assume ownership risk with agreements that did not fully recover investment and financing costs.

For example, a lessor might offer a 5-year term that recovers the purchase price—but not financing costs. Another might offer a 3-year term that recovers, say, 80 percent of the purchase price. In each case the lessor gambles that the residual earning power at the end of the initial agreement will provide full payout and a profit.

Such "near-payout" leases are neither clearly a debt equivalent nor clearly an expense, and their evaluation requires more subjective assessment of such factors as the noncancelable term of the lease and the estimate of residual value.

In some cases the noncancelable term of the agreement may be relatively more important than the relationship of the purchase price to the amount committed. Other factors aside, a contract to make a series of payments to a creditor for an extended period of time is a debt-like obligation. For example, an 8-year lease that commits for 80 percent of the purchase price may be held equivalent to an 8-year installment loan whose proceeds finance 80 percent of the cost. Regardless of the amount the lessor recovers, then, a long-term lease may well be held a capitalizable debt equivalent just because it is long term.

In other cases the estimate of residual value may be an important factor. If a three-year lease recovers 80 percent of the purchase price of equipment whose residual value is most likely well in excess of the residual 20 percent, the lessor assumes little of the risk of ownership; in effect the lessee pays for something he isn't getting—a shift in ownership risk. This may be the case, for example, in routine data-processing equipment of well-known manufacturers. In other instances, of course, say in a new large computer of a little-known manufacturer, the same lease terms may represent a significant assumption of risk on the part of the lessor.

Unequal terms.   If one lease offers a different noncancelable term than another—say five years compared with eight years—the analysis can proceed in either of two ways. One way is to assume that the five-year lease will be renewed for three years at the same or different rate at the end of the noncancelable term; the resulting eight-year cash flow can be compared with the eight-year lease. Another way is to assume that the eight-year contract has some "residual value" at the end of five years, so that five-year cash flows can be compared. Such a value might be realized, for example, if the eight-year lease enables the lessee to "save" the present value of the renewal payments on the five-year lease (in which case the solution should be the same as when eight-year cash flows are used), or if the lessee could sublet the equipment for the last three years of the eight-year term and earn rental income.

It may be very helpful in comparing leases of unequal lives to compute the break-even residual value: the value that the eight-year lease would have to have at the end of five years to make the user indifferent between the contracts. If the user foresaw a value higher than the break-even value, he would prefer the eight-year contract because the extra value would then accrue to him. If less, he would prefer the five-year contract to avoid the loss.

Summary

This chapter has reviewed some of the intangible considerations that affect the lease, rent, or buy decision, but has concentrated on ways to describe the economic consequences of the choice. The rent-or-buy decision can be viewed as an investment decision that seeks the less costly of two ways to obtain the use of an asset. The lease-or-buy decision, however, must recognize that the lease represents, in part, a means of financing; when the debt equivalent of the lease has been factored out of the lease the residual is an investment equivalent comparable with the buy alternative.

Supplementary measures are frequently helpful in the decision process, but these may be incomplete descriptions of economic consequences and as a rule should not supplant the analysis of least cost at the opportunity rate.

Bibliography

BIERMAN, HAROLD JR., and SMIDT, SEYMOUR.   "Buy or Lease," *The Capital Budgeting Decision,* chap. 12, 2d ed. New York: Macmillan Company, 1966.

VANCIL, RICHARD F. *Leasing of Industrial Equipment.* New York: McGraw-Hill, 1963.

WOODS, L. M.   "Evaluation of Leases," *Accounting for Capital, Construction, and Maintenance Expenditures,* chap. 3. Englewood Cliffs, N.J.: Prentice-Hall, 1967.

PART IV

Planning and budgeting

Environmental and competitive information

Patrick Conley*

How to find out about the external environment in which a firm exists and what to find out about it will be our primary concerns in this chapter. While data about the firm itself are commonly used in control of operation and in *tactical* decisions, data about the environment of the firm are important in strategic analyses and decisions.

In common with many other types of information, that on environment, including competitors, is characterized by superabundance rather than scarcity, and the task is usually that of selection rather than collection. Furthermore, each reader will have favorite sources with which he is comfortable and to which he frequently refers. For a truly comprehensive treatment, which would not be possible in a handbook, the reader is referred to Manley's *Business Information.*[1] Inevitably, in the discussion which follows some useful sources will be omitted, but the redundancy in the sources listed will partially compensate.

It hardly seems necessary to point out the extravagance in collecting information that will not be used. Before undertaking the collection and analysis of information, it is reasonable to ask, "For what decision is this information required?" For many decisions, rough estimates can be substituted for more precise data. Moreover, personnel engaged in collecting information which they suspect will not form the basis of deci-

---

* Vice President, The Boston Consulting Group, Inc., Boston.
[1] Marian C. Manley, *Business Information, How To Find and Use It* (New York: Harper and Brothers, 1955).

sions tend to become casual, and their information tends to become erroneous.

While this chapter lists many *sources* of information, the vitally important *uses* are discussed elsewhere. Chapter 22, "Forecasting and trend analysis," deals with techniques useful in analyzing the data; Chapter 23, "Profit planning and budgeting," is concerned with converting suitably anaylzed data into a budget; Chapter 27, "Capital budgeting procedures," describes an important use of these and other data; and Chapter 26, "Corporate long range planning," of course describes a key application.

Needs for environmental and competitive information

Formulating own stategy and plans

The plans of a corporation, whether they be formal or informal, rest on a set of data and assumptions about future data. Corporate budgets, forecasts of performance, and financial plans have validity only to the extent that their data bases are sound. Strategic plans, in particular, depend critically on assumptions about the economic and technological environment and about competitors' behavior.

Environmental and competitive information is needed not only in preparing plans and budgets but also as a background for judging the validity of those plans and budgets presented for approval. For instance, the validity of a forecast of increased unit sales can only be judged in the light of market growth rate and competitors' aggressiveness. In a slow-growth market with vigorous competitors, a significant sales increase will be unlikely.

An aggressive pricing strategy may, in another case, depend on strong financial resources. Unless the availability and cost of those resources has been evaluated, the strategy cannot be considered complete.

Detecting competitors' strategies

Almost as important as having clear and complete plans is the perception of those plans being employed by the three or four major competitors. Of particular interest are competitive policies regarding dividends, profitability, and debt since these determine the maximum growth rates competitors can sustain without new equity.

Competitors' pricing policies and productive capacities will be strong factors in influencing their reactions to any maneuver on your part to increase market share. A competitor's debt leverage will affect the margin he requires for a given return on equity and, as a result, will affect the price levels he can tolerate. From another standpoint, a competitor's use of debt financing will strongly affect the price he will bid for a desirable resource such as an oil lease or a timber tract.

Sensing changes in environment or competitors' strategies

While good environmental and competitive information is vital for constructing one's strategy initially, a continuous monitoring of such information is necessary to insure prompt identification of changes which require strategy modifications. A competitor's construction of new capacity might well presage a softening in prices that would, in turn, require major plan and budget revisions. A rapidly developing credit "crunch" would require complete revision of any plans based on highly leveraged operation. More prosaically, a shift in inflation rate must be factored into existing budgets. It is important to identify the characteristics of the environment and of competitors which are most critical for the success of plans and budgets. One may not wish to monitor all characteristics of the environment and competitors, but one must systematically monitor such high-sensitivity factors.

Techniques for acquiring environmental and competitive information

Direct information

Trade data, economic data, and much financial data are available directly from suitable publications. Identifying, selecting, and monitoring these direct sources will provide most of the information required. However, publication delays will cause most published information to be relatively stale.

Developed information

Current market information, financial analyses of industry and competitors, analyses of competitors' policies and strengths, industry and product growth rates, and many other interesting kinds of information are not usually available in published sources. Instead, information of this sort is obtained through research, or it is constructed or inferred from known data. Professional consulting assistance, often highly specialized, is frequently useful in developing many kinds of information, for example, market data. Since developed information is intrinsically expensive, it is usually produced only to satisfy a clearly defined need.

Predicted information

Information describing the economic or competitive environment at a time in the future is obtained by forecasts. Such forecasts are perhaps the most common. However, technological forecasts are now fairly frequently encountered as adjuncts to long-range plans.

Forecasts are intrinsically "soft" sources of information, and it is wise to seek confirmation whenever possible. If forecast information is incorporated as a critical part of a plan or strategy, then it is desirable to provide a mechanism for monitoring the developing accuracy of the forecast; the plan should be modified as soon as actual information becomes available.

Local and regional economic information

Typical sources of local statistical and economic information are shown in Exhibit 1. Many newspapers publish annual issues containing regional business and financial statistics in addition to a certain amount of current local statistical information.

EXHIBIT 1
Local and Regional Information Sources

Sources	Information Type
Federal Reserve Bank (12 regional banks —for example, Federal Reserve Bank of Boston, *New England Economic Review*).	Periodic analyses of business and economic conditions.
Chambers of Commerce (major U.S. cities).	Monthly bulletins containing indices of local business activity, labor rates, employment, manufacturers, bank clearings, etc.
U.S. Dept. of Labor, Bureau of Labor Statistics, *Employment and Earnings Statistics for States and Areas* (also Regional Director in larger cities).	Local employment and unemployment statistics, labor rates, etc., from cooperating state agencies.
State Department of Commerce (most states).	Labor rates, production indices, lists of financial and industrial institutions, land and facilities listings, transportation statistics, specialized manufacturer statistics, etc.
Regional Industrial Development Corporation (many regions—see, for example, The New England Council or Regional Industrial Development Corporation of Western Pennsylvania).	Brochures describing industrial features of region. Also assistance in site selection, financial connections, and sometimes information on financial aid programs for attracting industry.

Some of the larger cities have downtown business libraries, and in some locations university business school libraries can also be used. Correspondents or branches of your bank can be helpful in steering you to additional local and regional information sources. Do not overlook your own field sales force as guide to sources of information in its locales.

National economic information

Selected sources of national statistical and economic information are shown in Exhibit 2. The national economy has, particularly in recent years, been the object of intensive attention and measurement. The federal government remains the usual source of nationwide statistical material appearing in newspapers and business magazines. Since national economic data are commonly not needed immediately, the excellent summary reports published annually or quarterly by various government agencies can serve as basic references.

EXHIBIT 2

National Information Sources

Sources	Information Type
National Archives and Records Service, *United States Government Organization Manual.*	Lists activities, including information reporting functions, of all federal bureaus.
U.S. Government Printing Office, *Selected United States Government Publications.*	Bi-weekly listing of major studies and reports of any nature.
President of the United States, *Economic Report;* Council of Economic Advisers, *Annual Report.*	General summary. Economic statistical series for United States; sources are included for reference if primary detail is desired.
Council of Economic Advisers, *Economic Indicators.*	Monthly economic statistical series.
U.S. Department of Commerce, Office of Business Economics, *Survey of Current Business.*	General monthly economic activity, financial statistics, activity, indices, and data.
U.S. Bureau of the Budget, Special Analyses.	Brief summaries of federal budget items in categories of major interest, e.g., research and development.
U.S. Department of Commerce, Business and Defense Services Administration, *U.S. Industrial Outlook.*	Narrative and statistical trend analyses on industry and industry rates for major areas in U.S. economy.
U.S. Department of Commerce, Bureau of the Census, *Statistical Abstract of the United States.*	Annual summary of population, social, and business statistics and data.
U.S. Department of Commerce, Bureau of the Census, *Survey of Manufactures.*	Annual summary of industrial statistics.
U.S. Department of Commerce, Bureau of the Census, *Current Population Reports.*	Analyses of population, birth rates, death rates, etc. Population characteristics, technical studies, population estimates, and special censuses on consumer income and consumer buying indicators.
U.S. Department of Labor, Bureau of Labor Statistics, *Employment and Earnings and Monthly Report on the Labor Force.*	Monthly series on employment rates, weekly earnings, wage scales, etc.
Federal Reserve System, *Federal Reserve Bulletin.*	Monthly summary of banking data, interest rates, financial statistics, index of industrial production, etc.
Securities and Exchange Commission, *Statistical Bulletin.*	Stock transactions.

In addition to national economic statistical information, most corporations have special interest in detailed, frequently updated data in certain areas. A careful observation of current shareholder expectations available, at some expense, through direct inquiry or survey is sometimes of great value. The behavior of the stock market strongly affects acquisition plans. The Dow-Jones Index from the daily *Wall Street Journal* is a widely used measure of market trends. *The New York Times* Index is also well known. These are often available from other newspapers.

A regular culling of market comment, advisory letters, analysts' reports, and editorial material not only concerning one's own company but also concerning competing companies, the industry, and the economy can be assembled and analyzed periodically. Business and financial newspapers and journals are principal sources, while the reports of brokerage houses and market services are useful supplements. The corporation's investment bankers, or even its officers' brokerage houses, can be enlisted as regular sources for the kind of information about the "temperament" of that part of the financial community of particular interest to your corporation and industry. First National City Bank's *Monthly Economic Letter* is a good example of a source for this type of information.

From the financial news media it is simple to chart information concerning the cost of debt and equity capital and the cost and availability of labor. Changing labor rates can also be monitored by means of reported settlements in major contract negotiations as well as through statistical information from the Departments of Labor and Commerce.

International economic information

If corporate interests (or competition) extend abroad, the need to monitor selected foreign statistical information will be very similar to that for U.S. data. Unfortunately, foreign statistics are not as extensive as, and similar titles do not always mean the same as ours. A letter or telephone call to the embassy or trade mission of the appropriate country (addressed to Washington, D.C., if no local office is known) will initiate the development of those data sources which are available. Inquiries should also be made from the corporation's bank and, through it, the bank's foreign correspondents. More formal sources of statistical information are listed in Exhibit 3.

Usually foreign affiliates or international divisions of your own company can provide guidance to additional sources of information in a particular country or region.

Resource and commodity information

The plans of most corporations require or assume a forecast of the availabilities of various raw materials, feedstocks, process materials, com-

EXHIBIT 3

International Information Sources

Sources	Information Type
U.S. Dept. of Commerce, *Overseas Business Reports.*	Basic data on economies of various countries on trade with them.
*OECD, *OECD Economic Outlook.*	Monthly summary of economic trends and prospects in OECD countries.
OECD, *Main Economic Indicators.*	Monthly summary by countries of wages, prices, interest rates, and other indicators.
United Nations, *Statistical Yearbook.*	Annual summary of world population, production, consumption, finance, and similar statistics by country.
International Monetary Fund, *International Financial Statistics.*	Monthly summary of extensive list of financial statistics, including exchange and interest rates, prices, and production.
The Economist.	Weekly news magazine devoted to United Kingdom economic, business, and financial news.
Japan Economic Journal.	Weekly English language edition of newspaper devoted to Japanese and Asian economic, business, and financial news.

* A complete catalog of the extensive OECD publications is available from the OECD Publications Center, Washington, D.C. 20006.

ponents, and other resources. Key data in such forecasts are accurate predictions of the availability of particular materials. Even with gross forecasts of resources, it is important to apply carefully those restrictions, such as transportation availability or national policy limitations, which may practically limit the availability of various materials. In those instances where one seeks nonhistorical data, such as estimates of national or world supply, it is wise to try to find several sources. Usually there is a substantial spread in estimates obtained from several reliable sources, and the extent of the spread should be known and its implications recognized. Moreover, one must carefully assess the possibility and direction of bias which may exist in a given source. Typical sources of information on the supply and availability of commodity and resources are shown in Exhibit 4.

Tariff barriers, import quotas, defense or other priorities, and social or political pressures may all act to change practical resource availability or substantially increase cost. For instance, to predict the availability of, say, crude oil in Puerto Rico, one must not only know the probable world supply and distribution, but must also assess the effects of probable actions by the Texas Railroad Commission in setting allowables, the trend in national import quotas, the costs and availability of transportation, possible changes in depletion allowances, the success of the com-

EXHIBIT 4

Commodity and Resource Information Sources

Sources	Information Type
U.S. Dept. of the Interior, Bureau of Mines.	Supplies, production, and utilization of oil and metal ores.
U.S. Dept. of Interior Geological Survey.	Location and supply of minerals, ores, and petroleum.
U.S. Dept. of Interior, Bureau of Mines, *Minerals Yearbook*.	Annual production information on metal and mineral products in various stages of refining and finishing.
U.S. Dept. of Agriculture, *Agricultural Abstract*.	Annual crop production and yields; forecasts of current annual production.
U.S. Atomic Energy Commission.	Electric power production and forecast; present and future supply of uranium.
Resources for the Future (Foundation) *Resources in America's Future: Patterns of Requirements and Availabilities*.	Forecasts of availability of natural resources.
American Iron and Steel Institute, *Steel Facts*.	Supply and utilization statistics on metal ores, costs of production.
American Petroleum Institute, *Oil Facts*.	Supply and utilization of petroleum and its products, cost of discovery and production.

monwealth government in securing over-quota import permits, and—from a political standpoint—the likelihood of continuing availability of foreign sources.

National technology and markets information

The assembly and use of appropriate information to describe the technological environment is particularly frustrating and difficult. The fact that technological developments which will achieve great economic significance five, ten, or fifteen years hence are visible today only serves to make their study and identification more urgent. The recognition and anticipation of important technological innovations is not only desirable from a manufacturing and marketing standpoint, but also in order to forecast capital requirements and to plan expense timing and reported profits.

If the corporation has its own research and development group, the director may be charged with monthly or quarterly briefings for senior mangement on the subject of "external technology." He might cover not only technology which could affect his own product lines, but he could also review technology which may affect suppliers, customers, and the industry in general. Unless formally scheduled and regularly carried out, these briefings will not occur with adequate frequency, nor will they be sufficiently externally oriented.

Instead of, or in addition to, environmental information supplied by internal research and development staff, public and private organizations publish surveys and conduct studies. Some of these are listed in Exhibit 5. Appropriate departments in universities often are in a position to provide survey information or to encourage faculty members to perform studies on a consulting basis. It is worthwhile to collect the brochures of leading research institutes and university graduate schools in order to become familiar with their capabilities and specialties.

The technological environmental information is considerably more diffuse than economic statistics. Therefore, if required, its collection, assembly, and analysis should be carried out by a competent individual as a regular assignment. Left to haphazard means, the effort is likely to degenerate into the culling of occasional clippings and stories with limited complementary material and no analysis.

EXHIBIT 5
Sources of National Technology and Markets Information

Sources	Information Type
National Science Foundation, *Federal Funds for Research, Development, and Other Scientific Activities.*	Statistics on government support of research and development.
National Science Foundation, *Basic Research, Applied Research, and Development in Industry.*	Statistics on national research and development by industry.
National Science Foundation, *Scientific and Technical Manpower Resources.*	Statistics on employment, characteristics, and supply of technical manpower.
Non-profit research institutes, such as: Stanford Research Institute, Battelle Memorial Institute, The Franklin Institute, and Mellon Institute.	Special research projects, surveys, services, and studies.
U.S. Dept. of Commerce Clearinghouse of Government Publications, Springfield, Virginia.	Periodic listing, by requested categories, of government technical publications.
National Aeronautics and Space Administration Technology Utilization Program.	Periodic bulletins describing NASA-financed technical developments believed to have general applicability; also computer programmed searches of NASA data banks for information in specific technological areas.
Trade Associations,* such as: National Electrical Manufacturers Association, Gas Appliance Manufacturers Association, or The Virginia Crab Packers Association.	Industry statistics on markets, prices, sales, employment, competitors, and related annual series; also technological surveys, test and development reports, and special studies.
Subscription Statistical Studies, such as: *Starch Marketing Data Service* and *Dodge Construction Contract Statistics.*	Markets, market share, and related information by product, area, and competitor.

* Frederick G. Roffner, Jr., Editor, *Encyclopedia of Associations, Volume I, National Organizations of the United States* (Detroit: Gale Research Co.).

Marketing information, including current sales volume, prices, and share of market is equally obscure. Sometimes trade associations assemble such data at relatively frequent intervals. However, usually one must rely on privately financed statistical services and market surveys unless fortunate enough to be part of one of the industries served by regular subscription statistical studies. Examples of the latter are the various television and radio listeners' surveys and those shown in Exhibit 5. Consult your advertising agency for suggestions on this type of data service in your industry or inquire of local business or business school libraries.

A carefully organized and implemented program for obtaining current market information from the corporate sales force can prove highly effective. It is important and difficult to convince the field salesmen that the information requested is being analyzed and used. Someone at headquarters must have responsibility for collecting and analyzing the data, and he must provide regular summaries to decision makers.

Such data should, where possible, be correlated with other sources of statistics and with other scraps of market information to provide a current market intelligence service if its use will justify the expense. If left to an informal and haphazard system, the on-the-fly collection of current market data will almost surely provide incorrect and misleading estimates of market size, pricing behavior, and market share.

Competitive information

As with more general environmental information, it is usually ineffective and expensive to collect competitive information without some clearly defined idea of what is desired and how it will be used. Routing around bits and pieces of competitive intelligence will usually accomplish very little. Some corporations designate an individual of judgment whose responsibility is to collect and analyze the information flow about each competitor in such a way that he can respond effectively to top management's requirements, and can provide periodic management briefings. Assuming that the corporation has a healthy curiosity about the actions of its competitors and assuming that its competitive strategy is sufficiently well developed to *use* competitive information, the types available and the potential applications are extensive.

The problem is usually simplified because of the remarkable fact that there are usually only a very few significant competitors in any given product area. Since long-range plans and most corporate strategies must be closely associated with individual products, the need for competitive surveillance will arise naturally on product lines.

Financial condition and strength of competitors may be critical in timing a major challenge of market position or in transferring cash flows to a new venture. It is in the financial area that competitive information sources are usually well organized. These include annual reports (and sometimes more frequently published operating statements and balance sheets), proxy statements and prospectuses accompanying securities issues, Standard & Poor's and Moody's financial services, special analyses by investment services and brokerage houses (a personal investment banker can help here), Dun and Bradstreet reports, industry credit associations, bank references, and of course all of the usual—though more diffuse—informal information sources. Data contained in the *Fortune* Directory[2] is a particularly convenient brief summary of the characteristics of leading corporations.

Plant capacity and changes in plant capacity are of key importance in estimating a competitor's pricing behavior and capital requirements. Sources of this information include annual reports and newspaper announcements (in which the competitor will usually describe new additions in proud detail), stories in local newspapers where existing plants are located, feature articles in financial magazines and papers, direct inquiry, plant tours (frequently associated with an open house or stockholder's meeting), skillful analysis of external observations and photographs, and inquiries of former employees. Do not overlook papers in technical journals describing the solution of unusual process or construction problems.

Competitors products themselves provide a source of new ideas and a measure of relative cost advantage of a new design. The competitive product analysis can obtain its information directly by purchasing, testing, and dismantling products. On the other hand, since many product additions are of a minor nature and involve size additions or other "family" extensions, competitors' publicity, advertising, and catalogue releases are sources of additional product information from which adequate inferences may be drawn without physical examination. For some large products and systems it may be necessary to visit recent installations and discuss performance with recent customers.

Competitive technological strengths and potential must be known to estimate the lead time a new technological development can enjoy or to anticipate the size and nature of technological threats. Here one must rely fundamentally on the appraisal of an internal or external technical expert. He can be aided by information such as names and biographical data on key competitors' technical employees obtained from industry technical yearbooks and "American Men of Science"; lists of recent publications and papers presented by competitors' personnel; size and budgets of research and development activities, usually in the annual report and certainly disclosed to security analysts but always mentioned

---

[2] *Fortune* Directory, Part I, *The 500 Largest U.S. Industrial Corporations and The 50 Largest Banks, Merchandising, Transportation, Life Insurance, and Utility Companies,* and Part II, *The 200 Largest Industrials Outside the U.S.* (Chicago: Fortune Directory).

in connection with new facilities; laboratory tours in conjunction with regional meetings of technical societies; casual inquiry (often a grossly overlooked source), and recollections, of recent employees.

The same information collected to assess technical strength can be used to detect trends in technical interests. This is particularly visible from specialties and interests of newly employed scientists and engineers, whose movements are dutifully reported in the professional journals.

Management style, limitations, and reaction patterns can be inferred from stated policies and objectives carried in annual reports, revealed in officers' speeches, or published in corporation recruiting literature. Direct discussions with competitors' personnel, particularly officers, will usually unleash a proud list of "how we do things." Close observation over a period of time, however, cannot be replaced as the best guide for establishing characteristic behavior patterns and predicting reactions. Care must be exercised here in the event of a major management change, although the inertia of a large organization tends very strongly to make sudden changes in behavior patterns unlikely.

Gaming and sensitivity analyses provide guidance for assessing the operating limits for any strategy choice. They form the focus for the key decisions for which all environmental and competitive information is assembled. Unless the information is collected into one place, properly analyzed, and *used in arriving at a strategic or operating decision,* then its gathering is in vain.

Bibliography

American Iron and Steel Institute.   *Steel Facts.* New York, N.Y., five times a year.

American Petroleum Institute.   *Oil Facts.* New York, N.Y., every two months.

Council of Economic Advisers.   *Annual Report.* Washington, D.C. For sale by the Supt. of Documents, U.S. Government Printing Office, Washington, D.C. 20402.

Council of Economic Advisers.   *Economic Indicators.* Washington, D.C., monthly. For sale by the Supt. of Documents, U.S. Government Printing Office, Washington, D.C. 20402.

Economist. London, England, weekly.

Federal Reserve Bank of Boston.   *New England Economic Review.* Boston, Mass. 02106, every two months.

Federal Reserve System, Board of Governors.   *Federal Reserve Bulletin.* Washington, D.C., monthly. For sale by the Division of Administrative Services, Board of Governors of the Federal Reserve System, Washington, D.C. 20551.

First National City Bank.   *Monthly Economic Letter.* New York, N.Y. 10022.

International Monetary Fund.   *International Financial Statistics.* Washington, D.C. 20431, monthly.

Japan Economic Journal. Tokyo, weekly international edition.

National Archives and Records Service, Office of the Federal Register. *United States Government Organization Manual*. Washington, D.C., annually. For sale by the Supt. of Documents, U.S. Government Printing Office, Washington, D.C. 20402.

National Science Foundation. *Basic Research, Applied Research, and Development in Industry*. For sale by Supt. of Documents, U.S. Government Printing Office, Washington, D.C. 20402.

National Science Foundation. *Federal Funds for Research, Development, and Other Scientific Activities*. For sale by Supt. of Documents, U.S. Government Printing Office, Washington, D.C. 20402.

National Science Foundation. *Scientific and Technical Manpower Resources*. For sale by Supt. of Documents, U.S. Government Printing Office, Washington, D.C. 20402.

Organisation for Economic Co-operation and Development. *Main Economic Indicators*. Paris, France, monthly. For the U.S. there is the OECD Publications Center, Washington, D.C. 20006.

Organisation for Economic Co-operation and Development. *OECD Economic Outlook*. Paris, France, biannually. For the U.S. there is the OECD Publications Center, Washington, D.C. 20006.

[President of the United States.] *Economic Report of the President*. Washington, D.C., annually. For sale by the Supt. of Documents, U.S. Government Printing Office, Washington, D.C. 20402.

Resources for the Future, Inc. *Resources in America's Future: Patterns of Requirements and Availabilities, 1960–2000*. Johns Hopkins Press, Baltimore, Maryland, 1963.

Securities and Exchange Commission. *Statistical Bulletin*. Washington, D.C., monthly. For sale by the Supt. of Documents, U.S. Government Printing Office, Washington, D.C. 20402.

Statistical Office of the United Nations, Dept. of Economic and Social Affairs. *Statistical Yearbook*. United Nations, New York, N.Y.

U.S. Bureau of the Budget. *Special Analyses*. Washington, D.C., yearly.

U.S. Dept. of Commerce, Bureau of the Census. *Current Population Reports*. Washington, D.C., irregularly. For sale by the Supt. of Documents, U.S. Government Printing Office, Washington, D.C. 20402, or any U.S. Dept. of Commerce Field Office.

U.S. Dept. of Commerce, Bureau of the Census. *Statistical Abstract of the United States*. Washington, D.C., annually. For sale by the Supt. of Documents, U.S. Government Printing Office, Washington, D.C. 20402.

U.S. Dept. of Commerce, Bureau of the Census. *Survey of Manufactures*. Washington, D.C., annually. For sale by the Supt. of Documents, U.S. Government Printing Office, Washington, D.C. 20402, or any U.S. Dept. of Commerce Field Office.

U.S. Dept. of Commerce, Bureau of International Commerce. *Overseas Business Reports*. Washington, D.C., frequently. Numbers are devoted to the various countries. For sale by the Supt. of Documents, U.S. Government

Printing Office, Washington, D.C. 20402, or by any U.S. Dept. of Commerce Field Office.

U.S. Dept. of Commerce, Business and Defense Services Administration. *U.S. Industrial Outlook.* Washington, D.C., annually. For sale by the Supt. of Documents, U.S. Government Printing Office, Washington, D.C. 20402.

U.S. Dept. of Commerce, Office of Business Economics. *Survey of Current Business.* Washington, D.C., monthly, with weekly statistical supplements. For sale by the Supt. of Documents, U.S. Government Printing Office, Washington, D.C. 20402, or by any U.S. Dept. of Commerce Field Office.

U.S. Dept. of Labor, Bureau of Labor Statistics. *Employment and Earnings and Monthly Report on the Labor Force.* Washington, D.C., monthly. For sale by the Supt. of Documents, U.S. Government Printing Office, Washington, D.C. 20402.

U.S. Dept. of Labor, Bureau of Labor Statistics. *Employment and Earnings Statistics for States and Areas, 1939–1967.* Washington, D.C., August, 1968. For sale by the Supt. of Documents, U.S. Government Printing Office, Washington, D.C. 20402.

U.S. Government Printing Office, Public Documents Division. *Selected United States Government Publications.* Washington, D.C., bi-weekly, with supplements irregularly. For sale by the Supt. of Documents, U.S. Government Printing Office, Washington, D.C. 20402.

Forecasting and trend analysis

J. Marvin Forsberg*

The first and last step of any planning and budgeting process involve forecasting. Preliminary forecasts of orders, production, revenue, manpower, and expenses precede the planning and budgeting processes. Once the plans or budgets have been established, the evaluation should include a revised forecast. "Current outlooks" are intermediate forecasts which evaluate plans and budgets during the period of operations.

The terms projection, forecast, and plan are used interchangeably by most management personnel. Although the terms are interrelated, they are not synonymous. In this chapter, the terms will be defined as follows: *Projections*—mechanical, statistical, and econometric methods of mathematically extending past performance into the future. *Forecasts*—an estimate of the most probable course of events based on an evaluation of external factors such as markets, competition, product innovations, general business conditions, etc. versus current internal performance and plans for the future. *Plan*—the establishment of specific goals and objectives, and the detailed specific procedures for utilizing manpower, capacity, and capital to meet the goals.

This chapter is restricted to a discussion of projections and forecasts. It deals briefly with the various types of forecasts, and then goes on to describe the most commonly used forecasting methods in some detail.

* Manager of Long Range Forecasting and Analysis, Corporate Economic Planning, Burroughs Corporation, Detroit.

Types of forecasts

There are at least four forecast levels which should be considered.

1. The general business economy in which the firm operates. This level is as important, if not more important, to the small retailer in a "one industry town" as it is to the firm which operates worldwide. An analysis should be made to determine the effect, if any, of past changes in the business economy on the performance of the firm. A correlation analysis and comparison of trends will usually indicate any significant relationship. Large firms untilize an economist or consultant to evaluate and forecast this level. Smaller firms utilize secondary (published) data for forecasts at this level.

2. The industry level. An analysis and forecast of the industry of which the firm is a part begins to set the firm's own forecast limits. Past industry data are usually available from government or trade associations. In some instances, market surveys may be necessary to determine industry sales and potential. Industry trends may be forecast as a share of the economy, correlated with associated industry forecasts, related to population, employment, and buying power forecasts, or they may represent the opinion of experts in the industry.

3. The company forecast level. Past performance, market share and trend, new products, manpower and productivity, competition, organization, capacity, capital, and economic climate are factors to be considered in making company forecasts.

4. Forecasts at division, territory, and/or product levels. Some firms arrive at their company forecasts by combining forecasts made at a product, division, and/or sales territory level. Other firms forecast total company sales first and then divide the forecast between divisions, products, sales territories, etc. based on past performance and potential. The writer's experience indicates that forecasting by major product lines and then distributing these totals by districts, branches, and sales territories on the basis of past performance and potential gives the most satisfactory results.

Forecasts are usually catagorized by the time period covered. "Current outlooks" usually cover less than a year, and may be for a week, month, or quarter. Short range forecasts are usually for a year, and are the basis for budgeting. Intermediate range forecasts, four to five years covering one business cycle, may be used instead of a short range forecast for budgeting to assure that the budget will tie into plans for succeeding years. Long range forecasts of eight years or more are used to estimate market shares, facility requirements, product changes, and capital needs. Short range and intermediate range forecasts are usually done in greater detail than current outlooks and long range forecasts since they are usually used in the budgeting process.

Forecasts of one year or less place special emphasis on the firm's periodic or seasonal fluctuations, current irregular fluctuations, and the immediate economic outlook. Unless there is a major change expected in the firm's business pattern, a straight line can usually be used to describe the short range trend.

Intermediate and long range forecasts place special emphasis on sales and expense trends. These longer range trends usually cannot be described by straight lines. Growth curves reflecting introduction, growth, obsolescence, revision, and/or replacement of products are usually necessary. Changes in distribution, manufacturing, and service methods also must be reflected. Market trends and competitive factors are prime factors in the long range forecasts.

Four general types of forecasting methods will be discussed, with examples given of each type.

1. Grass root methods.
2. Mechanical methods.
3. Statistical methods.
4. Econometric methods.

In all methods, the basic procedure is to make a mathematical projection for use as a guide or benchmark, and then adjust the projection for anticipated deviations. It is always a good idea to use two or more forecasting methods to check the results.

Grass root methods

Many firms start their forecasting at a grass roots level by asking their salesmen what they expect to sell, or their customers what they expect to

EXHIBIT 1

SALES FORECAST					Salesman *J. P. Norton* Branch *Newark* Date *6/20/69*
CUSTOMER	Order Dollars				Remarks
	Last Year	Year to Date	Anticipated	Total Year	
C & P PRODUCTS	1050	510	600	1110	
JORDAN INC.	4500	-	-	-	*2 year Supply*
MAC-TO CO.	-	1100	500	1600	
TOTAL	125610	75350	81200	156550	
					Form No. XYZ

buy, over a specified time period. In the first instance, the salesman is usually required to fill out a form such as that in Exhibit 1 indicating, by customer, past, current, and anticipated orders. Potential, competitive, and/or product detail information may also be included.

Part or all of the historical data may have been entered by the branch or headquarters before issuing the form to the salesmen. The forecasts of the individual salesmen are evaluated, edited, and consolidated at each sales level (branch, district, region, and/or division). As an alternative or as a check, product order forecasts may be made at the branch, district, and/or regional managers level. This type of forecast tends to be biased. If things are going well there is a tendency to forecast high, and conversely. The pluses and minuses seldom cancel out. Some other type of forecast should be used as a check.

In some industries, a few consumers may represent the bulk of sales. A survey of these customers' buying intentions may be used as a basis for the sales forecast. There are published surveys of buying intentions for some consumer items such as homes, autos, and major appliances which, combined with a share of industry data, can be used for short range forecasts.

An introduction of a new product or marketing concept may necessitate a market research survey or a market test before a reasonable forecast can be made. Either of these requires trained researchers to evaluate the market and forecast the share that can be expected. Many consulting firms specialize in this area and are used by small firms, and by larger corporations to assist their market research departments.

Mechanical methods

Mechanical methods use simple mathematical relationships, or a pattern of simple mathematical relationships, to project the data. These are adjusted for any irregular patterns. The most common example is the percent change method. For short range forecasts, current year, month, or quarter figures are calculated as a percent increase or decrease over the same periods in the previous year. In Exhibit 2 the firm showed a 6

EXHIBIT 2

Sales Volume (Units)

	Last Year	This Year	% Change
1st quarter	250,134	264,932	6
2nd quarter	289,137	307,229	6
3rd quarter	261,120		
4th quarter	299,147		

percent increase in both the first and second quarters over the previous year. Unless major irregular factors were experienced in the third and/or fourth quarters of last year, or are anticipated this year, a 6 percent increase would probably be forecast for the last two quarters.

Percent change methods also can be employed on longer range forecasts or short range seasonalized data by observing percent change month to month, quarter to quarter, or year to year. Exhibit 3 displays a fairly stable sales picture. Sales are increasing at a slightly decreasing rate. Unless a major change is expected, a continuation of the trend shown would probably suffice for the short term. When seasonalized monthly or quarterly data are used, the percent increases are usually averaged after weighting the most current data. A popular method of projecting GNP is to average the last four quarterly percentage increases, weighting the last quarter by a factor of two. The result is the expected percent increase for the next quarter.

EXHIBIT 3

Year	Unit Sales	Percent Increase
1962	145,264	12
1963	162,986	12
1964	181,566	11
1965	203,353	10
1966	225,925	11
1967	249,421	10
1968	273,365	10
1969	300,975	10

Many industries have good published sales and forecast data. Firms within these industries or suppliers to these industries may use percent of market as their forecast base. Percent of industry figures are "sticky" numbers; that is, it is very difficult for a firm to change its market share radically over the short term. In Exhibit 4, the company sales range from 7 to 8 percent of the industry total. Any major change from the 7.8 percent in the near future should be justified before changing the market share forecast.

Firms in rapidly growing competitive industries often turn to productivity/manpower relationships. The rate of growth for these firms is based on their ability to obtain and train qualified personnel. The sales forecast is the result of a forecast of productive personnel and productivity. Productivity is usually based on a learning curve spread over experience levels.

Mechanical methods of forecasting are usually very successful in the short run. This is to be expected, since an examination of the methods indicates that they are merely procedures for extending or continuing trends. Major changes in trend do not occur often, and when they do, few forecasting procedures are correct.

"Short and dirty" is the term used for mechanical methods of forecasting. However, if a method giving 80 percent accuracy now is preferred to one giving 95 percent accuracy after six months of analysis, these are the methods to use for short range forecasting.

Statistical methods

Statistical methods center on time series analysis. Most of the methods used can be found in any basic statistics text. The advent of electronic data processing has simplified the once burdensome data handling and processing and allows selection of alternatives and greater depth of

EXHIBIT 4

Sales in Units

Year	Company	Industry	Percent of Industry
1962.............145,264		2,017,556	7.2
1963.............162,986		2,219,320	7.3
1964.............181,566		2,441,252	7.4
1965.............203,353		2,685,377	7.6
1966.............225,925		2,953,915	7.6
1967.............249,421		3,249,306	7.7
1968.............273,365		3,525,423	7.8
1969.............300,975		3,876,975	7.8
1970.............		4,264,672	
1971.............			
1972.............			
1973.............			
1974.............			
1975.............		6,861,800	

analysis. Most computer manufacturers, service bureaus, and software firms offer a wide variety of "canned" programs and/or services covering all aspects of time series analysis at a nominal charge.

Time series analysis aims at isolation and examination of four major factors:

1. Trends.
2. Periodic or seasonal variations.
3. Cyclical variations.
4. Irregular fluctuations.

An analysis of these four factors will assist the forecaster in making projections as a basis for forecasts. In addition, it will enable him to pinpoint major deviations in current data as they occur.

TREND ANALYSIS.   A trend is calculated to project future behavior, to compare one trend with another, and/or to isolate the deviations from trend—seasonal, cyclical, and irregular fluctuations. Trends may be drawn freehand or calculated using mathematical formulas depending on the needs and skills of the analyst. A time series may exhibit more than one trend over an extended period of time.

There are three basic trends which are of major interest to the forecaster. The time series will be increasing or decreasing by:

1. A constant amount. The changes in amount from one period to the next (first differences) are about the same. The points approximate a straight line when plotted on arithmetic paper. The formula for the line is $Y = a + bx$.

2. A constant rate. The percentage changes from one period to the next (first differences of the logs) are about the same. The points approximate a straight line when plotted on semi-log paper. This is an exponential curve, $Y = ab^x$.

3. An increasing or decreasing rate. The percentage changes in the raw data are themselves changing at a constant rate (the first difference of the logs is changing by about the same rate). When the points are plotted on semi-log paper a flattening out of the line (an asymptote) will be observed. These are growth curves, Gompertz $Y = ka^{b^x}$ or logistic $1/Y = k + ab^x$.

Each of these common trends will be illustrated below.

Straight line trend. To begin a time series analysis, place the data in a chart such as Exhibit 5. Units should be used, or else the data should be corrected by a price index. Calculate the first differences and the percentage change from period to period.

EXHIBIT 5

Year	Unit Sales	First Difference	% Change
1963	1,310		
1964	1,360	50	3.8
1965	1,408	48	3.5
1966	1,459	51	3.5
1967	1,506	47	3.2
1968	1,556	50	3.3
1969	1,605	49	3.1

The second step is to plot the time series on both arithmetic and semi-log graph paper. Based on the previous curve descriptions, choose the curve which best approximates the description. In some instances more than one curve will be necessary; in others, curves other than those described will have to be used.

The calculation of a straight line trend for the above data is illustrated in Exhibit 6. To calculate the formula for the line, the method of least squares can be used with the two normal equations

1. $$a = \frac{\Sigma Y}{N} = \frac{10,204}{7} = 1,458$$

2. $$b = \frac{\Sigma XY}{\Sigma X^2} = \frac{1,375}{28} = 49.$$

EXHIBIT 6

Years	X	X²	Sales Y	XY	Trend Values
Actual	*				†
1963..................	−3	9	1,310	−3,930	1,311
1964..................	−2	4	1,360	−2,720	1,360
1965..................	−1	1	1,408	−1,408	1,409
1966..................	0	0	1,459	0	1,458
1967..................	1	1	1,506	1,506	1,507
1968..................	2	4	1,556	3,112	1,556
1969..................	3	9	1,605	4,815	1,605
Total...............		28	10,204	1,375	
Projection					
1970..					1,654
1971..					1,703
1972..					1,752
1973..					1,801
1974..					1,850

* If an even number of years is used, start middle years with 1 and −1 and use odd numbers only (1, 3, 5, 7, 9, etc.).
† Estimating equation (origin 1966, X units 1 year) $Y_c = a + bx = 1,458 + 49x$.

A close approximation of the equation could have been calculated by averaging the years to determine a and averaging the first differences to determine b.

Exponential trend. An exponential curve can be used to describe the data in Exhibit 7.

EXHIBIT 7

Year	Unit Sales	First Difference	% Change
1963.............489			
1964.............544		55	11.2
1965.............610		66	12.1
1966.............680		70	11.5
1967.............762		82	12.1
1968.............845		83	10.9
1969.............945		100	11.8

The equation for an exponential curve is $Y = ab^x$. Expressed in logarithmic form ($\log Y = \log a + X \log b$), the formula is mathematically the same as the formula for a straight line, and calculation of the trend is similar to that discussed above. Taking the X origin in the middle of the period, the normal equations become

1. $$\log a = \frac{\Sigma \log Y}{N} = \frac{19.8270}{7} = 2.8324$$

2. $$\log b = \frac{\Sigma X \log Y}{\Sigma X^2} = \frac{1.3376}{28} = 0.0477.$$

EXHIBIT 8

Year	X	X²	Sales			Trend Values	
			Y	Log Y	X Log Y	Log Y_c	Y_c
Actual	*					†	
1963...........	−3	9	489	2.6893	−8.0679	2.6893	489
1964...........	−2	4	544	2.7356	−5.4712	2.7370	546
1965...........	−1	1	610	2.7853	−2.7853	2.7847	609
1966..........	0	0	680	2.8325	0	2.8324	680
1967..........	1	1	762	2.8820	2.8820	2.8801	759
1968..........	2	4	845	2.9269	5.8538	2.9278	847
1969..........	3	9	945	2.9754	8.9262	2.9755	945
Total......		28		19.8270	1.3376		
Projection							
1970..						3.0232	1055
1971..						3.0709	1177

* If an even number of years is used, start middle years with 1 and −1 and use odd numbers only (1, 3, 5, 7, 9, etc.).
† Estimating equation (origin 1966, X units 1 year) log Yc = 2.8324 + 0.0477X.

Growth trend. A growth curve, sometimes referred to as an S curve, best describes the introduction, growth, and peak of a product's life cycle. There are various forms of the curves. These curves are often used for long range projections. An analysis of such curves for existing products aids considerably in forecasting similar new product situations. The data in Exhibit 9 can be described by a growth curve.

EXHIBIT 9

Year	Unit Sales (MM)	First Difference	% Change
1961..................	8		
1962..................	13	5	63
1963..................	23	10	77
1964..................	39	13	70
1965..................	63	24	62
1966..................	93	30	48
1967.................124		31	33
1968.................148		24	19
1969.................164		16	11

The trend can be calculated by selecting three points equidistant from each other. These points are designated Y_0, Y_1, and Y_2. For this example Y_0 = geometric mean of 1961, 1962, 1963; Y_1 = geometric mean of 1964, 1965, 1966; Y_2 = geometric mean of 1967, 1968, 1969.

$$Y_0 = \sqrt[3]{8 \times 13 \times 23} = \sqrt[3]{2,392} = 13.4$$
$$Y_1 = \sqrt[3]{39 \times 63 \times 93} = \sqrt[3]{228,501} = 61.1$$
$$Y_2 = \sqrt[3]{724 \times 148 \times 164} = \sqrt[3]{3,009,728} = 144.4$$

The estimating equation is $Y = \dfrac{K}{1 + 10^{a + bx}}$.

The three constants are obtained by the formulas

$$K = \frac{2Y_0 Y_1 Y_2 - Y_1^2(Y_0 + Y_2)}{Y_0 Y_2 - Y_1^2} = 195.9$$

$$a = \log\left(\frac{K - Y_0}{Y_0}\right) = 1.1345$$

$$b = \frac{I}{n}\left[\log\frac{Y_0(K - Y_1)}{Y_1(K - Y_0)}\right] = -0.2658.$$

The balance of the calculations for computing the trend values is shown in Exhibit 10

EXHIBIT 10

Year	X	Unit Sales	Log μ $= a + bx$	$1 + \mu$	$Yc = \dfrac{195.9}{1 + \mu}$
1961..........	−1	8	1.4003	26.1	7.5
1962..........	0	13	1.1345	14.6	13.4
1963..........	1	23	0.8687	8.4	23.3
1964..........	2	39	0.6029	5.0	39.2
1965..........	3	63	0.3371	3.2	61.2
1966..........	4	93	0.0713	2.2	89.0
1967..........	5	124	−0.1945	1.6	122.4
1968..........	6	148	−0.4603	1.3	150.7
1969..........	7	164	0.7261	1.2	163.3

SEASONAL PATTERNS.   There are a number of ways to isolate the seasonal pattern. A recommended method will be illustrated in detail, and two other methods will be used to demonstrate the effects of using less elaborate procedures. To find the seasonal pattern, the past data are adjusted and smoothed to remove the trend, cyclical, and irregular fluctuations. These effects are eliminated in order to permit future forecasts to reflect different trends or cycles. For example, if the past sales had an upward trend, there would be a tendency for the last months of the year to be larger than the first months. The variation would be determined by the rate of increase. If this rate changed in the forecast period, the monthly seasonal fluctuation would be wrong.

The first step is to plot the past monthly orders. If the cyclical pattern is eventually to be calculated, at least three business cycles should be included. Use unit data or, if unit data are not available, adjust dollar values by some type of price index.

Method I: the average month.   If the plotted data do not show any significant trend or cyclical pattern, the actual monthly figures can be

EXHIBIT 11. Percent of Orders to Average Month

Year & Month (1)	Orders (2)	Average Month by Year (3)	% of Orders to Average Month [Col. (2) ÷ Col. (3)] (4)
1960			
Jan.	194.7	195.4	99.6
Feb.	176.2	195.4	90.2
Mar.	201.7	195.4	103.2
Apr.	201.1	195.4	102.9
May	197.4	195.4	101.0
June	191.1	195.4	97.8
July	174.9	195.4	89.5
Aug.	182.4	195.4	93.3
Sep.	189.6	195.4	97.0
Oct.	218.1	195.4	111.6
Nov.	211.6	195.4	108.3
Dec.	206.0	195.4	105.4
1961			
Jan.	185.2	204.6	90.5
Feb.	175.1	204.6	85.6
Mar.	202.8	204.6	99.1
Apr.	203.2	204.6	99.3
May	205.8	204.6	100.6
June	190.5	204.6	93.1
July	177.9	204.6	86.9
Aug.	202.9	204.6	99.1
Sep.	213.3	204.6	104.2
Oct.	236.9	204.6	115.8
Nov.	236.1	204.6	115.4
Dec.	225.4	204.6	110.2
1962			
Jan.	221.1	261.4	84.6
Feb.	223.2	261.4	85.4
Mar.	267.7	261.4	102.4
Apr.	259.0	261.4	99.1
May	261.5	261.4	100.0
June	259.3	261.4	99.2
July	243.1	261.4	93.0
Aug.	257.3	261.4	98.4
Sep.	265.6	261.4	101.6
Oct.	292.2	261.4	111.8
Nov.	291.5	261.4	111.5
Dec.	294.8	261.4	112.8
1963			
Jan.	266.4	297.1	89.6
Feb.	258.4	297.1	87.0
Mar.	302.7	297.1	101.9
Apr.	297.5	297.1	100.1
May	303.0	297.1	102.0
June	292.7	297.1	98.5
July	263.7	297.1	88.7
Aug.	281.1	297.1	84.6
Sep.	299.8	297.1	100.9
Oct.	339.3	297.1	114.2
Nov.	338.0	297.1	113.8
Dec.	322.1	297.1	108.4

used to determine the seasonal pattern. To remove the bias of large numbers, percentage figures are used.

a) Calculate the average monthly sales for each year by dividing each year's total by 12.
b) Divide each month by that year's average. (See Exhibit 11.)
c) Go to step (c) of Method III.

   Method II: percent of trend. If there is a significant trend but no cyclical pattern, the figures need be adjusted by the trend only.

a) Draw an estimate of the trend freehand (Exhibit 12) or calculate the trend.

EXHIBIT 12

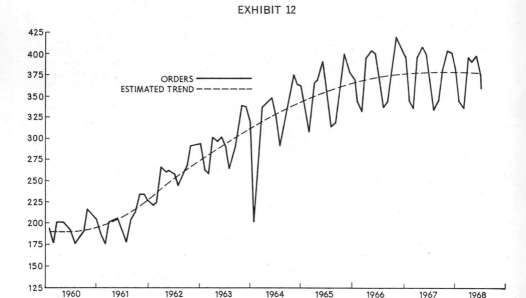

b) Divide the actual figures for each month by the trend figures for the same month (Exhibit 13).
c) Go to step (c) of Method III.

   Method III: moving average. If there are significant trend and cyclical patterns evident (or to play it safe), a 12-month centered moving average is used to adjust the data.

a) Calculate the 12-month centered moving average for the data as follows: multiply the first year total by 2; subtract January of the first year and add January of the second year; divide this total by 24. This is the average for July of the first year. To calculate the August value, subtract the total of January and February of the first year from the total of January and February of the second year. Divide the result

EXHIBIT 13

Year & Month (1)	Orders (2)	Freehand Drawn Trend (3)	Monthly % of Trend (4)
1960			
Jan.................194.7		190	102.5
Feb.................176.2		190	92.7
Mar.................201.7		190	106.2
Apr.................201.1		190	105.8
May.................197.4		190	103.9
June.................191.1		190	100.6
July.................174.9		190	92.1
Aug.................182.4		190	96.0
Sep.................189.6		191	99.3
Oct.................218.1		192	113.6
Nov.................211.6		193	109.6
Dec.................206.0		194	106.2
1961			
Jan.................185.2		195	95.0
Feb.................175.1		197	88.9
Mar.................202.8		199	101.9
Apr.................203.2		202	100.6
May.................205.8		204	100.9
June.................190.5		207	92.0
July.................177.9		210	84.7
Aug.................202.9		214	94.8
Sep.................213.3		217	98.3
Oct.................236.9		220	107.7
Nov.................236.1		224	105.4
Dec.................225.4		228	98.9
1962			
Jan.................221.1		232	95.3
Feb.................223.2		237	94.2
Mar.................267.7		242	110.3
Apr.................259.0		246	105.3
May.................261.5		250	104.6
June.................259.3		254	102.1
July.................243.1		258	94.2
Aug.................257.3		262	98.2
Sep.................265.6		266	99.8
Oct.................292.2		270	108.2
Nov.................291.5		274	106.4
Dec.................294.8		277	106.4
1963			
Jan.................266.4		280	95.1
Feb.................258.4		283	91.3
Mar.................302.7		286	105.8
Apr.................297.5		289	102.9
May.................303.0		292	103.8
June.................292.7		294	99.6
July.................263.7		296	89.1
Aug.................281.1		299	94.0
Sep.................299.8		303	98.9
Oct.................339.3		307	110.5
Nov.................338.0		310	109.0
Dec.................322.1		313	102.9

by 24 and add the July average. Continue the procedure for the time series. (See Exhibit 14.)

b) Divide the actual figures for each month by the moving average figures for the same month.

c) Plot the resulting index numbers on a graph—one graph for each

EXHIBIT 14

Centered 12-Month Moving Average and Percentages of Moving Average

Year and Month (1)	Orders (2)	Centered 12-Mo. Moving Avg. Col. (3) ÷ 24 (3)	% of 12-Mo. Moving Avg. Col. (2) ÷ Col. (4) (4)
1959			
Jan.	226.7	...	...
Feb.	208.1	...	...
Mar.	237.1	...	...
Apr.	243.3	...	...
May	248.3	...	...
June	228.4	...	...
July	212.3	225.4	94.2
Aug.	217.1	222.7	97.5
Sep.	222.7	219.9	101.3
Oct.	235.5	216.6	108.7
Nov.	222.3	212.8	104.5
Dec.	218.4	209.1	104.4
1960			
Jan.	194.7	206.0	94.5
Feb.	176.2	203.0	86.8
Mar.	201.7	200.2	100.7
Apr.	201.1	198.0	101.6
May	197.4	196.9	100.3
June	191.1	195.9	97.5
July	174.9	195.0	89.7
Aug.	182.4	194.6	93.7
Sep.	189.6	194.6	97.4
Oct.	218.1	194.7	112.0
Nov.	211.6	195.1	108.5
Dec.	206.0	195.5	105.4

month (Exhibit 15). If a changing seasonal pattern is evident, draw a freehand trend of the pattern. Post the values in an array, as at the bottom of Exhibit 16. Total the index numbers for each year. Each year should total 12. Adjust the trend values (on the graphs) until each year does total 12.

d) If the plot of the index numbers on the graphs did not indicate any trend, the seasonal index can be calculated as shown at the top of Exhibit 16 and in Exhibit 17. The index numbers for each month are averaged, leaving out the highest and lowest values or the two highest and two lowest values, depending on the quantity of data available.

The monthly averages are totaled, and any difference from 12 is pro-rated over all the months.

The same data were used in all three examples to illustrate the differences in results. Exhibit 18 shows a comparison of the results. The data had an increasing trend over the time period so that the results of Method I were too low for the first half of the year and too high for the last half of the year. There was little cyclical influence in the data, so that Method II and Method III using an assumed constant seasonal pattern came up with about the same results. There was some degree of change in the seasonal pattern so that plotting a trend of the index values gave the best result (line 4).

EXHIBIT 15

Changing Seasonal Pattern

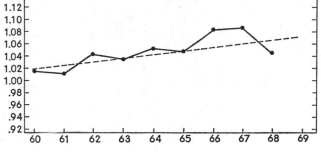

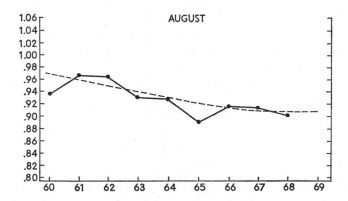

We can inspect how good our seasonalization is by dividing our actual monthly sales by the seasonal indices and plotting the results. Exhibit 19 illustrates the seasonally adjusted values (using the changing index values from Exhibit 16). The cyclical and irregular fluctuations are also seen in Exhibit 19 as the difference between the seasonally adjusted values and the trend.

EXHIBIT 16

A. Arrays of Ratios of Centered 12-Month Moving Averages and Computation of Seasonal Index
(assuming constant seasonal pattern)

Year	Jan.	Feb.	March	April	May	June	July	August	Sept.	Oct.	Nov.	Dec.	Mean
1960	.945	.868	1.007	1.016	1.003	.975	.897	.937	.974	1.120	1.085	1.054	
1961	.947	.891	1.022	1.015	1.019	.935	.863	.968	.995	1.080	1.054	.983	
1962	.942	.931	1.096	1.041	1.032	1.003	.924	.965	.986	1.072	1.057	1.057	
1963	.947	.913	1.060	1.030	1.035	.989	.885	.934	.986	1.104	1.086	1.024	
1964	.922	.931	1.049	1.052	1.061	.987	.871	.931	.995	1.119	1.059	1.049	
1965	.954	.883	1.046	1.048	1.109	.987	.881	.891	.993	1.104	1.041	1.020	
1966	.940	.902	1.069	1.083	1.071	.998	.890	.916	.987	1.111	1.076	1.051	
1967	.914	.890	1.043	1.087	1.069	.971	.887	.916	1.014	1.079	1.074	1.032	
1968	.918	.806	1.063	1.046	1.070	1.004	.871	.901	.998	1.115	1.087	1.004	
Total of middle seven	6.561	6.278	7.352	7.316	7.357	6.910	6.182	6.500	6.940	7.712	7.491	7.234	
Mean of middle seven	.937	.897	1.050	1.045	1.051	.987	.883	.929	.991	1.102	1.070	1.033	.998
Seasonal index	.939	.899	1.052	1.047	1.053	.989	.885	.931	.993	1.105	1.072	1.035	1.000

B. Arrays of Ratios of Centered 12-Month Moving Averages and Computation of Seasonal Index
(moving seasonal pattern from graphs)

Year	Jan.	Feb.	March	April	May	June	July	August	Sept.	Oct.	Nov.	Dec.
1960	.95	.91	1.05	1.02	1.01	.97	.90	.97	.99	1.11	1.08	1.04
1961	.95	.91	1.05	1.03	1.02	.98	.90	.96	.99	1.10	1.07	1.04
1962	.95	.92	1.05	1.03	1.03	.99	.89	.95	.99	1.09	1.07	1.04
1963	.95	.92	1.05	1.04	1.05	.99	.88	.94	.99	1.09	1.06	1.04
1964	.94	.92	1.05	1.05	1.06	.99	.88	.92	.99	1.10	1.06	1.04
1965	.94	.91	1.06	1.06	1.07	.99	.88	.92	.99	1.10	1.05	1.03
1966	.94	.89	1.06	1.07	1.08	.99	.88	.91	.99	1.10	1.06	1.03
1967	.93	.88	1.06	1.07	1.08	.99	.88	.91	1.00	1.10	1.07	1.03
1968	.93	.87	1.06	1.07	1.09	.99	.88	.91	1.00	1.07	1.07	1.03
1969 Projected	.92	.87	1.06	1.07	1.09	.99	.88	.91	1.00	1.10	1.08	1.03

EXHIBIT 17

A. Arrays of Ratios to Average Month and Computation of Seasonal Index
(assuming constant seasonal pattern)

Year	Jan.	Feb.	March	April	May	June	July	August	Sept.	Oct.	Nov.	Dec.	Mean
1960	.996	.902	1.032	1.029	1.010	.978	.895	.933	.970	1.116	1.083	1.054	
1961	.905	.856	.991	.993	1.006	.931	.869	.991	1.042	1.158	1.154	1.102	
1962	.846	.854	1.024	.991	1.000	.992	.930	.984	1.016	1.118	1.115	1.128	
1963	.896	.870	1.019	1.001	1.020	.985	.887	.846	1.009	1.142	1.138	1.084	
1964	.622	.913	1.033	1.051	1.070	1.004	.895	.964	1.035	1.171	1.118	1.116	
1965	.938	.870	1.034	1.040	1.105	.986	.882	.896	1.005	1.125	1.067	1.050	
1966	.912	.880	1.049	1.067	1.062	.995	.890	.916	.988	1.112	1.078	1.052	
1967	.919	.895	1.049	1.092	1.073	.972	.887	.916	1.015	1.078	1.071	1.032	
1968	.913	.890	1.055	1.040	1.068	1.004	.871	.903	1.004	1.126	1.102	1.022	
Total of middle seven	6.329	6.163	7.245	7.221	7.309	6.912	6.207	6.512	7.072	7.897	7.705	7.490	
Mean of middle seven	.904	.880	1.035	1.032	1.044	.987	.887	.930	1.010	1.128	1.101	1.070	1.001
Seasonal index	.904	.880	1.034	1.031	1.043	.986	.887	.930	1.009	1.127	1.100	1.069	1.000

B. Arrays of Ratios to Trend and Computation of Seasonal Index
(assuming constant seasonal pattern)

Year	Jan.	Feb.	March	April	May	June	July	August	Sept.	Oct.	Nov.	Dec.	Mean
1960	1.025	.927	1.062	1.058	1.039	1.006	.921	.960	.993	1.136	1.096	1.062	
1961	.950	.889	1.019	1.006	1.009	.920	.847	.948	.983	1.077	1.054	.989	
1962	.953	.942	1.106	1.053	1.046	1.021	.942	.982	.998	1.082	1.064	1.064	
1963	.951	.913	1.058	1.029	1.038	.996	.891	.940	.989	1.105	1.090	1.029	
1964	.639	.932	1.051	1.054	1.063	.991	.876	.935	.998	1.123	1.065	1.057	
1965	.933	.887	1.051	1.051	1.111	.988	.879	.888	.990	1.103	1.040	1.015	
1966	.938	.903	1.073	1.088	1.080	1.009	.901	.925	.997	1.119	1.085	1.059	
1967	.917	.893	1.046	1.087	1.067	.964	.880	.907	1.004	1.067	1.060	1.021	
1968	.909	.886	1.051	1.036	1.063	1.000	.868	.899	.999	1.121	1.097	1.017	
Total of middle seven	6.551	6.344	7.392	7.368	7.396	6.954	6.216	6.514	6.964	7.730	7.514	7.260	
Mean of middle seven	.936	.906	1.056	1.053	1.057	.993	.888	.931	.995	1.104	1.073	1.037	1.002
Seasonal index	.934	.904	1.053	1.050	1.054	.991	.886	.929	.993	1.101	1.070	1.035	1.000

EXHIBIT 18

Seasonal Index Comparison

	Jan.	Feb.	Mar.	Apr.	May	June	July	Aug.	Sep.	Oct.	Nov.	Dec.
Constant seasonal pattern using:												
(1) Average month	0.90	0.88	1.03	1.03	1.04	0.99	0.89	0.93	1.01	1.13	1.10	1.07
(2) % of trend	0.94	0.91	1.05	1.05	1.06	0.99	0.87	0.93	0.99	1.10	1.07	1.04
(3) Moving average	0.94	0.90	1.05	1.05	1.05	0.99	0.88	0.93	0.99	1.11	1.07	1.04
Changing seasonal pattern using:												
(4) Moving average	0.92	0.87	1.06	1.07	1.09	0.99	0.88	0.91	1.00	1.10	1.08	1.03

Above figures rounded and adjusted to total 12.00 for the year.

The same basic principles of analysis can be used for determining weekly and/or quarterly patterns. In some industries it is necessary to make further adjustments for changing holiday dates, such as Easter. A comparison of results of previously illustrated methods for the periods in question should determine the adjustments necessary.

CYCLICAL AND IRREGULAR FLUCTUATIONS. The cyclical pattern is calculated as a further step in isolating the irregular fluctuations, and/or so that it can be correlated with other national indices for which more

EXHIBIT 19

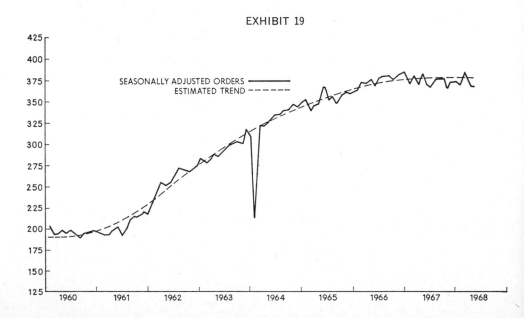

EXHIBIT 20

Cyclical and Irregular Fluctuation

Year & Month (1)	Actual Orders (2)	Seasonal Index (3)	Seasonally Adj. Orders (2) ÷ (3) (4)	Trend Value (5)	Cyclical Irreg. Pattern (4) ÷ (5) (6)	Cyclical Pattern (1–2–1 Avg.) (7)	Irregular Pattern (6) ÷ (7) (8)
1960							
Jan.	194.7	0.95	204.9	190	1.08		
Feb.	176.2	0.91	193.6	190	1.02	1.03	0.99
Mar.	201.7	1.05	192.1	190	1.01	1.02	0.99
Apr.	201.1	1.02	197.2	190	1.04	1.03	1.01
May	197.4	1.01	195.4	190	1.03	1.03	1.00
June	191.1	0.97	197.0	190	1.04	1.06	0.98
July	194.9	0.90	216.6	190	1.14	1.05	1.09
Aug.	182.4	0.97	188.0	190	0.99	1.04	0.95
Sept.	189.6	0.99	191.5	191	1.00	1.01	0.99
Oct.	218.1	1.11	196.5	192	1.02	1.02	1.00
Nov.	211.6	1.08	195.9	193	1.02	1.02	1.00
Dec.	206.0	1.04	198.1	194	1.02	1.02	1.00
1961							
Jan.	185.2	0.95	194.9	195	1.00	1.01	0.99
Feb.	175.1	0.91	192.4	197	0.98	0.99	0.99
Mar.	202.8	1.05	193.1	199	0.97	0.99	0.98
Apr.	203.2	1.03	197.3	202	0.98	0.99	0.99
May	205.8	1.02	201.8	204	0.99	0.98	1.01
June	190.5	0.98	194.4	207	0.94	0.97	0.97
July	177.9	0.90	197.7	210	0.94	0.97	0.97
Aug.	202.9	0.96	211.4	214	0.99	0.98	1.01
Sept.	213.3	0.99	215.5	217	0.99	0.99	1.00
Oct.	236.9	1.10	215.4	220	0.98	0.99	0.99
Nov.	236.1	1.07	220.6	224	0.99	0.99	1.00
Dec.	225.4	1.04	216.7	228	0.95	0.99	0.96
1962							
Jan.	221.1	0.95	232.7	232	1.00	1.00	1.00
Feb.	223.2	0.92	242.6	237	1.02	1.02	1.00
Mar.	267.7	1.05	255.0	242	1.05	1.04	1.01
Apr.	259.0	1.03	251.4	246	1.02	1.04	0.98
May	261.5	1.03	253.9	250	1.02	1.04	0.98
June	259.3	0.99	261.9	254	1.03	1.04	0.99
July	243.1	0.89	273.1	258	1.06	1.05	1.01
Aug.	257.3	0.95	270.8	262	1.03		

forecast data are available. If the major reason is to correlate with another index, partial correlation between the two series when time is constant can be used.

As a further step in isolating the irregular fluctuations and so that they may be correlated with another index, the following procedure can be used:

1. Adjust the actual data seasonally by dividing by the seasonal index.

2. Adjust for trend by dividing the results from step 1 by the trend values.
3. The results of step 2 represent the cyclical irregular percentages. To remove the irregular fluctuations use a three-month moving average (weighted 1, 2, 1) if the fluctuations are about one month in duration, or a five-month weighted moving average (1, 2, 4, 2, 1) if longer (see Exhibit 20).
4. The results of step 3 represent the cyclical pattern. The irregular fluctuations are evaluated by dividing the results of step 2 by the results of step 3.
5. If the cyclical pattern is not calculated as above, the irregular fluctuation can be calculated by dividing seasonally adjusted sales by the 12-month centered moving average (as in Method III for isolating the seasonal pattern).

The irregular fluctuations as calculated help to evaluate the effects of short term sales contests and promotions, manpower fluctuations, etc.

Econometric methods

The computer has allowed the development of complex cause and effect or input/output marketing models. On one side of the equation is the market or consumer, and on the other side are the suppliers. Economic factors are built in as an umbrella covering both sides of the equation. Each cause and effect is isolated and projected using one of the forecast procedures previously illustrated, and then combined to make up a marketing model. The major advantage of this procedure is that it allows considerable flexibility in trying and evaluating alternate assumptions.

Profit planning and budgeting

Jack A. Bump*

The purpose of this chapter is to elaborate on current *short-term* profit planning and budgeting techniques. Short-term is emphasized because of the necessity of distinguishing between short- and long-range profit planning (the latter is discussed in Chapter 26). The relationship of these two profit planning methods is as follows:

Long range. Profit planning of a long-range nature (beyond one or two years) is focused on the determination of corporate profit objectives and broad strategic plans for achieving these objectives.

Short range. Profit planning of a short-range nature (usually for the next 12 months) is concerned with developing operating programs which assure the effective implementation of long-range profit goals, but which also recognize the limitations and opportunities of present business resources and the current business environment.

Unless indicated to the contrary, subsequent references to profit planning in this chapter will refer to short-term profit planning only.

Need for profit planning

The reasons for profit planning are many and varied and depend to some extent on the nature of a particular business. Historically, however, most industrial corporations have subscribed to profit planning to assure a certain level of financial performance (earnings, return on equity, etc.)

---

* Divisional Controller, Coated Abrasive & Tape Division, Norton Company, Troy, New York.

and to enforce some degree of discipline with respect to the utilization of resources.

While the above reasons are adequate in themselves, profit planning today is receiving greater attention due to factors such as the following:

1. Information Technology.   The arrival of the computer age and the intensification of the information explosion.
2. Business Growth.   The growth of many corporations from a comparatively small base to a multidivisional structure with many major product lines, diverse organizations, and worldwide facilities.

These and other factors have complicated business management and have created a need for a more systematic means of identifying problems and opportunities. Profit planning, with characteristics such as management by exception and the use of dollars as a common denominator, represents a method for dealing with the complexity of current-day business and fulfilling the stated long-range corporate objectives.

Profit planning cycle

The establishment of a profit plan is a cyclical technique, due to the role of profit planning in the total planning and control process. The complete cycle consists of:

1. Adopting the plan or program.
2. Measuring actual performance against the plan.
3. Deciding on future action and adopting a new plan.

While this chapter is mainly concerned with the first step in the above cycle, i.e., the adoption of the plan, recognition must be given to the second and third elements. For example, the plan has to be comprehensive enough to permit an objective accountability of actual performance at each level in the organization—from the lowest spending unit, usually a department, to the highest profit center, usually a product division or group. In addition, the plan has to be responsive to change in order to provide current targets for an equitable evaluation of results under varying business conditions.

Adoption of the plan

Adoption of a profit plan for a specific period, say for the year 1969, starts several months in advance of the period to be planned and covers three major forecasts—a business forecast, a sales revenue forecast, and a cost and profit forecast.

Business forecast

Few companies are isolated from competition or are unaffected by changes in the national or international economy. Therefore, a general business or "environmental" forecast is necessary to establish a framework for the company's operation for the planning period. The business forecast should focus on three areas—an economic forecast, an industry forecast, and a market share projection.

Economic forecast. What is the course of the economy for the forthcoming year? This broad environmental question should be answered by an economic forecast (either prepared internally by an economist or based on one of the many external sources of economic projections). The economic forecast should include a short commentary on the basic underlying assumptions and also a projection of the various business indicators which reflect some degree of correlation with sales or orders of the company's major product lines.

Industry forecast. A sales volume forecast for the total industry represents the next stage in the business forecasting cycle. The primary reasons for an industry forecast are (a) to observe the industry's position in the overall economy and (b) to monitor the company's position within the industry.

Industry/economy. Even though major technological changes may consume a span of years, the fact that changes are occurring is important, especially if they represent a threat to a particular industry. In addition, an industry's sales volume for even a short planning period may be seriously affected by events in other industries (such as labor contract expirations) or by changes in government policy (such as tax increases).

Company/industry. Since market share growth or decline actually occurs each month of the business year, the profit plan should recognize the pattern of market share trends (as well as the necessary strategies for accelerating growth or arresting decline).

One of the most common techniques for developing a volume forecast for an industry is *correlation analysis.* The objective is to determine which economic indexes represent the best "fit" or behavior pattern with industry sales volume. Assuming a reasonably accurate economic forecast, a projection of the industry's sales for the forthcoming planning period can be accomplished on the basis of the correlation trend line of past experience. (Please refer to Chapter 22 for details on correlation and regression techniques.)

Market share. The third and final stage of the business forecasting cycle is development of a market share forecast.

Recent market share trends represent a logical bench mark from which to construct the market share forecast. However, since the company's planning process should continually generate explicit *strategies* (for the long range) and *programs* (for the short range) for each of its major product lines—with the objective of recapturing market share and penetrating new markets—the basic market share forecast, projected from recent trends, must be supplemented by the best available estimates of the impact of these strategies and programs.

Sales revenue forecast

Completion of the business forecast leads to sales revenue planning by product/market groups within each division. Although the structure of the product/market groupings will vary between divisions, the objective of each division is to "explode" the sales forecast to at least major product lines and markets in recognition of such factors as production planning requirements, manufacturing capacity, competition, customer purchasing trends, regional and district sales management objectives, etc.

Two areas associated with sales forecasting which are of importance are the special refinements or techniques employed and the organizational approach to the forecasting responsibility. The special refinements may consist of features such as (*a*) separation of the dollar forecast in terms of physical units and price per unit (advantageous in subsequent profitability analyses), (*b*) recognition of seasonal variations, and (*c*) utilization of daily averages.

Since the sales revenue plan represents the foundation of the entire profit planning activity, it deserves proper personnel staffing. While many diverse approaches exist, it is generally desirable to have personnel such as the divisional controller, divisional sales manager, and the corporate economist involved with the sales forecasting program. Final approval of the sales forecast normally resides with the product line or division manager, since he presumably has ultimate profit responsibility for the products or markets covered by the forecast.

The "state of the art" relative to sales revenue planning has undergone much change during recent years, and opportunities for further refinement certainly exist through use of the computer in areas such as input/output modeling, programs for seasonals, and a greater explosion of products and markets through an enlarged data base. However, the elements of judgment and realism should continue to occupy important roles in the sales forecasting function.

Cost and profit forecast

The final stage of the profit-plan development is the cost and profit forecast. Both terms are included in the identification of this stage because of differences in planning philosophy which result in the following extremes:

Bottom to top. The profit forecast represents the *residual* difference between sales revenues and total costs. Major emphasis is focused on cost forecasting, especially in short-range profit planning cycles. The consolidation of divisional forecasts constructed in this manner generally becomes an acceptable forecast for the corporation.

Top to bottom. In long-range profit planning, a more desirable method is to establish an acceptable *corporate* profit goal and then allocate goals to each of the divisions or groups. Given a sales revenue forecast and knowing its profit goal, the division then determines how to allocate its allowable expenses to each department, etc. This method may also be used in short-range planning but requires a greater-than-average degree of control of the business environment and also the ability to exert flexibility with respect to its internal resources.

Since the primary emphasis in this chapter is directed towards short-range profit planning, the cost and profit forecast methodology outlined below will essentially deal with the "bottom-to-top" approach.

The cost and profit forecast should include three major steps, as follows: (*a*) construction of the forecast, (*b*) evaluation of the forecast, and (*c*) reporting on performance.

FORECAST CONSTRUCTION.   Once a sales revenue plan has been generated, attention may be directed to development of the various elements of the cost and profit forecast. Generally, the cost forecast will be concerned with three elements, or inputs—(1) variable operating costs, (2) nonvariable operating costs, and (3) miscellaneous (nonoperating) factors such as "other" income and expense, investment credits, taxes, etc.

Variable operating costs. Regardless of the type of cost system or method of inventory valuation, i.e., direct or absorption costing, variable costs represent one of the major inputs in the cost forecast. Examples of certain of the major variable costs are:

Cost of goods sold (labor, material, etc.).

Cash discounts.

Sales incentive.

Freight.

Commissions.

Since these costs normally respond directly to changes in sales and production volume—in the short term at least—they should be expected to bear a permanent and automatic relationship to sales under any particular price, volume, and product-mix situation. Unless policy changes have recently occured, or are expected to occur during the planning period (changes involving price and/or wage levels, cash discount terms, sales incentive plans, commission rates, etc.), the percentage-to-sales relationship of these costs in recent periods should be adequate for utilization as forecast cost ratios in the forthcoming planning period.

Separate identification of variable costs has the major advantage of simplifying the overall cost forecast routine and also providing better information for profitability and break-even analyses.

While the "cost ratio" technique is generally superior to other cost forecasting methods, two cautions are advanced with respect to this approach—(1) it is necessary to explode the sales and cost ratio forecast to a greater level of refinement in order to avoid misclassification of volume and spending variances as mix variances, and (2) in the case of those product lines with fairly long production cycles, such as machine tools, it is necessary that the cost ratios (percentagewise to sales) reflect the *lag* between the occurrence of certain variable manufacturing costs (indirect labor, supplies, fuel, etc.) and invoicing.

Nonvariable operating costs. The other major operating cost category involves nonvariable costs, which, for the purpose of financial planning, may be classified as either "committed" costs or "managed" costs.

Committed costs. Committed costs are those which remain fixed, over the short term, regardless of the level of sales or production. They are primarily associated with costs of capital facilities such as depreciation charges, insurance, taxes, and rental charges for buildings and equipment. Over the longer range, these costs will inevitably vary as the result of changes in depreciation policies, the addition and retirement of assets, changes in insurance, and tax rates; however, they do not respond to fluctuations in volume within the limits of existing facilities.

Managed costs. Managed costs represent all other elements of overhead expenses. The distinguishing characteristic of these costs is that they are subject to management control, i.e., they are capable of being *planned* or *programmed* in advance of the forecasting period, depending on current economic conditions and business goals and objectives.[1]

Although conditions will vary between companies, a proper breakdown of managed costs will generally indicate that the majority of these costs are "personnel-related," as opposed to nonpersonnel costs. They include salaries, social benefits, and overtime which, in many businesses, account for 75%–80% of total managed costs. Therefore, close examination of personnel costs in the profit planning process represents an element of major importance. One method employed in the cost forecasting cycle is to require each cost center or department within the division or company to submit a "personnel cost summary," which projects forecast spending on personnel costs for the particular planning period. An example of this type of summary is shown by Exhibit 1.

Managed costs of a nonpersonnel nature (advertising, travel, entertainment, etc.) normally are best controlled by means of overhead or programmed budgets. Therefore, approved budgets for these costs should represent the basic input for cost forecasting.

Miscellaneous revenue and expense. Most nonoperating revenue and expense items are subject to the same programming type review and forecasting as managed overhead costs. Income taxes, of course, repre-

---

[1] The definitions for committed and managed costs are extracted from an article on "Profit Planning" by Marshall K. Evans, *Harvard Business Review*, July–August 1959, p. 46.

sent an exception, since they are generally a variable cost, depending on the level of pretax income.

FORECAST EVALUATION.   Although management participation in the *construction* of the cost and profit forecast may be somewhat limited (and perhaps confined largely to a review of managed overhead costs), management should assume the key role in the *evaluation* of the forecast before it is submitted to the next higher level and/or to the board of directors. Management involvement at the evaluation stage will probably

EXHIBIT 1

Personnel–Cost Forecast Summary, 1969
Department 32, Division A

	Number of Employees	Amount ($000)
A. Base salaries		
1. Base salaries of *present* payroll as of 12/31/68......................................	125	950
2. Adjustments		
a) Additions..................................	12	100
b) Reductions................................	7	50
Net adjustments (a − b).......................	5	50
3. Total base salaries (1 + 2).....................	130	1,000
B. Merit increases......................................	...	50
C. Total salaries (A + B).............................	130	1,050
D. Salaried overtime.................................	...	75
E. Total personnel costs (C + D).....................	130	1,125

Notes:
1. In actual practice, this summary would be prepared by quarters for the forthcoming year; in addition, supporting schedules would explain the reasons for personnel changes, etc.
2. Total personnel costs (line E) are *before* the application of social benefits.

fall into two broad areas—(1) evaluation of the realism of the forecast, and (2) evaluation of the adequacy of profitability. In the case of the former, management must have an understanding of the basic assumptions underlying the critical variables, i.e., whether cost reduction inputs are reasonable, whether a forecast increase in market share is overoptimistic, whether recent trends in purchased material prices may be expected to continue during the planning period, etc. The prime purpose of this phase of the evaluation is for management to satisfy itself that it can accept and be held accountable for the forecast results.

While management may pass favorable judgment on the *reasonableness* of the forecast in terms of likelihood of attainment, it also has responsibility to test the forecast in terms of *adequacy* of profitability. Although, as previously noted, short-term profit planning normally places more emphasis on the bottom-to-top approach (because of current business conditions and limitations in the short run of redirecting business resources), management should not accept a forecast, even for a short-term period, if the indicated profit results are inadequate. Rather, it should require that lower-level profit centers "recycle" the forecast's major variables to examine the impact of alternative programs for profit improvement—faster introduction of a planned price increase, accelerated development of a new product to increase market share, etc.

PERFORMANCE REPORTING.   Although reporting on actual results versus forecast performance obviously can not occur until after some portion of the planning period has elapsed (a month or a quarter), performance reporting is classified as a step in the profit forecast because of the previously described role of planning in the total planning/control process. In other words, decisions on future action and adoption of new profit plans are heavily dependent on feedback and on interpretation of actual results versus the current plan. If the profit plan has been properly constructed and evaluated, adequate reporting on performance against the plan should indicate the type and extent of corrective action.

Although reporting techniques will be expected to vary from company to company, it is essential that performance reporting explains the major variations from forecast and shows the influence of each of the factors normally responsible for forecast deviations—price, volume, mix, and cost performance. Exhibit 2 illustrates a "profit variation analysis" method which may be utilized to isolate deviations from forecast for each of the above-listed factors.

Financial planning

The completion of the cost/profit forecast represents the final element in profit planning; however, termination of the forecasting process at this stage is inadequate for the majority of industrial corporations because most companies are interested in several types of financial achievement, of which profitability is only one element. Therefore, consideration must be given to *financial*, as distinct from *profit*, planning. Some of the normal financial measurements, in addition to profitability, are:

Return on investment.

Asset turnover.

Leverage.

Earnings per share and dividends.

Since ROI (or its approximate equivalent) can be divisionalized, it may be desirable to incorporate ROI into the divisional financial planning process. This is particularly desirable for companies that:

Require a high level of working capital and/or plant and equipment investment per sales dollar.

Are involved in a fairly high dividend payout in relation to earnings.

Feel surplus cash may be limited in the future.

Recognize that all capital, whether debt, equity, or other, has a cost associated with it.

EXHIBIT 2

Operating Profit Report, January, 1969

Division A

($000)

P & L SUMMARY

	Forecast	Actual	Actual Better (Worse) Amount	%
Net sales..................	8,000	7,600	(400)	(5.0)
Variable costs.............	4,000	3,952	48	1.2
Variable contribution.......	4,000	3,648	(352)	(8.8)
% Variable contribution.....	50.0%	48.0%	...	...
Committed costs..........	300	305	(5)	(1.7)
Managed costs............	2,740	2,700	40	1.5
Total overhead costs.......	3,040	3,005	35	1.2
Operating profit...........	960	643	(317)	(33.0)
% Operating profit.........	12.0%	8.5%	...	...

OPERATING PROFIT VARIATION ANALYSIS
Actual Better (Worse) versus Forecast

	Sales Volume	Sales Mix	Price Yield	Cost Spending	Total
Sales..............	(500)	...	100	...	(400)
Variable costs......	250	(102)	...	(100)	48
Overhead costs.....	...	...	...	35	35
Operating profit....	(250)	(102)	100	(65)	(317)

The above analysis reveals the following facts on the month's operations for Division A:

1. Physical volume was actually $500,000 (6.3%) below forecast, but higher than forecast prices reduced the total sales variation from forecast to $400,000 (5%).
2. Although total variable costs were $48,000 less than forecast, the mix of sales adversely affected variable costs, and a sizeable unfavorable spending variation of $100,000 also occurred.
3. Overhead cost spending was favorable versus plan.

At the divisional level, ROI is usually modified to *return on net assets* (RONA), which is calculated as follows:

$$\% \text{ RONA} = \underbrace{\frac{\text{Income after taxes}}{\text{Sales}}}_{\text{(Profit margin)}} \times \underbrace{\frac{\text{Sales}}{\text{Net assets}}}_{\text{(Asset turnover)}}$$

Note: Net assets are defined as total assets at book value less liabilities other than interest bearing debt.

Net asset forecasting may be approached in the same general manner as the forecast of operating costs, i.e., recognition of both the variable and fixed elements. For example, forecasts of the major working capital items (inventories, receivables, and payables) should employ the ratio technique, since these items usually bear a constant relationship to sales. Plant and equipment, and certain other items, are similar to fixed costs, so that forecasting for these items should be of a programmed nature. The use of capital budgeting for plant and equipment (capital) spending fulfills the same role as overhead budgets for fixed costs.

Since sales and profit forecasts are generally exploded to at least major product lines within a division, it also becomes desirable to identify net assets with each major product line to determine RONA at a level below the division. Exhibit 3 demonstrates some of the allocation methods used

EXHIBIT 3

Bases of Allocations
Net Assets by Product Line

Item	Basis of Allocation
Assets	
Cash	Cash costs and expenses
Receivables	Sales
Inventories	Direct identification
Prepaid expense	Various
Plant and equipment	Direct plus allocated *
Liabilities	
Payables	Raw material purchases
Accrued expense	Payroll
Income taxes payable	Pretax income

* Certain plant and equipment asset values are directly identifiable by major product lines within a division; the balance are allocated to major product lines on the basis of a combination of items, i.e., direct floor space charges, number of employees, capital spending, etc.

in this respect. It should be noted from Exhibit 3 that major net assets, such as inventories and plant and equipment, may be directly identified with a profit center and this should be reflected in the accounting system to the extent possible.

The availability of divisional net asset forecasts provides one final financial forecast—that of cash flow which, for many corporations, has become as important as earnings, due to the multitude of project demands and also because of increases in the cost of money itself. Therefore, it is vital that the financial forecast include a section on cash flow.

Exhibit 4 summarizes a completed divisional financial forecast, which may be required by corporate headquarters at the beginning of each quarter, semiannually, or annually. Many companies ask division management to make a personal presentation of the annual forecast, whereas quarterly or semiannual revisions may be handled in a less formal manner.

EXHIBIT 4

Financial Forecast Summary, 1969

Division A

($000)

1. Net sales...100,000
2. Net income... 6,000
3. Net assets...
   Receivables...................................... 8,000
   Inventories...................................... 20,000
   Plant and equipment (net)....................... 25,000
   All other.. (3,000)
        Total....................................... 50,000
4. Turnover: Sales/Net assets....................... 2.0
5. Profit margin: Profit/Sales...................... 6.0%
6. Return on net assets: Profit/Net assets.......... 12.0%
7. Net funds generated/(consumed).................. 4,500
8. Capital expenditures............................. 5,000
9. Depreciation..................................... 4,000

Notes:
1. In actual practice, this summary would also reflect 1968 actual or estimated results.
2. Net funds generated/(consumed) figure is based on net income plus (or minus) change in net assets during the year.

Budgeting

While budgeting may be regarded basically as a management *control* tool (and more properly a subject for Part VI of this book), it also deserves reference within the general framework of *planning,* because of the previously outlined role of planning in the total planning and control process.

Budgeting in its broadest sense is a system or technique for overall financial planning and is sometimes referred to interchangeably with financial planning. However, since profit and financial planning have been covered in some detail in this chapter, and because certain of the major types of budgets (such as capital, cash, etc.) are dealt with in succeeding chapters, the primary emphasis on budgeting at this point will involve budgets of an *operating* nature which support profit plans and forecasts.

Two of the more common applications of operating budgets are (1) variable manufacturing budgets and (2) administrative or overhead budgets.

Variable manufacturing budgets

In most industrial corporations, manufacturing costs represent the largest single area of functional cost spending. Therefore, it is vital not only to provide a cost control tool to manufacturing management but also to afford the means of relating manufacturing activity to the profit forecast. The variable manufacturing budget, if properly constructed and maintained, should serve to fulfill these dual requirements.

EXHIBIT 5

Variable Manufacturing Budget
Mixing Department, Division A

BUDGET ALLOWANCE SCHEDULE

| | Fixed Allowance | | Variable Allowance per |
Item	4 Weeks	5 Weeks	Pound Mixed
Direct labor			
Product A............. ...	...		$1.00
Product B............. ...	...		.50
Indirect labor			
Supervision........... $480	$600		...
Utility................. 200	250		.02*
Departmental expense			
Supplies............. ...	...		.04*
Depreciation 1,200	1,500		...

BUDGET REPORT—JANUARY, 1969

	Budget	Actual	Gain (Loss)
Production (lbs.)			
Product A...................... ...		1,000	...
Product B...................... ...		4,000	...
Product A + B................. ...		5,000	...
Direct labor ($)			
Product A.....................1,000		950	50
Product B.....................2,000		2,100	(100)
Product A + B.................3,000		3,050	(50)
Indirect labor ($)			
Supervision.................... 480		475	5
Utility......................... 300		325	(25)
Total....................... 780		800	(20)
Expense ($)			
Supplies...................... 200		175	25
Depreciation.................1,200		1,200	...
Total.......................1,400		1,375	25
Total labor and expense ($).......5,180		5,225	(45)

* Variable allowance on total pounds mixed.

In constructing a variable manufacturing budget, one of the basic methods is to develop a correlation pattern for each cost category within a particular department to determine the relationship of each type of cost with some unit of physical output. Whether a sophisticated technique is employed, such as least squares, or a simple elastic-band (eyeball) approach, the objective is to establish an *expected* cost for a given production volume and product mix. (Refer to Exhibit 5 for an example of a variable manufacturing budget.)

Budget adjustments represent a source of concern and are worthy of brief comment. The budget must be kept current in order to provide a good target and to reflect variations from expected costs. At the same time, it loses significance as a measure of progress if adjustments are made for every small change which affects operating costs. While there is no specific "formula" for determining when a budget should be adjusted (and by how much), major changes in product mix and cost levels generally necessitate budget adjustments.

Since budget performance in the factory area should reflect the behavior of actual factory costs, budget gain variances should directly result in a P&L improvement in relation to forecast. The budget becomes, in effect, the individual foreman's P&L statement on a departmental basis and a net reduction in variable budget allowances is usually real proof of cost reduction, as long as good service, quality, and employee relations are maintained and equipment is kept in good shape.

Overhead budgets

As stated earlier, overhead costs are best controlled by budgets which arc directly linked to profit forecasts. Under conventional planning, operating budgets for the majority of overhead costs are usually developed and approved at the end of the year for the next calendar year. The "cconomic guideline" for the amounts to be budgeted is normally a sales forecast for the next twelve months.

Because of the fact that personnel-related costs (salaries, social benefits, and overtime) account for a large percentage of total overhead spending in most companies, and because of the desirability to relate departmental overhead budgets to long-range objectives, many companies are placing greater emphasis on the *personnel* element (via salaried head-count budgets, performance evaluation techniques, etc.) and its relationship to specific programs or accomplishments that are to be expected during the planning period if budgeted dollar amounts are approved. While "project" or "program" budgeting has existed in the area of *capital* budgets for some time, its development and utilization with respect to *operating* budgets has largely been limited to the R&D function. Many companies, for example, supplement the conventional overhead budget system in the R&D area with a breakdown and timetable of planned spending for each of several projects or programs; in some instances they require approval of a specific project prior to commencement of actual spending; and, in most cases, actual versus budgeted spending is examined monthly by project along with a review of target date attainments.

While other overhead areas of most businesses are not as suitable as

R&D for the implementation of project budgeting (due to the difficulty of measuring tangible contribution or output), many companies have improved overhead cost control by reducing the planning cycle—for both sales revenue forecasts and overhead budget reviews—from an annual to a quarterly basis. In addition, other techniques such as programs to "manage by objectives" (and appraisal by the results) have been effected independent of the budgetary system to monitor each individual's contribution to the company's goals. (See Chapter 24, "Management By Objectives.")

Conclusion

This chapter has attempted to identify the need for profit planning and has described techniques involved in adopting a profit (or, more broadly, a *financial*) plan.

Since planning is a forward-directed activity and is concerned with the identification of expected or desired results, two areas should receive greater attention in the future (in order to better identify the future): (1) the utilization of operations research and management science techniques in the planning process and (2) a proper definition of financial goals and their relationship to planning. The latter is especially important if top management is to give proper *direction* to the planning effort. For example, if corporate goals have evolved in terms of an annual earnings growth rate and a desired return on stockholders' investment, these goals must be explicitly understood by each major profit center manager in order to assure that strategies, plans, programs, etc., will be focused on helping each division attain the corporate goals. The absence of such guidelines or rules of the game makes financial planning an interesting, but wasteful, exercise in numbers.

In the final analysis, profit maximization accrues to those who can act quicker and expend available resources more wisely than their competitors can. Fulfillment of these attributes should be the overriding objective of the financial planning process.

Management by objectives

Donald P. Jones and Albert S. Martin, Jr.*

A key to successful management is an effective planning and control process, but the process itself presents one of the most difficult and challenging tasks for a manager.

Some of the contributing factors which make the planning and control process difficult are poor communication between superior and subordinate, lack of participation in the goal-setting and decision-making processes, and ineffective performance appraisal. The following complaints are classic:

The only guideline we get from top management is the annual letter requesting the budget.

Our budgets are extrapolations of past experience, not a reflection of plans for the future.

We have no direction from our superiors. Our goals are developed within the framework of what we think top management wants. We need company objectives and our responsibilities defined.

There should be some agreement between superiors and subordinates on how subordinates are to be judged. Some of the measures which my superior is currently using are meaningless and misleading.

We have no direction from the top so we arbitrarily decided in a group meeting to devote 50 percent of our effort to increasing production and 50 percent to increasing sales. We don't know whether this is right or not.

Management by objectives is a process by which the planning and control functions of a company can be improved tremendously. Odiorne

* Vice President, and Coordinator of Production Accounting, respectively, Sun Oil Company, Philadelphia.

describes the process as one in which ". . . the superior and subordinate managers of an organization jointly identify its common goals, define each individual's major areas of responsibility in terms of the results expected of him, and use these measures as guides for operating the unit and assessing the contribution of each of its members."[1]

This chapter is devoted to some of the broader aspects which should be considered in the initial development and implementation of a management-by-objectives program.

In order to simplify the discussion, the following organization structure is assumed:

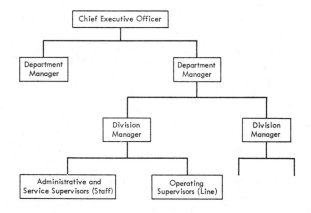

Three distinct levels of goal setting are recognized:

Corporate planning by top management in which the company's purpose is stated and broad objectives and strategies are formulated.

Goal setting by department and division managers within the framework of corporate objectives.

Operational planning in which specific projects and tasks are developed to carry out division goals.

Following the discussion of the goal-setting levels, the control function and the performance-measurement function are reviewed.

The goal-setting process

Setting broad objectives

The first level of goal setting in a management-by-objectives program should consist of the definition of the company's purpose; the formulation of broad objectives and strategies—and alternative strategies—for achieving the purpose; and the dissemination of this information

---

[1] George S. Odiorne, *Management by Objectives* (New York: Pitman Publishing Corp., 1965), p. 55.

throughout the organization. It is a job for the chief executive officer and his staff. This process is discussed in detail in Chapter 2, "Strategy Formulation and Implementation."

The first level of activity is the first step in the overall program because the dissemination of this information in the form of corporate planning guidance should trigger the lower level goal-setting processes and provide a framework within which lower levels of management can develop their goals.

Ideally, the dissemination of corporate planning guidance should be accomplished by means of a written memorandum and should contain such information as:

A concise statement of the company's purpose and basic philosophy.

Summary of long-range corporate objectives which will achieve the company's purpose:

> Share of market
> Rate of return on sales
> Rate of return on equity
> Financial policy
> Acquisition policy
> Production plans
> Manpower plans
> Etc.

A concise statement of short-range corporate objectives.

Evaluation of present position.

Changes in resources, organization, etc., to achieve the long- and short-range objectives.

Availability of funds and amounts tentatively allocated to each department.

Responsibilities to customers, stockholders, employees, and the community.

Since an effective management-by-objectives process requires a course of action to be plotted by top management before lower levels of management can define their goals, the existence of formal corporate planning procedures is essential. One method of insuring the existence of formal corporate planning is to delegate to one person or group of people the responsibility for corporate planning. Another method is to assign the task to a committee. Regardless of the person or persons responsible, the progress of the company should be reviewed frequently and modifications should be suggested which would change the course of action of the company when necessary.

Goals to carry out broad objectives

The second level of goal setting, which may be triggered by the corporate planning guidance memorandum, should be composed of two distinct phases:

1. The department managers should develop broad goals within the framework of the overall corporate objectives, and
2. The division managers should develop goals which will support and carry out the department goals.

It will be helpful if each department manager's broad goals are set out in a formal planning guidance memorandum. The memorandum should contain the following items of information:

Summary statement of corporate objectives.
Amount of funds tentatively allocated to the department.
Target rate of return on investment or other measure of profitability.
Summary statement of next year's goals for the department.
Review of long-term department goals.

Upon receipt of the department planning guidance memorandum, each division manager should develop a planning guidance memorandum for his division. The division memorandum is an extension of the department memorandum and should include the following additional information:

Summary statement of last year's performance.
Appraisal of competitive outlook.
Statement of next year's goals and major programs for the division.
Review of long-term division goals.

In the development of the division planning guidance memorandum, it is very important for the division manager to make certain that his goals and programs are realistic in terms of existing resources, e.g., manpower and equipment. Granger states that "establishing . . . a subobjective within the framework of a broader objective . . . involves the conceptual creation of a number of possible subobjectives, testing them against the realities of (1) consistency with internal resources, (2) consistency with environmental conditions, and (3) effectiveness/cost relationships in accomplishing the broader objective."[2]

The division manager must conduct a review with each of his line supervisors in order to test the realism of his goals and to establish tentative agreement.

In the goal-setting process this step is necessary in order for line supervisors to review in advance and tentatively agree to the goals for which they will later develop plans to achieve.

After tentative agreement has been gained, a group review session should be held with all staff managers in attendance. Since the function of staff personnel is to assist the line in carrying out the objectives of the organization, an exposure to these objectives makes it possible for them to set their own goals.

[2] Charles H. Granger, "Hierarchy of Objectives," *Harvard Business Review*, May–June, 1964, p. 69.

The final level of goal setting should include the development of projects for carrying out the division goals and the conversion of these projects into specific tasks. This is often referred to as operational planning and is illustrated by the next series of steps.

Operational planning

When the initial review sessions with the division manager are completed, it is essential that each line and staff supervisor be provided with a copy of the division planning guidance memorandum. Using the approved memorandum as a framework, each supervisor can then proceed to develop a written statement of his achievements so far this year, a list of short-range goals for the forthcoming year, a list of long-range goals for the next two or three years, and the job responsibilities and plans necessary to carry out his short-range goals. The plans which each supervisor develops should include a detailed description of each project and task.

In developing the projects and tasks for achieving the goals, alternative methods of reaching the desired goals must be worked out and evaluated.

Ideally, the plans should:

Be expressed in writing.
Include only actions that the originator can personally control.
Be broken down into detailed steps.
Be supported by a time schedule.
Include estimated costs.
Identify some means of measuring progress (activity indicators).

Each supervisor must review his past achievements and future plans with his respective division manager. Also the indicators which will be used to measure control and performance should be reviewed. During this review session all plans, alternative courses of action, and activity indicators should be modified until agreement is reached between superior and subordinate.

An example of how goals can be summarized at the department level can be seen in Exhibit 1. In this particular example, one objective is used for which three strategies have been developed. The goals for the strategies are also shown along with the various methods by which accomplishment of the goals will be measured.

After agreement is reached, all plans may be consolidated into a division summary, approved by the division manager, and submitted to the appropriate department manager.

The department manager should review all of the division programs and assess the different courses of action. He will also be able to

EXHIBIT 1

Management by Objectives

(retail marketing department)

Objective: To execute both profit and growth plans in a manner which will maximize the return on capital allocated to the department for accomplishment of short- and long-range company objectives.

Strategies	Goals	Method of Measurement (The Accomplishment of Goals)
I. A. Secure maximum results from TBA, jobbers, and advertising. B. Special gallonage building tools. Training. Sales building promotions and incentives. C. Improve existing operations. Effective use of credit. Control systems. Divestment. Product lines.	I. Achieve the profit and volume plan consistent with income and expense budgets.	I. A. Sales volumes, selling prices and expense budgets. Exercise cost management control. B. Improve unit gallonage through increased sales and divestment of low gallonage units. C. Market share in primary ____ state area of ____ %. D. Profit from credit-card promotions of $____. E. Issue a minimum of ____ credit cards.
II. A. Implement service station site-selection model. B. Concentrate efforts toward high-potential sites. C. Conform to minimal rate of return on capital expenditures. D. Evaluate existing units for possible divestment.	II. Achieve Market Development and Capital Expenditures plan. Realize long-range plan for return on investment.	II. A. Profitable investment of $____. B. On new facilities, a ____% DCF rate of return. C. Divest ____ service stations and ____ bulk stations. D. Study ____ key metro areas through use of the site selection model.

EXHIBIT 1 *(Concluded)*

Strategies	Goals	Method of Measurement (The Accomplishment of Goals)
E. Continue development of low cost units for individual ownership.		E. Finalize plans for new stations by ____.
F. Refine the ability to open stations on target dates.		F. Complete design studies and cost estimates for low-cost service station buildings by ____.
III. A. Utilize company cost-management training programs and improve ability of individuals to control cost.	III. Effectively implement and utilize sound cost management principles and systems throughout all phases of line and staff.	III. A. Operating expense not to exceed ____ per gallon.
B. Investigate cost-reduction possibilities through use of task forces.		B. Examine any item of expense varying ____% or $____ from budget for possible cost reduction.
C. Reduce credit losses.		C. Establish a committee within the general office to periodically review and determine cost saving ideas.
D. Refine and improve existing cost-management system.		D. Monthly reports from managers on expense variations from budget.
E. Study reduction of equipment investment at small volume accounts.		

determine whether resources can be shifted across division lines to provide a better mix of profitable opportunities for the company.

Review of company-wide goals and plans

At this point a company-wide budget review session is necessary with all of the department managers in attendance. If a corporate planning committee has been established, the review session should be conducted by this group. At this meeting it will be beneficial if each manager is given a reasonable length of time to make a presentation covering his achievements of the past year and a review of next year's plans, including alternative courses of action.

Departmental plans should be discussed, reevaluated, and modified until the most desirable course of action is determined for the company. Finally, the modified plans should be submitted to the chief executive officer for approval. After final agreement is reached the division managers can be notified by their respective department managers of the amount of funds available to them for the forthcoming year. At the same time the division managers officially should be delegated the responsibility for carrying out their plans. Reference should be made to Chapter 22, "Profit Planning and Budgeting," for additional discussion of these concepts.

The initial goal-setting phase is concluded when detailed plans for carrying out the goals have been established and authority to carry out the plans has been delegated. The next phase consists of controlling the events in order to carry out the plans.

Carrying out plans to achieve goals: control

Control has many meanings, but in relation to the management-by-objectives concept only one is important. Cass states that ". . . control may be understood negatively as the act of restraining or limiting. Or it may be understood positively as the action of initiating and directing activity in a definite manner for a definite purpose. It is in the latter sense that control is important to planning."[3]

The control function of a management by objectives system has three major steps:

Delegation of authority to carry out plans.
Carrying out plans.
Performance measurement.

Only two steps—delegation of authority to carry out plans, and performance measurement—will be discussed here.

Delegation of authority to carry out plans

Delegation has been appropriately defined by Dale and Michelon:

The principle of delegation is that authority should be delegated as far down the line as possible. The advantages of practicing delegation are those who are closest to the scene of action may be best able to deal with the prob-

---

[3] Richard T. Cass, "Pattern for Planning," *Management Services* September–October, 1964, p. 8.

lems that arise and time is saved by not sending information up the line and directions down again. Perhaps even more important, pushing responsibility down the line is one way of tapping the initiative of everyone in the organization and of keeping people interested in their jobs.[4]

For a management-by-objectives system to be effective, the expenditure approval limits should be in harmony with the responsibility for planning and control that is delegated to managers.

Consider as an example the exploration department of an oil and gas production company which has been delegated the complete authority for the planning and control of drilling prospects but does not have the authority to spend one single dollar on drilling without top management's approval.

If in this particular example the explorationists were given a range within which they could authorize the expenditure of previously budgeted funds without further approval, the management-by-objectives system of this company would be materially strengthened.

Some of the benefits of realistic expenditure approval limits are as follows:

It allows responsible individuals to become thoroughly committed to the entire management cycle.

Individuals are given the opportunity and incentive to become better managers.

It relieves top managment of the burden of reviewing and approving a large volume of appropriation requests which should be approved by the lower levels of management.

Performance measurement

Effective performance measurement is highly dependent upon a reporting system which will feed information back to each planner in such detail that he can measure and evaluate his performance in achieving his plans and take corrective action where necessary. The characteristics of this reporting system are discussed in greater detail in Part VI of this handbook.

It is very important that the reports which are provided to each planner should not be cluttered with cost and operating information over which he has no control. Also, the chances for a reporting system to be successful are increased when the user of the report fully understands the meaning of each item of information shown on the report. This can be accomplished in two steps:

Each report user should work out his own performance measures, review them with his superiors, modify them where necessary, and gain agreement in

---

[4] Ernest Dale and L. C. Michelon, *Modern Management Methods* (New York: World Publishing Co., 1966), p. 36–37.

advance of the report preparation process. The performance measures agreed upon should neither be difficult to develop nor difficult to interpret. The degree of accomplishment cannot be ascertained from broad subjective measures.

Training sessions should be conducted for the purpose of instructing each supervisor how to use the reports that he receives.

The first level of reports emanating from the system should be prepared for each operational unit or responsibility center and be directed to the supervisor in charge. The second level of reports should represent a summary of the first-level reports and be directed to the division manager. The third level represents a summary of the division reports and should be directed to the department manager. And of course the final report is a summary of the combined operations for top management. Each level of reports should reflect only those data representing the operations over which the manager has control.

In addition to reports covering his own activities, it might be extremely helpful in many instances if each division manager were to receive reports showing the overall results of other divisions within the department. If this is not practicable, he should at least receive additional reports reflecting the profitability of his department and the company. Information of this type will provide each manager with additional bench marks against which to measure his own performance and incentive for future goal setting.[5]

When the supervisor receives the report covering his unit, he should evaluate his performance relative to achieving his plans in terms of:

Why each significant variance occurred.
What corrective action is necessary.
What will it cost to take corrective action.
Whether replanning is necessary at this time.

In a regularly scheduled session, each supervisor should be given the opportunity to review with the division manager the evaluation he has made of his own performance. Agreement should be reached concerning the necessary corrective action.

After all review sessions have been concluded, each division manager should now have from his subordinates the information necessary to enable him to evaluate his own performance and thus prepare for a similar review session with his respective department manager. Likewise, department managers will be in a position to perform a self-appraisal before consulting with top management.

Under this approach ". . . no longer is the subordinate being examined by the superior so that his weaknesses may be determined; rather,

---

[5] Rensis Likert, "Motivational Approach to Management Development," *Harvard Business Review*, July–August, 1959, p. 81.

he is examining himself in order to define not only his weaknesses but also his strengths and potentials."[6]

Most of the emphasis in this section thus far has been on the performance measurement of line personnel, i. e., on those managers whose actions contribute directly to the realization of profit. There are certain staff groups whose primary purpose is to provide service to line personnel—purchasing, accounting, industrial relations, and legal, to name a few. Measuring the performance of these service groups is difficult because they do not contribute directly to the generation of profit.

Nevertheless, in the discussion of the planning cycle it was suggested that the staff groups be made completely familiar with the goals of the line supervisors. The reason for this is that such knowledge will enable the staff groups to plan their manpower needs in accordance with the projects recommended by the line supervisors. The manpower forecasts for the staff groups can then be used to prepare staff programs and program budgets. Carrying out the programs within the approved budget is an excellent measure of performance for staff groups.

Certain phases of the work performed by these groups can be measured in more detail by the use of activity indicators. The manager of each service group should be responsible for developing the indicators which are appropriate measures for the activity of his department. For example, the purchasing manager might choose as one indicator the total cost of purchasing as a percent of purchases; the accounting manager might choose the unit cost of processing customer invoices for mailing; etc. Each manager should review the activity indicators that he selects with his superior and gain agreement.

The reports which are prepared for each service group manager should reflect not only a comparison of actual costs with budget but also costs related to each activity indicator.

Each manager should perform his own appraisal of the results of his unit and meet with his immediate superior to review his progress. The budget comparison should be for the current period only, but an analysis of the activity indicators will have more validity if the indicators for the current period can be compared with the indicators of several prior periods. Any necessary remedial action should be discussed and agreed upon by the superior and subordinate.

To summarize the benefits received from performance review sessions between superior and subordinate, Hughes states:

Here the results-oriented philosophy of management by objectives achieves its fullest fruition and here, also, the benefits of organizational goal setting are realized most concretely. Here both organization and individual look back upon their accomplishments (or lack of them), measure the extent of their

[6] Douglas McGregor, "An Uneasy Look at Performance Appraisal," *Harvard Business Review,* May–June, 1957, p. 91.

success, and consider the activities that contributed to or detracted from that success. Such an analysis, not only of the results achieved but of the means employed in achieving them, can then be put to good use in the next goal-setting cycle.[7]

Summary

The purpose of this chapter has been to look briefly at what a management-by-objectives program has to offer and how such a program might be designed and implemented.

Management by objectives was defined as a process in which the superior-subordinate "team" work together to establish goals for a company and use these goals as guides in directing and measuring performance.

It was shown that a company's goals should be determined at three different management levels:

The corporate level (top management) defines the company's purpose and sets broad objectives and strategies to achieve the purpose.

Department and division managers set goals within the framework of corporate objectives.

Line and staff supervisors develop specific tasks and projects for carrying out division goals.

At each level the subordinate makes his plans and then reviews them with his superior. At these review sessions the plans should be modified until agreement is reached. After all plans are made and approved, each superior should delegate to his subordinates the authority to carry out his plans.

Since the plans serve as guides in operating the company, there must be a reporting system which will provide the planner with information which can be used in measuring and evaluating his progress in achieving those plans.

The content and format of these reports which are used to measure performance should have the approval of the person whose performance they measure.

Each person involved in the planning and control process should appraise his own performance by means of the reports and then discuss his self-appraisal with his superior. Agreement should be reached as to any corrective action recommended by either the subordinate or the superior.

The most important results of the technique described in this chapter are the full commitment of the employees to the company's purpose and a far better understanding of the management process.

---

[7] Charles L. Hughes, *Goal Setting* (New York: American Management Association, 1965), p. 111.

Bibliography

CASS, RICHARD T. "Pattern for Planning," *Management Services*, September–October, 1964.

COHRS, JAMES C. "Accountant's Responsibility for Effective Management Control," *The Texas CPA*, July, 1965.

DALE, ERNEST, AND MICHELON, L. C. *Modern Management Methods* (New York: World Publishing Co., 1966).

GRANGER, CHARLES H. "Hierarchy of Objectives," *Harvard Business Review*, May–June, 1964.

HUGHES, CHARLES L. *Goal Setting* (New York: American Management Association, 1966).

LIKERT, RENSIS. "Motivational Approach to Management Development," *Harvard Business Review*, July–August, 1959.

MCGREGOR, DOUGLAS. "An Uneasy Look at Performance Appraisal," *Harvard Business Review*, May–June, 1957.

MILLER, ERNEST C. *Objectives and Standards: An Approach to Planning and Control* (New York: American Management Association, 1966).

MYERS, M. SCOTT. "Conditions for Manager Motivation," *Harvard Business Review*, January–February, 1966.

ODIORNE, GEORGE S. *Management by Objectives* (New York: Pitman Publishing Corp., 1965).

Project scheduling and management

P. F. Muck*

During the past twenty years, more and more emphasis has been placed on corporate planning. Most of this planning starts with a set of basic long range objectives and develops through detailed analysis and appropriate revisions into plans of action which in turn satisfy the basic objectives. This chapter deals with the methods used to bridge the transitional period between objectives and accomplishment. This bridge is called project scheduling and management. Scheduling must outline the various steps leading to the ultimate goal, while management must control the pitfalls and delays which endanger the schedule. Although scheduling is not confined to projects, this chapter will restrict its discussion to the various methods used to schedule and manage projects, which for our purpose will be defined as one time, large scale endeavors.

A schedule can be considered a logical and systematic outline of the activities required to complete the project. It can include time, cost, manpower, or other elements which fit the overall plan of the user.

Few major projects are attempted today without some type of scheduling. First, time is always a significant factor, with overruns causing strained customer relations and impairment of future business. Delays tie up productive workers and jeopardize the future workload. Most significant of all, however, is the fact that overruns tie up capital. Therefore, the application of good scheduling techniques is closely coupled with the profit objective of the project. This objective is realized in terms of the

---

* Controller, Mesta Machine Co., Pittsburgh.

desired return on investment, or in the realization of the original profit goal.

Informal methods of project scheduling

Because of its minor nature, or because limited time and manpower do not permit a more formal method, it may prove expedient to adopt a relatively informal approach to project scheduling. Such scheduling can be left to the discretion of the management and operators involved, but there are certain basic factors which must be present before any form of reporting or control can be successful.

There must be a realistic completion date for the total project, and if major components are involved, a completion date for each component. In order to accomplish the overall completion date with a minimum of lost time, there should also be a recognition of the relationship between the major components.

In addition, there should be a firm estimate of total project cost and the cost of each major component. With this information, a time and cost schedule which measures current project status against targeted project goals can be developed and used for subsequent progress reporting at regular intervals. The form in which this information is presented is limited only by the imagination of the individual charged with the responsibility of reporting.

Gantt charts

One of the first formal methods of scheduling was developed in 1914 by Henry Gantt, who recognized the value of graphical analysis in project planning and scheduling. The method was first used to display plans and status reports for the U.S. Army Bureau of Ordnance munitions program in World War I. In this form of scheduling, as in all other forms, clear definition of the project objective and selection of an appropriate measurement system are imperative. The schedule is portrayed in bar chart form.

The basic approach requires a subdivision of the project into various elements which follow the chronological work flow of the entire project. An estimate is prepared for each element, using the measurement system selected. One of the most common systems uses material receipt dates as starting points, and lead time in man or machine hours as bar length determinants. Many elements are dependent not only upon material receipt dates, but also upon critical events in other elements. For example, a test fitting of one partially completed item may require the use of another partially completed item at some point in time. When all elements are plotted on the chart, an evaluation comparing the results with the overall plan objective can be made. At this point management can ascertain whether the individual elements can be completed within the overall time frame allotted to the project, and take the necessary action required to bring the schedule in line with the objective through adjustment of each element. This may be accomplished by trading man hours between a critical element and a less important element, authorizing overtime, improving material delivery dates, etc., depending upon the nature of the "bottleneck" encountered. The cost of such action can also

EXHIBIT 1

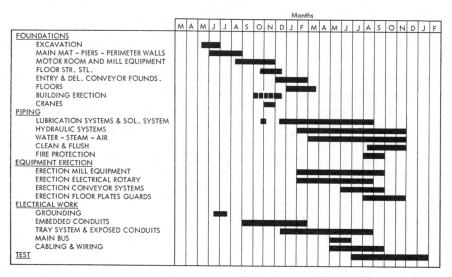

be evaluated. Summary charts, made up after detail charts are completed, are useful to management in the initial stages of evaluation.

As an example, Exhibit 1 shows the original summary schedule for the installation of a rolling mill for a basic metals processor. The various elements cover a wide spectrum of activities involving the erection of buildings, preparation of mill foundations, installation of utilities, delivery and installation of mechanical equipment, and final testing of the mill.

Although the original target completion date was August 31, the original work element schedule indicates that actual completion will be January 31. At this stage it is obvious that some action on the part of management is necessary if the desired completion date is to be reached. First attention must be given to the piping area, which shows overruns in the hydraulic system and water-steam-air piping installation, and in the cleaning and flushing of all piping. This work is performed by a subcontractor, who was asked to review his schedule. When the subcontractor determined that he could not significantly alter his schedule, the subcontractor who submitted the next highest bid was selected, as his time schedule fit the desired completion date. Management placed customer satisfaction above increased cost.

The next problem appears in the equipment erection area, where there is an overrun in erection of mill equipment, conveyor systems, and floor plate, which makes it impossible to meet the targeted completion date. These delays are caused by late deliveries from the manufacturer, and can only be resolved through an agreement between the manufacturer and the purchaser. In this case, the manufacturer agreed to work overtime on certain phases of the mechanical equipment in order to accom-

EXHIBIT 2

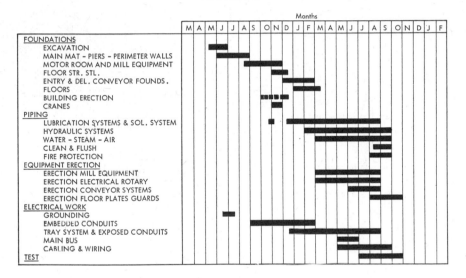

modate earlier shipment, while the owner agreed to accept an adjusted completion date of October.

The last item which requires adjustment is the testing procedure, which was originally estimated to require two months after final installation. Rescheduling of the owner's production and engineering personnel plus an increased manpower effort on the part of the contractor reduced this work to a one month period. The final result is an approved installation and start up schedule as displayed in Exhibit 2 which was acceptable to the machinery manufacturer, the contractor, and the owner.

Follow up is accomplished by plotting the actual progress of the work against the original objectives at regular intervals, carefully watching for any deviation in the plan and taking the necessary action to bring the work back in line with the agreed upon objectives. All schedules related to an overall plan must maintain a certain amount of flexibility to com-

EXHIBIT 3

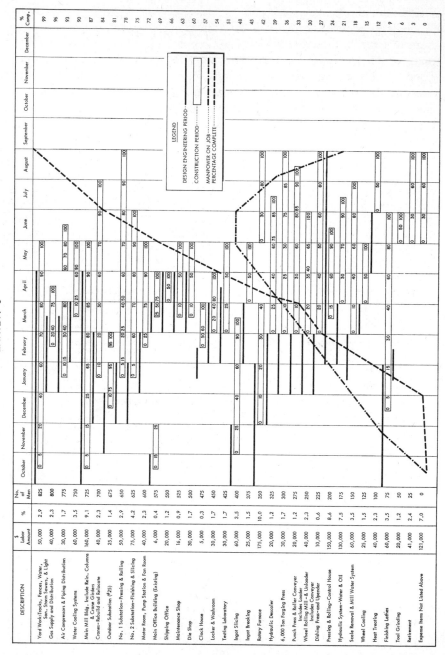

pensate for unanticipated contingencies, and this factor must be realized as part of the original planning and scheduling.

Exhibits 1 and 2 displayed a very basic summary Gantt chart schedule. Exhibit 3, also using the Gantt approach, shows a more complex summary of another project, with additional factors graphed for analysis and follow up. The schedule indicates the basic elements of the work necessary to complete a major mill alteration. Labor cost, the percent of total cost, and a manpower chart are shown, along with a schedule of engineering and construction work and a stage of completion indicator. A superimposed graph showing manpower requirements and the overall project stage of completion is also displayed. This chart, prepared and approved prior to the start of the project, is readily used for periodic measurement during construction. The exhibit is presented in a form representing the final completed status of the project.

Detail scheduling, using a modified Gantt approach, is shown in Exhibit 4. A complex fabricating, machining, and assembly operation is

EXHIBIT 4

	Description	Status	Feb.	Mar.	Apr.	May	June	July	Aug.	Sept.	Oct.	Nov.
1	Thermal Shield	At FF	HDP HBM FF			VB WS FF						
2	Lower Core Support	Wait 7" HBM	VB		HBM		NC HDP MM HDP FF					
3	Upper Core Barrel	Blending at Fitting Floor		HBM MM FF					VB			
4	Lower Core Plate		NC HDP	MM FF								
5	Lower Core Barrel	In Work on VBM			VB FF HRM VB FF							
6	Core Barrel Weldment					FF			WS MT FF / FF MT FF MS FF			
7	Formers	Complete										
8	Baffles	Burn & Inspect & Replace		MM RDP RDP	MM FF							
9	Baffles Assy.	Modification Required				FF		FF FF				
10	Access Port Plug Assy.								FF			
11	Lower Core Plate Assy.								FF			
12	Intermediate Plate	G & L & Slotter Oper. Comp. Wait VBM					HBM MM FF					
13	Core Barrel Assy.						FF IBM FF		FF FF			
14	Upper Core Plate	Semi Fin. Mach. Comp. on G & L Wait Jig for NC HDP		HB	NC HDP HB FF	MM						
15	Upper Core Plate Assy.	Checking on NC HDP Prior to HB							FF MM			
16	Upper Int. Shipping Std.								WS MT RDP			
17	Upper Internals Assy.								FF			
18	Upper Support Plate	Waiting VBM		MM	NC HDP HBM	MM FF						
19	Deep Beam Weldment	W Supplied Complete at NC					FF					
20	Upper Support Assy.							FF RDP FF HB FF				
21	Thermal Shield Fit Up										FF MT FF	
22	Thimble Guide Tube Assy.								FF			

LEGEND

FF – Fitting Floor
HBM – Horizontal Boring Mill
HDP – Horizontal Drill Press
MM – Milling Machine
MT – Miscellaneous Treatment
NC – Numerically Controlled
RDP – Rotary Drill Press
VB – Vertical Boring
WS – Weld Shop
V – Vacation

charted, showing the correlation necessary among many elements of a nuclear reactor assembly. Current status is shown by the solid black bars, and current date by the solid vertical line. Arrows mark the path of each component, and individual operations are identified with code letters. From this chart, critical operations can easily be identified and the amount of "slack" in less critical items determined.

The Gantt chart approach can be applied to almost every major project when some form of planning and scheduling is required. It represents a simple and inexpensive method of project scheduling and management. However, it must also be recognized as an approach which offers a minimum of control in comparison to the more sophisticated systems approaches developed in recent years.

Line of balance

As in all forms of project scheduling and management, a sound definition of objective, an ability to measure and report accurately, and a careful development of a basic plan are essential ingredients. Line of balance has been defined as an effective technique for measuring, collecting, interpreting, and presenting facts—time, cost, and accomplishment—all measured against a specific plan.

If used properly, line of balance can provide management with a tool which will forecast at regular intervals the development of a project and permit management to avoid future problems through a current decision making process. Line of balance scheduling will also encourage discipline and improve communications within an organization.

This method is usually composed of three levels of charts. *The level III,* or program chart, is developed by the line supervisors who are responsible for the accomplishment of the specific tasks. This chart usually takes the form of a flow chart, and includes time and cost estimates. Each flow chart should cover a component or subcomponent of the project, and be compatible in both data accumulation and line responsibility to the existing system. This will permit effective measurement. Level III charts provide line supervision with a technique for identifying and monitoring cost and performance.

Level II, or the progress chart, is a bar chart upon which the line of balance is plotted. The line of balance indicates the component accomplishment level necessary to meet the overall objective. Bars on the chart represent the actual status of each component. The Level II chart is directed to middle management, and can quickly reveal the status of the program and identify problem areas. The Level I, or objective chart, combines all the components and displays the project on a graph which compares the total actual progress with the basic project objective, usually in terms of cost, but sometimes in terms of other criteria which effectively measure progress. This chart is for top management use and provides a fast and effective summary, which can lead to timely action when necessary.

Line of balance, in its pure sense, is best suited for a production flow application where numerous like items must be produced within a given time frame. When so applied, all charts complement each other and the line of balance is determined by plotting the time remaining prior to overall completion for each component on the graph. This process automatically determines the line of balance.

In order to apply line of balance to a large one time project, some alteration must be made in the plotting technique. However, the effectiveness of the reporting system is not lost.

As an example, let us assume that the following schedule represents the cost and time required for the major components which comprise a project. Each of these components is supported by one or a series of Level III flow charts prepared by the line supervisor and coordinated by the project manager.

Component	Start Day	Complete Day	Elapsed Time—Days	Estimated Cost
A	1	60	60	$ 2,000
B	10	60	50	2,000
C	30	70	40	2,000
D	50	90	40	3,000
E	60	90	30	5,000
F	80	160	80	10,000
G	100	140	40	5,000
H	130	200	70	20,000
I	150	210	60	30,000
J	170	220	50	5,000
K	200	250	50	8,000
L	220	280	60	9,000
M	250	300	50	5,000
				$106,000

With these facts available we can now graph the project objective as shown in Exhibit 5. This calculation is made by determining the dollar value stage of completion at 30 day intervals. Example at 60 days:

Component	Planned Stage of Completion	Estimated Cost
A	100%	$2,000.00
B	100%	2,000.00
C	75%	1,500.00
D	25%	750.00
		$6,250.00

Similar calculations are made at each 30 day interval to indicate the desired project objective.

In addition to graphing the project objective on this chart, actual results are also plotted. We note that the project has been ahead of, or in

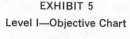

EXHIBIT 5
Level I—Objective Chart

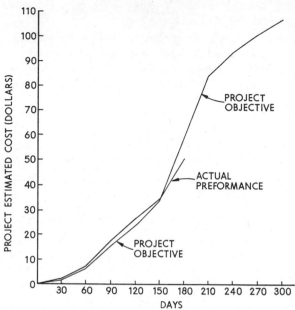

line with, the objective through the first 150 days, but that at the end of 180 days some problems have arisen.

The Level II, or progress chart will already have isolated the problem area as indicated in Exhibit 6. At the end of each 30 day period the line of balance is replotted on the chart. The line shows the level of each component's planned stage of completion at the time of analysis. Example, component H at 180 days:

Present elapsed time	180
Component H—start time	130
Component H—production time	50
Component H—-total estimated time	70
Desired % complete	71%

Therefore, for this line of balance analysis, component H should be 71% complete. This calculation is repeated for each component and plotted until the line of balance is complete. Actual component expenditures to date are then plotted in the hollow bars.

The next step is to determine an accurate actual stage of completion and place these levels on the chart in the solid bars. Determination of the actual stage of completion depends upon the criteria being measured.

The percentage of man hours completed to current man hour estimates may be applicable. The volume of material received related to total volume required may suit some components. Other components may require a combination of measurement devices. In any case, line supervision should be in the best position to supply the most accurate criteria to use.

Now the problem areas can be isolated and it can be determined that component A is causing much of the problem. An examination of the

EXHIBIT 6

Level II—Component Progress Chart

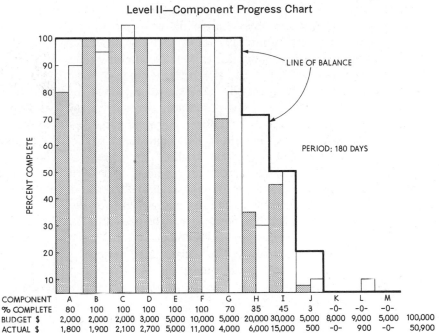

COMPONENT	A	B	C	D	E	F	G	H	I	J	K	L	M	
% COMPLETE	80	100	100	100	100	100	70	35	45	3	-0-	-0-	-0-	
BUDGET $	2,000	2,000	2,000	3,000	5,000	10,000	5,000	20,000	30,000	5,000	8,000	9,000	5,000	100,000
ACTUAL $	1,800	1,900	2,100	2,700	5,000	11,000	4,000	6,000	15,000	500	-0-	900	-0-	50,900

detail (Level III) flow charts may disclose that components G & H are behind because of a dependency on component A. In addition, unfavorable cost trends can be isolated and investigated.

As indicated earlier, this is just one approach for the use of line of balance scheduling and measurement. Each project can be different and can require different applications of the line of balance technique. However, certain basic facts must remain constant if the management of the project is to be successful. The project components and subcomponents must be compatible with the cost accumulation tools available and should avoid crossing responsibility lines.

The most severe disadvantage in the line of balance method is the inability of the system to adapt itself to uncertain time estimates or to changes made in time estimates during the project. However, in comparing the expenditure involved in the line of balance technique, as compared to that required for a more complex system such as PERT, it may prove the best approach for corporations with limited manpower or facilities.

Network scheduling

As both government and private projects have grown in complexity, the need for more precise and advanced methods of project planning, scheduling, and control has increased. In 1956, Du Pont, in conjunction with Remington Rand, responded to a need for better control of maintenance and engineering projects through the development of CPM (critical path method) scheduling. Du Pont was so impressed with the method that they kept it confidential until 1959, and only released it after the Department of Defense made the PERT (Program Evaluation and Review Technique) method public. Du Pont found CPM most effective when applied to projects where time estimates were fairly easy to predict.

About the same time, the Navy Office of Special Projects, in conjunction with Booz-Allen and Hamilton Co. and the Lockheed Aircraft Company, developed PERT for use in the Polaris project. Polaris involved approximately 3,000 contracting agencies, and required strong project control and measurement. The rationale behind the development of PERT was the vast uncertainty of the time required for the project. As the Polaris project proceeded, it became evident that PERT was capable of dealing with the uncertainties of completion times, and the method evolved as a basic accepted concept for government projects.

After both methods were made public in 1959, each copied various characteristics of the other, and by 1961, for all practical considerations, the systems were almost identical.

The fundamental benefit of network analysis is to provide the ability to determine the amount of resources needed to complete a project by a definite date. Network analysis is best adapted to a major project in a new and untried situation such as research and development work, or to those projects of a large and nonrepetitious nature. The application is expensive, as it requires continuous updating and analysis in order to identify problem areas, provide decision making information, and initiate the desired action. Proper application of the network approach to a major project usually requires a full time team of specialists.

The growing popularity of network analysis stems from the benefits which it affords the user. It provides a pictorial display of the interrelationship of many varied activities and points out the criticality of specific activities. In addition to the management and control features, it provides the individuals working on the project an insight into how they themselves fit into the overall framework of the project.

The general guidelines for the application of network analysis indicate that if a project has less than 50 activities, the network can best be prepared and updated manually, while 150 or more activities will make computer usage desirable. Between 50 and 150 activities can be handled efficiently in either manner. The possible applications are as broad as the spectrum of major projects carried on by government or industry today.

Definition of terms

With the development of network analysis, a number of associated terms also evolved. Some of the most common are: activity, event, arrow diagram, node, arrow, and slack. An activity is an operation of measurable time duration. An event is a specific point in time, when an activity has been completed, which has no measurable time duration. An arrow diagram is a pictorial representation of the activity list indicating the interrelationships of the activites. A node is a small circle which symbolically represents an event, while the arrow symbolically represents an activity.

The amount of slack in an activity is the amount of time an activity can be delayed from its earliest start date and still not extend the total duration of the project. Total slack is the cumulative allowable delay of an activity and its preceding related activities. Free slack is the amount of slack available to an activity which, if used up, will not affect the next activity. Free slack is not shared with other activities.

Float is a term which is sometimes used to describe the difference between the earliest and latest start times. Float and slack are synonymous in use and nature when applied to network scheduling.

Critical path method

As stated previously, the earliest form of network analysis developed was the critical path method (CPM). This method requires only one time estimate for each activity. The time must be the realistic expected completion time for the activity. The critical path network is an event-oriented network, with activity times listed in the node following the activity. The arrows do not, by length or notation, represent time. An earliest start time, which is the date an activity can be started if all preceding activities are completed in their estimated time, is calculated along with the latest start time for each activity. The latest start time represents the last day an activity can be started if the project time goal is to be met, assuming all succeeding events are completed at their estimated times.

Exhibit 7 indicates a partial list of activities required for the installation of a heavy rolling mill by a company in the heavy metals manufacturing industry. Each activity is placed in a sequence of earliest start and assigned an appropriate alpha character. Also indicated is the preceding activity which must be accomplished before the activity can begin and the realistic time required to complete the activity.

As can be seen from Exhibit 8, Activity W requires the completion of

EXHIBIT 7

Partial Activity Analysis for Installation of Mill by a
Company in the Heavy Metals Industry.

I.D. Code	Activity	Immediate Predecessor Activity	Estimated Time
A	Excavate for piers	None	3
B	Shore columns	None	7
C	Drive west pier piling	B	2
D	Sheet pile west wall	C, A	7
E	Excavate motor room	A	7
F	Drive east pier piling	E, D	2
G	Column piers	F, C	10
H	60" girder	G	6
I	Drive motor room piling	E, D	9
J	Modify row "C" piers	I	12
K	Ground motor room	I	5
L	Motor room mat.	I	14
M	Reinf. columns	G	4
N	Excav. mill area (partial)	D	8
O	Excav. mill area (finish)	N, I	20
P	Finish driving mill piling	O	25
Q	Mill material	P	32
R	Mill perim. walls	Q	21
S	Embedded conduit	Q	13
T	Mill foundations	Q	35
U	Embedded conduit	L, K	8
V	Motor room equip. foundations	L, K	28
W	Erect motor room steel	M, J, H	21
X	Roofing & siding	W	22
Y	Motor room floor slab	V, U	15
Z	Crane coll. rail bldg. lights	X	21
AA	Start conveyor found. mill housing	R, S, T, Y, Z	6

Activities J, M, & H before it can start. All of these activities are not on the critical path; therefore, they all have a certain amount of slack time. Activity H can be started anywhere from the 28th day to the 67th day without delaying the completion of the project. It therefore has a total slack of 39 days. Activity H has an earliest finish date of 34, and its successor Activity W has an earliest start date of 37; therefore, Activity H has free slack of 3 days. This means that if Activity H does not use the free slack of 3 days, no successor activity can use it because Activity W cannot start till the 37th day regardless of when Activity H is completed. However, the other 36 days of slack for Activity H can be used for successor activities, if not used by H, as long as activities J and M are

EXHIBIT 8

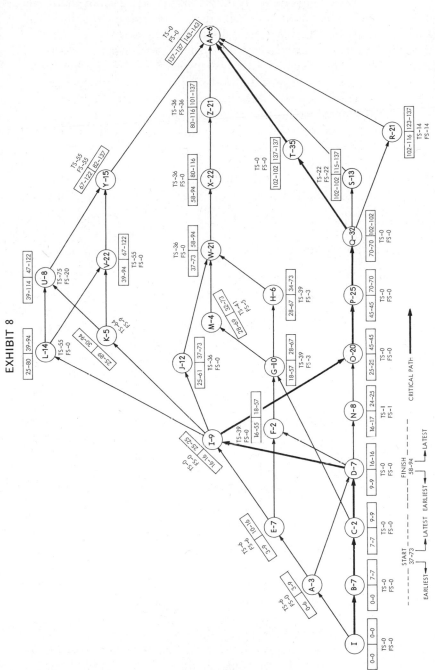

This is a network of the activity analysis listed in Exhibit 7 prepared following the critical path method. It is assumed that the project due date compares with the scheduled completion date; therefore, there is no slack on the critical path. TS represents total slack, and FS represents free slack.

complete by day 37. Conversely, if Activity H uses 21 days of total slack and is not completed until the 55th day, this will reduce the slack available to Activities W, X, & Z from 36 days to 18 days.

Activity M can be started anywhere from the 28th to the 69th day; therefore, it has a total slack of 41 days. However, M's earliest finish date is the 32nd day, and its successor Activity W has an earliest start date of 37, thereby giving M 5 days of free slack which no other activity can use. Activity J has a total slack of 36 days, but since J has an earliest finish date of 37 and W, its successor activity, has an earliest start date of 37, J shares all of its total slack of 36 days with successor activities and has no free slack.

The critical path (B, C, D, I, O, P, Q, T, AA) is the path of activities which have no slack at all. Any delay in these areas will cause a delay in the total project time.

Program evaluation and review technique

The program evaluation and review technique (PERT) method takes into consideration the probability that estimated time may not turn out to be the actual duration of an activity and calculated deviations are built into the technique. PERT is an activity-oriented method with the times identified on the arrows, and with dummy activities, symbolized by broken arrows, representing all activities whose culmination leads to the initiation of more than one event. Since all solid arrows must be represented by a time estimate, it becomes mandatory that only one of the arrows, representing the activity and leading to the events, can be solid. All dummy activities are allocated a time and cost factor of zero. The mathematical computation of the time estimates in PERT not only considers the realistic time, which is given a weight of four, but also considers the optimistic and pessimistic, which are each given a weight of one. The resultant equation to compute the time estimate is:

$$Te = \frac{To + Tp + 4\,Tr}{6}.$$

The following example will show the difference in estimated time by using PERT instead of CPM. Two activities have realistic times of 20, optimistic times of 16, and pessimistic times of 48. Using the CPM assumption, the realistic time of 20 would be used for each activity and the total elapsed time for both activities would be 40. Under PERT, a weight of 4 would be assigned to the realistic time of 20, and a weight of 1 each to the optimistic and pessimistic times of 16 and 48. Applying these in the above equation, a time estimate of 24 for each activity, or a total elapsed time of 48, would be derived. Although individual time estimates calculated under PERT and CPM will be different, it is generally felt that the sum of all the deviations, when applied to a total network, will serve to cancel out, and the total project estimate for each method will be almost equal. In its equation, PERT recognizes the uncertainties of time to reflect unexpected efficiencies or difficulties. Further refinements, involving the degree of probability of attaining estimated times, may be derived to provide useful information. For this, the standard deviation formula

$$Ds = \frac{Tp - To}{6}$$

is used.

The standard deviation sets the limits of time within which an activity can be expected to occur. An original estimate (Tr), refined by the formula above into Te, should have a 50 percent probability of attainment. Additionally, a standard deviation formula may be incorporated to further refine the estimate, as demonstrated by the following example. Assuming a realistic time of 24, a pessimistic time of 42, and an optimistic time of 18, the estimated time under PERT is

$$Te = \frac{To + Tp + 4\,Tr}{6}$$

$$Te = \frac{18 + 42 + 96}{6}$$

$$Te = \frac{156}{6} = 26.$$

The standard deviation is

$$Ds = \frac{To - Tp}{6}$$

$$Ds = \frac{18 - 42}{6}$$

$$Ds = 4.$$

The following statements can then be made:
1. There is a 50 percent probability that the job will complete in 26 days.
2. There is a 16 percent probability that the job will complete in 22 days (26 − 4).
3. There is an 84 percent probability that the job will complete in 30 days (26 + 4).

Thus, not only the expected time but also the probability that an activity can be performed within a specified time range can be determined.

Exhibit 9 displays the same activities outlined in Exhibit 7, but in a PERT network. The time estimates used in Exhibit 7 are retained for ease of presentation.

EXHIBIT 9

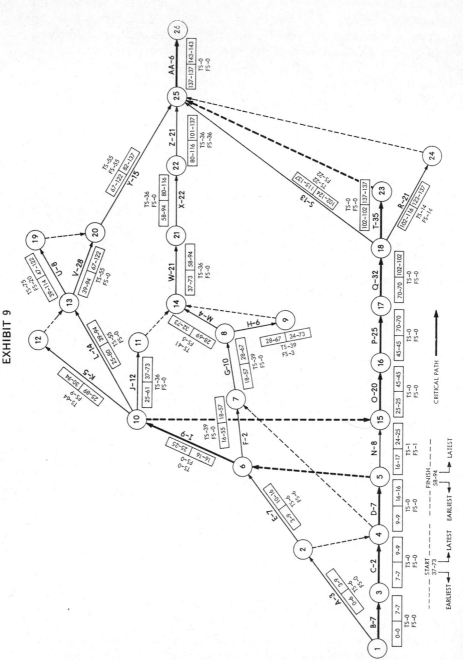

This is the deterministic PERT chart for the activities listed in Exhibit 7. It is assumed in the network that the earliest schedule completion date coincides with the due date.

It can be noted in Exhibit 8 that the culmination of Activity A leads to the initiation of Activities D and E. Since Activity C also precedes Activity D, it becomes mandatory to show a dummy activity arrow going from A to the tail of arrow D in Exhibit 9. It might be thought that the network could be shown as in Exhibit 10, but this would mean that

EXHIBIT 10

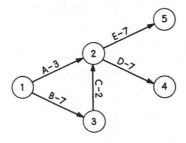

Activities C and A are not only precedent to Activity D's being initiated, but also to Activity E being started. This is not true, as C and A are precedent only to D, with just A being a precedent to E. The critical path for Exhibit 9 would be:

$$
\begin{array}{rl}
\text{B---} & 7 \text{ days} \\
\text{C---} & 2 \text{ days} \\
\text{D---} & 7 \text{ days} \\
\text{I---} & 9 \text{ days} \\
\text{O---} & 20 \text{ days} \\
\text{P---} & 25 \text{ days} \\
\text{Q---} & 32 \text{ days} \\
\text{T---} & 35 \text{ days} \\
\text{AA---} & \underline{6 \text{ days}} \\
& 143 \text{ days}
\end{array}
$$

The lines in Exhibit 9 from 5 to 6 and from 10 to 15 are dummy activities, but serve to show how the interrelationship will display the critical path. All dummy activities, such as the one emanating from A to D, have a time factor of zero.

Use of network analysis

ORIGINAL PLANNING. At this point, it will be beneficial to see how a network schedule is developed and used. For illustration, a PERT system will be examined.

First, a clear and concise definition of the project objective must be determined. (What is to be accomplished?) Next, the major steps which must take place to attain the objective must be identified. These steps should be cost related so that, along with a time schedule, a cost schedule can be prepared. A major consideration in defining the steps should be to include identification of the operating personnel who will be charged with the responsibility of carrying out these activities. All activities should be defined very specifically to prevent misinterpretation or duplication. After all the major activities have been listed, each major activity should be subdivided into smaller and more controllable activities, and the arrow diagram of the network prepared. This is normally accomplished by listing the last activity and working back to the first activity. The interrelationships must be shown, and all activities must be interconnected, except the first and last. In addition, the major decisions relating to the network should be documented to provide easy reference at a later date. Networks should be prepared in varying detail for different levels of management and control.

TIME ESTIMATES.   Upon the completion of the network, time estimates are obtained, usually from operating personnel, based upon past experience or some other available criteria. To achieve realistic estimates, it should be stressed to operators that the time estimates are just that, and are not commitments. The most successful way to achieve three good time estimates is to first obtain the optimistic, then the pessimistic, and last the realistic. The optimistic estimate should represent the time needed if everything goes right. The pessimistic should be the time needed if everything goes wrong (exclusive of low probability catastrophies), and the realistic should represent the expected time. The time estimates should be prepared viewing the activity as an isolated event; therefore, operating personnel should be unaware at this point of the time required for other activities. In originally determining the time estimates, a normal 40 hour work week is usually assumed. The appropriate unit to measure time should be based on the nature of the activity. Correspondingly, an activity such as digging the foundation of a building might be measured in days, while an extensive research or development project might be best expressed in weeks. Most imperative in the determination of time estimates is that they cannot be changed arbitrarily to fit a preconceived completion date, but must be a result of the reallocation of resources and manpower.

After completion of the arrow diagram and the time estimates for a project, the next procedure is to plot the time estimates into the network. The critical path can now be determined by the interconnected arrows having the largest total time estimates, and the earliest and latest start times can be developed. In calculating the earliest start time it is essential to remember that the earliest start time for an activity emanating from a node which receives more than one activity is the latest of the optimistic finish dates of the preceding activities. For example, in Exhibit

9, Activity V cannot begin until L and K are completed. K has an earliest completion date of 30, but L cannot be completed until the 39th day, which means the earliest start date for V must be the 39th day.

Conversely, the latest start time of an activity must be equal to or more than any of the latest finish times of the preceding activities. In Activity V, the latest start time is 94, which is equal to the latest possible finish times of preceding activities L and K.

At this point, the network should be reviewed and a comparison made between the scheduled completion date and the target completion date. The network should also be reviewed to ascertain the slack activities and their possible ramifications.

REVISIONS OF NETWORKS.   If the duration of the project schedule at this point does not compare favorably with the target date, the original estimates may have to be revised. As stated previously, time estimates cannot be changed arbitrarily. Manpower requirements previously established can be revised if the activity permits. Additional manpower needed on the critical path can be transferred from slack areas or taken from other projects if necessary. Scheduled overtime can be applied to the critical activities. Extra resources may be added, or the possibility of some work being subcontracted may be considered. It might be considered worthwhile to accept more risk, such as limiting quality control tests, performing series activities in parallel, or eliminating intermediate testing. If all of the above cannot reduce the scheduled date to the target date, then the scheduled date must be accepted.

Assuming the project being scheduled is of sufficient magnitude to require computer applications, the network revisions can easily be fed into the original network schedule and an updated schedule can be run. One form this schedule can take would display the following information: event—start, finish, duration; work area; activity description; earliest date—start, finish; latest—start, finish; total slack; free slack.

REPLANNING AND CONTROL OF NETWORK.   With the original planning phase of PERT completed, the control and replanning aspects of the system begin. As the performance of the project proceeds, actual results can be compared to estimates.

On a regular basis, operating personnel will report work completed and the current stage of completion, based upon time, and readily convertible into costs. As these results are received (daily, weekly, or monthly, depending upon the project structure) the network is updated and areas requiring special attention are pinpointed. Management, by exception, may be used to good advantage here.

If a computer application is used, the schedule displayed in the previous section can provide fast and accurate information by generating a printout of the updated network, and serve as the basis for progress reporting to various levels of management.

Once a trouble spot is indicated, information must be communicated to the particular level of management charged with the decision making function to determine the proper course of action. The personnel involved in making this determination should include the project manager, the operating personnel, and members of top management charged with overall corporate responsibility. This approach will provide a clear communications link and strengthen the bond between project personnel and operations.

In arriving at the proper course of action, management must take into account the target completion date which was originally developed, and the added costs necessary to reach that target under the revised and updated project schedule, if the revised schedule indicates a time extension. Profit planning and cost control must play an important part in this decision.

NETWORK SIMULATION.   A new method of network analysis called network simulation is now being explored. Network simulation is a mathematical sophistication of the CPM-PERT technique which uses as its basis Monte Carlo simulated sampling. Briefly, Monte Carlo simulated sampling simulates, through the use of random numbers, many possible actual lines to complete activities which could exist from the given time estimates. It then determines a "path criticality index" for each activity. This index represents the probability percentage that an activity could be on the critical path. The advantages of this method are the recognition of uncertainties in the total project time, and the consideration, stated as a percentage, that more than one path could be the critical one. The disadvantages of this method are the extensive computer time required to calculate the path criticality index, and the inherent assumption that management does not realize that the planned critical path is not always the actual critical path without the path criticality index.

Other modifications of the basic network system not covered in this article are: SCANS (scheduling and control by automatic network system), PACT (production analysis control techniques), and LESS (less cost estimating and scheduling). All of these are a sophistication of the basic network approach.

REVIEW OF NETWORK ANALYSIS.   With the inception of network analysis in the late fifties, a dynamic new tool became available to management. The tool had as its basis the principles of "management by exception" and "management from the bottom up." It applied management by exception because only when an activity falls outside of its acceptable range is it brought to management's attention. The principle of management from the bottom up is adhered to because the operating personnel, who actually perform the work, are the ones who are primarily responsible for setting the time estimates subject to management review.

The planning and preparation required to develop a network before a project is started enables management to consider many factors in advance. The manpower at the optimum time and place required will permit management to schedule the existing work force efficiently and, if necessary, to hire additional employees. The slack times in noncritical activities can provide the manpower needed to shorten the duration of the critical path. The network highlights the resources necessary and the dates needed, which permits management to schedule material receipts more efficiently, thereby reducing cash flow problems and holding storage and material handling costs to a minimum. The necessary planning also alerts management to the possibility of subcontracting work in order to meet deadlines. Most importantly, the network presents a clear and concise picture of all the project activities and enables management to revise the schedule to meet due dates or to determine why due dates cannot be met and have the necessary detail to back up its conclusions.

Network scheduling is not only an effective planning tool; it can also be a profitable control tool after the project has been started. With the system being revised constantly, the status of actual time as compared to the estimate is known promptly, and management can make decisions to insure compliance with the scheduled date. If the network is constructed to comply with the cost accounting system, actual costs can be related to estimated costs to ascertain the profitability of the project.

The major disadvantage of the network system is that it is difficult to use efficiently in production situations because it deals in time, not quantity. In mass production shops or assembly line operations, bar charts or line of balance methods, which were previously discussed, are more applicable. It must be recognized that there have been significant improvements in the network analysis scheduling technique in the past ten years; however, there is still extensive research being performed in order to strengthen some of the mathematical assumptions underlying the PERT-CPM calculations.

There is also extensive study being performed on improving the measurability of costs under the PERT-CPM technique; however, at its present state, PERT-CPM represents an effective and sophisticated technique in planning and controlling any major project.

Project management

The preceding description of network analysis showed how PERT scheduling could be applied to a complex project. With the application of this sophisticated scheduling technique to a project, a project manager is usually required for adequate planning and control. Depending upon the size of the project, the manager may have a central staff of thirty controlling a complicated PERT project, or, in a fairly simple task, he may be a one man control team.

One man projects

Although the words "project manager" and "project management" are not usually applied to a one man control project, one man from a functional department may work on a special assignment such as controlling the installation of a new roof on a plant. He would obtain the time estimates and cost estimates from the contractor at the start of the job, and plot the progress of actual against estimates at periodic intervals until conclusion. He would also periodically prepare reports for management as to the progress of the job, and would follow up any deviations from the estimates.

Requirements of a project manager

The title project manager, as generally used, refers to a manager of a complex project working with a sizable staff. A manager of this type must be highly qualified in the technical aspects of the project and have the necessary experience to command the respect of those with whom he works. These qualities are necessary because the project manager is often responsible for much of the design of the project and must provide the necessary communication with customers and suppliers. He also has the responsibility to provide his line personnel with assistance in logic and technique, and must have the ability to recognize current or potential problems and provide corrective action. He must be, in every sense of the word, a "manager." In fact, many project managers of large firms classify their duties as being very similar to those of the general manager of a small firm.

Need for a project manager

A project manager is needed under most situations requiring network scheduling applications, and the following conditions are usually present in the project.
1. High complexity or long duration.
2. A need for substantially more resources than are generally available in an organization or functional department. Some projects, such as the marketing of a new product, require an interrelationship between the production, sales, advertising, and marketing research departments.
3. An unusual or unfamiliar undertaking, such as the building of a new plant.

4. A project very important to a company's reputation and position, such as the introduction of a product into a competitive market.

Types of project management

There are basically three types of project managements—"pure" project management, "matrix" project management, and "influence" project management—with many variations of each type.

Under the theory of pure project management, the project manager has virtually full authority in all areas concerning the project. The project team is gathered specifically for the project, and they report directly to the project manager.

In matrix project management, the project manager shares authority with a functional manager. Our comments in this section will generally be tailored to the matrix method of project management. The project manager, basically, decides the "what" and "when" of the project, while the functional manager decides the "how" support aspect of the project. In this type of management the project manager operates horizontally and diagonally across the organization chart. In this situation, the respect that the other parties have for the project manager's abilities is important as it enables him to exercise informal authority over them. The project manager can also attempt to meet his goals by negotiating and trading off with the functional manager.

The third type of project management is the influence method. Under this method, the project manager functions only as a staff assistant. He exercises no formal or informal authority in the functional area, this being the full responsibility of the functional manager. Therefore, the project manager is basically a monitor or expediter. The remainder of this discussion does not pertain to the influence method of project management.

Organization of the project team

A project team gathered for a fairly complicated project will be organized along the following lines. It will consist of a project manager and a staff of up to thirty people. This is considered to be the maximum manageable staff. The staff is composed of people from the various functional departments participating in the project, and should be flexible so that it can adapt to the changing environment of the project. For example, as a project proceeds from the research and development phase to engineering and finally to production, the composition of the staff will change to meet the needs of the current phase of the project. However, while the majority of the staff will be oriented towards the current phase of the project, it will still consist of men from all pertinent functional departments.

Characteristics and operation of the project team

There are numerous characteristics of the project type of management which do not agree with the traditional concepts of vertical line management. The many functional departments included in the team have the same goals as those of the organization, instead of merely a functional objective. This unifying effect is very beneficial to the corporation. Another unique characteristic of the project team is the conflict of interests between the project manager and the functional manager. (This occurs due to the crossing of the functional lines of authority, and must be settled by negotiations, persuasion, or trade-offs.) Surprisingly, these conflicts are generally profitable to the corporation, because when the managers attempt to solve the problem together they generally achieve a more satisfactory solution than either could achieve individually. The project team also produces numerous dealings with peers, associates, and colleagues in the problem solving process, while traditional management concepts normally deal in superior-subordinate relationships. The project team is a complex and dynamic structure with no definite boundaries, exclusive of the project limits, which facilitates the coordination and integration of the project through all functional departments.

Once the project manager has been chosen and has assembled a staff, the project is ready to begin. The first step generally is to set up a project manual with all data pertinent to the project included, and as major decisions are reached, they should be documented in this manual. The requirements for the project, such as delivery date, budgets, and technical details relating to the product must then be developed. The project manager generally has control of the project funds, as it is his responsibility to produce the product efficiently. He participates in the design of the product and is often the chief engineer on the project. The project manager also has the chief responsibility for dealing externally with the customer, subcontractors, and suppliers.

At the outset of the project, it is necessary to develop standards, such as PERT time estimates, to be used as guideposts to evaluate the progress of the project. So that these standards may be used efficiently, they must be tailored to cost and other reporting systems. The development of an adequate feedback technique will prove useful for control purposes.

As the project proceeds, the project manager periodically will meet with his staff. The length of the period will vary with the stage of completion and the nature of the project, and may be daily, weekly, biweekly, or monthly. At these meetings, any problems or decisions relating to the project are discussed. To achieve adequate control of the project it is necessary for the reporting system to reflect revised forecasts of excessive time and costs at a date early enough to permit the necessary corrective action. The cost and time reports should be routed from the originating department to the project staff and then to the project manager. At his discretion, he should send appropriate reports to top management. This reporting, controlling, and replanning cycle will continue until the project is brought to a conclusion.

Project management summary

The project team is a very suitable management technique for use in conjunction with the more sophisticated scheduling methods. Project managers are able to operate across functional lines and thereby centralize control of their entire project. The separation of numerous complex jobs, and their assignment to specific project managers, enables top management to focus attention on the broad overall view of company policy and direction free from the burden of supervising in detail the various parts of each project. The smaller details are given the required attention by each project manager and his staff, thereby enabling the company to achieve sufficient control over a number of major projects simultaneously.

Bibliography

MARKS, N. E., and TAYLOR, H. L.   *CPM/PERT: A Diagrammatic Scheduling Procedure.* Austin, Texas: Bureau of Business Research Graduate School of Business, 1966.

MUNDORFF, GEORGE T.   Rear Admiral U.S.N. (Ret.), *PERT: A New Management Planning and Control Technique.* New York: American Management Association, Inc., 1963.

BLOOM, WILLIAM.   *PERT: A New Management Planning and Control Technique.* New York: American Management Association, Inc., 1962.

BUFFA, ELWOOD S.   *Production-Inventory Systems: Planning and Control.* Homewood, Illinois: Richard D. Irwin, Inc., 1968, Chapter 13.

DEAN, K. L.   *Fundamentals of Network Planning and Analysis.* St. Paul, Minnesota: Remington Rand Division of Sperry Rand Corporation, 1961.

RYAN, WILLIAM G., and STEINER, GEORGE A.   *Industrial Project Management.* Toronto, Ontario: Collier-Macmillan Canada, Ltd., 1968.

Corporate long range planning

William D. McEachron*

Rationale for corporate planning

Long range corporate planning is a highly personalized and subjective activity through which a company *charts* its future course of action; it contrasts sharply with the budgeting function, which *steers* the company along a prescribed path. For this reason the particular approach taken to planning must be sensitive to the nature of the company's business and its environmental setting, its organizational structure, its position relative to competitors, its resources and capabilities, and its own style of management.

In the broadest sense, corporate long range planning is a structured approach to the development of a strategy for the utilization of the resources of the firm within its projected environment so as to achieve the overall objectives of the enterprise. All of these elements are included within the broader context of planning as suggested by the schematic diagram shown in Exhibit 1.

It will be seen that corporate resources and environmental forecasts are inputs to the integration and evaluation that is at the core of the planning process, while corporate objectives and strategy can be both input and output.

Because of their interrelated nature and their relevance to corporate planning, a later section of this chapter deals specifically with corporate objectives and resources, environmental forecasting and analysis, and the determination of strategy even though most of these subjects are covered

---

* Manager, Planning and Economics, Standard Oil Company (Indiana), Chicago.

in greater depth elsewhere in this handbook.[1] Other portions of this chapter deal with the broad purposes and characteristics of planning, discuss factors which generally should be recognized in plans and planning, and cite some of the more important techniques that have been used in practice.

Most practitioners agree that the *process of planning* is more important than the plans themselves; it forces management to look further

EXHIBIT 1

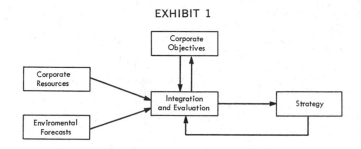

ahead than would otherwise be the case, and to recognize the futurity of current decisions. It also raises fundamental questions that all too often are simply unrecognized, particularly in the area of corporate objectives and strategy.

Corporate long range planning typically is but one of many forms of planning in the modern corporation. Other forms are discussed in Chapter 23, "Profit planning and budgeting" and in Chapter 27, "Capital budgeting procedures."

Purposes of corporate planning

Depending on the particular corporate circumstances at hand, long range planning may serve a number of purposes. More or less in decreasing order of importance, some of the more likely uses of planning are to:
1. Provide central direction and strategic control.
2. Identify potential threats and opportunities.
3. Preserve alternatives for future decision.
4. Evaluate possible programs for the future.
5. Evaluate and facilitate acquisitions and mergers.
6. Provide a common sense of purpose that integrates and motivates employees.
7. Orient management toward the future.

---

[1] Chapter 2 deals with strategy formulation and implementation, Chapter 21 with environmental and competitive information, and Chapter 22 with forecasting and trend analysis.

8. Stimulate new ideas and innovations.
9. Provide continuity and training at the executive level.

PLANNING VS. FORECASTING.   Planning and forecasting are often confused. In an engaging and oft-quoted paper presented in 1959, Peter Drucker distinguishes between the two and makes the point that planning in fact becomes necessary because of our inability to forecast with sufficient reliability.[2] The plan typically contains a forecast, but does not stop there; it goes on to chart a course of action.

The essential contrast between forecasting and planning can be illustrated by a series of dichotomies, as follows:

Forecasting	*Planning*
Objective	Subjective
Passive	Active
Openly available	Proprietary
Rejects uncertainty	Accepts uncertainty
Detail-oriented	Goal-oriented

Thus, forecasting is objective and passive in that it is an assessment of those elements of the future over which we have no control; planning is subjective and active in that it has to do with our intentions about those matters over which we do have control. Forecasts are often published; corporate plans are considered proprietary.

Uncertainty in the conventional forecast is usually handled by taking a definite position among possible alternatives;[3] the plan frequently copes with uncertainty by some form of hedging, such as taking a middle course of action to minimize losses among a variety of possible future events. Finally, forecasts are often built up from detail, in contrast to corporate planning in which the goals come first and the details are sketched in later.

Organization

SETTING WITHIN THE CORPORATION.   The most common ways of administering the planning function are through a top management committee or by delegation to a staff department or task force. In many companies the two coexist, with the management committee providing a decision capability and a vehicle for line involvement and the staff group providing analytical capability and continuity.

Top management committee.   Usually this committee is composed of line personnel, and reports to the chief executive officer. Alternatively, the board of directors can function as a planning committee under the

---

[2] Peter Drucker, "Long-Range Planning: Challenge to Management Science," *Management Science*, Vol. V, No. 3, 1959, pp. 238–49.

[3] More sophisticated forecasts may express the future in terms of a probability distribution.

guidance of the chief executive; this approach is usually confined to matters of broad strategy. On particular questions of strategy, outside management consultants may sometimes be used.

The use of the top management planning committee in conjunction with a planning staff avoids the need for complete delegation of planning responsibility, and at the same time provides the staff skills and continuing support that are essential for effective planning in today's complex environment.

Task force. This approach has several advantages: it is flexible, it can afford intense concentration on specific problems, and it is often a useful way to get started. Some practitioners favor the task force concept as a means of rotating personnel between staff and line positions, and for purposes of training. In most cases, however, this argument appears to be of dubious merit; the quality of technical analysis may suffer, and the confidence and hence involvement of top management in the planning function is likely to be impaired.

Staff department. This is the more permanent approach, and the one most widely adopted by large companies. Usually this department (it may be an individual) reports either directly to the chief executive officer or to another senior member of top management. Early in the development of corporate planning the function was frequently assigned to the financial vice president or to the controller, but more recently there appears to be a trend away from this;[4] even so, the financial executive is usually closely involved. Assignment of the corporate planning function to an individual operating department (e.g. marketing) is not likely to be successful because of its real or presumed lack of objectivity.

THE CORPORATE PLANNING DEPARTMENT.   The corporate planning staff per se is usually quite small, and even in a large corporation may number only half a dozen men. Frequently, however, corporate planning is combined with an economics function embracing environmental forecasting; the latter may in some instances involve a considerably greater staff. The planning department in some companies is also responsible for developing acquisition studies, and more rarely for conducting acquisition negotiations.

Except for the planning department's responsibility for environmental forecasting, most of the actual planning should be under the direction of those who carry the operating responsibility. Not only are they more familiar with existing operations, but their early involvement is the key to acceptance and implementation of the plan when it is completed. The

---

[4] Kirby Warren sees a basic conflict between the need for the controller to be guardian of corporate resources and the need for a planner to gain the confidence of line and staff personnel in the creative process of planning. E. Kirby Warren, *Long Range Planning—The Executive Viewpoint,* Prentice-Hall, Englewood Cliffs, N.J., 1966, pp. 43–45.

importance of line participation in planning is a major reason for keeping the planning department small.

Aside from the forecasting and acquisition functions mentioned earlier, the corporate planning department carries responsibilities in the areas of coordination, consolidation, evaluation, and planning research. *Coordination* is simply the mechanics of ensuring that the operating departments do in fact develop long range plans, and that these plans are reasonably compatible with each other. *Consolidation* is the assembly of the individual departmental plans into a single unified plan for the company. The *evaluation* of a corporate plan may take many forms, including various tests of its feasibility and its accord with company objectives, the determination of the relative attractiveness of alternate strategies, and the identification of problem areas within the company. *Planning research* refers to the continuing evolution of new planning systems and methodology; an example would be the use of subjective probability and discounted cash flow techniques in forecasting and evaluation.

Brian Scott[5] defines the four roles of the planning staff unit as integrator, forecaster, consultant, and instigator; the first two of these "appear to be adopted universally," while the other two are sometimes adopted and sometimes not. The role of *integrator* largely combines the coordination and consolidation functions mentioned previously together with the identification of any "planning gap" that may arise between the overall corporate plan and the company's long range objectives. The *forecaster* role is much more specific, and requires special analytical skills and a thorough knowledge of data sources. In some companies the central staff planning unit is responsible for detailed environmental forecasting for the entire company; the planning department of one large company numbers over 100 people, with most of them engaged in forecasting. Other companies place most of the detailed forecasting work with other staff departments or with the operating divisions most involved.

In its role as internal *consultant,* the staff planning unit provides to the operating people responsible for the development of corporate or divisional plans either written or interpersonal guidance ranging from the clarification of planning procedures and appraisal of planning methodology to the suggestion of new ideas. The *instigator* role calls for a more active participation in the planning process to ensure that it is successfully completed; it also includes the concept of planning research mentioned earlier.

Particularly in large multidivisional companies, the preparation of detailed operating plans may be handled by small planning units organized at the divisional level. These may be *ad hoc* committees made up of operating personnel, or the responsibility for planning may fall to a

[5] Brian Scott, *Long Range Planning In American Industry,* American Management Association, New York, 1965, pp. 181–186.

continuing staff group otherwise performing such functions as project evaluation or control budget development.

STAFFING.   Most men appointed to the planning staff are selected from within the firm. They range in age from 30 to 45 years,[6] and have had about ten years' experience with the company—frequently in research or administrative functions. Most have earned advanced degrees, either in technology or economics and business administration. Typically they have not had prior experience in planning on a corporate-wide basis.

The most essential qualifications of the staff planning group are (1) an ability to work and communicate effectively with both top and line management, and with other staff units, and (2) the capacity to combine broad-gauge thinking about the overall company and its total environment with the quantitiative and qualitative analysis of complex data. In order to meet these qualifications it may be necessary to staff the planning unit with two different types of people: those who relate to form and structure via analytical ability and attention to detail, and those with a wider spectrum of interests and contacts who can infer meaning from apparently unrelated events.

Line experience may be helpful in relating to line management, but it is no substitute for competence and attitude. The latter embraces not only objectivity but full recognition of the supportive role of staff planning and its boundaries in the operation of the company.

The planning framework

Corporate objectives

The dividing line between objectives and strategy is not clear cut, and some elements may fall into either category depending on the point of view. Fundamentally, however, objectives represent a subjective choice as to the quality, direction, and pace of the enterprise, while strategy is a considered judgment as to the broad routing by which the company can best realize those objectives.

NATURE OF OBJECTIVES.   In order to be meaningful, each corporate objective should reflect a conscious choice among reasonable alternatives. Most authorities agree that objectives must be articulated and preferably written in order to be effective; otherwise various members of the top management team are likely to entertain different and often contradictory notions of what the objectives of the corporation are. The interrelationship of the various items in the set of objectives under consideration should be given particular attention in order to insure that they are internally consistent.

---

[6] *Ibid.*, p. 189.

Most corporate objectives can be classified as follows:

Types of Corporate Objectives

Direction

Nature of business and its market
International vs. domestic
New markets
New types of business
Elimination of existing lines of business
Allocation of emphasis among major lines of business

Performance

Rate of return, margin, turnover, etc.
Stability in operations and earnings
Corporate image
Personnel competence, motivation, loyalty, etc.

Growth

Ultimate or target size
Minimum pace of growth in earnings, sales, assets, etc.
Market share goal
Acquisition vs. internal development

Survival

Limits to size and riskiness of new ventures
Exposure to takeover by other companies

Direction objectives define the scope of the business; they are the most basic and are usually rather subjective. *Performance* objectives relate to the health of the enterprise in contrast to *growth* objectives, which relate to its dynamics. *Survival* is so obvious an objective that it is rarely considered explicitly, except where survival may be threatened.

RELATIONSHIP TO PLANNING.   Determining a set of objectives for the company is not an easy or casual task. Although some sense of corporate direction is needed in order to initiate the planning process, the final resolution of objectives is as much an output of planning as it is an input.

Early in the planning process as parameters of interest are identified it becomes possible to define tentative objectives. Later these can be tested as to feasibility, and appropriate modifications made. In addition, new developments uncovered in successive plans may make it necessary to alter objectives previously established.

In spite of the intertwining of objectives and planning, the final responsibility for approving objectives must remain with top management—not with the planning staff. Indeed, stated objectives are a useful check on the planning function itself as to whether it is moving the firm in the proper direction. In addition, the give and take process of developing objectives constitutes a communication link of considerable importance between top management and the planning staff.

In a multidivisional company where operations are highly decentralized, the objectives established at corporate headquarters should be limited to those of corporate-wide interest. The strategy evolved for implementing these broad corporate objectives becomes the basis on which the divisions may develop their own operating goals and supporting strategy.

Corporate resources

Identification of the company's strengths and weaknesses is an essential ingredient in long range planning, and may in itself provide enough insight and understanding to justify the entire planning process. Corporate self-appraisal may be approached either on the basis of a total entity or functional components.

NATURE OF THE BUSINESS.   The key question in the total entity approach is "What is our business?" As posed by Peter Drucker,[7] this question is deceptively difficult and is rarely given the study needed for proper resolution. The nature of the business can usually be characterized in terms of product category, technology, and markets. It is often revealing to consider each at a higher level of abstraction, such as by taking the consumer's point of view and assessing how the product meets his basic needs. Explicit consideration of the life cycle of present products can also add breadth to the analysis.

It is all too easy to define the business too narrowly and thus be blinded to the threats and opportunities provided by changing behavioral patterns and new developments. One example often cited is that by considering itself in the movie business Hollywood rejected television when it should have recognized TV as an opportunity to expand in the entertainment business.

A somewhat different characterization of a company may be based on the skills and attitudes reflected by its operating, technical, and management personnel. Thus a company may be technologically or market oriented; it may seek major risks and large stakes or avoid them; it may evaluate new ventures with caution and deliberation or seize new opportunities with alacrity.

FUNCTIONAL STRENGTHS AND WEAKNESSES.   A more detailed identification of the principal strengths and weaknesses in a typical company might cover the following functions, both in the absolute and relative to competition.

1. *Physical facilities and other physical resources:* plants, mines, transportation equipment, retail outlets, etc.

---

[7] Peter Drucker, *The Practice of Management,* Harper & Brothers, New York, 1954, p. 49.

2. *Processes and technology:* patents, licenses, know-how, research capability, etc.
3. *Markets:* market share, customer loyalty, customer lists, market research, brand image, advertising, etc.
4. *Personnel:* knowledge and skills of key individuals, company recruiting capability, development programs, employee loyalty and motivation, age distribution, benefit plans, etc.
5. *Organizational structure:* corporate *modus operandi,* operating policies and procedures, communication links, staff support, corporate infrastructure, etc.
6. *Management:* management skills and attitudes, management style, replacement availability, etc.
7. *Financial resources:* capital structure, off-book obligations, borrowing capability, financial community's attitude, backing of stockholders, etc.
8. *Corporate image:* attitudes and beliefs held toward company on the part of its customers, employees, prospective recruits, vendors, the financial community, government (local, state, federal, and foreign), and the general public.

Environmental forecasting and analysis

Environmental forecasts and analyses may range from the total economy down to one or more individual competitors, and may embrace both continuous variables (such as volumes and prices) and isolated events (such as the passage of a law or a technological breakthrough). In order to define the corporate plan properly, major environmental assumptions should be identified and quantified; usually they are reviewed and approved by top management or the central planning committee. The need for such quantification does not necessarily equate with precision, and highly uncertain projections can often be of considerable practical use.

ECONOMIC FORECASTING. Most long range economic forecasts for relatively stable lines of business begin with a projection of the long range trends in population, the size of the labor force, labor productivity, gross national product, and similar broad parameters.[8] Total demand for products of interest is then derived from these underlying projections through correlations based on historical patterns.

Alternatively, product demand may be built up by projection of various use categories. As an example, total primary energy demand may be forecast through separate projections of the usage and unit demand of automobiles, jet planes, and other transportation media; heating and air-conditioning requirements for private homes and other buildings;

---

[8] For a more thorough discussion of trend analysis see Chapter 22.

industrial usage; and electric power generation. For some commodities, input-output analysis is gaining increased importance as a means of projecting demand by use category.[9]

Price projections are particularly difficult, and may require thorough analysis of competitive costs and the interdependence of costs and prices in the long run. Of particular importance is the forecast of wage and benefit costs per employee, which may generally be expected to increase more rapidly than the average price level in the total economy by an amount approximately equal to the annual gain in labor productivity.

GOVERNMENT ACTION.   The increasing impact of government on the private economy warrants recognition in environmental forecasting work. Government action is peculiarly responsive to social forces as well as those purely economic, and often occurs in quantum jumps.

Considered awareness of social and economic pressures and where they may lead is, of course, the principal resource of the planner in this regard. In addition, some of the techniques discussed in later paragraphs on technological forecasting and techniques for handling uncertainty are applicable.

TECHNOLOGICAL FORECASTING.   Initially applied to military and aerospace planning, technological forecasting is just beginning to gain acceptance in corporate long range planning. Its feasibility depends on the fact that technological progress is fairly steady, with even major breakthroughs dependent on a gradually evolving continuum of technology. Technological forecasting usually aims to assess the likely range and significance of technological progress in a given area without attempting to pinpoint the precise form of technology at some future date. An approach frequently used (so-called *normative* forecasting) is to define society's long range needs and desires and to work backwards to see how present capabilities may be extended to meet these needs.

Virtually all technological forecasting techniques depend on either an analysis of history or the insights of informed and creative people, and are closely coupled with long range socioeconomic forecasts. Careful consideration of internal relationships among different sets of variables is also very important. The principal techniques are trend and correlation analysis, historical and growth analogies, intuitive reasoning (e.g. "scenario writing"), analysis of structural constraints, and the construction of complete models similar to those used in econometrics.[10]

Consultants and private research organizations may be particularly helpful in technological forecasting because of their experience in partic-

---

[9] See Chapter 21.

[10] For a complete discussion of these techniques see James R. Bright, *Technological Forecasting for Industry and Government,* Prentice-Hall, Englewood Cliffs, New Jersey, 1968.

ular fields of interest. Some institutions specialize in this type of activity.[11]

ANALYSIS OF COMPETITION.   Many companies find it advantageous to make specific analyses of competition as part of their planning process; this may extend to explicit forecasts of the actions and performance of individual competitors.

There are three very good reasons for analyses of this type:

1. An understanding of competitive forces gives perspective to the environment in which the company operates.
2. It is useful for a company to compare its strategy with that of its competitors in response to the same environment.
3. Particularly for a company that is lagging within its industry, analysis of the performance (e.g., rate of return) of its more successful competitors can be an important element in setting its own corporate objectives.

MONITORING.   Environmental forecasting is a continuous process, keeping abreast of changes in outlook as they occur. To insure adequate monitoring, critical points in the forecast should be identified in advance. Changes in successive forecasts can also constitute a check on the adequacy of the forecasting process itself.

Determination of strategy

Although the actual determination of corporate strategy rests with the chief executive, the plan may assist in its formulation by identifying and evaluating alternate courses of action. Once formulated, strategy becomes a constraint on planning similar to that of corporate objectives. As noted earlier, objectives and strategy in a multidivisional company may form a hierarchical pattern in which the strategy of the parent constitutes the objectives of the divisions.

FORMS OF STRATEGY.   Corporate strategy may either evolve from the company's historic course of action or represent a climactic change of direction. The first type is relatively straightforward and is often implicit in the way the company conducts its affairs; however there is a real need to make it explicit thus insuring a common understanding within management. The second type of strategy is usually ill-structured and less predictable; it does not fit easily into the formal long range corporate planning process.[12] An acquisition is an example of a strategic move of this type.

---

[11] A notable example is the *Long Range Planning Service,* a multiple client service conducted by Stanford Research Institute, Menlo Park, California.

[12] Robert Anthony argues that the long range planning process more closely resembles management control than it does strategic planning of the climactic type.

Not all strategy has to do with specific operations. Setting acceptance standards for investment evaluations (e.g. the minimum acceptable discounted cash flow rate of return for any project) is an element of strategy that may limit the pace of growth in favor of profitability or vice versa; a variation in acceptance standards among different areas of the business may be used to effect some change in the direction of growth as well.[13] Capital structure and the pattern of new financing fall within the category of financial strategy,[14] as does the company's policy toward leasing and other off-book commitments.[15] Another facet of strategy may relate to organization structure and personnel.

RELATIONSHIP TO PLANNING. At the beginning of this section it was stated that strategy is both an input and an output of corporate long range planning. Strategy may be formulated early in the planning process, either *a priori* or in response to a need identified as the plan is developed, or the plan itself may examine the consequences of a number of alternative strategies. In either case, the plan is likely to be the vehicle by which strategy is articulated and communicated.

As noted previously, the choice of major corporate strategy is a responsibility of top management that should not be delegated to staff planners. It is equally important that top management avoid the opposite extreme of choosing strategy arbitrarily and without staff consultation. The corporate long range plan constitutes a useful testing ground for evaluating a proposed strategy in the context of the total company.

It should not be inferred from this that strategy can reliably be chosen solely on the basis of its economic results as indicated by the plan. Strategy is too open ended and estimates of the future too uncertain to permit this. Nonetheless, the plan does rough out the long run picture in a quantified way that provides a point of departure for the judgment and insight of an informed management.

NEED FOR FLEXIBILITY. Good strategy of necessity provides for some degree of flexibility to allow for the deviation of actual events from the forecast pattern. This can take the form of hedging in the operating strategy itself, or laying plans for alternate courses of action so that a final commitment may be safely delayed until additional information is available.

Nonetheless, he feels that the long range plan is a useful starting point for testing proposed strategies. See Robert N. Anthony, *Planning and Control Systems: A Framework for Analysis,* Graduate School of Business Administration, Harvard University, Boston, Mass., 1965, pp. 57–58.

[13] See Chapter 19, "Analysis of capital expenditures."

[14] See Chapter 46, "Capital structure determination."

[15] See Chapter 20, "Lease, rent, or buy decisions."

Planning practice

Structure and content of corporate plans

Surprisingly enough, a rather large minority of long range plans are still not prepared in written form on any comprehensive basis. Divisional plans may not be consolidated, or substantial gaps may be left in the total picture. Such practice diminishes the effectiveness of the plan; there is considerable merit to one planner's observation that if you cannot write it down, you have not thought it through.

Most long range corporate plans are financially oriented. In part this reflects the economic character of the business enterprise, and the fact that its broader decisions are fundamentally economic. A second consideration is the fact that the diverse activities covered by the corporate plan can frequently be integrated on a quantitative basis only in financial terms.

ELEMENTS OF A TYPICAL CORPORATE PLAN. Comprehensive top management plans vary in size from less than 10 to over 300 pages, with the median ranging from 51 to 100 pages.[16] Because of the importance of trends, major parameters are usually shown not only in tabular but also in graphical form, frequently (where rate of growth is of interest) with logarithmic scales. Many such charts provide perspective by including as many or more years of history than the time period of the plan.

Most long range plans include all or most of the following elements:

Statement of objectives.	Operating program.
Environmental forecasts.	Development program.
Appraisal of corporate resources.	Financial results.
Statement of general strategy.	Personnel requirements.

The first four of these have been discussed previously and need not be considered further here.

The *operating program* is a comprehensive summary of the physical program proposed by line management to meet the objectives and follow the strategy previously laid out. It typically includes the markets to be captured, anticipated sales, required facilities and their throughput, a statement of raw materials requirements and sources, and estimated capital expenditures. The program may be segregated by product group, marketing regions, and/or major functions. Where appropriate, attention may be given to product life cycles. The timing of new programs and facilities is usually spelled out. Some plans also include a table of

---

[16] Kjell-Arne Ringbakk, "Organized Corporate Planning Systems," Ph.D. dissertation, University of Wisconsin, June, 1968, pp. 54–55. Major findings repeated in *Organized Planning in 40 Major U.S. Corporations*, Long Range Planning Report No. 365, December, 1968 (Menlo Park, Calif.: Stanford Research Institute), page 11 (available only to SRI Planning Service Clients).

decision points, which indicates the latest point in time at which significant decisions (e.g. make or buy) can be made without jeopardizing freedom of choice.

The *development program* may or may not be included in the operating program. It describes and quantifies new products and new markets and the route and timing of entry. It includes the cost, magnitude, and direction of the research program. A major consideration may be mergers and acquisitions. Particularly with the latter, the development program is more conjectural than the operating program and in some planning systems is developed as a separate document.

Virtually all corporate plans contain a section on *financial results*, usually including on a year-by-year basis and in a more or less abbreviated form a profit and loss statement, source and application of funds, and a balance sheet. Financing may be an important consideration. Because of the span of time covered, many parameters considered constant in a one-year budget must be treated as variables; examples include working capital requirements, dividends, wage rates, and benefit plan costs. To assist in management's evaluation of the plan, extensive use of ratios such as rate of return, margin and turnover, dividend payout, debt ratio, labor productivity (e.g. sales per employee), and the annual rate of growth in significant parameters (e.g. profit, or profit per share) on a year-by-year basis is often desirable.

Relatively few companies analyze long run *personnel requirements* in depth. Among those that do, some make explicit projections of retirements, terminations, and the changing age profile of their employees in order to estimate future recruiting and hiring requirements and to provide insight into the future availability of experienced personnel for promotion to management vacancies.

COMPARISON WITH PRIOR PLANS.   Many companies which follow an annual planning cycle find it of value to include in each plan a comparison with similar plans issued in prior years. This may be simply a comparison of successive estimates of profits and other key parameters for some common year or group of years in the future, or it may be a more sophisticated comparison, such as discounted present value, that seeks to combine variations in profit and capital in a single measure. The primary purpose in making such a comparison is to check the validity of the planning *process* and guard against continual slippage in projected performance from plan to plan. In no sense is it a check on the validity of the *new* plan; presumably those who developed it were perfectly well aware of the earlier plans and exercised their best judgment in this context and in the light of later developments.

TIMING AND FREQUENCY.   A question frequently asked is "How long is long range?" According to Kirby Warren,[17] most companies have settled

[17] Warren, *op. cit.*, p. 23.

on five years as their long range planning period. However, exceptions to this are common and have good cause; paper and pulp companies concerned with forest management claim to plan forty years ahead, while situations involving rapid changes in style may preclude meaningful planning beyond a year or two.

Where long range plans are prepared on a routine basis (this would be true of most corporate plans), they are normally updated or revised once each year. The primary reason for this frequency is that it coincides with financial and environmental reporting practices.

Special plans, particularly those covering a greatly extended period of time, are developed and revised less frequently as the need arises. The annual plan serves to integrate such studies into the context of the total corporation.

Techniques for handling uncertainty and unknowns

Most corporate planning at the present time is based on "most likely" estimates of the future, with little or no explicit recognition of the uncertainty involved. However, there is increasing recognition of the inadequacy of this approach, particularly for those factors that are critical to corporate strategy.

Although uncertainty is rooted primarily in the forecasts of the environment, it carries over in chain reaction fashion to alternate strategies. For this reason more advanced techniques for handling uncertainty cover both environmental alternates and decision alternates in an interlocked sequence.

SUBJECTIVE PROBABILITY. Within the environmental sector, a probability cannot be assigned (in the strictest sense) to a future event that will happen but once; it is not like a repeatable situation such as the tossing of a coin. However, it is possible to determine the odds that an informed person would require in order to bet on a future event—hence the term *subjective probability*. Usually the subjective probabilities assigned by several individuals are combined to determine a probability profile.

Estimates of probability in environmental forecasting are particularly significant in situations where uncertainty is high—as in forecasting technological changes or government actions—or where strategy is assymmetrical to the probability distribution or sensitive to its extremes. Although the explicit assessment of subjective probabilities may be of some help in determining the "most likely" forecast, its principal use is in corporate plans that are designed to handle it, through either sensitivities or decision analysis as discussed below.

SENSITIVITIES. The most common way of treating environmental uncertainty in the plan is through the development of sensitivities, in which a given change in one or more critical environmental assumptions is traced through to its impact on financial results, usually profit. In the case of continuous variables, such as price and volume, for which subjective probabilities have been prepared, it is more useful to develop sensitivities in terms of a probability distribution; e.g., the plan might show the impact on profit of a variation up or down in price within prescribed statistical confidence limits.

ALTERNATES. Alternates may be defined as discretionary differences in strategy. They may simply reflect an increase or decrease in the pace of growth, or they may cover changes in timing or in the allocation of emphasis (e.g. capital) to different facets of the business. A common situation is to project current lines of business and internally developed new ventures as a base plan, and show as one or more alternates the base plan plus a given acquisition. This approach has particular merit when the acquisition is relatively uncertain.

There is a caution to be observed, however; the development of a number of alternates in full detail may make the plan so unwieldy as to be a disservice to the management group for whom the plan is intended. Sometimes this can be avoided by presenting the detail for only the base plan and possibly one or two alternates, and limiting the remainder to a few key parameters. It should be recognized that the utility of an alternate plan in evaluating a given strategy usually lies in considering that strategy in the context of the total company, not in examining the difference between the alternate plan and some other; the latter is better assessed by the techniques of incremental evaluation.[18]

DECISION ANALYSIS. Decision analysis is a management tool of fairly recent origin for combining subjective probability and discretionary alternates into an overall strategic decision process. In effect, benefits and costs of a given strategy are assessed over the full spectrum of possible environmental variations weighted by the probability of their occurrence. The combined economics of this given strategy can then be compared to the economics of an alternate strategy similarly computed on the basis of the same set of environmental variations. The resulting comparison thus takes into account forecasting risks to the extent that they can be identified and quantified. Although simple in concept, this type of analysis can become quite complex, especially since some of the changes in environment are likely to induce different corporate decisions and different competitive responses down the road.[19]

---

[18] See Part III of this Handbook, "Financial and Economic Analysis."

[19] For further reading on this subject see Howard Raiffa, *Decision Analysis*, Addison-Wesley Publishing Company, Reading, Mass., 1968. Some of the basic concepts are covered by John F. Magee, "How to Use Decision Trees in Capital Investment," *Harvard Business Review*, September–October, 1964.

USE OF MODELS.   At the present time, it does not appear that the development of a comprehensive optimizing model to cover the entire corporate long range planning process is a practical exercise. However, less ambitious models of the simulation type can be quite helpful.[20] An assumed acquisition might be treated in this way, or some new product line that has only broadly been defined. Some plans tend to "fall off" in capital growth during later years because of the inability of those doing the planning to anticipate specific investment opportunities that far ahead; it may actually be more realistic to "model in" unspecified investment projects to fill in this gap. There is an obvious danger, of course, that this may simply cover up a growth problem that really exists, and this possibility must be considered when such plans are evaluated. As noted in the succeeding section on implementation, the existence of such a planning gap may warrant increasing the pace of development to insure that it will in fact be filled.

Another use of models is in exploring relationships within the corporation that are not evident in normal operations. Major changes in growth rate or capital allocation outside the range of past experience require analysis of the impact of investment decisions over time in a way that is best handled by a series of simulation models. A less complex example is the determination of the equilibrium growth rate of the firm under various assumptions as to dividend policy, debt ratio, and rate of return on various operating investments. Models such as these are equivalent to laboratory experiments and provide insight into the behavior of the firm under different test conditions.

Finally, models may be used to simulate the environment in order to give explicit recognition to interrelationships among the various environmental factors on which the plan is premised. The input-output table is an obvious illustration of this.

Implementation

Obviously, the corporate plan is of little value unless it improves the quality of current decisions. Because of the pervasive nature of long range planning, however, it is not easy to identify its impact. Attempts to audit the utility of corporate planning—and many firms do not even try —have not been very meaningful.

LINK TO THE CONTROL BUDGET.   In general, the corporate plan is too broad a tool for blueprinting near term action and controlling short run operations. Implementation of this type is best achieved through the control budget.

In some companies, selected parameters from the first year or two of the plan are modified by top management to reflect near term considera-

---

[20] See Chapter 14, "Systems analysis and simulation."

tions and then used as targets against which operating management prepares a more detailed control budget, subject to a final top management review. Other companies prepare the first year or two of the long range plan in sufficient detail to serve directly as the control budget; even in this case, however, provision is made for top management adjustment to give more specific consideration to the short run situation.

FAILURE TO MEET GOALS.   In some respects a long range plan is most useful when it projects an undesirable situation, for then a change of strategy is clearly indicated. One illustration of this is the *planning gap,* in which the growth of the firm over the period of the plan falls short of the growth objective. If this gap is real, further development may be called for to see what new product lines can be added to maintain growth at the desired rate. One company assigns growth goals to each of its major divisions; to the extent that a division projects such a gap and cannot find a way to fill it, a central development group is given the responsibility of finding a new line of business to solve the problem.

Similar corrective action may be required with respect to other key parameters of the business, such as profitability or capital requirements versus capital availability. Sensitivity analyses in the plan may show undue reliance on doubtful factors in the environment and warrant a strategic shift to safer ground. In some instances where plans are developed on a decentralized basis, interdivisional relationships may be inconsistent and require straightening out.

INDIRECT IMPLEMENTATION.   Considerable corrective action takes place within the planning process itself. Identification of strengths and weaknesses, and the determination of objectives and strategy, all of which may be triggered by the need to develop a plan, are of value in their own right. In addition, the plan constitutes a common and agreed upon background for the evaluation of strategy and investment proposals throughout the firm.

Start-up of a formal planning program

Assuming that planning is to be formally implemented through the appointment of a staff director of planning, the most important prerequisite for success is the willingness of the chief executive to share his planning responsibilities and the readiness of line management to support the total planning effort. There must also be a recognition of the need for planning and its relevance to corporate affairs.

ORIENTATION.   For those inexperienced in corporate planning, a review of the planning literature will be helpful, but not totally satisfactory because of its emphasis on theory. Planning seminars, such as those conducted by the American Management Association and by Stanford Research Institute may also be of value.

A great deal can be learned by intensive study of the firm itself and its planning problems. This is particularly useful in establishing priorities as to which areas should be tackled first. In this connection the planner should make every effort to tap the thinking of others throughout the firm.

It is important at the outset that a satisfactory working relationship be established between the staff planning director and the chief executive or other top management man to whom he reports. This includes a mutual understanding of the job itself and the responsibilities that it includes, the extent to which planning will be insulated from crash programs and recurring crises, and the role that planning is expected to play within the organization structure of the firm.

Good relations with line managers and other staff functions are also essential to a successful planning effort and need to be developed early. The supportive role of planning and its relevance to line activities are key elements in establishing satisfactory rapport in these areas.

In order for planning to be meaningful and creative, both the staff planners and those whom they contact must come to recognize the distinction between the charting function of long range planning and the steering function of budgeting. This is not easy to achieve, and may well evolve only through a protracted period of study and education. The planners themselves must have clear ideas about what they are trying to accomplish with planning and communicate these ideas effectively to all areas of the company which are involved.

THE INITIAL PLAN.   Ideally, a long range plan should be developed within the context of stated objectives and some degree of explicit strategy. For an initial plan this is usually not possible. This chicken-and-egg dilemma is often resolved by focusing the first plan on problems confronting the company.

In some situations, this may take the form of a diagnostic report which sets forth problem areas as developed through staff planning analysis. This may be followed by appointment by the chief executive of management-staffed task forces to study these problem areas and evolve provisional plans to resolve them. Such a procedure not only provides impetus to the planning effort but may also serve to enlarge the interests of divisional management toward corporate-wide issues.

Other companies have used special top management seminars to analyze problem areas in depth as a focal point for the development of long range plans designed to resolve the specific problems identified. Particularly in small companies, the initiation of a planning system may be facilitated by the use of management consultants who are experienced in the field of corporate planning.

The important thing is to make a definite start without waiting for all the information that it would be desirable to have. Mistakes will be made but can be corrected as the procedure evolves. Initial plans in particular should be kept simple without being superficial, and should avoid too deep an entry into the theory of planning. It is quite possible that the first plan will pose more questions than answers; this is typical and provides a basis on which later plans may be built. It may also provide a springboard for the explicit consideration of corporate objectives and strategy.

SUCCEEDING PLANS. By the time the second corporate plan is in process, the general planning structure should be fairly well defined. The relative responsibilities of division and central planning units should have been established, and an appropriate time schedule developed. At least tentative agreement should have been reached as to general objectives and strategy, some of which may be tested in the second plan.

After the initial period of trial and error, further modification will prove desirable as later plans are developed. Most companies with considerable planning experience find that continual evolution and improvement of the planning process is the norm.

Problem areas

Even among companies that have engaged in corporate planning over a number of years, it is frequently the case that the practice does not measure up to its potential. Most of the difficulties encountered fall into one of three categories: (*a*) insufficient interrelationship between management and the planning effort, (*b*) unwillingness to take planning seriously, and (*c*) inadequate performance in the planning process itself.

Specific problem areas, arranged roughly in order of decreasing frequency and importance, are listed below.

1. *Insufficient top management support.* Planning requires top management involvement and support on a continuing basis, and a consistent management orientation toward the long range point of view in the face of recurring short term crises is essential. It is important that good two-way communication be maintained between management and the planning staff. It should be recognized that planning is hard work on the part of both management and the planning staff.

2. *Inadequate line involvement.* Operating management must be committed both to the development and to the implementation of realistic and challenging long range plans. Such commitment becomes particularly difficult if too much emphasis is placed on short term operating performance. Line management must be willing to share its problems and its aspirations with the planning staff.

3. *Lack of relevance.* Plans should be addressed to the problems that

actually confront the firm. It is all too easy for planners to lose contact with the realities of the business.

4. *Lack of use.* Corporate plans should provide the focal point for management decisions on a continuing basis; they have little utility if they are forgotten between plans.

5. *Lack of direction.* Indecisiveness and vacillation among successive plans may reflect inadequate or conflicting objectives, or a failure in communication from top management as to what the objectives really are. Special studies of strategically sensitive areas may be necessary.

6. *Lack of realism in the plans.* This may stem from inadequate forecasting and insufficient information used as input to the planning process, weakness in analytical reasoning, a general lack of objectivity, or insufficient attention to the practical politics of corporate organization.

7. *Inadequate thinking through.* It is all too easy to extrapolate both internal and external trends without making conscious choices among future alternatives and considering the underlying interrelationships among the factors involved.

8. *Insufficient recognition of contingencies.* No matter how excellent the environmental forecasting may be, there is always the possibility that events will turn out to be different than anticipated. The development of alternate plans and hedging maneuvers may be indicated. Plans should be used with due regard for the uncertainties involved.

9. *Inadequate feedback and control.* Control of long range plans is more than a question of how well the plans prove out in practice; it also includes the larger question of how well the plans carry the company in the direction of its objectives.

10. *Poor communication.* Clear and continuing three-way communication among top management, operating management, and the planning staff is essential if plans are to be timely, realistic, effective, and oriented toward the objectives of the company.

11. *Lack of integration.* Effective corporate planning cannot be done on a piecemeal basis, nor without integration of major components. In terms of goal-oriented planning, the total has more meaning than the sum of its parts.

12. *Too much attention to detail.* A penchant for detail in long range planning is not only a waste of time and effort, but can obscure important trends and undermine confidence. It frequently reflects a failure to distinguish between planning and budgeting.

13. *Overconcentration on short term and undue rigidity.* Too much emphasis on achieving the precise results shown in a plan tends to undermine creativity and cause successive plans to be less challenging. Again, planning may be confused with budgeting.

Bibliography

The literature in recent years on long range corporate planning has been quite voluminous. A few selected references for further reading are listed below.

ANSOFF, H. IGOR.   *Corporate Strategy*. McGraw-Hill Book Co., New York, 1965. An analytic discussion of business policy for growth and expansion.

ANTHONY, ROBERT N.   *Planning and Control Systems: A Framework for Analysis*. Graduate School of Business Administration, Harvard University, Boston, 1965. Rigorous theoretical definition of planning and control system concepts.

BRIGHT, JAMES R.   *Technological Forecasting for Industry and Government*. Prentice-Hall, Inc., Englewood Cliffs, New Jersey, 1968. Comprehensive review of methods and applications.

HENRY, HAROLD W.   *Long-Range Planning Practices in 45 Industrial Companies*. Prentice-Hall, Inc., Englewood Cliffs, New Jersey, 1967. General discussion of interview results plus description of planning at International Minerals and Chemical, Motorola, and a major automotive company.

STANFORD RESEARCH INSTITUTE.   *Long Range Planning Service*. Menlo Park, California. Series of confidential research reports, available only to client-subscribers, covering planning theory and practice, and forecasts of selected technological, economic, social, and political patterns.

STEINER, GEORGE A.   *Top Management Planning*. The Macmillan Co., New York, 1969. Comprehensive analysis of corporate planning, including basic concepts, the planning process, tools for rational decision-making, and a discussion of planning in various functional areas.

WARREN, E. KIRBY.   *Long-Range Planning: The Executive Viewpoint*. Prentice-Hall, Inc., Englewood Cliffs, New Jersey, 1966. Broad discussion of problem areas based on interviews with 15 companies.

Capital budgeting procedures

Frank L. Linton*

This chapter will attempt to describe the procedures by which proposals for capital expenditures pass from initial ideas through analysis to final approval and implementation. It will not attempt to discuss in detail the criteria for analyzing proposals; this is the subject matter of Chapter 19, "Analysis of capital expenditures." The chapter assumes that the reader recognizes the need for integrating capital expenditures with corporate strategy (see Chapter 2, "Strategy formulation"), and understands the way in which this need is reflected in the formulation of long-range plans, as described in Chapter 26.

There are some types of decisions that are so critical to the existence of the firm that they *must* fall within the purview of top management. These are decisions where either the magnitude of the decision in relation to the firm's total operations or resources is great, or where even though the magnitude of the resources currently involved is small, the effect of today's decisions on tomorrow's operations is large. This chapter will be primarily aimed at firms where capital expenditure decisions are critical for either of these two reasons.

Capital intensive firms are more likely to find relevant the procedures described in this chapter than are other firms. In firms where a few investment dollars can produce a relatively great increase in sales dollars, capital budgeting will receive less attention from top management and the real decision-making process on capital expenditures may be decentralized. For example, although capital assets (those whose useful life usually exceeds one to three years) costing a few thousand dollars

---

* Vice President (Retired), Allied Chemical Corporation, New York.

may be included in the profitability evaluation of a proposal to introduce a new multimillion dollar sales product line, orientation of the decision-making process would probably de-emphasize the effect of the capital investment required in favor of expected marketing variables. This would be true, for instance, for a carpet manufacturer for whom tufters and looms have fairly universal application. For the low sales/capital ratio firms, however, and for firms which evince a high degree of techno-logical specialization, the outlay of capital funds may be an issue of critical importance. The bench mark for comparison here is the electrical power company, for which the size, location, and type of capital assets acquired can have a marked effect on profitability for decades. Even for the power company, however, the use of a capital budget in its most sophisticated form may not be a necessity. A chemical company with a diverse product line, roughly a one-to-one sales/fixed-capital dollar ratio, and a multiplicity of rival investment opportunities, provides a classic example of the usefulness of capital budgeting.

RELATIONSHIP TO LONG-RANGE PLANS. It is important that the capital budgeting procedures relate the firm's capital budgets to its long-range plans. Capital budgets are really one of the ways of implementing the long-range plans, and so they must be consistent with those plans.

The firm that has a reasonably clear idea of what its business is—and will be—should be able to draw broad parameters covering general economic conditions, potential markets for its products, probable market shares and prices, and the costs that must be incurred in order to achieve market objectives and subobjectives. However, the experience of most firms shows that use of the capital budget as the primary investment decision tool provides less than satisfactory results, since the scope of activities related to the "capital project" is frequently too narrow to take into consideration the broader ramifications of related decisions. Stated another way, capital projects tend to lose the quality of independence when viewed over a longer span of time, and for this reason the top managers of many larger companies have shifted emphasis toward greater use of the long-range plan. Accordingly, capital investment itself has been relegated to a subsidiary role in the planning process, and capital budgeting per se has become, or can be expected to become, a decision tool of lesser importance in relation to the firm's total planning process. Thus, in a company with a reliable long-range planning process, the capital budget's greatest usefulness lies principally in enabling op-timization of the long-range plan, as well as helping to achieve certain objectives outlined in this chapter.

Objectives of capital budgeting

1. *Establishing priorities.* Nearly every growing firm is able to envi-sion more uses for investment funds than it can possibly implement due

to constraints on availability of funds, manpower, and other resources. When the time comes to prepare a detailed budget, firms with viable long-range plans will have already restricted investment plans to manageable levels; these companies, for which investment decisions have already been made in principle, can restrict the use of the capital budget to that of a short-range planning tool. In the absence of meaningful prior long-range planning, however, management is confronted with the additional problem of making a rational selection of the businesses which it would prefer to emphasize. For such firms, the capital budget can serve the function of helping to establish strategic investment objectives.

2. *Cash planning.* An integral part of the financial executive's job ordinarily assigned to the treasurer is that of ensuring availability of funds in sufficient quantity to meet the firm's cash needs, including outlays for acquisition of capital assets. Inclusion of a capital expenditures estimate in the capital budget on a period-by-period basis helps to serve this need.

3. *Construction planning.* The capital asset acquisition period is normally one in which funds are being expended, but no income is being generated. Since all funds have a cost, it is important to minimize the acquisition period. An accurate expenditures forecast is an indication that construction plans are being formulated in advance of funds requirements. (However, this forecast by itself, even if accurate, does not ensure that the construction period is actually being minimized.)

4. *Eliminating duplication.* Centralized consideration of capital budgeting activities in a decentralized organization may reveal duplication of effort at local levels or potential synergism among different product lines or plants. An example of a function which has experienced growing management attention is distribution. It has been found time and again that requirements for distribution facilities can be reduced when the distribution system is viewed as an entity.

5. *Revising plans.* Periodic reviews of the capital budget may indicate changes in the basis for authorization of investment projects, including expected profitability, construction cost, and the timing of start-up where coordination with related activities is essential. A good capital budgeting system will illuminate such problems and can lead to a timely response to changing environmental factors.

A capital budgeting system

This section explains a practical capital budgeting system and illustrates commonly used forms. Each firm, of course, uses forms and procedures designed to suit its own requirements, and so alternative ways of accomplishing similar ends are included in the discussion. In creating or using a capital budgeting system, one should keep in mind not only the requirements of one's own company but also a broad understanding of the philosophy and objectives underlying the application of sound budgeting procedures.

Budgeting

Periodically (usually once a year) budget requests are submitted— that is, requests to include in the corporate budget capital projects which are felt to be desirable by lower organizational levels. These requests are usually consolidated at lower levels (at division, for example), though they may be submitted directly to the company's head office. As a group, these requests constitute the preliminary budget. Top management then establishes priorities and eliminates undesirable projects. Finally, management may submit its recommendation to the board of directors for adoption in principle, after which most companies require submission of a detailed study of each project individually in the form of an appropriation request prior to approval of expenditure of funds.

A changing environment necessitates periodic review of the assumptions and justification underlying approval of a capital project. Progress reports may be required in the interim between approval and start-up in order to ensure continuing viability, to evaluate execution procedures and to keep expenditures forecasts up to date. Furthermore, to improve the company's capital investment processes and as a continuing test of the reliability of information submitted in substantiation of individual requests, it is desirable to require a detailed study of at least the major projects undertaken. Such a review is usually initiated shortly after project start-up.

INCLUSIVENESS OF BUDGET.   The capital budget should include all resource outlays with protracted payout periods, including, for example, long-term investments in other companies and leased assets with extended useful lives. In this connection, due to the growing trend toward leasing of assets, it is desirable for the company to establish policies covering the types of assets to be leased, and to provide for sound lease-versus-purchase analyses. See Chapter 20 for a discussion of the lease-versus-purchase decision.

The budget often includes projects to be submitted during a one- to three-year period. If the time period is restricted to one year for formal budgeting purposes, a forecast of requirements for the subsequent year or two will enable management to view current budget requests in a broader context, especially where long-range plans are not considered fully viable.

THE PRELIMINARY BUDGET.   Virtually any member of the organization may participate in the preparation of the preliminary budget, since it represents basically a "basket of ideas." Top management must formulate from this compendium a viable short-range plan whose implementation is both desirable and feasible. The usefulness of the capital budget will reflect the emphasis placed on it by top management. Although virtually any member of the organization *may* participate in preparation of the preliminary budget, certain members almost always play specific roles in the preparation of both the preliminary and final budgets, as outlined below:

1. *Chief financial executive.* Authority for preparation of procedures, instructions, and forms—as well as coordination of budget-related activities—is part of the general area assigned to the chief financial executive. While he alone will not ordinarily be responsible for approving the budget or determining its composition, his recommendations regarding its magnitude and alternate methods of financing will certainly be required.

2. *New business staffs.* Of growing importance in many corporations are staffs representing a concentration of entrepreneurial talent. Normally positioned near the top of the structure, they serve the dual purpose of identifying broad opportunities for the corporation and helping to organize projects in their formative stages. Such groups can be expected to provide ideas for new capital projects and to provide recommendations enabling the formulation of the firm's capital budget.

3. *Product-line manager or chief marketing executive.* In order to ensure that customers receive products and services as required, the product-line manager or chief marketing executive must provide accurate sales forecasts. Additionally, he must understand that management will be reluctant to budget plant expansions for products which do not provide sufficient profitability.

4. *Plant manager.* The role of the plant manager in preparation of the capital budget is critical. With the aid of company engineers, he must determine how to achieve output requirements at minimum cost, which includes outlays of new capital. He should be able to identify situations where substitution of capital for labor will improve efficiency and should attempt to optimize the relationship between repair and replacement costs.

5. *The controller and his staff.* Usually, the controller performs the task of compiling the preliminary budget, under the direction of the chief financial executive. He provides interpretations of instructions and procedures during preparation. Later, he is responsible for accounting for the costs incurred in instituting the individual projects and for recommending appropriate depreciation methods. He is also responsible for reporting significant deviations from plans to top management.

CONTENT OF THE BUDGET REQUEST. The quantity of detailed information included in the preliminary capital budget depends primarily upon the relative emphasis placed upon the long-range plan and final approval procedures. When the capital budget is used as a decision-making tool, it is usually necessary to provide at least the following items of information in the budget request (see Exhibit 1):

EXHIBIT 1

Budget Request

MISCELLANEOUS PRODUCTS COMPANY

Budget Request
($000)

Title Expand XYZ Plant				Priority	2	of	8	
Appropriation Amount $5,000				Product	XYZ			
Location Smithville, U.S.A.				Project Classification	Revenue-Producing			
Profitability				Timing		Month	Year	
Net Present Value			$1,300	Submission		Mar.	19x2	
Discounted Rate of Return			22 %	Initial Expend.		June	19x2	
Profitability Index			1.26	Final Expend.		Aug.	19x3	
Payback			3.7 Years	Start-up		Sept.	19x3	
Net Income/Total Investment			10.0 %	Production		Nov.	19x3	

Project Cost	Total	19X1	Carryover	19X2	Carryover	19X3	Carryover
Fixed Assets	4,400			3,900	500	500	-
Working Capital	400			-	400	400	-
Expense	100			50	50	50	-
Other	100			50	50	50	-
Total	5,000			4,000	1,000	1,000	-

Financing Method		Total	19X1	Carryover	19X2	Carryover	19X3	Carryover
	Cash	4,800			4,000	800	800	-
Stock	Lease	200			-	200	200	-
Debt	Stock	-			-	-	-	-
	Technology	-			-	-	-	-
	Other	-			-	-	-	-
	Total	5,000			4,000	1,000	1,000	-

Narrative

    Project provides for expansion of the Smithville XYZ Plant by 50,000 units per month.

    Principal objective is that of maintaining current market share of 27% in the Smithville marketing region. Incremental flows due to proposed expansion yield a rate of return estimated at 22%.

    Profitability estimates assume stable and moderately rising variable costs over 15 year project life. No other major changes are expected. Profitability is sensitive to changes in price only; probability of price change is dependent upon Competitive Products Company's decision to construct an XYZ plant as rumored. This is considered rather unlikely, however.

    This project is in accord with long-range plans for development of XYZ markets, plants and distribution systems.

Corporate Office Use Only

1. *Project title.* This is for purposes of identification. A code may also be used, though a brief title has the advantage of enhancing communications and should cover what is to be done and where.

2. *Cost.* Project cost should include all relevant resource allocations

—that is, any outlays required to prepare the product for sale other than annual operating and other current costs. Thus, the following elements of cost should be included in the project cost estimate:

Fixed Capital.   Includes new items of equipment to be purchased, regardless of the method of financing involved. Assets to be leased should be included on a capitalized or "if-purchased" basis.

Working Capital.   Includes raw material and finished-product inventories and an estimate of increases in accounts receivable. May also include an estimate of incremental cash balance and expected accounts payable.

Expense.   Refers to nonoperating outlays deductible in the year expended for tax purposes, or generally not required to be depreciated.

Other.   Includes the opportunity cost for the use of resources already on hand that can be used for some other purpose or sold. The cost of a project may differ from the amount to be appropriated, especially in cases where delegation of authority for final approval purposes must be based on some objective and controllable measure of cost, such as "fixed assets to be purchased."

3. *Priority.*   Frequently, operating divisions will propose inclusion of several capital projects in the budget. Priority ratings constitute, in the preliminary phases, the division manager's judgment of the importance of the particular project in relation to other projects proposed for his division. Priorities should be based on the following factors:

Longer range objectives for the business or plants involved.
Profitability and risk of project and business involved.
Operating needs.
Timing.

In recent years, considerable literature has been devoted to the problem of ranking projects. The preferred method, by and large, is one of the methods discussed in Chapter 18 (net present value, profitability index, discounted [internal] rate of return). In a practical sense, however, management tends to introduce additional factors into the ranking process. This makes sense, since the individual capital project is, more often than not, too narrow in scope to enable evaluation of the broader, long-term impact of accepting it at the cost of eliminating another. This pattern implies that even in companies which lack formal viable long-range plans, management usually has a fair idea of its longer term objectives and will consciously or subconsciously take them into account at some stage of the investment decision process. Priorities may be expressed either by listing projects in sequence or by some quantitative measure of their importance. (See Exhibit 2—Priority Schedule.)

4. *Profitability.*   Some measure of profitability is usually indicated. The sample budget request form shown in Exhibit 1 includes five. In firms which have established minimum profitability standards, it would be rare indeed to find a project submitted on a preliminary basis with profitability below cutoff. Since profitability is always defined in terms of

alternatives, care should be taken to note the particular alternative against which the proposal's profitability has been measured.

5. *Timing.* The ability to adhere to a construction schedule is evi-

EXHIBIT 2

Priority Schedule

PRIORITY SCHEDULE

($000)

Priority	Profit-ability Index	DCF Return	Project Title & Location	Appropriation Amount	Year of Approval
1	1.31	27%	Build new XYZ Plant - Detroit	$10,000	19x0
2	1.26	22%	Expand XYZ Plant - Smithville	$ 5,000	19x2
3	1.23	19%	Modernize ABC Plant - Louisville	$ 6,000	19x1
4	1.19	16%	Rehabilitate Widget Plant - Wilmington	$ 9,000	19x1
5	1.15q	14%	Install automatic process coated equipment - Buffalo	$ 2,000	19x0
6	1.13	13%	Replace worn-out process machinery Cleveland	$ 700	19x2
7	1.08	11%	Renovate plant warehouse - Knoxville	$ 850	19x2
8	1.02	10%	Lease 5 Railroad Cars - Knoxville	$ 125	19x2

dence of an effective planning effort. Achieving and maintaining an edge on the market, combined with the need to minimize the construction period and to avoid prolonged severe overcapacity situations, places a premium on effective prior planning and organization.

6. *Financing method.* For many reasons, it is frequently desirable to specify the method of financing to be utilized for a capital project—first, *corporate policy* may dictate an alternate form of financing. For example,

all railroad cars may be covered under blanket lease agreements. Second, *cash considerations* may indicate the desirability of a leasing arrangement, industrial revenue bond financing, or use of stock (for example, in acquisitions).

7. *Project classification.*   Companies often classify projects according to purpose. An example of such a classification system follows:

Service.   New facilities or expansion of existing facilities for the purpose of accommodating employee needs, expediting administrative functions, or satisfying governmental regulations. Examples include office buildings, cafeterias, furniture and fixtures, wash and locker facilities, and pollution-control facilities.

Cost Saving.   Projects which increase income by reducing manufacturing costs and/or selling and administrative expenses.

Additions and Expansions.   New facilities, expansions of existing facilities, and acquisitions to increase production of existing lines or generally to provide for additional product sales and corresponding income streams.

New Products.   Generally, where wholly new products and/or manufacturing or marketing processes are required, these projects would be categorized for special attention as they would normally be considered high-risk ventures.

Replacement.   Projects involving the substitution of one piece of equipment for another, principally to keep a larger unit in operation.

EXHIBIT 3

Expenditures Forecast

MISCELLANEOUS PRODUCTS COMPANY

Expenditures Forecast
($000)

Priority	TITLE AND LOCATION	Approp. Amount	Carryover to Current (19X1)	Expend. Current Year (19X1)	Carryover to Budget (19X2)	Expend. Budget Year (19X2)	Carryover to Forecast (19X3)	Expend. Forecast Year (19X3)	Carryover to Future Year
1	Build new XYZ Plant-Detroit	10,000	9,000	7,000	2,000	2,000	-	-	-
2	Expand XYZ Plant-Smithville	5,000	-	-	-	4,000	1,000	1,000	-
3	Modernize ABC Plant-Louisville	6,000	-	2,000	4,000	2,000	2,000	2,000	-
4	Rehabilitate Widget Plant-Wilmington	9,000	-	3,000	6,000	4,000	2,000	1,000	1,000
5	Install automatic process control equipment-Buffalo	2,000	1,000	500	500	500	-	-	-
6	Replace worn-out process machinery-Cleveland	700	-	-	-	370	330	330	-
7	Renovate plant warehouse-Knoxville	850	-	-	-	250	600	600	-
8	Lease 5 Railroad Cars-Knoxville	125	-	-	-	125	-	-	-
	Total	33,675	10,000	12,500	12,500	13,245	5,930	4,930	1,000
	Other Minor Projects	4,040	1,200	1,500	1,500	1,590	710	590	120
	Grand Total	37,716	11,200	14,000	14,000	14,835	6,640	5,520	1,120

8. *Project narrative.* To complete the request, it is necessary to provide a clear statement of the proposal and a decision-oriented discussion of the objectives, benefits, assumptions, and relationship to long-range plans. The narrative may also include mention of the sensitivity of project profitability to possible changes in major variables and an analysis of the degree of risk inherent in acceptance of the project.

THE EXPENDITURES FORECAST. The preliminary budget usually includes a forecast of expenditures (see Exhibit 3) on at least a year-by-year basis. If budgeting takes place well before the time period under consideration, it is normally necessary to forecast expenditures only on an annual basis, since many of the projects subject to preliminary consideration may not be included in the budget finally adopted by the company. In any event, the ultimate decision on this point should rest with the treasurer, as he perceives his requirements for adequate cash planning. Although the forecast of project cost includes several types of costs, a common practice is to limit the expenditures forecast to fixed capital, as working capital and expenses can often be introduced into the cash budget via the operating budget. The use of assets already on hand does not normally constitute a budgetable item, since accounting systems do not readily handle opportunity costs. The profitability evaluation, however, should reflect all such costs.

The approved budget

After the preliminary budget has been prepared by the controller, top management must decide which projects it will recommend to the board of directors for inclusion in the approved capital budget. A rational selection at this point depends heavily upon the accuracy and completeness of the budget requests, as well as a good concept of the objectives and long-range plans of the company. Naturally, profitability of individual projects and the priorities recommended at division level will play important roles in the selection process. Following board of directors approval of the budget as a plan, top management must inform project sponsors of the action taken on their projects.

The appropriation request

Management may either authorize the expenditure of funds when the budget is adopted, or it may delay authorization until funds are actually required. The latter approach is usually followed in the expectation that many budget requests will be rejected by management; a comprehensive study of each would be a waste of manpower. Thus, efforts in the interim between budget adoption and appropriation request approval can be focused upon those projects initially exhibiting greatest promise.

The decision to include any given capital project in the capital budget is usually that of top management. Individual projects whose cost is less than some minimum amount can be lumped together and included in the budget as a single major project. Authority to expend funds tentatively authorized by virtue of the capital budget can be delegated among management after adoption of the capital budget. While the exact limits of authority differ substantially from company to company, generally board of directors approval is required for appropriations exceeding a certain amount. Below this amount, individual managers may approve appropriation requests falling within preestablished limits. The President of the corporation may have a limit of $2 million for any single project, while a division president's limit may be $100 thousand. Some types of appropriations may not be delegated at all; an example would be a situation involving issue of stock which ordinarily would require board of directors authorization. The reasons for delegating authority to spend funds for capital projects are fairly obvious. First, those occupying the highest positions in the organization have only so much time to spend on various activities, so there is an obvious need to allocate this time in the most productive manner possible. Second, relatively small projects are usually specialized in purpose, and those most intimately associated with the problem should be able to arrive at the correct decision without further review.

The appropriation request usually consists of several forms, although in some companies presentations and authorizations are made orally or by informal letter. For companies utilizing a standard format, the following elements generally comprise the appropriation request:

REQUEST AND AUTHORITY. The first page of the appropriation request (see Exhibit 4) serves to identify the originator and the project, and may include a brief summary of the project's justification. In addition, space is normally provided for the signatures of the recommending and authorizing personnel.

NARRATIVE. The narrative section details the requesting entity's justification for undertaking the proposal, and frequently follows a prescribed format. The reader would be likely to find the following elements of information included in the narrative:

1. *Proposal.* A clear statement of what is to be done.

2. *Objectives.* The beneficial results of undertaking the project, including the profitability.

3. *Conceptual framework.* Contains the necessary background information, an analysis of the relevant environment (e.g., markets, competition), the present and required capabilities of the company to achieve the objectives, and finally, if possible, a comparison of the project to

EXHIBIT 4

Request and Authority

APPROPRIATION REQUEST

REQUEST AND AUTHORITY

Originator	Date	A.R. No.
Product Manager - XYZ	23 March 19x1	0627

Amount $5,000,000	Budget Status Project Budgeted in 19x1

Project Title

Expand XYZ Plant - Smithville

Summary of Justification

Project provides for expansion of the Smithville XYZ Plant by 50,000 units per month.

Principal objective is that of maintaining current market share of 27% in the Smithville marketing region. Incremental flows due to proposed expansion yield a rate of return estimated at 22%.

Profitability estimates assume stable and moderately rising variable costs over 15 year project life. No other major changes are expected. Profitability is sensitive to changes in price only; probability of price change is dependent upon Competitive Products Company's decision to contruct an XYZ plant as rumored. This is considered rather unlikely, however.

This project is in accord with long-range plans for development of XYZ markets, plants and distribution systems.

Requested By Product Manager	Date 23 March 19x1
Recommended Plant Manager	Date 30 March 19x1
Recommended	Date
Recommended	Date
Approved By Chairman of the Board	Date

Approver's Remarks

---

objectives outlined in the company's long-range plans (as well as discussion of special short term needs).

4. *Alternatives.* The problem with alternatives is that of determining which ones may be of interest to top management. Every company's approach is different. Minimally, however, top management should be

informed of the course of action the project sponsor would recommend if the proposal were rejected. Other alternatives of frequent concern include make-versus-buy, location, and smaller (larger) plant size.

5. *Sensitivity and risk.* Discussions of alternatives also imply the existence of certain underlying assumptions. The chief purpose of sensitivity analysis is to isolate those variable factors which are most likely to have the greatest effect on profitability and achievement of other objectives. If top management disagrees with the assumptions made by the project sponsor, it may recommend alternative courses of action. Furthermore, careful analysis of the probability of deviations from projections may indicate that the proposal would involve bearing risks not commensurate with project size and expected profitability.

SUPPORTING DOCUMENTATION. The final section of the appropriation request is comprised of other supporting documents, including cost estimates and the results of market studies and financial analysis. While standard forms may be provided for such presentations, it is frequently desirable to leave format as flexible as possible, since the elements of importance and the framework of the analysis tend to vary considerably from project to project.

Progress reports

Progress reports are submitted at regular intervals during the course of implementing the capital budget in order to review the accuracy of expenditures forecasts; to provide updated expenditures forecasts; and to verify the assumptions and economics underlying the acceptance of individual projects.

In order to achieve objectives pertaining to cash and construction planning, companies often require submission of periodic reports containing actual expenditure and commitment information. Expenditure delays revealed by such reports are indicative of construction slowdowns and incorrect planning. Of added importance is the fact that as a result, estimates which had been used by the treasurer in preparing his comprehensive cash budget will have proved to be incorrect. Such reports may also include revised forecasts of expenditures to reflect the effect of both previous and expected variations from budget. Lastly, where construction must be coordinated with related functional activities, it may be necessary to reschedule such activities.

The prolonged lead times required for installation of multimillion dollar projects also necessitate periodic review of these projects during the construction period. Status reports should provide information relating to both the progress of project execution and the critical underlying assumptions. Changes in expectations can lead to shifts in plans to meet new contingencies; severe reversals may even dictate scrapping a project in the middle of construction. Admittedly, such action is difficult for management to take if only because of the human tendency to avoid admitting errors in judgment. Also, large cancellation penalties for equipment already ordered and/or the "sunk cost" aspect of the situation may justify continuation in spite of major reductions in profitability forecasts. Nevertheless, it should be remembered that creative management is required even during the construction period to avoid "throwing good money after bad."

Postapproval reviews

1. *Objectives.* It was suggested above that a comprehensive capital budgeting system encompasses the life of the product in the broadest sense, and the life of a particular plant in a more narrow sense. Evaluation of the performance of individual capital projects is part and parcel of any broadly based performance evaluation system. Postapproval reviews ideally would go beyond the construction-in-progress reviews mentioned above, and would include evaluation of projects which have reached the commercial production stage. The objectives of postapproval reviews include the following:

a. To provide management with a standard method of evaluating the abilities and judgment of project sponsors.

b. To identify errors or patterns of error in judgment which can be avoided in future similar situations.

c. To help ensure that the quality and accuracy of information attains the highest feasible standards.

2. *Use of accounting systems.* The results of the capital budgeting decision are ultimately reflected in the operations of the firm. However, the accounting system that automatically provides the results of a specific capital investment project is a rare one indeed. In fact, the profitability of some types of decisions never appears as an increment to total profitability. Typical of these is the make-versus-purchase decision discussed in Chapter 15. Only by comparing the production cost of a produced product with an estimate of its purchase cost can the firm determine the wisdom of the investment decision. Thus, while the company's accounting system can provide a certain amount of the information required, a meaningful and consistent postapproval review must also include some judgmental factors.

3. *Scope.* Some firms require reviews for virtually every project approved by top management, while others restrict efforts to an intensive analysis of only a few of the larger projects—those which are expected to have the most profound effects on future operations. The scope of coverage is primarily a function of the investment mix of the particular company.

4. *Responsibility for preparation.*   Postapproval reviews may be prepared by those responsible for the project or by an outside staff, usually from the controller's office. The advantage of using the former lies in their greater familiarity with the project and associated technical aspects, whereas the latter would tend to exhibit greater objectivity. The best approach probably involves preparation by the project sponsor combined with review of his study by independent staff personnel.

5. *Timing.*   Many companies perform only one audit during the one- to two-year period after construction. While such an approach may be valid for certain types of projects (e.g., cost saving), there are others which should be subject to scrutiny for a longer period.

6. *Format.*   The format of the postapproval review should essentially follow that used in the original presentation for approval, in order to achieve comparability. The analysis should be aimed at understanding the extent to which the initial objectives were attained and the validity of the principal underlying *assumptions.*

PART V

Information technology

Evaluation of economic feasibility

John W. Richy*

Electronic data processing (EDP) has become a major contributing factor in our nation's continued ability to conduct its affairs. With the tremendous growth and rapidly accelerating pace of our economy, practically every segment of our society has found it necessary to avail itself of the amazing data handling and storage capabilities provided by this relatively new technology. Even in those areas where EDP has not yet manifested itself, the question is no longer whether an organization needs the assistance of an EDP installation, but rather what kind of a system it needs, when it can be implemented, and at what cost?

This section of the *Financial Executive's Handbook* will cover some of the more important considerations involved in the selection, implementation, and operation of an EDP system. It is organized into six related chapters. This first chapter deals primarily with the initial feasibility study for a new or radically changed installation. It includes an evaluation of the basic requirements and the initial analysis to determine whether the economic potential of the EDP system justifies its installation. Chapter 29, "Development of system specifications," considers the development of both hardware and software specifications to the point where a formal request for proposal (RFP) can be made to potential vendors. Chapter 30 deals with the techniques for "Information storage and processing." Chapter 31, "Selection and installation of data processing equipment," focuses on the problem of selecting a vendor from those

* Manager of Technical Services, Computer and Data Communication Systems, United Air Lines, Chicago.

who have submitted formal proposals, and discusses some of the problems that occur in the physical installation of EDP hardware. Chapter 32, "Program development and management," is concerned with the process of translating detailed software specifications into working programs. Finally, Chapter 33 is devoted to "Managing the data processing function." It covers staffing, the selection and implementation of new applications on existing hardware, and the manufacturing-like production aspects of the operating EDP center. In connection with the implementation of new applications, it discusses the problems of the transition from one system to another. This discussion is relevant to both new applications on existing hardware and to total new systems that include new hardware.

The technology of computer systems has been subject to rapid change throughout its existence, and the pace of change does not appear likely to slow down in the near future. If these six chapters were to concentrate on the specific technology available today, they would rapidly become obsolete. Instead, an effort has been made to concentrate as much as possible on the problems and techniques of managing information technology. Today's good techniques of EDP management are likely to continue to be relevant for many years after today's technology becomes ancient history.

This chapter deals with the preliminary economic feasibility evaluation using a feasibility study approach describing the types of data that should be considered. The objective of the feasibility study is to define, in terms readily understandable to corporate management, the need for an EDP System and its economic potential for the company. This is an important first step, as it will apprise management of the costs in terms of dollars and manpower commitment involved in proceeding to each stage of the EDP implementation process.

Although the conclusions reached as a result of the feasibility study are not expected to result in a final commitment on the part of management, they will involve significant decisions regarding the scope and direction of the project. These decisions could have a significant long-term effect on the company's future, and a decision not to proceed should be given as much consideration as would a decision to proceed. Either decision may be very difficult to reverse at a later stage without incurring added costs, loss of time, or both. Management should therefore be fully aware of the significance of the feasibility study, and be prepared to devote time and attention to this important first step.

Drawing up the feasibility study

The study team

To assure that the process of evaluating the need for an EDP System will result in a complete and meaningful report to management, a study team should be established for this specific purpose. The team members should be relieved of their other duties for the duration of the study to enable them to devote their full time and attention to the study.

The study team should be headed by a company representative from a fairly high level to add prestige and importance to the study. The team leader should also have broad company experience and knowledge of the organization's structure, and have access to planning information which may indicate potential changes in organization that should be known to the study team. Some familiarity with data processing techniques is necessary, but need not include expert knowledge or experience in hardware or software. The primary function of the team leader is to organize the thoughts and ideas of the group into a clear, concise report to management. He should have the persuasiveness and authority to direct the study towards an unexaggerated statement of the problems in terms readily understandable to management, and to present a realistic appraisal of the potential economic advantages. The overriding qualification of the team leader is an objective outlook and an appreciation for the potential impact of a new data-processing system on the company's present organizational structure, personnel procedures and overall business policies.

Supporting the study team leader, a representative will be needed from each of the using departments to define the problems and describe the expected benefits to be derived from their solution. Each user representative should have recent experience in the functional activity under study in order to guide the team's efforts in analyzing current problems. Knowledge and experience in data processing concepts is not necessary; in fact, too much knowledge of data system limitations might tend to inhibit the user from presenting his problems for solution, or dispose him to accept ready-made hardware solutions too quickly.

Sufficient freedom and authority should also be delegated to the user representatives to make decisions and commitments for their departments during the day-to-day development of the study team's report. They should not feel it necessary to interrupt the study team's discussions to check with department heads each time a decision is encountered. A departmental review of the report prior to submission to top management will enable the using elements to finalize their department's position. Part time participation by experienced data processing technical personnel will be needed to guide the study team in determining the feasibility of achieving satisfactory solutions through automation and to assist in the cost development. Even with the tremendous advances in data systems technology, there are still many problems that do not lend themselves to data processing solutions. An optimistic, but realistic, knowledge of software and hardware capabilities and possible state-of-the-art future developments is, therefore, essential input to keep the study team concepts within the realm of practical and economic possibility.

If in-house technical capability is not available, or cannot be diverted to the study project, consulting services are available to furnish this support to the study team. Consulting firms can also be called on to conduct and direct the full study. In most instances, however, the leadership and direction of the study can be adequately handled from within the company, particularly in this initial phase where the experience and knowledge of the company's problems and operational needs are the essential ingredient to a meaningful report to management.

Coverage of the feasibility study

The goal of the study team effort is to present an advisory report to corporate management explaining the potential economic advantages of a new system and apprising management of the types of cost elements that will be involved in its implementation and operation. The main emphasis should be directed towards enabling top management to gain a basic understanding of the assumptions and estimates that have been made in evaluating the profit potential of a new system. Based on this information, management will be in a position to support commitments of manpower and resources for the further development of a total system implementation plan. It is highly desirable that top management understand the scope of the proposed plan and be prepared to follow developments in each of the subsequent stages. A steering committee with top management representation might also be established to periodically review progress of the study team and provide the necessary guidance on a continuing basis.

FUNCTIONS OR ACTIVITIES CONSIDERED. The methods of performing current functions should be described. Are they manual, semiautomatic, or fully automatic? Any new functions should be described. The informational or operational interrelationships of the various functions should be identified.

PROPOSED SYSTEM CONCEPT. The sources of information under the proposed system should be described, highlighting changes from the present information flow. The procedural or operational changes needed should be identified.

The informational or operational interrelationships of the various functions should be identified. A summary statement of the relationship of each function to other functions should be drawn up to establish dependencies and commonalities.

The value of each function to the company and to other related functions should be rated. This step is needed to establish relative levels of priority in the event certain requirements have to be deferred or deleted.

ECONOMIC EVALUATION.   The benefits expected from the new system should be listed, highlighting the potential for added revenue, reduced costs, and improved performance. The probable cost elements should be listed, along with an estimate of the possible range of costs for each item. The present system costs should also be listed to make direct comparisons possible.

Since the feasibility study does not commit management to the new system, but merely orients top management to the scope of the full project, the cost and benefit figures can be a little rough. An accuracy of plus or minus 15 percent is completely acceptable as a goal. In fact, it is not possible to be really precise about the costs and benefits of the new system without doing a lot of the detailed system's specification work and getting specific proposals from vendors. It is costly to go this far with the project, so one of the prime purposes of the feasibility study is to enable management to get a rough idea of whether the project is worthwhile before incurring the costs necessary to develop precise cost estimates. If management decides to proceed further with the project, precise cost estimates will be available as a byproduct of the system's specification effort and the vendor selection process. The factors to be considered in developing estimates of costs and benefits are described later in the chapter.

Once the cost and benefit estimates are derived, they should be analyzed according to the company's normal methods of evaluating capital investments. The most common possible methods are described in Chapter 19, "Analysis of capital expenditures." The payback method, concentrating on the time when the break-even point will be reached, is more useful in the analysis of this type of capital investment than of other types because of the high potential for rapid technological obsolescence if a long period of time is required to reach this point. In determining the break-even point, it is useful to estimate expenditures on a month-by-month basis during implementation as well as over the useful life of the system.

PROJECT SCHEDULE.   The length of time necessary to accomplish each of the following steps should be estimated:

a) Initial management review and approval.
b) Development of the request for proposal (RFP).
c) Vendor proposal preparation.
d) Review of vendor proposals and vendor selection.
e) Major implementation elements and time estimates covering programming, site preparation, equipment installation, system tests, training, and transition to the new system.

MANPOWER AND ORGANIZATIONAL REQUIREMENTS.   The organization of the present data system should be described and the number of personnel listed by job category. Then the manpower and the specific skills needed to implement and operate the new system should be listed and compared with the current personnel and skills. The expected sources of new manpower should be described, with consideration to overlapping requirements to operate both systems during the transition period.

A long-range organizational plan for the implementation and operation of the new system should be developed. Specific attention should be given to the continued operation of the existing system during the implementation phase. This can be a real problem if the new system is going to eliminate a number of the jobs essential to the old system.

An important management consideration at this time is a review of present data processing organizational responsibilities within the company to determine whether restructuring of the data processing activities can be made more effective under a new system concept. The new generation data processing systems, oriented towards multiprocessing and time sharing by remote data terminals, will enable company-wide multidepartmental sharing of a powerful centralized data processing complex.

More and more companies are finding substantial cost/performance advantages by concentrating computing capability into one or more interconnected communications-oriented systems rather than continuing operation of several independent systems. A number of companies has recognized the advantages of a separate data processing organization and established data processing departments or divisions with top-level administrative authority to manage and operate their EDP systems.

In addition to the cost/performance advantages achieved by combining computer power into fewer more powerful and versatile systems, EDP systems are becoming a vital and essential part of a company's operation, contributing substantially to the company's success and profitability. The EDP resource must, therefore, be controlled and prudently utilized. Many examples can be cited where jobs are run, reports prepared, or applications implemented on a system with little thought to the value in relation to the computer resource allocation. In other instances, one system may be struggling to keep up with demand while another independently-administered system may have idle time. These and other similar inefficiencies can be overcome by concentrating the data processing resources, which include the programming manpower skills as well as hardware, into one organization charged with the responsibility for company-wide development, implementation, and operational performance of all computer systems.

Such a change in a company's data processing organizational responsibilities, developed over the years as one or more separate departmental responsibilities, is not easily accepted at the outset. It may take a firm and unilateral approach by top management before traditional organization lines can be changed, and the sooner the matter is introduced and settled, the greater will be the likelihood of cooperative company-wide effort towards implementation and transition to a new major system within a projected time schedule.

Economic factors

This section will describe the types of cost and savings factors to be considered in determining the economic justification for a new system. No attempt will be made to discuss methods, such as rate of return on investment or payback, for analyzing these factors. These methods are discussed in detail in Chapter 19.

Although management will not be expected to commit to a new system based on this preliminary study, it is still necessary to develop a reasonably good economic prediction to place the project in proper perspective in relation to other company activities and demands on resources. One of the difficult tasks is developing this economic prediction prior to receipt of actual vendor proposals and costs. This can be accomplished, however, by obtaining cost guidance from one or more representative vendors who will be more than willing to assist.

Vendors may be reluctant to engage in discussion of costs without detailed specifications. However, since this information is for preliminary planning purposes, there should be no objection to providing representative standard component prices and ballpark estimates of programming and other costs. It should be made clear that no vendor preference is implied by the request for cost guidance, and that all interested vendors will be given an equal opportunity to present system proposals after this initial exploratory stage is concluded.

Another avenue of obtaining cost guidance is to contact other users who have already implemented systems with similar operational considerations. There are a number of system user organizations through which such contacts can be initiated.

Described below are representative cost and saving factors that will be encountered in one form or another in the implementation and operation of a data system. The degree to which any element enters into a particular evaluation is dependent on the size of the system and the specific application under consideration. Likewise, the magnitude, or range of cost/savings figures, will have to be gauged by the reader, depending on his detailed knowledge of the conditions involved.

The same cost and savings elements covered in this section apply to subsequent analyses, where more precise figures will be developed for final determination of economic feasibility and for selecting a particular vendor system.

Implementation costs

SYSTEM'S DEVELOPMENT.   The system's development phase includes the initial manpower necessary for the development of detailed specifications for submission to vendors as a request for proposal [RFP], and the preparation of final cost/savings figures and detailed evaluation of vendor proposals. Man-month estimates should be developed for project leader, user representatives and programmer, hardware and data communications technical assistance, as well as any direct costs for consulting services.

Also included are the man-hours needed for interviews and discussion with company personnel to finalize functional requirements, and for vendor meetings to review specifications and proposals. One of the purposes of isolating this particular expense item is to apprise management of the commitment involved in proceeding to the next phase. This will enable management to determine whether economic potential warrants this commitment of time and manpower resources and, if the potential is good enough, to augment the subsequent efforts to reduce the time frame for completion of the overall project.

Negotiation leading towards final vendor selection will entail legal counsel and possible outside consultant costs. This involves the development of a legal contract document covering the terms and conditions under which the system is to be implemented and operated. A performance specification and detailed description of the vendor system is also developed as an appendix to the contract.

IMPLEMENTATION MANPOWER.   *User analysts.*   User analysts will be needed to further develop general user specifications into detailed functional and procedural definitions based on the known operational capabilities and features of the selected vendor system.

Programmer analysts.   The programmer analysts will translate the detailed user functional and procedural specifications into computer programming specifications. They will act as liaison between user analysts and programmers, verifying the logical relationships implied by the functional specifications.

Application programmers.   Application programmers will convert programmer specifications into appropriate compiler language as source programs. They will debug and analyze the object code programs produced and estimate running times.

System control programmers.   This level of programmer effort is needed to work with vendor programmers in adapting vendor-furnished system control and executive programs to the system being implemented. This includes checkout and acceptance of these vendor routines, and subsequent maintenance and modification by user programmers.

Training.   The vendor generally provides training for programmers, analysts, and computer operators. Man-day estimates for attending classes should be developed with the vendor.

Functional operation and procedural training for users will be required where remote input/output equipment will be operated by department personnel. A training staff generally attends the indoctrination sessions conducted by the vendor. These trainers will then train various user personnel as part of an on-the-job training program. New mechanized systems can cause significant changes in procedures and job skills. This will require training present personnel to acquire the new skills, or hiring new personnel with these skills. The man-day requirements for this training, as well as system cutover data consideration, can be a *major* cost. The lack of early recognition of these requirements on the part of user organizations can cause significant problems in implementing a new system.

Technical support staff.　Large scale on-line systems with many remote terminals require a technical staff to coordinate site preparation, equipment delivery and installation, communication facility installation, and system check-out and acceptance. Budgeting and cost control of hardware, communications, and facilities costs are also performed by this group.

Supervision and project control.　Any moderately sized project will require organization and manpower to coordinate and schedule the activities of the various groups. This may require the use of project control techniques such as PERT to follow project progress.

Managerial and clerical.　Management, secretarial, and clerical requirements should be considered in determining total manpower costs. Clerical assistance to document specifications and programs and to keep these documents updated can require a sizable clerical staff.

OTHER IMPLEMENTATION COSTS.　*Site preparation.*　This includes architectural and contractor costs for building construction, office modification, electrical power systems, signal cable conduit, air conditioning, lighting, and other requirements for equipment installation at central and remote sites.

Shipping.　Shipping and drayage costs are generally charged to the customer f.o.b. the vendor's factory. Special charges may be incurred to effect inside delivery to customer offices, particularly where access problems require the use of rigging equipment.

Installation.　In most cases, vendor lease and purchase prices include normal equipment installation and checkout at no additional cost. Where unusual installation conditions exist, or cable runs exceed those normally provided, vendor may engage an electrical contractor. Contractor costs and excess cable costs are charged to the customer at direct cost, or with overhead and handling charges previously agreed to.

Taxes.　Sales, property, use, excise, or other taxes imposed by local, state, or federal taxing authorities on the delivery, installation, use, and maintenance of equipment components are passed on to the customer. Property improvement taxes, resulting from site preparation, can also become a system cost factor. The application of taxes can vary widely throughout the country, but is usually a significant cost item, particularly initial sales taxes.

Materials and supplies. Initial outlays for machine supplies, particularly magnetic tape and punch cards, should not be overlooked as potentially significant cost factors.

Removal and refurbishment. Replacement of existing systems will require removal and disposal of equipment and cabling, and refurbishing of the affected locations to their original condition. In some leased system agreements, removal and shipping costs are borne by the vendor. This responsibility should be spelled out in the original contract to eliminate later misunderstandings. Refurbishment, however, is strictly a customer problem. Where an in-service transition is to take place from an old to a new system, dual installation equipment will be necessary. Installation of a new system under these conditions, and subsequent removal of the old system, will entail somewhat higher costs than a first-time installation.

Transition costs. In the transition process from an existing system to a new system, there is usually an overlapping period when manpower and operating costs are being incurred for both systems. Estimates should be made to determine the period of overlap and the extent of concurrent costs. Cross-utilization of manpower between old and new systems can help to reduce manpower costs. Where the existing system is to be terminated before contract expiration, termination charges should be included in the transition cost figure.

Conversion and testing costs. Transition to a new system will also require establishing a new data base. Converting existing files to the new data base, testing and validating the data, and keeping the new data base updated until the transition is completed and the previous files are completely phased out can be very significant in both cost and time.

Operating costs

Many of the one-time implementation costs described above will continue to be incurred throughout the life of the system. These costs, however, will vary from month to month and require averaging to obtain a continuing monthly cost. In addition to these costs, there are other continuing monthly operating costs to consider.

COMPUTER OPERATIONS. This involves customer staff to operate the equipment. Operation may require multi-shift or 24-hour 7-day week staffing with computer operators and clerical and supervisory personnel.

Additional operating personnel may be required to enter changes in system parameters periodically, or introduce new data to keep a dynamically changing data base updated. Where data processing application activity is a continuous 24-hour process, applications specialists may also be needed to handle rejected activities, take corrective action, and analyze any user operational problems that may arise during the course of the day.

EQUIPMENT LEASE OR PURCHASE AMORTIZATION. *Lease.* Equipment lease arrangements are available from vendors to meet customers' needs for one or more operating shifts. Short-term and long-term leases can be negotiated. Third party lease arrangements whereby a bank or other financial organization purchases the equipment and then leases the equipment back to the using company might be considered. Certain tax and other savings realized by the financing organization which can be passed on to the user could result in lower monthly costs over a term suitable to the user's requirements.

Purchase. The subject, "Lease, rent, or buy decisions" is covered in Chapter 20. Monthly cost figures will depend on the particular plan adopted. Purchase arrangements provide maintenance service as a separate monthly cost item which must be added to the equipment amortization cost. Where the user assumes ownership of equipment, added costs for insuring the equipment against fire or other damage should be determined in keeping with the protection desired.

MAINTENANCE. Lease agreements generally include routine and emergency maintenance during the specified shift or shifts covered at no additional cost. Maintenance service during off-shift periods is generally charged at an agreed hourly rate, with a two-hour minimum, which includes the maintenance engineer's usual travel time from home office. Travel costs, meals, and other expenses may be added to the hourly figure to arrive at a total charge for the call. In some cases, overhead or handling charges are also added. The method of computing these charges and the conditions under which they are incurred should be agreed to beforehand and covered in the system contract. Fixed fee total maintenance coverage can be arranged with a number of vendors.

Maintenance coverage in a purchase/maintenance arrangement is identical in most respects to lease maintenance coverage. There are some differences, however, which should be recognized as potential added costs in the purchased system. Where equipment is purchased, the owner assumes certain cost responsibilities for major damage requiring replacement with new equipment. Under a lease arrangement, the vendor, as equipment owner, assumes these costs.

Equipment manufacturers have a continuing program for improving equipment performance. The resulting improvements are accomplished as routine field changes on vendor-owned equipment. These same changes are, in many cases, made at no cost to customer-owned equipment to maintain uniformity for maintenance purposes, but may also be made at the customer's option as a cost item.

DATA COMMUNICATION FACILITIES.   Monthly rental and installation costs for lines and line termination equipment will depend on transmission speeds, distance, and quality of lines. More expensive channel conditioning and data subsets are required as the transmission speeds increase. Dial-up dataphone service may be more economical than private line services for applications where periodic high-volume data transfers are involved. Fixed fee inward and outward wide area telephone service [WATS] may also be economical for handling data transfers on a dial-up basis.

FLOOR SPACE.   This covers lease or allocated cost for computer room and remote control equipment space. To be included are work and storage space for vendor maintenance personnel and spare parts.

FUTURE EXPANSION.   System growth over the expected system life will require additional equipment components. Cost for added components, facilities, and installation should be projected to obtain a long-term cost picture.

Savings and benefits

Although numerous examples where EDP systems have produced outstanding efficiencies and contributed substantially to the profit capability of a company can be cited, there are also those little-heard-of-cases where the results have fallen short of expectations. One reason for such failures is a mismatch of the system selected and the application or job the system is expected to perform. This mismatch could be an oversized system for the application, resulting in higher than necessary cost, or an undersized system, limiting full realization of the savings potential. Subsequent chapters describe the process of organizing application requirements into a specification for vendor bidding and evaluating proposals. This approach will assist in achieving the best cost/performance value for the particular application.

A more common reason for disappointment in data system economic performance is an over-optimistic prediction of the magnitude of the benefits that can be achieved, or the time frame in which the benefits can be realized. This section will highlight the types of tangible and intangible benefits to look for in predicting the economic outlook for a data system, pointing out those areas where caution should be exercised to avoid overstating the potential returns.

DIRECT COST REDUCTIONS.   *Manpower savings.*   Improvements in employee productivity and elimination of manual work functions have been a major source of economic justification for a new system. A direct reduction in number of employees, however, is frequently not realized, or is realized only as a result of normal employee turnover or attrition over a long period of time. Benefits from increased employee productivity may likewise be delayed, resulting in a higher expansion rate in number of employees needed to accommodate future business growth than predicted.

Capital equipment savings. This saving involves reductions in capital equipment and plant expenditures through better utilization of available facilities, resulting in postponement of future capital equipment acquisitions. Building and facility expense reductions can likewise be attributed to manpower and capital equipment reductions.

Existing systems costs. Lease, maintenance, and operating cost reductions through replacement of existing systems should be fairly straightforward and easy to determine. Requirements for dual system operation during the transition period can be treated as an added cost item as noted under transition costs. Termination charges on contract items must be similarly treated. Residual value or sale of owned equipment is a source of revenue to be included as a potential benefit. The sale price, however, could very well be substantially lower than the residual value placed on the equipment, depending on depreciation techniques used and current market demand for a particular type of equipment.

Inventory reductions. Where an EDP system is utilized in an inventory control application, savings in reduced inventory through more precise and current knowledge of inventory status can be projected fairly accurately.

Reference materials and manuals. Where an EDP system utilizes a large number of remote data terminals for on-line interrogation of a centralized data storage bank, reductions in cost for printed reference material can be significant. Reductions in distribution and updating costs should also be considered in the value of expedited information distribution.

INCREASED REVENUES. *Product sales.* Consumer product inventory control systems can contribute directly to increased sales through more positive commitments for customer delivery. More efficient order and billing systems allowing earlier presentation of invoices for payment can effect an improvement in the cash flow for the company, with obvious economic advantages.

Data processing services. Most large-scale systems are designed to handle peak activity occurring during a limited number of months during a year and/or hours of a day. The excess capacity during off-peak periods can be utilized to sell data processing services to other companies. The possibility of companies with similar or complementary data processing requirements combining their requirements into one time-shared system is a potential cost reduction or source of added revenue if one company undertakes the venture and sells service to the participating companies.

Related to the subject of data processing services is the possibility of obtaining the desired service from a data service bureau or from an organization with excess capacity for sale. Such arrangement have proven to be quite successful, as evidenced by the rapidly expanding number of service bureaus and companies offering this type of service. To the user, such an arrangement offers the advantage of minimizing development and implementation problems, but does not change the requirement to develop a comprehensive application specification. Data communications techniques enabling on-line or batch-processing services to be performed remotely from the service center have greatly facilitated the use of such service arrangements.

INTANGIBLE BENEFITS. *Customer relationships.* General improvements in customer relationships through more efficient and businesslike operations have been derived from the use of EDP systems. Customer-contact employees with accurate up-to-date information readily available to answer customer questions regarding product availability, status of customer accounts, and other requested information, should not be overlooked as a potential competitive advantage.

Market forecasts. More comprehensive and timely information about a company's day-to-day operation will enable management to project market and profit goals more precisely, and to monitor the progress toward achievement of these goals.

Company growth. In many industries, expansion pressures to accommodate increased business activity cannot be accomplished practically or economically by adding more manpower and supporting facilities. The introduction of EDP systems has opened up new methods of operation and enabled such companies to expand market capability. In some cases, this consideration of maintaining and improving the company's business position is overriding, with other savings and benefits added as secondary factors.

Economics summary and recommendations

A pictorial presentation of costs and savings as a function of time would be useful as a summary of the project economics and implementation time schedule. Such a chart or table will highlight the periods when high costs will be incurred with no return, and indicate when savings will first begin to accrue. A third curve on the chart should depict the cumulative net cost/savings for each increment of time so that the break-even point for the project can be readily seen. To be strictly accurate, the early costs incurred should be calculated to reflect the cost of money. The significant point to note is that substantial funds will have to be expended before any savings are realized. Also, savings may not begin until some months after system implementation.

With such a table or chart as a point of reference, a summary of conclusions and specific recommendations can be presented to corporate management in a clear, concise manner. Further supporting data in the form of supplementary charts could also be prepared for each major cost and savings element. These detail charts would be helpful to management in their assessment of the validity of the cost and savings estimates and the likelihood of realizing these figures in the time frame depicted.

Development of system specifications

John W. Richy and Charles K. Scott*

Once top management has decided, on the basis of the feasibility study (see Chapter 28), to go ahead with the development and implementation of an EDP system, the next step is the development of system specifications. This is an iterative process, with each iteration leading to a greater level of detail. The first part of this chapter will deal with the development of software specifications only through the gross design stage, leaving the discussion of the development of detailed specifications and of the programming to Chapter 32, "Program development and management." This chapter will also deal with the development of specifications for vendor-supplied software and hardware for presentation to vendors of a request for proposal (RFP).

The system specifications development described in this chapter should be done by a team composed both of future users of the system and of technicians who understand system analysis and the capabilities of the hardware and software available. This team is similar to the team which prepared the feasibility study, and often the feasibility study team forms its nucleus.

At the start, it is important to avoid imposing strict hardware or programming limitations on the development of the system to meet user requirements. A certain amount of "blue sky" thinking is desirable to push the state-of-the-art, and in many cases will encourage vendors to discuss new system concepts which are under development but not yet announced. One should be cautious about expected results, however, if

---

* Manager of Technical Services, Computer and Data Communication Systems, United Air Lines, Chicago; and, Operations Research Analyst, Department of Health, Education, and Welfare, respectively.

one is the initial user of a new system concept. They invariably have bugs in them when first released, and the correction of these can be expensive for both the user and the vendor.

The main idea is to avoid limiting the initial definition of system requirements to known hardware and software solutions, concentrating instead on desired operational capabilities necessary to satisfy the present or future needs of the user. The entire process of formulating requirements will undergo several iterations before a final design is established, and there will be ample opportunity to narrow down requirements in keeping with their value, costs, and technical feasibility.

Development of software specifications

Stages of software design

After the feasibility study, the design of the software for the system must go through at least three iterations before an operational system can be produced.

The first stage is the gross design of the overall system. It should involve both the users and the technical system analysts. User involvement at this level is very important, as decisions will be made here which can be extremely important to the business, and which only an executive with an intimate knowledge of the business is competent to make. The output of this first stage should be a simple flow chart defining the key logic of the system and the nature of the key information files.

The second stage is the detailed system design. It requires only the involvement of technicians (system analysts), unless questions come up which were overlooked in the first stage. It translates the simple flow chart produced in the first stage into detailed flow charts and detailed specifications of file layout and input/output design.

The third stage is the programming stage. It is a completely technical job. The specifications developed in the second stage should be detailed enough so that the programmers can write the programs directly from them.

This chapter will cover only the first stage of software design. The second and third stages are discussed in Chapter 32, "Program development and management."

Integrated versus modular design

One of the first choices that the system design team is likely to face in developing the gross system design is whether to have an integrated system or a modular one. In an integrated system, all the operations that are at all significantly related are made part of a single computer run. Data and results are transferred automatically from one application to another. There is no need to write out data and manually transfer it. A modular system, on the other hand, is composed of a number of independent, although related, computer operations. There is no automatic transfer of data from one module to another. The results of one module must be read out of the computer and then, if needed for the next module, they must be read back into the computer.

It is not clear that either the modular or the integrated design concept is generally superior. Each concept has its partisans. Which system is best for a given company probably depends on its particular circumstances. Furthermore, if the decision is to use the modular design, there is then a question of the degree of modularity that tends to obscure the distinction between the two concepts.

When compared to the modular design, the integrated design has a number of advantages. It takes less time, both elapsed time and computer time, to run because less time is spent reading data in and out. This same feature makes it cheaper to operate. Also, fewer expensive data files will be required, because all applications use the same set of files.

The integrated design has, however, a number of disadvantages compared to the modular design. It is more difficult to program than the modular design. It requires more computer capability than the modular design. It makes it easier for errors in the input to get all the way through the system and cause mistakes in a number of widely separated areas.

A major disadvantage of the integrated design is that it is a lot less flexible than the modular design. Changes are much more difficult to make. In a modular design, changes will generally necessitate reprogramming parts of one module. In an integrated system, changes can require reprogramming large segments of the entire system.

Either design can be implemented in pieces, although the modular system is easier to implement. Modular segments can be programmed and operated independently. With the integrated design, data that are supposed to go to a routine as yet unwritten can be removed by a simple strip routine, but there are difficulties if a routine requires data from another routine which is not yet operating.

The fact that the modular segments can be operated independently does not mean that they can be designed and programmed without reference to the other modules. It is essential that the various modules be planned and coordinated so that the data that have to be transferred from one module to another will be in a form compatible with the requirements of the next module. If the various modules are not designed in the context of some reasonable overall plan, there will be failures at the interfaces.

Development of the gross system design

The most important job of the system design team is to develop a gross design for the system. User involvement in this task is very important. Only the users know enough about the applications under consideration to properly identify the key decisions involved and understand their implications. This stage of the system design cannot, therefore, safely be left to outside consultants, internal technical system analysts, or vendors.

The design team should draw up a simple flow chart of the proposed system. The flow chart should be one which operating management can

EXHIBIT 1

Sample Systems Flow Chart

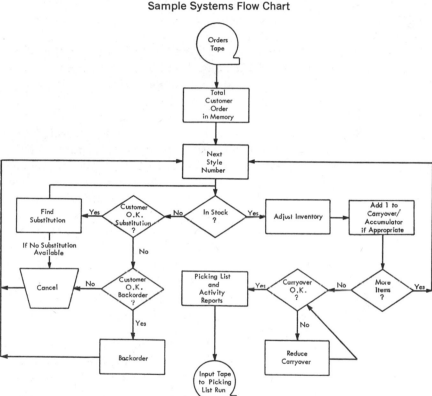

understand. An example of such a flow chart is shown in Exhibit 1. It is a chart of the order processing system of a greeting card company.[1]

The first step in the system shown in Exhibit 1 is to read the orders into memory. The orders are for standard qualities of a number of different cards, the different cards desired being specified by style numbers. As it goes through the order, the computer checks each style number to see if it is in stock. If it is, the inventory is adjusted. If the

---

[1] This example, and the flow charts in Exhibits 1 and 2, are taken from the "Carver Greeting Card Company" case, Harvard Business School. The flow charts in Exhibits 1 and 2 were prepared by Professor F. Warren McFarlan.

card is one carried over from a previous year, this is noted in an accumulator which keeps track of the percentage of the order which consists of carried-over items. If the item is not in stock, there are procedures for finding substitutes or back ordering if the customer permits. Once the order has been processed, there is a procedure for removing carried-over items if they exceed a certain fixed percentage. The computer than prints out a picking list that the pickers in the warehouse can use to make up the order for shipping. It also prints out various sales reports and creates an input tape which is used in a later computer run to prepare a profit and loss statement. (This creation of an input tape shows that the company's overall system is modular rather than integrated).

A number of subsidiary flow charts will be required at this stage. Exhibit 2 shows one for the substitution subroutine for this same system. It shows the procedures used to substitute other merchandise if the style number ordered is not available.

INTERFACE WITH USERS.   The flow charts must be accompanied by a list of the key assumptions and decisions made. For example, in this greeting card order processing system, a key decision is what percentage of the order can be items carried over from the last year. If the percentage is too small, the company will be unable to get rid of its excess inventory. If the percentage is too large, the customer will get angry because he is getting too many items that are a little out of style, and probably are left over because they didn't sell very well the year before. This is a prime example of the need for user involvement. This decision cannot be left to the systems analyst, but rather should be made by the marketing department. Another example of a key decision would be the means of determining the related styles for substitution purposes and their order in the substitution table shown in Exhibit 2.

If the assumptions and decisions are not adequately thought out and discussed with the users, there will be difficulties. In this example, user involvement was inadequate and a faulty assumption in the flow chart [Exhibit 1] was found only after the system was running. It was assumed that if no substitute was found within certain constraints, that portion of the order still unfilled would be cancelled. However some customers, such as supermarkets, were more interested in receiving the total amount they ordered rather than in receiving specific styles ordered. Therefore, the system had to be modified to include a fill-to-dollar total subroutine for these customers to insure they got the quantities ordered.

It is important to think the gross design through carefully and get it done right before moving on to the next stage, because modifications can be very expensive once the detailed design work and the programming have started. In this greeting card example, some of the early programming had to be scrapped because, after the programming had started, someone had the bright idea that it would save a lot of expense to drop back orders under $10 in size.

It is also important at this stage to develop rough estimates of the run times involved. In the greeting card case, the company did not do this,

EXHIBIT 2

Flow Chart of Substitution Subroutine

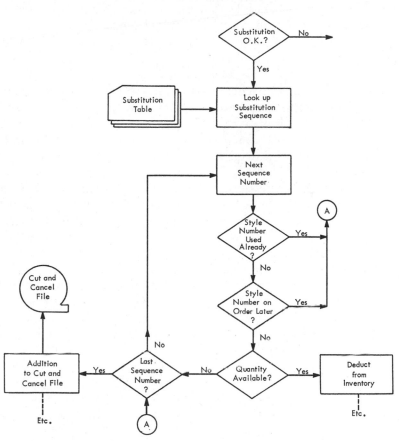

1. Entire substitution table stored in internal memory.
2. Entire order in internal memory.
3. Finished goods inventory on disk.

and incurred the unforeseen expense of purchasing additional internal computer memory capacity to store inventory status information. Referencing the inventory status on random access storage proved to take too long. In another example, a major oil company found itself faced with a costly system modification effort when a system which had to produce output twelve hours after the input was received actually took eighteen hours to run.

The system specification team should specify the basic procedures for off-line data storage, for security of the information, and what to do in case of hardware failure, although this is not really part of the system design. The procedures for off-line storage and for protection of data against accidental destruction can be very important because the loss of some key data, for example the tapes containing records of orders received but not yet shipped, could be disastrous. These procedures are discussed in greater detail in Chapter 30, "Information storage and processing." Preserving the security of the information would, if necessary, involve limiting access to stored information to authorized individuals.

Some contingency plan for failures is necessary because computers are like any other kind of machinery—they break down. If the resulting delay in the operation of the system is unimportant, the contingency plan can be to call the repair man and wait. If necessary, back-up systems can be developed. Their cost should be balanced off against the importance of running the application in question promptly.

INTERFACE WITH HARDWARE SELECTION.   The available hardware and its cost will, of course, limit the gross design of the system as will the nature of the available vendor-supplied software. Problems with the detailed design of the system will influence the selection of the hardware and of the vendor. In general, however, the selection of the basic hardware and a particular vendor should be dictated by the requirements of the system developed in the first stage of the software design. The request for proposal should be based on the requirements of this first stage. The second stage should take the hardware largely as a given, and the third stage, program writing, should take it entirely as a given also.

Preparation of the request for proposal

The following paragraphs will describe a specification format which can be followed in developing a system specification for presentation to vendors as a request for proposal (RFP).

System objectives

The functions to be performed by the new system should be described in general terms. A brief description of present systems and procedures used to carry out these functions should be included with a summary of the deficiencies and problems which the new system is expected to correct. A discussion of growth possibilities and anticipated useful system life will aid the vendor in judging expansion possibilities based on the long-term expectations for the system.

The application specifications portion of the system specification contains the description of user information requirements to enable the vendor to establish specific design features and system capabilities. A guideline is suggested which will subject each application to a type of screening analysis which will help to assure that only those applications worth considering are included in the RFP. Although the initial RFP may not require this level of detail, it will be required for final system design and program development. For the users, the development of this information will serve as critique of the applications and help to insure a sound statement of requirements. In many instances, such an analysis will result in immediate improvements in existing procedures and methods and may enable early introduction of new procedures based on anticipated changes under a new system. This is a reflection of the fact that many of the benefits of introducing a new computer system can come from the required logical and rigorous thinking-through of procedures used, rather than from the use of the computer itself.

Contents of the application specification

The application specification prepared for the RFP should include statements of the purpose of the application, its environment, and its major inputs and outputs. The statement of purpose should include a description of the objectives to be accomplished by the information flow defined in this specification. The summary of the inputs and outputs should indicate in general terms how the specification objectives are to be accomplished. The description of the concept should include descriptions of the types of hardware needed, the system interdependencies, and the constraints on the system. A statement of organizational responsibilities for preparing input information and taking action, or otherwise using output information, is useful, and this stage will be necessary at later stages of system specification development.

CONCEPT. *Hardware.* Provide a detailed description of the number and type of computer peripheral and remote input/output devices required for this application, regardless of whether or not these devices are also defined for use with other applications.

System interdependencies. There should be cross references to all other application specifications, by name, providing input to, or receiving output from, this specification.

Constraints. Include a statement of any significant conditions or assumptions which limit the scope of this application specification. Such contraints may be imposed by company policy, hardware capabilities, or limitations of other application specifications.

INPUTS. Each input operation should be described individually by the following:

1. Title of input.
2. Purpose of input.
3. Input hardware device or devices utilized and whether remote or processor site.
4. Special input hardware requirements, including a description of unique equipment functional capabilities and purpose.
5. Description of each input item, including the average and maximum number of characters for each item and whether the item is mandatory or optional. For each pure numeric item, include the range of values. For example, a pure numeric item with a maximum of four characters might have a range of values 0001–2999.
6. Input message format, including detailed samples, and the average and maximum number of characters per input transaction.
7. Average and maximum number of input transactions per hour by time of day for both normal and nonroutine demand situations.
8. Job turnaround or response time requirements during peak periods for normal and nonroutine demand situations.
9. Source of input information, form at source, and description of source document, if any.
10. Physical location of hardware and responsibility, by job title, for input operation.

OUTPUTS.   Each output operation will be described individually by the following:
1. Title of output.
2. Purpose of output.
3. Output hardware device or devices utilized and whether remote or processor site.
4. Special output hardware requirements, including a description of unique functional capabilities and purpose.
5. If output information is automatically generated, describe triggering condition, e.g., time of day, receipt of certain information, control limit reached, etc.
6. Description of each output item, showing format and average and maximum number of characters for each item. Include the range of values for each pure numeric item. For reports generated, detailed samples should be included to show format.
7. Frequency of report preparation, such as daily, weekly, monthly; or, for remote locations, the average and maximum number of output messages per hour by time of day for both normal and nonroutine demand situations.
8. Job turnaround or response time requirements during peak periods for normal and nonroutine demand situations.
9. Physical location of hardware and responsibility, by job title, for acting on output information.

10. Multiple copy or special hard copy forms required at output location.
11. Distribution of hard copy output information.

DATA STORAGE. The following is not intended to be an exhaustive treatment of data storage, and the reader is referred to Chapter 30, "Information processing" for further discussion.

A description of the random access data files should include the following:

1. Title of data file.
2. Purpose of data file.
3. Description of each item in a record to be stored. This must include the maximum number of characters for alpha or alpha-numeric items, and the range of values, such as 001–999, for numeric items.
4. Maximum number of records stored. If number of records varies hourly or daily, provide average and maximum number of items stored by time of day for normal and nonroutine demand situations.
5. Length of time data to be retained in random access storage, such as "until one hour after input," or "until revised by new input operation."
6. Disposition at end of retention period, such as "destroy" or "store off-line." Off-line storage refers to magnetic tape, disk packs, punch cards, or hard copy media.
7. Definition of key item in each record of the data file for accessing the record.

USE OF TABLES. The various statistical data regarding input/output volumes, record lengths, storage, equipment and location requirements, job turnaround time, response time, reliability, etc. should be summarized in appropriate tables for easy reference. The need for tables and their design can be determined by the reader, based on the requirements of the system under consideration.

System organization

PROCESSOR CONSIDERATIONS. Any preference for a centrally located data processing complex or regionalized systems interconnected with data communications channels should be stated.

The vendor should be provided with guidance regarding the need to consider system redundancy in meeting the reliability performance requirements defined in this specification. The need for alternate commercial or auxiliary generator power systems should be indicated.

Any processor configuration preferences, such as multiprocessor or multiprogram capability, shared high-speed core or low-speed bulk core, accessibility of mass storage and peripheral devices to multiprocessors, etc., should be stated.

COMMUNICATIONS CONSIDERATIONS. If remote on-line terminals are planned, provide a list of the offices to be equipped and their location addresses within each city. The range of data communications line speeds required, information code preferences for interfacing with the various types of input/output devices and other computer systems should be described.

Any preference for error detection and correction capability should be stated. Possible schemes in use are character parity and/or block parity, cyclic error checking, and automatic retransmission of input and/or output.

The desirability for standby communications line capability for ready fallback in case of line failure should be stated. Vendor equipment interfaces can be provided to enable standby lines to be connected in an active state and used directly for overflow during peak traffic periods. Also standby dial-up capability might be utilized as a means of establishing communications in the event of primary channel failure. A general statement that vendor equipment design must be compatible with normally available common carrier facilities and must be able to operate within the characteristics specified for such facilities should be included.

REMOTE INPUT/OUTPUT TERMINAL CONSIDERATIONS. The RFP should state types of input/output devices required, i.e., cathode ray tube sets, hard copy printers, teletype send/receive units with or without paper tape, card readers, card punches, data collection devices, etc. Specific operating speed and functional capabilities desired for each type of device, particularly any unique operating functions or operator visual/audio alerts, should be detailed. Character set, special symbol requirements for display and printing units, and any special format control considerations should also be described.

The need for free-standing, self-contained units, or for multiple units which can share a common control unit at a given location, should be indicated. The RFP should describe maximum cabling distance preference, and any status-assurance provisions desired to determine operating condition of remote units.

Any size, weight, mobility, or other physical constraints related to input/output terminal installations, as well as associated control units, should be indicated. The RFP should also include temperature and humidity environment ranges under which equipment is expected to operate satisfactorily. Any noise limitations necessary for operator comfort or ease of operation should be indicated.

Standards for system performance

Specific performance standards which the vendor would be expected to guarantee should be described for each part of the system—central processor site, remote control equipment, and remote input/output terminals. The description should include the hours of operation under which each location on the system will be operated. The three basic performance categories to be considered are: accuracy, reliability, and speed. It should be recognized that high performance in one or more of these categories will add cost to the system. Any performance requirements should, therefore, be carefully considered in keeping with actual needs and impact on the use of the system. It is idealistic to set high standards of performance, but the added costs should be compared against the losses, if any, that may result if lesser performance were realized.

ACCURACY. The RFP should define the allowable level of errors not automatically detected and corrected by the system. This level can be expressed as a percentage of total daily transactions. With a minimum of hardware and/or software protection, an undetected error rate of 1 in 100,000 characters can readily be realized at a reasonable cost for this protection capability.

The RFP should also indicate the variations from normal in data communications line quality under which this level of performance is to be maintained. Since this depends on the types of lines, line speeds, and, to some extent, on the local conditions involved, telephone company assistance should be requested to establish the range of conditions that might be expected on the telephone data facilities to be ordered.

The extent to which programming, hardware, or operator action can be used to assist in maintaining this performance, level should be indicated. In the more sophisticated systems, a minimum of operator intervention is necessary. Programming and hardware provisions are used to achieve system performance, with cost of hardware versus programming load on the system determining which method would be most advantageous in the given system.

RELIABILITY. The RFP should define the number of outages allowable and the return-to-service time permissible for each part of the system over a given period of months. A clear definition of what constitutes an outage chargeable to the vendor should be developed to delineate between operator, environment, or communications causes.

Outage rates and return-to-service times are determined to a great extent by the quality of electrical components used and redundancy provided. Availability of maintenance service is also an important factor. Since each of these affects costs, care should be used in attempting to achieve trouble-free operation. Inherent reliability of business equipment can be expected to achieve at least 2,000 hours, or approximately three months, of trouble-free operation between failures without incurring excessive costs. Maintenance service to effect return-to-service in two to four hours is also not unreasonable to expect.

Installation environment also has an effect on equipment reliability. Temperature and humidity environment control requirements for computer equipment are quite critical and are specified by the vendor. Remote control equipment and input/output devices, however, should be designed to operate over a wider range of conditions, depending on the local facility conditions expected from the customer's application. The RFP should specify the variations in power and environment under which the equipment is expected to operate. Equipment capability to withstand momentary and long-term power variations of ± 10 percent in voltage and ± 0.5 cycles frequency are standard. Environment ranges covering temperatures of 40° to 95° F. and relative humidity of 5 to 95 percent are also tolerable conditions under which equipment should be expected to operate satisfactorily. Ranges beyond these are also achievable in equipment design at some added cost, which may be less than the cost for a controlled environment.

The locations where alternate power, fallback equipment, and line fallback capability are to be utilized should be stated, and the conditions under which routine maintenance and equipment shutdown will be permitted at specific locations should be specified.

SPEED.   Speed, as defined here, refers to response time at remote input/output terminals under given transaction volumes, and to production rates or job turnaround times of off-line processor batch or data base updating operations.

Remote terminal response time is usually stated in average seconds or minutes, with a percentage of calls allowed to exceed the average. Response time can be defined as answer time from moment of input request, or as delivery time from entry of information, from one terminal to receipt at another. Response times of less than ten seconds are readily achievable, with three to five seconds quite commonly available at a nominal cost.

Central site production time can be stated by describing the various types of reports, batch jobs, and operations in a given period of hours, or over a 24-hour period. This requirement can also be stated by indicating the reports required at a given time of the day, assuming all inputs are provided by a certain preceding hour, i.e., inputs received by 0000, reports available by 0800.

System tests

The RFP should contain a description of the type of performance tests the vendor will be expected to demonstrate before the system is accepted and placed in operation. These tests can be generally categorized as: *component and subsystem tests* to check the functional capability and individual unit design specifications; *programming tests* to demonstrate that various vendor-supplied programs are operating properly and to determine processor overhead; and *overall system tests,* including application programs, under controlled traffic conditions to measure accuracy, reliability, and response time performance capability.

The end objective of these tests is to observe and measure actual performance of the job expected of the system under as near a live environment as possible. Vendor diagnostic routines and simulations should not be accepted as adequate demonstration of system performance. The final applications and vendor-supplied programs on the equipment configuration to be utilized is the best assurance that the customer is getting what he is buying. These tests should be developed jointly and agreed to as early as possible to avoid any last minute disageements. If any disagreements do arise, customer satisfaction should be the governing factor.

Vendor support

The type and extent of manpower support the vendor will be expected to furnish during the implementation period, as well as during the expected life of the system, should be described. As part of the RFP, the vendor should be requested to furnish a complete rundown of manpower and other support that the vendor is willing to commit to the project.

An important consideration is the early availability of processor equipment for program debugging and system checkout. Obtaining vendor commitment to make available adequate system capability for program checkout and system tests well in advance of the planned implementation date at readily accessible locations is absolutely essential. This requirement should be spelled out beforehand, and the extent of vendor commitment should be a major consideration in vendor selection.

Vendor programming support in the form of standard routines for random access storage and magnetic tape file control, punch card and line printer input/output operation, operating system control, and communications line control are generally provided as part of the computer system. There is a trend lately for these programs to be furnished as extra cost items. A review of available vendor-supplied programs, their cost and suitability for use in the system under consideration should be determined. These programs can usually be used with little or no modification at substantially lower cost than can be realized by user development. In many cases, the vendor will also undertake to write the applications programs and provide the total software and hardware package as a turnkey operation.

Contract considerations

Final acceptance of a vendor proposal will involve developing a contractual document which incorporates all the ageements, terms, and conditions under which the proposed system will be furnished. As part of the vendor responses to the RFP, the vendors should be asked to submit a copy of the contract they would propose to use for this propose. An alternate approach would be for the user's legal staff to submit a draft copy of contract for comment by the vendor when he submits his proposal. It is advisable to explore the contractual positions of both vendor and user early in the evaluation process since satisfactory terms and conditions could become a significant influence in the final selection of a system.

Following are a number of areas for consideration in a contract document. The objective is to put in writing the understandings of both party's commitments and responsibilities in legal terms to minimize any later differences of interpretation.

1. Intended use of the system and range of possibilities.
2. Conditions under which the system will be furnished, and any limitations that the vendor feels are reasonable.
3. Guarantees of performance.
4. Delivery, installation, and acceptance.
5. Maintenance of the system.
6. Terms and conditions under which additional components, modifications of components, or removal of components will be accomplished.
7. Title to equipment purchase option.
8. Payment of sales and use taxes.
9. Liability, indemnity, and insurance.
10. Patent indemnity.
11. Default by seller or buyer and definition of excusable delays.
12. Priority rights, advertising, and promotions.
13. Assignment.
14. Entirety of agreement—description of all documents comprising the agreement and an understanding of which document takes precedence in the event conflicting terms arise.

Information storage and processing

John F. Dudas*

As a company grows there is a corresponding growth in the volume of business data which must be processed. And as a company's operations become more complicated, as competitive pressures increase, and as government reporting requirements become more extensive, there evolves a need for processing more varied and more complex data, and for processing it in a manner which will produce useful analyses and summaries more quickly. Thus the normal development of a company is accompanied by a need for processing more rapidly and more efficiently a larger and more complex mass of business information.

How best to meet this need will depend upon the problems and circumstances of the particular company, but in each case the best solution will require an evaluation of the various methods which can be used to collect and process data, including consideration of the cost and capability of the various types of data communication and data processing equipment.

In general the solution to the problem of more rapidly processing this larger and more complex mass of business information requires one or more of the following:

1. A more powerful central processor with larger and faster core memory.
2. Faster input/output transfer rates for devices such as magnetic tape drives and mass storage units.
3. Effective use of alternative input/output devices in application programming.

---

* Manager Technical Planning, Westinghouse Tele-Computer Center, Pittsburgh.

4. Independent utility functions of card reading, card punching, and printing, operating concurrently with main task processes.
5. More efficient sort/merge software utilizing the media of mass storage devices.
6. A more efficient software control system to reduce the central-processor overhead required for job scheduling, job flow and input/output device control.

In much the same manner that excessive overhead cost acts as a profit detractor to a manufacturing plant, so does excessive control-system overhead act as a production detractor to a data processing installation. Also of significance is a substantial reduction in the amount of central-processor core memory required for the control system, thereby making more core memory available for productive tasks.

Since most users must depend upon the software control system supplied by the computer manufacturer, only Items 1–5 will be discussed in this chapter, with emphasis on concurrent utility functions and efficient sort/merge software.

The key to the solution of the problem of collecting, processing, and making available to management more current data lies in the integration of the following concepts:

1. Advanced application system design.
2. Data bank structure.
3. Communications-oriented central processors.
4. On-line inquiry devices.
5. Data collection/dispersal networks.

To cover the important aspects of these concepts requires background information on data storage devices and their usage.

Information storage and files

In a computer system all data must be recorded in a machine-sensible form of storage before it can be read into the central processor for manipulation. Storage media may be thought of as a completely indexed, easily accccessible electronic filing cabinet. The most widely used machine-sensible storage media are punched cards, magnetic tape, punched paper tape, and mass-storage magnetic disks and drums.

Taken individually, the read/write speed of devices that interface the storage media with the central processor is relatively slow when compared to processor core speed. However, many processing tasks require data from and to a number of storage devices. These needs can best be satisfied by the concurrent operation of devices through separate data paths (called data channels) or through a multiplexed data path (called a multiplexor channel) that permits simultaneous transmission of two or more independent data signals. The number and type of data channels should therefore be a serious consideration in the selection of a central processor system.

Storage media characteristics

A. PUNCHED CARDS. The punched card is one of the most successful media for communication with computers. Information in cards is recorded by a card punching machine and read or interpreted by a card reader. Data resulting from computer processing are punched into cards by a computer-controlled punching device. Cards are generally considered to be a fixed data length medium—27, 51 or 80 columns (alphabetic or numeric characters) per card. Information is updated or modified by punching new cards. Large data files of punched cards for manual and/or machine manipulation may be practical depending on:

1. Need for visual reference. (Punched holes can be interpreted and printed in alphanumeric representation.)
2. Need for interim updating. (Repunching manually only the new information and automatically reproducing the unchanged data.)
3. Care and orderliness in handling to permit re-entry of cards into a computer as desired.
4. Needs and economics that dictate a card processor installation is all that is required. This type of computer installation usually consists of a small central processor with a card reader, card punch and line printer.

Computer-controlled card reading and punching equipment is considered to be in the low speed data transfer range of from 100 characters/second to 2700 characters/second (80 to 2000 cards/minute.)

Punched cards are also used extensively for preparation of both data transactions (such as receipts and issues for an inventory control application) and program instructions for all sized computer systems.

B. MAGNETIC TAPE. Magnetic tape units have for many years filled the need for high speed input/output devices to satisfy the ever-increasing internal speeds of computers. One reel of 2400 ft. magnetic tape can store in excess of 400,000 80-column card images which can be transferred to or received from a central processor at a rate of up to 320,000 characters/second. Information, which is recorded as magnetic spots on the reel of tape, may be variable in data record length. Since writing on magnetic tape is destructive, that is, old information is destroyed, data update requires reading (which is non-destructive) the old information from one reel of tape and writing the desired combination of unchanged and updated information on a new tape. This characteristic provides the means for master data file preservation frequently called the "Grandfather-Father-Son" system where the "Grandfather" tape is two generations removed from the currently updated tape ("Son"). In order adequately to protect information whose loss would be disastrous, the more recent of the outdated master files should always be stored in a physically separate location, together with the source transactions necessary to update that data file to current status ("Son").

The mode of processing data using magnetic tapes is in sequential order, much the same as a personal tape recording unit. When a specific item of data is desired, the tape must be passed serially until that recording spot has been reached. Hence all transactions to be processed against a magnetic tape data file must be presequenced (sorted) to the key (called the argument) of the master data file.

The data transfer rate for magnetic tape devices ranges from 10,000 characters/second to 320,000 characters/second. Information on tape is structured on the basis of an arbitrary number of logical records (called items) grouped into one physical record (called a block). The decision on this blocking factor is critical in attempting to obtain optimum tape read and write rates, presuming the central processor's core size and instruction execution rate are adequate.

A number of keyboard-to-magnetic-tape units called "inscribers" have been marketed in recent years to replace manually-operated punched-card machines. Either "inscribers" or punched cards can be used effectively to get the initial data onto magnetic tape for subsequent processing.

Magnetic tape, then, is an accepted and effective storage medium,

1. For inexpensive off-line storage of large data files in machine sensible form. Tape costs less than one-tenth that of an equivalent number of cards and can be used over and over. However, the relatively inexpensive and one-time cost of tape should not be confused with the relatively expensive monthly rental charge for magnetic tape processing units.
2. For high speed transfer of sequenced data to and from a computer.
3. For reasonably efficient temporary storage of data during computerized sort/merge processes. These temporary storage tapes are generally referred to as "scratch" tapes as the data recorded on them is no longer useful after the computer run has been completed. Scratch tapes may then be reused at the operator's discretion.

C. Punched paper tape. Punched paper tape may be effectively used as a data storage medium in some instances. Paper tape is cheaper and more compact than punched cards (although not as compact as magnetic storage) and consequently less expensive to store and to transport.

And, like magnetic tape, it does not have the card's fixed length dimension. As few characters as desired may be used, and if more than 80 characters are required no trailer card penalty is incurred as in punched cards where space and time are expended to duplicate identification and codes prior to continuing the data.

Paper tape may frequently be produced as a by-product from the following sources without incurring the delay, expense and errors of the key punch/key verify steps:

a) Shop data collection stations.

b) Adding machine punches.

c) Flexowriter or computyper hard copy printers.

In addition, paper tape can be used to store data for operating numerically controlled machine tools. These paper tapes can be manually keypunched or can be an output from a highly sophisticated computer program. In many small computer installations, paper tape is also used to store programs and constants for scientific analyses.

Paper-tape reading and punching equipment ranges in speed from 10 characters/second to 1,000 characters/second.

D. Optical Character Recognition (OCR). No discussion on computer input media would be complete without at least mentioning character recognition devices. Since the first optical scanner was put into service in 1955, the industry has been heralding optical character recognition as the breakthrough that would eliminate keypunching and verification—the input bottleneck of data processing. Yet today OCR input only equals about 1 percent of the present keypunch volume. Specialized systems such as magazine subscription, airlines ticket data gathering, and health/insurance service account for the great majority of installations. However, past performance is not necessarily an accurate indicator of future growth. It is almost impossible to find an area of volume paper flow related to data processing that would not benefit from OCR. Even the banking industry, though presently committed to magnetic ink character recognition (MICR), looks with favor on the greater flexibility of OCR.

The key to growing use of OCR is lower cost machines, and they will be coming. Coincident with lower cost machines will probably be a trend toward the use of large-scale OCR systems on a service-bureau basis, enabling many companies that may not have enough input volume of their own to enjoy the economic benefits of optical reading.

Basically, there are three types of optical character readers on the market today, with each involving its subsystems of paper transport, optical scanner and recognition.

1. Document readers, primarily used in "turnaround" systems where the output form becomes the input to the system at a later time.

2. Page readers, with greater reading flexibility.
3. Journal tape readers, which have wide appeal for the retail trade, perform a high-speed scan of cash register and adding machine tapes.

Making a case for page readers, one industry representative contends that a typist, with her typewriter, costs 20 percent less than a conventional key entry station and can produce up to 30 percent more data in the same period of time. Even critics of OCR generally agree that typists are easier to hire and train. They are not as unanimous in accepting sight verification as a replacement for key driven verification. Nor are they convinced of the necessity for the stringent document requirements imposed by OCR.

E. MASS STORAGE FILES.   For purposes of this chapter, mass storage files are designated to be computer-controlled devices, generally considered to be on-line (that is, under the direct control of the central processor) although many also have the valuable facility of serving as off-line storage (for example, removable disk packs). All are presumed to be capable of direct access, which means that the next position from which information is to be obtained is in no way dependent on the previous one. Therefore specific data can be referenced directly without the delay of serially processing (passing) unwanted data as required by magnetic tape. It is important to note, however, that these devices may also be used for sequential, partitioned sequential, indexed sequential, and address linkage processing.

As a simple analogy:

1. Sequential processing may be likened to starting at the beginning of a phone book and calling every number in sequence to find the ones you want.
2. Partitioned sequential processing may be likened to starting at the beginning of any desired alphabetic letter in a phone book and calling every number in sequence under that letter to find the ones you want, then continuing to any other desired letter. Another analogy might be the yellow pages of a phone book where independent groups of sequentially ordered data are identified by member names which in turn are in sequential order.
3. Indexed sequential processing may be likened to starting at the beginning of any desired alphabetic letter of a phone book, then searching each page heading for the desired page, then searching each page for the desired name. In addition, this organization also lets you insert new names by an overflow method without rewriting the entire book. With indexed sequential organization, numbers can be called sequentially as in 1. above, or individual numbers can be called directly through the search mechanism described.
4. Address linkage may be likened to being given the first number in the

string, from the first number obtaining the second, etc. This method is also frequently called chaining.

5. Direct address processing may be likened to specifying an actual address (or a relative address that can be converted to an actual address) for each name in a nonsequential phone book.

The available types of direct-access mass-storage devices may be divided into three general categories largely according to access time required and storage capacity. The small magnetic drum devices on today's market have storage capacities of up to ten million characters of data with the average access time (average time required to locate a given piece of data) ranging from 3½ to 20 milliseconds (thousandths of a second). These devices are the fastest and most expensive units per volume of storage in the categories referenced. Therefore, strict management control should be exercised over their use. They are generally used as auxiliary main computer memory for purposes of storing operating systems software routines, application program libraries, and queues of frequently referenced and dynamic data for real-time systems. They are also used to store address indices referencing larger, slower file systems.

The second level of mass-storage devices are the 20 to 200 millisecond access devices such as disk files, disk packs, large drums and other rotating electro-mechanical elements. These devices fall into the storage-capacity area between 20 and 170 million characters of information and cost considerably less per character of storage than the small magnetic drums. Usually data is recorded in fixed block or sector length. These units are used for the large file applications where access time requirements, the number of accesses and the time-conscious need for the information preclude the use of slower, less expensive mass storage devices or magnetic tape units. Another criterion for use is when a small percentage of the total file items require updating on a given application cycle and where output is predicated upon updated data only—for example, an inventory-control system with a daily processing cycle. Typically 10 percent or less of the master data file is affected by a day's transactions, and reports are prepared on an updated, exception, or trouble-indicator basis. In this example, only the specific file items to be changed are referenced and updated with no time wasted for passing and rewriting the 90 percent of file that is unchanged. Most of the discussion of mass storage files in this chapter will focus on this critical category.

The third category, bulk storage, has storage capacity from the hundreds of millions to billions of characters per unit and relatively slow access, usually in excess of 300 milliseconds. They are best applied in systems where very large files have relatively low access requirements, such as government records of Medicare participants or policy-holder records of large insurance companies, where only a very small number of the millions of records stored are required for a given processing cycle. An example of this type of device is the data cell.

Data bank concept of mass storage files

Construction of an effective data bank requires broad knowledge of management needs combined with technical knowledge of systems design, computer software (control system, device handlers, languages, etc.) and data control characteristics. Presuming that technical knowledge is resident or can be acquired on the open market, the key ingredient is the definition of needs by top management. These needs can then be categorized into (a) immediate accessibility, (b) short-term interrelationships and (c) longer term analyses, where immediate response may be measured in seconds and longer term analysis in weeks. Files structured from a common data base must be able to serve a variety of information needs in terms of content and time response. The problem with the common data base approach is that individual data files, which were previously engineered to minimize processing time, may become inefficient in the generalized restructuring. This can occur if, in the restructuring, (a) data records become excessively large and unwieldy, (b) numerous records are updated in a single transaction cycle irrespective of when the updated information is needed, or (c) an additional order of magnitude of data file accesses is imposed on the system. In view of today's technology and experience, a cautious approach is recommended.

A multi-file concept, linked by a common number, may satisfy management's needs better for the immediate future and still provide application interrelationship and sufficiently time-conscious reaction. This interim step could also supply valuable experience for future data management systems. A common numbering system would provide the base for an index file stored on a direct access device. Each common number record would contain the identification, location and storage device of each of the separate application file records that relate to the number. Each independent data file would be structured for the most efficient processing of that application considering the size of file, access requirements, response time for data requests, nature and frequency of processing, etc. Any application could have different levels of files depending on requirements. For instance, an on-line order-entry application could have separate data files for customers and master parts with lower level files for warehouse inventories, quantity discounts, alternate warehouses and general statistical data (which would be used to generate invoices, back orders, replenishment stock orders, sales statistics and cost and billing distribution). To further simplify the transition to the multi-file concept, input data transactions could continue to contain only the key of the specific application file to be processed. Initially then, the common number index record would provide only the means of gathering together all of the diverse pieces of data related to that number. The later transition from this multi-file concept to a pure data bank concept may then become more orderly, effective and definitive.

These comments are not intended to be a guide to the implementation of an advanced data bank concept. Books, seminars, and complete conferences are attempting to develop this controversial and complex subject.

Mass storage file protection and recovery

When properly used, magnetic tape by the nature of its recording, provides an automatic data file recovery. Not so with mass storage data files where newly updated data records are written in the same physical location previously occupied by the old record. Device malfunction, worker program error or systems software error may destroy data files. These files should be protected by periodic "dumping" or recording on an independent storage medium such as magnetic tape or mass storage. The main criterion in deciding the frequency of the file dump should be the amount of time needed to reconstruct the file should it be completely destroyed. Two points to consider are the size of the file, and the volume of daily transactions. Some methods for protecting and recovering daily updated files are as follows:

1. Record the "after image" of an updated item on an independent secondary storage device as well as on the primary file as each transaction is processed. Dump the secondary storage file to magnetic tape each night. Dump the entire primary data file, or progressive sections of it, on a weekly basis. Rotate these dump tapes through a physically separate storage location for added protection.
2. Record both the "before and after image" on an independent secondary storage device and follow remaining steps outlined in 1.
3. Dump the transactions periodically during the day and the entire data file nightly onto magnetic tape, thereby providing the ability to update the prior night's file in case of emergency. Rotate the dump tapes for both the transactions and the data file through a physically separate location.

Dumping data files alone, or both data files and transactions, may still not be sufficient to effect full recovery. Some installations capture transactions on two independent storage devices during the course of the day as a further safeguard. This procedure assures the ability to reprocess an entire day's transactions where critical data, such as product prices, have been incorrectly maintained on the master file. The decision on what procedure to follow becomes a matter of weighing cost and other facets of the problem against the calculated risk of failure.

The time to think about recovery programs is during systems design of the first on-line application. The time to fully implement these programs and procedures is before any application process using on-line files has been cut over to production status. File protection may be costly, but file destruction can be catastrophic.

Another aspect of file protection worthy of consideration is file security, or the procedure for assuring that only specifically designated personnel have access to confidential data files. Identification key or password codes are the most commonly accepted methods. Since any password can be broken, a readily changeable code should be structured to monitor periodically for unauthorized intruders.

Standards

With the continuous and rapid evolution of the field of computer processing the need for standards has become apparent. All computer installations cannot possible conform to the same standards, but it is recommended that a code of standards be established within a company or at least within an installation. That code should be unique, and consistent with requirements and environment. Standards are the rules under which systems analysts, programmers, and operators work. These rules should be in writing for the benefit of the new members of the organization. They should be rigidly enforced to assist in (a) changes to existing applications and computer systems, (b) maintenance of programs by new or existing staff personnel, (c) planning, costing, and time estimating of new work, (d) better understanding of existing work and (e) reduced errors and confusion in computer operations. Standards encompass languages, common numbering systems, library subroutines, utility programs, character sets, data transmission codes, flow chart symbols, vocabulary, data elements, programming practices, file labels, terminal identifications, and literally anything that contributes to quality control and continuity and uniformity of operation.

Where national or international standards exist, an organization should adopt these standards or at least work diligently toward their adoption. The United States of America Standards Institute[1] has approved and published many standards that are available upon request. In addition, many worthwhile seminars are conducted by consulting firms to aid in the establishment of sound standards.

Batch processing

In a batch process, similar transactions for an application are prepared in machine-sensible form and collected (batched) over a set time. At a predetermined time all transactions are processed against a master data

---

[1] United States of America Standards, 10 East 40th Street, New York, N.Y.

file to update files and prepare the required printed or card outputs. If the data file is recorded on magnetic tape, the updating transactions must first be sorted to the sequence of that file. If data is mass storage oriented, processing can take place on a direct access basis without sorting.

Growth of requirements

In view of the desired objective of having the best available price/performance equipment which is adequate for actual requirements, an installation may start with a card-oriented computer system, including only a card reader, line printer, and card punch. Master files are kept on punched cards and updating transaction cards are sorted to the prescribed sequence by off-line sorters prior to entry into the computer system. If the system does not have multiple card reader hoppers, the master file cards and the transaction cards are merged by an electro-mechanical collator.

The next stage of growth usually includes adding magnetic tape units and/or direct access mass storage units for storing and updating master information files. This stage usually requires (a) a more powerful central processor to utilize better the higher input/output speed of the added devices, and (b) a larger and faster core memory to control the new devices and to handle the longer and more inclusive data records. The reader, printer, and punch may still function under the direct control of the worker program. This means that the processing is hindered by the speed of the slowest device on the system—in this case a reader, punch, or printer that operates in tens of milliseconds impeding a central processor operation that executes in units of microseconds (millionths of a second).

When the operation of magnetic tape processing with direct reading, printing and punching is no longer adequate, two significant information-processing concepts should be implemented:

1. Direct card reading, line printing, and card punching should be removed from the worker programs for more effective throughput of data.
2. Sort/merge processing should become mass storage oriented to permit faster sequencing and merging of data.

Concurrent utility functions

The most effective and flexible way to divorce reading, punching, and printing (frequently called utility processes) from worker programs is by use of intermediate storage devices such as magnetic tape and mass storage.

As an example of this concept, printer line images which had previously been transmitted directly to the line printer from the worker program would instead be recorded on an intermediate storage device that operates at a far greater speed. Then at a later time, a utility program would perform the print image-to-printer function concurrent with the processing of another worker program. Three important advantages to this concept are:

1. The worker program executes far more rapidly because the relatively slow line-printer has been removed from its control. The fastest line-printer available today requires nearly 40 milliseconds per print line, during which time a central processor can execute from 1,500 to 30,000 program instructions depending on its internal cycle rate.
2. The worker program operates in a more reliable environment because it no longer is dependent on an electro-mechanical, trouble-prone printing device.
3. The utility printing function can be scheduled to meet specific demands better because the print data can be retrieved and printed on a priority basis irrespective of the worker program currently being processed.

Utility programs for reading, punching, and printing in this manner should be provided as a part of the computer manufacturer's software support. The manufacturer's software control system should have the capability of performing all utility functions at the rated speeds of the reader, punch and printer devices concurrent with at least one worker program.

Efficient sort/merge software

Generally, business reports are required to be printed in a detailed sequence different from that of the master data file. Take the example of a payroll system. The master data file is usually stored in sequence by Social Security Number; the payroll checks are printed in pay station and name sequence; union lists in union, location and name sequence; state Form 941A in state and Social Security Number sequence; internal distribution of pay in budget number sequence, etc. As a result of these requirements, approximately 70 percent of all computer programs for business applications must include data sort/merge routines. The software should be provided by the computer manufacturer, and must possess two key abilities in order to be efficient.

1. The ability to (a) audit the input data for errors and inconsistencies and to edit it to the desired format and content prior to sorting and (b) to rearrange the sequenced output from the sort into the final printer format. These three phases of (a) input audit and edit, (b)

sort and (c) output edit should be automatically linked to give the effect of one operating program.

2. The sort routine itself must have the ability to capitalize on the unique advantages inherent in direct access, mass storage devices. Sorting efficiency is a function of (a) internal processor speed for sequencing strings of data (items to be sorted) (b) processor main memory size for number and length of strings and, (c) storage media for interim recording, collecting and merging of strings. With magnetic tape the number of strings recorded is limited to the physical number of magnetic tape units available. Mass storage devices with direct access capability are limited only by their capacity, speed of access and data transfer rates. As many data strings as are practical without unbalancing the key input/output elements in the system may be stored for merging. Performance improvements over magnetic tape of from 1.5/1 to 8/1 are achievable.

Communications-oriented processing

One of the first considerations of communications-oriented processing is whether or not it is needed. Assuredly, this mode of processing adds dollars of cost to both central and remote sites in the form of communications lines, line interfaces and communications data sets. Only the management of today's complex businesses can make this decision. The choice becomes obvious when rapid collection, processing, and subsequent use of business data is imperative for serving customers and for maintaining close management surveillance over critical activities. However, before designing a computer-oriented data communication system a study should be conducted to question the real purpose and need for each type of data.[2] Only then can the most suitable configuration for a data communications system be determined.

Terminal equipment capabilities must be referenced within the general speed groupings offered by the common carrier.

1. *Teletype or telegraph*—low-speed channel capable of transmission rates up to 10 characters/second. These lines can be interfaced to computers on one end and to teletypewriters, paper tape transmitters, paper tape punches, punched card converters and teletype message generators at the remote end. Information can usually be prepared off-line, and can include automatic preparation of hard copy and punched paper tape for on-line transmission after visual verification. Completely off-line devices for paper tape to card or card to paper tape are also available.

2. *Voice grade or telephone*—medium-speed channel capable of transmission rates up to 1200 characters/second although current technol-

---

[2] Refer to Chapter 29. "Development of system specifications."

ogy limits transmission to 600 characters/second. This should be a significant area of growth because of the wide range of devices and small computers currently available for terminal use. Character and line printers, magnetic tape readers and recorders, key depression machines, paper tape readers and punches, card readers and punches and cathode ray tube displays are all available as stand alone devices for direct communication with a central computer installation. If greater capability is required, a number of small computers are available to serve as remote terminals. Printing speeds up to 600 lines per minute and card reading speeds up to 600 cards per minute are achievable today.

3. *Wideband*—high-speed channel capable of transmission rates up to 6800 characters/second. This rate implies terminal use of a small-to-medium scale computer capable of simultaneously driving two 1100 line per minute printers, a 1000 card per minute reader and a 300 card per minute punch at rated speeds. Since a terminal computer system of this type implies a cost roughly equivalent to that of a free-standing small/medium computer, a thorough study is required to determine that the linkage to a more powerful central computer is desirable, economical and practical.

Types of communications-oriented processing

A. ON-LINE REAL TIME SYSTEMS.   On-line real time systems have been defined many different ways by many different people. For purposes of this chapter "on-line" pertains to local or remote terminal equipment which is connected to a transmission line under control of and in direct communication with the central processing unit. "Real time system" is the ability to process incoming transactions on a transaction-by-transaction basis as that transaction occurs, to update on-line files, and to respond in accordance with the need for current data.

For effectiveness and efficiency, on-line real time systems are usually associated with a computer operating under a multiprogramming monitor and control system. Multiprogramming provides the ability to process concurrently, within one computer, diverse incoming transactions as well as other related or unrelated tasks under a predetermined priority scheme.

A productive multiprogramming real time system that can serve as an example is one which concurrently performs teletype message switching, and many other real-time and batch data gathering and processing functions. Two primary disciplines were imposed on this system. First, no real-time process was permitted to directly reference central site magnetic tape units, readers, punches, or printers for reasons of reliability, speed, and stability. Only the very reliable and fast mass-storage devices were used for real-time processing. In the opinion of the management of this installation, magnetic tape did not qualify, even though this storage medium had been used effectively at other real-time installations. And second, no batch worker program was permitted to directly reference readers, punches, or printers, implying that these devices functioned under utility processes. This system features fixed memory partitions and a processing priority structure as follows:

Priority	Process	Type of Process
1.	Message Switching Input	Real-Time Demand
2.	Message Switching Output	Real-Time Queue
3.	On-line Inquiry	" " "
4.	On-line Order Entry	" " "
5.	On-line Finance	" " "
6.	⎧ Any combination of three	Utility
7.	⎨ card-to-tape, tape-to-printer,	
8.	⎩ tape-to-card type operations	
9.	Any magnetic tape or mass storage task	Batch

Each of the above tasks was assigned a fixed portion of central processor memory, hence the term "fixed partition."

In this example, teletype message switching is the primary real time application although voice-grade communication capability is also provided for certain inquiry devices and remote computer linkages. A message is either "administrative" to be forwarded or "data" to be processed. Appropriate action is taken by the programs, based upon analysis of the message heading format. Since incoming messages enter the system at the discretion of remote terminals, they demand priority over outgoing messages that are under the complete control of the central processor.

Inquiry messages from any station on the network are initiated through use of a teletype machine keyboard, a teletype message generator, or a cathode ray tube device, then queued to the On-line Inquiry process for immediate access to currently updated data contained in on-line mass storage files. Answers are formatted and routed back through message switching where they are queued ahead of all waiting administrative traffic on outgoing lines. The teletype message generator used extensively in this system is a dial device supplied by the common carrier that (a) permits visual verification of data prior to transmission (b) automatically generates the encodement necessary to identify the station and to enter a specific teletype system and (c) properly terminates the message. Typical inquiries are for stock status of any part at any warehouse, or for any of the financial or order data contained in on-line files.

The fourth priority covers actual processing and filling of orders entered from remote sales offices. Once the order passes the initial editing checks, other routines are automatically brought into the same partitioned area to execute the main processing required to fill the order. The customer's record is looked up in the mass storage file and validated, the product identifications are checked and validated, and the warehouse record is checked to determine if sufficient stock is available at the preferred warehouse, normally the warehouse nearest the customer. If sufficent stock is available, the record is updated, the order review point checked for a possible break, and the item is priced and costed. If stock is not available at the preferred warehouse, the program automatically calls in an alternate warehouse procedure that searches additional warehouses between the preferred warehouse and the manufacturing plant.

After the order has satisfied all of the conditions of the main processing run, another routine immediately generates complete shipping instructions in teletype message format and transfers this information into the message switching program, which in turn queues it with other messages for the line that services the designated warehouse.

Certain necessary controls are built into this and other real time applications. For instance:

1. Each transaction transmitted has a unique data number assigned to protect against loss.
2. The customer number has a precalculated self-check digit attached to the basic five digit customer identification. The customer file is sought using only the five basic digits of the transmitted six digit number but validated against all six digits.
3. Both a part number and an independent part identifier are transmitted so that one is used for file seeking and the other for validation.
4. All outgoing transmissions are numbered in sequence by receiving stations and are centrally logged and available for automatic retrieval and retransmission upon request.

Priority number five is for a similar type of on-line file update process for financial applications such as Cash Management and Financial Closings.

Next are utility functions oriented to magnetic tape or mass storage devices and used for printing, card reading and punching. Note that these functions are independent of the worker programs that processed and formatted the data. Therefore, these relatively slow devices have not inhibited the speed with which the worker tasks could be completed. The last priority is used for either a magnetic tape or a mass-storage-oriented batch process.

The keys to the effectiveness of this multiprogram processing are (a) sufficient central processor memory for effectively partitioning, (b) balancing of independently channeled on-line mass storage devices with central processor speed, and, (c) designing and implementing applications that have a favorable balance of input/output and internal compute requirements. Periodic analysis of the data flow is necessary to uncover potential bottlenecks before they adversely affect processing.

B. Remote entry with centralized control of batch processes. In this category, transactions are collected or prebatched at a number of remote points and transmitted in controlled lots to a central computer system. The transactions are used as inputs to centralized applications that are systemized, programmed, scheduled, initiated and controlled by a central group. Output reports may be transmitted as a part of a computerized collection/dispersal system or may be mailed depending upon urgency of need and volume.

Examples of this type of batch process are a centralized accounts payable application and a centralized payroll application. While these specific applications are usually magnetic tape oriented tasks, other applications may be better suited to mass-storage batch processing, with real-time inquiry into frequently updated files.

C. Remote entry with remote control of batch processes. With this concept the central facility is available to the remote user as though it were located at his site. Each user develops, codes and debugs programs, and schedules his own application processing. Programs, data files and batched transactions may be transmitted by the remote user at his discretion using processing priorities assigned to him. Programs and data files may also be stored centrally and called by the remote user as a part of his transmission of data transactions. The user may encounter scheduling conflicts at the central site but these are usually no more severe in terms of elapsed time than if he used a less powerful processor at his own site. The input card reader at the remote site is treated by the system as equal in priority to a card reader at the central site.

Examples of this remote control type of batch process are Factory Labor Distribution and Factory Production Scheduling/Material Breakdown/Inventory Control[3] systems where problems may be best known and solved at a local plant level, but where processing efficiencies may best be achieved by using the power of a centralized computer facility.

D. Integration of on-line and batch processes. As a part of the study and development of on-line real-time processes, all applications related to the real-time transactions should be reviewed. In an order-entry system, for example, statistical data from the processing of each transaction may be stored (batched), then extracted and used as direct input to allied informations systems for:

1. Invoice preparation (several times daily)
2. Disposition lists of filled and unfilled orders (several times daily)
3. Replenishment stock requisitions using order review point and economical order quantity formulae (daily)
4. Order Follow (daily)

---

[3] Refer to Chapter 43, "Inventory management and control."

5. Accounts Receivable (semi-weekly)
6. Cost and billing distribution (weekly)
7. Sales statistics (weekly)

The ability to pass data mechanically from one computerized application to another eliminates a high percentage of the errors prevalent in a manual-intervention system. Moreover, with a communications-oriented processor, selected data outputs from any application may be transmitted to remote locations. This combination of systems integration and communications capability provides a mobility of products, data and people heretofore unknown.

E. TIME SHARING.   Before we leave communications-oriented methods of processing, one rapidly growing segment called "time sharing" must be discussed. Time sharing is a way of making the power of large computers directly available to a number of users, using low-cost typewriters for input and output, and standard voice-grade or sub-voice lines for communications. In effect, the processor power is split equally among a large number of widely separated users so that each user has the illusion of having the central computer at his immediate disposal. Thus the delays in service that normally accompany the use of batch processing systems are eliminated. Perhaps even more important to the remote user is the elimination of messenger and mail service delays.

Time sharing services today are primarily directed toward the solution of small-to-medium sized scientific problems. The services are provided by (a) entrepreneurs who establish computing centers within the reach of desirable geographic areas, (b) universities for education and training, and (c) large companies for in-house capability. The languages used to communicate the problem to the computer are usually mathematics-oriented, designed for ease of learning and of statement of the problem. The man-machine interaction of these systems provides direct and instantaneous answers designed to assist and stimulate the user in the solution of his problem. With these tools, he can write and debug his own problem solution without the risk of programmer misinterpretation and the delay in programmer scheduling. Once debugged, programs and data may be stored at the computer site by a simple instruction, and recalled in a matter of seconds at any later time for modifications and processing. Private files of programs and data are protected from unauthorized access and destruction. To further assist the user, libraries of preprogrammed mathematical routines are available for common calculations. And, perhaps most important of all, no capital investment and no added personnel are required. The user pays only for the terminal, the actual computer time used plus storage space, and a nominal connect time charge. In summation, this type of service is geared to better utilization of the user's time and to extension of the power of large computers to more users.

To what extent this concept will be applied to the solution of business problems is difficult to evaluate today. While this concept is competitive with traditional batch and remote job entry batch processing of scientific problems, its place in the solution of business problems is not as evident. Engineers in their normal work develop mathematical equations and determine a range of variables for solution to problems encountered. Time-sharing systems provide a language to permit easy expression of these equations and variables in a machine-understandable form. The business man on the other hand does not have a language available that permits him to compose readily a computer program. Nor, in fact, does the nature of his problem usually lend itself to this type of solution. Most conventional business applications require high volumes of input/output data and intricately structured master data files. However, simple modeling of business problems can assuredly be accommodated through use of a time-sharing terminal. Other specialized business applications (such as inventory control and accounts receivable) and appropriate languages are also being developed for man-machine interaction. When and to what extent they will become a significant factor in business processing is a function of need and marketability. In all probability time-sharing service for business problems will be only a small part of a complete commercial computer utility service that will include real-time, remote batch entry and traditional batch processing. Even then, the problem of providing business systems programs to a variety of users will be so large that the provider may have to specialize by either industry or narrow data processing function. A combination of supplied computer utility services and own-company tailor-made programs may provide a better solution to the problems confronting the small-to-medium data processing user.

Conclusion

Unquestionably, effective solutions to the information processing problems encountered in any computer installation offer great opportunities, benefits, and challenges to today's management. In order to realize these advantages, a broad set of problems must be solved through the concerted efforts of the best available technical and administrative manpower.

Selection and installation of data processing equipment

John W. Richy*

Selection of vendors for bid

Upon completion of the system specification (Chapter 29), the next step is to select the vendors to whom the specification will be transmitted as a request for proposal (RFP). This step should be considered carefully to avoid involvement with too many vendors, but at the same time not exclude those who have the potential of meeting the requirements. In the past, the determination of vendor potential has, in many cases, been based simply on the vendor's past experience and success with systems of the type under consideration. Although this is a relatively easy approach with a minimum of risk involved, it does not always result in the best cost/performance acquisition. Also, with the rapid advances being made in the field of information technology, today's tried and proven systems are already obsolete and will become more so if a long-term operation is planned. One method of determining which vendors to consider is to start with the multitude of data processing magazines which cover almost every aspect of present state-of-the-art hardware, software, and systems development. These publications also provide periodic listings of manufacturers showing types of data processing systems installed and on order with representative cost ranges. User case histories are presented regularly, and provide a source for establishing contacts with companies having similar EDP system requirements. The vendors will also furnish a

* Manager of Technical Services, Computer and Data Communication Systems, United Air Lines, Chicago.

list of customer installations which can be used to establish such contacts.

Vendor's conference

Within two or three weeks after transmittal of the RFP to those vendors selected for bidding, a vendor's conference should be scheduled with those vendors who have indicated their intention to bid. The purpose of the conference is to review the specifications and answer questions regarding the content and intent. Since this information is of general interest to all vendors, an open meeting with participation by all vendors will save time and enable a more uniform understanding by all.

Evaluation team

As was suggested for the development of the system specification (Chapter 29), an evaluation team, consisting of user and technical representatives with possible outside consulting support, will be needed to review the proposals and compile the pertinent cost and performance data for comparison and evaluation. One of the first objectives of the team is to narrow the field quickly to two, or possible three, vendors to save time and effort on the part of all concerned.

Evaluation factors

The following guideline describes the types of evaluation factors to be considered in selecting a data processing system. Since the significance of any factor or factors is dependent on the specific type of data system under consideration, no attempt is made to assign specific weights to the factors. For those factors which are likely to have particular significance in the evaluation and selection process, a more in-depth discussion of considerations is provided to assist the reader in applying his own weights for these factors.

System management factors

VENDOR CAPABILITY. Summarize each vendor's background and past experience with the type of system proposed. Determine how much reliance will be placed on subcontractors for providing major system hardware or software components required to implement the system. The ability of a vendor to deliver the system in the time frame required can be influenced a great deal by his dependency on subcontractors. This could be an asset or a hindrance. It should be recognized, however, that extensive use of subcontractors will require considerable coordination to assure that all of the major system components are delivered in time for checkout and integration with other components. Alternate sources of components should be known beforehand in the event it develops that a subcontractor furnishing a critical component is unable to deliver in time, or possibly not deliver at all.

VENDOR MANAGEMENT SUPPORT.   Describe vendor's top management knowledge of, and expressed support for, the project. The main point here is to determine whether the proposed system is important enough to the vendor to assure commitment of adequate manpower and other resources to the project, and to increase these commitments in the event of schedule slippage or other problems.

VENDOR MANPOWER.   Prepare a list for each vendor showing the specific manpower commitments proposed for the project. Indicate the number of vendor support personnel to be provided in the areas of training, programming, installation, maintenance, sales, and engineering. Summarize the experience and background of the key personnel in each area. An understanding of the possible sources for replacements should be reached in the event any of the key vendor personnel are not able to continue with the project.

HARDWARE AVAILABILITY.   List each vendor's stated commitment to provide on site, or to make available at vendor's site, hardware for program debugging and system checkout. Determine how much total computer time will be available, when, and with what configuration of hardware. Determine at what point in time remote input/output devices will be made available for operator training and system checkout, and in what quantities. An understanding of system checkout availability is important since the user must be furnished sufficient capability early enough to program and train for the use of the system. A misunderstanding on this point could result in delivery of the system before the user is ready, with the expectation of payment on the part of the vendor.

SOFTWARE AVAILABILITY.   This factor is probably one of the most important in assessing vendor capability to deliver a usable system in the time frame required. Vendor-supplied software generally includes executive and control routines which assign priorities and control the internal operations of the system, file access and control routines which control the storage and retrieval of programs, records and data stored on the various types of peripheral storage devices, standard batch processing routines, and many other programs which the vendor provides for general usage in customer systems. Operating system programs for multiprogramming, multiprocessing, and time sharing systems are quite complex and have been found difficult to implement in the time periods established. A clear understanding of which software the vendor will furnish, how much modification will be required for the particular system and configuration, and a realistic assessment of the time frame to develop, check out, and integrate this software into the system will help to avoid later delays and disappointments.

PERFORMANCE GUARANTEES. Describe each vendor's position regarding guaranteeing accuracy, speed, and reliability. Indicate willingness of the vendor to submit the system to extensive acceptance tests for measurement of actual performance before acceptance and payment. Describe simulation programs or other techniques available to predict system capability and to check adequacy of the system proposed well in advance of actual system tests.

IMPLEMENTATION AND CUTOVER. Determine how well each vendor understands your company's business operation and to what extent each recognizes how the implementation and cutover will be influenced by operational considerations. Describe how the proposed installation plans and schedules reflect this understanding.

System concept

PROCESSOR CONFIGURATION. Determine whether the proposed configurations reflect the preferences and conditions stated in the system specification. Describe any quantity differences in like components between proposals and indicate the reason for any differences.

DATA COMMUNICATIONS PHILOSOPHY. Determine whether the proposed configurations reflect the preferences and conditions stated in the system specification. Describe the differences in number and speed of lines proposed and indicate the reason for any differences.

REMOTE INPUT/OUTPUT TERMINALS. Determine whether the proposed I/O terminals cover the range of activities described in the system specification. Compare the types and quantities proposed, and describe the reason for any differences.

EVALUATION OF DIFFERENCES. Prepare a summary of the above differences, indicating to what extent they influence the costs. The primary objective is to equate proposed systems to be sure that comparisons of capability and costs are made on an equal basis. There is a possibility that in order to present an attractive cost proposal, a vendor will propose a bare minimum system with the expectation that additional components will be added during implementation, if needed. There is some merit to the approach, but it could also present a distorted cost comparison. There is also a possibility that a weakness in the proposed configuration, such as inability to share peripheral devices by multiple processors, is being compensated for by added hardware. On the other hand, the higher cost proposal with greater quantities of hardware may reflect a better understanding of the job to be performed and the guarantees to be met. The effect of stringent performance guarantees on proposal costs should be considered in the evaluation of differences to assess whether the level of performance specified is worth the added costs.

System performance capability

CAPACITY AND LOADING. Determine how much margin the estimates of capacity and loading allow for unknowns in usage predictions and programming difficulties. Depending on the complexity of the job to be performed and the confidence in the accuracy of forecasted usage statistics, a margin of 30 percent to 50 percent, and possibly higher, is not excessive. It is much better to overdesign and use any excess capacity for growth than to underdesign and find a system that will not handle the job. Reconfiguring and reprogramming of an underdesigned system could be quite costly in man hours already spent and in time lost.

FLEXIBILITY FOR EXPANSION. Determine how the system can be expanded. Will the expansion require changes in software, and to what extent? Will the introduction of additional hardware shut down the system, and for how long? Upgrading to a more powerful computer is facilitated if the vendor has available a program-compatible family of computers through which additional capability can be provided with little or no changes in software. It should be recognized, however, that certain features in the next level in the computer family may not be usable without software changes. The extent to which software changes will be necessary to achieve certain levels of increase in capability should be reviewed carefully by technical programmers before any judgments are made on ease of upgrading through the computer family approach.

FALLBACK PROVISIONS. Summarize how each of the proposed systems provides fallback capability. Determine how failures in the system will be detected, and how recovery will be handled. Will standby hardware require manual switching into the system, or will this hardware be accessed automatically through software? Is the standby hardware exercised continually to assure its availability when needed? What is the cost for providing the higher levels of fallback, and are the added costs in keeping with performance requirements?

OPERATOR CONSIDERATIONS. Determine whether each of the proposed systems has given adequate consideration to human engineering factors in the design of computer consoles and remote input/output devices. The provision of an adequate number of control keys, switches, indicator lights, and alarm features is an important consideration if efficiency of operation and operator satisfaction with the system are to be achieved. Well-planned physical locations of these controls and their ready identification will reduce the amount of operator fatigue and resultant operator errors encountered in usage.

Hardware summary

The more significant hardware capabilities affecting system capability and performance will be evident from the results of the previously described system concept and overall performance reviews. It might be helpful, however, to prepare comparison tables listing the certain specific hardware capabilities of like vendor equipment. This summary table will provide a means to further compare capabilities of the proposed systems, and will assure that all factors have been considered by each vendor. Examples of such tables are shown in Exhibits 1, 2, and 3.

Other general considerations regarding hardware that should be noted are the initial and maximum expansion capabilities, as well as the increments by which this expansion can be achieved. These considerations have been highlighted for a number of items shown in the comparison table. Other pertinent items could also be subjected to this type of itemization and covered in separate tables, if deemed necessary.

Certain hardware factors which should be looked for, but which do not lend themselves to table comparisons, include storage protection features, bit-character-word manipulation capability, priority interrupt techniques, programming assist registers, and features which enable programming to increase the throughput of the system. Ease of programming and low overhead hardware features can be a major system advantage.

Software considerations

In most third generation data processing systems, and particularly the larger systems with on-line, off-line, and batch processing functions performed in a real time or time shared mode, an efficient and comprehensive system of programs is needed to manage the movement of data throughout the processor complex. The development of such operating system or executive control programs can run into hundreds of man-years, and as such is a major item of vendor-provided system capability. The state of development of control system logic and executive software must be evaluated carefully if any realistic implementation schedule is to be established and valid estimates made of system capability. It should be noted that this system control software is above and beyond the

EXHIBIT 1

Processor Equipment Comparison Table

	Vendor		
	A	B	C

PROCESSOR
    Internal core
        Size
        Word length
        Cycle time
        Shared (yes or no)
    I/O channels
        Number
        Transfer rate
    Instruction execution time
        Minimum
        Maximum
        Average

PROCESSOR PERIPHERAL EQUIPMENT
    External core
        Size
        Word length
        Cycle time
    Random access storage (per type)
        Number of units
        Number of words or char./unit
        Access time
            Minimum
            Maximum
            Average
        Transfer rate
        Block size
            Minimum
            Maximum
    Magnetic tape
        Bit/inch densities
        Tape speeds
        Transfer rates
    Other equipment
        Card read/punch speeds
        Line printer speeds
        Line printer char./line

standard programming packages available from the libraries of computer equipment manufacturers. However, depending upon the programming capability of the customer and the type of system to be implemented, the availability of other programs, such as automatic programming languages, compilers, assemblers, translators, file control, and other support routines, is an important consideration in the selection of a system for a given job.

One of the major items to look for in evaluating vendor-supplied

EXHIBIT 2

Communications Comparison Table

| | Vendor | | |
	A	B	C

COMMUNICATION LINES (PER TYPE)
  Number of Lines
  Line Speed
  Number of Data Subsets
  Character code
    Name
    Bits/char.
  Line control
    Name of technique
    Maximum number of units/line
    Delivery assurance (yes or no)
    Outage monitor (yes or no)
    Automatic fallback (yes or no)
  Error control (yes or no)
    Character parity
    Block parity
    Cyclic check
    Automatic retransmission
  Message envelope
    Number of header characters
    Number of ender characters

COMMUNICATION INTERFACE EQUIPMENT
  Maximum number of high-speed lines/unit
  Maximum number of low-speed lines/unit
  Maximum number of medium-speed lines/unit
    Speed/no. relationship (yes or no)
    Minimum unit of expansion (no. of lines)
    Line buffer storage
      Type
      Number char./line

software is the size of executive, control, and other operating system software, and where in the system these programs will reside. Core storage, for example, is quite costly and generally limited in maximum size, and large vendor programs residing in core could have an impact on core available for user applications. On the other hand, moving portions of these programs to a lower speed and less expensive type of storage will slow down the throughput capability of the system. In on-line or real time systems in particular, working core size is a very important factor where the processors must have fast availability to a large number of programs. Too much reliance on retrieving programs from slow bulk storage in effect reduces processor efficiency because of waiting. This can be overcome to some extent by multiprogramming and multiprocessing techniques, but processor hardware capability and a proper equipment configuration are required to accomplish this.

EXHIBIT 3

Remote Equipment Comparison Table

	Vendor		
	A	B	C

INPUT/OUTPUT DEVICES (PER TYPE)
   Number of units
   Operating speed
   Characters/line (if applicable)
   Total characters (if applicable)
   Power requirement (voltage and amps.)
   Heat generated (B.t.u./hr.)
   Physical dimensions
   Weight
   Environment
      Temperature range
      Humidity range
   Noise level (db.)
   Stand-alone capability (yes or no)

I/O DEVICE CONTROL EQUIPMENT
   Maximum number I/O devices/unit by device type
   Device/no. relationship (yes or no)
   Type of storage
   Size of storage
   Programable operation (yes or no)
   Fallback capability (yes or no)
      Control equipment
      Communication line
   Maximum line speed capability (bits/sec.)
   Power requirements (voltage and amps.)
   Heat generated (B.t.u./hr.)
   Physical dimensions
   Weight
   Environment
      Temperature range
      Humidity range
   Noise level (db.)
   Maximum direct cabling distance to I/O's

Maintenance considerations

The type and quality of vendor maintenance support will determine the up time and return-to-service experienced in actual operation. An understanding of the following maintenance factors will provide an insight into the vendor's capability to meet the performance levels expected.

MAINTENANCE ORGANIZATION. Outline the management levels, showing the placement in the vendor organization and titles of individuals comprising the organization.

FIELD MAINTENANCE SUPPORT. Determine specific city and location addresses of each organizational unit (division, region, branch, local office). Indicate the number of personnel assigned to each office and hours when staffed. Determine which offices will stock major components and spare parts.

PREVENTATIVE MAINTENANCE.   Describe the daily or periodic preventative maintenance requirements of each vendor. When will this maintenance be performed and how long will it take? What impact will this have on use of the system and how will the vendor accommodate to customer preferences?

Installation considerations

A comparison of vendor environmental requirements can highlight potential site preparation cost differences to a customer. Following are the main points to look for in making an "ease of installation" comparison:

1. Floor space for equipment, including clearances to permit maintenance access.
2. Floor space required for expansion units.
3. Physical dimensions and weight of equipment components.
4. Type of power required, i.e., 115 volt single-phase, or 208 volt three-phase and variation tolerances.
5. Current and wattage ratings.
6. Heat dissipation in B.t.u./hr.
7. Noise level of equipment.
8. Equipment mobility and positioning constraints.
9. Temperature and humidity ranges.
10. Interequipment cable sizes, types, maximum permissible lengths, voltage and current levels carried.
11. Shielding or special conduit requirements for signal cabling.

Cost comparison

The various cost factors were described in Chapter 28 under the section "Economic Evaluation." The reader is referred to that section for developing the necessary cost comparison data. A few words of caution are offered regarding proposal costs as an evaluation factor. Although cost is certainly a prime consideration, a more important factor is the assurance that a system will satisfactorily meet the specified requirements within the time frame desired. In many instances, this is not the minimum cost proposal. There is also the tendency of originally-proposed costs to increase as system requirements are refined. The extent of this increase is a function of margin built into the originally proposed system and the costs for component expansion increments. All of these somewhat intangible factors have to be equated to arrive at a true cost comparison between proposed systems.

Before considering proposed vendor system costs as final, the matter of lease versus purchase and third-party lease possibilities should be investigated. Based on this investigation, the company can decide on the most advantageous financial arrangement to pursue. Each vendor's proposal should be studied to determine whether there are any potential difficulties in accomplishing the desired financial arrangement. The subject of lease versus purchase and third-party lease is discussed briefly in Chapter 28, with a more in-depth discussion presented in Chapter 20.

Equipment installation

Implementation of a data processing system requires close coordination between a number of parallel activities such as personnel recruiting and training, applications and vendor support programming, site preparation, equipment manufacture and delivery, equipment installation and checkout, communications facilities installation and checkout, system testing, and finally, transition and cutover to the new system. The relationship and dependencies between these activities should be thoroughly examined and charted to arrive at an overall implementation plan with completion dates for each activity as they relate to other activities. Timely completion of each activity must be assured to avoid hampering the progress of dependent activities. On the other hand, undue acceleration in one activity may be unnecessary and costly if other activities are not ready to use the activity's output. See Chapter 25, "Project scheduling and management," for a discussion of the formal methods of scheduling the project so that all activities mesh and are accomplished on time.

Site preparation and equipment installation are closely related. This section will discuss some of the problems and pitfalls to consider in planning for these two activities to minimize the possibility of their becoming a stumbling block in meeting the objectives of the overall implementation schedule.

Site preparation

Preparation of customer locations for installation of vendor equipment is primarily a customer responsibility and expense. Vendors, however, provide considerable guidance and support to assure that their requirements are understood and properly implemented. Vendor installation planning engineers will work with customer representatives and provide the necessary environmental and electrical specifications as well as typical floor plans and equipment layouts. The customer representative will be expected to take the specific site requirements and arrange with contractors to have the work accomplished.

There are a number of potential problems that might be encountered in preparing sites such as adequacy of floor space, capacity of electrical power and air conditioning plant, and structural support capability of floors and beams. Acquisition of additional floor space, adding to main power source capacity, increasing existing air conditioning plant, or relocating an office to a new location are generally long lead time items. Detailed site planning should, therefore, be initiated as soon as possible to allow sufficient time to investigate and implement alternatives with a minimum of expense and delay to the implementation schedule.

CUSTOMER RESPONSIBILITIES.   Customer site preparation generally involves the following types of activities:

1. Arranging for architectural and contractor services.
2. Providing power wiring, ground wire, conduit, wireways, switches, and circuit breakers from main power source to each unit of vendor equipment.
3. Providing external voltage regulators where required to compensate for deviations and fluctuations beyond equipment design tolerances.
4. Providing adequate air conditioning and control to meet vendor environmental requirements.
5. Arranging for cutouts through existing ceilings, walls, floors, and desks for signal cabling and power cords, and for subsequent refurbishment.
6. Removing of existing wall panels and ceiling tiles to allow access for cabling.
7. Providing work areas for vendor service personnel and space for parts and test equipment storage.
8. Scheduling of contractor work and arranging for receipt of equipment deliveries.
9. Complying with building, fire protection, and electrical codes as they relate to site preparation. For detailed information, refer to the "National Electric Code (NFPA No. 70)" and the "Standard for the Protection of Electronic Computer Systems (NFPA No. 75)." Code compliance should be stated as a requirement in all contractor work agreements. Vendor equipment compliance with electrical codes is a vendor responsibility but should be verified prior to manufacture to avoid later problems in attempting to correct compliance deficiencies.

VENDOR RESPONSIBILITIES.   The vendor normally assumes the responsibility for arranging equipment shipments and for supervising the loading and unloading at origin and destination. Shipping costs are passed on to the customer and it is advisable to consult with the vendor's shipping representatives to determine the cost alternatives for various shipping and on-site delivery arrangements. The need for fast shipping times and use of bulk shipments are cost variation factors to be considered in arriving at the most desirable shipping plan.

The vendor is expected to furnish all interconnecting data cables and connectors and assumes the responsibility for their installation and connection to equipment cabinets. Vendor personnel will also assemble, install, and level equipment cabinets and perform system checkout.

At certain locations, local labor agreements or unusual installation conditions may require the employment of qualified subcontractors to perform part or most of this work. The vendors, however, will usually reserve the right to make final connection of data cables to their cabinets.

System conversion

After all equipment is installed and operationally checked out as a total system with vendor and customer programs, the job of system conversion and cutover to the new system begins. This subject is covered in Chapter 33, where the reader can obtain an insight into the considerations and pitfalls in planning for this important, and sometimes most difficult, phase of implementing a new data processing system.

Program development and management

Dorothy Walsh*

For the financial executive, program management is a twofold task:
ensuring communication between the applications and technical staffs,
and evaluating the work of the technical group. Communications are
based on specifications and plans. Evaluation is carried out in review
meetings. This chapter gives some guidelines for preparing specifications
and conducting reviews. Such guidelines are oriented toward the applications area. The technical management of program development is
described elsewhere in this section. Therefore, this chapter begins with a
discussion of the basic steps in setting up a programming project:
preparation of specifications and work plans. The second part of the
chapter describes some means of ensuring and evaluating the quality of
the finished application.

Specifications for the application

The program specification

A programming effort originates in the recognition of the need for the
use of EDP to perform some task. A specification for the program which
will do the required job is the starting point of the programming project.
The quality of the final product is directly dependent on the quality of
this specification. Therefore, ample time should be given to preparing
clear and complete descriptions of the processing that is to be done. The

---

* Vice President, Advanced Computer Techniques Corporation, New York.

first step in specifying an applications program is the most important because it directly determines the kind of end product that will be produced. The basic need at this point is meaningful communication between the applications and programming staff. The responsibility for that communication rests with financial management. A good specification is the first step. Continued review by management and interchange of information between the financial staff and technical staff must mark its development.

Properly performed, the specification activity should be valuable as a means of determining the feasibility of proceeding with a proposed system. It should reveal whether an application is really programmable, i.e., totally defined and able to be done by means of a systematic procedure.

The following procedure is suggested as a guide to specifying programs:

1. Design a standard specification format (see below) for use by all applications groups.
2. Choose personnel thoroughly familiar with the application to write the program specification.
3. Add an EDP man as technical consultant to the specification team. If needed, add an expert in the applications area who can introduce new techniques being employed in the field.
4. Make guidelines clear. Spell out the magnitude of the effort to be undertaken. Indicate which, if any, features may be eliminated, deferred, etc.
5. Set a reasonable, definite deadline to the job.
6. Ensure that the group works together. If advisors are used, establish a pattern for regular communication.

A standard format, covering all required classes of information, is a must. Such a format serves as a basic contents checklist for the categories of information to be provided. It should be general and expansible. At the same time, it should not be so detailed as to be self defeating and rigid. The list given in Exhibit 1 is suggested for basic minimum content. It is also a guide to the organization of the material. Any particular data related to the application, required for company standards, etc. should be included where pertinent.

The purpose of a program specification outline is to serve as a guide for applications personnel in preparing the description of a system to be programmed. Applications oriented staff ordinarily prepare such specifications. However, they should be assisted by data processing staff who can advise on the interfaces between the application and the processing environment.

The activity of preparing the program specification serves to identify the ill-defined areas and to indicate where more information is needed. The applications group preparing the program specification, by working with programming staff, can ensure that the information given is at once

EXHIBIT 1

A Program Specification Outline and Checklist

```
NAME (of Program) _____
DATE _____
PREPARED BY _____

Description and Background (of the System Being Converted)

     1.  Block Diagram of the Application System as Currently Performed
     2.  Block Diagram of the Application System To Be Automated

             Input
                   Type A (card, invoice, bill, etc.)
                        Origin
                        Source (for the system)
                        Medium
                        Format - with sample lay/out; thoroughly detailed
                                 description of fields
                        Content
                        Use - including frequency
                        Volume
                        Disposition
                   (repeated for each distinct input item)
                                      :
                                      :
                                      :

             Output
                   The same headings apply - origin will be some
                   part of the program system.  Disposition may
                   include a distribution section for printed
                   documents.

Processing

     1.  Manual
     2.  Automated

Hardware and Software System Requirements

Error Detection and Correction
Back-Up Procedures
Limitations or Restrictions
Procedures for Manual/Automated Interfaces
Applicable Standards
     (refer here to any corporate publications)
Documentation
```

adequate for a program design and faithful to the requirements of the application itself.

In constituting a specification team and initiating the work they will do, the financial executive must be careful to give necessary guides for filling in specification details. Thus, he should set a reasonable time limit to avoid an endless effort at specifying the unspecifiable. Where pertinent, he should give some gross cost limit to provide insight into the magnitude of the effort he anticipates. Such an estimate is another ·ndication of feasibility for the specifying team. It can save time that might otherwise be wasted in specifying a programming effort that cannot be carried out within current budget constraints. This does not mean that, in every such case, the entire effort should be abandoned. A vital application unrealistically costed by management may have to be rebudgeted. Providing a limit and maintaining communication with the specifying team enables the manager to know quite early in the game that he must rethink his budget or his commitment to the application.

Providing limits and definitions is not enough. Communication must be maintained so that an entire specification effort is not carried through before word that it is unrealistic reaches the applications management. Communication between the team and management must be maintained on some regular basis. Meetings should be scheduled periodically throughout the time allotted to the specification effort. Frequency depends on the length of the time allowed to complete the specification. Such meetings need not be time consuming, and can be restricted to the manager and a representative of the specifying group. Communication within the specification group should also be provided for, especially if the group is made up of staff from several different areas.

The tremendous potential represented by electronic data processing technology can only be realized by informed and directed use of the capabilities it presents. The financial executive can ensure informed use by choosing his staff wisely. His next responsibility is that of planning the task they will perform and directing its completion.

Having initiated a programming project, the financial manager has certain well-defined responsibilities for directing it. These vary at each stage.

1. Design a standard specification format (see Exhibit 2) for use by all applications groups.
2. Choose personnel thoroughly familiar with the application to write the program specification.
3. Add an EDP man as technical consultant to the specification team. If needed, add an expert in the applications area who can introduce new techniques being employed in the field.
4. Make guidelines clear. Spell out the magnitude of the effort to be undertaken. Indicate which, if any, features may be eliminated, deferred, etc.
5. Set a reasonable, definite deadline to the job.
6. Ensure that the group works together. If advisors are used, establish a pattern for regular communication.
7. Constitute a qualified review panel to assess the program specification before design is undertaken.

The design specification

The design phase of program development begins when an acceptable product specification has been produced. The design phase also yields tangible results by which the proposed program may be evaluated. These are:

1. The programming design for implementing the specified system.
2. A work plan showing time schedules and estimates of the resources required for the implementation effort.

Both are documented and presented at the design review.

A design specification, like a program specification, must be completely detailed. It differs from the program specification on which it is based in two aspects: orientation and degree of detail.

The design specification builds upon and expands the program specification, including technical detail. However, as has been stated, this technical detail is dependent upon assumed characteristics of the application and its environment. The financial manager is responsible for constituting a design team capable of producing a good design. He is also responsible for knowing what a good design specification should contain. As in the case of the program specification, the best approach is that of drawing up a standard form. Such a standard form can be based on the program specification shown in Exhibit 1.

There are, however, certain fundamental differences between the two. In the design specification emphasis shifts from the applications system characteristics to the structure of the program system that will process the application. A good design specification is characterized by:

1. Completeness.
2. Clarity.
3. Comprehensibility.

A complete specification implies that all contingencies are foreseen and planned for. This means, then, that the manual parts of the system have been considered, and the interface between them and the automated parts clearly defined. For example, in a system which prepares checks for disbursements, if expenditures beyond a certain amount must be approved by a particular corporate officer, then this manual step in the processing must be planned for.

A manual step may impact the overall design of the automated parts of a system in a number of ways. In the case cited above, it could be undesirable to set up a plan of processing which resulted in all checks being printed in a continuous process with no indication given of amounts beyond the limiting value. Recognizing the amount at which approval is needed and taking appropriate action is a necessary program step. The program design must show what disposition is made of requests for checks beyond the limit—whether they are never prepared by program, prepared in a special run, etc.

This kind of information comes from the program specification and appears in the design specification as a break in the program flow, or as an additional program. The design specification is, thus, closely related to the program specification but, as has been noted, in far greater detail and in more technical terminology.

Completeness requires that both the application and the program be fully described. This means that each step in the application process has a corresponding program, routine, etc. in the design specification. Completeness means that all interfaces between the application and the program have been resolved.

The resolution of all interfaces must be planned for by the financial manager. A program system designed to run 12 hours and print checks at 12:00 midnight to be left in a computer center till 9:00 the next morning might be an efficient technical design. However, it could be undesirable from other points of view.

Thus, while the financial executive does not participate in the technical program design per se, he must interact with the design staff throughout their effort. Such interaction may be minimal. The major requirement is that it be regular and timely.

Completeness has yet other implications when applied to a design specification. It means that the final specification must be in a form for use by a group of programmers. Therefore it must contain full details about all of the topics outlined in Exhibit 1. In developing a program design specification the following information is added to the system specification:

1. Overall system flowcharts showing the relationships of all subsystems.
2. Overall charts of the subsystems showing the relationships of the component parts.
3. An information flowchart showing the source and use of all input records, files, etc., and the origin and disposition of all output reports, etc.
4. Pictorial layouts of every record to be input or output.
5. Detailed description of the support hardware/software system.
6. Outlines of all documents that will be produced.
7. Brief descriptions of all component programs.
8. Descriptions of methods used, where such are pertinent.
9. A statement of the criteria of acceptance for the finished system.

Clarity and comprehensibility refer to format and language. Clarity requires that graphic displays—flow diagrams, etc.—be used wherever possible to replace narrative text. Comprehensibility requires that standard terminology and standard forms be employed so that any programmer may read and use the finished specification.

The work plan

The second tangible result to be expected from the design phase is the work plan. A work plan includes estimates of the expected resource expenditures required to achieve the programmed system.

Together the program design specification and the work plan constitute a contract made between the implementation group and the group requesting the program. Both must be quite clear about what such a contract calls for.

To ensure that he knows what he is agreeing to, the financial manager should require a thoroughly documented plan of work from the technical manager. Time and cost as well as all necessary support facilities should be spelled out. A time chart of program development should be included to give the manager checkpoints by which he may gauge the completeness and timeliness of the effort. Tangible results—documents, partial systems—should be planned for release at stated intervals during program development. The financial manager can then schedule reviews at the time such results are due to enable continual quality control to be performed.

The best way for a financial manager to make certain he has all of this information is to design a standard document form showing the various categories of data he needs. Exhibit 2 illustrates a work plan form.

Two important categories of information are assumptions and resource estimates. All assumptions on which the programming staff is proceeding should be stated. Thus, for example, if they are anticipating procedural changes in the application area to generate input, it is clear that the program completion date is directly dependent upon the smooth transition to those new procedures.

Time and cost estimates are also important. The financial manager should be fully aware of the expected cost of any system he requests, and the date he may expect to have it.

Once the program design and work plan have been accepted, the manager has agreed to meet costs and to accept risks implied in the assumptions. In addition, he has agreed to accept the program system described. Thus it is vital that he be both aware of the commitment he is making and satisfied with the proposed system.

Specification review

The opportunity to evaluate the contract he is making is provided to the manager by the specification review. This review takes place when the design specifications and the work plan are complete. It has as its purpose the determination of:
1. Conformance of design to original program specification.
2. Feasibility and acceptability of the work plan.
3. Clarity and acceptability of the completion criteria for the programming effort.

The financial executive should set up a review, inviting representatives from all groups who interface with the system in any way. Additionally, he should bring in any consulting staff in the applications or technical area who may assist him in understanding the nature of the

EXHIBIT 2

Work Plan for Programming Projects

```
┌──────────────────────────────────────────────────────────────────────┐
│                    WORK PLAN for (Application Name)                     │
│    DATE _____                                │
│                                                                        │
│                                                                        │
│    I.   INTRODUCTION                                                    │
│                                                                        │
│    II.  COMPONENT TASKS                                                 │
│              PROGRAM DESIGN                                             │
│              PROGRAM DEVELOPMENT                                        │
│              TESTING                                                    │
│              DOCUMENTATION                                              │
│                     ⋮                                                   │
│                                                                        │
│                                                                        │
│    III. STAFFING PATTERN                                                │
│              ASSIGNMENTS                                                │
│                     DURATION                                           │
│                     SPAN                                                │
│                     ⋮                                                   │
│                                                                        │
│                                                                        │
│    IV.  FACILITIES REQUIRED                                             │
│              HOUSING                                                    │
│              COMPUTER CONFIGURATION                                     │
│                     ⋮                                                   │
│                                                                        │
│                                                                        │
│    V.   TARGET DATES                                                    │
│                     ⋮                                                   │
│                                                                        │
│                                                                        │
│    VI.  PROJECT NETWORK                                                 │
│              (Pert Chart)                                               │
│                                                                        │
│    VII. DISCUSSION                                                      │
│              (all assumptions, risks, etc. should be thoroughly explained) │
│                                                                        │
│    ATTACHMENTS                                                          │
│          TIME AND COST ESTIMATE                                        │
│                     ⋮                                                   │
└──────────────────────────────────────────────────────────────────────┘
```

design and the feasibility of the work plan. It is at this point that he must make a realistic decision about the proposed effort. He may find all aspects acceptable, or he may require modification. He may have to recognize the basic infeasibility of a proposed system. This review is a crucial point for, once having signed off on the design and the work plan, the manager is committed to accept what they represent in terms of finished product and resource expenditures. If he requires modification after this review he may save time or money. That would be all to his good. More likely, he will incur added cost or delay the work. This should be clearly understood by him before the programming proceeds.

Implementation and review

Staffing and support facilities

Once the initial review has been passed and the programming effort is under way, there are three major areas of concern to the nontechnical executive. They are related to ensuring the quality of the finished product. The first of these is who will do the work and what support will be required.

Choosing technical staff is the responsibility of technical management. The applications manager is responsible for certitude about the qualifications of his technical counterpart, and a wise choice of applications staff who will work with the programming group. There are certain characteristics he should look for in such personnel:

1. A thorough competence in the applications area.
2. An openness to the use of EDP in the applications area.
3. The ability to learn new techniques in the applications field.
4. Willingness and ability to adapt applications knowledge to an EDP context.
5. Willingness to work with the technical group in a working pattern that might differ from the normal one, e.g., different hours, more meetings.

Should it be apparent that no one possessing these qualities is available, the manager should attempt to constitute a small liaison team to work with the technical staff. However, especially at design time, it must be remembered that too many people can hinder rather than help get a job done.

An alternative is to seek an outside consulting group versed in the application. In this case the qualification of competence in EDP techniques should be added. Having chosen staff, the manager should see to it that all support required is given them.

Securing technical personnel is but a part of the staffing job. There may be a wide range of service staff required to support the activities of the programming group. In all cases some secretarial assistance must be provided. Internal documentation—specifications, layouts, etc.—are developed by programmers on a continuing basis throughout project implementation. Having such documentation typed and distributed can be a valuable means of making sure program interfaces are smooth.

The size of the programming project determines how large a secretarial staff is needed to prepare internal documents, progress reports, and the like. The nature of the external documentation to be produced determines the size and composition of additional support staff.

Technical writers and editors may be needed to prepare references and user manuals. Draftsmen and layout designers may be needed to assist in formatting finished documentation.

The importance of support staff in the documentation area cannot be overemphasized. The nature of programming, the dynamic character of the development of the final program system, makes timely information vital at every step. Programmers should be encouraged to document as they go along, submit the documentation for typing, and then update from draft copy. It can be a costly mistake to assume that all documentation can be done comparatively late in the program development and to plan availability of secretarial staff on that basis. Development details not written down and circulated can be overlooked. Leaving documentation until late in the implementation activity can result in having programmers spend additional time after program completion attempting to prepare adequate documentation. There are two major flaws in this procedure. The first is the cost of programmer time. The second is the impossibility of recapturing all necessary information. It is far less costly to have typists retype and correct specifications and internal systems material on a continuing basis.

Where required, technical writing staff should be added to the project as early as possible. This is true even if they cannot begin writing until certain information is developed as a result of implementation experience. An adequate familiarization period is especially important in the area of financial system documentation. It must be clear and concise and written in terminology familiar to its readers. The writer who has too little time to finish his task may be unable to translate from technical to applications language and may have to rely too heavily on the technically oriented material supplied by programmers.

Keypunch operators and data processing machine operators are another group to be integrated into the programming project. Here again the keywords are adequate size of staff and proper availability. Valuable time can be lost because input cards are not punched. Valuable programmer time can be misspent operating a computer because operating staff is not supplied on all shifts. The programming manager should consult the work plan to determine when such staff will be needed. Progress reports will help him keep current on any shift in the time at which the programmers will be ready to utilize keypunch and machine services. The manager must utilize these two sources of information to make certain that requirements and availability coincide.

It is necessary that the financial manager recognize the dependence of programming efforts on such support services. No attempt should be made to economize on these auxiliary services in the expectation that programmers will assume some of them. Time spent in performing auxiliary services is time not spent in technical development. It can mean the difference between timely completion of a project and schedule slippage.

The same importance attaches to facilities provided for the project staff. The nature of programming is such that a quiet, private place to work is necessary. The nature of program system development, especially for systems which necessitate large staff, is such that good communication facilities are required. Thus, housing staff in small, separate offices in close proximity is a good method of meeting both needs.

At the time that computer use becomes a major activity, the programming staff should be given adequate housing near the computer. Adequate housing implies sufficient space to retain, in an orderly fashion, the often cumbersome tools of the program testing activity—boxes of cards, disk packs, large program listings.

Any member of special supplies may be valuable to a programming group. These may range from color coded cards to small metal tabs to mark errors in test listings. It is not possible to foresee each specific need that might arise. It is possible, however, to provide for having such needs filled quickly. A standard procedure for requesting special supplies should be set up by the manager to permit requests to be met without the usual time lapse encountered in large corporation supply procedures.

Progress reporting and documentation

From the inception of the programming project regular progress reports should be required of the staff. Together with specifications, review reports, and work plans they form part of the project archives, its historical record.

The essence of a good progress reporting technique is simplicity. It must be simple to use, not time consuming or complex in any way. It must be simple to understand, not requiring laborious interpretation. The value of project control boards makes the board format a good basis for project reporting techniques; a scheme of reporting which allows information to be transcribed onto the board can relieve the financial manager of a large burden in assessing reports.

Progress reporting techniques are worth time devoted to studying alternatives and selecting the one that gives the most information for the least effort. A regular progress reporting plan should be drawn up before the project begins and then put into effect immediately.

Each programmer should make a weekly report to his group leader, project leader, or whoever is his immediate supervisor. Group leaders or the project leader can then combine the information for presentation to their manager. The progress of making composite reports from a number of related reports can be continued through the applicable number of levels of management for a particular programming effort.

The frequency of composite reports depends upon the project time frame. Weekly reports are advisable because they allow the financial manager timely notice of situations that may require some action on his part. However, when weekly reports are found to be unfeasible for some reason another schedule, bi-weekly for example, can be used. Weekly reports from programmers should be required.

Exhibit 3 illustrates the format of progress report technique suggested because it is clear, easy to use, and easy to transfer to a project control board.

In this scheme each expected task is listed across the page. Ten boxes are allowed under each task. This is done to permit representation of the status of a task in terms of percent complete. There are various ways in which percent complete may be represented. For example, an X might be put in the box that most nearly corresponds to percent complete at a given time. Tasks for which no X appears might not as yet be started. Completed tasks could be shown each week with an X in the last box. Or, the number of the week in which the report is made might be entered in the box. More than one week should be shown on a given report form to impart a dynamic character and to emphasize the information provided. Thus, for example, a 40 percent in one week for a given task followed by a 30 percent the week after would be brought to the attention of the manager who could then determine the cause, and whether or not action was needed. The "remarks" section permits special situations to be described and commented upon.

Project documentation includes all such reports as well as notes about what action was taken in any special situations that developed. The project historical record is the documentation of the programming effort. It must be distinguished from documentation of the programming product, discussed elsewhere in this handbook.

Project documentation also serves as a means of evaluating the program development effort itself. A project record can be used as a guide in planning similar efforts. Therefore, in order to be useful, project documentation should include annotated copies of all specifications, reports, the minutes of review meetings, and any applicable inter-project memoranda.

Evaluating the results

The results of a programming project are more than the product system itself. What must be evaluated encompasses as well the task of implementing the program system. This means determining the accuracy of the resource estimates made for the project and the time estimates made for each component task.

Thus, evaluation is not a one-time activity performed at the completion of the programming project. The financial executive must do his own on-going assessment of the implementation, using project documentation as his source material. Then, when the product system is ready for release, a review team carries out the overall evaluation.

To evaluate progress on an on-going basis, the financial executive

EXHIBIT 3

Weekly Progress Report Form

(Programmer's Name) _____

PROJECT NAME _____
MANAGER _____
DATE _____

SPECIFICATION | USER'S GUIDE | INTERNAL SYSTEM SPECIFICATION | FLOWCHARTS | CODING | CHECKOUT | SYSTEM INTEGRATION must use the information supplied in progress reports. Such information enables him to determine when certain tasks are late, or early, when additional resources are needed, etc. Any great disparity between an estimate, whether it be time or cost, and actual requirement for a task is indicative of a possible area of nonconformance. The financial manager should investigate any such instances to determine where the problem lies so that he may take remedial action.

EXHIBIT 4

Documentation Checklist

```
┌──────────────────────────────────────────────────────────────────┐
│ Documentation Checklist                                            │
│                                                          YES    NO │
│ Is The Project Documentation Complete                    ☐      ☐ │
│      SPECIFICATIONS                                                 │
│      WORK PLAN                                                      │
│      PROGRESS REPORTS                                               │
│      REVIEW MEETING MINUTES                                        │
│                                                                    │
│                                                          YES    NO │
│ Is The Product Documentation Complete                    ☐      ☐ │
│      SYSTEM DESCRIPTION                                             │
│      USER INSTRUCTIONS                                              │
│      OPERATING NOTES                                               │
│      MAINTENANCE MATERIALS                                         │
│                                                              NOT   │
│                                   GOOD  FAIR  POOR  APPLICABLE     │
│ SYSTEM DESCRIPTION                 ☐     ☐     ☐       ☐          │
│      Completeness                                                  │
│      Clarity                                                       │
│      Organization                                                  │
│      Use of Tables, Figures Etc.                                  │
│      Glossary Supplied                                            │
│      Indexed                                                       │
│      Provision Made For Modifications                             │
│                                                                    │
│ USER INSTRUCTIONS                                                  │
│         ·                                                          │
│         ·                                                          │
│         ·                                                          │
│         ·                                                          │
└──────────────────────────────────────────────────────────────────┘
```

A second gauge of quality, during program system development, is the tangible milestones set up in the work plan. These might be documents, or partial systems. In any case they are results which can be submitted to applicable quality tests. Arrangements should be made for a review group to read documents and a control group to test systems as soon as possible after the milestone date. Thus, any discrepancy between expectation and the actual product can be detected, and corrective action begun.

Finally, before the programming system is accepted for use, a series of reviews should be planned. All aspects of the product system should be evaluated against applicable criteria. This is best done by staff well versed in the area under consideration: documentation, technical efficiency, performance of the application processing, and competence of the implementation staff. The financial executive thus will have to seek specialized personnel in areas with which he is not familiar. Such specialized personnel should be given an orientation to the specific application under review. They should be asked to prepare checklists for the review task. The financial executive can request any changes to the criteria before review takes place. Exhibit 4 illustrates a checklist that might be made up for reviewing documentation in connection with an applications system. The existence of required items is the first check made. Then individual items are rated on a scale which is shown going from good to poor, but which might have excellent to poor or simply acceptable/unacceptable as the range for rating. The not applicable classification permits a generalized checklist to be drawn up for documents which have common characteristics to be checked.

A similar rating list can be prepared for conformance of product to design, conformance of project to planned duration, cost, etc. The technical efficacy of the product system is tested by its performance of the task it is designed to do. Such testing is carried out by the technical product test staff, who report their findings at the performance review.

The synthesis of all review reports provides the basis on which the financial manager can make his overall judgment about the product and the project. Should the results be less than satisfactory in some aspect, corrective measures can be taken and the results reviewed again.

All checklists and the final evaluation report form part of the project documentation to be used in carrying out similar efforts.

Managing the data processing function

David W. Packer and Harry S. Mann*

Traditionally, responsibility for data processing has been assigned to the chief financial executive. This assignment stems more from history than from the particular skills or knowledge of chief financial executives. The early uses of data processing equipment were largely in handling large volumes of accounting data. Today, the data processing function has long since passed that original and rather straightforward application and has progressed to processing large quantities of data for a variety of operating and management purposes.

Managing the data processing function involves all the ingredients of managing an entire manufacturing company. Success, therefore, requires a broader view than that usually possessed by those steeped in the tradition of controllership or treasurership. This does not mean that such breadth of vision cannot be attained by people with this type of education and experience. It merely means that the financial executive must broaden his perspective if he is to manage it effectively and to assure that end products are profitable to the business as a whole.

The electronic data processing function begins with system design and, in one sense, ends with the distribution of edited, legible, easily understandable information. In reality, however, there is no end to the data processing function, since much of the data being produced relates to the most dynamic aspects of a business. Thus, systems and formats are

* Manager, Systems and EDP, and the late Vice President, Finance, respectively, of Digital Equipment Corporation, Maynard, Massachusetts.

constantly changing, and feedback loops are constantly introducing new inputs which, in turn, require new programming, new processing techniques, and new reports.

Systems design requires an initial intensive research of the existing state of affairs and inquiries of operating people to determine how they would like the state of affairs changed. This activity compares to that of marketing research. System planning follows, with the objective of establishing data, system, and program specifications, so that the result will give the user what he believes he wants. This step is analogous to the specification of product characteristics which result from a market survey.

Technical analysis and programming translate the specifications into the steps which are necessary for the system to accept the data and produce the desired finished product; namely, a set of reports or calculations. EDP analysts and programmers must have not only an intimate knowledge of the requirements of the hardware and software with which they are to work, but also a realization of the demands for input data that their systems require. Since most input data is largely dependent upon many people, the analyst is constantly striving to minimize demands in this sector through his design work. The analogy between this operation and those of a product engineering department is apparent. The building of test runs, test data, etc., and the acceptance by the user of the model thus produced, completes the analogy between programming and engineering.

The training of operating personnel in new procedures and the layout of step-by-step machine functions is comparable to the start-up activities of a manufacturing unit when a new product is introduced to production. Scheduling each new job and interleaving it with jobs already being processed through the data processing center forms a close analogy with the scheduling function of a manufacturing unit. The problems of cycle-time, allowances for downtime, manpower loading, deadline dates, and relative priorities of different jobs are almost identical to the factors facing a scheduler in a manufacturing unit.

Quality control is an essential ingredient in effective data processing and encompasses input data, intermediate steps of processing, as well as output data of the finished product. Quality control, in this regard, also encompasses the effectiveness of meeting schedules as well as the accuracy of the work.

Finally, all of these activities, like any manufacturing entity, must be evaluated from the standpoint of economics. Is the end product worth the cost? Are there less expensive or quicker ways in which the same task can be performed? Are modifications in specifications possible which will meaningfully reduce cost or time and not unnecessarily compromise the goal of the customer or user? Thus, we see that the management of the data processing function does in fact encompass all factors which the chief executive of a manufacturing company must oversee in carrying out his role for the company as a whole.

This chapter bypasses the initial conversion to EDP systems and equipment, which has been covered in Chapter 28. Instead, it treats the management of an ongoing EDP function by discussing the two main components of the EDP effort—the creative unit responsible for the design and development of electronic data processing systems, and the production unit which is responsible for processing the data and generating the required outputs from these systems.

Managing the creative effort

The systems and programming organization

Staffing an electronic data processing function is one of the crucial problems of any business organization today. The intense shortage of programmers and technical people has been made evident by both raw statistics and rising salary levels. The EDP staff consists of a mix of capabilities. The three major capabilities are:

1. *Business analysis.* The capability for business analysis implies personnel with the ability to comprehend the problems of operating departments, so that they can effectively design possible solutions to these problems through data processing. It implies an ability to work with operating managers; to understand their motivations, their operations, and procedures; and to design computer-based systems which will aid them in accomplishing their business objectives.

2. *Technical analysis.* This involves the conversion of business system ideas to the most effective technical structure for implementing these ideas. Problems of what hardware to use, whether files should be randomly accessible on disk or be sequential in nature are highly technical considerations which, to some degree, are often independent of the business considerations in the system.

3. *Programming.* The capability to convert business and technical analysis results into operating programs which are well-designed, capable of being easily changed and maintained over a long period of time.

Most EDP organizations are staffed in one of two ways. First is the functional approach which involves a staff of business and possibly technical analysts, who specify and design systems, and a functional programming group that is responsible for the actual programming, coding, testing, and debugging of the programs required to implement the system. Second is the project organization, where a single project team has the capabilities of business analysis, technical analysis, and programming, and can be made responsible for the entire design through conversion process.

Exhibit 1 shows simplified functional and project organization charts.

The functional organization has a systems group (business analysis) that interacts with users to plan and propose systems. After a new application is agreed upon, the specifications are turned over to the technical group for technical analysis and programming. In some organizations, the technical group assumes full responsibility from this point on, with the systems people serving as staff consultants. Another alternative is for the systems group to retain systems responsibility; in this case, the technical effort becomes a service function to the systems effort.

The project organization typically has a number of teams, consisting of business and technical capabilities. Each team, normally led by the senior business analyst, has capabilities for designing, programming,

EXHIBIT 1

Managing the Creative Effort
(the systems and programming organization)

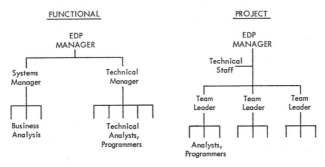

installing, and maintaining applications for a segment of the business. Areas of team responsibility are often defined by data flow, not organizational structure. For example, one team might be responsible for "Marketing Applications" that cut through a number of departments, from sales offices to general accounting, and include sales forecasting, new orders, backlog, sales analysis, invoicing, and accounts receivable.

The functional organization has the obvious advantage of specialization in duties and supervision. Enforcement of good programming standards and programming training, for example, becomes easier when all programmers operate through a single organization. The project organization often requires a senior technical person, operating in a staff role, to effectively coordinate and control activities taking place in numerous project teams.

Inherent in the functional organization, however, is the problem of communications between business analysts, technical analysts, and programmers. Characteristic symptoms of its deficiencies are the large number of programmers who feel that they are forced to write programs for poorly designed systems, and business analysts who are frustrated about the quality of programming that influences the total operation of the systems they have designed.

Many detailed systems considerations become evident during the programming phase. If the technical effort is too highly disassociated from the design effort, not only will poor programs be written, but many opportunities for substantially improving the design of the system may be lost. When a programmer prepares a flowchart, precision is essential; every decision point must have a clear-cut output path for every possible state of affairs. When a path appears for which there is no specification, it is highly probable that a flaw exists in the technical or business design of the system.

The extensive need for detailed communications between programmers and analysts, I believe, makes the strongest argument for a project rather than a functional organization. The advent of higher level compilers, such as COBOL, make programming neither drudgery nor a highly technical activity. Thus, many people in the business have capabilities which now range all the way from business analysis to programming. Because the entire process is so precise, an organization requiring highly formal communication among capabilities runs the risk of overall inefficiency and the creation of dissatisfaction among the people involved.

Project control

Once an electronic data processing project is undertaken, the EDP manager takes responsibility for controlling its progress and assuring that it will be finished on time and meet the objectives initially specified.

Projects normally proceed through several interacting and often overlapping phases. Detailed systems analysis produces firm specifications for programs, new hardware, forms, etc. Program writing commences and may run parallel with development of new procedures, training, and ordering of forms or hardware. Then comes a period of full system testing, followed by system conversion.

Techniques for controlling project progress range from simple bar charts to computerized PERT analyses. Whatever technique is used, it should clearly identify activities and end points so that actual progress can be posted and slippage identified as early as possible, insuring that corrective action can be taken or potential users informed that implementation will be later than planned.

Programs are primarily an extension of human logic; their scheduling often defies the most competent techniques applied. It is possible to have a program problem which even highly skilled people will take days or even weeks to solve. Programming is too creative a process to be automatically accelerated by the injection of additional effort into the system. This does not mean that effective scheduling cannot be done, but rather that it becomes a relatively statistical process. Some programs will be completed earlier than expected, and some programs will take longer. On an average, however, a solid base of estimating rules can be established which will avoid gross over or under estimates of the magnitude of the task.

At our installation, for example, we have sampled several programming activities performed by people of various competence and experience levels, and have developed some good rules of thumb for effective scheduling. These rules of thumb take the form of estimates of the number of man-hours required for programs of various complexities. For example, we know that a report writing program should take approximately 15 to 20 hours of programming effort. Note that this is not elapsed time, but instead total effort required for program implementation. Once a set of rules such as this is available, it is possible to look at a major project which involves a large number of programs and, at minimum, assure that the total number of man-months of effort available on the project stand a good chance of producing the results required by the project schedule. If, for instance, there are 20 new programs required in an application, and a very rough analysis of their complexity leads to the result that 50 man-weeks of programming effort will be required, then you know that the programming phase of the project with two people assigned to the job should take approximately six months.

Most applications that are badly executed suffer from two problems:
1. Initial commitments on the project are made before detailed analysis has been completed.
2. Even with good analysis, there is a great tendency to underestimate the amount of time required to make the system operational. This occurs particularly in the programming phase when good rules for estimating both total and elapsed time are not available. Thus, good scheduling becomes impossible. Experience has shown that programmers will, perhaps like most creative people, tend to underestimate the length of time that a given job will take, simply because they consider the way they want to do the job; *i.e.* that there will be no problems to solve when finished. Every major project should have a realistic schedule of all activities, from initial systems analysis to a schedule for each program to be written, tested, and debugged, and a schedule for full systems testing. Such schedules should be updated on a weekly basis and should provide the groundwork for meaningful summary reports on progress. These should be presented to the operating managers for whom the work is being done and to EDP management to enable them to recognize the need for more effort or for design review of the system.

Coordination with users

The concept of making electronic data processing work visible is of key importance, simply because such work, once started, tends to become highly technical. Thus, while the work is proceeding, often over an extensive period of time, there is no easy way for the nontechnical user to see exactly what is being done. Too often this leads to programs and systems that are technically sound, but which fail to do the job for which they were initially defined. A continuing flow of user-oriented documentation will help achieve the goal of effective coordination between the user and the EDP staff. For example, every report to be produced by the system should be reviewed by the user. The report is something that he can readily understand, and often will enable him to see items which have not been taken into account or areas that will lead to future operational and procedural problems at his end.

In addition to formal documentation, there should be intensive contact between users and system developer, in the form of periodic review meetings and informal contacts. EDP personnel should be extremely sensitive to the user's requirements. They should make every effort, not only to receive feedback from the potential user, but to stimulate such feedback by such procedures as reviewing report formats, reviewing questionable areas within the system, and generally discussing the new system's operation.

The challenge here is to avoid selecting a project, starting to work on it on the basis of an initial set of fairly broad specifications, and then, when implementation occurs many months later, finding that the system does not do what the user had expected it to do. The most effective way of combating this communication problem is extensive contact with the user and a real effort on the part of the EDP staff to take the initiative for such contact. The EDP staff knows both the user's job and the technical job, while the user only knows his job and often is not able to really sense what will happen in the context of the new system.

System conversion

At the end of the project development process comes the conversion from the existing system to the EDP system. The existing system is often manual, while the new system is highly automated. The new system will automatically change the procedures of one or more operating departments, as well as those of the EDP operation itself. There is no question but that the conversion process is one that is often handled badly and that it creates most of the problems of the entire project development process.

The reasons for this are clear. The conversion itself imposes peak loads throughout the whole system. If the prior system was manual, a vast amount of data transcription may be necessary before the EDP system can become operational. Operating personnel must learn new procedures, often not clearly and simply related to the ones they now follow. The EDP operation must adjust to new schedules, which may require the revision of existing schedules. All of these factors must be planned for by laying out in detail the steps that will be necessary in the conversion process and by making realistic plans for handling the peak loads that will be generated. In addition, because the system is new and has not been used extensively, it is quite likely that unforeseen problems will develop, that program "bugs" will crop up, and that a number of situations which require extremely responsive corrective action will develop.

Thus, the entire organization involved in the conversion must be mobilized to recognize the possibility of such occurrences and to develop the capability for handling all problems that will occur. An atmosphere of mutual sympathy is desirable, so that the EDP staff recognizes operational problems and the operating departments recognize EDP problems. This can be achieved by intensive contact between the EDP staff and the user departments in the weeks or even months before conversion takes place.

The two extremes of conversion strategies are:
1. Parallel operations for a significant time period.
2. Immediate cutover to the new system after intensive volume testing.

Although the concept of running parallel is widely heralded as being desirable, it has features all its own which often preclude its effective use. Its key weakness is that the new system may not be (usually, is not) exactly comparable to the old system. The appealing idea in parallel running is that data can be processed through both the new and the old system, and that the end results of this processing can simply be compared to verify that the new system operates properly. The problems here are obvious. First is that to run simultaneously *two* systems, which may have different input formats, different operating procedures, and even different outputs, imposes a gigantic load on the organization. The operating departments must do close to double their normal work. When there is no time left to solve problems in the new system, parallel running may continue for a prolonged period or until the new system is dropped, simply because there are no resources to devote to its effective operation. Second, the existing system may operate with much less precision than the new system, so its end results look different from the EDP system. To trace back a variety of differences on a continuing basis requires a tremendous amount of effort.

The immediate cutover strategy avoids the problems of parallel operations, but creates a more risky situation should the system fail to operate properly.

Here, the important factor is full-scale volume testing before the system is converted. For example, in a payroll system, a good test may be to take one week's payroll a month or more before system conversion is scheduled and use it as a full test. An intensive run of the new system on one week's payroll will provide the users with a full set of outputs for complete verification of the system. Verification can be done at a moderately leisurely pace because of the time interval between the full-scale volume test and the cutover point. Thus, there is time in the process to correct problems and assure that the new system is meeting specifications. Then, when cutover is made, the likelihood of substantial conceptual or program problems is minimized.

I believe that, in most cases, the best approach to conversion is that of full-volume testing and then immediate cutover. Full volume testing provides several fringe benefits, such as a thorough test of the new system and an example to users of what the system will really do.

A period of initial system operation follows system conversion. This is a crucial period in the system's life, when most system flaws will make themselves evident. It is also a time when users lack complete confidence in the new system and are overloaded with problems of changeover. The EDP staff must not lessen its efforts during this period, for it is here that the highest response activity will be required, particularly if the corporation is now committed to operating under the new system. Too often, systems projects are scheduled so that immediately upon conversion few, if any, resources are available for handling postconversion problems.

A final note on the first postconversion operation is that, during the system's initial running, the EDP staff will often be subjected, not to hurrahs from users, but to intense criticism because of problems encountered in the conversion process. Often, for example, the new system points up user problems that have never been obvious before. It is possible for a rather depressive psychology to develop at this point, and the only way of overcoming it is by effective action and management support for the new system at all levels.

Planning for systems and programming work

Heavy EDP project backlogs and user frustration at the long lead times required for development of EDP systems characterize most companies today. There exists no lack of ideas on what to computerize; what is scarce is the means to turn these ideas into smoothly operating systems.

In this context, project selection and planning becomes an item of key importance. Out of a mass of ideas for justifiable projects, management must build a realistic and attainable schedule of projects that are, in fact, to be undertaken. Ideally, those with the highest rate of return will be selected.

Planning for the systems and programming effort must take into account several different kinds of work that are going on at all times.

1. DEVELOPMENT OF NEW SYSTEMS.   This requires design, initial analysis, and programming for new EDP applications.

2. MAJOR REVISIONS TO EXISTING SYSTEMS. This entails changes to operating systems that are necessary because of major organizational changes, new data processing requirements, etc.

3. MAINTENANCE OF EXISTING SYSTEMS. This is the effort that is required on a continuing basis to keep systems in operation. At the lowest level, it involves removing program "bugs" that arise even in systems that have been in operation for a long period of time. Obviously, as time goes on, maintenance work for an application which is not itself changed should decline and require less and less effort. However, in most operations, there is always substantial flow of effort still required in this area. Many organizations have set up a separate group called maintenance programming simply to handle such work.

4. UNPLANNED WORK. Electronic data processing plans should always allow for effort to satisfy short-term system requirements. This means the implementation of fairly simple jobs that rely on an existing data base and for which requirements are impossible to predict.

Data processing applications can be best viewed as capital investments. They require initial expenditures for analysis and programming effort, with no effective results. Later, after implementation, they produce a flow of cost savings or better decision-making capability in the whole system that pays for initial development and creates a return to the corporation.

The investment consists of:

1. Analysis and design of the system. The cost here is primarily that of the human effort required to look at the proposed application in enough depth to determine what information will be processed, how the system will operate, what programs and equipment are required, etc.
2. Programming of the application. Again, a major commitment of human resources.
3. Computer time required for programming, testing, and conversion.
4. Training of operating and EDP personnel, development of procedures, etc.

The time pressures exerted on the EDP manager often create an environment where projects are accepted without reasonable estimates of total development cost. This is obviously a mistake and a tendency which must be counteracted. Developing such an estimate requires time, primarily in initial analysis of the system, to see what really is involved and what, in fact, will be the impact on other systems and procedures within the corporation. It is highly unlikely that a good estimate of project development cost can be made until enough analysis has been done to determine, as a minimum, precisely what programs will be required and what operating procedures will be necessary. For a major project, this may require several man-months.

This means that the project selection process should be broken into two phases. At the end of the first phase, the EDP manager must know how much total effort will be required to implement the proposed system. Operating management must know precisely what the results of the proposed system will be, what new reports will be available, how much clerical time will be saved, what new information will be produced to aid in more effective decision making. At this point, the project decision—go or no-go—should be made, based on sound business judgements of costs and returns.

The fact that many more EDP ideas are available than there are resources to achieve them makes the rational evaluation of new projects even more important. Management must have the means to weigh project proposals against each other, so that a truly meaningful set of commitments will be made. The process of comparing a project which will save the accounting department clerical money to a project which will improve marketing resources is a very sophisticated one requiring real management judgement. If sound business judgement is not injected into the project selection process, projects which have the most tangible savings (often clerical cost elimination) or those which are the most exciting to the EDP staff (such as those requiring sophisticated use of the computer) will be selected. This selection may be correct, but it is important that the process be strongly influenced by managers concerned with business objectives and the importance of making the company more successful. This means that a formal or semi-formal method of project selection is extremely desirable to assure that major projects are effectively analyzed and that project commitments are not made without considering all the factors relevant to the decision.

Once the investment in a new system has been made, there may be striking opportunities for relatively simple new projects that were not conceived at the time that the major system was planned. Since these projects are high rate-of-return items, it would appear unwise to put them into long project backlogs. They are usually small enough in nature so that a detailed analysis of their return may not be justified. Therefore, the EDP organization should include enough capability for doing a reasonable amount of unplanned work on a fast turnaround basis.

The most effective way of planning the creative effort is to isolate and make reasonable estimates for work of the four varieties previously described. The planning must be highly sensitive to overall corporate plans. New systems and required major revisions to existing systems are of utmost importance, if the EDP staff is to be capable of meeting these requirements. As discussed in earlier sections, the desirability of good overall estimating rules for determining the level of effort necessary to achieve a set of objectives is absolutely essential to good estimating, planning, and budgeting. Without such rules, the EDP staff and its budget are likely to be such that it will provide inferior service to the organizational users of this capability.

The EDP creative staff is a key organizational service unit. Its plans, budgets, and staffing must be of adequate quality and quantity to satisfy requirements placed on it by a wide variety of users. Such planning requires aggressive projections of what needs to be done. The EDP staff must recognize and account for sound ideas of new projects, changes, and other types of work. A mode of operation as a responder only, with no real comprehension of fundamental requirements, precludes both good planning and high level professional service to the organization.

Managing the production effort

The EDP production effort, commonly called Operations, is a facility equivalent to a manufacturing assembly department. It converts raw date to finished products, normally reports, via a series of well-defined operations. These operations consist of steps, such as data transcription, unit record processing, and computer processing. In addition, strong quality control must be exercised, taking the form of internal and external controls on data, to assure that the outputs truly reflect the impact of raw data submitted as input.

Organization and staffing

The operations organization typically contains these subunits:

1. The data transcription section, normally a key-punch operation, responsible for receiving raw data, transcribing and verification, and delivering machine processible data to the operation.

2. The scheduling and control section, responsible for setting up standard runs, for maintaining tape and disk library records, and for logging and controlling run results to assure their accuracy.

3. The machine operations section, responsible for physical operation of the computer and other types of equipment.

The heart of the operation lies in the scheduling and control area, where available machine time is allocated, records are kept, and quality control is maintained. Ideally, machine operators always run fully prepared jobs from clear operating instructions, and no machine time is lost by decision making at actual run-time.

A smooth running and efficient operation requires a sound set of procedures enforced in each section and good supervision of all tasks. Key jobs, such as maintenance of the tape library, should be audited frequently to assure strict compliance to established standards. Mistakes, requiring reconstruction of previous data, are extremely costly and make precision, even under intense production pressure, a vital component of every EDP operations job.

The EDP operations area is a fine training ground for programmers and analysts. One company puts new programmers into operations for several months for training. The gain is threefold: close exposure to many EDP applications, familiarity with hardware, and a feeling for how to write programs that are easy for operations to run.

As might also be expected, EDP operations offers a source of programming talent for the future, which should not be overlooked or restricted by organizational barriers involving transfers from one type of job to another. Machine operators are more available than programmers, and much of the experience in this area is directly applicable training for a programming career.

Basic production techniques—scheduling and control

The bulk of EDP work involves scheduled production: producing outputs on a regular, known basis. Scheduling is a highly critical factor, because most EDP operations are operating close to the limit of available capacity; the massive capital outlays for equipment preclude built-in excess processing time. Also, capacity cannot be increased easily or quickly; in the short term, schedules must conform to the capacity constraint, if acceptable service is to be realized. Unlike a manufacturing department, there is no buffer inventory that can be utilized to smooth output in the face of input or processing variations.

Scheduling the EDP operation requires knowing all requirements and a constant analysis of workloads in the light of volume changes and changing systems. Of major significance are peak loads, such as those generated by monthly or quarterly closing operations. The operations staff must plan for peaks, assure that time is available to meet them, and plan for non-critical jobs in such a way that time requirements are smoothed.

The keys to effective control are realistic scheduling techniques and sound understanding of the schedules throughout the organization, so that every operating unit is sensitive to the end product requirements and is in a position to provide feedback on internal problems or late data that could cause delays in output. As in any production operation, it is important to know early that data will be late, so that corrective action can be taken or, at minimum, so that this fact can be communicated to the key users of the data. In other words, the information about schedules is nearly as important as meeting the schedules themselves, and the service organization must be geared up and sensitive to the overall need for determining its position relative to schedules. In many applications, there is so much dependence on EDP operations that a major organizational crisis can develop if schedules are not met, without advance communication and an effective method for rescheduling these operations.

The EDP production operation is a key service organization. As such, it must be sensitive to multiple users' needs, and willing to work out compromises to compensate for various types of problems as they arise.

Analysis of performance

The production unit is evaluated on several factors, including:
1. Performance versus schedule.
2. Quality of output.
3. Cost of output.

Adequate information for assessing trends in these factors must be maintained within the EDP area.

Of particular importance to the EDP area, as a source of control information, are computer-run logs. Such logs usually show what jobs have been run, how long they have taken (both in machine-time and in total elapsed time), and what amount of reruns were necessary during any given time period. Analysis can show many of the problems of the production organization. It can indicate when peaks are so heavy that schedules cannot possibly be met, when rerun time is causing excessive workloads, and which jobs have heavy setup times relative to run-times. All of these factors may be a result of poor production operations, *i.e.* inexperienced operators or ineffective production controls. They may indicate that the system's planning and development has been faulty, so that jobs, which have a high tendency for error, are being run or are set up in such a way that they become extremely difficult to run.

Records in the production area should also include good volume data on all jobs currently being processed, so that changes in volumes can be seen before they impose heavy loads on the production operation. By using such records consistently and effectively, the EDP manager can gain a good feeling for the personnel and equipment requirements within the computer area and can start to develop a sound body of data which will play a key role in determining new hardware requirements, new personnel requirements, and weaknesses in both the production and the creative organization.

Feedback to systems and programming

The EDP production area should be extremely sensitive to feeding information back to the systems and programming group. The types of information that are most useful are suggestions on how to improve the operations of existing systems, recognition of changes in data volumes and input characteristics that make additional system design desirable, and information about control problems where programming work could significantly simplify or improve the control of data through the processing runs.

It is essential that a good channel of communication exist between the production group and the systems and programming section, so that such feedback can be effective both in improving existing systems and designing new ones. It is also essential that information on new systems be given to the production section in advance of their initial operation. Quite often the operations group will be able to improve on the design and also will be able to learn the concepts of the new system, so that their ability to solve initial problems and effectively control and process the data will be enhanced.

Documentation from programmers should be highly formal, so that operations can run most jobs without reference to the systems and programming area. All new jobs should be approved by the operations section before they are accepted for running. Complete documentation of these jobs should be required before such approval is given.

Security

Many EDP operations have experienced explosive growth over the past decade, compounded by numerous hardware and software changes. One result has been a general lack of attention to basic security precautions. While the accounting department regularly locks valuable corporate data in security files, often vastly more data in more compact form are left loosely attended in the computer room.

The objectives of a security system should be:

1. To insure day-to-day control and availability of data, *i.e.* normal retention of past files, so that if data is destroyed by program, machine, or operator errors, rapid recovery can be made.

2. To insure that EDP operations can continue on all necessary jobs in the event of destruction in the EDP area itself caused by fire, vandalism, etc.

A security system, then, normally involves both adequate operating control of data and programs, and either "second location" storage of key files, programs, and documentation or fire and theft-proof storage in the primary location. The ingredients of a sound system are regular rotation and updating of material earmarked for recovery, and periodic review of the system to assure it is operating effectively in the light of changing EDP requirements. Such a system should be critically assessed to make sure that:

1. Everything absolutely necessary is included.

2. Unnecessary items are not included. Often the temptation is to store everything, which creates an expensive operation or one that crumbles under its own weight.

Planning production capacity

In order to successfully meet its service requirements, the EDP operation must have the capacity for several types of jobs.

1. SCHEDULED PRODUCTION. This is the running of normally scheduled jobs as discussed in the preceding section. In most operations, this accounts for the bulk of production time.

2. SPECIAL REQUESTS. Sufficient capacity should be available to run special request jobs which are required by the organization on a high response basis. The magnitude and number of such jobs can be determined from past records and from the type of organization involved. At any rate, in most operations, some jobs of this nature are required, and the service of running them on a rapid turn around basis is an important ingredient of the total service factor.

3. SYSTEMS AND PROGRAMMING TIME. The EDP operation must supply adequate time for programming and systems testing of programs. Some operations are closed shops, where all testing is done by the operations staff itself. Other operations are of an open shop nature, where programmers are allowed on the machine during specific times of the day for testing. However test-time is handled, specific consideration must go to the amount of it required for supporting the programming staff.

4. RERUN AND DOWNTIME. Adequate capacity must also be allowed for a normal volume of reruns and for times that the computer system is down. To schedule an operation to the hilt, assuming no reruns and no downtime is courting disaster. Again, the computer logs can be used to determine historically how much rerun time and how much downtime is required. The point here is that it is essential to allow for imperfect input data and operations performance, if realistic planning is to be done.

Planning the EDP capacity involves continual monitoring of the production operation and good liaison with new systems that are being developed, so that their impact on production time can be combined with the impact of volume changes in existing operations to determine when new capacity must be added. The capacity planning problem is increased because of the long lead times for acquiring new EDP equipment and the tremendous conversion costs for shifting from one system to another.

Chapter 31 discusses many of the problems inherent in evaluating the acquisition of new computer hardware. The only comment necessary here is that such an evaluation will be much more effective if the operation is well-controlled so that information on current processing requirements are readily available. In such an evaluation, the operations information system becomes of key importance. By using it, one can develop a model of the current mix of EDP jobs and isolate various critical factors in evaluating what type of new equipment is best for handling the corporation's EDP jobs. Essentially, evaluating capacity involves analysis of existing operations, new systems requirements, and a feeling for overall corporate plans.

PART VI

Control,
measurement,
reporting, and
evaluation of
operations

Reporting to operating management

E. B. Rickard*

The purpose of this chapter is to examine the problems involved in developing a reporting and control system for operating management and describe the principal factors which ought to determine the structure and content of such a system. It is not our intention to deal with this subject by describing operating reports which can or should be used in specific situations. Such a discussion of specialized reports would have limited general application. Business situations are so varied and the informational needs of operating management so highly personal that standardized reports are not likely to meet the desires or needs of different managements. A reporting and control system needs to be custom tailored to the specific environment.

This individuality of any particular reporting and control system does not mean, however, that no ground rules exist or no generalizations can be drawn with respect to the premises or concepts on which such a system rests. The reporting and control systems of successful companies usually have certain well defined characteristics. In this chapter, we will deal with the more important of these characteristics.

Preceding chapters have dealt with various responsibilities of the financial executive which are primarily oriented toward the future, such as planning and budgeting. Succeeding chapters in this part of the Handbook deal with the control, measurement, and evaluation of performance, and to an important degree, are concerned with analyses or evaluations of past performance.

---

* Marketing Services Manager, Ford Motor Company, Dearborn, Michigan.

Basic concepts and philosophy

Obviously, a major share of the time and attention of operating management must be directed toward planning for the future in addition to monitoring the performance of the organization in the recent past. Since actions taken to improve the future position of the company eventually, through the passage of time, find their way into historical performance reports, management has a right to expect that the reporting and control system will provide for a logical and understandable bridge which will permit it to deal with future problems and examine past problems within the confines of a single, comprehensive, internally consistent reporting system. There cannot be two unrelated systems, one facing the future, the other facing the past. One of the important purposes of this chapter is to examine this interrelationship between the past and the future, and indicate how management decisions relative to the future of the business affect the system for measuring and evaluating past performance.

Operating management defined

The term "operating management" needs some clarification for purposes of this discussion. Everyone in a business organization who is charged with a supervisory responsibility is a part of operating management and has a need for information which will tell him whether he is discharging his responsibilities well or poorly. The general manager of a business (including the general manager of a division within a larger corporate entity) is clearly part of the group which "operates" the business. So are the key subordinates of a general manager who are in charge of such areas as marketing, manufacturing, engineering, purchasing, public relations, finance, and similar functional activities. In the same vein, regional or local sales managers, plant managers, plant foremen, and unit supervisors in finance, purchasing, or engineering have operating responsibilities which will condition the development of an effective reporting and control system for operating management.

In brief, operating management embraces everyone from a general manager to the lowest supervisory employee. The reports used by this group represent the foundation of the control system used by these various organizational components. This system of reports gives tangible expression to the management control concepts which have been adopted by the company.

Effect of basic corporate objectives on the reporting system

If a business enterprise is to succeed it must define its basic objectives concisely and unambiguously so that individual members of the organization can have a clear frame of reference in which to develop plans or programs and make operating decisions. Obviously its objectives must be understood and pursued by operating management in the day-to-day operation of the business. It is equally clear that its objectives will have a major bearing on the reporting and control system used by management. However, individual companies can and do state their basic objectives in a great variety of ways. Some companies have adopted lengthy statements of objectives, while others have simply stated that their principal purpose is to make money. In this discussion, we shall assume that the principal reason for forming the particular business enterprise was to prosper financially and, therefore, the company wishes to

a) maximize, in the long run, the return on investment which it realizes from the economic resources which it presently has at its disposal, and

b) seek opportunities for the investment of additional capital resources on which a satisfactory return can be realized in the long run.

The reports used by the general manager must relate directly to these basic long-run objectives of the business. He and his superiors must know whether the long-run profit position of the business is, in fact, improving. He must also know whether the managers of functional areas are making an effective contribution to profits within their separate areas of responsibility. The reports prepared for his benefit must be designed to assist him in forming these judgments. The reports prepared for managers of separate functional areas of the business, such as marketing, manufacturing, purchasing and engineering, will inevitably be more detailed than the reports given to general management, but these reports need to be developed on a basis which is entirely consistent with the reports given to general management. They should generally employ the same analytical, accounting or financial conventions; they must use the same basic assumptions in areas of uncertainty; and they must tell a story which is consistent with, albeit more detailed than, the story told in the reports given to general management. Otherwise, general management can have a different view of the basic problems of a functional area than does the manager of that area. In the same vein, the reports used by subordinate areas within a functional activity, such as a plant foreman, local sales manager or a supervisor of a research and development project, may be more detailed than the reports used by their supervisors but the two sets of reports must be mutually consistent.

In brief, there is a "pecking order" in a reporting and control system. The overall pattern is set by the reports used by general management. At each successively lower level of organization, there is a need for more detail, but there is also a need for compatibility and consistency with the reports used by higher levels of management. Since the main interest of a general manager will center on how to improve the future profits and return on investment of his business, he must have available reports which describe the performance of his subordinates in terms of their contribution to the improvement of long run profits. How he should do so will be an important part of this discussion.

To bring a discussion of this broad spectrum of reports into manageable proportions, we shall concentrate our attention on the reporting and control system as it applies to the general manager of a product division or "business," the managers of key functional areas of the business (such as marketing, manufacturing, engineering and purchasing) and their principal subordinates. We shall not deal with the reporting and control problems associated with the more routine functions of the business. The reports needed for effective control and supervision in routine areas is a matter of considerable importance but, since the operating responsibilities in these areas are clearly defined and operating results can usually be expressed in objective terms, the design of an appropriate reporting and control system is not too difficult. Such reports can consist of some relatively simple description of performance such as physical units produced or sold compared with an approved budget or spending plan.

Basic concepts underlying reports for general management

If a general manager is expected to maximize profits from the products which are under his control, he must, as we have indicated, receive reports which permit an evaluation of the quality of his profit performance, past, present, and future. However, such a need requires that a decision be made as to the criteria to be used in deciding whether his performance is acceptable or not. It is clear that return on investment, taken alone, is not an adequate measure, since it can be maintained or increased even when profits are declining provided the investment in the business is reduced commensurately. Return on investment can be used to measure the effectiveness with which the existing resources of the business are being utilized, but it needs to be supplemented by some indication of the adequacy of the absolute level of earnings. In many companies, this latter measure is achieved by establishing a target level for sales (such as a given absolute level of sales volume or a percentage share of the market) together with a planned level of profit on those sales. In other words, the general manager is expected to maintain or improve his total sales or his share of the market, maintain profit margins commensurate with or better than his competitors (allowing for the effect of differing levels of vertical integration), and earn a competitive rate of return on the investment for which he is responsible. If he succeeds on all three counts, he should be given credit for doing an excellent job.

The foundation of a reporting and control system consists of those reports which describe a general manager's profit performance in these terms. Moreover, these reports should not only describe his past performance but should indicate his probable future performance. But this is by no means enough for a general manager. It is also essential that he be well informed as to the impact which various factors are likely to have on his future profit performance. From this point of view, the most important unit of information for a general manager is "the decision." There is nothing a general manager can now do to alter the results which have been produced in the past year, month, week or day. His only opportunity for improving profits is through the development of a better input of decisions than his competitors. The quality of those decisions will be virtually the sole determinant of the quality of his future profit performance.

Decisions determine the operating plan of the business

It was suggested at the beginning of this chapter that there should not be two separate control systems, one of which relates to the impact of the decision-making process on future profits, and a second which deals with historical information and after-the-fact performance evaluations. It is not uncommon in practice, however, to see reporting systems which appear to have been developed on an *ad hoc* basis with no attempt to integrate the past and the future into a unified and comprehensive management control system.

Decision making is the essence of managerial responsibility. However, one of the more perplexing problems which can face a general manager after he has made his own decisions, or has reviewed the plans and evaluated the decisions of his subordinates, is how to keep himself adequately informed as to the profit position he will occupy in the future as a result of all of these determinations. Obviously, some simple workable system must exist for summarizing their cumulative financial effect in a readily digestible form. Otherwise he is flying blind.

The solution to this problem is not difficult if the expected financial consequences of the more important decisions have been described clearly as part of the decision-making process. As a matter of fact, if management was told the probable financial consequences of a decision *before* the decision was made, all of the information needed for accumulating and summarizing the effect of that decision is readily available. Of course, if decisions are made with no adequate attention to the financial consequences of those decisions, it is apparent that there will be no timely way of summarizing their financial effect.

The summarizing technique can be illustrated by a somewhat oversimplified example. Assume that a decision has been made to build a new plant which will permit the company to replace several obsolete plants and expand its product line by producing a new group of products. If this decision is made in an orderly and financially responsible manner, the estimated effect of the decision on future profits will have been determined in advance, along with the added investment which will result from the decision. Hence, if the decision is approved, these representations become, in effect, a set of commitments on the part of the managers of the functional areas who are responsible for the execution of the decision. These commitments should cover all the important aspects of the decision and will include:

Timing of all physical aspects of the decision.
a) Beginning and end of the design and construction phase of the new plant, supported by a detailed timing plan for the total construction project.
b) Duration of new plant launching and rate of acceleration of production.

Financial consequences of the decision (time-phased by month or quarter).
a) Estimated profit and return on investment from the new product line.
b) Estimated monthly or annual volumes of production and estimated production costs to permit a determination of the production costs of the new product and the production cost savings expected from existing products to be manufactured in the new facility.
c) Cost of the new facility, fully equipped, and the effect on investment as well as variable and fixed manufacturing costs.
d) Launching costs of the new plant, including employee training requirements and related costs.
e) Advertising and promotion program for the new product.
f) Tooling and engineering costs.

Nonfinancial or quasifinancial considerations.
a) Quality level planned for the new product and the effect of the new plant on the quality level of existing products.
b) Union relationship problems, if any, resulting from opening the new plant and closing the old plants.
c) Community relations at the new location and at the location of the plants to be closed.

The data used in arriving at this decision can be readily incorporated into a pro forma financial statement showing how future years will be affected.

This example over-simplifies a complex decision but it illustrates two points of fundamental importance to a general manager. First, as decisions are being made, he needs to know whether the decision appears to be sound financially and will produce profits in the long run which are commensurate with the added investment required by the decision.[1]

---

[1] Stated more precisely, there must be an evaluation of the risks of possible failure versus the rewards which flow from success. A decision to proceed is not an assurance of success. It merely indicates that the manager feels the potential rewards justify the risks.

Second, he must be sure that an effective system exists for controlling the execution of the decision. Of course, the only way such a decision can be executed effectively is to make sure that each participant has a clear idea as to what his contribution is to be and then establish a reporting system which indicates whether each is performing according to plan.

Financial Effect of New Plant/New Product Decision
(in millions)

	Annual Profits	Total Assets (or Assets Less Related Liabilities)
Current Financial Position	$1,000	$10,000
First Year		
Tooling & engineering costs for new product	(100)	
Production planning costs related to activation of new facility	(30)	
	$ 870	
Second Year		
Net savings in fixed cost associated with closing obsolete plants	50	
Cost of new plant		1,000
Adverse effect on production costs during launching of the new plant	(75)	
Advertising program for new product	(50)	
Net loss realized on sales of the new product (excluding costs shown elsewhere) due to low volume in startup period	(100)	
Added inventory of new product		75
	$ 695	
Third Year		
Increased sales, inventories and profits from new product	400	25
Reduced production costs due to end of launching and increased efficiency from new plant	200	
Financial Position at End of Third Year	$1,295	$11,100

The importance of controlling the execution of a decision explains why the financial and timing elements of a decision should be viewed as a firm commitment on the part of the managers of the functional areas which are responsible for execution. In the example given above, the expected profits may not materialize if, for example, the plant is not completed approximately on time, if production costs and launching costs greatly exceed the original estimates, if sales of the new product are well below expectations, or if the quality of production in the new plant is unsatisfactory. Representations which cause a general manager to approve a commitment of funds should be good enough to be used as a target, budget or performance objective for measuring the performance of the responsible functional activities in executing the decision.

This concept is the crux of an effective reporting and control system. A general manager is essentially a decision maker who must not only have better ideas than his competitors, but must also have a system for assuring that these ideas are effectively executed by his subordinates.

The decision to build a new plant which was just discussed illustrates the manner in which a specific decision can be related to the future financial position of the business. This not only needs to be done for important product or facility decisions but should be done for all important decisions. For example, the general manager needs to know the financial results which can reasonably be expected from a planned expansion of the sales force to cover new territories, or an expansion of manpower and promotional expenditures to secure a larger share of the market in areas presently served by the company. The same applies to decisions affecting production processes, production scheduling, product quality or production inventories. The research and development program of the company also needs to be projected in these terms so that the overall dimensions of the program can be defined, including the future level of expenditures, the types of projects to be explored and the expected output of commercially feasible product ideas which will be of future benefit to the company.

Every organizational component in the company needs to have an operating plan for the future. The plan for a given component may simply be to continue to operate in the future as it has in the past. For example, the public relations activity may have no plan to change its manpower or operating practices. In this situation, the financial projects for future years will presumably be the same as in the past. Other activities which handle routine functions such as payrolls, inventories or accounts receivable may plan to continue unchanged, or may, for example, decide to automate their operation through new data processing techniques. In the latter instance, the effect of this decision will require a careful evaluation of the benefits of the new system in terms of cost effects as well as the impact on the accuracy and timeliness of the work done by these activities.

Structure of general management reports

In most companies, the operating plans of each organizational component are the subject of an annual review and evaluation which results in the establishment of specific operating budgets. These budgets describe the results expected from these organizational components in terms of actions to be taken, money to be spent, and results to be produced. The individual budgets, when taken collectively, describe the expenditures and results which are projected for the business as a whole and constitute the financial plan or financial budget of the business. The existence of such a financial plan clearly makes it possible to develop financial summaries which set forth the estimated future revenues, costs, profits, assets, and liabilities of the business. Information of this type which would be shown to the general manager is set forth in Exhibit 1. A

EXHIBIT 1

XYZ Division of the ABC Company
Sales and Profits

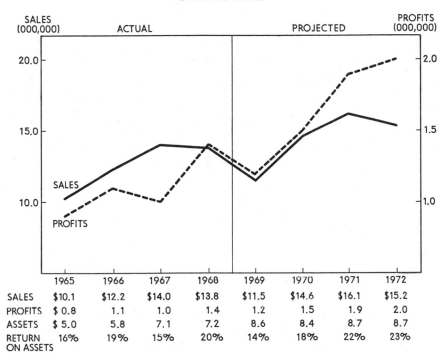

	1965	1966	1967	1968	1969	1970	1971	1972
SALES	$10.1	$12.2	$14.0	$13.8	$11.5	$14.6	$16.1	$15.2
PROFITS	$ 0.8	1.1	1.0	1.4	1.2	1.5	1.9	2.0
ASSETS	$ 5.0	5.8	7.1	7.2	8.6	8.4	8.7	8.7
RETURN ON ASSETS	16%	19%	15%	20%	14%	18%	22%	23%

general manager needs more detailed information than is provided in this summary. In particular, he needs to have actual and planned profits by product line, including a description of the factors which cause profits to change from year to year.

Reports on product line profits

The most sophisticated method of performance evaluation cannot overcome an unsound and uneconomic product concept and, therefore, general management must consistently devote time and attention to an evaluation of the attractiveness and profitability of its offerings to customers.

The profits shown on Exhibit 1 can, by applying appropriate alloca-

tion techniques to fixed and semi-variable costs, be subdivided to show
the trend of profits on each product line in terms of absolute profits,
profits per unit, and return on investment. Presumably, product lines
which have reached planned volume levels, have produced an adequate
level of profit and resulted in a reasonable return on investment, will be
given less attention while detailed analyses may be made of products
which generate losses or a low return on investment.

There are a variety of ways for the senior management of a company
to motivate a divisional manager to pay adequate attention to product

EXHIBIT 2

Sales by Product Line

(in millions)

Product Line	Actual				Projected			
	1965	1966	1967	1968	1969	1970	1971	1972
Current Product								
A—Units								
Dollars								
B—Units								
Dollars								
C—Units								
Dollars								
etc.								
Future Products								
AA—Units								
Dollars								
BB—Units								
Dollars								
etc.								
Total Dollar								
Sales								

problems, but one of the most effective is to see to it that the reporting
system clearly identifies such problems. The reports which are discussed
below are typical of those found in many companies where product
problems are given intensive and continuing review.

A summary report is illustrated in Exhibit 2 and shows past and
projected future sales volumes for each of the product lines offered for
sale. It also shows new products which are under development and
indicates when those products will be on the market. The data are shown
on a unit basis as well as total sales dollars and the figures may be
projected as far as five or ten years into the future. The report should be
expanded to show information on the market share secured or planned
for each product line if that information is available and is deemed to be
important. This particular report would be prepared at least annually,
and probably quarterly, for review by the general manager of the

interested division and for review by the senior management of the company.

A second product report represents a summary of sales profits and return on investment by product line. This report would usually be prepared at least quarterly and would show actual data for the past several years as well as projected profits and returns for the next three to five years. The report would presumably be similar in format to Exhibit 1 except that it would cover individual product lines rather than summarizing all product lines.

This report needs to be supported by analyses which describe in some detail the factors which are expected to affect the future profits of each product line. The general manager is then not only aware of the anticipated changes in future profits but is also aware of the factors which will cause those changes. These supporting analyses can begin by setting forth the changes anticipated in future profits in the manner shown in Exhibit 3. The information shown in Exhibit 3 can be further subdivided to show the effect of these profit changes by product lines (Exhibit 4).

EXHIBIT 3

ABC Company

Analysis of Profit Changes

1969 to 1972

(dollars in millions)

	Actual Profits 1968	Projected			
		1969	*1970*	*1971*	*1972*
Prior Year Profits	$15.0	$ 15.0	$ 15.3	$ 18.9	$ 17.2
Profit Changes					
Product Programs		1.0	2.5	(3.0)	1.7
Changes not reflected in product programs					
Economics (general changes in cost of wages & materials)		(0.5)	(0.5)	(0.5)	(0.5)
Planned price increases on existing products		0.2	0.4	0.2	0.2
Facility changes— manufacturing and ware- housing		0.2	0.5	0.7	0.1
Sales expansion, excluding product program effect		0.6	0.6	0.6	0.6
Cost reduction plans					
Administrative expense		0.2	0.1	—	—
Engineering (excluding product program effect)		0.1	0.2	—	—
Other programs		(0.5)	(0.2)	0.3	—
Total Profit Change		$ 0.3	$ 3.6	$ (1.7)	$ 2.1
Profits at Year End		$ 15.3	$ 18.9	$ 17.2	$ 19.3
Assets Allocated at Year End		$175.0	$186.5	$190.2	$193.0
Return on Average Annual Assets		9.0%	10.1%	9.1%	10.1%

EXHIBIT 4

ABC Company

Product Line A—Profit Changes

1968–1972

	Actual Unit Profit 1968	1969	1970	1971	1972
Prior Year Unit Profit	$4.50	$4.50	$4.77	$5.20	$4.68
Product changes					
Material cost—design changes		.35	(.10)	(.20)	.13
Tooling		(.10)	.05	(.10)	.40
Engineering		(.13)	(.10)	.18	.20
Other		.05	.08	—	—
Effect of product changes on volume and mix		.25	—	—	—
Economics (general changes in cost of wages and materials)		(.60)	(.60)	(.60)	(.60)
Planned price changes		.35	.20	.10	.10
Effect of new facilities					
Launching		(.20)	.20	—	—
Other		.10	.40	—	—
Effect of other company programs		.20	.39	.10	—
Unit profit change		$ .27	$ .43	$ (.52)	$ .23
Unit Profit		$4.77	$5.20	$4.68	$4.91
Normal Volume					
Units		100,000	103,000	106,000	109,000
Dollar sales (000)		$2,020	$2,106	$2,184	$2,250
Total Profit (000)		$ 477	$ 536	$ 496	$ 535
Assets (Allocated) at Year End (000)		$4,562	$4,860	$5,006	$5,289
% Return on Average Assets		10.1%	11.2%	9.5%	10.3%

A third type of product report is designed to focus attention on products with low profit margins. Products which produce a return on investment of less than a stipulated percentage would be listed on this report. A divisional manager could be expected to review this report with senior management of the company each time a formal review was held of the operation of his division. He would be expected to have a full understanding of the profit problems on each of these product lines and have a recommended course of action for dealing with those problems.

The precise form and content of these reports are not important since they presumably would be modified in some respects if they were adapted to a particular company. However, they illustrate a general approach and describe the general content of a product reporting system for use by general management.

The profit problems of a product line are uniquely the problems of the general manager and he must secure analyses or arrange for special studies which will help him to understand these problems. The analyses may indicate that the problems are due to the quality or styling of the product, lack of adequate breadth in the product line, noncompetitive selling prices which have had an adverse effect on sales volume, excessive production or marketing costs, and so on. The precise nature of the profit problems may not be apparent and may prove to be a complex mixture of many things. However, the general manager is the final diagnostician and is the only person who can decide what corrective actions need to be taken and what the relative priority of those actions should be.

A point worth emphasizing is that the recurring financial reports used by the general manager can identify problems—but they cannot provide solutions. Solutions require a different perspective. The corrective plan of action will rely heavily on special studies and reports which are nonfinancial in content. Product problems are repaired by physical actions such as improved quality, more efficient production, improved facilities or increased manpower. The general manager must form his own judgment, with assistance from the financial executive and others as to whether these physical actions will produce an improved financial result which may ultimately be acceptable.

Performance reports for functional areas

It is axiomatic that delegations of responsibility to functional areas must be accompanied by the authority to guide and direct these activities within the limits of the delegation. However, that authority must also be accompanied by a system of accountability which permits a general manager to develop meaningful reports on the stewardship of the individual in charge. A delegation of authority from a general manager with no effective system of accountability is not a delegation; it is an abdication on his part. The general manager should know what he expects from each functional area on as precise and quantitive a basis as possible and should have a reporting system which describes performance in those terms.

The interest of a general manager in having an effective system of accountability stems from his need to motivate subordinates to further *his* basic objective of improving the long run financial position of the business, rather than pursue their more provincial interests. Clearly, if he is to achieve this, the system of accountability must be tied into *his* financial plan for future years. The budgets, operating targets and performance objectives which he approves as part of that financial plan must be clearly assigned to specific functional areas so that, to the fullest extent possible, the responsibility for executing that plan is clearly placed.

The recurring reports used in any system of performance evaluation will ordinarily compare actual or estimated actual performance with an assigned objective, budget, target, or goal. This is the essence of the message which is found in financial and business literature on the subject of budget administration. The concept that budgets are the performance standards or the plan with which actual results are compared is well understood. Financial and business literature is less clear on how those performance standards or plans should be established in order to assure that functional areas are assigned a task which is a well defined, discrete segment of a total financial plan.

The interdependence which exists between functional areas is one of the principal complications which affects this assignment of financial responsibility. Consider the problem of evaluating performance of the purchasing activity with respect to the cost of raw materials or purchased components used in production. These costs may change because of changes in sales volume or mix changes. However, that type of cost change would reflect neither credit nor discredit on the purchasing activity. Also, purchased costs may change because of higher prices for basic raw materials, higher wage rates in supplying industries or similar changes in the economic situation which are beyond the control of the purchasing activity. Moreover, design or specification changes proposed by the engineering activity can have an important impact on the cost of purchased items.

If the performance of the purchasing activity is to be evaluated, it is apparent that an effort must be made to segregate the effect on the cost of purchased items of changing sales volume and mix, economic changes, and specification or design changes. If this can be done, the residual cost changes would represent a far more precise description of the contribution of the purchasing activity to the profit position of the business. By the same token, such analyses would permit the cost increases or decreases caused by the engineering or marketing activities to be isolated and assigned to the responsible functional area.

In the same vein, the manufacturing activity can have its performance affected to a significant degree by cost changes which are caused by others, such as changes in sales volume or mix, launching new products, capacity expansions, design or engineering changes and basic economic changes in the cost of labor and material. These extraneous factors need to be identified and their effect eliminated if the performance of the manufacturing activity is to be evaluated realistically. Performance reports which fail to allow for such adjustments not only generate frustrations within the management system but will eventually fail to motivate the individuals who find they cannot meet the goals which have been set because of factors beyond their control.

How are these factors to be taken into account? First, let us examine the practices to be followed in setting the goals for the year just ahead. The sales quotas, expense budgets, and other elements of the operating plan for the coming year ordinarily must have the approval of the general manager before inclusion in the overall financial plan. The financial executive, as part of the process of securing general management's approval, should be expected to indicate to the general manager how the decisions which have been previously approved should be segmented and assigned to each functional area in establishing budgets or performance objectives. For example, assume that the manufacturing activity has spent $10 million in the past year to produce a given volume and mix of products. A variable budget system can be developed which will allow for changes in volume or mix during the following year, so that the $10 million cost level can be more or less automatically adjusted to accommodate those two factors. Supplemental allowances can also be added to or deducted from the proposed budget, to allow for the effect of decisions involving new facilities or the cost of launching new products. Also allowances can be made for the effect of product design changes on labor, material, and overhead costs. Such allowances will presumably be in line with the commitments previously made by the manufacturing activity when it provided the information which was used to reach the decision to build new facilities or to introduce new product designs.

In summary, the financial executive must maintain a reporting system which keeps track of commitments as decisions are made and permits him to incorporate those commitments in the budget recommendations he submits to the general manager. This closes the circle and assures that commitments made by the manufacturing activity on earlier decisions will not be forgotten but will finally be converted into clear-cut performance standards in the operating budgets of that activity.

The general manager may approve departures from the past cost level of $10 million, plus or minus the effect of the special factors. He may ask for further cost reductions or may approve a larger budget because it appears that the earlier commitments will not or cannot be met. Obviously, the financial plan must be realistic and attainable even though it means a departure from earlier commitments by managers of functional areas. However, it is important that these earlier commitments be reviewed as part of the budget approval process. An important aspect of the performance of a manager of a functional area is his ability to provide reliable and accurate estimates of the probable effect of a particular decision on his activity. If he is unable to meet the cost estimates which were submitted when a decision was made, the effect on the business can be as serious, if not more serious, than a failure to meet his operating budget in the current year. He could easily have misled management into making unwise decisions affecting the entire organization because he seriously misjudged the effect of these decisions on his organization.

In brief, the most important part of the budgetary control system is that part which relates to the initial establishment of the budget (or the approval of subsequent changes to the initial plan). After the general manager and the manager of a functional area have agreed on the task for the coming year, the reporting problems are clear. The reports need to (a) permit the manager of a functional area to monitor performance by plant, by department, by sales district, or by other such organizational segments, and by element of cost within such segments to identify the deviations which should command his attention, (b) permit the general

EXHIBIT 5

Status Report of a New Product Program
Current Estimate Versus Objective
(as of December 31, 1968)

	Profit Per Unit	Allocated Assets Per Unit	Return After Taxes	Fixed Expendi- tures[a] (millions)
Product Plan	$33	$365	9%	$18.0
Current Estimate	29	368	8	19.5
	$(4)	$ (3)	(1)%	$(1.5)
Design changes and related tooling (Specific design changes would be described)	$(3)	$ (1)		$(1.0)
Engineering (Causes of principal deviations would be listed)	(1)	—		(0.8)
Launching costs (Reduced due to simplification of design)	1	(1)		0.3
Economic cost increases	(2)	(1)		
Revised pricing assumption	1	—		
	$(4)	$ (3)	(1)%	$(1.5)

[a] Fixed expenditures include facility modification costs, tooling, engineering, and launching costs.

manager to monitor the performance of the functional area in sufficient detail to be able to evaluate the overall quality of performance, and (c) provide such information on a timely basis.

It should also be pointed out that budget performance need not be confined to the reporting of actual costs versus budget. The past is important in budget administration—but it is frequently less important than estimated future performance. An activity may be over its budget for the first six months of the year but that is no assurance that the unfavorable performance will continue for the remainder of the year. The performance reporting system needs to cover actual performance to date but should also include estimates from the functional activity as to its probable performance for the balance of the year.

Most of the details of budget administration relate to operating performance for the current year. However, it is also necessary that periodic readings be taken on the probable financial performance of each functional area in future years. Exhibits 1 and 2 described the planned profits for the years 1969 through 1972. Obviously, it is not necessary to wait until these future years arrive to determine whether these results can be achieved or not. If the execution of a particular program is not going according to plan in a particular area that fact needs to be known. Hence, there should be periodic (monthly or quarterly) reevaluations of the status of major plans or programs. If these reestimates indicate that a particular program is lagging behind its objectives, management's attention can be directed to the unfavorable areas by a report similar to that shown in Exhibit 5. The unfavorable areas shown on this report would receive direct management attention to correct the problems. If this failed, other aspects of the profit situation would be examined in an effort to find ways to offset the unfavorable developments and maintain profits and returns at planned levels. In brief, performance reporting needs to be prospective as well as retrospective. Management should learn of unfavorable developments far enough in advance so that it can change its future plans on a timely basis before the bad news becomes an actuality.

Multiple indicators of performance

The performance reporting system cannot be just an array of budget performance reports. There are some aspects of performance which are important to the long run strength of a company which cannot be subjected to precise financial measurement. It may be a matter of some importance to limit customer dissatisfaction as evidenced by customer complaint rates. Quality levels measured from returned merchandise, warranty costs, or product quality audits may also be significant in protecting against product problems which could alienate customers but might not be reflected in lower sales volumes for several years in the future.

The management reporting system should see to it that such interrelationships are covered adequately. In one company with a number of large warehousing locations, the budget performance reports for each location took the form shown in Exhibit 4. However, this was accompanied by charts in similar format showing the trend for each warehouse of the following performance factors:

a) Percent of orders filled within the standard time allowance of three days.
b) Back orders as a percent of all items ordered.
c) Errors in filling orders, such as shipping the wrong item.
d) Accounting errors in billing customers as evidenced by sales adjustment accounts.

Exhibit 7 sets forth an illustration of such a nonfinancial measure of performance covering the first item, orders not filled on schedule.

This type of nonfinancial performance objective can be applicable in many areas. For example, a manufacturing activity has a complex set of responsibilities which embrace manufacturing costs, quality levels, pro-

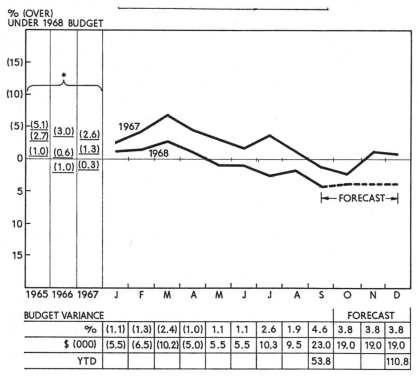

EXHIBIT 6

MNO Company

Warehousing Cost Performance—All Locations

(9 months ended September 30, 1968)

BUDGET VARIANCE											FORECAST		
%	(1.1)	(1.3)	(2.4)	(1.0)	1.1	1.1	2.6	1.9	4.6	3.8	3.8	3.8
$ (000)	(5.5)	(6.5)	(10.2)	(5.0)	5.5	5.5	10.3	9.5	23.0	19.0	19.0	19.0
YTD									53.8			110.8

ᵃ Prior year data shows the highest and lowest budget off standard for three consecutive months as well as the average variance for the year.

duction scheduling, equipment maintenance, inventory control, and so on. To some extent, these objectives are inconsistent in the sense that improvements can be made in any one area at the expense of the other. A well considered system of operating reports for the manufacturing organization should, at least, report on the trend of all such elements and should, if possible, develop a weighting of each element so that an overall summary of performance can be developed.

Similarly, the marketing organization should seldom, if ever, be evaluated on the basis of changes in the absolute level of sales or changes in market penetration. Usually the marketing activity is responsible for

   a) sales volume or market penetration.
   b) advertising, sales promotion and marketing strategy.
   c) pricing of the product and related discount structures.
   d) manpower and related costs in the marketing area.
   e) customer relations.

EXHIBIT 7

MNO Company

Percent of Orders Shipped after Standard Schedule Date

(9 months ended September 30, 1968)

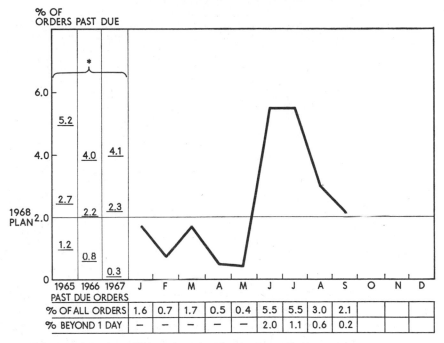

PAST DUE ORDERS	1965	1966	1967	J	F	M	A	M	J	J	A	S	O	N	D
% OF ALL ORDERS	1.6	0.7	1.7	0.5	0.4	5.5	5.5	3.0	2.1						
% BEYOND 1 DAY	—	—	—	—	—	2.0	1.1	0.6	0.2						

ª Prior year data shows highest, lowest and average month.

Changes in sales levels can be induced by price changes, expansion or contraction of the advertising and promotion program, or by changes in the level of marketing manpower. However, these elements can be mutually inconsistent in their effect on profits. The general manager is interested in having the marketing organization arrive at a mix of policies in these several areas which will produce an optimum long run effect on profits.

In one company, this interaction of policies was covered in the reports shown in Exhibits 8 and 9. Exhibit 8 shows unit and dollar sales volumes primarily for informational purposes. The marketing organization was evaluated on the basis of a synthetic "net profit" on sales which was calculated by assigning the marketing organization a modest commission or royalty, based on the planned gross profit of the product lines sold. This commission was based on only a portion of the total gross profit realized on the sale of the product, but it gave the marketing organization an incentive to arrive at an optimum balance between sales volume on the one hand and selling prices on the other. Advertising and promotion costs and the cost of operating the marketing organization were

EXHIBIT 8

MNO Company
Marketing Profit Performance
(dollars in millions)

	Sept. 1968		Year to Date	
	Actual	Favorable (Unfav.) vs. Plan	Actual	Favorable (Unfav.) vs. Plan
Sales Volume—Units	1,658	62	18,928	493
Sales Volume—Dollars	$ 568.2	$(13.6)	$6,875.5	$198.6
Commission on Sales	$ 54.9	$(1.0)	$ 584.7	$ 15.2
Operating Expenses				
Advertising	12.1	1.9	121.2	13.8
Promotions	2.0	2.0	64.0	16.1
Personnel	24.3	(1.1)	227.3	(10.6)
Other Operating Expense	10.6	0.3	113.6	(3.5)
Total	$ 49.0	$ 3.1	$ 526.1	$ 15.8
Marketing Net Profit	$ 5.9	$ 2.1	$ 58.6	$ 31.0

deducted from this commission to arrive at the "marketing net profit" shown at the foot of the schedule. The marketing organization was assigned a "marketing net profit" objective at the beginning of the year and was free to change the mix of elements as long as it achieved this objective.

Exhibit 9 is a report of the trend of customer complaints. As long as the marketing organization achieved its results on a basis which customers found acceptable, management ordinarily would not get involved. However, if customer complaints showed an adverse trend, any favorable financial results would be appropriately discounted. If the trend were serious enough, management could get directly involved in determining the cause of the trends.

This approach was not only used to evaluate the total marketing organization but was also useful in evaluating performance differences between the sales branches located in different areas of the country.

If the factors taken into account in establishing a performance report for the marketing activity give proper weight to the principal areas of responsibility of that activity, the chief executive will have available an evaluation of performance which is more likely to be consistent with his own objective than if he relies on some more limited measure such as mere changes in sales volume or market penetration. Perhaps of equal importance is the fact that the existence of such an evaluation system

EXHIBIT 9

MNO Company
Customer Complaint Rates
1967 and 1968

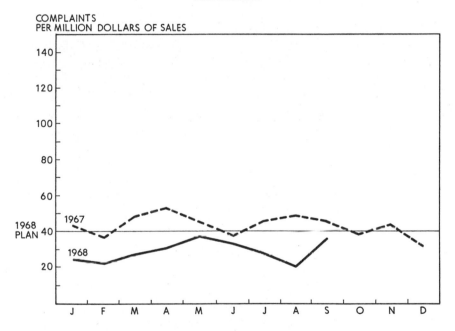

permits the chief executive to reduce the time he must spend in reviewing the manner in which the marketing organization is discharging its basic responsibilities. He can reduce the frequency of his detailed reviews and can place greater reliance on the formal evaluation system to assure that the marketing organization is conducting its affairs in his best interest.

It is beyond the scope of this chapter to examine the analytical pitfalls and the reporting complexities which can lie behind the development of a performance reporting system which is able to provide a reasonably complete and accurate description of the performance of a functional area. Such matters will be discussed in later chapters in this part of the Handbook.

The performance reports given to the general manager are the most important single device in the corporate environment for motivation of key people. Everyone wants to be shown in a favorable light when his performance is described to his superiors. This motivation is so powerful that it is important for the general manager and the financial executive to make sure the performance reports will, in fact, provide a well-rounded evaluation of the overall performance of a functional area and will cause key people to strengthen the long-run financial position of the business. To do otherwise may cause these key people to concentrate on one or a few aspects of their job at the expense of their overall responsibilities.

Special non-recurring financial reports

The reports to operating management discussed to this point have consisted primarily of those reports which would be provided on a recurring basis to interested members of management. They are generally prepared by the financial executive (except for those reports which deal with wholly non-financial measures of performance) as an essential part of his responsibility for managing an effective system of financial control. However, the financial executive must, from time to time, also submit to operating management special non-recurring reports dealing with special problems. These reports generally grow out of the financial executive's participation in the decision making process or result from analyses or evaluations which he may prepare concerning profit problems or profit opportunities.

Special reports relating to the decision making process. Most of the decisions made by operating management are relatively clear cut in their impact on the business, and the financial effect of the available alternatives can be readily determined. However, there are many situations in which the financial consequences of alternative courses of action are obscure or cannot be readily determined by general management or the manager of the functional area involved. Hence, situations frequently arise in which the financial executive must prepare special analyses or reports for management to assist them in their decision making role. This is particularly true of major decisions which must be made at the general management level. Such decisions usually involve a sizeable expenditure of funds and the financial executive is usually expected to provide analyses and evaluations which will confirm or question the adequacy and reliability of the supporting data. Such reports would indicate whether the proposals appear to cover all the feasible alternatives, whether financial estimates used in support of the various alternatives appear to be realistic and attainable and whether the financial estimates have been developed in sufficient detail to permit effective control over the execution of the alternative which may finally be chosen. All general management decisions are not exposed to this type of financial counsel or advice but the more important the decision, the more important that it be scrutinized from these points of view.

The financial executive is in a unique position to serve the managers of functional areas in a similar manner. He can offer an expertise in financial analysis which the functional manager may be unable to duplicate in his own activity. Also, the financial executive can bring an independence and objectivity which may or may not be found in the recommendations made by the manager's subordinates, who are involved in the day to day operating problems and may have little enthusiasm for changes or innovations which can complicate their existence. Finally, the manager of a functional area recognizes that his plans, programs, or decisions must eventually be integrated with those of other segments of the organization. He needs to be sure that the financial results attributed to his decisions will be in line with his expectations. The financial executive can help to assure that the manager's decisions are properly evaluated and will not, when reflected in financial projections for the future, reflect adversely on the soundness of his judgment in making those decisions.

Special reports on profit problems. A second type of special non-recurring report frequently issued by a financial executive is an outgrowth of special studies or intensive analyses of specific operating problems or profit opportunities. If significant cost problems arise with respect to a particular product or a specific operation, it is essential that someone in the organization undertake a study of the factors which seem to have generated the problem. Such analyses can frequently point the way to an appropriate solution. Since the profit problems or profit opportunities which confront an enterprise can be numerous and should have continuing attention, there is a real advantage in having a single activity with good analytical ability and broad business judgment act as the focal point for such analyses. In many companies, the financial executive is expected to play this role because he occupies a position of detachment as far as line operating responsibilities are concerned and can take an objective and impartial position. Also, he is the custodian of current information about all the important plans and programs which will affect the future so that he can properly relate his analyses to these anticipated developments.

If the financial executive is expected to undertake such special studies, it represents a heavy responsibility. He must assure that problems are clearly perceived and carefully analyzed, and he must be able to suggest sound and feasible steps for dealing with those problems. He should not merely "view with alarm"; he must also suggest how to begin dealing with the problems.

In particular, there can be a temptation, in analyzing profit problems, to concentrate excessive attention on cost-reduction opportunities. Costs incurred are highly visible and there is an understandable temptation to propose cost reductions which will make a measurable and immediate contribution to profits. It is more difficult but far more important for a financial executive to orient his financial analyses toward profit improvements. For example, it is possible that some cost reductions will have an adverse effect on profits in the long run. This latter result is difficult to perceive and is easy to ignore. Whether a financial executive serves management well depends on whether he helps the business to improve its long run *profit* position. A financial executive who concentrates on cost reductions is not unlike a credit manager who has never had a bad debt loss. He can be an expensive luxury that the business can ill afford.

This does not mean that cost controls are unimportant—merely that they are not the entire story. A financial executive must take a broad view of business problems and have the good business judgment needed to recognize profit opportunities which flow from cost increases as well as those which flow from cost reductions.

Effect of computers on management reporting

The advent of computers have had a major impact on the entire area of management reports. Management can have, and should have, an inexhaustible appetite for information which is relevant to the affairs of the business. Computers have broken a major bottleneck in supplying such data. It becomes possible for a financial executive to supply far more detailed information on the profit and investment problems of the business than has ever been possible before.

The financial status and timing of specific plans or programs can be made available to management with a frequency, timeliness, and penetration of detail never before possible. One company has gone so far as to convert its financial plans for the future into a computer model which is modified quarterly. All the key inputs are reexamined on a regular basis so that every three months a complete restatement is available for management review in any degree of detail desired. This had been patently impossible for the company under any system of manual data accumulation.

However, computer programs make it possible to confuse quantity with quality. Management is not interested in infinite detail about everything, nor does it wish to sort through computer runs to find those matters with which it should be concerned. Management reports must still be incisive and permit "management by exception." In part, the effect of computers has been to make it possible for someone to sift through vastly increased quantities of data to find more exceptions, and find them on a more timely basis. Because of computers, reports can be prepared today on many aspects of performance which could not be economically evaluated before. In the automobile business, for example, computers have had a major impact on sales analyses and vehicle registration data. Also, they have made it possible to analyze warranty costs with a high degree of sophistication so that product designers and manufacturers can approach quality problems with far more precision and assurance.

Responsibility accounting

Erich A. Helfert*

This chapter is directed toward a specialized application of accounting —the use of a system of data gathering and reporting for purposes of evaluating objectively the financial results of management efforts. As the name implies, the process involves accountability by area of responsibility; that is, an accounting for revenues, expenditures, and profits by assigned responsibility.

Responsibility—a key concept of management control

Seen in perspective, there are three interrelated purposes of accounting, serving distinctly different ends:
1. Accounting for financial reporting.
2. Accounting for the costs of products and services.
3. Accounting for performance evaluation.

Each of these accounting purposes supports the basic function of appraising the "stewardship" of the management of a business, but each from a different viewpoint. The first is addressed to the financial community to present the past and current financial position and earnings results; the second is directed toward the internal users of information to track costs and expenses and to relate these to output of goods and services; the third is pointed toward the various levels of management concerned with measuring the results of individual and group efforts as reflected in revenues, or costs, or profits, or combinations of these.

The third area of measurement has become an increasingly important function of the accounting process. It is closely allied, at an operational level, with the notion of management by objectives as discussed in

* Assistant to the President of Crown Zellerbach Corporation, San Francisco.

Chapter 24. Several key concepts and criteria of the process should be described, however, before engaging in a detailed discussion. *Responsibility* in this setting has a meaning broader than mere accountability. It encompasses the degree of delegated authority which a manager or individual has been assigned at any level of an organization. This responsibility may extend only to the operation of a single machine or it may be the chief executive's responsibility for a whole enterprise.

Accounting for the respective range of responsibility of a manager at any level thus must be selective and responsive to the *degree of control* he can exercise over the activities he supervises. It must *reflect the results* he has obtained within the framework of the authority and responsibility he has been assigned and which he has achieved through his efforts. Since performance cannot be measured in absolute terms, the responsibility accounting process must be tied to management's expression of *expected performance.* This may take the usual form of unit output standards, sales quotas, cost budgets, profit goals, etc. Moreover, the system must permit successively higher levels of management to concentrate on *key indicators* of performance and thus permit "management by exception," an attribute of good reporting as discussed in the previous chapter.

Responsibility accounting, in short, measures performance by a selective comparison against a plan; reflects the degree of success a manager had in dealing with his assigned responsibility; and provides indications for corrective action by establishing a cause and effect relationship between effort and results. It concentrates selectively on those revenue, cost, profit, or output data over which a manager has control.

For emphasis it should not be overlooked that the main orientation of the accounting function is generally that of recording the changes in the assets and liabilities of a business entity over time. The accountant reflects profit or loss as an increase or decrease in ownership equity, and additions or deductions of assets or liabilities are properly recorded at the cost incurred. In cost accounting he attempts to assign costs and expenses incurred to identifiable units of output under carefully spelled-out assumptions about allocations of costs encountered jointly or independent of the volume of output. In contrast to these common accounting processes, responsibility accounting introduces a *segmentation* of a business operation into distinct *responsibility centers* and a measurement process of comparing *results obtained against goals established* prior to the accounting period. The recording and allocation process is thus expanded into a *critical evaluation,* keyed through *careful selection of data* to the responsibility area being measured.

The importance of the goal-setting process and the assignment of clearly defined responsibilities cannot be overstressed. It is as basic as the art of management itself—one of the pillars of successful operation of a business or any other organization. Without clear responsibility and delegated authority commensurate with the assignment, there can be no consistent efforts towards established goals and objectives. Similarly, there can be no responsibility accounting without these.

For example, the manager of a marketing division in a manufacturing organization cannot really appraise his or his organization's performance unless he has made an estimate of the volume of product to be sold, the number of people needed to sell this volume, the cost of selling, advertising, and marketing staff support, and the profit to be generated for the company. Moreover, if he is not free to set prices, or to vary the product mix, or must accept changes in the cost of product transferred to him— that is, if his responsibility in operating the division is limited—an accounting for the total profit or loss of the division in absolute terms will not be a very meaningful set of figures with which to appraise his performance. It will represent a mixture of the effects of different spheres of responsibility beyond his own.

It is obvious that responsibility accounting, to be useful, must be tailored to the needs of a particular organization. First, the accounting mechanism must be *adjusted to fit the pattern of responsibilities,* and data collection will likely have to be made in much greater detail. It will not do, for instance, to record expense information such as power use for a factory as a whole when there are several distinct departments in the factory with different requirements under the management of different foremen. It may even be useful to isolate power use for individual machines if there is a significant relationship between this use and the efforts of the people manning it. Thus, revenue and expense categories must be fitted to spheres of responsibility which management has elected to monitor.

Second, successive levels of responsibility involve a *pyramid of information.* While the data collected at the lower levels of responsibility will be quite detailed, the proper concept of responsibility accounting involves a successive summarization of the information commensurate with the level of responsibility. Selectivity in the choice of data, highlighting the key information reflecting on performance, and interlocking reports designed to permit the analysis of variances from expectations must be observed. More details will be given on this aspect later.

Responsibility centers

The activity or group of activities for which responsibility has been assigned in an organization is commonly called a "responsibility center." The size or nature of this center can vary almost infinitely—from a single machine tool or salesman to a major division of a diversified international company. In fact, the total corporate entity is a single responsibility center for which the chief executive is held responsible by the owners. Within an organization of any reasonable size, however, there can be literally hundreds and even thousands of responsibility centers which, when grouped together, make up the total responsibility sphere of the chief executive.

A business enterprise will normally have a *hierarchy* of responsibility centers pyramided one upon the other, following the functional line and staff groupings of the organization. Several such pyramids can exist side by side, each layer having an increasingly wider "span of control" or reach of authority.

To illustrate, the manufacturing pyramid of responsibility may begin with a machine as the elementary unit, several of which are grouped under the supervision of the department foreman. Several of these department heads—some responsible for producing departments and some responsible for staff services such as maintenance, production planning, and methods engineering—will report to the factory manager. Several factory managers report to the vice president of manufacturing who, together with other vice presidents in charge of other functions (sales, finance, engineering, research, etc.), reports to the chief executive. While this typical structure is quite straightforward, the pattern of responsibilities can be quite complex, of course, in a diversified multiproduct organization.

The key to responsibility accounting in such a framework is accountability for the activities and/or resources entrusted to each responsibility center. As will be clear from the examples just cited, the nature of the responsibility center can differ as follows:

a) A responsibility center is a *"cost center"* if the person in charge is held responsible for the costs incurred in the operating unit. Examples of cost centers are a production department in a factory or a staff department such as public relations. While the responsibility of a producing unit extends to quality, promised volume of output, and timely shipment, the focus is often on the cost of producing goods or services, in conjunction with other physical measures.

b) A responsibility center widens into a *"profit center"* when the operating unit is held accountable for the profit contribution it makes to the enterprise. An example would be a selling division or an entire product or service division of a corporation, a branch bank, or a retail store in a chain. An individual salesman can be considered a profit center as well. The criterion is the calculation of the profit contribution on the basis of clearly defined rules under which management measures revenue-producing effort and the costs to be apportioned against the revenue.

c) A responsibility center can, in its broadest sense, be an *"investment center"* if the manager in charge is held responsible for *both* the profit *and* the investment required to produce the profit. The added step, which is applied to the kinds of responsibility centers under (*b*), is the introduction of a rate-of-return concept to measure the relative success

EXHIBIT 1

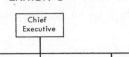
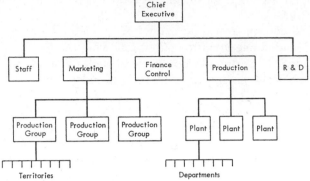

with which committed capital has been employed. The manager of an investment center thus must have a large degree of control over the current and future investments to be committed to his operation. In this sense the investment center is most akin to the overall responsibility implied in the total enterprise—as each manager of a clearly defined investment center "runs his own show" and should be judged accordingly. This type of responsibility center is rapidly gaining wide acceptance as an organizational concept.

The principles just enumerated are quite straightforward, but their application in practice brings a variety of complications to which the remainder of this chapter is devoted. Before proceeding with this discussion, however, simplified organization charts are presented to show the various types of cost centers and their interrelationship. Exhibit 1 dem-

EXHIBIT 2

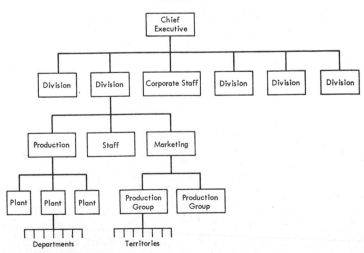

onstrates a typical "functional" organization of a manufacturing company, where production and marketing are separate and where all staff services are structured along functional lines. Most of the units on the chart will have to be cost centers, the only exception being marketing which, however, can be judged on profitability only to the extent that it can influence or negotiate the transfer prices of the goods from manufacturing to marketing.

Exhibit 2 shows a typical "divisionalized" organization, where each product or service division is essentially a self-contained unit. Only a few central staff personnel serve all of these. Each of the divisions could be structured as an investment center with profit-centered marketing functions. Furthermore, if sales organizations were attached to individual factories the manager there could run an investment center with limited direction from headquarters. Within each of the divisions there would naturally be many individual cost and profit centers at the lower levels of management.

Accounting aspects of responsibility accounting

As stated earlier, the main issues in adjusting cost accounting and financial accounting to conform to the needs of responsibility accounting are as follows: (1) the realignment of the gathering of revenue and cost data by responsibility center instead of the usually wider boundaries of the accounting structure; (2) the separation of revenue and cost elements into "controllable" and "noncontrollable" categories commensurate with the sphere of influence of the head of a responsibility center; and (3) the incorporation of performance standards into the accounting and reporting system.

The realignment of data gathering usually involves nothing more than a broadening of the chart of accounts and the addition of subgroupings built around the responsibility center. For instance, departmental accounts for labor, materials, and direct overhead items may be established for each foreman in a factory, where before there were accounts only for broad areas or sections of the productive manpower and key service sections headed by superintendents. The realignment of accounts is a relatively minor matter and the increasing use of electronic data processing for routine accounting chores makes the additional detail required available with little extra effort.

The separation of controllable and noncontrollable elements of revenue and cost poses more of a challenge. In essence, the concept reflects the ability of a manager to influence the size and nature of revenues and costs connected with his area of responsibility. The issue is closely related to budgeting and performance evaluation. Difficulties arise in proportion to the complexity and interrelationships found in the organization structure, where products or services may pass through several successive responsibility centers and where separate areas of responsibility such as central purchasing, central engineering, etc., may limit the free choices of managers of responsibility centers. Two examples will serve as illustrations here.

In a small independent unit of operations, such as a single plant which buys its raw materials and sells products to outside customers, it is quite easy to differentiate between controllable and noncontrollable items since practically all revenue and expense items will be controllable by the plant manager. Only such elements as property taxes—assessed outside the sphere of influence of the manager—will not be controllable. Otherwise, the actions of the manager will reflect themselves in the profit obtained in a fairly close cause-and-effect relationship. An analysis of the operations thus should encompass the full range of revenues and costs.

The contrast is obvious when this situation is compared with one of the product sales groups in Exhibit 1. While selling expenses can probably be directly controlled in each territorial responsibility area, the costs of the products made by the supplying plants—separate responsibility centers—are not controllable by the sales management. This is so unless the transfer price is based on current market prices, if available, or is negotiated with some give and take. Moreover, if advertising is handled by the central staff, the allocation of this expense can be problematic since the advertising program may only be partly influenced by the desires and decisions of the sales management. A negotiated formula, never completely satisfactory, for allocating advertising on the basis of sales dollars or physical units is often made to charge sales management for a reasonable share.

As a rule it can be said that the separation of controllable and noncontrollable revenues and expenses is desirable in principle—since responsibility accounting attempts to ascribe responsibility to the *originator* of revenue or expense. Where intertwined organizational arrangements make this difficult, it is common to set out and highlight such items in the performance reports so that, while an item may show up in the report on a responsibility center, it is clearly understood that the item is only partly controllable. The same rule applies to allocated common overhead items, which the cost accountant has apportioned to various units on the basis of some reasonable measure, such as floor space, direct labor dollars, etc. Generally, such overhead items are controlled by others than departmental operating management, and will appear in the operating report of the plant manager responsible for them. If allocated costs are to be reflected in departmental reports, they must be clearly labeled as such.

For example, a performance report for a plant may take the form illustrated in Exhibit 3.

The third accounting aspect—the incorporation of performance standards into the responsibility accounting system—is intimately connected

EXHIBIT 3

XYZ Company Budget Report for Factory C

(month of July and year-to-date)

	July			Year-to-Date		
	Budget	*Actual*	*% Vari-ance*	*Budget*	*Actual*	*% Vari-ance*
A) *Controllable direct costs*						
Direct labor........						
Operating supplies.						
Repair labor........						
Repair parts........						
Heat, light power...						
Subtotal........						
B) *Costs transferred in*						
Raw materials—						
primary..........						
Product for						
processing.......						
Subtotal........						
C) *Period costs*						
Supervisory salaries						
Property taxes,						
insurance........						
Depreciation ex-						
pense...........						
Subtotal........						
D) *Allocated costs*						
General corporate						
overhead.........	xx		xx	xx		xx
Total.........						

with the previous aspect. Performance can be judged only on those revenue and cost elements which are reasonably under the control of the operating unit. Once a proper breakdown of revenue and expense categories has been established and a reasonable separation has been made of controllable elements, a performance plan for the next operating period is necessary to establish the goals of the responsibility center. Each item of revenue and expense controlled must be forecast in relation to the operating goals—that is, a budget must be developed which reflects volume, quality standards (through allowance for required materials, labor time, supplies, etc.), and monetary aspects of the forecast. It should be stressed here that under responsibility accounting *all* costs are controllable by one manager at least, with each unit controlled at its appropriate level of responsibility. Thus budgets for successive responsibility "layers" will encompass all corporate costs—fixed, variable, and in between.

From an accounting standpoint, the forecast must be stored to appear later in the performance reports, to be able to compare actual versus plan. More important, however, the budget by responsibility area must be designed to allow for volume and price fluctuations beyond the control of the responsibility center. The principles of variable budgeting described in Chapter 23 apply here; in other words, the budget mechanism incorporated in the accounting system should be flexible, reflecting at all times a reasonable standard of operating efficiency against which the controllable revenues and expenses can be measured. This by no means implies that the system is intended to provide convenient excuses for nonfulfillment of goals; rather, it is attempting to place the blame at the unit or units where it belongs.

Proper systems design can achieve the three aspects discussed. The growth of the concept of the "corporate data base"—computer-stored price, output, and cost standards in elementary detail—greatly eases the task of establishing variable budgets and of combining basic revenue and expense data to conform to any responsibility-center pattern desired. Because electronic data processing takes the time and drudgery out of report preparation, many companies have found profitable a rethinking of the different information needs as they have adjusted their systems to the newer types of computers available. The use of responsibility accounting has been advanced through these efforts as the recognition of different uses of the same basic and detailed input information has grown.

Operational aspects of responsibility accounting

The basic purpose of responsibility accounting is to motivate managers in charge of an operating unit to perform in accordance with the goals established. The discussion so far has stressed the need for defining the area of responsibility and for developing a budget and accounting system which conforms to these definitions. The very compromises and problems encountered in developing such a system in concept, however, also exhibit themselves in the operations of the system. Research into the experiences companies have had with responsibility accounting systems has shown that problem areas are quite common and not necessarily related to industry or company size. Several principles relevant to the best utilization of the advantages of responsibility accounting have been derived from that research.

To achieve proper motivation, a cardinal rule for managers of responsibility centers—costs, profit, or investment centers—is *to participate in the establishment and maintenance of the system.* Those to be measured under any system must have a good understanding of how it operates and must agree that the goals are attainable through specific efforts on their part. This principle applies in general to all motivational situations, within or without the sphere of business. Nevertheless it has often been neglected, with the result that serious stresses have developed in a management group operating under responsibility concepts.

To illustrate, the sales quota established for a territory must be reasonably attainable, and the individual salesman responsible should have the opportunity to express his views when the budget for the operating period is set, (working with his manager who is intimately familiar with the opportunities and problems of the territory). Similarly, the manager of a manufacturing plant must be consulted and must agree to the output, quality, and cost goals under which he will operate his cost center. If this rule is not observed, excessive efforts to "beat the system" through manipulation of necessary but postponable outlays, for example, will be the result. Worse yet, the adverse effect on morale and cooperation among the various responsibility centers can be severe.

The second commonly encountered condition is the *systems compromises* necessary to have an operable system and the effect these have on the people operating under the system. The most difficult condition is in the establishment and use of transfer prices for intracompany movements of raw materials, work-in-process, finished goods, and various services performed by specialized departments. It is not always possible to use market value as an absolute standard of value, since sometimes there is no ready market for the transfer in question; or higher management, for various reasons, wishes to use the internal sources of supply which may be costlier for a responsibility center compared to what is available on the outside. Even if a market alternative is available, it is often difficult to establish a transfer price satisfactory to both responsibility centers if market prices tend to fluctuate widely and no actual transactions have been made on the outside. Negotiated transfer prices also contain conflict elements and may cause friction.

Other conflict situations develop from the degree to which *controllable expenses* have been *isolated,* and from the extent to which the *budget mechanism* has been *refined.* In the endeavor to foster motivation it can happen that a department or other operating unit is judged partly on costs which are only influenced but not controllable, and which the budget system has not allowed for sufficiently.

For example, if sharply increased production output requires the use of costlier materials available from another division not usually supplying it, and if the decision to use this source is largely dependent on a central planning decision to increase volume, some careful analysis must be made of the using unit's costs to eliminate the effect of decisions made outside the limits of its responsibility. Such considerations lead to the third problem area, that of having the separate results of responsibility centers *conform to the interests of the overall organization.* Hopefully, the parts should total up results greater than their simple sum.

While profit or investment centers especially give the individual manager responsibility for operating his unit as if it were his own business, and provide motivation accordingly, these types of responsibility centers also harbor the greatest possibilities for conflict with the overall corporate interests. The preceding discussion has already foreshadowed this difficulty. If given complete choice, the manager of a profit or investment center may prefer to go to the outside to obtain raw materials, product, and services, and in turn may also prefer outside customers over other corporate divisions. Yet the circumstances can be such that the exercise of free choice will bring economic losses to the corporation as a whole. If this is the case, a change in the rules of the system is indicated and certain decisions will have to be removed from the responsibility center and made centrally.

For example, the price for a raw material from a supplying division may be higher than competitive bids on the outside, yet the out-of-pocket cost to the corporation may be higher on the outside. A policy decision may force the manager of a responsibility-centered division to buy from another division of the corporation unless the price outside is some minimum percentage under the corporate level. While such a change would destroy some of the responsibility of the unit manager, it could have a net economic benefit for the corporation. The key question would be whether this economic relationship has been properly analyzed and understood, and if justified, the system would have to be adjusted as indicated.

In the light of the economic realities of the multifaceted organization, a responsibility accounting system is subject to continuous adjustment and top management review to ensure that the desirable incentive of focused responsibility will direct the efforts of the subunits in the interest of the total corporation.

A fourth area of consideration should be raised. In the administration of a responsibility accounting system, care must be taken to *avoid staff-line conflicts*. If the system is administered through the accounting area of the business, as it most commonly is, there exists the risk that staff personnel overstep their authority and direct the line management to take actions to correct performance deviations. The accounting staff can be most helpful in the analysis of variances from budget in the reports prepared by them and can even suggest areas for improvement, but the line of authority in responsibility accounting extends from the chief operating executive down through successive levels of narrower responsibility areas to the smallest operating unit. Each of the operating managers reviewing the results of his area must, with the assistance of analyses by the accounting function, take action to see that the decisions of his subordinates will bring results closer to expectations. Since ideally the operating managers have participated in the setting of the performance goals, they will be in a position to adjust their actions to secure better results if the system has been designed so that it reasonably reflects the results of the efforts put forth.

Illustrative system of responsibility accounting

For purposes of demonstrating the advantages and problems of responsibility accounting, the following hypothetical company will be described to show the interaction of a responsibility-accounting system.

The XYZ Company is a fully integrated nationwide manufacturing

EXHIBIT 4

XYZ Company Organization Chart

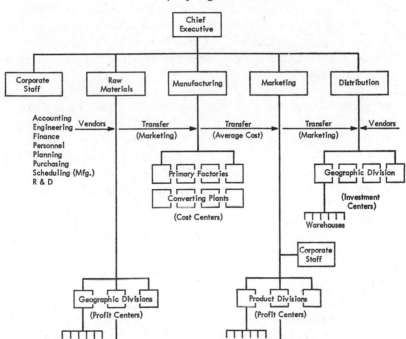

concern which produces thousands of different end products from a primary product, which in turn is developed from company-owned basic resources. The company owns facilities to gather and refine the raw materials, primary factories to produce the base product, and manufacturing plants to produce secondary products interchangeably. The company also owns a distribution subsidiary with warehouses and delivery fleets.

The organization structure is shown in Exhibit 4, and it is clear that the company has a basically functional organization with a mixture of cost centers, profit centers, and an investment center. Transfers take place between most of the operating divisions, and some divisions supplement their needs from outside suppliers. Purchasing of all needs other than primary raw material is done centrally, manufacturing operations are scheduled centrally, and the product sales divisions are assisted by a central marketing staff. The Raw Materials Division is semiautonomous, while the distribution subsidiary is self-contained with its own full complement of functions.

The advantages of the responsibility accounting used in XYZ Company are numerous:

A. The Raw Material Division operates its various locations as profit centers, which are thereby encouraged to upgrade the raw materials and sell to the best market. In supplying the corporate factories they are free to purchase substitute materials of specified quality. Transfer is at market, periodically set from published data in joint conference with factories. This division operates aggressively, much like a separate business.

B. Both primary factories and multipurpose manufacturing plants are cost centered with detailed variable budgets based on volume and product mix. All products are scheduled centrally in response to demand from Marketing. Cost standards are closely administered; budget reports by cost responsibility area are used extensively for efforts in cost reduction. Quality fluctuations of raw material provided by Raw Materials are adjusted for in the transfer price to reflect responsibility. Transfers to Marketing are made at a weighted average standard cost of all supplying points based on yearly production plan. This avoids penalizing market divisions when sources change through central scheduling. Plants are extremely cost conscious; they look for constant improvement in those areas they can control.

C. Marketing Product Divisions are profit centered, with sales plans and budgets built up in layers from the field. Focus is on price and volume; the divisions analyze profitability by product line, emphasize upgrading of mix to raise total profit, and attempt to maximize profit contribution. Average standard transfer cost protects product divisions from fluctuations in cost not caused by them and puts cost responsibility where it belongs, in the factories and plants.

D. The Distribution subsidiary acts essentially as a separate business with responsibility both for capital tied up and operating profit. It purchases from product sales divisions and outside vendors alike at prevailing market prices. Geographic locations are investment centers, complete with warehouse and delivery fleet. Each branch manager operates his own business with minimum guidance from Distribution.

Here are some of the problem areas likely to arise in the XYZ Company:

A. There can be friction between the Raw Material Division and the using factories over the quality of raw material to be delivered to them. The setting of the transfer price is problematic because of a limited market for the material in some locations.

B. Cost concentration at the factories and plants eliminates them as "profit watchdogs," that is, they may not decide on the desirability of products or product changes. No decisions are made by manufacturing management on product mix, yet the cost performance of the operating units is affected by the mix of products requested. The system cannot fully overcome this. Variance analysis is made very difficult because of multiple variables; and production scheduling's effect is hard to measure.

C. Marketing's decisions on product mix are difficult because of multiple plant options with different costs. Average standard cost smooths out fluctuations in profit performance but also tends to delay impact of product cost changes caused by marketing demands.

D. The distribution subsidiary has the clearest picture of all, because of the specialized nature of its business. The pyramid of investment centers in its structure works well, except that central product-policy decisions may unevenly affect some of the responsibility centers.

The selected highlights of pros and cons in a specific situation should point up the fact that responsibility accounting must be tailored to the

EXHIBIT 5

Reporting System—XYZ Company

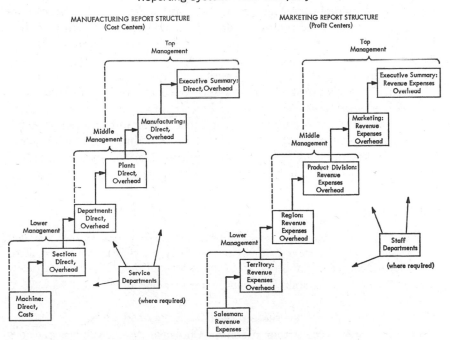

All statements show actual versus budgeted revenue and expense, and state differences.

needs of each enterprise. No absolute answers are possible but the system described above works better on balance than would a highly centralized structure with actual cost transfers between divisions and little decision-making power at the local level.

The report structure of XYZ Company is developed along responsibility lines. Successively higher levels of management receive increased summarization of results of the lower responsibility centers. Two schematic representations follow which assume that the results of each center have been broken into controllable and noncontrollable elements, and show how the relevant totals are carried over to the next higher level of responsibility to be joined by the results of similar centers (Exhibit 5). As the span of control widens, layers of overhead elements controllable by the respective managers begin to appear. Invariably, the controllable elements on each report are set opposite current budget phases, and deviations are indicated.

Summary

The preceding comments have pointed up the key aspects of a performance-centered accounting approach, in which all elements from data gathering through the reporting and analysis stages are viewed with respect to specifically assigned responsibility in an organization. Experience has shown that properly designed and administered systems of this type have provided increased motivation and improved results. Importantly, the systems relate to management by objective and plan and thus heighten recognition of the need for orderly approaches to any administration task.

Since any measurement process cannot be fully objective, responsibility accounting must rest to some extent on compromises, especially in complex organizations. As the preceding chapter on reporting and the ensuing chapter on divisional performance point out, proper systems design can largely overcome these problems and thus assist in realizing one of the key missions of the accounting process: the measurement of performance in relation to stated goals and responsibilities.

Bibliography

The following references are intended as suggestions for further detailed discussions of the concepts in this chapter. Only a few key works are listed here; further materials can be found in the indexes of these books and articles:

BEYER, ROBERT.   Profitability Accounting for Planning and Control. New York, 1963.

DEARDEN, JOHN.   *Cost and Budget Analysis.* Englewood Cliffs, N.J., 1962.

HIGGINS, JOHN A.   The Arthur Andersen Chronicle, "Responsibility Accounting." April, 1952.

HORNGREN, CHARLES T.   *Cost Accounting: a Managerial Emphasis.* Englewood Cliffs, N.J., 1967.

MCFARLAND, WALTER B.   *Concepts for Management Accounting.* National Association of Accountants. New York, 1966.

MOORE, CARL L., AND JAEDICKE, ROBERT K.   *Managerial Accounting.* South-Western Publishing Co., 1963.

PEAT, MARWICK, MITCHELL & Co.   *Responsibility Reporting.* K. S. Axelson, Ed. New York, 1961.

Measuring divisional performance

Richard N. Stillman*

Measurement of divisional performance is a systematic procedure for aiding corporate management in identifying the company's major points of operational strength and weakness, and for stimulating divisional management toward attainment of optimum profits. The objective is to measure *both* the manager and the business. Techniques stem from the development of organization and control systems in multi-product and multi-service corporations. An effective program of performance measurement incorporates responsibility concepts, profit-planning and budgeting, and return-on-investment and residual income yardsticks. In practice, the procedure is likely to represent a pragmatic compromise that is closer to the functional than to the academic ideal.

The importance of the subject is heightened by growing pressures to compel disclosure of product-line profits by publicly owned companies.

Responsibility centers

At first in the largest and most complex corporations, and now in companies of medium and smaller size, organizing operations into natural business segments has proven to be sound policy. Such segments are usually based upon a compatible set of products, services, or markets, and each one is headed by a profit-responsible manager who is given ample authority, within limits, to influence the performance of his unit.

The term "division" is commonly and sometimes loosely applied to

---

* Controller, Stauffer Chemical Company, New York.

such separately accountable organizational units. Various types of responsibility centers exist within each division. However, we are here concerned with the division itself as a collective responsibility center. The term "profit center" is properly applied to the division when some measure of profit performance is determined periodically. With the development of return-on-investment (ROI) and residual income concepts, the term "investment center" has been devised to describe the division or profit center which is measured by use of ROI or residual income techniques.

Measurement of divisional performance is indispensable, if top management is to assess all major strengths and weaknesses of the company as accurately as possible and to take corrective action as the need is indicated. When properly presented, the yardsticks of divisional performance also serve to motivate division managers toward attitudes of self-evaluation and self-improvement, maximizing both divisional and corporate earning capacity.

The fundamental concept of profit-responsibility holds the division manager accountable for generating sufficient earnings from the assets that are—at least theoretically—in his custody. The word "sufficient" is a necessary generalization. Built-in, long-standing competitive factors and operating efficiencies or defects—over which the manager may be able to exercise little or no current control—can cause divisional profits to depart widely from normal or desired rates of return. Likewise, short-term aberrations will erupt from external events that are uncontrollable, or almost so—from new or intensified competitive forces, from fire, explosion, strikes, material shortages, and so forth. Thus, problems are clearly inherent in measuring the *manager* as opposed to measuring the *business*. Additionally, decisions in areas of the company outside of the individual division will have an effect on divisional operations and results, further complicating the measurement mechanism.

It is often advocated that a division or profit-center manager should not be accountable for operating results that are significantly affected by corporate activities beyond his own area of responsibility. In the framework of this proposition, the divisional measurement procedure would restrict itself to the profit and loss data and to the investment data of the division alone—the responsibility center. No allocation would be made of any portion of non-divisional operating profit and loss or of non-divisional investment, except, perhaps, that charges might be made for measurable central-staff services specifically required and requested by the division. Further, in adherence to this precept, it would be in order to segregate variable expenses of the division from so-called controllable divisional overhead and further to segregate so-called non-controllable overhead, in order to calculate a "variable profit," a "controllable profit," and a "contribution margin." Divisional investment would be similarly classified, in order to effect legitimate responsibility measurement.

The trouble with this concept is that it embodies sharp departures from conventional financial-statement presentation and complicates appraisal of the *business*. It often compels corporate and divisional management to acquire or pretend some esoteric technical and academic skills which are normally the trade of the accountant. Moreover, strict adherence to the responsibility principle may produce results which blur the ultimate comparability of one division within the corporation with another, with other companies within the industry, with other industries, or with other standards of corporate profit criteria.

It may be argued that divisional performance measurement is not intended to provide such business comparisons—that its purpose is *only* to evaluate the effectiveness of divisional *management*. However, the pragmatic corporate executive is looking for a dual-purpose tool. He wants to equate the performance of a division and its management with the performance of other divisions in the company, as well as with the performance of the total company and with other companies. Such a dual-purpose tool requires the allocation of non-divisional operating income and expense, and non-divisional operating investment to the divisions.

Accordingly, many companies have incorporated allocation techniques into their divisional-measurement practices, thus vitiating the classic principle that interlocks responsibility with accountability. The typical division is likely to be, in statistical terms, a structure that consists of a responsibility center base with an artificially contrived super-structure completing the investment center concept. The resulting apparition may please neither the divisional manager who toils within it, the corporate manager who is asked to appraise it, nor the financial-executive–architect, unless considerable forethought is given to design and use of the yardsticks that serve to measure the structure's soundness and the division manager's stewardship.

Profit yardsticks

The financial executive has available to him a number of yardsticks—both traditional and innovative—for measuring divisional performance.

However, it should be said at the outset that even the most sophisticated principles and techniques of performance measurement must be viewed as requiring much flexibility in their application and in the interpretation of results. In short, a considerable degree of discreet judgment is required of the financial executive as well as of other members of the corporate hierarchy, if profit-center reporting is to be more than a token genuflection toward modern management methods. The professional financial man has yet to develop procedures that are more vital than the simple virtues of knowing the business and working at it.

Moreover, few businesses are so simple that statistics alone will tell the story. Skill in editorializing—verbal and written—is a necessary adjunct for a successful program.

The development of modern measurement techniques was spurred by the corporate manager's realization, perhaps belatedly, that the customary reporting of sales, and of gross or operating profits and profit margins, by products and product groups, does not do the job; profits as a percent of sales are a useful equation, but profits in relation to capital employed and to stockholders' equity are the most revealing gauge. Without firm commitment to this concept by top management, the financial executive may be able to launch a measurement procedure initially, but its long-term effectiveness must be suspect.

Once management support is assured in principle, the approach will require, first, the determination of report content and format and its approval by users. Concurrently or later, accounting policies should be reviewed to assure that proper and consistent practices are followed in the development of information. Finally, the data-processing system must be programmed—and often tortured, unless the measurement procedure is to be dovetailed with an overhaul of existing data-processing methods—to assemble the required raw material for reporting purposes.

A conventional one-page format for divisional profit measurement is illustrated on the following page. This example for the *Mini-Widget Division of Maxi-Widget Corporation* will be used as a point of reference for discussion in this chapter. The format presents the "top-layer" view of the division's operations. A similar format can be used for "sub-layers" of major products and plants, and additional "sub-layers" in varying format for detailed analyses of revenues and expenses. Additional columns may be provided for "Current Month," "Variances," and so forth, as desired. Significant variances should be indicated with an asterisk, or otherwise highlighted, in order to provide an effective "management by exception" tool.

The format includes virtually all of the customary yardsticks of profitability, ranging from "profit-as-a-percentage-of-sales" to "residual income." Additionally, two non-traditional indicators are included: "Earnings Per Share" and "Cash Flow Per Share." Each one of these yardsticks has a place in the apparatus of measurement and control.

Profit-as-a-percentage-of-sales.   Together with the measurement of sales-volume increases and decreases, profit-as-a-percentage-of-sales is perhaps the oldest and still the most widely used indicator of corporate and divisional well-being. The utility of this yardstick is incontestable. For example, if sales volume increases and if margins are firm or trend upwards, profits will expand commensurately—unless there is a substantial breakdown in the efficient utilization of investment. This "unless," although a small word, is a formidable *sine qua non,* for impairment of investment is more than a casual mishap. Nevertheless, the profit margin expressed as a percent of sales remains one of the better early-warning devices in the financial executive's arsenal. Its usefulness is restricted to gauging relative progress in each division unilaterally. It has almost no value in judging results of one division versus another, or in determining the essential profitability of each division.

The illustration in Exhibit 1 would motivate the financial executive to develop an analysis of volumes and unit sales prices and costs to explain the unfavorable variance in gross profit margin; that is, the actual 40.8 percent versus the forecast 42.2 percent.

Return-on-investment. The limitations inherent in profit-as-a-percentage-of-sales were recognized early in this present century. In his book, *My Years with General Motors,* Alfred P. Sloan described the attempts to develop more meaningful measures of divisional performance, which culminated in the return-on-investment measure. Today—decades later—return-on-investment is a firmly established management principle, although the specifics of its use and computation will vary widely among individual companies.

The book authored by David Solomons, *Divisional Performance: Measurement and Control,* makes the point that management views the return-on-investment indicator as a simple and effective measure of operating efficiency, whereas the large number of variants in common use are clear evidence that the concept and its application are really somewhat complex. Many companies tend to oversimplify the procedure, with only passing attention given to possible alternative practices in treatment of such items as divisional investment computation, fixed asset valuation, shared or corporate assets, controllable and noncontrollable income and expense, and the like. In most cases, it will be expedient to make an effort to keep the format and content of divisional performance reports consistent with the company's customary financial statements. This effort recognizes that the corporate executive typically has little time to spare for a financial re-education. If the approach to ROI and residual income is to be oversimplified for this or any other reason, the financial executive must satisfy himself that he has not introduced an intolerably low level of statistical accuracy. There should be an acceptable middle ground that accommodates a reasonable standardization of report content and format together with a fair degree of precision.

In the case of the Mini-Widget Division, as shown in Exhibit 1, it would be desirable, following the gross profit analysis described above, to analyze the divisional selling, general, and administrative expense as well as the trend of receivables and inventories. All of these have contributed to the below-budget ROI.

Residual income. The principal drawback of the return-on-investment procedure is its tendency to cause divisional personnel to overemphasize the *ratio* of profits to investment, rather than the *total* of dollar profits. Focus on the profit ratio may discourage the sponsorship of

EXHIBIT 1

Sample Format
for Divisional Measurement

		Maxi-Widget Corporation	
		Division	Mini-Widget
		Month	June 1969
	*Year-to-Date**		
	This Year		*Last Year*
	Actual	*Budget*	*Actual*
Trade Sales—Domestic...................	$26,738	$27,500	$23,942
Export.......................	3,291	3,000	3,469
Total.......................	30,029	30,500	27,411
Intercompany Sales......................	1,122	1,000	1,029
TOTAL SALES........................	31,151	31,500	28,440
Cost of Goods Sold.......................	18,429	18,200	16,924
GROSS PROFIT......................	12,722	13,300	11,516
% TO SALES.....................	40.8%	42.2%	40.5%
Divn.—Sell. Genl. Admin..................	3,375	3,200	3,123
Research & Development...........	1,239	1,250	1,140
Divn.—PROFIT FROM OPERATIONS.......	8,108	8,850	7,253
Corp.—Sell. Genl. Admin..................	1,326	1,350	1,232
Research & Development...........	209	200	185
PROFIT FROM OPERATIONS.............	6,573	7,300	5,836
% TO SALES.........................	21.1%	23.2%	20.5%
Taxes on Income........................	3,615	4,020	3,210
NET EARNINGS.......................	$ 2,958	$ 3,280	$ 2,626
Depreciation............................	$ 2,732	$ 2,700	$ 2,502
Cash Flow.............................	$ 5,690	$ 5,980	$ 5,128
Capital Expenditures....................	$ 4,382	$ 4,500	$ 3,794
Investment:			
Gross Plant........................	$35,672	$35,600	$32,147
Receivables.......................	6,970	6,800	6,423
Inventories.......................	7,256	7,000	6,452
TOTAL.......................	$49,898	$49,400	$45,022
RETURN ON INVESTMENT...............	11.9%	13.3%	11.7%
RESIDUAL INCOME (DEFICIT)............$	(42)	$ 280	$ (124)
Per Share:			
NET EARNINGS.....................	$.30	$.33	$.28
CASH FLOW........................	.57	.60	.54
Receiv.—Collection Period (Days).........	42	41	43
Inventory Turnover......................	5.1	5.2	5.2

* ($–000)

projects that promise less than average rate of return, even though they
will effectively increase total corporate earnings. To overcome this deficiency, a profitability index has been developed to which the General
Electric Company assigned the label "residual income."

The index is applied by establishing the company's current cost of capital, determining the portion of that cost which is attributable to each division and computing the consequent positive or negative amount of divisional residual income.

With properly charted amounts of residual income established by corporate management, emphasis will be shifted from the ratio return-on-investment to the desired level of total dollar profits. This transfer of emphasis is obviously warranted, since the proper company objective is maximization of earnings on the stockholders' equity.

For purposes of illustration in Exhibit 1, the cost of capital employed in the Mini-Widget Division has been assumed to be $6.0 million for the year 1969 and $5.5 million for the year 1968, or just one-half of these amounts for the illustrated six-month periods.

Earnings per share. A practical and unsophisticated approach to divisional appraisal can be achieved by the use of "earnings per share." While the corporate chief executive is intent on raising the return on stockholders' investment and in building up the total profit level, he is necessarily concerned day-in, day-out with per-share earnings performance. This indicator—more than any other, probably—is responsible for the ultimate valuation accorded to the company's stock in the marketplace. The real worth of vibrant market performance has been demonstrated many times over, and "for instances" are too numerous to describe here.

Additionally, the earnings per share figure will guide the executive to directing energies into the proper channels. A 50 percent return-on-investment is admirable, certainly. However, little time should be wasted on congratulations if the division accounts for only a nickel of the company's two-dollar per share of profits, and if prospects for its expansion are anything less than splendid. Better to tackle the division that accounts for half the company's earnings, yet is mired in a seeming morass of sub-par profitability.

Cash flow per share. Had Gertrude Stein addressed herself to the subject, she might have written that earnings is earnings is earnings. But the equality of this expression is increasingly in dispute. Apart from the elasticity of "generally accepted accounting principles" that may cause the reported profit to be a dubious figure, the "quality" of earnings and the relative size of the non-cash deductions from earnings now receive increasing scrutiny.

For years, spokesmen for industry have advocated the viewpoint that depreciation allowances are inadequate because they are based on the original cost of the depreciable assets and do not, therefore, provide sufficiently for asset replacement at current higher construction costs. In this context, one dollar of reported earnings must really be less than one dollar, since depreciation expense—if it is intended as a fixed asset replacement fund—is understated. On the other hand, many analysts contend that existing plant is generally kept in good repair and its life prolonged by maintenance projects that are charged to current expense. In *this* context, a large portion of the depreciation costs recorded by industry will really have no relevance to the actual wear-and-tear or obsolescence of existing property and may, in fact, provide a means of future expansion of and additions to existing facilities, as well as providing funds for construction of entirely new facilities.

The difference in viewpoints is provocative. In any event, the ascendancy of the "cash earnings" or "cash-flow" index provides something more than just a plaything for security analysts. It is a meaningful tool in measuring divisional performance, if only because, with all other things being equal—which they never are, of course—the division with the highest sustained cash-flow is the one most contributive to the company's well-being. At the very least, the cash-flow indicator—usually expressed on a per-share basis—is a useful measurement device.

Both the "cash-flow per share" and "earnings per share" figures are computed by dividing the divisional earnings and cash-flow by the number of outstanding common shares of the company. The divisor, in Exhibit 1, is ten million shares in 1969 and 9.5 million shares in 1968.

Budget and industry yardsticks. Properly focused, divisional performance measurement will give a good view of both management capability and the intrinsic business entity. The use of budgets for monitoring actual results, as described in Chapter 23, provides the principal tool for evaluation purposes. Comparisons of current results with prior periods continue to be widely used. In addition, comparisons among divisions of the company and, to the extent that data are available, with competitors and with other industries can be helpful, particularly in determining whether the business itself is one that should be expanded, cut back, or abandoned.

Once again, it must be emphasized that the financial executive carries the burden of interpreting the yardsticks—of distinguishing the variances that are or should be controllable by management from those which are to be found in the business itself.

Problems of profit measurement

Profits are conventionally computed according to generally accepted accounting principles, which may or may not produce results that are suitable for use in measuring divisional performance. Examination of the profit and loss data in Exhibit 1 will serve to highlight some of the problem areas, such as:

Sales and transfer prices. Ordinarily, the recording of sales to trade is straightforward. All domestic trade sales can be readily identified with a profit-responsible division or center in most multi-line companies. Sales of domestically produced goods in the export market may be made or administered by the same selling group that handles domestic business, or the marketing may be under the jurisdiction of an export or "international" group within the company that is set up as a wholly or partially profit-responsible division. Alternative methods of measuring the international division are described later in this chapter. In the exhibit the export sales and profits remain identified with the domestic division.

The separate display of intercompany sales is usually advisable, in order to portray the magnitude of interdependence among the divisions of the company. It is in this area that transfer-pricing practices come into play.

If a competitive outside market exists for the transferred product, the latter should be transferred to the receiving division at market price. More specifically, the receiving division should enjoy a cost which is no greater than the aggregate cost were the product purchased from the most competitive outside supplier. Any freight or other delivery penalty inherent in adverse location of the supplying division's plant should fall upon the supplying division. Conflicts of interest between the supplying and receiving divisions may require intervention of a corporate official, group, or committee, and should be resolved in the corporate interest regardless of divisional impact. However, in many companies a laissez-faire policy still prevails in transfer pricing.

When an effective competitive market for the transferred product is lacking—and this condition often occurs—another basis for interdivision pricing must be found. Solomons is a strong advocate for use of the marginal cost rule, whereby the transfer price will be set at the transferor division's incremental cost at that level of volume for which the incremental cost equals the transferee division's net incremental revenue from use of the transferred products. The formula is not easy to grasp and would, in practice, require frequent surveillance and updating. For these reasons, as well as several others suggested by Solomons, the marginal-cost rule is little used.

In a typically simplified resolution of the transfer-price problem when a genuinely competitive outside market is non-existent, most financial executives will settle for the use of negotiated prices or for arrangements that provide for profit sharing between the producing division and the consuming or marketing division. These practices are equitable enough if the transferred product does not bulk large within the total scope of operations of the divisions involved. However, if the product's pricing is a major determinant of either division's profitability, a degree of artificiality will necessarily be introduced into that division's profit measurement.

Under such circumstances, it may be preferable to treat the division —or both divisions, if both are affected materially—as only a quasi–profit-responsible division, with the measurement techniques restricted to financial data that exclude or obscure the effect of the transferred product. One method of achieving this result is to price the transfer at average or incremental cost and to "rollover" the related portion of the producing division's investment into the investment of the transferee division. The comparative efficacy of the alternatives—that is, whether to accept the artificiality of a contrived transfer price, or to opt instead for only a partially profit-responsible division—must be considered in the light of the specific circumstances in each instance.

In the most highly integrated corporations, subtle and not-so-subtle distinctions in design, engineering, metallurgy, chemistry, fabrication, assembly, packaging, and the like will create a host of intermediate products that have no competitive counterparts in the marketplace. Under these conditions, even with artificiality of transfer pricing at its extreme, a majority of company executives are inclined to favor the use of negotiated prices or profit-sharing in order to permit a full display of divisional profit data.

Similar transfer-pricing problems will exist within a single division when efforts are made to calculate the earnings contribution of individual products and plants.

Cost of goods sold. The generally accepted cost of sales as reported for a division may include a number of elements that render the amount unacceptable for measurement purposes.

First, of course, the pricing of products or services received from other divisions of the company will affect the cost of sales and reported profits of the transferee division. The elimination of unrealized profit in the inventory of the transferred product itself or of any upgraded material of which it is a constituent should be accomplished as a corporate (non-divisional) transaction, except where the profit has arisen from pricing of transfers within the division itself. In the latter case, the elimination should be reflected in the division's own operating results, of course.

If direct costing methods are followed, it may be advisable to make an adjustment to the divisional income statement for period costs. That is, if there has been a significant increase or decrease in the quantity of the in-process or finished inventories from the beginning to the end of the accounting period and if period costs are substantial, an adjustment of inventory values may be required to reflect proper absorption of the period costs which would otherwise be excluded.

The adoption of the last-in, first-out (LIFO) method of inventory valuation as an income tax device may cause distortion of divisional profit results. The aberration occurs when low-cost inventories are substantially depleted by withdrawals in excess of current higher-cost additions to stock. Under this condition, the division's profits will be inflated, unless the inventory is valued on a first-in, first-out basis, or by an alternative "current cost" method. The adjustment should be made if distortion of divisional results would otherwise be material.

Depreciation policy can have a significant effect on reported divisional profitability. There may be very little relationship between the amount of depreciation charged to a division's current operations and the "normalized" depreciation of the assets employed. That is, the assets in service may include fully-depreciated assets, facilities constructed or acquired years earlier when costs were substantially lower than today, facilities subject to accelerated depreciation methods, and so forth.

The financial executive should apply at least subjective judgment to assure himself that the divisional depreciation charges when computed according to generally accepted accounting principles are reasonable. In this instance, "reasonable" means that the indicated depreciation charges, together with expensed maintenance, are adequate to sustain and ultimately to replace the subject facilities, or alternatively to provide funds for other investment purposes. Without such reasonableness, the financial man must determine whether he is going to attempt to negotiate a more realistic charge with the division manager's agreement; or, alternatively, whether he will deal with the subject in editorial comment accompanying the periodic divisional performance measurement reports.

Overhead expense. In the vernacular, overhead is any element of non-productive costs—usually encompassing selling, general, and administrative expense, and research and development expense in manufacturing companies. Exhibit 1 illustrates an appropriate method of displaying these costs for divisional measurement purposes.

In this area of expense, more than in any other, differences of opinion continue to exist as to the desirability of assessing the divisions with "non-controllable" costs—and particularly with respect to the practice of charging divisions for expenses of central corporate administrative groups. The prime argument in favor of making such charges is to permit the development of a full-scale statement of profit and loss which will disclose—with possible imprecision—the complete divisional profitability in a format that is tied-in with the company's customary financial reporting system, and that has reality in terms of the final earnings outcome of the business. The principal reason for avoiding such assessments of expense is to hew to the responsibility concept, whereby the division is to be freed insofar as possible from items of bookkeeping that are beyond divisional control and whereby the division can be more readily evaluated and motivated in an incremental earnings framework.

Financial managers, for the most part, cling to the full-allocation procedure. In many cases, they will establish detailed methods for determining the costs of services rendered to the divisions by the various central groups in order to make charges as accurately as possible. However, if the allocation technique is to be used, a short-cut method may as well be adopted whenever practicable, on the premise that all central corporate expense is the result of executive management's decision or need to establish and maintain the particular corporate functions that are in being. Accordingly, each division will be expected to contribute (or absorb) a prorata share of the total expense based on total divisional investment, regardless of the individual cost or value of corporate services rendered or received, with adjustment of such allocations to be made only for those services in which the division itself is largely self-sufficient.

The allocation procedure may motivate a division manager somewhat negatively, in that the allocated corporate overhead can be so large as to cause him to profess indifference for controlling his own divisional overhead. On the other hand, the practice of allocation gives the division manager the opportunity to suggest to corporate officials their victimization by Parkinson's Law.

Income Taxes. It is observed by some authorities that income taxes are non-controllable and consequently should not be charged to the divisions for performance measurement purposes. This position is unreal, since it results in omission of one of the major costs of doing business.

Moreover, income taxes are partially controllable at the divisional level, specifically in repair-versus-replace decisions.

In many industries, percentage depletion allowances are a factor of income tax liability, and omission of the income tax effect—which may vary widely from division to division—misrepresents comparative earnings contributions.

A simple procedure is to estimate each division's combined federal, foreign, state, and local income tax rate and to apply the rate to pre-tax income. A 55 percent rate is used in the exhibit.

The investment tax credit is excluded from the calculation. No negative income tax provision is shown when a division operates at a loss, despite the effective reduction in the company's liability for taxes. No income tax provision should be shown when loss carry-forwards are available.

The "corporate" division. On occasion, it will be desirable to classify certain items of operating income or expense to a "non-divisional" or "corporate" category, in order to avoid impact on the operating results of any division, either directly or by allocation. For example, it may prove expedient to charge abandonment losses to this "corporate" division, in order to encourage the disclosure and elimination of uneconomic facilities and to avoid distortion of current period results by large write-offs which may be principally applicable to prior periods. Revenues or expenses may still derive from former divisions that have been sold or liquidated, and they are rightfully "corporate."

The international division. Companies with significant overseas activities will usually find it advisable to organize such functions within an "international division."

Difficulties may be encountered in applying measurement procedures to foreign affiliates, because of delays in receipt of complete reports and because of problems involved in realistic translation of foreign currency amounts.

The measurement of profits attributable to the export sales of products that are produced by the domestic divisions of the company may be accomplished by transfer of the product to the international division at market or negotiated price, or by profit-sharing arrangement, or by the "rollover" technique that transfers a prorata share of product cost and investment from the domestic to the international division.

The period.   The reporting period will generally be one month, or multiples thereof. The investment amounts should be averaged for the period. When the period is less than a fiscal year, the return-on-investment and residual income calculations may be meaningless in seasonal businesses. The seasonal factor can be overcome if credible forecasts are available, by adding forecasted results for the remainder of the year to the actual year-to-date figures.

Problems of investment measurement

The profit-center concept has evolved from the assumption that the manager's control over divisional assets is custodial and that he should be expected to generate sufficient earnings from his custodianship. In fact, the current division manager will be inclined to look upon the clutch of plants, products, customers, et al. which has been, in most instances, thrust upon him as being a mixed grab-bag, with the recorded values often being at odds with his own judgment of what they should be. Nonetheless, the assets are there, and the manager's responsibility is established by executive fiat.

The divisional performance measurement procedure (Exhibit 1), as applied to the profit and loss statement, is terminated at the operating profit level, after assessment of income taxes. Consistently, the investment base includes fixed assets and working capital required for divisional operations, with other assets and liabilities excluded.

Fixed assets—attribution.   The fixed assets of a multi-product or multi-service corporation will usually consist of facilities operated by one division and wholly dedicated to the requirements of the operating division; facilities operated by one division, but wholly or partly dedicated to serving the requirements of one or more other divisions; and facilities not under the jurisdiction of any one division, and serving the requirements of more than one division.

No problem of fixed-asset attribution exists in the first instance, when, for example, Division A is wholly responsible for the operations of a plant or a portion of a plant that turns out product which is marketed by Division A entirely to customers outside of the corporate structure. All of the applicable fixed-asset value is clearly assignable to Division A, with appropriate allocations of joint facilities if the total plant is shared with one or more other divisions.

In the second instance—when all or a portion of the product of a Division A plant is transferred to Division B for further processing or upgrading by the latter division, or for sale by Division B to outside customers—the attribution of the plant asset value will generally be dictated by the practice observed in transfer pricing of the product. If the product is transferred to Division B at a market-related value, or at some price negotiated or established higher than cost, it will be appropriate to include the plant asset value in the investment base of Division A.

If the product is to be transferred to Division B at cost, the prorata portion of the plant asset value will be "rolled-over" into the investment base of Division B. In some instances—when Division A is small relative to Division B and when the transferred product is all or a major part of Division A's output—it may be logical to meld the two divisions for reporting purposes. The "rollover" is most often made as an accounting worksheet calculation, although some companies have found it practical to effect the entry on the books of account in order that investment values may be developed as an integral part of financial statement preparation.

The attribution of corporate non-divisional assets involves questions of accounting and managerial philosophy which are widely debated. However, having resolved the procedure in a manner that allocates corporate overhead expenses among divisions, it is consistent to similarly allocate the corporate assets that are supportive of divisional operations. These assets will include executive, administrative, research, engineering, and other facilities which are operated as central staff activities.

In the event that the company enjoys a significant income from non-operating sources—for example, interest and dividends on investments—some portion of the central fixed assets should be attributed to these non-operating functions, thus being excluded from allocation to the divisions. In practice, the computed fixed-asset value will often be relatively small, with negligible effect on divisional results if overlooked.

The divisional investment base will include idle plant facilities, if any, as distinguished from non-operating property. By definition, idle plant is categorized as productive or service facilities which are under divisional jurisdiction and which are expected to be utilized once again in the foreseeable future. On the other hand, non-operating property will generally have been removed from divisional control, and will be in the hands of a corporate staff group for disposition or development.

As with the allocation of central corporate expenses, a strong case can be made for inclusion in the division investment base of only those assets which are directly controlled or controllable by the division, and excluding shared and corporate-service assets. However, this position introduces difficulties when one division houses functions such as research, warehousing, engineering, data-processing, and so forth, and another division shares common facilities or secures services from central corporate groups. Although the difference in modus operandi may account for only a point or two on the return-on-investment scale, the discrepancy exists, and it should be corrected by an allocation formula.

The total allocated amount of fixed assets—as compared to specific divisional asset values—will generally be small enough to preclude any drawn-out controversy. Moreover, allocations invariably can be carried out in a simple and straightforward manner: Shared warehouses in relation to proportionate floorspace occupied; shared or corporate laboratories in relation to research and development budgets; corporate headquarters assets based on total divisional investment; and so forth.

Fixed assets—valuation. Problems of fixed-asset valuation arise mainly from the year-by-year upward spiral in fixed-asset costs, running the gamut from the acquisition of raw land all of the way to the last embellishments on the equipped structure. Inflation has played hob with the validity of the dollar as a measuring device. Yet no alternative method has met with any wide acceptance to date.

Most companies continue to use the gross or net fixed-asset values as entered in their property records, with no adjustment for variations in price-levels and usually with no regard to whether an asset was constructed by the now-owning company, acquired by direct purchase, or acquired in a pooling of interests. This method has the advantage of simplicity, at least, and will obviate difficulties inherent in any price stabilization or appraisal technique.

The controversy over the use of net book value versus original cost (e.g., gross book value) still rages. A preference for use of net value is triggered by two rationale: First, it produces a higher, more comfortable return-on-investment percent; second, it satisfies the debatable conception that accrued depreciation represents a specifically identifiable recapture of funds that has effectively reduced divisional investment. For all that, and in this writer's opinion, the cost basis is the more logical, considering the uneven pattern of capital spending, the happenstance of the depreciation cycle, the high productive order in which most plants are maintained during their working life, and the resulting simplification of financial analysis. Admittedly, the cost basis fails to screen out purchasing power and acquisition-type distortions of the fixed-asset base. However, it is not evident that the considerable effort required by the alternatives produces enough added accuracy to justify the trouble and expense.

Two principal methods are advocated by some for overcoming the garblings that arise from asset age and from the method of asset acquisition. The first is the use of index numbers to translate fixed-asset values to a common price-level, hopefully approximating replacement cost. The second is by means of appraised values, to determine the "real" worth of the facilities. Either one of the two methods will be accompanied by suitable adjustment of depreciation charges, in order to restate the amortization of fixed assets consonant with their revised valuation.

The first method—that is, the use of index numbers—has the presumption of logic that is the essence of constant-dollar valuations. Yet, it may compound distortions by applying index factors to numbers which are already unrepresentative because of "bargain" purchases, wasteful construction practices, expense versus capital accounting policies, and the like. Moreover, the procedure applies the highest multiple to the oldest asset and leaves the division burdened with today's construction cost— purportedly—attached to a unit that preferably might be, with 20–20 hindsight, reconstructed in a different size (capacity) with different technology and different materials at a different location.

Appraisals have their place for insurance purposes, but their validity in arriving at a divisional investment base for measuring performance is obscure. The appraisal necessarily conjures a value that is evoked from earning power. The rate of return later calculated from the appraised value becomes a function of the capitalization rate originally employed in the appraisal. Thus, the arithmetic comes full circle to little avail.

All of the foregoing points to the conclusion that valuation of the fixed-asset component of the investment base can be one of the most unsettling elements in the measurement process. The difficulty may be further intensified when the fixed-asset figure includes a healthy block of fully depreciated assets still in service, with no current depreciation charges reflected in the company's records.

Working capital.   In balance-sheet context, the working capital necessary to support divisional operations will consist of cash funds, accounts receivable, inventories, and prepayments, reduced by ordinary short-term liabilities.

In many multi-division companies only the accounts receivable and inventories will be readily identifiable with specific divisions. When data-processing is conducted centrally, the cash balances, prepayments, and current liabilities will generally lose their divisional label. For this reason, it is a common practice to include only trade accounts receivable and inventories in the investment base, rationalizing that cash funds and prepayments, were they identifiable, would be offset by current liabilities —if the latter were identifiable. Some companies, alternatively, compute cash-fund requirements and current liabilities by formula methods.

In practice, the exclusion of working capital other than trade accounts receivable and inventories may introduce a comparative inequity in the investment base, if one or less-than-all divisions have secured extended payment terms from major suppliers or if an appreciable portion of sales are made to other divisions. In such case, adjustment of the investment base may be required.

The inclusion of trade accounts receivable and inventories as separate items in the investment base permits a ready calculation of their turnover rates, as shown in Exhibit 1.

The financial executive's role

The preceding sections of this chapter have described the financial executive's part in divisional performance measurement.

He is, first of all, the architect of the system. He is, most of all, the interpreter of its output.

At the risk of repetition, a point to be emphasized is that performance measurement requires much more that carte blanche acceptance of computer printouts. Off-line analysis of the data is essential if the full significance of the indicated results is to be unveiled. Only then will it be possible to evaluate *both* the manager and the business, thus achieving the objective of the procedure.

Little has been said heretofore as to just how the financial manager is to conduct his analysis in such a way as to distinguish the variances attributable to divisional management's performance from those that are intrinsic to the business itself, or that otherwise arise from wholly or partially uncontrollable factors. The evaluation obviously must be conducted as objectively as possible, but it will at times inevitably require subjective and intuitive judgment. In particular, judgments as to the division manager's performance may cause highly sensitive and emotional reactions, unless extreme tact is exercised.

There are no specific mathematical rules to observe, apart from the traditional analyses of volume, price, and cost variances. Once again, success will hinge ultimately upon the financial man's knowledge of the business and its managers. This understanding is essential to the development of accurate conclusions and effective decisions.

Bibliography

An extensive bibliography on this subject is appended to the David Solomons book, *Divisional Performance: Measurement and Control*. Of particular interest are:

MAUTZ, R. K.   *Financial Reporting for Diversified Companies*. Financial Executives Research Foundation, 1968.

SLOAN, ALFRED P.   *My Years with General Motors*. New York: Doubleday & Co., Inc., 1964.

SOLOMONS, DAVID.   *Divisional Performance: Measurement and Control*. Financial Executives Research Foundation, 1965.

Also recommended for practicality and directness of approach are three books by Ronello B. Lewis, published by Prentice-Hall, Inc., but unfortunately not recently updated: *Accounting Reports for Management*, 1957; *Financial Analysis for Management*, 1959; and, *Financial Controls for Management*, 1961.

Control of research and development costs

Paul R. Langdon*

The financial executive does not "control" research costs. Research costs are a result of the decisions made by the research director and other members of top management. Just as the financial executive leaves production decisions to the production manager and marketing decisions to the person in charge of marketing, he leaves technical evaluation of the research program to the research director. Whether emphasis on one part of the program rather than on another will produce better technical results is a decision for the research director.

The financial executive's function is to give service by furnishing correct and current cost information to the research manager just as he does to the production and marketing managers. He cooperates with them in preparing estimates of the financial results of possible future actions. He is also a part of the top management team and summarizes the projected financial results based upon decisions which the various components, including research, have made.

Although various functions are discussed in this chapter, it is not implied that the financial executive performs all of them. This is especially true in the area of evaluation of technical performance. These operations are described here in order to give perspective to the financial executive's contribution to the entire process.

---

* Assistant Treasurer, Battelle Memorial Institute, Columbus, Ohio.

The approach to R.&D. operations

The area of controlling R.&D. costs, as contrasted with the control of other costs of operating companies, is characterized by several unique factors which the financial executive must constantly keep in mind.

Research is the exploration of the unknown, which follows an unknown number of unknown steps. Manufacturing, sales, and general administration, on the other hand, are the performance of known steps. Manuals are often written to describe these latter processes in detail so that each person involved knows what is expected of him. The accountant has enough information about these steps so that he can prepare a classification of cost accounts to pinpoint the expenses for the benefit of management. In research these steps are not known; research is the process of determining them.

Other procedures of a company are generally repetitive. Standard costs can be applied in many areas. It is thereby easy to determine when costs are out of line in certain operations. In research many of the basic steps are new and not repetitive. Repetitive procedures are usually found only in service departments, such as the analytical laboratory and report reproduction.

In research, one cannot predict with certainty the results or end product; its primary purpose, in fact, is to determine what the results might be. In manufacturing, the research has already been performed and the results are reasonably predictable; otherwise, the process would not go into manufacturing.

The research process

For effective financial control of R.&D. costs, understanding the research process is essential. Research has been defined as all scientific, engineering, and related activities that are directed toward the conception and development of technical ideas. Thus research involves many different activities.

The relationship between research costs and this wide range of activities can be pictured as an inverted triangle:

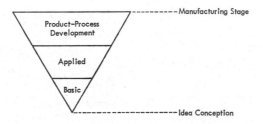

The conception of the technical idea (basic research) is at the apex of the triangle. The idea then goes through the applied stage to the area development and manufacturing. These stages tend to overlap. The financial executive would need to know only that these general areas exist. There are disagreements about the definitions of basic and applied research because of the complexities involved.

As discussed above, it is difficult to predict the effort required to achieve the desired results. This makes cost control of research different from normal cost control methods. The process of research is the testing of hypotheses and the discarding of unacceptable ones until the desired result is obtained. One cannot guarantee that he will secure the answer before the budgeted amount is expended. Every experiment that is unsuccessful will at least reveal the path *not* to follow under the chosen experimental conditions. Management desires to know the cost and the time required. The best that can be done in most instances is to predict what *probably* will happen. While sales predictions are uncertain, in research the degree of uncertainty is even greater.

In research it is also difficult to measure performance. Usual indices such as monthly sales per salesman, sales expenses related to sales volume, cost per unit produced, etc., are not available. The number of ideas produced cannot be equated to research costs, although some attempts have been made to evaluate the efficiency of a research department by the number of patents secured. Even here, whether or not an idea is patentable may relate little to its value to the company profits. Although other techniques have been tried, there is no sure method of determining how effectively the money was used.

Equipment costs for research are also different. Equipment used is, itself, experimental at times and must be manufactured to order. It may be required to perform to certain specifications which never have been met before. Development of such equipment is itself research, which adds to the uncertainty of its costs. Also, with the constantly changing conditions and developments in the field of research, equipment rapidly becomes obsolete. Decision as to what equipment is necessary must be left to the research manager, even though this is a large part of the budget. The accounting system should help a manager to measure the results of his decisions and make it possible for the president of the company to hold him responsible for his decisions.

The public thinks that most research discoveries are accidental research findings. The contrary is most generally true. Most discoveries result from careful planning based on sound reasoning, skillful and persistent work, and sound methodology.

The research worker

The type of personnel is another important factor in controlling R.&D. costs. One is dealing with the scientists or the engineer, professional men.

Many scientists and engineers desire to do basic research only, and the necessity for doing applied research or developmental work requires an adjustment in thinking on their part.

The research worker must have a minimum of direct supervision and great freedom to plan the details of his work. The necessary rules and regulations should be devised keeping that thought foremost; and, they should assist him in his work. The financial executive must be prepared to explain the necessity for the rules when they must be applied. Interruptions should be minimal, and the opportunity to discuss the work with colleagues is essential.

The research worker needs to know what is expected of him. Being a combination of curiosity and logic, he wants to know why things are as they are and then to search for the logic behind the "why." When a reasonable explanation is not apparent, his acceptance is reluctant and evasive. Naturally such a reaction has an effect on the cost control efforts. For this reason the logic of the necessary procedures, forms, and techniques should be demonstrated to the research worker. He needs to be shown how they can serve his purposes.

The research worker is often little concerned with management problems. His technical problems are paramount. He therefore expects for the solution of such problems the minimum of supervision, competent technical assistance, well-maintained and up-to-date equipment, plenty of laboratory space, and prompt delivery of supplies and materials. He is less interested in the procedures required to supply his technical tools. This includes time reporting and other items of an accounting nature.

It is easy to see the need for modern and efficient equipment in a manufacturing process. Professional development of the research worker is just as important but more difficult to justify. Tools for this purpose include advanced educational opportunities, professional society activities, seminars, publications, literature surveillance, training programs, travel, and personnel counseling. Provision for these activities must be included in the research budget either as direct cost, departmental burden, or general overhead.

Research organization

The organization of the research staff is an important part of the environment affecting cost control. The estimate of project costs must come from this organization, and the control techniques are carried out within this organization.

The research director is the key person in the organization. He participates in planning the research program and he manages the research organization. The exact titles of the research director and the one to whom he reports may vary depending upon the organization structure of the company.

The office of the research director is responsible for the decision to accelerate, slow down, or stop effort on phases of the overall research program. Responsibility for individual projects and for the assignment of researchers' time to these projects is best delegated to the department head or division supervisor. The latter makes a preliminary estimate of time and cost factors, including project potentials. This is submitted to the research director for review.

Reporting to the research director are division heads. The divisions may be organized on the basis of (1) scientific discipline such as physics, chemistry, metallurgy, (2) type of research, such as basic, applied, product or process development, or pilot plant, or (3) product group, or field of investigation. Responsibility centers for cost control may be located at division level or at the next lower level. The accumulation of costs may be made at the division level and it may be a burden center.

Financial control of R.&D.

It cannot be overemphasized that financial control in research does not directly control how the research will be performed. Control of research per se is exercised by the research worker. Budgeting and financial measurements are simply tools which assist management in making "go–no go" decisions on undertaking, continuing, or terminating research projects.

Of course, there is financial control of research in that the flow of money through a research operation is predetermined. Provision must be made as to who establishes its volume, how the funds are utilized, and how the flow of funds is measured, as well as what feedback or control action is to be taken. A research operation is pictured as a system wherein a tangible input of money generates an output of intangible ideas, with a proper feedback so that one can stop the flow of money to less promising ideas and increase it to the more promising. The secret of success lies in determining which is promising and which is not.

It is the function of top management to determine the type of research to be conducted and the amount to be invested in the program. The areas of research must be compatible with the corporate policies and objectives. The financial resources of the company will limit the amount to be invested and control the areas for future research. The estimated benefits from the program are an important determining factor.

At one time, it was felt that the management of research meant giving the scientist an entirely free hand in spending money. In fact, it was thought that if top management would just release so many dollars in manpower over a reasonable period of time, the company should get results. In more recent years, the management of research has leaned toward the idea that more control is possible, but a different type of control than that provided for other operations of the organization. It must be recognized that the evaluation of research results is more subjective, and that decisions to invest in research cannot be based on specific expected financial return as can be done for other operations of the company.

The research budget

While the research budget is helpful in planning the research program, *it does not control the costs*. Top management and the research worker control the costs with the help of the budget. Nor does the budget measure and evaluate research. It only establishes the amounts of money which may be spent on various research programs. Just as in any budgeting, the budget serves its primary role as a planning tool.

An industrial research program must be regarded as a business investment. Therefore, in the long run, it is expected to provide some sort of profit for the company. Yet, it is often difficult to establish in precise financial terms just how this profit is to be realized and when. Some have attempted to set gross budgetary amounts by formula or arbitrary rules in establishing the amount for research. Examples of such approaches are:

1. Percentage of sales.
2. Percentage of net profit.
3. Percentage of investment in capital assets.
4. Overall cost of an established research staff.
5. Percentage of cash flow.
6. Programmed.
7. Total cost of selected projects.

The percentage-of-net-profit base produces more violent fluctuations in research projects than does the percentage-of-sales method. Since research can be used to decrease costs as well as increase sales, this does give profits an advantage over sales in determining the research budget. The percentage-of-investment-in-capital-assets method has little relationship to the actual cash needs for research, although it does have the advantage of keeping the research activity in step with the overall activity.

The basis for the cost-of-research-staff method is using an arbitrary or estimated figure for the size of a research staff in determining the budget. The advantage is that it permits stability of the research staff.

Cash flow is directly correlated with the financial ability of the organization. It is more stable than the sales or profits methods.

The programmed method uses a long-range plan determined by comparison with competitors, by industry practice, by funds available, or by arbitrary executive decision. There is a distinct disadvantage in comparing one company's creative research with that of other companies even within the same industry because financial reporting may be different, and some companies may tend to capitalize research more than others. For valid comparisons it would be necessary to have a working knowledge of all the accounting methods. Furthermore, conditions within the other companies may vary considerably because of differences in the development of their various research programs.

The cost-of-selected-projects method is more useful because it is based on consideration of the value of each project to the overall company objectives. This method is becoming the preferred one. In addition, the research budget should be large enough to maintain a reasonable staff, and there should be enough research to make the overall program interesting for them; otherwise they will leave. If the research is to be done inside the plant, there must be allowance for adequate capital investment for the plant and the equipment needed to support the research staff.

The maximum amount of research, of course, is limited by how the funds may be used in other areas of the company budget. Furthermore, it is important to keep in mind that once research is begun on a certain project funds should be available to carry it on through the development stage to marketing and manufacturing. There is also danger in suddenly increasing R.&D. expenditures. In such instances care may not be exercised in spending the funds, and other aspects of corporate operations may not be able to absorb the benefits of the research.

Several general areas must be considered in determining the amount to be spent on research:

1. *Determine how much should be spent to develop new products.* Accounting information on the amount the company has spent on research in the past is helpful in this area. Management should examine the cycle of the research expenditures for new products over a five- or ten-year period. It generally takes at least five years for the proper development of a new product. While the sales on existing products are being reviewed, attention should be given to those whose sales have declined. If there are quite a number it would indicate the need to invest in the development of new products.

2. *Determine the amount to be spent to lower the cost of existing products.* Consideration should be given to lowering the cost of existing products and to what extent this would result in increased sales.

3. *Determine the amount to be spent on the problems in present products and processes.* A part of every R.&D. budget should be allocated to this effort; often the results are dramatic. Providing for research expenditures in this area may be a means of getting a plant back into efficient operation in a much shorter time than normal. Again, this can be overdone. If an inordinate amount of the total costs is in trouble-

shooting, this may indicate that an overall review of the manufacturing process may be in order.

4. *Determine the amount to be spent to develop new applications for existing products.* Records on the cost of past research to develop new product applications should be used. Comparisons of these costs with sales and profit figures will guide the allocation of future funds in this area.

5. *Determine the amount to be spent to help customers make better use of their own products.* R.&D. personnel may be assigned to help customers develop new uses for the company's products. This is important with respect to R.&D. and can result in a considerable amount of new business.

6. *Determine the amount to be spent to develop know-how in areas of major importance to the company.* It may be difficult to determine how much should be spent in this area, but if the company wants to be a leader in the industry it will be necessary to keep ahead of its competitors. At the same time, it should be investigating other technologies that may make inroads upon the company's present position. Expenditure in this area is a good way to develop capabilities in new technological fields, and research for this purpose may be basic.

7. *Determine the amount to be spent to improve existing products.* Product improvement is essential to maintain or increase the company's share of the market. Consideration should be given to how sensitive the product's market position is to technical advances, how heavily the competitors are committed in a given area, and the technological maturity of a given product.

Research projects should make a positive contribution to profits. Above all, research projects should be in line with the objectives of the company and the goal should be compatible with a company need. Research expenditures can be made in many areas. If they are not directed by company-oriented goals and the needs of the product line so that they add to the company profits, these funds may afford little return even if the research is considered successful. There is need for constant surveillance of the planned projects.

Consideration should also be given to the probability of the success of the project and to whether the results are reasonably obtainable. If these are negative the funds may be better spent elsewhere.

In making an examination of the costs of the various proposed programs, the time factor should also be considered. The costs for a given program may be reasonable, but the time needed to complete it may be so long that realization of profitability may not be probable. Consideration should also be given to availability of facilities and to what plant and equipment may be needed in the event the research is successful. Availability of personnel should also be considered, including personnel who are educated and experienced in the discipline that may be needed.

In determining whether or not to invest in a given project, some companies make an extensive effort to develop probable future costs for bringing the results of the research to market and to estimate the probable return on the investment. Every six months they prepare estimates on the following:

1. Cost and time to complete the research.
2. Cost and time for development and engineering.
3. Tooling and start-up costs.
4. Marketing costs.

In summary, it is unrealistic to set arbitrary amounts for the research budget. Various considerations must be taken into account so that it is a true planning process. Using the team approach, the research staff and the financial executive can be expected to produce a reasonable estimate of the amount required. Of course, the financial executive will be strongly influenced by how these expenditures will affect the financial position of the company and by its ability to continue such research programs in the future, in view of the equipment and the current expenditures that may be required.

When preparing estimates for the budget, all costs should be taken into account. These include the staff time, services of various departments, travel, supplies, and capital equipment. The technical man should take the initial step in preparing these estimates. The staff of the financial executive can assist by supplying the rates and historical costs on similar items in the past. One should not overlook the application of departmental burden and general overhead as they may be used in the accounting system.

Authorization for research

No research should be started without authorization through a work authority or work order. Numbers should be assigned to these, which will be the basis for the accounting control. As the program develops, research subaccount numbers may be established through such work authorization. This phase should be closely controlled.

The individual responsible for maintaining the control should be identified on the work authorization or order. Other information such as the scope of the work, the terminal date of this phase of research, and other instructions should be on the authorization.

Of course, such work authorization is a part of the accounting system and costs are collected under the assigned number.

Theoretical or educational research studies can also be authorized with similar work authorization. These studies are used to improve the capabilities and scientific knowledge of the staff. Cost limitations and time periods should be established for such studies just as they are for regular research projects.

Main attributes of control of R.&D. costs

The purpose of the accounting system in controlling R.&D. costs is to report the expenditures back to the research manager in a manner that is meaningful to him. While it is recognized that a uniform system of accounting must be used for the entire research operation and that different research managers may have different desires, it is possible to have a cost accounting system that gives the desired information to all.

For effective control of R.&D. costs, the techniques and procedures should provide the means to hold costs within budget limits and to apply corrective measures when needed.

Hence, there is the need to clearly define lines of cost authority and the relationship between the financial executive and the research manager. While the latter has the authority to incur costs within the budget, the financial executive has certain responsibilities.

Here it must be stressed that it is well to keep in mind that the accounting is a service to the research manager. When adequate information is not given to him, he will tend to keep his own side records of various costs for which he is held accountable. One must also stress the need for early reporting of costs, as a delay in cost reporting encourages such separate informal systems of accounting.

The accounting system must be integrated with the budget system just as the cost accounting system should be integrated with the general ledger. There is no one best system that can be devised to fit the requirements. Generally speaking, a job-cost system is preferable since this most closely fits the project situation.

Cost information does not measure results of research. It merely measures the expenditures for research and tells in what areas they have been incurred. The use of computers has made possible better information for the research manager. In the past, research expenditures might be classified into only a few general categories. If the manager wanted more specific information it was necessary to go back to a detailed listing of the costs. Now, with the computers, it is possible to have more classifications of these costs; the manager can quickly examine them and ask for details only in those areas which he feels require further study.

The accounting system should be designed for responsibility accounting so that the one with authority to make decisions has the resultant costs assigned to the accounts for which he is responsible. Care must be exercised in designing the accounting system, because it is possible for an accounting system to inadvertently encourage a researcher to use a less efficient method of research. Sometimes, for example, the researcher must decide between using manpower or equipment (which may be more efficient). One method of costing a computer is to assign all its costs to the projects using it, and, if there is little actual use of the computer, this could result in such a high use rate that the project leaders would tend to use the manual (less efficient) methods. A better costing method would be to have a reasonable use rate for the computer and to assign the remaining costs to burden or overhead accounts, thus encouraging the use of the more efficient equipment by ensuring that the costs charged to the project are less for the equipment than for the manpower. The accounting system should be designed with this in mind.

Here, as mentioned above, it is important for the financial executive to keep in mind the personnel with whom he is dealing. They are not factory workers, but scientists and engineers who are hired for their ingenuity. An enterprising engineer may try to circumvent the accounting system to gain an advantage. He may attempt to operate so that certain costs will go to a burden or overhead account and be borne partially by others, rather than directly to his own project.

Cost information and budgets do not by themselves measure and evaluate the results of research. Keeping costs within the budgeted amounts does not mean that a good research job has been done. The accountant cannot judge the effectiveness by cost data. He can only provide financial information to help the research manager direct the program. *Effective controls in the utilization of research funds are a well-planned research budget, good financial reporting, and the systematic evaluation and redirection of the research effort by management.*

The accounting system should provide:

1. *Assignment of responsibility for all costs.*
2. *Authorization of work.* Accounts should not be opened without a proper work authorization. This is just like a production order. It is important that research management fully support this concept.
3. *Advance estimates of the time and cost for each project at each phase before it is authorized to begin.* It is recognized that in any area of research the estimate must of necessity be, at times, very rough. Such an estimate is the basis for the authority to spend the specified amount of money. When these funds are expended, it is the time for reappraisal and a management decision as to whether to go ahead and, if so, in what direction.
4. *Cost reports in sufficient detail to be meaningful to the research manager.* The categories should be such as to be of value to him in making decisions. Here is the opportunity to make comparison with the budget, but it must be kept in mind that since this is research, there may be a considerable difference by categories between amounts budgeted and amounts actually spent. The research manager often decides to go in a different direction after he has had the preliminary results from his research.

5. *Charging of all research department personnel to projects by work authority numbers or to overhead accounts as may be indicated.* It is better to have a separate account for leave time than to charge vacation or illness to the project on which one may be working at the time.

6. *Direct charging as much as practicable.* Costs should go directly to the research project or to the particular research department burden account for materials, travel, time, and facilities. This is one of the primary methods by which the cost system can pinpoint the areas of research effort. Direct charging can, of course, be overdone, especially on small expenditures when the cost of accounting for them may greatly exceed their value.

7. *Prorating to research-work authorizations the indirect costs charged to research department burden accounts.* There are quite a number of indirect costs incurred by various departments or subdepartments of a research activity. Projects within a department should have the current costs incurred by that department charged to those projects. In addition, if it is consistent with the over-all accounting system, a fair share of the company overhead cost for the facilities and services furnished should be included. It should be kept in mind that, if the research is an overhead activity in itself, it should not bear general G and A costs.

8. *Reports for research and management designed to help achieve the objectives of the research program.* Accounting and budgeting systems should be kept simple and coordinated with management planning. Such planning and evaluation may be quite effective in achieving a sound research program, as planning and evaluation are, by far, the most important factors; the accounting system can be designed to provide the information that management needs.

Accounts are established for each work authorization described above. These also establish the responsibility for the costs.

Labor costs

Since labor is the largest cost element in research, special attention should be given to its allocation. Time records are essential for proper record keeping. The scientist's resistance to the keeping of a time record may be minimized by the fact that he may not be working on many projects, so that the allocation of his time among them is not much of a burden.

From a practical standpoint, it is not reasonable to attempt to record overtime of staff members who are exempt from wage- and hour-law regulations. Naturally, the exact time record must be kept of those who are not exempt. For those in the exempt category, time would be kept according to the standard working day, such as 8 hours, and for the standard week, such as 40 hours. Any hours in excess of such standards would not be entered, and the time recorded would conform to the standard working hours which would be allocated in proportion to the hours the scientist or engineer worked on the respective projects.

Many companies use monthly or weekly timecards. When more frequent time reporting is desired, daily cards may be required. This may be especially true of the service departments such as the machine shop or analytical laboratories.

It is preferable to allocate fringe benefits, including vacation, to all the projects on which the individual works over a period of time. If vacation time is charged only to the project on which the individual would have worked during the time he takes a vacation, distortion results. For this reason, a common practice is to add the costs of the various fringe benefits of insurance, payroll taxes, and similar items to the base salary. This total is then divided by the *net* working hours, which are determined by subtracting from the total working hours in the year the vacation, holidays, and estimated average sick leave. This calculation produces an hourly rate. Of course, overtime of nonexempt personnel will be costed at a straight rate or at one and one-half times the straight rate, depending upon the amount of the applicable compensation.

Departmental burden accounts

Accounts must be provided for time spent by research personnel on work other than projects. This may include nonproductive time for which the appropriate department burden account is provided. If the individual is working on certain studies for which there are appropriate accounts, they should be used. An account should be provided for the operating costs of each department within the research organization of the company. This account will cover administrative costs, nonproductive time, and secretarial and other costs that are not directly applicable to research projects.

The burden from each of these accounts is charged to the projects for which the department is responsible. This is done in the same ratio as the productive time charged for such projects.

Materials

As is done with other costs, all materials and other items should be charged directly to projects as far as is practicable. Those items which cannot be charged directly to projects may be distributed as a burden. The latter costs will go into an account to be distributed to those projects for which that department is responsible, as described above.

Materials and other items from vendors are assigned project numbers as they are purchased. When these items are sizable and it may be a long time between the time they are ordered and delivered and the invoices are actually submitted for payment, some companies make a commitment against the project. The purpose of this is to prevent the expenditure of money which has already been committed for another purpose. In such instances, when the invoice arrives, the charge is made to the project and the amount of the original commitment is removed.

Items of common use and those required on several projects and by different organization units may be placed in the storeroom to be charged out to the projects as they are used. These costs are often charged directly to the project concerned.

Service departments

The various service departments may be called upon for work in connection with research projects. Direct labor from the machine shop is collected by shop order; the burden is applied as a percentage of direct labor. Materials may be charged directly to the shop order. In the analytical laboratory, standard costs may be used for each analysis.

Since technical reports are an important research item, and many copies of a technical report may be required, standard costs may be set per page, and cost per impression may be used. Time for typing, editing, and similar items may be a direct charge to the project. The per-unit standard costs can include administrative time of the report-processing department, duplicating, and machine costs, and costs for paper, ink, etc. The other service departments charging to the project may require different accounting methods.

An instrument laboratory may be established to service the various instruments throughout the research laboratory and to act as a repository for general-purpose instruments. Such instruments can be placed on use rate to be charged to the various projects as they are used. The instrument laboratory can also be in charge of calibrating various instruments even though they may not belong to the instrument laboratory but to a department of the research laboratory assigned to the project. In such cases, the charges for the cost of calibration would go directly to the project.

Other direct costs could include long-distance calls. Telephone service, including instruments, attachments, switchboard, and operator's salary costs, may be allocated to the department burden account.

Overhead

Overhead is best distributed as a percentage of the direct-labor cost as it is accumulated on the projects. Overhead would include the cost of the facilities, such as depreciation on the building, maintenance, heat, light, and power, and other appropriate general overhead items. Other overhead accounts might include staff education and development, and internal research of a basic nature. Since internal research of a basic nature is an overhead item, it should not bear general overhead itself.

Technical equipment

Often technical equipment which may be used on many projects is required. This equipment can be rather expensive and may require special facilities. The depreciation for such technical equipment is determined on the basis of the estimated life of the equipment for research purposes and also on the basis of the estimated number of hours that it will be actively used on projects. From this information, which is best secured from the technical staff, one can determine the depreciation factor and the use rate. To this amount should be added maintenance costs on the equipment. An amount equal to the depreciation cost has been a good estimate. To determine whether the use rate collected on technical equipment is in balance with the costs, it is necessary to have a separate account for each department. All technical equipment assigned to a department has its charges and credits to a single account.

Capital equipment procured solely for a project and to be consumed in the course of it is charged directly to the project. Other technical equipment for utilization on more than one project is placed under use rate as described above. Budgeting for technical equipment is done by the various departments that will have the equipment assigned to them. Such equipment will be under use rate, and it will be the responsibility of each department to keep its own income and expense account on its equipment in balance. Such accounting will readily point up those items of equipment that have been procured but not used.

Generally, building alterations made to rearrange space between the various organization units are an expense that follows normal accounting procedure. A more difficult accounting problem arises when facilities are built solely for certain projects. The costs that are of a housing nature will be considered as a part of a building, and the depreciation will go into general overhead. Following normal accounting procedure, the cost of installing equipment is part of the cost of equipment and capitalized as such, and depreciation of such equipment is included in the use rate. Costs of supplying utilities other than those which are supplied generally to the research laboratory should be a part of the cost of the equipment. Of course, these costs may be divided between real and personal, depending upon the property-tax law and regulations in the state in which the equipment is located. Utility services installed for general use throughout the laboratory, although they may be a bit unusual when compared to normal plant construction, will be depreciated in the general overhead.

Reports of research costs

The timing of reports of research costs is important. The reports should be submitted in good form at regular intervals. With the use of computers and electronic equipment, such costs should be available around the fifth business day following the close of the accounting period. For a closer control of costs, reports are submitted weekly; in such instances only staff time may be included, with a more complete statement of costs showing on monthly reports.

As discussed above, it is desirable to supply as much detail by categories as is practicable. As many as 10 to 15 categories may be used, including separate costs for each of the various service departments, storeroom issues, purchases, etc. Extensive as it is, this level of detail is useful to the research director in making estimates in the future. The reports should show the current allocation, the total cost to date, and the unexpended balance; preferably there should be a column on the report for each month, and the cost for the last several months may be listed for comparative purposes.

Also, reports may be prepared on the backlog of work. This should include the unexpended balance and take into account the number of months the project is yet to run. One can then determine what the average projected expenditures will be by the month. Reports of this nature help the research manager make effective use of the staff.

Cost reports should go to the individual responsible for operating within the project budget, to the immediate supervisor, and to others who have supervisory responsibility.

Evaluation

The preparation of the budgets and the compilation of the research costs are not the end of the story. Research cannot be properly evaluated solely from conventional accounting data. Dr. Ray Villers has emphasized this fact in his book, *Research and Development; Planning and Control*. Not only must past performance and costs of the research project be evaluated, but considerable attention must be given to the present program and staff and to appraising the future.

One important aspect to be kept in mind is that there is apt to be a considerable variance between the actual expenditures for various categories of the research program and the budgeted amounts. One must remember that research is a development of the new. The researcher is expected to change his program to reflect the results of the research. For this reason he may use more equipment and less time or vice versa; he may use more consultants or other methods as the program may dictate.

Comparison of budgeted and cost figures in these categories may be of some benefit, but pointing out these differences to the researcher may produce few benefits.

When evaluating research, some of the first questions are: Will the R.&D. be productive in terms of the company's profit and goals in the future? and has the project contributed to the company's profit and goals, judged by the recent performance? Again, one must keep in mind that often five years is required for the proper development of the research.

Methods that have been used in the past to evaluate research include determining the number of new products developed, the number of patents, and the number of publications, and making a general appraisal of the value of the research and development program.

Experience has shown that no single method of evaluation is sufficient by itself. Elements of a program for evaluation of research are:

1. The evaluation of people and the quality of their contribution.
2. The evaluation of the individual research projects relative to company objectives, etc.
3. The evaluation of how well the objectives were achieved as originally planned.
4. The evaluation of how well the company has been able to utilize the innovations of research.

Various other general factors are to be considered. The evaluation of a man's performance is easy when it can be related to the dollar value of the research results, as is the case when his work is in support of existing products and processes. If, however, the technical man's work is exploratory and directed toward new technology, another method of evaluation must be used.

Research is concerned with the development of new ideas leading to the development of hypotheses and the testing of such hypotheses. Accordingly, a man's performance can be judged on the basis of how well the work was conceived, planned, and conducted, and how well the results were interpreted.

It cannot be expected that all members of the research group will be top producers of new ideas; however, they must be in sufficient number to stimulate the research. Productivity can be measured but to some extent is controlled by the area of research. Some types of research can result in definite dollar benefits, but with others it is not possible to take a proprietary position in the results.

It must also be recognized that the cooperation of marketing personnel is necessary to develop the results of the research. The effectiveness of marketing efforts must be included in the analysis if the evaluation of R.&D. is to be meaningful.

Market research is one method of securing information necessary to promote the products of research. To avoid useless expenditure of research effort on processes which are not novel, it is well to check the market possibilities of a potential new product.

The operating departments should define markets and the development. Of course, it is up to the researchers to find the solutions.

Some basic research may be very good. It is occasionally desirable to conduct research in areas outside the line of products of the company, research which may not produce the dollars as soon as does other support research. If a company does choose to diversify its product line through research, it must be able to utilize the output of the research program.

In the discussion of the research process early in this chapter, the statement was made that it is difficult to predict the effort required to achieve the desired results. On the other hand, many industrial companies are spending more dollars in the area of development which is closer to the top of the inverted triangle shown on page 665, than on research. In the development area it is easier to relate expenditures and elapsed time to other historical data. Yet periodic evaluation of the technical accomplishment is particularly important at this stage. One other point is that the researcher must be kept on the path to the objectives, as he may tend to be sidetracked by a by-product idea which is scientifically intriguing but not oriented to the objectives of the company. All of this points to the fact that constant evaluation is therefore essential.

Bibliography

COLLIER, DONALD. "How Much Should Your Company Spend on R.&D?," *Business Management*, p. 57, Vol. 34, No. 2, May, 1968.

ENGLES, EARL S. "Evaluating a Company's Research Program," *Research Management*, p. 147, Vol. X, No. 3, 1967.

HARBRECHT, ROBERT F. "Designing a System for Control of Research Costs," *National Association of Accountants, Bulletin*, p. 3, June, 1964.

QUINN, JAMES BRIAN. *Yardsticks for Industrial Research*, New York: *The Ronald Press Co.*, 1959.

REDMOND, JOHN C. "The Essential Elements of Research in Industry," *Research Management*, p. 175, Vol. X, No. 3, 1967.

SLOWTER, E. E. "Budgeting and Financial Control of Research," *Financial Executive*, p. 17, October, 1964.

VILLERS, R. "Research and Development; Planning and Control," New York: *Financial Executives Research Foundation*, 1964.

Control of manufacturing costs

Mario R. Funari*

Few successful companies can sustain a profitable existence in today's fiercely competitive environment without the use of some hard-nosed and practical control over their manufacturing costs. Some companies have been fortunate enough to have their profits carried along by new product breakthroughs, technological advances, proprietary products, etc., but the day eventually approaches when they too must adopt sound cost control techniques in order to maintain or enhance their profit structure.

Companies utilizing sound cost control techniques have seen their value proven in strong profit results, consistent growth, and excellent management depth.

Presently, we are witnessing unprecedented expansion in the size of business units as the result of mergers and acquisitions, which, in turn, is placing an added control burden on an already busy top management group. Far-flung and often diverse operations must frequently be controlled from a central point which emphasizes the need for the best possible control techniques to aid management.

This chapter will describe and illustrate various management tools designed to aid local plant foremen, superintendents, and managers—as well as top management—in initiating corrective cost action of manufacturing costs on a daily basis. Numerous cost control techniques have been developed by industry over the past 50 years and more recently exploited by the computer. However, the success or effectiveness of these

---

* Vice President-Controller, The Weatherhead Company, Cleveland.

techniques is in direct proportion to management's willingness to accept and adopt them as part of the daily way of life.

The discussion in this chapter will be confined to techniques for controlling direct material, labor, and manufacturing expenses. In addition, the simple daily control of productive inventories will be illustrated.

Bases used for controlling manufacturing costs

Basic tools typically used for controlling manufacturing costs are:

1. Standard costs.
2. Estimates.
3. Budgets.
4. Learning curves.
5. Break-even analyses.
6. Interpretive reports highlighting problems.

Standard costs

The most widely used basis for controlling manufacturing costs is standard costs established in complete detail for all parts, subassemblies, and assemblies. See Exhibit 1, "Standard Cost and Routing Sheet," for a manufactured component.

A standard cost, in essence, represents a commitment by the entire manufacturing organization to what a part or assembly should cost to produce, assuming a given level of productive activity (i.e., 70, 80, or 90 percent, of normal operating capacity). To operate without standard costs can be likened to flying an airplane without a compass or radio.

Estimates

In some industries the practical use and application of standard costs is not possible owing to the long cycle time of product manufactured. However, in the absence of formal standard costs, reasonable estimates can and should be used to control manufacturing costs by stages. In most cases the original cost estimate used to obtain the order affords the best practical approach to cost control under such circumstances. Rarely does one knowingly quote a job to lose money, and, if manufacturing can produce at no higher than the cost used in quoting, a profit can be assured if initial margin was sufficient to cover general, administrative, and selling costs.

Budgets

Variable manufacturing expense budgets (which are discussed in greater detail in Chapter 23 "Profit planning and budgeting") are an

EXHIBIT 1

STANDARD COST AND ROUTING SHEET

PLANT	FOR QUANTITY	SET-UP SEQ.	CATALOG NO.	PAGE	P/C	DATE	PART NUMBER	TYPE
04	DR PRESS			1	001	06/01/67	100-40216	

PART NAME: TUBE ELBOW

	PART NUMBER MATERIAL CODE	CC MODE	PART MATERIAL DESCRIPTION	PRICE PER/M	QUANTITY WEIGHT/M	STANDARD COST PER/M LABOR	BURDEN	MATERIAL
041	0412082	R	1/2" HEX BRASS BAR	4100 0	1862			76342
041	0419999	R	BRASS SCRAP	2500 0	1049			26225CR

TOTALS:
- TOTAL COST 647.89
- MATERIAL 501.17
- LABOR 47.66
- BURDEN 99.06
- WORK IN PROCESS 574.53
- CUMULATIVE TOTAL

COST CENT	OPER NUMBER	MACHINE DESCRIPTION	OPERATION DESCRIPTION	M B	SEC. PER/PC	HOURS PER/M T/S	STD./COST	STD. RATE LABOR	BURDEN	SET UP COST	LABOR	BURDEN	OUTSIDE OPERATION COST AS MATERIAL
1530	0012	HSAW	SAW TO LGTH			186	186	220	635		409	1181	
1420	0102	H ALLEN	MACH PIPE END			850	850	220	460		1870	3910	
1520	0202	A ALLEN	SEAT 200X16			315	315	195	400		614	1260	
1520	0302	DR PRESS	BURR THRU PIPE			190	190	195	400		371	760	
1520	0402	TAPPER	TAPI 5/16-16			300	300	195	400		585	1200	
1520	0502	TAPPER	THRD I PIPE+BURR			280	280	195	400		546	1120	
3010	0602	BENCH	BLOW CLEAN+PAK			190	190	195	250		371	475	

SET-UP	LABOR	BURDEN	MATERIAL	TOTAL
	4766	9906	50117	64789

SC/L REV-10/63

important and integral part of good standard costs since they establish the spending rate for manufacturing expenses at varying levels of production. The manufacturing expense element of costs is the most difficult to control since it has numerous inputs that are influenced by many individuals throughout the organization.

Learning curves

Learning curves are often used to estimate the cost of new products where prior cost experience is of little benefit. In the production of

EXHIBIT 2

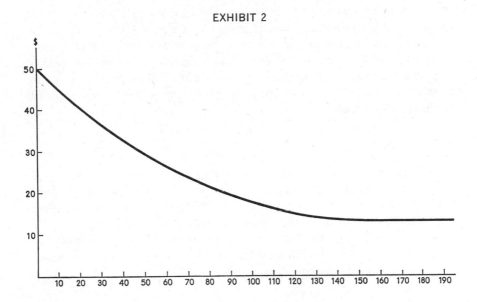

practically any new item, the labor and manufacturing expenses are unusually high for the first units produced since there is a learning period involved before production begins to flow smoothly, with the bugs worked out of the equipment, and the operators attain the rhythmn or pace necessary for efficient output. Determining at what point such costs will level off in their downward slope is important in pricing the product. The government has frequently used the learning-curve technique in negotiating contracts for new weapons, planes, etc., and this same technique can be useful to industry in guiding the orderly reduction of costs for a new product as well as in projecting the future cost.

Learning curves are especially helpful where new major single product lines are produced in large quantities and the labor and manufacturing costs per unit can be charted periodically to establish a realistic curve. This, in turn, can be the basis for establishing standard labor and manufacturing expense allowances based on experienced cost levels after the learning period has been completed.

Exhibit 2, "Learning Curve," shows the simple charting techniques of such curves.

Break-even analyses

Break-even analyses can be prepared for entire plant operations or individual product lines. Their use graphically displays the point at which costs lines bisect sales lines to determine the break-even point. Those companies operating at or near their break-even points recognize the need for corrective cost action to avoid slipping into the red. At this point, companies find that "fixed" costs are really not fixed but can be reduced to accommodate a break-even point lower than was previously thought possible. The disposal of certain fixed assets and their depreciation charge against income can become a reality. Likewise, discontinuing a product line or even an entire facility sometimes is the only practical solution to the problem.

Standard cost system

A standard cost accounting system must be simplified so as to be readily understood by all who will be measured by the results it reflects. Purchasing must know how its efforts in the form of price variance affect profit and loss. Likewise, the superintendent and foremen must appreciate how labor and manufacturing expense variances erode the standard gross profits. Exhibit 3, "Standard Cost Accounting System," reflects a basic system in use by many companies.

Composition of standard costs

To properly control any cost, one must first understand its source and composition and the factors affecting its behavior.

Standard costs are merely the extension of standard quantity—whether it be for material, direct labor, or manufacturing expenses—times the respective standard material price, standard labor rate, and standard manufacturing expense rate.

The quantitative elements of standard costs are determined by product engineering and industrial engineering departments. From the drawings, the product engineer determines and specifies the quantity and type of material to be used. In establishing the standard quantity, proper allowance is made for gross amount of material required and includes provision for cutoff scrap and other unavoidable losses resulting from processing.

From the same drawings, the industrial engineer will establish the

EXHIBIT 3

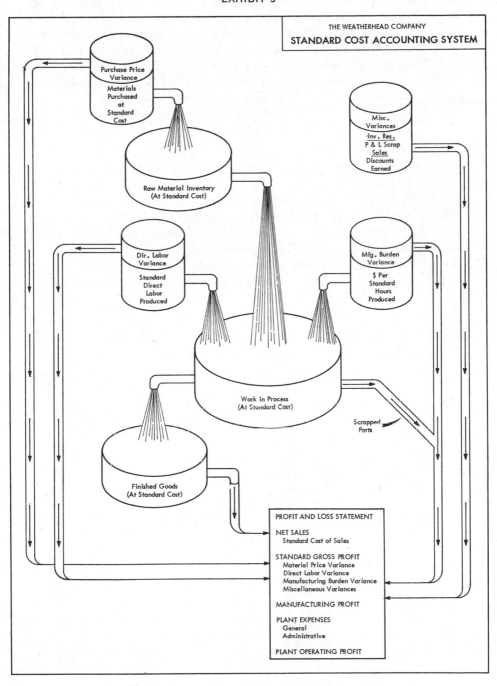

THE WEATHERHEAD COMPANY
STANDARD COST ACCOUNTING SYSTEM

Purchase Price
Variance

Materials
Purchased
at
Standard
Cost

Misc.
Variances
·Inv. Res.
P & L Scrap
<u>Sales</u>
Discounts
Earned

Raw Material Inventory
(At Standard Cost)

Dir. Labor
Variance

Standard
Direct
Labor
Produced

Mfg. Burden
Variance

$ Per
Standard
Hours
Produced

Work in Process
(At Standard Cost)

Scrapped
Parts

Finished Goods
(At Standard Cost)

PROFIT AND LOSS STATEMENT

NET SALES
    Standard Cost of Sales

STANDARD GROSS PROFIT
    Material Price Variance
    Direct Labor Variance
    Manufacturing Burden Variance
    Miscellaneous Variances

MANUFACTURING PROFIT

PLANT EXPENSES
    General
    Administrative

PLANT OPERATING PROFIT

proper sequence of manufacturing operations by routing the part or assembly over the most economical and efficient equipment available. At this point, it might be determined that a more sophisticated machine should be devised or purchased to achieve a more economical overall cost. Standard allowed hours, which are also used as the basis for applying standard manufacturing expenses, are finally determined for each operation by the industrial engineers using time study data along with standard data available for various types of equipment.

MATERIAL COSTS. Standard prices for materials are established by the purchasing department which contracts with vendors to supply specified quality and quantity of materials at a fixed price and delivered as requested. The control of material costs, therefore, is the result of quality buying at right prices plus the judicious use of materials in production processes to minimize both the avoidable and unavoidable scrap losses.

The establishment of standard material prices should be reviewed by the accounting department, comparing standards with actual prices paid in the past for similar quality, size, and quantity. The approved standard

EXHIBIT 4

The Weatherhead Company
PRICE VARIANCE ANALYSIS BY MATERIAL CODE OR PART NUMBER
Month December, 1965

Material Code Part No.	Vendor Code	Rec. PLT.	Quantity Purchased		Standard Cost		Var. Code	Variance			
			Month	Year to Date	Month	Year to Date		Current Month		Year to Date	
								Favorable	Unfavorable	Favorable	Unfavorable
150073	92305	07	2,100	5,600	142	344	06		7		18
150074	90153	07	12,028	37,028	826	1858	04		13		30
150120	12109	09	23,349	61,938	355	915	01	54		59	
150157	78012	05	12,260	92,817	668	10720	06		10		46
210011	92305	06	44,736	226,839	2169	10239	06		27		144
210041	20850	05	25,175	98,676	4985	20412	05	556		2147	
211024	18701	05	3,000	6,753	569	1043	02		23		39
412082	44462	04	29,540	44,790	340	515	06		12		19
412840	44462	04	1,221	58,127	195	9076	06		3		180
415307	20954	04	3,795	3,795	1689	1689	07				
416075	49093	04	4,234	137,661	150	4950	01	10		330	

material prices become the established yardstick for the price variance analysis of all productive material purchases.

It is not always possible or wise to buy materials at lowest prices, because of problems concerning quality, delivery, and so forth on the part of suppliers. Nevertheless, when purchases are made either above or below the established standard price, justifiable reasons should be noted on the purchase order via a coding technique which can be analyzed in a price variance report. Purchasing's primary objective is to buy at the lowest price and still maintain necessary quality and delivery. One of the best methods of assuring that the price is right (where two or more sources are available) is periodically requesting new quotes on major purchased-material items. This technique also applies to the purchase of other items, such as supplies, tools, etc.

Another method of reducing material costs involves the "value analysis" approach used by numerous companies. This combines cooperative studies and analyses made by both the supplier and customer to determine if substitute materials, revised designs, etc., can achieve an equal or better product at a reduced cost. Many times a slight revision in tolerance, that does not interfere with proper functioning of a part or assembly, can result in substantial savings in machining, scrap, and inspection costs.

Exhibit 4, "Price Variance Analysis," is the report card that Purchasing receives and which reflects the effectiveness of their buying efforts; it is further translated in the P&L (profit and loss) statement under the heading "Variances—Material Price."

However, material costs are also affected by usage variance which represents the cost of materials used in excess of the standard allowed.

All variances under a standard cost system are the result of either price-rate variation or quantity variation and can be analyzed as indicated below:

Price or Rate Variance	*Quantity Variance*
Material price	Material usage
Direct labor rate	Direct labor hours
Manufacturing expense rate	Manufacturing expense efficiency

It should be noted here that scrap costs resulting from errors in processing are usually considered as part of manufacturing expense, except that portion which may be considered normal and is included as part of the standard cost.

DIRECT LABOR. The industrial engineering department is normally charged with the responsibility for determining the most economical routing of a part or assembly through its various operations—indicating manpower, machines, tools to be used, speeds of machines, feed of material, and standard hours required for each operation. A standard hour represents time allowed a normal operator working at normal speeds to produce a specified quantity of production. Allowances are made in the standard hour for personal and fatigue time, tool allowances such as minor regrinding or setup adjustments, and other recurring work delays that are small enough not to warrant punching out on downtime. See Exhibit 5, "Operation Routing Sheet."

The accounting department determines the average direct labor rate per hour to be used as the standard rate for each operation. Determination of the rates is based on a historical review of past costs adjusted for any impending wage costs during the succeeding fiscal year.

With computers and punched card equipment, numerous analyses can be prepared to reflect the efficiency and productivity of the labor force.

Exhibit 6, "Daily Direct Labor Performance Report," is a typical analysis of direct labor operators' efficiency, which can be prepared by part number, by operation, by operator, by shift, etc. A report of this type is of considerable help to an industrial engineering department charged with the responsibility of establishing standard hours of work, whether used for incentives purposes or not. The report will show how effective the standards are as well as the relative efficiency of all operators. It will also reveal situations where the standards are set too loosely

EXHIBIT 5

The Weatherhead Company

OPERATION ROUTING SHEET

Part No.: 100-40216		Material: ½" Hex Brass Rod SAE 72		For Quantity 5000	Weight Per M PCS. Gross 1862 / Scrap 1049 / Net 813			Date 6-1-67	
Cost Center	Oper. No.	Operation	Machine	Std. Hours Set Up / Per M	PCS. Per Hr.	Length of Cut	Spindle Feed	Feed	Tool Number	Tool Description
1530	0012	Saw to Length	Hand Saw C	1.86 540	.350					
1420	0102	Machine Pipe End	H. Allen C	8.50 118		554	.004	602-71906	Kirksite Jaws	
1520	0202	Seat	H. Allen C	3.15 317		900	.045	816-4-115	Seating Tool	
1520	0302	Burr thru Pipe	Drill Press C	1.90 528		600	.045	DRILL	14/64"	
1520	0402	Tap 1 5/16"	Tapper C	3.00 333		750	.050	5163-6-R	Tap	
1520	0502	Thread Pipe End & Burr	Tapper C	2.80 355		700	.060	816-6-115	Tap	
3010	0602	Blow Clean & Pack	Bench	1.90 528						

EXHIBIT 6

The Weatherhead Company
PLANT "B"
DAILY DIRECT LABOR PERFORMANCE REPORT
Date December 13, 1965

Cost Center	Clock Number	Shift	Part Number	Oper. No.	Quantity	Std. Hrs. Per M	Labor Class	Actual Hours	Paid Hours	% Effic.	Downtime Hours	Daywork Hours	Indirect Hours	Downtime Reason Code
1530	50118	1	100-40216	0012	1500	1.86	01	2.40	2.79	116				
	50118		103-32606	0012	670	1.20	01	.50	.80	160				
	50118		141-27203	0012	2000	2.40	01	3.50	4.80	137				
	50118		141-27205	0012			01	1.10	1.10		1.10			3
	50118						20	.50	.50				.50	
								8.00	9.99					
	50312		600-30078	0012	1000	1.00	01	.80	1.00	125				
	50312		103-32704	0012	4000	2.10	01	6.50	8.40	130				
	50312		100-10657	0012	100	3.00	01	.20	.30	150				
	50312						20	.50	.50				.50	
								8.00	10.20					
	50371		101-20008	0012	3000	1.20	01	3.60	4.32	120				
	50371		600-72309	0012	1000	.90	01	.90	1.00	111				
	50371		100-23804	0012	2000	1.50	01	3.00	3.75	125				
	50371						20	.50	.50				.50	
								8.00	7.57					

LABOR CLASS LEGEND: 01 INCENTIVE   03 REWORK   10 INDIRECT   20 PAID LUNCH
                     02 NON-INCENTIVE 04 SETUP   19 TRAINEES   21 CLEAN UP

and have to be tightened. Tight standards are quickly brought to management's attention, but unfortunately loose ones are rarely reported by the operator.

A further analysis of direct labor performance involves the determination of "rate" variance as contrasted to "efficiency" variance. Rate variance applies to that portion of direct labor whose rate of pay is either higher or lower than the rate used in determining the standard cost.

Referring to Exhibit 1, "Standard Cost and Routing Sheet" (page 684), assume that operation 0102 "mach pipe end" was performed by an operator earning $2.30 per hour and that he expended 9.0 hours to produce 1000 pieces. The rate and efficiency variance would break down as follows:

	Hours	Rate	Cost
Actual	9.0	$2.30	$20.70
Standard	8.5	2.20	18.70
	.5	$ .10	$ 2.00

Rate variance = 9.0 hours × 10¢ or $ .90
Efficiency variance = .5 hour × $2.20 per hour or   1.10
    $ 2.00

In addition to controlling labor rate and efficiency, management must be cognizant of the importance of utilizing skilled direct labor, particularly when skilled labor is hard to replace in today's tight labor market. If a skilled worker is spending only 50 percent of his time on direct productive work, an extremely costly situation can result. Skilled labor must be utilized to the fullest possible extent. There are times when for reasons of machine breakdown, setup corrections, etc. this is not possible, but when utilization as a whole drops below 75 percent of theoretical optimum performance—that is, when less than six out of eight hours are devoted to productive effort—some serious investigation is needed to determine why more hours of direct labor are not being used to produce company products.

MANUFACTURING EXPENSES. Manufacturing expenses comprise those costs (other than productive materials and direct labor) necessary to manufacture a product. They generally fall into two major categories as outlined in Exhibit 7, "Budget Standard Rate Sheet"—namely, "Indirect labor costs" and "indirect materials and other expenses."

The cost element most difficult to control is manufacturing expenses, since the responsibility for them cannot be easily defined as it is in the case of productive materials or direct labor. However, with the aid of variable budgets established by department or cost center, these costs also can be brought under reasonable control. Some companies shy away from establishing variable budget programs because they expect such budgets to be scientifically prepared and hence perfect. Those taking the "perfectionist" approach finally give up because of the sheer volume of work involved in drawing scatter charts or in other mechanical techniques used to prepare flexible budgets.

Any company with a reasonable cost history broken down by department can establish a variable budget program in a very short period of time if it adopts a philosophy of having reasonable budgets which can be later refined as the company gains more experience with budgets as well as with the actual cost data.

In approaching a budget program, maximum time should be spent in analyzing the major expenses which, in most cases, account for 80 percent of the cost and only 40 percent of the items.

A budget program as discussed above must represent the combined thinking of the accounting, industrial engineering, and factory supervision departments. In other words, if you intend to measure a man's performance by a budget, give him an opportunity to either agree or disagree with the yardstick. It has been proven repeatedly that when an individual participates in the planning of a project, his interest is much greater than if it is forced upon him. See Exhibit 7, "Budget Standard Rate Sheet," which establishes both fixed and variable cost levels for a given cost center.

EXHIBIT 7

The Weatherhead Company

BUDGET STANDARD RATE SHEET

Cost Center __1530__ Name __Hand Saw__   Plant __"B"__

Foreman __J. Doe__   Normal Capacity Hours Per Month __1200__   Effective Date __1-1-65__

	ACCOUNT CLASSIFICATION	Date 6-1-65		Date	
Number	Description	Variable Cost Per Hour	Fixed Cost Per Month	Variable Cost Per Hour	Fixed Cost Per Month
	INDIRECT LABOR COSTS				
03	Rework				
04	Setup	0500			
05	Material Handling				
06	Supervision & Clerical		1600		
07	Inspection				
08	Maintenance	1500			
09	Tool Room				
10	Other Indirect	3000			
11	Overtime Premium	0200			
12	Downtime	0800			
13	Vacation & Holiday Pay		200		
14	Bonuses		100		
15	Retroactive Wage Adjustment				
16	Provision for Pensions		200		
17	Night Shift Premiums	0200			
18	Retirement Savings	1000	70		
19	Training New Employees				
20	Paid Lunch Periods	2000			
24	Suggestion Awards				
	TOTAL INDIRECT LABOR	9200	2170		
	INDIRECT MATERIALS & OTHER EXPENSES				
25	Oils, Greases, Cutting Compounds	2000			
26	Auto & Truck				
27	Office Supplies				
28	Other Indirect Proc. Materials	0200			
29	Sundry Supplies	0500			
31	Experimental Material				
35	Utilities	1200	150		
38	Dies, Jigs, Fixtures, Patterns				
39	Perishable Tools	2700			
42	Maintenance—Buildings & Grounds				
43	Maintenance—Other Capital Equipment	3500			
46	Depreciation & Amortization		1250		
51	Insurance—General		100		
52	Insurance—Life, Health, Accident	0500			
53	Insurance—Compensation	0400			
55	Taxes—Payroll	2500			
56	Taxes—Property & Corporate		50		
60	Rentals		100		
61	Outside Work & Services				
62	Legal & Professional				
66	Postage & Freight				
67	Telephone & Telegraph				
77	Scrapped Parts	1200			
78	Traveling				
83	Membership & Dues				
87	Welfare				
92	Unclassified Expense				
93	Labor Transfers				
94	Expense Transfers				
95	Expense Transfers to Divisions				
96	Expense Transfers from Divisions				
	TOTAL INDIRECT MATERIALS & OTHER EXP.	1 4700	1650		
	GRAND TOTAL	2 3700	3820		

Variable cost per hour is determined from an analysis of past cost history by comparing the actual expense level with the productive labor hours. In Exhibit 7 it is noted that various types of indirect labor totaling 92¢ are needed to support every hour of productive labor in the hand saw cost center.

Standard manufacturing expense rates are developed jointly by the accounting, industrial engineering, and factory supervision departments. A review is made of all manufacturing expenses by department or cost center to establish those costs that are of a fixed nature versus those whose cost level would vary with a change in production levels. Normal operating levels are then established to determine the fixed costs per hour or dollar of standard labor as well as the variable costs, to arrive at the total standard manufacturing expense per machine hour or standard labor dollar. The variable budget for manufacturing expenses, therefore, provides a practical control tool over those costs that are most susceptible to control in most manufacturing companies.

Computer impact on manufacturing cost controls

No other area of accounting for a manufacturing concern has been more profoundly affected by the computer than the area of standard costs. As a tool of management, the file of detailed cost data is most vital to the daily operations of a manufacturing company. Basically, standard costs are used primarily to perform the following functions:
1. Promote and measure efficiency.
2. Control and reduce costs.
3. Prepare cost estimates.
4. Calculate standard cost of shipments.
5. Evaluate inventories.

The computer's impact on the usefulness of standard costs has been substantial because of the flexibility of the standard cost file once it has been established and because of the relative ease with which the file can be updated at periodic intervals, whether daily, weekly, monthly, or annually.

FLEXIBILITY OF THE FILE. One of the greatest benefits derived from computerized standard costs lies in the extreme flexibility of data on file. Once standard cost information has been properly captured, whether on disk or tape (but preferably on disk because of greater flexibility), numerous operations can be performed, among them:
1. Costing shipments.
2. Preparing cost estimates using bills of materials.
3. Extending inventory balances.
4. Printing out "where used" file of parts and subassemblies.

5. Measuring efficiency of purchasing function.
6. Measuring efficiency of direct labor by operator, part, department, etc.
7. Calculating standard gross profit by part, customer, territory, etc.
8. Determining machine loads for scheduling and manning purposes.
9. Preparing proposed selling prices based on revised standard costs when market conditions permit.

With a manual system, standard costs compiled on sheets or cards afford little or no flexibility, and the desired information has to be secured through a laborious hand-search process; hence, the file is not very useful. Today, however, with the fantastic seek, read, and print speeds available in computers, this file has taken on greater stature not only in the accounting area, but throughout many other departments of the company as well.

UPDATING AND REVISING STANDARD COST FILE. Another area where the computer has had great effect in accounting is in the updating of the standard cost files, whether they are maintained on tape or disk.

To be effective as a cost control tool, all standard costs should be revised at least annually, immediately preceding the physical inventory which can be extended by the revised as well as the old standard costs. The task of revising thousands of standard costs manually can be a costly and laborious process. With a computer, however, the job is considerably simplified. Whereas the task of manually revising standard costs for over 60,000 different parts took one company more than 10,000 man hours annually, the task today is accomplished in approximately 90 computer hours plus the time taken during the year to keypunch only quantitative changes to the master files as they occur.

Aside from the fact that the job is done much more quickly, the most important aspect is that the standard cost file on the computer has greater flexibility than heretofore thought possible.

Daily cost controls

Once the yardsticks (standard costs) by which all manufacturing costs will be monitored have been established, the next major step is the development of a practical tool designed to measure actual operating results to assist responsible individuals such as foremen, superintendents, and plant managers, as well as top management, in initiating corrective cost action on a daily basis.

With the ever-increasing complexities of managing a manufacturing company, aggressive and creative managers are constantly striving to develop one or more concise reports that will permit top management to quickly evaluate the overall performance of the particular operation on a daily basis. They know that if good cost controls are maintained throughout each day of the month, the overall monthly performance should yield the forecasted profit results. Most businesses today have grown beyond the owner-manager size—they have more than a single plant and sales office—and the problem is how to restore the owner-manager touch to daily business decisions. It is not unreasonable, therefore, for management to expect information concerning the day-by-day progress toward achieving its monthly profit goal, indicating where and why profit results will either exceed or fall short of the forecast. Such areas as manufacturing expenses, direct labor costs, and inventory changes are volatile and subject to daily control, provided that management is furnished the tools with which to carry out its responsibilities.

A simple daily plant control report embodying the foregoing is feasible and, when coordinated with a monthly profit forecast, will quickly reveal to management where and why projected profit results will exceed or fall short of the forecast any time during the month.

Cost control, with resulting profit control, is not a once-a-week or once-a-month program. It is achieved only by dynamic and unceasing day-by-day surveillance of formal, well-recognized, and forcefully administered cost controls leading to the desired profit levels.

Most companies employ accounting reports that accurately reflect the company's operating results for a given accounting period are available within a reasonable time after that period. However, to advise management that a certain plant or operation did not achieve its cost or profit budget after month end, or that certain expenses were out of line, does nothing to correct that month's results. As financial executives, we question what our month-end statements have done to enhance that month's profits. However, the data necessary to forewarn management of similar pitfalls in the following month is available.

To be effective, daily cost controls must be preceded by monthly profit forecasts which reflect anticipated shipments, direct labor to be generated, and manufacturing expenses to be incurred as indicated by the variable budget allowances mentioned earlier. The forecasts should be reviewed by top management and revised where necessary, after which the approved forecasts become targets for the month with all planning and control centered on these figures.

As stated earlier, the simplicity of the standard cost system is a major factor contributing to the ease with which daily cost controls can be employed. Standard costs and variances move through the various accounts and eventually into the profit and loss statement. Cost controls center directly on those areas of excess costs commonly referred to as variances. Management has neither the interest nor the time to delve into the reams of reports that can be produced today, particularly with the advent of the computer. They want to be told quickly, and shown by very few reports prepared on an exception basis, where the significant trouble areas are and who is responsible.

Daily profit control

The daily control of profits can best be accomplished through the medium of a daily control report on costs which eventually translates into either higher or lower profits.

Utilizing all the tools and thoughts mentioned heretofore, a daily plant control report can be prepared with comparative ease. As shown in Exhibit 8, "Daily Plant Control Report," four major categories of costs are treated:

1. Manufacturing expense items.
2. Direct labor costs.
3. Manufacturing expense absorption.
4. Productive inventory analysis.

The accounting department prepares this report daily for submission to local plant manager and superintendent as well as to the budget department at company headquarters. The budget department then summarizes the data from all plants on "Daily Plant Control Summary" (Exhibit 9) for top management use at headquarters. The control summary provides totals comparing projected figures for direct labor and manufacturing expenses with those on the profit and loss forecast, plus information about shipments and inventory levels. It indicates not only which plants are on target, but also those which are not—and why they are not. It is amazing to see the accuracy with which costs can be projected when such a control is used over a period of time.

Although preparation of the "Daily Plant Control Report" (Exhibit 8) may seem complicated it is actually relatively simple, and requires little extra effort in gathering results of the previous day's operations. An explanation of the sources of data follows.

CONTROL OF MANUFACTURING EXPENSE. Indirect labor costs are obtained from daily distribution of hourly payrolls. A detailed breakdown by types of indirect labor, both actual and budgeted, can also be presented for an entire plant as shown in Exhibit 9.

Perishable tool and supply requisitions are processed daily for withdrawal of these items from inventory, and the costs are entered on this form.

Expense and supply purchases are recorded as the expense vouchers are processed for payment through the accounts payable department.

Machine Repair parts requisitions are processed daily in same manner as perishable tooling tickets.

Scrapped parts costs are the result of daily processing of all scrap tickets. It is extremely important that scrap tickets be processed daily so that large scrap losses can be analyzed and brought to the attention of responsible parties for immediate correction. Scrap losses for the reasons

EXHIBIT 8

THE WEATHERHEAD COMPANY
DAILY PLANT CONTROL REPORT
FOR THE DAY OF _December 14, 1965_   WORKING DAYS THIS MONTH __20__

PLANT ___"B"___   WORKING DAYS THIS REPORT __10__

MANUFACTURING EXPENSE ITEMS		TOTAL			MONTH TO DATE		
		ACTUAL COST	TARGET	VARIANCE FROM TARGET	ACTUAL COST	TARGET	VARIANCE FROM TARGET
INDIRECT LABOR	(A)	7,400	6,500	900	68,000	65,000	3,000
PERISHABLE TOOL AND SUPPLY REQUISITIONS	(B)	2,200	2,000	200	20,500	20,000	500
EXPENSE AND SUPPLY PURCHASES–VOUCHER REGISTER	(C)	7,700	7,400	300	75,000	74,000	1,000
MACHINE REPAIR PARTS	(C)	900	900	—	9,000	9,000	—
SCRAPPED PARTS	(D)	800	700	100	7,500	7,000	500
FIXED CHARGES	(E)	11,000	11,000	—	110,000	110,000	—
TOTAL MANUFACTURING EXP.		30,000	28,500	1,500	290,000	285,000	5,000
% OF VARIANCE FROM TARGET				5.3%			1.8%

DIRECT LABOR COSTS	TODAY	MONTH TO DATE	TARGET TO DATE
ACTUAL DIRECT LABOR	12,000	120,000	126,500
STANDARD DIRECT LABOR	11,850	118,000	125,000
LABOR VARIANCE	150	2,000	1,500
% OF INCENTIVE COVERAGE	91%	92%	92%
% OF LABOR EFFICIENCY	125%	124%	125%

TOTAL MANUFACTURING EXPENSES FOR THE MONTH ARE PROJECTED AT THE RATE OF __600,000__.

AT THIS RATE MANUFACTURING EXPENSE WILL BE UNABSORBED AT THE RATE OF __30,000__ FOR THE MONTH BASED ON STANDARD DIRECT LABOR PRODUCED.

MFGR. EXPENSE ABSORPTION	TODAY	MONTH TO DATE	TARGET TO DATE
MFGR. EXPENSES ABSORBED	28,200	275,000	275,000
MFGR. EXPENSES UNABSORBED	1,800	15,000	10,000
TOTAL MANUFACTURING EXP.	30,000	290,000	285,000

UNABSORBED MANUFACTURING EXPENSE AMOUNT FORECASTED FOR THE MONTH WAS __20,000__.

PRODUCTIVE INVENTORY ANALYSIS

ADD:	MONTH TO DATE	PROJECTED FOR MONTH	TARGET FOR MONTH
RAW MATERIALS VOUCHERED AND INTER PLANT RECEIPTS	1,000,000	2,100,000	2,200,000
STANDARD DIRECT LABOR PRODUCED	118,000	240,000	250,000
STANDARD MFGR. EXPENSES ABSORBED	275,000	562,000	585,000
TOTAL INVENTORY INPUT	1,393,000	2,902,000	3,035,000
DEDUCT: STANDARD COST OF SALES	1,431,000	2,980,000	3,088,000
MATERIAL USAGE VARIANCE	4,500	8,000	8,000
SCRAPPED PARTS	7,500	16,000	14,000
NET INVENTORY INC.–(DEC.)	(50,000)	(102,000)	(75,000)

SIGNED _R. J. Martin_
PLANT MANAGER

DATE ISSUED _December 15, 1965_

REMARKS: _____

EXHIBIT 9

The Weatherhead Company

DAILY PLANT CONTROL SUMMARY
MONTH TO DATE

Date Issued ___December 15, 1965___

As of ___December 14___, ___, ___1965___

Working Days This Month ___20___

Working Days This Report ___10___

Particulars	A	B		E	F	G	H	J	Total Weatherhead Parent
SHIPMENTS—TO DATE									
Actual Shipments	600,000	2,000,000	1,500,00	0,000	1,200,000	700,000	1,200,000	2,000,000	10,200,000
Scheduled Shipments	550,000	2,100,000	1,450,000	0,000	1,220,000	720,000	1,120,000	1,960,000	10,100,000
Shipments—Over (Under) Schedule	50,000	(100,000)	50,000	0,000	(20,000)	(20,000)	80,000	40,000	100,000
LABOR HOURS—TO DATE									
Actual Direct Hours	32,000	40,000	52,000	20	35,000	18,000	45,000	35,000	292,000
Actual Indirect Hours	30,000	41,000	57,000	18	40,000	15,000	35,000	40,000	293,000
DIRECT LABOR COSTS—TO DATE									
Actual Direct Labor	87,000	120,000	160,000	30,000		40,000	60,000	50,000	617,000
Standard Direct Labor	78,000	118,000	165,000	27,000		6,000	52,000	41,000	599,000
Variance	(8,500)	(2,000)	5,000	(3,000)		,000	(8,000)	(9,000)	(18,000)
% of Variance	(10.8)	(1.7)	3.0	(11.1)			(15.4)	(22.0)	(3.0)
Standard Direct Labor Forecasted	75,000	125,000	168,000	29,000	21.0	0	51,000	43,000	609,000
Labor Variance Forecasted	(4,500)	(1,500)	4,000	(2,000)	2.0		(6,000)	(9,000)	(11,000)
MANUFACTURING EXPENSES									
Actual Mfgr. Expenses—To Date	240,000	290,000	450,000	80,000	50,00		160,000	97,000	1,677,000
Mfgr. Expenses Projected for Month	480,000	600,000	1,000,000	150,000	100,000		9,000	190,000	3,380,000
Mfgr. Expenses Forecasted for Month	470,000	590,000	1,050,000	130,000	70,000	23	,000	200,000	3,210,000
Projection—(Over)—Under Forecast	(10,000)	(10,000)	50,000	(20,000)	(30,000)	(70,0		10,000	(170,000)
UNABSORBED EXPENSES									
Actual Unabsorbed To Date	70,000	15,000	150,000	20,000	10,000	50,000	30,	15,000	490,000
Actual Unabsorbed Projected for Month	140,000	30,000	275,000	35,000	21,000	95,000	60,000	28,000	934,000
Actual Unabsorbed Forecasted for Month	120,000	20,000	290,000	40,000	15,000	106,000	45,000	,000	902,000
Projection (Over) Under	(20,000)	(10,000)	15,000	5,000	(6,000)	11,000	(15,000)	00)	(32,000)
Inventory Increase (Decrease)	119,000	(50,000)	27,000	54,000	(98,000)	(210,000)	(90,000)	(100	(250,000)

indicated on scrap tickets can then be minimized. If scrap is reported only weekly, or less often, it is possible that errors in manufacturing could continue throughout the entire period before being caught. In the preparation of a daily scrap report, sufficient detail must be included to establish the cost of the scrap by reflecting number of pieces scrapped, part number, operation, operator and reasons for rejection.

Since scrap cost can be a volatile expense, it is singled out for attention on the daily plant control report.

Fixed charges shown on the daily plant control report cover such items of manufacturing expense as supervision and clerical salaries, property insurance and taxes, depreciation, pension costs, vacation and holiday pay, bonuses, and other fixed expense accruals. Detailed analyses of fixed charges should be maintained for every manufacturing operation to establish break-even points when needed. From such an analysis the fixed charges are applied to the report at a constant daily rate throughout the month.

CONTROL OF DIRECT LABOR. With the introduction of data collection systems, computers, etc., the daily processing of even large hourly payrolls has become practical. From the daily hourly payroll distribution, numerous exception reports can be compiled relative to direct labor costs, as indicated on Exhibit 6, "Daily Direct Labor Performance Report" (page 691). The summarization of all direct labor performance is posted to the direct labor sections of the daily plant control report as follows:

> Actual direct labor dollars.
> Standard direct labor dollars.
> Labor variance dollars.
> Percentage of incentive coverage.
> Percentage of labor efficiency.

Any unusual variations from budget, standard, or normal can be traced in detail by shift, department, part number, operation, or operator since the details will have been previously exploded by the computer or punched card equipment.

The percentage of incentive coverage indicates the number of direct labor hours that were performed with an incentive pay standard. In plants employing some incentives, productivity on day-work (or nonincentive basis) jobs ranges from only 50 to 60 percent. Therefore, if incentives are employed, it behooves management to get the incentive coverage as close to 100 percent as possible.

Labor efficiency relates to the productivity of the direct labor that is measured by an incentive pay standard and is determined by dividing actual hours worked into the hours of work produced. Even if a plant does not employ incentive standards, it still can determine the efficiency of its direct labor if it uses measured day-rate standards which, in essence, are no different from incentive pay standards since they both establish the expected normal level of production for each operation per hour or per day.

MANUFACTURING EXPENSE ABSORPTION. Whether a plant is utilizing direct or absorption costs, the daily absorption of manufacturing expenses can have a profound effect on monthly profit results as well as on inventory levels. As mentioned earlier, standard costs employ the use of standard manufacturing expense rates by cost center based on standard direct labor hours produced. The rates are used to charge manufacturing expenses into, as well as relieve them from, inventory. Since the standard direct labor generated daily by cost center is compiled in the hourly labor distributions, the computer can also extend the standard manufacturing expenses chargeable to inventory based on standard rate per hour times hours of work produced.

Exhibit 8, "Daily Plant Control Report," compares the manufacturing expense absorption forecasted at the beginning of the month with that projected from the latest actual cost incurred. Likewise the unabsorbed manufacturing expenses projected are compared with the forecasted amount. It is in this area that top management must focus its attention to note any significant variations between forecasted and projected amounts because the level of manufacturing expense variance and labor variance, along with sales volume and mix are, in most companies, the four largest factors influencing profit results.

PRODUCTIVE INVENTORY ANALYSIS. The bottom section of the daily plant control report deals with productive inventories. The control of inventories is one of the major responsibilities of local plant management. As an aid in achieving better control, a month-to-date analysis reflects the effect that purchasing, production, and shipments are having on the inventory levels as shown on the bottom of the report.

This section allows for recording, at standard cost, receipts of raw materials from outside vendors as well as from sister plants. This is accomplished via the regular accounts payable distribution mentioned earlier. The standard direct labor produced and standard manufacturing expenses absorbed on a month-to-date basis are taken directly from the preceding lines of this report and the sum of the material, labor, and manufacturing expenses results in the total inventory input.

The relief to inventory is determined by the daily extension of all shipments at standard cost. Usage variance is compiled from excess material requisitions, and scrapped parts costs are taken from the top section of the report. Total input, minus total relief to inventory, indicates daily whether inventories are rising or declining. Once again, the simplicity of the basic standard cost system lends itself very well to the calculation of daily inventory changes.

A quick profit check

The primary objective of daily cost control reports discussed throughout this chapter is to provide a simple technique for controlling manufacturing costs and inventories and quickly evaluating profit results against forecast. In order to check performance for a single plant or an entire company at any time during the month, similar calculations are made. For example, in checking profit performance of Plant "B" as of the middle of December, the following analyses are made from Exhibit 8, "Daily Plant Control Report" and Exhibit 9, "Daily Plant Control Summary."

Shipments
Scheduled shipments (Exhibit 9)................................$2,100,000
Actual shipments (Exhibit 9).................................... 2,000,000
Under schedule... 100,000
Standard gross profit (assumed)................................ 30%
  Loss in gross profits..$30,000
Direct labor variance
Projected actual for month
  $2000 = 10 days (Exhibit 8)...................................... 4,000
Standard forecasted for month
  $1500 = 10 days (Exhibit 8)...................................... 3,000
  Loss in profits—excess labor variance....................................... 1,000
Manufacturing expense variance
Unabsorbed manufacturing expense projected for month
  (Exhibit 8)... 30,000
Unabsorbed manufacturing expense forecasted for month
  (Exhibit 8)... 20,000
  Loss in profits—excess manufacturing expense variance.................... 10,000
    Total profit loss..$41,000

Assuming that mix of product sold will be in accordance with forecast and that material price and usage variance are likewise in line with the forecast, the quick check on profits reveals a projected profit deficiency from forecast of $41,000 for the month. Unless shipments improve during the last half of the month and pick up to equal the schedule, loss in gross profits will be $30,000. Without an improvement in present rate of labor efficiency and reduced spending levels for manufacturing expenses, profits will fall short of forecast by $11,000 ($1,000 + $10,000).

In the example cited for Plant "B," a portion of the increased unabsorbed manufacturing expenses of $10,000 can be attributed to "volume variance" or failure to absorb the full portion of fixed expenses that would have been absorbed by operating at normal capacity level, which is the basis used to develop standard hourly burden rates by cost center.

Referring to Exhibit 8 note that the inventories for Plant "B" reflect a decrease of $50,000 through December 14th, and projected will indicate a total decrease of $102,000 for the full month versus $75,000 targeted.

Daily commitment report

To control the expense voucher portion of manufacturing expenses, some companies, which regularly commit for expenditures considerably in advance, utilize a daily commitment report indicating how much the company is bound to spend on outside purchases for such expense items

EXHIBIT 10

PLANT "B"

DAILY MANUFACTURING EXPENSE COMMITMENT REPORT

Month _December; 1965_

| DATE | COMMITMENTS | | VOUCHERED | | |
	Daily	Month to Date	Daily	Month to Date	Balance
1					10,000
3	5,000	5,000	6,000	6,000	9,000
4	7,000	12,000	8,000	14,000	8,000
5	2,000	14,000	3,000	17,000	7,000
6	8,000	22,000	4,000	21,000	11,000
7	5,000	27,000	3,000	24,000	13,000
10	3,000	30,000	5,000	29,000	11,000
11	6,000	36,000	8,000	37,000	9,000
12	10,000	46,000	4,000	41,000	15,000
13	4,000	50,000	1,000	42,000	18,000
14	2,000	52,000	3,000	45,000	17,000

as tools, supplies, indirect materials, etc. Without a measure of control over the open commitments, the expenses cannot be cut off readily without incurring possible cancellation charges. Exhibit 10, "Daily Manufacturing Expense Commitment Report," illustrates a simple form that shows at all times how far out one is committed for such expense items. The system requires that all requisitions for expense purchases be cleared through the accounting department for proper account distribution as well as for cost calculations of the commitment. As expense vouchers are paid they are reduced from the commitments so that at any time management is aware of what it is "on the hook for." It is too late to decide that the budget for the period has been overspent when the invoices begin to roll in. Control must precede the commitment rather than the payment of the invoice.

Conclusion

The use of daily plant control reports as described can instill into operating management a measure of confidence and faith in its abilities to maximize profits. Such a system will also give the accounting and financial departments greater stature in the profit structure of a manufacturing establishment. More important, however, such a system can save many thousands of dollars in manufacturing expenses and labor costs, as well as aid in keeping inventories at minimum by pin-pointing trouble spots as they occur. These savings, though, are not possible without the sincere support of top management for a program of daily controls. As stated earlier, this has to be a way of life and, if management does not encourage it, such daily control reports can be "just another" accounting report.

Many reports flow across a manager's desk and each must catch his attention if it is to be of value. The "Daily Plant Control Summary," Exhibit 9, brings together the daily reports for all plants and is of great value to management in its responsibilities for increasing profits. It is in no way intended to be a substitute for good management, but rather to aid and direct its efforts.

Most financial executives will have to "sell" management on the merits of such a program. However, once management has had the opportunity to compare some of the key figures from the summary report for all plants with the forecast they will realize, "If they continue at this pace, we will miss our forecasted profits by $100,000." In short, management will know if and where they are in trouble. Day by day, as the "barometer" rises or falls, they can tell which way the month-end fortunes will go. To find out only after the books are closed that profits did not equal the forecasted levels is of little help in recouping such losses.

With this reporting tool, the plant should be able to project labor and manufacturing expense variances quite accurately after some experience in daily reporting techniques and procedures. Flash profit and loss statements can be compiled at any time during the month once the system for assembling the data expediently has been established.

One may wonder if daily profit and loss statements are possible under this system; the answer is "Yes." However, there are several reasons why they are not practical or necessary. First, in many plants throughout our country there exists a significant difference between actual shipments and production on a daily, as well as month-to-date, basis, resulting in a buildup of shipments during the latter part of each month when production people like to "sweep the plant clean." Therefore, a profit and loss statement prepared daily during the first few days of a month can be misleading and meaningless.

The second reason for not preparing daily P&L statements is the ease with which the results for the entire month can be projected from the daily plant control reports compared to the forecast—a calculation that takes but a few minutes to prepare.

It may seem that the operating tool presented herein requires considerable clerical effort. Experience has proven, however, that such reporting techniques need not increase accounting personnel. The most difficult task is reorganizing the data collection system to provide for orderly assembling of control figures on a daily basis. One extremely beneficial side effect resulting from this change is that the plant accounting departments become aware of the importance of performing certain accounting functions daily and thereby minimize the peak month-end loads for which many accounting departments have been notorious.

Control of administrative costs

William J. Robinson

Administrative cost, in its broadest sense, is a classification often applied to the cost of activities and functions applicable to a business as a whole, as contrasted to costs pertaining to more specific functions, such as manufacturing and selling.

Declining profits or periods of stability traditionally lead members of top management to become more vitally interested in cost reduction and control. Faced with leveling off or diminishing profits, executives typically turn to administrative cost reduction as the surest way to improve profit margins. The active leadership of senior management is indispensable to the success of broad-scale cost cutting. Unfortunately, even in the better-managed businesses, the interest in this subject seems to fluctuate. During prosperous times, efforts are devoted to expanding sales volumes; and only when business turns downward is there a sudden reawakening to the fact that cost reduction is a responsibility that must be faced on a daily, continuing basis.

Although, admittedly, the objectives of cost reduction are the same throughout a company, the problems encountered in attempting to economize in office or administrative areas are vastly different from those met, for example, in manufacturing. In the administrative area, clerical salaries and related costs and the presence of marginal functions constitute the major problems. Product design, materials, and machinery matters are of primary concern in the production area.

Typical examples of administrative expense accounts are:

---

* Vice President-Controller, Insurance Company of North America, Philadelphia.

1. Data Processing Equipment (D.P.E.)–Rental.
2. Depreciation–Office Furniture and Equipment (including D.P.E. if owned).
3. Directors' Fees.
4. Donations.
5. Dues and Subscriptions.
6. Legal and Auditing.
7. Postage.
8. Salaries–Executives.
9. Salaries–General Office.
10. Stationery and Office Supplies.
11. Travel Expense.

In a business organization, the administrative function generally embraces departments, such as:
1. Accounting Department.
2. Data Processing Department.
3. General Executive Departments.
4. Internal Audit Department.
5. Legal Department.
6. Personnel Department.
7. Purchasing Department.
8. Treasurer's Department.

Several writers on the subject have viewed manufacturing and sales expenses as the two major activities of a producing organization, and administrative expenses as facilitative.

It is not uncommon, particularly in financial institutions, to have the president designated as the chief administrative officer, and the chairman of the board designated chief executive officer. It is apparent from this that the administrative function is not an unimportant one, and also suggests the probability that the financial field may offer some worthwhile methods for controlling administrative costs. As a matter of fact, the administrative costs of insurance companies, banks, and other financial institutions are significantly higher than in the nonfinancial field, in relation to product or service and selling costs. Certainly this, coupled with the constantly increasing and sophisticated use of electronic equipment by the financial community, has somewhat revolutionized the processing and reporting techniques during the past decade, resulting in substantially reduced costs.

An interesting article, appearing in the January 3, 1963 issue of the *Wall Street Journal,* by Albert R. Karr and headlined "White Collar Cutback," focused attention on the rising cost created by corporate bureaucracy. Evidently numerous American corporate giants at that particular time recognized that white-collar worker payrolls had ballooned beyond reason. Compared with 15 years earlier, office workers employed by manufacturers had climbed 65 percent, whereas the total production force had shrunk seven percent. Obviously, most of the companies had attempted to reduce expenditures and improve efficiency on the assembly line, ignoring the administrative costs. This same trend exists even today, but, fortunately, there is a keener, healthier concern over administrative cost reduction.

Management and personnel attitudes

Organization structures, in many cases more elaborate than necessary, seem to become rather permanently anchored in place by the sheer weight of the vested interests they support. Management, of course, is at fault for failing to detect the situation and take corrective action. There may even be cases where top management has taken the path of least resistance, and purposely ignored the additional cost factor to avoid offending associates or employees of long-standing.

Many executives indicate that they would welcome an opportunity to economize, but are uncertain where to begin and also shy away from possible unfavorable consequences.

Middle management executives usually agree on the desirability of reducing costs. However, their prejudices are very often similar to their superiors and, furthermore, are prone to believe that "the other department" is responsible for any waste or inefficiency. Frequently, they are embittered with the impression that a cost reduction program concentrates on trivial matters and completely ignores the significantly wasteful areas.

Top and middle management executives are certainly not against cost reduction, but are so overly concerned about the adverse effects on employee morale that they very often choose to evade the situation entirely. Most corporate executives admit that, even in efficient organizations, there are unexploited ways and means of saving substantial amounts of money, if only everyone can be influenced to cooperate in achieving a well-thought-out continuing cost reduction program.

Quite true, certain of the economy measures may well include cutting salaries, dismissing below-calibre employees, requiring greater. output per employee, and other incidental employee and employee-benefit cost curtailment. All of this is probably conducive to opposition by the rank-and-file employee. This is not desirable and, in most instances, can be avoided, if carefully planned and communicated right down to the lowest level employee.

The early communication of management's desire to maintain job security for all personnel presently on the payroll is of paramount importance. If a positive and confident attitude is adopted by every officer and employee involved, there should be minimal opposition. The important points to keep in mind include: creating cost consciousness, promoting cooperation, maintaining a spirit of competition, providing proper incentives, communicating results.

Case after case proves that the serious consequences predicted by those opposing cost reduction have never materialized.

Cost emphasis geared to profitability

Unfortunately, management's interest in administrative cost is in direct relationship to the climate of profitability in a specific industry. In exceptionally good times, there is not much interest in the subject. When hard times fall on an organization, whether it is caused by government regulations, severe competition, or internal problems, the question of administrative cost receives the undivided attention of corporate management. As the national economy continues to climb at record levels, company managements are forced to face up to the question–Why are our sales and earnings at less than optimum levels?

Comparisons with other companies within a particular industry frequently spark energetic action on the part of top management. About seven years ago, the American Management Association conducted a formalized program for companies within designated industries to submit data covering manpower by established functional groupings according to concise definitions. The resulting comparative data enabled a participating company to readily detect vulnerable areas where worthwhile savings might be possible. Apparently, due to the difficulty of arriving at mutually satisfactory definitions and terminology to satisfy the variety of industries involved, the AMA abandoned their activities in favor of having each individual industrial organization pursue its own project.

One of the advantages of regulated industries is the readily available and uniform presentation of detailed revenue and expense analysis for every company required to render reports required by the authorities.

Nonregulated businesses must rely on trade organizations, cooperative and voluntary exchange of information between companies, or perhaps the imaginative initiative of the corporate controller to obtain meaningful comparisons to aid in the detection of substantial variances from an acceptable expense standard.

Once in a while, the attitude displayed by some disinterested executives, upon being notified of areas where the comparisons reveal significant overages, is so what, our company is different. Quite possibly it is, but that unto itself is not sufficient reason for ignoring the situation and exploring other possible basic reasons for the poor comparison.

Employees must be made aware of apparent efficiencies and economical operations of competing companies. Significant suggestions emanate from thoughtful and concerned employees. Too often, the attitude prevails that only managerial personnel and those specifically trained in cost reduction matters can contribute to a successful solution of the excess expense problem.

Management consultants can be very helpful, both in identifying problem areas, as well as charting a course of action. The best use of management consultants finds them in the role of planning and guiding the program, with client personnel doing most of the work and getting training value from working with the consultants.

Frequency of effort

Once it has been recognized that there is a need for better control of administrative costs, management must determine the most ideal approach to coping with the particular circumstances then in existence. There are at least three approaches: (1) crash programs, (2) long-range programs, and (3) continuing programs. A long-range plan, incorporating all three approaches, might in certain instances be desirable.

Crash programs, although sometimes rather harsh on employee morale, require very little advance planning. Usually such programs involve the issuance of ultimatums directing everyone to eliminate or reduce certain expenses. Notices and posters throughout offices are quite often utilized to create an awareness of company goals for reducing costs. Unfortunately, sporadic contractions of expenditures rarely produce lasting benefits.

Long-range programs on the other hand require skillful planning and complete top management backing and participation. Many organizations use corporate planning departments or management consultants to formulate the program and chart the necessary and desired progress.

Astute executives are alert to the fact that there is no substitute for continuing and controlled management of overhead costs to assure maximum profits.

It should be emphasized that not every situation will require elaborate revamping and expansion of control procedures. One company, for instance, merely decided to solicit cost reduction ideas from employees, and offered cash rewards for the best suggestions. The highest award went to an employee who came up with the elimination of unnecessary details on supply requisitions. His entry was simple and to the point:

> To:　Supply Department
> From:　ABC
> Re:　Form XYZ
> Send some.

The president of a medium-sized company, alarmed by increasing costs, adopted the procedure of having supervisors submit a daily report listing each and every expense he authorized. This simple procedure reminded the supervisor that he was being held responsible for the costs incurred by his department.

In spite of the glaring lack of sophistication inherent in the foregoing illustrations, both companies received significant benefits from the procedures. This, of course, is the key to the situation—Have maximum profit potentials been realized?

Specific techniques for controlling administrative costs

There are numerous techniques for controlling administrative costs available to modern businesses. From a rather broad, general viewpoint, they would include continuous profit consciousness throughout the organization, corporate advance planning programs, clearly defined and communicated expense policies, specifically stated objectives and responsibilities, adequate expense approval procedures, work simplification and measurement, staff balancing and reorganizing, budgetary controls, responsibility accounting, and, finally, adequate internal and external auditing.

To attempt to identify and discuss every possible type of administrative cost control, both formal and informal, would be a sizeable undertaking and far beyond the scope of a handbook chapter. Therefore, discussion is limited to the four interrelated, most currently popular, and universally accepted savings opportunities:
1. Work simplification.
2. Work measurement.
3. Adjust staff and reorganize.
4. Budgetary control.

Work simplification

The first step in simplifying the work is to study each clerical function as it is actually being performed. This is essential to understanding exactly what the job entails, why it exists, how it meshes with other parts of the organization, and, finally, whether or not it is a vital function. A "task analysis sheet" (Exhibit 1) is used during the interview, with each individual worker to outline briefly the present procedures. Ideas and improved procedures emanating from either party are noted on the form. The work sheets later serve the purpose of piecing together the existing work flow of that particular unit.

Frequently, during the course of the interviews and the preparation of analysis sheets, recommendations for altering or even eliminating certain activities are noted. "Action Memorandums" (Exhibit 2) are issued, and the change implemented when approved within an allotted time by the department manager.

The knowledge and experience background of the analysts assigned to the program must be broad enough to assure recognition of better work flows, new and improved forms and reports, and possibilities for eliminating manual processing.

During the work simplification procedure, serious consideration should be given to transferring appropriate clerical functions to electronic data processing, after comprehensive studies confirm complete feasibility and justification.

All management reports should be carefully reviewed, both as to content and distribution. In many instances, it will be discovered that a rearrangement of data will make the report more meaningful. Time after time, reports are distributed to individuals who have no interest or responsibility whatsoever in the matter being reported. The establish-

EXHIBIT 1

Task Analysis Sheet

TASK ANALYSIS SHEET

Name: Henry Daniels   **Task:** Examining Invoices
Position: Clerk   **Department:** Purchasing

Description:	Suggestions:
Receives #3 Copy of invoices from Mail Unit. Sorts by Field Office	Why sort? No sort would speed up examining.
Examine invoices as instructed by Sec IV of Purchasing Manual. List errors and questions. Send to Fields for explanations. Record in log for monthly report.	Sort here for questions. Discontinue. Use copy of above list
Daily, photostat invoices $500.00 and over. Give to Mail Clerk.	
Twice daily delivers invoices to Coding Unit.	Insert in Pre-printed envelope and place in inter-company mail.

Remarks: _____

EXHIBIT 2

Action Memorandum

UNIT *Disbursement*   ACTION MEMORANDUM NO. *34*

DEPARTMENT *Purchasing*   DATE SUBMITTED _____

I.   **JOB:** *Senior Disbursement Clerk*

II. **TASK:** *Collect State Tax worksheets from clerks, total and forward to typist. Check typed Form C-27, post totals to Tax Ledger and send Form C-27 to Tax Department.*

III. **ACTION:** *Total worksheets, attach tape, and send to Tax Department. Discontinue Tax Ledger and typing Form C-27.*

IV. **REASONS FOR ACTION:** *Tax Department has indicated that Ledger and Form C-27 no longer required. Original worksheets provide necessary information.*

ment of report control procedures will produce worthwhile savings, particularly in larger organizations.

Annual savings of over $200,000 were recently reported by a major oil company, resulting from improvements made from a work simplification analysis alone.

Work measurement

Work measurement usually follows the work simplification program. This measurement determines work load which, in turn, is the basis for evaluating staffing requirements. Thomas C. Pitney, of Arthur Young and Company, claims that clerical activity eligible for work measurement usually exceeds 75 percent. The remaining 25 percent, customarily involving nonrepetitive activities, can be controlled by budgeting or random sampling. There are various measurement methods in use today, but the most popular seems to be a time study applied to each step of an entire operation. This analysis results in what is commonly referred to as the time it "should take" to perform a particular function. Predetermined time systems are used by some consulting management engineers for many elements of clerical and other office work. Many authorities oppose that method on the grounds that the measurement program must be precisely tailored to the requirements of the company, rather than installing canned office standards. Regardless of the method employed, it is important to determine that reasonable and completely equitable standards are adopted.

The foregoing determination is not a simple one, and extreme care must be exercised to avoid employee apprehension and mistrust. If everyone looks upon work measurement simply as a means of establishing a fair day's work, the problems will not be staggering. Allowances are usually made for training time, absence from work (illness, vacations, etc.), and personal time (coffee breaks, rest stops, fatigue, etc.), aggregating at least 25 percent of the measured working time. Furthermore, the standard should be developed from as many observations and studies as possible, in order to reflect the average time required for an employee to complete the tasks assigned.

Adjust staff and reorganize

Although staff reduction is of considerable importance in any work measurement program, it is essential that each department be organized so as to obtain the utmost efficiency.

Throughout the work simplification and measurement programs, the ultimate organization should be kept in focus. It will no longer be necessary to staff the department solely on judgment. With the facts at hand, it will be feasible to match work loads with manpower required. Conceivably, it will be possible to combine or regroup several functions. It is also beneficial, particularly in large organizations, to help maintain the realized gains in order to establish some means for reporting and evaluating staffing requirements of each department. The illustrated report (Exhibit 3) serves the dual purpose of revealing the personnel requirements of the department and the achievement in staff reductions against projected goals.

In reorganizing, it must be realized that personnel have a tendency to revert to old ways of doing things. Therefore, it is imperative that measures be anticipated and steps taken to prevent carry-over.

The process of developing the organization structure merely involves the identification of functions, the relationship of those functions in and outside the unit, and the most desirable grouping. This process must be clearly distinguished from other related aspects of modern management principles—motivating, delegating, and establishing employee relationships that foster effective teamwork.

It should also be noted that there is considerable danger in considering the agreed upon organization as fixed and permanent. People, circumstances, practices, and economic conditions change during a given period of time and, sometimes, faster than most people realize. It follows,

EXHIBIT 3

Staffing Report

STAFFING REPORT

_____Purchasing_____ Division

As of the last day of the month of: _____

Section/Unit	Recommended Staff	Actual Staff		
		Time of Study	Previous Month	Present Month
Purchase Order	30	36	35	34
Disbursement	23	30	29	27
Mail	3	5	3	3
Packaging	4	5	5	5
Typing	6	8	6	6
Filing	8	12	9	9
Totals	74	96	87	84

then, naturally, that managers and executives must be flexible in their work and be fully cognizant of the fact that organizing in business is a continuous process.

Budgetary control

Following the implementation of the programs of work simplification and measurement, budgetary control procedures will be significantly improved. Unfortunately, expense budgets, prepared without the benefit of standards or measurements, are arbitrarily predetermined on the basis of past performance. Furthermore, the deficiencies of past performance become entrenched and, in many instances, compounded each year by at least 10 percent.

Having identified work loads and the most efficient organizational arrangement, it is in order to determine personnel counts and payroll dollars for each unit or department. With this basic starting point, it is not too difficult to project other direct and indirect administrative costs. The type of budgetary control adopted is of minor importance compared with the thoroughness required for its preparation and maintenance. Conformance reports must be available at least on a quarterly basis.

Continuous programs

Earlier in this chapter, in the section dealing with the various approaches to administrative costs, mention was made that continuing programs are the most desirable. This is of outstanding importance and most deserving of the repetition afforded it. The entire program outlined must be kept on a current and continuing basis by way of planned maintenance and careful audit. Otherwise, the old way of doing business will be resumed in very short order.

To guard against the possibility of slipping backwards with its administrative cost reduction control, a large insurance company recently created a permanent organizational unit within the controllership function named the ACR department. The major responsibilities of the department are as follows:

1. *Develop and execute annual and long-range plans* for the periodic review and restudy of all key elements of company clerical and administrative expense.
2. *Take the initiative in continuously studying all clerical and administrative systems and procedures.* Recommend and assist in installing improvements that will cut clerical and other administrative costs, reduce errors, strengthen operating or management controls, and improve service.
3. *Assist in the establishment of Administrative Cost Reduction Units* that may be set up in certain large functional divisions, providing assistance in staffing, training, project-planning, and technical supervision on a continuing basis. These units should be kept as small as practicable.
4. *Develop and maintain an information system* that will permit appraisal of the performance of clerical units with respect to:
   (a) The effectiveness with which the clerical staff is being utilized.
   (b) The quality of clerical performance as measured by service times, error rates, etc.
   (c) The trend in unit costs for major administrative functions.
5. *Make work-measurement studies* as the basis for determining the required clerical staff at varying volumes of work.

Effect on quality of work performance

The true success of any cost reduction program must be measured, in some way, against its effect upon the excellence of performance in each position and department throughout the company. If success in reducing administrative costs by 10, 20, or 30 percent is achieved by merely reducing the quality of the work performed, then very little indeed has been accomplished. As a matter of fact, ground may have been lost, if management cannot accept operating reports and financial statements with the highest level of confidence. Sacrificing effective systems of quality control is false economy, and must be carefully avoided. This

EXHIBIT 4

Corporate Quality Control Coordinator
(duties and responsibilities)

A. Develop and maintain a companywide system for investigating significant questions regarding the accuracy of data in reports to management.
   1. Investigate and resolve all problems involving the quality of data in reports.
   2. Develop and coordinate corrective actions with quality control representatives in each department.
   3. Provide appropriate reports or explanations to executive management.
B. Evaluate quality controls over the preparation and processing of data in all areas of the company; secure cooperation of department managers in *strengthening* and *policing checks* on quality of data, where needed.
   1. Prescribe and coordinate effective quality improvement programs, utilizing the most up-to-date techniques for quality control, such as statistical sampling, computer edits, job engineering, etc.
   2. Identify data quality problems and focus special attention on data quality related to: agency relations, statutory financial reports, management reports, policyholder relations.
C. Develop and implement programs to motivate employees toward improved quality of data preparation and processing.
   1. Improve quality through better training and development programs, "quality-mindedness attitude" education, company projects and promotion, etc.
   2. Establish and administer appropriate employee incentive programs.
D. Periodically prepare a comprehensive evaluation of quality control of data, and coordinate implementation of approved recommendations and planned actions.
E. Nurture and coordinate the activities of quality improvement program representatives in each department.
F. Evaluate the quality control aspects of administrative cost reduction action memorandums, to insure that quality is not sacrificed by eliminating vital and important tasks of jobs and functions.

does not, by any means, suggest that costs should be disregarded entirely to provide excessive controls over inconsequential absurdities.

Department managers frequently believe that work measurement programs only cause clerks to speed up their work and increase the error ratio. This is not the case, because it has been proven that employees usually work at a satisfactory pace. Increased output, resulting from the program, is attributable to streamlining the operations and to employees working more continuously. Specific quality improvement programs (QIP) have been successfully carried out in the insurance industry. One large organization has appointed a corporate quality control coordinator who, along with QIP representatives from each department, handles all matters relating to this important activity. Their duties and responsibilities are indicated in Exhibit 4.

In financial institutions, large dollar transactions usually constitute a small percentage of the total number of items but a relatively large percentage of dollar income processed. A recent insurance company survey, of premium transactions over $5,000 and loss transactions over

EXHIBIT 5

Stop for Quality Control

E R R O R

C A U S E   No. *107*

R E M O V A L   Date *1/27/69*

TO: *Mr. J. A. Jones*

FROM: *W. R. Brown*

SUBJECT: E.D.P. Document # *3207*

        The following quality control problem was called to my attention by the *Investment Acctg. Dept.* . Please investigate, complete the form below and distribute the necessary copies.

ERROR – *(Briefly describe nature of error and impact on a particular financial statement and/or report.)*
The 12/31/68 E.D.P. Document #3207 is less than our year-to-date input control record for Dividends Received in the amount of $6,300.00. We cannot complete investment exhibits for management until the discrepancy is resolved.

CAUSE – *(Briefly describe why the error occurred.)*
Difference represents dividends received in 1968 on I.D. #1473, Food Fair Stores, which was sold at the close of the prior year. The EDP Utility System cannot accept dividend input for securities disposed of prior to the current accounting year.

REMOVAL – *(Briefly describe steps taken to prevent this or a similar error from happening in the future.)*
The new investment accounting program (now in a parallel testing stage) will avoid this problem as the new system develops a permanent history file which will accept input transactions such as described above.

J. A. J.   *1/27/69*
Management Systems Coordinator   Date

W. R. B.   *1/28/69*
Computer Systems Analyst   Date

$25,000, indicated the items to be substantially less than one percent, whereas the dollars were in excess of 30 percent of the total processed in a given month. It is important, therefore, to make certain that they are processed as promptly and accurately as possible. It has been highly beneficial to specially flag the large transactions with bright-colored slips attached to the documents. Before the document is passed along for processing, it must be carefully examined and verified for completeness and initialled by the supervisor.

Exhibit 5 is a copy of a form found useful for cataloging and correcting errors.

Results of good controls

Throughout the chapter, mention has been made of the underlying benefits resulting from implementation of various controls. Of primary importance, of course, is the reduction of operating costs. Improved profits can obviously come from only two sources—increased income and decreased expenses. Very often it becomes difficult to increase income, and the only available solution is expense reduction. A $50 thousand-a-year reduction in operating expense can have a similar effect on profits as adding $1 million of income.

The improved measurable efficiency throughout the organization, after installing these controls, is beneficial to all employees. Each person is judged on the quality and quantity of work performed. Everyone knows exactly what tasks are to be performed. Supervision is made easier, and salary administration proves more equitable. Additional time is available to supervisors to do a creditable job of supervising and improving procedures. The main advantage to management is the availability of complete and accurate information to evaluate and appraise performance. Comparisons should result, highlighting the before and after results of procedural change and reorganization.

With proper installation and administration, the various programs outlined can provide the most effective control media currently available to enterprising management.

Bibliography

The broad scope of the subject, coupled with the fact that each business organization will require controls that are unique and tailored to its own needs, limits detailed discussions herein. Recommended reading includes:

HECKERT, J. BROOKS, and WILSON, JAMES D.   *Controllership*, Chapter 18. 2d ed. New York, 1963.

IDLAS, ALLAN R.   (Kemper Insurance Company).   "Work Measurement—A

Tool in Expense Control," *Insurance Accounting and Statistical Association Annual Proceedings,* 1967.

PITNEY, THOMAS C. (Arthur Young and Company). "A Proven Plan for Controlling Administrative Costs." Reprinted from the *Proceedings of the Thirteenth Annual Conference and Convention of the American Institute of Industrial Engineers;* "Bank Approaches to Controlling Clerical Costs," *Burroughs Clearing House,* November, 1960; and, "Clerical Cost Control," *Best's Insurance News,* February, 1960.

POLLACK, JACK HARRISON. "Your Office Costs Can Be Cut," *Nation's Business,* March, 1968.

SPOAR, GEORGE K. (Aetna Life Affiliated Companies.) "Work Measurement and Quality Control," *Insurance Accounting and Statistical Association Annual Proceedings, 1965.*

PART VII

Asset management and control

Cash management

J. T. Hackett and G. R. Thurston*

Since the early 1960's, increasing emphasis has been placed on the management of the cash resources of corporations. The development of improved cash management techniques is a result of higher opportunity costs in the form of higher interest rates, and programs to improve asset utilization. All of these programs are designed to help achieve a more efficient utilization of resources and improve the return on the shareholder's investment.

Nonproductive cash tends to collect in several areas within a firm's financial framework. The first, and most obvious, area is in the company's demand deposits in commercial banks. The cash kept on hand in the bank serves two purposes: it is a buffer which absorbs the variation in the daily inflow and outflow of funds, and it serves as one form of compensation to the bank for services rendered.

Nonproductive near-cash assets may also accumulate in the form of accounts receivable and inventory. Today's financial executive must be as deeply involved in monitoring and improving his working capital turnover as he is in controlling his cash balances.

This chapter will focus on determining the proper size of cash balances; on increasing the turnover of the firm's accounts receivable and inventory; and finally, on investing the surplus funds that will be generated from improved cash management.

---

* Vice President—Finance, and Manager—Corporate Cash Management, respectively, Cummins Engine Company, Inc., Columbus, Indiana.

Determining appropriate size of cash balances

The key to reducing the required cash balances is the improvement of the predictability of the company's cash flow and an understanding of the relationship between balances and the bank's cost of servicing the account. If the company has more than one bank account because of its widespread operations, an additional element affecting the size of overall bank balances is introduced, that is, the efficiency of intercompany cash control. Each of these three areas—predicting cash flows, understanding the cash balance/cost relationships of the bank, and controlling intercompany cash balances—will be covered separately in the following three sections.

Improving the predictability of cash flows

Good cash forecasting is the key to improved predictability. The short-range cash forecast is a basic tool in the financial management of the company: it provides the finance staff with the ability to:
1. Determine operating cash requirements, i.e., the "buffer."
2. Anticipate the need for short-term financing.
3. Select appropriate maturities for short-term investments.

In addition, a good cash forecasting system provides valuable input to the financial executive who must plan the timing of certain quasi-discretionary expenditures such as capital expenditures, repayment of long-term debt, and dividend payments.

The time period covered by the cash forecast is determined by two general factors: (1) the particular purpose of the forecast, and (2) the general business characteristics of the company.

If the purpose of the forecast is to determine the adequacy of short-term credit lines, a twelve-month forecast, subdivided into months with some estimate of potential mid-month peaks is most appropriate. For the executive concerned about what to do with his "surplus" cash, a three-month forecast subdivided into weeks will help in planning the maturities of his short-term investments.

The business characteristics of the company have a definite, and sometimes more limiting, influence on the length of a forecast period. Some businesses are inherently more unpredictable than others. A company subject to the wide, irregular fluctuations in sales and cost of raw materials would be unwise to forecast for more than a short period, because a longer forecast would be too inaccurate potentially to be useful. Conversely, the financial executive of a company with a stable business environment could utilize a twelve-month forecast, or perhaps an even longer one, and still obtain the desired degree of accuracy. Where business characteristics allow, many companies make several forecasts in varying lengths with various subdivisions depending on a particular need.

Two basic methods of short-term cash forecasting can be used. One is based on the *receipts and disbursements* (cash flow) approach, and the other on the *adjusted net income* method. Some companies use both methods since each has its inherent advantages.

RECEIPTS AND DISBURSEMENTS METHOD. The cash receipts and disbursements method is essentially a projection of the company's sources and uses of cash. Collections of receivables, sale of assets, and interest income are projected as well as payments for payrolls, supplier invoices, and dividends. This approach is favored by companies more for the day-to-day control of cash and is generally limited in length to 30 to 90 days. Exhibit 1 reflects a typical receipts and disbursements forecast format.

The details of items included under this approach will vary from company to company depending upon the relative significance of each or upon the degree of accuracy required. Once the items are selected for forecast, it is essential that each item be projected carefully. Some items such as dividends, taxes, payrolls, insurance, and scheduled debt repayments are easy to calculate; but others, particularly receivable collections and material purchases, often require considerable judgment.

Several methods can be used in estimating sources of cash. One technique is to take recent collection activity in absolute dollars and project it forward, adjusting for any known or suspected deviation in the sales trend. Companies which monitor the average number of days that their customers take to pay invoices can use a slightly different approach. If the company's recent history indicates that customers have been paying, on the average, within 36 days of invoice date, then the forecaster may assume a particular month's collections will equal 80 percent of last month's sales plus 20 percent of the sales of the preceding month. If the forecaster is forecasting a particular week's collections, he can refer to invoices issued five to six weeks previously.

In cases where sales and collections tend to fluctuate widely or where the company has a diversified and decentralized operation, the financial executive may turn to the local credit managers for the collections forecasts. Since the credit managers tend to be closer to the day-to-day financial problems of the customers, they can often peg irregular payments more closely. For example, the credit manager would probably know that major customer X normally pays on the 25th of each month, but lately has been almost a week late because of cash availability problems.

However, a company with a large number of accounts would find this individual account approach overly burdensome on their credit men. This company could segregate receivables into separate categories, such as international, government, regular customer, and irregular customer, and project collection patterns based on the expected sales and individual characteristics of each category.

To exercise tight control over cash, the financial officer may wish to forecast collections on a daily basis. To do so, it is necessary to develop a

EXHIBIT 1

Cash Forecast for March, 19—

	Week ending			
	3/7	3/14	3/21	3/28
Beginning balances				
Cash	$1,100	$ 610	$ 520	$ 700
Marketable securities	2,400	1,900	—	500
Total	$3,500	$2,510	$ 520	$1,200
Cash receipts				
Collections on A/R	$ 700	$ 400	$1,800	$2,100
Sale of fixed assets	—	—	200	—
Receipts from subsidiaries	250	200	—	400
Interest income	—	20	20	—
Other	150	110	150	100
Total receipts	$1,100	$ 730	$2,170	$2,600
Cash disbursements				
Supplier invoices	$1,800	$1,500	$ 800	$1,100
Payroll	200	800	200	800
Operating expenses	20	20	20	20
Advertising and sales expense	20	—	20	20
Capital expenditures	—	150	—	150
Interest payments	—	—	—	—
Scheduled debt repayment	—	150	—	—
Dividends	—	—	250	—
Advances to subsidiaries	50	100	100	—
Total disbursements	$2,090	$2,720	$1,490	$2,090
Net funds available	$1,510	$ (520)	$1,200	$1,710
Additional borrowings/(repayment)	—	1,000	(—)	(—)
Balances—end of period	$2,510	$ 520	$1,200	$ 710
Probable breakdown				
Cash	$ 610	$ 520	$ 700	$ 510
Marketable securities	1,900	—	500	1,200
For reference only				
Short-term borrowings at end of period	$ —	$ —	$ —	$ —

working knowledge of the daily billing pattern of the firm plus any particular payment patterns of significant customers. An investigation of the payment policies of all major customers will be worth the initial effort; the continuing effort of periodic monitoring to detect any shifts is also worthwhile.

Forecasts of payments to suppliers are based on the sales forecast for the particular period, which in turn must be translated into a production schedule. Based on the production schedule, material quantities and delivery dates are estimated. Then, by projecting the supplier's standard payment terms from the expected delivery date, a good estimate of that period's dollar payments can be made. If the company has a standard payment schedule, such as every Friday, or on the 10th and 25th of every month, the timing can be pegged even more closely.

Forecasting expenditures for capital assets for the near term (three to four months) can generally be tied to a particular purchase order since most major capital purchases have lead times of approximately this length. In forecasting further out, the estimate of when payments are to be made should be conditioned by the availability factor. Operating division personnel often underestimate the time necessary to procure the capital asset needed. When the capital asset is equipment which must be custom made and/or is technologically unproven, allowances should be made for the possible delay in payment until the equipment is installed and operating to specifications.

Estimating payments to contractors for a new facility is even more uncertain. Construction progress can be significantly altered by material shortages, strikes, and weather. A good forecaster really needs a crystal ball in trying to time the payments for a major facility. The arrangement of a temporary construction loan line might be worthwhile in that it buffers the general operating funds from the irregular payment requirements.

Since the receipts and disbursements method is the approach most commonly used in forecasting *daily* activity, it might be wise here to point out the following caveat. *The shorter the time span of a forecast, the less likely that random variables will average out.* That is, the shorter the incremental period being forecast, the greater the potential inaccuracy. For example, a snowstorm in the east, a fogged in airport in the south, or a delayed mail delivery to the local post office can produce a high degree of inaccuracy in a two-day forecast of collections, while these random factors will tend to work themselves out over a longer forecast period. Therefore uncertainty is magnified as one moves closer to a daily forecast from a monthly forecast.

Advocates of the receipts and disbursements method of forecasting point out that it provides a fairly complete picture of all expected cash transactions and thus provides an excellent means of controlling the company's cash for the short run. The method is flexible and can be used for longer term forecasting. However, the receipts and disbursements method is best within a 60 or 90 day period. Its accuracy beyond 90 days is hampered by the fact that it does not focus on the subtle changes in the balance sheet items affecting working capital, most notably, receivables and inventory. Over a six-month period, a modestly growing level of receivables may not be reflected in the receipts and disbursements approach, yet will surely drain away cash. Because of the tendency of this method to overlook these changes in working capital, some financial executives prefer the adjusted net income method, which focuses directly on working capital.

ADJUSTED NET INCOME APPROACH.   This method, sometimes referred to as the sources and application of funds method, focuses on changes in the balance sheet, particularly the working capital accounts. *Since this method does not focus directly on the cash accounts, its usefulness to a company that faces acute day to day cash problems is questionable.* Companies concerned only with the general outlook for funds over a month or quarter or year (in order to plan shifts in expenditures or the arrangement of credit lines) may be more comfortable with the adjusted net income approach.

EXHIBIT 2

Projected Sources and Uses of Funds First Six Months, 1968
(thousands of dollars)

Sources of funds	January	February	March	April	May
Net income after tax	$ 1,100	$ 800	$ 900	$ 800	$1,100
Depreciation	200	200	200	200	200
Increase in accrued federal tax	500	400	(900)	400	550
Increase in federal tax reserve	100	100	100	100	100
Increase/(decrease) in other liabilities	20	20	(40)	20	20
Increase/(decrease) in accounts payable	400	600	(300)	(100)	300
Increase/(decrease) in short term borrowings	(670)	(430)	1,800	(850)	(950)
Other (specify)	—	—	50	—	—
Total sources	$ 1,650	$ 1,790	$ 1,760	$ 570	$1,320
Uses of funds					
Capital expenditures	$ (100)	$ (200)	$(1,100)	$ (250)	$ (200)
(Increase)/decrease in accounts receivable	(1,400)	(1,300)	(1,100)	(200)	(300)
(Increase)/decrease in inventory	(100)	(100)	(200)	(100)	100
(Increase)/decrease in other assets	(50)	(50)	(50)	(50)	(50)
Long term debt repayment	—	—	(150)	—	—
Dividends	—	—	(200)	—	—
Total uses	$(1,650)	$ (650)	$(2,800)	$ (600)	$ (450)
Cash position—beginning					
Cash	$ 50	$ 50	$ 100	$ 150	$ 120
Securities	—	—	1,090	—	—
Total	$ 50	$ 50	$ 1,190	$ 150	$ 120
Cash position—ending					
Cash	$ 50	$ 100	$ 150	$ 120	$ 90
Securities	—	1,090	—	—	900
Total	$ 50	$ 1,190	$ 150	$ 120	$ 990
Short-term debt					
Beginning	$ 1,100	$ 430	$ —	$1,800	$ 950
Increase/(decrease)	(670)	(430)	$ 1,800	(850)	(950)
Ending	$ 430	$ —	$ 1,800	$ 950	$ —

Parentheses () reflect uses of funds.

Exhibit 2 presents a typical format of sources and uses of funds forecast. The common items generally reflected in such a forecast include:
1. Net income—optional whether before or after tax.
2. Depreciation—a non-cash expense to be added back to profits.
3. Change accrued income tax—if income is shown after tax, the change in the tax accrual should be reflected; actual tax payments will be reflected as a decrease in the accrual.
4. Change in net working capital—can be subdivided into major categories or treated in aggregate: increase in net working capital is a *use,* a decrease is a *source.*
5. Debt repayments and/or additional borrowings.
6. Capital expenditures.
7. Dividends.

The forecasting of each of these items varies significantly in difficulty. Such items as dividends, required debt installments, depreciation, and other accruals are generally fairly easy to peg for the short term. Income and the resulting tax liabilities can be determined by studying forecasted sales, manufacturing costs, and operating expenses. Pegging the changes in working capital accounts is more of a challenge, and practices do vary.

Two basic techniques are used for forecasting the changes in such balance sheet items as receivables, inventories, and payables: historically developed ratios and direct estimates. For a company not subject to significant seasonal influences, a common technique is to compute a ratio for each major item to sales. Based upon the sales forecast for the periods being projected, changes in the different working capital accounts can be computed via the ratio. The second method is the direct estimate, taking into account not only the sales trends but also the seasonal and historical patterns of each item of working capital. The financial executive may wish to consult directly with the credit, production, and purchasing departments in preparing these direct estimates.

The primary advantage to the sources and uses of funds method is that it tends to produce a more accurate estimate of the cash position in the intermediate term (three to nine months) because it takes into account the effect of working capital changes and other non-operating balance sheet items. *The primary limitation of the sources and uses of funds method is in the short term for day-to-day control over cash.*

For a strong cash management system, a combination of the receipts and disbursements method and the sources and uses method is desirable. By using the sources and uses method for the three- to twelve-month forecasts, the financial executive can determine the adequacy of his credit lines or other borrowing reserves. By focusing the receipts/disbursements method on a 90-day period, the cash manager can vigorously control his cash balances and aggressively invest his temporary cash surpluses.

The administration of the short-range cash forecasting function gener-

EXHIBIT 3

Cash Forecasting Calendar for 1970

Forecast Required	Due Date(s)	Instructions	Preparer
Annual forecast—1970	Nov. 15, 1969	Sources and uses of funds format; subdivided into months; estimate mid-month peaks.	Operating divisions' financial control departments; consolidation by treasury staff.
Quarterly revisions to annual forecast	April 15, 1970	Sources and uses format; subdivided into months; add next quarter not previously forecasted; estimate mid-month peaks.	Operating divisions' control departments; consolidation by treasury staff.
60-day cash forecast	25th of each month for subsequent 2-month period	Receipts/disbursements format; subdivided into days.	Operating divisions' control departments; consolidation by treasury staff.
Annual forecast—1971	Nov. 15, 1970	Sources and uses format; subdivided into months; estimate mid-month peaks.	Operating divisions' control departments; consolidation by treasury staff.
Forecast review: Annual forecasts and quarterly revisions	Jan. 10, 1970 Apr. 10, 1970 Jul. 10, 1970 Oct. 10, 1970 Jan. 10, 1971	Compare actual balance sheet changes with forecast for previous quarter.	Treasury staff.
60-day forecasts	10th of each month	Compare actual daily receipts and disbursements with previous 60-day forecast.	Treasury staff.

ally is the responsibility of the treasurer because of his traditional responsibility for company funds. Depending upon the organizational emphasis of the particular company, the treasurer and his staff may prepare the actual forecast in its entirety, or he may delegate the preparation to the various operating departments after establishing the basic format and assumptions.

If the company has more than one operating division, the treasurer may direct that each division prepare its own forecast with the treasury serving to consolidate the individual inputs. An important aspect of administering the cash forecasting function is the periodic testing of accuracy. The actual cash records of the company will provide the basis for testing the accuracy of the receipts/disbursements method. The company's balance sheets will provide the basis for testing the sources and uses forecasting method. It is generally recommended that the receipts/disbursement forecasts be tested at least monthly, and sources/uses forecasts at least quarterly. Timely feedback to those persons involved in the preparation of the forecasts is essential to identify improper assumptions or shifts in major trends or relationships.

Exhibit 3 presents a common cash forecasting system found in many large companies today. Note that both the receipts/disbursements and sources and uses approaches are used. With this system providing accurate and timely information, the treasurer and his staff can:
1. Plan for borrowing reserves.
2. Determine the level of balances needed on any given day to meet the outflow of funds.
3. Invest surplus funds at appropriate maturities.
It must be pointed out that both of the above forecasting techniques produce estimates of cash balances *per books*. A further refinement reflecting the day to day *float* on funds received and disbursed could be made for a company in a critically short cash position. A discussion of float is included in the next section.

ESTIMATING THE COST OF BANK SERVICES. Generally, banks look to a company's cash balances for compensation for the various services rendered. Common services include:
1. Check clearing for both deposits and withdrawals.
2. Credit checks for potential customers or business associates.
3. Information pertaining to the local and national economic conditions.
4. Custody accounts for certain of the company's negotiable instruments.
5. Broker or dealer for company's short-term investments.
If the company has international dealings, a qualified bank can provide a wide range of services. If the company is also a borrower from the bank or maintains unused lines of credit, balances are required as a part of credit compensation. However, this form of compensation is unique to U.S. banking relations.

Banks differ on how they "charge" for services rendered. Some banks have developed an elaborate fee schedule that charges the company a fixed amount for each of the services rendered during a particular time period. One bank may charge 7 cents per check, 3 cents per deposit, a 2 percent commission on all investments handled. Another bank may provide these services "free," but insist that a minimum balance of $1.5 million be maintained. These differences between banks often reflect a definite difference in the philosophy of banking, but more often reflect the varying abilities of each bank to "cost out" each of its services.

How does the financial executive determine whether his company's cash balances are appropriate? Can he assume that if he has heard no complaints from the bank his balances are too high? If so, should he judiciously reduce balances to the point where the bank complains and then, during the confrontation, reach a mutually agreed-upon minimum? Or should he decide to leave the balances as they are, in the belief that he will be accruing goodwill that may become valuable in the future? Generally, it is recommended that the financial executive develop his own "account analysis" to determine the probable profitability of his balances to the bank. Having done his homework, he will have an idea of whether his balances are satisfactory.

Just how should the financial executive prepare his account analysis? Exhibit 4 shows a format useful in analyzing one's bank account. From the company's own check book, the analyst can find the actual number of checks written during the period. He then estimates as best he can the bank's average cost per check handled. A good reference is the price per check that the bank charges to individuals holding checking accounts. Adding an additional 20 percent per check may be fairer, since many banks view the individual checking accounts as "loss leaders."

The volume of checks deposited can be picked up from the cash receipts journal. Costing deposits is a little more difficult since there is generally no outside reference. Generally, each deposit will cost a bank roughly one-third to one-half as much as handling a check.

Special services such as a bank newsletter, credit references, and investment-custody accounts should be costed at the discretion of the analyst. He should estimate roughly the amount of time and expense involved in each service and enter the cost. This latter analysis points out the need of having all the company's dealings with the bank coordinated through the treasury function.

The analyst then determines the average daily balances as shown on the bank's ledger. He then must adjust for the deposits credited to the company but not as yet collected by the bank. Generally, a two business day collection period adjustment will realistically reflect the general level of float.

Having established the collected funds balance, the analyst must subtract the reserve requirement of the particular bank. The Federal

Reserve requires that a certain percentage of a bank's demand and time deposits be kept on reserve at the Federal Reserve Bank. This reserve requirement will vary by type of deposit, i.e., demand or time, and will be determined by reserve city or country bank classification, so the analyst should ascertain the appropriate reserve requirement.

Having deducted the reserve requirement from the collected funds balance, the analyst now sees what amount the bank had available to invest. He must then select a measure for the earning potential of these

EXHIBIT 4

Account Analysis
bank: Home Town National   period: 1/1—3/31, 1969

Cost of services rendered

Service:	Quantity	Cost/unit	Total cost
Payroll checks	1,400	$ 0.085	$119.00
Regular checks	2,200	0.085	187.00
Deposits—in town	400	0.030	12.00
—out of town	1,100	0.040	44.00
Special:			
Credit reference checks	3	10.00	30.00
Bank newsletter	3	1.50	4.50
Custody acct.—investments		3.00/mo.	9.00
Total cost			$405.50

Compensation from actual balances		
Bank's average daily ledger balances	$ 40,850	
Less: float-funds in collection process	(12,050)	
Collected funds balances	$ 28,800	
Less: reserve requirement—12.5%	(3,600)	
Investable funds	$ 25,200	
Bank's daily earnings rate, (prime)/365	.0001918	
Average daily earnings	$ 4.833	
Earnings for period		$434.97
Net profit/(loss) to bank		$ 29.47
Percent above/(below) cost		7.3%

funds. The most common rates used are prime rate, the current daily Federal Funds[1] rate or the current yield on 91-day Treasury Bills. Another technique is to ask the bank for an average interest rate figure. By adjusting one of these rates to its daily basis, the analyst can calculate the earnings of the bank on the company's deposits for the period in question. Comparing the earnings with the cost of service, he can estimate the bank's profit or loss on the account during the period.

If the financial executive is satisfied that the general level of the bank's service will not fluctuate from period to period, he can "peg" the mini-

---

[1] Federal Funds is the term used for excess reserve requirements of one Federal Reserve member bank that may be loaned to another that is experiencing a short-term reserve deficiency.

mum service balance that he will maintain. However, in doing so, he must remember that the amount of investable funds that the bank requires needs quite a bit of translation to tie into the *company's book balances*. The following diagram reflects the various elements which must be accounted for in this translation.

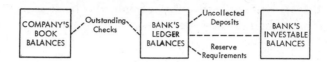

Since the company's cash forecasting techniques are tied to *book balances*, it is imperative that some adjustment be made so that the financial executive can monitor the investable balances at the bank through his regular cash forecasts. Perhaps the best approach is to calculate for a reasonable period of time the estimated level of outstanding checks on a daily basis versus the uncollected deposits. This "net float" plus the reserve requirement can then be used as the adjustment between book balance and the bank's investable funds balance.

It is interesting to note that many banks are willing to prepare the "account analysis" for review by the company. In these cases, the financial executive will probably negotiate with the bank on the appropriate collected funds balances to be maintained over the next period. He must still, however, be able to translate this collected funds requirements into his book balances format.

To these services funds required, the level of compensating balances for outstanding loans and/or credit lines should be added. With this deposit target and a good forecasting system, the financial executive can begin to hold the actual daily balances to the minimum, aggressively directing all surplus funds in income-producing investments.

Hopefully, in the future much of this work can be eliminated as the compensation of banks for services can be made on a direct fee basis. However, this will require better cost accounting techniques among commercial banks. Many financial executives are urging the banks to adopt a fee basis and eliminate the compensating balance technique.

Controlling intercompany cash balances

A financial executive of a company with decentralized operations faces an additional concern in managing the company's overall cash position. Should he let each operation manage its own cash autonomously, with the corporate finance staff serving merely an audit function, periodically testing the efficiency of cash control at each location? Or should the central finance staff tightly control all company funds, distributing funds to the operating entities as needed?

Despite the general move to decentralized business responsibility for "profit center" entities in multidivisional companies, the cash management function has generally been maintained as the closely controlled responsibility of the corporate finance staff. The benefits of coordinated bank relations, concentrated borrowing power, and a centralized investment procedure outweigh the organizational advantages of delegating the responsibility to the operating units. The centralized management of cash also eliminates the potential of an uneconomic cash imbalance within the system; that is, when Division A is investing surplus funds at 6 percent while Division B is borrowing funds from their local bank at 7.5 percent.

EXHIBIT 5

Centralized Cash Management System Banking Network

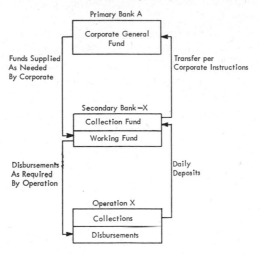

Within a centralized cash management system, the corporate finance staff can control funds through one or more primary banks. These primary banks serve as the reservoir through which all the company's funds flow. The secondary banks serve each of the operating entities through the operation of a working fund account and a collection fund account. The working fund account is a "disbursement only" account for the use of the operating entity. Cash is transferred from a primary bank to this account as needed for day-to-day disbursement activities. The collection fund account is actually a corporate-controlled account at the secondary bank. All collections and other cash receipts by the operating division are deposited to the collection fund account daily and transferred to the nearest primary bank when the corporate finance staff directs. Exhibit 5 shows schematically how such a system might work.

The corporate finance staff can direct the secondary bank to transfer funds from the collection fund account to the working fund account rather than back to the primary bank in cases where the operating units inflows and outflows for a particular day are fairly equal. The important element in this system is that the corporate staff retains control over cash balances throughout the system.

The one disadvantage to this system is the potential cost of monitoring the balances continually from the corporate staff level. There is an increased need for communication between the corporate staff and the operating unit for accurate daily forecasts of disbursements and receipts. The corporate staff might also have to be in daily communication with the primary and secondary banks with instructions on when and where to transfer funds. The difficult decision for the chief financial officer is whether the improved efficiency of centralized cash control warrants the expense. Implicit in this centralized approach is the assumption that operating units are not adequately staffed to provide their own cash control and management.

In cases where the financial executive believes that each of his operating units does have the capability to manage its cash tightly on a day-to-day basis, he need only establish a minimum balance target for the operating unit and instruct it to transfer excess funds to the corporation's primary bank account. In the event that the operating entity expects to run short of cash for a period of time, the corporate finance staff will arrange an advance from its primary banks.

Regardless of whether a centralized or decentralized approach is used, the corporate finance staff will still require forecasts of the operating units' cash generation or utilization to properly manage the primary bank accounts.

Increasing the turnover of receivables and inventory

Thus far, the discussion has focused on effectively managing the company's cash within an established cash flow. Two additional areas that offer opportunity for improved cash flow are collections on accounts receivable and inventory control. A secondary area, the proper control of payables, will also be reviewed.

Speed up of the receivable collection process

Two general approaches for speeding the collection of receivables are:
1. The utilization of area concentration banking.
2. The implementation of the lock box system.
Both of these approaches concentrate on the collection process *after* the customer mails his check.

1. AREA CONCENTRATION BANKING.   After the customer remits the funds, the financial executive's goal is to convert it into usable funds as quickly as possible. Two general causes of delay are the mail system and the internal cash handling procedures of the company itself. For a company with many local operating entities, each serving a particular locality, the area concentration banking method will reduce both the mail time and the internal cash handling time. Under a system of area concentration banking, the customer mails his remittance directly to the operating units serving his locality. Each local operation in turn deposits the remittance immediately in its local bank; from the local bank, usable funds are immediately transferred by wire to the nearest regional bank. A one-day delay in the wire transfer may be necessary to allow the local bank to clear the deposited checks and receive collected funds. If the mail time from the local operation to the regional bank is only one day, the system may dictate that the manager of the local operation draw a depository transfer draft at the time the deposit is made and mail it immediately to the regional bank. The bank depository draft is advantageous in that it is less expensive and provides documentation of each transfer. In either case, the regional bank will receive collected funds one business day after the deposit is made.

Upon receipt of funds, the regional bank could either transfer them automatically to the company's headquarters bank, or invest them in short-term securities if the company uses a standard instruction. In cases where such standardized instructions are deemed impractical, the company may request that the regional bank notify them daily of the balances and then instruct the bank on the proper disposition of the funds the next day. Allowing the bank the opportunity to invest these funds overnight will generally provide adequate compensation for the services.

The area concentration banking network is advantageous in that it generally holds the mail delivery time of the customer's check to one day, the collection time on the check to one day, and keeps idle funds from collecting in the local bank accounts. Requiring the customer to mail his remittance to the headquarters bank could involve two or three days delivery time and another two days for check clearing. If a weekend falls within the five-day cycle, the company would have to wait as many as seven days before it could use the funds.

2. LOCK-BOX SYSTEM.   The lock-box system also reduces the mail delivery time and check clearing time of a company's collections. This is effective where the company has a geographically diverse customer base for which the mail delivery time to the company's office would be several days. This approach differs from the area concentration network in that the company will not have many local operating units to collect and

initiate the processing of the remittances. A lock-box system involves a locked post office box (hence the term) and a designated banking agent at one or more regional locations.

The determination of where to locate each of these lock-boxes generally involves a study of the mail delivery times within a particular zone. Many banks in recent years have published maps detailing which cities can receive mail from which areas within one day. By overlaying the distribution of the company's customers on such maps, the financial executive can determine the locations for the minimum number of lock-boxes required to cover the maximum number of customers.

EXHIBIT 6

Lock-Box Analysis

	Zone A	Zone B	Zone C
Average monthly collections	$140,000	$1,840,000	$2,160,000
Average number of items per month	1,100	2,300	3,800
Average size of check	$ 127	$ 800	$ 568
Estimated number mail days saved with lockbox (including weekends)	2.3	2.5	2.3
Estimated collection time saved with lockbox (including weekends)	1.3	1.5	1.3
Total days saved per check	3.6	4.0	3.6
Effective daily yield at 7 percent	0.0192%	0.0192%	0.0192%
Potential yield per check*	$ 0.087	$ 0.616	$ 0.392
Cost per check	$(0.120)	$(0.115)	$(0.110)
Potential gain/(loss) per check	$(0.033)	$ 0.501	$ 0.282

* Calculated as average size per check x days saved with lock-box x effective daily yield.

Once the locations of the lock-boxes are determined, the company may rent a locked post office box and appoint a bank as agent at each location. The customers are then instructed to remit to the post office box in their zone. The bank, as agent for the company, collects the remittances several times a day from the post office box, deposits the checks, clears them locally, and credits the company's account. Depending upon prearranged instructions, the bank will wire transfer funds to the company's prime bank or notify the company and invest the funds daily, pending specific instructions.

Remittance details necessary to post the accounts receivable journal of the company are forwarded immediately to the accounting department at the company's headquarters. Organizations that maintain receivable records on the computer may establish a data processing link with the bank which allows the bank to transmit the collection details directly into the company's computer. This eliminates the delay between the actual collection and the eventual account posting.

The agent bank can be compensated in either of two ways:
1. Negotiate a per item charge for each remittance handled by the bank.
2. Maintain a minimum balance of collected funds with the bank.
In either event, the basic cost of a lock-box system must be weighed against the benefits.

Exhibit 6 shows the type of calculation that a financial executive might make in deciding whether a lock-box was justified in particular zones. In this example, he would establish lock boxes in Zones B and C; the amount of each item in Zone A does not warrant the cost. The cost or saving per check is not necessarily the only determinant, since the cost per item will generally decline with volume. However, there is still a large percentage of individual handling cost that will prevent the cost per item from declining too far.

The decision on whether to utilize the lock-box approach should not be approached solely on the basis of preceding analysis, however. The delay between the time the actual collection is made and the time the credit manager is notified can be disruptive to a tightly controlled credit management department. The additional handling of the remittance advice by the bank causes delays which can embarrass the credit manager who may be following up with a supposedly late-paying customer.

The introduction of the lock-box can have negative ramifications from a customer relations standpoint. Customers with tight cash positions who had been depending upon the traditional three-to-five day float on their checks may turn to competitors where the inherent payment terms are not so harsh. Or these same customers may merely adjust their payment pattern back to recoup the two or three days lost, negating all the benefits of the lock-box.

Reducing the investment in inventory

Inventory accumulates in three general areas within the company— raw materials, goods in process, and finished goods. Generally, each of these areas is controlled by operating functions not under the direct control of the financial executive.

The purchasing and material control functions are responsible for maintaining raw material levels and goods in process. Marketing is largely responsible for the finished product. The details of purchasing control, production planning and procedures, and finished goods stocking and distribution will not be discussed here. However, the financial executive should develop standards that permit him to determine whether the company's inventory-to-sales relationship is appropriate. Most of the time, he will have to rely on industry ratios or the company's own performance history. When it becomes apparent through periodic review that one or more areas of the inventory have begun to absorb a disportionately high percentage of the company's capital, he should notify the appropriate function and require an explanation and remedial action. Chapter 43 discusses inventory management and control in some detail.

Controlling payables

The financial executive can also conserve the company's cash through a properly administered payment program. Four possible methods that can generate additional funds are:
1. Centralizing the payable function.
2. Carefully timing disbursements.
3. Taking discounts when offered.
4. Payment by draft rather than check.

A centralized payables function can reduce the level of cash balances required at the subsidiaries and divisions and reduce the chance that these funds are not being aggressively managed. The centralized payable section also facilitates the control over the following three methods.

Timing. The proper timing of payments within a month, a week, or a day can conserve the company's cash. By matching disbursements with expected collections during a month, the company can avoid the excessive and rapid build-up and drain-off of cash which is difficult to manage. By timing disbursements for the last day of a week, the company benefits from the additional delay in mail delivery from the two-day weekend. By mailing checks in the afternoon rather than in the morning the company can gain an additional day of mail time before the check is deposited.

Discounts. The advantages of taking offered discounts are obvious. Yet the financial executive should be satisfied that his company's accounts payable function (either centralized or decentralized) can process the supplier's invoices quickly enough to take advantages of such discounts.

Payment by draft. Use of the payable-through-draft method rather than a regular check offers some additional flexibility, but only in a technical sense. A company utilizing a payable-through-draft is not considered to have made payment until the bank through which the draft is payable contacts the company for settlement. Upon being contacted by the bank, the company still need not honor the draft for any reason whatsoever or, if the draft is to be honored, the company can take one business day to raise funds to satisfy the draft. With a regular check, the company is considered to have made payment when the check is delivered to the payee, and funds must be on hand when it clears.

A company prevented from running negative cash balances per books by the "kiting laws" could technically do so with a draft system of payment. A more acceptable purpose for the payable-through-draft, and the real reason that it was first developed, is to provide a company's decentralized operations a means to draw against the central bank account for expenses without usurping the right of the central finance group to control all disbursements. If the draft were drawn for a legitimate and approved expenditure, it would be honored; if not, the draft would be refused. Obviously, if the company is to be assured that its payable-through-drafts are accepted as payment by the payees, it must not fail to honor them.

Investing surplus funds

The three basic elements that concern the financial executive in the selection of appropriate short-term investments are yield, risk, liquidity and/or maturity. Corporate financial executives have traditionally been satisfied with the low risk of the following investments, selecting between them on the basis of yield, marketability, and maturity:

1. U.S. Treasury bills and other Treasury obligations.
2. Federal agency issues.
3. Federal funds.
4. Bank time deposits and negotiable certificates of deposit.
5. Tax exempt obligations.
6. Banker's acceptances.
7. Commercial paper.
8. Repurchase agreements.
9. Canadian time deposits.
10. Eurodollar deposits.

U.S. Treasury bills and other U.S. Treasury obligations

Treasury bills are non-interest bearing obligations, issued at a discount, with original maturities of three months, six months, nine months and one year. Theoretically no credit risk exists, but bills are subject to market fluctuations if sold prior to maturity. There is a broad secondary market maintained by registered government security dealers and dealer banks creating maximum liquidity.

The U.S. Treasury also issues interest bearing obligations which differ largely in terms of the initial maturities—bonds (more than seven years), notes (one to seven years), and certificates of indebtedness (one year or less). These other Treasury obligations are essentially the same as bills in terms of risk and liquidity. U.S. Treasury obligations are considered to be the most conservative investment possible when held to maturity.

Federal agency issues

Interest bearing obligations of federal agencies created by Congress are essentially the same as treasury obligations in credit risk, although the U.S. government has no explicit obligation to prevent default. There is a broad secondary market providing access to almost any maturity sought. This same secondary market, maintained by government security dealers and dealer banks, provides excellent liquidity. Examples of federal agency issues are Federal Home Loan Bank notes, Federal National Mortgage Association notes and Tennessee Valley Authority 126-day notes.

Federal funds

The Fed Funds market arises daily as banks who are members of the Federal Reserve System "trade" funds to meet the Federal Reserve's legal reserve requirements. Banks holding excess reserves will "sell" (lend) funds to banks having deficiencies. This is a daily market whose rates can fluctuate greatly depending on the relative balance between banks with excess reserves and banks with deficient reserves. During June, 1969, rates reached over 3.5 percentage points above the Federal Reserve discount rate.

A non-bank investor cannot directly place funds into this market through a commercial bank that is a Federal Reserve member bank. Certain non-member banks will, on occasion, act as an agent for a non-bank investor and place the funds through a Fed member bank for a small commission. The inherent one day maturity and the standing of the Federal Reserve System makes this a virtually riskless investment, if a reputable agent is used.

Bank time deposits and certificates of deposit

Time deposit certificates are interest bearing deposits in a commercial bank with a fixed maturity date. Rates and maturity are regulated by federal and state authorities, and in recent years have tended to be non-competitive vis-à-vis other short-term investments. Credit risk is measurable directly with the credit standing of the bank accepting the deposit. Liquidity is limited by the fixed maturity and the nonnegotiability of the instrument.

Negotiable certificates of deposit are interest bearing obligations of commercial banks, similar in most respects to the time deposit except for the negotiable feature. Because they are negotiable, the CD's of major banks are considered relatively liquid because of an active secondary market maintained by dealer banks and dealers in government securities.

Tax exempt obligations

Non-federal governmental bodies and their agencies can issue bonds and notes whose interest is exempt from U.S. income tax. There is a wide range of credit risk which can generally be determined by referring to one of the standard bond rating tables. Liquidity is totally dependent upon the existence of a secondary market for a particular obligation. Entry into this specialized market is recommended only under the counsel of a reputable dealer or dealer bank.

Prime banker's acceptances

A prime banker's acceptance is a draft instructing a major commercial bank to make payment to a party at a future date—with the bank's prior approval (acceptance) of its obligation to do so. Original maturities on prime banker's acceptances range up to six months, but 90-day terms or less are most prevalent. The party to whom the draft is payable can sell the banker's acceptance at a discount into an established secondary market via his endorsement. The creditworthiness of this instrument rests on the standing of the accepting bank, although the purchaser also has recourse against any endorsers and to the original maker. Bond dealers and most large commercial banks maintain an active market in these instruments, assuring excellent liquidity.

Commercial paper

Commercial paper is unsecured, interest-bearing promissory notes issued by finance companies and industrial companies to obtain working capital. There are three classes of commercial paper, each with its own range of initial maturities:
1. *Direct finance paper* (3–270 day maturity)—issued directly to investors by high-quality major finance companies.
2. *Dealer finance paper* (30–270 days)—issued through dealers by less than highest-quality finance companies.
3. *Industrial paper* (30–180 days)—issued through investment banking firms for major industrial companies.

The credit risk does vary between the classes of paper. All direct finance paper is generally considered prime; the rating of the other classes depends upon the financial standing of the particular issuer. Independent bond ratings of major industrial companies give a meaningful comparison if other public debt financings have been make. Liquidity is limited, so commercial paper should be purchased with the expectation of holding it to maturity. In some cases, for a premium, some dealers will buy or sell prime paper for their own account.

Repurchase agreements

A repurchase agreement consists of a sale of a money-market instrument (the collateral) with the simultaneous commitment by the seller to repurchase it and by the buyer to resell it at a certain price at a later date. The difference between the first selling price and the repurchase price produces the yield for the investor (original purchaser). Depending on the availability of collateral, the short-term investor can tailor the maturity to suit his own needs. The investor is protected from credit risk both by the quality of the basic collateral and the contractual obligation of the seller to repurchase it at a fixed price. This investment is totally illiquid and should be entered into only when it is certain that it can be carried to maturity.

Canadian time deposits

Canadian bank time deposits are similar in most respects to U.S. commercial bank time deposits. The basic difference is that the maturities and rates are not presently bound by U.S. regulations. Rates in recent years have tended to be higher than yields offered by U.S. banks on their time deposits or CD's. The deposits are made in U.S. dollars; therefore, no currency hedging is required.

Interest earned on time deposits in Canadian banks is currently subject to a 15 percent withholding tax by the Canadian government. However, this tax can normally be used to offset U.S. income taxes. The provisions of the U.S. Interest Equalization Tax do not apply as long as the maturity on the time deposits is less than 12 months.

Eurodollar deposits

Foreign banks and foreign branches of U.S. banks accept time deposits in U.S. dollars from U.S. companies. These dollars then become part of the Eurodollar market, and yields to the short-term investor reflect the short-term market conditions. Since the deposit is in U.S. dollars, no currency risk exists. The credit risk is relative to the financial standing of the bank accepting the deposit. Liquidity is nil since the deposit is made for a fixed maturity.

In recent years, Eurodollar deposit yields have outpaced domestic money market yields to the extent that the U.S. government has placed limitations on a U.S. company's ability to invest in this market in order to protect the U.S. balance of payments. The Office of Foreign Direct Investment of the U.S. Department of Commerce has strict limits on the level of liquid investments a U.S. company can hold abroad. Before a U.S. company seeks to invest in this market, it should consult the OFDI Regulations.

41

Consumer credit appraisal, administration, and collection

Linden E. Wheeler*

In contrast to trade credit which "oils" the wheels of the productive economy, consumer credit has the function of procuring goods, money, and services for consumption by individual consumers or their families.

Definition of consumer credit

In discussing the management of accounts receivable representing consumer credit transactions, it is important to define the types of debt covered under consumer credit. The Board of Governors of the Federal Reserve System publishes statistical data on consumer credit and, in their terms, consumer credit represents short and intermediate term credit used to finance the purchase of commodities and services for personal consumption, or to refinance debts originally incurred for such purposes. Credit extended to governmental agencies and non-profit or charitable organizations, as well as credit extended to businesses, is excluded.

Consumer credit is further broken down into two main classes—installment credit and noninstallment credit. Installment credit includes all consumer credit, held by financial institutions and retail outlets, that is scheduled to be repaid in two or more installments. Revolving credit, soft-line budget, and coupon accounts are treated as installment credit.

The four main classes of installment credit in descending order of outstanding volume are:

---

* Vice President–Credit, Sears, Roebuck and Co., Chicago.

1. Automobile paper
2. Personal loans
3. Other consumer goods paper
4. Repair and modernization loans, including FHA insured loans

Noninstallment credit is subdivided into "single payment loans," "charge accounts," and "service credit" used by individuals to pay for services rendered by professional practitioners and service establishments.

Growth and evaluation of consumer credit

The spectacular growth of consumer credit since World War II has been the subject of much discussion and deliberation among economists, businessmen, sociologists, and government economic experts. Starting at $7.2 billion in 1939, the amount outstanding dropped to $4.9 billion during World War II. In 1946, it climbed to $8.4 billion and has surged up to $99.2 billion as of the end of 1967!

The enormity of consumer debt has not only been discussed but has caused some concern among observers who are optimistic about the growth of the gross national product, the high level of employment, and increase in purchasing power, but seem to worry about the high level of consumer indebtedness. Is there cause for alarm? The answer is not simple and requires comparisons and evaluations of consumer credit debt with other economic factors or segments. For the sake of brevity and to try to analyze current trends, let us examine several relationships during selected years from 1957 to 1967.

First, let's look at the amount of consumer debt in relation to the total debt structure of the economy. Exhibit 1 shows the distribution among the three main segments of the economy . . . public, corporate, and individual. As shown, from 1957 to 1967 the percentage of public debt to the total decreased from 36.7 percent to 28.0 percent. The percentage of corporate debt to total, however, increased from 33.4 percent to 37.2 percent. During these same years, the percentage of consumer credit debt increased from 6.1 percent to 6.9 percent. The table shows that the volume of consumer credit debt carries much less weight than the public and corporate debt. In the 1968 Survey of Consumer Finances, Statistical Report Number Two, published by the Survey Research Center at the University of Michigan, it was reported that among the American families with installment debt the mean amount of debt early in 1967 was $1,260.00. Public and corporate debt, however, represent greater amounts owed by fewer units; changes in any individual unit's debt management policy could have a broad impact on the economy.

In interpreting statistics on debt, it is important to understand that when the consumer incurs a debt he generally also acquires an asset. Debt, in other words, has two faces and the National Consumer Finance

Association, in its "Finance Facts" 1968 Yearbook, concludes that the consumer's balance sheet looks very sound and shows an 18.8 to 1 asset to debt ratio of all assets and debts excluding net equity in home ownership.

This favorable ratio should be qualified to give recognition to the elusive possible influence of "other consumer debt" including second mortgages, insurance loans outstanding, etc.; however, best estimates indicate that this total is approximately one-half of the readily recog-

EXHIBIT 1

U.S. Net Public, Corporate, and Individual Debt
for Selected Years, 1957–1967

	1957		*1962*		*1967*	
	$ Billions	*% of Total*	*$ Billions*	*% of Total*	*$ Billions*	*% of Total*
Public[1]	*271.1*	36.7	*331.2*	32.6	*400.0*	28.0
Corporate[2]	*246.7*	33.4	*348.2*	34.2	*533.0*	37.2
Individual	*221.1*	29.9	*337.3*	33.2	*497.3*	34.8
Farm[3]	20.3		30.2		45.4	
Mortgage	131.6		206.3		294.0	
Comm. & Financial[4]	24.4		37.6		58.7	
Consumer Credit[5]	44.8	6.1	63.2	6.2	99.2	6.9
Total	738.9		1,016.7		1,430.3	

Note: Underscored figures are estimates.
[1] Federal, state, and local government—state and local debt as of June 30
[2] Long term and short term
[3] Farm mortgages and production loans
[4] Debt owed to banks for purchasing or carrying securities, debt to brokers and debt owed to life insurance companies by policyholders
[5] Total installment and non-installment debt
Sources: Department of Commerce (Office of Business Economics and Bureau of the Census), Treasury Department, Department of Agriculture, Board of Governors of the Federal Reserve System, and Federal Home Loan Bank Board

nized consumer goods obligations. Considering this additional consumer debt, the asset to debt ratio is still a favorable 12 to 1.

Another objective method of analyzing consumer credit debt is to measure it against disposable personal income, personal savings, and retail sales. When we look at consumer credit in this manner, we find that its growth is closely associated with the general growth of our economy. The American consumer, anxious to improve his standard of living, has naturally responded with the purchase of a greater variety and quantity of goods as his income and savings have increased.

In evaluating the quality of consumer credit debt, economists and statisticians frequently compare this debt with disposable income. During the ten year period from 1957 to 1967, the percentage of consumer credit debt to disposable personal income increased from 14.5 percent to 18.2 percent . . . a change of 3.7 percent of disposable income. During the previous decade (1947 to 1957), however, consumer credit debt as a percentage of disposable personal income had a more significant increase from 6.8 percent to 14.5 percent or an increase of 7.7 percent! This should be attributed to the fact that the consumer during the post-war years had to purchase badly needed durable goods which were not produced in the wartime economy. After the war-time shortages were filled, the consumer moderated his buying.

These trends are put in truer perspective when we recognize that their effect on the family budget has been reduced by a general lengthening of available repayment terms. For this reason, another comparison commonly made in determining how well the American consumer has controlled his installment-buying commitments is that which relates installment repayments as a percentage of disposable personal income. The increase in these ratios or percentages was 1.4 percent during that decade (12.9 percent to 14.3 percent). Two of the main reasons for this satisfactory condition are (1) the American consumer has shown both his ability and willingness to regulate his own installment buying in line with his ability to repay; and (2) the credit grantors have, in general, assumed their responsibility for credit counseling and limiting, where necessary, the extension of credit to consumers.

Responsibility for sound credit management

While the preceding evaluations may indicate a general soundness in the total volume of consumer credit, we must remember that the data used was for the entire economy. Analysts of credit must remember that a debtor-creditor relationship exists in each and every credit transaction and, while there may be an inherent soundness in the total volume of consumer credit, there must be a continued emphasis on the administration of sound credit and collection policies. These policies must provide for procedures whereby the debtor-creditor relationship is closely analyzed so that changes in income, personal circumstances, and individual desires do not put a strain on the relationship of the debtor and creditor. If the soundness of the total volume of consumer credit is to prevail for individual accounts, it is mandatory that top management, financial management, and credit managers deeply concern themselves with the management of the Credit Department and continually review and refine credit and collection policies, procedures, tools, and controls.

The emergence of professionalism in credit management

Consumer credit management has come a long way over the years and so have the credit managers who are responsible for the planning, organization, and control of credit activities.

The dynamic growth of the credit economy, the great waves of technological change connected with electronic computers, the expansion of credit legislation, and the need for improving customer relations have created new and serious challenges for the credit executive. The alert, well educated, and imaginative credit executive is accepting these challenges as opportunities to develop into a well rounded, management-oriented executive. More than ever before, he is working closely with sales, legal, advertising, and merchandising executives in planning to achieve company objectives and to improve the corporate image.

With the encouragement of management and in his eagerness to learn more about his job and his profession, the credit executive generally joins a trade association which assists him in dealing with problems in the areas of standardization, business ethics, statistics, trade promotion, and relations with the government and general public. He attends local and regional meetings and seminars, he participates in national conventions, he diligently keeps up to date with many trade publications and tries to take advantage of the special educational courses and research facilities provided by the professional credit associations.

Through these facilities and with experience on the job, many credit executives have become very professional. They have been asked by government agencies, elected officials, and others to serve as consultants on important consumer-oriented credit educational programs, family-counseling services, and legislative matters. As professionals, they have merited the recognition and acceptance of top management and have become very important in the total impact the firms' operations make on society as a whole and the communities in which they do business.

Establishment of sound credit policies in retail outlets

Thus far, we have discussed general aspects of the consumer credit industry which includes retail outlets, and financial institutions such as commercial banks, sales finance companies, credit unions, consumer finance companies, mutual banks, and savings and loan associations. In covering the particular subjects of credit policies, procedures, tools, and so on, we will confine the material to retail outlets.

Retail businesses engage in the sale of goods and services on credit because this is a corollary function essential to the dynamic growth in total company sales volume. Accordingly, credit plans and credit management functions have been developed in line with clearly conceived and defined principles and policies and are continuously refined and improved through experience in order to compete more successfully in the market place. Credit policies are generally formulated in terms of two objectives: maximizing sales and minimizing costs and bad debt losses.

Credit policy statements usually include: direction in new account and business development; a description of the credit plans and terms applicable to each; delineation of credit quality standards used in accepting business; and the specific procedures to be used in following up delinquent accounts. Policy statements should reflect positive thinking in harmony with the over-all objectives of the business.

Implementation of policy in day to day business practice

Irrespective of the size of the retail unit or the kinds of credit plans offered, the three main functions of the Credit Department are:
1. Establishing new business (interviewing, investigating, appraisal, and decision)
2. Controlling the account
3. Collecting the balance

The credit interview

The methods of conducting the interview in which the credit application is completed vary among retailers. Some prefer to conduct the interview in the Credit Department where a credit interviewer develops and records answers to questions on the application. This works well where there is adequate space and sufficient numbers of qualified interviewers.

Most credit managers prefer to conduct the interview in the Credit Department because they feel they can do a more effective job in training their own interviewers to counsel with the credit applicant in setting up a credit plan which will be tailored to the customer's needs. Since they will be responsible for controlling the account, they also feel that they should have the opportunity for opening the account.

In some stores, as a convenience to the customer, the salesmen are permitted to complete the credit application. This situation requires special training and careful supervision of the salesmen in order to prevent insufficient or inaccurate information or a misunderstanding of the credit terms established in the credit agreement.

Where a shortage of space and skilled interviewers has been a problem, management has permitted the credit applicant to complete the credit application. Many times, the applicant furnishes a more complete application and feels more comfortable in answering personal questions.

What is more important than who should do the interviewing is the development of the proper attitude toward the interview. The interviewer should be courteous, friendly, businesslike, and should regard the interview as an opportunity to convert the credit prospect into a credit customer, and to influence the customer in such a way that he will be well disposed toward the company.

Finally, a successful credit operation works on the premise that an account well opened is half collected; it knows that an incomplete

EXHIBIT 2

Credit Application

(Please Print)
Mr. First Initial Last (Wife's Name)
Mrs.
Miss.

Limit | Authorized Purchasers
1.
2.

Address

SRC ☐
EP ☐
MCP ☐

Interviewer | Authorized
(Date) | (Date)

City State Zip Code

Age Married ☐ Widowed ☐ Number of Dependents How Long at Present Address Own ☐ Rent ☐ Board ☐ Monthly Rent or Mortgage Payments $
Single ☐ Divorced ☐

Phone No. Former Address (If Less than 2 Yrs. at Present Address) How Long

Employer Address

How Long Occupation Social Security No. Time Card or Badge No. Earnings $ Monthly ☐ Weekly ☐

Former Employer (If Less than 1 Yr. with Present Employer) How Long

Account No.

Name and Address of Bank ☐ Savings ☐ Checking ☐ Loan Acc't No.

Explain Other Income, if, Any

ACCOUNTS AT OTHER STORES or BANK LOANS, FINANCE, ETC. Name of Firm Street Add. City & State Acct. No.		Date Opened	High Credit	Present Balance or Date Closed	Monthly Payments	How Paid
1.	Open					
	Closed					
2.	Open					
	Closed					
3.	Open					
	Closed					

Relative or Personal Reference (If No Credit References) Address City and State

application slows down the authorization, creates unnecessary work and expense, and could result in unnecessary later expense and bad-debt losses.

Credit applications vary among retailers, but all contain specific questions which will help to answer basic questions concerning the applicant's identity, location, ability to pay, and willingness to pay. A typical application is shown in Exhibit 2.

Planning the credit investigation

Generally, retailers follow the policy that no customer will be allowed a charge privilege or possession of merchandise until the credit application has been investigated and approved.

Under restricted conditions, however, some credit policies permit "on sight" approvals where the credit order is released immediately to expedite delivery. In those cases, an investigation is made at a later time to verify pertinent information, confirm the decision, and set the proper credit limit.

Most customers demand and have every right to expect prompt action on their applications, and failure to meet their expectations will often result in lost sales and lost permanent customers. It is necessary, then, to organize the credit-investigation section properly, and to set up standards specifying how much to investigate and where to check for verification in order to expedite the approvals.

How much is enough? Sources of credit information

In setting up guidelines for credit investigations, recognition must be given to certain facts. First, it is possible to over investigate or under investigate. Errors of judgment can result from having insufficient information. The credit decision could be different if the investigation revealed all the pertinent data.

On the other hand, extensive investigation is costly and may involve delaying the decision and thereby prompt the cancellation of a credit order and loss of customer goodwill. On many of the over-investigated applications, credit analysis may be difficult because the pertinent information may be buried under a mass of less important details.

As a general rule, the amount necessary to investigate is just that needed to make a decision. There can be no hard and fast rules since credit orders represent assortments and mixtures of credit prospects, merchandise, and credit terms all of which are important in making a decision. The experience and judgment of the credit executive is vital here since he will make the final decision.

Credit information is generally verified in four ways involving different sources:

1. Checking the firm's own records. The best source of credit history is a customer's past record with the merchant. Obviously, this verification can be done when the customer has an open or closed account in file.

2. Direct investigation. One of the quickest methods of checking facts on the application is directly contacting the employer, bank, business reference, etc. This information obtained is current and may contain additional details which the investigator skillfully obtained from the direct contacts. This method is frequently less costly.

3. Other lending institutions. Retail credit establishments, as a general rule, are willing, on reciprocal basis, to exchange information with other grantors with whom their credit customers wish to do business. This exchange provides up-to-date information which benefits the retailers involved.

4. Local credit reporting services. When speed is required and other direct sources of information are not available, credit information may be obtained (purchased) from credit-reporting services. These services include two kinds: 1) local retail credit bureaus, mutually or privately owned; 2) national reporting services like the Retail Credit Company of Atlanta, Georgia, and the Hooper-Holmes Bureau, Inc. Local retail credit bureaus are highly regarded and recognized as the most important sources for the exchange of credit information among retailers dealing with consumer credit.

Credit or risk analysis and decision making

The decision to use credit originates with the consumer and, whether it is right or wrong, it is his decision. The credit manager's problem is to screen out the acceptable risks from the unacceptable risks. This process is called credit analysis or risk analysis. Many credit executives consider credit analysis and credit decision making to be the most important credit activities in the department. All the efficiencies and economies realized through hard work in other credit activities may be offset by the loss of good business resulting from rejecting acceptable risks, or by bad-debt losses resulting from acceptance of bad credit risks.

3 C's of credit

Weighing and analyzing the credit risks is often very difficult and always requires sound judgment which improves with experience and a detailed study of the principle that a person's credit worthiness is related to the long-established and recognized 3C's of credit which are: Character, Capacity, and Capital. Briefly, *Character* involves the customer's reputation and behavior patterns and relates to willingness to pay. *Capacity* concerns the debtor's ability to pay from cash-flow specific obligations when due, and *Capital* deals with the financial strength of the customer, available if the customer were unable or unwilling to pay.

These 3C's are not independent of one another. For example, Capital is the result of past Capacity and, in some, evidence of Capacity for the future. Also, Capacity for producing income relates to Character, because obviously an unreliable person seldom attains a position commanding a high salary.

With the 3C's in mind, the credit analyst realistically determines what the verified credit facts reveal in regard to income, employment, payment habits, residence, marital and dependency status and reserve assets. These are referred to as "credit qualities."

Credit judgments must be made on specific cases and the weights placed upon the credit qualities must relate to the circumstances of the individual. In other words, the importance of these credit qualities varies with the individual.

Analyzing the consumer's capacity and character

In retail credit analysis, more weight and emphasis is generally placed upon Capacity and Character than on Capital. Accordingly, two factors must be established prior to approval:

1. The ability to pay based upon income versus commitments against that income (Capacity).
2. The willingness to pay based upon the reputation and behavior of the applicant—how he handles his obligations and responsibilities (Character).

In analyzing the applicant's ability to pay (which includes earning ability to generate sufficient income for the life of the credit contract) the analyst considers the amount of "take home" wages or salary (disposable income), the prospects for continued earnings, and the regularity of income. Additional income may include dividends, pensions, rental income, etc., and generally should not include the wife's wages if she is of child-bearing age and employed. The sudden withdrawal of a wife's income could cause a family financial problems which would affect repayments. In evaluating income, the analyst must also assess the economic outlook for the community and for the particular business from which income is derived.

Another factor to be analyzed is the extent of the debtor's obligations. The retail credit man looks at how many accounts the customer is committed to pay, how old the accounts are, and how the applicant is paying on current balances. He also projects the approximate amount of fixed expenses for the home mortgage or rent, the miscellaneous living expenses for food, utilities, etc., and relates them to income.

If trade information was purchased, and contained notices of repossessions, suits, judgements, or garnishments, the credit grantor would conclude that the applicant's ability to pay may have already been exceeded.

In reviewing these credit facts, the analyst is very much aware of the importance of establishing that the income is sufficient to cover existing payments as well as the new commitment since he is aware that buying in excess of ability to pay is the most common reason for bad-debt losses.

If the credit information evaluated thus far looks favorable, the analyst proceeds to examine the credit qualities which relate to the applicant's willingness to pay. Careful examination is made of verified credit references to determine how the debtor has paid or is currently paying his obligations. If credit bureau reports are purchased, they will be scrutinized for legal information concerning attorney action or referrals to collection agencies; both are indicators of the customer's unwillingness to pay.

Paying records on smaller bills for utilities and 30-day charge accounts are also reviewed. If these are not paid promptly the analyst would safely assume that the applicant may be involved in deeper financial problems.

Willingness to pay is closely related to character and the analyst studies credit facts including the address, marital status, and whether the customer owns, rents, or leases his dwelling. Experience has proven that home-owners are generally better credit risks than unestablished renters, and that settled married applicants rank higher in willingness to pay than unsettled single persons.

While there is disagreement on the importance of the applicant's occupation, most credit analysts do consider the classes of occupation in their risk appraisals. Some still feel that professional persons (physicians, engineers, dentists, etc.), are among the better risks, while seasonal workers or applicants employed for short periods in questionable businesses may be less desirable risks.

Final decision to accept or decline the credit applicant

The credit analysis has been made and the applicant meets the requirements for approval established in the credit policy. The credit manager has satisfied himself that the verified information clearly indicates that the customer has sufficient and steady income to meet his obligations and has demonstrated his willingness to pay; the application is approved. Generally, these cases represent approximately 75 to 80 percent of the total number of applications in retail stores operating with sound credit policies. Another 5 to 10 percent represent unacceptable risks which must be rejected. Obviously, these percentages will vary depending on the market and the objectives of a company's credit policies.

The remaining group represents cases where the credit information appears contradictory and reflects equal amounts of plus and minus factors. Good business would dictate that not all of these cases should be rejected because there is some doubt about the risk. Experience has shown that there are good risks among these applicants, but further efforts are necessary to discover who they are, and to separate them from the undesirable risks. This includes rechecking the information to determine if it is complete or whether facts stated in a general manner might, if made specific, solve the problem. For example, information regarding the applicant's business, job or amount of income may be vague or of a general nature. It may be, in these cases, that if the precise kind of business or job and exact income were ascertained, the credit manager could definitely decide more readily whether to accept or decline the credit order.

Also, in re-examining doubtful risks the credit manager seeks to determine whether or not a different interpretation, other than that originally made, might be placed on certain factors. An example would be interpreting credit-bureau information showing the applicant to be slow and undesirable at one retailer and prompt at another. There are differences as to what is regarded as prompt or slow by different lines and different retailers in the same line. The credit manager should always consider the source of information and recheck derogatory information in doubtful cases.

Rechecking of credit information to determine if it could be interpreted differently may show, after all, that many of the apparently contradictory facts may be disregarded or that, in reality, they are not contradictory at all. Also, from the recheck it may develop that the information does not add up to a fifty–fifty chance but clearly indicates an acceptance or rejection of the applicant.

Necessity for a second interview

In some of the doubtful cases, it may be necessary to interview the customer a second time to secure additional information, to get more precise information, or to work out a specific understanding on the use of the account. In such cases, the credit manager must carefully guard against being too willing to hear the applicant explain away the questionable facts. He should, instead, closely analyze the doubtful factors and make up his own mind that the customer's credit is acceptable.

Once the credit grantor has decided to accept or decline a credit applicant, he should never allow himself, except on receipt of new or corrected information, to be talked into changing his decision by the customer, by the salesman, or by anyone else. When he does, he not only exhibits a lack of courage and conviction, but invites trouble; experienced credit men claim that a substantial percentage of such decision reversals prove to be undesirable accounts.

Setting credit limits

Retail credit limits generally refer to the maximum amount of a credit a customer may charge or a maximum monthly payment he may not exceed. A better term would be "credit guides," as limits are generally not considered as absolutes, but merely as guides in handling the account; they may be changed as circumstances warrant.

The best time to establish limits is at the time the account is opened, since at that time the credit information is subjected to the most intensive review on the basis of current verification. Also, if the credit manager must approve a specific limit, he will necessarily make a more careful and penetrating analysis of all the credit facts.

There are definite advantages to establishing credit limits. From the credit department viewpoint, it relieves key credit personnel from constantly making credit decisions on credit purchases which will not cause the balance or monthly payment to exceed the limit. If good judgment is used in establishing the original limit, the account can be effectively controlled without further reexamination by the credit manager. This is especially helpful in the case of a doubtful credit risk where the account should be carried on a restricted basis.

From the customer's viewpoint, credit limits are desirable because they tend to restrict his temptation to overbuy or commit himself beyond his ability to repay.

While the use of credit limits is well recognized, and their advantages are very evident, it is difficult to recommend any one method for establishing limits. Some retailers use a limit which refers to the total amount which may be charged; others use a monthly payment limit. Some businesses start with a low limit and increase it with ledger experience, while others establish a limit which is the maximum a customer could charge at any time in the future. This could even be an "unlimited amount." Some retailers encourage the customer to fix his own limit; others mention that there will be a limit established after the credit analysis and approval have been made.

Credit selection by statistical evaluation

The determination of a credit risk has been largely a function of the credit manager's training, experience and judgment. The broader and lengthier the exposure of the credit manager, the better his credit decisions.

However, we also know that this area of judgment was not always consistent due to, in some cases, emotional factors.

Recently, however, many companies have been researching techniques which will provide the credit managers with a quantitative rating system for the evaluation of credit risks. These systems or processes have been called "point scoring," "credit scoring," "numerical scoring," "discriminate analysis" and "credit evaluation." Whatever they're called, they are simply a sort of mathematical evaluation of credit risks based upon the law of averages. The use of such systems reduces the possibility of judgment being influenced by irrelevant factors.

Statistical evaluation is not new. Insurance companies have used mathematical techniques to predict insurance risks for some time. Many personnel departments have used similar processes in personnel selection, through applying weighted numerical values to personal characteristics obtained from information on the employment application.

In determining the point scores, modern statistical techniques are employed to find the characteristics which, in fact, distinguish poor and good risks. These techniques result in the number of points that the presence of a characteristic (for example, having a telephone) should be assigned. The points are then totaled to get an overall score for the application and a "cutting score" is set which, on the average, eliminates a large number of poor risks, while keeping a large number of good risks.

Briefly, the process of developing a point scoring system involves the following:

1) Collecting random samples of the two classes of accounts that the system will distinguish, namely, the "good" accounts and the "bad ones" (delinquent and charged-off accounts).
2) Determining which characteristics are consistently associated with one or the other class of accounts.
3) Weighting the risk factors by assigning high weights to those characteristics associated with the good accounts and low weights to negative characteristics associated with the bad accounts.
4) Checking the weights against independent samples of good and bad accounts to determine whether the results hold up.

While the general principles guiding the development of a scoring system are straightforward, there are many complex technical problems that must be overcome. For example, the orientation of the system to profit (defines the score below which applications should be rejected) involves detailed cost studies. Costs and profit margins vary; each company has its own appeal and attracts its own clientele; legislation varies from state to state; financing costs fluctuate; all of these factors must be scrutinized by each company in setting up its scoring system which, obviously, will be different from that of its competitors.

An important fact to remember is that each system must fit the company's credit and sales philosophy and the geographic area in which it operates. These factors are subject to change, and therefore the basic characteristics that make up the scoring system must be periodically checked and updated.

Members of retail and financial institutions using point scoring have cited the following advantages:

1) Credit policy can be intelligently revised to meet the changing economic and merchandising situations.
2) It may provide guidance to less experienced credit managers in arriving at a credit decision.
3) It may reduce investigation costs, (credit bureau checks, especially) and work loads of credit investigations.
4) It provides for constant monitoring and control over the risk grade of new accounts.

From the experience gained thus far by firms now using a credit scoring technique, it would appear that a well-planned and developed scoring technique can be an invaluable aid to the credit manager and to the store management in providing consistent guides for approving credit, and assignment of a limit on the account. While the credit sales manager should always have the prerogative of "overriding" the system where unusual factors are encountered, a record should be kept of these exceptions and periodic checks made of the account workout. This will point out the accuracy of the system, or highlight a need for revision. It should be kept in mind that the key characteristics and their assigned weights are based on an analysis of past history of the accounts themselves, in the same location. The average credit manager will have added confidence if he is involved in developing the basic model.

Collection policy, system, procedures, and methods

The collection policy of any credit grantor is the other side of the coin of credit policy. Each is a part of the other and cannot be *unrelated* nor disconnected.

Credit policy is influenced by many considerations including resources available to the grantor, quality of the credit organization, the state of progress in technology, etc. Once an account is established there can be only one reasonable collection policy and that is to carry out the terms of the agreement.

The question of severity of tactics used to encourage payments is receiving considerable attention. While indiscriminate resort to legal remedies available is always less than desirable, on the other hand it should not be assumed that undue leniency is a service to either the customer in question, the grantor, the future of consumers, or the consumer-credit industry. The United States economy, which includes an annual cash flow of $95 to 100 billion in payments on consumer receivables, would be significantly influenced even by a modest deterioration in consumer paying habits.

Each grantor should accept his share of the ever-present need to educate new credit users to buy or borrow wisely and to repay faithfully according to the agreement. While discipline is not the only end in view, there is a growing awareness that the want of adequate personal discipline is often a forerunner of difficulties. The customer benefits from being educated to pay promptly because this habit contributes to sound family financial management and is conducive to a trouble-free family life.

Collection systems

Systems and procedures utilized by the credit department in implementing collection policy generally embody the following fundamental requisites:
1. Accurate records of the balance, debits and credits;
2. Routine and inexpensive methods of issuing casual reminders;
3. Definite procedures for identifying and following up on more serious accounts;
4. Written record of special collection follow-up;

5. Provision for classifying and recording the extent and stages of delinquency.

An effective collection system must provide for promptness and regularity of follow-up and must be organized to make maximum use of routine, less expensive, and less time-consuming methods of communication with those customers who require only casual contact. This frees the credit manager and his key personnel to devote appropriate time and attention to those problems which require skill and mature judgment to handle effectively.

Collection sytems utilizing electronic data processing equipment

Many retailers have converted their manual credit operations to mechanized systems using electronic computers. They have realized efficiencies and economies in bookkeeping and credit approval activities, and are becoming aware of the many advantages of a mechanized collection system. Electronic computers are discussed in Part V, "Information Technology" of this handbook.

Experience has shown that effectively managed mechanized systems, with rigid schedules and inspection of the flow of input detail, consistently produce and release statements with greater speed, accuracy, and economy than does a manual operation. This is particularly true during heavy selling periods before Easter, beginning of fall school terms, and Christmas when it is frequently impossible to handle manually the volume of billing media.

Promptness in dunning is also an important feature in a successful mechanized collection operation. Many systems provide for a printed collection message on the billing statement and at a definite time between statements during the early stages of delinquency. These procedures save postage, maintain collection follow-up on schedule, and allow collection personnel to concentrate on more serious collection problems which require aggressive and personalized handling.

Another important requirement of any sound collection system is the "aging" of accounts. The computer manages this accurately and with greater speed, and eliminates the errors and costs inherent in a manual operation. Helpful management reports may also be produced to indicate the number and "age" of the delinquencies for each collector or group on a weekly or monthly basis.

Under most manual systems, the collector follows up on delinquencies by reviewing all the ledgers assigned. In contrast, several mechanized systems provide for a monthly listing of only those accounts which need attention. In addition, there are "daily" programs which produce "activity messages" and alert the collector that a transaction took place on the delinquent account (a payment, a sale, or credit). These messages also cover customers who are "over-loading" and may need counseling.

There are many other refinements which have been programmed into the collection systems to assist the collection personnel to follow up on promises to pay, on account adjustments, and on other service work which is required.

Also, in some automated systems, as accounts are referred to collectors, attorneys, collection agencies or charged off as bad-debt losses, controls are set up in the computer. These controls are periodically and automatically reviewed, and ticklers may be generated automatically; eventually, cost and recovery figures are analyzed to provide a report of performance and to assist management in modifying credit and collection policies.

Although the computer has been a valuable tool in relieving collection personnel from routine and time-consuming activities, it has not been a substitute for aggressive, persistent, personal, and professional follow-up which rehabilitates debtors and profitably liquidates delinquent balances.

Helping the American consumer in financial difficulty

Because man is human, he suffers from social, economic and physical ills which may result from causes he cannot control nor foresee, or from conditions he himself creates through ignorance or carelessness.

Consequently, the users of credit and businesses offering credit services become involved in serious credit problems which require understanding, counseling, justice and legal remedies. Of serious concern is the steady growth of personal bankruptcies. In 1967, approximately 192,000 Americans sought relief in the bankruptcy courts. Millions of dollars were literally evaporated from the cash flow of the economy and everyone was a loser—the consumer, the creditor, and the community.

In an effort to perfect the consumer-credit mechanism and to do something before the government steps in, responsible leaders in the consumer-credit industry have supported programs involving remedial and preventative consumer-credit education, which appears to be the best approach to consumer-credit problems.

Remedial education is best provided through credit counseling which, in itself, is not a new idea. Retail credit men, bankers, and consumer financial businessmen have always counseled their customers on an individual basis. The new approach is to provide counseling through Consumer Credit Counseling Services which are non-profit, community organizations making adjustments with creditors and, when necessary, establishing adjusted-payment distributions within the income limits of families with financial problems. All of this is done with creditor cooperation and through counseling centers wholly supported and managed by responsible public-spirited professional civic leaders.

The National Foundation of Consumer Credit has taken an active and leading role in helping communities to start these counseling services.

While this organization neither establishes nor operates the counseling centers, it does provide "blueprints" for setting them up, and assigns staff members to consult with local founders and operators of counseling services.

Presently, there are over 100 centers throughout the country. They are encouraged with the results, and proud of the fact that they have brought back thousands of American families into responsible citizenship without the stigma and demoralizing effects of bankruptcy.

While credit counseling has been effective, it is not the final answer since it is mainly a remedial measure. An even more important approach is the expansion of preventative educational programs aimed at teaching young American students how to manage money, to budget, and to use credit wisely. Unfortunately, thousands of junior high school, high school, and college students never receive credit education.

In approaching this deficiency the National Foundation for Consumer Credit has undertaken the task of providing texts and outlines for courses now being taught in some 3,000 high schools. The Foundation is also designing new material for junior high and college students, and for adults who have missed this type of education in their schooling. Finally, the Foundation is working on courses for training teachers who will teach money-management subjects.

Leaders in the consumer-credit field strongly feel that the remedy for errors of poor judgment and disorder in our economic life is not found in legislation but in the leadership of those who care. They also realize that the key will be found in the way business makes good its responsibilities.

Trade accounts receivable and credit management

Bernard Kopel and Lloyd Sinnickson*

Accounts receivable are a major item in most business balance sheets. Depending upon the type of business, they may be the largest individual asset. To illustrate the range, a recent balance sheet of a leading grocery chain listed accounts receivable amounting to less than three percent of total assets, while a major chemical manufacturer had more than 15 percent of its assets in receivables, and a small company distributing industrial explosives had 48 percent. The SEC *Quarterly Report on Net Working Capital of U.S. Corporations* shows that accounts and notes receivable increased between December 31, 1950 and September 30, 1966 from 34 percent of current assets to 47, and from 68 percent of net working capital to 106. Receivables, as of September 30, 1966, totaled $202.8 billion. This does not include receivables of banks or insurance companies or amounts due from the U.S. government.

Most businesses both extend credit to customers and receive credit from their suppliers. Manufacturing corporations, as a group, extend more credit than they receive. The reason for this is apparent: The item for which they extend credit (their sales) far exceeds the principal item for which they receive credit (their purchases). The FTC-SEC *Quarterly Financial Report on Manufacturing Corporations* indicates that these corporations were net creditors to the extent of $40.5 billion, as of June 30, 1968.

During the past 20 years, corporate receivables have increased faster

---

* Vice President, The First National Bank of Boston, and General Credit Manager, American Cyanamid Company, Wayne, New Jersey, respectively.

than sales. Measured from 1950, sales rose 155 percent by 1965, while receivables were up 261 percent (Internal Revenue Service–*Statistics of Income*). Obviously, trade credit has become increasingly important in moving goods in the U.S. economy. How much further the trend can continue, without creating dislocations in the economic system, has not been established in the rather meager literature on the subject.

The magnitude of these figures suggests that credit management is an important aspect of financial management. The turnover rate of accounts receivable and the level of bad debts can have significant impact upon the earnings of a business. Dun & Bradstreet lists "receivables difficulties" among the major causes of the thousands of business failures they review each year. In addition, the way credit relations with customers are handled will add to or detract from customer goodwill.

Credit policies

Among the policy matters to be considered are the standards customers must meet in order to obtain credit, terms of payment offered, and the approach to collection of overdue accounts. The decisions made on these points will largely determine the rate of turnover of accounts receivable and the level of bad debt losses.

The standards of financial strength, payment performance, and credit reputation to be used in making decisions to grant or withhold credit

Competitors' standards, availability of the product in the market, and the credit quality of the typical customer are among the factors to be considered. A firm whose principal customers are major corporations will have few credit problems, while one selling extensively, for example, to retailers of infants' and children's apparel or to furniture manufacturers (in both of which the failure rate is very high) can expect a full quota of problems.

There are a number of possible approaches to minimizing credit problems. The extent to which these approaches are used will depend, to some degree, upon the size of the average transaction and the average account balance. If they are very small, it may be profitable to establish a blanket policy of approving all orders, up to a certain amount, without investigation, thus eliminating the expense of buying credit reports on small customers, reducing the order processors' and credit men's workloads, and speeding up service to customers.

If most orders from new accounts result from solicitation by salesmen and many of them involve more than minimum credit risk, it may be desirable to require the salesman to submit, with the order, a form on which he supplies information about the customer that will assist the

EXHIBIT 1

Salesman's Credit Information Report

SALESMAN'S CREDIT INFORMATION REPORT

FULL NAME OF CUSTOMER OR PROSPECT

DATE PREPARED

NAMES OF OWNERS IF PROPRIETORSHIP OR PARTNERSHIP

STREET ADDRESS

CITY & STATE

☐ CORPORATION   ☐ PARTNERSHIP   ☐ PROPRIETORSHIP   HOW LONG IN BUSINESS?

LINE OF BUSINESS

ESTIMATE OF AVERAGE MONTHLY BUSINESS WE MIGHT DEVELOP   WHEN IS FIRST ORDER ANTICIPATED?

APPEARANCE OF PREMISES   ☐ ABOVE AVERAGE   ☐ AVERAGE   ☐ POOR

YOUR OWN OPINION OF MANAGEMENT   ☐ ABOVE AVERAGE   ☐ AVERAGE   ☐ POOR

BANKS OF ACCOUNT	LOCATION
1	
2	
3	

MAJOR SUPPLIERS	LOCATION
1	
2	
3	
4	
5	

FINANCIAL STATEMENT: ☐ ATTACHED   ☐ WILL BE MAILED   ☐ OTHER

OTHER COMMENTS:

SALESMAN'S NAME

DIVISION

ADDRESS

credit department. This would include such information as references, any financial data the customer will provide, and his own impressions (for example, see Exhibit 1). This may help to discourage the salesmen from spending time on prospects with poor potential and avoid some very slow accounts and bad debts. There are many situations, though,

EXHIBIT 2

An Example of Order Limits

(based on Dun & Bradstreet ratings)

D & B Rating	Max. Order Limit	D & B Rating	Max. Order Limit
Aa A1	$15,000	Aa 1	$10,000
A + A1	12,000	A + 1	7,500
A A1	10,000	A 1	7,500
B + 1	10,000	B + 1½	5,000
B 1	7,500	B 1½	4,000
C + 1	7,500	C + 1½	2,000
C 1½	5,000	C 2	1,000
D + 1½	3,000	D + 2	1,000
D 1½	2,500	D 2	1,000
E 2	1,500	E 2½	750
F 2½	1,000	F 3	500
G 3	500		
−1	7,500		
−2	2,000		

EXHIBIT 3

An Example of Credit Limits

(based on Dun & Bradstreet ratings)

Rating	Amount	Rating	Amount
AaA1	$35,000	Aa1	$20,000
A + A1	25,000	A + 1	20,000
A A1	20,000	A 1	15,000
B + 1	20,000	B + 1½	12,000
B 1	15,000	B 1½	10,000
C + 1	15,000	C + 1½	10,000
C 1½	10,000	C 2	7,500
D + 1½	7,500	D + 2	5,000
D 1½	3,500	D 2	2,500
E 2	2,500	E 2½	1,500
F 2½	1,500	F 3	1,000
G 3	750	G 3½	500
H 3	500	H 3½	300
−1	10,000		
−2	2,500		

where the benefits do not justify burdening the salesmen with another reporting chore. A decision in this area should be thoroughly thought out.

Another area, in which a policy decision can be considered, is the possibility of using credit agency ratings (such as Dun & Bradstreet) without any further investigation, to permit approval of orders (Exhibit 2) and establishment of credit limits (Exhibit 3). This procedure will contribute to efficient use of credit department manpower, by quickly separating the orders or accounts which do not require study and individual judgement from those that do, provided that a substantial percentage of customers have agency ratings good enough to justify approval of their orders and the credit lines they require.

Banks are an excellent source of credit information. Arrangements should be made with each depository bank to provide the names of several people who will handle telephoned or written credit inquiries. To avoid imposing upon the banks or incurring an obligation to maintain unnecessarily large balances with them, this source should be used only when the amount of credit in question cannot be justified by the agency rating or, going one step further, the agency report. The inquiry should specify the amount of credit being considered and give some idea of what information is sought, to guide the bank in providing a reply that will be adequate, but not take more of their time and effort than necessary. An obviously routine inquiry will get a routine response. Sometimes, this is all that is needed.

Where the amount involved is substantial and the information available from all other sources is not adequate or suggests caution, communication directly with the customer is in order. He is the best source of information about himself and/or his firm. Usually, it is a good idea to talk to the salesman or someone in sales management before going directly to the customer. They may have information, which will help in the credit decision, or some thoughts about how best to approach the customer. Where the facts obtained from the customer still do not warrant extension of credit on the usual terms, the credit man may be able to arrange for the sale to be made on a secured or guaranteed basis. If not, either the sale will be declined or, sometimes, the general management may decide that other factors make it desirable to conclude the sale on a credit basis, despite the greater-than-usual risk. Such cases should be very rare, or the basic credit policy changed.

Some limit should be set on toleration of slow payments. Such accounts are expensive to the creditor in two ways–loss of use of the money and increased bad debts. The longer that financially weak customers are carried, the more there will be owed by those that fail to pay. It is unrealistic to expect that every customer will pay when due. This could be accomplished, in most cases, only by sacrificing sales that still are profitable even with somewhat delayed payments. The problem is to determine the cut-off point, beyond which the loss of use of the money and risk of bad debts wipe out the profit. It is good practice to periodically analyze the profitability of the slowest paying accounts, to see whether there are some that should be dropped if they cannot be induced to pay more promptly. Not all customers, upon whom this pressure is brought to bear, will be lost; some will pay more promptly.

Terms of payment offered to customers

A firm will be unable to offer terms less favorable to customers than those prevalent in the market, unless it enjoys a dominant position in its industry, its product is in short supply, its quality or service is superior, or its price lower. It sometimes is advantageous to offer a cash discount for prompt payment, to reduce the investment needed in receivables and potential bad debts. This is especially apt to be true in a field characterized by a high percentage of slow-paying customers, a situation which may create problems, not only in accounts receivable turnover, but also in customer relations. When poor adherence to terms becomes generally known, prompt-paying customers resent the advantage some of their competitors enjoy, of free working capital furnished by the supplier through toleration of slow payments.

Rarely is it possible to justify incurring the expense of a cash discount, by the cost-of-money value of the reduction in receivables. For example, if customers paying in an average of 60 days on net terms can be induced by a two percent discount to pay in an average of 30 days, the supplier is paying two percent to get his money one month sooner or 24 percent per annum. This is too high a price to pay. However, at the time of a price change, upward or downward, the price can be set higher than otherwise planned, by an amount sufficient to provide for a cash discount. In this case, it costs the supplier nothing, the discounting customer pays the same amount he would with the lower price and no discount, but pays sooner, and the slow-paying customer pays a higher price, which is appropriate.

Some trade creditors do not favor cash discounts, citing the difficulties of dealing with customers who pay after the discount period has expired but take the discount anyway. To rebut this, it can be pointed out that it is no more difficult to deny such a customer unearned discount than it is to induce him to pay within, or closer to, net terms. There is no question that discount terms can bring in the money sooner and are more equitable in cases where compliance with net terms has deteriorated.

Another question to consider is whether to use credit aggressively, as a means to improve the firm's competitive position, or restrict credit accommodations to the customary practices in the trades in which the firm is engaged. In the former case, there is the danger that competitors will offer customers the same facilities, so that no supplier gains any competitive advantage, but they all find themselves with larger investments in receivables. Needless to say, the antitrust laws do not permit any discussion between competitors of credit terms any more than of price. It is up to each supplier to find out for himself what is going on in the market, then decide whether to meet all competition, go beyond it, or try to hold the line.

Apart from *terms* of payment, some underfinanced customers use all they can of their suppliers' money for working capital, and become quite expert in getting suppliers to accept their payments late without cutting off further credit. Frequently, a supplier cannot be sure to what extent an existing or prospective customer is bluffing about his ability to get a greater degree of tolerance from a competitive supplier. His decision about how to react to such pressure will be affected by how much he needs the sales volume, whether the margin of profit will permit the additional cost of a larger receivables investment, his evaluation of the buyer's credit, and the adequacy of his own working capital.

Getting back to credit *terms* rather than the way they are administered, it sometimes is possible for a total market to be enlarged by liberal credit extended by suppliers. A notable example has been the fertilizer market. The use of fertilizer on crops grew very rapidly in the United States during the 1950's and 1960's. Presumably this was due, in part, to the willingness of fertilizer manufacturers to permit farmers to pay a large part of the bill after selling the crops. (Unfortunately, production facilities for fertilizers were expanded even faster than sales, prices declined, and manufacturers' earnings did not reflect the market growth.) A happier picture, and a very familiar one, is presented by the appliance and automobile industries, whose growth was made possible by credit extended to consumers, retailers, and distributors by banks and finance companies. This, however, is not trade credit.

The question may arise whether the firm will factor its accounts receivable or carry the investment itself. There are certain fields, such as garment and carpet manufacturing, in which tradition will encourage a decision to factor. The availability of factoring concerns well acquainted with customers, with industry practices, and with sources of information in these fields tends to facilitate such a decision. Chapter 48, "Short-Term Financing," discusses in detail the decision whether or not to factor.

Collection of overdue accounts

Questions include: how long after the due date an account will be followed and how frequently thereafter, at what stage to turn accounts over to collection agencies, and whether to use company attorneys in the collection procedures. How diligently and effectively accounts are followed will have a bearing upon the rate of turnover and the size of the investment in accounts receivable, as well as the amount of bad debt losses. The collection policy also will affect, and be affected by, the approach to staffing. To illustrate, one major manufacturing firm operates with a very low ratio of credit staff to sales volume and number of accounts. They refer overdue accounts to collection agencies, after relatively few requests by their own people for payment. The collection agencies eagerly solicit this company's business, because they have a high percentage of collections on the company's accounts referred to them. Another manufacturer, of about the same size, has a far larger credit staff. They hate to give up on an overdue account, and the ones that reach the collection agencies have little life left in them. There may be other reasons for the difference in size of these two companies' credit departments, but the collection policy almost certainly is part of the story. Either of these approaches can be overdone, but, as a general statement, the first is preferable. It permits the credit staff to concentrate on those accounts with better potential, both for collection and for future sales.

Many companies extending trade credit think accounts should be followed 10 to 15 days after the due date and at two-week intervals thereafter. Form letters generally are used for the first two or three reminders, after which the credit man composes letters, he thinks will be effective in the particular situation, or telephones the customer. Copies of the specially composed letters are sent to the salespeople concerned, to keep them advised of collection problems approaching the serious stage. They may attempt to assist, if they wish, but most companies do not require salesmen to involve themselves in collection problems, leaving it to their judgement to volunteer where they see fit. If the credit man hears nothing from the salesman, he proceeds with his collection efforts. It is not desirable for him to get bogged down in a series of reminders to the salesman, while the customer hears nothing of any request for payment.

Some companies involve their own legal staff in collection problems, before sending them to collection agencies. There may be cases where this is desirable, but it is questionable whether it is a good general practice. Most corporation attorneys can be used more effectively on higher level legal work. The collection agencies and most attorneys working with them are specialists, and generally, are quite effective.

Organization and administration

These comments concern manufacturers, wholesalers, and retailers with large enough credit functions to require the full-time services of several people. The credit activity in banks and other financial institutions requires somewhat different organization. In many such institutions, every officer functions, to some extent, as a credit man; and the role of the credit department is to gather facts, which are presented to officers to aid in decision making (or, sometimes, to customers as a service, in the case of banks).

In most manufacturing or trading companies, the credit function reports to the treasurer. A publication of Credit Research Foundation, entitled "Credit Department Profile," reports that, among companies surveyed in 1967, the top credit man reported to:

	Number	Percent
Treasurer*	78	55
Financial vice president	12	9
President	11	8
Comptroller	16	11
Assistant treasurer	9	6
Vice president	5	4
Other	10	7
	141	100

* Including officers with titles "vice president and treasurer" and "secretary and treasurer."

Line or staff responsibility

The credit department may have either line or staff responsibility. Most commonly, it has line responsibility for credit extension, collections, credit relations with customers, turnover of the investment in accounts receivable, bad debt losses, and, sometimes, accounts receivable bookkeeping. These responsibilities, except the last mentioned, may be shared, to some degree, with management of operating divisions or departments.

There are companies, including some very large ones, in which a central credit department has a purely staff role. It advises operating divisions or departments regarding their credit activities, which are administered by credit people reporting to the operating management. General Electric Company is an example of this type of credit organization, which grows out of a corporate philosophy of decentralizing to the fullest possible extent, making managers of operating divisions and departments responsible for every aspect of their operations. Other companies, while decentralized, think that credit belongs with such things as taxes, insurance, banking, and employee benefits, under corporate rather than divisional control.

Areas of responsibility

Areas of responsibility for credit people in a large company may be delineated by product line (*i.e.*, operating divisions, departments, or subsidiaries), by geographical territory, by degree of credit risk, or by marketing level (*i.e.*, sales to manufacturers, wholesalers, retailers, farmers, consumers, government). Some of the larger companies employ a combination of areas of responsibility, in an effort to achieve maximum efficiency in each of a variety of product lines. A refinement, employed in some companies, is to classify accounts by degree of risk, for the purpose of assigning the highest risk accounts to their most experienced, best qualified credit men and the relatively risk-free accounts to clerks or junior credit men, with perhaps one or two gradations between. In a company with a large number of accounts, varying in size and quality, this approach will contribute to efficiency. As in any other area of the business, the objective is to maximize earnings by getting the best combination of quality of results with costs.

Staff development

Most young men going into credit today have bachelor's or master's degrees in finance, business administration, economics, or, occasionally, marketing. As in all areas of business, they are better educated than the previous generation. Hundreds of trade credit people, mostly on the management level, and hundreds of bankers have attended the Graduate School of Credit and Financial Management sessions at Dartmouth, Stanford, Harvard, and Tulane. The three-year program requires attendance two weeks each year and completion of a thesis. The curriculum includes: financial management, economics of money and credit, marketing, managerial psychology, computer applications to credit and financial decision making, and a management policy seminar.

A career in credit can be quite rewarding for an able man or woman with the right temperament. Credit people enjoy the mixture of financial analysis, a certain amount of routine administration, and negotiations with customers.

Evaluating the credit function

Why do businesses spend, on this activity, sums ranging from a few thousand dollars a year, in small companies, to several millions in very large organizations? The role of the credit department is to collect accounts as rapidly as possible with minimum bad debts, without significant loss of profitable business to competitors for credit reasons. The goal is to achieve the optimum blend of sales, turnover of investment in receivables, bad debt expense, and credit department operating costs.

TURNOVER OF INVESTMENT IN RECEIVABLES. One way to measure turnover of investment in accounts receivable is to calculate the number of days sales outstanding. There are a number of ways to make this calculation, most of which are satisfactory, if applied consistently. The Credit Research Foundation, in its quarterly surveys of domestic trade receivables, uses the following method:

$$\frac{\text{Average A/R Balance Last 3 Month-ends} \times 90}{\text{Sales for Last 3 Months}} = \text{Days Sales Outstanding (D.S.O.)}$$

However it is measured, turnover of receivables by U.S. corporations as a whole has been slowing down during the entire post-World War II period. The CRF surveys of manufacturers' D.S.O. show a steady increase since their inception:

Annual Averages

Year	D.S.O.	Year	D.S.O.
1959	33.9	1964	36.3
1960	33.8	1965	38.6
1961	33.8	1966	39.5
1962	34.7	1967	40.1
1963	36.5	1968	40.6

The rate of increase has not been uniform in all industry groups. Presumably, the differences in rate of increase arise from variations in competitive pressures in the various industries.

BAD DEBT EXPENSE. Factors affecting the level of bad debt expense include:
1. The number of days sales outstanding. Obviously, the larger the investment in receivables, the greater the exposure to possible bad debts.
2. Effectiveness of the collection follow-up. Customers with overdue accounts should be promptly and regularly reminded. If four or five reminders do not produce payment or some satisfactory response, the account probably should be referred to a collection agency.
3. The quality of the accounts approved for credit. This will depend, in part, upon the industry or trade involved. In some industries, where materials are in plentiful supply and competition between suppliers is intense, buyers exact concessions from their suppliers in the form of extra time for payment. They tend to become dependent upon generous trade credit as a source of working capital. In such cases, the typical customer may have a high ratio of debt to equity, and a supplier with a financially distressed, perhaps bankrupt, customer may be owed for a number of months' purchases.

In the consumer credit field, a number of companies have developed scoring systems which enable them to rate credit applicants and refuse credit to those falling below a minimum score. They have been able, in many cases, to reduce their bad debt losses below the level experienced with a less structured approach to credit screening.

Some attempts have been made, with little success to date, to use the scoring technique in trade credit. The main obstacle is the absence of sufficient criteria uniformly available for all customers, comparable to criteria available for consumer credit applicants, such as "how long in present job," "how long at present address," "owns or rents," and "annual income."

OPERATING COSTS. A median figure for total credit department overhead, not including bad debts, is about one-tenth of one percent of sales.

Seventy percent of this figure is centered in payroll and related expense, with an additional eight percent in costs of credit reporting services, five percent in travel and entertainment, four percent in fees for collection agencies and/or attorneys, about four percent in communications expense, and five percent for various office services. The remaining four percent includes: supplies, forms and printing; memberships; employee relocation; educational grants and programs; and miscellaneous expense. (See Credit Research Foundation, "Credit Department Profile.")

Use of computers in accounts receivable bookkeeping and production of credit reports

There has been a strong trend in this direction, as there has been in using computers in other areas of business. The timing, in converting accounts receivable and credit records to the computer, may be influenced by such factors as: availability of electronic data processing equipment and people; integration with other systems, such as billing; the number of invoices, payments, and accounts; and the relative complexity of the system required. On the last point, a firm with numerous divisions or product lines, wishing to keep records of accounts receivable investment by division or product line, and, with many variations in terms of payment, will require a relatively complex system, the design and programming of which may require several man-years effort by systems analysts and programmers. Where a simple system is adequate, it may be possible to use one of the systems available at computer service bureaus, perhaps with minor modifications. The reader is referred to Part V for a general discussion of the design and implementation of computer systems.

Many credit people feel that use of computers has great potential for helping develop better systems of credit management information. Such usage is in its infancy; most systems so far developed do little more than substitute for the old ledger cards or tabulating equipment. Some progress has been made, however. One company, for example, has included in its system classification, by the computer, of each account as high risk or normal risk. The computer compares the amount owed and the Dun & Bradstreet rating with a schedule indicating the maximum amount a customer in each Dun & Bradstreet rating bracket ("High" and "Good" credit appraisal only) may owe and be considered normal risk. If the total owed exceeds that amount, the computer puts the account into the high risk category.

This is a rough system of classification, intended to provide a census of customers in each division. It has no significance so far as action taken in handling any customer's account is concerned. It does provide tangible and consistent information about "marginal accounts," which usually are talked about in a subjective way, without providing any objective stand-

EXHIBIT 4

Monthly Report of Accounts Past Due by Department

DEPT UAT   DATE 02 28 69

(Handwritten annotations)
- *Includes only high risk accounts owing at least $3,000 and more than 30 days past due.*
- *add up 7 days past due* (circled, pointing to CURRENT)
- *Credit assignment field / needs to effect the account receivable is assigned* (pointing to CR ASSIGN 40)
- *Credit Risk B indicates a high risk account* (pointing to CR ASSIGN 76 · CR-B)

CUSTOMER NO	Name / CR ASSIGN	BALANCE	CURRENT	PAST DUE 8-30	PAST DUE 31-60	PAST DUE 61-90	PAST DUE 91-120	PAST DUE OVER 120
0092690	██ INCORPORATED · CR ASSIGN 40 · CR-B	86,672.65	46,984.64 BLVD	39,011.51	676.50 CAL			
0093783	CORP · CR ASSIGN 14 · CR-B	20,343.64 ST	10,215.69	3,272.14 NEW YORK	6,855.81 N Y 10019			
1647250	CORPORATION · CR ASSIGN 42 · CR-B	106,972.55	85,377.85 AVENUE SOUTH	18,152.00	OHIO			3,442.70
2967110	CORPORATION · CR ASSIGN 74 · CR-B	13,315.08	1,363.50	6,185.84	5,765.74 WASH			
3145659	CO · CR ASSIGN 74 · CR-B	3,280.00			CAL			3,280.00
3443830	██ CORPORATION · CR ASSIGN 18 · CR-B	74,592.87 ROAD	50,328.19	23,700.38	CONN	45.40		818.90
3826740	██ INCORPORATED · CR ASSIGN 44 · CR-B	101,648.01	103,045.48	125.83	197.53- TEX	1,606.50		57.73
7041945	CO · CR ASSIGN 76 · CR-B	53,045.56	34,754.24	19,799.79	2,370.63- CAL	862.16		
7167910	██ CORPORATION · CR ASSIGN 76 · CR-B	223,046.21	195,730.87	14,200.00	5,453.22 CAL	5,977.98		1,684.14
7173367	██ INDUSTRIES · CR ASSIGN 76 · CR-B	9,765.11	3,208.54	•1,776.40	4,780.17 CAL			
DEPT TOTAL		692,681.68	527,709.00	126,223.89	20,963.28	8,492.04		9,293.47

ards for determining which accounts are marginal or measuring the overall impact in the creditor firm. This company knows, by department, how much of its sales are to high risk customers, how its receivables investment breaks down between high risk and normal risk accounts, and how the accounts in each risk category turn over. Its computer produces monthly reports for each operating department management showing overdue high risk accounts above a certain amount (Exhibit 4). This keeps the managers informed as to where their credit problems are and which customers' accounts need to be improved or eliminated in order to improve the department's turnover of accounts receivable. These reports also help credit management forecast the company's investment in receivables, as well as highlighting the areas most in need of attention.

Bibliography

Securities and Exchange Commission, *Quarterly Report on Net Working Capital of U.S. Corporations.*

U.S. Government Printing Office, Division of Public Documents, *Quarterly Financial Report on Manufacturing Corporations.*

Treasury Department, Internal Revenue Service, *Statistics of Income.*

Credit Research Foundation, Inc., Lake Success, N.Y., *National Summary of Domestic Trade Receivables.*

Credit Research Foundation, Inc., *Credit Department Profile.*

Inventory management and control

John N. Hart*

This chapter presents current practice in inventory management and control. In it, policy decisions necessary for effective inventory management are discussed, as are other facets such as planning and organizing for inventory management and the use of budgets as an aid to management and control. Note is taken of the expanding use of computers and operations research techniques. Other chapters in this *Handbook* discuss accounting for inventories, the use of models and simulation, make or buy decisions, and forecasting—all topics important to the most effective inventory management.

Planning for inventory management

Policy decisions

The types of policy decisions to be made about inventory management are similar regardless of the size and complexity of the business. However, all decisions may be made by one man in the simpler businesses, while a separate level of top management will usually be concerned with policy decisions in the more complex businesses.

The decisions to be made will be used as guides by the organization in establishing its program and controls so that a suitable rate of return will be earned on the inventory investment. The policy decisions will cover:
1. Products to be sold, including a periodic review of existing or proposed lines to consider additions, deletions, or a change of emphasis within existing lines.
2. Markets to be served, including consideration of new market opportunities or withdrawal from unsatisfactory markets.

---

* Vice President and Controller, The B. F. Goodrich Co., Akron.

3. Distribution methods, including the appraisal of the use of field sales forces, dealers, agents, or others. Warehousing and transportation should be considered in establishing the policies on distribution.
4. Inventory investment, which should be guided by the establishment of a goal or goals in total dollars or in turns in sales that will set top-management limits on capital invested in inventory.
5. Speculative purchasing, which requires the establishment of limits to control the amount that is permissible. This policy will require continual review.

Organization

The highest level of policy and authority should be exercised at a senior executive level. In some instances this function is assigned to a committee made up of the senior executives responsible for sales, manufacturing, and purchasing. The senior financial officer or controller is also a member of this committee. Whether the responsibility for inventories is assigned to an individual or to a committee, the interests of all the major functions of the business must be considered. The policies and decisions should balance the interests of each function so that the best overall results are realized for the entire business. A basic organization chart, indicating also the source of data for planning and controlling inventories is shown in Exhibit 1. The corporate staff positions, as well as that of divisional president, would be eliminated in a company that is not divisionalized. The staff functions would be assumed by the functional executives and their staffs.

EXHIBIT 1

Organization for *Inventory Management*

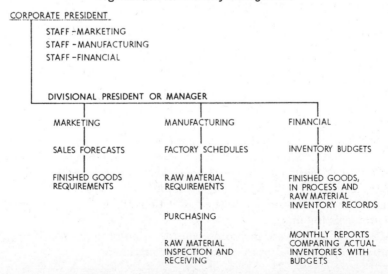

CORPORATE PRESIDENT
   STAFF -MARKETING
   STAFF -MANUFACTURING
   STAFF -FINANCIAL

DIVISIONAL PRESIDENT OR MANAGER

MARKETING	MANUFACTURING	FINANCIAL
SALES FORECASTS	FACTORY SCHEDULES	INVENTORY BUDGETS
FINISHED GOODS REQUIREMENTS	RAW MATERIAL REQUIREMENTS	FINISHED GOODS, IN PROCESS AND RAW MATERIAL INVENTORY RECORDS
	PURCHASING	
	RAW MATERIAL INSPECTION AND RECEIVING	MONTHLY REPORTS COMPARING ACTUAL INVENTORIES WITH BUDGETS

The committee or individual should furnish guidelines to be followed in organizing the inventory management and control function. Any guidelines should clearly define authority as well as responsibility. The larger and more complex the organization, the more likely it is that both authority and responsibility will be joint rather than individual.

Consideration should be given to careful selection of the people who will actually perform the management and control function. Failure to achieve effective inventory control can often be traced to inadequately trained or unqualified people. In some instances, it may be desirable to establish a training program that will not only include a review and explanation of policy decisions but will also teach the control methods that are to be used or that are available for use.

The above committee or individual will decide the reporting that will be required to allow the discharge of the assigned responsibility for the actual management and control performances.

Budgets

To implement an effective inventory management program, it is necessary to devise a means of measuring the results of actual operations. Current practice includes many measures, such as dollars invested; turns in sales; days, weeks, or months of coverage; and minimum-maximum inventory levels.

A business with a complete budget program can use any of the above measures to coordinate inventory control with the budget. Many of the factors which must be considered in establishing supplementary goals, such as turnover, coverage, or minimum-maximum inventories, are also necessary in budgeting purchases, production, and inventories.

Exhibit 2 shows a typical finished goods inventory budget. The inventory amounts and turns are shown for January, December, and average for the year. In actual practice, the same data are shown for each month. While dollars have been shown in this exhibit, units may be used where applicable. Turns are based on the budgeted sales.

EXHIBIT 2

Finished Goods Inventory Budget

Item	January Amount	Turns	(show for each) (month in year)	December Amount	Turns	Average Amount	Turns
Finished Goods							
Product A	$3,600	5.4		$3,800	5.2	$3,700	5.3
Product B	1,000	3.8		1,200	3.3	1,100	3.5
Product C	1,250	7.2		1,350	7.1	1,300	7.1
Product D	1,700	2.3		1,900	2.8	1,700	2.9
Total	7,550	5.0		8,250	4.8	7,800	4.9

Top management is thus provided with a means of assuring that the decisions regarding inventory are reflected in the budget. The budget then permits the comparison of actual performance with top management plans and desires. Whether control is accomplished by inventory budgets or supplementary reports of actual dollars, coverage or turns as compared to goals will depend generally on which method produces the desired result at the lowest cost. Any of these methods may be supplemented at the inventory management level by the development and use of economic order quantities and reorder points.

Organizing for inventory management and control

Select the organization

The responsibility for inventory management is generally assigned to the executives responsible for marketing, production, and financial control or to their delegates. It is their responsibility to understand the policies established to guide their operation and to organize so that effective management of inventory is achieved.

Here, as at the policy level, it is essential that the needs of the sales, manufacturing, purchasing, and financial functions be given careful consideration. The manager of one of these four functions or his delegate may be made primarily responsible for the management of inventories. Another option is to name an inventory manager who is primarily responsible for the management and control of inventories, working with the sales, manufacturing, purchasing, and financial managers. In either case, it must be understood that the end purpose is to obtain the best results for the whole business rather than any of its parts.

In selecting the organization, it is advisable to have available, either as a member of the organization or in a staff position, a person or persons proficient in the use of operations research techniques. Such people can aid in finding solutions to inventory related problems. They can also help to familiarize the inventory management with operations research techniques that can be used to aid in making inventory management decisions. Examples are economic order quantities, which are concerned with how much to order or make, and reorder points, which are used to decide when to order.

Establish authority and responsibility

It is important that responsibilities and authority for inventory management and control be clearly defined. Primary responsibility will differ for the different types of inventories. Purchasing or production managers will usually control raw materials and supplies. In process inventory is the responsibility of production management. Finished goods inventory is usually the responsibility of sales management with the production management being responsible for producing the schedule provided to them; and the purchasing management having the responsibility for obtaining the products purchased for resale.

To aid in clarifying the authority and responsibility of the various people involved in this function and to provide instructions for performing the assigned responsibilities, many companies develop inventory procedural manuals. If a decision is made to do this, it will be necessary to provide staff to keep the manual on a current basis.

Establish reporting practices

The reporting required will depend to some extent upon the organization that is established. Reporting needed for the more detailed management and control functions is discussed in the inventory management section of this chapter.

The reporting selected should provide top management with the means of observing actual performance in relation to a goal or budget. In addition to any periodic reports of performance, a report of trends of that performance is also desirable. A trend is more indicative of long range adherence to top management policies and goals than is the performance in any one period.

EXHIBIT 3

X Y Z COMPANY

INVENTORY CONTROL REPORT

19___

	Jan.	Feb.	March	April	May	June	July	Aug.	Sept.	Oct.	Nov.	Dec.
Product A	3,800											
Turns - Goal	5.4											
Actual	5.2											
Product B	1,000											
Turns - Goal	3.8											
Actual	3.9											
Product C	1,150											
Turns - Goal	7.2											
Actual	7.1											
Product D	1,600											
Turns - Goal	2.3											
Actual	2.5											
Total Finished Goods	7,550											
Turns - Goal	5.0											
Actual	4.9											

The goals in turns are taken from the finished goods inventory budget shown in Exhibit 2.
Each month is added to the report as actual results are available.

Reporting should be a periodic, usually monthly, comparison of actual inventory position to expected inventory position. Reports can show actual dollars of inventory, in whatever detail is considered desirable, as compared to actual dollars of inventory in a budget. The comparison can also be made to goals expressed in months of coverage or turns in cost of sales. Exhibit 3 on page 5 is an example of such a report.

One effective method of reporting is to chart dollars of inventory by major classification, that is, finished goods, in process, and raw materials. The same chart can also show a 12-month moving average of turns, or months coverage, or any period other than 12 months that may be appropriate. Turns or coverage based on actual results for each month can also be shown. This provides a trend and also indicates the deviations from that trend in any month. In multiproduct companies, charts by product line will also be useful.

If a budget program is in use, the actual inventory turns can be compared with the planned inventory turns used in developing the budget for return on capital employed.

Inventory management

Advantages of inventory management

A well-organized and efficiently operated inventory management program will have many advantages. Some are:

1. Inventories are kept at a level that provides the desired customer service in relation to the cost of providing the service.
2. Costs resulting from excess handling, storage, obsolescence, and so forth, are reduced.
3. Raw materials are available as required, minimizing production delays.
4. Manufacturing efficiency is improved by leveling production through absorbing demand fluctuation in inventory.
5. Information on inventories and their handling costs permits better purchasing decisions.
6. Investment in storage facilities may be reduced.
7. Inventories can be standardized and simplified.

Inventory levels

Inventory levels are determined by the person or persons responsible for inventory management, acting within the limits established by top management policy. Any decisions about inventory levels are usually preceded by a classification of the various items in inventory in relation to usage. It is probable that a small number of items in the inventory will account for a large share of the total usage, while the larger share of the items in inventory will support a small share of the total usage. It is not uncommon to find that 20% to 25% of the items in inventory account for

75% to 80% of the usage. The classification of inventory into levels of activity can be expanded to recognize the high-cost and low-cost items in each activity layer.

The fast-moving, high-cost items require the most attention and should be reviewed more frequently than other inventory categories. As activity or value diminishes, the controls can be relaxed, so that the slow-moving, low-cost items will be controlled by judgment based on limited records without the necessity of a more elaborate control system.

To determine inventory levels, information is required that will normally include forecasts of demand or sales, cost of carrying inventory, costs of obtaining inventory (order costs), and costs of not having inventory (stock-out costs).

Sales forecasts

Sales forecasts are very important to the proper operation of an inventory control system. Forecasts may be made by averaging the previous 12 months' sales and assuming that the subsequent months will equal the average. This approach is valid only if demand is constant, which rarely happens. The forecast can be improved by adjusting for seasonality or for any other known or expected deviation from the average.

Sales forecasts are used to determine the amount of inventory required to meet future demand. Inventory budgets established in turns or coverage permit revisions in inventory levels as sales requirements change. To the extent that forecasts are inaccurate, sales will be lost or inventory excesses will develop, either of which condition will cause unfavorable deviations from the inventory control plan and will affect the company's profit.

This subject is discussed in depth in Chapter 22. Suffice it to repeat here that, all other factors being equal, the more accurate the forecast, the better the control procedure will function.

Inventory related costs

INVENTORY CARRYING COSTS. The costs of carrying inventory, which increase or decrease in relation to the amount of inventory carried, include taxes (primarily personal property), insurance, obsolescence, handling and storage, and the cost of money.

1. *Taxes.* Tax costs will be a combination of the rate at the location being considered, the valuation of the inventory for tax purposes, and any policy which provides for reducing inventories on tax declaration dates.

2. *Insurance.* These costs are usually readily available from the insurance policies or accounting records of the business.

3. *Obsolescence.* Inventories of items with a style life, a seasonal pattern, or which are perishable, probably have the greatest risk of obsolescence. Highly engineered products also have a greater obsolescence risk than standard items. This cost cannot be readily determined from the usual records unless the company has recognized the importance of this cost in their particular operation, in which case accounting procedures may have been developed to determine the cost of obsolescence.

4. *Handling and Storage.* These are the costs relating to getting inventory into and out of storage and to providing space for storage. While these costs will normally increase or decrease with inventory, there is more likely to be a step relationship than a straight-line relationship to inventory dollars. To the extent that higher priced items require additional care or protection, the relationship may be more direct. The concern of inventory managers is the change in this cost as compared to the amount of inventory ordered or carried. This relationship may be more difficult to determine for these costs than for other inventory carrying costs.

5. *The cost of money.* This should be either a minimum amount representing the interest cost on the investment in inventory or the amount that could have been earned had this money been invested in the best alternative use.

ORDER COST. While normally considered to be the costs of ordering an item or the setup and change costs for a manufactured item, other costs, such as receiving and inspection of the goods, the accounts payable function, and the scheduling function, are also a part of this cost category.

Usually a business that is operated under a budget system will have data on the cost to issue a purchase order, to receive and inspect a unit or dollar of product, and to audit and pay an invoice. These costs should exclude all costs which do not change as activity changes. These data can be used to calculate order costs.

STOCK-OUT COSTS. Stock-out costs can result either from not having a product available for sale when required or, in a manufacturing operation, from being out of raw materials or component parts needed in the manufacturing process. In the latter event, excess costs that result from disruption of the manufacturing process are a part of stock-out costs.

Stock-out costs that result from not having a product available for sale when required, whether the product is produced or purchased, while readily defined, are nearly impossible to determine.

These stock-out costs include the incremental profit that would have been earned on the lost sale if the customer goes elsewhere to satisfy his needs. If he agrees to wait for delivery, stock-out costs are limited to the costs of issuing back orders plus any additional costs that are incurred to expedite delivery. If the customer accepts a substitute, the stock-out cost would be limited to the difference in profit on the item sold as compared to the item preferred. The ultimate cost could be that, having taken his business elsewhere, the customer never returns. Too many of these events, and the firm's reputation for service (goodwill) could be damaged.

Computers—operations research

Proper inventory management has always been a difficult problem. The larger and more complex the inventory, the more difficult it is to manage and control.

Computers and operations research are discussed in Chapter 14 of this *Handbook*. The advent of computers has provided the capacity to accumulate the inventory detail and associated costs, so that they are readily available for use in making decisions about the inventory.

Computers also provide the capacity to rapidly solve equations that if done manually could not be completed in time to be of use. This has permitted the use of operations research techniques to aid in making decisions about inventory management.

Two techniques that are specifically designed to aid in the solution of inventory management problems are economic order quantity (E.O.Q.) and reorder point (R.O.P.). These two equations are designed to help in the solution of two important inventory management decisions:
1. How much to buy or make.   2. When to order.

ECONOMIC ORDER QUANTITY. This formula is designed to aid in deciding how much to buy. The formula adds the cost of ordering inventory and the cost of carrying inventory. The order quantity which results in the total of these two costs being at a minimum is the optimum quantity to order. The costs which make up carrying costs and ordering costs have been discussed above.

To demonstrate the use of this formula, assume that inventory management wants to decide whether to order an item annually or monthly.

	Purchase Monthly	Purchase Annually
Quantity on each order......................	15	180
Investment in inventory		
First of period.............................$1,500		$18,000
End of period..............................	0	0
Average.....................................	750	9,000
Annual costs		
Carrying cost...............................	188	2,250
Ordering cost...............................	240	20
Total Cost.............................$	428	$2,270

The annual usage is 180 units. The unit price is $100. The carrying cost is 25% of the average investment, and the ordering cost is $20 per order.

The better of the two options is to purchase monthly. Whether this is the optimum decision can be determined by calculating the other options open to the inventory managers.

Consider the following tabular presentation, which elaborates on the above data by extending the choices to nine rather than the two shown above. All assumptions made in the first table remain unchanged.

Annual Usage $18,000 180 Units		Carrying Cost 25%		Order Cost $20		
Orders per Year for Inventory	Order Size	Average Inventory	Annual Carrying Cost	Annual Ordering Cost	Total Annual Costs	E.O.Q.
1................	$18,000	$9,000	$2,250	$ 20	$2,270	
2................	9,000	4,500	1,125	40	1,165	
3................	6,000	3,000	750	60	810	
4................	4,500	2,250	562	80	642	
5................	3,600	1,800	450	100	550	
6................	3,000	1,500	375	120	495	
9................	2,000	1,000	250	180	430	
10................	1,800	900	225	200	425	18 units
12................	1,500	750	188	240	428	

This table indicates the optimum order quantity is 18 units per order. Exhibit 4 is a graphic presentation of combined order and carrying costs.

EXHIBIT 4

Graphic Presentation of Combined Order and Inventory Costs

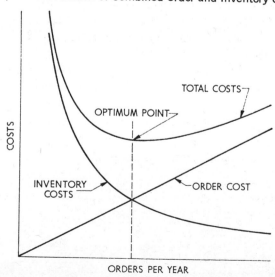

While useful for illustrative purposes, the amount of detail and calculations required makes this approach impractical for the purpose of reaching an economic order quantity decision.

A simple formula can be used to calculate the economic order quantity. The formula is stated as:

$$E.O.Q. = \sqrt{\frac{2\,AO}{PC}}$$

where:

E.O.Q. is the economic order quantity.
A is the annual usage in units.
O is the ordering cost per order.
P is the cost of carrying inventory expressed as a percent of cost or invoice price.
C is the cost or invoice price per unit including inbound freight.

The values used in the preceding table were:

A, the annual usage, was 180 units.
O, the ordering cost per order, was $20.
P, the carrying cost, was 25% of cost.
C, the cost per unit, was $100.

The optimum quantity can be obtained from the formula as follows:

$$E.O.Q. = \sqrt{\frac{2\,AO}{PC}}$$

$$E.O.Q. = \sqrt{\frac{2 \times 180 \times \$20}{25\% \times \$100}}$$

$$E.O.Q. = \sqrt{\frac{\$7,200}{\$25}}$$

$$E.O.Q. = \sqrt{288} = 17 \text{ units}$$

The E.O.Q. of 17 units differs from the 18 units in the table shown earlier, since the table assumed ordering in quantities that would equal the annual usage of 180 units. A comparison of the total cost of ordering 9, 10, or 12 times indicates that the optimum quantity is less than 18 units.

ECONOMIC LOT SIZE. This formula is designed to aid in deciding how much to make. For a produced item the inventory will increase in steps as the product is manufactured. In addition, the inventory will never reach the same maximum as for a purchased item, since usage and production will both be taking place at the same time. The formula can be adjusted for these conditions as follows:

$$E.L.S. = \sqrt{\frac{2\,AO}{PC} \times \frac{B}{(B-A)}}$$

where:

> *E.L.S.* is the economic lot size.
> *B* is the annual production rate.
> *A* is the annual usage rate.

This formula assumes that production will always exceed usage. If it does not, there is no choice to be made, since all production will be devoted to the one item.

REORDER POINT.   One equation that can be used as an aid in deciding when to order is dependent on the existence of an economic order quantity. It matches the cost of carrying inventory against the cost of being out of inventory, or stock-out cost. It determines the optimum quantity to have on hand immediately following replenishment so that the cost of carrying the inventory balances the stock-out cost. Coupled with the economic order quantity, the point to reorder is determined.

To determine the reorder point with this formula, it is necessary to know:

1. Economic order quantity.   4. Carrying cost.
2. Demand or usage.   5. Unit cost of the item.
3. Stock-out cost.   6. Usage during lead time.

If the demand or usage and the lead time are known and the desired customer service level permits no stock-outs, then the reorder point will be set to equal the lead-time usage. For example, if daily usage is 10 units and the lead time is 20 days, usage during lead time will be 20 days × 10 units per day or a lead-time usage of 200 units. The reorder point will be equal to the lead-time usage of 200 units. This is not necessarily the optimum quantity to order, since it is based on the decision that no stock-out will be tolerated.

If, in addition to the other known data, the stock-out cost is also known, and it is decided that a stock-out will be acceptable if it is to the economic advantage of the business to be out of stock rather than incurring the costs of carrying stock, the optimum amount can be determined by using the following formula:

$$R.O.P. = E.O.Q. \times \frac{S}{(C \times P) + S} - LTU$$

where:

> *E.O.Q.* is economic order quantity.
> *S* is the cost of being out of stock by one unit for one year.
> *C* is the carrying cost for one unit for one year as a percent of the value of the item.
> *P* is the unit cost of the item.

LTU is the units sold or used during lead time.

Assume that the economic order quantity for an item has been set at 200 units. If demand or usage is 50 per week and the lead time is two weeks, lead-time usage (LTU) will be 100. If the cost of a stock-out is about $10 per year for each item out of stock, the unit cost of the item is $5 and the cost of carrying one unit in inventory for one year is 20% of the unit price, the solution is:

$$R.O.P. = 200 \times \frac{\$10}{(0.20 \times \$5) + \$10} - 100 = 82 \text{ units}$$

The higher the cost of a stock-out is in relation to the carrying cost, the higher the reorder point will be, so that the number of stock-outs will be reduced.

The above formula provides the best answer when stock-out costs, lead-time, and demand usage are known. However, in actual practice, stock-out costs are nearly impossible to determine, while both lead times and demand or usage tend to vary. Stock-out costs may be replaced by an acceptable customer service level established by management. This may be defined as the willingness to accept the risk of not having a particular item at the proper point once in a given time period. Also, the distribution of the variations in lead time and demand or usage can be determined.

When establishing reorder points, normally about a 50–50 probability of having a stock-out can be expected if the reorder point is set equal to lead-time usage. However, the lead-time usage can be increased by an amount which will reduce the probability of stock-outs from about 50–50 to a customer service level more acceptable to management. In many cases, the distribution of varying lead-time usage is closely approximated by the normal distribution. In these cases, if one standard deviation of lead-time usage is added to the average lead-time usage, the probability of a stock-out drops to 16%. If two standard deviations of lead-time usage are added to the average lead-time usage, the probability of a stock-out drops to 2%. The amount of this increase is called "safety stock." Therefore, the reorder point is equal to the lead-time usage plus safety stock.

Based on these conditions, the reorder point can be determined by the following formula:

Reorder point = Lead-time usage (*LTU*) plus some factor (*F*) times the standard deviation (*S.D.*) of the lead-time usage.

The factor *F* indicates the acceptable customer service level. Setting it implies some awareness of stock-out and carrying costs, for example, the larger the stock-out costs are in relation to carrying costs, the larger the factor will be. If the lead-time usage is 100, the standard deviation of lead-time usage is 10, and the desired customer service level is 84%, then, using this formula, the reorder point will be:

$$R.O.P. = 100 + 1 \times 10 = 110$$

To further simplify the application of this formula, in those cases where lead times are very nearly constant, the standard deviation of lead-time usage can be approximated by taking the square root of lead-time usage and:

$$R.O.P. = LTU + F \times \sqrt{LTU}$$

Inventory records and reports

This is the second area in inventory management and control where the computer offers the possibility of making major improvements. The ability of computers to handle and process large amounts of data rapidly makes them especially suitable for processing the voluminous details associated with large, dispersed inventories. The decision about whether the use of computers is justifiable for inventory control will depend on many factors, including the size and complexity of the inventory, the location of production plants, the location of inventory points, and the geographical areas serviced. In any event, the value of information obtained from a computerized system must be balanced against the cost of obtaining the information.

Depending on the size of the company and the inventory, these data should be obtained by the most economical means, which include:

1. Manual records.
2. Electromechanical record-keeping machines and calculators.
3. Computers.
4. Any combination of the above.

To realize the advantages that can be gained from a well-designed inventory management system, it must basically provide for each item at each location:

1. Actual quantity on hand.
2. On order from supplier or production.
3. Receipts.
4. On order from customers.
5. Shipments or disbursements.
6. Uncommitted quantity available for use or sale.

In addition, the following information should also be available:

1. The unit cost of materials and supplies used in the manufacture of products.
2. The unit cost of manufactured products.
3. Transportation from warehouse or factory to customer, from factory to warehouse, and between warehouses, which is often a major cost of having inventory.

4. A summary by item of shipments from factories or warehouses to customers. This is needed to measure the effectiveness of warehouse locations.

5. Costs related to the handling and storage of inventory.

Companies that have inventories widely dispersed geographically are using computers and wire reporting to keep aware of what products are available at each location so that the most efficient use may be made of the total inventory. Systems of this type can improve customer service and reduce stock-outs, obsolescence, and deterioration losses, which will generally aid in attaining a faster turn of capital invested in inventory.

Some larger companies are now obtaining the information required for an inventory control system as a by-product of the Purchasing, Accounts Payable, Receiving, Production, and Sales Order Entry and Billing functions.

The flow of work through this type of system is shown in Exhibit 5. The flow is a normal one and can be either accomplished manually, with

EXHIBIT 5

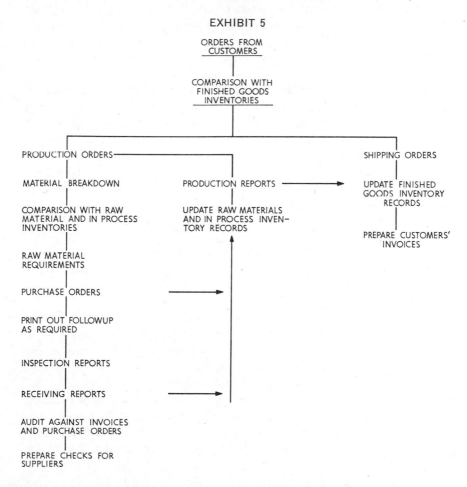

a combination of mechanical and manual operations, a combination of manual and electronic operations, or a completely computerized operation.

Assuming a computerized system is decided upon, all repetitive data, including products, selling prices, terms, specifications or bills of material, customers' names and codes, and suppliers' names and codes, will be stored in the computer.

Customers' orders are entered in the computer after editing. The material ordered is compared with inventory records to determine availability. Production orders are issued for required products in economic order quantities if the reorder point has been reached. Shipping orders are also issued. These orders update the finished goods inventory records which are maintained in the computer.

Material breakdowns are calculated from production orders and compared with raw material and in process inventories to determine raw material and in process requirements. Purchase orders are written for raw material requirements. As materials are received and pass inspection, receiving reports clear open purchase orders and update raw material inventory records. Invoices from suppliers are audited against the purchase orders and receiving reports, and checks are prepared to pay the invoices if in order.

As production proceeds, reports update the raw material, in process, and finished goods inventory records. As shipments are made, finished goods inventory records are updated and customers' invoices prepared.

Reports from such a system show exceptions to the system based on rules stored in the computer to control the operation of the system. These reports, in addition to special-purpose reports required by the company, will normally include:

1. Purchased material not delivered as scheduled.
2. Differences between quantities ordered and received.
3. Exceptions to prices, quantities, or terms on suppliers' invoices.
4. Differences between scheduled and actual production.
5. Materials to be reordered based on reorder points, economic order quantities, minimum-maximums, or whatever guides have been established to control reordering.
6. Differences between actual and book inventories.
7. Report of slow-moving stock by location based on appropriate rules that can be applied to determine what constitutes slow-moving stock.
8. Out-of-stock report by item and location.
9. Backordered stock by customer, item, and location.

In addition to the above exception reports, the system should produce total inventory value reports for accounting purposes. For a manufacturing company, the report should segregate raw materials and supplies, in process, and finished goods. The data in these reports should be grouped as required for inventory control purposes, for federal, state, or local government reports, including tax reports and those for insurance purposes or for other special uses required by the company.

For further information on the uses and limitations of computers, the reader is referred to Part V, "Information technology" and especially to Chapter 30, "Information storage and processing."

Inventory control

Control procedures

The methods used for the detailed control of inventory will essentially be determined by the total inventory system established by those responsible for inventory management.

In order to understand the system and their part in it, personnel performing this function should be provided with written instructions or a manual that explains what is to be done by the control people to make the system operate as planned. The duties or the way in which they are to be performed may vary due to various factors, for example, the type of inventory being controlled, the market being served, and so on. Exhibit 6 is a copy of control instructions from an inventory manual.

EXHIBIT 6

X Y Z Company
(excerpt from inventory manual)

Finished Goods Inventory Control
1. Establishment of inventory control levels for fast-moving high-unit-volume products.
    The basis for establishing control for high-unit-volume products is the monthly average of units sold calculated from the prior 12 months' sales figures. The inventory analyst establishes review points by number of months' coverage desired. These are then processed and retained by the computer. The computer uses the review levels in conjunction with the average monthly usage previously determined to calculate review control levels.
2. Exception reporting and following.
    When the quantity on hand plus quantity on order less quantity on back order, is equal to, or less than, the review control levels, the product is reported on the Daily Inventory Exception Report. The inventory analyst will investigate each item on the report and initiate the required action.

Essentially, control personnel will need to respond to any exception reporting furnished by a computerized system or to any exception to desired conditions noted from the review of records maintained by or for the control personnel. The usual exceptions that will occur will arise from the rate of demand or usage developing at a rate different from that expected or the failure of suppliers or production plants to deliver as scheduled.

Replenishment

The control function is essentially concerned with decisions regarding the replenishment of inventory. In order to avoid improper accumulation of inventory, the acquisition of inventory is most important since, once acquired, profits can be adversely affected by the costs of carrying excessive inventory for long periods of time or by discounting to dispose of the excesses.

The formulas for determining the economic order quantity, economic lot size, and reorder point, which are discussed above, are designed to aid in making better replenishment decisions. In order to make these formulas more useful, especially where there are a large number of items in inventory, tables can be designed for use by control personnel.

Tables for economic order quantity determination will require the preparation of a table for each combination of ordering cost per order and carrying cost rate. The tables will show the calculated economic order quantity for selected annual usage rates in units on one axis and the unit cost per item purchased on the other. The figure at the intersection of the applicable annual usage and the cost per unit purchased is the economic order quantity. A table based on an ordering cost of $20 per order and a carrying cost of 20% of unit cost is shown in Exhibit 7.

EXHIBIT 7

Economic Order Quantity Table
(quantity per purchase order)

Usage per Year in Units	Cost per Item Purchased		
	$5	$50	$500
10	20	7	2
50	45	14	5
100	64	20	7
200	90	28	9
300	110	35	11
400	127	40	13
500	142	45	14

Tables can also be designed to determine safety stocks which, when added to lead-time usage, establish the reorder point. Whether tables will serve a useful purpose will depend on the complexity of the inventory and the variety of different ordering costs, carrying costs, and desired customer service levels.

Physical inventories

Actual inventories should be taken as often as required to verify the accuracy of the stock records and the adequacy of the control and protection procedures. Accurate inventories are more likely to result if stock is carefully stored in well-planned warehouse facilities.

The tendency is to take cycle inventories so that the cost of taking inventory is kept to a minimum and delays in receiving or shipping stock during the inventory are reduced or eliminated. Actual inventory counts are being speeded by the use of voice recorders instead of written records. The recorded counts are summarized, priced, and extended by office personnel or by service bureaus. The important consideration is that the correct counts be recorded and, where differences between the physical count and the stock records exist, that the count and the record be verified and appropriate adjustments made. If inventory records are maintained on a computer, a recap of all transactions since the last inventory can be printed for any item where the physical count does not agree with the stock record. This is an aid in determining if the reason for the difference is in the maintenance of the stock records, if receiving or shipping procedures are being properly followed, or if an actual stock disappearance has occurred. The amount of verification done will depend on the value of the item and the quantity involved as well as the number of differences that develop.

Warehousing facilities

Well-planned warehousing facilities are necessary for good inventory management and control. The inventory must be stored so that both inbound and outbound movements can be readily accommodated, that actual inventories can be taken easily, and that the stock is open to observation to aid in protecting against spoilage or obsolescence.

Warehousing arrangements will depend upon the product, how it is packaged, whether it is subject to shelf spoilage, and how it can be handled in and out in the most efficient manner.

With the high lift power trucks available today, the use of pallets for storage and shipment, and the use of racks or shelves that make pallet loads readily accessible to power equipment, the emphasis is placed on designing the warehouse with proper ceiling heights and increased clear areas not obstructed by building columns. This type of warehouse building, properly equipped with power handling equipment, permits maximum utilization of the total volume or cubic feet available rather than just the floor space or square feet available. The current tendency is toward the automation of the warehousing function.

The warehouse design should provide for flexibility in handling both inbound and outbound shipments by either rail or truck. A rectangular warehouse with loading and unloading facilities on the long sides of the building will provide good access. Dock space should be separated from the warehouse and from adjoining dock area so that merchandise to be shipped by truck can be isolated on the dock for loading by the carriers' employees without allowing them to have access to the entire warehouse.

Bibliography

Except where it was thought necessary to the discussion, detailed information has not been included because of the many variations in types of businesses and inventory management and control requirements. For those interested in additional reading the following are recommended:

HECKERT, J. BROOKS, AND WILLSON, JAMES D. *Controllership*, Chapter 21. 2d ed. New York, 1963.

HOFFMAN, THOMAS R. *Production Management and Manufacturing Systems*, Chapters 12 and 13. Belmont, Calif.: Wadsworth Publishing Co., Inc., 1967.

NATIONAL ASSOCIATION OF ACCOUNTANTS. *Techniques in Inventory Management*. New York, 1964.

Fixed assets

William H. Lowe*

The management of fixed assets is the process of investigation, evaluation, and decision-making involved in evaluating, acquiring, controlling, utilizing, maintaining, and disposing of these assets. The financial executive, as a part of the management team, participates in all of these functions. In addition, he is particularly qualified to provide special expertise in the areas of evaluation and control. For the purposes of this chapter, fixed assets are defined as tangible property, such as land, land improvements, buildings, and machinery and equipment which are not held as the "stock-in-trade" of the business.

The various methods of economic evaluation of acquisitions, are covered in Chapter 19, "Analysis of Capital Expenditures." Control through use of budgeting techniques is covered in Chapter 27, "Capital Budgeting Procedures." Insurance considerations are covered in Chapter 45, "Property and Liability Insurance." Accounting policy considerations, including methods of depreciation, valuation, and tax questions are covered in Chapter 55, "Accounting for Property, Plant, and Equipment."

The portion of the financial executive's time which should be devoted to the management and control of fixed assets depends to a considerable extent upon the type of business involved. Some industries, such as steel and railroads, have a tremendous portion of the company's capital invested in fixed assets. Other industries, such as clothing and drug manufacturers, have a relatively small proportion of capital invested in fixed assets. Therefore, the specifics of a particular business will dictate the

* Vice President-Finance and Chairman of the Finance committee, Inland Steel Company, Chicago.

materiality of fixed asset management and control in relation to the total business. However, large or small, the principles apply to all. Only the degree of application varies.

This chapter presents concepts and principles rather than attempting to detail a specific step-by-step method of operation. By adopting these principles as policy, the financial executive can then proceed to tailor a program suited to the needs of his organization to implement these policies.

This chapter is divided into two principal sections:

1. Management decisions. This section discusses the broad areas of management of fixed assets which have not been covered elsewhere in the Book.
2. Control. This section discusses in some detail, the control of fixed assets.

Management decisions

Many of the management decisions and responsibilities for fixed assets have been discussed in previous chapters. However, there are three areas which often are not commented on as specific topics in discussions of fixed assets, although they may be incorporated into other topics. It is felt that there should be some brief comment here on each to emphasize that the financial executive should keep them in mind as he plans his function with respect to fixed assets. These areas are: (1.) Obsolescence; (2.) Sale of unneeded items, and (3.) Destruction.

Obsolescence

Detection and determination of obsolescence is not a primary responsibility of the financial executive, but rather the responsibility of the engineering and production staffs. However, the financial executive and his staff can provide help in this area.

Obsolescence can be one of two types. First, a piece of equipment, although in good mechanical condition, may become obsolete because of new technology. Finance is usually not involved here until it reaches the stage of a proposal of the economic benefits of old versus new.

Second, a piece of equipment, which may be technologically current, may be so worn out that it causes increases in manufacturing costs. Frequently, there is a tendency among operating people to keep using a machine until it falls apart and can be no longer repaired. In the meantime, the maintenace crew keeps repairing and repairing and, in some cases, literally tying it together with baling wire.

This phenomenon occurs because local plant management wishes to spend as little money as possible, and maintenance expenditures, because they are spread over a period of time, psychologically appear smaller than a large sum spent for a replacement. Also, most companies have appropriation procedures requiring high-level approvals for acquisitions, while repairs can often be approved locally.

The financial executive's representative at the plant should be alert to the signs of obsolescence, such as:

1. Excessive downtime.
2. Increasing repair costs.
3. Increasing quantities of scrap.
4. Decline in quality—indicated by an increasing number of rejects and increasing returns by customers for specific types of defects.

Any or all of these conditions will be reflected in increasing variances from budgets and standard costs. A good plant production and financial reporting system will aid in spotlighting the trouble area. While such deviations could be due to any number of causes, the operating management is alerted to investigate.

If the rising cost is due to equipment, then the local finance people should assist the operating people in collecting specific data and preparing comparisons to possible alternatives, including replacement.

Sale of unneeded items

Almost every company which has been in operation for more than a few years usually has some surplus fixed assets. These might range from an unused machine sitting in a corner of the plant to a complete facility standing idle because the capacity or process is not needed

All facilities and equipment, of course, constitute "tied up" capital. The financial executive is responsible to see that a company's capital is being utilized in the most effective and profitable maner possible. Therefore, he should periodically and systematically review the utilization of the company's fixed assets, and bring to the attention of the rest of management any which are not being utilized.

This policy can be implemented through use of techniques, such as:

1. Institution of a procedure whereby a surplus equipment report is prepared for each piece of equipment that is taken out of production. This report would then be reviewed by affected departments, such as production, engineering, and possibly sales, so that a decision can be made as to what to do with the item.
2. Periodic inventories of fixed assets which, among other things, would spot items not being used. These could then be cross-checked with management reports to determine if these items have been reported as idle and if a decision on disposition has been made.
3. Provision for periodic management review of idle property held for some future purpose. Such a review should reexamine the future purpose to see if it is still valid, and also should point out the total cost (including the cost of capital) of continuing to hold the property.

In all cases, the ultimate objective should be to determine if the asset is to be utilized for a definite future purpose. If not, it should be sold and the capital recovered.

Destruction

Fixed assets, being physical things, are in constant danger of being destroyed as a result of many different perils, from fire or flood to riot or war. The destruction of vital fixed assets has many times been the cause of a company's collapse because it lacked adequate records to prove for insurance purposes the value of the loss. (See Chapter 45, "Property and Liability Insurance.")

The financial executive is responsible for maintaining adequate detailed records of the company's fixed assets. He is also responsible for protecting these records. The finest set of records in the world are of no use if they are destroyed.

Some executives may feel that an elaborate record protection system is a needless expense. Others may feel that implementation of a records protection system is a low priority item and can be put off.

Disaster can strike at any time. The financial executive who has detailed property records and who has executed a plan for protecting them may well be the one who saves his company from financial ruin.

Control

Control over fixed assets is vital to a company's economic health. Frequently, substantial sums of money can be lost through lack of control over the acquisition and utilization of fixed assets. The financial executive is primarily responsible for implementing and maintaining much of this control.

This discussion of control over fixed assets is divided into five basic aspects: (1.) Control procedures; (2.) Adequate records; (3.) Reports; (4.) Physical safeguards; and (5.) Comprehensive internal auditing.

Control procedures

Establishment of procedures is basic to any good system of control. It is especially important in the case of fixed assets, because the money involved, in many cases, is too large to risk handling on a "seat-of-the-pants" basis. Written procedures provide a step-by-step plan for implementation of management's plans and policies.

ACQUISITION AND/OR CONSTRUCTION. Procedures for acquisition and/or construction of fixed assets insure that funds committed to projects are in line with management's overall policies and plans for capital investment.

Procedures controlling acquisitions and/or construction break down into four principal groups: (A.) Instituting the project; (B.) Controlling the project; (C.) Closing the project; and (D.) Post-audit of the project.

A. Procedures for instituting the project.

Procedures for instituting the project are discussed at length in Chapter 27, "Capital Budgeting Procedures."

B. Procedures for controlling the project should include:

1. Specification of responsibilities for commitments to vendors, technical supervision, and for record keeping and reporting.
2. Specification of the type of records to be kept for projects.
3. Specification of the type of progress reports, both financial and technical, to be prepared, and for the frequency of their issuance.
4. Provision to notify appropriate persons of material deviations from plans as soon as such deviations become known.
5. Standards for physical safeguards and controls to be in effect for the duration of the project. The amount of control, of course, will vary substantially with the type of project. A large project, such as building a plant, will require substantial control measures, such as guards, inspectors, etc.
6. Provision for notification of changes in the scope of the project. This should include specification of an appropriate form requiring approval of the *same* authorities who initially approved the project.

   While this point is not followed now by many companies, it is one that should be given very careful consideration. It is one of the weakest points in a project. Oftentimes, engineers, regardless of the best of intentions, become infatuated with doing the project in the fanciest way possible without too much regard to the costs involved. Management must exercise careful control to prevent the engineer from embarking on a "frolic of his own" to the detriment of the company's overall plan for capital investment.
7. Provision for an inspector or auditor from the finance department. Obviously, such a person would not be qualified as an engineer, but a layman can observe a lot, especially in the areas of scope changes and physical controls at the building site. This would be principally used on projects of large installations or constructions.
8. Provision for examination and audit of contractor's procedures and records on projects where contractors are used.

C. Procedures for closing the project should include:

1. A formal notification of project completion. This should provide for all pertinent data and appropriate approvals necessary to formally close the project and change its status from in-progress to completed fixed asset.

2. Specification of the method of preparation, routing, and approvals required for the notice of project completion. As a minimum, this should include:

a) Approval of the technical personnel responsible for implementation of the project.

b) Approval of the accounting personnel controlling the records of the project who must verify that all outstanding commitments have been paid or cancelled.

c) Acceptance by the operating personnel who will be responsible for the facility from this point on.

3. A formal project result report which compares actual expenditures and results accomplished with the original proposal and estimated costs.

Formal closing procedures such as these are used in some companies, but are not common for industry in general. Consideration of using such procedures is strongly recommended as a control over capital spending. Among the advantages of such procedures are:

1. It will prevent loading completed projects with continuing charges which more properly belong to another project or to operating costs.

2. It will assist in the recapture of unexpended funds.

3. It will act as a deterrent to unnecessary delays in completing a project.

D. Procedures for postaudit of the project should include:

1. A requirement for auditing a project sometime after its completion.

2. Providing management with a report evaluating the actual results of the project with the original proposals. Particular emphasis should be placed upon the project's economic evaluation, with explanations of any material deviations occurring in actual operation.

Postaudits are not needed for all acquisitions, but should be considered for substantial and complex acquisitions and/or constructions. Usually, they will be confined to projects involving cost savings, quality improvement, or profit improvement.

Also, the word audit may imply use of the audit department. In companies where projects are few and infrequent, the audit group may be the most logical unit to conduct these evaluations. However, for companies with numerous projects, this task is probably best undertaken by a special unit. This unit should have available engineers, industrial engineers, and other appropriate technical specialists, as well as accountants.

REPAIRS AND MAINTENANCE.   Expenditures for this category could range from fifty cents to a million dollars and more. Some formal procedures are needed to insure that substantial expenditures are approved by responsible executives who can evaluate the expenditure in light of the company's long range capital investment program.

Procedures for repairs and maintenance should include:

1. The company's official definition of what is to be considered normal repairs and maintenance, and therefore charged to operations; and of what is to be considered extraordinary repairs and maintenance, and therefore capitalized as an addition to fixed assets. This distinction is not easy to make. Any one particular project might be considered either way, and the decision would have to be based on the specifics of the company's size and type of operation and on the applicable income tax and property tax situations. This definition would probably take the form of a set of guidelines on which to base a decision about a particular project.

2. For projects that fall in the category of being additions to fixed assets, procedures should provide for formal evaluation and approval routines similar to those described under "Acquisitions and/or Constructions." Many companies do use the same routines for both.

3. Also, for projects adding to fixed assets, procedures should provide for control, closing, and, if appropriate, postaudit of the project similar to those discussed earlier.

It must be emphasized that procedures covering repairs and maintenance must be mentioned specifically, because material expenditures for fixed asset repairs are an important part of the overall planning of capital investment and must be evaluated and approved by those responsible for capital planning.

RETIREMENTS, SALES AND OTHER DISPOSITIONS. Disposal of fixed assets is just as important as their acquisition. Again, management should assure itself that such activities are under its control. Formal procedures can be very useful in maintaining this control. Such procedures should include:

1. A formal request for disposition. This should provide all details necessary for a complete evaluation, including:
   a) Description of the item.
   b) Proposed method of disposal.
   c) Estimated gain or loss on disposal. This must include consideration of current book value, dismantling and other related disposal costs, and revenue expected, if any.
   d) Reason for disposal.
   e) Alternatives to disposition, if any.
   f) Estimated time required for the project.
   g) Space for appropriate approvals.
2. Specification of the method of preparing the request for disposition

and the routing of the request through the various levels of the organization.
3. Specification of various responsibilities. For example, the accounting department would be responsible for determining the net book value.
4. Authority for approval of the method of disposition. Many companies have certain types of unique machinery and process equipment which the company would want to prevent falling into the hands of competitors. Sometimes companies may not want certain things to be sold even within the same country.
5. Authority for approval of the project. This authority may or may not be separate from the authority approving the method of disposition. As with acquisitions, this may be stratified through several layers of management by type of project and by dollar value of the project.

If a company were to prepare all of the procedures just discussed they would come up with a fairly sizable volume. They would also provide for good control by opening lines of communication between management and operating personnel. An investment in the preparation of such procedures could be substantial. The return on that investment can be lower costs, improved efficienty, better control, and improved chances for success in the company's capital investment program.

Adequate records

The second element of control over fixed assets is the maintenance of records. Detailed fixed asset records should be maintained to the maximum extent practicable under the circumstances of the value of the investment and the cost involved. Records are needed for: (1) the asset units; (2) depreciation and depletion; (3) investment credit; (4) acquisitions in progress; and (5) repairs and maintenance.

ASSET UNITS. The foundation of fixed asset records should be a unit record for each principal item. That is, there should be an individual record for each item of property, such as a machine, a vehicle, a parcel of land, etc. In most cases, these records would be maintained at the location where the item is situated.

A typical unit record should be structured to show at least the following:
1. Description of item.
2. Accounting classification.
3. Company identification number.
4. Date acquired.
5. Cost.
6. Specific location.
7. Subsequent cost added (*i.e.*, major repairs and improvements capitalized).

8. Manufacturer's name and identification number, if applicable.
9. Reference to legal documents, where applicable (deeds, contracts, etc.).
10. Disposition information, including date, authorization, value received, etc.

The maintenance of adequate unit records provide the following benefits:

1. A sound basis for insurance valuations and claims in the event of loss.
2. Substantiation for property tax valuations, depreciation computations, and investment credit computations.
3. Control over the location and utilization of items.
4. Provision of data for budget preparation and allocation of departmental costs.
5. Provision of data for the planning of future capital investment for replacement.

Some companies maintain unit fixed asset records separately from the accounting records. However, such records will be considerably more valuable if they are maintained as an integral part of the accounting records in a subsidiary ledger. In this way, the certainty of their being complete and up-to-date will be enhanced.

When incorporated into the accounting system, these records would be grouped into logical classifications and controlled by one or more control accounts for a location. These control accounts may, in turn, be controlled by master control accounts for the entire corporation. Usually, the top series of control accounts will number five to ten, and will probably parallel the current Internal Revenue Service *Guideline Classifications*, such as land, land improvements, buildings, fabricating equipment, transportation equipment, etc.

DEPRECIATION AND DEPLETION. The records required for depreciation and depletion need not be as detailed as the records for the properties themselves. Internal Revenue Service regulations permit depreciation computations to be made for groups of assets. Therefore, it is recommended that the depreciation accounts parallel the asset accounts from the point of location control accounts upward.

By adopting this approach, a company can maintain all of the necessary detail data with a minimum number of accounts. Under this system, the net book value of a specific asset cannot be computed. However, when an asset is disposed of by a company using group depreciation, Internal Revenue will permit the assumption that the item is fully depreciated.

INVESTMENT CREDIT. The AICPA currently recognizes both the deferred method and the flow-through method of accounting for investment credit. Under the flow-through method, no additional records would be needed. Under the deferred method, it is desirable to establish two sets of accounts—one set for the investment credit earned and one set for the amortization of the investment credit. As with the depreciation accounts, these accounts need not be in any greater detail than the *Guideline Classifications* by location.

ACQUISITIONS IN PROGRESS.   As mentioned before, the process of acquisition, either through purchase or construction, is critical and in need of close, complete control. This is especially important in large complex projects spanning a long period of time.

A subsidiary ledger should be established with one or more accounts for each project. For large projects, it is often helpful to establish a separate subsidiary ledger for a specific project. In this area, it is a virtue to have too many accounts rather than too few. When too few accounts are used, project accountants will be spending many hours analyzing accounts to segregate large amounts into smaller and more identifiable pieces.

The account structure should parallel the types of costs projected in the original appropriation request. This will then facilitate preparation of progress reports comparing actual versus projected cost. In some appropriation requests, there may be some combining of costs, *e.g.*, 3—XYZ machines—$45,000. In this case, it would be desirable to go even further and provide an account for each machine. This will then facilitate transferring the specific cost of an individual item to the unit records at the close of the project.

In addition to recording actual costs during a project, it is also important for complete control to maintain records of commitments. Especially in large projects, commitments to purchase are made months, even years, before the money is actually expended. In order to evaluate the status of a project and to evaluate the timing of future capital requirements, management must be kept informed of commitments as well as actual expenditures.

The responsibility for maintenance of commitment records varies from company to company, but it would seem most logical to incorporate it into the rest of the record keeping function in the finance area. Then it is readily at hand to be incorporated into project progress reports.

The commitment record system, of course, would be external to the accounting ledgers. Their organization, however, would be most effective if they paralleled the breakdown used in structuring the project accounts. These records would then be charged when a formal commitment is made, such as a purchase order or a contract, and relieved when an invoice is processed for payment.

MAINTENANCE RECORDS.   Regardless of what type records of fixed assets are maintained by the finance area, the maintenance department will also have records of fixed asset information which is pertinent to its function. These records may range from a simple box of 3 × 5 file cards to an elaborate system maintained by several clerks.

The records kept by maintenance people can be a very useful source of information for finance and for management in general. This source of information can be especially useful if the financial executive participates in the establishment and maintenance of these records.

In many cases, it may be practical to combine the unit asset records with the maintenance records. This would automatically eliminate some duplication and possibly provide some cost savings.

In addition to the various items of identification, location, and cost, maintenance records would probably include, where applicable:
1. Weight.
2. Horsepower.
3. Utility demands (power, gas, etc.).
4. Inspections made.
5. Preventive maintenance and lubrication.
6. Repairs made—parts replaced.
7. Description and location of principal spare parts.

If finance participates in the maintenance of these records, it becomes possible to more accurately forecast future budgets for maintenance costs and to prepare reports showing maintenance cost trends with specific reasons for variances highlighted.

Reports

Once control procedures have been established and the data collected and recorded, the next step is to assemble the key points of information and report them to management. Effective management and control of fixed assets requires reports in three principal areas: (1) Acquisitions and/or constructions; (2) Repairs and maintenance; and, (3) Obsolete and surplus equipment.

ACQUISITIONS AND/OR CONSTRUCTIONS REPORTS. Once management has approved the purchase or construction of a fixed asset, they must be kept informed of the project's progress. This can be accomplished by periodically issuing a status report on the project. This report may take on a variety of formats, but should include four key items:

1. Original amount appropriated. For any report of expenditures to be meaningful, it must contain some sort of bench mark against which actual expenditures can be measured. In the case of acquisitions, the amount which management has approved for expenditure is that bench mark.
2. Actual amounts expended.

3. Commitments for future expenditures. Because of timing situations occurring in such projects, this information is vital, if a true picture of a project's status is to be given. Also, it is necessary information for management to have in the rare event that they must decide to discontinue a project in midstream.

4. Estimated cost to complete. As a project progresses and engineering details become more refined, it is often discovered that a project cost will differ from the original estimate. Management must be made aware of this development as soon as it becomes apparent, so that they can revise their planning for capital investment accordingly and, in extreme cases, reexamine the feasibility of the project.

The first three items are available from accounting records. The fourth must be provided by the engineering staff. Because of this dual function, some companies may have two reports—one from each area. However, it is more desirable that the information be presented in one report, so that management can view the entire situation at once.

It is also desirable that a status report show information on the progress of the project in point of time. Such information is not always indicated by the financial information, because the expenditure of funds does not necessarily parallel the timing. A project might be only half completed, yet 90 percent of the money may have been expended. Reporting of the timing progress can be accomplished in one of several ways, such as:

1. A statement on percent completed.

2. Comparison of budgeted completion date with current estimate of completion date.

Theoretically, all expenditures connected with a project are a cost of doing the project and should be included as a part of the final evaluation of the asset. However, due to the effect of accounting principles, tax laws, and sometimes due to the difficulty of segregating costs within an organization, a portion of the project cost will be assigned to regular operating costs instead of being capitalized as part of the value of the asset.

The costs assigned to expense can be substantial in some projects. If management is to exercise complete control over a project, it must be able to control *all* of the costs of the project. Therefore, it is recommended that requests for projects and reports on projects disclose total costs, not just those costs to be capitalized.

REPAIRS AND MAINTENANCE REPORTS. The continuing cost of repairing and maintaining fixed assets can often represent a material portion of a company's operating expenses. Also, the level of repair costs can give an indication of how well the company's investment in fixed assets is being cared for and when certain fixed assets have deteriorated to a point where they should be replaced.

Repair costs fall into two principal categories—(1) preventive maintenance and upkeep and (2) repair of worn, broken or damaged facilities. It is desirable for management control that reports on repair costs be structured along these lines.

One possible technique of accomplishing this is to consider the upkeep and preventive maintenance as a fixed cost and repair as a variable cost. Cost accounting theoreticians may have all sorts of arguments against this, but it is an approach that can work.

Under such a system, budgets would be prepared for each type. For the fixed portion, maintenance management would review the normal upkeep requirements of its facilities in terms of man-hours and supplies. This is then translated into dollars and used as the bench mark for measuring these types of expenditures as they actually occur.

Next, other repairs would be projected against some flexible measurement, such as machine hours, units produced, etc. Then this, adjusted to the actual measurement of the period, can be used as the bench mark for evaluation of these costs.

A report showing these two comparisons would enable management to gain a fairly good indication of the status of their facilities. Variances in the fixed portion might indicate possible neglect of normal maintenance which could result in the shortening of an asset's useful life. Variances in the variable portion might indicate facilities which should be considered for replacement.

OBSOLETE AND SURPLUS ITEMS.   The section on control procedures discusses procedures for recognizing and disposing of obsolete and surplus items. In addition to such procedures, it might be useful to issue periodic reports showing the status of surplus equipment notices in process. Such a follow-up report could provide additional control, by highlighting reluctant decision-makers and encouraging more prompt action.

Physical safeguards

In addition to procedures and systems the financial executive can also improve control over fixed assets, by recommending and assisting in the implementation of physical safeguards. Physical safeguards include: (1.) Plant protection; (2.) Identification systems; (3.) Physical inventories; and, (4.) Inventory systems for spare parts.

PLANT PROTECTION.   The financial executive is not usually responsible for plant protection and security. However, because of his close association with internal control and because he usually is responsible for the audit group, he is in a good position to review and recommend improvements in plant protection.

When one thinks of plant protection and security, it is usually in terms of inventory protection. However, the basic principles also protect the fixed assets.

A good plant protection and security system will include consideration of the following:

1. *Perimeter security.*   Is the outside boundary of the facility protected by fences, walls, or natural obstacles to prevent people and/or vehicles from gaining access at will?

2. *Access control.*   Are points of access limited and controlled? Are all persons and vehicles checked in and out? Are all strangers conducted to and from their place of business by an employee? Are employee's automobiles kept outside the security perimeters?

3. *Guard forces.*   Are there sufficient well-trained guards?

4. *Protection systems.*   Are there protection systems such as ADT for facilities which can't be guarded? Are there adequate fire and explosion control systems? Are employees trained for the possibility of disaster?

5. *Hiring and firing.*   Are potential employee's backgrounds checked so as to avoid hiring trouble? Is stealing dealt with promptly and severely?

IDENTIFICATION SYSTEMS.   The financial executive should encourage the installation of a good system for identification of fixed assets. Especially in the area of equipment, companies will often have several identical pieces of equipment. Identification by name, motor number, etc. might often not be sufficient to identify a specific item.

One good system is to assign a company serial number to each item, and to permanently affix a metal tag bearing this number to the item. This number should be recorded on the asset unit record, so that the two can be positively related.

Establishing a tagging system requires that, insofar as practical, a standard location be designated for affixing the tag. This will save considerable time in the future when someone wants to locate it. Also, the tag should be affixed to the main frame or some other basic part of the item. It should not be attached to items such as a switch box or motor that may be replaced, or exchanged with another machine.

PHYSICAL INVENTORIES.   It is recommended that physical inventories be taken periodically, say every five or ten years. This particular control is in dispute among financial executives. Some consider it not worth the effort and expense, while others consider it worthwhile.

It is felt that there are benefits to be gained from taking an inventory. These include:

1. Verification of the accuracy and reliability of the unit asset records.
2. Verification of the effective operation of the surplus equipment procedure.

3. Possible reduction of property taxes, if less assets exist than the records show.
4. Avoidance of costly appraisals.
5. Better acceptance of unit asset records by insurers as proof of loss.

One of management's most vexing problems is unrecorded retirements. The procedure for disposition discussed earlier would prevent this. However, a physical inventory will help by disclosing possible failures of the procedure.

INVENTORY SYSTEMS FOR SPARE PARTS.   Modern industrial machinery is often highly complex, and may involve parts that are quite unique. Recognizing this, a company will often acquire one or two sets of spare parts at the same time the machine is acquired. The investment in these spare parts can often be substantial. In addition, and more importantly, unavailability of a spare at the time of a breakdown can cause serious losses due to interrupted production.

Many operating people recognize that lack of a spare part at a critical time can be disastrous to them. Therefore, they will tuck away spares in hiding places all over the plant. Then, as time moves on, personnel changes and the spares become lost in their hiding places. As a result, a company can wind up with an investment in spares that is twice or more than what it needs. Or, a breakdown can bring production to a halt, because the spare can't be located.

An inventory system for spares will avoid these situations, enable the company to keep its investment in spares to a minimum, and insure that critical spares are on hand at all times. Such an inventory system should include:
1. Provision for specific controlled areas for spares storage.
2. A record-keeping system providing all pertinent data for spares in stock, their location, their usage, and their acquisition.
3. Assignment of responsibility for maintaining the inventory in accordance with company needs and policies.

The record-keeping system can often be incorporated into and operated as an integral part of the unit asset record system discussed earlier.

Internal auditing

All of the finest controls in the world are worthless if they are not used. Thus, the financial executive is faced with the problem of determining whether his carefully planned system of control is functioning. The best assurance is the existence of an internal audit group performing comprehensive internal audits.

The previous sentence may appear to be somewhat redundant but the mere existence of an internal audit group within an organization is not enough. Even today, in the era of modern business enlightenment, too many companies use their audit groups merely as accuracy checkers instead of as an essential element of internal control and as a source of suggestions for improved, more effective, and sometimes, more economical procedures.

The internal auditing function is discussed in detail in Chapter 12, "Internal Auditing." However, some of the general aspects of internal auditing for fixed assets are briefly discussed in the following paragraphs.

For fixed assets the internal audit group should:

1. Physically inspect the fixed assets.
2. Determine the adequacy and reasonable accuracy of the property records.
3. Determine that construction contracts have been properly audited and recorded.
4. Determine that acquisitions and dispositions were properly authorized.
5. Determine that established internal controls are adequate and are functioning properly.

PHYSICAL INSPECTION.　As a part of the overall program of examination, some portion of the fixed assets should be physically examined. Some items should be selected and traced to the property records and, conversely, some items should be selected from the property records and traced to their physical location. In both cases, the accuracy of the property records should be verified as to description, location, etc. In addition, some observations should be made as to appearance and apparent condition. These tests provide an evaluation as to the adequacy and reliability of the property records as a tool of control. Property records which are allowed to go out of date are not worth the cost of the space in which they are stored.

PROPERTY RECORDS.　As discussed earlier in this chapter, the records maintained for the properties are a key factor in adequate control. The audit examination should include a careful examination of these records to determine that they are functioning as intended and that they are up-to-date and accurate.

The importance of the accuracy of these records cannot be stressed too much. These records are the source of basic information about the company's property, depreciation, and investment credit. This information is frequently called on by top management for use in basic decisions of corporate management and policy.

CONSTRUCTION CONTRACTS.　Many companies construct large facilities. They may hire a general contractor to provide a so-called "turn key" job, or they may act as their own general contractor. In either case, it is quite important that the progress of the work be closely audited.

The auditor in this case watches to see that financial provisions of the contract are adhered to; that expenditures are properly classified and recorded; that billings are for legitimate work performed and materials received; and that adequate security measures for protection of the site and materials are taken by those responsible.

In companies where large construction projects are frequent, special organizations are formed within the finance department to provide this control. In companies where such projects are infrequent, the audit department usually provides this control. In the first case, the audit department should verify that the special group is providing the financial control needed.

In any event, it is very important that the financial executive, through his audit group, exert close watch over large construction projects.

AUTHORIZATIONS.   The auditors should verify that *all* acquisitions and dispositions are properly authorized by the level of management specified in the company's procedures. Plant managers as a group are a determined lot and will go to great lengths sometimes to acquire a fixed asset which they feel they must have. Sometimes, they will even go to the extreme of buying an item without the required higher management approval. This disrupts the overall financial planning of the company and cannot be tolerated.

The verification of authorizations is a part of the overall examination of the functioning of internal control discussed next, but also is of such importance that it deserves special emphasis.

ADEQUATE AND FUNCTIONING INTERNAL CONTROLS.   The internal auditor is in the best position to examine internal control and make recommendations for its improvement. This examination is to determine both its adequacy and whether it is functioning as intended. Internal control is a vital tool of the executive needed to assure him that his policies and directions are being carried out in the manner which he intended.

Property-liability insurance

Stanley L. Wallace*

This brief chapter attempts to permit the reader to view corporate property and liability insurance through the eyes of a professional buyer. It will not make him an expert in a complicated field. However, it does make available in plain language the necessary thought vocabulary to aid him in supervising the development and maintenance of a sensible corporate insurance program adjusted to his company's needs at minimum cost.

The principal subjects discussed include the nature of insurable risk, the concept of risk recognition, and a brief discussion of a hypothetical manufacturer's property-liability insurance program. The same thinking applies to any business; the risks to which other businesses are subject vary only in dimension.

Also covered are control of losses, including prevention and minimizing of their effect, and self-assumption, together with methods to help avoid paying for unnecessary insurance company overhead. The last section is a discussion of administration of the insurance function.

Insurable risk

Much has been written on the subject of risk. Virtually every business decision contains some element of risk. For our purposes, we need concern ourselves only with a special class of business risk called *insurable* risk. Every insurable risk is a business risk. However, we generally

---

* Vice President, Johnson & Higgins, New York.

think of business risks as involving a possible profit, whereas insurable risks involve only a possible loss.

Every business risk involving a possible loss is not insurable, although the scope of insurability widens constantly. "Insurable" does not necessarily mean it can be insured, either; this takes a willing underwriter. It does mean, however, that the particular hazard or peril which might cause loss or damage to the insured would be fortuitous as to the insured were it to happen. This is the test. There is nothing fortuitous as to the employee who steals from his employer, but the event is quite fortuitous as to the employer.

Insurable also means that the risk for which insurance is sought can be described clearly with words and that any loss or damage resulting from the hazard or hazards insured against can be expressed in money. An insurance policy, then, is nothing more than a contract entered into in good faith and at arm's length between two parties, the insuror and the insured, wherein the insuror, for a consideration called *premium,* agrees to indemnify or pay on behalf of the insured up to a specified sum of dollars in event of loss, damage, or liability caused by an occurrence covered by the policy, subject otherwise to its terms and conditions.

Generally speaking, the loss or damage must involve tangible property, something you can see or feel, or someone or his feelings or reputation must be injured. But there are enough exceptions that no such narrow definition would be adequate. For example, a common liability insurance is Advertising Liability which covers, among other things, liability for unauthorized use of material. Advertising creates a risk of a demand for damages because, as an example, someone neglected to obtain proper releases for material used. This doesn't fit the preceding definition because the property damaged was not tangible. Still, it's an insurable risk. Common sense is often as good a criterion for insurability as any. Risks which were not considered insurable years ago are routine today, e.g., *personal* (as opposed to *bodily*) injury, which brings in libel, slander, etc. Directors' and Officers' Liability is another example.

What about the risk of liability for damages for bodily injury or damage to tangible property (called property damage, generally) from *use* of the product? Suppose it arose out of an error in manufacture? Let's assume an employee did not use the prescribed insulation (a *bench* error) and a user was electrocuted. Insurable? Of course. As far as the insured is concerned, it was an accident and quite unexpected. The specifications were not followed, but the insured was unaware of the fact. This was fortuitous as to the insured. What about proper workmanship but faulty specifications (a *design* error)? Suppose the prescribed insulation was simply insufficient. Would a loss be unexpected? From the company's point of view it would certainly seem to be. Presumably no management would permit manufacture and sale of a product where the specifications were faulty if management *knew* they were faulty. So from the company's point of view, there was an unexpected event which subsequently led to injury. Suppose the design error originated within the insured's own staff. Insurable? Why not? Coverage in either case would depend on the wording of the policy; coverage is available for design errors. But don't assume you have it—it's not that available. Although injury may be inevitable with use of an improperly designed product, such inevitability does not rule out insurability; neither will it rule out coverage unless the insuror can prove the insured knew of the improper design or the policy excludes design or formulation errors. Naturally, if the insured knew of any improper design or formulation, the result could hardly have been fortuitous.

The word loss is used variously in insurance. Used without qualification, it generally refers to a claim under a policy. If an underwriter feels a loss is inevitable under a specific policy requested, he may not be willing to insure the risk of such loss. It really isn't a risk at all in his opinion. Risk implies a possibility, not a certainty. Yet there are many exceptions where some losses are expected, such as in workmen's compensation, transit policies, etc. However, the "expected" losses in these policies are of a frequency type, as opposed to those involving severity. The underwriter in many cases is really providing services[1] beyond indemnification. Of course, severity losses may occur, which is the principal reason the insured buys insurance. However, the underwriter expects to take in more than he pays out. He expects losses but also expects a net profit. This thinking applies to many policies involved in the program of a large company. Few are expected to be completely loss free.

If, after a loss, an insuror can prove the insured was aware of conditions which would have made an underwriting loss under the policy inevitable, the insuror may deny liability for a subsequent loss. In many cases, if the insuror can prove the insured was aware of conditions whose disclosure would make the insurance *undesirable* to a prudent underwriter, such as unseaworthiness of the vessel, an inoperable water supply to a sprinkler system, etc., he may deny liability. There have been numerous such denials upheld by the courts. Policies generally specifically protect the underwriter against fraud, but public policy would probably make the contract unenforceable anyway. Lack of full disclosure of material information to an underwriter can sometimes have the same result.

Keep the underwriter in mind. He's the one who pays the losses. Other than certain underwriting pools or syndicates, and underwriters of certain classes of insurance where the emphasis is on loss prevention, most insurance is an application of the law of large numbers. It performs the function of reducing the impact of losses. At the other end of the

---

[1] Safety services, defense, etc. in liability claims; pursuing subrogation rights against carriers or other third parties, etc., in property insurance.

spectrum, when a risk is unique, or nearly so, there is no spread of risk. This risk becomes unattractive to an underwriter because he cannot use the law of large numbers. He will gain a very little or lose a great deal. If he accepts the risk, he will almost certainly charge a premium far in excess of that for a common risk on which he has a "book" of business. Underwriting a "single shot" risk is more like gambling than insurance.

Insurance, like most everything else, is going through a constant evolution so that too precise a definition of insurable risk would only confuse the issue. If there is a risk of financial loss because of some unexpected but possible future event which can be clearly described, the risk is theoretically insurable. Coverage may not be available today, but tomorrow it might.

Risk recognition

Risk recognition for our purposes means *insurable* risk recognition. The average business executive becomes involved in a wide array of risks, most of which have to do with possible profit and have nothing to do with insurable risk. Yet failure to recognize and take proper action on insurable risks continues to bankrupt many companies.

This section will not make the reader an expert on insurable risk recognition, but it should help throw some light on a difficult subject. Ideally, a company could decide how many dollars, or perhaps how many cents per share it could afford to self-assume each year, and could then transfer to insurors all losses from insurable risks beyond this figure. Transfer of some specific risks over x dollars per occurrence or subject to an annual aggregate self-assumption is possible, but the risks remain identifiable. Transferring all insurable risks is not presently possible. Although we have come a long way, we are far from the ideal expressed above. Tomorrow it may be different, but we must try to solve today's problems with today's tools.

Insurable risks involve potential loss of, or damage to, property or the loss of its use on the one side, and potential liability to others including expense of investigation, defense, etc., on the other. As you read insurance contracts, you will see the words "peril" and "hazard" from time to time. These words refer to the potential causes of loss, damage, or injury.

Property risks

Property insurable risk recognition is really a combination of the following: identification of the types of property potentially exposed to loss, damage, or loss of use; consideration of the perils which could create a loss; and the types of loss that could eventuate. For example, a factory is subject to damage by fire. It could also be destroyed or seriously damaged by any of a long list of other perils. The result would be direct loss to or destruction of the property and, depending on the extent of damage, possible loss of use of the property in addition.

Let's consider a serious fire. Direct loss or damage caused by the fire would be covered by the fire insurance policy subject otherwise to its terms and conditions. The loss of profit and continuing necessary expenses would be covered by the business interruption policy, if any, subject to its terms and conditions. But suppose that particular plant was the company's only one, at least for that product, and it was not only a matter of collecting the dollars representing lost profits and continuing expenses throughout the period of down time but also, and possibly more important, a matter of protection of market position and therefore possible survival. You would then be forced to use every means to deliver the product *no matter what the extra expense.* This would probably include accelerated reconstruction *no matter what the extra expense.* However, it could also mean the use of any other available means temporarily, for example, having the product manufactured by others *no matter what the extra expense.* These extra expense dollars could be staggering. To the extent, *but only to the extent,* that they reduce the business interruption loss, they are covered by the business interruption policy subject otherwise to its terms and conditions. But the extra expense dollars beyond those recoverable under a business interruption policy represent a large potential risk for some companies who must continue to deliver their product or suffer serious long term problems. This is not always recognized as an insurable risk. Coverage is available under an extra expense policy.

So we must look at each type of property and try to evaluate its insurable risk characteristics as to direct and indirect or consequential loss possibilities. This is quite an order. The following list is not complete; it could go on and on. However, if you will read it slowly and ask yourself in each case what perils could directly or indirectly affect each type of property; what types of loss could result (direct damage, loss of use, extra expense, etc.); and how many loss dollars could be involved in each case, the scope of the problem will become more evident.

Types of property (not intended to be complete):
1. Buildings and structures if owned, used, or liable by contract.
2. Leasehold improvements to leased premises.
3. Machinery, furniture, and fixtures.
4. Molds, patterns, tools, dies, jigs, etc.
5. Raw materials and supplies.
6. Work in process.
7. Finished goods.
8. Property of others in your care, custody, or control.
9. Boilers, machinery, and electrical apparatus where the perils originate within the property itself, e.g., explosion, disintegration, short circuit, etc.

10. Data processing equipment and media.
11. Money, securities, bullion, rare stones, jewelry, furs, fine arts, etc., where highly concentrated values are involved.
12. Valuable papers and records where what is on the paper constitutes the value.
13. Accounts receivable.
14. Scientific, photographic, radio and television broadcasting equipment.
15. Salesmen's samples.
16. Property on lease, loan, exhibition, consignment, or conditional sale to others.
17. Property on the premises of others for processing.
18. Property in transit domestically.
19. Property in warehouse.
20. Property in transit to or from a foreign country.
21. Property located abroad.
22. Motor vehicles.
23. Plate glass.

It must be apparent that most of the above have different hazard characteristics, e.g., money is exposed to theft, but a building is not. Fire is a potential hazard to all property, wind, water, explosion, earthquake, and flood to most, internal breakdown to some, theft to some, etc.

Ideally, we could lump all property into one policy and not have to select the perils. But it's not that simple, although much progress has been made in the direction of blanket, broad peril coverage.

Let's look at the policies making up a typical manufacturer's property program, assuming reasonable sophistication.

MANUFACTURING LOCATIONS
1. *Fire.* This will be a policy covering direct damage to real (principally buildings and structures) and personal (other property except money, etc.) property, blanket over all locations. Perils will be fire, extended coverage,[2] vandalism, and sprinkler leakage.

2. *Business interruption.* This will cover loss of profits and continuing necessary expenses on the same locations and for the same perils as in 1.

3. *Boiler and machinery.* This policy will also be blanket and should include coverage on all equipment, including electrical, whose use creates a potentially serious loss from explosion, disintegration, or breakdown. Business interruption is usually included in the same policy, often

---

[2] Extended coverage extends coverage to direct loss from windstorm, hail, explosion, riot, riot attending a strike, civil commotion, aircraft, vehicles, and smoke. Each peril is defined in the endorsement. The words cannot be taken literally.

subject to less broad coverage and also to either a dollar deductible or a waiting period.

4. *Difference in conditions.* This is an "all risk"[3] policy on real and personal property covering manufacturing locations. Naturally it excludes perils already covered by the fire and boiler and machinery policies. It can be written to include warehouses, etc., and can include business interruption. D.I.C. policies generally have deductibles well into five figures to make the risk palatable to underwriters and the cost acceptable to insureds. (They are also useful where buildings are in course of construction.)

PROPERTY NOT AT MANUFACTURING LOCATIONS

1. *Manufacturer's output.* This is a blanket "all risk" policy covering personal property in transit and elsewhere, e.g., in warehouse, at distributors, at processors, etc. There is generally automatic coverage for locations not listed in the policy subject to a negotiated limit of liability.

2. *Ocean cargo.* This is a blanket policy on imports and exports. Coverage is usually "all risk," but may be more restricted in some cases, e.g., bulk shipments.

SPECIAL HAZARD COVERAGES

1. *Blanket crime or dishonesty, disappearance, and destruction.* These are the two principal types of blanket bonds covering employee dishonesty, depositors' forgery, credit card forgery, and money and securities.

2. *Electronic data processing.* This is an "all risk" policy including breakdown. It covers hardware and software and can include extra expense coverage.

The key to risk recognition lies in an understanding of the property policies in force to determine what is being self-assumed. Read the policies, particularly the insuring agreements, limitations, warranties, valuation clauses, and exclusions. Self-assumption can be deliberate or unavoidable. Unfortunately, it is often unintentional, sometimes through accident, frequently through ignorance.

Let's take a closer look at the indirect or consequential loss possibilities. These are generally less obvious and consequently less well understood. Direct and/or contingent coverage is available for most exposures.

BUSINESS INTERRUPTION.   A business interruption loss can arise from many causes:

---

[3] "All risk" is always in quotes because the coverage is not standard nor does it ever cover all perils. There are always exclusions and limitations, some of which are negotiable but all of which must be read and understood. The term cannot be taken literally.

1. Direct damage to manufacturing (or sales) premises, or damage while in course of construction. This damage and consequent loss of use can result in loss of profits, obligation for continued payroll expense,[4] and continued contractual obligations, e.g., heat, light, power, advertising, rent, telephone, etc. Keep in mind also that use of some equipment, e.g., boilers, turbines, etc., creates special hazards with severe potential but frequently unrecognized business interruption problems.
2. Direct damage to the premises or contents of an exclusive supplier of a product, or of a key ingredient or component part, or of new machinery on order, or of a key supplier to him.
3. Direct damage to the plant or store of a purchaser, or all or an important part of output or sales, or direct damage of a key customer of his. Either could result in cancellations.
4. Direct damage to key machinery, component parts, or ingredients in storage or in course of delivery or installation.
5. Shutdown of manufacturing premises or of a supplier or customer by loss of off-premises power, by civil authority or strike.
6. Additional delay in reconstruction because of required demolition of undamaged portion due to changed building regulations.
7. Direct damage to key research facilities. This is a situation where the loss will be difficult, perhaps impossible, to prove. An agreed-in-advance daily amount of indemnity is the acceptable solution.

EXTRA EXPENSE. When part or all of an operation is shut down because of fire, explosion, etc., it sometimes is necessary or desirable to spend a great deal more than otherwise would be required in order to accelerate a return to normalcy. To the extent, but only to the extent, that the business interruption loss is reduced, these extra dollars are considered part of the business interruption loss. However, if it is a matter of delivering the product no matter what the cost in order to protect market position, or because of a contractual obligation, a problem exists which a business interruption policy alone cannot possibly solve.

Sometimes it is a matter of extra dollars, not to accelerate getting back into business or contracting the work out, but rather to get on schedule in new construction which has been damaged, irrespective of overtime, etc., or to accelerate manufacturing, delivery, and installation of new and more efficient machinery or equipment which has been destroyed or damaged prior to installation. Remember, the damage causing the delay

---

[4] Payroll for business interruption insurance purposes is considered as either "key" and "ordinary." "Key" represents executives and other personnel necessary to be kept on the payroll even though operations are curtailed. "Ordinary" is the rest, all presumably easily replaceable. Where ordinary payroll is deducted on the worksheet, it is up to the insured as to the distinction. Be sure a copy is retained in event of loss.

may occur during manufacture and well before title transfers, maybe even at some remote component supplier's. Or it may occur in transit, but the loss is just as real.

Sometimes direct damage to nonproduction facilities, research labs, executive offices, etc. creates a need for immediate substitute space, equipment, help, etc. The possibilities of an extra expense loss are broader than is generally realized.

Demolition and increased cost of construction. Building codes change over the years. Some buildings are of construction outlawed since they were completed. In many areas the building code requires demolition of outlawed construction if they are damaged in excess of, say, 50 percent. With buildings like this, there is a twofold risk of loss which must be considered. The extent of loss at risk is not only the cost of demolition of the undamaged portion, but the increased cost of construction of an entirely new and probably more costly building.

Other risks of potential indirect loss which should be recognized are loss of rents on property leased to others, liability for continued rents on leased property, loss of a valuable leasehold, and loss of royalties or license fees where the licensee is shut down.

Liability risks

There are two kinds of potential insurable liability for damages: liability for torts and liability by contract. A tort is a civil wrong, other than a breach of contract, for which the court will provide a remedy in the form of an action for damages. Thus tort liability is created either by negligence or by statute. However, for insurance purposes, we must separate liability exposures into *statutory, negligence,* and *contractual.*

STATUTORY LIABILITY.   There are a few statutes which create liability on the part of an employer to its employees which it might not otherwise have.

Workmen's compensation.   All 50 states and Puerto Rico have workmen's compensation acts which cover most employment and most employees. These acts vary from state to state, but all create a liability on the part of most employers. In addition, most states make employers liable for workmen's compensation benefits payable to employees of contractors who fail to provide coverage and who cannot pay themselves. This latter is a widely unrecognized risk which can be avoided by obtaining certification of insurance from the contractor.

There are other statutory liabilities, less frequently found, but just as binding on the employer. The principal ones are the Longshoremen's and Harborworker's Act applying to casual employment on navigable waters and nonpublic employees in the District of Columbia, and the Jones Act applying to seamen.

Reimbursement of directors and officers.   Many states have statutes which enable a company to reimburse anyone under qualified circumstances who is or was a director or officer. Most statutes are simply enabling statutes. They enable a company to reimburse *under certain qualified circumstances,* principally when the individual was acting in good faith and in what he reasonably believed was the best interest of the company. Several states confer qualified reimbursement rights directly to the individuals, in which case the reimbursement liability, to the extent provided by the statute, becomes a statutory liability. From a risk point of view, most companies have changed the nature of the liability by granting the right to reimbursement under qualified circumstances in their charter or bylaw. This establishes the company's risk. However, an important and often unrecognized risk here is the risk of insurable yet unreimburseable liability on the part of one or more of the individual officers and/or directors. The principal, but by no means exclusive, example is the risk of an unsuccessful defense of a stockholder's derivative action. In this case, the award (less legal fees) goes to the corporation and reimbursement would obviously not be proper. This is a risk which has become widely recognized only in recent years. Coverage is available under a directors' and officers' liability policy. The policy has two sections. One covers the company for its reimbursement liability; the other covers the directors and officers for their insurable but not reimburseable liability.

Statutes policed by the S.E.C. A number of court actions have highlighted the statutory civil liabilities of companies, their directors, officers, and other "insiders" under the Federal Securities Acts. The principal risks arise from errors or omissions in the registration statement of an original or secondary securities issue, and from distribution of information in the form of proxy statements or publicity releases. Specific insurance is designed for registered offerings although coverage is not always available. Most large secondaries are insured. The securities underwriter who also has a statutory liability usually insists on it as well as being named as an insured.

Other statutory risks. Many states have statutes making the user strictly liable for damage through use of explosives. Some states have "Safe Place To Work" statutes covering, for example, construction, where the owner or general contractor may have an absolute and nondelegable liability for bodily injuries arising out of failure to provide a safe place to work. Many states have "Blue Sky" or other securities laws which apply to securities sales. Counsel should be consulted to ascertain whether there are other statutes in the states in which the company operates which can affect its liability for civil damages to third parties. Risks may exist which have not yet been recognized.

Negligence liability. This is the most common type of liability. With the increasingly successful activity of plaintiffs' attorneys in the negligence field, it is difficult to feel comfortable that any activity in which a company is engaged will be free of alleged negligent damage to the person or property of others. And since the employer is liable for the acts of its employees and also more and more for damages arising out of the use or consumption of products manufactured, sold, or distributed by it, the risk potential of any company is considerable.

There are countless risks of potential liability for damages because of personal[5] injury or property damage from operating a business. These can arise out of operations at or from occupied premises or the premises of others; ownership of nonoccupied premises; use, ownership, or control of machinery, equipment, or other property such as vehicles, aircraft, or watercraft, or railroads or other operations or activities away from owned or occupied premises; and the manufacture, sale, or distribution of products or the performance of services for others. Liability policies should be inspected carefully to be certain adequate coverage exists.

Liability for damages arising out of the manufacture or sale of products seems not only to be approaching being absolute in many cases, but additional, sometimes quite unexpected, problems may arise. A company may be obligated to recall or have destroyed all similar products at its expense. Or the product may be a component part or an ingredient of someone else's product where liability may involve not only the initial damages sought by allegedly injured third parties but, in addition, the liability to the customer for damage to his product including his cost of recall, sorting, etc. If a product is an advertised consumer product this could have far-reaching implications. The publicity could be such as to require complete withdrawal of the trade name. This could create additional loss beyond lost sales because of the need for the introduction of a new product with possibly large start-up expense. Additional research, development, testing, advertising, etc., can run to large figures. These risks, a mixture of property and liability, are real. Coverage can sometimes be tailored to the need if there is one.

CONTRACTUAL LIABILITY.   Here is an insufficiently understood field of liability exposure from a risk recognition point of view. Oral or written contractual responsibility can create a liability in the eyes of the law which is independent of any statutory or negligence liability. We may not be negligent or have any statutory liability, but we may be liable nevertheless because we, or an employee acting within the scope of his employment, agreed to be before the fact. Employees, by orally agreeing to or by signing a contract, can create this liability. Contractual liability can be found in all the myriad types of contracts accepted or

---

[5] "Personal" injury is distinguished from "bodily" injury. It includes "bodily," and also libel, slander, defamation, invasion of privacy, false arrest, and other specific injuries to the person which are not injuries to the body. Unfortunately for the insured, "personal" injury is defined when insured. Definitions vary and often leave coverage gaps.

agreed to by representatives of companies. These include but are not restricted to leases of premises, machinery, equipment, vehicles, watercraft, aircraft; construction, delivery, service, or maintenance contracts; easement agreements; permits with city, state, or federal government or authorities; sales or purchase agreements; sidetrack agreements, etc.

The odds in favor of any company's existing without some potential contractual liability someplace along the line are about nil. The coverage afforded by the standard comprehensive general liability policy is very limited.

Errors and omissions. Some businesses are exposed to a special type of liability. Their potential liability for damages because of alleged personal injury or damage to tangible property can be the same as most other businesses. But there is an additional risk of liability. Accountants, actuarial firms, architects, attorneys, data processing companies, engineering firms, insurance agents and brokers, management consultants, etc. all can create a civil liability for damages where there is no personal injury, nor is any tangible property damaged. Yet there can be a loss because of an error or omission, poor advice, wrong information, or failure to advise, with a resulting potential action for substantial damages. These are genuine risks not only to professionals but also to companies employing professionals and on whose advice others rely or whose design errors may create liability. Generally, special coverage is needed.

Package policies

It is possible to combine many property and nonstatutory liability coverages into one policy. There is a potential saving, but it generally works out better for smaller companies than larger ones where separate insurors may be desirable.

UMBRELLA LIABILITY. Most manufacturers buy an umbrella liability policy. This is an "all risk" liability policy covering in excess of the usual specific policies or a deductible of at least $10,000 where there is no underlying coverage. Yet, broad as the coverage is, it is restricted to claims for damages for personal injury, damage to tangible property, and advertising liability. Policies are not standard and should be reviewed carefully.

Loss control

It should be obvious that the better the loss experience, the better the insured's bargaining position with underwriters from the point of view of broader coverage, lower cost, and leverage in loss adjusting. Loss control is an absolutely vital part of any effective insurance program. Less obvious is the fact that the hidden loss factor is frequently higher than the actual loss itself. The National Safety Council reports workmen's compensation losses paid are only 20 percent of the actual loss. The hidden loss factor is thus four times the apparent figure. Some professionals feel it is more like six times. The average accident is not an isolated event. Consider the combined effect of down time, damaged products and/or machinery, reduced production because of emotional impact on fellow employees, particularly witnesses, discussion time, report filing, testimony, etc., plus the insurance company's expenses in handling and the future effect on insurance expense because of experience rating. All losses have hidden loss factors. Unless there is fraud it is impossible to come out even.

Loss control pays off, not the slightest question about it. The larger the company, the more credibility is attached to its loss experience. Thus, as a company grows, the value of loss control grows. What is surprising is that more companies don't see the obvious and do more about it. Keep in mind loss control embraces more than prevention. It includes prompt and effective reporting procedures, minimizing of effect, and efforts to prevent recurrence. Alert companies solicit help from their own personnel, their representatives, and insurance carriers. They listen carefully to all recommendations. They don't discard any lightly. They know loss control is cost control.

Loss prevention

Every plant, warehouse, hotel, store, exhibition, construction area, etc. where machinery is used, merchandise is handled, or where the public is involved, and every fleet of vehicles, trains, ships, or aircraft should have a formal accident prevention program. It should not be left to chance.

All employees, wherever employed, should have pre-employment physical examinations. The company's workmen's compensation and benefit plans should not be exposed to a new employee's pre-existing medical problems without prior knowledge and appropriate records.

Third party liability losses can be reduced by avoiding assuming liability of others through acceptance of contracts containing hold harmless provisions. Try to assume nothing except liability for sole negligence. Consider having contractors and suppliers assume all liability arising out of their supplying goods or services. Counsel should be asked exactly how this can be accomplished. Be certain certificates of insurance are supplied in every case. They should be for workmen's compensation, comprehensive general, and products and/or completed operations, and also comprehensive automobile liability if applicable. It is vital that any assumed liability be certified; it may otherwise be excluded, since it is a standard exclusion. A bankrupt contractor or supplier is of little use.

The subject of contractual liability is not widely understood; yet it provides potentially serious loss possibilities often overlooked and therefore frequently uninsured. Every contract should be reviewed with the preceding comments in mind before it is accepted. All liability insurances should be properly endorsed to cover potential liability. A word of caution: companies should avoid accepting leases, particularly in sole tenancies, where the lessee agrees to return the property in the condition received, wear and tear excepted. This makes the lessee an "all risk" insuror but probably without insurance, other than a properly written umbrella liability policy; fire legal liability policies exclude contractual liability. The point is to avoid potential loss-producing situations.

Every occupied premises where values are high or loss of use could cripple the operation should have a property loss prevention program starting with a trained fire brigade. This includes new construction where all plans should be reviewed by the company's insurance representatives and carriers in the draft stage. Even where old buildings are involved, there are effective loss prevention steps which can be taken. Get help—it's available. Establish a program.

As to recommendations offered, ask "Why not?" not "Why?" These people are generally skilled in their trade. Some insurance companies are particularly skilled in certain types of risks. This is where knowledge of the marketplace comes in. If you have doubts that the present insurance carrier is best for your company, ask your representative to explain. Maybe it isn't.

Minimizing loss effect

In most cases, losses or claims will develop even with the most elaborate prevention program. Still, an effective program to minimize the after effects will be highly productive. Fire losses cannot be totally prevented, but if there is a well designed fire protection system, proper fire fighting equipment, and a trained fire brigade, they can be minimized. All unsprinklered properties should be evaluated as to the advisability of a sprinkler system. A properly designed sprinkler system with adequate water supplies will not prevent a fire, but it will control one and minimize its effect. Also, the expense can frequently be amortized through savings in insurance expense through reduced rates.

Duplicate programs, time sharing agreements, fireproof storage, etc. will help minimize EDP, valuable paper, and accounts receivable losses.

Transit losses cannot be totally prevented. They can be reduced in number and effect, however, by careful packing, by selling f.o.b., by avoiding labels which advertise the contents if they are susceptible to theft, by shipping on a declared value bill of lading where the additional cost over a released bill of lading can be passed on to the consignee, by accuracy in preparation of packing slips, by careful inspection of incoming shipments to disclose external evidence of shortage or damage and noting any shortage or damage on receipt before signing.

Dishonesty losses cannot be completely prevented. Their incidence and severity can be reduced by an awareness of how embezzlers work, and by realizing that it is usually a trusted employee who is involved. Having all new employees who have any possible access to money or merchandise complete individual fidelity bond application forms has been found to be helpful.

Probably the most common opportunity to minimize loss effect comes in workmen's compensation and third party accidents. Insurance cost on workmen's compensation, general, products, automobile, and other liability is directly related to loss experience. Most loss dollars used in experiencing rating formulae are the result of someone's guess. It's an educated guess, to be sure, but a guess nevertheless. Insurance companies have claims examiners who estimate the value of all workmen's compensation and third party liability claims not finally settled. Few claims involving bodily injury are settled immediately. These estimated amounts are called "reserves," and are used in experience rating plans. It must be clear that the loss experience in workmen's compensation, etc., although directly affecting prospective insurance expense, is usually only an *apparent* loss experience and can be influenced by changes in reserves. It follows that all reserves should be reviewed carefully before being used in any rating formula. This review should be done by someone representing the insured competent to argue with the insurer's claims people on *their professional level.* This is a big order.

Another excellent loss control device is to allocate premium expense, self-assumed risks, and deductibles on the basis of each profit center, division, or subsidiary's own losses. There are countless possibilities, but remember to use a sensible dollar limit per event and per year in order that the plan be reasonable. There should always be a minimum, even with no losses. In some cases this will not take care of all the dollars needed. The excess can be pooled. These internal allocation plans are effective motivators and are highly recommended.

Loss reporting

Prompt notice of loss or claim is not only required but is also in your company's best interest. This is particularly true in liability claims where witnesses may disappear. A reporting procedure for all claims should be established with your insurors so that everyone knows what is expected. This procedure should be part of the insurance manual. Where there is an internal allocation plan based on losses, it is most important that a coding plan be established and that the reports be properly coded. Sometimes special report or enclosure forms are desirable to ease the flow of papers. Be certain that if there is a possibility that a third party, e.g., a supplier, may be liable, the report calls attention to it. If his coverage has previously been certified, this should be noted.

Loss control is an important program. It is nothing to take for granted.

It should not be static. It should expand and be refined as time goes on. The company which seeks constantly to improve in all facets will probably develop a more effective loss control program with resulting broader insuring provisions and lower costs than one which ignores opportunities. Like any other goal, it takes planning, organization, and cooperation both from within and without. However, it's worthwhile and can usually be achieved.

Self-assumption methods

Why should an insured pay an insuror to return the insured's *money* less the insuror's *overhead?* As companies grow, so do premiums and probable losses, thus creating opportunities for self-assumption.[6] Many companies self-assume the entire property risk where there is no catastrophe involved, e.g., collision on private passenger cars, plate glass, parcel post, etc. This is sensible. The risks which can probably be safely self-assumed over the long pull will vary from company to company, but be alert to the savings possibilities.

Self-assumption of all or a portion of the risk takes on different forms with different risks. One or more methods of self-assumption are available in most cases where the annual property premium is in five or more figures. In liability, most professionals feel higher annual premiums are required. Middle five figures are considered to be the minimum, with very few exceptions. Let's look at the most common types of self-assumption.

Deductible

This is the most common form of self-assumption in property coverages. In boiler and machinery business interruption, the deductible can be expressed in time (first midnight, etc.). Normally, deductibles are not available in statutory liability coverages. When they are used in other third party liability insurances, it is usually either at the insuror's insistence to avoid the expense and nuisance of small claims, e.g., property damage liability in chain stores (ripped clothing, etc.), or in umbrella liability where deductibles start at $10,000.

Disappearing deductible

These are used only in property, principally fire insurance. They are growing in popularity. Here the net loss, after application of the deductible, is increased by a fixed percentage, thus partially or totally offsetting the deductible. The larger the loss, the larger the dollar offset. For

---

[6] "Self-assumption" and "self-insurance" are used interchangeably, although technically the latter implies a formal plan of setting aside (nondeductible) reserves.

example, with a $10,000 disappearing deductible, the factor is 25 percent. A $20,000 claim would generate a payment of $12,500 ($20,000 less $10,000 is $10,000 plus 25 percent, or $2,500, totals $12,500). A $10,000 deductible would thus disappear on a gross claim of $50,000 or more ($50,000 less $10,000 equals $40,000 plus 25 percent, or $10,000, equals $50,000). Naturally, the discount is less than for a straight deductible.

Retrospective rating

Retrospective plans are most commonly found in the liability field, principally workmen's compensation. What follows is over-simplified, but essentially the concept is unlike guaranteed cost, the usual liability premium computation method. In this method the rates are established at the outset. Thus, final cost is "guaranteed" once the exposures are determined for the policy period, usually by physical audit after expiration. Retrospective rating plans use losses occurring *during* the policy period. What is retrospective is the method of calculation of the premium subject to the retrospective agreement. There are a number of plans available, but the operation is essentially the same. The final retrospective premium (subject to a minimum and a maximum) consists of:

a) State premium taxes (tax multiplier).

b) Limited[7] losses and claims handling costs (limited losses × loss conversion factor).

c) All other expenses (basic premium).

Annual adjustments are made until all claims are closed out or until insured and insuror jointly agree to close out the particular year. These are really cost-plus plans, the degree of self-assumption lying in the size of the loss limit, minimum and maximum premiums. All things being equal, the higher these factors, the more self-assumption.

Let's take an example. Assume (subject to "retro" rating) standard premium of $100,000; basic premium 25 percent; loss conversion factor 1.14; minimum premium 75 percent; maximum premium 110 percent; tax multiplier 1.03; and losses $50,000. Indicated retrospective premium would be $25,000 (25 percent of $100,000) plus $57,000 ($50,000 times 1.14) or $82,000 times 1.03 or $84,460. This would also be the final retrospective premium since it falls between minimum ($75,000) and maximum ($110,000).

Most retro plans are tabular and are designed for workmen's compensation only. There are a variety of tabular plans, each with different self-assumption characteristics. Plan D allows other liability coverages and is extremely flexible as to the factors. There are other rating plans using current losses, but beware any glib talk on the subject; it is one for

---

[7] Losses are generally limited to $10,000 or more per accident. The cost to buy this limitation is added to the basic premium. If other liability insurance is subject to "retro" rating, the cost for that limitation is charged separately.

the top-drawer professionals only. Also beware of three-year plans—one poor year can destroy the benefit of two good ones. Underwriters naturally like three year plans.

Self-insurance

The distinction between self-insurance and other self-assumption is that self-assumptions generally are simply expensed, whereas self-insurance involves setting aside (nondeductible) reserves. It is rarely found outside workmen's compensation. The trend is distinctly away from liability self-insurance. Modern liability rating plans allow sophisticated buyers an almost unlimited choice of combinations of self-assumption and insuror services, the latter of which the insuror can generally perform more efficiently. Self-insurance is no bargain in most cases. Most self-insurors have been so for a long time, often where habit has taken over and many of the true expenses have long since lost their original visibility. More companies come out of it than go into it. Companies involved or tempted to be should take a hard look at all the costs. It is the exceptional case which is justifiable today. Where it is found, there is always the risk of a catastrophic loss for which excess insurance is generally arranged. Excess is a term used to describe liability insurance in excess of self-insurance or of other (primary) insurance. Complete self-insurance is a risk few self-insurors take unless coverage is unavailable.

Captive insurance companies

There has been a recent resurgence of interest in captives, particularly the foreign or offshore captive. The domestic captive, while occasionally logical, has less to recommend it because of the difficulties in setting it up, administering it, and satisfying the various state insurance departments. Offshore captives are most frequently domiciled in Bermuda. It is nearby, start-up and administrative costs are low, and only a relatively modest amount is required to be kept on deposit locally. Premiums paid the captive are deductible here, but retained earnings are not taxed unless premiums on U.S. exposures exceed 5 percent. They can be used anywhere. Of course, if profits are exported to the U.S. they will be taxed.

Essentially, the offshore captive is useful where there are large, concentrated foreign property exposures, including offshore drilling rigs, and where the loss experience has been good. Offshore captives are useful also where they are jointly owned or where domestic coverage is unavailable, i.e., for flood, strikes, etc. Where liability exposures are involved or where insuror loss control services are required, captives begin to lose their attractiveness. Their principal proponents are those selling a captive insurance company administrative service, and the prospective president is often its most ardent supporter. However, sometimes they make a great deal of sense. Often they are best set up as reinsurors, at least initially, but only a feasibility study will tell. It is important that this be made by one of the very few organizations who are capable of and who can be relied on to make an objective study.

The insurance function

Because of potential, possibly disastrous, lawsuits arising out of events whose financial consequences are insurable, and because of potential loss, damage, destruction, or reduction in value or loss of use of company assets, it seems obvious that the insurance function should be in capable hands both internally and externally. The insurance function should not be treated as routine by senior management, as it too frequently is. The billions of dollars of uninsured yet insurable losses each year attest to the validity of this conclusion. It can't happen here? It can, and does.

Administration

Most companies have the insurance function directly or indirectly under the chief financial officer. The insurance responsibility can be full or part time depending not only on the size and complexity of the insurance program, but also on the quality, capacity, and interest of the broker or agent, if any. Where there are full-time people, they are often called risk managers; many prefer this title. However, most companies retain the title insurance manager or manager—corporate insurance on the basis that the chief executive is the real risk manager. The title is less important than recognition by management that effective administration is vital. As companies grow, the insurance program is likely to grow also, both in size and in complexity. Hopefully, the insurance manager, whether he be the treasurer, assistant treasurer, controller, assistant controller, or whoever has had the function on a part time basis during this growth period, is above average in capability. If, in addition, he has had the wholehearted cooperation of a professionally oriented and well staffed brokerage or agency firm on his side of the bargaining table, he will have increased his grasp of a subject that is anything but simple. If, further, he has had the good fortune of being part of the kind of management team where maximum use of personnel at their optimum capacity is one of the corporate ground rules, he will have been able to delegate an increasing amount of the insurance workload to a capable clerk, still retaining overall control. And if the clerk has been carefully chosen and trained, he or she will gradually have taken over enough of the load to delay the need for a full time insurance manager.

Ideally, employment of a full time manager will be deferred until the additional overhead necessarily created by hiring a fully qualified insurance manager represents only a small percentage of the insurance budget. Actually, the clerk may easily end up qualifying as insurance manager in many cases, at least in title, if he or she had the raw material in the beginning and has been given the opportunity to grow in stature and encouraged to become more educated both in insurance and in other areas. Insurance management is a function where poor selection may not be known until too late. It should not be treated casually.

The value of independent expertise on the buyer's side of the table is obvious. It has to come from someplace. This is not to imply anything unflattering about insurance companies. It must be presumed every insurance company intends to do the right thing. Yet potential differences of opinion between the best intentioned parties is a fact of life which it is better to be aware of. The fact is simply that the interests of insured and insuror are not always the same. Any other conclusion would be naive. This is presumably the basis of the steady growth of the large, fully staffed brokerage and agency firms and of the independent consulting field.

Brokers, agents, and consultants

Whereas some corporate insurance is purchased directly from insurors through full time salesmen, most is handled through brokers and agents. The legal distinction between broker and agent is that the broker represents the insured and theoretically is not limited to any particular insurance companies, whereas the agent represents the insuror and can offer only those insurors represented. As a practical matter, most brokers and agents are independent businessmen or organizations, many of whom deal with or represent enough insurance companies to make the distinction unimportant as it relates to the buyer. What is important to consider is that there are all levels of competence, ranging from part time salesmen of little or no competence to large, professionally oriented organizations staffed with qualified experts in all phases of coverage and loss control. In addition, several have an international network of branches and correspondents.

Consultants theoretically provide independent advice. They vary from practitioners of little competence but great salesmanship, sometimes with elaborate picture and graph-laden reports, to highly competent effective organizations. Consultants charge a fee for services rendered. Some are really brokers or agents willing to waive the fee in return for being named broker or agent. Services vary from a single assignment, e.g., a review of a corporate insurance program, to an annual retainership.

The name broker, agent, or consultant by itself is no guarantee of anything. The stockholders' interest is best served if competence in administration of insurance protection of corporate assets is not taken for granted. It may not exist.

Consolidation of policies

Consolidation of a company's insurance program into as few policies with as few insurors as practicable is an obvious goal. Yet the frequent failure to do this, thus losing the opportunity to develop broader coverage and lower premium and administrative costs, as well as more effective leverage for service and losses, hurts many companies unnecessarily.

The proliferation of policies resulting from a corporate merger, consolidation, or purchase of more than 50 percent of another company's voting stock or of part or all of its assets already covered by separate policies, presents the same type of opportunity. Unfortunately this opportunity is also often missed.

When an opportunity to consolidate policies exists, a study should be made including a complete listing of all policies, showing after each its ultimate disposition, i.e., "leave in force"; "change name of insured to _____ as of _____"; "add coverage under policy #_____ as of _____"; "cancel and add coverage to policy #_____ as of _____"; etc. No policy should be without a notation. This should include the date of change or cancellation, if any. Advance planning is important and can help prevent later problems.

Where a policy is cancelled, its return or a signed release is required. Choose the latter; its just as legal, and a dispute may arise later as to the wording of the policy.

EMPLOYEE BENEFITS. At some point along the line, consideration should be given to a split-off in the administration of the employee benefits plans. Some companies find this can be done more effectively through Personnel or Industrial Relations. Many who do this still leave the negotiating of contracts to the insurance functionary, who may have more effective access to insurors and be better able to watch over costs. They can get together prior to anniversary dates when rates and retentions may be subject to change, or anytime in between when negotiations with the insuror may be required.

Company policy

Company policy should be set by the board. It should not be left unexpressed. This policy should be in broad but definite terms. A good example is Westinghouse Air Brake's Business Insurance Policy as outlined below:

1. "The Company's policy regarding the assumption or insuring of hazards to which the Company and its Divisions and Subsidiaries are exposed is:

   a) To assume losses which, because of the size and spread of risk present little, if any, catastrophe exposure and, therefore, would not significantly affect the financial position of the Company, and

   b) To purchase insurance of the type and amount which will adequately protect those risks not assumed, and

   c) To eliminate or reduce, as far as practicable, through an effective loss prevention and safety program, the conditions and practices which cause losses.

2. _____, located at _____ and reporting to the Treasurer, has the responsibility of administering the insurance program for the Company, its Divisions and Subsidiaries, in keeping with established policy. His duties shall include the determination of risks to be insured; the selection of insurance brokers and carriers; the negotiation of insurance contracts and rates; the coordination of the loss prevention and safety program; and the establishment of the procedures necessary to carry out a sound insurance program. An Insurance Manual outlining coverages and procedures will be prepared and distributed to the Divisions and Subsidiaries as a reference.

3. Each Division and Subsidiary is asked to designate a person, preferably a Treasury Department employee, to handle insurance matters for that activity and provide liaison with _____ at _____."

The administration of the policy should be somewhere under the chief financial officer who, together with the insurance manager or intermediate financial officer, if any, should establish guidelines which form an operating policy. This should be flexible and subject to change on accepted recommendation of the insurance manager. The point is that management's policy should be expressed in writing. This is fairer to the insurance manager, and applies regardless of the size of the company. The guidelines should embrace the following elements of policy.

1. *Annual insurance report.* The guidelines should call for an annual insurance report to management by the insurance manager. This should include a schedule of all policies with very brief description of type and amounts of coverage, limitations, and exclusions. It should also include all coverage recommendations by the insurance functionary, broker, agent, consultant, or direct writer which could seriously affect the financial position of the company, but on which no action has been taken, together with approximate costs.

2. *Authority of insurance manager.* In addition to the above, the

guidelines should include what authority the insurance manager is given to act on behalf of the company. This might involve:

a) Incurring additional expense for coverage.

b) Selection of insurors.

c) Selection of brokers, agents, or consultants.

3. *Contracts.* The guidelines should establish policy as to company position in accepting liability of others to third parties (hold harmless clauses) and in freeing others from liability to the company (exculpatory clauses). The guidelines should establish which company officer is to approve which types of contracts (leases purchase order agreements, etc.), and should establish that copies of all contracts must be sent to the insurance manager, in draft stage, if possible, to be certain any assumed liability is recognized or can be insured.

4. *Insurance Manual.* An insurance manual is good only if there is a built in system to keep it up to date. Any manuals given subsidiaries or divisions should be procedure and information manuals rather than coverage manuals. Local managers should not become involved with trying to interpret coverage, generally speaking. It and the guidelines should be reviewed by the chief operating financial officer together with the insurance functionary at least annually. The manual should cover what local managers should know about:

a) Internal premium allocation plans.

b) Pooling of uninsured losses.

c) Loss control.

d) Loss reporting.

5. *Loss control.* See section on loss control earlier in this chapter.

6. *Loss records.* Detailed loss records should be kept by policy for five full policy years, each year adding the latest and dropping the oldest. These data are important in premium negotiations.

7. *Loss reporting.* See loss control section.

8. *Premium Allocation.* See loss control section.

9. *Pooling of uninsured losses.* See loss control section.

10. *Self-assumption.* This was discussed above in the section on self-assumption methods. Recognition of sensible self-assumption should come from the board. Some buyers think a limit should be expressed in dollars and be a reflection of cents per share. If a dollar figure is used, it should be evaluated annually. Refinement of this policy in the form of self-assumption of risk decisions and of cost-plus rating plans should be made or approved by the chief operating financial officer. Self-assumption of, for example, plate glass, parcel post shipments, etc., can be considered where there is no catastrophe exposure —all exposures less than x dollars.

Conclusion

It should be evident that a corporate insurance program is nothing to take for granted, although too many are. Shortcomings can result in unnecessary and possibly crippling financial loss. Many now bankrupt companies would be in business except for an inadequate insurance program. Where there is any self-assumption there should be an awareness of it. Unfortunately, self-assumption is not always intentional. It frequently exists because of ignorance of the availability of coverage. Every company should know what it has and what it doesn't have. Don't assume anything. This requires considerable thought, as well as knowledge on somebody's part. Where a company is represented by a truly competent broker or agent (don't assume it), help should be solicited to modernize and streamline the program. If there is any question, find one or hire a competent consultant. The material presented above will not make an expert of the reader, but it should be helpful in evaluating the corporate program and working with the experts.

Bibliography

Long, John D. and Gregg, Davis W. (Eds.). *Property and Liability Insurance Handbook* (The Irwin Series in Risk and Insurance), (Homewood, Ill.: Richard D. Irwin, Inc., 1965).

MacDonald, Donald L., *Corporate Risk Control* (New York: The Ronald Press Co., 1966).

The Hold Harmless Agreement, A Management Guide to Evaluation and Control (Chicago: The National Underwriter Co., 1968).

PART VIII

Financial
structure

Capital structure determination

J. N. Philips*

The appropriate capital structure for a business enterprise depends largely upon (a) the nature of the assets it employs and the way it manages them, and (b) the availability and cost of different types of capital (as discussed in the next six chapters in this handbook).

Needs determined by nature of business

As an illustration of the first of these determinants, consider the contrasting types of assets and the management of them in a natural gas pipeline company and in a wholesale produce firm.

The natural gas pipeline company needs a large amount of long-lived fixed plant capital and little working capital. It customarily purchases and sells under long-term contracts. New competitors can enter the market only by proving that they are needed to serve some public convenience or necessity. The company is financed principally, therefore, by long-term debt calibrated not only to the value of its plant investment but also to the expected revenues from the long-term sales contracts. The pipeline company deals with national underwriting firms, mostly located in New York City, and sells long-term bonds by private placement or by public sale.

By contrast, the company wholesaling fresh fruit and vegetables trades in spot markets and needs working capital for inventory rather than long-term capital for plant. Anyone able to obtain some working

---

* Executive Vice President, Eastern Gas and Fuel Associates, Boston, Mass.

capital, including the employees, can instantly become a competitor. The long-term publicly held bonds suitable for the pipeline cannot be justified for the produce wholesaler either on the basis of fixed plant as collateral, or on cash flows of sufficient certainty and timing to assure debt service; they cannot even be justified by the likelihood of a reasonably long-term continuation of the business enterprise based on its size, franchises, depth of management, and contracts.

The produce wholesaler, therefore, must use short-term bank loans, and, in most cities, bank branches will be found in the produce centers for the convenience of both the wholesaler who must make frequent visits to his banker and the responsible bank lending officer to keep a daily watch on his borrowers. If the produce wholesaler is incorporated, he may be required to guarantee personally his company's bank loans. The debt, therefore, is essentially a character loan to an individual, and the capital structure is really all equity.

Most business enterprises, of course, fall somewhere between our two extreme illustrations, and management has considerable discretion in determining the capital structure between the extremes of mostly long-term debt and mostly equity. This discretion often is not used because of inertia, prejudice against debt, and difficulty in making changes in existing capital structures.

Internal considerations

The interplay between management on the one hand, and the capital suppliers of loaned funds and of equity money on the other hand, thus involves many interconnected issues in trying to achieve the optimum capital structure of the firm. There are internal considerations which affect the desires of the management and there are external constraints which must be taken into consideration by the capital supplier.

The principal internal factor is the degree to which the business is capital intensive. Particularly because interest is deductible for tax purposes and dividends are not, businesses which require substantial capital require a significant amount of debt in order to produce a reasonable rate of return on the equity. For example, in transportation and utility firms, the total physical plant may very well exceed the annual sales volume by as much as 100 percent. If the entire plant is financed with equity, and a reasonable equity rate of return is to be achieved, the pre-tax margin of profits on sales volume would have to be considerably higher than if a reasonable amount of debt capital were used to finance the physical plant. Businesses with such relationships between plant and sales often have perpetual franchises, long-term contracts, and/or physical assets with sufficiently long lives that mortgage financing has become customary.

With more complicated corporate structures, additional internal considerations come into play. If a company is in several different businesses, it may be simpler for each subsidiary to finance itself along the lines of the practices current in its own trade rather than to try to have the parent corporation finance a mixture of businesses which confuse the analyst. Of course, the rise of the conglomerates and the readier acceptance of debentures relying on the general credit of the conglomerate parent instead of bonds which fasten on the specific physical assets of the subsidiaries has meant easier financing for those conglomerates which have succeeded in attracting a favorable investor attitude. The more widely known parent can then sometimes sell securities which its lesser known but technically more creditworthy subsidiaries cannot as easily do.

Foreign subsidiaries raise special and complex and continuously changing problems of finance. Wholly aside from restrictions on funds both exported and imported, many domestic lenders are doubtful about the security of mortgage money on assets held abroad. Since they would demand on such debt almost an equity rate of return, companies such as the United Fruit Company with substantial land holdings in Central America have traditionally been only slightly leveraged.

Responding to change

When the nature of an industry changes and historic attitudes of lenders lag behind the realities of the industry, it may be difficult to change established customs. The coal industry, for example, moved into a very capital intensive pattern when John L. Lewis accepted mechanization but demanded high hourly wages. Sales patterns were not concurrently changed, and coal was still sold on a spot basis. Only in recent years has the coal industry established a pattern of long-term sales contracts and, thereby, changed investor attitudes so that long-term debt financing could become possible.

The rapidity of growth of an industry also affects its attitude towards debt. If earnings are constantly reinvested and the rate of growth does not exceed the capital available from internal financing, there will be no need to incur debt, and often, no real consideration of the advantages or disadvantages of an underleveraged equity for the particular firm. This comes, in part, as a result of the tax burden if dividends are declared, taxes are paid, and then the funds are reinvested. The internal dollars available for growth are not reduced by an income tax payment by the owners.

Managerial decisions on debt to equity ratios are increasingly subject to rigorous analysis; they should reflect the degree to which the management is prepared to expose the stockholders' equity to some additional risk in return for enhanced profit possibilities on the equity. Too often, the management has not even considered this issue, or has done so in a rather unscientific way. Professor Donaldson's book, cited in the bibliography, states the modern approach, which is to consider a dynamic rather than a static test of debt capacity. Just as physicians took a fresh look at their ideas of the functioning of the human body following Harvey's discovery of the circulation of blood, the greater importance of cash flow in larger, more capital-intensive enterprises has meant that a different look must be taken at corporate capacity for debt.

Significance of cash flow

The true measure of debt capacity is a comparison of the size, timing, and certainty of the cash flow into the enterprise as compared with the cash flow out. As management increasingly relies upon sophisticated cash flow projections in policy determination, it increasingly realizes that the cost of a pure equity capital structure can actually be very great, and the risk of incurring debt can actually be very small.

Net cash flow, by which is meant not only the usual elements of net income plus depreciation, but also such regular and predictable items as deferred tax provisions, should be given frequent cool appraisal by management. This is particularly true, of course, when planning new financing. It is too easy to predict only constant forward progress, and good managers will not permit themselves the luxury of this sort of trap.

One obvious answer is to plot a disaster course, in order to have a balanced view of the degree of certainty in the estimates of future cash flow. There is nothing new about "best-worst" projections, but too frequently they are forgotten.

Even though the business may be largely supported by long-term contracts or other apparently certain streams of revenue, things can happen and customers can disappear, temporarily or permanently, for a multitude of reasons. And those can so often be the times when expenses, at least on a unit basis, will rise. So management should evaluate its expected cash flow on a "gloom and doom" basis, and if it will still support the contemplated fixed charges while maintaining other necessary expenditures, there can be a basis for feeling relaxed about its leveraged condition. This will be true even though the more traditional ratios of debt and fixed charges may cause raised eyebrows.

External considerations

There are, however, external traditions and constraints which may hamper a management in trying to develop an optimum debt to equity capital structure. For one thing, banks and rating bureaus still use, to a great extent, the kind of debt capacity standards which look only at the balance sheet. Although these institutions are beginning to request modern cash flow analyses, these often are used only as a background for comment upon more traditional ratio tabulations.

In addition, there often are complex tax considerations in revising a capital structure. Careful planning is required if the equity investment is to be reduced without the distributed cash being treated as ordinary income to the shareholders. Furthermore, from time to time new tax concepts develop such as that of "thin capitalization" in which interest payments may be treated as dividends, "unreasonable accumulation of capital" where internal financing may be regarded as a form of tax evasion, and other complex tax traps for those who would alter capital structure. Recently, the use of convertible debentures for acquisition purposes has been seriously discouraged by proposed changes in the tax treatment of them.

There may also be government controls or government guarantees to be considered. For example, the establishment of preferred ship mortgages by the federal government greatly facilitated marine financing, and the availability of FHA mortgage guarantees has been the principal source of capital for low and middle income housing. Non-government constraints may also be important. For example, until a change in membership rules in the summer of 1969, member firms of the New York Stock Exchange were not permitted to have public ownership; thus, most stock exchange equity capital is in the form of short-term partnership interests.

There are also styles and moods. The saying goes that "Wall Street is a village," and this village is subject to the rumors, fears, and hopes of any small in-group. In the 1960's convertible debentures became extraordinarily popular, not only because the debentures had a higher cash yield than the underlying stocks, but also because of a general mood of optimism about rising stock prices. Further, there were many managements who had not anticipated the requirement that their earnings be stated on an "as if converted" basis.

Flexibility of opportunity

Underwriting firms and other financial advisors keep themselves current on the mass of constraints that apply and opportunities that are available, so management's principal problem is to solve a jigsaw puzzle of fitting its internal needs and desires into the external constraints and opportunities of the marketplace. In all this, two issues are of prime importance—timing and flexibility. To the extent that management can build in options to prepay, forgiveness periods for delay, flexible sinking fund requirements, and other opportunities to change course, it will have greater command of its destiny. It will also have the flexibility to adjust to altered circumstances in the future and to take advantage of moods as they ebb and flow, interest rates as they go up and down, and tax laws as they change.

In short, an astute management at regular intervals will review both the changes in its internal circumstances and the changes in the external markets to reappraise the degree to which its existing capital structure is an optimum one. In making such an analysis, management has a fairly wide selection of "models" of capital structure from which to choose.

Choices of capital funds

On the question of what type of debt security to employ, one of the first decisions will be between a secured or an unsecured issue. The former looks to assets, the latter to the general credit and, particularly, to the future net cash flow of the enterprise. The secured lender looks to cash flow also, but is more influenced by the bricks and mortar of the properties involved. It appears that, as technology advances and a greater number of industries find they must periodically modernize their plants and adjust facilities to the demands of more rapidly changing markets, the mortgage type of debt financing becomes less attractive. There are just too many strictures and too many mechanical problems for both borrower and lender. Thus we have the growing popularity of the debenture in industrial debt financing. For utilities, real estate, and transportation concerns (with fungible collateral), the secured issue will probably remain an economical financing vehicle. Industrial firms, whose plants become economically obsolete faster than they deteriorate physically, are finding that even secured lenders are emphasizing general credit and cash flow.

We have referred to the recent popularity of convertible debentures, particularly for purchase money financing, but also for more general purposes as well. In a sense, this is a means for the issuing company to have some part of the best of both worlds—at least for a while. If convertibles are subordinated, and this is usually the case, they are really part of the equity base of the company. And upon conversion the company must continue to match or improve its equity performance upon this wider base or fall back in the eyes of its shareholders. But prior to conversion they offer all the advantages of debt, with tax deductibility of a fixed interest obligation on a discounted basis since convertibility permits a lower coupon. In a sense they are a means of selling equity at a premium while borrowing at a discount.

Straight preferred issues are seen less and less as time goes on, except for utilities which must issue them from time to time to keep down their debt ratios while avoiding the greater expense of a straight common equity issue. Even for utilities, the marketplace will accept only a minor proportion of preferred relative to the entire capital structure. For most industrial concerns, though, a preferred stock is just too expensive a form of fixed income security, largely because the dividend is paid out of after-tax profits.

The convertible preferred, like its cousin the convertible debenture, is seen increasingly often as a purchase money device, and for many of the same reasons. In this usage, it can have the additional important advantage of permitting a non-taxable merger transaction, assuming all the proper conditions are met.

There are further specialized ways of arranging financing, on or off the balance sheet. For example, the investment tax credit of recent years has been one of the factors in popularizing arrangements for "sale and leaseback" of certain types of equipment. The basic advantage of this procedure is the ability to borrow most or all of the cost of the equipment without *directly* affecting company credit, and where a company has more investment tax credits than it can utilize, it can probably find a lender who will share the benefit by lending at a discounted rate. As the practice spreads, however, it is recognized increasingly by accountants and analysts as a type of "borrowing" for special purposes.

Another specialized type of financing is the sale of commercial paper as a means of obtaining short-term money. This is largely restricted to finance companies, but has seen increasing use by other companies, often as a means for facilitating the financing of installment sales. It has even been used by utilities in recent years, in order to meet heavy seasonal borrowing requirements beyond those handled through more traditional bank borrowings. One advantage, not too palatable to the banks, is the absence of any necessity to maintain corresponding demand deposit balances. This makes it cheaper borrowing, but no financial manager should ignore his traditional banking relationships; they are far too valuable to be tossed aside lightly.

Special considerations

One thing to be remembered is that there are certain possibilities and economies of scale. That is to say, a small one- or two-man business does not have the range of options in the financial marketplace that are open to a large corporation. Nevertheless, some of the same principles of borrowing versus investing equity can and do apply to small and medium sized concerns.

Earlier in the chapter we mentioned some of the widely accepted views on debt capacity and debt-to-equity ratios. One often hears that for an industrial enterprise a debt ratio of 40 percent of total capitalization (long-term debt plus equity) is on the high side. This may or may not be the true case. It depends largely on the nature of the enterprise. Are there long-term contracts with price escalation? What are depreciation, depletion, and amortization policies? Is there "pass-through accounting," whereby the tax benefits of accelerated depreciation are in reality transferred into the equity account? Does the stock market put a value on the equity at something close to stated book value, or at a figure many times book? Does the company establish and maintain reserves for special obsolescence and the like? These are all questions whose answers have a material effect upon the true debt capacity of the business, to a far more meaningful extent than any traditionally accepted ratio, for they affect the size, certainty, and timing of cash flow.

By this time, one may be wondering if a debt-free capital structure is as desirable as many traditionalists would have us believe. It clearly is not. Leverage is merely the means by which the best use can be made of the owner's equity capital through sensible and safe employment of borrowed capital. This will be true so long as decisions as to capital structure take into account the realities of the particular business and the various factors that impact upon it.

Management preparedness

In brief, the appropriate capital structure with which to clothe a business enterprise, like the appropriate attire for a businessman, depends upon a balancing of many considerations—the physical assets to be clothed, the current styles, the customary dress for a particular occasion or activity, the habits and future plans of the wearer, the freedom of action he feels necessary, the price he feels he can pay, and a multitude of other more or less significant factors. The financial clothing should, above all, be adjustable; the capital structure must be able to change as the business grows, changes, or even shrinks, as tax considerations are altered, and as capital markets and other external factors come into play.

The optimum capital structure of any particular firm is always about to change. Good financial management is ready for such changes, and can even anticipate them.

Bibliography

DONALDSON, GORDON. *Corporate Debt Capacity* (Boston, Massachusetts: Division of Research, Graduate School of Business Administration, Harvard University, 1961)

GRAHAM, BENJAMIN, DAVID L. DODD and SIDNEY COTTLE. *Security Analysis, Fourth Edition* (New York: McGraw-Hill Book Co., 1962), particularly Chapter 40 on "Capitalization Structure" which, interestingly enough, comes in a part of the volume captioned "The Valuation of Common Stocks."

Relations with capital suppliers

William M. Cockrum*

Capital suppliers are sources of and intermediaries for both short- and long-term debt and/or equity capital. Capital suppliers have several requirements and needs which may be viewed as common denominators for initiating or maintaining good relations. These requirements are discussed broadly in the early part of this chapter. Later, specific aspects of relationships with various capital suppliers are covered in chapter sections devoted to the several types of capital suppliers—commercial banks, commercial-paper dealers, factors and commercial finance companies, institutional investors, SBIC's and venture-capital companies, investment bankers, and securities dealers. The problems of choosing among these capital suppliers when financing is needed are discussed in the three chapters immediately following this one.

Common denominators

Initially, the capital supplier requires a basic understanding of the history and operating environment of the business enterprise as well as specific detailed information about its operating results and forward plans, both good and bad. This background and business information, coupled with adequate exposure to management, will serve as the basis for the capital supplier's representative to make a personal judgment about the desirability of investing capital in the business. The representative's judgment and his knowledge of the role expected of the supplier

---

* Vice President, A. G. Becker & Co., Incorporated, New York.

will start a framework for the development of a business relationship. The commitment by the capital supplier to establish a business relationship will typically be determined by a "committee" of the capital supplier. These elements—adequate background information, the impression and judgment about management, the expected role of the capital supplier, and the "committee" decision—are common to relationships with capital suppliers.

Background information

The existing or potential capital supplier and its representative(s) must make a judgment about the adequacy and appropriateness of supplying capital to the business entity. This judgment is based primarily upon written and numerical information about the business. Thus, the financial executive's initial and continuing responsibility is to communicate as much information as is required by the supplier to reach sound conclusions about the business entity. A clear, simple, and frank dialogue is therefore the primary objective in providing information to the capital supplier.

The typical capital supplier deals with business entities through representatives organized along geographical or industry bases. The representative will be faced with recasting the information about and peculiarities of the business entity into a standardized format for use with his superiors and "committee" in reaching a decision to supply capital. This format usually requires extensive explanatory and descriptive material about the company and its industry as well as the arrangement of financial data into a consistent format for review by others. The financial executive, therefore, must initially seek to provide this background data to the representative in a simple, clear, and consistent format. Later, if capital is provided, monthly, quarterly, or annual updating and review of this information will be required by the capital supplier.

Initially, the supplier should receive historical audited and other financial data about the business entity. This information should include detailed income statements, balance sheets, and other pertinent statistics (all on a comparative basis for at least the last five fiscal years). The other statistical data are especially important and might include, for example, an analysis of loss experience and loss reserves for finance companies, inventory accounts for commodity traders, drilling experience and reserve information from oil companies, or rate and customer data for utilities. The information is best presented in exhibit form which contains all historical information on one page, i.e., all five income statements should be shown on one page.

Further, in establishing a relationship with a capital supplier, written material which describes the company's business, and its operating results should be included to the extent requested or required by the supplier. Later, as a relationship is established, the descriptive material and operating statistics will need to be continuously provided to the capital supplier on a comparative basis with prior years' experience.

Most capital suppliers will request audited statements from the business entity at the time of establishing a relationship as well as on a continuing basis thereafter. These statements will necessarily contain appropriate notes by the firm's auditors about the accounting procedures used in preparing the statements. Nevertheless, the capital supplier should be provided with a more detailed explanation of the specific accounting practices used by the business entity. For example, the details of inventory valuation, charge-off policies for accounts receivable, the determination of loss reserves, and any significant depreciation and depletion practices are areas of accounting which vary greatly and usually need an expanded explanation for the capital supplier. Of equal importance to the specific business entity is a summary of the peculiarities of the accounting system. Why the system is appropriate for the business and how it compares and contrasts with accounting practices used by similar businesses are significant.

The analysis of accounting practices among businesses within a particular industry is only the beginning of the comparisons which the capital supplier may make. Various numerical comparisons can be made which could include inventory turnover, return on sales, return on net worth, loss experience on receivables, and return on gross assets. These numerical comparisons will vary by industry but nevertheless will be employed to varying degrees by representatives of the capital supplier. Further, comparisons of geographical territories, suppliers, customers, etc. will also be drawn. The financial manager can act with certainty about the use of comparisons by capital suppliers, and, as a result, should take every opportunity to inquire about these comparisons and thus to try to be certain that appropriate and correct comparisons are made.

As noted later, some capital suppliers place special emphasis on historical operations yet others look equally to forward plans. Expected operating results for monthly, quarterly, or annual periods into the future need be provided to many potential and existing capital suppliers. (Some managements follow a policy of not releasing earnings forecasts. In such cases, sufficient information on expansion plans and capital requirements will probably suffice.) The plans will necessarily be comparable to and in the same detail as the historical information which has been provided to the supplier. It is important that future plans be presented fairly, pointing out positive and negative aspects, and, again, be provided in both numerical and descriptive form. One specific forward plan which is usually required by all short-term capital suppliers is a cash forecast which is necessary for suppliers to determine how their capital will be used and repaid.

The background information outlined in the preceding paragraphs is necessarily more detailed than the data usually provided to credit rating agencies, employees, or stockholders. Nevertheless, the information is required by the capital supplier as background for reaching a sound decision. However, his relationship with the business entity will (in most companies having public shareholders) place the supplier in the position of an "insider" as defined by the Securities Act of 1933 and the Securities and Exchange Commission. There is nothing irregular about the supplier being placed in this position although he should be notified specifically of his position and its legal ramifications and prohibitions against his using the position to personal advantage.

Finally, there are two generalities which apply to unfavorable operating results or publicity. First, few capital suppliers prefer to learn of unfavorable information after the fact. The early disclosure of unfavorable information is a must for sound relations with capital suppliers. Secondly, capital suppliers lose confidence in management when learning about significant business developments through news media rather than from the Financial Executive. More broadly, in any business entity with public shareholders, relations with capital suppliers are vastly improved when information which is reported in news media has been previously provided to that supplier or at least at the same time as the media release.

In summary, background information which capital suppliers require includes the numerical and descriptive explanation of historical results and forward planning, the peculiarities of the business entity's accounting, how and why comparisons should be made with competitors, and the anticipation of unfavorable or publicly disclosed information about the business. This background information typically makes the supplier an "insider."

Personal contact with management

The Financial Executive is the focal point for personal contact between the business and representatives of the capital supplier. The Financial Executive's duties require that he communicate through the background information noted earlier as well as personal visits with the capital supplier. The Executive should determine early what number of visits or pattern of personal exposure each capital supplier requires and prefers. Personal contact gives the Financial Executive an opportunity to create and build an image of the business entity which he represents and also permits him to evaluate the availability (and durability) of capital which can be provided by the supplier.

Adequate personal contact can not be overemphasized and, in almost all cases, an annual personal visit to each capital supplier is a minimal requirement for strong relations. Moreover, good relations with capital suppliers are usually based upon a broad exposure to several members of management. Financial Executives frequently overlook the importance of exposing capital suppliers to other members of management. Capital suppliers rely heavily upon their impression and judgment about management depth and experience in making capital available to the business entity. A Financial Executive improves the view of his company by exposing suppliers to key members of the management group. On the other hand, through visits with capital suppliers, non-financial managers can learn about the impact of their decisions and operations upon capital availability, and about what parts of their operations seem to be especially important and emphasized by capital suppliers.

Of special importance to the Financial Executive is the exposure of the chief executive officer to the capital supplier. The chief executive officer should have annual exposure to capital suppliers not only to reinforce the suppliers' impressions of management but also to confirm the financial officer's description of policy. Further, exposure to capital suppliers provides an opportunity for the chief executive officer to learn information which he may use in his management decisions. If the number of capital suppliers required by the business entity is extensive, time may not permit the chief executive officer to visit all suppliers, but he should meet with the "key" suppliers at least once each year.

Personal visits by the capital supplier to the business entity provide another excellent opportunity for representatives to meet operating management. Also, the Financial Executive should encourage representatives of the capital supplier to visit the company's headquarters and various operating locations, if appropriate.

Business relationship

A clear understanding of the exact and specific relationship which the business entity and capital supplier expect is a necessity in building a strong relationship. Certainly, such items as interest rate, dividend yield, maturity, sinking funds, or the dollar amount of capital available will be easily developed. However, often overlooked are the many other services which capital suppliers may have available or may wish to supply. All aspects must be clearly defined for an effective relationship.

For example, the availability of counsel about business direction and objectives, referral of merger and acquisition candidates, specific services related to cash management, or other services to the business entity must not be overlooked. These added services each have costs for the capital supplier. The capital supplier and the business entity must understand clearly the expectation of the other in order to define an adequate, sound, and profitable business relationship. Importantly, unstated expectations and assumptions by either the capital supplier or the business entity have over time weakened and broken many relationships because one party was disappointed in the other.

As businesses grow and begin to deal with a number of suppliers of the same type (for example, twenty or more commercial banks) the concept of "key" suppliers will evolve. A small number of the sources in each capital category will become relatively more important in providing not only funds but also added services to the corporation. Further, other suppliers will tend to note these key relationships and follow the lead established by the key suppliers. Special attention must thus be directed to the key suppliers not only in the form of exposure to management and adequate background information, but also, in many cases, with added compensation for the services provided.

As a company grows in asset size and earning power, the business entity may have less dependence on any single capital supplier. Further, many functions or services formerly provided by capital suppliers may be performed more economically inside the business. However, nothing replaces friendly, informed, and imaginative capital supplier relations, even though a firm policy of requiring adequate services and compensation is expected from and by the supplier. The Financial Executive must constantly remember that he has a responsibility first, to raise capital, and second, to raise it at the lowest possible long-term cost to the corporation. Rigid and tough policies about relationships and especially the compensation to the supplier may not produce the desired result of raising capital at the lowest possible long-term cost. One eighth of one percent per annum saved when money is generally available may preclude the business entity from borrowing urgently needed capital during tight money. Thus, a delicate balance of firm yet reasonable relationships is required to insure the availability of capital under all market conditions.

The committee

Most capital suppliers deal with business entities through representatives which have a general knowledge of the capital availability of the supplier. Typically, the final decision for placing capital rests with a number of senior executives or directors in the capital supplying institution. These men usually have extensive experience in supplying capital and a broad range of experience in dealing with various types of business endeavors. Through this group of individuals, "the committee," the capital supplier seeks to reach consistent judgments as well as protect itself against mistakes or poor judgment by any one representative. Generally, the larger the capital supplier the stronger the role of the committee, although small amounts of capital may be left to the discretion of an individual representative.

The Financial Executive is thus faced with circumstances wherein the availability of capital from the supplier is controlled by a group of individuals whom he does not know or with whom he has no direct relationship. A close association with the representative of the capital supplier therefore becomes all the more important in order for the Executive to be sure of the supplier's view of the business entity as well as the supplier's availability of capital. These circumstances reinforce the requirement for a continuous and strong personal relationship with the representative in order to adequately judge the availability of capital from each source and, in turn, to determine the total availability of capital to the business entity. While the representative may be quite willing to provide capital to the business, his ability to perform may at some times or in some circumstances be completely limited and the actions of his committee beyond his control. A strong relationship should expose these circumstances. Usually, the representative will make clear his position vis-a-vis his committee and the supplier's availability of capital for the business entity.

Commercial banks

Commercial banks are usually the first, longest lasting, and most intimate capital supplier to a business entity. The continuous counselling and advice provided by commercial bankers in the process of extending short and intermediate credit to business entities represents the most basic credit supplier relationship. Because of their importance, commercial banking relationships must be constantly fostered and improved.

The operations of commercial banks and the pattern which has evolved over many years cause certain aspects of a commercial banking relationship to be similar for all banks. The process of continuing or "renewing" the relationship is common in most banks. The commercial bank, like other short-term capital suppliers, will place emphasis upon future cash requirements. In addition to short-term capital, commercial banks provide a vast array of other services, all of which need to be known and surveyed in order to be certain that the business is receiving the best service available. Finally, a close relationship with commercial banks is especially important because of the sponsorship they can provide other non-banking capital supplier relationships.

Line renewal

A commercial bank extends credit typically on the basis of a "bank line" which is stated in terms of dollars and represents the maximum dollar amount of credit which the business can expect to obtain. These bank lines are approved by the loan committees of individual commercial banks both initially and then on a renewal basis after receipt of an audit from the borrower. For all but the very smallest of bank lines, the line of credit is usually renewed on an annual basis.

In the annual renewal process, the representative of the commercial bank is expected to put together the historical operating figures for the borrower as well as its projected cash requirements over the coming 12 to 24 months. Therefore, in the renewal process, the representative is required by his associates to assemble the background information which has been supplied by the corporation along with his other comments. The committee then reviews this information prior to a reaffirmation by the commercial bank of the extension of credit to the business entity.

The Financial Executive should determine the renewal dates of his business' bank lines and plan to visit with his banker prior to the annual review of the line by the loan committee. The visit should enable the Executive to be certain that the banker has all the information necessary for the renewal process and that the banker has been completely brought up to date about the operations and plans of the business. It is especially important at least annually to provide an opportunity for a personal visit at the time of a line renewal in order to be sure that all of the appropriate facts are placed before the loan committee.

Projections

Unlike almost every other type of capital supplier, the commercial bank relies heavily upon projections of operations both in the form of net income objectives and cash flow requirements. The banker is interested in projected operations primarily in the 12 to 24 months immediately ahead because he interprets his function primarily as extending short-term capital to the business. The banker extends capital with a view that it will be properly employed and at the same time that there are adequate means by which the capital can be repaid. In short, the commercial bank feels that a turnover of its capital and a fair return for its use is the most important objective of the commercial bank (as contrasted later with the equity investor or the long-term creditor who seeks to put funds to work over a much longer period of time and is less interested in early repayment).

Given the banker's orientation to the turnover of his capital, cash forecasts as well as net income projections become important in maintaining a sound commercial banking relationship. A discussion about future plans and cash flow requirements leads naturally, of course, into a business counselling or consulting relationship between lender and borrower. The Financial Executive will thus find that his commercial banker can provide many excellent suggestions about the direction of operations and how the business might improve its performance in the utilization of cash or in achieveing net income objectives. In many cases, the larger the business entity becomes, the less its dependence or need for the counselling of the commercial banker. Nevertheless, the commercial banker generally stands ready to provide this added counselling advice, and, at the same time, to extend credit as appropriate to meet the corporation's short- and intermediate-term needs.

Services

Unlike any other capital supplier, the commercial bank offers a wealth of services which can be made available to the Financial Executive and his business entity. Typically, the corporation initially views the commercial bank as only a source of short-term capital. The natural adjunct to extending short-term credit to the business entity is an intermediate credit extension through revolving credit plans or term loans, thus placing the commercial bank much nearer the suppliers of long-term capital. Other financing available through commercial banks today include two special purpose forms: factoring of accounts receivable, and leasing of chattels and real property. Also, many commercial banks today have special departments which can serve as advisors or idea creators in mergers and acquisitions by providing both the names of candidates as well as attractive introductions to either prospective buyers or sellers.

In addition to extending both general and special forms of financing and assisting in mergers and acquisitions, a commercial bank can provide credit information. A bank can be of untold assistance in seeking credit information about suppliers and customers of the corporation to determine how much credit should be extended to these particular sources or how good their performance in the past has been in delivering and meeting the needs of other customers. Further, in seeking new personnel as well as in dealing with suppliers or customers, the banks can provide information about the reputation and backgrounds of the individuals involved.

The Financial Executive can in some cases arrange loans to other members of management or to key employees through a commercial bank. Also, the trust departments of commercial banks provide extensive services in the management of capital and trusts and estate work which should not be overlooked for other members of management and key personnel. These services are profitable for the bank and provide some extra compensation for it.

All of these services added to the extension of short- or intermediate-term credit must be weighed into the total relationship with the commercial bank. As noted earlier, the Financial Executive must be especially attentive to learn what services the commercial bank thinks are appropriate in the circumstances and what he intends to seek for the corporation. Only after these points are determined can a proper working and compensation relationship be established. The commercial bank also provides sponsorship to other capital suppliers in advising them about the bank's relationship with the business and indicating its satisfaction with the business. Therefore, this makes formation of a strong bond between the business and its commercial banks especially important.

As the business expands, and it may rely on many commercial banks, the concept of key commercial banks becomes applicable. Some banks may choose only to extend limited credit to the corporation and not be interested in or expect to provide large amounts of credit or other services to the business. However, the key banks will expect to provide many services to the business and by placing many of these other requirements in the hands of a few key commercial banks, a stronger and closer relationship may be established.

Commercial paper dealers

The commercial paper dealer assists the business entity in raising short-term capital (having a maturity of less than 270 days) by purchasing notes of the business which are then resold to other investors. Commercial paper is purchased by investors who do not have the time and are not compensated for extensive credit investigation. These investors thus base their credit reliance upon either the size and history of the business entity or the reputation of the commercial paper dealer. Because of this "disinterested" market, the credit of the borrower in the commercial paper market must be of the highest quality and typically only the largest corporations have commercial paper market available to them.

Most commercial paper issuers provide investors and the commercial paper dealer with the same types of information which are provided commercial banks although because of their size, the same detail may not always be required. The commercial paper dealer will be interested in forward plans but typically will not take the same counselling position as the commercial banker. Since commercial paper is normally a supplement to, as contrasted with a replacement for, commercial bank credit, the primary credit available to the business entity is determined by its commercial banking relationships and not its commercial paper relationships.

Finally, only companies in excellent operating condition should use the commercial paper market. Any significant complication within the business entity requires a withdrawal from the commercial paper market. Complications being exposed to disinterested investors usually is undesirable, and unwanted public knowledge of unfavorable information might also result.

Factors and commercial finance companies

The factor or commercial finance company is also a short-term creditor, who chooses to extend credit either through the purchase of receivables or by lending on the security of receivables, inventory, or fixed assets of the business. Through the security (collateral) arrangements, a factor or commercial finance company might extend more credit to a business than a commercial bank, or might even lend to a business otherwise ineligible for bank credit for some reason. A relationship with either of these sources of credit will usually preclude any credit relationship with a commercial bank unless the factor or commercial financing arrangement is effected through the special service facilities of a bank. The ability to extend a greater amount of credit to the business is especially important to smaller businesses and can not be overlooked. The advantages of bank versus finance company financing are discussed in detail in Chapter 48, "Short-term Financing."

The requirements for a relationship with a factor or commercial finance company are essentially the same as those for a commercial bank although these creditors will typically impose more controls in the relationship. Quarterly field audits, a quarterly review, and perhaps even some participation in management decisions may be required. The typical representative of a factor or commercial finance company is very experienced in the extension of credit and as such can best serve as a strong advisor to the Financial Executive and the business entity.

Institutional investors

Within the heading "institutional investors" are included many savings vehicles—trust departments of commercial banks, insurance companies, pension and profit-sharing trusts (corporate, union, and governmental), mutual funds, and foundations. These institutional investors usually supply capital to the business entity in one of two forms, long-term debt or equity capital. Further, institutional investors have two common characteristics whether they are interested in debt or equity securities—they tend to have small staffs and, like the commercial bankers, they generally operate through a committee.

Common characteristics

Because many institutional investors operate with a small staff, the investment department personnel of the institution will have a heavy work load and can devote little time to any single investment. Therefore, its representatives need and prefer extensive preparation of materials for their review. Depending on whether the institution is being approached for debt or equity capital, the materials which will be required will be quite similar to those that would be used in either a presentation to a bank (although the time period reviewed may be longer) or the same material that would be available to research analysts or equity capital investors. The material should be well prepared and carefully documented. Most of the work should be done for the representative of the institutional investor so that little more is necessary than reading and reviewing the materials which have been presented to him.

Like commercial banks, most institutional investors operate with committees. The investment committee has one characteristic which is different from the commercial banking situation—some or even a majority of the committee may be outside, non-affiliated directors who have a rather broad and extensive exposure to business activity but who are not employees of the institution. These committees tend to have foibles which may be related to the outside business experience of one or more of the committee members. It is therefore important to have a good understanding with the institution's representative about your business and its future. The representative may be faced with a difficult set of circumstances unless he can clearly explain the difference between the business entity seeking capital at the time and another entity which may have for one reason or another created an unfavorable impression in the mind of any committee member.

Long-term debt

All of the institutional investors noted earlier supply long-term debt to business entities in one form or another. The maturity of the indebtedness typically runs from 10 to 25 years although some investors, especially the foundations, pension funds, and casualty insurance companies may purchase debt securities with maturities of three to ten years. The debt instruments may have an equity feature (conversion or warrants) included in the financing package, in which case later comments about equity financing also apply. Finally, these institutional investors purchase debt securities in both the public and private placement markets.

Institutional investors among capital suppliers seem to place the greatest emphasis on a business' operating history and therefore tend to look backward at operating results as opposed to forward in reviewing a company's operations when debt securities are involved. As contrasted with commercial bankers, there is less emphasis, perhaps short sightedly, upon forward plans although there will always be a requirement to substantiate to the institutional investor the use of proceeds from the issuance of securities. Fundamentally, the institutional investor purchasing debt securities having a maturity of 10 to 25 years is "locked into" the investment. Therefore, the representative must look at the company's operating history in the five to ten years immediately prior to purchasing the securities as the best indicator of what the company's operations may be for a longer term in the future. As a result, the background information supplied institutional investors may be more extensive and more detailed than that supplied commercial bankers. The Financial Executive may expect a request for solid explanations of any unfavorable historical results.

Because the institutional investor is "locked in" the investment and has no way to be repaid other than through the provisions laid out in the contractual arrangement between the debtor and creditor, the contract itself is used to document the business relationship and the expectations of the investor when a security is purchased. In most cases there is a debt agreement which contains covenants by the borrower as well as representations and warranties about the company's business. Generally, the smaller the borrower, the more covenants will be included in the debt agreements. These covenants are designed to insure that the investor is protected on such matters as the issuance of additional indebtedness, the basic business of the borrower, and the future operating results of the borrower. If the business entity does not meet the covenants set forth in the debt agreement, the entity can be "in default," which may either accelerate repayment of the indebtedness or provide the institutional investor with increased control over the activities of the business.

A close personal relationship with the representatives of institutional investors is quite important to facilitate amending outstanding debt or equity agreements between the business and the investor. Generally, amendments are not difficult to effect assuming there is a sound business purpose for such action. Typically, the financial covenants of a debt agreement (rate of interest, maturity, prepayment provisions, etc.) cannot be amended more favorably to the business entity. However, certain required financial ratios or business covenants can be altered as business conditions change. But, the ease of altering or amending the agreement will also be heavily weighted by the exposure of the institution to the borrower's management and the resulting confidence in that management. If the business entity has a large number of institutional investors, a close relationship should be developed with the key investors who will make the fundamental decisions which smaller investors will tend to follow.

A close personal relationship with representatives of institutions does not have the same implication, however, as with commercial banks. At any particular time when a business entity is seeking additional capital, a particular institution may not have funds available for investment. Institutions tend to allocate their funds among three basic portfolios—a real estate mortgage portfolio, corporate debt securities, and corporate equity securities. This allocation is based upon the balance among these three types of investments that the institution thinks will best meet its objectives and obligations. Therefore, in many cases, a historical investor in the debt securities of a business may not have funds available at each precise time the business seeks to raise additional capital in the debt market. Thus, for the acquisition of additional debt capital, a close relationship with the institution has less importance than with commercial banks, although the relationship may at any specific time spell the difference between additional investment and none.

Stated in other words, in seeking long-term debt capital, the Financial Executive must search the market for the best combination of rate, terms, and covenants. An existing investor may not provide that package. As a result, the use of a broker or investment banker becomes more important in seeking long-term debt. A broker or investment banker with substantial market knowledge will direct the business to the institutional investor(s) which has the most attractive set of terms available in the market place.

Equity investments

The development of institutional investor interest in the equity securities of a business entity is usually a combined effort of the Financial Executive and an investment banker, broker, or financial public relations firm. In approaching the equity market the business entity seeks to develop investor interest for two objectives: new securities to raise additional capital or outstanding securities which are trading in the public market. The equity investor, meanwhile, usually is looking at a great number of alternatives from which he tries to select the most attractive alternatives which meet his investment objectives.

There is generally a wealth of information available about equity securities traded in the public market place. The institutional investor needs good information and a vehicle to focus attention on attractive equity opportunities. The Financial Executive is not the best vehicle for this purpose. The use of an intermediary, an investment banker or broker, will tend to attract more attention from the equity institutional investor. The investor knows that these intermediaries have either a reputation and/or knowledge about a particular industry or type of security and thus attaches significance to the sponsorship. Thus, when the intermediary is involved in seeking additional purchasing interest in the securities of a corporation, the institutional investor realizes that the intermediary is placing its reputation and knowledge on the line and will tend to be more objective in his analysis and appraisal of the business enterprise. These aspects of reputation and knowledge serve as a filter for the institutional investor in finding good ideas.

In addition, the intermediary is in a rather interesting position if he is either an investment banker or a broker. The intermediary will probably develop substantial business from the institutional investor in executing the orders of the institution. On the other hand, the intermediary may be paid a fee in the process of raising capital for the business entity. As such, he is a true middle man and cannot compromise his judgment and reputation in trying to provide too much service to either side of the transaction or his reputation will suffer accordingly. Finally, because of the other business relationships between the investment banker or broker and institutional investors, these intermediaries will tend to attract more attention from the representatives of institutional investors than the business executive may find directly.

SBIC's and venture capital suppliers

Small Business Investment Corporations (SBIC's) and venture capital suppliers can provide the business entity with funds ranging from short-term debt to long-term debt and equity securities. Typically, these suppliers are investing in smaller companies and seek primarily to realize a return on the capital supplied through appreciation of whatever equity securities may be received.

The informational requirements of both the SBIC and the venture capital concern will tend to be the same as those of commercial banks and institutional investors. However, because of the size and condition of the companies using their capital, they tend to impose more controls (covenants) to protect themselves and their investments. Further, any capital extended to the business enterprise may be secured by collateral. Finally, anyone seeking to use capital from an SBIC or a venture capital firm may expect automatically a greater participation in management and planning decisions by these institutions than by either the commercial bank or the institutional investor.

For the smaller business enterprise, both the SBIC and venture capital represent logical sources of capital. The SBIC will typically require a lesser return on its investment than private venture capital. In exchange for a lower return, the SBIC will tend to be more restrictive in terms of controls, security, and participation in management decisions than the venture capital firm. Because of the equity aspects of a relationship with either an SBIC or a venture capital firm, the use of an investment banker to handle the relationship from its initiation and to negotiate the terms may be a good approach. By using an investment banker, the Financial Executive will be exposed to and have available the market knowledge of the investment banker in negotiating the investment by the SBIC or venture capital supplier.

Investment bankers

Investment bankers provide three basic services that can be made available typically to larger business entities which have sufficient size and earning capacity to seek admission to the public debt and equity markets. First and foremost, investment bankers have distribution capacity for selling or placing the securities to be issued by the corporation and market knowledge about the securities' markets. Secondly, and in some cases of most importance, the investment banker may have a reputation for or history of dealing with a particular industry, size of company, or type of security which can be vital to the business entity in raising the desired type and amount of capital. Third, investment bankers, especially the larger ones, offer a broad range of other services which may include counselling about the capital structure, sources of short-term debt, mergers and acquisitions, the sponsorship of equity securities, trading in either the over-the-counter or listed markets, and recommendations to equity purchasers through their research departments. All of these assets need to be closely analyzed in developing a relationship with an investment banker.

Since most investment bankers offer a broad range of services and as such have the capacity of handling most securities distribution and marketing problems, the investment banker as well as the business entity tend to look at the other aspects of the relationship. Investment bankers prefer an exclusive relationship which means that they will act as the sole investment banking source for the business entity. Exclusivity provides investment bankers with a known continuous stream of income for their services and, at the same time, provides the business entity with much more attention than might be received if the business continually sought and discussed plans with other investment bankers. The process of trying to induce competition in the investment banking relationship even through the honest objective of looking for alternative advice may well reduce the quality of service provided by any one investment banker. Unlike the commercial bank or institutional investor who has capital to provide the business entity, the investment banker is a purveyor of services in the form of individuals, their ideas, knowledge and skills, and he needs adequate compensation for them.

Distribution

The distribution process involved in marketing either debt or equity securities in the public or private markets can normally be effected by any of the larger investment bankers. As mentioned later, the larger the business entity, the more attractive any single security issue or business entity will be to investment bankers. Nevertheless, there are many types and forms of investment banking. The Financial Executive must look closely at the distribution process followed by any investment banker under consideration in order to be sure that the process satisfies the desired pattern.

For example, in private placements a business entity may seek to have only four or five large institutional investors involved in the purchase of debt security; on the other hand, a large number of much smaller institutions may be desired. Unless the operations of the investment banker in the private placement field and in that industry are quite broad, it may not provide the desired distribution.

In another case, with equity securities the business entity may seek a very broad distribution and at the same time desire that the number of shares purchased by any one buyer be quite small. Meeting these objectives may require careful selection of an investment banking firm because in many firms distribution is concentrated. A careful analysis of the historical results of distribution effected by any investment banker can, however, enlighten and inform the Financial Executive about its distribution pattern.

As can be seen from these examples, the Financial Executive should have carefully established the distribution objectives as well as requirements for the terms of the securities to be sold. One investment banking house may specialize in a particular type of security and be selected because its reputation is more important than a distribution network; a careful balancing of these factors is significant in selecting an investment banker for the distribution of public or private securities.

Reputation and specialization

Investment bankers tend to have reputations for particular types of services and/or securities. Therefore, the selection of an investment banker requires close scrutiny of the investment banker's reputation for not only integrity and sound business judgment but, more importantly, for dealing with the best companies in a particular industry or with specific financing arrangements. For example, Goldman Sachs has long been associated with the textile field, Eastman Dillon with sale leaseback transactions, and White Weld with oil and gas pipelines. Similar reputations have been developed by other firms for most types and varieties of business endeavor. Therefore, these reputations should be researched carefully in making a decision about an investment banking relationship.

Further, as noted earlier, the reputation of the investment banker is quite important since he will serve as a focal point for making recommendations to capital suppliers and purchasers of outstanding securities issues. The investment banker's reputation is intimately involved in the success of these recommendations.

Counseling and other services

Because of the number of businesses and securities reviewed by an investment banker, he tends to have very broad market knowledge about securities and industries. Further, through a close relationship, the investment banker can assist in planning and raising capital for the corporation. Of course, the market information supplied by the investment banker can be vital for planning the capital structure and the securities package to be sold by the corporation in raising capital. Through this process, the Financial Executive can gain the benefit of the investment banker's overview and span of many industries and corporations.

The investment banker will usually develop a long-term capital plan for use by the corporation in its own internal planning as well as for reviewing prospective terms and covenants of securities to be sold. The investment banker also may be involved in the planning of short-term capital requirements, especially if it has knowledge of the short-term markets through the commercial paper distribution process.

Investment bankers provide other services which can be used by the business entity and which are unrelated to the process of distributing securities. Most large investment bankers have the facilities for assistance in the search for acquisition candidates, and later, handling the negotiation of terms in the acquisition process. Investment bankers can provide sponsorship to publicly traded securities through their research departments or corporate information services—both being designed to broaden the knowledge in the market place about the business entity.

Further, many investment bankers have large over-the-counter trading departments or specialist's operations on the securities' exchanges and in either form can assist the corporation through this knowledge. Also, an investment banker can make recommendations of security purchases to other dealers which are in a network working with the investment banker or to institutions or individual purchasers of debt or equity securities.

As noted previously, most large investment banking firms have the capacity to distribute securities. Therefore, the need of the business entity for the pure distribution process provided by any one investment banker diminishes markedly as the corporation grows. The sheer size and magnitude of the business entity will automatically be attractive to any number of major investment banking firms and investors. However, the specialized services and reputation of the investment banker usually continue to be important to the business. (The use of investment bankers and the criteria for selecting them are also discussed in Chapter 50, "Dividend Policy and Equity Financing.")

Securities brokers

Brokers in securities are involved in the public distribution of new debt or equity securities by making sales to their customers and in the redistribution of outstanding securities through the same process. Therefore, the interest of securities brokers in a company can be quite important to the process of distributing new or outstanding securities. Securities brokers have the responsibility of recommending to their clients the best alternatives available to meet the clients' investment objectives. In meeting this responsibility, the best assistance which the business entity can provide the broker is information—full, plenty, and continuous.

The securities broker must have sufficient information available to him to reach a decision about the prospects for the business entity in relation to other alternative investments. Therefore, the need for a continuous flow of detailed, broad, and sound information about the history, current operations, and future plans of the corporation is essential. Performance, in terms of earnings and other criteria, will determine the price of an outstanding public security, but information, including its accuracy and accessibility, improves the trading market and the activity therein. An active market involves a broad interest by many different types of investors in the securities of the corporation, and, with better information, closer comparative pricing with comparable companies is possible.

The types and forms of information which can be made available by the business entity to securities brokers and other investors in public securities of the corporation is covered in Chapter 63, "Financial Public Relations." Financial public relations firms are in many cases best used for advice and counsel about the format, design, and approach to the corporation's annual and quarterly reports (see Chapter 62, "Published Annual Reports") and other information provided for investors as well as the distribution of these materials.

There are other vehicles than the printed word and periodic dissemination of information which can be used in order to broaden the knowledge about a business entity among securities brokers. For example, small informal presentations to representatives of institutions, research analysts, and/or to securities brokers who are interested in the corporation's publicly held securities can and should be organized by the investment banker, the broker, or the financial public relations firm. These meetings can be scheduled on an annual or periodic basis through a continuous program which should involve meetings in a number of the major cities in the United States. In determining who should be present at any of these small and informal meetings, the Financial Executive should choose carefully among research analysts and registered representatives, either of which may have big or small followings. Analysts with a broad following and reputation for securities in that company's industry are important. Equally significant are registered representatives who do a substantial business and who therefore can make a sizeable commitment in terms of numbers of purchasers to the securities of the business entity if convinced about the investment merit of the securities.

Conclusion

Strong capital supplier relationships depend upon sound knowledge of business objectives, adequate information, strong personal contact, and knowledge about the supplier and its representative. The information and techniques outlined above should assist Financial Executives in seeking capital. As each Executive's experience and wisdom about capital suppliers improves, so should capital availability to the business increase.

Short-term financing

John A. Kingston*

The responsible financial officer of any business establishment large or small constantly stands face-to-face with the obligation of providing his management with adequate funds and credit to meet his company's foreseeable money needs. Moreover, he recognizes a duty to accomplish this at the lowest possible cost that is consistent with the financing services he requires and in a way that will insure continued maintenance of a reliable relationship with his sources of credit. Finally, he is aware he must always be prepared for a call for funds to meet *unforeseen* needs for cash and must respond both quickly and with maximum effectiveness when such a call comes.

The primary challenge facing any financial executive is to determine, with his associates, the timing and amounts that must be borrowed and to establish an effective program for the eventual liquidation of the debt created. Most needs for funds that occur in the ordinary course of business, and thus can be foreseen, involve borrowings for which the purpose is clearly defined, as are the amounts required and the anticipated duration of the need. Normally, the means of liquidating the debt also will be foreseeable. To anyone familiar with the money market, the presence of these three conditions—a reasonable and limited term, a determinable amount and a predictable and reliable means of liquidation —will identify the solution as one calling for *short-term financing*.

By the same token, *unforeseen*, or relatively unexpected, calls for additional working capital will normally have to be met, at least at the

---

* President, Meinhard-Commercial Corporation, New York.

outset, through short-term financing because time is likely to be of the essence and short-term funds normally can be obtained much more promptly and readily than funds that are to be advanced for long periods.

In this study of the overall functions of the financial manager, it will be the purpose of the present chapter to focus on one of his most important areas of responsibility—short-term financing. We shall examine the sources of such financing, what they are, how to reach them, how to use them, and how to manage and evaluate this type of credit efficiently in combination with a company's intermediate and long-term financing requirements.

Short term defined

In adopting the conventional definition of short-term financing, this discussion will attempt to make clear that such a definition is a highly theoretical one; under actual money market conditions, a marked intermingling occurs among the various forms of credit, even though they may be categorized as "short," "intermediate" and "long." Under a frequently accepted breakdown, short-term credit is usually said to be any type of financing that is negotiated for, and expected to be paid within, a one-year period. Similarly, intermediate credit is said to cover obligations of from 1 to perhaps 10 years, while any obligation having an original maturity of 10 years or longer is considered long-term financing.

In point of fact, however, many of the forms of short-term credit take on a semipermanent quality, involving a relationship that extends as *functional financing* (i.e., as an integral, continuous operating procedure) from year to year virtually without interruption. A typical accounts receivable or factoring arrangement illustrates this in that the client is never "off the books" of the financing house despite the short-run nature of the individual underlying receivables, which are created and then collected in a matter of weeks or months, only to be replaced by others. The same can be said for the regular flow of commercial borrowing in the form of notes or commercial paper. As will be seen later, except for the possibility of temporary "clean-up" periods, such a borrower-creditor relationship between a company and its regular financing source may go on indefinitely, even though individual notes involved in the dealings carry near-term dates of maturity.

Borrower's requirements

There are certain fundamental principles that guide the borrower of short-term money. He is well aware that lenders, desirous as they are of putting their funds to work profitably, nevertheless establish individual criteria to which he will be expected to accommodate himself. The requirements of the lender and the steps the borrower will take to qualify for credit are two sides of the same coin. The borrower makes it his business to anticipate what the lender will want from him and to be ready to supply what will be asked. Although, as has already been said, different lenders will have their special requirements or idiosyncrasies, a list of the basic requisites for entering into any borrowing transaction follows:

The borrower's operations must be technically sound. He must be able to forecast his normal needs. In considering any type of financing, he must carefully estimate the number of dollars involved, the whole cost of borrowing, both stated and hidden, and the period of time over which the funds will be required.

He must know how and where he will obtain the money to repay the loan.

He should be entirely familiar with his own accounting system and able to explain it or answer any questions. If he finds it difficult to interpret his company's accounting practices, he should have his staff accountant participate in his discussion with the lender.

His books must be in order. He must be ready to present a short- or long-form comparative balance sheet and profit and loss statements for several recent periods and to give answers to such questions as: Has your company shown steady progress? Or, conversely, have there been severe losses, or a slowdown in collections of accounts receivable? Has the company loaned money to any of its officers? Is the debt already too heavy? Is the ratio of current assets to current liabilities a satisfactory one?

In negotiating with his selected source of funds, the seasoned financial officer expects to be judged against certain basic criteria set up by the financing institution. Indeed, as has been said, he welcomes their appraisal procedures and cooperates fully with them. He must be prepared to answer such questions as these—indeed, if his organization and he personally are not well known to the potential lender, he will probably volunteer most of the information before he is asked:

1. Why do you need the money and how soon must you have it? Is your proposition soundly and thoroughly thought out?
2. Where do you expect to get the money to repay us?
3. Has your business a record of successful operations? If you are in temporary difficulties, what is going to change the present trend?
4. Are you supplying us with reliable financial statements?
5. What is your business actually worth? Are you capitalized so that we will be fully secured, or what will be the basis of our security position?
6. What specific collateral are you offering?
7. What are the reputation, character, and business qualifications of the principals in your company?

8. What personal, business, and financial references can you give us?

The borrower must understand that the lender can better appraise the loan request and be influenced favorably if the loan applicant welcomes all questions and deals with them in a spirit of candor.

Analyzing the need for credit

Each working day presents four problems to the financial executive and his associates: How to finance current operations or expansion? What type of financing does the problem require? Where can the money be found? Will the cost of borrowing the money be less than the additional profits obtained from making the loan?

Since businesses need money to pay wages, purchase supplies, and extend credit to good customers, every businessman has a list of legitimate needs that must be met from his available cash resources in combination with short, intermediate, or long-term borrowing.

These include the following:

Buying—or leasing—additional plant or office space, delivery vehicles, warehouses, machinery, office equipment.
Borrowing to get cash discounts.
Paying taxes.
Adding employees.
Expanding advertising and promotion.
Enlarging inventory or work-in-progress.
Adding new lines, enlarging old lines.
Buying out a partner.
Supporting research or development projects.

To meet such demands, he and his associates will first ask themselves if the required funds can be generated within the enterprise itself. Here are a few of the ways businessmen often avoid additional borrowing and, by revisions in their present business practices, create increased income or turn available and under-utilized assets into cash:

Reduce costs through increased efficiency or production.
Step up sales and collection procedures.
Discontinue unprofitable products.
Cut down on inventories.
Utilize installment selling methods.
Sell off assets not needed in the business.
Eliminate marginal personnel.
Cut down on dividends or cash withdrawals.
Raise prices to enhance profits or reduce them to increase sales volume.

To help him determine the best course of action—to seek credit or choose some alternative course—a businessman can obtain guidance from any of the following sources:

His bankers.

Industrial and commercial finance companies.

A factoring firm.

U.S. Small Business Administration. (Individual consultants are prepared to review overall problems and offer guidance in obtaining a share of government business. An affiliate, SCORE, diagnoses business ills and provides solutions for small firms free of charge. It is staffed by 3,000 volunteers, all retired business executives.)

Small-business investment companies.

State and local development authorities.

Trade associations.

Management consultants.

Attorneys and accountants.

Major suppliers and major customers. (They are often willing to share broad experience in seeking solutions to common problems.)

Entering the money market

Once the potential borrower decides to enter the money market, however, he must decide where to apply. He will compare available rates of interest or other charges, giving consideration to the range of services he requires and the conditions he is willing to accept. What he will appraise is not only the stated interest rate but the absolute cost in dollars of the loan and all accompanying services.

For example, if he can borrow just the amount he needs at a given time, then the money cost is only for the exact amount of the funds used, with the financing charges levied only against what is actually outstanding. If credit approval, collection, or billing services are to be provided, the internal saving achieved by the elimination of these functions within the borrower's organization can be considered a clear offset against a part of the financing cost.

The manager will also wish to determine what security he can offer and what restrictions on his financial structure or operations he is willing to accept. In his negotiations, he will make certain that the terms of his obligation are sufficiently flexible and contain no covenants that are unduly limiting. His rights of prepayment should be spelled out, including any favorable concessions or any penalties that may be incurred in this event. Similarly, the document should set forth any privileges he can negotiate allowing the possible extension of the loan beyond the original date of maturity, with the penalties for this or any late installment payments clearly defined. Whatever the procedures are, they should be convenient and be simply documented, and should list supplemental services the borrower has been offered, such as marketing assistance, budgeting, collection, or accounting services.

It is axiomatic that he will investigate the competence, dependability, and scope of available credit sources. Is the bank or the finance or leasing company equipped to augment his own hard-earned experience with well-thought-out advice, to help him analyze to the fullest his immediate problem, and to pursue, if necessary, alternative and imaginative answers?

The answers to questions such as the foregoing will give the executive an early indication of the type of institution that can serve him best. Moreover, the far-seeing manager will look beyond his immediate needs. He rightfully will expect his business to grow. Therefore, his appraisal of financing sources must include this further consideration: Even if these particular lenders will fill the bill today, is there any likelihood that he will outgrow them in the foreseeable future? If a borrower's expansion leads to impairment of service from his established financial source unnecessary hardships will be created, and the enforced severing of long-established and friendly ties when a source is outgrown can be decidedly painful for everyone.

A decision must also be reached on the relative merits of secured and unsecured borrowing.

Unsecured borrowing may well require, of necessity, higher interest rates, demonstrated financial strength, and management ability of a high order.

Secured borrowing offers greater credit potential, possibly lower interest rates, and more liberal terms.

The principal disadvantage involved in secured borrowing is that the pledging of collateral may create a financial risk for the borrower in addition to the normal risk of doing business. The collateral, once committed, is no longer available for future credit needs. A firm that ties up all its attractive security has committed all its reserves, and yet further unforeseen needs may develop that must be met. In addition, many firms depend heavily on continued trade credit from suppliers, extended on an unsecured basis. As a firm commits more and more of its assets as security for loans, the trade creditors must increasingly depend on the shrinking amount of assets left unpledged. Excessive pledging of assets can result in the impairment or the loss of credit from alert suppliers and other unsecured creditors.

In every instance, the financial executive must decide whether or not it will be more advantageous for him to offer collateral or to seek an unsecured loan. His decision will often dictate the choice of the financial institution to which he will apply.

Sources of funds

The following evaluations of the principal sources of short-term credit are based on general knowledge of the field and are treated in the order of total magnitude of loans extended insofar as such information is available.

1. *Bank loans.* The acceptability of a traditional unsecured loan application by a commercial bank is measured by the borrower's profit and loss statements, his current balance sheet, his reputation and credit rating with other lenders, suppliers, etc., and his projected capacity to repay the loan out of cash income. As is often said, the borrower will be judged by the three C's of credit: Capital, Character, and Capacity. These cover unsecured loans.

A fourth "C" is added in the case of secured loans, or those granted for pledged assets: Collateral. These assets may consist of equipment, real estate, or personal assets such as securities or life insurance. In the event of a default, the lender has the expectation of discharging the debt by taking possession of, and usually liquidating, the collateral. It is readily recognized that no one, neither the borrower nor the lender, anticipates a default and the collateral is posted simply to protect the lender from wholly unforeseen difficulties.

A prudent banker, when asked for a loan, will consider the current and anticipated economic situation, and such matters as: Should he discourage inherently speculative ventures? Should he deny loans that might unfavorably affect the nation's international balance of payments? Should he shift the customer to other channels of borrowing? Is the action he proposes to take consistent and fair in the light of his obligations to this, as well as every other, customer of the bank? These are but a few of the questions bankers must ask, but all of them emphasize to the borrower that he must have maintained a good credit rating—by seeking money only for highly worthwhile purposes—and that it is essential for him to maintain a continuing and mutually profitable relationship with his bank.

When the demand for credit is great and money becomes "tight," banks may run short of funds to make all the good loans available to them. With such a heavy loan demand in these periods, a bank may be forced to reject or suggest a postponement to customers with sound projects to finance. On the other hand, astute bankers will often escape this unpleasant choice by arranging a participating loan with another source of funds, such as a finance company, thereby maintaining their basic relationship as the customer's "regular bank."

A bank will consider a loan either on a "demand" or a time basis, the latter typically calling for a fixed maturity of 90 days, 6 months, or a year. Interest rates will range from the prime rate—the lowest rate, which is offered only to strong borrowers such as major corporations—to a substantially higher rate that is intended to compensate the lender for the amount of risk and handling expense he assumes. Time notes are more common than demand notes and are usually made with the understanding that the loan may be considered for renewal on maturity if the borrower qualifies at that time. Required reductions in the amount of the loan are not uncommon on renewals, however. Any loan balance must be "cleaned up"—completely paid off—about once a year in a typical case.

Normally, short-term financial arrangements are liquidated out of the cash flow that the company generates in the regular course of its business. An obvious example would be that of a company that makes Christmas greeting cards. It borrows in the spring and summer in order to purchase paper, inks, art work, and other materials that it uses in its manufacturing. After the cards are made, they are shipped to retail outlets for the Christmas season, but the terms of the sale do not call for payment until January or later. After the retailer sells the cards, he pays the manufacturer, who uses the cash to retire the loan. The cash that was borrowed has become raw materials, finished products, accounts receivable, and, finally, cash again. The transaction is self-liquidating.

Many concerns use short-term loans as interim financing for major projects in their early stages, progress payments to the contractors for construction costs of a plant or factory, for example. After construction has been completed and all costs have been incurred, long-term financing through a mortgage or the issuance of bonds, debentures, or equity is arranged.

Those business enterprises that regularly use bank credit usually do so through a "line of credit" arrangement with a given banking institution. Such a line of credit represents a formal or informal commitment by the bank to lend to the borrowing firm any amount up to a stipulated limit. This line can be drawn against at the pleasure of the borrower, assuming no material deterioration has occurred in his financial situation. The arrangement may call for payment of a standby fee by the holder of the line. In addition to any such standby charge, the customer is nearly always expected to keep on deposit with the bank a balance that bears a specified relationship to the amount of the credit line. This minimum compensating balance is likely to range between 10 and 20 percent of the amount of the line, which means that, when the line is in use, the customer is actually receiving from the bank a lesser amount than that which he has borrowed and on which he is paying interest. Credit-line arrangements frequently require a borrower to keep a higher compensating balance on deposit when he is using any part of his line than when the line is dormant.

As mentioned previously, a "compensating balance" is always required to support a bank line of credit. This will vary between 10 to 20 percent of the total line. For example, a loan of $200,000 that called for a $40,000 balance to be maintained will give the borrower the use of only $160,000 of the bank's money. Since the borrower receives no interest on the $40,000 in his account, but is paying interest on the full $200,000, the return to the bank and the cost to the borrower are higher than the stated interest on the loan. As a rule of thumb, the effective rate for borrowing from a bank, when a 20 percent compensating balance is required, will range between 1½ percent and 2 percent higher than the rate on the face of the note. (This does not take into account balances left on deposit from time to time *in excess of the compensating balance minimum,* which may be said to have the effect of further increasing the effective rate.)

It is very important to calculate the "true cost" of such borrowings, especially if the funds are not used continually throughout the full year.[1]

For example, Exhibit 1 shows the actual cost of borrowing under a conventional bank line of credit arrangement, which requires that the borrower keep a minimum of 10 percent of his line of credit on deposit as a compensating balance when he is not borrowing and 20 percent on deposit when he is borrowing.

EXHIBIT 1

Actual Cost of Borrowing versus Stated Interest Rate

Average Number of Days of Use of Full Line Stated Interest Rate, 6%	Actual Interest Cost per Annum
60	12.19%
90	10.31%
120	9.38%
150	8.81%
180	8.43%
210	8.16%
240	7.97%
270	7.81%
300	7.69%
330	7.59%
360	7.50%

It is to be noted that the true cost of borrowing declines significantly as a borrower increases his use of the "line."

Another important factor in determining the actual amount of interest being paid on a loan is the form which the payment of interest takes. If the institution deducts periodic interest payments at the beginning of the period—discounting the loan—the effective rate of interest will be significantly higher than if interest due is billed or charged for at the end of the period. It will be readily recognized that if the loan is discounted, the actual amount available for the customer's use is less than the amount on which he is paying interest, which results in an increase in the rate.

2. *Accounts receivable financing.* A new or rapidly expanding business with a limited capital base may generate a need for larger amounts of money than an unsecured bank loan can provide. Such companies

---

[1] "The vast majority of executives cooperating in a survey said they were generally well satisfied with their commercial banks as a source of short-term funds, while several expressed dissatisfaction that their bank's compensating balance requirements were too high, thus unduly increasing the cost of short-term bank financing." Edwin P. Harkins and Francis J. Walsh, Jr., "Current Corporate Debt Practices," *The Conference Board Record,* June 1968.

have long relied upon accounts receivable, also called "commercial," financing. By taking accounts receivable as collateral, financing institutions are able to put cash into the hands of such concerns as an alternative to the latter's carrying receivables for customers and thus tying up large amounts of capital on terms of 30, 60, or 90 days, or longer. The lenders recognize that such open-account sales spell out a completed but as yet unpaid-for transaction and are willing to advance a liberal amount of money at the time the merchandise is shipped. As fast as goods or services are invoiced, funds are loaned against the pledge of the receivables created. As collections are made by the seller, the advances are paid back. This process continues as goods are shipped, and a permanent flow of funds thus is made available on a revolving basis. The financial burden of carrying receivables is eliminated and the money derived can be put to immediate use in the seller's business.

As this type of financing became understood, it was realized that it could be used not only to obtain more operating cash than from any other source on a continuing and flexible basis, but that there were certain other advantages. To name a few: the increase of capital turnover, a greater return on invested capital, the ability to make advantageous purchases requiring cash, and the improvement of credit standing by discounting suppliers' bills. It eliminated the undesirable alternative of seeking equity capital or taking in partners and diluting the owners' control of the business. Financing accounts receivable gave significant leverage to limited investment capital at a sustainable and recoverable cost.

The mechanics of financing accounts receivable are simple:

a) A contract is drawn up between the business concern and the financing institution under which it is agreed that funds will be loaned to the business firm on a continuing basis, secured by the pledge of its open accounts receivable as well as of new receivables as they are created.

b) The loans are made "with recourse" to the firm but without notice to its customers. "With recourse" means that if a client's customer becomes delinquent or his account becomes uncollectible, the client must supply the financing institution with additional current accounts of equal value to replace it, or actually repay the amount involved. "Without notice" means that to accommodate to certain trade conditions and the wishes of certain clients, their customers are not notified that their receivables have been pledged.

c) The client passes on its own credits, makes deliveries on regular trade terms, handles its own collections, and takes the credit risk. As it renders invoices to customers for its goods or services, it sends copies assigning each account to the financing institution and reports the total amount of the receivables created each day on a form provided by the financing institution, along with evidence of shipment. Money is then made available to the client up to a maximum percentage agreed to in advance.

d) The percentage amount of each invoice to be advanced is arrived at after the client's business has been analyzed, taking into consideration the selling terms, the number and nature of the customers sold, their average credit standing, the firm's previous credit loss and collection experience, and the amount of discounts, credits, and allowances given. A maximum of 80 percent might be considered an average figure, although anywhere from 60 percent to 90 percent might be established for various reasons. Of course, the full face amount of each receivable is credited to the client when payment of the receivable occurs.

e) The client agrees to turn over to the financing institution all checks in payment of its invoices and these are deposited in a bank account carried under a code number so that the name of the financing institution does not appear on the checks.

The cost of carrying receivables under a commercial financing arrangement, often regarded as a part of the cost of sales, is represented by a single charge, namely interest at a fixed rate on the actual amount of money used for the length of time it is used. It is charged daily on the amount of money in use each day and might be expressed, for example, as $\frac{1}{30}$th of 1 percent per day. At the end of each month an accounting is sent indicating what the interest charge amounts to on the average daily balance for the month. The daily charge can vary with the nature of a client's business; for the purpose of discussion, a rate of $\frac{1}{30}$th of 1 percent amounts to 12 percent per annum. In addition, such sources of funds may also supplement accounts receivable financing with seasonal inventory advances as well as term financing secured by a lien on machinery and equipment.

Among the examples of businesses that have prospered through the employment of commercial financing of this type are National Air Lines, The Diners' Club, The Jim Walter Corporation, Buitoni Foods and United Artists.[2]

3. *Factoring.* This term describes another specialized and important form of credit and collection service. It is essentially the extra service of credit protection that differentiates factoring from accounts receivable financing.

The factor checks the customer's credit for the seller, advances cash as the goods are shipped, keeps accounts receivable ledgers on the customer, and absorbs all credit losses. The factor also supplements these

---

[2] "Commercial Finance Companies and Factors," *Dun's Review,* January 1966. Among the largest firms offering commercial financing in the United States are C.I.T. Corporation, Commercial Credit Corporation, James Talcott, Inc., W. E. Heller and Co., and Meinhard-Commercial Corporation.

services with seasonal inventory financing as well as term financing of equipment.

Factoring houses started in the U.S. about 150 years ago.[3] "Old-line factors" represented European textile mills by selling their goods and by collecting money from the buyers in this country. Modern factoring has abandoned the selling of its clients' goods, but continues to offer clients the privileges of realizing cash income on the shipment of goods and avoiding exposure to credit losses. The other recognized advantages of factoring are:

a) Eliminating the expense of personnel, agency reports, and overhead in operating a credit department and a collection department.

b) Permitting the client to do business for cash, while providing his customers with the credit terms they require.

c) Providing money prior to the shipment and invoicing of goods sold in order to finance a preseason buildup of inventory for the client. The factor also will finance machinery purchases.

d) Providing advisory service, marketing surveys, and management and production counseling.

For these services, a factor is paid a commission in the range of ¾ of 1 percent to 2 percent of the volume of the clients' sales. Users of factoring also pay interest for money actually used. Usually, this rate is directly related to, but higher than, the bank prime rate. Clients are not required to maintain compensating balances such as are required in connection with most bank loans.

The commission and interest charges vary with the type of industry involved, the annual sales volume, the average amount of sales, the number of customers, the trade involved, and the terms of the sale.

Factors divide their clients into two classes, "wholesale" and "retail." A client who sells raw materials to manufacturing customers is called a wholesale client. A retail client is one who sells his product to stores, chains, and mail order houses. Since each class of business entails different handling problems, the rate of commission varies accordingly.

Many large and well-capitalized firms use factoring primarily to obtain credit investigation, protection, and collection services, while firms with lesser financial strength rely more heavily on the ability of factoring to provide working funds in excess of their own resources.

The mechanics of factoring are simple:

a) A business firm signs a contract in which it agrees to factor all its sales. Such contracts are usually on a continuing basis, subject to termination by either party on 60 days notice.

b) As orders are obtained, the client submits the customers' names, dollar amounts, and terms for credit approval. If a client wishes, it may

---

[3] See "Factor," *Encyclopaedia Britannica.* This article written by J. S. Fechteler, C.I.T. Financial Corporation, gives a comprehensive explanation of the subject.

obtain credit information before soliciting business. This credit service is provided by the factor's large credit department, with its vast resources of industry-wide and continuous credit investigation of the status of customers. Skillful credit services call for travel and negotiation, and involve the recording of the factor's experience with thousands of customers. The factor's policy is not to restrict credit but to extend it beyond the client's individual ability to do so. Factoring agreements are intended to create growth and to build sales volume.

c) As shipments are made, a concern bills its customers in the usual manner, except that each invoice carries a printed notice requesting payment be made directly to the factor.

d) A client may draw cash against these invoices immediately, or leave a credit balance until funds are needed.

e) Bookkeeping is greatly simplified for the business concern that factors. It maintains just one account on its books—that with the factor, who takes full responsibility for handling the accounts receivable and for collecting them. Once the goods are shipped, the client is no longer concerned with when or how the customer pays, or whether he pays at all, as the customer is instructed to make payment directly to the factor and the factor assumes the credit risk. The client's only responsibility arises if the goods are claimed to be defective, or some dispute occurs concerning the shipment.

f) A periodic acknowledgement of all invoices received is sent by the factor to the client, and a monthly recapitulation of all sales is rendered. The latter also shows interest charged on advances made, interest earned by the client on his credit balance, the factor's commission, and the exact amount of the credit or debit balance on the last day of the month.

g) The factoring agreement provides that a client may draw money in advance of actual shipments in order to finance preseason inventory buildup or other unusual financial needs. Such advances are liquidated as goods are shipped and the invoices credited to the client's account. Such advances may be unsecured or secured.

Factors usually enjoy a close business relationship with their clients and are frequently called on for counsel in areas beyond financing and credit. These may involve such areas as acquisitions and mergers, improved sources of supply, expanded distribution of a client's products, and the recruitment of sales or other executives.

When he operates with a factor, a manufacturer's balance sheet shows one account receivable from a company (the factor) of outstanding financial integrity, instead of numerous accounts receivable due from variously rated customers. Because the volume of credit business handled by the factor is so much greater than that of the individual business firm, and because of more comprehensive information, services and standardization of credit procedures, the factor is in a position to be more liberal in granting credit than his client. This broadens the client's sales opportunities.

4. *Maturity factoring.* Many factored concerns have no immediate cash needs but they elect to use a factor in order to get the benefit of a factor's credit service. These firms do not take advances from a factor on their receivables, nor do they require other financing. The factor simply remits to them their monthly sales. The cost of the service is the factoring commission. There are no interest charges. Some clients leave their funds with a factor on a demand basis, on which the factor pays interest.

5. *Export-import factoring.* Since American manufacturers are looking more and more to foreign markets to increase sales, and foreign customers at the same time are offering increased business to American exporters who are willing to sell on terms of credit up to 90 days or more, old-line factoring concerns can check and approve credit for foreign customers. They provide cash upon shipment of goods and assume full responsibility for collections with protection against losses due to faulty credit or political upheavals. The factoring procedure is as follows:

a) The exporter signs a contract with the factor covering all his foreign sales.

b) The contract provides that all orders are to be submitted to the factor for approval of customer credit; the factor's worldwide contacts make for speedy credit approval.

c) Once an order is approved in writing for credit, the shipment is made and the goods are billed by the shipper on an invoice indicating that payment is to be made directly to the factor by the foreign customer. Copies of all invoices and shipping documents along with the assignments of invoices are sent to the factor. Some foreign countries (Japan is a prime example) insist that their manufacturers use letters of credit when exporting goods to the United States. In such cases, the American importer uses his factoring concern to arrange for letter-of-credit financing with his bank in the United States. When the goods are shipped, the factor accepts the documents on behalf of the client and pays the bank according to the terms of the letter of credit, whether the draft is "on sight" or 60 to 90 days.

6. *Inventory loans.* Most business firms have a substantial portion of their resources invested in inventory, and many in need of credit have inventory on hand that can readily be used as collateral to raise cash in cases where an unsecured loan is not available. The method by which a concern can use its inventory as collateral is extremely simple because of recent changes that have been made in the laws of most states. Today, under the Uniform Commercial Code, all that is necessary is for a simple financing agreement to be drawn up and a brief financial statement to be filed with the proper filing officials.

7. *Customers or suppliers.* A businessman may have customers who are in a position to help him financially by making advance payments on goods supplied either before or immediately upon shipment.

Financial aid from indulgent suppliers is important to producers of large, specialized equipment, where the time and expense involved in manufacture is great. A machine such as an enormous newspaper printing press may take months to complete. Obviously the supplier must be prepared to supply materials and await payments to the manufacturer. Similarly, an oil company will help finance the building and equipment of a filling station long before the first automobile drives in; or a maker of dairy products may help his milk suppliers acquire refrigeration equipment. On the negative side, reliance on suppliers for unusual credit arrangements can have such disadvantages as a loss of bargaining power on price, rate of delivery, and other terms. It depends on how anxious the supplier is to develop new customers; the more competitive the business, the greater pains the suppliers will take to make sure the customer is completely satisfied.

8. *Trade credit.* Credit has been described as man's confidence in man, and as the lifeblood of our economy. Instead of cash dollars changing hands at the conclusion of each selling transaction, most goods and services are exchanged upon a promise to pay in the future.

Manufacturers and wholesalers offer a variety of credit terms at no interest charge. Terms up to 90 days are common. When discounts are offered for prompt payments in cash, a good businessman will frequently borrow the money to take advantage of the bargain, since the interest he will pay on the loan costs him less than the amount he will save by earning the discount for cash.

From the seller's point of view as well as from the buyer's, the extension of trade credit terms is desirable. When management is sales minded and production oriented, it is likely to be disinclined to devote effort to collecting cash from customers on a C.O.D. basis. Instead, established billing procedures are followed, which means the seller must find other ways to forecast and finance his operation. If the businessman allows his customers 30, 60, or 90 days to pay a bill without penalty, then he must have adequate working capital, obtain additional short-term financing, or establish similar "dating" privileges with his own suppliers.

From the buyer's viewpoint, the credit granted by the seller represents an integral part of his financial structure, for the grace period serves to bridge or effectively narrow the gap in time between his receipt of the goods and the day when he in turn disposes of them and receives payment.

The following basic elements make it possible for an estimated 90 percent of American business to be conducted on credit terms:

An accepted code of conduct. It must be anticipated that debtors will pay their obligations without costly collection effort.

Legal machinery for enforcement of claims. Creditors with claims against nonpaying debtors must be enabled to bring to bear the force of law to effect collection. This assists the creditor and also helps preserve the credit system.

A reasonably stable monetary unit. The money received by the creditor next month or next year must have a purchasing power approximating that money's present purchasing power. Otherwise, the credit cannot project the future value of the present promise and is therefore understandably disinclined to extend credit.[4]

9. *Commercial paper.* Commercial paper refers to short-term promissory notes, generally unsecured, which are sold through commercial paper dealers or directly to investors. A firm entering the commercial paper market is likely to do so first through a dealer, as a greater sophistication and an established position in the commercial paper market is required to market paper directly. Investors in commercial paper include banks and other financial institutions, but in recent years, nonfinancial concerns with excess funds to invest on a short-term basis have become major buyers of commercial paper.

Recently, public utilities have been issuing commercial paper to an increasing extent to provide a portion of their short-term debt requirements for construction, inventory, and other current purposes. With the relaxation in the requirements of the Securities and Exchange Commission and the tightness at times in bank credit, this has provided a ready source of funds on an economical basis. Care should be taken, of course, to limit commercial paper issuance to amounts that are not so large that they cause unhappiness in bank relationships.

Notes sold in the commercial paper market are usually written in denominations or multiples of $5,000, with maturities of from one to nine months. Ninety-day maturities are common. Some firms sell commercial paper on a continuing basis. Others use it only to borrow to meet seasonal or temporary needs. Interest rates on commercial paper usually are lower than the prime bank rate and, of course, no compensating balances are required.

The organization of the commercial paper market is such that it is at the disposal only of borrowers with highest credit standing, good earnings over a period of years, and a strong working capital position.

According to a leading commercial paper dealer, prospective users of commercial paper should be able to show a practical minimum worth of $25 million. Credit records must be first-rate and the firm name should be one recognized immediately by investors as an excellent credit risk. Commercial paper is sold on either a discount or an interest-bearing basis and the dealer commission varies from ⅛ percent to ⅜ percent on a per annum basis.

---

[4] Monroe R. Lazere, *Commercial Financing* (New York: The Ronald Press, 1968), p. 4.

10. *Banker's acceptances.* The financing of foreign trade involves many distinctive instruments and practices, and is best left to specialized books on the subject—of which there are many.

One such instrument, the banker's acceptance, commonly used in foreign import and export trade, may also be found in certain domestic transactions. It begins as a draft, or demand for payment by a bank of a certain amount. The bank marks "accepted" on the draft, provided it is satisfied that the customer has a good line of credit and that he will pay his bills. The customer then receives the goods he has ordered from his domestic or foreign supplier, who presents the draft to his local bank. It forwards the draft along with the shipping papers to the originating bank, which presents it to the ordering firm for acceptance. If all the papers are found to be in order, the bank accepts the draft, and it becomes a banker's responsibility to collect the funds. The only risk involved is to the accepting bank, which must rely heavily on the credit standing of its customer. Depending on the quality of the customer's credit, the bank charges 1½ percent to 3 percent for the use of its name and credit. In addition, the customer pays a rate of interest on the note to the bank.

11. *Individual lenders.* The individual private lender, who might also be a relative or friend, is an important source of cash for growth. There are always some individuals who want to take a chance on a business venture, because the risk promises more excitement than better known investment possibilities do.

Informal syndicates of Wall Street financiers often put free time and excess cash to profitable use in this way. Many, but not all, demand an equity position in the companies in which they invest and insist upon passing upon major policy decisions. Some will pull out as soon as they see a chance to take a profit. Cautious experts feel that borrowing from these sources, like borrowing from your mother-in-law, should be "the source of last resort." It may be so, but enormous investments are made each day by individuals who risk their funds based upon their faith in the potential success of business enterprises.

Summary

In the final analysis, the execution of a program to meet the financial requirements of a going business is an exercise of *discrimination* and *decision.* When confronted with any situation calling for the employment of a firm's credit, only the very smallest of enterprises or one with its financial condition in a truly parlous state will not have a number of courses of action available to it. A well-managed, active business always has a number of options open, for there is no more competitive area in the American economy than that devoted to providing business credit.

As we have seen, having first decided with his associates that funds ought to be borrowed, the financial executive must next determine whether his needs in the given set of circumstances call for him to "go short" or "go long" in his borrowing. That decision made, he will know the types of lending institutions to which he wants to turn.

Assuming that the particular requirement for funds, and perhaps cost considerations as well, dictate recourse to the short-term money market, our financial officer has a whole new series of decision to make. If these are made correctly, they will lead him to the financing institution best suited to serve him and his company. He must first objectively appraise the credit worthiness of his company and of the application for which the funds are to be used. If these are high, he will have access to the most economical sources of funds in the market. If these are less than A-1, he will be realistic and apply elsewhere, prepared to pay a higher rate.

He will ask himself if he has a pure money need—simply for so many dollars at a certain schedule of maturity—or whether collateral services, such as credit passing, collections, or an open or flexible line of credit, are as important as the money itself. Again, that decision, correctly made, will narrow the area of choice to the one group of institutions or the one type of financing most appropriate to fill his company's requirements.

Now, he must choose between individual institutions that are prepared to offer the precise accommodations he has specified to himself. The influences that can come into play in the course of making a final choice of a single institution are innumerable—convenience, personal loyalty or "chemistry," reputation, recommendations from other businessmen, past experience, comparative rates, advertising, and size or stature in the business community are just a few of the considerations he may weigh, often in consultation with executive associates or other financial advisors.

In certain situations it is entirely acceptable and appropriate to discuss his requirements with several competing institutions. In other cases, the confidential nature of his requirements, his long-standing and valued relationships with an institution that has served him well, the demands of time, or the need for close-at-hand, highly convenient service may lead him to a single first-choice source.

Finally, he must exercise his expertise and negotiating ability to see that, from among several competitors or from a single, predetermined institution, his needs are fulfilled on the best and most suitable terms for his firm. Again, a multiplicity of alternate solutions may arise.

The ability to practice discrimination and decision making of the highest order is the primary test of competence for a successful financial executive. Because of the many choices, both as to the sources and forms of financing, that are normally available to him in the highly competitive field of short-term financing, no part of his responsibilities is likely to be more demanding than the subject covered in the present chapter.

Long-term debt financing

William G. Nelson IV*

Long-term financing involves the accumulation of cash resources for use by the corporation in its quest to maximize profits within the markets it has chosen to serve.[1] The long-term financial requirements of the business should evolve from a business plan.[2] A key challenge for the financial officer is to adapt long-term financing in a creative manner to serve the business, rather than unduly constrain the business by "conventional" financial considerations. It cannot be emphasized too strongly that long-term financing simply involves the exchange of a claim by a financial intermediary (e.g., a bank) or saver against the business in return for money. The characteristics of a particular claim may be selected to serve almost any reasonable financial requirement.

Strategic framework

The strategic financial framework within which the corporation should operate must be fully considered before the financial officer can assess the specific tactical attributes of financing that might be most appropriate to his particular corporation. The capability of the business

---

* Monsanto Company, Manager, Planning and Commercial Development, St. Louis.

[1] The discussion in this chapter is limited to tax-deductible forms of long-term financing. That is, the discussion concerns corporate long-term debt, including long-term leases. Preferred stock is discussed in Chapter 50, "Dividend Policy and Equity Financing."

[2] See Part IV, "Planning and Budgeting," particularly Chapter 26, "Corporate Long Range Planning."

to service debt must be considered.[3] The "degree of business risk" must be evaluated in order to establish an appropriate "degree of financial risk." Lowest cost financing (i.e., the lowest weighted average cost of capital) may be associated with a unique debt-equity ratio range.[4] The financial officer should be aware that there may be an optimum capital structure which would maximize the long run value of each share of common stock.

Of course, the financial officer should carefully determine how much, and when, external funds will be required. Perhaps the very first charge of the financial officer is to insure that the corporation is never technically bankrupt because of a temporary shortage of cash in an otherwise healthy business. On the other hand, too much idle cash is expensive because of the opportunity cost of money. Thus the financial officer's perpetual dilemma—liquidity versus profitability—must be considered. Throughout all financing the financial officer must maintain financial flexibility for the corporation. That is, the corporate capability to obtain still more funds, if required (because of adversity or in case an unusual opportunity occurs), must be preserved. In no event should the debt level be permitted to reach a point necessitating the issuance of equity regardless of the conditions of the equity market.

In all likelihood the corporation should utilize professional assistance.[5] Usually such assistance comes from the corporation's commercial bankers (with whom the corporate financial officers should always maintain good rapport—just in case!); however, it may come from investment bankers.

Public distribution or private placement

A long-term debt issue may be sold through investment bankers, who act as underwriters, to the public. The cost of such public distribution includes the underwriters commission as well as the various expenses incurred in order to comply with the Securities and Exchange Commission (SEC) registration requirements and the actual public flotation.[6] Much of this cost is fixed in nature and, as a result, the cost of public distribution is scale sensitive. Unless the long-term debt amounts to at least $4 or $5 million, public distribution is probably too expensive. However, if the borrowing corporation is well known and the issue is

---

[3] See Chapter 46, "Capital structure determination."

[4] Some of these issues, such as "business risk," "financial risk," and "cost of capital," are discussed in greater detail by me in the article: Nelson, William G., IV, "Cost-of-Capital Standards with Debt and Equity Financing," *Financial Executive*, January, 1966.

[5] Professional assistance includes more than just financial expertise. It includes tax experts, lawyers, and accountants. See Chapter 13, "Use of professional services."

[6] Such expenses typically include printing and engraving, state taxes, trustee fees, and SEC fees, in addition to the usual legal and financial fees.

large, public distribution may be the low-cost route. A public distribution of long-term debt does establish a market for the issuing corporation's debt which may result in lower cost with future financing. Further, public trading of the debt issue may enable the issuing corporation to retire some of its debt under favorable conditions by repurchasing such debt whenever the price of the debt is low.

On the other hand, long-term debt may be privately placed by selling it directly to financial intermediaries. In fact, most corporate long-term debt is now privately placed. Private placement has several advantages for the borrower. First, the loan can be negotiated quickly, because the several-week time period associated with an SEC registration (required for public offerings) is avoided. Second, the terms of the loan can be specially tailored more readily because only a few people are involved in the negotiation. That is, a desirable but none-the-less peculiar term does not have to be explained and sold to many, many prospective buyers as would be the case with a public offering. Third, the cost may be lower, particularly for debt issues under $5 million. Incidentally an investment banker's service may be valuable as the borrowing corporation's agent in a private placement even though he is not required as an underwriter.[7]

Sources of long-term debt[8]

By reputation, commercial banks are sources of short-term and intermediate-term loans. In fact, however, they may well be the most frequently utilized source of long-term debt funds for corporations.[9] The trend toward the availability of bank funds on a longer term basis has been affected in recent years by the tightness of credit. Commercial banks have been more selective in extending credits and have oftentimes required a time schedule for repayment. Bank financing is apt to be more expensive than, for example, an issue of bonds, especially after taking compensating balances into account. However, the ease and speed of negotiations coupled with the flexibility associated with bank financing probably accounts for its popularity.

Life insurance companies are perhaps the next most popular source of long-term-debt funds. Costs of such financing are moderate for high quality issues. And recently life insurance companies have increasingly

[7] See Chapter 47, "Relations with Capital Suppliers" for discussions of investment bankers' services in placing long-term issues.

[8] See Chapter 47, "Relations with Capital Suppliers," for a fuller discussion of fund sources and the kinds of analyses that the various types of institutions will want to perform before supplying funds.

[9] In a survey of 257 corporations by the National Industrial Conference Board, commercial banks were cited as ". . . the financial institutions most frequently resorted to by surveyed companies when they look for long-term funds." Harkins, Edwin P., and Walsh, Francis J., Jr., *Corporate Debt Management*, The Conference Board, Managing the Financial Function, Report No. 2. (New York: National Industrial Conference Board, Inc. 1968), p. 6.

emphasized decentralized or regional loan administration in an effort to more satisfactorily serve smaller businesses. Recently insurance companies have tended to shun corporate debt issues (even with ten-year call protection) in favor of mortgage investments. There is also a trend toward participation in the equity side of commercial mortgage situations (commonly called "a piece of the action").

Mutual savings banks, which are located for the most part in the Northeast, are a low-cost source of long-term debt funds provided the issues are of high quality.[10]

Other sources of long-term debt funds include finance companies, investment companies, pension funds, foundations, educational and religious funds, and, for small companies, the Small Business Administration and Small Business Investment Corporations, if the borrowing company will also offer some equity consideration.

Timing

Of course, a corporation should not issue long-term debt in order to obtain funds unless and until it needs the funds because of the continuing interest costs associated with debt. However, even when the time has arrived for the corporation to utilize funds for long-term purposes it may not be an appropriate time to issue long-term debt. For example, at the particular time the corporation will need the funds the interest costs associated with long-term funds markets might indicate that interest costs should be significantly lower within a one, two or three year horizon. Then the corporation probably should utilize short-term debt as an interim source of funds until long-term interest rates decline, rather than becoming locked-in with high interest costs for the duration of the long-term financing.[11]

There are, however, limitations on the ability of corporations to postpone long-term debt financing. This is particularly true of public utilities, which require substantial amounts of capital on a continuing basis, and short-term debt must, therefore, be converted into long-term financing from time to time without undue delay. Obviously, commercial banks are unwilling and perhaps unable to carry indefinitely substantial amounts of short-term or intermediate-term borrowing.

In order to avoid the undesirable impact of a lock-in with high interest rates, some long-term debt issues have provided for refunding at any time with no restrictions except the high cost of call provisions. For example, the SEC has required such freedom to refund in the case of Registered public utility holding companies. This requirement often has been costly in terms of interest but has obviously given complete free-

---

[10] However, mutual savings banks as well as savings and loan associations primarily invest in home mortgages.

[11] See Chapter 48, "Short-term financing," for a discussion of interim financing.

dom to refund in the event of more favorable interest rates. The trend in recent years has been toward restrictions on refunding for a period of five years with insurance company investors and some others requiring ten years. This becomes a matter of balancing cost of money against refunding flexibility in the event of a future lower interest level.

As a practical matter the forecasting of interest costs has become extremely difficult in recent years. The operations of the Federal Reserve System, government fiscal policies, private investment demand, and international money flows all influence interest rates. Furthermore, any one of these may affect interest rates dramatically. A review of the fluctuation in the prime level for commercial borrowing in recent years provides ample evidence such as volatility and unanticipated levels which indicate the difficulties inherent in forecasting interest rates. A review of bond market trends supports the same conclusion.[12]

Fundamental terminology

Six technical terms which involve concepts that are fundamental to long-term debt financing will now be discussed before describing several forms of long-term debt in detail. To repeat, long-term financing simply involves the exchange of a claim by a financial intermediary or saver against the business in return for money.

Funded debt is simply long-term debt. That is, "funded" is a synonym for "long-term." Funding of the debt means replacing short-term liabilities with long-term liabilities.

A *bond* is a long-term promissory note. It is a contract that states that the corporation will pay certain specified sums at specific times to designated financial intermediaries (who may merely be the person holding the bonds at the specific times).

A *mortgage* represents a legal claim against a designated real or personal asset. That is, the corporation pledges real property as security behind the promises to repay made in the bond. The pledge of security is a necessary condition of a mortgage loan.

A *debenture,* on the other hand, is long-term debt that is not secured by a pledge of some designated specific piece of real property. Rather, it is secured by the general credit of the corporation. The security behind a debenture, then, is like that of general creditor claims.

An *indenture* is a document which details the contractual relationship between the corporation which is borrowing money, the lender, and the

---

[12] Current information about interest rates is readily available from the Federal Reserve System. The financial officer might find it useful to read some of the recent monthly publications from some of the Federal Reserve district banks, particularly the New York District Bank and the St. Louis District Bank before going to see his bankers.

trustee. A bond indenture may be a document containing several hundred pages because it must detail a relationship between borrower and lender that will last for a long time. The bond indenture is considered a part of the package represented by the single-page bond certificate actually received by the bondholder. The indenture discusses the form of the bond, provides a complete description of any property pledged, and specifies the authorized amount of the bond issue. The indenture then details the protective clauses or covenants. These clauses can contain almost anything, provided that it is negotiated between the borrower and the lender (assuming that neither borrower nor lender "slips in a clause"). Some examples of what these clauses may cover follow: a pledge (i.e., a covenant) that certain officers will remain with the company; a pledge to maintain the property in good repair; a pledge to pay all taxes levied by the government against the property; restrictions on dividends; limits on further indebtedness; redemption or call provisions; sinking fund provisions; minimum current-ratio requirements; financial statement provisions; the rights and responsibilities of the trustee.

The *trustee* is the representative of the bondholders. The trustee has three main responsibilities:

1. The trustee certifies the issue of bonds, insuring that all legal requirements for drawing up the bond contract and indenture have been met.
2. The trustee polices the behavior of the corporation in its performance with regard to the indenture provisions.
3. The trustee is responsible for taking appropriate action on behalf of the bondholders if the corporation should default on payment of interest or principal.

A trustee may be any legal person but is usually a commercial bank. Interestingly, the trustee who represents the lenders is in fact usually selected by the borrowing corporation. The business necessity to place the debt tends to insure the selection of competent trustees. The Trust Indenture Act of 1939 provides that trustees must be given sufficient power and information to act in behalf of bondholders. The act further provides for an arms-length relation between the borrowing corporation and the trustee. The act also provides that at least one trustee shall be a corporation authorized by law to exercise corporate trust powers and be subject to regulation.

Types of long-term debt financing

The principal types of debt issues will now be discussed, proceeding from secured to unsecured forms of debt. Because convertible bonds are considered by many to be a way of selling common stock at a price above the market with a tax deductible cost in the short run, convertibles are discussed in Chapter 50, "Dividend Policy and Equity Financing."

Real estate mortgage

The real estate mortgage loan is just like a mortgage loan on a home. Two types of legal instruments are involved: the note describing the amount of money involved and the terms associated with repayment; and the mortgage which pledges a specific piece of real estate as security for the loan. There is no indenture to be administered by a trustee because this sort of debt financing is not suitable for public offerings. Rather, such financing is obtained from one or a few large institutional investors.

The advantages inherent in a private placement are available. Such advantages include relatively quick, hopefully low-cost arrangement, and ease of negotiation with respect to special terms. In addition, there may be no restrictions on the corporation's general financial policies and there is usually no after-acquired clause attaching to other separate projects of the corporation because the real estate in question has some market value. This market value is the ultimate security to the lender in that if the corporation defaults, then the real estate can be sold in order to satisfy the lender.

The amount of money that can be borrowed from most institutions in this fashion is limited by law to a percentage of the appraised value of the real estate. This limit ranges from two thirds to three fourths of the value of the property depending upon the institution. The note provides that the corporation will satisfactorily maintain and insure the real estate. The repayment schedule is usually rapid enough to assure that the market value of the real estate remains above the amount still due on the mortgage.

Mortgage bonds

A mortgage bond has assets pledged as security and has a lien on those assets.[13] It differs from a real estate mortgage, described above, in that the mortgage on the property is held by a trustee for the benefit of the bondholders. There is an indenture administered by the trustee. Frequently the mortgage will include all the properties of a company rather than just a specific building. It may include just a single building, however. This type of financing is designed to allow many investors to

---

[13] There are several forms of mortgage bonds such as: purchase money mortgage bonds, general and refunding mortgage bonds, divisional mortgage bonds, terminal mortgage bonds, and mortgage and collateral trust bonds (the collateral part refers to securities which are pledged in addition to property in order to offer the investor more security). These forms are all variants of the same type, with the specific name indicating the purpose for which the financing was undertaken, e.g., terminal mortgage bonds were issued so that railroads could build terminals.

share in the financing; in fact, this type of financing can be used for a public offering.

It is usually desirable for the borrowing corporation to have its mortgage bond open-ended. This permits the corporation to issue additional bonds up to a certain percentage of new property additions, provided certain tests as to the company's financial strength are met. The mortgage will usually include an after-acquired property clause so that subsequent additions come under the mortgage. A corporation, particularly a growing corporation, can be severely constrained by a closed-end motgage bond, which forbids the issue of new bonds with a similar lien, or by a limited open-end mortgage, which limits the issue of new bonds to a specified amount.

Mortgage bonds can be expensive to administer because liens must be recorded in all the counties in which the properties to be secured are located.[14] Further the form of the mortgage will have to comply with the state laws associated with each state in which secured property is located.

Even though mortgage bonds may be expensive to administer, the additional security they offer to investors may be necessary to place the issue at all. Of course this additional security should result in lower interest charges than the corporation might have paid if it issued debt unsecured by specific, identifiable real property. Another reason for using this type of financing is associated with maintaining financial flexibility as discussed in the opening paragraphs of this chapter. That is, the use of mortgage bonds will preserve the capability of the corporation to issue another type of debt, e.g., debentures, at a future time, when more outside funds are desired, under less limiting circumstances than if the future issue were a subordinated debenture.

Equipment trust certificates

Equipment trust certificates are chattel mortgages on specific units of equipment. Title to the equipment is transferred to a trustee to secure the debt represented by the equipment certificates. The certificates are then sold in the market to obtain investors' funds. The user of the equipment, i.e. the borrowing corporation, usually makes an initial payment of approximately 20 percent of the purchase price of the equipment and further agrees to a serial repayment schedule that is at a faster rate than the equipment is actually depreciating. The user further agrees to maintain the equipment, pay any pertinent taxes, etc. As a result there is a satisfactory equity position throughout the life of the equipment trust certificate. Hence, equipment trust certificates are usually regarded as very safe loans. Because of their strong security position, they usually

---

[14] If personal, rather than real, property is used as security for the loan then the lien may have to be recorded at other locations.

result in low interest charges for corporations using them and they are one of the few types of financing available to corporations with poor credit ratings. Because of the usually rapid paydown feature, equipment trust certificates are not a very permanent source of long-term funds, and this may be significant disadvantage, particularly to a growing corporation.

In order to maintain the strong security position, it is essential that the equipment be free from all liens except the one represented by the equipment trust certificate. If a corporation has a mortgage bond outstanding with an after-acquired property clause attaching to new purchases of property, then one of the following two methods is used to keep the title to the equipment otherwise unencumbered:

1. With the most frequently utilized scheme, the so-called Philadelphia plan, title to the equipment is passed to a trustee by the manufacturer. The equipment is leased to the user and upon final payment title to the equipment passes to the user.
2. The other scheme, a conditional sales agreement, involves selling the equipment to the user on a conditional sales basis with the title remaining with the manufacturer. The manufacturer passes the title to an agent. The agent may be the lending institution. Upon final payment by the user to the agent (and then by the agent to the certificate holder) the title passes to the user of the equipment as all conditions of the sale then will have been met.

Lease financing

Conceptually lease financing is quite analogous to other forms of debt.[15] However, in lease financing the title rests with the supplier of capital, not with the user of the property. With respect to costs and other advantages or disadvantages it should be compared with other types of debt.

Lease financing can be a straightforward lease of real property or equipment from an investor. Or leasing can involve the original ownership of the real property or equipment; the sale of the property or equipment to an investor; and the subsequent leasing back of the property or equipment by the investor to the original owner. This latter form of leasing may involve a dummy corporation to hold the property in order to facilitate such financing.

Some forms of leases cover only the financing charges, i.e., the return of capital and interest for the use of the money. The corporation using the property has to maintain it, insure it, pay taxes on it, etc. Such leases

---

[15] For the purposes of this chapter leases are an alternate among many types of long-term debt financial instruments. It is recognized that corporations frequently lease for business reasons other than financial, e.g., to obtain the use of one office in a large office building.

are called net leases. Other forms of leases may include payments to the investor, or lessor, for maintenance or insurance, etc. Such leases are more complex with respect to the lease-or-not-lease issue than are net leases. The financial and the nonfinancial considerations must be evaluated separately.[16] From the point of view of the borrowing corporation, a lease is an obligation to pay a fixed amount periodically. If this is not paid, the corporation will have to forego the use of the property under lease. Further the investor, or lessor, has a legally enforceable claim for the full lease except in bankruptcy.[17]

Because at the expiration of the lease the corporation (i.e., the lessee) using the real property or equipment no longer has the property or equipment, the loss of any remaining value of such assets must be considered a cost of financing when compared with alternate types of financing. As a matter of fact, based on interest costs alone, lease financing is usually an expensive financing method compared to alternate types of financing. Therefore the use of lease financing probably should be based on some nonfinancial considerations.

Some of the nonfinancial considerations are associated with net leases. Because lease payments are deductible before income taxes, the tax considerations must be considered. The lease-payment tax deduction must be compared with the depreciation tax deduction and the interest tax deduction assuming the real property or equipment were owned by the corporation and financed by some alternate means. Renewal and forfeiture privileges of the lease must be considered. Any rights with respect to eventual purchase of the property or equipment must also be considered.

Some advantages attributed to lease financing are of questionable value. For example, it is suggested that a corporation is in a more flexible position under a lease arrangement because the corporation is not burdened with the ownership of the property. Essentially all the burden of ownership is in fact associated with a net lease. Other forms of leases could avoid this burden only if there were a low-cost, anytime bail-out provision in the lease, not a very likely circumstance with a reasonably priced lease. Another advantage of questionable value is that such a type of financing does not show up on the corporation's balance sheet. Investors are increasingly sophisticated, and sophisticated investors are well aware of the debt-like commitment associated with lease financing.[18] They are also thorough enough to probe for any significant lease commitments. Furthermore, the trend among public accounting firms, stock

---

[16] See Chapter 20, "Lease, Rent, or Buy Decisions" for a discussion of such considerations.

[17] Even in bankruptcy the lessor usually has a claim for one year's worth of lease payments. In financial reorganizations the lessor has a claim to three year's worth of lease payments.

[18] In fact, the SEC requires disclosure of lease commitments.

exchanges, and regulatory agencies is to require disclosure of lease obligations in financial statements. See Chapter 59, "Accounting for Liabilities and Capital" for further discussion.

Debentures

A description of debentures and associated indentures and trustees is included above in the "Fundamental Terminology" section of this chapter.

As indicated above, a debenture is not secured by a pledge of some designated specific piece of real property. Rather, it is secured by the general credit of the corporation. For this reason the indenture almost always contains a negative pledge clause—a provision which prevents subsequent debt issues from placing liens prior to the claim of the debenture in question.

Particularly with growing companies, it is consistent with the financial-flexibility concept discussed earlier to provide for subsequent debenture issues in the indenture of the original debenture. That is, the original indenture can be drawn in a manner that permits subsequent issues under the same indenture by means of a supplemental indenture. When it becomes desirable to raise still more money from outside the corporation, such a provision should save the corporation considerable effort and associated expense, compared to an entirely new issue. An extension of the existing debenture issue is viewed by lenders much more favorably than a junior debenture.

In fact, a considerable amount of effort should be expended to insure that the indenture of any particular debenture issue does not shut out other sources of funds. For example, access to unsecured bank credit should always be preserved (and nurtured!).

Subordinated debentures are designed to maximize a corporation's capability to utilize other sources of debt funds such as banks. Subordinated debentures are subordinated in the event of bankruptcy, liquidation or financial reorganization to any existing or future debt that is defined as "senior debt" in the indenture. Senior debt almost always includes bank loans. It may also include specified long-term debt. The key feature is that in the event of insolvency or liquidation, etc., the holders of the subordinated debentures receive no payments until the holders of the senior debt (as defined in the indenture) have been paid in full. By contrast, without subordinated debt, each debt holder would share in the "corporate remains" to the same percentage of his nominal claim against the corporation. In effect then, the subordinated debt holders turn their percentage of the spoils over to the senior debt holders. Thus, the subordinated debt materially improves a corporation's borrowing power because it supplies funds which increase the asset base upon which senior debt may be issued. In this respect it functions as preferred stock, but it has an advantage over preferred stock in that the interest payments are a tax-deductible expense, whereas preferred dividends must be paid out of after-tax income.

Some other general concepts associated with bonds, whether they be debenture, mortgage or other types, follow. Bonds can be coupon bonds. Coupon bonds literally have attached to them coupons which are clipped and submitted to a designated paying agent—a coupon for each date on which interest is due. Such bonds are bearer instruments and therefore are negotiable and transferable without any registrar intervening. A fully registered bond contains a statement indicating the dates and amounts of interest payments instead of coupons. The registrar for the bonds maintains a record of the bond's owner and address and sends him the interest checks. Such a bond is nontransferable without endorsement. A coupon bond may be registered as to the principal, which means that the principal amount of the bond is nontransferable without endorsement while the coupons are transferable by delivery alone. Most bond issues actually combine the latter two forms—i.e. both registered as to principal only, with coupons attached, and full-registered bonds are offered interchangeably to the lenders.

In recent years the trend has been toward the issuance of bonds in registered form only. This not only has the advantage of cost saving and simplicity, but also provides the issuer at all times with full knowledge of the names and addresses of the holders. Such information is invaluable when it is necessary to communicate with the holders to obtain approval for indenture changes or for any other reason.

The maturities of bonds can be any term including perpetual. At least two considerations are pertinent to the decision with respect to maturity. One involves the current level of interest rates in the bond markets. This consideration is discussed in the "Timing" section above.

The other consideration involves the corporation's requirement for funds now and during the lifetime of the bond issue. Resolution of the future cash requirements will have a major bearing on decisions with respect to retirement of the issue via serial call or sinking fund. Then the decision, serial maturity or sinking fund, can be based on consideration number one—i.e., current level and structure of interest rates. The serial-maturity feature turns the bond issue into an issue with a spectrum of maturities from short term to long term, and these various issues may command significantly different interest rates.

Bonds may contain regular call provisions. Call provisions enable the corporation to eliminate a particular bond issue in whole or in part at its option. However, the corporation pays a premium over the principal amount of the bond when it elects to exercise its call options.

Income debentures

With income debentures the interest is paid only when earned in a manner similar to dividends on preferred stock. Income debentures appear to have an advantage for corporations compared to preferred stock in that interest is deductible before taxes while dividends on preferred stock are not tax deductible. Income debentures are not commonly used.

Long-term notes or loans

Particularly with private deals, notes can be negotiated much less formally between two parties than is possible for bonds issued under an indenture. Bank loans are in fact a popular source of long-term funds for corporations, as indicated in the section on "Sources of Long-Term Debt" above.

Suggested further readings

CHILDS, JOHN F. *Long Term Financing*, Chapter 7. Englewood Cliffs, N.J.: Prentice-Hall, Inc., 1961.

DONALDSON, GORDON. *Corporate Debt Capacity*. Boston: Harvard Business School, 1961.

GUTHMANN, HARRY G. and DOUGALL, HERBERT E. *Corporate Financial Policy*, Chapter 25. Englewood Cliffs, N.J.: Prentice-Hall, Inc., 4th ed. 1962.

JOHNSON, ROBERT W. *Financial Management*, Chapters 12, 15 and 16. Rockleigh, N.J.: Allyn & Bacon, Inc., 2d ed. 1962.

O'DONNELL, JOHN L., and GOLDBERG, MILTON S. *Elements of Financial Administration*, Selection 13. Columbus, O.: Charles E. Merrill Books, Inc., 1962.

WESTON, J. FRED. *Managerial Finance*, Chapter 18. New York: Holt, Rinehart & Winston, Inc., 1962.

Dividend policy and equity financing

John K. Castle*

Cash dividends, equity financing, stock dividends, and stock repurchases are key tools available to corporate management in maximizing short term and/or long term common stockholder values. The tools directly affect the total funds a corporation has available for investment. They also directly influence its current and future stock price. The greater the funds spent on cash dividends or stock repurchases, the higher the immediate stock price and the more likely that the firm in the future will have to dilute the ownership of its shareholders by going to the equity market. Conversely, retaining cash or selling equity shares now may reduce the current stock, but it also increases its long term values—assuming that management effectively invests the retained or new funds.

The balance between cash dividends, stock repurchases, and equity financing is (or at least should be) a reflection of a corporation's total strategy. In establishing a dividend and/or stock repurchase policy, a corporate management determines which segment of the investor market will be most attracted to its securities. Managements which pay out 45 to 60 percent of their earnings in cash dividends, keep their debt to equity ratio under 50 percent, and invest in activities closely related to their current businesses are following the traditional American pattern and tend to attract more conservative, income-conscious investors. Managements that have lower dividend payouts, incur higher debt to equity ratios, and invest their internal cash in new and perhaps unproven and unrelated businesses, will probably attract more aggressive investors.

---

* Vice President, Donaldson, Lufkin & Jenrette, Inc., New York.

Dividend policy

Despite the fact that it is largely a matter of management strategy which markets a corporation's securities attract, businessmen, stockholders, and academicians hotly dispute the optimal balance between cash dividends, equity financings, stock dividends, and/or stock repurchases. Several growth company managements and academicians, such as Miller and Modigliani, think that cash dividends are less advantageous to common shareholders than the reinvestment of the funds within the corporation or the repurchase of the company's stock.

Disadvantages of cash dividends

It is argued that the tax structure favors repurchase of stock or retention of earnings. If a company has excess funds, it can buy its own stock in the open market with the prospect that the selling shareholders will receive capital gains treatment and the remaining stockholders will have an increased market value for each share they continue to hold. If the company does not have excess funds, it is to the shareholder's benefit to leave earnings in the corporation rather than receive dividends, pay taxes, and subsequently reinvest in the corporation through a stock rights offering.

Some members of this nondividend-paying school would even contend that corporations should always be able to invest excess cash on more profitable bases than individual stockholders, who must pay federal taxes before they reinvest their funds.

Advantages of dividends

The proponents of cash dividends which include (by action, if not by verbal expression) most American corporate managements, textbook authors Graham, Dodd, and Cottle,[1] and academicians such as Gordon Donaldson[2] have equally incisive arguments why stock repurchases and/or retained earnings are not substitutes for cash dividends.

These experts give the following factors to support the benefit of cash dividends:

1. Cash dividends historically have indicated that a company is financially healthy and has represented a return to shareholders for the use of their capital.

2. A cash dividend creates a floor on the price of common stock. Most

---

[1] Benjamin Graham, David Dodd, Sidney Cottle, *Security Analysis: Principles and Techniques.* (New York: McGraw-Hill Book Company, Inc., 1962), p. 480.

[2] Gordon Donaldson, *Corporate Debt Capacity.* (Boston: Harvard University Graduate School of Business Administration, Division of Research, 1961), p. 42.

portfolio managers and many private investors will purchase a common stock when its yield reaches a high level, e.g. 5 percent—even in a major stock market collapse or a corporate earnings decline if they think that the dividends will be continued. Thus, a high yielding common stock may have less downside risk than lower yielding common stock.

3. Many stockholders prefer regular cash payments. In the case of retired people, dividends may be an important part of their current income, and they value being able to plan on a specific cash flow for living expenses.

4. A good dividend payment increases a company's price-earnings ratio, which is important in the event that the firm must regularly raise equity capital. Utilities, which sell common stock frequently, seem to accept this argument and pay high dividends. Conglomerates, by contrast, which have heavily issued common shares for acquisition in recent years, generally pay low dividends (see Exhibit 1).

EXHIBIT 1

Conglomerate Dividend Payout Policy

Name	Dividend per Share	Earnings per Share	Payout Ratio
AMK Corp.	$0.15 + Stock	$1.90	8%+
"Automatic" Sprinkler Corp.	0.11	1.43	8%
Glen Alden Corp.	—	0.61	—
Gulf & Western Industries	0.26	3.91	7%
International Telephone and Telegraph	0.75	2.27	33%
Ling-Temco-Vought	1.17	7.69	15%
Litton Industries	2½% Stock	1.83	—
Teledyne, Incorporated	3½% Stock	2.66	—
Textron, Incorporated	0.62	2.07	30%
TRW, Incorporated	0.80	2.03	39%
U.S. Industries	0.35	1.58	22%
Walter Kidde	3% Stock	3.20	—
White Consolidated Industries	0.08 + Stock	1.41	6%+

5. Finally, many state laws, e.g., Texas and Minnesota, require a company to pay a cash dividend to be included on the state's legal lists, or have tax penalties on non-dividend-paying stocks, e.g., Ohio. These state laws can restrict the potential purchases of non-dividend-paying common stock.

The purpose of this chapter is not to resolve the arguments on cash dividend payout policy, to which many articulate authors have devoted thousands of pages. Rather, recognizing that a good dividend policy is affected by subjective factors such as management's corporate strategy as well as purely objective criteria, our purpose is to examine and understand current corporate practices and the reasons why such practices vary among different corporations. The corporate financial executive, who plays a key role in helping his company formulate its dividend policy, knows that his company cannot simply adopt someone else's policy; his obligation is to formulate a policy that is best for his company, given its particular objectives and its particular group of stockholders.

Standard dividend practices

The standard practice for American corporations is to pay annually 45 to 60 percent of net earnings in equal quarterly dividend checks. In recent years, the 88.8 percent of the companies in S&P's 425 that pay only cash dividends on their common stocks have sustained an average yield of 3.1 percent. A smaller group of corporations, 5.1 percent of stocks in S&P's 425, have paid stock dividends (in some instances in addition to cash dividends), and 6.1 percent of the companies have not had a cash or stock dividend.

There are many rules which corporations utilize when they establish their dividend policy. Some of these rules are almost mythological, but others can be helpful in establishing a dividend policy. Some of the more commonly used dividend rules are cataloged below:

1. Firms with a high growth rate and a high price/earnings ratio on their stocks can be more stingy with cash dividend payouts than low price/earnings ratio companies. For example, an electronics firm selling at 50x earnings which would have a yield of 1 percent if it paid out half its earnings in dividends will not significantly affect its stock price by increasing the dividend payout. Conversely, a company selling at 10x earnings yielding 5 percent with a 50 percent payout will very significantly affect its stock price by increasing the dividend. In between these two extremes, a company with a price/earnings multiple of 20x yielding 2½ percent probably would be modestly affected by a substantial increase in the dividend payout ratio (see Exhibit 2).

An underlying hypothesis of this analysis is that an investor buys a high price/earnings ratio stock for something other than dividend, such as a company's rapid growth. A company with a low price/earnings ratio is more frequently purchased for its dividend payment, and the investor is more interested in the downside protection afforded by the increased dividend.

2. Cash dividends are normally not more than 75 to 80 percent of earnings in a good year, and seldom exceed 100 percent of earnings in a bad year. The historic reasoning is that earnings per share is only an estimate of what a company is actually earning. Therefore, prudent management reserves some of its reported earnings in the event that they proved to be overstated.

In bad years, companies seldom pay out more in dividends than they have realized in net income despite the fact that they have retained earnings from a substantial number of years of good profits. This posture is usually based on a concern that the company's adverse circumstances may not be corrected quickly.

3. The dividend payout of earnings is frequently established as that portion of earnings which is not required for long term growth. For

EXHIBIT 2

Price Earnings Ratio

	High	Medium	Low
Stock price (50% payout)	$100	$100	$100
Earnings per share	$2.00	$5.00	$10.00
P/E ratio	50x	20x	10x
Dividend (50% payout)	$1.00	$2.50	$5.00
Yield (50% payout)	1%	2½%	5%
Dividend (75% payout)	$1.50	$3.75	$7.50
Estimated stock price (75% payout) after dividend increase	$100	$110	$140

example, a company with a long-term growth rate of 4 percent (gr) and a return on equity (roe) of 10 percent would have a payout ratio (pr) of 60 percent of its earnings.

$$\text{pr} = \frac{\text{roe} - \text{gr}}{\text{roe}} = \frac{10 - 4}{10} = \frac{6}{10} = 60\%$$

Assuming that the corporation had adequate equity capital when this policy was established, theoretically it should not need to sell additional common stock at any time in the future.

4. Common stockholders prefer, and many corporations have established, dividend policies which are regular nondeclining payments. The principal benefit of a cash dividend is that it provides a shareholder with a reasonably predictable cash flow. If the company changes its dividends substantially (up and down), most of the value of consistency is lost to the common shareholder. In the event that a company's earnings base is highly cyclical, and the company wants to pay out more dividends than it could expect to sustain in a poor economic year, the company can pay an extra dividend. Such a practice puts the stockholders on notice that the cash dividend cannot be maintained in a period of adversity. Another practice is for the corporation to repurchase its stock with excess cash, thus reducing the number of outstanding shares and hopefully increasing future earnings per share.

5. Companies with a few high-tax-bracket stockholders frequently have lower cash dividend payout ratios than firms with a broader group of public stockholders. Unless a company's major stockholders intend to

liquidate their holdings in the near future, or are concerned about current income, maximization of near term stock price is not as important as effective investing of the corporation's funds in order to maximize the long-term corporate values.

6. Various legal agreements and contractual arrangements may limit dividend payments. Legal restrictions, for example, may be found in indentures, bank loan agreements, and restrictions of state laws on capital surplus.

A company, once it has established a dividend policy, should articulate its program to investors. Such steps reduce the risk that shareholders will be disappointed by the company's dividend action. It also increases the probability that investors whose investment goals concur with the company's dividend strategy will buy its stock.

Steps in establishing dividend policy

Within these general guidelines, corporate management has great latitude in establishing a specific dividend payout rate. In many instances, the decision is intuitive. In other cases, it is derived after months of study of industry competitors, corporate cash flows, and analysis of the prospective return on investment from additional dividends.

Industry dividend analysis

Most companies begin their study of dividend policy with an analysis of practices of major competitors or similar firms. The study includes an examination of the price/earnings ratios of various competitors as compared to their corporate dividend payout ratios.

An example of such a comparative analysis for the electrical equipment industry is presented in Exhibit 3. The current practice for a typical electrical equipment industry member is to pay out between 40 and 50 percent of its earnings. A highly profitable company such as Square D, with no apparent intention to expand by cash acquisitions, pays out an above-average proportion of earnings. A company such as I.T.E., with plans for expansion through acquisition, pays a lower dividend as compared to net income.

In recent years, the electrical equipment companies have paid, considering their sales growth, a greater proportion of their earnings in dividends than would be sustainable without an infusion of external capital. In other words, each company's sales growth rate has exceeded retained earnings as a percent of beginning equity. This liberal dividend policy was reflected in substantial new debt issues by General Electric, Westinghouse, Cutler Hammer, and I.T.E. Imperial during 1967.

A new member of the electrical equipment industry would want to consider whether to match the industry's policy, which could require raising external funds to pay dividends. He might conclude that the

EXHIBIT 3

Analysis of Electrical Equipment Companies

	General Electric Co.	Westinghouse Corp.	Square D Co.	Cutler-Hammer, Inc.	I.T.E. Imperial Corp.	Emerson Electric Mfg. Co.	Reliance** Electric	McGraw-Edison Co.
P/E ratio 8/19/68	22x	21x	19x	22x	21x	27x	16x	15x
Yield 8/19/68	3.2%	2.5%	5.2%	3.0%	1.6%	1.8%	2.5%	3.9%
Redundant cash (millions)	$27	—	$24	—	—	$21	$20	—
Debt to equity	31%	36%	—	33%	38%	26%	18%	2%
Avg. dividend payout (5 yrs)	68%	52%	71%	45%	23%	45%	44%	50%
Net income margin (5-yr avg)	4.9%	3.8%	12.6%	4.2%	4.3%	7.1%	6.8%	5.9%
Dividend/sales	3.4%	2.0%	9.0%	1.9%	1.0%	3.2%	3.0%	3.0%
Earnings retained/sales	1.5%	1.8%	3.6%	2.3%	3.3%	3.9%	3.8%	2.9%
Growth rate-sales								
5 years	9.2%	8.2%	9.1%	12.8%	11.2%	12.8%	11.0%	9.7%
10 years	7.0%	4.9%	8.8%	12.5%	8.0%*	21.0%	7.4%	9.7%
EPS growth (5 yrs)	6.8%	15.5%	9.5%	7.0%	63.0%	14.9%	28.0%	13.6%
Return on beginning equity								
5-year avg.	15.5%	8.8%	24.8%	10.9%	11.8%	19.6%	15.6%	13.3%
10-year avg.	16.4%	8.1%	22.7%	8.4%	9.3%†	20.4%	13.5%	12.0%**
Retained earnings as a % of beginning equity (5 yrs)	4.8%	3.8%	7.1%	6.0%	9.1%	10.8%	8.7%	6.3%

* 7 years.
† 9 years.
** Including Dodge Mfg. but excluding Toledo Scale.

rapid industry sales growth of the early 1960's would not continue, and that the amount of increased retained earnings would be adequate to finance sales growth in the future.

There are several other ways an electrical equipment management might deviate from the industry pattern. A highly profitable firm similar to Square D might choose to repurchase some of its stock with its redundant cash rather than pay dividends, thereby achieving a capital gains tax treatment for its shareholders. Square D's multiple at 19x only partially reflects its high dividend payouts when the stock is compared to other industry members' price/earnings ratios. A firm such as Emerson Electric, with a substantial price/earnings ratio, probably could justify making a lower payout, permitting the firm to invest more of its cash in other corporate activities.

Cash flow analysis

Another approach to establishing a dividend policy is an application of the technique of determining corporate debt capacity, as developed by Gordon Donaldson.[3] Management can estimate its future cash inflows, assuming a variety of economic, industry, and corporate operating conditions. Using these various assumptions, management can determine the amount of cash dividends it can reasonably maintain over the long term, after servicing its debt requirements and providing for capital expansion.

Stock price appreciation analysis

A recent concept for evaluating alternative cash dividend policies is to analyze dividend increases as a capital investment decision. Gary Mac-Dougal, in the *Harvard Business Review*,[4] details a method whereby a corporate management can evaluate additional cash dividends versus the reduction in the number of shares of stock the company will have to distribute in a new equity offering or in acquisitions. This approach permits management the opportunity to view dividend policy as a return on investment.

Outside opinion analysis

Finally, in defining its dividend payout policy, a corporation might well seek the opinion of its investment bankers, large individual stockholders, institutional investors, and/or a pool of all stockholders. These

---

[3] *Ibid.*

[4] Gary MacDougal, "Investing in a Dividend Boost," *Harvard Business Review*, Vol. 45, no. 4, pp. 87–92.

parties have a vested interest in their company's dividend program, and their comments on the program which they prefer should be of great value to management.

Stock dividends

Some corporations pay low cash dividends because of poor earnings, high internal demands for cash, or a corporate philosophy that cash dividends are inappropriate, given the income tax disadvantages of paying dividends versus the repurchase of common stock. In instances where the lack of a cash dividend is due to high cash demands or philosphical considerations, companies sometimes pay stock dividends as a substitute for cash payments.

The arguments for a stock dividend are manifold. A stock dividend symbolizes the earnings which a corporation retains for the benefit of the common stockholders. Stock dividends further provide shareholders with

EXHIBIT 4

Companies' P/E Ratio

No dividends 39x
Stock dividends only 28x
S&P 425 ....18x

Sources: Donaldson, Lufkin & Jenrette on June 30, 1968; S & P 425 common stocks.

small-denomination stock certificates which they may sell on a capital gains basis to raise cash. Stock dividends also increase the number of a company's shares in circulation and increase the company's cash dividend payout, if it has one, by increasing the number of shares receiving a specific dividend. With the exception of a few conglomerates, stock dividends have generally been used when a company is reducing its cash dividends due to a decline in net income.

Despite their wide application, many authorities believe that stock dividends have little or no economic value and several disadvantages. Studies at Donaldson, Lufkin & Jenrette indicate that the stock price declined for all but two companies that substituted stock for cash dividends in the period 1959–1966. Further studies indicated that non-dividend-paying stocks in the S&P 425 had higher price/earnings ratios (excluding securities with losses) than stocks of companies that paid stock dividends (see Exhibit 4). Some statistics indicate that few stockholders take advantage of stock dividends by selling their new shares. For instance, 57 percent of stock dividends paid by mutual funds are automatically reinvested. Of course, if stockholders do sell their stock they tend to depress its market price.

The payment of stock dividends may also retard the company's apparent growth rate. Many financial services do not restate earnings per share until the accumulated impact of stock dividends is 5 percent. A corporation's apparent growth rate could be understated to this extent.

Theoretically, the economic advantages of stock dividends are completely illusory unless accompanied by a higher effective cash payout. A stock dividend simply splits the corporate ownership into a greater number of pieces. It also lacks the benefit of offering the shareholder a specific dollar payment, in contrast to cash dividends, because the value of the stock dividend is a function of the stock price on the day the shareholder decides to liquidate.

Finally, stock dividends create administrative complications. The company and its agents are burdened with the responsibilities of sending certificates to its shareholders and liquidating fractional shares as authorized by shareholders.

Despite these objections, some managements will decide to pay stock dividends. If they so choose, their first consideration is the determination of a dividend rate. Usually the company will select a rate which is similar to a typical cash dividend yield. For instance, management would normally select a rate somewhere between 2 and 5 percent. For mechanical reasons, management should consider the effects of fractional shares when establishing a stock dividend rate. Integer percentages (i.e., 2, 3, 4 percent) do not create fractional shares for round lot common stockholders. Fractional percentages ($2\frac{1}{2}$, $3\frac{1}{2}$ percent, etc.) create a fractional share for each round lot stock dividend paid, thereby greatly increasing the problems of disposing of fractional shares.

Traditional practice, intended to preserve the symbolism between stock and cash dividends, is to select a stock dividend rate that is no greater than net income. In other words, a company's earnings should be large enough so that stock dividends do not dilute book value each year. For example, a company with a $10.00 book value would be expected to earn at least $0.50 a share if it were to pay a 5 percent stock dividend. Some would even argue that the symbolism between stock and cash dividends is destroyed if the stock dividend rate is not somewhat less than 5 percent.

Management, in addition to the specific stock dividend rate, should also develop and disclose a stock dividend policy to its shareholders. The policy should complement its cash dividend policy, and be consistent with the company's overall corporate strategy.

Equity financing

Corporations, particularly rapidly growing ones, require new equity capital from time to time. The methods of determining a corporation's needs for funds and what proportion should be equity capital are based upon a multitude of standards, some of which are traditional rules of thumb, while others are based on more sophisticated analytical techniques.

Most managements determine their total fund requirements by a cash flow projection. This analysis can be expanded by examining the fund requirements assuming a variety of economic, industrial, and corporate operating circumstances. After determining its total fund requirements, management must determine what proportion of external requirements should be supplied by debt rather than equity capital.

The standards for selecting a debt to equity ratio are multitudinous, including some with long-standing traditions. A conventional standard is that debt to equity should never exceed one for one, and usually should not exceed one for two. Another historic standard is that pretax earnings plus interest payments should "cover" the interest requirements at least three times, and normally should cover them at least six times. (See Chapter 45 for a more detailed discussion.)

Companies frequently have used the lending limitations established by their commercial banks and other institutions as a principal method of determining what their borrowing limits should be. This latter criteria has merit only to the extent that the lenders are not too lenient or too tight in providing funds. Ultimately it is corporate management that must accept responsibility for the decision of how much debt is appropriate for the company.

As noted previously, the most sophisticated way to approach the problems of determining a company's equity needs is Gordon Donaldson's method of analyzing cash flows under various economic circumstances and operational assumptions. Using this analysis, a company can estimate the total amount of debt which it can properly service, given management's attitudes toward risk and desire to maintain freedom of action. The fund requirements in excess of this "debt capacity" are the new equity funds needed by the firm.

A company, once it determines its equity financing requirements, can obtain funds from a variety of total or partial equity sources including:

1. An acquisition of a company with an excess equity base.
2. An issue of warrants usually attached to debt.
3. A convertible debentures issue.
4. A preferred stock issue.
5. A convertible preferred stock issue.
6. A common stock issue.

The selection of one or several of these methods to raise equity funds is dependent on the cost of capital, accounting practices, and several qualitative factors, such as servicing costs and the problems of retiring debt from a convertible debenture/or debt with warrants issue in the event the common stock does not appreciate sufficiently to make conversion of the debt or the exercise of the warrants attractive. At the time of this writing, the accounting practices for computing earning per share when various equity forms are included in a company's capitalization are under major review by the AICPA. That review could significantly alter which alternative forms are most attractive for raising equity funds.

Purchasing an equity rich company

One of the cheapest methods of raising new equity funds is through the acquisition of an equity rich company. Frequently, a company is able to acquire such a firm and still increase its own earnings per share. For instance, a company with a 15x price/earnings ratio and a debt-heavy balance sheet can acquire a debt-free company with a 10x multiple and improve its balance sheet if the transaction is done with an equity security (see the example in Exhibit 5).

EXHIBIT 5

Combination of Companies*

(pooling of interest accounting)

	Premerger Acquirer Company	Premerger Acquired Company	Postmerger Combined Companies
Income statement			
Total common mkt. value	$150	$100	$250
Net income	$ 10	$ 10	$ 20
Shares outstanding	3	2	5
Stock price	$ 50	$ 50	$ 50
EPS	$ 3.33	$ 5.00	$ 4.00
P/E ratio	15x	10x	12.5x
Total assets			
Current assets	$100	$100	$200
Fixed assets	50	50	100
Total	$150	$150	$300
Total liability/equity			
Current liabilities	$ 50	$ 50	$100
Long term debt	50	—	50
Equity	50	100	150
Total	$150	$150	$300

* The acquiring company is purchasing the acquired firm on a share for share basis.

The acquisition of an equity rich company, which is frequently the only method of raising equity without diluting earnings per share, may be quite attractive, assuming that the acquisition conforms to a company's corporate business strategy and growth goals.

Warrants with debt

The second cheapest method of raising equity funds is warrants with debt, which usually requires options for about half as many shares as are required with convertible debentures (see example). The disadvantage of warrants is that a company may have to retire a portion of the debt outstanding even if the common stock appreciates sufficiently to justify exercise of the warrants. For this reason, warrants combined with debt have risks not associated with a convertible debenture or common stock issue.

Example: Common share options required for debt with warrants versus convertible debentures. *Problem:* Assume a company burdened with debt requires $100 which can be raised from debt with warrants or convertible debentures. Assume the firm's common stock price is $45.00. *Alternative solutions:* Such a firm might have either of the two following alternatives to raise funds. (1) The company could issue $100 of 20-year 6½ percent debentures and a warrant to buy one share of common stock for $50.00. (2) The firm could issue a 6½ percent 20-year debenture convertible at $50 per share. The debentures, if converted, would have the effect of selling common stock at a price 11 percent higher than the current price. *Impact of solutions:* The debt and warrants package would require that the firm ultimately issue only one share of stock for every two required for the convertible debenture issue. The debt with warrants package would have the disadvantage that the company would still have $50.00 of debt outstanding after the warrants were exercised as opposed to none if the debentures were converted.

Convertible debentures

Convertible debentures always result in less stock dilution when raising equity than common stock. A convertible debenture can normally be sold at some premium over conversion value, and therefore a firm can raise a greater number of dollars for a given number of shares of common than if it sold common stock directly. Using our example of warrants with debt, a company with a stock price of $45 must sell 2.2 shares in order to raise $100 versus giving options on two shares for convertible debentures, and one share for debt with warrants. Of course, convertible debentures, like debt with warrants, suffer from the risk of retiring debt in the event the common stock does not appreciate sufficiently to make conversion attractive.

Preferred issues

Straight preferreds, seldom used today because the dividends are not tax deductible, are a form of equity financing whose cost relative to common stock is really dependent on the common's price/earnings ratio. A straight preferred usually has a coupon between 5 and 8 percent, or a price to dividend ratio of 20.0 to 12.5x (i.e., 100/5 percent and 100/8 percent). For that reason, a company with a price/earnings ratio below 12 may find a straight preferred an inexpensive method of raising equity. On the other hand, a company management with a multiple above 20x might argue that its common stock is a cheaper method of financing than preferred, a judgment which may or may not be true when one considers the prospective growth of the company. In fact, management might decide that even with a price earnings ratio of 50x a common stock issue is more expensive than a preferred issue because of the growth which they anticipate for their common earnings per share.

Convertible preferred stocks, which suffer from the same tax problems as straight preferreds, have seldom been used except in mergers and acquisitions in recent years. Most corporations prefer convertible debentures whose interest cost is tax deductible. Convertible preferreds have been used in mergers and acquisitions because they can be used in tax free exchanges.

Common stock issues

The final and most straightforward method of raising equity funds is through the sale of common stock. The sale of common is usually the most expensive form of obtaining funds for a corporation. It does have the advantage that it does not create any service or other burdens (except dividends) for the corporation. Sometimes a corporation's debt structure is so great that corporate management has no alternative but to sell straight common stock. In other instances, the company's P/E ratio may be so great that its apparent cost is lower than straight debt—a situation which is probably illusory when long-term growth factors are considered. However, a company with a very high multiple may find that new equity will affect immediate earnings per share less than debt.

Underwriter fees

The underwriter's fee will be a percentage of the price of the securities underwritten, a schedule of which is detailed in Exhibit 6 for recent underwritings. The company will also have to pay legal fees associated with the preparation of the prospectus. A company will be able to determine the current market for underwriting fees by examining the prospectus of recent offerings by other similar companies. (See Exhibit 6.)

Mangement will be called upon for much support when the investment bankers and lawyers prepare the prospectus. This support will include the gathering of extensive financial, operating, and other data on the company for filing with the Securities and Exchange Commission. The bibliography at the end of this chapter lists several references which detail all steps in an underwriting.

EXHIBIT 6

Cost of Underwriting Common Stock Issues
(Jan. 1966 through March 1968)

Market Value of Issue	*Cost of Equity Underwriting as a % of Total Value*
Under $10 million	6.4%
$11–20 million	4.7%
Over $20 million	4.3%

Source: Donaldson, Lufkin & Jenrette, 1968.

Stock splits

A stock split may be appropriate after a company's stock exceeds $60.00 or $70.00 per share. The purpose of a split is to expand a stock's liquidity by decreasing the price so that more shareholders can participate in the market by purchasing round lots.

In making the decision for a stock split, management must decide some specific price which is most appropriate for its shares. The usual price range, with notable exceptions, for which management aims is between $25 and $50 per common share. A stock price below $25 per share has disadvantages. In a bad economic period for the company, or a declining stock market, such an issue can easily fall into the teens. At that price level, the public may stop relating the stock price to any meaningful standard of the company's current or prospective earnings or dividends. In fact, if the price of a stock falls below $10.00, its price may have no relationship to corporate performance. At such a low price, many naive and uninformed stockholders purchase the issue just because they can afford to purchase a round lot. At the other extreme, a company with a common stock price over $70.00 that fails to split may be cutting off many prospective investors who could add liquidity to the company's issue.

There are several exceptions to these general rules. For example, many high technology companies with very high multiples, including IBM and Xerox, let their stock prices seek levels over $100 per share and do not split the shares. In the cases of these firms, the stock might assume absurd multiples because of masses of investors purchasing round lots in order to participate in the company's unique technological position.

Selecting the ratio for a stock split is a matter of determining a stock price which seems reasonable and deducing the proper division of the current stock which is necessary to get the stock to that price level. Management normally uses an integral number or some simple rule to determine the ratio for a split. For instance, ratios such as 5 for 4, 4 for 3, 3 for 2, 2 for 1, 3 for 1, etc., would be considered good; a more complicated mathematical relationship would be unnecessarily complex.

Management traditionally has selected a period of enthusiasm to split the stock. Such a time would be when the earnings outlook is good, the stock has had a major upward move, and the split may be accompanied by an upward adjustment of the cash dividend. It would be unusual to split the stock when the outlook is poor, primarily because the issue might decline into the price region where the stock does not reasonably reflect the economics of the company.

The mechanics of a stock split are usually simple.

1. A sufficient number of shares must be authorized, a step which normally requires a stockholder vote. For this reason, stock splits are often timed to coincide with an annual meeting when additional shares can be authorized.

2. Management must determine whether the transaction should take the legal form of a stock split or stock dividend. For example, a firm with 5,000,000 shares of $5 par value stock could split the stock, the result of which would be to give them 10,000,000 shares of $2.50 par value stock; or they could have a 100 percent stock dividend, which would increase the outstanding shares to 10,000,000 shares of $5 par value common. The latter alternative would increase the company's capital account by $25,000,000 and reduce retained earnings by the same amount.

The selection of one course versus the other is normally a matter of form and of certain legal restrictions which vary from state to state. The economics of either alternative are usually unimportant, except in states where cash dividends cannot be paid from capital reserves.

A management seeking advice on a stock split can look to its investment banker, institutional investors, and general stockholders to determine what type of policy most shareholders would prefer and what type of practices appear most intelligent within the context of a company's specific situation.

Stock exchange listing

A company with publicly traded securities should consider listing its securities on a national exchange assuming that it can qualify. Although intangible, a securities exchange listing may significantly affect a firm's cost-of-capital by its impact on the corporation's price/earnings ratio.

Listing common stock, particularly on the New York Stock Exchange, is viewed by many investors as a certification of investment quality. The Exchange listing normally assures investors that a company has a certain minimum net income and that other financial criteria were achieved before the securities were admitted for trading on the exchange. Further, listing assures investors that a corporation's stock has a certain liquidity since Exchanges require that a corporation have at least a minimum number of shareholders and trading volume prior to admission for trading.

Exchange listing has additional advantages for investors. The stockholder can receive the prices and volumes of actual daily stock transitions, whereas the quotation for over-the-counter markets does not reflect the actual price of transactions or indicate the volume in a security. A stock exchange is a double auction market where the highest bid and lowest offering are the prices for transactions at any given instant; the result is that investors should get the best possible price in the market. In an over-the-counter market, by contrast, investors may get less than the best price if they purchase through the wrong dealer.

An important, although not inherent, disadvantage of securities exchange listing is that it may reduce the liquidity professional traders will provide for a given common stock. Many over-the-counter investment houses have greater capital and are therefore able to assume greater positions in a given security than the specialists on the floor of even the New York Stock Exchange. As a result, some stocks may have even greater liquidity when traded over the counter than after listing on a major securities exchange.

When weighing the advantages of listing a stock versus over-the-counter markets, most managements seem to prefer having their securities listed. Usually, corporations seem to make preparations and become listed within a year or two of meeting exchange listing requirements. Management evidently thinks that a securities exchange listing is attractive for investors and an effective method to reduce cost-of-capital.

Bibliography

ROBINSON, GERALD J., *Going Public Successful Securities Underwriting.* (New York: Clark Boardman Company Ltd., 1962).

WHEAT, FRANCIS M. and BLACKSTONE, GEORGE A., "Guideposts for a First Public Offering," *The Business Lawyer,* April 1960.

WHITE, K. K., *Financing Company Expansion.* (New York: American Management Association, Inc., 1964) Chapter 7.

WINTER, ELMER L., *A Complete Guide to Making A Public Stock Offering.* (Englewood Cliffs, N.J.: Prentice-Hall, Inc., 1962).

Financial aspects of acquisitions and mergers

James S. Smith and Larry L. Chamberlin*

This chapter serves as a brief summary of the financial aspects of mergers and acquisitions. It does not discuss the analysis of potential acquisitions, since that is the province of Chapter 18. Although the accounting aspects of mergers and acquisitions are covered in detail in Chapter 57, "Accounting for Business Combinations and Goodwill," they are also briefly discussed here. A familiarity with their basic aspects is necessary to an understanding of the various financial forms a merger can take. The principal section of this chapter is concerned with the various methods of financing and consummating a merger or an acquisition.

Accounting and tax aspects

Purchase versus pooling accounting

A business combination is accounted for, either as a purchase or pooling of interests or a combination of the two. A detailed definition and discussion of purchase and pooling accounting is developed in Chapter 57, but since the whole concept of pooling accounting is being reexamined at the time of this writing, a brief definition and discussion is presented below.

Purchase accounting may be selected as a method of accounting for virtually all business combinations. Under purchase accounting, the sep-

---

* Partner, and Consultant, respectively, of Peat, Marwick, Mitchell & Co., New York.

arable assets and liabilities of the acquired company are recorded, as assets and liabilities of the acquiring or surviving company, at their fair values on the date of the combination. The difference between the total value of the consideration given and the fair values assigned to the assets and liabilities represents goodwill, an asset. If the total purchase price is less than the fair value of the separable assets and liabilities, negative goodwill is created. Generally, goodwill must either be charged against income over a reasonable period of time, or carried as an asset until it is determined no longer to have value, at which time it would be written off.

Pooling of interests accounting is considered an acceptable alternative to purchase accounting, for most business combinations effected by issuing common or voting stock. Under the pooling of interests concept of accounting, the business combination is not viewed as the purchase of one company by another, but as a joining of the companies. The assets and liabilities of the acquired or merged companies are carried forward at historical costs into the accounts of the surviving entity. Pooling of interests accounting does not recognize or assign any value for goodwill; it has enjoyed a recent upsurge of popularity, partly, because no goodwill, which must be charged against future earnings, is created.

As was stated earlier, purchase accounting may be selected for virtually all business combinations. However, pooling of interests accounting is often the method preferred by the businessman. While several conditions have been spelled out, as required for pooling of interests accounting, some of them have been loosely interpreted. Most important of these conditions is that holders of substantially all ownership interests in the constituent corporations should become the owners of a single corporation, which owns the assets and businesses of the constituent corporations. In effect, there should be a continuity of ownership. In determining the extent to which a new ownership, or continuity of old ownership, exists in a particular business combination, consideration should be given to the attendant circumstances and the parties' intentions at the time of the transaction.

SELECTION OF PURCHASE VERSUS POOLING ACCOUNTING. In situations where a businessman may select between purchase and pooling accounting, the decision is sometimes based on considerations other than accounting. One major factor, affecting the selection of purchase versus pooling accounting, is that when purchase accounting is selected or dictated, the operation of the constituent companies are combined only for periods subsequent to the date of the transaction. With the pooling, the operations of the constituents are combined for the entire year. Furthermore, when pooling of interests accounting is used, prior periods' comparative statements must be restated to report operating results, as if the entities had been combined during the periods. Purchase accounting is sometimes chosen to improve reported operations, when stated comparatively to prior periods. For example, Company A acquired Company B, which is a profitably operating company, and the combination is reported on a purchase basis. The operations of Company A would be favorably reported, when comparatively stated to prior periods' operations, because the results of A's prior periods are not restated and the current year's reported results include the profitable operations of B. Another situation, in which a businessman might select purchase accounting as opposed to pooling accounting, is the situation in which negative goodwill is generated. Hence, if a company does purchase another company, and the consideration for the purchase is less than the book value of the acquired company after adjustments are made to reflect the fair values of the separable assets and liabilities, negative goodwill is generated. The amortization of this negative goodwill increases the reported earnings over future periods, as compared to reported earnings if pooling accounting were selected.

Other than avoiding the disadvantage of having to amortize goodwill against earnings in future periods, pooling of interests accounting can sometimes hide poor performance of the parent company, by the acquisition of a rapidly growing subsidiary. For example, assume the following earnings record:

	Earnings	
	Year 1	Year 2
Parent company	100	90
Subsidiary	40	80

Assume parent acquired the subsidiary during Year 2. Then, the consolidated comparatively reported earnings would be as follows:

	Year 1	Year 2
Earnings	140	170

Hence, the poor performance of the parent is not so readily apparent, because of the progress of the subsidiary.

Summary of tax aspects

Tax treatment for the many various types of business combinations is a very complex subject, and this section only serves as a broad explanation. Certainly, before any transaction is contemplated or consummated, the businessman should consult his tax advisor. The principal tax aspect of mergers and acquisitions is whether or not the transaction results in recognition to the selling company, or to its stockholders, of a gain or loss, subject to immediate capital gains taxation. The general rule is that all mergers and acquisitions result in taxable transactions, unless the transaction qualifies as a corporate reorganization. The Internal Revenue Code outlines six types of corporate transactions which qualify as nontaxable corporate reorganizations, three of which are most applicable: (1) the *A* type, statutory mergers and consolidations; (2) the *B* type, acquisition of one corporation's stock control by another with the consideration being solely voting stock; and (3) the *C* type, acquisition by one corporation of substantially all of the assets of another, with the sole consideration usually being voting stock.

The introduction of any consideration, other than voting stock, voids the tax-free status of *B* and *C* types. One exception to this is that cash may be issued in lieu of fractional shares. For *A* types, consideration other than voting stock, up to certain limits, subjects only this proportionate amount to taxable status. The primary test for nontaxable status is the continuity of proprietary interest concept. Thus, the shareholders of the selling corporation must continue to participate in its ownership. This participation can only be satisfied by an equity interest, *i.e.*, voting stock.

Generally, the selling company and/or its stockholders prefer a nontaxable transaction, *i.e.*, an exchange of voting stock. However, the selling stockholders may wish to receive cash for diversification purposes. In this situation, the stockholder must weigh the advantages of receiving cash for his personal investment diversification objectives versus the disadvantages of being immediately subjected to capital gains taxation. A taxable transaction may also be preferred by a selling company's stockholders, when the purchase price of the company is less than the tax basis of the company, so that a tax loss may be generated to apply against current capital gains for taxation purposes.

Another important tax consideration revolves around the fact that, in a taxable transaction, the purchasing company may acquire a new tax basis for assets acquired. The purchase price may be allocated to the fair market value of the assets purchased. Often, the fair market value is higher than the book value. The result is that, for tax purposes, future depreciation for the acquired company can be greater than for the company prior to the acquisition. However, in a tax-free exchange, the purchaser generally assumes the seller's tax basis.

Methods of financing mergers and acquisitions

This section deals with the various methods of financing a merger or acquisition transaction, the ramifications of each method, and why businessmen use each one. The instruments of purchase may be cash, common stock, preferred stock, debentures, warrants, or some combination of the above. Also briefly covered are the modified arrangements to meet special situations and objectives. These arrangements include payments on a contingent basis, tender offers, and other miscellaneous transactions. For proper understanding of the financial aspects of mergers and acquisitions, one must have a familiarization with the concept, treatment, and effect on earnings per share of common stock equivalents. Therefore, this section begins with a discussion of common stock equivalents and earnings per share. For a more detailed treatment of this topic, the reader is referred to Chapter 59 "Accounting for Liabilities and Capital."

Common stock equivalents

Certain securities are treated as the equivalent of common stock in computing primary earnings per share. Common stock equivalents are securities which, because of the terms or circumstances under which they were issued, are, in substance, equivalent to common stock. These securities may participate in the appreciation or other economic benefits resulting from the underlying earnings and earnings potential of the corporation, if the value of the common stock rises or is expected to rise.

This opportunity to participate in economic benefits, resulting from improved operations or growth potential, is essentially the same as that of a common stockholder, except that the residual security may have a specified dividend or interest rate different from that of the common stock. The value of this type of security is often primarily based on the potential right to share in increases in the earnings potential of the issuing corporation, rather than on its fixed return or other senior security characteristics. Hence, its value is derived from the value of the common stock to which it is related or into which it is convertible. Changes in the market value of such securities tend to reflect changes in the market value of the common stock. Common stock equivalents may take the the form of convertible preferred stock, convertible debentures, a second class of common stock, and options or warrants to purchase common stock.

The concept of common stock equivalents is important because of its role in the calculation of earnings per share. Earnings per share data have become a very significant factor in evaluating the past performance of a business, in forming an opinion as to its future potential, and in making investment decisions. Hence, the effect of common stock equivalents has a substantial impact on the financial community's decision-making process. Exhibit 1 illustrates the concept of common stock equivalents and why proper reporting of their effect on earnings per share data is important.

Opinion No. 15, of The Accounting Principles Board of the American Institute of Certified Public Accountants, states that two types of earnings per share should be reported for corporations with capital structures which include securities having a potentially dilutive effect on earnings per common share. These two amounts should be primary and fully diluted earnings per share. Primary earnings per share is the amount of earnings attributable to each share of outstanding common stock, including comcon stock equivalents. Fully diluted earnings per share is the amount of current earnings per share, reflecting the maximum dilution that would have resulted from conversions, exercises, and other contingent issuances that individually would have decreased earnings per share and, in the aggregate, would have a dilutive effect. All such issuances are

EXHIBIT 1

Illustration of Dilution of Earnings Per Share, When Convertible Securities Are Outstanding

Year 1

	Company	
	A	*B*
Earnings	$1,000,000	$500,000
Common stock shares outstanding	500,000	400,000
Earnings per share	$2.00	$1.25

Market value of *A's* common stock
 $40 per share
 No preferred stock or long term debt

Year 2

Assume:
 (1) *A* acquires *B,* by issuing $5,000,000 of 4 percent convertible debentures, each $1,000 bond convertible into 20 shares of common stock; and
 (2) no change in operating results.
 If no effect is given to potential dilution, the reporting of results would be as below:

Consolidated operating earnings	$1,500,000
Interest expense (less tax benefit)	100,000
Net consolidated earnings	$1,400,000
Common shares outstanding	500,000
Earnings per share	$2.80

Year 3

Assume conversion at the beginning of the year and no change in results:

Consolidated operating earnings	$1,500,000
Interest expense	–0–
Net consolidated earnings	$1,500,000
Common shares outstanding	600,000
Earnings per share	$2.50

assumed to have taken place at the beginning of the period (or at the time the contingency arose, if later).

The concept of primary earnings per share is based on the existing relationship between earnings and outstanding common stock and common stock equivalents. Fully diluted earnings per share is based on potential dilution of earnings per share. The actual calculations of primary earnings per share assume the exercise of conversion privileges of options, warrants, or convertible securities, which are considered common stock equivalents at the beginning of the period, and using any funds so generated to purchase (and retire) during this period common stock at the average market price. This "use of funds" rule, commonly called the treasury stock method, is applicable only to the extent of assuming purchase of a number of shares, not to exceed 20 percent of the

EXHIBIT 2

Illustration of Computation of Primary Earnings Per Share When Common Stock Equivalents Are Involved

A. Assumed reporting, if no effect given to common stock equivalents:

Operating earnings, before income tax	$1,000,000
Interest on $5,000,000 4 percent debentures, convertible into 50,000 of common stock	200,000
Earnings after interest, before income tax	800,000
Provision for income taxes	400,000
Preferred dividends on $2,000,000 of $3 preferred stock, convertible to 20,000 shares of common stock	60,000
Available to common stockholders	340,000
Shares of common stock outstanding	100,000
Earnings per share	$3.40

Also, 5000 warrants to purchase one common share, each at $100, are outstanding; common stock average price during period — $125

B. Calculations of primary earnings per share:

Assume convertible debentures, and preferred stock, in addition to the warrants, are common stock equivalents.

Operating earnings, before income tax	$1,000,000
Less: interest or preferred dividends on noncommon stock equivalents	—
Appropriate provision for income taxes	500,000
Available to common stock and common stock equivalent shares	$ 500,000

Number of common shares and common stock equivalent shares:

Common shares	100,000
Debenture conversion	50,000
Preferred conversion	20,000
Exercise of warrants	5,000
	175,000
Less: treasury shares purchased with proceeds from exercise of warrants*	4,000
Common shares and common stock equivalent shares	171,000

Primary earnings per share — $500,000 ÷ 171,000 =	$2.92

* 5000 warrants × $100 = $500,000 proceeds; $500,000 proceeds ÷ $125 average market price of common stock = 4000 shares

outstanding shares. The balance of such funds would first be applied to reduce borrowings. Any remaining funds would be assumed to be invested in short term notes. Appropriate recognition must be given to any income tax effect. (See Exhibit 2, for an illustration of the calculation of primary earnings per share.)

Opinion No. 15, of the Accounting Principles Board of the American Institute of Certified Public Accountants, states a specific test for determination of common stock equivalents. This determination should be made only at the time of issuance, and should not be changed thereafter, as long as the security remains outstanding. Specifically, the board states that a convertible security should be considered as a common stock equivalent, if, at the time of issuance and based on market price or fair value of the security, it has a cash yield of less than 66⅔ percent of the then current bank prime interest rate. Furthermore, stock options and warrants should always be considered common stock equivalents.

The reporting of earnings per share becomes quite complicated in certain situations, such as business combinations based on contingent payouts and in situations with more than one class of common stock. In such circumstances, one should seek qualified expert advice to determine the proper treatment.

Earnings per share considerations

One of the most important elements, governing the feasibility of a possible corporate combination and the particular form of such a combination is the effect on earnings per share, and possible dilution or increase of such for the surviving corporation. Reference to the example shown below illustrates the problems and possibilities.

	A	B
Sales	$100,000,000	$ 50,000,000
Earnings	5,000,000	4,000,000
Shares outstanding	1,000,000	500,000
Earnings per share	$5	$8
Market price per share	$50	$200
Price earnings ratio (PER)	10	25
Total market value of company	$ 50,000,000	$100,000,000

Such a situation is a realistic example of a large company in a mature industry (Company *A*) and a smaller, faster growing company (Company *B*). These facts are reflected by their price earnings ratios of 10 and 25, respectively.

At first thought, one would expect that the larger company (in sales and earnings) would acquire the smaller company. Assuming no premium being paid for *B's* stock, *A* would have to issue $100,000,000 of its stock. At $50 per share, thos would be two million shares. Therefore, the combined results would be as follows:

Earnings	$9,000,000
Company *A* shares outstanding	3,000,000
EPS	$3

Thus, *A* shareholders, even though they have acquired a "good" company which has potential for rapid growth, suffer immediate dilution in earnings per share of 40 percent, from $5 to $3. Assuming annual growth of earnings rates of five percent for *A* and 20 percent for *B* (as reflected in their respective PER's), five years will elapse before *A's* EPS of $5 is reestablished.

EXHIBIT 3

Total Earnings

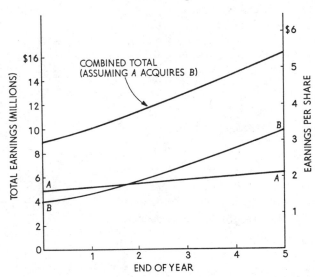

End of Year	Company A	Company B	Combined
0	$5,000,000	$4,000,000	$ 9,000,000
1	5,250,000	4,800,000	10,050,000
2	5,512,500	5,760,000	11,272,500
3	5,788,000	6,912,200	12,700,200
4	6,077,500	8,292,000	14,369,500
5	6,381,500	9,953,200	16,334,700

Furthermore, if *A* maintained the same PER, after the combination as before (this is not probable), the value of *A's* stock would also be reduced by 40 percent. More likely, the resulting combination would command a PER somewhere between *A's* and *B's* PER's before the combination.

However, let us assume that *B* acquires *A*, again assuming no premium, *B* would issue $50,000,000 of its stock, 250,000 shares. The combined results would produce EPS for *B* stockholders as follows:

Combined earnings........................$9,000,000
Company *B* outstanding shares............ 750,000
EPS...................................... $12

Thus, B shareholders' EPS immediately appreciate 50 percent, but it is unlikely that the market price of B would immediately appreciate 50 percent. The slower growing A would act as a drag on future earnings growth of the surviving, combined company B. This slower growth

EXHIBIT 4

Comparative EPS Figures

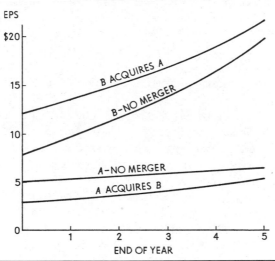

End of Year	EPS A No Merger 5% Growth	EPS B No Merger 20% Growth	EPS A acquires B 3,000,000 shares	EPS B acquires A 750,000 shares
0	$5.00	$ 8.00	$3.00	$12.00
1	5.25	9.60	3.35	13.40
2	5.51	11.52	3.76	15.03
3	5.79	13.82	4.23	16.93
4	6.08	16.58	4.79	19.16
5	6.38	19.90	5.44	21.78

potential for combined B would probably result in a lower PER than the PER of 25, which the market assigned to B prior to the merger.

However, it should be pointed out that whatever the form of the merger, if the exchange is based upon market price, A's shareholders are going to get $3 of earnings for each share of A they originally held, and B's shareholders are going to get $12 of earnings for each share of B they originally held.

If company B decided it wanted to purchase A and increase its reported earnings per share, the likely prospect is that B would have to pay a premium over the market value to A shareholders, in order to generate sufficient interest in the deal. Assuming a 20 percent premium, the result would be as follows:

```
Purchase price.........................$60,000,000
Number of B shares issued..............   300,000
Combined earnings......................$ 9,000,000
Company B outstanding shares..........    800,000
EPS....................................$    11.25
```

Therefore, at any PER, in excess of 17.7 ($17.7 \times \$11.25 = \$200$) for the surviving company B, the value of the shares held by original company B shareowners would be increased. In fact, if B were to continue to command a PER of 25, the market price of B stock would move from $200 to over $280. Each original shareholder of company A would receive 0.3 shares of B for each share of A stock held. Thus, B stock would have to have a market value of $166⅔ for A stockholders to be at least as well off at the time of transaction. This would necessitate a PER of slightly under 15.

The scope of this discussion is designed solely to show the mathematical results of various types of combinations and the possible resulting effect on EPS and, consequently, the market value of stock. It is not within the scope of this chapter to deal with the determinants of PER's and, consequently, market price of the stock. It deals only with the immediate mathematical impact on EPS, PER, and market value. However, the financial executive must give consideration to both the immediate impact on EPS and upon potential growth of EPS with regard to an acquisition strategy. He must especially consider the possibility that acquiring a company with a lower PER, and probably less growth potential, may act as an anchor on future earnings growth of the combined company.

Marvin May has likened the tactics of conglomerates to a chain letter. Regarding chain letters, May reflects the sentiments of many financial analysts toward conglomerates. He states, "While it is generally agreed that chain letters cannot create wealth, it is well recognized that they are a very effective means of transferring and redistributing wealth."[1] As illustrated in the above example, a company can exhibit a growth in earnings per share (from $8 to $12), although neither the company nor its acquisition(s) experience any comparable "real" growth. By continually expanding through acquisitions of this type (exchanges of stock, with the higher PER stock being the survivor), a company can produce a substantial growth image. Furthermore, a growth image commands a high PER. Mr. May also illustrates that acquisitions of this type must continue to expand at a rapid rate, in order to maintain the trend. Otherwise, the trend will be reversed. This is the reason for his reference to the chain letter effect.[2]

In summary, one can see that the form of a merger can drastically

---

[1] Marvin M. May, "The Earnings Per Share Trap," *Financial Analysts Journal*, (May–June 1969), p. 113.

[2] *Ibid.*, pp. 113–117.

affect the picture of reported operations, even though actual economic results are the same. Basically, the true growth of a company, expanding by acquisitions, depends, in the long run, upon the real growth potential of its business. In the event the growth trend is not maintained, the shareholders may well become disillusioned with a resulting adverse market impact.

Instruments or vehicles of purchase

CASH. Cash to effect a merger or acquisition is available from normal channels, such as: (1) cash on hand, (2) short-term borrowing, (3) long-term debt, or (4) a public offering of common stock. The use of cash dictates that the combination must be accounted for as a purchase or partial pooling, and the transaction is taxable. A cash transaction has the advantage to the seller that he can immediately diversify his personal investment portfolio. Cash offers the advantage to the acquiring company that, as opposed to a common stock transaction, no large block of stock is placed in the hands of one or a few stockholders. In other words, this advantage revolves around a control aspect. Closely held corporations, with a substantial accumulation of cash, can often avoid a tax on excess accumulated earnings by using cash for an acquisition. Furthermore, the effect on EPS of amortizing goodwill may not be such a large problem for a closely held corporation, as it is for a publicly held company.

COMMON STOCK. If all of the common stock issued in the transaction is voting, then the transaction is nontaxable, and pooling of interests accounting may generally be elected. Exchanges of stock transactions have an important impact on recorded earnings per share, based upon the price earnings ratios of the stocks exchanged. This aspect is discussed in detail in another section of this chapter. Common stock exchanges often involve control problems. Management of the acquiring company may be blocked in many of its pursuits, because of a large block of stock in unfriendly hands. The stockholders, of the selling company receiving common stock, do not have a personal investment situation which would be as flexible as if they had received cash.

PREFERRED STOCK. Convertible preferred stock has become a frequently used instrument in corporate acquisitions. As an investment, convertible preferred offers the protection of a senior security with fixed income and the growth potential of common stock through its conversion provisions. If the convertible preferred is voting, then the transaction is nontaxable, pooling accounting usually may be elected, but the earnings per share of the acquiring company may be subject to dilution, because of the earlier discussed concept of common stock equivalents.

The use of convertible preferred represents a compromise between cash and common stock. If an acquiring company wishes to purchase with cash to avoid dilution of earnings per share, but the selling company would like a tax-free exchange, then convertible preferred may be the answer. As will be discussed below, convertible preferred does not eliminate or even postpone dilution, but can minimize or reduce it. Also, using voting convertible preferred can provide the tax-free advantage to the selling company.

Using convertible preferred offers several advantages to the acquiring company. The dividend requirements of the acquired company's stockholders can be met, without the acquiring company's having to change its dividend policy. Below is an example to illustrate the problem and solutions:

	Company A	Company B
Shares outstanding....................	1,000,000	100,000
Market price per share................	$100	$50
Market value of company..............	$100,000,000	$5,000,000
Total earnings........................	$ 4,000,000	$ 500,000
Earnings per share....................	$4	$5
Dividends per share..................	0	$3

If *A* acquired *B* and paid a 20 percent premium for a total of $6,000,000, *A* would have to issue 60,000 shares of common stock to acquire the stock of *B*. If *B*'s shareholders demand continuance of their dividend income, a total of $300,000 ($3 per share × 100,000 shares), then *A* would have to pay dividends of $5 per share ($300,000 ÷ 60,000 shares) on all of its common shares. As *A* is only earning $4 per share, such a transaction would not be feasible. However, a deal might be structured whereby *A* could issue 60,000 shares of $5, $100 par value, preferred, each convertible into 0.8 shares of common stock. There is no guarantee that *B* will accept these terms, but *B* stockholders would enjoy several advantages.

1. They would receive their desired $300,000 of dividend income.
2. They would, most likely, receive securities with a value in excess of the then current market value of $5,000,000. The market value of the convertible preferred would principally be determined by:
   (a) The conversion aspect.
   (b) The cash yield or investment value.
   (c) The likelihood of conversion.

As discussed earlier, these securities would be classified as common stock equivalents if, at the time of issuance, the cash yield, based on the market price or fair value of the security, is less than 66⅔ percent of the then current bank prime interest rate.

Assuming that the terms of this transaction are agreeable to and accepted by *B* stockholders, then *A* common stockholders would suffer less dilution of earnings per share, as compared to the straight common stock deal. If the convertible preferred is classified as a common stock equivalent, then the dilution would be calculated on the basis of an additional 48,000 shares of common stock (60,000 shares of convertible preferred shares × 0.8 conversion rate) as opposed to 60,000 shares, if common stock is the consideration for the transaction. Another benefit, paralleling this reduced dilution, is the control element involved. By ultimately issuing fewer shares of common stock, less voting power is dispersed to original stockholders of B.

Furthermore, if the convertible preferred does not qualify as a common stock equivalent, a leveraging effect is exerted upon income to common shareholders, to the extent which earnings of the acquired company exceed preferred dividends that must be paid. In the above example, this leveraging effect would be as follows:

```
Company B's earnings acquired by A.........$500,000
Less preferred dividends to be paid..........  300,000
Additional earnings for A's common
     shareholders.............................$200,000
```

DEBENTURES. Purchasing with debentures generally produces a taxable transaction. The bond may be convertible, nonconvertible, callable, noncallable, etc., but the transaction remains taxable. Also purchase accounting must be used. If the debentures are common stock equivalents, then dilution may occur. The acquiring company may issue debentures directly to the selling company, rather than incur the expense, time, and effort of a public offering of debentures to raise cash to effect a business combination. One advantage of debentures over preferred stock is that, at least at the time of this writing, the interest on debentures is deductible as an expense for tax purposes, while preferred dividends are not. Also, the interest income to the recipient of the debentures is not taxable until received.

However, the House Ways and Means Committee is now seriously considering major legislative action, which would hit hard at the tax advantages in acquisitions involving debt instruments. More specifically, a corporation would not be generally allowed to claim a deduction for interest paid on bonds and debentures, issued in exchange for at least two thirds of the stock of another company. This would apply to bonds which: (1) are subordinate to a significant segment of the corporation's other creditors, (2) are convertible into stock or warrants, and (3) result in the corporation's pro-forma debt-equity ratio exceeding a specific rate.

WARRANTS. Warrants are options to purchase common stock at a fixed price intended to be favorable in the future. Basically, they have the same effect on merger or acquisition transactions as do convertible bonds. The transaction is taxable, purchase accounting must be used, and present shareholders are subject to dilution of earnings per share, as warrants are considered common stock equivalents. They are usually part of a financial package, and inclusion of warrants would have the same effect on the tax status as inclusion of cash. With the exception of a statutory merger, the transaction would be fully taxable and would be accounted for on a part purchase, part pooling basis. The portion attributable to warrants would be accounted for as a purchase.

COMBINATIONS OF PURCHASE VEHICLES.   To meet the various objectives of the parties to corporate mergers, various combinations of purchase vehicles, or financial packages, may be used to make acquisitions. The ingenuity of financial executives in designing these financial packages is constantly producing innovations. This chapter does not attempt to describe all of the possible combinations; rather, some basic general ground rules are outlined. With the exception of a statutory merger, the introduction of any consideration other than voting stock, common or preferred, will produce a taxable transaction. Thus, using a combination of ten thousand shares of common stock, having a total value of $75,000, plus $25,000 in cash, bonds, or warrants (fair market value), would result in a taxable transaction. The pooling of interest would not be completely lost, because the transaction could be accounted for as 75 percent pooling and 25 percent purchase.

Often, the valuation of, and subsequent purchase price for, a company with an erratic earnings history, tax-loss carryover, or attractive earnings projections presents a hindrance to the consummation of a merger or acquisition. The answer to such a situation may be a fixed initial price, with additional future payments contingent upon future earnings, acceptance by the Internal Revenue Service of a tax-loss carryover, or some other projected occurrence. The terms or formula for these contingent payments can be negotiated, and should be carefully spelled out in the agreement. There is no typical type of formula, but the following hypothetical situation will serve as an example of one possible type of contingent payment.

Assume Company A's (100 percent owned by one person) earnings have been as follows, for the last three years:

1	2	3
$150,000	$50,000	$250,000

For the next three years, Company A projects earnings of:

0	1	2
$300,000	$350,000	$400,000

B, the acquiring company, is a large company, with its stock currently trading at $20 per share. Company B wishes to issue $3 million worth of stock (150,000 shares), but A thinks his company is worth $4 million, or

200,000 shares. Ultimately, the two compromise on a contingent payout type of exchange. *B* will initially issue 100,000 shares. Also, *B* will issue additional shares of stock equal to ten times *A*'s next three years' average earnings in excess of $250,000. In no case will the number of these additional shares exceed 100,000. For purposes of the value of additional shares of *B*, current market price of $20 per share will be used. Therefore, if *A*'s next three years' average earnings are $250,000 or less, *B* will pay out no additional shares. If *A*'s next three years' average earnings are $450,000 or more, *B* will have to pay out an additional 100,000 shares. For any average earnings, between $250,000 and $450,000, *B* will issue a proportionate number of shares. For example, if the average three-year earnings are $350,000, *B* will issue an additional 50,000 shares, as calculated below:

> Average earnings in excess of $250,000 = $100,000
> Ten times $100,000 = $1,000,000
> $1,000,000 ÷ $20 per share = 50,000 shares

As was pointed out earlier, this is only one method of structuring a contingent payout. Many variations are possible.

It is especially important, in the case of payments contingent upon future earnings, that the method of accounting be specified and arrangements be made for extraordinary gains and losses. In fact, payments may be contingent upon net operating profit before taxes, depreciation, or even on sales. Contingent payout transactions result in complicated taxation treatments; therefore, the businessman should contact his tax advisor. However, it should be noted that the transaction can qualify for deferred tax treatment, if not more than 30 percent of the purchase price is paid in cash during the first year. Such contingent payouts result in imputed interest income to the seller and expense to the purchaser, unless the effective interest rate is at least four percent. Also, for exchanges of voting stock involving contingent payouts to qualify as tax-free exchanges, the following conditions usually must be met:

1. A maximum number of shares to be issued must be stated.
2. At least 50 percent of these maximum number of shares must be issued on "the front end."
3. The contingent shares must be paid out within five years of the date of the acquisition.

The accounting for contingent payouts also involves some unique treatments, which are briefly touched upon below.

If the contingent payout is based upon the maintenance of a level of earnings that is currently being met, then the additional shares payable in the future should be considered as outstanding, for the purpose of computing both primary and fully diluted earnings per share. If attainment of increased earnings, reasonably above the present level or increased earnings over a period of years, is the condition, then the additional shares should be considered as outstanding only for the purpose of computing fully diluted earnings per share (but only if dilution is the result). For this computation, earnings should be adjusted to give effect to the increase in earnings specified by the particular arrangements.

The number of shares contingently issuable may depend on the market price of the stock at a future date. In such a case, computations of primary earnings per share should be based on the number of issuable shares, based on the market price at the close of the reported period. Furthermore, if the payout is contingent upon both earnings and market price, then the accounting is a combination of the above two methods.

Modified methods of exchange involving securities

To meet objectives of many varied situations, financial executives have designed many modified methods of mergers and acquisitions involving exchanges of securities.

In the situation where the stockholders of the acquired company wish to receive some cash and yet maintain the tax-free status of the combination, two basic techniques have been employed. (1) The merger may be consummated by the normal exchange of stock. Then, some of the shares that were transferred to the selling company's stockholders can be sold to provide the cash. In fact, the sale of these shares could even be a public offering. Care must be taken, in such a disposition of the shares, not to nullify the tax-free status and the pooling of interests accounting, if used. Basically, the continuity of proprietary ownership should not be lost. (2) Prior to the combination, the company to be acquired can redeem part of its stock with cash or other assets, before the remaining shares outstanding are exchanged for stock of the acquiring company. Therefore, some of the shareholders of the selling company could receive some cash. Again, care must be taken not to eliminate the tax-free status and the pooling of interests accounting, if desired. Both of these techniques can be used to give a partial cash payment to all stockholders, or to give all cash to some and all stock to others.

Dilution of control or voting power is often a worry to acquiring companies, especially in acquiring a closely held corporation. To combat that problem, and again maintain the tax-free status and the pooling of interest accounting, two principal methods have been developed. The acquiring company may issue common and voting preferred in exchange for the common stock of the selling company. If the par value of the preferred stock is substantially above the market value of the acquiring company's common stock, then the voting power of the selling company's stockholders will be diluted, as opposed to the issuance of only common stock. Another technique used is to issue different classes of stock. For example, a high-dividend class of stock may be issued with substantially less voting power. However, to maintain a continuity of ownership interests necessary for nontaxable transactions and pooling of interest accounting, such a class of stock may have to be convertible into common stock. Hence, the effect usually is a postponement of the dilution of control, rather than a permanent avoidance of such.

When one company desires to purchase another that is experiencing depressed earnings or a deficit, with the intention of turning it around, exchange of stock would dilute the earnings of the acquirer and a cash deal would make the transaction taxable. Hence, to avoid dilution of earnings and produce a tax-free transaction, the acquiring company can effect a normal exchange of stock and, at the same time, purchase its own stock in the market and retire these treasury shares. In effect, the acquiring company reduces or eliminates any increase in outstanding shares by issuing new shares, while simultaneously repurchasing and retiring previously outstanding shares.

The technique known as a "downstream merger" is used to reduce the creation of goodwill, when the stockholders of the company to be acquired wish to receive cash. For example, assume that P wishes to acquire S, but a substantial portion of S's stockholders wish to receive cash. If the market value for S stock would result in an acquisition by P in which substantial goodwill were generated, then the combination might not be feasible, unless a downstream merger is implemented. Company P may acquire, say, 30 percent of S stock for cash, from those stockholders desiring cash. Then, the combination could be effected by having S issue its shares for all of the outstanding shares of P. As the combination could be accounted for on a pooling basis, no goodwill would be generated.

Also, a company not wishing to issue additional stock, but desiring to have a tax-free transaction and pooling accounting, may purchase its own stock in the market and then reissue these shares for the acquisition. This method suffers the disadvantage that the acquiring company may substantially drive up the market price of its shares by such purchase. Hence, the total cost of the acquisition can be substantially increased.

Tender offers

Tender offers, the offer of a company to the shareholders of another to take over their company, serve the business community as a means whereby incumbent management can be replaced when other methods are not available.

Tender offers are effected by the acquiring company's announcing their offer to the target company's shareholders, in such media as: newspaper announcements, direct mailings from a shareholder list to the shareholders, or personal solicitation of the shareholders. They are a means whereby an aggressive, acquisition-minded company can acquire companies not particularly agreeable to selling out. Practically, the only alternative for an aggressive company, in such a situation, is to gradually buy shares of the target company in the open market. This has the disadvantage of possibly driving up the market price to the point of being too costly or taking so much time that intentions may become known, thus giving hostile incumbent management the opportunity of utilizing defensive tactics. Such intentions will also become known because of the SEC requirement, providing that each officer, director, and beneficial owner of more than 10 percent of any class of registered equity security must file with the SEC reports showing his holdings of such stock. In addition, he must report each month thereafter any change in these holdings. Conversely, such an accumulation could result in a smaller overall cost of acquisition, by purchasing some of the stock in the market rather than at the tender offer price, which can be substantially above the market price.

Once the decision has been made to proceed with a tender offer, the company must decide upon an offer of cash or stock. A study by Samuel L. Hayes, III and Russell A. Taussig indicates that ". . . for the years 1956 through 1966, not only has the number of offers shown a recent and impressive climb, but the relative popularity of stock and cash bids has been reversed during the 1960's with cash offers accounting for the great majority of tenders in 1965 and 1966."[3] There are two principal reasons for this preference of cash offers. Cash offers the advantage of surprise and speed, because the use of the stock calls for time-consuming registration with the SEC. Also, the use of cash reduces the risk of dilution of earnings per share for the acquiring company's shareholders. Cash tender offers are subject to purchase accounting and are taxable transactions, whereas stock tender offers may be accounted for on a pooling basis, if they meet the criteria for poolings. The tendering company must also decide whether or not to acquire part of the target company's stock in the open market, before making the tender offer. The Hayes-Taussig study outlines several advantages, to the acquiring company, in achieving a substantial holding in the target company, before the date of the tender offer:

1. Getting a shareholder list will be facilitated.
2. Possibly, the shares bought in the open market will be at less than the tender price.
3. Fewer shares will be required through the tender offer to ensure success.[4]

Such an accumulation has the following disadvantages, however:

1. The price of the target company's stock may be driven up so as to make the tender offer price prohibitive.
2. The accumulations and, thus, intentions of the "raiding company" may become known. This could give the target company time to

---

[3] Samuel L. Hayes, III, and Russell A. Taussig, "Tactics of Cash Take-Over Bids," *The Business of Acquisitions and Mergers,* ed. by G. Scott Hutchinson (New York, 1968), p. 258.

[4] *Ibid,* p. 139.

formulate a successful defensive strategy, which it otherwise would not be able to do.

A sufficiently attractive premium (an offer above the current market value of the stock) usually is necessary to produce a successful tender offer. A general rule of thumb is to offer a 20 percent premium, but the Hayes-Taussig study found a large variation in the size of premiums offered. Furthermore, the study produced no particular correlation between success and the size of the premium. Hence, the design of the successful tender offer must be left to the financial executive, after he considers all of the relevant factors, such as the degree of incumbent management's resistance, general status of the stock market, and general expectations for the future of the target company. Like any other investment decision, the cost can reach the point of producing a negative return on the purchase investment.

In addition to the purchase premium, the financial executive must decide upon the terms of the offer. A first-come first-served basis, for a certain number of shares, may be used to induce target shareholders to react before giving incumbent management an opportunity to resort to defensive, resistive statements. Also, the offering company may retain the right to accept or reject shares if the size of the response is not satisfactory. An important factor to consider is that, if the target company has cumulative voting, the offeror can possibly achieve sufficient control with fewer shares.

The Hayes-Taussig study lists several warning signals to companies that they may be tender offer candidates: poor performance and operating results, declining dividends, surplus liquid assets, fixed assets which can be liquidated, accumulation of stock ownership by individuals or brokers, and abortive merger talks. In fact, one merger and acquisition consultant has said that an acquisition-minded company, which has a string of three or four unsuccessful merger discussions, becomes a takeover target.

When the management of a target company becomes aware of an impending tender offer, it may resort to various defensive tactics. The management may issue resistive statements to stockholders, warning them that accepting the terms of the tender offer is not in their best interests. The company may also repurchase shares to reduce holdings in the hands of possible acceptors of the tender offer. This tactic also tends to increase the price of the stock, and this may discourage the aggressor. Also, the target company may quickly resort to a merger with a more friendly company, or it may make an acquisition with stock so as to place a larger portion of stock in friendly hands. Some raided companies change the certificate of incorporation to provide for cumulative voting. This makes it more difficult for the tendering company to replace the existing board of directors. The financial executives' ingenuity in fending off raiders has shown an imagination comparable to that exhibited in structuring the terms of mergers and acquisitions.

Financing foreign operations

Herbert C. Knortz*

The international firm must govern its financing with due consideration of all of the cost and timing factors that are important to the domestic corporation. In addition, it must be aware of the incentives and controls which are provided by foreign governments, and also of the aids and restraints which have been established by the U.S. government. These have been discussed in Chapter 4, "Operating in the Foreign Environment" and should be considered as an integral part of any plan for the financing of foreign operations.

In this chapter attention will be given to more specific approaches to providing the capital for carrying on the international activity. Since currency devaluation is a major factor in establishing the financial plan, some brief consideration is given to this subject along with a view of special sources of credit and of some special techniques for financial operations in the foreign world.

Growth by local investment in equity

Prior to the mandatory balance of payments program of 1968, a domestic corporation which wished to "go international" customarily thought of providing all of the long-term capital, other than that covered by mortgages, from its domestic resources. However, with the new program, this alternative no longer appears as readily available for

---

* Senior Vice President and Comptroller, International Telephone & Telegraph Corporation, New York.

general use as it was previously. Instead, there will have to be a greater reliance on foreign sources of capital, and perhaps an increase in the use of the equity securities of foreign subsidiaries.

Managerial considerations

Operation in a foreign economy inevitably requires the solicitation of financial or political support. Such support is customarily more accessible when there are national shareholders involved. Obviously, if this shareholding can be broadly held without sacrificing managerial control, it has additional values from the viewpoint of labor and market relations.

Many companies have found in the course of their international acquisitions that an experienced minority interest can provide an insight into the market and its problems that can only be alternatively acquired by years of experimentation. For the most part, it is found that the minority interests which have a significant stake in the profitability of an enterprise can be relied upon to balance satisfactorily the corporate and the national interests.

The increased use of stock to provide the capital for private enterprise tends to improve profitability measurement in many firms. Too often in the past, the capital of a subsidiary was obtained on open account from its parent. The loan might be free of interest or it might be for an excessive part of the capital structure. In either case, the customary measures of profitability were distorted. A reasonable use of "equity investment" tends to normalize reporting and the executive actions stemming from such reports.

On the other hand, a minority interest restrains the independent action of the management. The consistent pressure for dividends makes it impossible to forego short-run profits in order to assure higher profits later.[1] Nor may the international management freely deploy its business throughout its system when the individual subsidiaries have private interests. For these reasons, some of the major international firms have bought out minority holdings where this was feasible.

Flotation of securities

The major international firms are usually in a position to borrow funds in foreign countries, either in their own names or in those of their foreign subsidiaries. However, this should not rule out the flotation of equity securities, since it is important that the financial planners retain a choice of future alternatives.[2]

---

[1] Howe Martyn, *International Business,* Collier-Macmillan Ltd., London, 1964, p. 58.

[2] K. K. White, *Financing Company Expansion,* American Management Association (1964), p. 100.

The trading of stocks is less common in Europe and other foreign areas of the world than it is in the United States. This reflects the periodic military disturbances which have taken place and also a smaller disposition on the part of investors to move away from traditional equity holdings. This constraint is gradually changing, and the local stock exchanges are becoming increasingly active as people more fully satisfy their demand for real goods (e.g. houses, autos, TVs). To many of the potential investors, stock begins to look more desirable than cash—providing that it is easily marketable.

The surge in the acquisition of European firms by Americans has played a major role in increasing activity on the stock exchanges. In most acquisitions involving stock, the deal frequently involves a company with stock selling at high earnings multiples buying one selling at low multiples.[3] It is useful, in preparing for a series of such negotiations, to submit shares to the market place for establishment of the inherent trading values. Obviously, Europeans will feel more confident when this market evaluation takes place within their local financial circles.

For some years American firms chose to offer securities of the American parent in setting up acquisitions since they avoided the involvement of the minority interests in the management of the subsidiaries. However, the mandatory program for the U.S. balance of payments treats stock transfers in the same way as cash. Since they are, thus, brought under the tight overall restrictions on direct investment, the use of parent-company stock will no longer be possible for most firms.

However, prior to the mandatory program the swapping of shares was an acceptable technique. If the shares were listed only on a U.S. exchange, it meant that foreigners were faced with paying a 30 percent U.S. withholding tax when the shares were sold.[4] If listed on European exchanges, the shares could be sold without U.S. tax, and since there is no capital-gains taxation in some European countries, the 30 percent withholding could be overcome. Fortunately, the stock-listing expenses were not heavy, and many major firms chose to list on several European exchanges. In many cases, certain shares of large foreign subsidiaries were also listed, and it is possible that these will become more active as an offset to the restraints of the balance of payment program.

Growth through borrowing

The financing of foreign activities is primarily accomplished through borrowing. Such borrowing has been particularly active during 1968 as corporations have sought to carry out their growth programs while living within the strictures laid down by the Office of Foreign Direct Invest-

---

[3] J. K. Lasser, *Business Management Handbook,* McGraw-Hill Book Company (1952), p. 109.

[4] *Acquisition Abroad,* Business International (1963), p. 22.

ment. Although interest rates have risen, the supply of credit is still adequate for current and foreseeable needs.

Use of credit forms

In international affairs, as in domestic financing, the smallest possible equity investment and the greatest amount of debt is likely to produce the greatest return on investment while maintaining the highest opportunity for capital appreciation.[5] Furthermore, in inflationary situations borrowing for repayment in local currency stands as a hedge against currency devaluation. For these reasons, borrowing has been a popular means of financing foreign subsidiaries.

In general, foreign subsidiaries in Europe carry between 40 percent and 60 percent of their capital as debt. Although this is somewhat higher than the figures reported by most American corporations, it is quite in line with the 52 percent shown by major European firms.[6] In any event, it is unlikely that the balance of payment controls will permit any near-term reduction in foreign borrowing, and it is probable that borrowing in the United States for investment abroad will be sharply curtailed from the levels of 1966.

In addition to borrowing at the level of the local foreign subsidiaries, U.S. firms have been forced, in order to conform with the repatriation demands of the mandatory balance of payment program, to turn to foreign markets for the parent-company funds needed for investment in their international operations. As a result the value of Euro-dollar issues floated or announced in January 1968 was ten times that of the comparable period in 1967, and such borrowings were in excess of $2.2 billion for the 1968 year as compared with $500 million in 1967.[7]

In 1967, U.S. corporations invested over $4.1 billion in foreign countries other than Canada. Of that amount approximately 88 percent represented direct outflows from the United States, while 12 percent was borrowed abroad. In addition, it is estimated that foreign subsidiaries borrowed between $500 million and $1 billion beyond their usual credit levels because of the pressures of the voluntary balance of payments program. It was recently calculated by the Office of Foreign Direct Investment that as of mid-1968 over $4 billion in credit facilities had been arranged for use in 1968.

Don C. Cadle, Deputy Director of the Office of Foreign Direct Investments reported in 1968 that an analysis of data filed with his office indicated that about two-thirds of the total credits are denominated in

---

[5] J. K. Lasser, *Business Management Handbook,* McGraw-Hill Book Company (1952), p. 55.

[6] Dr. A. Schaefer, *Economic Penetration and Business Concentration,* Union Bank of Switzerland (1966), p. 7.

[7] *World Financial Markets,* Feb. 1969, Morgan Guaranty Trust Co.

U.S. dollars, with the balance in various foreign currencies. He also reported that 40 percent of the $4 billion credit facility was raised in the form of long-term bonds; that U.S. banks provided 30 percent in the form of medium-term credits; and that the balance was contributed by foreign banks, insurance companies, pension funds, and other lenders. Convertible issues have represented a large portion of the total debenture offerings during the year.

Alternative forms of borrowing

Borrowing for the purpose of financing foreign operations may be carried out in the United States or in the foreign area. Consequently, the variety of borrowing forms and possible interest costs are far greater than those available to corporations seeking normal domestic financing. In general the policies of the U.S. government have kept domestic money costs below those available in Europe. On the other hand, the interest costs incurred in Brazil and other inflationary environments have been so extreme at various times that the ordinary manufacturing operations became far less important than the risks and costs involved in the daily financing of the business.

The following paragraphs comment on some of the more common forms of borrowing arrangements. In general, money costs which are quoted at the mid-1968 levels are representative of recent years and indicate that interest charges are lowest in Switzerland and Germany. Costs for money in Latin America are likely to be geared to the expected rate of inflation.

1. Debenture issues. Debentures provide capital at a fixed interest cost and are repayable at a fixed face value which takes advantage of inflationary trends. Where the debenture is convertible into equity securities, the bond holder is given a chance to share in corporate growth. Public issues may require government approval in some countries. In Germany the costs will run about 7 to 8 percent, while in Switzerland available issues cost 5.5 to 5.75 percent.

2. Mortgage loans. Mortgages are generally a cheap source of working capital. Because they have specific claims on real property, they may inhibit flexibility in disposing of such assets. Usually about 70 percent of the appraised asset value can be borrowed.

3. Long-term loans. Funds are available for companies with sound credit ratings. However, countries such as Italy, Netherlands, Spain and France restrict borrowing to some percentage of total investment. In Germany the usual costs come to 7.5 to 8 percent. Switzerland offers few long-term loans but costs run 6 to 6.75 percent.

4. Medium-term loans. Except in Denmark and Spain where all money is currently tight, medium-term money is generally available but carries the same restrictions as applies to long-term money and has similar

costs. However, because of the generally rising level of interest costs, medium-term loans have been more popular recently than has been true of longer issues.

5. Short-term loans. Short-term money is readily available except in Denmark and Spain. Fewer countries place restrictions on these loans than is done with longer borrowings. In Germany the costs range from 4 to 7.5 percent while in Switzerland the costs run from 4 to 6.5 percent.

Corporations wishing to finance their local European operations should give special attention to their practices regarding trade credit. In general, most European suppliers are willing to offer longer settlement terms than is customary in the United States, and there is, in most cases, less vigor exerted in the credit and collection activities. Attention should also be given to obtaining advance payments and progress payments from customers. In the early 1960's most customers dealing in large orders were willing to offer early payment to support the working capital needs of the supplier, but in more recent years there is a reluctance (except for government agencies) to offer such money.

The discounting of customer and dealer notes (e.g. Italian cessione) and the offering of customer invoices as note security (e.g. Brazilian duplicatas) are common practices. In general the lender is likely to require full recourse back to the supplier, but in any event banks are usually quite willing to deal in such paper.

Credit lines are easy to arrange with foreign bankers, and activity in this area has increased as companies cope with a tightening of available money sources. Offerings are made which involve "a three-to-five year commitment on the basis of three-month revolving notes carrying the prevalent Euro-dollar rate at time of issue plus a commission."[8] Some companies will find it necessary to pay a fee to obtain a binding commitment from banks on a line of credit arrangement. In general, companies would be well advised to use credit lines with several banks rather than to concentrate all activity with one lender.

Current literature makes frequent reference to the Euro-dollar market, but the international executive should be aware that there is no such special security. Instead of being a security, the term connotes the existence of a need for the investment of international funds, a desire to negotiate in the long-established European centers, and a current willingness to accept the U.S. dollar as a reasonably reliable currency in which to satisfy a debt on maturity. Obviously, where such claims are held by foreigners, they represent a potential call on U.S. currency reserves. At the present time the claims are considerably in excess of

---

[8] Pierre Haas, *The Role of Continental Bankers in the International Capital Market,* Management Bulletin No. 95, American Management Association, 1967, p. 6.

available gold stocks, but the internationalists continue to deal confidently in the issues offered.

Banks and banking systems

Any American company which is actively engaged in foreign operations will develop an increased appreciation of the treasurership function and of the banking world. When faced with problems of inflation, devaluation, credit restrictions, selective credit policies, differential interest rates, exchange regulations, and balance of payment restraints, the responsible corporate executive will be appropriately grateful for the expert assistance of domestic and foreign bankers.

To a greater or lesser degree the foreign countries of the world have government-related banks which supervise the flow of international exchange. For the most part these central banks maintain currency reserves, administer the regulations on security issues, and represent the government in respect to international exchange rates. At the present time, the central bank in a foreign country takes a more noticeable position in industrial affairs than that to which the American executive became accustomed in the days prior to the Office of Foreign Direct Investment.

On the other hand, the private foreign bank also appears strange to the American financial manager. This largely stems from the fact that there is no required separation between the affairs of the investment banker and those of the commercial banker as there is in the United States.[9] The European banker tends to be a very sophisticated money manager with wide international interests. In many cases, he may also hold active equity investments in industrial operations.

Because of the structure of the banking system, straight debt issues have been a prevalent form of financing. Since there is no equivalent of the U.S. Securities and Exchange Commission, listing has been easily accomplished in most instances. However, since 1967, European investment funds have shown an increasing interest in the equity securities and the convertible bonds of U.S. corporations.

In the placement of large international loans the continental bankers seek a greater share in the management of such issues and point to their long experience in underwriting the Swiss issues. Since the local bankers are likely to control the accounts of the major investors, their request has a basic propriety. From the viewpoint of the American investor, it is probably desirable on major financings to have a major American international bank and a continental European banker as co-managers of the issue.

---

[9] John H. Hickman, *International Financing,* Management Bulletin No. 95, American Management Assn., 1967, p. 2.

Decapitalization through devaluation

The financing of foreign subsidiaries cannot be organized intelligently without a continuous consideration of inflationary trends and of the probability of currency devaluation. Generally accepted accounting techniques provide instruction on the reporting of foreign currency statements but, in addition, the indicated operating conditions must be carefully reviewed to be certain that inflation and devaluation are not resulting in the insidious decapitalization of a subsidiary. The protection of the inherent values, maintenance of profit margins, and the avoidance of decapitalization require sophisticated planning, an energetic attack on pricing strategies, and the use of certain protective financial approaches.

Reporting of foreign currency statements

Generally accepted accounting practice acknowledges three acceptable procedures for handling the translation of foreign accounts:

a) The most commonly used procedure is that of translating current assets and liabilities at the current rate of exchange and all other assets and liabilities at the rates of exchange in existence when they were originally recorded.

The items in the income statement are translated at the average exchange rate during the period except for depreciation where historic rates are used.[10]

Realized conversion losses and gains are recorded as current operations in addition to unrealized translation losses. Unrealized gains are deferred.

The method presumes that long-term effects are the concern of future periods, and it makes no distinction between a definite receivable value and an inventory value that is still subject to monetary correction.

b) An alternative approach emphasizes the difference between accounts of a "financial" nature and those which have inherent "physical" values.

In this approach inventory and fixed assets are translated at historic values on the theory that, through increased sales prices, the original values will still be realized. In other words, prices will appreciate to the same extent that the foreign exchange value of currency depreciates.

Under this technique all locally denominated debts are translated at current rates—not only those due within one year. As a consequence, the financing program can deal with maturities in a more normal manner than is true under the previously described approach.

c) A third method of translation has also been suggested. This technique accepts the basic principles of the first method identified, but adds to it the concept of translating both the current and non-current locally denominated liabilities at the current rate.

---

[10] NAA Research Report No. 36, *Management Accounting Problems in Foreign Operations,* National Association of Accountants, 1960, p. 44.

In this method, all locally denominated liabilities represent a reduced "exposure" to the losses incurred in devaluation. The method fails to recognize the distinctive character of inventory values. However, because it translates inventory at current rates it is particularly appropriate under price-controlled circumstances.

The foregoing comments are not intended to be a full discussion of the accounting techniques used in translating foreign currency statements, which are more fully dealt with in Chapter 60, "International Accounting." Instead, the several methods are introduced as a means of identifying the need for sophisticated consideration of devaluation and its effect on the financial plan. It is important to recognize that fluctuations in foreign exchange are an inherent risk of foreign operations and to identify the protective approaches which are available in minimizing the risk.

Exchange rates

Inherently, the exchange rate used in translating accounts is the expression of the realization or conversion value of the local currencies in terms of the U.S. dollar. However, it should not be assumed that a single definitive rate is in existence at a given time. Many countries have authorized multiple rates. For instance, a preferential rate may be used to stimulate investment in plant, while a penalty rate may be used as a means of discouraging imports or dividend remittances.[11] In such countries, the nature of the transaction must be identified before the truly applicable rate can be selected.

In addition to recognizing the multiplicity of rates, the international accountant must acknowledge the conditions of exchange which existed at the time that certain past transactions occurred or those that will apply when future activity takes place. Thus, in the case of fixed assets, it is said that they retain relative values during inflationary periods. As a result, the translated values at the date that the original costs were incurred are said to be appropriate in establishing both the balance sheet values and the depreciation charges which are derived therefrom.

Current accounting practice deals with the translation problem on the basis that all accounts will be converted into dollars. In practice, only dividends and international payments are actually converted. Insofar as the residual assets are concerned, they are retained locally and are more affected by changes in purchasing power than they are by official exchange rates.

Exchange rate changes normally recognize the devaluation of local currency in terms of the U.S. dollar. These devaluations are usually only

---

[11] George C. Watt, *Management Accounting Problems in Foreign Operations,* Mathew Bender & Co., Inc. (1960), p. 505.

the delayed official recognition of inflationary conditions that have existed for some time. Nevertheless, none of the accepted techniques of translating foreign statements gives any recognition to the loss in comparative purchasing power prior to its reflection in the exchange rate. Since no effective system of recording has been identified there is a tendency in international management to ignore the slippage and thus to permit an insidious decapitalization of the enterprise. It is recommended that some form of replacement index be used for both inventory and fixed assets to assure that prices are fixed with due consideration of the long-term needs.

Avoiding devaluation losses

Companies which have been active in South America have learned to make continuous provision for the devaluations caused by policies of currency inflation. In Brazil, inflation has averaged 50 percent per annum over the five years 1964–1968 and 49 percent over the 10 years 1959–1968.[12] To understand the relative loss of purchasing power this must be compared with the 3 to 5 percent per annum experienced by most industrialized countries. Those companies which have not adjusted to the environment have had extremely trying years.

The continuous devaluation of Latin American and Asian currencies must be viewed as a going cost. In Europe, however, the relatively rare official devaluations (i.e. the pound sterling in late 1967) are extraordinary events and may require unique and special approaches.

Keeping in mind that devaluation is the delayed expression of inflationary conditions and that the accountants have identified certain procedures for recording and measuring the costs of devaluation, it is appropriate to identify some of the more common ways of avoiding potential devaluation losses. These are presented as follows:

1. To the greatest extent possible, remit cash promptly when settling the bills of international suppliers.
2. Make early remittance of all dividend payments due to parent.
3. Insist on an early collection of all receivables giving consideration to cash discounts and penalty interest.
4. Reduce all local currency assets (except plant) to a minimum.
5. Borrow local money to finance working capital even though interest costs appear high.
6. Purchase fixed assets and goods for resale instead of holding idle cash or other financial assets.
7. If possible, build escalator clauses into sales contracts.
8. Employ an accounting technique which isolates the true costs of

---

[12] *International Financial Statistics,* Dec. 1967 and Feb. 1969, International Monetary Fund.

carrying receivables and inventories in terms of interest charges and exchange exposures.

9. In establishing sales prices, use a current replacement cost rather than a book cost.
10. Where the cost of forward exchange contracts is not excessive in terms of the risk of devaluation, purchase such contracts to cover assets exposed to devaluation, and also the expected profits for a future reasonable period.
11. Produce locally so as to minimize the need for foreign currency payments for imports.
12. Where possible increase export sales payable in hard currencies.
13. Increase sales prices as an offset to devaluation.
14. Translate accounting reports locally so as to make local managers completely aware of the impact of inflation and devaluation on the parent company statements.
15. Recover "real" rather than "historic" fixed asset values in current pricing.
16. Where possible, revalue assets to take full advantage of tax savings.
17. Pay off hard currency obligations promptly.
18. Use techniques such as currency and credit swaps to provide needed funds.

The above techniques are representative of the steps that should be taken in all cases of impending devaluation. Needless to say, any early warning of the exact timing of a devaluation can be used to good financial advantage.

Credits, insurance, and guaranties

The successful financing of a foreign business involves an awareness of all sources of funds and particularly those credit instruments and credit agencies which facilitate the day-to-day operation of the international activity. In particular it should be noted that international companies are often required to find financing for their major customers and distributors, thus increasing their normal business exposures. However, in their pursuit of favorable balances of trade, most of the industrialized western governments have provided credit arrangements which protect their exporters from political and currency risks.[13]

Credit agencies of the U.S. government

Export-Import Bank. The principal aid which the U.S. government offers for the support of exporters is the Export-Import Bank which has a

---

[13] Howe Martyn, *International Business,* Collier-Macmillan Ltd., London, 1964, p. 204.

$6 billion borrowing capacity and capital stock of $1 billion owned by the U.S. Treasury.[14] The Eximbank does not compete against private capital but attempts to provide capital which would not otherwise be available. It lends for specific rather than general projects and requires appropriate assurance of repayment. Its charges reflect the risks which it bears.

The Eximbank offers long-term (5 to 20 years) loans for the most part, providing the funds to a foreign borrower but requiring that the proceeds be spent in the United States. It also makes available non-recourse discounting of medium- and short-term credits, thus relieving the exporter of significant contingent liability. This is executed by providing a commercial bank with an Eximbank guarantee usually covering 85 percent of the political and credit risk. The Eximbank also participates with the Foreign Credit Insurance Association and the American War Risk Agency in insuring exporters against specific types of losses.

Agency for International Development.   AID is the organization which is most actively mentioned in respect to foreign operations. This agency is concerned with encouraging and facilitating "those private U.S. investments abroad which further the development of the economic resources and productive capacities of a less-developed country or area."[15] It does this by a program of technical services, investment guaranties, and loans.

The technical services of this agency include an extensive catalogue of investment data and a subsidy program on investment surveys. The guaranty program covers specific risks, extended risks, and housing guaranties. The specific-risk coverage protects against non-convertibility, expropriation, and war. The extended-risk covers all risks (except fraud or misconduct of investor or commercially insurable exposures) up to 75 percent of long-term loans and sometimes 50 percent of equity investments. The housing guaranties cover 100 percent of certain housing projects which stimulate private home ownership.

Under Title I of Public Law 480, foreign currencies received in payment for surplus agricultural commodities (popularly known as "Cooley" funds) may be lent to either U.S. or foreign firms for specific purposes (particularly those not competing with U.S. production). The Private Investment Fund and dollar loans under the Foreign Assistance Act of 1961 are other programs of AID.

In 1966, AID spent $1.1 billion for shipments to underdeveloped countries.[16] For the future the linking of AID financing to a 90 percent

---

[14] John G. McLean, "Financing Overseas Expansion," *Harvard Business Review*, March-April 1963, p. 56.

[15] "Where to Get Export-Import and Investment Assistance from the U.S. Government," *Business Abroad*, Jan. 22, 1968, p. 14.

[16] Hyson and Stout, "Impact of Foreign Aid on U.S. Exports," *Harvard Business Review*, Jan.-Feb. 1968, p. 63.

level of domestic procurement avoids an unfavorable impact on the balance of payments but, in addition, the agency continues to favor loans that result in "additional" exports rather than those which replace goods that would have moved in any case.

Foreign Credit Insurance Association. The FCIA was founded to stimulate export by putting U.S. businessmen on an equal credit footing with foreign shippers. The association consists of the Eximbank and over 75 qualified insurance carriers.[17] The member companies provide short- and medium-term insurance for 90 percent of the commercial risks of receivables and Eximbank insures 90–95 percent of the political and transfer risks. The program is available to manufacturers and exporters who are residents or do business in the United States or its territories, for goods with specified U.S. content, under invoices payable in U.S. dollars. The insurance cost averages less than 1 percent of most credit sales.

International and foreign credit agencies

World Bank. The International Bank for Reconstruction and Development (IBRD) was originally concerned with aid to war-torn Europe, but more recently it is concerned with economic development. Most of its loans deal with infrastructure development and are made to governments or large enterprises of member countries operating with a government guaranty.[18] The bank is capitalized by subscription from members of which $20.4 billion is subscribed and $2 billion paid in. IBRD sells its own bonds and also sells off portions of the loans which it has acquired. Loans are normally of 15 to 25 years duration. Although the World Bank makes a profit, it has never paid a dividend.

International Finance Corporation. The IFC aims at stimulating productive private enterprise in less developed member countries. It is an affiliate of the World Bank, was formed to get around the requirement of a government guaranty, and deals only in the private sector. It is capitalized at about $100 million from member countries and holds both loan and equity investments (usually in common with other private interests) which it sometimes sells to other financial institutions. Loans are usually for 5 to 15 year periods.

International Development Association. IDA is another affiliate of the World Bank which typically offers credits to member governments or subdivisions thereof. Its loan requirements, particularly in respect to repayment, are easier than those of IBRD. Loan maturities run to 50 years with 10 year extensions. There are no interest costs and only ¾ of 1 percent service charge. The subscribed capital is in excess of $1 billion. Competitive bidding on project expenditures is required.

---

[17] Sylvester F. Majestic, "Financing International Trade," *Handbook of Business Administration,* McGraw-Hill Inc., 1967, p. 16–85.

[18] *Industrial Development at Home and Abroad—Problems and Prospects,* Financial Management Series 101, American Management Association, 1952, p. 22.

Inter-American Development Bank.   IDB extends loans or guarantees to member governments, subdivisions, or enterprise within member countries. It covers 20 countries of the western hemisphere. It makes no working capital, refinancing or acquisition loans, but lends for purchase of capital assets or technical services. Its Ordinary Operations Loans have maturities between 10 and 20 years, while Special Operations Loans run from 10 to 50 years. (Its affiliated Social Progress Fund has maturities between 15 and 30 years at low interest and covers education, housing, community water, and sanitation.)

International Monetary Fund.   IMF is aimed at providing currency stability by monetary cooperation and a balanced growth of world trade. Its resources consist of gold and currencies amounting to about $15 billion. Member borrowings are repaid within 3 to 5 years. "Under IMF, exchange regulations and restrictions have been relaxed and exchange rates have shown a higher degree of stability."[19]

Foreign credit agencies.   The need to provide financing for customers is not necessarily applicable only to large projects. In almost all countries, low-interest cost credit facilities are available to finance export sales. The low interest is made possible through government guarantees provided by such organizations as:

> U.K.—Export Credits Guarantee Department (ECGD)
> France—Compagnie Francaise d'Assurance (COFACE)
> Germany—Hermes Kreditversicherung (Hermes)
> Belgium—National Credit Guarantee Bureau (Ducroire)

Development banks.   The industrial development bank, of which there are about 100 throughout the world, has been widely accepted as an aid to financing the less developed countries in their program of local industrialization and employment of national resources. They mobilize needed credit but also provide technical and economic information. The banks are sponsored by the government but are largely capitalized with low-cost loans on a long-term basis. However, interest earnings, profits on equity holdings, and profits on portfolio sales provide additional resources for relending to qualified private borrowers.

Special techniques for foreign operations

A fundamental objective of international operation is that of participating in all potentially profitable markets while minimizing the risks inherent in such operation. As shown in the foregoing paragraphs, the governments of the world have established or supported institutions furthering the basic effort, but businessmen, through their normal operations, can also prevent unwarranted exposure to international risk. This may be done by use of appropriate instruments of credit or by the employment of special techniques applicable to foreign operations.

---

[19] W. A. Muriale, "A Blueprint for Banking in Developing Nations," *International Handbook of Management,* McGraw-Hill Book Co., 1965, p. 281.

Instruments of credit

Exporting to foreign countries usually involves some unfamiliarity with the credit position of significant customers. Overcoming the risk inherent in this lack of specific awareness, while easing the financing requirement, has caused the evolution of specific instruments of international trade. Some of these are listed below:

1) *Bill of Exchange*—This is a written order in which the initiator (drawer) instructs another party (drawee) to pay a sum of money at a specific time to a third person (payee) or his order, or to bearer. Several variations are:

> Sight draft—Payable on demand.
> Time draft—Payable at a given period after preparation or presentation.
> Arrival draft—Payable on arrival of goods.
> Bank draft—Check drawn by one bank on another.
> Clean draft—Drafts without shipping documents permitting early acquisition of goods.
> Documentary draft—Draft accompanied by shipping papers which must be held until acceptance or payment.

2) *Letter of Credit*—A formal letter issued by a bank which authorizes drafts against the bank up to a limit as specified. The bank, in effect, substitutes its credit for its customer's credit. Several variations are:

> Commercial Letter of Credit—A letter in favor of the seller of goods authorizing the drawing of drafts against the buyer's bank.
> Travellers Letter of Credit—A letter in favor of a traveller authorizing the drawing of drafts by a beneficiary upon identification.
> Revocable Letters of Credit—The term of credit is specified after which the letter of credit cannot serve as authority for new drafts.

3) *Bill of Lading*—A document issued by a carrier which serves as a receipt and authorization for later delivery to a designated person or his order. Several variations are:

> Straight Bill of Lading—Non-negotiable and for specified person.
> Order Bill of Lading—Negotiable and for person named or his order.
> Clean Bill of Lading—Goods are described as in good order on receipt.
> Unclean Bill of Lading—Goods are noted to have defect on receipt.
> Stale Bill of Lading—Presentation occurs only after unreasonable time.

4) *Certificate of Origin*—A document stipulating the place of manufac-

ture of goods submitted for export and used usually for the administration of tariffs.

Techniques applicable to foreign operations

Throughout this chapter there has been an emphasis on the reduction of the risk inherent in international affairs. Various concepts have been explored but fundamentally the problem reduces itself to one of measuring international risks and, in respect to monetary uncertainties, determining the degree to which one can afford to hedge those risks. These hedges can be achieved in several recognized ways:

1) *Swaps*—This technique refers to the exchange of unusable local currency for usable currencies on a promise to restore the local currency at a specified future time. Characteristically the central banks permit the repayment to take place at the original rate of exchange. Thus, a firm, needing local currency, deposits dollars against a local-currency loan from a central bank. Upon repayment of the loan, the dollar deposit is released and exchange conversion takes place at the rate in existence at the time when the loan was made.

2) *Deposits*—This aspect of foreign-exchange dealing requires that a local-currency deposit be placed with a central bank before an import license is granted. The money stays on deposit until the goods are received and payment made. In some cases the loss in value because of inflation during the period of deposit falls to the account of the depositor.

3) *Related company loans*—Proposed borrowings by subsidiaries from affiliated companies should be screened from the viewpoint of the host country. It is conceivable that the host country may refuse foreign exchange when repayment is attempted on the grounds that the affiliated loan is really an investment. To avoid confusion, it may be wise to go through a third party bank.

4) *Parent company guarantees*—Most international parents wish to avoid guarantee of bank loans of subsidiaries so as to avoid contingent liabilities and difficulties with parent company borrowing indentures.

5) *Letter of Awareness*—Instead of requiring a guarantee, most banks have been willing to accept a letter indicating the parent company awareness of the subsidiary's borrowing. It has been felt that the parent would honor a moral obligation to redeem the debt even though it had no legal obligation. The actions of Raytheon in Italy have cast some doubt on this reliance.[20]

6) *Escalation clauses*—International sales cannot always be made in U.S. dollars. It is therefore often necessary to provide in the sales contract for an increase in the foreign currency price if a currency

---

[20] "Raytheon and the Mayor of Palermo," *The Economist,* June 22, 1968, p. 69.

devaluation takes place. This is particularly important when the settlement is made over an extended period.

7) *Forward exchange contracts*—A hedge against foreign exchange devaluation can be accomplished by transactions aimed at retaining the present relationship between two currencies. Through the execution of a contract a party customarily pledges to deliver a specified amount of local currency at a future time. In return the other party (usually a bank) agrees to purchase that local currency at a specific rate which is normally close to the current rate. The bank charges a fee for its service which varies in accordance with the relative strengths of the currencies concerned.

8) *Switches*—When local funds are blocked as to remittability, subject to high tax upon conversion, accumulating in a currency which is depreciating, or represent an otherwise unwanted currency balance or excess trade credit, a "switch" may be arranged after obtaining approval of the appropriate central banks. The excess local currency or trade credits may be sold to a third party who will arrange to exchange them for hard currencies, local commodities, or commodities located abroad.

9) *Barter*—This approach is like a switch except that it exchanges the local commodity for a foreign commodity which may be in greater demand either in world markets or for use in the local area.

10) *Hard goods protection*—In countries faced with devaluation, it may be wise to invest in hard goods as a temporary storer of values. When funds are required the hard goods (farms, ships, hotels, factories) can be sold so as to yield needed local currency. Because hard goods escape most of the incidence of devaluation the fiscal amount of local currency (even after costs) can be greater than if liquid funds had been retained.

11) *Link deposits*—The availability of local funds can be assured or costs reduced by making a deposit in an alternate currency. Thus to get Italian lira, dollars may be deposited in London. The lira remain available while the link deposit is maintained.

12) *Overdraft*—This banking approach is merely a form of unsecured borrowing in which the borrowing fluctuates as business needs and deposits are processed through the bank. It is a salient feature of British banking relations and currently costs about 6% per annum.

The above techniques indicate some of the opportunities which are available to the international financing expert. The details of the related programs can be worked out with the international executives of any of the major banks throughout the world. In each case the reduction of risk or increased availability will be accomplished at some cost to the international company. However, by using these techniques properly, many of the serious risks of international trading can be reduced to a tolerable, known expense which can be provided for in established prices.

PART IX

Financial
accounting
policies

Nature and objectives of financial statements

O. L. Luper*

The focal point of this chapter, as indicated by its title, is the nature and objectives of financial statements.[1] In general, an attempt has been made to explain the theory of financial statements, what they are, and what they include. An effort has also been made to discuss the purposes of financial statements and some of their more important characteristics and limitations. Views have likewise been expressed as to the basic responsibilities of users and preparers. Moreover, in view of the fact that financial statements are a product of the financial accounting process, it is difficult to see how a discussion of the former can be considered complete without some reference to the latter. For this reason, the brief introductory section on financial accounting was considered necessary to place the discussion of financial statements in perspective.

Nature of financial accounting

The sheer immensity and variety of human activity has forced man to divide it into a large number of parts in order to comprehend it. Thus,

* Vice President and Director, Humble Oil & Refining Company, Houston; member of Accounting Principles Board and Chairman of Committee on Fundamentals of Financial Statements.

[1] This chapter relies substantially for its content on the ideas and subject matter contained in research material prepared by the Accounting Research Division of the American Institute of Certified Public Accountants for the Committee on Fundamentals of Financial Statements of the Accounting Principles Board. An expression of thanks is extended to the Accounting Research Division for its help and for granting the necessary permission to use some of the material presented herein.

broad categories of endeavor, such as physical and spiritual, and social, political, and economic, are identified; and each of these is further divided and subdivided into narrower and more specialized (though not completely mutually exclusive) categories. Accounting is one of these subdivisions concerned primarily with economic endeavors, and financial accounting is a part of accounting.

Financial accounting is a service activity that provides information intended to be useful in economic activity. The information provided is a continual history, quantified in money terms, of those aspects of the economic activities of an individual business enterprise which form its financial position and changes in its financial position, with emphasis on those changes which directly affect the profitability of the enterprise. It has been demonstrated that there are a large number of ideas basic to financial accounting—that they are not few in number, as was previously believed by some. Moreover, these ideas are most easily and effectively understood if they are classified according to certain similarities. This procedure enables relationships to be discovered that might otherwise be overlooked. These ideas upon which financial accounting is based may be divided into two broad categories—basic concepts and generally accepted accounting principles.

The basic concepts of financial accounting may be defined as observations about aspects of the environment in which financial accounting operates and the effects of the environment on the financial accounting process. These environmental influences can be observed and described, but not readily changed. They are conditions which are almost completely beyond the control of businessmen and accountants. However, to the extent that businessmen and accountants make the observations, their perceptions of the environment might be considered by some as an indirect form of control.

For explanatory purposes, these basic concepts may be classified into two major groups. The first group includes those concepts which are observed to be inherent in the environment of financial accounting. The second group includes those which establish the broad objectives of financial accounting.

The first category of basic concepts pertains to (1) the uses and users of financial accounting information, (2) the nature of economic activities of individual business enterprises, (3) the characteristics of the business environment in the United States, and (4) the problems involved in quantifying economic activity in terms of money.

While this first category consists primarily of observations about the environment, the second category—the broad objectives of financial accounting—is concerned with the impact that the environment has on the financial accounting process. Again, for purposes of clarity, the basic concepts of the second category may be divided into two classifications. The first deals with the basic features of financial accounting, and the second is concerned with the broad objectives of financial accounting.

The concepts identified as features of financial accounting include accounting entity, going concern, time periods, money measurement, accrual, materiality, and several others. These basic features indicate some of the important strengths and limitations of financial accounting. The number and complexity of the relationships that exist among these basic features and the effect that these relationships have on financial accounting point up the need for specific objectives for financial accounting, and for guidelines and rules for performing financial accounting operations. This leads, therefore, to the second category of basic concepts which pertains to the broad objectives of financial accounting.

The broad objectives represent the goals which, if achieved, promote the usefulness of financial accounting as a service activity. Some of the broad objectives that have been identified are: relevance, completeness, objectivity, neutrality, reliability, comparability, regularity, timeliness, verifiability, intelligibility, adequacy of disclosure, and reasonableness of cost. Each of these concepts is related to, and has its roots in, broad ethical goals: truth, justice, and fairness.

Observing and describing the basic concepts of financial accounting does not alone solve accounting problems. The basic concepts *describe* —they do not *prescribe*—financial accounting. Although they are essential to an understanding of the financial accounting process, and ultimately to improvement of financial statements, they do not directly indicate what is "good" and what is "bad" accounting. Their importance lies in the fact that they provide a bridge between the forces that shape financial accounting, which are primarily environmental forces, and generally accepted accounting principles, which determine how financial accounting is done.

In contrast to the basic concepts, generally accepted accounting principles reflect decisions of businessmen and accountants. As such, they represent a consensus at any point in time as to how the financial accounting process should operate to achieve the objectives embodied in the basic concepts. Also in contrast to the relatively stable basic concepts, generally accepted accounting principles are continually evolving as new accounting procedures and practices are agreed upon to reflect changing business conditions.

In October of 1964, the Council of the American Institute of Certified Public Accountants issued a bulletin which stated in part:

1. "Generally accepted accounting principles" are those principles which have substantial authoritative support.
2. Opinions of the Accounting Principles Board constitute "substantial authoritative support."
3. "Substantial authoritative support" can exist for accounting principles that differ from Opinions of the Accounting Principles Board.[2]

---

[2] American Institute of Certified Public Accountants, "Special Bulletin: Disclosure of Departures from the Opinions of the Accounting Principles Board," (New York, 1964).

Thus, the general acceptability of accounting principles is based upon the idea of substantial authoritative support. At present, authoritative accounting literature contains no formal definition of "substantial authoritative support." Over the years, accountants have relied upon the general meaning of the words and a general understanding as to how to find substantial authoritative support. However, situations have changed and business developments have occurred which present new problems that the profession had not been called upon to address in earlier years. Today's situation demands that we sharpen the idea of substantial authoritative support so that it will be more useful to a larger profession facing new and more complicated problems. The profession recognizes this problem and is working on a solution.

There are two ways to approach substantial authoritative support. One would be to construct a definition of the term based upon the fundamental meanings of the words *substantial, authoritative,* and *support.* The other would be to develop guidelines on how to look for substantial authoritative support. Currently, many members of the profession feel that guidelines as to how one should look for substantial authoritative support would be more useful than an academic definition of the term.[3]

Obviously, Opinions of the Accounting Principles Board are one source of substantial authoritative support. However, it is evident from the preceding quotation that these Opinions are not the only source of substantial authoritative support. The accountant must therefore take other steps, including surveying the relevant literature, in a search of support for a given accounting practice. The author would not attempt in this space even a partial listing of such other sources of substantial authoritative support. The important point is that ideas and procedures become "generally accepted accounting principles" by agreement. The principles are based on experience, reason, custom, usage, and—to a significant extent—practical necessity. The ideas of "general acceptance" and "substantial authoritative support" relate to the propriety of the practices, as viewed by informed, experienced accountants and businessmen in the light of the purposes and limitations of the financial accounting process.

Purpose and objectives of financial statements

The term "economic activity" has been applied to man's attempts to satisfy his needs with scarce (economic) resources. Thus, economic activity involves decision-making. Quantitative information is helpful in making rational economic decisions, that is, in making reasonable choices among alternative courses of action. Numerous variously affected groups

---

[3] Marshall S. Armstrong, "Substantial Authoritative Support," *The Journal of Accountancy,* April 1969, pp. 45–50.

have an economic interest in the activities of each and every business enterprise. There is therefore a great demand for quantitative information about the economic affairs of business enterprises from which necessary judgments can be made. Financial accounting furnishes certain types of this quantitative information useful in making rational choices among economic alternatives and in evaluating economic progress and results.

The basic, overall purpose of financial statements is to communicate to the user the quantitative information generated by the financial accounting process. Since the information is intended to be useful in making economic decisions, financial statements seek to present it in the manner most suited to the user's needs. Within the framework of this basic purpose, there are a number of specific objectives. These are related to the informational needs of the user groups to whom the statements are directed.

One objective of financial statements is to communicate information in "general-purpose" form. Certain groups often display significant common needs for information about the activities of individual business enterprises. Quantitative information about the enterprise's financial position and changes in its financial position is a basic need of almost all groups, and is of prime importance to investors and creditors. The general-purpose financial statements which are intended to meet the needs of a wide variety of users reasonably well are the most important product of the financial accounting process.

It is appropriate to mention at this point that financial accounting also provides many special-purpose reports. These are commonly prepared for (1) those who have highly specialized information needs and/or (2) those who occupy a position of economic or legal power with respect to the reporting enterprise. Tax returns and financial statements submitted to regulatory authorities are examples of such special-purpose information. Inasmuch as these special-purpose reports are prepared to meet the needs of specialized users, they are not often suited to the needs of other users. Therefore, such reports are not the primary product of financial accounting, and the term "financial statements" as used in this chapter refers to the general-purpose statements.

Another objective of financial statements, and one of prime importance, is to provide reliable information about the earnings of a business enterprise. Almost all of those who are directly concerned with the economic activities of business enterprises are interested in the enterprise's ability to operate at a profit. Creditors, suppliers, and employees provide funds, materials, and services necessary to the operations of the enterprise and expect payment in return. Investors expect either money incomes in the form of dividends, or capital gains in the form of increases in the value of ownership shares, or both. Taxing authorities base a major portion of their taxes on profits. Management must report to owners and others on its stewardship of the enterprise's resources. An adequate level of profits is essential over the long run to the very survival of the enterprise.

A related objective is to provide, to the extent practicable, quantitative information useful as an assistance in predicting the future earning power of the enterprise. It is not an objective of financial statements to be predictive; they communicate information about the past and present, not about the future. They do, however, seek to reflect proper trends which may be extrapolated and used, perhaps with supplementary data, to predict future earning power.

Financial statement users also need information suitable for evaluating the financial strength and distribution of ownership of the enterprise. In recognition of this need, a related objective of financial statements is to provide information which aids in assessing such matters as the enterprise's capability to finance operations out of earnings, its ability to repay obligations when due, and its capacity for obtaining additional funds from investors and creditors.

A further objective of financial statements is to disclose, to the extent possible, certain other information which is relevant to the statement user's needs but which is not suitable for presentation in financial terms. Examples of such nonfinancial disclosures are information about the enterprise's accounting policies and changes in those policies, and information about contingent liabilities of the enterprise.

Inherent in the preceding discussion is the fact that the decisions of financial statement users involve the process of choosing among alternative courses of action. Investors must choose among various enterprises in which to invest and make decisions as to retention or termination of their holdings. Creditors must choose enterprises to which to extend credit and establish terms for repayment. The financial statement user wants to be able to compare performance both among enterprises and among reporting periods for the same enterprise. Comparability is thus an important objective of financial statements.

In summary, then, the purpose of financial statements is to provide general-purpose, historical, quantitative information, intended to meet the needs of several user groups (but primarily the needs of investors and creditors) for information relevant to the financial position, changes in financial position, and earning power of a business enterprise. Meeting these needs implies that the financial statements are prepared so as to provide a basis for comparison both among different accounting periods for a given enterprise and, to the extent practicable, among different enterprises.

Nature of financial statements

As indicated earlier, financial statements are the medium for periodically communicating the information accumulated and processed by financial accounting to potential users. Through the financial accounting process, myriad and complex details of the effects of economic activity on an enterprise's economic resources and the interests in those resources are accumulated, analyzed, quantified, summarized, and reported as information of two basic types: (1) that which relates to financial position, implying a point in time, and (2) that which relates to changes in financial position, implying a period of time.

A statement of financial position, or *balance sheet,* normally contains three major categories. First, there are reflected the "assets" of the enterprise, these being financial representations of the enterprise's economic resources as recognized and valued in conformity with generally accepted accounting principles. Second are the enterprise's "liabilities," which are financial representations of the economic obligations of the enterprise as recognized and valued in conformity with generally accepted accounting principles. The third category, "owner's equity," is the representation of the ownership interest in the assets of the enterprise which remains after recognition of the liabilities. A statement of financial position reflects, at a specific date, the cumulative financial effect of all the recorded changes in the assets of the enterprise and the interests in those assets since its inception.

The most important statement of changes in financial position is the *income statement.* It shows those changes (positive or negative) in the financial position of the enterprise which have resulted from its profit-seeking operations or activities during a stated period. The principal components of this statement are "revenue," "expenses," "gains and losses," and "net income" or "net loss." Revenue in an income statement means increases in assets or decreases in liabilities from operating sources (as opposed to owner's contributions or borrowing) as recognized in conformity with generally accepted accounting principles. Expenses in an income statement represent the increases in liabilities or the decreases in assets which result from matching costs with revenue or with proper time periods also in conformity with generally accepted accounting principles. Under generally accepted accounting principles, gains and losses are the net result of the revenue and expenses from events which are not an integral part of the normal profit-seeking operations of the enterprise, and which are disclosed separately in the income statement. Finally, as might be expected from the caption, net income or net loss in an income statement is the net result of totaling all revenues, expenses, and gains and losses for the period indicated.

Since profitability occupies a central position to those interested in the economic activities of the enterprise, the information presented in an income statement is usually considered the most important information provided by financial accounting. Yet a statement of income alone is normally not sufficient to explain the change in owner's equity during a period because changes arise from sources other than profit-seeking operations. The total change in owner's equity is normally presented by a combination of statements: an income statement, a *statement of retained earnings,* and, if appropriate, a *statement of other changes in owner's equity.* A statement of retained earnings reflects not only net income (as shown in the income statement) but adjustments or corrections of the net income of prior periods, and distributions of assets to owners, usually as dividends. A statement of other changes in owner's equity reflects all other changes; for example, owner's contributions of assets, retirements of owner's interests (except for the part representing a "distribution of earnings"), and similar events. If these "other" changes are simple, they are often presented in notes to the other financial statements rather than in a separate statement.

Certain other statements of changes in financial position are often presented as supplemental information to the financial statements. These generally take the form of analyses of changes in certain individual balance sheet items. Among the more popular of these statements are those dealing with sources and applications of funds, changes in plant and equipment, changes in long-term liabilities, and receipts and disbursements of cash.

Technically, every asset, every liability, and every item of owner's equity might be analyzed, singly or in any conceivable combination, to determine how and why it changed during a period, and a statement setting forth the results of the analysis could be prepared. For the most part, however, the usefulness of the information would not justify the time, expense, and effort involved, and statements of changes in financial position in addition to those discussed are seldom presented.

Influence of basic concepts and accounting principles

Many forces are simultaneously at work to define the form and content of financial statements. Financial statements are vitally affected, for example, by (1) the nature of the economic activities about which they provide information, (2) the requirements of useful information, (3) the characteristics of the environment in which the financial accounting process operates, and (4) the decisions and judgments of businessmen and accountants in gathering, processing, and communicating financial acounting information. In other words, they are directly affected by those basic concepts and accounting principles discussed in the section on financial accounting.

For example, financial statements are most valuable as an aid in making rational economic choices and evaluating economic progress if the information communicated by them is relevant to the purpose for which it is prepared, is as complete as is reasonably possible to avoid misleading implications, and is communicated as soon as is reasonably possible following the close of the time period being reported upon. These goals of relevance, completeness, and timeliness are examples of the objectives of financial accounting discussed earlier.

Further, an enterprise's assets, liabilities, owner's equity, revenue, expenses, and net income or net loss (all financial statement items), as well as the extent of disclosure, are largely determined by generally accepted accounting principles, in that these principles determine which economic resources and obligations should be recognized as assets and liabilities, which changes in these resources and obligations should be recorded, when and how they should be valued, what information should be disclosed and how it should be disclosed, and which financial statements should be prepared. A brief discussion of some of the more important principles of financial accounting measurement and financial statement presentation should help the reader reach an adequate understanding of the derivation of the amounts appearing in the financial statements.

Financial accounting is transaction-based. This means that two-party events in which the enterprise acquires and/or gives up assets or incurs or satisfies liabilities in dealing with another entity are the events recorded by financial accounting. Transactions, then, underlie the dollar amounts appearing on financial statements.

With few exceptions, financial accounting measures or values assets and liabilities involved in transactions through the use of exchange value, which is the amount of some other asset that a given asset commands in a market, quantified in money terms.

It must be recognized that financial statements can never portray with infallible and irrefutable accuracy an exact picture of a business enterprise. Even in a relatively small enterprise, the number of transactions represented is simply too large, too varied, and too complex. However, certain principles of financial statement presentation are used to insure that the financial statements meet a standard of "fair presentation." This means that within reasonable and acceptable limits, the financial statements do depict fairly the financial position and results of operations of the business enterprise as indicated. Fair presentation is a subjective benchmark against which the independent public accountant judges the propriety of the communication of financial accounting information.

Although it is a difficult concept to define, most would agree that fair presentation results if a number of conditions are met: (1) appropriate generally accepted accounting principles have been consistently applied (or changes have been appropriately disclosed) in accumulating and processing the financial accounting information; (2) the information in the underlying records is accurately reflected and described in the financial statements; and (3) a proper balance has been achieved between the conflicting needs to disclose important features of the conventional concepts of financial position and results of operations and to summarize the voluminous underlying data into a limited number of financial statement captions and supporting narrative notes.

Principles of financial statement presentation require that a balance sheet, a statement of income, a statement of changes in retained earnings, and disclosure of changes in other categories of stockholders' equity be considered the minimum presentation necessary to present fairly the financial position and results of operations of an enterprise. These principles also require that such financial statements be complete, that is, that they include all known assets, liabilities, revenue, and expenses as defined by generally accepted accounting principles at the time.

Financial accounting, of course, contains many more detailed principles of both financial accounting measurement and financial statement presentation. The principles briefly discussed are only examples of the way in which generally accepted accounting principles influence the preparation of financial statements. This discussion should, however, aid the reader in understanding how and why the basic financial statements are prepared and how the amounts displayed in the statements are derived.

Characteristics of financial statements

If it is accepted that the basic concepts and accounting principles influence, shape, and otherwise serve to define financial accounting, and if it is accepted that financial statements are an important end-product of financial accounting, then it seems only logical that financial statements should have observable characteristics which are closely related to the factors defining the process by which they are prepared.

Financial statements as they are prepared today do, in fact, exhibit numerous characteristics and limitations which flow from the environment, the nature of the financial accounting process, and generally accepted accounting principles. Some of these characteristics and limitations are inherent in the nature of financial accounting and change only slowly, if at all. Other characteristics reflect the necessity for using judgment and conventional procedures in the face of uncertainty and impreciseness, while still others result from the complexities of the situations and of the interrelationships involved. This section concentrates on an enumeration and description of some of these observable characteristics. The limitations of financial statements are discussed in the succeeding section.

The following are some of the more important observations about financial statements which are necessary for an adequate understanding of the subject. These observable characteristics of financial statements concern:

Intended audience.	Historical nature.
Articulation.	Legal and economic consequences.
Technical terminology.	Summarization and classification.
Money terms.	Various valuation methods.
Accrual basis.	Need for estimates and judgment.
Verifiability.	Conservatism.

Certainly there may be characteristics of financial statements in addition to the ones covered here. This list is not intended to be exhaustive.

Any type of communication presupposes an audience to receive it. It has been indicated that financial statements are general-purpose reports intended for those who have an interest in a given business enterprise as a whole, and to whom special-purpose financial information is not readily available. Financial statements are prepared on the assumption that the user is generally familiar with business practices and financial statement preparation, as well as with the meaning and implication of the terms used and the nature of information reported.

It has also been indicated that the purpose of financial statements is to report what has happened in the past; they are therefore historical in nature. Although investors and creditors often make judgments as to the future prospects of an enterprise based on the information provided by its financial statements, the statements themselves are not intended to provide estimates of the effect of future economic activity on the financial position and results of operations.

As has been demonstrated in this discussion, the basic financial statements are interrelated and therefore are said to be "articulated." To illustrate, the income statement shows the financial results of operations and represents an increase or decrease in resources that is reflected in the asset and liability accounts on the balance sheet. Also, many of the items of costs included in the income statement represent the portions of various assets that are used during the accounting period for income-producing purposes.

It can be observed also that financial statements reflect elements of both economics and law. However, they do not reflect the subject matter of either discipline completely. In fact, to do so would probably be impossible since legal form does not always reflect economic substance and economic events may not always have discernible legal effects. Suffice it to say that financial accounting, and therefore financial statements, are conceptually oriented toward economic substance, but many of the underlying conventions have their origin in legal rules.

It is a fair statement that technical processes generally give rise to technical terminology. Financial statements are the product of a technical process and involve the use of technical terms. Unfortunately, many of the terms so employed are additionally words in common usage to which accountants have applied technical meanings. It is important for users of financial statements to be aware of the proper interpretations of such terminology.

Some of the characteristics of financial statements have been influenced greatly by the necessity for meeting practical expedients. For example, the volume of transactions affecting the financial position and results of operations of a business enterprise is so large that providing meaningful information is not possible without summarization and classification.

The presentation of financial information likewise necessitates a unit of measurement. It is characteristic of financial statements that transactions are measured and reported in money terms. In the United States this means the dollar. Fluctuations in the purchasing power of the dollar are not generally taken into account in preparing financial statements. Moreover, the valuation method is not uniform for all statement items. The various financial statement items are stated at different exchange values. Cash is stated at current exchange value, receivables at net realizable value, inventories basically at lower of acquisition cost or replacement value, productive assets at acquisition cost adjusted for depreciation and depletion, and so on. The foregoing is not to imply that the existence of different valuation methods is undesirable. It is nonetheless an observable characteristic of financial statements that various methods of valuation are employed.

A further characteristic of a related nature is the fact that most financial statements are prepared on an accrual basis rather than on a cash basis. In other words, an attempt is made to recognize revenue and expense in the period to which they relate and not necessarily in the period in which cash is received or paid.

Finally, periodic reporting requires making determinations before full outcomes of past events are known. When this condition is accepted, estimates and allocations become necessary parts of financial accounting. The same is then true of informed judgment since the exercise of informed judgment is essential to arriving at rational estimates and allocations.

The reliability of financial statements is so important that, to the extent possible, the data presented in them should be susceptible to objective verification. To enhance verifiability, financial accounting measurements are, so far as practicable, based on completed transactions, and the recognition of increments in value is deferred until the estimates of management are corroborated by verifiable outside evidence. Sales, purchases, and other events which are independently measurable are therefore the basic data of financial accounting measurements. Some kinds of events, especially those wholly internal to the enterprise such as depreciation, are not verifiable by transactions to which the enterprise is a party, and their verifiability therefore must be based on the consistent application of rational and systematic procedures.

An added restriction on estimation and judgment stems from the fact that financial statements are conservatively prepared. This characteristic of financial statements results from a general agreement on the premise that some risk of understatement, particularly of assets and net income, must often be accepted in order to avoid any possibility of results being overstated, an even less desirable alternative.

Limitations of financial statements

In the past few years, considerable criticism has been directed toward financial accounting and financial statements. Moreover, the source of this ciriticism has not been confined to those outside the accounting profession. In fact, members of the accounting profession may well number among the more vocal of the critics, for they—better than anyone else—know the limitations of financial statements, and they are constantly working with financial accounting problems.

Reducing the number and the effect of financial statement limitations is certainly a worthwhile goal. However, some of the limitations of financial statements stem from the very characteristics of the information —the same characteristics discussed in the preceding section. It would appear that the profession need not be particularly apologetic concerning limitations of this type. That observable characteristics may assume the role of limitations when viewed in a different context is by no means peculiar to financial statements.

The fact that financial statements are, by definition, general-purpose reports intended for use by several different audiences has been stressed previously. Thus, they cannot be expected to completely fulfill the requirements of any one of the audiences. For example, many users would like more information about the future prospects of an enterprise. However, financial statements reflect a sequential history. They do not *directly* provide information about the future, although, as Patrick Henry remarked for another purpose in another time, "I have but one lamp by which my feet are guided; and that is the lamp of experience. I know of no way of judging of the future, but by the past." The trends reflected in properly prepared financial statements may be valuable indications of the enterprise's future prospects.

Financial statements are the end-product of a great deal of summarization and classification, and no one denies that a certain amount of detail is thereby lost. One may recall that achieving a proper balance between the conflicting needs to disclose important features and to summarize voluminous underlying data is one of the major conditions of fair presentation. The presentation of raw financial data in an unclassified and unsummarized state would certainly not require much of the statement preparer, nor would it be likely to provide a product which would be of much value to anyone else.

These are not the only such limitations of financial statements. For instance, because financial statements are expressed in money terms, they do not take into consideration changes in the size of the measuring unit over time. Because financial statements are generally prepared on the accrual basis, supplementary analyses must be supplied to explain fluctuations in cash. Because financial statements are prepared periodically and not as the full outcomes of past events become known, estimates and allocations cannot be avoided. One could go on, but these examples should be sufficient to show that certain limitations are inherent in financial statements.

Certain financial statement limitations, however, do not stem from the characteristics of financial statements. The most serious and probably the most discussed of these is the existence, in some cases, of alternative accounting principles and practices. Where different underlying circumstances exist for similar transactions, alternative accounting practices are required for fair reporting. However, in cases where the underlying circumstances are not significantly different, the existence of such alternatives may lead to a lack of comparability that tends to invite misleading conclusions.

The major portion of the efforts of the Accounting Principles Board since its inception has been directed toward eliminating alternative accounting practices which cannot logically be justified by differences in the underlying circumstances. Significant progress has been made in several areas, and much work is being done to eliminate unwarranted alternative practices in other areas. However, until the accounting profession is able to identify and deal with this problem in all areas of financial accounting, the financial statement user should be aware that, to a certain extent, financial statements of different enterprises may reflect differences related to the choice of accounting method and not to basic differences in the enterprises and their transactions.

Responsibilities of users and preparers

It almost goes without saying that information prepared in a given way and for a given purpose probably cannot be used in other ways and for other purposes without incurring some risk that it may do more harm than good by leading the user to false inferences. Information in financial statements is no exception. Inasmuch as the preparers of financial statements cannot control the uses to which the information is put, then it is incumbent on users to accept certain significant responsibilities in drawing conclusions from financial statements.

Knowledgeable users must recognize, for instance, that financial statements are the result of the application of rules and procedures which are basically conventional in nature, that is, sanctioned by or growing out of custom and usage rather than natural laws. Moreover, the language used in the statements is primarily technical. They should, therefore, have some understanding of accounting terminology and generally accepted accounting principles, which describe the rules and procedures pertaining to financial accounting and thereby govern its implementation. Another basic responsibility of users is that they refrain from limiting their study of financial statements to an analysis of one or two statement items. Many users tend to place undue reliance on single measures. In this regard, net income and earnings per share of a single period are unfortunately often overemphasized.

Trends usually (though not invariably) are more reliable aids to prediction than the results of a single year. Likewise, estimating results which are remainders, such as net income, is usually better accomplished by estimating the components, such as revenue and expenses, than by attempting to predict the remainder directly. Furthermore, meaningful extrapolations of financial data can be made only in conjunction with the use of the best nonfinancial information available regarding the enterprise and its circumstances.

In light of the preceding, it appears advisable, as a minimum, for users of financial statements to (1) study the detailed information in financial statements, including notes, (2) study information for a number of consecutive periods, (3) use financial statements in conjunction with other information, and (4) keep the characteristics and limitations of financial statements well in mind.

In the hands of a knowledgeable user, financial statements can be of considerable assistance in making informed economic decisions. As indicated in the discussion of the purpose and objectives of financial statements, this decision-making generally takes the form of choosing among alternative courses of action which, in turn, presupposes that the choices are presented on a basis so as to be substantially comparable. Comparability is thus vital to the utility of financial statements.

Comparability in financial statements is primarily of two basic types: (1) interperiod comparability, or comparability within the given enterprise over time, and (2) intercompany comparability, or comparability as among different enterprises. Achieving reasonable comparability in financial statements is an important responsibility of the preparer. He is inhibited in this effort, however, not only by restrictions inherent in the environment of financial accounting and the composition of generally accepted accounting principles, but also by the fact that "comparability" means different things to different people. Nevertheless, reasonable interperiod comparability is usually achieved when the following conditions are present:

1. The presentations are in the same form.
2. The content of the statements is identical.
3. Changes in accounting practices, including the financial effects thereof, are disclosed.
4. Changes in circumstances or in the underlying nature of transactions are disclosed.

Conceptually, reasonable intercompany comparability involves all of these conditions, plus the important added condition that differences reflected in the financial statements of enterprises should arise from basic differences in the underlying circumstances related to the enterprises themselves, and not merely from differences in the accounting practices employed.

Discussion of comparability necessarily introduces two other important areas of responsibility in financial statement preparation—the responsibilities for consistency and disclosure. Consistency is an essential ingredient in achieving reasonable comparability since it, above all else, facilitates valid comparisons over time. Moreover, since adequate disclosure comprehends that all situations in which there is a material loss of comparability should be described in a clear and concise manner, it likewise is closely associated with the concept of comparability. Disclosures fit into one of the following four categories: (1) customary or routine disclosures, such as the basis for stating inventory, (2) disclosures of changes in accounting practices, (3) disclosures of changes in circumstances, and (4) disclosures of subsequent events.

Finally, the use of financial statements by those who are not in a position to evaluate either their accuracy or their validity makes it essential that the basic reliability of the financial statements not be subject to question. The primary responsibility for the reliability of an enterprise's financial statements rests with management. To discharge that responsibility, management has an obligation to adopt appropriate accounting practices, to maintain an adequate system of accounts, and to install and operate an effective system of internal control.

In addition, there are other sources to which the user of financial statements may look to satisfy himself as to the reliability of the information presented therein. One source is the report of an independent auditor. This report indicates that the financial statements have been examined by external experts who have satisfied themselves that the information is presented fairly and in conformity with generally accepted accounting principles. Another is the regulations of the Securities and Exchange Commission and the stock exchanges, which contain accounting and disclosure requirements. Still another positive factor in promoting reliability, and one that should not be underestimated, is the constant pressure for more and better financial information on the part of statement users themselves.

In the final analysis, however, the responsibility of management underlies the success of the entire system, and no amount of auditing or regulation can fully protect the public from the unscrupulous. Fortunately, the American business community has an excellent record for providing fair and reliable financial reports. Differences of opinion can and do arise from time to time as to what constitutes fair presentation in a specific situation or a specific enterprise, but these controversies arise primarily from the nature of the financial accounting process and generally accepted accounting principles, and do not represent questions of integrity.

Financial statements and change

Shakespeare wrote in *The Tempest*, "What's past is prologue." The past does indeed lay a foundation for the future. Thus, while the task of this chapter is primarily to describe and explain financial statements as they exist today, it seems fitting to conclude with at least a glance at tomorrow. Although members of the accounting profession are often characterized as being somewhat overly concerned with maintaining the status quo, few accountants really express the view that financial accounting will or should remain unchanged for any significant period of time.

Quite the contrary, financial accounting is dynamic and accounting practices are continually changing. They change for several reasons: to meet changing conditions, to reflect improved valuation methods, to embrace better ways of meeting the broad objectives of financial accounting, to reflect a better understanding of financial accounting and its environment, and many more.

A number of proposals have been made in recent years which have not been fully evaluated to date but which, if accepted, would result in significant changes in generally accepted accounting principles and the resulting financial statements. An enumeration or description of these proposals would not be appropriate here. Suffice it to say that the accounting profession is continually considering a wide variety of such proposals in an effort to continue the improvement in financial accounting and reporting.

What course future financial accounting will take, as well as what the form and content of tomorrow's financial statements will be, is anyone's guess. Perhaps some of the proposals currently being discussed will become generally accepted. Or perhaps others not even presently contemplated will determine what goes into future financial statements. All that can be said with any degree of certainty is that tomorrow's financial statements will be somewhat different from today's. For, in the end, only change itself is really predictable.

Accounting for inventories

Bertrand J. Belda*

Inventories, in an accounting sense, represent values assigned to goods or services acquired or produced by an enterprise for the purpose of subsequent sale, but not yet transferred to customers. Inventories include elements of raw material or components not yet processed or assembled, items in process of manufacture or refinement, finished products, and merchandise intended for resale. Also included in inventories are values of services applied to customer orders on projects or engagements not completed or invoiced. Throughout this chapter, the term *value*, as applied to inventories, represents the monetary quantification assigned for accounting purposes.

The nature of inventories

Inventories may also include various supplies (cutting oils, fluxes, equipment repair parts, etc.) ordinarily used or consumed in the operations of a business, but not comprising a part of the products produced for the purpose of eventual sale to customers. Although many of the criteria for evaluation of product, service, or merchandise inventories intended for sale to customers also apply to supplies inventories, the latter are sometimes treated and valued, for accounting purposes, in a manner similar to that of a deferred charge or prepaid expense. The principal thrust of this discussion relates to inventories of items acquired or produced for eventual sale.

---

* Partner in charge of Management Consulting Services, Ernst & Ernst, National Office, Cleveland, Ohio.

Inventory valuation concepts and accounting methods used in a business are important in measuring period income and asset dollar amounts at a given point in time. Accordingly, inventory accounting may have a significant impact upon interpretations of economic and financial results and status. Such interpretations affect income and other tax levies and are, therefore, important in the determination of funds extracted from businesses under laws and regulations applied by various taxing authority.

Inventories (with some exceptions) are usually valued at cost, or a modification thereof. Inventory accounts in the bookkeeping system of an organization are usually structured to facilitate the accumulation of cost values of materials, processes, and services as they are acquired or produced, and relieved of the values applicable to goods or services as they are sold. Thus inventory accounts, at a particular point in time, represent a "snapshot" view of the total values applicable to the inventory items on hand or in process. As a corollary, the amounts extracted

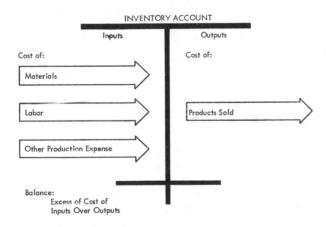

(deducted) from the inventory account during a period of time constitute the basic data for determining the cost of items sold during that term.

In summary, the inventory accounting process represents a key feature in the reckoning techniques applied to business operations. The inventory accounts, and the input and output elements to and from those accounts, represent the values assignable to the fundamental sequences of business operations in which goods are first acquired and then, after any processing, are later delivered to customers.

This sequence of flow is depicted in the chart above, in the form of a "T" account.

The determination of amounts of costs that should be assigned to inventories as such costs are incurred (inputs), and which costs or expenses should be excluded from inventory inputs (and charged off as incurred), is often a key factor in accounting for inventories. Also, the determination of the amounts of costs to be extracted (inventory outputs) upon sale of items, or when product damage, obsolescence, or other loss occurs, usually requires considerable information and an effective system to gather, summarize, and develop the needed data. The valuation of inventories (pricing) is, therefore, essentially concerned with allocations of costs incurred (historical costs) relating to materials, components, processes, and services acquired or produced during an accounting period into two categories, namely:

1. That portion which should be deferred to future periods as inventory costs and which is expected to be realized through revenues derived from subsequent sale.
2. That portion which should be charged off as an expense of the period.

A great number of larger companies, and many other smaller organizations having expertly devised accounting systems, maintain inventory accounts by capturing, summarizing, and recording inventory cost inputs and outputs as the transactions occur, and developing resulting balances. Others find it easier to accumulate only the costs of inventory inputs (purchases, production costs incurred, etc.), and to determine the outputs (cost of items sold) by tabulating and valuing the physical inventory quantities on hand at the close of a period. Both methods are aimed at similar results, and reflect the application of a basic accounting equation:

Beginning inventory plus purchases and other (inventoriable) cost incurred, minus cost of items sold, equals ending inventory.

In the case of accounting systems providing for entry of inputs to and outputs from inventory as they occur, including eliminations of costs applicable to spoiled or damaged products, obsolete items, etc., all of the elements needed for the equation are determinable, and the accounts can reflect the appropriate amounts of costs applicable to a period and/or to the inventory on hand at the end of that period. In situations where the measurement of cost of sales is not made on a continuing basis, the inventory tabulation at the close of the period, properly evaluated, can produce the aggregate amount of cost of sales. This is accomplished by a simple manipulation of the above equation, as follows:

Beginning inventory plus purchases and other (inventoriable) costs, minus ending inventory, equals cost of sales.

Regardless of the extent of the accounting system for inventories, it is prudent and customary to test the accuracy of book records by periodic checks of physical quantities actually on hand from time to time.

Inventory valuation concepts

Although "costs" constitute the principal bases for inventory valuation for accounting purposes, the extent to which they may be recognized and the methods used in applying them may vary extensively. These variations extend from industry to industry and, sometimes, between companies in the same industry.

The principles of inventory valuation, as set forth in *Accounting Research Bulletin 43*, Chapter 4, of the American Institute of Certified Public Accountants, provide some broad guidelines to costs to be considered. The pertinent sections of this bulletin are reproduced below:

The definition of cost as applied to inventories is understood to mean acquisition and production cost, and its determination involves many problems . . . encountered in the allocation of costs and charges. For example, under some circumstances, items such as idle facility expense, excessive spoilage, double freight, and rehandling costs may be so abnormal as to require treatment as current period charges rather than as a portion of the inventory cost. Also, general and administrative expenses should be included as period charges (against income, and excluded from inventory costs), except for the portion of such expenses that may be clearly related to production and thus constitute a part of inventory costs. Selling expenses constitute no part of inventory costs. It should also be recognized that the exclusion of all overheads from inventory costs does not constitute an accepted accounting procedure. The exercise of judgment in an individual situation involves consideration of the adequacy of the procedures of the cost accounting system in use, the soundness of the principles thereof, and their consistent application.

These general statements of inventory valuation can accommodate a wide range of cost elements that may be applied. In summary, these ranges may be bracketed in the following manner:

Maximum limitations on costs includable in inventory. All costs incurred, except selling expenses, and only that portion of general and administrative expenses that may be clearly related to production or acquisition of goods.

Minimum costs to be recognized in inventory. Delivered cost of materials and goods acquired, plus direct production costs, including recognition of some overheads related to such production, and excluding any "abnormal" costs of procurement and production.

Regardless of the method for determining which costs are to be recognized in inventory valuation and how they are to be applied, it is important to note the admonition in *ARB 43* relative to consistency. It should be evident that consistent policies and methods of inventory valuation are imperative to useful measurements of profitability between periods, and for interpretations of financial position at various dates.

Underlying these expressions of inventory valuation concepts is the notion that the particular methodology adopted by a business should be one that is most likely to present fairly the operating results and financial position of the enterprise. This implies that the effect of major changes in inventory quantities that may occur between periods should result in minimum distortions in measurement of income. Included in the considerations relating to the inventory values to be "carried over" from one period to another are such factors as the prospective recoverability of inventory values through subsequent sale, as well as the allocation of appropriate costs thereto.

In establishing an inventory valuation policy most suitable to a particular enterprise, the following elements may be of importance.

1. *The relative size of the inventory in relation to the business.* If inventory constitutes a major portion of working capital, and has relatively slow turnover, the costs to be recognized in valuation are likely to be more inclusive than if it is small in size and rapid in turnover.

2. *The magnitude of product profitability.* In cases where the difference between customary realized selling prices and cost (normal profit margin) is relatively high, the risk of subsequent loss on inventory carried forward is likely to be minimal. In such situations, the extent to which costs are included in inventories may be greater than in cases where product lines have low profit margins.

3. *The regularity and stability of sales patterns.* In situations where the operating volume and marketing pace is consistent from month to month, and inventory quantities are held to required levels, the fluctuation in total inventories on hand is not likely to vary extensively from year to year. In such cases, the method of determining costs used in inventory valuation may not be as critical as in companies in highly volatile, cyclical businesses. In the latter circumstance, the costs used for inventory valuation may require particular consideration of the impact of costs incurred as a result of idle or underused facilities, and other fixed charges. It is usually advisable to exclude excess costs attributable to low operating volume.

4. *Industry practice.* Companies comprising segments of a particular industry often tend to adopt inventory valuation policies comparable to those used by others in that same field. This approach often reflects the considered judgment and experience of seasoned organizations that have evolved a technique which appears to be the most satisfactory. Moreover, investment bankers and others who rely on income and other measurements displayed in financial statements can more readily understand and compare results of competing members of an industry if inventory valuation procedures are based upon a common method.

As stated in the previous section, inventory accounting is concerned with two important elements of financial statement presentation: (1) the asset value of goods on hand and in process, and (2) the flow of values from inventory into cost of sales as deliveries are made to customers. In cases where inventory quantities increase during a period, the thrust of the equation (beginning inventories, plus purchases and production, less ending inventories equals cost of sales) serves to decrease amounts stated for cost of sales when inventory values are calculated on the basis of full, all-inclusive costs. Of course, the opposite is true when inventory costs are determined through use of limited cost factors (more "conservative" values). When a decrement occurs in inventory quantities during a particular period, the impact on income resulting from applying these differing cost concepts would, of course, be contrary to that observed in the case of increasing inventories.

Of the foregoing two elements, the effect upon cost of sales is generally regarded by leading accounting and financial authorities to be more important than residual inventory asset value.[1] This view undoubtedly stems from the concern about profitability of companies as the major indicator of business success. Profitability, in turn, is measured most effectively when costs are appropriately matched against items sold.

Alternatives to cost

In a major sense, therefore, inventories are in the nature of a deferred charge—that is, the asset value of costs incurred that are applicable to anticipated future sales. However, other factors (in addition to the elements of costs recognized and applied) are important to inventory valuation. These may be classified under the general category of "utility" values which, under certain circumstances, may require some modification of costs.

Utility values are alternatives to cost which may require application under accounting convention in situations where accumulated inventory cost is in excess of estimated realizable values, or which could produce other incongruities in financial statements. Notwithstanding the objective of matching costs against related revenues, the traditional accounting axiom of "anticipate no profits, and provide for all losses" serves as a limitation on computed costs that should be carried forward in inventories. Any prospective losses on inventory items that appear likely upon subsequent sale of the goods should be calculated, and inventory values should be reduced accordingly.

Another factor that may affect utility values of inventory items is a significant reduction in acquisition or production cost due to changes in market prices or other events that reflect some deterioration in economic

---

[1] A CPA's *Accounting Research Bulletin 43* states, "A major objective of accounting for inventories is the proper determination of income. . . ."

value of incurred or accumulated costs ascribed to inventory. In such instances, consideration may be given to utilizing the lower replacement costs in lieu of the higher inventory values based on incurred costs.

In situations where products are periodically modified or changed, and new models supplant the old, it is important that the company develop and consistently apply a valuation method to price inventories of obsolete components and units in a manner that gives adequate recognition to their prospective deterioration in sales values. In the automobile, home appliance, and other similar industries, the policy relating to obsolete items usually gives consideration to probable sales of repair or replacement parts for obsolete models still in use by customers.

The use of utility values as a substitute for cost is generally referred to as the "lower of cost or market" theory, commonly used in inventory valuations for accounting purposes. This concept is also described in *Accounting Research Bulletin 43* which is quoted, in part, below.

Cost (for inventory purposes) is satisfactory only if the utility of the goods has not diminished since their acquisition; a loss of utility is to be reflected as a charge against the revenues of the period in which it occurs. Thus, in accounting for inventories, a loss should be recognized whenever the utility of goods is impaired by damage, deterioration, obsolescence, changes in price levels, or other causes. . . .

In describing "market" as a means of developing a utility value for inventories, as an alternative to cost, *ARB 43* provides these broad guidelines concerning the determination of maximum and minimum to be considered:

. . . the term market means current replacement cost (by purchase or reproduction, as the case may be) except that:
1. Market should not exceed the net realizable value (i.e., estimated selling price in the ordinary course of business less reasonably predictable costs of completion and disposal); and
2. Market should not be less than net realizable value reduced by an allowance for an approximately normal profit margin.

ARB 43 observes that these guidelines are subject to some exceptions and that judgment must be exercised in applying them. For example, the bulletin states

Replacement or reproduction prices would not be appropriate as a measure of utility when the estimated sales value, reduced by the costs of completion and disposal, is lower, in which case the realizable value so determined more appropriately measures utility. Furthermore, where the evidence indicates that cost will be recovered with an approximately normal profit upon sale in the ordinary course of business, no loss should be recognized even though replacement or reproduction costs are lower (than inventory costs).

These admonitions concerning utility value of inventories serve as a major restriction upon cost as a basis for stating assets of a business.

Moreover, the calculation of such values and consideration of the extent to which they are to be used instead of cost are frequently among the more difficult and significant accounting problems to be resolved in many situations.

Among other things, "replacement cost," in the case of manufactured goods, involves consideration of the method of applying fixed, or nonvariable cost elements to products. This matter is discussed more fully in subsequent sections of this chapter. For purposes of the "lower of cost or market" determination, however, it should be noted that the replacement cost calculation should ordinarily be determined on the basis of fixed costs as applied to quantities of products normally produced, rather than some lower level of output that might have actually occurred during the period of manufacture applicable to the goods on hand. This approach to a measure of utility value avoids the otherwise illogical result which might attribute greater inventory values to products made in lesser quantities than would have resulted if normal plant utilization had been achieved.

Sequence of cost flow

Concepts of inventory valuation, as they are geared to the determination of cost and the application thereof to goods on hand (except as modified by "utility" values), require some theory or convention about the *time* or period that the inventory costs were incurred. Since the inventory accounts constitute residual values attributable to goods on hand, receive inputs from materials purchased and processes applied, and expel outputs as sales are made to customers, the *sequence* of reckoning costs incurred is an important consideration. Among the generally accepted methods utilized in determining the time sequence of costs for inventory accounting are: (1) first-in, first-out; (2) average cost; (3) last-in, first-out; (4) specific lot; and, (5) base stock.

The *first-in, first-out* method (FIFO) of determining costs for inventory accounting assumes that the "flow" of costs through the inventory is sequenced in an order whereby the earliest costs incurred are attributed to the goods first sold. The resulting inventory costs are, therefore, based upon the most recent costs incurred. In companies where various lots of goods are commingled with others, the FIFO technique can provide a practical means of identifying cost of inventory items on a relatively current basis and, quite often, it tends to coincide with the physical movement of goods and processes through the company's plants and warehouses. While this method ordinarily tends to produce inventory asset values at current costs, any advantage derived from a balance sheet presentation on this basis may be offset by the impact on the cost of sales determination. In situations where prices of materials and other costs are subject to change (through fluctuations in price levels or otherwise), the first-in, first-out method is not likely to result in matching costs against revenues on a current basis. This is caused by the time delay occurring between the acquisition and/or production of inventory, and the date of sale. Thus, this method may produce greater or lesser profit determinations than current costs would develop in relation to current revenues.

Average costs for inventory pricing are used extensively in extraction and processing industries where changing volumes and varying sources of raw materials may cause significant fluctuations in incurred costs from time to time. By averaging the high and low costs over a representative period of time, the inventories and cost of sales determinations tend to reflect a kind of cost stability that may be useful for certain management purposes and financial presentation convenience. In developing average cost calculations, it is customary to use the aggregate of the opening inventory plus incurred costs for a representative period, divided by the total of the units on hand at the beginning of the period and the units produced during the period.

The last-in, first-out method (LIFO) of inventory costing is predicated on the assumption that the costs of products sold should reflect the most recent costs, and that the earliest incurred costs should be retained in the inventory. It should be noted that this procedure is based upon a concept of cost flow through the inventories, and not the actual physical movement of goods. The LIFO method generally provides a useful means of matching current costs against current revenues, and it is particularly effective in reducing the impact of continuing price inflation upon profitability determinations. The virtues of LIFO as a means of measuring operating income may be offset by some limitations upon the resulting asset value of the inventory in presenting financial position. Since the LIFO method results in valuations of inventory goods at the close of a period at the same costs as used in the opening inventory (to the extent that quantities are equivalent), the balance sheet inventories tend to retain costs at price levels extending back to the time the LIFO method was adopted. Thus, after some years of progressive price inflation, an enterprise using this method is likely to evaluate its inventories at prices considerably below current replacement costs.

Use of the LIFO method imposes certain technical accounting problems, especially when this inventory technique is used for income tax, as well as financial reporting purposes. These are discussed later in this chapter.

The *specific lot inventory* valuation method is frequently used by companies engaged in producing custom-made products to customer order. Under this method, costs incurred in connection with each order are accumulated in separate accounts, and inventories are evaluated by totalling the costs for all unbilled orders at a particular point in time. The identification and recording of individual items of material and production costs according to specific order is not particularly difficult where the quantity of orders in process is relatively small. However, in situations where large numbers of orders are frequently in process, classification of incurred cost by job-lot can be a difficult data processing problem. Other difficulties in job-order inventory systems include identification and purging of abnormal costs due to errors in procurement or processing. Also, the calculation of the cost of partial shipments from orders not fully completed can pose some complex problems of identifying that portion of the order costs applicable to the sales made.

The *base stock method* of inventory valuation resembles the LIFO method in that a determined quantity of "normal" inventory requirements is consistently valued at a constant price—usually at a historical cost incurred when such quantity was originally required. Increases in quantity over the base stock level at any given inventory date are valued at one of the other conventional cost-determining methods. If actual inventory quantity levels fall below the base stock quanity, a provision for any loss upon replenishment, based upon the difference between base stock price and replacement cost, is charged to income.

The base stock method is a relatively old concept of inventory accounting that may have certain pertinence in industries such as pipelines or continuous processing companies where the physical system usually contains a relatively constant quantity of inventory at all times. The base stock quantity is not usually changed until plant or processing capacity is changed. Although regarded as an acceptable accounting practice for financial statement purposes, the base stock inventory method is not permitted for federal income tax purposes.

Other variations from the cost concept, in addition to those relating to utility values, are occasionally used for accounting purposes. For example, dealers in securities and producers of precious metals frequently value their inventories at market prices. Agricultural and livestock enterprises may use a type of equivalent market value for inventories of crops and animals. However, these exceptions are relatively rare in commercial and industrial enterprises. The major differences in inventory valuation techniques among various businesses usually are due to varying methods used in determining cost and, sometimes, to interpretations of "market" or other modifications of cost occasioned by utility value differences. These are discussed in following sections of this chapter.

Cost for inventory purposes

The assignment of costs to products for inventory, as well as for other purposes, involves determinations of product components, production, processing, fabrication or other conversion efforts applied, establishment of appropriate units of measure, identification of the cost factors to be considered, and, finally, an understanding of the purpose of the cost-finding process.

Many of the technical problems associated with the determination of product costs relate to fundamental differences in the manner in which inventories are actually acquired, as compared to the manner in which they are sold. The acquisition of raw materials and components or merchandise for resale, as well as the processing of such items, usually occurs in quantities that are economical and efficient from a purchasing or production viewpoint. The specific lots of merchandise purchased or production quantities run, except for custom-designed orders, are seldom coincident with quantities shipped to customers. Moreover, in the case of manufactured products fabricated from various components, the form of the physical items and the quantity in which incurred cost transactions enter inventories are usually different from the form and quantities of products sold which leave the inventories.

Another troublesome aspect of product cost determination stems from the integration of purchasing and production activities where quantities of merchandise or materials acquired, and fabrication processes applied, are related to numerous varieties of products. Sheet steel, for example, may be acquired in sizable purchase lots, but used in making many different products. Similarly, a machine tool forming or cutting process may be used in shaping components of diverse dimensions which are used in several kinds of products.

Thus, the cost identification process is often concerned with *separating* common costs among products, as well as with *accumulating* those costs applicable to specific products. Cost accounting as applied to products, or work in process (unfinished products, components, etc.), is usually developed in terms of quantities of goods normally purchased or produced, but applied to *portions* of such quantities sold or on hand in inventories.

With these general observations in mind, let us consider costs for inventory valuation from several distinct viewpoints, all of which bear upon the determinations. These are:
1. Costs to be recognized (those to be included or excluded).
2. Treatment of capacity costs (consideration of the effect of acquisition or production volume on product costs).
3. Cost accounting methods.

Costs to be recognized

Accounting Research Bulletin 43 states that cost, in accounting for inventories, is ". . . the price paid or consideration given to acquire an (inventory) asset. . . . (This) means . . . the sum of the applicable expenditures and charges directly or indirectly incurred in bringing an article to its existing condition and location."

Federal income tax regulations relating to inventories set forth a definition for inventory cost as follows:

In the case of merchandise on hand at the beginning of the taxable year, (the ending inventory cost shall be) the (same as the opening) inventory price of such goods. . . .

In the case of merchandise purchased since the beginning of the taxable year, (the cost shall be) the invoice price less trade or other discounts, except strictly cash discounts approximating a fair interest rate, which may be deducted or not at the option of the taxpayer. . . . To this net invoice price should be added transportation or other necessary charges incurred in acquiring possession of the goods. . . .

In the case of merchandise produced by the taxpayer since the beginning of the taxable year, (costs shall be) (1) the cost of raw materials and supplies entering into or consumed in connection with the product, (2) expenditures for direct labor, (3) indirect expenses incident to and necessary for the production of the particular article, including in such indirect expenses a reasonable proportion of management expense, but not including any cost of selling or return on capital, whether by way of interest or profit.

In the case of merchandise purchased for resale (without further processing), cost for inventory purposes is usually limited to the vendor's invoice price, plus the charges for freight-in or other delivery services required to bring the goods to the buyer's warehouse or shop. Although expenses associated with receiving, inspecting, handling, and warehousing might be considered a part of the cost incidental to "bringing an article to its existing condition and location," these are seldom recognized as inventory costs. Generally, receiving and other costs are minor in relation to the invoice charges from the purveyor, and are not readily identified with the merchandise items to which the receiving effort has been applied.

Raw materials, components, and other goods acquired for the purpose of fabrication, mixing, assembling, or otherwise producing other items are also valued in inventory at the purchase price paid, plus the cost of transporting the goods to the buyer's location. However, receiving, handling, and storage expenses associated with obtaining such materials are frequently included in "factory overhead," and a portion of these costs may be included in inventory costs, depending upon the cost accounting methods employed in the business. Sometimes a "material handling" overhead charge, including warehousing, intra- and inter-plant transportation, etc. is developed and applied to raw materials inventories. This charge may be applied on the basis of a percentage of raw material purchase cost, weight, or some other appropriate measure. In some instances, the materials-based overhead charge is added to the raw material at the time acquired; more often, the overhead applicable to material content is added only as it physically moves into production. In the latter case, the material-based overhead is included in inventory costs for work in process or finished goods, but not on raw material or components as acquired. In cases where expenses associated with receiving of raw materials are combined with other factory overhead costs, the inclusion of these items in inventory also occurs at the time the process-ing of raw materials occurs, since the method of applying overhead is usually based upon direct labor or some other measure of production.

Raw materials inventory costs, whether determined for unprocessed items or for elements of semi-processed or finished products, may present certain accounting problems when large or diverse quantities of these elements are on hand. Occasionally, some purchases of certain raw materials may be made from alternative suppliers (other than "normal" sources) at invoice prices differing from the customary source. For example, some quantities of commercial-grade steel may be bought from a warehouse to meet an unusual emergency, instead of from the regular mill supplier. Similarly, certain components may be purchased from a substitute supplier when the usual source is temporarily unable to pro-vide them due to labor difficulties, a plant casualty, or other disturbance of production. Often, such purchases are made at prices, or involve transportation costs, above those usually paid. In these circumstances, the price premium is often written off as a period charge against income, and only the normal purchase price and freight are included in inventory values.

Determinations of costs of raw materials in the state originally ac-quired is relatively simple as compared to the task of cost assignment for such materials as they may be cut, shaped, or otherwise fabricated or assembled into semi-finished and finished products. Oftentimes, there is a normal waste or processing loss of physical dimensions, and measure-ment of quantities remaining in the product may need to be recast in order to obtain appropriate equivalents of original raw material content and its cost. Thus, the weight or other measurement of raw material as represented in the product should be converted to the dimensions of such materials normally required to produce the article, and this is usually based upon its production specifications.

In the event of any significant salvage that can be realized from other use or disposal of processing scrap or residuals, these values may be taken into account in developing the appropriate raw material cost applicable to the product. For example, a household appliance cover, fabricated from sheet steel, may be cut, formed, pierced, and trimmed into a product component which may weigh only two-thirds that of the original raw material blank. In addition, the processing techniques may result in some spoilage through imperfect machining or improper han-dling. In such a situation, the raw material cost may be determined in the manner illustrated in Exhibit 1.

Costs applied to conversion of raw materials and components into finished or semi-finished inventory values are usually termed "conver-sion" or "processing" costs. Traditionally, in companies where production or fabrication of products are primarily paced by human effort, the measure of conversion cost has been "direct" labor applied. The direct labor term is normally used to designate the effort of workers whose task can be specifically related to the production of the product or its components—and where the extent of that effort is in direct proportion to the volume of output. Although the measure of direct labor applicable to product cost has, in some instances, been payroll dollars paid or accrued to such workers, a more common method is the use of direct labor time, usually man-hours.

The cost of direct labor incurred and applied to finished or semi-fin-

EXHIBIT 1

Appliance Cover—Raw Material Cost

Made from
    20 ga. 1020 sheet steel blank 20″ x 30″
    Original weight—2.4 lbs. per piece
    Final weight   —1.6 lbs. per piece
    Cost per cwt:
        Invoice $12.50
        Freight-in   .50
        Total $13.00

Processing loss: 2% spoiled components

Cost per 100 finished components		
102 blanks @ 2.4 lbs. each		244.8 lbs.
Cost per cwt. @ $13.00		$31.82
Deduct scrap salvage (244.8 lbs. original weight,		
less 160 lbs. final weight = 84.8 lbs., less 10%		
unrecoverable) 76.3 lbs. @ $0.015/lb. =		1.14
Net material cost per 100 pieces		$30.68

ished products for inventory purposes is subject to certain inclusion and exclusion conventions that are similar in character to those mentioned for raw material costs. Thus, excess direct labor costs due to abnormal errors, whether caused by a temporary lack of appropriate skills, design, or other specification mistakes, or by use of less efficient substitute equipment or of workers commanding a pay rate above the normal required skill levels, are frequently segregated and charged off as period costs and excluded from inventory values.

With the ever-increasing extent to which automated equipment and labor-saving devices are being applied in manufacturing, more and more production activities are being paced by the rates of feed and speed of machinery. The role of the production worker has thus become more of an equipment attendant, and his tasks are not so closely related to production output. This development has promoted the use of "machine-hours" of operation as the more appropriate method of applying conversion or processing costs to products in inventory. In companies engaged in producing large volumes of bulk products from other bulk materials, the measure of production is frequently one of weight or other quantity dimensions of throughput of materials, coordinated with output measures of products made.

Regardless of the measure used to develop product costs, and whether direct labor is dealt with as a separate element or as an integral part of the total conversion costs, a wide range of alternatives may be considered in determining which costs should be included in inventory valuations, and which should be written off as period charges.

It is a general practice to consider all costs and expenses classified as "manufacturing" or "production" as elements to be recognized in inventory valuation. However, there are a number of expense categories that might initially be regarded as a part of manufacturing cost, but on more searching examination, appear to relate more appropriately to the "administrative" expense designation. Overhead elements such as the expenses of the payroll, personnel, cost accounting, estimating, standards, production control, purchasing, engineering, expediting, inventory control, and similar departments may fall into this category. Some organizations may classify all or some of such expense items as manufacturing, while other businesses treat them as a nonproductive overhead and exclude them from recognition in inventory valuation. In part, these differences in treatment may occur because organizational responsibilities for these service functions are sometimes under the direction of a manufacturing executive and, in other cases, they are supervised by the controller or other administrative official.

Other expenses, such as receiving of raw material, incoming inspection, material handling and storage, and similar functions concerned with the receipt and maintenance of a supply of usable materials for processing may be overhead elements that may be appropriately related to inventory cost. However, these types of expenses do not ordinarily pertain to the production process, but rather to the raw material cost itself. As indicated earlier, these expenses may be applied to product costs as a "material overhead" element. The dollar value, weight, or other dimensions of the items are sometimes used to assign such overhead costs to the material or component purchase costs.

Manufacturing or processing overhead, like material and labor costs, sometimes reflects unusual charges incurred as the result of major problems in operations or special nonroutine events. Unusual amounts of spoiled work may bring about more intensive inspection techniques, or key equipment breakdowns may result in special repair costs. A major rearrangement of factory layout or a major clean-up and painting of the plant could increase overhead costs temporarily. These kinds of expenses may be so abnormal as to merit exclusion from inventory costs, or may be given consideration as an element to be recognized as having "benefits" beyond the short period in which the cost is incurred.

In summary, the accounting problems to be considered in determining which costs are to be recognized in inventory relate both to the *nature* of the costs (classification) and to the *amount* of such costs incurred as they may or may not be appropriate to inventory values. Businesses employing the "standard cost" method are likely to have a valuable systematic means of identifying any abnormal amounts of cost incurred. Under a typical standard cost system, the differences between the planned and actual costs are expelled into "variance" accounts which facilitate analysis of the exceptions and determination of which unusual costs should be excluded from inventory or which cost changes should be recognized in the inventory. In companies not using the standard cost method, the principal signal indicative of possible abnormal costs incurred is usually a significant change in overhead rate from traditional levels.

Capacity costs

Another major factor affecting the inventory inclusion or exclusion of incurred costs is the impact of manufacturing or processing volume upon incurred costs. A significant portion of the expenses normally associated with the production of goods relates to the costs of providing the facilities and organization needed to operate the plant or establishment. Many of these charges occur on a routine, regular basis and, although their amounts may change in response to price level fluctuations or management policy decisions, they do not ordinarily increase or decrease in proportion to the level of production activity in the business. These costs are commonly referred to as "fixed" or "standby" expenses.

Rents, depreciation, local taxes, salaried clerks and supervisors, casualty insurance, and certain kinds of maintenance expenses are typically among those in the fixed cost category. In the determination of costs to be included in inventory valuation, it is usually appropriate to consider and deal with those of a fixed nature in a manner that will eliminate any excesses attributable to unused capacity.

Unless due recognition is given to the impact of fixed costs, it is quite possible that major changes in production volume could result in product cost determinations that are illogical and incompatible with sound value. The behavior characteristics of fixed costs, and the paradox that might result if they are not properly considered, is illustrated by the following example of product cost calculations for two periods experiencing different production volumes.

The $0.27 cost increase (approximately 9 percent) between the two periods, as shown above, may be largely attributed to the reduction in quantity.

If the experience of these two periods reflects the costs to be reckoned with for inventory valuation, and if no consideration is given to the capacity cost factor, the value assigned to products on hand at the close of the second period would be significantly greater than that assigned to the inventory at the close of the first period. To increase inventory values merely because of lower volume of output would seem to be inconsistent with any sound concept of inventory pricing.

The solution to the capacity cost problem in determining appropriate inventory values involves the quantification of two factors: (1) establishing "normal" capacity measures, and (2) identifying the "fixed" costs.

Normal capacity is frequently based upon levels of production output that may be expected under operating conditions that fully utilize the

	Period I	Period II
Fixed costs incurred................................	$ 32,000	$31,000
Variable costs (those that tend to fluctuate in relation to production volume).....................	68,000	59,000
Total..	$100,000	$90,000
Production volume (quantity of products made, in units)..	34,000	28,000
Cost per unit..	$ 2.94	$ 3.21

plant facilities on a schedule customary in the type of industry or in the company's own traditions. The measure of capacity may be units of product or equivalent (in single-product organizations); more frequently, direct labor hours, machine hours, or processing hours are used. Usually, these volume measures are determined for key operating departments or facilities that represent the critical limits of output. These are calculated to reflect the normal plant schedules for the number of work shifts regularly employed, and give consideration to periodic shut-downs for maintenance, vacation and holiday programs, etc. These and other pertinent considerations may produce a *theoretical* capacity measure. Another alternative is to use the actual output achieved during a sustained period of prior experience to determine a level of *practical* capacity. Many other variations, using combinations of these approaches, or especially tailored methods, can be devised to accommodate this determination.

Fixed expenses of the category previously mentioned (depreciation, rent, insurance, etc.) may be identified fairly easily. Other expense account classifications, such as indirect labor, utility charges, factory supplies, etc., may include certain elements of both a fixed and variable nature. Some portion of these kinds of costs is likely to increase or decrease in proportion to operating activity, and the remainder may be incidental to providing or maintaining the organization and facilities in a functional condition. The separation of the fixed and variable segments may be accomplished by analysis of the composition of each account according to the purpose of the various functions. For example, the electric utility expense may be segregated into the portion of power used for plant lighting and similar stand-by purposes, and the portion used to operate productive machinery. Often, a study of historical behavior patterns, observing the extent to which increases or decreases in certain overhead expenses tend to respond to changing volumes of plant activity may provide worthwhile statistical evidence of the degree of fixed and variable elements included in the account.

The fixed expense amounts are related to capacity measures, rather than to actual operating volumes, in determining the appropriate inventory cost rates. This technique may be illustrated by using the information shown in the previous example, together with the added element of practical capacity. Assuming plant capacity to be 40,000 units per period, the cost for inventory purposes might be computed as follows:

	Period I	Period II
Fixed costs..................	$32,000	$31,000
Capacity in units..............	40,000	40,000
Fixed cost per unit............	$ 0.80	$ 0.78
Variable costs................	$68,000	$59,000
Production in units............	34,000	28,000
Variable cost per unit.........	$ 2.00	$ 2.11
Total cost per unit (Fixed plus variable cost)....	$ 2.80	$ 2.89

The results shown above for Periods I and II are respectively $0.14 and $0.32 per unit less than the original cost computations, and these differences are due to the elimination of unused capacity costs from the inventory values.

Direct costing

Proponents of the direct costing theory prefer to limit inventory values to those manufacturing or production costs that tend to increase or decrease in proportion to production volume. Thus, only the "variable" costs shown in the foregoing example would be included in inventory under the direct cost method. This technique tends to simplify analyses of operating results and may contribute to more effective short-run decisions on product pricing.

For inventory valuation purposes, however, elimination of all fixed costs may present some problems. The accelerating practice of substituting automated equipment for human labor, common in industrial companies, tends to decrease the portion of variable cost, and to increase the fixed cost applicable to manufactured products. Thus, by confining inventory values to variable costs alone, the inventory asset amounts for a given quantity of products tend to become lower for each period in which automation innovations occur, and the fixed costs charged to current operations tend to increase. Moreover, costs identifiable as being directly applicable to specific products are not necessarily limited to those that vary with production volume. In a number of situations, certain processes of production are clearly applicable to particular products, even though much of the cost of those processes is "fixed" in behavior tendencies. The omission of these costs from inventory values may significantly affect the measure of profitability at the time of sale of the products and fail to adequately match costs against revenues—a major objective of financial accounting.

Notwithstanding these problems, some companies, particularly those in the machine tool and glass industries, have adopted the direct costing method for inventory valuation for internal management purposes. In many of these instances, the direct costs are supplemented by the addition of allocated fixed costs to evaluate inventories for published financial statement and income tax purposes. A few companies use direct costing for inventory for all purposes and, where consistency in policy is paramount, and there is little significance to the impact on earnings, this practice has found acceptance for tax and financial accounting purposes.

Retail method

The determination of "cost" for inventories could be especially difficult in businesses dealing in an extremely wide variety of merchandise, such as full-line department stores. This problem has been traditionally handled by use of the "retail method" for inventory valuation, and is based upon the premise that the selling price for all merchandise is readily identifiable from price tags attached to or displayed with the stocks on hand. By maintaining statistical information about the relationship of selling price to cost for various classes of merchandise, the quantity of goods on hand valued at retail (selling) prices may be reduced to cost by applying appropriate percentages based upon such statistics.

The key to this procedure is to develop totals of retail prices, as well as costs, for all merchandise purchased, and to classify all purchases according to department or section (usually based upon managerial responsibility and general category of merchandise, e.g., ladies ready-to-wear, men's clothing, housewares, etc.). The excess of retail prices over cost of purchases, in relation to the retail price of such acquisitions, is used to arrive at a percentage of "mark-up." By combining the opening inventory and merchandise purchases for a given accounting period, and valuing all elements at both retail prices and at cost, the departmental mark-up percentage may be applied to the unit's inventory at retail prices in order to eliminate the dollar amount of mark-up and arrive at a composite cost.

The original mark-up assigned to merchandise purchased is frequently adjusted by additional mark-ups and by mark-downs, mark-down cancellations, and similar changes as merchandising tactics may require. However, in determining the mark-up percentage for purposes of calculating inventory cost, based upon retail value, only additional mark-ups (and similar retail adjustments) are normally recognized. Mark-downs (net of mark-down cancellations), special discounts, etc., are usually ignored. Although this practice may result in a cost amount lower than incurred purchase price for any marked-down items that remain in inventory, the presumption is that this result serves to recognize a loss in utility value comparable to a write-down to market.

Application of these general principles of the retail method may be illustrated by Exhibit 2.

EXHIBIT 2

	Retail	Mark-up %	Cost
Beginning inventory	$25,000	40 %	$15,000
Purchases	40,000	40 %	24,000
Freight in			500
Additional mark-ups	300		
Total	$65,300	39.5%	$39,500
Less			
Mark-downs (net of cancellations)	$ 700		
Employee and other discounts	600		
Total reductions	$ 1,300		—0—
	$64,000		$39,500
Less sales	34,000		
Closing inventory—retail	$30,000		
Closing inventory—cost		39.5%	$18,150

With the aid of computers and sophisticated systems, many department stores are turning to more precise cost identification than that offered by the averages used in the retail inventory method. In developing detailed item costs, the department stores are able to achieve better marketing strategies, improved buying methods, and sounder merchandising practices. By matching item costs so developed against sales, profitability may be measured more accurately for diverse items having different mark-ups and varying turnover volumes in each department. For the most part, however, the large retail establishments use item cost data for managerial planning and control, and continue to use the retail method for inventory costing.

LIFO

The specific provisions of the Internal Revenue Code and Regulations, together with some other complexities in calculating inventories under the last-in, first-out method, merit further discussion in this chapter. Although isolated applications of the LIFO principle occurred in prior years, it was not until 1938 that it was recognized as an acceptable inventory pricing method for tax purposes. In the following year the "elective method" embracing the LIFO concept became a part of the 1939 Revenue Code and established the basic tax provisions generally applicable ever since.

Income tax law and related regulations and other interpretations are important to all inventory accounting, but this is especially true of the LIFO method. It seems likely that the opportunity for long-term, if not indefinite, postponement of income taxes which might be achieved through the use of LIFO in a protracted period of continuous monetary inflation has been a major factor influencing corporate decisions to adopt this method. The requirements of the various income tax rules relative to the use of LIFO include the following:

1. In the year that the LIFO method is adopted, the opening inventory (based upon whatever previous method might have been employed) must be stated at "cost." Thus, if the company had formerly used "cost or market" (cost being based upon the first-in, first-out method), and any portion of that inventory was valued at market, the market write-downs must be eliminated.

2. The records and reports of the company must use the LIFO method in conformity with the valuation of inventories used for tax purposes. Unlike many other accounting policies where tax and financial reporting methods may differ (depreciation, deferred research, development, etc.), the stipulations about LIFO impose this conformity requirement.

3. In calculating LIFO inventory values, no write-downs to market value are permitted for tax purposes. However, in financial statement preparation for shareholders, creditors, or others, a reduction in inventory value, where current market prices are lower than LIFO cost, may be given effect, but not recognized for income tax purposes (an apparent inconsistency with point 2 above).

Growing investor interest in profitability trends as a leading measure of corporate success has probably dampened interest in LIFO as an instrument of business policy. The tax savings potential and the traditional virtues of conservatism in accounting, as provided through the use of LIFO, may be difficult to maintain in the face of strong pressures to report increased earnings per share of common stock. Nevertheless, LIFO continues to have strong representation as an inventory valuation policy in major industrial enterprises. Among 83 industrial companies having sales in excess of $1 billion annually (*Fortune* magazine 1968 listing), 39 used the LIFO method for all or a portion of their inventory valuations. Six of the top ten of these businesses utilized LIFO.

Originally, LIFO was conceived as a means of valuing inventories of bulk materials where physical quantities of such goods on hand at the beginning and end of the accounting period could be readily determined. Since the method of assumed cost flow contemplated that the cost of goods most recently acquired was the cost of most recent sales, it followed that the cost of goods remaining in inventory was that applicable to the goods earliest acquired. Thus, the inventory values to be assigned at the close of the period were identical to those at the beginning of the period—to the extent that quantities were the same. Any increase in inventory quantities was valued at costs incurred during the period. Any decrease in quantities was eliminated from inventories at cost levels relating to the latest acquisitions included in the opening inventory. The effect of this costing process may be illustrated in a simple case of a series of LIFO inventory calculations that might be applied to bulk materials as shown in Exhibit 3.

EXHIBIT 3

	Quantity	Cost per unit	Amount
Year I			
Opening inventory	10,000 lbs.	$1.00	$10,000
Acquisitions	30,000 lbs.	1.20	36,000
Total available	40,000 lbs.		$46,000
Sold-from acquisitions	25,000 lbs.	1.20	30,000
Closing inventory comprised of opening inventory	10,000 lbs.	1.00	$10,000
Year I increment	5,000 lbs.	1.20	6,000
Total closing inventory	15,000 lbs.		$16,000
Year II			
Acquisitions	35,000 lbs.	1.30	45,500
Total available	50,000 lbs.		$61,500
Sold			
From Year II acquisitions	35,000 lbs.	1.30	$45,500
From Year I acquisitions	2,000 lbs.	1.20	2,400
Total sold	37,000 lbs.		$47,900
Closing inventory comprised of			
Opening inventory—Year I	10,000 lbs.	1.00	$10,000
Acquisitions—Year I	3,000 lbs.	1.20	3,600
Total closing inventory	13,000 lbs.		$13,600
Year III			
Acquisitions	40,000 lbs.	1.40	$56,000
Total available	53,000 lbs.		$69,000
Sold from acquisition	35,000 lbs.	1.40	49,000
Closing inventory comprised of			
Opening inventory—Year I	10,000 lbs.	1.00	$10,000
Acquisitions—Year I	3,000 lbs.	1.20	3,600
Acquisitions—Year II	5,000 lbs.	1.40	7,000
	18,000 lbs.		$20,600

The LIFO inventory valuation at the close of Year III ($20,600) may be contrasted with the valuation that might have been determined under the first-in, first-out method which would be based upon most recent cost:

$$18,000 \text{ lbs. } @\$1.40 = \$25,200$$

From this example, it may be noted that the cost of sales for the three-year period shown would be $4,600 greater under the LIFO method than would have been determined under the FIFO method. This difference is, of course, the amount of the difference between the respective inventory valuations at the close of the period.

The above illustration also displays the manner in which the inventory composition at the close of each period is classified according to the year of acquisition (frequently termed "layers"). This procedure would continue indefinitely and, accordingly, some of the layers for companies having adopted the LIFO method twenty or thirty years ago are likely to be comprised of costs incurred at that time.

Use of the specific quantities of materials as a means of determining LIFO values for inventory purposes is commonly referred to as the "unit" method. This technique has some rather apparent disadvantages. Among other things, over a long period of time technological changes tend to affect the quality and nature of materials and products used or produced. For example, the growing use of pelletized or highly beneficiated iron ore concentrates during recent years has made it difficult to compare these materials with mine-grade ores generally used in iron and steel production a generation ago. Moreover, in fabricated products, new materials are being used and traditional materials are being eliminated in the evolution of product design. The result of these changes in material and product specifications has been to exhaust one variety of inventory and supplant it with a new one. When this occurs, and where the company uses the "unit" method of calculating LIFO inventory values, the various cost layers comprising the old materials are eliminated—usually involving the recording of an increased profit as the lower, pre-inflationary costs move out of inventory and into cost of sales. At this same time, the continuing enterprise begins its buildup of the new substitute materials at cost levels current at time of acquisition.

An alternative to the unit method of computing LIFO inventories is the *dollar value* method. This technique was developed for use by companies having a large variety of materials or merchandise in inventory and where the unit method was impracticable. The historic precedent for the dollar value method was the Hutzler Brothers case, in which that department store's use of this method was upheld in the U.S. Tax Court in 1947. In 1949, Income Tax Regulations were amended to recognize the dollar value method specifically as an acceptable LIFO technique for general application.

The dollar value approach to LIFO inventory calculation utilizes money value as the measure of equivalent quantity changes in inventory, instead of the physical quantities utilized by the unit method. Dollar amounts, appropriately employed, permit the combination of a wide variety of items into a single group or pool where money values can be applied to each inventory element and provide a common measure of equivalents. The advantages of this system are evident in manufacturing companies having many thousands of different inventory components, or in retailing and wholesaling establishments carrying an equally large variety of merchandise items. However, some of these same advantages are also present in enterprises having a limited number of inventory items, but where the specifications of materials or products are subject to change over a period of time. It is important to note that the dollar value method embraces labor and other conversion cost elements, as well as physical materials or components of the inventory. Accordingly, as the production process may be extended to include manufacture of parts formerly purchased, the substitution of conversion cost for purchase cost may be accommodated through application of the dollar value method.

This method is implemented essentially through the use of consistent costs which are used to develop current inventories in terms of values extant at the date the LIFO method was adopted. These values are usually referred to as the "base" prices or costs. By comparing the dollar totals of beginning and ending inventories of a single pool, both priced at the same base costs, a determination may be made of the extent of any increase or decrease in such inventories. Any increase in dollar amounts of inventories, computed through application of such base prices, are converted to current costs by use of index numbers representing the relationship of current costs to base prices. These indexes may be determined by pricing and extending the entire inventory at both current and base costs, or by a suitable representative sample. By relating the totals of current costs to base cost to obtain the price index, the current cost for any increase in inventory may be determined by applying that index to the portion of inventory increase as measured by base cost amounts. This technique may be illustrated by the example shown in Exhibit 4.

The inventory elements to be included in a single pool for computing LIFO may be of a heterogenous nature but, according to Income Tax Regulations, should be limited to items comprising a "natural business unit." If, for example, a business is comprised of two divisions, one involved in producing household appliances and the other concerned with manufacturing chemicals, the inventory items for each might be classified into separate pools. In such a case, the LIFO calculations for each pool would be made independently.

Some caution in creating separate pools is necessary. In situations where separate natural business units utilize common materials or components, the inventory asset values and income determination could be artificially affected by the caprice of having an increase in one LIFO pool, but a decrease in the other, simply because of the divisional status of the common materials at the reckoning date. In such a case, the decrement in one of the pools is likely to result in a variation in

EXHIBIT 4

Year I

Opening inventory at current cost (base price)..............$100,000	
Closing inventory	
at base price.. 110,000	
at current (year-end) cost $132,000.......................	
Inventory increase (at base price).........................$ 10,000	
Price index (relationship of current cost to base price)	
$132,000 ÷ $110,000...................................... 1.20	
Current cost of inventory increase $10,000 × 1.20 = ...$ 12,000	
LIFO value of closing inventory	
Base quantity at base price............................$100,000	
Year I increment at current cost.......................... 12,000	
Total...$112,000	

Year II

Closing inventory at base price............................$106,000
Opening inventory at base price............................ 110,000
Inventory decrease at base price (no current cost calcula-
  tion necessary because of decrease in inventory).......$ 4,000
LIFO value of closing inventory
  Base quantity at base price............................$100,000
  Year I increment at Year I closing inventory cost—re-
  maining base price value of original layer ($10,000
  less $4,000 = $6,000) at price index of 1.20............. 7,200
    Total...$107,200

Year III

Closing inventory
  at base price..$130,000
  at current (year-end) price $169,000
Opening inventory at base price............................ 106,000
Inventory increase at base price...........................$ 24,000
Price index (169,000 ÷ $130,000)............................ 1.30
Current cost of inventory increase $24,000 × 1.30 = ...$ 31,200
LIFO value of closing inventory
  Base quantity at base price............................$100,000
  Year I increment (remaining after Year II decrement).... 7,200
  Year III increment....................................... 31,200
    Total...$138,400

reportable income, merely because of an intra-company transfer of materials.

Other LIFO problems may arise in developing base cost data for items currently used, but not available at the date LIFO was adopted. Many department stores overcome this dilemma by utilizing index numbers as published by U.S. Government agencies to convert current costs of inventory items back to base costs (instead of pricing and extending the inventory at base cost amounts). Some companies use the "link-chain" method of developing base costs by developing year-to-year price relationships. Inventories at current cost will be converted to base cost by application of the cumulative effect of each of the several years' price changes in arriving at equivalent base year costs. This method, however, is not the preferred one according to Internal Revenue Regulations.

Inventory quantity determination

Inventory values, as used in determining asset values and, in turn, income for a period, are based upon costs or other amounts assigned to goods on hand at the beginning and end of the period. Ascertaining the quantities of items on hand is often a complicated and demanding task.

Many businesses determine inventory quantities by count, weight, or other measurement at the close of each fiscal year. By identifying the quantities so determined in a suitable manner, costs can be applied to each group of items, extensions made, and totals determined. Other businesses choose a "physical" inventory reckoning date at a point prior to the end of the fiscal year and, after determining the cost value at that date, adjust the total for additions and deductions for the interval between that date and the end of the year.

Companies maintaining detailed perpetual quantity records take physical inventories of selected items during the course of the year, adjust the records as necessary to reflect accurate quantities at that date, and use the "on-hand" balances of the quantity records at the year end to provide the quantities for inventory valuation.

Many variations of these methods for quantity measurement may be used, depending upon the efficacy of internal control measures and the significance and nature of inventories and other pertinent factors. The importance of inventories, the variety of items, and the need to ascertain the condition of stock as well as quantities for operating and financial purposes usually impose a requirement for some kind of physical verification and reconcilement with book records at reasonable intervals.

Careful planning and coordinated execution is essential in taking physical inventory. Errors in count, improper identification, omission of items, or duplications of the same items can result in serious misstatements of inventory values. Similarly, the application of wrong costs, calculation errors in extensions, footings, and summary totals must be guarded against.

When taking physical inventories of an entire plant area, encompassing a wide variety of inventory items ranging from raw materials and components to semi-finished parts and assemblies, as well as finished products, the program should be developed well in advance and communicated to all personnel who are to take part. The plan should give particular attention to the following matters:

1. Preferably, the plant should cease operations, and no inventory should be moved from one location to another during the counting process.

2. Prior warning to production supervisors concerning physical inventory plans should include suggestions for stacking items in a manner that will facilitate measurement and, to the extent feasible, separation of items into convenient batches of common components in similar stages of completion.

3. Production or routing tickets pertaining to each batch of items should be placed in accessible places, attached or adjacent to the items, to facilitate identification by counters.

4. Inventory tickets or lists, providing blank spaces to insert quantities, unit of measure, item identification, degree of processing completed, condition of stock, etc. should be provided to counters and necessary instructions given to assure proper completion of needed information.

5. Counters should be assigned specific plant areas and move through them in an organized fashion to facilitate coverage of all items on hand.

6. When original counters have completed a section or area, other personnel should review the inventory lists or tickets, and by appropriate test checking ascertain that the counts and other information have been satisfactorily and accurately recorded, and that no errors of omission or duplication have been made. (Usually, this test checking process is coordinated with the inventory tests made by the company's independent public accountants.)

7. Upon completion of physical determination, care should be exercised to assure that all inventory lists or cards are accounted for, and then assembled or arranged to facilitate pricing.

8. Pricing bases should be test checked against appropriate cost sources, and arithmetic calculations also tested to determine that all elements of totals are accurate.

9. Precautions to assure proper "cut-off" should be taken. This involves ascertaining that appropriate consideration is given to the impact of "in transit" items covering incoming items billed by vendors and not received, or other items received but not billed. Similar steps should be taken with respect to products shipped and billing to customers.

10. Inventory value totals so determined should be compared to book records and the book amounts adjusted as appropriate. Significant differences between the books and physical inventories, if any, should be carefully investigated. Such differences may be symptomatic of serious flaws in the accounting system or inadequate source information or control, or of unrecorded losses due to pilferage, unreported spoilage, or other physical deterioration.

Among the more important considerations in the physical inventory process is the careful assessment of condition of the stock being counted. Shopworn merchandise, corroded parts, broken or damaged products, and similar evidence of limited utility are not readily identified any other way. These kinds of items are likely to need some downward adjustment of value. Quantities of items in excess of readily usable or salable levels may be determined from usage or sales records, and consideration given to appropriate valuation adjustments through such analyses. A careful perusal should be made of item quantity totals as shown on physical inventory listings, with particular attention given to large numbers of high unit value items, as errors in such items may be significant to the total inventory valuation.

In some companies having appropriate records, and where the quantities and varieties of items are extensive, physical inventory determinations may be satisfactorily accomplished through the use of statistical sampling techniques. The particulars of this approach should be worked out by a competent statistician and be organized so that the company's accountants can make adequate tests of the procedures.

Financial statement presentation of inventories

Accounting Research Bulletin 43 of the American Institute of CPA's observes that "The basis of stating inventories . . . should be disclosed in the financial statements . . ." (Chapter 4). Also, ". . . it is important that the amounts at which current assets are stated be supplemented by information which reveals . . . for the various classifications of inventory items, the basis upon which their amounts are stated and, where practicable, indication of the method of determining the cost—c.g., average cost, first-in, first-out, last-in, first-out, etc." (Chapter 3).

Regulations S-X of the Securities and Exchange Commission, which govern the form and content of financial statements of companies required to file with that Agency, prescribe certain disclosures concerning inventories in Rule 5–02, item 6. This provision calls for substantially the same information as *ARB 43*, and adds the requirement to state separately (in the balance sheet or footnote), if practicable, "the major classes of inventory such as (1) finished goods; (2) work in process; (3) raw materials; and (4) supplies." In Rule 5–03, these regulations pertaining to income statements require that the registrant "indicate the amount of opening and closing inventories used in the computation (of cost of goods sold), and state the basis of determining such amounts."

In some instances, companies using the LIFO method to determine cost for inventory purposes have indicated (usually in a footnote) the total current cost of the inventories. This disclosure may be of assistance to investment analysts and others who seek to compare asset values and earnings of a LIFO-using business with another using cost methods for inventory resulting in a more current value.

Inventory accounting system

The structure of the accounting system relating to inventories should be developed to "balance" the following basic objectives:

1. To yield inventory data useful to management in determining the amount of inventories at the close of each interim account period (monthly, quarterly, etc.) by categories that permit evaluation of:
   a) Turnover velocity by product lines.
   b) Trends in stock status (raw materials, work in process, finished goods).
   c) Potential problem areas, such as failures to process source data concerning materials received, scrap generated, etc. through the accounting system.
2. To minimize data processing effort involved in obtaining and recording input and output to and from the inventory accounts, and to establish the means to develop a high degree of reliability.

By careful consideration of these two factors, a business may develop a plan that suits its particular needs. With regard to the data processing matter, it should be noted that accounting system accommodation of transfers of inventory from the raw material status to work in process to finished products frequently involves massive amounts of paperwork which can multiply the number of required entries many times. In some situations, useful classifications of inventories in the accounting records can be developed by using groupings based upon the *nature* of the costs, as opposed to the status of the physical items. Thus, categories such as (1) material, (2) labor, and (3) factory overhead may be used to obtain approximations of inventory status useful for internal analytical purposes.

A major problem in maintaining accurate accounting records for inventory purposes is the constant fluctuation in costs of materials and labor moving into the inventories. The task of monitoring these changes and recognizing their impact upon costs extracted from inventory and charged to cost of sales, or to scrap or rework expense, can be a tremendous one, especially where the variety of components, operations, or products is extensive. Unless the inputs and outputs to inventory are appropriately matched, in dollar as well as quantity measures, it is evident that the resulting monetary balance in inventory accounts will not reflect the true quantities on hand and evaluation thereof.

By keeping a watchful eye on the inventory accounts, their balances at the close of each interim period, as well as the volume of inputs and outputs in dollars, a corporate controller can gain considerable insight about the business. Moreover, by analyzing other facets of operations (sales-order-production volumes, etc.) he can sense whether or not the inventories are in line. It is not unusual to find occasional lapses in processing vital source information through the inventory accounts. Problems of unreported scrap, errors in production reporting, and failures to charge out supplies or materials actually consumed may, for example, cause an overstatement of interim inventories. Failure to detect these circumstances may result in substantial year-end inventory adjustments at the time physical inventories are taken.

In many companies, particularly those having complex, multiproduct operations, the controller may establish appropriate inventory reserves during the periods between physical inventory determinations. These reserves may be related to the size of operating volume and be created on the basis of a percentage of calculated cost of sales as a "cushion" against possible inventory shortages. The percentage or amount of reserve provision may be based upon shortage experiences of the past and adjusted to recognize unusual circumstances that may be troublesome. Introductions of new products, special difficulties with certain raw materials, suspiciously high inventory balances, and similar clues can be useful in arriving at sound judgments about the amount of inventory shrinkage reserve appropriate in the circumstances.

Standard costs

A large number of industrial companies maintain inventory accounts and develop product and process costs through the use of a standard cost system. Standard costs are predetermined or planned costs, established through industrial engineering and other analytic techniques, for all materials, components, and productive effort normally required to complete salable products. Thus, the specifications of raw material and parts needed for each product, both as to quantities and purchase cost, together with quantities and cost of productive labor and applicable overhead required to manufacture or produce each such product are established in advance as standard costs.

As raw materials or components are purchased, the standard cost per unit is applied to the quantities so acquired, and the standard cost is used as the inventory input amount. Any differences between actual purchase cost and the standard are expelled into "variance" accounts as an income or expense element for the period. Similarly, as the productive or manufacturing processes are applied to raw materials to convert them into products, the standard cost of such processing is also treated as an inventory input, based upon the operations or processes completed. Differences between the standard costs and actual incurred costs are charged or credited to a variance account as a period item.

By charging only the standard costs of materials and productive effort to inventory as an input, the task of extracting costs of products sold or otherwise disposed of can be simplified. Standard costs of all materials and production processes required to make or produce a finished item can be compiled for each such product in advance. Thus, the predetermined standard cost of each product sold can be applied to the quantities delivered and obviate the need for a cost analysis that might otherwise be necessary to develop the inventory output information.

In addition to the simplification of identifying costs for inventory purposes, the standard cost approach has many other advantages over other forms of cost accounting. Since these are not directly related to the subject of this chapter, only brief mention is made, as follows:

1. Costs are stabilized at standard amounts, thus facilitating analyses of profitability of sales by territory, product line, customer or other category without penalty or benefit that might occur if fluctuating cost measures were used.

2. Identifying and summarizing variances by type and by managerial responsibility (plant, department, etc.) and reporting them to concerned executives can provide valuable intelligence about critical operating matters. In this way, the extent to which operating costs are varying from planned levels can be quickly ascertained, and the principal causes readily determined.

3. Unusual costs incurred due to errors or other abnormal events or circumstances can be eliminated from the inventories, thus avoiding the capitalization of these period expenses.

When standard costs are employed, it is customary to analyze variance accounts carefully to determine which, if any, of the differences between actual and standard costs should be included in inventory values. Variances caused by price changes in raw materials, wage rate adjustments, or changes in manufacturing methods are among those which should be considered. Often, these occurrences are recognized by revising the standards to reflect the changes. In other cases, the standards may be adjusted for inventory valuation purposes by applying a percentage increase or decrease to reflect the appropriate variance amounts to arrive at approximate incurred costs suitable for inventory pricing.

Accounting for property, plant, and equipment

Robert S. Kay*

This chapter discusses the principles of accounting for property, plant and equipment—their acquisition, expiration of assigned carrying amounts, their disposal, and several other related matters.

The term "property, plant and equipment" comprises tangible assets held for the services they yield in the production of other goods and services, or wasting assets (natural resources) which upon extraction become part of the product.

Criteria for capitalization

Usually, it is not difficult to determine whether a particular item is a capitalizable addition or an expense item. However, there are situations where the nature of the item is on the border line (such as machinery overhauling), and it is advisable for a company to have a set of rules created to cover as many of these situations as possible.

One very common criterion involved in most companies is that no property expenditure is capitalized if it represents an expenditure of less than a specified amount, perhaps ranging from $50 in small companies to $500 in large companies. This very practical policy avoids cluttering up

---

* Partner, Touche Ross and Company, Chicago.

the records with excessive detail. Also, it is generally agreed that, except in rare instances, property expenditures which are calculated to expire within one year are not considered to be capitalizable as property, plant and equipment, and if they are deferred, they may best be classified in a prepaid expense account.

Some companies have taken the position that, depending upon the nature of the item involved, it is not advisable to record it as a property addition even if it has a life of up to three years. An example of this might be small tools, where their control is so difficult that it is simpler merely to record these as a deferred charge to be written off ratably. It should be noted, however, that such decisions are made on a practical, rather than a theoretical, basis. It would be perfectly appropriate to record tools, dies and other short-lived property assets within the property accounts, so long as there could be some reasonable assurance as to their being on hand and in productive use, in the amounts net of accumulated depreciation or amortization at which they are carried on the books.

Despite any well-intentioned criteria a company sets for itself internally, it may run into situations where the Internal Revenue Service will, upon examination of its tax returns, disagree with something which has been expensed instead of capitalized. A question arises as to how to reflect this adjustment in the records.

Theoretically speaking, such capitalizations by the IRS would not be recorded on the books since the IRS should not be in a position to dictate generally accepted accounting principles which resulted in the original expensing of the item. However, from a practical standpoint, companies have taken either of two approaches:

1. Capitalization of the item taken exception to by IRS and depreciating it over its remaining useful life. The capitalization amount, less related income tax assessed, would be treated, if material, as an extraordinary item in presenting results of operations. If not material, the net amount would be included in earnings before extraordinary items.
2. Treatment of the related additional income tax expense as a deferred tax charge to be amortized over the assigned remaining life.

Consistency

Whatever methods are chosen to record property accounts and to depreciate them, such methods should be consistently applied. When changes occur, depending upon their magnitude, it may be necessary to disclose in published reports that such changes were made, and what effect they have, presently or prospectively, upon earnings.

The remainder of this chapter is divided into sections on acquisitions, depreciation and amortization, disposals and retirements, wasting assets, and other matters.

Acquisitions

Property, plant and equipment should be carried in the accounts of commercial enterprises at the cost of putting the asset in the condition and location for its intended use. When several assets are acquired at a group price, an allocation of such price must be made based on their relative fair values. In the case of land, demolition costs relating to pre-existing structures are often properly includible in the land cost. The elements of cost vary somewhat depending on the manner in which the asset is acquired.

Purchase for cash

Cost is represented by the net cash purchase price (after all discounts), plus incidental costs such as freight and installation. Such incidental costs should be included in the capitalized amount whether paid for to others or performed with company facilities and labor. The appropriate amount to be capitalized in the latter instance is governed by the principles discussed in a subsequent section on self-construction.

In general, sales and other non-income taxes are a part of the capitalizable cost, but these may instead be charged directly to an expense account (and deducted for income tax purposes as incurred if the tax is one which is assessed directly on the purchaser).

Investment tax credits on purchases of eligible equipment, realized as a reduction of income taxes payable, have been in many situations regarded as a reduction in or offset against the cost of the related acquired asset. This subject is discussed further under "Other Matters" later in this chapter.

Purchase on contract

In many cases, properties are acquired under a conditional sales or other installment contract, and the elements of cost basically follow the principles outlined above. However, the interest charges included in the total payments should, of course, be excluded from the capitalized amount. Where properties are acquired under an installment or other delayed-payment contract which does not separately state the financing charges, a determination should be made of the excludible amount using an appropriate discount rate. Normal trade terms for payment, even if somewhat extended, will not ordinarily require the imputing of a discount.

Purchase for equity securities

If a company's own equity securities are used to acquire properties, the par or stated value cannot be assumed to represent cost, although by coincidence this might be the case. The preferred method of assigning cost in this situation is to ascertain the amount of money which could have been obtained through the sale of the securities for cash. Should this evaluation of the securities not be possible, the fair value of the property acquired should be used.

In some cases an entire business, including its properties, is acquired by the issuance of equity securities. If such an acquisition has been treated as a pooling of interests for accounting purposes, the net assets, including properties, of the acquired company should be recorded at the amounts at which they have been carried theretofore. If such an acquisition is treated as a purchase for accounting purposes, the net assets, including properties, of the acquired company should be recorded at their fair values. If the acquisition has been treated as a partial pooling (part-purchase, part-pooling) the excess of fair market value over cost of net assets may only be recorded in the proportion the purchase part of the transaction bears to the entire transaction. A discussion of accounting for business combinations may be found in Chapter 57 of this *Handbook*.

As a practical matter, such fair value adjustments are difficult to apply to the individual acquired assets, if for no other reason than the task of revising property records. Accordingly, the excess usually is adequately handled if it is split according to depreciation life categories, to permit the proper recording of depreciation.

Trade-ins and other exchanges

When part of the consideration given in the acquisition of a property is a similar property traded-in, it is preferable to record as the cost of the new property its net cash purchase price plus the unexpired cost of the trade-in, where the new item is to fulfill basically that function performed by the trade-in. Of course, the traded-in item should be specifically removed from the accounts in conjunction with the re-entry of its unexpired cost as part of the cost of the new item.

Alternatively, it is permissible to treat trade-ins as dispositions not related to the newly acquired item, considering the proceeds on disposition to be the trade-in allowance granted. The cost of the new item would, therefore, be the stated price before trade-in allowance. This approach is often not realistic because the trade-in allowance may be inflated to reduce an equally overstated selling price for the new item, the net cash purchase price being the controlling figure. Considerable care must be exercised to avoid the misstatements which can occur under this approach.

Exchanges of property which are not trade-ins require an evaluation of the fair value of the property relinquished, or less preferably, the fair value of the property received. Using either of these fair values as the cost of the acquired property will result in the recognition of a gain or loss if unexpired cost of the relinquished property is not the same amount. As a practical matter, in such exchanges the cost of acquired property may be considered to be equal to the unexpired cost of the relinquished property, in the absence of reasonably ascertainable fair values.

Self-construction

Technically, the cost to be assigned to self-constructed property, plant and equipment is much the same as that applied to purchased assets, i.e., they are recorded at the net price paid to get them in condition and location for use. As a practical matter, there is usually some difficulty in determining the cost of self-constructed property, because of the need to accumulate itemized direct costs of materials and labor, as well as to determine some appropriate method of charging indirect costs to the construction. Overhead costs include supervision, engineering and interest during construction. To the extent these costs are specifically identifiable with the project, they should be added to its cost. It may also be appropriate to allocate certain overhead costs not specifically identifiable with the project, if the existence of a portion of these costs can be attributed to the project.

A common practice for companies which do not normally construct their own properties is to add in only the incremental overhead, that is, that amount which can be directly attributed to the construction. Further, in the case of industrial companies, capitalized interest is generally limited to interest incurred during the construction period on amounts borrowed specifically for construction purposes.

In accounting for construction in progress, it is desirable to maintain separate accounts for each individual project. In a large project, it may also be desirable to maintain separate accounts for identifiable major portions of the project, especially where there will be a further need to know separately the cost of such components—such as where differing depreciable lives might be attached to the various components.

In certain situations, a company may produce a product which, in addition to being sold to the company's customers, is also utilized within the company as a capitalized item. Generally speaking, profits recorded internally, based upon normal trade customer selling prices, should be eliminated. This is discussed in more detail under "Unrealized Profits in Property, Plant and Equipment" later in this chapter, as are "Transfers" of property assets.

Properties leased from others

While leased properties are not generally accounted for as a portion of property, plant and equipment, there are certain circumstances under which such properties should be capitalized.

The property should be recorded as an asset, and the related obligation as a liability, if the terms of the lease result in the creation of a material equity in the property. Such an equity is presumed to exist, in a non-cancelable lease or in a lease cancelable only upon the occurrence of some remote contingency, if either of the two following conditions exist:

1. The initial term of the lease is materially less than the useful life of the property, and the lessee has the option to renew the lease for the remaining useful life of the property at substantially less than the fair rental value; or

2. The lessee has the right, during or at the expiration of the lease, to acquire the property at a price which at the inception of the lease appears to be substantially less than the probable fair value of the property at the time or times of permitted acquisition by the lessee.[1]

Obviously, it is often difficult to determine when lease payments result in the creation of an equity. Unless it is clear that no material equity in the property will result from the lease, the existence of one or more of the following factors will tend to indicate that the lease should be accounted for as a purchase:

1. The property was acquired by the lessor to meet the special needs of the lessee, and will probably be usable only for that purpose and only by the lessee in the "special purpose" situation.

2. The lease is a net lease, and its term corresponds substantially to the estimated useful life of the property.

3. The lessee has guaranteed the obligations of the lessor with respect to the property leased.

4. The lessee has treated the lease as a purchase for tax purposes.

When the lessee and the lessor are related, leases should often be treated as purchases even though they do not fall into the categories mentioned above. When related parties are involved, a lease should be recorded as a purchase if the primary purpose of ownership of the property by the lessor is to lease it to the lessee and:

1. The lease payments are pledged to secure the debts of the lessor; or

2. The lessee is able, directly or indirectly, to control or influence significantly the actions of the lessor with respect to the lease.

As illustrations, these conditions are frequently presented where:

1. The lessee and the lessor have common officers, directors, or shareholders to a significant degree.

2. The lessor has been created by the lessee and is substantially dependent upon the lessee for its operations.

3. The lessee has the right to acquire control of the lessor.

Leases which are clearly, in substance, installment purchases of property should be recorded as purchases. The property and the obligation should be stated in the balance sheet at an appropriate discounted

---

[1] "Reporting of Leases in Financial Statements of Lessees," *Opinions of the Accounting Principles Board, Opinion No. 5* (New York: American Institute of Certified Public Accountants, 1964).

amount of future payments under the lease agreements. The method of amortizing the capitalized amount of the asset should be determined by reference to the nature and use of the asset, without reference to the period over which the related obligation is discharged.

Therefore, in summary, the cost of an asset at the time it is acquired by lease is equal to the initial prepayment amount, if any, and the present value of future rental payments (and future lump-sum payments, where applicable), and such cost is to be depreciated over the useful life of the property, regardless of the term of the lease.

In general, sale-and-lease-back transactions are not considered to be independent transactions. Therefore, material gains or losses resulting from the sale of the properties which are the subject of sale-and-lease-back transactions should be amortized over the life of the lease as an adjustment of the rental cost or, if the leased property is capitalized, as an adjustment of depreciation. There may be unusual circumstances in which it is appropriate to recognize the gain or loss in such a transaction, but such cases would be rare.[2]

Commencing with fiscal years beginning after December 31, 1966, subsidiaries must now be consolidated, regardless of when such subsidiaries were created, if they are primarily engaged in leasing property or facilities to their parent or other affiliates. Such consolidation, of course, most effectively accomplishes the capitalization of property leased from a related party.

Additions or betterments to existing assets

There are situations in which significant changes are made to existing assets, without necessarily retiring the entire asset. Examples might be the cost involved in revising a machine to perform more efficiently, reroofing of a building, or an overhaul of a machine. While considerable discretion must be used in differentiating between capitalizable costs and expense amounts in such situations, the basic principle to be followed is that expenditures which are expected to extend the useful life or productivity of the property should be capitalized.

Capitalizable expenditures of this nature should be recorded as additions to the asset account, and if there is any retirement of assets associated with the expenditure, the cost of such retirement and the accumulated depreciation related thereto should be removed from the accounts.

Where a company maintains its assets in composite accounts, the cost of the retired assets should be charged to the accumulated depreciation account, and the addition or betterment added to the asset account. There are some situations in which the expenditure in connection with an addition or betterment (situations probably more aptly described as

---

[2] For further information see publication cited in footnote 1.

renewals or major repairs), may be charged against the accumulated depreciation account.

Donated assets

Occasionally property of a reasonably estimable value is acquired without cost. Fair value should be used in recording this property on the books, with the credit going to an appropriately titled paid-in capital account. However, where the donation is made by an affiliated person or company, it is usually required that the donor's cost be carried through to the donee.

Depreciation and amortization

Depreciation accounting is a system of accounting which aims to distribute the cost of tangible capital assets, less salvage (if any), over the estimated useful life of the unit, which may be a group of assets, in a systematic and rational manner. It is a process of allocation, not of valuation. Depreciation for the year is the portion of the total charge under such a system that is allocated to the year. Although the allocation may properly take into account occurrences during the year, it is not intended to be a measurement of the effect of all such occurrences.[3]

Simply stated, depreciation and amortization are designed to charge operations with the cost of capitalized assets (except land), less the related estimated salvage value, over the estimated life of the asset. Guideline lives have been promulgated by the Internal Revenue Service in Revenue Procedure 62–21, and such lives purport to give actual experience of taxpayers. Guideline lives should be carefully considered when establishing lives on depreciable assets.

Often, as a practical matter, salvage value is ignored in depreciation computations if it is less than ten percent of the asset amount, since for federal income tax purposes, salvage may be ignored to the extent of ten percent even if it is greater.

With the prevalence of different methods and rates of depreciation for book and tax purposes, there is no compelling reason to ignore salvage for book purposes. For a discussion of accounting treatment of differences between book and tax depreciation, see "Income Tax Allocation" later in this chapter.

Depreciation methods

1. Straight-line method. Under this method, the cost of the capitalized asset, less its estimated salvage value, is spread evenly over its estimated useful life. Useful life connotes the period over which the asset

---

[3] "Review and Resume," *Accounting Terminology Bulletins, Bulletin Number 1* (New York: American Institute of Certified Public Accountants, 1953).

can be expected to be used by its owner, even though the asset might physically exist longer than the period; the salvage value should give appropriate effect to those situations where the asset will still have utility to someone other than its present owner at the end of its depreciation span.

Certain conventions must be adopted as to when to begin and end the charging of depreciation with respect to a particular asset. One common method is to record a half year's depreciation in the year of acquisition, and a half year's depreciation in the year of retirement. In other situations, where depreciation is calculated on a monthly basis, the charge might begin with the month following acquisition and end during the month of disposal. Criteria adopted should be consistently followed.

2. Declining-balance method. This is an accelerated method under which considerably heavier depreciation is recorded early in the life of the asset, and lesser amounts in the later years, as compared with the straight-line method. Under this method, the depreciation rate which would exist under the straight-line method for the particular asset involved would be increased by a multiple (usually double in the case of new assets and one-and-a-half times in the case of used assets), and the resulting rate would be applied to the net undepreciated cost. In theory, there will always be a small "tail" of undepreciated cost, since the same rate is always being applied to a lesser amount. As a practical matter, this is usually not a problem, inasmuch as declining-balance depreciation charges should cease when the net undepreciated cost is reduced to estimated salvage value. Alternatively, if there is no salvage value to be recognized, a switch may be made from declining-balance depreciation to straight-line at any point in the process to eliminate the "tail" over the then-estimated remaining useful life.

As an example, the $1,000 asset having a ten year life and a salvage amount of $200, would be depreciated as shown in the following exhibit:

Year	Net Undepreciated Cost	Depreciation for the Year
1	$1,000	$100*
2	900	180
3	720	144
4	576	115
5	461	92
6	369	74
7	295	59
8	236	36

* A half year's depreciation was taken in the year of addition.

Note that this asset was depreciated down to salvage value of $200 in slightly under eight years.

3. Sum-of-year's digits method. This method is also an accelerated method in that a considerably higher portion of depreciable cost is charged to operations early in the life of the asset, and less later in the life, as compared with the straight-line method. Under this method, the depreciation charge is calculated by determining the sum of the individual years of useful life. For example, an asset with a ten-year useful life has a sum-of-year's digits of 55, this being the total of the individual numbers 1 through 10. A simple formula for obtaining sum-of-the-years digits for any useful life is as follows:

$$n\left(\frac{n+1}{2}\right)$$

where n signifies the length in years of useful life.

Depreciation for the first year is based upon a fraction which uses the remaining years of life as a numerator and the sum-of-the-years digits as the denominator. Salvage value is deducted from the cost of the asset in calculating the amount subject to depreciation, unlike the declining-balance method. An example, again using an asset having a cost of $1,000, a salvage amount of $200 (and therefore a depreciable base of $800) and an estimated life of ten years, is as follows:

Year	Depreciation for the Year Fraction	Amount
1	10/55	$145
2	9/55	131
3	8/55	116
4	7/55	102
5	6/55	87
6	5/55	73
7	4/55	58
8	3/55	44
9	2/55	29
10	1/55	15
Total depreciation over ten years		$800

For simplicity, a full year's depreciation is shown for the year of addition. Taking a half year's depreciation would require a fraction of 5/55 (one-half of 10/55) in the first year, 9.5/55 in the second year (5/55 + 4.5/55), 8.5/55 in the third year (4.5/55 + 4/55), and so forth.

4. Unit of production method. Under this method, the useful life of a property, usually an item of machinery, is stated in terms of the

number of units produced by it, or hours of its operation, rather than in years. For example, it might be estimated that a particular machine is capable of producing 100,000 units of a product before it reaches the stage where it is no longer useful to the owner. The depreciation during a given year would be based upon the units produced during that year as a proportion of total estimated units, perhaps with a minimum annual depreciation charge if the units are not running up to expectations. This method does not appear too often because of the difficulty involved in estimating total units.

5. Sinking fund method. Under the sinking fund method, depreciation is a lower amount in earlier years, increasing to a higher amount in later years. In theory, it provides depreciation equal to the sum of a periodic provision, accumulating over useful life at a specified rate of interest, and interest on previous accumulations of periodic payments. This method has little use in commercial practice because of what seems to be a lack of correlation of depreciation provisions with the incidence of wear and tear on the asset, and the unacceptability to the Securities and Exchange Commission of the use of this method in filings.

Amortization of leasehold improvements

This is simply a manner of recording the expiration of an asset installed in leased property, which asset may not be removed at the expiration of the lease. Leasehold improvements in rented premises are the most common type of asset amortized over the life of a lease.

In determining the amortization period, due consideration must be given to the likelihood of exercising renewal options under the existing lease.

To the extent that leasehold improvements have a useful life less than the lease term, they should be depreciated over their shorter useful life.

Variations within depreciation methods

1. Unit basis. In this instance, each individual asset is depreciated, ordinarily under some system of identification which records the depreciable cost of the individual asset. Often such a system takes the form of individual asset cards showing depreciation to be charged by period, and the sum of the amounts shown on each individual card for a particular period will equal depreciation expense for that period. The unit method is advantageous in arriving at net undepreciated cost in the event of sale or other disposal, and it is also quite valuable for purposes of physical accountability for individual items, as it presents a detailed record against which the items may be counted or

inspected. It is also quite useful for insurance considerations. With present-day data processing systems, the considerable detail involved in a unit-record system does not seem to present the problems that sometimes exist in manual-unit systems.

2. Composite accounts. In this variation, assets usually of the same general class are grouped, even though individually they would have varying lives. A single life (composite life) is applied to the entire account, such rate being a weighted average of the rates for the various items in the account.

A composite account may have individual assets with lives varying, for example, from ten-year assets to fifty-year assets, as in the case of an entire building. However, only a single rate, say 2½ percent, would be used in depreciating these assets.

3. Lapse schedules. This is simply a grouping of all assets acquired within a particular period, usually a year, each group consisting of assets of the same class and life. Depreciation is calculated and laid out on a schedule which will show the "lapsing" of the cost of each group over its assigned life.

Each of the three variations indicated above generally can be used with the methods of depreciation described earlier. For example, composite accounts may be depreciated on straight-line, accelerated, or other methods of depreciation.

Only on the unit basis is it possible to know, without specific calculation, the net undepreciated cost of a particular asset. If lapse schedules are used, it is necessary to make a computation on a lapse basis for the individual asset when such information is required. In the case of composite accounts, it is usually not necessary to know the net undepreciated cost of a single asset, but should this be required, the presumption is that the rate which would have been applied to the individual asset had it not been in a composite account is the one which will be used in determining its presently undepreciated cost—rather than the rate which has been applied to the entire composite account.

Obsolescence and other extraordinary diminishment in usefulness

There are situations in which an asset built or obtained for a particular purpose at a time when its useful life was readily estimable, is somewhat suddenly found to have lost all or a large part of its originally estimated usefulness. Often this occurs because of considerable improvements in technology, or changes in the nature of or demand for the product to which the asset contributes.

In the case of a suddenly shortened useful life, the remaining undepreciated cost should be spread over the remaining useful life. In a case where an asset suddenly has no remaining useful life as the result of an extraordinary occurrence, the undepreciated cost, less salvage value, will have to be charged against operations.

For situations which fall into the classification described in this section, the circumstances involved in each individual case will determine whether the charge against earnings is an extraordinary item, or is simply another charge used in arriving at earnings before extraordinary items.

Changes in depreciation methods and lives

The method and rate of depreciation chosen should, in theory, be suitable to the nature of the assets involved, resulting in a reasonable matching of cost with the benefits derived from the use of the assets. As a practical matter, a method is often chosen because of its simplicity and the projected effect it should have upon earnings over future years.

Accordingly, changes in depreciation methods are often made for practical reasons, such as the lessening of recordkeeping detail, the facilitation of depreciation computation, or the permissible accomplishment of a desired effect in the operating statements. A very common change observed lately is the switch from accelerated depreciation for book purposes to straight-line depreciation for book purposes, notwithstanding that accelerated depreciation will continue for federal income tax purposes (with tax allocation).

When a change in method is made, the net undepreciated cost at that point should be spread over the remaining period of original life in a fashion dependent upon the nature of the change. For example, a change from an accelerated method to a straight-line method of a ten-year asset at the end of its seventh year would be accomplished by taking the net undepreciated cost at the end of the seventh year and spreading this evenly over the remaining three years. A variant on this might be to determine what the original straight-line charge would have been, and to merely charge that amount for such periods after the change as will expire the undepreciated cost; of course, under this variation, the asset will be fully depreciated prior to the end of its useful life.

In the somewhat unusual change from straight-line to an accelerated method on existing assets, it would be appropriate to take the net undepreciated cost and depreciate that over the remaining years of original life using the assumption that the asset was just put into use at that time. For example, a ten-year asset being changed from straight-line to double-declining balance at the end of the fifth year would subsequently be depreciated as if it were a five-year asset with a cost equal to the undepreciated cost at the end of the fifth year. In a change from straight-line to sum-of-the-years digits in the example described, the digits would be determined on the basis of a five-year asset.

While depreciation is a method of allocation rather than valuation, it is possible that situations will arise where the depreciation life assigned to a given asset is subsequently found to be significantly inappropriate. When this occurs, it is usually advisable to "relife," if an important portion of total property assets are in this position.

Earlier, under "Obsolescence," there was some discussion of what effectively amounts to a reduction in depreciation lives. For a stretch-out of depreciation life, under a straight-line method, the net undepreciated cost would merely be spread over the presently estimated years of remaining life. In an accelerated method, the double-declining rate to apply, or the rate equivalent of the sum-of-the-years digits fraction, would be determined on the basis of the revised estimated remaining life.

Disposals and retirements

Ultimately, property assets will be disposed of, either by sale, scrapping, exchange or abandonment. Because depreciation expense charged over the period of usage of the asset was merely an allocation of the cost, it is probable that a gain or loss will occur at this point in time. Also, price-level changes will certainly have an effect upon gains or losses, and, in recent years, such changes have had a tendency to create gains.

Generally, gains or losses on the disposal of property assets are treated as income or expense. However, where assets have been maintained in composite accounts, a gain or loss should not be reflected unless the disposal is considered extraordinary, since by its very nature a composite account contains some assets which will expire before the life-span set for the entire account. When recording a disposal in composite accounts, the cost of the asset is removed from the asset account and charged to the accumulated depreciation account, and the proceeds or other consideration received upon disposal are credited to the accumulated depreciation account.

Sales

When a property asset is sold, its cost should be removed from the asset account, the applicable accumulated depreciation should be removed from the accumulated depreciation account, and the difference between the net undepreciated cost and the proceeds received upon sale will be the gain or the loss. This computation is quite simple to make when assets are carried in the records on a unit basis. When assets are maintained on lapse schedules, there is a presumption that the original cost of the asset being disposed of can be found by reference to subrecords of vendors' invoices; to determine accumulated depreciation, a computation will have to be made for the individual asset based on the assigned life and method being used on the lapse schedule.

As indicated above, ordinary disposals of assets maintained on the composite basis will not result in gain or loss, and should be treated as indicated. However, in the case of extraordinary disposals, such as an entire plant, the asset cost is identified and accumulated depreciation is calculated based on the individual life of the asset involved, without regard to the life assigned to the entire composite account. When this is completed, the cost and accumulated depreciation are removed, as in the case of unit-basis accounts, and a gain or loss is calculated, based upon the proceeds received.

Trade-ins and other exchanges

Earlier in this chapter, trade-ins and exchanges were discussed from the standpoint of the new asset acquired. There it was indicated that, under the preferable method of handling trade-ins as having a cost equal to the net cash purchase price of the new asset plus the unexpired cost of the trade-in, the item traded in should be specifically removed from the accounts in conjunction with the re-entry of its unexpired cost as part of the cost of the new item.

Therefore, in a trade-in situation, the entry required above is effectively accomplished by charging accumulated depreciation for the amount therein with respect to the traded-in asset, and crediting that amount to the asset account, preparatory to recording the new acquisition at its net cash purchase price.

Under the alternative method of treating trade-ins as dispositions not related to the newly acquired item, of course, such disposition would be treated simply as a sale, as indicated in the preceding section. Other exchanges, or "swaps," would require, under preferred treatment, the recording of the acquired property at the fair value of the property relinquished, or, alternatively, at the fair value of the property received. Accordingly, it is possible to have a gain equal to the difference between the fair value of the relinquished property (or, alternatively, the new property) and the undepreciated cost of the property relinquished.

Involuntary conversions

On occasion, property assets are destroyed or effectively removed from the owner's usage by actions beyond his control. A few examples would be fires, floods, or condemnation proceedings under a governmental unit's powers of eminent domain. In general, a gain or loss will occur upon involuntary conversion, and this is measured by the difference between the insurance or other proceeds and the net undepreciated cost of the property.

However, an alternative approach, where the affected property is replaced, would be to defer the gain or loss by either adding the loss to the cost of the newly acquired property or deducting the gain from its cost. In this circumstance, the cost as adjusted for the gain or loss becomes the cost for future depreciation purposes. This alternative method, which is common for tax purposes, is rarely considered acceptable for financial-statement purposes, since the converted assets have in fact been replaced by assets which will now last longer than the original assets would have had they not lost their usefulness. Also, the replacement assets are not being stated at cost under this method.

Retirements

While, in the broad sense, any removal of a property asset from service is a retirement, this term is meant here to signify those instances where (1) an asset has become fully depreciated, and (2) it is the policy of the company to treat such items as retirements, removing them from the accounts. If no salvage value has been assigned, the accumulated depreciation will equal the cost of the asset, and a charge to the accumulated depreciation account and a credit to the asset account will accomplish the retirement. Of course, to the extent any salvage value has been assigned to the asset involved, it cannot be removed from the accounts, since it will still have some cost residual. On the other hand, as indicated earlier, should an asset continue to be used beyond its originally estimated depreciable life, consideration should be given to continuing the depreciation, up to the extent of the salvage value originally assigned.

If a lapse schedule is in use and it is desired that fully depreciated assets be removed from the records, this would have to be done annually with respect to an entire year's acquisitions. In such a case, problems are created to the extent that salvage values were assigned to any of the items.

Composite accounts, even when maintained by year of addition, should not have retirements reflected because of the fact that some portion of the assets in the account will remain in use, and this factor was originally contemplated in using composite accounts.

Particularly because of income tax regulations, the removal of fully depreciated assets still in use is becoming more infrequent. The practice also makes it extremely difficult to account physically for property assets.

Abandonments

An abandonment represents the disposal of a property asset without receiving any consideration, except perhaps for salvage or other reclamation of parts. In some instances, this takes the form of simply giving up title to the property, and its ownership would escheat under legal rules. Abandonment is somewhat different from scrapping, in that the latter presumes there is no utility left in the property, whereas an abandonment permits the possibility that there could be some utility left, but not to its present owners.

Transfers

There are occasions in which property assets are transferred from one unit of a company to another, or from one classification of accounts to another. In general, transfers among company units should be performed on the basis that original cost and accumulated depreciation to date of transfer are recorded on the acquiring unit's books, so that depreciation can continue according to the original plan. For income tax purposes, this might not be possible if transfers are among entities filing separate returns. If the transfer creates such changes in circumstances as would suggest a relifing, this matter should be handled as indicated earlier in this chapter.

Transfers of property assets among account classifications should likewise have both original cost and depreciation transferred to the respective new classifications, rather than having net undepreciated cost transferred.

Wasting assets

Wasting assets are natural resources which, when extracted from their natural state, become salable merchandise either just as extracted or after further processing. The extraction process causes physical exhaustion of the property, and depletion, as distinguished from depreciation, is the term used to describe the provision for such physical exhaustion.

The acquisition of land containing valuable mineral deposits or other natural resource should be accounted for by allocating its cost between the residual value of the land and the depletable natural resource. In the normal situation, considerable amounts are often spent for exploration, options, and other investigatory costs, without assurance that a successful discovery will result. Even if it were reasonable to assume that discoveries would be made, there is the further problem of making estimates of extractable quantities. This uncertainty characteristic creates some difficult problems of cost determination and allocation. It is acceptable either to capitalize or expense the investigatory outlays, but the prevailing practice is to capitalize costs which can be identified with successful acquisitions or developments and to expense the others.

Depletion is usually computed by the unit-of-production method. The carrying amount of the asset is divided by the estimated number of recoverable units to determine the charge per unit to be made upon extraction. The unit measurement to be used is, preferably, the marketing unit, but where this is not feasible, the extracting unit may be used. An example of a marketing unit is board feet of lumber, whereas an example of an extraction unit is a ton of ore. In instances where there is no further processing after extraction, the extracting unit is equivalent to the marketing unit.

Depletion rates should be adjusted as it is determined that the extent of the natural resource is more or less than was previously estimated. In effect, the unexpired cost assigned to the wasting assets should be spread over the remaining units to be obtained, such computation being updated whenever better information presents itself.

For income tax purposes, depletion allowances will ordinarily be based upon income from the property. It is not considered acceptable to use such income tax allowances for financial reporting. Assuming that the tax depletion will be greater than book depletion, there is no need to provide for any deferred income taxes, unless the total depletion for tax purposes is limited to the cost basis of the property. In this case, of course, book depletion will ultimately catch up with tax depletion, and thus, deferred taxes should be provided (except in rare circumstances) against the timing difference relating to the deductions for book and tax purposes.

Other matters

Appraisals

At present, it is not considered acceptable to carry properties at appraised valuations. This is distinguished, however, from the situation where appraisals are used in determining the allocation of cost to a group purchase of properties, or where properties are being acquired through the issuance of equity securities. These situations are covered earlier in this chapter.

Undoubtedly, appraisal valuations based on market values or replacement costs are quite useful in the determination of salvage values, insurance values, and tax-assessment figures. Also, appraisal figures could be useful in determining, in those situations where the property asset is a very important element in the cost of a finished product, what selling price should be attached to the product.

Where an appraisal is to be recorded in the financial statements despite its nonconformity with generally accepted accounting principles, the excess of the appraisal valuation over net undepreciated cost at the time of such valuation should be credited to "paid-in capital arising from appraisal" or, more succinctly, "appraisal surplus." Subsequently, depreciation should be computed on the written-up amounts. It would be inconsistent to claim higher valuations in the balance sheet for the appraised property, but not to record depreciation on the new basis.

Somewhat akin to appraisal valuations is the adjusting of financial statements, including property assets, to current price levels, generally by the application of price indices. While presentations of financial statements restated for general price level changes are becoming more prevalent, they are not now generally accepted in place of cost-basis financial statements, but may be shown as supplementary information.

Investment tax credit

The Internal Revenue Code of 1954, as amended, provides for an investment credit equal to a specified percentage of cost of certain eligible depreciable assets acquired and placed into service in 1962 and thereafter. There are certain statutory limitations on the maximum amount of the investment credit which may be used in any one year to reduce the income tax payable for that year. Once an investment credit is allowed, it is subject to recapture should the property not be held for the required length of time.

The Accounting Principles Board of the American Institute of Certified Public Accountants has concluded that the investment credit is a reduction in or offset against the cost of the acquired asset, thereby reducing the depreciation otherwise chargeable in a greater amount to future accounting periods. However, also generally accepted (and undoubtedly more popular) is the practice of crediting investment tax credits directly to income, as a reduction of income tax expense for the period during which such credits are realized. This is generally referred to as the "flow-through" method.

When the deferral method (reduction of asset cost) is adopted, it is appropriate to either directly reduce the cost of the individual assets, or to create an offsetting account, included under the property section. Where the asset cost is directly reduced, of course, the depreciation calculated against such assets will be directly affected. When an offsetting account is used, it might be appropriate simply to amortize this account over a suitable period, depending upon the life of the related assets.

Most companies are on the "flow-through" method because of its simplicity, and because of the immediate benefit it has upon earnings. It must be emphasized, regardless of the method in use on the books in accounting for the investment credit, investment tax credits are available for tax purposes only when there are taxes otherwise due from which it may be deducted, and then only within specified limitations.

At present there is active consideration of the repeal of the investment tax credit and of its carry-forward utilization provisions.

Income tax allocation

It is a common practice for companies to use a different depreciation method for tax purposes from the one which is used for book purposes. In general, such variances exist to increase cash flow to the company by minimizing taxes payable currently, although theoretically, such differences will be paid up in the future. The classic example is the use of straight-line depreciation method for book purposes, and an accelerated method for tax purposes.

To the extent there is a greater deduction for depreciation in the tax return than on the books, the effect of this timing difference should be measured, and the related tax, computed at rates currently in effect, should be credited to a deferred tax account. The amount of tax to be credited to the deferred account is determined by calculating the tax on income both before and after the deduction of the timing difference, and the difference between the two tax amounts thus calculated is the deferred tax applicable to the timing difference.

In calculating the deferred tax applicable to the timing difference, the investment tax credit should be taken into account as a reduction of the two tax figures calculated, any limitations on the amount of investment tax credit being observed.

The requirement that income tax allocation be applied to timing differences, such as depreciation, became effective for fiscal years beginning after December 31, 1967, under pronouncements of the Accounting Principles Board. This opinion does not require retroactive adoption, and therefore some companies will find themselves in the position of not having provided deferred taxes on all timing differences in the past, but now being required to do so with respect to similar transactions subsequent to the effective date of the opinion. To the extent that a one-time adjustment is made providing for such "back" deferred taxes, then the tax effects of timing differences may be calculated on a grouped basis— that is, reversals of prior-period items may be offset against creation of new similar timing differences in the current period, in determining the deferred tax to be applied at current rates. However, if the company chooses not to provide for the "back" deferred taxes, it may not use this net-change method—instead, the effects of timing differences upon income tax provision, as such prior-period differences reverse, must be considered independently of the creation of new timing differences. In this way, ultimately a company will work off its old timing differences and be fully on tax allocation accounting. For further discussion of income tax allocation, see Chapter 59 of this *Handbook*.

Unrealized profits in property, plant, and equipment

Earlier in this chapter under "Self-construction" there was a brief reference to profits created internally by a company utilizing its own products as capitalizable assets, such products also being sold to the company's customers. Profits recorded in such transactions should be eliminated in preparing financial statements, on the premise that the profit is not realized (except in the sense of reduced depreciation over the life of the asset). The profit-elimination amount should be such, at any point in time, that it reduces the net carrying value of the asset to what it would have been had the asset been recorded at manufacturing cost, and depreciated on that basis.

While there may be some situations where it is appropriate to consider the profit on self-constructed assets to be realized at the time the assets are put into service, such situations become less frequent as the asset involved moves further into a special-purpose classification.

Intercompany profits on property, plant, or equipment may also be created in the transfer of an existing asset from one unit to another at an amount in excess of its undepreciated cost. In these circumstances, the general rule of elimination still applies. Where the acquiring unit uses a different depreciation method than the relinquishing unit, the amount of profit elimination will be measured, after transfer, based on the depreciation method of the acquiring unit.

Reference should also be made to the discussion of "Transfers" earlier in this chapter.

Diverse practices

Extensive activities in mergers and acquisitions, particularly those treated as poolings of interests, have resulted in the combining, in consolidated financial statements, of property, plant, and equipment accounts of a number of units, which accounts may be maintained on different bases from unit to unit. For example, the acquiring company may maintain its property accounts on the basis of not capitalizing any individual expenditures under $200, and depreciating assets capitalized on a straight-line method. The acquired company may have followed the policy of capitalizing all asset acquisitions which individually were in excess of $50, and may be using accelerated methods on the books.

While the capitalization policies are usually not radically different so as to require retroactive adjustment, it might be desirable, in recording the acquisition, to restate the property accounts of the acquired unit in terms of what the depreciation accumulated would have been had the acquired company followed the acquiring company's policies. This is a fairly normal "pooling" adjustment. More often, however, no retroactive adjustment is made. In this circumstance, it would be advisable that the acquired company conform its policies to that of the acquirer, effective at the date of acquisition; as a practical matter, this conformance usually takes some period of time.

The foregoing discussion presumes that there is no compelling reason for the use of a different method of depreciation in the acquired company. It is possible, however, that, because of the nature of the business of the acquired company, a certain method of depreciation may be appropriate for its assets, notwithstanding the method used by the parent.

It is also possible, in an acquisition not treated as a full pooling of interests, for the assets of the acquired company to be carried at a different amount than they were carried on the books of the previous owner before acquisition.

Quasi reorganizations or corporate readjustments

In situations now relatively infrequent, a corporation may decide to write-down its plant accounts to more realistic amounts, in conjunction with a revaluation of all of its assets. Such write-downs should result in plant account figures which are fairly stated at the time of the adjustment, and should not be unduly conservative where estimates are required.

Should such a quasi reorganization occur, it is preferable to eliminate the accumulated depreciation account in the readjustment.

Subsequent to a quasi reorganization, it is likely that the tax basis of the revalued assets will be the same as before the revaluation, resulting in greater depreciation being permitted for tax purposes than for book purposes. Ordinarily, the company performing such a readjustment will have been in a loss position, and will probably have loss carry-forwards for tax purposes. Once the "reorganized" corporation begins the recording of profits, the tax benefit from utilization of loss carry-forwards— to the extent not recognized in the recording of the reorganization— should be credited to capital surplus.

Idle or standby facilities

A financial-statement classification for property, plant, and equipment should generally include only property held with reasonable expectation of its being used in the business. Should there be temporarily idled plant or standby equipment, it is not necessary to segregate this equipment. However, should there be important amounts of property still owned but no longer expected to be used in the business, such assets should ordinarily be written-down to estimated realizable value.

Facilities leased to others

Accounting for properties leased to others depends upon the nature of the lease. If it is an operating lease, where the risks and rewards of ownership lie with the lessor, the property should be carried at its cost in a classification separate from but probably just preceding or following property, plant, and equipment used in the business, and depreciation should be recorded based upon the estimated useful life of such properties. If the lease is a financing lease, where the risks and rewards of ownership lie with the lessee, the total lease payment should be recorded as a receivable in the financial statements, and the unearned income (total lease payments less residual value and, in some cases, lease acquisition costs) should be deducted therefrom.

Also, the residual value of the leased property, that is, the estimated realizable amount upon termination of the lease, should be shown in a separate caption in or near the property accounts.

Financial statement presentation and disclosure

The following items should be dissclosed in financial statements, with respect to property, plant, and equipment:

a) Total amount of depreciation expense for the period
b) Balances of major classes of depreciable assets
c) Accumulated depreciation, either by major class of depreciable assets or in total and
d) A general description of the method or methods used in computing depreciation with respect to the major classes of depreciable assets.

Generally, this information has been shown by most companies in their published reports, but it is now required by an Accounting Principles Board Opinion, effective for fiscal years beginning after December 31, 1967.[4]

In reporting under requirements of the Securities and Exchange Commission, it has been general practice to give considerable detail on property accounts. This is not necessarily suggested for published financial statements, especially that portion of the SEC footnote which gives ranges of lives applicable to particular classes of assets. It would not seem to be informative disclosure to show a wide range, such as 5 to 40 years for buildings, in a published report. However, to the extent it is possible to show some fairly close ranges applicable to particular classes of assets, this would be desirable.

The SEC also requires schedules covering property, plant, and equipment (Schedule V) and accumulated depreciation (Schedule VI) to be included in certain filings, such as forms S–1 and 10–K. These schedules show, for each year required, beginning and ending balances by major classes, with intervening transactions, in columnar form. Specific information is available in Regulation S–X of the Commission.

Disclosures other than those required by the APB Opinion have been suggested throughout this chapter and will therefore not be repeated.

---

[4] "Omnibus Opinion," *Opinions of the Accounting Principles Board, Number 12* (New York: American Institute of Certified Public Accountants, 1967).

Intangible assets (other than goodwill)

Oscar S. Gellein and H. G. Robinson*

Accounting for intangible assets continues to be one of the more unsettled aspects of corporate financial accounting today. The unsettled condition arises mainly from the difficulty of valuing such assets, particularly those developed internally, and of selecting an appropriate amortization policy. In this chapter, these and other considerations concerned with accounting for intangible assets (other than goodwill) will be discussed under the general headings of nature and characteristics of intangible assets, initial valuation, revaluation, amortization, and financial statement presentation.

The nature and characteristics of intangible assets

An intangible asset has been defined as "a capital asset having no physical existence, its value being dependent on the rights and benefits that possession confers upon the owner."[1] The words capital asset[2] are important to the applicability of this brief definition. Otherwise, it would not be meaningful, because, for accounting purposes, the lack of physical existence alone does not establish an asset as an intangible. Assets such as accounts receivable lack physical existence, but because they are not

---

* Partners, Haskins & Sells, New York.

[1] Eric L. Kohler, *A Dictionary for Accountants* (3d ed.; Englewood Cliffs, New Jersey: Prentice-Hall, Inc., 1963) p. 269.

[2] A capital asset has been defined by Kohler, ibid., p. 82, as "an asset intended for long-continued use or possession, common subclassifications being . . . (b) goodwill, patents, trademarks, franchises (intangibles). . . .

capital assets they are not considered intangibles. Prepaid expenses and deferred charges are sometimes referred to as intangible assets; but this class of assets generally is limited to deferrals of expenditures chargeable to operations of future periods. Accordingly, prepaid expenses and deferred charges do not have certain characteristics, such as those referred to in the next paragraph, normally ascribed to intangible assets.

Intangibles as a class of assets have either protected or owned rights and privileges that are expected to give rise to future income. Some intangibles such as patents and copyrights stem from governmental grants of monopolistic privileges. Other intangibles, such as secret formulas, name lists, and trade routes, are privately created and controlled. The value of intangible assets is derived solely from their potential earning power. Thus, unlike tangible assets, a disparity between cost and value may arise immediately upon their emergence in the accounts. The valuation of intangibles is surrounded with uncertainty because the basis of value—future earnings—is likewise subject to uncertainty.

Accounting Trends and Techniques, 1968 Edition, published by the American Institute of Certified Public Accountants, classified intangibles in the 600 corporate reports surveyed into several categories (see Exhibit 1). Although the tabulation in Exhibit 1 includes goodwill, this intangible asset is discussed in Chapter 57 on business combinations and goodwill. Certain intangibles (leaseholds, for example) represent rights to use tangible property. The accounting problems are therefore similar to those encountered in accounting for plant and equipment. For this reason, such intangibles will not be treated here. Other intangibles are peculiar to mining and extractive industries and likewise are not treated in this chapter.

Initial valuation

Intangible assets may be acquired for cash or noncash consideration, with or without contingent payments, from related or unrelated parties, individually or as part of a basket purchase. Intangibles may also be developed internally. Irrespective of the manner of acquisition, it is a general principle that the initial value assigned to all types of intangibles should be cost. The general principle is simple enough; it is the application in specific circumstances that is often difficult.

Externally developed intangibles

The initial valuation of an externally developed intangible acquired from an unrelated party in an outright purchase for cash does not present any unusual accounting problems. Frequently, however, intangibles are acquired as part of a lump-sum purchase, for consideration other than cash, from related parties, or under agreements providing for con-

EXHIBIT 1.* Intangible Assets—Presentation

Type of Intangible Asset	Balance Sheet Presentation					Total 1967
	Separately Set Forth	Under Fixed Assets	Under Other Assets	Under Deferred Charges	Shown Only in Notes to Financial Statements	
Goodwill re subsidiary	88	2	30	1	4	125
Goodwill (source not indicated)	59	—	18	2	4	79
Patents, patent rights and applications	65	3	40	4	—	112
Trade marks, brand names	40	1	15	1	—	57
Copyrights	4	—	2	—	—	6
Licenses, franchises, memberships	11	3	6	—	—	20
Formulae, processes, designs	6	—	4	—	—	10
Various other	24	20	9	3	2	58
Intangible assets (not otherwise described)	20	1	10	—	—	31
Total	317	30	134	11	6	498

Intangible Assets—Valuation

Type of Intangible Asset	Amortized Value			Unamortized Value	Nominal Value	Not Determinable	1967 Total
	Shown	Charge for Year is Not Shown	Total				
Goodwill re subsidiry	5	25	30	60	1	34	125
Goodwill (not otherwise indicated)	5	8	13	12	30	24	79
Patents, patent rights and applications	9	40	49	14	25	24	112
Trade marks, brand names	5	13	18	7	16	16	57
Copyrights	—	1	1	2	2	1	6
Licenses, franchises, memberships	1	10	11	3	2	4	20
Formulae, processes, designs	1	4	5	2	2	1	10
Various other	7	27	34	6	2	16	58
Intangible assets (not otherwise described)	4	11	15	10	1	5	31
Total	37	139	176	116	81	125	498

Number of Companies:

	1967
Presenting intangible assets	289
Not presenting intangible assets	311
Total	600

* Source: AICPA, Accounting Trends & Techniques—1968 edition.

tingent payments. Any of these conditions may give rise to unusual accounting problems.

A cash outlay representing a payment for the use (as opposed to the purchase) of intangible assets, such as rights or processes, should be charged to production costs or to other income accounts on the basis of use. Payments made to an independent organization to finance research that may lead to the development of intangibles are discussed later under the heading of research and development costs.

LUMP-SUM PURCHASES.   When several tangible and intangible assets are acquired in a single transaction for a lump-sum consideration, an allocation of the purchase price among each of the assets purchased is required. (Acquisition of entire businesses as going concerns are discussed in Chapter 57 on business combinations and goodwill.) In the absence of agreement between the parties to the transaction concerning prices paid for specific assets, a reasonable basis should be used to allocate the total purchase price to specific tangible and intangible assets. A procedure commonly used in such cases is to allocate the total cost among the assets acquired in the ratio of the value of each asset to the total value of all assets acquired. Some may contend that values should be assigned first to tangible assets purchased and that any remaining portion of the purchase price should be attributed to intangibles. This procedure ordinarily would not be appropriate since it does not give proper accounting recognition to the fact that when specified assets are acquired in a basket purchase, a cost was incurred with respect to each asset, whether tangible or intangible.

ACQUISITIONS FOR OTHER THAN CASH.   The accounting principle applicable to the initial valuation of intangibles acquired for consideration other than cash is stated in *Accounting Research Bulletin No. 43*, Chapter 5, of the AICPA, as follows: "In the case of non-cash acquisitions, as, for example, where intangibles are acquired in exchange for securities, cost may be considered as being either the fair value of the consideration given or the fair value of the property or right acquired, whichever is the more clearly evident."

If intangibles are acquired for marketable securities or other consideration that can be valued readily, initial valuation of the intangible may be based upon the consideration given by the buyer. If the consideration given cannot be valued readily, the initial valuation should be based upon the value of the intangible acquired. In the latter case, consideration should be given to such guidelines as a reasonably current, bona fide cash offer by a financially responsible person to purchase the assets for cash or its equivalent; responsible independent appraisals; capitalization of earnings attributable to the intangibles; and the transferor's cost.

The par or stated value of shares of stock issued to acquire intangibles should not be used arbitrarily. The proscription against such arbitrary valuation is clearly documented in the Securities and Exchange Commission's *Accounting Series Release No. 73*, issued in October, 1952. The following excerpts from a note to the financial statements of Olme Precision, Inc., which appeared in Fawick Corporation's listing application dated July 10, 1967 to the New York Stock Exchange, describe the changes made in Fawick's financial statements to eliminate from the assets an amount that arose from using the par value of capital stock as a basis for valuing intangible assets.

. . . 28,000 shares of $5 par value common stock were issued in January, 1961 in exchange for all licensing rights to produce and sell Power-Max clutches in the United States and Canada with options for Western Hemisphere licensing rights outside North America. Aggregate par value of shares issued in exchange for such licensing rights exceed transferors' costs to the extent of $140,000. The total par value of 28,000 shares of $5 par value common stock, issued in exchange for these licensing rights was previously reported as an asset under the caption "Other Assets and Deferred Charges." The accompanying statements have been restated to eliminate this amount from the assets and to reflect it as a reduction of total capital stock less deficit.

ACQUISITION FROM RELATED PARTIES.   Noncash transactions involving intangibles frequently are effected by affiliated parties—that is, the transferor is affiliated with the transferee. In a common situation, intangibles are transferred to a newly formed corporation in exchange for shares of common stock. In the absence of a fair market value for the stock (such as a value established by a simultaneous sale of a substantial block of stock to unrelated parties for cash), one must look to the intangibles as a means of assigning a value to the transaction. Where there have been no recent bona fide cash offers to purchase the intangibles, and where there is no demonstrated earnings history as a basis for valuation, the transferor's cost should be used as the basis of valuing the intangibles in the absence of evidence indicating a lower valuation.

The question has frequently arisen whether departure from cost is justified when partnership or corporate reorganizations are effected without substantial changes in ownership. Contrary to some authorities, the prevailing view is that in the absence of a material change in the effective and beneficial ownership or unusual circumstances, there is no basis for an upward restatement of intangible assets.

CONTINGENT PAYMENTS.   Provision for contingent payments in cash or stock are frequently incorporated in agreements for the acquisition of intangibles. The contingent payments may be based on sales or income from the intangibles or on the future market value of shares given. Depending upon the terms of the agreement, any additional payments made should be added to the original cost or charged to income. The following cases illustrate the differing treatments afforded payments made under contingency provisions of purchase agreements:

Xerox Corporation in its Annual Report for 1965 disclosed that additional contingent payments (cash and stock) for the acquisition of patents are recorded as patent assets and amortized over the remaining years of average useful life (14.28 years from January 1, 1959 in the case of U.S. patents purchased); the payments were based upon a percentage of domestic xerographic net sales, rentals, and royalties in the years 1959 through 1965. On the other hand, Electrolux Corporation in its 1963 report stated that it had purchased certain Canadian patents (under which its Canadian subsidiary was licensed on a royalty basis) for a contingent sum not to exceed $1 million calculated in accordance with a formula based on the annual earnings of the Canadian company for the years 1962 to 1968. Payments made were charged to income as amortization of patents.

Since the variety of individual types of contingent-payment agreements is virtually unlimited, the propriety of the accounting practice adopted would obviously depend on the circumstances in each case. It is the authors' opinion, however, that if the contingent payments are deemed to be in the nature of a profit-sharing arrangement with the seller, as in the Faradyne case cited below, they should be charged directly to income. Otherwise, such payments should be added to the original cost. In deciding upon the appropriate treatment in each case, consideration should be given to such factors as fair value of the intangibles, intent of the parties, and the nature of the contingency. The following case involving the Faradyne Electronics Corporation (*Securities Act Release No. 4469*, March 21, 1962) illustrates some of the considerations bearing on the accounting for contingent payments.

Faradyne acquired the business and assets of a partnership for $1,550,000 and agreed to make additional maximum contingent payments of $2,500,000 representing 50 percent of the net profits of the acquired business beginning in the year following the purchase (loss years would serve to extend the 20-year period for which payments could be required). In holding that the contingent payments should be charged directly to income, the SEC observed that the total of the fixed and maximum contingent payments was more than eleven times the book value of the assets acquired as shown by the books of the partnership. The SEC also reasoned that "since Faradyne obtained for an indefinite period in the future only 50 percent of the net income of the business, we conclude that it is improper to inflate the carrying value of total assets by setting up payments on the contract . . . ; or to report as net income the earnings before deducting the payments under the contract."

Although the Faradyne case concerned the purchase of an entire business, the principles applicable to that case would also apply to the acquisition of individual intangible assets as well.

Internally developed intangibles

Internally developed intangible assets include only capital assets and accordingly do not include, for example, deferred charges representing expenditures carried forward for writing off in one or more future periods merely to effect a matching of costs with revenues. Such expenditures lack one of the essential characteristics of intangible assets—that is, they do not result in an asset providing protected rights and privileges expected to give rise to future income.

Intangible assets (other than goodwill) developed internally include formulae, secret processes, patents, trademarks, trade names, copyrights, name lists, trade routes, scripts, and scenarios.

Accounting for intangibles developed in the regular course of business by research, experimentation, advertising, or otherwise is especially difficult because of the doubt that generally exists at the time the expenditures are made about whether the expenditures will give rise to intangible assets. Also, because of the joint efforts frequently involved, difficulties may be encountered in allocating cost to the research, developmental, or other activity that could produce intangible assets.

RESEARCH AND DEVELOPMENT COSTS.   Since important internally developed intangibles, such as patents and processes, frequently result from expenditures for research and development, it seems appropriate to discuss in this chapter some of the considerations pertinent to the accounting for such expenditures.

The principal accounting question concerning research and development expenditures incurred by a company operating as a going concern[3] is whether such expenditures should be charged to income as they are incurred, or deferred and amortized by charges to income during the periods when revenues are expected to be enhanced as a result of the research and development efforts. Collateral questions concern methods of amortization and matters of financial statement presentation; these questions are dealt with later in this chapter along with similar questions concerning intangible assets in general.

Uncertainty of future revenues from research and development efforts is a factor bearing heavily on the accounting question of whether or not expenditures for these efforts should be deferred. Deferral is appropriate if the expenditures result in the creation of an asset. It has been said that three conditions apply to the listing of items as assets:

[3] The accounting treatment of R & D expenditures incurred by development-stage companies is governed by concepts that differ in some respects from those applicable to going concerns. A discussion of these concepts is not included here. Development-stage companies are generally considered to be new companies contemplating speculative or promotional ventures from which no substantial revenues from the sale of products or services have been realized.

1. The business in question *owns* them.
2. The business has acquired them at a *cost*.
3. They are of *value* to the business.[4]

Although research and development efforts meet the first two conditions for listing as assets, generally there is a question at the time the expenditures are made of whether or not the results of the efforts will be of value to the business. While there is a presumption that value is created (otherwise the expenditures would not have been made), the value actually created is dependent upon the future economic benefits resulting from the R & D efforts, and often is fortuitous. The degree of uncertainty of future benefits becomes, then, one of the principal determinants in deciding whether R & D expenditures may be deferred. The generally accepted accounting principle in this regard has been stated as follows: "To the extent that the rate of asset expiration is either erratic or unpredictable, reliable measurement is tempered or replaced by judgment as the basis by which cost is allocated between expenses and assets. Substantial uncertainty as to whether benefits may reasonably be expected to be realized in the future are resolved by charging the costs against current revenues."[5]

Nature of research and development. In considering the matter of uncertainty of future benefits, it is helpful to identify the nature and purpose of the research and development activity. Current practice would seem to indicate that the following types of activities are classified under the broad heading of research and development:

1. Basic research—fundamental, pure, exploratory research.
2. Applied research—invention, technological research.
3. Development—new product, new process, major improvements or new uses.

Applied research takes over where basic research ends and attempts to direct basic ideas into more profitable channels. Development extends from the point where research ends to the point where production begins. Some companies also include the cost of technical support activities (application of engineering, cost reduction, product maintenance, product engineering, technical information, quality control) in research and development costs. This classification may result from the fact that technical work supporting ongoing production or sales activities often is performed by research scientists or engineers, perhaps even in a central laboratory. There is a presumption that the costs of technical support activities benefiting current, ongoing operations should be accounted for

[4] Thomas Henry Sanders, Henry Rand Hatfield, and Underhill Moore, *A Statement of Accounting Principles* (American Institute of Accountants, 1938), p. 58.

[5] Paul Grady, *Inventory of Generally Accepted Accounting Principles* (American Institute of Certified Public Accountants, Accounting Research Study No. 7) (New York, 1965), p. 101.

separately as a part of manufacturing or selling overhead. This approach may, however, require an allocation of costs where support activities are not clearly distinguishable from other R & D activities.

The basic alternatives as to whether R & D expenditures should be capitalized and amortized against future revenues or charged against the revenues of the current period should be examined in the light of the types of research—basic, applied, and development—and the kinds of programs in which the research efforts are applied. For purposes of this discussion, the following programs are recognized: (a) continuing research programs, (b) substantial or special projects. Continuing research would include all three types of R & D. Substantial or special projects would generally include only applied research and development.

Continuing research.   With respect to a continuing research program, the concept of matching costs with revenues is an argument in favor of deferral, since there is an obvious implication that these expenditures give rise to future value to the business. The arguments for immediate write-off, on the other hand, rest mainly on the propositions that (a) such costs are principally business-preserving costs, and (b) uncertainty of future benefits and the periods that may be benefited are so significant that deferral is questionable. It is the authors' view that, as a general proposition, the arguments for immediate write-off are more compelling than those for deferral. This view apparently is shared by a major segment of the business community, since the dominant practice by a substantial margin is to charge to income as incurred the cost of continuing R & D programs.

Single major project.   When a company commits itself to substantial research and development expenditures for a single product or process, a situation somewhat different from that of a continuing research program exists. There is likely to be more extensive advance design and planning for a major project than for a continuing research program; and there would seem to be a greater tendency, in considering a large project, to identify expenditures with the end product or process and to associate the recovery of expenditures more directly with anticipated revenues. The presumption that future value to the company will be created would appear to be more justified, therefore, with major projects than with a continuing program. Nevertheless, the matter of uncertainty of future benefits remains an important consideration.

Since uncertainty is an important consideration, it seems necessary to establish criteria for distinguishing situations in which the extent of uncertainty is reduced to a level that would justify deferral of the cost of major projects. Our view is that presence of the following conditions, taken as a whole, would tend to indicate reasonable certainty of future benefits and therefore justify deferral of cost of major research and development projects:

1. The existence of a significant and well-defined project or series of projects.
2. A determination of technical feasibility for the product or process.
3. A reasonable certainty about the amount and timing of expected revenues.
4. An allocation of deferred costs to specific future periods or contracts.
5. An expected excess of revenues over completion costs (plus selling costs).

Situations in which the foregoing conditions, or other equally effective conditions, are present generally are rare. In our opinion, therefore, most research and development expenditures for major projects should be charged to income as the expenditures are incurred. Current practice in accounting for research and development costs remains unsettled, however, and the above-mentioned conditions, which we believe should be present to justify capitalization of R & D costs, may not necessarily exist in companies that defer such costs.[6]

Costs includible in R & D. If R & D expenditures are shown separately in the income statement or are deferred in the balance sheet, it is necessary to define and classify these expenditures properly. The usual primary classification of costs by nature of expense does not pose any insusmountable problem in connection with research and development. Payments made to outside parties for research and development work should, of course, be classified as R & D costs. As salaries and wages constitute a major portion of research costs, it seems particularly important to treat fringe benefits as part of R & D costs. Materials, supplies, and equipment may be a significant factor in research activities. It is not uncommon for equipment purchased for research purposes, which would otherwise be capitalized, to be expensed currently. This practice should be followed when use or disassembling renders such equipment inoperative for other purposes, or when the company has no regular use for it. The extent to which applicable overhead costs are attributed to research and development activities varies in practice, depending upon the degree of refinement desirable or practicable.

Patents. Research and development efforts sometimes result in products or processes that are patentable. In these cases, a company that has been charging R & D expenditures to income as they are incurred, may wish to capitalize the cost of the patent as an intangible asset. Ordinarily, the capitalized costs would include legal and other expenses incurred after the decision to apply for a patent is made (see discussion concerning reinstatement of costs under the heading of Revaluation of Intangibles).

---

[6] A research study on accounting for research and development costs is being conducted under the auspices of the Director of Accounting Research of the AICPA.

Illustrations. The following excerpts from annual reports illustrate the accounting treatment given to patents and research and development costs.

A subsidiary company has a six-year research agreement, expiring August 31, 1971, under which it is required to make payments of $120,000 per year; such payments through August 31, 1968 (aggregating $360,000) are shown as deferred costs relating to patent applications and research and product development. The company plans to amortize such costs (beginning with the commencement of the marketing of each specific product or the grant of a patent, whichever comes first) over the shorter of eight years or management's estimate of the market life of the particular product. In the event a specific research project is abandoned or a management decision is reached not to market the product or to cease marketing it, for whatever reason, all unamortized deferred costs relating to such product or project will be charged to operations in the year of such occurrence.

Other research and product development costs, such as clinical testing and improvements to existing products, also were deferred in prior years. Effective September 1, 1967, such costs are being charged to operations as incurred. . . . (Sperti Drug Corp. 1968 Annual Report to Shareholders)

The Company has acquired rights to, and is itself and through independent research agencies, conducting research into and developing an automatic closed-chest resuscitator ("heart machine"), a cigarette treating device designed to reduce possible health hazards of smoking, and head rests for automobiles. The Company has deferred the costs incurred on these projects through independent research and testing agencies, and has charged to current expense the salaries of its own engineering and technical staff. Such deferred costs are to be amortized over a period not to exceed five years from date of completion of the specific project. (American Safety Equipment Corporation 1966 Annual Report to Shareholders)

It is the practice of the Company to carry forward product development costs of those products which have passed the prototype stage, and for which initial production orders are being solicited. Management of the Company expects that production orders or direct repayments will provide reimbursement for the product development costs presently being carried forward. (Mite Corporation 1967 Annual Report to Shareholders)

In general, only the legal and filing costs relating to patents developed by the companies are capitalized; other costs are charged to expense as incurred. Costs of purchased patents, patent rights, drawings, and other intangible assets are capitalized and amortized by charges to expenses over their estimated useful lives. (Microdot Inc. Proxy Statement dated December 16, 1968)

OTHER INTANGIBLES. The legal costs and registration fees incurred to perfect trademarks and trade names are capitalizable. These costs in relation to the promotion and advertising costs incurred to establish these values generally are nominal, however. Advertising costs incident to developing consumer preference for commodities identified by trade-marks, trade names and brands, as well as so-called institutional advertising will, in many cases, result in value to the future. It is generally impossible, however, to determine a reasonable basis for allocation of advertising costs to future periods. It is the common practice, therefore, to charge such costs to income as they are incurred.

The capitalizable cost of copyrights may include legal and filing fees and expenses as well as the costs incurred in developing the copyrighted material. The accounting problems associated with the development costs are somewhat similar to those encountered in accounting for research and development expenditures. Similarly, the accounting for name lists, subscription lists, and trade routes is influenced by the same considerations affecting other internally developed intangibles. The costs incurred to develop assets of this type are promotional in nature and include advertising, sales promotion, etc. In theory such costs may be deferrable. From a practical standpoint, however, in the light of the uncertainties of future benefit, it is common practice to charge such costs to income as they are incurred.

Intangible assets in the category of scripts, scenarios, and story and film rights are generally treated in the financial statements of companies in the television and film industry as "inventory" and are therefore subject to valuation principles applicable to inventory in general. For example, Warner Bros.–Seven Arts Limited in its 1968 Annual Report shows among current assets:

Inventories, not in excess of cost
Film productions for theatrical and television
  exhibition:

Released, less amortization	$ 20,383,000
Completed, not released	39,219,000
In process	9,232,000
Film rights for television, less amortization	47,453,000
Rights and scenarios	3,280,000
Other	2,759,000
Total inventories	$122,326,000

The company discloses its method of accounting for assets in this category as follows:

a) Film rights for television:
This caption on the consolidated balance sheet includes (i) a portion of the cost of released feature film productions which is allocated to television exhibition based upon the net income expected to be derived therefrom and (ii) exclusive licenses acquired by the companies to distribute certain feature motion pictures for television exhibition, a substantial number of which expire from 1973 through 1993.

b) Film amortization:

The cost applicable to both the theatrical and television release of each film production is amortized on a basis designed to provide annual amortization charges in the proportion that each year's actual theatrical and television income bears to management's estimate of the total income that will be realized from each of such sources. Such estimates are continually reviewed by management and are revised, if warranted.

c) Interest:

Interest charges incurred with respect to film productions are capitalized until the companies release such films for exhibition.

Film productions are not usually entirely liquidated within one year; however, it is the practice of this industry to include them among current assets.

Expenditures to maintain intangibles

Expenditures to maintain intangibles are generally expensed in the period incurred. The difficulty of establishing any meaningful relation between such expenditures—for example, promotion and advertising—and any enhancement in value of related intangibles—trademarks and trade names—justifies the practice. In connection with an inquiry concerning the deferral of advertising and circulation promotion expenditures, Ingalls, in *Practical Accounting and Auditing Problems,* (Inquiry No. 125), refers to the point that "the distinction is sometimes drawn between advertising and promotional expenditures made to increase the circulation structure and those made to maintain or support the circulation structure, the former being deferrable, the latter being deemed current expense."

Revaluation of intangibles

Appraisal increase. The Accounting Principles Board in Opinion No. 6 reaffirmed the principle ". . . that property, plant and equipment should not be written up by an entity to reflect appraisal market or current values which are above cost to the entity." Although the reference is to fixed assets, it is generally accepted that the principle applies to intangible assets as well.

Reinstatement of costs. A change in accounting policy to reinstate expenditures for intangibles previously written-off as incurred is not desirable. Financial statements are not deemed to be tentative and subject to revision as uncertainties concerning the classification of expenditures are resolved. Such revisions could lead to disorder in the financial reporting process.

When costs of the type discussed in this chapter are to be incurred, careful consideration should be given to the adoption of an appropriate accounting practice in light of the particular circumstances, including the expected benefits. This procedure generally should preclude a future change in accounting policy. When changes in the practice of accounting for costs of the type discussed here are made, however, the usual procedure is to commence the capitalization of costs with expenditures incurred in the current accounting period. This procedure is illustrated by the practice adopted by Data Corporation of America during its year ended March 31, 1967 with respect to internally developed computer programs. In Note 1 to its financial statements for that year, the company stated that "Since the latter part of its 1967 fiscal year, when the Company began to reflect charges to customers for the development of computer programs in monthly billings for data processing services, the costs of the programs, which are considered by the Company to have general utility, have been deferred and are being amortized over a three-year period on a straight-line basis."

Amortization of intangibles

For financial accounting purposes it is important to distinguish intangibles for which the term of existence is limited by law or economic factors, and hence subject to amortization, from those having no such limited term of existence. Chapter 5 of *Accounting Research Bulletin No. 43* classifies intangibles broadly into two types:

a) Those having a term of existence limited by law, regulation, or agreement, or by their nature (such as patents, copyrights, leases, licenses, franchises for fixed terms, and goodwill as to which there is evidence of limited duration);

b) Those having no such limited term of existence and as to which there is, at the time of acquisition, no indication of limited life (such as goodwill generally, going value, trade names, secret processes, subscription lists, perpetual franchises, and organization costs).

Limited term of existence

Limited-life intangibles [type (a)] should be amortized by systematic charges to income over the period benefited, as are other assets having a limited period of usefulness. If it becomes evident that the period benefited will be longer or shorter than originally estimated, recognition thereof may take the form of an appropriate decrease or increase in the rate of amortization, or a partial write-down may be made by a charge against income.

Methods of amortization. Intangible assets may be amortized under the straight-line method or, where more appropriate, under methods that attempt to match the amortization with revenues derived from the assets. As a practical matter, intangibles are most commonly amortized under the straight-line method, which in most cases is the only method acceptable for federal income tax purposes.

Research and development costs. As stated previously, under certain circumstances research and development costs may be deferred. In the absence of good evidence to the contrary, such costs should be amortized over a relatively short period, generally not exceeding five years. In an address presented on May 24, 1966 at Dallas, Texas, Mr. Walter Mickelsen, Chief Accountant, Division of Corporation Finance of the Securities and Exchange Commission, stated that "As to research and development expenses, we feel that five years is usually the top time limit, this coinciding with the maximum allowed if deferral and later amortization is chosen for both financial reporting and federal income tax purposes. We believe also that the amortization should be on a unit of production or sale basis which could amortize the deferrals over considerably less than five years, with a minimum flow, as say 20 percent, in a five-year time period, for each year."

Patents.   A patent's legal life in the United States is seventeen years from the date of grant. The capitalized cost of the patent may be amortized over that period or, if the circumstances indicate a shorter useful life, a lesser number of years. Where auxiliary patents effectively extend the useful life of existing patents, the amortization period of the old patents may, under proper conditions, be extended to correspond to the remaining life of the new patents.

Copyrights.   These intangibles are rarely, if ever, amortized over the legal copyright life of twenty-eight years. From books, as well as other copyrighted materials, the bulk of the revenue is realized in the early years. Hence, the costs are amortized over the first few years—sometimes in the first year of publication.

Franchises.   The costs of securing a terminable franchise should be amortized over the initial period of the franchise unless renewal for a nominal additional cost is likely.

No limited term of existence

Generally accepted accounting principles sanction the discretionary amortization of [type (b)] intangibles. *Accounting Research Bulletin No. 43*, Chapter 5, states that—

When a corporation decides that a type (b) intangible may not continue to have value during the entire life of the enterprise it may amortize the cost of such intangible by systematic charges against income despite the fact that there are no present indications of limited existence or loss of value which would indicate that it has become type (a), and despite the fact that expenditures are being made to maintain its value. Such amortization is within the discretion of the company and is not to be regarded as obligatory. The plan of amortization should be reasonable; it should be based on all the surrounding circumstances, including the basic nature of the intangible and the expenditures currently being made for development, experimentation, and sales promotion. Where the intangible is an important income-producing factor, and is currently being maintained by advertising or otherwise, the period of amortization should be reasonably long.

Among the types of intangible assets (other than goodwill) for which amortization is discretionary are name lists, routes, franchises having no limited term, network affiliation contracts, and circulation structure. Practices vary with regard to amortization of intangibles having no definite limited life. For example, McGraw-Hill, Inc., in its 1967 Annual Report shows: "Publication Titles, Copyrights, Subscription Lists, and Goodwill—Substantially at cost . . . $42,963,829." A footnote in a 1967 Prospectus issued by the company disclosed that "the publication titles, copyrights, subscription lists and goodwill, as shown by the consolidated balance sheet, do not purport to reflect actual present value of these intangibles. No amortization is being made of this amount because management considers the value to be of a permanent nature. The value will be reviewed by management on a periodic basis, with an amortization program to be established in the event that future results render it appropriate."

Consolidated Laundries disclosed in its 1967 Annual Report on Form 10K to the SEC that it is "the Corporation's policy (a) to amortize the portion of the cost of purchased service routes allocable to restrictive covenants (generally the major portion of entire cost) over the period of such covenants and (b) to amortize the portion of the cost not allocable to restrictive covenants over a period of twenty-five years. Periods of restrictive covenants do not exceed ten years."

Scripps-Howard Broadcasting Company, in its 1968 Annual Report to shareholders, stated that "intangible assets consist of the portion of the purchase price assigned at the time of acquisition to a station's network affiliation contract, licenses, and goodwill. It is the Company's present intention not to amortize amounts carried in this account."

Some believe that the position taken in *Accounting Research Bulletin No. 43* with respect to voluntary amortization is open to question because intangibles may be written off against income over a period when their value and earning power are as high or higher than at date of acquisition, with the result that net income may be understated by the amount of intangible amortization in years when there is no diminution in the value of intangible assets. Nevertheless, a number of companies systematically amortize the cost of intangibles having no limited term of existence. Ordinarily, the decision to amortize is based mainly on conservatism and a belief that the appearance of intangible assets in the balance sheet casts a shadow over the financial position. This belief is substantiated, to some extent, by the fact that many lenders ascribe no value to intangibles in determining financial statement ratios that must be maintained by the borrower.

If a decision is made to amortize intangibles having no limited term of existence, the amortization method and period selected should be such that income for any single period is not distorted by the amortization. In this connection, *Accounting Research Bulletin No. 43* states: "The plan of amortization should be reasonable; it should be based on all the surrounding circumstances, including the basic nature of the intangible and the expenditures currently being made for development, experimentation, and sales promotion. Where the intangible is an important income-producing factor and is currently being maintained by advertising or otherwise, the period of amortization should be reasonably long."

Lump-sum write-offs, or accelerated amortization in the absence of evidence of loss of value, are not in accordance with generally accepted accounting principles. Although an appropriate amount of conservatism in accounting is thought by most to be a virtue, it should not be used to sanction lump-sum write-offs and thereby result in distorting income in the period of write-off.

The SEC is known to frown on lump-sum write-offs of intangibles in the absence of any indication of loss in value. We noted one instance (Sprague Electric Company, 1963) when goodwill written off in prior years was reinstated at the suggestion of the SEC. A footnote to the financial statements indicated that "goodwill arising in connection with the acquisition of subsidiaries during 1960 through 1962, which previously had been charged to retained earnings in the years of acquisition, has been reinstated retroactively in the accounts at December 31, 1962, at the suggestion of the Securities and Exchange Commission." Although Sprague's intangible was written off in the year of acquisition, we understand that the SEC would take a similar view toward lump-sum write-offs in subsequent years.

When it becomes evident that the term of a type (b) intangible has become limited, its cost should be amortized by systematic charges to income over its remaining useful life. In certain circumstances, a partial write-down to income may be warranted, with only the remainder being subject to amortization.

When a decision is made to discontinue periodic amortization of intangibles having no limited term of existence, the amortization accumulated to date ordinarily should not be reversed (see the discussion concerning reinstatement of cost under the heading Revaluation of Intangibles).

Termination of utility

When any intangible asset becomes worthless, it should be written off to income.[7] In this connection, *Accounting Research Bulletin No. 43*, Chapter 5, cautions that:

---

[7] Accounting Principles Board Opinion No. 9, effective for years beginning after December 31, 1966, changed the formerly permitted practice of charging worthless intangibles directly to retained earnings.

In determining whether an investment in type (b) intangibles has become or is likely to become worthless, consideration should be given to the fact that in some cases intangibles acquired by purchase may merge with, or be replaced by, intangibles acquired, or developed with respect to other products or lines of business and that in such circumstances the discontinuance of a product or line of business may not in fact indicate loss of value.

Tax status

The tax treatment of intangibles as depreciable property is provided by the regulations promulgated under the Internal Revenue Code of 1954. Regulation 1.167 (a)–3 states that:

If an intangible asset is known from experience or other factors to be of use in the business or in the production of income for only a limited period, the length of which can be estimated with reasonable accuracy, such an intangible asset may be the subject of a depreciation allowance. Examples are patents and copyrights. An intangible asset, the useful life of which is not limited, is not subject to the allowance for depreciation. No allowance will be permitted merely because, in the unsupported opinion of the taxpayer, the intangible asset has a limited useful life. No deduction for depreciation is allowable with respect to goodwill.

Mertens' Law of Federal Income Taxation, at paragraph 23.10, identifies patents, copyrights, licenses, franchises, and, perhaps, the "premium" value of a favorable lease as intangibles having definitely limited terms of existence. Goodwill, trade names, trade brands, newspaper subscription lists, and formulae are cited as examples of intangibles not ordinarily subject to depreciation or obsolescence allowances due to the indefinite duration of their effective usefulness.

Essentially, to be depreciable, the tax law requires that the intangible have a determinable useful life. In the case of *Commissioner* v. *Indiana Broadcasting Corp.* (16 AFTR 2d 5465 7th Cir. 1965), the taxpayer acquired, along with the other assets of two television stations, network affiliation two-year-term contracts that were automatically and indefinitely renewable for successive two-year terms unless either of the parties gave six months' written notice of its intention to terminate. On appeal, the Tax Court was reversed, and it was held that, there being no reasonable basis for the prediction of expected life (industry statistics were held not applicable as each contract was deemed to be unique), the intangibles were therefore not subject to depreciation.

In earlier cases, it was established that television licenses granted by the Federal Communications Commission for three-year terms and renewable upon approval were not subject to depreciation. In one case, the court stated that the FCC had never denied a renewal of its three-year license.

Research and experimental expenditures. Sec. 174 of the IRC and the related regulations permit taxpayers to elect to treat expenditures for research and development costs as current deductions or as deferred charges subject to amortization ratably over a period of not less than 60 months. When the election is not made, the expenditures must be charged to a capital account and treated in the usual manner—depreciated if related to an asset with a determinable life, deducted as a loss if the project is unsuccessful, or not depreciated if related to an asset having a life of indefinite duration.

Trademark and trade-name expenditures.   Similarly, Sec. 177 of the IRC allows a taxpayer to elect to treat as a deferred charge any trademark or trade name expenditure paid or incurred during a taxable year beginning after December 31, 1955. Such deferred expenditures may be deducted ratably over a period of not less than 60 months. When the election is not made, the expenditure must be charged to a capital account probably with no amortization permitted because of the indefinite life of a trademark or trade name. The term "trademark or trade name expenditure" includes any expenditure that:

(1) is directly connected with the acquisition, protection, expansion, registration (federal, state, or foreign), or defense of a trademark or trade name;
(2) is chargeable to capital account; and
(3) is not part of the consideration paid for a trademark, trade name, or business.

Financial accounting and tax accounting may differ

The IRC does not specifically require that financial accounting practices for intangibles conform to the tax methods elected under the IRC. Thus, a company may capitalize and amortize intangibles, such as research and development costs, for purposes of financial accounting, and for tax purposes elect to treat the expenditure as current deductions. Such differences between financial accounting and tax accounting are referred to as timing differences.

Accounting Principles Board *Opinion No. 11* defines timing differences as: "differences between the periods in which transactions affect taxable income and the periods in which they enter into the determination of pretax accounting income. Timing differences originate in one period and reverse or 'turn around' in one or more subsequent periods."

Deferred Taxes.   Under APB *Opinion No. 11,* the deferred method of tax allocation should be followed. Thus, the tax effects of current timing differences are deferred currently and allocated to income tax expense of future periods when the timing differences reverse. Deferred taxes are determined on the basis of the tax rates in effect at the time the timing differences arise, and are not adjusted for subsequent changes in tax rates or to reflect the imposition of new taxes.

The tax effects of transactions that reduce taxes currently payable are treated as deferred credits and are not to be offset against the asset (research and development costs, trademarks, etc.) giving rise to such tax effects. Amortization of these deferred taxes to income tax expense in future periods is based on the nature of the transactions producing the tax effects, and on the manner in which these transactions enter into the determination of pretax accounting income in relation to taxable income.

Financial statement presentation

Intangible assets are generally set forth separately in the noncurrent section of the balance sheet with reference being made to the specific assets. The 1968 edition of *Accounting Trends and Techniques,* published by the AICPA (see Exhibit 1 on page 1028), shows that 289 of the 600 surveyed companies disclosed intangible assets in their 1967 annual reports. In presenting its survey of practices regarding intangible assets, *Accounting Trends and Techniques* commented:

1. *Type.* The most common types of intangible assets were "goodwill," representing the excess of book values of subsidiaries acquired over the cost of acquisition; "goodwill" not otherwise identified; patents; and trade marks, etc. Leaseholds and leasehold improvements which most frequently are included among property accounts, are excluded from these tables.
2. *Presentation.* Intangible assets shown separately in the noncurrent asset section of the balance sheet was the most frequent method of presentation though it was not uncommon to find such terms grouped with "other assets."
3. *Valuation.* Intangible assets were frequently shown in the balance sheet at an amortized value. A nominal-value (usually $1, or $1,000 for companies "rounding" to the nearest $1,000) presentation was also favored as a method of valuation for goodwill (not otherwise classified) patents, and trademarks. Goodwill, representing the excess of book values of subsidiaries acquired over the cost of acquisition, was frequently shown at unamortized cost.

Exhibit 1 reveals that there were 176 instances of intangibles shown in the balance sheet at an amortized value. *Accounting Trends and Techniques* states that:

. . . the companies classified as valuing intangible assets at "Amortized value, charge not shown," include only those which specifically indicate that the assets are being amortized, such as: "Goodwill, net of amortization," "Goodwill, unamortized balance," etc. Companies classified as valuing intangibles at "Unamortized value" include those which show no change in carrying value from the previous year and no specific indication that the asset is being amortized. Included in "Not determinable" are those which show only the title of the intangible in the balance sheet caption with values other than nominal value.

which indicate a change in valuation from the previous year without any information regarding such change.

More extensive disclosure with respect to amortization is required in reports filed with the SEC. Rule 3–20 (c) 2, of Regulation S–X, requires that the income statements, or a note thereto, must state for the period of the statement the policy followed with respect to the provision for amortization of intangibles, or reserves created in lieu thereof, including the methods and, if practicable, the rates used in computing the annual amounts.

Nominal value. Exhibit 1 discloses 81 instances of intangibles stated at nominal value (usually $1). This practice is unique with intangible assets and does not conform with the general principles of accounting for tangible assets. Undoubtedly, this presentation is intended to disclose the existence of intangible assets, amortized over a relatively short period, or not capitalized at all, having continuing value to the company. This form of presentation may very well have developed as a means of emphasizing to the reader the potential disparity between the cost and value of intangibles, the great uncertainty in which intangible values stand, and the difficulty of determining the cost of internally developed intangibles.

Initial acquisition. Upon the initial acquisition of significant intangibles, disclosure should be made in the financial statements of the circumstances surrounding the purchase. If the consideration is other than cash, the basis of valuing the intangibles should be stated. When amounts allocated to intangibles in lump-sum purchases are based on appraisal value, disclosure of that fact should be made. If there is any relation between "insiders" and persons from whom intangibles were acquired, this condition should be disclosed.

Research and development costs. Exhibit 1 does not list deferred research and experimental costs as intangible assets. These assets are classified by *Accounting Trends and Techniques* as deferred charges or other assets. Generally, deferred research and development costs should be shown separately and should not be included in product inventories or other tangible assets. The 1967 report of Xerox Corporation and subsidiaries describes a change to the preferred method of classification. Note 5 to the financial statements states that "prior to 1967, a portion of research and engineering expenditures was added to the capitalized value of rental equipment and depreciated as part of the cost over the life of the equipment. Beginning in 1967, the Company changed its method of accounting for these expenditures by charging the deferred portion to a separate account and amortizing this portion on a straight-line basis over three years. This change had no material effect on net income."

Accounting for business combinations and goodwill

Charles F. Axelson*

The financial accounting policies associated with the broad area of business combinations, including the treatment of goodwill arising from such combinations, are complex, varied, and, in some cases, unsettled at the time of this writing. The purpose of this chapter is to cover the financial accounting matters, whether settled or not, that may pertain to a business combination. Since most business combinations represent an acquisition of one company by another, we can think of the subject matter of this chapter as primarily relating to the accounting problems faced by the acquiring company in an acquisition. It is not intended that this chapter cover the analysis of potential acquisitions, covered in Chapter 18, the nonaccounting financial aspects of acquisitions and mergers, covered in Chapter 51, nor accounting matters more strictly related to consolidations and intercorporate investments, covered in Chapter 61.

The methods of combination, the tax considerations, and the accounting considerations in the merger agreement will have a bearing on the accounting approaches that will be taken and are first briefly reviewed in this chapter before proceeding to a discussion of the problems relating to the actual recording of the acquired company on the books of the acquiring company.

---

* Controller and Assistant Treasurer, United States Gypsum Company, Chicago.

Methods of combination

The various methods of combination will ordinarily have been considered during the negotiations and one specific method selected; the accounting treatment is often affected by the specific method selected. Chapter 51 contains a thorough discussion of the economic and financial aspects of the various methods.

Obviously the choices will be affected by the tax, legal and economic positions of both the buyer and seller.

Purchase of assets versus purchase of equity

Whether the acquiring company acquires the assets or the stock of the selling company, the accounting treatment on the books of the purchaser will ordinarily be the same, depending on whether the "purchase" or "pooling-of-interests" policy (as described later in this chapter) is followed.

Purchase in entirety versus purchase of components

When assets are being purchased, they may be purchased in their entirety for a lump sum price, or the various assets may be purchased separately. Thus the acquiring company may purchase the fixed assets, and possibly certain deferred charges, for a price agreed upon in advance, with the inventory to be paid for on the basis of the values existing at date of acquisition. Accounts receivable may be purchased at net value at date of acquisition or not purchased at all, in which case the selling company continues to collect accounts receivable and liquidate its liabilities. Infinite combinations are possible and care must be taken that the accounting treatment on the books of the purchaser reflects the exact arrangements that were made.

Purchase for cash versus purchase for stock

Whether a purchase is paid for in cash or in the stock of the acquiring company will have a bearing on the values recorded on the books of the purchaser. Tax considerations are usually an important factor in this determination.

Tax considerations

Any acquisition requires the services of a thoroughly knowledgeable professional tax expert. There are too many variables for an amateur to attempt to apply tax rules to his own particular situation. However, some general rules can be laid down.

Nature of taxation on profits made by the combination

ACQUISITIONS PAID FOR IN CASH. An acquisition for cash will normally involve an immediate taxable profit to the seller and (with the tax on the profit having been paid) the right to the purchaser to bring the assets onto his books at the full purchase price. Whether any of the purchase price is allocable to goodwill or other intangibles depends on each situation, but generally every effort should be made, of course, to allocate as much of the purchase price as possible to the *fair value* of the tangible assets acquired. For fixed and other amortizable assets this will provide a high depreciation or amortization basis to the acquiring company for tax purposes. When an acquisition is made partially for cash and partially for stock, the Internal Revenue Service will regard the transaction as a taxable combination if more than 20 percent of the purchase price is paid in cash (including buyer's assumption of liabilities). If cash is paid to acquire stock rather than assets, there are tax requirements relating to the liquidation of the acquired company which must be observed to obtain the maximum tax base.

ACQUISITIONS PAID FOR IN STOCK. An acquisition paid for in stock will normally represent a tax-free sale by the seller, so that the seller will not have to pay any immediate tax on profit associated with the sale. The stock received by the seller will have a tax basis equal to that of the property sold, and any tax otherwise payable will be deferred until later disposition of the stock which was received. Likewise, the tax bases of the properties purchased by the acquiring company must be the same for that company as those which were applicable to the seller, and these values may be below the purchase price. In these circumstances, the excess of the purchase price over the net value for tax purposes will not be allowed as additional tax basis to the acquiring company. Where voting stock is exchanged for assets, the acquiring company must receive substantially all of the assets of the seller; however, up to 20 percent (including the assumption of liabilities) of the purchase price of the assets may be paid for in cash and still normally represent a tax-free sale by the seller.

Tax rate

While the income tax paid by the selling company or its shareholders on a taxable transaction is normally computed at capital gains tax rates, certain portions of the profit (e.g., recaptured depreciation since January 1, 1962) may be taxed at ordinary income tax rates.

Recaptured depreciation

In the case of the purchase of assets for cash, where there is an overall taxable gain, such gain is taxed to the seller at ordinary income tax rates to the extent of depreciation applicable to machinery and equipment included in the acquisition and taken since January 1, 1962. When cash is paid for the *stock* of the seller, however, it is the *buyer* that is liable for such tax when he disposes of the assets. However, if the buyer under these circumstances liquidates the acquired company within two years and obtains a stepped-up basis for the depreciable property, the step-up may be taxed (as ordinary income) at that time to the buyer. In each of the preceding situations, the gain on real property is also, in certain instances, subject to tax as ordinary income. In the case of an acquisition paid for with the stock of the buyer (involving no change in the basis of assets for tax purposes) such tax is imposed on the buyer (when disposition of the assets is made).

Loss of investment tax credit

A consideration that should not be overlooked is that on the purchase of assets for cash the seller may lose portions of the investment tax credit previously claimed because certain assets may not have been held by the seller for the qualifying period. In the case of a purchase of the stock of the seller, such loss of investment tax credit is borne by the buyer when he disposes of the assets. The buyer may also lose the investment tax credit if he has purchased stock for cash and liquidates the acquired company within two years.

Other considerations

Whether the acquisition is for cash or for stock, careful analysis of the components of the purchase price should be made to make as many items as possible fit the category of tax-deductible items to the purchaser. On tax-free acquisitions, the amount of acquisition or reorganization expense is not ordinarily deductible for tax purposes. Such expenses should be written off on the books as quickly as practicable. Some payments made by the seller may require escrow arrangements which may pose special tax problems. Needless to say, the tax basis of all assets being acquired must be reviewed thoroughly regardless of what the books show.

Accounting considerations in the merger agreement

Valuations

Merger agreements often contain references to accounting considerations and the most common of these relate to inventories and reserves.

Where inventories are to be purchased separately (or where a lump-sum purchase price is to be adjusted if certain inventory provisions are not met) the merger agreement should clearly state the basis of valuing the inventories and whether or not the basis is consistent with prior periods. The basis may be the normal basis used by the selling company (Fifo, Lifo, average, direct cost, etc.) or it may be the actual built-up purchase price plus freight (and possibly inbound handling) for every item or group of items in the inventory. Particular attention should be paid by the acquiring company to the value to be assigned to obsolete, slow moving, or used inventory items if they exist. If the inventory is to be physically counted at or near the acquisition date, provision should be made for the makeup of the inventory counting teams and how disputes in counting or valuation are to be resolved. Whether or not maintenance items, spare parts, general stores, and the like, which are normally charged to cost upon receipt, should be included in the inventory being paid for should be resolved. Of course, the tax basis for all inventory items should be evaluated.

The merger agreement may contain specific provisions for the handling of reserves. The reserve for doubtful receivables may be agreed upon at the time of acquisition, based on all known factors at that time, or it may be desirable to have this valuation tentative and subject to final determination after a specified period of time for collections on accounts existing at the time of the acquisition. Likewise, reserves for income taxes may be agreed upon at the date of acquisition or may be regarded as tentative until the passage of a specified period of time, or until the taxes for certain years in question have finally been resolved by the taxing authorities. Reserves for depreciation, depletion, and other amortizable accounts are normally susceptible of final determination as of the date of acquisition. Merger agreements often provide that the purchase price will be reduced for any pension, insurance, or vacation liabilities being assumed by the acquiring company. It may also provide that the purchase price include a value for certain assets not carried on the books of the selling company, such as patent rights or development expense.

Withheld amounts

The merger agreement may provide for the acquiring company to withhold a portion of the purchase price (or place it in escrow) to pay for unanticipated claims, contingencies, or adjustments in values at acquisition date. The amount may be withheld (often for a period of up to three years or more) at which time cash will be paid or stock issued to the seller in the amount of the sum withheld less any claims or adjustments applicable thereto. Another possibility is to withhold a portion of the purchase price with the provision that the withheld amount will be paid only if a certain level of projected earnings is attained. Where the amounts withheld and contingent payouts *could* have a material effect

on the overall earnings and financial position of the buyer for any given
year or years, there may be serious accounting and reporting complications with which to contend. An article in the June, 1968, *Journal of
Accountancy* on "Contingent Pay-Outs In Mergers and Acquisitions"
explores this subject in considerable depth.

Recording the acquired company

Purchase versus pooling

In accounting for acquisitions the term "purchase accounting" refers
to the practice of recording on the books of the acquiring company the
full purchase price paid for the assets or stock being acquired. This
practice is normally followed only for the portion of the acquisition paid
for in cash. The term "pooling-of-interests" refers to the practice of
recording on the books of the acquiring company the underlying net
book value of the assets of the selling company rather than the value of
the stock issue. Pooling-of-interests accounting has become acceptable
in most situations where voting stock is issued although there may be
exceptions, particularly where there is no continuity of management or
ownership interests in the company being acquired. When an acquisition
is partially for cash and partially for stock it is normal practice, irrespective of tax considerations, to record the cash portion on a "purchase
accounting" basis and the stock portion on a "pooling-of-interests" basis.
In any tax-free combination where the selling company has a net asset
value for tax purposes that is different from its net book value, only the
net tax value can form the tax basis for assets in the hands of the
acquiring company.

Since most acquisitions for stock are concluded at a value in excess of
the underlying book or tax value of the selling company (with the tax
value becoming the tax base for future depreciation deductions, thus
permitting tax-free sale by the selling company) the actual "excess
purchase price" (excess of the price paid by the acquiring company over
the net book value for the selling company) is never recorded. The stock
issued by the acquiring company is valued on its books at less than its
total fair market value at date of acquisition. The par value of the stock
issued in the acquisition is credited to the capital stock account and the
amount *over* par value, if any, is credited to capital received in excess of
par value and/or retained earnings, depending upon circumstances.
Thus, of the amount *over* par value, a portion (up to the amount of
retained earnings carried by the seller) would normally be credited to
retained earnings, with the excess credited to capital received in excess
of par value. In most states, the buyer cannot be in the position of having
the value acquired less than the par value because the stock would not
be considered fully paid. However, if state law permits and there is an

amount *under* par value to account for, the charge should normally be made to capital received in excess of par value (first to the extent carried on the books of the seller, then to the extent available on the books of the acquiring company) with the excess, if any, charged to retained earnings. If no-par stock is available for issuance by the buyer, many of these problems can be avoided, however, since then the net value acquired is credited to the no-par capital stock account. No-par value convertible preferred stock is sometimes used to effect a tax-free acquisition and, in the process, minimize the requisite carrying value of the assets acquired. The alternatives and the circumstances should be thoroughly reviewed before the entries are made on the books.

The practice of accounting for acquisitions for stock on a pooling-of-interests basis, which results in less than the total fair market value of the stock being issued ever appearing on the acquiring company's balance sheet, should not, however, form the basis for economic analysis of return on investment. While the excess purchase price does not appear on the books of the acquiring company, the true economics of the situation suggest that the future earnings contributed by the company being acquired should be related to the total purchase price, which would be the fair market value of the stock being issued. Amortization of the excess purchase price, even though not recorded on the books, should be considered in calculating the annual contribution of earnings from the newly acquired business and the consequent return on investment.

Purchased goodwill

The subject of accounting for goodwill is, at the time of this writing, the most controversial and unsettled area pertaining to the accounting problems broadly asssociated with business combinations. Purchased goodwill, often referred to as excess purchase price, refers to the excess of the purchase price paid for an acquisition over the values that can be assigned to asset and liability categories on the balance sheet. In the case of acquisitions for stock of the acquiring corporation, it is now common practice to record such acquisitions on a pooling-of-interests basis that omits the recognition of purchased goodwill (if applicable) by not recognizing the excess of the price paid in the acquisition over the book value of the assets acquired. Under these circumstances, purchased goodwill is now normally recognized only on acquisitions for cash where the purchase price exceeds the fair value of the assets being taken over. Of course, there are those who say that under any basis of accounting the total market value of the stock being issued should be recorded and, where this value exceeds the fair value of the assets being acquired, purchased goodwill should appear on the books of the acquiring company. Even here, it should be recognized that the purchased goodwill recorded on the books may be different from the excess of the purchase price over the *tax* basis of the assets being acquired. This would be particularly true if the selling company had taken accelerated depreciation for tax purposes and a lesser rate of depreciation for book purposes. Every effort should be made by the acquiring company to avoid the dilemma of accounting for purchased goodwill by assigning the entire purchase price to recognizable assets if this is possible, even though the asset values thus assigned may not be fully allowable for tax depreciation purposes. Thus, where a company has been acquired because of its manufacturing facilities or natural resources, it may be proper to allocate the full purchase price (up to the fair value of the assets) to the definable assets acquired for purposes of recording values on the books of the acquiring company.

Where purchased goodwill exists, however, the acquiring company has the problem of accounting for this goodwill. This purchased goodwill (for which a tax deduction cannot be taken by the acquiring company) represents an economic cost which has been acquired and which must always be considered in measuring the return on the investment in the acquired company even though, as under pooling-of-interests accounting, the purchased goodwill is not recorded on the books. If purchased goodwill has been recorded there are three principal avenues open for subsequent handling of this purchased goodwill:

1. Leave the purchased goodwill on the books indefinitely as a permanent asset.
2. Amortize the purchased goodwill against future earnings, either on a predetermined regular basis or on some special basis.
3. Write off (in a year following acquisition when no further values appear to exist) the purchased goodwill against current income or, in case the loss of value was due to unusual events or developments within the period and the amount is material, as an extraordinary charge against income after first arriving at a figure representing income before extraordinary items. Immediate write-off in the year of acquisition is not now sanctioned under current accounting practice.

Factors to consider in accounting for purchased goodwill.

Retain as a permanent asset.   This handling recognizes that the purchased goodwill has been bought and paid for and represents a valid asset that contributes to the success of the business. As long as this goodwill contributes to the business in an amount at least equal to its value, the continuation of it as a permanent asset prevents a dilution of earnings which would occur if the goodwill was amortized and retains the cost of the acquisition on the books of the acquiring company. Unlike land, however (which is not normally depreciated), the value of purchased goodwill is apt to lose its identity after a period of merged operations. In such cases, care must be taken to be sure that the value assigned to purchased goodwill in later years really represents a valid company asset. In this connection, identifying the reason for paying the excess purchase price in the first place may help to indicate the subsequent accounting treatment. Thus, if the excess purchase price was paid for intangible know-how, the purchased goodwill account should not be retained as an asset beyond the period when this know-how has lost its identity or ceased to benefit the acquiring company. If the excess purchase price was paid for superior future earning power, it probably should be written off in those years in which the superior earning power has been demonstrated.

Amortization of purchased goodwill. A theoretical case can certainly be made for amortizing purchased goodwill over some predetermined period (such as 10 or 20 years) or on some special basis, such as relating the amortization in any given year to a superior earning power emanating from the acquired company. Those who believe that purchased goodwill should be amortized against future earnings in some manner believe that it is an inescapable cost that must be charged against the earnings of the business, and not to do so will result in a misleading overstatement of the earnings of the business. Those opposed to this view hold that by amortizing purchased goodwill against the current earnings of a given year tends to introduce a charge that is irrelevant to current year's operations and unnecessarily reduces reported earnings available to stockholders. This group argues that financial statements are prepared largely for the benefit of investors and would-be investors, that purchased goodwill (if shown) is normally subtracted by sophisticated financial analysts from equity accounts in analyzing a balance sheet and that the stockholders' equity is really not affected by amortizing the excess purchase price. They hold that purchased goodwill really represents an equal subtraction from stockholders' equity at both the start and end of the amortization period and that to reduce earnings during the amortization period by a write-off of excess purchase price is unrealistic and unnecessarily clutters up the earnings picture.

Write-off of purchased goodwill all at one time. If purchased goodwill is not to be retained on the books indefinitely or is not to be amortized, then it should be written off and current accounting practice requires that the write-off be made against current income or (if this would materially distort income and is caused by unusual events or developments within the period) as an extraordinary charge against income at such a time as no further value appears to exist. Immediate write-off of purchased goodwill in the year created is not now sanctioned under current accounting practice. Furthermore, the regulations of the Securities & Exchange Commission specifically prohibit the write-off of purchased goodwill against capital received in excess of par value.

Although it is not now sanctioned, there are those in the accounting profession who believe that a strong theoretical case can be made for the immediate write-off of purchased goodwill or, as an alternative, a lump-sum deduction of goodwill from the stockholders' equity accounts. In holding these views, they maintain that purchased goodwill is not a tangible asset that should be continued on the balance sheet of the acquiring company. They maintain that purchased goodwill represents an adjustment of the equity being contributed to the overall enterprise by the company being acquired and should be left out of the accounts of the continuing enterprise so that these accounts will reflect earnings based on current performance, not cluttered with a controversial item representing a transaction of the past. In immediately writing off purchased goodwill against stockholders' equity accounts, they recognize that there may be a distinction between which equity account should be charged. Thus, in the case of acquisitions for cash, they state that no particular logic or reason requires that payments for purchased goodwill be deducted from either capital surplus or retained earnings to the exclusion of the other, and that this decision might best be made by the company's board of directors after considering applicable state laws. In the case of acquisitions for stock, they state that goodwill must have been purchased with the proceeds of the stock issued and hence the write-off of purchased goodwill may most appropriately be deducted from the capital received in excess of par value (to the extent available) created by the stock issued. These same people feel that pooling-of-interests accounting is not sound and that all acquisitions should be recorded on a purchase accounting basis. Thus purchased goodwill would always be booked, even though it might be written off immediately against surplus accounts (if large enough to permit) so as to furnish a complete record of the acquisition transaction. It must be emphasized, however, that the contents of this paragraph are not now sanctioned under current accounting practice and are presented only as opposing views now receiving attention by the accounting profession.

Minority interests

When an acquiring company purchases less than all of the stock of the selling company a continuing minority interest exists, and if the accounts of the acquired subsidiary are consolidated (normal when a 51 percent or more interest is held by the parent company) the minority interests of the subsidiary are set out in a separate category between the liabilities and stockholders' equity accounts on the consolidated balance sheet. Earnings applicable to the minority stockholders must be deducted from the total earnings of the subsidiary before determining the earnings applicable to the parent company and its stockholders. The existence of minority interests puts a greater responsibility on the parent company to observe separate-entity accounting for the subsidiary than would be the case if the minority interests did not exist. This means that a subsidiary should be treated as a completely independent profit center with "arm's length" charges made for all goods and services rendered in either direction between the parent and its subsidiary. Separate-entity accounting for the subsidiary may also be necessary wherever an independent determination of subsidiary profits is necessary for bonus, management contract, or other purposes. Tax considerations may also have a bearing on how precisely the subsidiary is accounted for on a separate-entity basis.

Negative purchased goodwill

Where an acquiring company pays less than the net book value for the assets of another company, negative goodwill (sometimes called surplus from consolidation, or excess of book value over cost of investment) arises. This account, normally classified on the consolidated balance sheet between the liabilities and stockholders' equity accounts, may be written off against the asset accounts to which it most nearly relates, carried as a reserve, or amortized to income over some period of time. If not material, it may best be deducted as a reserve from fixed-asset values. Even if it is material, the existence of such an account is confusing to many people and tends to clutter up the balance sheet. It would seem to be the better practice, therefore, to dispose of this account as rapidly as possible, preferably by writing it off against assets acquired or carrying it as an asset reserve. For tax purposes, of course, the handling of the negative goodwill account and its subsequent amortization, if any, will have no significance.

Preparing for takeover of the acquired company

Separate operating arrangement

Where one company acquires another for a lump-sum predetermined price, and it is the intention to continue the acquired company as a separate operating entity with its own accounting staff, reports, books and records, etc., it is usually possible for the acquiring company to account for the newly acquired division or subsidiary with a minimum of additional effort. Since the purchase price has been settled in advance, there is nothing to be done at the date of acquisition (such as counting inventory, valuing accounts receivable, etc.) that will affect the arrangement. If the company acquired is continued as a subsidiary, the acquiring (parent) corporation will be faced with consolidating problems at the end of each accounting period. These problems are discussed at length in Chapter 61, "Consolidations and Inter-Corporate Investments."

Integrated operating arrangement

Where it is not the intention to operate the company being acquired on a separate-entity basis, considerably more responsibility is placed on the acquiring company to bring the newly acquired company into the fold. If the inventory is being purchased separately, it may be necessary to plan for physical inventory counts in considerable detail in advance of the acquisition date. Even if the inventory is not being purchased separately, it will normally be desirable for the acquiring company to take a physical inventory as a start for its cost accounting and inventory-control system, particularly if the accounting bases are different. Depending on the merger agreement and the circumstances, it may be desirable to have an exacting cut-off on the date of acquisition for taxes, utilities, purchased materials, and the like. Where the acquiring company is completely taking over the seller for an agreed-on price regardless of conditions as of date of acquisition, however, such exactness may not be necessary.

Where the parent company's accounting system is to be installed, decisions will be required as to whether the newly acquired entity is to conform to the parent company's accounting practices in all respects or whether exceptions (which may be necessary or desirable for tax or other purposes) shall be permitted. Installing a parent company's accounting system can involve a considerable amount of effort which must be weighed against the advantages of having all consolidated reporting on a uniform basis. The systems aspect of installing the parent company's accounting system will be a dominant factor, involving, as it does, decisions on the mechanics of receiving and disbursing cash, order handling and invoicing, purchasing and receiving, cost accounting, etc. Arranging for the printing and delivery of the necessary forms that will be involved can often become a major undertaking, particularly if existing company forms do not fit the situation.

It will normally be desirable for the newly acquired entity to at least conform to the acquiring company's chart of accounts to facilitate consolidation, even if the acquiring company's accounting system is not installed in all details. Deadlines for having accounting data at the point of consolidation will have to be established. Where time does not permit meeting usual deadlines, such as with foreign subsidiaries in remote locations, the subsidiary accounts may have to be brought into the consolidation as of an earlier date.

After merger

Reporting considerations

Pooling-of-interests accounting (used in certain acquisitions where stock is issued for the purchase price) requires that the acquiring company restate its balance sheet, statement of earnings and other financial statements published in reports to outsiders on a pro forma basis which includes the accounts of the acquired company in the current and all past years portrayed on the statements. The theory here is that a merged enterprise should be portrayed in historical consolidated figures as though the merger had been in effect throughout the period displayed. Including the financial data retroactively prior to acquisition is sometimes omitted if the amounts involved are not material. In the case of purchases paid for in cash, it is not the usual practice to portray financial data prior to the acquisition on a retroactive pro forma basis.

Profit center considerations

If a newly acquired entity is to be operated as a separate profit center (whether a division or a subsidiary), certain additional accounting considerations arise which do not exist if the entity is not to have an exact net profit separately calculated. Reasons for setting up separate profit center accounting on a newly acquired entity include management, tax, and legal considerations. Management considerations include the ability to appraise the performance of the entity separately, bonus and incentive programs relating to the separate profits of the entity, and continuation of pension, labor, insurance, and fringe benefit arrangements which may be different from those of the parent entity. Tax considerations could be important where the entity is continued as a separate subsidiary, whereas legal considerations might be important where the acquired entity was in a completely unrelated line of business or located in another country. Of course, an estimate of the profit contribution of a newly acquired entity can be made without actually keeping separate records on a profit center basis, and the additional cost of keeping records on a profit center basis should be weighed against the benefits to be derived therefrom.

SERVICE CHARGES.   When an entity is operated as a profit center, the parent company or division may want to make some charge for corporate services rendered. The type of charge will depend upon the nature of the services. The charge for services may be made as incurred, or on an estimated basis as a flat monthly sum, or at an estimated percentage of sales. Where services are charged for as incurred, this may involve a considerable amount of timekeeping if it is to be done right. The problems of allocating common costs to profit centers are discussed in Chapter 36, "Measuring Divisional Performance."

INTERCOMPANY DIVIDENDS.   Where an entity is operated as a subsidiary, dividends to the parent company will be paid from time to time. The timing of these dividends, particularly from foreign subsidiaries, involves complicated tax, legal, foreign exchange, and policy questions and normally requires the services of expert counsel.

TRANSFER PRICING.   When the new entity is operated as a separate profit center, it is necessary that shipments from and to the new entity be priced on some reasonable and applicable basis. The question of transfer pricing is discussed at length in Chapter 36.

Summary

Business combinations normally involve many accounting decisions that depend on the specific facts of the case and that are heavily influenced by tax, legal, economic, management, and possibly other considerations. Expert advice should be sought before proceeding too far with any aspect of a business combination. Persons involved in business combinations should understand the rules applicable to pooling-of-interests accounting, the choice of rules pertaining to accounting for purchased goodwill (when it exists), and the principal financial considerations to appraise in an acquisition situation.

Compensation and employee benefits

Ernest L. Hicks*

A company's compensation program ordinarily reflects both the objectives of the employer (obtaining competent people, keeping them, and motivating them) and those of the employees (enjoying a reasonably high standard of living and providing security for themselves and their families in the event of illness, retirement, or death). In pursuit of these objectives, the compensation program may, and usually does, comprise both current compensation (usually a salary or an hourly wage) and supplementary compensation (incentive payments and/or fringe benefits). Current practice in accounting for the costs of these elements of employee compensation is the concern of this chapter.[1]

Compensation programs vary considerably from company to company and industry to industry, especially with regard to those elements of compensation that are not specifically covered by the Internal Revenue Code. As a result, this discussion may omit certain elements of compensation included in a particular company's program. It is hoped, however, that any such omitted elements will be sufficiently similar to those discussed in order to permit the appropriate accounting treatment to be inferred by analogy. For a discussion of questions involved in compensating executives, readers are referred to Chapter 5, "Executive Compensation."

---

* Partner, Arthur Young & Company, New York.

[1] The author thanks J. F. Cerny and E. O. Wood, two of his partners, for their permission to use or paraphrase, without acknowledgment in each instance, portions of their book *Tax Aspects of Deferred Compensation,* Second Edition, (Englewood Cliffs, N.J.: Prentice-Hall, Inc., 1969).

The principal accounting questions that arise with regard to any element of compensation or employee benefits are:

1. At what point in time should the related liability be recognized, in determining the employer's financial position?
2. To what period of time should the related cost be assigned, in determining the employer's results of operations?

To simplify the following discussion, it will be assumed, unless otherwise stated, that the cost of an element of compensation or employee benefit is included as expense in the employer's books, and enters into the determination of the employer's results of operations during the calendar period when the related liability is recorded. This assumption makes it unnecessary to discuss here the effects of cost accounting procedures, through which costs of compensation or employee benefits may be assigned to other time periods. (If assigned to inventory, for example, a compensation or benefit cost may affect an employer's results of operations in a later period than that in which the liability is recorded.) Such procedures are dealt with elsewhere in this volume.

The discussion in this chapter of the deductibility of various types of compensation and fringe benefits by the employer for income tax purposes and the taxability of benefits to the recipients is limited primarily to matters pertinent to the accounting questions considered, and is not intended to be a comprehensive treatment of the related tax questions that may arise.

The accounting discussion that follows is, for the most part, in terms of charges to expense in financial statements for a full year. Separate sections, appearing at the end of the chapter, discuss charges to expense in interim financial statements and the disclosures that may be required in notes to annual or other financial statements.

A further preliminary word of explanation may be helpful, concerning classification of compensation and benefit cost elements. It should be recognized, at the outset, that categorizing elements of compensation is, to some extent, an arbitrary process. For example, pension plans and hospitalization insurance programs are usually viewed as fringe benefits, but either employer or employee may look upon them as compensation. Similarly, a stock option plan may be, in some instances, considered a form of incentive compensation and, in others, a fringe benefit. Furthermore, deferred compensation may be payable in cash or in shares of the employer's stock. Nevertheless, it is useful to have some structural classification, however arbitrary, on which to build a discussion such as this. Consequently, the following arrangement has been chosen:

1. Compensation payable when earned:
   (a) Basic compensation.
   (b) Incentive compensation.
2. Deferred compensation:

(a) Deferred incentive compensation plans.

(b) Deferred salary arrangements.

3. Fringe benefits:

  (a) Stock option and stock purchase plans.

  (b) Shadow stock plans.

  (c) Retirement programs:

    (1) Pension plans.

    (2) Other retirement programs—deferred profit-sharing plans, money purchase plans, stock bonus plans, and employee savings plans.

  (d) Compensation for time not worked:

    (1) Vacations, sick leave, and holidays.

    (2) Layoffs.

  (e) Groups insurance—life, accident, hospitalization, medical, surgical.

  (f) Social insurance—social security, state unemployment, workmen's compensation.

Compensation payable when earned

In most companies, the greater part of total compensation is payable when earned. In this context, "when earned" implies, in most instances, some degree of delay—usually not more than two or three weeks—between the earning and the payment. Compensation involving relatively long intervals between the earning period and the time of payment is discussed below under "deferred compensation." Compensation payable when earned is mentioned in this discussion primarily for the sake of completeness; it poses few, if any, accounting problems.

Basic compensation

Basic compensation consists principally of salaries and wages, both measured by the passage of time. Salaries are fixed payments made periodically, ordinarily by the week, half-month, or month. Wages are variable payments ordinarily equal to the product of an hourly pay rate and the number of hours worked in a given pay period, usually one or two weeks. Either type of compensation may include payments for overtime—typically, all hours worked in excess of 40 per week or eight per day. The liability and the related expense are ordinarily recognized during the period in which the compensation is earned; in the usual case, the period is specified in making the payment.

Incentive compensation

Incentive compensation is a means by which the employer appeals to the financial self-interest of the employee, in order to obtain a higher quantity or quality of output than would otherwise be achieved. For the employee, incentive compensation has the appeal that his expenditure of effort has a more or less immediate and direct effect on the amount of his compensation. Piecework payments to factory production workers (based on output) and commission payments to salesmen (based on sales) are examples of incentive compensation payable when earned. Such payments may be made in addition to a basic salary or wage measured by the passage of time, or they may be the sole form of compensation. Ordinarily, incentive compensation payments apply to a specific period of time. The liability is recognized, and the compensation is included under expense in the incentive period. If the incentive period is not coextensive with an accounting period, appropriate procedures should be developed to permit determination of the amount applicable to the accounting periods involved.

Deferred compensation

Deferred compensation arrangements fall into two catgories: deferred incentive compensation plans and deferred salary arrangements.

Deferred incentive compensation plans

Some types of incentive compensation are related less directly to the employee's performance than in the case of piecework or commissions. Incentive payments falling into this category include those commonly referred to as additional compensation, extra compensation, and bonuses. For the most part, such payments are made to salaried employees only— ordinarily those classed as executives. A profit-sharing plan is another type of incentive compensation arrangement, which frequently includes hourly-rated employees and salaried employees not in the executive group, in addition to those classed as executives.

Programs of deferred incentive compensation may vary in a number of respects, including the following:

1. Degree of formality. The range is from a simple situation, in which amounts are determined arbitrarily by the president of a small company, to a formal plan of a large company, administered by a committee of the board of directors.
2. Basis of determining the total amount to be allocated among employees. The amount may be determined arbitrarily, by the president of a small company or, more formally, by the board of directors of a large company. One of the more common methods of determination is a formula in which the principal variable is the employer's profit for a specific fiscal year. In any event, the amount of the company's actual or expected earnings for a specific period usually influences the determination.

3. Basis of determining which employees will receive payments and the amount each should receive. Sometimes this determination is arbitrary; in other instances, a committee awards amounts on the basis of its appraisal of the contributions of individual executives to the success of the company. Again, a formula approved by the board of directors may be used. For example, each employee (or each participating employee) may receive an amount equivalent to:

(a) two weeks' salary or wages (an average may be used for hourly workers).

(b) one, two, or three weeks' salary or wages, depending on length of service (an average may be used for hourly workers).

(c) two, four, or six percent of earnings for the year, depending on length of service.

PROFIT-SHARING INCENTIVE PLAN. In a profit-sharing incentive plan, the aggregate amount to be divided among participating employees is determined by a formula in which the principal variable is the employer's profit for a specific fiscal year. The amount may, for example, be:

1. 10 percent of net income (as defined).

2. 15 percent of net income (as defined) in excess of a specified return (for example, 12 percent) on stockholders' equity.

3. 25 percent of earnings (as defined) before income tax.

A formula for allocating the total amount among participating employees is also given in the plan. The allocation is usually based on the employees' compensation or on a combination of compensation and length of service. Fund earnings and, in most instances, forfeitures (amounts becoming available because of the withdrawal of participants before their rights have vested) are also allocated among participants.

It is essential that terms about which there may be uncertainty be carefully defined in the plan. Thus, net income may be defined as the amount reported in the employer's annual report to stockholders, with one or more adjustments. For simplicity, one of the adjustments may be to add the provision for payments under the plan. It is also common to exclude certain types of extraordinary gains and losses from the incentive earnings base, because they usually are not the result of the efforts of employees participating in the plan. The method of handling adjustments of operations of prior periods may be stated. If a return on stockholders' equity is specified, the plan should point out whether the base is the amount at the beginning of the fiscal year, the average amount for the year, or an amount determined in some other way. This type of plan is closely related, in its accounting consequences, to a profit-sharing retirement plan discussed later in this chapter.

ACCOUNTING CONSIDERATIONS. As with other forms of compensation, the principal accounting problem is to identify the point in time at which the liability for deferred incentive compensation arises, and the period to which the expense applies. Usually the amounts awarded are understood, by employer and employee alike, to be compensation with respect to a specific fiscal year. Awards are often authorized, usually in the aggregate, by the employer's board of directors, whose resolution may specify the period (usually a fiscal year) to which the awards apply. Typically, the liability is recognized at the end of the fiscal year—to the extent not recognized earlier (see the discussions later in this chapter of interim financial statements)—and the additional compensation is included in expense for the year.

Payment in shares of stock.   If payment of all or part of additional compensation is to be made in shares of the employer's capital stock, the number of shares is usually determined by the market value per share on a specific date. The accounting result depends on whether the shares used are: (1) treasury shares, carried at cost (including shares purchased for use in paying additional compensation), or (2) unissued stock or treasury stock, carried at par or stated value.

If treasury stock carried at cost is used, an acceptable procedure is to: (1) reduce the carrying value of treasury stock by the cost of the shares issued, (2) reduce the liability for compensation by the value (usually fair value) assigned to the shares, and (3) increase or reduce capital in excess of par value, by the difference between the assigned value and the cost.

If unissued stock or treasury stock carried at par or stated value is used, the usual procedure is to: (1) reduce the liability for compensation by the value (usually fair value) assigned to the shares issued, (2) increase capital stock by the par or stated value, and (3) increase capital in excess of par value by the amount by which the assigned value is greater than par value.

In either event, an adjustment of the related income tax accounts may be required, if the resulting deduction for income tax purposes differs from the amount of the liability extinguished. In general, the employer has a deduction for tax purposes, at the time the shares are distributed, in an amount equal to their fair value at the date of distribution.

Delayed payment.   In some instances, especially in the case of executives, payment of all or part of additional compensation awarded for a given year is delayed. For example, one fourth of the amount may be payable immediately and an additional one fourth may become payable at the end of each of the three succeeding years, but only if the executive is in the company's employ at each of the succeeding payment dates. Such a period of delay is commonly called the "earning-out" period. In this type of arrangement, a question may be raised as to whether some or all of the additional compensation should be allocated to the earning-out period, since the effect of the requirement of continued employment may be to keep the executive from leaving the company's employ. Customarily, however, accounting recognition is not given to the earning-out requirement; the entire amount is included in expense for the year in which it was awarded.

Deferred salary arrangements

The deferred salary arrangement, usually with an individual executive, is what is often meant when the unqualified expression "deferred compensation" is used. In most deferred salary arrangements, there is a tax saving for the executive, because part of his compensation becomes taxable after his retirement from active employment, presumably at rates lower than those applicable during his earlier years of higher income. Ordinarily, the payments are deductible to the employer when taxable to the executive.

Typically, a deferred salary arrangement is a contract of employment; among other matters, it specifies the duties the executive is to perform and the compensation he is to receive during his period of active employment. The contract provides that the executive will receive periodic payments, after his retirement, for the remainder of his lifetime or for a stated number of years, and may also provide that payments will be made to a beneficiary, in the event of his death. With the intent of making the payments forfeitable, and hence not immediately taxable, the executive may also agree that, following his retirement, he will: (1) refrain from competing with the employer; and/or (2) perform consulting services, during the retirement period, when requested to do so by the employer. His right to receive the deferred payments may be contingent upon his fulfilling these or other conditions.

ACCOUNTING CONSIDERATIONS. The contingencies introduced into deferred salary arrangements have raised some troublesome accounting questions. Prior to 1968, various methods were used in accounting for the cost of deferred payments. Late in 1967, the Accounting Principles Board issued an Opinion[2] dealing with, among other matters, deferred salary arrangements (referred to in the Opinion as "deferred compensation contracts"). The Opinion (in paragraph 6) provides as follows:

The Board believes that . . . deferred compensation contracts should be accounted for individually on an accrual basis. Such contracts customarily include certain requirements, such as continued employment for a specified period and availability for consulting services and agreements not to compete after retirement, which, if not complied with, remove the employer's obligations for future payments. The estimated amounts* to be paid under each contract should be

---

[2] Opinion No. 12, "Omnibus Opinion—1967," issued in 1967 by the Accounting Principles Board of the American Institute of Certified Public Accountants.

* The amounts to be accrued periodically should result in an accrued amount at the end of the term of active employment which is not less than the then present value of the estimated payments to be made.

accrued in a systematic and rational manner over the period of active employment from the time the contract is entered into, unless it is evident that future services expected to be received by the employer are commensurate with the payments, or a portion of the payments, to be made. If elements of both current and future services are present, only the portion applicable to the current services should be accrued.

Applying this provision calls for a careful appraisal of the circumstances surrounding each contract, including the circumstances expected to prevail after the retirement of the executive. Essentially, the procedure required is to estimate the value of the actual services, if any, which the executive is expected to perform after retirement, and to include currently in expense a provision for the cost of future payments in excess of such value. The Opinion also includes paragraphs dealing with contracts which provide for mimimum lump-sum settlements and contracts with executives who were actively employed at the effective date of the Opinion (January 1, 1968), or the first day of the employer's fiscal year beginning thereafter.

Fringe benefits

In the following paragraphs, various types of compensation elements, classified for purposes of this chapter as fringe benefits, are discussed.

Stock option and stock purchase plans

To attract and hold executives and other employees, and to give them an incentive for superior performance, many companies issue stock options. Ordinarily, such options give an employee the right to purchase shares of the employer's capital stock at a stated price during a specific period of time. If the stock rises in value (in theory, at least in part as a result of the efforts of the employee), the employee may profit by purchasing the optioned shares at a price less than the fair market value.

QUALIFIED STOCK OPTION PLANS.   Usually, options granted to executives are issued under a plan which meets the tests for "qualified stock option plans," imposed by the Internal Revenue Code. If the requirements of the Code are met, the executive receives favorable tax treatment and is deemed not to realize income at the date of exercise. If the executive does not dispose of the shares within three years after he purchases them (the holding period), and if he later sells the shares, any gain is taxed as a long-term capital gain and any loss is a long-term capital loss.[3]

---

[3] Similar tax benefits are available to employees who exercise options that were issued before 1964, under a plan meeting the tests prescribed for a "restricted stock option plan."

If the employee sells shares, acquired under a qualified stock option plan before the end of the three-year holding period, any gain is compensatory income, and the employer may obtain a tax deduction. Otherwise, neither the issuance of the options nor their exercise results in a deduction for the employer for federal income tax purposes.

Accounting considerations. The principal accounting question that arises, with respect to stock options, is how to measure the compensation, if any, that has resulted from their issuance. The widely recognized use of options as an element of compensation suggests that an expense results in every instance. This notion could be given effect, on a theoretically sound basis, by recording as expense the fair value of options issued (the offset being an increase in capital in excess of par value); the fair value of options, although obscure, could be determined by appraisal. That procedure, however, has not been adopted, presumably because it was not considered practical.

In practice, most companies follow the principles outlined in Chapter 13(b), "Compensation Involved in Stock Option and Stock Purchase Plans," of ARB No. 43.[4] Under the provisions of that chapter, compensation is recorded only if, and to the extent that, the price at which optioned stock may be purchased is less than the fair value of the stock at the date the option is granted. Since it is a requirement of the Internal Revenue Code that the option price under a qualified stock option plan be at least equal to the fair value of the stock, it is clear that no compensation (for accounting purposes) can result under ARB 43 from the issuance of options under a qualified plan.[5] Reference is made to Page 19, for a discussion of the employer's procedures in accounting for tax benefits arising in connecting with employee stock option plans.

EMPLOYEE STOCK PURCHASE PLANS. An employee stock purchase plan also calls for the issuance of options, but it differs from a qualified stock option plan in important respects. Among other requirements, an employee stock purchase plan must avoid discrimination, by making options available generally to all employees (certain categories may be excluded). In some instances, the employee stock purchase plan is designed to raise capital, rather than to provide an incentive, although the latter may result. The employee stock purchase plan has two holding periods: (a) two years from the date on which the option was granted, and (b) six months from the date on which the stock was transferred to the employee. The option price may not be below 85 percent of the lower

---

[4] Committee on Accounting Procedure, "Restatement and Revision of Accounting Research Bulletins," *Accounting Research Bulletin No. 43*, The American Institute of Certified Public Accountants, 1953.

[5] Compensation was recorded only rarely under "restricted stock option plans" entered into prior to 1964 under the Internal Revenue Code as then in effect. Although the fair value under such options was permitted to exceed the option price, the aggregate excess was seldom material, and so was ordinarily disregarded.

of the fair market stock value at the option grant date or the fair market stock value at the option exercise date. If the option price is less than the fair market stock value on the date of grant, the individual may have taxable income upon disposition of the stock; the employer, however, does not receive a deduction.

Accounting considerations.   Because the option price may be less than the fair value of the stock at the date the option is granted, compensation may be deemed to have been incurred under the provisions of ARB 43, cited above. If the difference is material, in relation to the employer's financial statements, it is recorded as a compensation cost, and there is an offsetting increase in capital in excess of par value. In most instances, the compensation cost is immediately recognized as an expense; less frequently, the amount is recognized ratably over a period of time following the date of grant.

NONQUALIFIED STOCK OPTION PLANS.   The tax consequences of stock option plans which do not qualify for special tax treatment are significantly different from the tax consequences of the plans already discussed. Usually, with a nonqualified option, the employee has taxable income at the date of exercise, and the employer a tax deduction, equal to the amount by which the option price is less than the fair market value of the stock at that date. This income and the employer's deduction are ordinarily measured at the exercise date (except as to restricted stock, for which different rules may apply). If later the stock is sold, capital gain or loss results.

Accounting considerations.   Nonqualified option plans are relatively rare, and there is some variation in the practices in accounting for them. In general, compensation is recorded as described earlier for employee stock purchase plans. In addition, the tax deduction expected to be available to the employer when the employee exercises the option is considered in recording the compensation expense. If compensation is not recorded, and a related tax benefit is later realized, it is viewed as a consequence of a capital transaction; hence, it is added to capital in excess of par value, rather than to retained earnings by inclusion in net income. If compensation and the expected tax benefit are recorded, but the tax benefit when realized exceeds the amount initially recognized (as might occur if the fair value of the stock increased between the date on which the option was granted and the date on which it was exercised), the excess is added to capital in excess of par value.

Shadow stock plans

The expression "shadow stock" is used to describe plans in which employees receive credit for units which are, in some ways, equivalent to shares of the employer's stock.

The provisions of shadow stock plans vary widely. One such plan operates essentially as follows: An amount determined by a formula specified in the plan (a stated percentage of defined earnings in excess of a stated percentage return on defined invested capital) is made available each year for the purposes of the plan. The amount is allotted in memorandum form among the participants by an administering committee. The company's liability to each participant is contingent on his continuing employment until retirement.

Each participant's annual allotment is translated into a number of shadow shares, by dividing the market value per share at the date of the allotment into the amount allotted. Each participant receives credit, based on his number of shadow shares, for amounts equivalent to any dividends subsequently declared by the employer on its outstanding common shares.

Upon retirement, or in installments thereafter, a participant receives an amount equal to the sum of: (a) the market value, at his retirement date, of the number of shadow shares standing to his credit (based on the market value of the employer's real shares outstanding), and (b) the total of the dividend equivalents previously credited to his account.

Other plans take a different approach in determining the amounts payable. In these plans, a retiring participant receives an amount equal to the excess, if any, of the total market value of his shadow shares at his retirement date, over the aggregate of the market values of such shares at the earlier award dates. Thus, the participant receives only the increase in market value, instead of the entire market value. He may also receive credit for dividend equivalents applicable to the number of shadow shares assigned to him.

For income tax purposes, the compensation under shadow stock plans is ordinarily taxable to participants when received, and deductible by the corporation when paid.

ACCOUNTING CONSIDERATIONS.   Appropriate financial accounting for compensation under shadow stock plans has not been authoritatively defined; since the amounts involved are frequently immaterial, companies having such plans often do not disclose the related accounting procedures. The procedures described in the following sections are considered to be those most frequently used.

At the time awards are made, the amount allotted is included in compensation expense and a liability to each participant is recorded for the amount of his allotment. The expected future deductibility, for income tax purposes, is ordinarily recognized at this time. Memorandum records, showing the number of each participant's shadow shares, are established. When dividends are declared on outstanding (real) shares, compensation expense is recognized in the amount of the dividend equivalents, and the liability balance is increased correspondingly.

If a shadow stock plan contains antidilution provisions, the participants' memorandum accounts must be adjusted for stock splits, stock dividends, and other dilutive transactions. For a stock split, entries are necessary only in the memorandum record. For a stock dividend, however, the equivalent fair market value of the shadow dividend shares is recognized as compensation expense, the liability balance is increased correspondingly, and appropriate notation is made in the memorandum record of shadow shares.

Inasmuch as the amount payable will depend on the value of the shadow shares at the time employees retire, it may be appropriate to record additional amounts of compensation, as the market value of the employer's stock increases, recognizing, in most instances, the expected future deductibility for tax purposes.

Retirement programs

A planned retirement program is an important part of the compensation structure of many companies. Most companies, that have retirement plans, tailor the provisions of such plans to meet the requirements for qualification under the Internal Revenue Code. If the plan is qualified: (1) the employer's contributions are deductible, within specified limits, for federal income tax purposes; (2) earnings on funds accumulated under the plan are not taxed; and (3) employees are taxed under the plan only when they receive benefits, ordinarily after retirement, when their income will be in lower tax-rate brackets. Under some circumstances, payments received under a qualified retirement plan may be taxed as capital gains.

PENSION PLANS. A pension plan is a type of retirement program in which an employer undertakes to provide retirement benefits that can be determined or estimated in advance, usually according to the provisions of a document that is made available to employees. The benefits of such plans are usually monthly annuity payments; in some instances, benefits include payments upon death or disability.

Pension plan provisions.[6] The provisions of a pension plan reflect the interaction of many factors. Some of these factors relate to the employees—for example, whether they are represented by a labor union, their average age and length of service, their willingness and ability to set aside funds for their own retirement. Other factors relate to the employer—for example, the employer's ability to finance pension benefits and management's point of view as to how large benefits should be. As a result, provisions vary markedly.

A pension plan may be expressed in one or more of several different

---

[6] Much of the descriptive material in this section has been taken from *Accounting Research Study No. 8*, "Accounting for the Cost of Pension Plans," by Ernest L. Hicks, (American Institute of Certified Public Accountants, Inc., 1965).

kinds of documents. The *plan* itself may be expressed in a separate document, or it may be incorporated in the *funding instrument,* which may be a trust agreement or a contract with an insurance company. In a trust fund plan, the trustee may, in turn, purchase insurance or annuity policies. A collective bargaining agreement, covering such matters as wages and working conditions, may incorporate a pension plan by reference.

Among the matters typically covered in a pension plan, are the following:

1. *Eligibility*—the conditions an employee must meet, in order to be covered under the plan.
2. *Retirement ages*—the ages at which employees (a) normally will retire, (b) may choose to retire (early retirement), or (c) may retire by reason of physical or mental disability ("disability retirement").
3. *Benefits*—the method of determining the amount of a retired employee's pension payments (one consideration is whether, and to what extent, social security or other benefits are to be deducted).
4. *Credited service*—the number of years of employment to be considered in determining an employee's entitlement to benefits and, usually, the amount of the benefits.
5. *Vesting*—the time and extent to which an employee's right eventually to receive a retirement benefit is *no longer* contingent on his remaining in the service of the employer.
6. *Contributions by the employer*—the manner in which the benefits are to be funded by the employer.
7. *Contributions by employees*—the extent, if any, to which employees will bear part of the cost of providing pensions.
8. *Limitation of employer's liability*—provisions, present in many plans, to the effect that: (a) the obligation of the employer is to be limited to amounts previously contributed to a trust or an insurance company, and (b) the employer may terminate the plan at any time.

Accounting considerations. Most companies, in accounting for pension cost, follow the provisions of Opinion No. 8 of the Accounting Principles Board ("APB 8").[7] That Opinion treats pension cost in considerable detail, reflecting in part its complicated nature. This chapter can deal with the subject only in broad outline.

Several overriding considerations need to be kept in mind, in applying the provisions of APB 8.

1. *Accounting versus funding.* It is important to be aware that the Opinion is concerned exclusively with *accounting* for pension cost; determining the amounts to be *funded* is a financial matter not within the purview of the Opinion.
2. *Actuaries.* The Opinion recognizes that the computation of pension

---

[7] Opinion No. 8, "Accounting for the Cost of Pension Plans," issued by the Accounting Principles Board of the American Institute of Certified Public Accountants (1966).

cost for accounting purposes requires the use of actuarial techniques and judgments. It provides that pension cost should generally be determined from a study by an actuary, giving effect to the conclusions set forth in the Opinion.

3. *Consistency.* The Opinion contemplates that, once a method is developed, combining one or more of various alternatives, the method will be followed consistently.

4. *Materiality.* The detailed accounting specifications set forth in the Opinion need not be followed, if the effect of the departures on the financial statements is immaterial.

Although not explicitly stated, the central philosophy of APB 8 is that pension cost is incurred, and consequently should be recognized, over the period between the hiring and retiring of an employee. In part because of the long-range nature of pension cost and the involvement of actuarial science in computing it, there are different points of view as to its composition. APB 8 evidences a compromise on the fundamental issue of accounting for prior service cost. As a matter of actuarial convenience, pension cost is divided, in many determinations, into *prior service cost* and *normal cost.* Prior service cost is the cost assigned, under the actuarial cost method in use, to service credits for years prior to the date of determination; it includes *past service cost,* the cost assigned to service credits for years prior to the inception of the plan. Normal cost is the cost assigned to service credits of the current and subsequent years.

The compromise, on prior service cost, is expressed in the requirement that the chosen accounting method result in an annual provision for pension cost between minimum and maximum amounts, which are described in the Opinion (paragraph 17).

1. *The minimum* annual provision comprises: (a) the normal cost, (b) interest on any unfunded prior service cost, and (c) if required, a provision for vested benefits (benefits not contingent on the continued performance of services for the employer).

2. *The maximum* annual provision comprises: (a) the normal cost, (b) 10 percent of the initial amounts of past service cost and any prior service cost increments (increases or decreases in prior service cost arising upon amendment of a plan), and (c) interest on any difference between expense provisions and amounts funded.

In the calculations, actuaries use techniques called "actuarial cost methods," or "funding methods" (examples are the "entry age normal method" and the "unit credit method"). Cost computed under the various methods can differ substantially. APB 8 accepts all of the methods currently in use, other than the one known as the terminal funding method. It rejects this method and also the pay-as-you-go procedure, neither of which provides for the cost of an employee's pension during his period of active service.

The Opinion allows for alternative procedures in accounting for actuarial gains and losses—the adjustments that arise when experience in matters such as mortality and fund earnings differs from the actuary's estimates or the estimates change. These are handled in one of three ways: (a) spread over the current year and future years, (b) recognized on the basis of an average, or (c) applied, in the case of gains, to reduce prior service cost. If spreading is the procedure chosen, the Opinion specifies a period of from 10 to 20 years, unless an actuarial cost method which spreads gains is used (for example, the entry age normal method). Under the averaging procedure, gains and losses that have occurred in the past are averaged with those expected to occur in the future, to develop an adjustment factor which is applied to the normal cost. Applying gains to reduce prior service cost indirectly accomplishes a semblance of spreading. Actuarial gains and losses are to be immediately recognized, if they arise from a single occurrence not directly related to the operation of a pension plan, and not in the ordinary course of the employer's business. Examples of such occurrences are plant closings and certain business combinations.

Unrealized appreciation and depreciation in pension fund investments are considered to be, respectively, actuarial gains and losses, and are to be recognized on a rational and systematic basis that avoids giving undue weight to short-term market fluctuations.

The Opinion accepts the widely followed practice of omitting, from pension cost calculations, those employees likely to leave the company within a short time after employment, if the cost omitted is not material. This practice may not be acceptable, if the waiting period for coverage under a plan is unusually long (for example, in excess of five years) or, if employees are excluded from the calculations until a fairly advanced age (for example, age 45) under a plan which does not deal with eligibility to participate. (Such a plan may deal with eligiblity only in connection with benefits.)

For defined-contribution plans (plans in which benefit payments are based solely on the amounts accumulated from contributions), the employers' payments applicable to a particular year determine the pension cost provision for the year. Some plans have both defined contributions and defined benefits, and such plans may raise complicated questions. If contributions are made to a fund administered by a labor union or by representatives of a group of employers and of one or more labor unions, the contributions applicable to a particular year should be the pension cost for the year. If the plan covers employees of a single company (or of a group of related companies), it would be unusual for there to be a need at the plan's inception for an accrual pattern different from the payment pattern. If the defined contributions subsequently appear to be inadequate or excessive for the purpose of funding the benefits on the basis originally contemplated (for example, because of a change in the level of the employer's operations), either the contributions or the benefits, or both, may have to be adjusted, usually through negotiation. Under such circumstances, or if the defined contributions differ from an accounting provision conforming with the criteria set out in the Opinion, determining an appropriate accounting accrual requires careful analysis, based on the facts of each situation.

APB 8 applies to insured plans as well as to plans funded by other means. For plans funded through individual annuity or life insurance policies or group deferred annuity contracts, special consideration should be given to three factors:

1. *Dividends.* Usually the procedure by which insurance companies arrive at the amounts of dividends to be made available meet the requirements of the Opinion as to spreading or averaging actuarial gains; in the absence of wide year-to-year fluctuations, dividends are recognized in full in the year allowed.

2. *Termination credits.* It is not acceptable, under the Opinion, to recognize material termination credits in the year of termination; they are to be accounted for in accordance with the requirements of the Opinion for actuarial gains.

3. *Employees not yet covered.* Unless the period from date of employment to date of coverage is so long as to have a material effect on pension cost, no provision need be made for employees expected to become covered under a plan. If such a provision were made, it would not necessarily be based on the application of an actuarial cost method.

The employer's policy, as to funding, influences the computation of accounting provisions for pension cost. For unfunded plans, the accounting provision includes an amount equivalent to the interest that would have been earned in the current year if prior-year provisions had been funded. For funded plans, the accounting provision includes an amount equivalent to interest on prior-year accounting provisions not funded, or is reduced by an amount equivalent to interest on prior-year funding in excess of accounting provisions.

If a pension plan becomes overfunded—that is, if it has fund assets in excess of prior service cost—the amount of the overfunding is usually spread over a number of future accounting periods.

When a change in pension accounting is made, the effect on pension cost for prior years is applied prospectively, and not retroactively (as an adjustment of retained earnings or otherwise). The change and its effect are disclosed (see page 1082). The effect on pension cost for prior years of any changes in accounting methods, made as a result of the issuance of the Opinion, are also applied prospectively.

The Opinion also discusses the following matters, which have not been covered in detail in this chapter: informal plans, certain plans outside the United States, deferred compensation contracts (if, taken together, they are equivalent to a pension plan), deferred profit-sharing plans (if they are equivalent in substance to pension plans), balance sheet presentation of pension cost, companies with more than one plan, allocation of income taxes, transition to recommended practices.

OTHER RETIREMENT PROGRAMS.   There are other types of retirement programs, which are not subject to the provisions of APB 8 but which are, for the most part, qualified under the provisions of the Internal Revenue Code. Under these plans, the benefits are not determinable in advance. Each employee's benefits are the amounts that can be provided, often through purchase of an annuity, by the sums contributed for him. Thus, as to the method of determining benefits, these plans differ significantly from pension plans. Many of the other provisions found in pension plans, such as those dealing with eligibility and vesting, may be found in other retirement plans.

Deferred profit-sharing plans.   The aggregate amount of an employer's contribution, under a deferred profit-sharing plan for a given period, is ordinarily determined, and allocated among participating employees, on the basis of formulas stated in the plan. For further discussion of this procedure, readers are referred to the discussion of profit-sharing incentive plans (page 1065).

Money purchase plans.   A money purchase plan is similar in its effects to a deferred profit-sharing plan. The essential difference is in the manner of determining the employer's contributions. In a money purchase plan, the employer's profits are not a factor. The contribution is, instead, ordinarily determined as a percentage of the compensation (sometimes excluding bonuses and overtime compensation) of participating employees. A typical contribution formula calls for annual payments to a fund of 10 percent of the aggregate compensation of covered employees.

Stock bonus plans.   A stock bonus plan provides benefits similar to those of a profit-sharing plan. Contributions by the employer, however, are not necessarily dependent upon profits, and the benefits are distributable in stock of the employer.

Employee savings (thrift) plans.   Under an employee savings plan or employee thrift plan, both the employees and the employer make contributions to a trust. An employee makes an election as to the amount of his periodic contributions, or the basis of determining them, when he first qualifies under the plan and, usually, has a right to change his contribution level. The contribution is ordinarily made by means of a payroll deduction, and is usually determined as a percentage of compensation. A plan may provide for employee contributions, which may be as much as six percent on an involuntary basis and 10 percent on a voluntary basis, making a permissible total of 16 percent of his compensation put into the plan in the form of his own contributions.

The employer's contribution usually is determined as a percentage of each employee's contribution—50 percent is common, but percentages up to 100 percent are encountered.

Accounting considerations. Deferred profit-sharing plans, money purchase plans, and employee savings plans do not ordinarily raise significant accounting questions. The cost is recognized on the accrual basis—that is, the amount contributed *for* an accounting period (although not necessarily paid *in* that period) is the measure of the expense for the period. The accounting for stock bonus plans follows the procedures described in the discussion of deferred incentive compensation (page 1066).

Compensation for time not worked

Some companies pay their employees for two categories of time during which they do not work. Vacations, sick leave, and holidays comprise a category applicable to most companies; in some companies, periods of unemployment during layoff are another category.

VACATIONS, SICK LEAVE, AND HOLIDAYS. The formula for determining the number of days or weeks allowed for vacation and sick leave, and the specific holidays to be observed, are ordinarily set forth in collective bargaining agreements, and may be specified in a policy statement applicable to nonunion employees. Since any period of twelve months includes a full cycle of vacations and holidays, the related cost is ordinarily recognized in the fiscal year when paid. In some instances, the period which determines eligibility for vacations does not correspond to the employer's fiscal year. For example, employees may "earn" vacation time on the basis of the number of hours they have worked during a twelve-month period and their number of years of employment. In such a situation, the employer may recognize the vacation expense in the year when it is earned, rather than in the year when the vacation is taken. (For federal income tax purposes, the expense is not deductible until paid, or unless there are liabilities to specific employees.) In some instances, employees are permitted to carry accumulated sick leave allowances forward from one year to the next. It would be rare, however, for a company to recognize sick leave expense in a year prior to that in which the employee's illness occurs.

LAYOFFS. Some collective bargaining agreements include provisions for supplemental unemployment benefits (SUB) or a guaranteed annual wage (GAW). Provisions of either type are intended to avoid or cushion the sharp drops in the incomes of wage earners (hourly-rated employees) that would otherwise occur during periods of layoff. The terms of the arrangements vary. Generally, the employer pays into a fund amounts based on the number of hours worked by employees who are members of the collective bargaining unit (for example, 10 cents per hour). Employees may receive benefits from the fund, usually, to the extent it is adequate, if they are paid for fewer than 40 hours in any week or are laid off. An employee's compensation, when laid off, is typically a percentage of his normal earnings, subject to a limitation as to amount. The compensation may consist of three components: payments from an unemployment compensation fund administered by a state government, payments from an SUB fund provided by the employer, and payments from a GAW fund provided by the employer. The components may be available for differing periods of time, depending on the employee's length of service. The expense of SUB and GAW plans is ordinarily recognized as hours are worked, based on the specified payment rates.

Group insurance

Most companies provide insurance for their employees, usually on a group basis, against various types of risks. The types of such coverage provided include: life and accident insurance and policies which defray all, or part of, the cost of hospitalization and the fees of doctors (including, in some cases, surgeons). Usually, the premiums on such insurance are included in expense when incurred. In some instances, premiums are calculated on a retrospective rating basis; under this type of arrangement, substantial adjustments may be made, from time to time, applicable to premiums paid for earlier years. Some companies estimate the adjustments that will be made and record them in the year to which they apply, so that each year's expense is stated as nearly as possible on a basis which gives consideration to the expected adjustments.

Social insurance

Employers are required to contribute to federal and state funds, which provide security for employees in the event of certain contingencies. One such program is the federal old-age, survivors and disability insurance, often referred to as "social security." Its principal purpose is to provide retirement benefits. Another program provides benefits for covered individuals who become unemployed; these benefits are provided under state laws. Under the federal social security law, both employer and employee pay a tax, at a specified rate, on each employee's earnings up to a stated level. In the case of state unemployment insurance, a similar tax is paid to both the state and federal governments, but only by the employer.

Various states also have programs to provide death and/or disability benefits, when employees are killed or injured while at work. In some instances, the benefits are financed through insurance premiums, usually determined by applying varying percentages to compensation for different categories of employment, levied by the state upon the employer. In some states, employers are required to provide such benefits through insurance policies purchased from private companies.

ACCOUNTING CONSIDERATIONS. Without significant exception, the cost of social insurance programs is included in expense during the fiscal year for which it is paid.

Interim financial statements

Earlier sections of this chapter have described accounting procedures from the standpoint of a fiscal year. The importance of interim financial statements (monthly statements used by management in controlling operations and quarterly reports to stockholders), has led many companies to adopt interim accounting procedures which differ in some respects from those described earlier.

Some compensation costs are customarily determined at, or near the end of, the employer's fiscal year but, nevertheless, are part of the expense of each interim period. These costs include various forms of incentive compensation, and provisions for deferred compensation, for compensation under stock option and other stock plans, and for pension and other retirement benefit plans. Payments, under guaranteed annual wage plans, if required, may not occur until the latter part of the year to which the guarantee applies (which may not coincide with the employer's fiscal year).

Another category of compensation, requiring special recognition in interim financial statements, comprises elements which tend to be incurred during one part of a fiscal year, but which are, nevertheless, applicable to the entire year. Vacations, for example, tend to be concentrated in the summer months. Some months have no holidays. Both the federal social security tax and the state unemployment insurance tax apply only until a specified compensation level has been reached for each employee. Consequently, they are highest in the early months of the year, and may be eliminated, or virtually eliminated, in later months. Group insurance premiums are sometimes determined (and paid) once a year.

Many companies have adopted procedures for spreading such compensation costs over the fiscal year. Some costs are spread, using an estimate, evenly over the interim accounting periods. Others are spread as a percentage of total compensation, or on some other reasonable basis.

Disclosure and reporting requirements

The disclosures to be made regarding compensation are determined, for the most part, under principles of disclosure applicable to financial statements in general. There are, however, several specific requirements for disclosure concerning compensation, as discussed below.

Stock option and stock purchase plans

Paragraph 15 of Chapter 13 of ARB 43[8] provides the following with respect to disclosure:

15. In connection with financial statements, disclosure should be made as to the status of the option or plan at the end of the period of report, including the number of shares under option, the option price, and the number of shares as to which options were exercisable. As to options exercised during the period, disclosure should be made of the number of shares involved and the option price thereof.

The form of listing agreement, presently in use by the New York Stock Exchange, includes the following paragraph:

6. The corporation will disclose in its annual report to shareholders, for the year covered by the report, (1) the number of shares of its stock issuable under outstanding options at the beginning of the year; separate totals of changes in the number of shares of its stock under option resulting from issuance, exercise, expiration or cancellation of options; and the number of shares issuable under outstanding options at the close of the year, (2) the number of unoptioned shares available at the beginning and at the close of the year for the granting of options under an option plan, and (3) any changes in the exercise price of outstanding options, through cancellation and reissuance or otherwise, except price changes resulting from the normal operation of antidilution provisions of the options.

The pertinent disclosure requirements of the Securities and Exchange Commission, applicable to financial statements, appear in Rule 3–20, "General notes to profit and loss statements," of the Commission's Regulations S-X[9]:

(d) Capital Stock Optioned to Officers and Employees.
(1) A brief description of the terms of each option arrangement shall be given, including (i) the title and amount of securities subject to option; (ii) the year or years during which the options were granted; and (iii) the year or years during which the optionees became, or will become, entitled to execise the options.
(2) State (a) the number of shares under option at the balance sheet date, and the option price and the fair value thereof, per share and in total, at the dates the options were granted; (b) the number of shares with respect to which options became exercisable during the period, and the option price and the fair value thereof, per share and in total, at the dates the

---

[8] See citation on page 1069.

[9] Regulation S-X, "Form and Content of Financial Statements," United States Securities and Exchange Commission (as in effect September 1, 1968); Code of Federal Regulations, Title 17, Part 210.

options became exercisable; and (c) the number of shares with respect to which options were exercised during the period, and the option price and the fair value thereof, per share and in total, at the dates the options were exercised. The required information may be summarized as appropriate with respect to each of these categories.

(3) State the basis of accounting for such option arrangements and the amount of charges, if any, reflected in income with respect thereto.

In formulating and administering a stock option plan, stock purchase plan, or thrift plan, the employer should consider whether the stock to be offered under an option or purchase plan or the units of ownership in a thrift plan, must be registered under the Securities Act of 1933. This is a legal question.

The employer should also consult legal counsel as to the requirements under Section 16 of the Securities Exchange Act of 1934 for: (a) reporting changes in beneficial ownership of securities of the employer corporation by officers and directors, and (b) recapturing profit accruing to an officer or director, as a result of certain transactions in securities.

Pension plans

Opinion No. 8 of the Accounting Principles Board[10] includes the following paragraph, with regard to disclosure about pension plans:

46. The following disclosures should be made in financial statements or their notes:
   (1) A statement that pension plans exist, identifying or describing the employee groups covered.
   (2) A statement of the company's accounting and funding policies.
   (3) The provision for pension cost for the period.
   (4) The excess of the actuarially computed value of vested benefits over the total of (a) the pension fund and (b) any balance-sheet pension accruals, less (c) any pension prepayments or deferred charges.
   (5) The nature and effect of significant matters affecting comparability for all periods presented, such as changes in accounting methods (*e.g.*, actuarial cost method, amortization of past and prior service cost, treatment of actuarial gains and losses), changes in circumstances (*e.g.*, actuarial assumptions) or adoption or amendment of a plan.

Welfare and Pension Plans Disclosure Act

The federal Welfare and Pension Plans Disclosure Act requires the filing of reports with the Secretary of Labor in respect to plans (except those covering a small number of employees) providing for participants or their beneficiaries, medical, surgical, or hospital care or benefits;

---

[10] See citation on page 1073.

benefits in case of sickness, accident, disability, death, or unemployment; or retirement benefits. A report, giving descriptive information, must be filed when such a plan is established or amended, and a report giving information as to transactions, assets, and liabilities must be filed annually.

Accounting for liabilities and capital

Merle S. Wick*

Accounting for the liabilities and equity of a corporation is a matter of particular relevance to the financial executive's job. The asset side of the balance sheet analyzes a company's total resources; the liabilities and equity reflect the manner in which these resources have been financed—a clear reflection of the financial manager's performance. While problems of valuation arise more conspicuously in the case of assets, the liability and capital accounts are by no means free of estimation, especially where complicated income tax problems are involved. However, in general, the principal difficulty is in being sure that all liabilities are recorded rather than in determining the amount at which they should be entered.

In the past several years the series of opinions issued by the Accounting Principles Board of the AICPA has had a profound effect upon generally accepted accounting principles as they pertain to liabilities and capital. Some of the more far reaching were the opinions relating to pension accruals, tax deferrals, convertible debt, and debt issued with stock warrants. And Opinion 9, "Reporting the Results of Operations," radically changed the types of charges and credits that may properly be entered directly to retained earnings.

The interaction of the APB pronouncements and the accelerated rate at which they have been issued makes cross reference to individual APB opinions difficult. Recognizing this problem, the AICPA arranged for Commerce Clearing House to publish a two volume looseleaf set entitled

* Vice President, New York Stock Exchange, New York.

Accounting Principles. This publication is an official composite of currently effective AICPA Accounting Principles.

Current liabilities

Liabilities classified as current are those that are due to be paid within the operating cycle—ordinarily one year. Because of the importance given to financial ratios which include current liabilities as a factor, it is important that care be exercised in segregating liabilities as between current and long term.

Accounts and notes payable

Trade accounts payable represent the obligations of the company to its suppliers. In recording these obligations, it is important to give attention to the problem of cut-offs. Under the accrual basis of accounting, liabilities for goods and services are properly recognized at the time legal title to the goods passes or the services are rendered. If the company ordinarily records a purchase at the time an invoice is received, an adjusting entry will have to be made at the end of the accounting period whenever title has passed or services have been received and no invoice has been received.

Credit balances carried in asset accounts should normally be reflected as liabilities in financial statements. Credit balances in accounts receivable, for example, should be treated as accounts payable.

Notes payable represent the obligations of the company under legal instruments in which there is a promise to pay a specified amount at a specified time. Short term bank loans are probably the best example. Where obligations are secured by specific assets, the pledged assets should be identified and the extent of the security disclosed in the balance sheet or notes.

Accrued expenses

When an expense has been incurred by virtue of benefits having been received but the liability is not due or payable, the obligation should be recorded as an accrued expense. The most common such expenses are employee compensation, rent, interest, and taxes. Estimated liabilities for product warranties would also be included under this heading.

Accrued pension costs

Most pension plans are funded, i.e., administered by trustees who receive periodic payments from the company and administer the investment of the funds and the eventual payments to retired employees. The assets and liabilities of such a pension trust are not reflected in the company's financial statements.

The following disclosure with regard to employee pension plans is called for in the financial statements:

1. Description of the employee groups covered.
2. Accounting and funding policies followed.
3. Pension cost for the period being reported on.
4. The excess, if any, of the actuarially computed value of vested benefits over amounts provided in the fund or financial statements.
5. Any significant changes in the plan or accounting or funding policy.

The ground rules for the accrual of pension costs were substantially revised for fiscal periods beginning after 1966 by APB Opinion Number 8, which discusses the matter in great detail. In summary, pension costs must be recorded on a consistently applied accrual basis using an acceptable actuarial cost method. The "pay as you go method" and the terminal funding method previously used in some cases are no longer acceptable.

In determining the periodic pension provision, appropriate recognition must be given to actuarial gains and losses, including investment gains and losses. In addition, unfunded past service cost and prior service cost arising out of amendments to the plan must be handled in a manner consistent with the long range nature of pension plans so that the annual cost provisions are reasonably stable in amount.

The credit balance of accrued pension cost will normally appear among the current liabilities, and represents the amount to be funded or paid over to the pension trust shortly after the fiscal year ends. Federal income tax regulations encourage prompt payment of pension provisions. However, where there are timing differences as between the financial accounting and tax reporting, interperiod tax allocation adjustments would be required.

Deferred income

Under the principle of matching costs with related revenues, it is sometimes necessary to defer the recognition of income to a period subsequent to that in which cash is received. Income should be deferred until the period in which goods or services are provided and the related costs incurred.

Some items of deferred income are deducted from their related assets in the balance sheet. Examples are advance payments on uncompleted contracts and unearned finance charges.

More commonly, however, deferred income items are carried among the current liabilities or just above the stockholders' equity section, as appropriate in the individual case. Unearned royalties, subscription income, production payments, and unused rail and air tickets are examples of the wide variety of transactions that may result in deferred income.

Other current liabilities

Other liabilities that may be carried under the current caption include dividends declared but not distributed, customers' deposits, drafts, and the portion of any long term debt falling due within one year.

Long term liabilities

Long term leases

Ordinary leases which convey only the right to the use of property over a limited period require only appropriate disclosure in footnotes to the financial statements. On the other hand, lease agreements which are in essence installment purchases of property create assets and liabilities which must be accounted for in the corporate books.

Key portions of AICPA Accounting Principles Board Opinion No. 5 relating to leases requiring capitalization are quoted below:

The property and the related obligation should be included in the balance sheet as an asset and a liability, respectively, at the discounted amount of the future lease rental payments, exclusive of payments to cover taxes and operating expenses other than depreciation (if the terms of the lease result in the creation of a material equity in the property). Further, in such cases, it is appropriate to depreciate the capitalized amount for property over its estimated useful life rather than over the initial period of the lease.

The presence, in a noncancelable lease or in a lease cancelable only upon the occurrence of some remote contingency, of either of the two following conditions will usually establish that a lease should be considered to be in substance a purchase:

    a. The initial term is materially less than the useful life of the property, and the lessee has the option to renew the lease for the remaining useful life of the property at substantially less than the fair rental value; or

    b. The lessee has the right, during or at the expiration of the lease, to acquire the property at a price which at the inception of the lease appears to be substantially less than the probable fair value of the property at the time or times of permitted acquisition by the lessee.

One or more circumstances such as those shown below also tend to indicate that the lease arrangement is in substance a purchase.

    a. The property was acquired by the lessor to meet the special needs of the lessee and will probably be usable only for that purpose and only by the lessee.

    b. The term of the lease corresponds substantially to the estimated useful life of the property, and the lessee is obligated to pay costs such as taxes, insurance, and maintenance, which are usually considered incidental to ownership.

    c. The lessee has guaranteed the obligations of the lessor with respect to the property leases.

    d. The lessee has treated the lease as a purchase for tax purposes.

When lessee and lessor are related corporations, or have common ownership or control, capitalization of leases may be required even though they are not covered by the ground rules outlined above.

Sale and leaseback transactions require detailed disclosure in the financial statements in the year in which they occur. Leasebacks usually require capitalization. Also, any material gains or losses, and the related tax effect arising from such transactions, should be amortized over the life of the lease.

Where leases not requiring capitalization are material in amount, adequate disclosure of the present and prospective impact of the lease commitments upon the financial position and results of operations should be given. Generally, these are given in footnotes and should include the period of the leases, the minimum annual rentals thereunder, the kind of property, and any other important provisions such as restrictions or guarantees.

Bonds and debentures

Long term negotiable corporate notes or certificates of indebtedness are usually referred to as bonds. When a bond is not secured by the pledges of specific assets of the corporation, it is appropriately referred to as a debenture. However, the term bond is often used in a generic sense.

The provisions of bonds are set forth in contracts known as indentures. When bonds are publicly offered, the requirements of the Trust Indenture Act of 1939 must be followed. These are administered by the Securities and Exchange Commission and require, among other things, the designation of an independent trustee to protect the interests of the bondholders.

Most bonds provide for fixed interest payments on a quarterly or semiannual basis. The traditional practice of issuing bonds in bearer form with coupons to be detached and presented for payment is rapidly being replaced by registered bonds with interest paid by check to the record owner. Income or revenue bonds may also be issued, with the interest payable only when an earnings formula is complied with.

Convertible bonds, bonds with warrants attached, or separate warrants issued in a package with bonds are all currently popular in view of their potential equity characteristics. The accounting required in connection with various transactions involving bonds is discussed below.

BOND DISCOUNT AND PREMIUM. The proceeds in cash or the value of other consideration received in connection with the issue of bonds often differs from their face (par) value. When sold at a premium, the excess over par is credited to a premium on bonds account, and when sold below par value the deficiency is recorded in a discount on bonds account. The usual balance sheet presentation is to include bond discount in deferred charges and bond premium in deferred credits. Since the discount or premium is in effect an adjustment of the interest rate on the face of the bond, the periodic amortization of the premium or discount should be reflected in the interest expense account.

An exception to the foregoing would be where convertible securities are issued at a substantial premium. Under such circumstances, the premium would be credited directly to paid in capital.

There are three common methods for amortizing bond discount and premium. The most commonly used is the straight-line procedure whereby premium or discount is amortized in equal amounts over the life of the issue.

The second method, known as the interest method, spreads the interest charges over the life of the issue based on a constant effective interest rate applied to book value of the bonds (face amount minus unamortized discount or plus unamortized premium). As a result, where bond discount is involved, the dollar amount of interest expense will be lower at the start but will gradually increase over the life of the issue. The opposite effect results when there is a premium. The difference between the actual interest payments and the amounts charged to expense, as calculated above, are applied to reduce the unamortized discount or premium accounts. The mathematical calculations are greatly simplified by using published tables of yield rates.

The third method, the bonds outstanding method, is akin to the straight-line method and is frequently used for issues having serial maturities. The face amounts scheduled to be outstanding as of the beginning of each bond year over the life of the issue are totalled. This total is divided into the balance actually outstanding at the beginning of the year to arrive at a percentage which is then applied to the remaining discount or premium to determine the current year's amortization. The bonds outstanding method tends to provide heavier charges in the early years of discount amortizaton than the interest method would provide.

In the event that bonds are refunded before their normal retirement date, a question arises as to how to treat unamortized discount or premium. The several alternatives are: an immediate write-off to income, amortization over the remaining period of the original life of the issue retired (the preferred method), or amortization over the life of the new issue. If the refunding results in a new term that is less than the remaining years of the original issue, then amortization should be over the lesser number of years.

CONVERTIBILITY. Convertible debt securities have become increasingly popular in recent years, especially for use in connection with acquisitions and tender or exchange offers. Debt securities with nondetachable warrants, or cases when the debt must be surrendered in order to exercise a warrant, are treated as convertible securities for accounting purposes. Normally, no portion of the proceeds from the issuance of such convertible debt securities should be accounted for as attributable to the conversion feature. However, when a substantial premium is involved, the premium should be credited directly to paid-in surplus. Accounting for the conversion of such debt varies depending on the attendant circumstances.

When convertible bonds issued at par are converted into equity securities at par on a dollar-for-dollar basis, the accounting consists merely of a transfer of the amounts involved from the bonds account to the stock account. Where the conversion price is higher than the par value of the stock, the excess would be credited to the paid-in surplus.

Where the bond issue has related unamortized premium or discount at the time of conversion, the unamortized amount is regarded as an adjustment of the consideration for the securities being issued. Accordingly, it would normally be written off to paid-in surplus.

BONDS USED IN EXERCISE OF WARRANTS.   Bonds sometimes provide that they may be used at their face value in connection with the exercise of long term warrants for the purchase of common stock. The accounting entries upon exercise would be essentially the same as those outlined above for convertible bonds.

SINKING FUNDS.   Many bond issues provide for the retirement of bonds at their maturity or earlier by creation of a retirement (sinking) fund. The fund may be administered by the issuing corporation. Alternatively, this function may be carried out by an outside party, generally a bank, acting as a trustee. The fund may be set aside or deposited with the trustee in periodic fixed amounts or amounts based on a percentage of income (either gross or net) with a stated maximum or minimum. The procedure to be followed is set forth in the indenture covering the particular issue.

The sinking fund payments made to a trustee are charged to a properly identified asset account. The fund accumulated by the trustee, including both the deposits and any earnings thereon, should not be treated as a reduction in the bond liability, but should be shown as an asset of the issuing company. Not until bonds are actually acquired by the trustee is there a reduction in the outstanding bond liability. Periodically, usually once each quarter, the trustee will make a report of his activities. When the trustee reports the purchase of bonds through his sinking fund operation, the company will reduce the bond liability outstanding and refrain from paying interest at the next interest due date on such bonds. Any earnings of the sinking fund during the period will be recorded as earnings of the corporation. Similarly, the trustee's expenses and fees will be recorded as a corporate expense.

At the time of recording the reduction in outstanding bonds, the corporation will also reduce the amount of any applicable unamortized bond discount or premium that it may be carrying on its books relative to the particular issue by a charge or credit to current income. Where bonds are purchased by the trustee for less than their face amount, the difference will be recorded as income. Likewise, any premium paid in excess of the face amount in the case of called bonds would be expensed.

Disclosure. The maturity dates, interest rates, priorities, call price, conversion features, assets pledged, restrictive covenants, and other provisions of long term debt of material significance should be adequately set forth in the financial statements, usually in tabular form in the footnotes.

Other obligations

Deferred income taxes

Income tax laws permit and/or require reporting for tax purposes of certain classes of income and expense in different fiscal periods than generally accepted accounting principles permit and/or require. When timing differences of this nature are material in amount, an adjustment is required so that there may be a proper matching of the tax expense provision with the costs and revenues included in the income account for this period. This procedure is referred to as interperiod tax allocation.

Simply stated, the income tax applicable to income[1] which is reported for financial statement purposes but not reported for tax purposes in a given period is recorded as tax expense in the income account and as a credit in the deferred tax account in the balance sheet. When the timing difference reverses, the deferred amounts are likewise reversed. The amounts shown as deferred income taxes are not liabilities in the true sense of the word. As a result, no change is made in the amounts recorded even though tax rates may change materially before the reversal. Any such differences become an additional cost or reduction at the time the reversal is recorded.

The foregoing is obviously a very simple statement for a very complex subject. APB Opinion No. 11 and an interpretation[2] of that Opinion subsequently published by the AICPA are lengthy, detailed, authoritative statements on the matter. In addition to setting forth the ground rules for income tax allocation accounting, the Opinion also requires fairly detailed disclosure in financial statements including:

---

[1] "Income" is used here in the "net" sense. Reported income could be higher than taxable income due to *lower expense deductions* (straight lines vs. accelerated depreciation) or *higher income reported* (total gross profit vs. installment method).

[2] "Accounting for Income Taxes—An Interpretation of APB Opinion No. 11," by Donald J. Bevis and Raymond E. Perry.

1. Income statement.
   a) Taxes estimated to be payable.
   b) Tax effects of timing differences.
   c) Tax effects of operating losses.
2. Balance sheet
   a) Deferred charges and deferred credits relating to timing differences.
   b) Refunds of past taxes or offsets to future taxes arising from tax effects of carrybacks and carryforwards of operating losses and similar items.

The balance sheet items should be classified as either current or noncurrent depending on the classification of the asset or liability to which they relate. In addition, certain general disclosures are required:

1. Significant amounts of unused deductions, credits, or loss carryforwards together with their expiration dates.
2. Reasons for significant variation in the customary relationship between income tax expense and pretax accounting income.

Disclosure of significant differences between book and tax income is also recommended.

Many regulated public utility companies do not follow deferred tax accounting procedures, but use the so-called "flow through" method. They record as expense only the actual tax payable, even though that amount is reduced by the use of higher depreciation or similar deductions for tax purposes than those used for book purposes. Briefly stated, the rationale for this procedure is that only the taxes actually paid are considered by the regulatory agencies in setting rates. Thus, when and if higher taxes become payable in the future, they will be recovered by the utilities from their customers through higher rates to be approved by the appropriate regulatory agency.

Deferred compensation contracts

These contracts are generally entered into with a limited number of key executives. They typically provide for continued employment for a defined number of years, an agreement not to compete thereafter, and continued availability thereafter as a consultant.

Such contracts should be accounted for individually on an accrual basis. Methodical, periodic accruals throughout the active employment period should provide by the end of that period an amount not less than the then present value of the estimated payments to be made following retirement. Where it is evident that future services expected to be received would be commensurate with a portion of the payments to be made, the portion clearly applicable to the future services need not be accrued.

Since many companies had not provided for such compensation costs prior to the issuance of APB Opinion No. 12, that Opinion provides for an alternative 10-year transition period for fiscal years beginning after December 31, 1967. This alternative can be used when material amounts are involved and the remaining term of active employment was less than 10 years at that time.

Where a large number of deferred contracts are involved, which taken together would be equivalent to a pension plan, the accounting rules for pension costs would be applicable, rather than the foregoing.

Negative goodwill

The unallocated excess of the net assets over the cost of a subsidiary acquired in a so-called "bargain purchase" is sometimes referred to as negative goodwill. This deferred credit is amortized into income over some reasonable period. See Chapter 57, "Accounting for business combinations and goodwill."

Minority interests

Consolidated financial statements present the statements of a parent company and one or more subsidiaries as though they were a single operating entity. When any subsidiary is less than 100 percent owned within the combined group, the outside ownership is referred to as a minority interest. The portion of the equity attributable to the outside shareholders is not shown as a part of the stockholders' equity section. It is carried immediately above that section as a separate item among the long term liabilities. Similarly, the portion of the income or loss of the subsidiary attributable to the minority interest is eliminated before arriving at consolidated net income. For a discussion of this subject, see Chapter 57.

Commitments and contingencies

AICPA Accounting Research Bulletin No. 50 defines a contingency as

an existing condition, situation or set of circumstances, involving a considerable degree of uncertainty, which may, through a related future event, result in the acquisition or loss of an asset, or the incurrence or avoidance of a liability, usually with the concurrence of a gain or loss. A commitment which is not dependent upon some significant intervening factor or decision should not be described as a contingency.

Contingent assets are relatively infrequent. Examples would be claims against others for patent infringement or upward price redetermination. The financial executive is far more concerned with the recognition and treatment of contingent liabilities.

Basically, contingencies involve an ambiguous situation in which the outcome is not sufficiently predictable to quantify in the accounts. On the other hand, there is a reasonable possibility that the financial position or the results of operations could be materially affected. The general rule is to describe the situation and to evaluate the outlook for its resolution. To the extent that specific amounts are susceptible to estimation, the range of these amounts should be disclosed.

Sometimes companies disclose various commitments and contingencies only in the president's letter or another narrative section of the annual report to stockholders. Even where this is permissible under the materiality concept, full disclosure of all aspects of a company's financial position would usually make it desirable to cross reference this information in the notes to the financial statements. An excellent technique for providing disclosure when more material amounts are involved is to enter a "commitments and contingencies" caption on the liabilities side of the balance sheet, with a reference to the footnote in which these situations are described.

Among the conditions that are more commonly disclosed in a "commitments and contingencies" footnote are the following: pending litigation; proposed assessments of additional taxes; sales subject to renegotiation; guarantees of the indebtedness of others, such as affiliated companies; notes discounted; agreements to repurchase receivables sold; purchase agreements; long term leases (if they are not capitalized); pledged assets; commitments for fixed asset acquisitions; and obligations to reduce debts, maintain working capital, or restrict dividends.

In describing any of these conditions, it is well to disclose the period of time over which the situation is expected to continue unresolved and, where appropriate, an opinion of counsel or of management giving their best evaluation of the outcome.

Stockholders' equity

The excess of the assets over the liabilities of a corporation represents the stockholders' equity or the capital of the corporation. The ownership interests in the net assets may be divided among several issues of equity securities. Common or capital stock, preferred or preference stock, and a new hybrid type known as "special stock" (discussed later in this chapter) are the three broad classes of equity securities.

The number of shares authorized for each class of stock that may be sold or issued is specified in the charter. Any increase in the authorized amount requires approval by shareholders and an amendment to the charter which must be filed with the secretary of the state of incorporation. Previously issued stock which has been reacquired by the corporation but not yet formally retired is referred to as treasury stock.

In addition to the securities accounts, the equity section includes the accounts for paid in surplus and retained earnings.

Par value and no par stock

The par value of an equity security has no direct relationship to its real value or the price at which it was or may be sold. However, at the time of original issuance, the cash or other consideration received must be at least equal to the par value in order for the stock to be fully paid and nonassessable.

No par stock may be carried in the accounts at a stated value or at the proceeds from the original issue. The recent trend has been towards a low stated value in order to provide maximum flexibility. There is very little practical distinction between par and no par stock at the present time. Its historical importance was largely related to the World War II Federal Capital Stock Tax and the discontinued Federal Stock Transfer Tax, which penalized no par and high par stocks.

LIQUIDATION PREFERENCES—REDEMPTION OR CALL PRICES. If a senior stock has a preference in involuntary liquidation considerably in excess of the par or stated value, the aggregate amount thereof should be shown on the face of the balance sheet. In addition, aggregate or per share amounts of the call and redemption prices and other pertinent details should be shown on the balance sheet or in the footnotes.

ACCOUNTING UPON ORIGINAL ISSUANCE OF STOCK. The particular equity account may be credited with the par, stated, or assigned value with the balance of the proceeds credited to paid in surplus. Another alternative is to credit the particular security account with the entire proceeds of the issue. For accounting to be followed in pooling of interests transactions, see Chapter 57.

It is appropriate to deduct the directly related expenses of the issue from the gross proceeds before recording the transaction. These would include underwriting fees and expenses, professional fees, printing costs, etc. Using a low par or stated value will avoid the problem of having to deal with net proceeds lower than those amounts.

Whichever procedure is followed, it is important to keep a detailed record of each transaction affecting the equity accounts so that future analyses may be made, if necessary, in connection with retirements, redemptions, merger, new tax laws, new accounting rules, etc. For example, some of the aforementioned expenses may be deductible for tax purposes upon liquidation.

Preferred or preference stock

Classes of stock that have privileges ahead of the common stock carry this title. Most frequently, the preference takes the form of a fixed cash dividend which has a priority claim over dividends payable on the common stock.

Preferred dividends may or may not be cumulative, or may be cumulative only if earned. Another variation, participating preferreds, may be entitled to participate along with the common stock on some formula basis in the earnings remaining after the deduction of their fixed dividend or after the common has been paid a specified dividend. In any case, however, the dividend must be declared by official action of the board of directors before it is payable. When such action has been taken, the dividend is recorded by a charge to retained earnings and a credit to a current liability account for dividends payable.

The aggregate and per share amounts of arrearages in cumulative preferred dividends should be set forth either on the face of the balance sheet or in the notes. Normally, such dividends would not have been declared payable by the board of directors, and hence not recorded as a current liability.

Preferred stocks were rapidly losing investor interest in the late fifties and early sixties. However, in the late sixties convertible preferred issues began to be used extensively in pooling of interests transactions and the "blank check" preferred came into vogue. Stockholders were asked to authorize a maximum number of shares of a class of preferred stock and to give the board of directors a "blank check" to issue all or any part of such shares in separate series with such terms as they deemed appropriate. Usually, these issues were of the no par or very low par variety to provide maximum flexibility. These securities could be tailored to meet a particular situation and the traditional relationships between par value, dividend rate, redemption and liquidation value, convertibility, and voting rights were often abandoned.

For the rationale behind the use of the various forms of preferred issues, see Chapter 50, "Dividend policy and equity financing," and Chapter 51, "Financial aspects of acquisitions and mergers."

Special stock-increasing conversion ratio

During 1968, a number of companies[3] issued new classes of stock which were essentially hybrid common stocks. These special stocks had a steadily increasing annual or semi-annual conversion ratio into common stock, but were not entitled to cash dividends or else cash dividends were nominal as compared to the dividend rate on the regular common stock.

Securities like the foregoing might be especially attractive to investors primarily interested in capital gains, especially if the conversion increments are not taxable as cash dividends would be. A number of companies that contemplated such issues abandoned their plans when

---

[3] Braniff Airways Incorporated, Holiday Inns of America, International Utilities Corp., Ling-Temco-Vought, Inc., Winn-Dixie Stores, Inc.

they were unable to obtain favorable tax rulings on this point. The tax status is still unclear.

From the issuer's standpoint, these securities would be useful where a dividend-paying company was acquiring another company that did not pay cash dividends and whose cash flow was not adequate or available for such dividends.

The accounting for special stock is essentially the same as that accorded common or capital stock. No accounting is required for the increment in the conversion ratio as would be required if a stock dividend had been declared. Disclosure of the nature and rate of the changes in the conversion rate should be made in notes to the financial statements. Also, these increments would enter into the calculation of earnings per share.

Because of the potential conflict of interest between these special stocks and the common stock, the New York Stock Exchange adopted certain requirements for such issues including the following:

1. The number of shares of all series of the special class outstanding at any time should be limited so that the number of votes applicable to such shares will not exceed 95 percent of the vote applicable to the common stock.
2. Where each accumulating share is currently convertible into at least one whole share, the voting right of each share of accumulating stock should be at least equal to the voting right of the number of whole shares into which it is currently convertible.
3. The automatic increase in convertibility should be limited to a period of not more than 25 years.
4. Cash dividends on common stock under normal conditions should not exceed earnings per share on both classes on a current conversion basis.
5. The corporate charter should not preclude equalizing the change in equity between the common shares of stock and the special stock which may occur in any one year because of the effect of the change in the special stock's conversion rate.
6. The terms of the initial series should be set by action of the common stockholders and if an additional series is created which has a higher rate of conversion into common stock, such series also should have the approval of common stockholders.

Common or capital stock

The basic equity security of a corporation is its common or capital stock. The ownership of the corporate net assets is represented by the stock account and the paid in surplus and retained earnings accounts after any priorities applicable to preferred stock have been eliminated. As previously pointed out, these preferences may be substantially higher than the amounts at which the preferred stocks are carried on the balance sheet. The common stock may be carried either with or without par value, as discussed earlier in this chapter.

STOCK DIVIDENDS AND STOCK SPLITS.   Stock distributions of less than 20 to 25 percent made to shareholders on a pro rata basis require a transfer from earned surplus to the capital stock and paid in surplus accounts of an amount equal to the fair value of the shares distributed. Fair value is deemed to closely approximate the current share market value adjusted to reflect the issuance of the additional shares.

Stock distributions of 25 percent or more are regarded as stock splits and in the absence of legal requirements need not be capitalized. When it is desired to maintain the existing stated or par value the necessary amount may be transferred from paid in surplus or retained earnings.

Common stock equivalents

APB Opinion No. 15, issued in May 1969, introduced a new term into the financial reporting vocabulary: "common stock equivalents." In describing the nature of such equivalents, the Opinion states:

The concept that a security may be the equivalent of common stock has evolved to meet the reporting needs of investors in corporations that have issued certain types of convertible and other complex securities. A common stock equivalent is a security which is not, in form, a common stock but which usually contains provisions to enable its holder to become a common stockholder and which, because of its terms and the circumstances under which it was issued, is in substance equivalent to a common stock. The holders of these securities can expect to participate in the appreciation of the value of the common stock resulting principally from the earnings and earnings potential of the issuing corporation. This participation is essentially the same as that of a common stockholder except that the security may carry a specified dividend or interest rate yielding a return different from that received by a common stockholder. The attractiveness of this type of security to investors is often based principally on this potential right to share in increases in the earnings potential of the issuing corporation rather than on its fixed return or other senior security characteristics. With respect to a convertible security, any difference in yield between it and the underlying common stock as well as any other senior characteristics of the convertible security become secondary. The value of a common stock equivalent is derived in large part from the value of the common stock to which it is related, and changes in its value tend to reflect changes in the value of the common stock. Neither conversion nor the imminence of conversion is necessary to cause a security to be a common stock equivalent.

Convertible debt, convertible preferred stocks, stock options and warrants, stock purchase contracts, participating securities, two class common stocks, and shares subject to contingent issuance may all be classified as common stock equivalents under the guidelines set forth in the Opinion.

When a corporation has securities outstanding that fall under the common stock equivalent classification, they must be included in the primary earnings per share computation if they have a dilutive effect. They would also enter into the computation of fully diluted earnings per share. Opinion No. 15 requires that both these computations be shown on the face of the income statement. Also, that financial statements should include a description in summary form sufficient to explain the pertinent rights and privileges of the various securities outstanding when complex securities are part of the capital structure. Dividend and liquidation preferences, participation rights, call prices and dates, conversion or exercise prices or rates and pertinent dates, sinking fund requirements and unusual voting rights are cited as examples of the kind of information called for.

TREASURY STOCK. Treasury stock is stock which has been previously issued by the corporation and subsequently reacquired and not formally retired. It is generally shown as a deduction from the aggregate of the capital and retained earnings accounts at par or stated value under the retirement method or at cost. It may be carried as an asset at cost when it is purchased under a specific plan for sale to employees, although this treatment is infrequent and not required. It is a rule of long standing that gains or losses on transactions by a corporation in its own stock may not be reflected in the income account.

Cash dividends are not usually paid on treasury stock. Stock dividends may or may not be paid on such issues. Where such dividends are paid, the accounting should follow the treatment afforded the dividend to the public holders.

Retirement method of valuation. Stock purchases for constructive retirement, stock formally retired, and stock to be re-issued in pooling of interests transactions must follow the retirement method of accounting.
1. Where there is a gain involved—an excess of par or stated value over purchase price—the excess should be credited to paid in surplus.
2. Where there is a loss—an excess of purchase price over par or stated value—the excess may be charged entirely to retained earnings. Alternatively, it may be allocated between paid in surplus and retained earnings. The portion allocated to paid in surplus should be limited to the sum of any such surplus previously arising out of sales or retirements of treasury stock of *the same issue* or the pro rata portion of paid in surplus applicable to *the same issue* arising out of surplus paid in on original issue, voluntary transfers of retained earnings, capitalization of stock dividends, etc. Where formal legal retirement takes place, the laws of the state of incorporation govern. Generally, the par or stated value is eliminated against the equity account and the corresponding shares are eliminated from both the authorized shares

in the charter and the issued and outstanding shares in the stock records.

Cost method of valuation. Stock purchased for undetermined purposes or purposes other than retirement may be carried on an interim basis at its cost.

STOCK SUBSCRIPTION RIGHTS—SHORT TERM. Stock purchase rights are short term warrants—usually ranging from 14 to not more than 90 days in life—issued to shareholders permitting them to purchase specific additional securities being offered by the corporation to raise new capital. The exercise price of rights is usually lower than the existing market price of the securities being offered. This gives value to the right. A shareholder who does not wish to make the additional investment necessary to purchase the additional securities and thus preserve his proportionate equity in the corporation may sell his rights. No accounting recognition is given to the value of rights at issuance. The financing is recorded, based on the additional securities being offered. Normally, substantially all short term rights are exercised before they expire, either by the shareholder or his transferee.

Long term warrants

Long term warrants, those with a life of 90 days or more, are frequently issued along with an offering of new debt securities as a "sweetener." Using such warrants results in a lower cash interest cost or makes possible financing that would otherwise be unacceptable to underwriters. See Chapter 49, "Long term financing."

The fair value of the warrants at the time of issue is credited to paid in surplus. Where warrants are not detachable from a debt security, no such recording is necessary. Instead, the security package is treated as a convertible debt issue.

Long term warrants to purchase common stock are essentially "call" options. They enable the holder to participate in appreciation in the market value of the common stock without making a commensurate investment at the present time. Normally, long term warrants will not be exercised until near their expiration date because the value of the call option remains open until expiration. Historically, only a minor fraction of the long term warrants issued have ever been exercised before their expiration, and a considerable number of "perpetual" warrants have been eliminated in reorganizations. Thus, warrants with lives of five or ten or more years are not likely to be current sources of new capital. Further, stock that may be issued eventually through the exercise of warrants may have to be issued at a price very much lower than it would otherwise bring in the market. Also, warrants are built into the capital structure and normally cannot be called, as would be true of most convertible securities. Nevertheless, very recently they have come into vogue as part of securities packages used for acquisitions or takeovers.[4]

WARRANT DISTRIBUTIONS OR "DIVIDENDS." A development in late 1968 and early 1969 was the direct distribution of warrants to shareholders in much the same manner as a stock dividend. One of the purposes of these distributions was to set up a wide market by the initial distribution so that a dollar market value was available for merger discussions in which warrants might be part of the package. In addition, it has been suggested that this is a "something for nothing" opportunity. The first such distributions did, in fact, add a substantial market value to the aggregate value of the company's securities in the market.

There was no precedent for the type of warrant distribution outlined above, and thus nothing in accounting literature dealing with the subject. However, the New York Stock Exchange has indicated that it will require the fair value of warrants so distributed to be capitalized by a transfer from retained earnings to paid in surplus in the same manner as is required for stock dividends. Generally accepted accounting principles do not presently require nor prevent such capitalization.

Retained earnings

Retained earnings (sometimes called earned surplus) represents the cumulative total of the net profits and losses of the corporation after deducting distribution to shareholders and amounts transferred to other capital accounts.

Since APB Opinion Number 9 was issued in December 1966, all items of profit and loss with the exception of prior period adjustments must be reflected in the income account. Such adjustments are expected to be rare, and must meet rigid requirements. This pronouncement eliminated many of the items that previously were accounted for by charges or credits directly to retained earnings.

In the light of the foregoing, charges for stock and cash dividends and for the retirement of treasury stock are the principal entries to be entered in this account. Generally, a separate statement of retained earnings is used in order to simplify the balance sheet presentation.

Disclosure is also required of any restrictions on the use of retained earnings for cash dividends or any other use contained in loan agreements, debt securities, contractual arrangements, legal requirements, etc.

Occasionally, retained earnings is segregated into so-called "surplus reserves." Such practice is not favored, as it is largely meaningless. Such reserves are, of course, no substitute for liabilities that need to be

---

[4] Samuel L. Hayes III and Henry B. Reiling, "Sophisticated Financing Tool: the Warrant," *Harvard Business Review,* January-February 1969; "Rebirth of the Warrant,"*Forbes,* February 15, 1969.

recorded, and cannot be used to relieve the income amount of charges. There is a danger that shareholders may fail to understand this fact.

Paid in surplus

This account reflects permanent capital of the company that arises in a number of ways. The most common source is the excess of consideration received on original issue over the par or stated value of common stock or other equity securities. Other sources would be amounts transferred from retained earnings as the result of a voluntary decision of the board of directors, capitalization of stock dividends, excess arising from conversion of securities with higher carrying values than those into which converted, and similar transactions which relate primarily to the equity capital of the corporation. Transactions relating to treasury stock purchases, sales, and retirements may also require entries to this account as described earlier in this chapter. Charges and credits may arise in connection with pooling of interests transactions. See Chapter 57.

Disclosure should be made of any changes occurring during a reporting period in the paid in surplus account, along with any related changes in the outstanding shares in the equity accounts. There is a growing trend to use a separate statement for this purpose, though footnote disclosure is also acceptable. In this connection, disclosure should also be made of commitments to issue additional equity securities in connection with "earn out" provisions of acquisition and merger agreements.

Bibliography

Because of the far-reaching impact of the opinions by the Accounting Principles Board of the AICPA and the large number being issued, reference to these pronouncements may often be necessary. They are published in a two volume loose leaf codified version as follows:

APB Accounting Principles published for the American Institute of Certified Public Accountants by Commerce Clearing House, Inc.

There are many matters discussed in this chapter not covered in APB announcements. For those interested in additional reading, the following are recommended:

AMERICAN ACCOUNTING ASSOCIATION. *Accounting and Reporting Standards for Corporate Financial Statements and Preceding Statements and Supplements,* 1957.

ANDERSON, C. D. *Corporate Reporting for the Professional Investor,* Financial Analysts Federation, New York, 1962.

GRADY, PAUL. "Inventory of Generally Accepted Accounting Principles for Business Enterprises," *Accounting Research Study No. 7.*

MAURIELLO, J. A. *Accounting for the Financial Analyst,* C.F.A. Monograph Series Number 1, Richard D. Irwin, Inc., Homewood, Illinois, 1967.

RAPPAPORT, LOUIS H. *SEC Accounting Practice and Procedure,* The Ronald Press Company, New York, 1963.

International accounting

Joseph E. Connor*

It has been tersely stated that "the world belongs to those who think and act with it, who keep a finger on its pulse." The quotation has particular relevance in narrowing a subject as broad as international accounting to those few aspects which may effectively be dealt with in the limited space available in this Handbook. The pulse, in this case, is the measurement process reporting and controlling in dollars the financial position and results of operations of a worldwide business.

No attempt has been made in this chapter to cover other aspects of the financial executive's responsibilities, such as communications, staffing, and training, which are not unique to the financial function in foreign operations. These added responsibilities obviously are magnified in a foreign area and require more of the manager's attention than is the case with domestic operations. The special problems of foreign operations are discussed in Chapter 4, "Operating in the Foreign Environment."

Three principal problems in applying the usual measurement and control techniques of financial accounting to foreign operations are the substance of this chapter:
1. Accounting for differences in accepted practices as between countries.
2. Measuring foreign financial operations in terms of U.S. dollars.
3. Controlling the added business risk from foreign exchange in overseas operations.

---

* Partner, Price Waterhouse & Co., New York.

Accounting for differences in accepted practices

In his *Inventory of Generally Accepted Accounting Principles for Business Enterprises,* Paul Grady has said:

. . . accountants are generally agreed that accounting principles cannot be derived from or proven by the laws of nature. They are rather in the category of conventions or rules developed by man from experience to fulfill the essential and useful needs and purposes in establishing reliable financial and operating information control . . .[1]

Grady, of course, was discussing divergence in practice within the United States. Divergence in need, which has produced divergent accounting principles in this country, has also resulted in far greater deviations in the accounting practices followed as between countries.

Factors influencing development of accounting principles

Generally, four prime factors influence the development of those accounting conventions followed in a particular country. First, accounting principles of debtor nations usually follow those of the particular creditor nations which supply capital. Second, legal traditions have a marked influence on accounting; the effect of Roman law and the Napoleonic code, for example, has produced far different accounting requirements in Latin America than is the custom in the United States. Third, tax legislation and regulations are of overwhelming importance; these are frequently the vehicles through which governments express their divergent programs for economic development, and many foreign countries require conformity between tax and financial accounting. Lastly, differing accounting philosophies and business customs contribute to the variations in accounting principles.

Exhibit 1 lists some of the major accounting practices of other countries, which differ from U.S. practices. The compilation of accounting principles set forth has been drawn from material contained in a recent publication of the Committee on International Relations of the American Institute of Certified Public Accountants.[2]

Adjustment of foreign accounting to a U.S. basis

The presence of numerous divergent accounting conventions as between countries presents a unique problem to financial management of a U.S. parent company. Where the foreign accounting practices fall outside the range of practices acceptable in this country, consideration must

---

[1] Paul Grady, *Inventory of Generally Accepted Accounting Principles for Business Enterprises* (Accounting Research Study No. 7, American Institute of Certified Public Accountants, [New York, 1965]), p. 23.

[2] AICPA Committee on International Relations, *Professional Accounting in 25 Countries* (American Institute of Certified Public Accountants [New York, 1964]).

be given to adjusting those having material effect when a U.S. reporting purpose is involved.

REQUIRED BY THE SEC AND THE U.S. ACCOUNTING PROFESSION FOR SHAREHOLDER REPORTING. It is neither practical nor desirable to attempt to enforce across international boundaries a set of accounting principles

EXHIBIT 1

Foreign Accounting Principles Different from Those of the
United States and Countries Following Them
(not all inclusive)

Recognition of currency inflation through recording appraisal values, revaluations on the basis of coefficients or otherwise, and/or current provisions for replacement costs.
   Argentina, Brazil, Chile, Colombia, Mexico, Peru, Belgium, Denmark, France, Italy, Sweden, Netherlands, South Africa, Australia, India, Japan, New Zealand, Canada and the U.K. (permitted but rarely practiced).
Use of reserves to achieve ultra conservative results or to equalize profits between years:
   a) excessive bad debt provisions established on the basis of statutory allowances.
      Brazil, Colombia.
   b) provisions made for replacement of inventory and/or fixed assets.
      Argentina, France.
   c) contingency reserves or generally excessive provisions for known items.
      Belgium, France, Germany, Italy, The Netherlands, Sweden, U.K., India.
   d) "secret" reserves, generally relative to inventory.
      Argentina, Belgium, Denmark, Germany, Italy, Sweden, Switzerland, The Netherlands.
   e) unrealistically accelerated or excessive depreciation.
      Denmark, France, Germany, Italy, Sweden.
   f) deferral, either temporarily or permanently, of profits on sales of fixed assets.
      France.
   g) write-off of extraordinary items to reserves previously established.
      U.K., South Africa, New Zealand.
Differing concepts of what constitutes assets, liabilities, equity, income, and expense, or as to the amounts at which these are recorded:
   a) mandatory establishment of legal reserves (appropriations) out of earnings.
      Argentina, Brazil, Chile, Colombia, Mexico, Venezuela, Belgium, Denmark, France, Germany, Greece, Italy, Sweden, Switzerland, Japan.
   b) nonacceptance of LIFO as an inventory cost method, either for financial and/or tax purposes.
      Canada, Brazil, Belgium, Denmark, France, Sweden, U.K., Philippines.
   c) absence of accrual accounting, in whole or part, for pensions and/or severance allowances.
      Canada and U.K. (divergent practices followed), Brazil, Colombia, Peru, Belgium, France, Sweden, Japan.
   d) prohibitions (usually tax regulations) restricting establishment of valuation reserves such as allowances for estimated bad debts, inventory write-downs to market, etc.
      Peru, Venezuela.
   e) absence of tax effect accounting (where books and tax differ frequently).
      Belgium, Denmark, Switzerland.
   f) immediate write-off of bond discount or premium.
      Denmark, Netherlands, New Zealand, U.K.
   g) absence of depreciation or depletion, in whole or for some fixed assets.
      Brazil, France, U.K., South Africa, Australia.
   h) deferral and amortization of unusual losses.
      Japan

intended to achieve blind conformity. On the other hand, to be meaningful, consolidated accounts of an international company must reflect accounting principles which are reasonably consistent and generally understood and accepted by the management or investment public to which they are directed. Where that management or public is in the United States, principles of accounting generally accepted for U.S. purposes should be controlling. Accordingly, for U.S. reporting purposes, it is common practice to assess material differences in accounting principles and adjust the financial statements of foreign companies for significant items to a basis of accounting and reporting accepted in this country.

There have been many cases of prominent Japanese, Swedish, and Dutch companies which, in order to sell securities in the United States, have publicly restated their financial statements to a basis of accounting acceptable in this country. A common device, for this purpose, is shown by Exhibit 2, an extract from the combined summary of earnings of Philips Industries (a Netherland organization) and United States Philips Trust, filed with the U.S. Securities and Exchange Commission.

The same requirement, to restate foreign accounting principles to a basis acceptable in the United States, extends to subsidiaries included in the consolidated accounts of a U.S. company. Accordingly, when differences in accounting principles are material, it is common practice to adjust the foreign statements, usually through consolidating entries, to reflect principles accepted in this country.

REQUIRED UNDER FOREIGN DIRECT INVESTMENT REGULATIONS. In addition to SEC reporting requirements and those of the U.S. accounting profession, conformity of accounting principles for international companies is required by the regulations published by the Office of Foreign Direct Investments, U.S. Department of Commerce. These regulations set forth ground rules for assessing the base period investment and repatriation ratio, as well as current year compliance with the U.S. government mandatory program for improving this country's balance of payments. Under these regulations, the earnings of foreign affiliates "shall, where appropriate, be computed . . . and other proper adjustments made in accordance with accounting principles generally accepted in the United States and consistently applied." In practice this will mean that adjustments made in consolidation to conform consolidated financial results to U.S. generally accepted accounting will have to be applied in preparing Department of Commerce reporting forms to each area where an adjustment applies.

REQUIRED UNDER TREASURY REGULATIONS. Foreign currency statements must also be restated in accordance with U.S. accounting principles for

EXHIBIT 2

Extract from Combined Summary of Earnings of Philips
Industries and United States Philips Trust
(illustration of adjustment of foreign accounting
principles to a basis accepted in the United States)

Extract from Income Statement: (000's omitted)
Net income (on basis of accounting principles customarily followed
  by Philips Industries and the United States Philips Trust)............Nfl.326,242
Deduct:
Profit-sharing with supervisory board, board of management, and
  employees...   25,109
Cash dividends to participating preferred shares..........................   11,520
Balance of net income...   289,613
Estimated adjustment to state the aforementioned balance of net
  income on the basis of accounting principles generally accepted
  in the United States (Note 1)...   7,916
Adjusted balance of net income..Nfl.297,529

Extract from Notes to Financial Statement

Note 1: The accounting principles customarily followed by Philips Industries differ
in the following principal respects from those generally accepted in the United States:
  a) Provision for depreciation of fixed assets is based on their replacement value.
  b) Fully depreciated fixed assets, if they are still in use, continue to be depreciated
     on the basis of their replacement value.
  c) Inventories are stated on the basis of replacement value, and such amounts are
     used in determining cost of goods sold.
  d) Gain on sale of shares of the parent company (Philips N.V.) is included in income.
  e) Profit-sharing with management and employees is shown as a deduction after
     net income.
  Philips Industries has attempted to estimate what adjustment, in addition to the
deduction for profit sharing, would have been required if Philips Industries had employed accounting principles generally accepted in the United States, in lieu of the
principles set forth above; that is, computing depreciation on the basis of historical
cost, computing inventories on a cost basis, eliminating depreciation on fully depreciated assets, and eliminating the gain on sale of shares of the parent company. In
the opinion of Philips Industries, this would have required the estimated adjustment
shown in the summary. There are other respects in which the accounting principles
followed by Philips Industries differ from those generally accepted in the United
States, but they would not have materially affected net income.

certain U.S. tax purposes. Under the Internal Revenue Code provisions
(subpart F) dealing with controlled foreign corporations (CFCs), U.S.
shareholders of CFCs must apply U.S. accounting principles to the
operating results of their CFCs as the first step in computing the "U.S.
tax earnings and profits" of these corporations, including many that have
elected to avoid subpart F taxable income by electing the minimum distribution relief provisions. They must also make computations of the
U.S. tax earnings and profits of their foreign subsidiaries, for presentation to the Internal Revenue Service.

The computation of the foreign tax credit of a U.S. corporation may
also involve the restatement of foreign earnings of subsidiaries in accordance with U.S. generally accepting accounting principles. Thus, for

U.S. tax purposes, adjustment of foreign statements to an acceptable U.S. basis is a must.

Measuring foreign operations in terms of U.S. dollars

Translation of foreign currency financial statements, after adjustment to a U.S. basis of accounting, should not be regarded as a task of applying a set of rules. Application of traditional translation procedures, line by line, is a starting point; along this way, judgment must be applied to reach results which are realistic.

This section will discuss and illustrate the translation rules generally followed. Comments will also be made as to situations where application of these translation rules mechanically, without judgment, can produce unrealistic results.

Translation rules—general case

Generally, a basic distinction is made in the translation process between monetary items in a balance sheet (such as cash, accounts receivable) and nonmonetary items (such as inventory and fixed assets).

Monetary items are acutely susceptible to the risk of foreign exchange fluctuations, and their value vis-a-vis the U.S. dollar will tend to vary in proportion to the exchange rate. This is not invariably the case. For example, governments may take actions which artificially hold the relationship of local currency to the dollar disproportionate to the rate of local inflation vis-a-vis U.S. inflation. None the less, current exchange rates are usually the best available measure of relative values and are considered appropriate for measuring local currency monetary items in dollars at year end.

The value in dollars of nonmonetary items is not considered to be diminished by devaluation. The intrinsic values of these physical items will generally tend to be recovered over the years, through increased selling prices in local currency. In cases where it is expected that these assets will produce increased local currency revenue sufficient to cover the dollar cost of the nonmonetary asset, the asset is usually carried forward at the historic cost in dollars.

The above distinction is of overwhelming importance in translating foreign currency financial statements. It is the translation of year-end assets and liabilities which "fixes" the resulting (residual) shareholders' equity amount. The translation rules applied to shareholders' equity, particularly the change from one reporting period to the next, are merely conventions to arrive at an amount already determined in total by the translation practice for assets and liabilities at yearend. The usual rules for translation of foreign currency financial statements and the recognition of gain or loss on foreign exchange are summarized in Exhibit 3. This is only a brief summary of the subject.

The translation process and the accounting for a loss on foreign exchange are illustrated in Exhibit 4. A somewhat detailed analysis of the exchange gain or loss arising from the translation process is also shown

EXHIBIT 3

Translation Practices for Financial Statement Items

Item	*General Rule*
Assets and liabilities:	
Monetary items (subject to exchange "risk")—cash, short-term and long-term accounts and notes receivable, accounts payable, accrued liabilities, short-term and long-term debt	Current rate, except for items which are to be settled in dollars for which the same dollar basis should be maintained
Nonmonetary items (not subject to exchange "risk")—fixed assets, inventories, deferred charges and prepaid expenses (represent costs already incurred and not subject to further exchange fluctuations)	Historical rate, subject to a "cost or market" test that value will be recovered through increased local selling prices
Shareholders' equity:	In total an amount contra to that determined for net assets
Capital stock and surplus	Historic dollar-cost (to match parent company investment)
Retained earnings at beginning of the year	Dollar value assigned previously as earnings accumulated
Dividends paid	Rate prevailing at date of transaction
Income statement:	
Depreciation, inventories included in cost of sales, amortization of deferred charges or prepaid assets carried at historic dollar cost in the balance sheet	Historic rate
All other items	Average rate for each month applied to the local currency amounts for that month; monthly results aggregated for the year

in Exhibit 5. Under Opinion No. 9 of the Accounting Principles Board, gains or losses from changes in exchange rates are included in net income; only material amounts which relate to major devaluations are reportable as an extraordinary item before net income. These illustrations have been prepared to highlight the fact that gains or losses on exchange relate to monetary items, and are measured by the extent that these monetary items are exposed when exchange rates change.

EXHIBIT 4

The Translation Process—First Year of Operation
(an illustration of a loss on foreign exchange resulting from a weakening
of foreign currency in relation to the U.S. dollars)

Balance Sheet

	Local Currency	LC Units	U.S. Dollars	Rate Used
Net assets at risk (monetary items):				
Cash	LC 2,800,000	.1450	$ 406,000	C
Accounts receivable	2,000,000	.1450	290,000	C
Bank loan payable in local currency	(2,000,000)	.1450	(290,000)	C
Income taxes payable	(450,000)	.1450	(65,250)	C
	2,350,000		340,750	
Net assets not at risk (nonmonetary items or those with fixed dollar equivalent):				
Inventory	1,800,000	.2090	376,200	H
Fixed assets	7,500,000	.2500	1,875,000	H
Accumulated depreciation	(2,500,000)	.2500	(625,000)	H
Long-term debt payable in dollars	*(1,000,000)	.2100	(210,000)	H
	5,800,000		1,416,200	
Net assets	LC 8,150,000		$1,756,950	
Shareholders' equity:				
Capital—beginning and end of year	LC 8,000,000	.2500	$2,000,000	H
Retained earnings	150,000	below	(243,050)	
	LC 8,150,000		$1,756,950	

Income and Retained Earnings Statement for the Year

	Local Currency	LC Units	U.S. Dollars	Rate Used
Sales	LC 10,000,000	.2300	$2,300,000	A
Cost of sales:				
Purchases	6,100,000	.2150	1,311,500	A
Less—Closing inventory	1,800,000	.2090	376,200	H
	4,300,000		935,300	
Salary and wage costs	2,200,000	.2050	451,000	A
Depreciation	2,500,000	.2500	625,000	H
	9,000,000		2,011,300	
Income from operations before taxes	1,000,000		288,700	
Taxes on income	450,000	.2000	90,000	A
Income from operations after taxes	550,000		198,700	
Loss on foreign exchange			361,750	
Net income (loss)	550,000		(163,050)	
Dividends	400,000	.2000	80,000	T
Balance carried to retained earnings	LC 150,000		($ 243,050)	

Rates Used

"C"—current rate, the rate prevailing on closing date for the period.

"H"—historic rate, i.e., the rate prevailing when fixed assets were acquired (.2500), investment made in the subsidiaries' capital stock (.2500) or, in the case of inventories, the rate prevailing during period of accumulation.

"A"—average rate during the period; in practice each month's total is translated at the average rate for that month–only the average rate for the year is shown here for simplicity.

"T"—transaction rate, i.e., the rate prevailing when a dividend was paid.

* It is preferable practice to increase local currency debt, following devaluation, to the amount necessary to settle the dollar obligation at current rates; the recorded local exchange loss would not be assigned a dollar equivalent. This preferable practice is, however, not followed in many instances when such an exchange loss is not recognized for tax purposes until the debt in dollars is settled.

EXHIBIT 5

Analysis of Loss on Foreign Exchange Resulting from
the Translation Process, First Year of Operation
(an illustration of the calculation of exchange loss based on an
analysis of net monetary assets at risk during the year)

	(1) Net Monetary Assets At Risk (Local Currency)	*(2) Exchange Loss or (Gain) (U.S. Currency)*
Net monetary assets at risk at beginning of year (1) and loss from exchange (loss measured by change in rate from .2500 to .1450) during the year (2)..LC	8,000,000*	$840,000
Additions to net monetary assets at risk during the year:		
a) Net addition from operations (1) and exchange loss therefrom (2)..............................	1,250,000	266,250

Operating transactions affecting net monetary assets	LC	Exchange Rate†	Exchange Loss or (Gain)
Sales................	10,000,000	.0850	$850,000
Purchases...........	(6,100,000)	.0700	(427,000)
Salary, wages........	(2,200,000)	.0600	(132,000)
Taxes................	(450,000)	.0550	(24,750)
	1,250,000		$266,250

b) Additional cash resulting from dollar financing (1) and loss on exchange measured at difference between rate at date of borrowing (.2100) and year end (.1450) (2)........................	1,000,000	65,000
Reductions in net monetary assets at risk during the year (1) and corresponding exchange loss (2)...	(7,900,000)	(809,500)

Nonoperating transactions affecting net monetary assets	LC	Exchange Rate‡ Difference	Exchange Loss or (Gain)
Purchase of fixed assets.........(7,500,000)	(7,500,000)	.1050	($787,500)
Payment of dividends...........	(400,000)	.0550	(22,000)
	(7,900,000)		($809,500)

Transactions not affecting net monetary assets at risk:		
Local currency bank loan obtained (increased cash and local borrowing offset)...............	—	—
Net monetary assets at risk at end of year (1) and loss from exposed position during the year (2)...LC	2,350,000§	$361,750

* Consists of cash initially paid in for capital by the parent company.
† Difference between average transaction rate used in the income statement and year end rate of .1450.
‡ Difference between transaction rate and year end rate of .1450.
§ Detail snown in Exhibit 4.

Gains or losses on foreign exchange

The imbalance created by applying the above rules to net assets, on one hand, and shareholders' equity, on the other, is the foreign exchange gain or loss, accounted for as follows:
1. Realized gains or losses should be recognized in income.
2. Unrealized losses should be recognized in income, whereas unrealized gains should be deferred to the extent they exceed prior losses.

Commentary on illustration (Exhibit 5)

In brief, exchange gain or loss can arise only when *both* of two conditions exist:
1. A change must occur in exchange rates, and
2. A net monetary asset or liability position must exist at that time.
Exhibit 5 illustrates the interplay between changes in exchange rates and the amount of net monetary assets on hand at the time.

In this illustration, net monetary assets existed at the beginning of the year and constituted a potential foreign exchange loss situation if an exchange rate decrease were to occur. Additions to net monetary assets (occurring in the illustration from cash flow from operations and additional dollar financing) increased the exposure; decreases in net monetary assets (occurring in the illustration from purchase of fixed assets and payment of dividends) decreased the exposure.

In this situation, the general weakening of exchange rates throughout the year would usually be expected to produce an exchange loss. The opening amount of net monetary assets were exposed for the entire period; accordingly, the loss on exchange is measured by the full decrease in rate during the year applicable to the beginning amount of net monetary assets. Increase and decrease in the amount of net monetary assets added to or reduced exposure during the period; accordingly, the loss or gain on exchange resulting from these transactions is measured as the difference between the rate of exchange when the transactions occurred and the year end rate.

Translation rules—the special problem of deferring unrealized gains

The preceding comments and illustrations have not dealt with a situation where a net liability position exists as to assets and liabilities at risk. This commonly is the situation where a balance sheet sets forth both a significant investment in fixed assets (translated at historic rate) and a substantial local currency debt position (translated at current rate). The translation of the bank loan, at the weaker closing rate, gives rise to a potential (presently unrealized) foreign exchange gain, as shown below:

Balance Sheet

(after devaluation from L.C. .50 to L.C. .30 to $1)

	L.C.	Rate	$
Cash	100	.30	30
Fixed assets	500	.50	250
Depreciation	(100)	.50	(50)
	500		230
Bank loan payable in local currency	300	.30	90
Deferred gain			40*
Capital	100	.50	50
Retained earnings:			
Beginning	50	.50	25
Current year	50	.50	25
	500		230

* Potential foreign exchange gain resulting from the excess of local currency liabilities (bank loan LC 300) over assets (cash LC 100) at risk at the time of devaluation (LC 200 × .20).

In a situation where the foreign company had no prior history of exchange losses, the accepted accounting convention, as set forth on Exhibit 3, is to defer the recognition of income. This is realistic.

Two observations are pertinent to this conclusion:

1. The potential foreign exchange gain arises largely from continuing to value fixed assets at historic rates. This has been done following the presumption in translation practices that nonmonetary assets do not lose their intrinsic value following the devaluation, and that they will produce through operations increased local currency revenue sufficient to continue dollar profitability. This is, however, a presumption and judgment would indicate caution in continuing to use historic exchange rates in a situation where fixed assets constitute a very large segment of total assets. If dollar profits are earned in the future, the validity of continuing to value fixed assets at historic rates, following a devaluation, will have been proved. With only the potential of a gain on exchange of $40 at date of devaluation, it would be unrealistic to immediately increase dollar statement earnings by transfer of all or part of the deferred gain to income.

2. Retained earnings in local currency at date of devaluation is significantly less when converted to dollars at the new rate than at historic rates. If total local currency retained earnings (LC 100; $50 at historic value) were declared as a dividend, it would have yielded only $30 (LC 100 at $.30). This is a temporary situation, if dollar profits continue to be earned in the future. Depreciation in the future will produce a heavy dollar charge to earnings. Local currency equity will increase at a rate faster than dollar equity. Local currency equity translated to dollars, following traditional rules, will, over future years, tend to approach the new, weaker, current rate of exchange. In this situation, it would be unrealistic to write down accumulated dollar

earnings to their present local currency value at the date of devaluation.

Existing AICPA literature[3] can, however, be overconservative in dealing with deferred exchange gains, and would not permit, in the absence of prior exchange losses, recognition of the unrealized gain in dollars. For example, when the fixed assets are fully depreciated in future years, the only asset left is cash. Obviously, cash can be converted to dollars, and realized. There could, at that time, be no unrealized gain remaining in the company's financial position. It is ultraconservative to wait until all assets are realized to recognize the exchange gain in income. A more practical approach has recently been suggested.

The suggested approach:

. . . postpones recognition of the realization of the gain (only) until there is measurable proof in the equity section of the balance sheet of the reasonableness of the release of a portion of the deferred gain into the income statement—namely, there is sufficient local currency at the new weaker current rate to support the dollar translated equity as it stood when the devaluation occurred.[4]

This technique is shown in Exhibit 6. The author views this timing of income recognition as more appropriate than delaying until the later year, when the fixed assets are fully depreciated. Under this approach, an additional L.C. 134, without any dollar counterpart, would be necessary at the current rate to equal the historic dollar net worth (L.C. 334 × .30 = $100). Realization in local currency cash of L.C. 134, in excess of dollar earnings, would be necessary before any of the deferred credit were regarded as realized and appropriately included in dollar net income. In the illustration, this point in time is reached at the end of the second year following devaluation. Actual local currency earnings were 234 during this period. Dollar earnings for those two years were $30, or L.C. 100, at current rates. Accordingly, the inclusion in income of a portion of the deferred gain becomes desirable in the third year.

Translation rules—the special case of multiple rates

Systems of multiple exchange rates have developed in a number of foreign countries, either permanently or in certain years. Very briefly, a multiple exchange system consists not only of an exchange rate (the free market rate) at which most transactions between countries are permitted, but also special rates prescribed for certain transactions. These additional rates are frequently designed to discourage (penalty rates) or encourage

---

[3] American Institute of Certified Public Accountants, *Restatement and Revision of Accounting Research Bulletins,* Accounting Research Bulletin No. 43, (New York, May 1953), p. 113, 1961 Final Ed.

[4] George C. Watt, "Unrealized Foreign Exchange Gains and Losses," *Management Accounting,* Volume XLIX, Number 8, April 1968, p. 34.

(preference rates) the importation or exportation of items to which they apply. Preferential rates for imports are a form of government subsidy which maintains lower selling prices in the foreign country, For example, a preference rate favorable to the current rate may be used to encourage the importation of mechanized farming equipiment. Conversely, penalty rates make it more expensive to resell certain other imports, effectively

EXHIBIT 6

Illustration of the Realization Concept–Deferred Exchange Gains
(an illustration of timing the inclusion of exchange gains in
income to coincide with the accumulation of local
currency equity)

Assume: Local currency sales prices increased sufficiently following devaluation to maintain historic dollar profit of $15 per year

	1st and 2d year after devaluation			3d year after devaluation		
	L.C.	Rate	$	L.C.	Rate	$
Income statement						
Sales	434	.30	130	217	.30	65
Depreciation—only expense	200	.50	100	100	.50	50
	234		30	117		15
Realization of exchange gain						20
Net income	234		30	117		35
Balance sheet:						
Cash	534	.30	160	751	.30	225
Fixed assets	500	.50	250	500	.50	250
Depreciation	(300)	.50	(150)	(400)	.50	(200)
	734		260	851		275
Bank loan	300	.30	90	300	.30	90
Deferred gain			40			20
Capital	100*	.50	50	100†	.50	50
Earned surplus	334*		80	451†		115
	734		260	851		275

* Local currency equity of 434 times the current rate .30 results in dollar equity of $130, just equal to historic dollar equity and, accordingly, not justifying transfer of a portion of the deferred exchange gain to dollar earnings.
† Local currency equity of 551 times the current rate .30 results in dollar equity of $165, the third year being the first one in which local currency equity, when multiplied by the current rate, exceeded dollar equity and permitted recognition of a portion of the deferred exchange gain.

constituting a tax on imports. Exhibit 7 shows one technique for dealing with a multiple exchange structure.

This exhibit is concerned largely with a translation problem unique to dealing in multiple exchange rates. Unless additional dollar accounting is undertaken, exchange profits may, for example, arise when preferential imports are paid for, rather than when they are resold locally.

Controlling the risk of foreign exchange losses

Management's responsibility for minimizing foreign exchange losses requires threefold action: (a) measuring exposure to exchange losses,

(b) forecasting weakening of foreign currencies, and (c) initiating protective measures to avoid or mitigate unacceptable exchange losses. Each of these are considered in turn.

EXHIBIT 7

Multiple Rate Translation
(an illustration of translation practice when
more than one currency rate is involved)

The illustrated technique permits all sales and cost of sales (whether applicable to preference rate items or otherwise) to be translated at the free rate. More importantly, it prevents incorrect exchange profits and losses from arising because of (a) the payment for imports at a preference rate in advance of sale (incorrect exchange profit situation), or (b) realization of local currency cash as sales are made in advance of liquidating the preference liability (incorrect exchange loss situation).

	Opening trial balance transactions		Current operations transactions		Closing trial balance	
	L.C.	$	L.C.	$	L.C.	$
Cash	1,000 (a)	10	230 (d)	2.30	1,080	10.80
			(150)(e)	(1.50)		
Preference rate inventory	300 (b)	3	(75)(d)	(.75)	225	2.25
Free rate inventory	400 (c)	4	(100)(d)	(1.00)	300	3.00
Deferred charges	(b)	1	(e)	(.50)		.50
Intercompany payable	(300)(b)	(4)	150 (e)	2.00	(150)	(2.00)
Accounts payable	(400)(c)	(4)			(400)	(4.00)
Capital stock	(1,000)(a)	(10)			(1,000)	(10.00)
Sales			(230)(d)	(2.30)		
Cost of sales			175 (d)	1.75	(55)	(.55)

Transactions:
(a) Cash received for capital stock at free rate—LC 100 to $1.
(b) Products imported at preference rate—LC 75 to $1; the liability is translated at the preferential rate (to conform to the actual dollar debt), but the inventory is charged at the free rate, the dollar difference being carried as a deferred charge. The dollar cost of the inventory in the United States ($4) is thus shown in two asset accounts in the foreign company accounts, inventory ($3) and deferred charges ($1). (If the deferred charge account were not used and dollar inventory cost accumulated in one inventory account, subsequent sales realized in cash would have been translated at the lower free rate and would have caused an incorrect "exchange loss" to arise later, to be offset by an incorrect "exchange gain" as the preference liability is liquidated.)
(c) Products imported not subject to preference rate–LC 100 to $1.
(d) Sales and cost of sales at free rate–(one preference rate item sold for which local currency equivalent to the dollar cost of the item in the United States is allowed, and one free rate item sold at a 30 percent markup).

	Preference rate item		Free rate item		Total	
	L.C.	$	L.C.	$	L.C.	$
Sales	100	$1.00	130	1.30	230	2.30
Cost of sales	75	.75	100	1.00	175	1.75
	25	.25	30	.30	55	.55

(e) Payment is made of $2 preference liability.

Measuring exposure

As commented on earlier, foreign exchange gains or losses result from financial type assets being subject to a decrease in value when local currency deteriorates. Measuring exposure to foreign exchange losses is, simply stated, a matter of segregating those assets and liabilities which contribute to a net risk position, and estimating the probable weakening of the exchange rate during the forecast period.

One type of report, for this purpose, is shown by Exhibit 8, using local currency amounts from earlier illustrations in this chapter.

EXHIBIT 8

Exposure Report
Local Currency Net Assets Subject to Exchange Risk
(an illustration of a reporting form for measuring and
initiating action to control foreign exchange losses)

Section 1–Exposure Calculation

	Local currency
Assets exposed:	
1. Cash..	LC 2,800,000
2. Accounts receivable, less allowances..............................	2,000,000
3. Inventory (only amounts subject to price control).................	—
4. Investments to be recovered in fixed amounts of local currency, less allowances...	—
5. Long-term receivables due in local currency, less allowances.......	—
6. Other (describe)...	—
7.	4,800,000
Less exposure coverage provided by:	
8. Local currency liabilities.......................................	2,450,000
9. Pension reserves, etc., payable in local currency.................	—
10. Deferred income or credits......................................	—
11. Other (describe)..	—
12.	2,450,000
13. Net assets exposed to exchange risk at period end...............	2,350,000
14. Forecast change in net assets exposed by time of next expected significant change in rate–explain: Cash flow from operations....................................	1,000,000
15. Total expected exposed position, if no action taken...............	LC 3,350,000

Section 2–Probable Exchange Loss Forecast

	U.S. dollars
16. Net assets expected to be exposed to exchange risk, expressed in dollars at period-end exchange rate (.1450).................	$485,750
17. Forecast change in exchange rate by next report (present .1450 less forecast .1000 = change)................................	.0450
18. Loss forecast if no action taken (lines 15 times 17)...............	$150,750

Section 3–Actions Planned to Reduce Exposure

(Local management should insert in this section their comments relative to the degree of confidence in the local currency and the treasury actions planned to reduce exposure by the time of expected next devaluation.)

This type of exposure report is expected to come into increasingly wide usage, as additional companies become more astute in foreign exchange matters. One author envisions:

. . . a worldwide management information system that would periodically (at least monthly) open its real time, on line circuitry to accounting needs (relative to translation of statments) . . . and a program that will report exposed assets to management on a weekly basis, for trouble spots only, and instantaneously on an exception basis, when revaluation or devaluation is imminent. This report will be designed to reflect simply and understandably to top management the potential loss expected, compared to the cost of risk coverage.[5]

Forecasting weakening foreign currencies

Obviously, an exposed foreign currency position is a relative risk of all business, higher in certain countries than in others. The cost of protective action, like all other business decisions, can be better evaluated when the likelihood of loss is well-appreciated. Financial executives, alert to recognize the following early warning signs of exchange devaluation, are the first line in initiating corrective actions.

Warning signs of currency weakness

1. Continuing inflationary spirals or an increase in money in circulation which foreshadows inflation.
2. Recurring and/or growing adverse balance-of-trade.
3. Unfavorable balance-of-payments over a period of time.
4. Recurring national budget deficits.
5. Rising interest rates.
6. Inadequate or declining gold, and hard currency reserves.
7. Rising costs of hard currencies for future delivery.
8. Existence of a higher rate black market for hard currencies.

Initiating protective measures

The treasury function of minimizing net assets at risk, and subject to exchange loss, is a balancing proposition—weighing the feasibility, cost and benefits of each possible action-reducing exposure. A number of common protective actions are set forth below and should be considered.

Protective actions

1. Draw down foreign cash balances by conversion to hard currency, and
   (a) payment of provisional dividends.
   (b) advancement of loans to affiliates.
   (c) advance payment of royalties.
   (d) deposits on purchases.
2. Intensify collection of trade and other receivables or discount re-

---

[5] American Management Association, *Management Bulletin No. 103*, pp. 35 & 36.

ceivables to maximize the cash needed for the above suggestion.

3. Pay hard currency obligations promptly.
4. Pay local currency obligations slowly (including delay of tax payments, whenever possible).
5. Borrow locally, whenever possible (consider after tax interest cost).
6. Arrange currency or credit swaps where local finances cannot be arranged.
7. Sell, wherever possible, for hard currency.
8. Purchase foreign exchange forward for known hard currency obligations.
9. Accumulate inventory, not subject to price control, with excess funds or on local currency credit.
10. Invest in fixed or other assets which will not deteriorate, or, at least, not as deeply as the value of local currency.

In considering these actions, the impact of local tax regulations must be borne in mind. High interest costs and immediate local currency expenditures may, when considered on an after-tax basis, be economically advantageous.

Summary

This chapter has briefly covered several aspects of accounting for and controlling foreign operations. Where a U.S. reporting purpose is involved, accounting for international operations on a meaningful basis requires adjustment of foreign financial statements to conform accounting principles to those in the United States. Translation of the adjusted foreign currency financial statements involves the application of judgment to arrive at realistic results, not merely the application of a set of rules. Multiple-rate translation is a specialized problem, growing in importance as governments increasingly regulate economic policy through foreign exchange mechanisms. In the final analysis, foreign exchange gains and losses result from certain types of foreign assets being subject to diminution, as local currency decreases in value vis-a-vis the dollar. It is necessary and practical for the financial executive to measure exposure to adverse foreign exchange movement, forecast weakening of the exchange rate, and initiate protective measures.

Consolidations and intercorporate investments

Frank T. Reid*

The financial executive must deal with financial as well as accounting factors when concerned with business consolidations. The financial aspects of a business combination at the time of occurrence are covered in Chapter 51 "Financial Aspects of Acquisitions and Mergers" and the accounting aspects are covered in Chapter 57 "Accounting for Business Combinations and Goodwill." This chapter will deal only with matters related to consolidated business organizations on a day-to-day basis.

Nature and objectives of consolidated financial statements

Consolidated financial statements are designed to report the financial position and results of operations of a group of companies operated under the control of a parent company, as if the group of companies were a single business organization. It is of prime importance to shareholders, potential shareholders, creditors, and others to be properly informed of a company's total financial position and results of operations. Normally this can best be accomplished through presentation of consolidated financial statements.

It is also extremely important to present separate or non-consolidated financial statements to company management and, where significant, to shareholders and others, covering each diversified or separate activity of

---

* Treasurer and Assistant Secretary, Western International Hotels Company, Seattle.

a group of companies which are involved in many differing types of business. This is necessary in order that each separate organization's performance be properly reviewed by management or, where appropriate, by others.

Under some circumstances it may be unwise to consolidate and may be preferable to account for the investment in some subsidiaries at equity and to report the earnings of such subsidiaries as a one-line item in the statement of earnings.

The Accounting Principles Board of the American Institute of Certified Public Accountants states that disclosure of financial data relating to separable industry activities of a diversified company has not been considered essential for fair presentation of financial position and results of operations in conformity with generally accepted accounting principles. The Board recognizes, however, that financial reporting practices are not static and should be responsive to changes in the business environment. The increase in industry diversification, represented by the conglomerate organization, is one aspect of the rapidly changing business environment which indicates a definite need for re-examination of present financial reporting practices. At this writing the Accounting Principles Board is studying the situation and intends to issue a definitive pronouncement on the subject. There is, however, a wide area of research required before any conclusions can be reached concerning the extent to which additional information is, in fact:

1. Needed by investors.
2. Reliable for investment decisions.
3. Not harmful to the company (that is, its present shareholders).
4. Necessary for fair presentation of financial position and results of operations.
5. Meaningful in light of the many alternative methods of apportioning the general expenses of the parent company.

On an interim basis, the Board has urged diversified companies to review their own circumstances carefully and objectively with a view toward disclosing voluntarily supplemental financial information as to industry segments of the business. On February 18, 1969, the SEC, after long deliberation, proposed to amend registration forms so that companies registering securities with the Commission would be required to furnish more detailed breakdowns of the sources of their revenue and earnings. The changes would require a separate breakdown for those products or services that, during the previous two fiscal years, contribute at least 10 percent to total sales and operating revenue, or to income before taxes and extraordinary items have been deducted. For those products and services falling into this category, the SEC would require companies to specify the "approximate amount or percent" that each contributed to revenue and net income during each of the previous five years. However, if it isn't possible to indicate the contribution to net income, companies should disclose as specifically as they can how much profit or loss resulted from the particular product line. The proposed rules would also require "to the extent practicable" the approximate amount of assets employed in each segment of the business.

A more detailed analysis of the situation can be found in *Financial Reporting by Diversified Companies* by R. K. Mautz, published by the Financial Executives Research Foundation.

There are limitations with respect to the usefulness of consolidated statements. Separate statements should be prepared, in certain circumstances, such as where there are large minority interests or where large creditors are involved. In addition, separate statements may be more meaningful to certain readers than consolidated statements. This would be the case where activities of the various subsidiaries differ greatly. Examples would be those cases where an insurance company or a bank may be owned by a manufacturing company, or where the parent company is essentially a holding or investment company owning interests in many different types of business activities. Separate statements would appear to be mandatory for corporate management if such management is to assess properly the responsibility of operations and financial position of individual subsidiaries.

Consolidated statements may not disclose to an investor or shareholder conditions of an adverse nature that could be discovered in the statements of one of the companies included in the consolidation. For example, the solvency or insolvency of a single entity may not be revealed. In addition, dividend policy may depend upon retained earnings of each separate company, state laws, etc. Consequently, a large consolidated retained earnings and a strong consolidated working capital may not be considered assurance that dividends can be declared by any of the individual companies included in consolidated financial statements.

When to consolidate—financial reporting

A majority voting interest generally indicates controlling interest of a company, therefore, ownership of more than 50 percent of the outstanding voting shares of a company owned directly or indirectly would generally require preparation of consolidated financial statements. There are, of course, exceptions to this general rule, some of which are as follows:

1. Subsidiaries of insignificant impact upon financial condition (for example, a newly organized subsidiary with little in assets and liabilities and insignificant earnings or losses).
2. Investments, where control is likely to be temporary, such as a subsidiary in the process of reorganization where upon completion of reor-

ganization, the subsidiary will no longer be majority owned, or a subsidiary in process of being sold.

3. Subsidiaries where control rests not with the shares owned, but elsewhere, such as a company in the process of bankruptcy, etc.

4. Foreign subsidiaries under certain circumstances discussed later.

Basically, the criterion for consolidation must be that which results in presenting financial statements which are most meaningful to the reader, and which best tell the story of the financial condition and results of operations of the business entity being reported upon.

It is also important to bear in mind the regulations of the Securities and Exchange Commission, because companies regulated by the SEC must observe the SEC regulations relating to financial statements. In general, the regulations provide that consolidated statements of the registrant and its subsidiaries which are to be filed, must clearly exhibit the financial condition and results of operations of the registrant and its subsidiaries. This has been interpreted (where there are significant minority interests in the subsidiaries) to mean a separate statement for the parent company and a consolidated statement including the parent company and its subsidiaries. The regulations also state that:

1. The registrant shall not consolidate any subsidiary which is not a majority-owned subsidiary.

2. If statements of the subsidiary are as of a date or for periods different from those of the registrant, such subsidiary may be consolidated only if certain conditions exist.

3. Considerations shall be given to the propriety of consolidating foreign subsidiaries with domestic corporations, where the operations of such foreign subsidiaries are affected in terms of restricted foreign currencies.

When to consolidate—federal income tax reporting

Whether or not to consolidate for federal income tax purposes is dependent upon the method by which total income taxes payable by the combined group of companies can be reduced in the greatest amount. This generally demands a long-term look at the company's tax position in order to establish whether or not it would be advantageous to consolidate for tax purposes.

Internal Revenue Service regulations provide that ownership of 80 percent or more of the voting stock in another corporation is necessary in order to allow consolidated reporting of income and expenses for income tax purposes. Some of the advantages and disadvantages of reporting on a consolidated basis for tax purposes are mentioned below. It is important to assess these advantages and disadvantages in determining whether or not to consolidate for tax purposes.

Advantages of filing consolidated income tax returns include the following.

1. Losses of subsidiaries can be offset against profits of other subsidiaries thereby not losing the tax benefits of loss operations.
2. Dividends may be passed from a subsidiary to its parent company free of income taxes.
3. Intercompany transactions can be eliminated without recognition of profit for tax purposes.
4. Assets can be transferred between subsidiaries and/or the parent with retention of the same depreciation base for such assets.
5. The allowance of potentially greater tax deductions or credits for (a) contributions; (b) Western Hemisphere Trade Corporation deduction; (c) foreign tax credit limitations.

Disadvantages of filing consolidated income tax returns include the following.

1. Only one surtax exemption is allowed, consequently the effective tax rate may be greater.
2. Only one $100,000 accumulated earnings exemption is allowed. Use of this exemption has application only to small, closely-held groups.
3. The company would be required to conform all domestic subsidiaries which have differing fiscal years to the same fiscal reporting period.
4. Election to file consolidated income tax returns is difficult to revoke once consolidated returns are filed.

In making any decision to file or not to file consolidated income tax returns, the corporate financial executive should use expert tax counsel in order to avoid potentially costly pitfalls.

Consolidation of different forms of business entities

Although consolidation generally is thought of in connection with the corporate form of business activity, it may be appropriate to consolidate other forms of business entities and to consolidate noncorporate forms of entities with corporate forms. The business enterprise, not the form of organization, should be the main criteria used in determining whether or not to consolidate. For example, if an income-producing asset such as real property is owned in fee by several owners, one of which has majority ownership, it may be appropriate that this entity be included in the financial statements of the majority owner, just as though it were a corporate organization. Likewise, it may be appropriate to consolidate the partnership or joint-venture form of organization where one corporate partner has majority ownership of the partnership or joint venture.

In other instances, corporate organizations may organize joint ventures for specific undertakings, such as contractors for construction of a particular facility, or developers for the development of large tracts of land. If this becomes a standard procedure within the business organization, it may be appropriate to apply some consolidating principles. Generally speaking, each member of the joint venture or partnership would record his interest in such venture at his equity in the net assets of the particular venture and would reflect (preferably on a segregated basis) in the statement of earnings his share of total revenues, expenses, etc. In some cases, separate statements of the enterprise operated jointly should also be included, particularly when such enterprise has assets and liabilities and revenues or expenses which are material in relation to those of the partner that is reporting its financial condition and results of operations.

Foreign subsidiaries

Careful consideration must be given with respect to including foreign subsidiaries in consolidation with domestic corporations. Because of foreign exchange restrictions, governmental controls, etc. and the resultant uncertainty of the value of assets and availability of these assets, consolidation of foreign subsidiaries may result in unrealistic financial statements. Whether foreign subsidiaries are consolidated or not, adequate disclosure of foreign operations should be made in financial statements. The Accounting Principles Board of the American Institute of CPA's states the following possible ways of providing information relating to foreign subsidiaries:

1. To exclude the foreign subsidiaries from consolidation and to furnish (a) statements in which only domestic subsidiaries are consolidated and (b) as to foreign subsidiaries, a summary in suitable form of their assets and liabilities, their income and losses for the year, and the parent company's equity therein. The total amount of investments in foreign subsidiaries should be shown separately, and the basis on which the amount was arrived at should be stated. If these investments include retained earnings of foreign subsidiaries and such retained earnings had previously been included in consolidated retained earnings, the amount should be separately shown or earmarked in stating the consolidated retained earnings in the statements suggested. The exclusion of foreign subsidiaries from consolidation does not make it acceptable practice to include inter-company profits which would be eliminated if such subsidiaries were consolidated.

2. To consolidate domestic and foreign subsidiaries and to furnish in addition the summary described in 1(b) above.

3. To furnish (a) complete consolidated statements and also (b) consolidated statements for domestic subsidiaries only.
4. To consolidate domestic and foreign subsidiaries and to furnish in addition parent company statements showing the investment in and income from foreign subsidiaries separately from those of domestic subsidiaries.

If foreign subsidiaries are consolidated, disclosure should be made as to the effect of any major foreign exchange restrictions and war conditions on the consolidated financial statments. The SEC states that if inclusion of foreign subsidiaries in consolidated statements will not prevent a clear and fair presentation of the financial condition and results of operations of the registrant and its subsidiaries, their inclusion is ordinarily permissible.

All foreign accounts must, of course, be converted into United States dollars. Working capital would generally be converted at the rate of exchange prevailing on the date of the balance sheet. Property and equipment and similar assets should be converted at rates of exchange in effect at the date the assets were originally acquired. Long-term liabilities should be converted at rates in effect when the debt obligation was incurred unless, under certain circumstances, it would be appropriate to reflect changes in exchange rates by making adjustment to the assets acquired from proceeds of the debt obligation. If unsettled economic and political conditions exist or where exchange restrictions make it difficult to transfer money out of a foreign subsidiary, appropriate disclosure of such information would be required in the footnotes to consolidated financial statements in which the foreign subsidiary is included.

Major changes in exchange rates resulting from devaluation, etc. must be carefully reviewed, and if the impact of such devaluations is material, such impact should be set out separately in statements of earnings as a one-line item.

The problems of accounting for foreign subsidiaries are discussed in greater detail in Chapter 60, "International Accounting."

Inter-company accounts

Consolidated statements represent the financial position and operating results of one business entity. Consequently, such statements should not include the results of transactions among the companies included in the consolidated group. All inter-company balances including open account balances, accrued interest payable or receivable to or from a subsidiary, security holdings, and all income and expense items between companies included in the consolidated statements should be eliminated.

However, in certain regulated industries it would not be appropriate to eliminate certain inter-company items. The general rule in such cases with respect to elimination of inter-company profit is not intended to require the elimination of such profits, where the profit results from the sale of items which are capitalized by the purchaser and resultantly enter into the basis for the rate making structure of the particular regulated industry.

The cost of a parent company's investment in its subsidiaries, plus or minus its share of subsequent changes in the subsidiaries' equity (if recorded) must be eliminated against the equity of such subsidiary or against the related debt obligation if debt securities are involved. See Chapter 57 regarding differences between the cost of such investments to the parent and the carrying value of the related item in the records of the subsidiary.

Subsidiary statements at date different than parent company

As a general rule, it is best to use the same date and to cover the same period of time for all companies included in consolidated financial statements. However, a difference in fiscal periods between a parent and its subsidiary is not justification for exclusion of the subsidiary from consolidation. In instances where communications are slow or difficult, it may be more feasible to consolidate a subsidiary with a different fiscal year. Examples would be, a foreign subsidiary whose statements must be converted to United States standards or when a time lag results from the fact the subsidiary is located a substantial distance from the parent company thereby making quick communication or transmittal of information difficult. Difference in dates should not be more than three months, however, and the SEC allows for consolidation of subsidiaries for different periods than the parent, provided the following conditions exists:

1. Such difference is not more than 93 days.
2. The closing date of the subsidiary is expressly indicated.
3. The necessity for using different closing dates is briefly explained.
4. Any changes in the respective fiscal periods of the registrant and the subsidiary made during the period of reporting are clearly indicated, together with manner of treatment.

Indirect ownership

Indirect ownership results when more than one company in a consolidated group owns an interest in another company, or when a subsidiary owns the majority of stock in another corporation in which the parent company has no direct interest, the total of all such interests equaling majority control on the part of the parent. This means the parent company may have to include in consolidated statements a company in which it has no direct ownership interest. Some examples of indirect ownership in situations under which consolidation is approporate or not are as follows:

1. Company A owns 30% of Company B.
   Company A owns 60% of Company C.
   Company B owns 20% of Company C.
   In the above circumstances, C would be consolidated with A and 66% of the equity of C would be included in consolidated net worth of A (60% plus 30% of 20% equals 66%). Company B would not be consolidated.

2. Company A owns 51% of Company B.
   Company B owns 51% of Company C.
   Although Company A's equity in Company C is only 26% (51% times 51%), C would be included in the consolidated financial statements of A because B (which is majority-owned by A) owns more than 50% of C and therefore would be required to consolidate C.

3. Company A owns 20% of Company B.
   Company A owns 100% of Company C.
   Companies B and C each own 50% of Company D.
   Company D is 60% owned indirectly by A, however D should not be consolidated because the 80% minority shareholders of B control 50% of D, therefore majority control of D is not held by the parent even though its total direct and indirect ownership of D is 60%.

4. Company A owns 11% of Company B.
   Company A owns 100% of Company C.
   Company C owns 45% of Company B.
   Company B would be included in consolidated financial statements of A because A owns directly 11% of B and indirectly through 100% ownership of C holds an additional 45% of B making a total of 56%.

5. Company A owns 11% of Company B.
   Company A owns 51% of Company C.
   Company C owns 40% of Company B.
   Company C would be consolidated with Company A because A owns and controls directly 51% of C. Even though A controls (directly and indirectly) 51% of B (40% through its control of C and 11% directly), its ownership interest is only 31%, consequently B would not be consolidated with A.

6. A owns 40% of each of Companies B, C, D, E and F.
   Companies B, C, D, E and F each own 20% of Company G.
   None of the above companies would be consolidated with A because A does not own majority interest in any company. However, if A owned 51% of each B, C, D, E and F, then G would also have to be consolidated, as well as all other companies in the group.

The above illustrations show only a few possibilities of the many potential combinations of direct and indirect ownership. The basic criterion needed to determine whether or not consolidation is required is that majority control of a company's voting stock can be voted as determined by the parent company and, in addition, that majority ownership by the parent company actually exists. The parent company in this case could also be a subsidiary (the case illustrated in 2. above). Even though majority control of a company's voting stock is held directly and indirectly, majority ownership may not exist as indicated in illustration 5. above. Also, even if direct and indirect ownership may result in more than majority ownership, such voting control may not exist as illustrated in 3. above.

Changes in ownership interest

When a company acquires controlling interest in another company at various dates and eventually gains control, the date of acquisition depends upon circumstances surrounding each situation.

If the acquisition is made over a relatively long period of time, and involves a number of small purchases, and then a purchase is consummated which results in gaining control, the date of the latest purchase should be considered the date of acquisition and the date from which consolidation begins. This means that consolidated income for the year in which control is acquired would include post-acquisition income of the acquired subsidiary and consolidated retained earnings would include post-acquisition income of prior years attributable to each block of stock acquired prior to gaining control. For example, if a 10 percent interest were acquired in 1954, a 20 percent interest in 1960, a 10 percent interest in 1963 and a 30 percent interest on June 30, 1966, consolidated income for 1966 should include 40 percent of the subsidiary's earnings for the entire year and an additional 30 percent for the last six months of the year. In addition, consolidated retained earnings at beginning of period being reported upon should be credited with the proportionate share of earnings of the subsidiary in prior years applicable to previously-held mniority shares (10 percent of the earnings for 1954 through 1959, 30 percent from 1960 through 1962 and 40 percent from 1963 through June 30, 1966). However, if the original purchases are relatively small and then a purchase is made which results in gaining control, retained earnings may not be credited on a step-by-step basis. The date at which control was actually obtained would be used as the date of acquisition, and no credit would be made to retained earnings at that date for any earnings of the acquired company prior to that date.

When a purchase of a subsidiary occurs between balance sheet dates, alternate methods for recording income of the subsidiary are available.

The preferable method, but not commonly used, is to include the subsidiary's earnings in consolidation as though control had been acquired at the beginning of the year with a deduction at the bottom of the statement of earnings for pre-acquisition earnings of the subsidiary. This facilitates future comparisons of operations and shows results more in line with the current situation. Another acceptable method, and most common in practice, is inclusion of the subsidiary's income from the actual date of acquisition or the month beginning closest thereto if acquired during the month.

When a subsidiary is sold or otherwise disposed of during the year, it would be preferable to exclude from operations for the entire year the earnings of the subsidiary and to show its earnings to date of disposal as a separate item.

Ownership of common stock, preferred stock, and debt obligations of a subsidiary

In most instances, when a subsidiary company is organized to engage in business, it will be capitalized with both equity and debt securities. Often times a company will be capitalized with a minimum dollar investment in equity and a large dollar investment in debt. This is done primarily in instances where the ownership interest is to be retained wholly or mainly in the hands of the organizer, but where the total investment is financed in addition, by others through debt securities, mortgages and equity without common share ownership. This procedure is used to set up a subsidiary, the purpose of which is to maintain operating and financial control, but to minimize or spread to others the risk inherent in any new venture. In addition, good business reasons may require a minority interest be given to those making a contribution specifically involved in the new operation, but not involved in any way with other functions of the parent organization.

Also, the acquisition of one company by another may require, in addition to purchase of common stock, the purchase of preferred stock and retirement of debt obligations, although the latter would be rare.

The accounting ramifications of the above-described situations (other than those applicable to the initial purchase of a company—which are covered in Chapter 57), insofar as consolidation is concerned, are not particularly difficult, if one keeps in mind the basic principle of eliminating inter-company items.

Let's assume the following for illustrative purposes:
1. Company A owns 90% of Company B common stock, 40% of its preferred stock, 50% of its 5½% convertible debentures and all of its 8%—20 year debentures.
2. Condensed (unconsolidated) balance sheets of Company A and Company B are as follows:

Assets	Company A	Company B
Current assets	$ 1,110,000	2,200,000
Investment in Company B:		
Common stock	900,000	—
Preferred stock	240,000	—
5½% convertible debentures	250,000	—
8½%—20 year debentures	2,000,000	—
Property, plant and equipment	6,000,000	10,000,000
Other assets	500,000	800,000
	$11,000,000	13,000,000

Liabilities & Equity		
Current liabilities	$ 1,000,000	900,000
5½% convertible debentures	—	500,000
8½%—20 year debentures	—	2,000,000
Preferred stock	4,000,000	600,000
Common stock	2,000,000	1,000,000
Retained earnings	4,000,000	8,000,000
	$11,000,000	13,000,000

3. Condensed (unconsolidated) statements of earnings and retained earnings of Company A and Company B are as follows:

	Company A	Company B
Net earnings	$ 500,000	2,500,000
Retained earnings at beginning of period	4,000,000	7,036,000
	4,500,000	9,536,000
Dividends paid	500,000	1,536,000
Retained earnings at end of period	$4,000,000	8,000,000

Upon consolidation of Company A and Company B, the following adjustments would be made:

1. Company A would eliminate its 90% interest in Company B ($900,000) against Company B's common stock and the $100,000 remaining common stock of Company B would be shown as a minority interest.

2. Company A would eliminate its 40% (or $240,000) interest in Company B preferred stock against Company B's preferred stock totaling $600,000 and the remaining $360,000 would be shown as preferred stock of a subsidiary held by others and included in minority interests.

In addition, the dividend income from Company B preferred stock would be offset against a dividend paid as shown by Company B in the amount of $214,400—40% of 6% of $600,000 ($14,400) plus the amount equal to half the dividend paid to common shares (one half of $1,000,000 times 40%) or $200,000. The remaining dividends paid on preferred stock acounting to $321,600 would be included with dividends paid.

3. Company A would eliminate its 50% investment of $250,000 in Company B's convertible debentures totaling $500,000 and the remaining $250,000 would be shown as long-term debt upon consolidation.

The 5½% interest income received by Company A ($13,750) would be eliminated against a like amount of Company B interest expense.

4. Company A would eliminate all of its $2,000,000 investment in Company B 8% debentures against the $2,000,000 liability shown in Company B statements. In addition, the 8% interest income received by Company A ($160,000) would be eliminated against a like amount of Company B interest expense.

5. Company A would include in its retained earnings, its 90% interest in the retained earnings of Company B (assuming Company A has always owned the 90% interest in Company B common stock) amounting to $7,200,000 (90% of $8,000,000) and the remaining $800,000 of Company B retained earnings would be shown as minority interest.

Further, if Company B's preferred stock shared in the retained earnings of the company, then that portion of Company B earnings applicable to the other 60% shareholders of Company B stock would have to be shown as a liability to such other shareholders.

6. Company A would include in its earnings 90% of Company B's earnings or $2,250,000.

7. Company A would eliminate the $900,000 dividend income from Company B against the like amount paid by Company B. The remaining $100,000 paid by Company B would be inlcuded in dividends paid.

After the above adjustments have been made, the consolidated statements of Company A would be as follows:

Balance Sheet

Assets

Current assets		$ 3,310,000
Property, plant and equipment		16,000,000
Other assets		1,300,000
		$20,610,000

Liabilities and Equity

Current liabilities		$ 1,900,000
5½% convertible debentures		250,000
Minority interests in subsidiary:		
In preferred stock (represents majority interest thereof)	$360,000	
In common stock	100,000	
In retained earnings	800,000	1,260,000
Preferred stock		4,000,000
Common stock		2,000,000
Retained earnings		11,200,000
		$20,610,000

Earnings and Retained Earnings

Earnings before minority interests	$ 1,885,600
Minority interests	250,000
Net earnings	1,635,600
Retained earnings at beginning of period	10,332,400
	11,968,000
Dividends paid:	
Paid to parent company shareholders $500,000	
Paid to outside shareholders of preferred and common stock of subsidiary, less portion of preferred allocatable to minority interests share of common stock of such subsidiary 268,000	768,000
Retained earnings at end of period	$11,200,000

From a management viewpoint, Company A should review its investments in Company B in accordance with proper financial analysis as though Company B was an investment and that the investment in Company B is in accordance with the investment policy of Company A, as well as its operating policy.

Reciprocal or cross holdings

When two or more affiliated companies own stock in each other, the result is reciprocal or cross shareholdings. In most instances, this situation arises when one company acquires another company, which company happens to own stock in the acquiring company. Even though, from a legal standpoint, a subsidiary owning shares of its parent corporation is entitled to vote such shares, the practical implications require that such shares be treated as treasury shares upon consolidation.

In the event a subsidiary acquires or disposes of shares in its parent company, such transactions should be accounted for as a purchase or sale of treasury stock.

As indicated above, the accounting treatment is relatively simple, that is, reporting transactions in each other's shares as treasury share transactions. However, if the cross holdings represent control of each other's shares, a determination of proper earnings of the entire entity must be considered. Assume the following facts:

1. Company A owns 90% of Company B common stock which cost $800,000 (same as the book value of the stock on Company B's books at the time purchased).
2. Company B owns 20% of Company A's common stock which cost $500,000 (the same as the book value of Company A stock at the time purchased).
3. Nonconsolidated earnings of Company A for the most recent fiscal year amounted to $4,000,000 and nonconsolidated earnings of Com-

pany B amounted to $1,000,000 including $200,000 of dividends received from Company A.

4. Retained earnings (before considering earnings for the most recent fiscal year) amounted to $8,000,000 and $4,000,000 respectively for Companies A and B.

Consolidated earnings of Company A would be determined on the same basis as if the reciprocal shares did not exist because, as previously mentioned, the 20% ownership of Company B in Company A would be considered as treasury shares. Therefore, consolidated earnings would amount to $4,700,000 (nonconsolidated earnings of Company A amounting to $4,000,000 plus 90% of Company B's earnings of $800,000 after deduction of the dividend received by Company B from Company A).

The equity section of Company A's balance sheet would be shown as follows:

Common stock	$ 2,500,000
Retained earnings	15,500,000
	18,000,000
Less treasury stock	500,000
	$17,500,000

Retained earnings of $15,500,000 represent Company A's retained earnings of $11,000,000 plus 90% of Company B's retained earnings of $5,000,000. The treasury stock of $500,000 represents Company B's 20% interest in Company A stock.

Consolidated earnings of $4,700,000 for A can be shown as follows:

Company A earnings	$4,000,000
Company B earnings	1,000,000
	5,000,000
Less dividend paid by Company A, received by Company B	200,000
	4,800,000
Minority interest in B (10% of $1,000,000)	100,000
Consolidated earnings	$4,700,000

Since Company B is consolidated with Company A, the dividend of $200,000 paid by Company A to Company B must be eliminated in its entirety as required by normal principles of consolidation. Therefore, Company A's dividend paid would, upon consolidation, be reported as $800,000 ($1,000,000 paid less $200,000 received by Company B).

The point here is, B should not include any portion of its 20% of A's earnings as it does not control A's activities. This would be true even if B owned 60% of A's outstanding shares because consolidated earnings of both Companies A and B must be the combined earnings of the two companies less the amount of such earnings attributable to minority shareholders. In this instance, where B's ownership of A is 60%, consolidated earnings would be determined as follows:

Company A earnings	$4,000,000
Company B earnings (additional $400,000 in dividends received from Company A)	1,400,000
	5,400,000
Less dividend paid by Company A, received by Company B	600,000
	4,800,000
Minority interest in B (10% of $1,400,000)	140,000
Consolidated earnings	$4,660,000

The reason consolidated earnings are $40,000 less than shown in the first example above, results from the fact that Company B would receive 60% of the dividend paid by Company A ($600,000), rather than the 20% ($200,000), thereby increasing its earnings $400,000, 10% of which would be attributable to minority shareholders of Company B—$40,000.

Income taxes

When consolidated federal income tax returns are filed by the parent company, problems of tax allocation to companies included in the consolidation arise. No problem exists insofar as consolidated statements themselves are concerned; however, proper allocation has an impact on each individual company included in the consolidation, to the extent of properly allocating such taxes in a manner which truly reflects the net income of each individual company. For federal income tax purposes (in determining taxability of dividends which are dependent upon the amount of earnings available for dividends), the following methods may be elected:

1. *Taxable income method*—allocation made in accordance with the ratio that the portion of the consolidated taxable income produced by each member having taxable income bears to the consolidated taxable income.
2. *Separate return liability method*—taxes are allocated in the respective percentages which the separate return tax liability of each member is to the aggregate of the separate return tax liability of all members.
3. *Special allocation of tax increases method*—income taxes allocated, exclusive of tax increases of individual members arising from consolidation, in proportion to the consolidated taxable income produced by each member of the group. Allocate the increases arising from consolidation in proportion to the tax reductions of individual members arising from consolidation. The reduction of any member is the excess

of its separate return liability over its proportion, based on consolidated taxable income produced, of the consolidated tax exclusive of the 2 percent additional surtax, namely, for taxable years beginning before 1964.

4. *Discretionary methods*—allocation is to be made in accordance with any other method which the group may select with Treasury Department approval. Use of such a method may result in an inter-company dividend or an inter-company capital contribution. Where members of an affiliated group are engaged in distinctly different types of operations, the commissioner has approved a discretionary method proposed by the group.

Where statements filed with the Securities and Exchange Commission include the financial statement of the parent company alone and the parent company and consolidated subsidiaries together, proper allocation is necessary. The most widely used methods are as follows:

1. Allocation on the basis of the ratio of normal tax and surtax of each company which would have been paid on a separate return basis to the aggregate amount of such taxes for the companies included in consolidation.

2. Allocation on the basis of the ratio of that portion of consolidated normal tax net income attributable to each member of the affiliated group to consolidated normal tax net income, leaving out of consideration any member of the group having no income.

Some authorities believe it is not good practice to assign to each subsidiary a portion of the consolidated tax equal to the tax of the subsidiary on an individual company basis, and to allocate the remainder to the parent company. Offhand, it would appear this may be correct at a specific point in time (especially with a new corporation having early period losses). However, it would also appear that such might not be the case and it would be appropriate to determine the tax on a separate return basis, and give the subsidiary credit (at a future date) for tax benefit on its losses deducted by the parent not otherwise deductible by the subsidiary, but actually recoverable by the subsidiary over the period prescribed by tax regulations. This assumes future earnings of the subsidiary are sufficient to cover such early period losses within the required time period.

In case separate returns are filed, Accounting Research Bulletin No. 51 of the American Institute of Certified Public Accountants states the following:

When separate income tax returns are filed, income taxes usually are incurred when earnings of subsidiaries are transferred to the parent. Where it is reasonable to assume that a part or all of the undistributed earnings of a subsidiary will be transferred to the parent in a taxable distribution, provision for related income taxes should be made on an estimated basis at the time the earnings are included in consolidated income, unless these taxes are immaterial in amount when effect is given, for example, to dividend-received deductions or foreign-tax credits. There is no need to provide for income tax to the parent company in cases where the income has been, or there is evidence that it will be, permanently invested by the subsidiaries, or where the only likely distribution would be in the form of a tax-free liquidation.

The Accounting Principles Board of the American Institute of Certified Public Accountants in its Opinion No. 11 has deferred any modification of the above position until the accounting research study on accounting for intercorporate investments is completed and an Opinion is issued on that subject.

The amount of income taxes to be reported in consolidated financial statements should be the total income tax payable by the consolidated group whether or not the group files consolidated income tax returns. In the event that a noncorporate entity is included in consolidated financial statements of a corporate entity, and if such noncorporate entity includes a minority interest, the entire income tax payable (by both the majority and minority owners) should be shown in the statement of earnings as income tax expense. The liability for income taxes applicable to the minority ownership would be credited to the minority interest in the statement of earnings, thereby reducing the minority interest that is shown as a deduction from net earnings in such statement of earnings.

Minority interest

Simply stated, minority interests represent the share of equity in a company's net worth or earnings held by others than the parent company. It should be pointed out that elimination of profits on inter-company transactions is not affected by the existence of a minority interest because consolidated financial statements represent the financial condition and result of operations of a single business organization.

If a deficit applicable to a minority interest in a subsidiary exceeds the minority interest in capital of the subsidiary, such excess should be charged against the majority interest as there is no obligation insofar as minority shareholders are concerned, to reimburse the subsidiary for such losses. If future earnings reverse the deficit situation, the majority interest should be given credit for any deficits previously charged to such majority interests.

Footnotes to consolidated financial statements

In general, consolidated financial statements should include footnotes explaining the basis of consolidation and any other pertinent data resulting from consolidation or nonconsolidation of subsidiaries.

The basis of consolidation is an explanation of the consolidating principles used and should include, in the case of subsidiaries not consolidated, the reasons therefor. If such subsidiaries are a material factor in relation to the cost of the investment in the subsidiary, its financial condition, and/or the results of its operations, summary information should be given regarding assets, liabilities and operations of such nonconsolidated subsidiaries in a footnote or a separate schedule. In addition, it may be appropriate to give comparisons of the carrying value in the financial statements of unconsolidated subsidiaries and the equity in the undistributed earnings and capital of such subsidiaries should be indicated.

Other pertinent data which should be disclosed in footnotes to consolidated financial statements would include, but not be limited to, the following:

1. Disclosure, if material, of the impact of any subsidiaries acquired or disposed of during the period covered by the financial statements.
2. The accounting treatment, if material, given to differences in cost of investments in subsidiaries and the book value of the assets of such subsidiaries. Refer to Chapter 57 regarding proper accounting treatment of these items.
3. Treatment of inter-company accounts and transactions.
4. Appropriate information regarding foreign subsidiaries should be included and if foreign subsidiaries are consolidated, a statement as to method used in making conversions to United States dollars.
5. In the case of unconsolidated subsidiaries, appropriate reference to any parent company contingent liabilities or guaranties connected with such unconsolidated subsidiary should be described.
6. Reference to income taxes as to whether or not consolidated, and periods that the company's tax returns have been examined by the Internal Revenue Service preferably should be disclosed.

Unconsolidated subsidiaries

As previously mentioned herein, it may be appropriate not to consolidate certain subsidiaries, such as foreign subsidiaries under certain circumstances, or subsidiaries where such subsidiaries' business is unrelated to that of the parent company.

As a matter of fact, from a management viewpoint, it may not be necessary to prepare consolidated financial statements every month, but rather to prepare such statements only when needed, such as on a quarterly, semi-annual, or annual basis, dependent, of course, on the circumstances in each individual case. However, it is important under most circumstances to be aware, as quickly as possible, of net earnings of the consolidated group every month. This can be accomplished without going through the whole consolidating procedure, by use of the most accepted method of accounting for unconsolidated subsidiaries. This method, commonly known as the "equity method," is the preferable or recommended method and requires adjustment of the investment in a subsidiary to reflect the parent company's share of changes in the equity of such subsidiary. This method would require the parent company to increase its investment in its subsidiary for its (the parent company's) share of earnings and extraordinary items of the subsidiary with a credit to earnings and extraordinary items. Dividends paid by the subsidiary to the parent would be credited to the investment in the subsidiary. In cases where exchange restrictions or other factors raise a question as to whether or not the increase in the equity of the subsidiary is real, it would not be advisable to follow the "equity method" of accounting for unconsolidated subsidiaries. An alternate method would be to provide for an adequate reserve in the parent company's accounts.

Another method of accounting for unconsolidated subsidiaries (which method should not be used for domestic subsidiaries, unless the conditions mentioned earlier herein under the caption "When to Consolidate —Financial Reporting" are existing), is to carry the investment in the unconsolidated subsidiary at cost, and to record, as income, dividends received from the subsidiary. If this method is used, provision should be made for any material impairment of the investment, such as losses of the subsidiary, unless it can be ascertained clearly that such losses are only of a temporary nature.

If the investment in an unconsolidated subsidiary includes the difference between cost of the investment and the book value of such investment at the time acquired, consideration must be given to amortization of such differences as mentioned in Chapter 57.

In addition, recognition of adjustments necessary to properly reflect inter-company profits must be considered. In other words, consolidating principles should be applied so that amortization of differences in cost and book value and inter-company profits or losses are eliminated from consolidated earnings and equity in the event the "equity method" of accounting is followed. No such adjustment is necessary if the investment in the subsidiary is carried at cost, unless the gain on such inter-company sales exceeds the unrecorded equity in undistributed earnings of the subsidiary.

Combined statements

As indicated earlier herein, consolidated statements require that a controlling interest rests directly or indirectly in one of the companies in the consolidated group. However, combined financial statements of individually controlled companies may well be more meaningful than separate statements. For example, assume that an individual owns more than a 50 percent interest in ten different companies, all with related types of operations. Although none of the companies is controlled by another, combined statements would be much more meaningful and would present more realistically the financial condition and results of operations from the viewpoint of the controlling owner.

In addition, combined statements of companies under common management may be appropriate in order to assess the financial condition and results of operations of the companies under common management, irrespective of the ownership interests.

Combined statements may also be prepared on a pro forma basis to assess financial conditions and results of operations of companies considering a merger or acquisition by one company of another company.

When combined statements are prepared, they should be prepared in accordance with consolidating principles and inter-company items should be eliminated. In addition, such matters as income taxes, foreign subsidiaries, unconsolidated subsidiaries and minority interests must be considered, just the same as when consolidated statements are prepared.

Consolidating process

Procedural problems often outweigh consolidating principles in completing the preparation of consolidated financial statements, particularly when operations of the consolidated group are far-flung and when many companies are included in the consolidation. Even though consolidated statements are prepared, it is essential that separate and complete records of each subsidiary be maintained. This is necessary from a legal standpoint, and also to provide management with accurate information on each individual subsidiary, as well as to properly reflect the interests of minority shareholders in such subsidiaries.

The importance of using a uniform accounting system and the same accounting principles for each subsidiary must be considered. Many practical problems would arise in the event different systems and different principles were used among the subsidiaries included in consolidated financial statements.

It is essential that consolidated statements be prepared quickly, as the value of early review by management is obviously important. Equally important is the necessity of meeting deadlines imposed by SEC regulations or by other regulatory agencies. In addition, shareholder requirements must be met. Therefore, the most efficient methods of consolidation must be employed and put to use, particularly where there are many inter-company transactions between companies included in the consolidation.

When circumstances also require certification of consolidated financial statements by independent public accountants, coordination and cooperation with the accountants can materially affect the speed with which the consolidated statements are completed, and the cost of the audit performed by such independent public accountants. It is therefore essential that maximum coordination and cooperation be accomplished. In addition, maximum cooperation and coordination among subsidiaries and parent company personnel must be accomplished.

Quite often, because of deadlines or because mistakes are made, adjustments are proposed by the independent public accountants, and if they are material, it is necessary to record such adjustments. It would be advisable to have the subsidiary companies, as well as the parent, complete their financial statements as quickly as possible without regard to any possible adjustments, applying such adjustments at a later date to the consolidated statements and subsequently to the individual statements of the subsidiaries. This procedure can speed up materially the completion time of the consolidated financial statements because the consolidating process allows the subsidiary companies, as well as the parent company, to complete their closing without waiting for completion of the audit examination and any adjustments arising from such audit.

Summary

Accounting for consolidations and intercorporate investments requires the utmost consideration be given management, economic, legal, tax and other related matters and requires, in most instances, that expert advice be sought in order to preclude the possibility of making costly mistakes.

Shareholders, investors, creditors, and others make important decisions on the basis of financial statements they examine and, accordingly, the financial executive responsible for such statements must understand the principles involved and know where the answers to important questions can be found when such financial statements involve consolidations.

PART X

External relations

Published annual reports

LeBaron R. Foster*

Picture, if you will, a well-dressed woman of 50 sitting across from you at your desk, attentive, interested in her company. Curious, but untutored in the language of finance, she requests, "Please tell me in plain words how my investment is doing."

This woman comes as close to being the typical stockholder as any one person can. She must have the story simply, if she is to get it at all. Every query of stockholders on how best to improve the annual report brings out the same demand, "Simplify it!"

If that were the only requirement, the report could be streamlined to eight pages. But as every financial executive knows, a bare-bones report would invite a barrage of inquiries from investment experts demanding facts, facts, and more facts. To say nothing of urgings from the SEC and the exchanges for compliance with increasingly rigorous demands for "full disclosure."

Planning the report: a team effort

The powerful report is neither an aseptic set of statistics, nor a tour de force of the graphic arts. At its best, it is an articulate accounting of management stewardship—philosophy, goals, performance record, and prospects.

The best read of all communications to name-of-record stockholders,

---

* Vice President, Opinion Research Corporation, Princeton, New Jersey.

and a resource highly valued by studious security analysts,[1] the annual report affords to executives their best opportunity in any given year to expound their story broadly to the investing public.

On the chief financial officer rests the responsibility for accurate and complete financial reporting. Jealous of the company's integrity, he must design or review the formal financial statements, the accompanying notes, and all supporting tabulations, exhibits, and charts. His foremost aim is that the data presented be accepted as reliable, without question.

On the other hand, it is the chief executive who is accountable to the owners for the conduct of the enterprise. In the eyes of rank-and-file stockholders, the annual report is, in fact, the company head speaking.

The report writer faces the necessity of satisfying an army of critics. Furthermore, the annual report is but one part of a continuous, year-long communication effort directed to the financial community.[2] It must be coordinated with the other parts if it is to speak with a consistent voice and capitalize on the power of repetition.

It is therefore essential that the executive team in charge reach advance agreement on the salient facets of the company's character, the concepts to be projected, and the most significant recent events. Only when these are set down boldly, in writing, can writers and designers be held accountable for their translation in text, table, and illustration. Companies find that taking time for this step at the outset reduces argument in later stages and effects important savings in the executives' time investment.

Selection of reporting objectives

In effect, management is asking the shareowners to understand the factors that underlie past operating performance and the steps taken to build a bright future. These will differ radically for, say, a food processor and an airline. Accordingly, each year the planning team will single out the appropriate objectives that deserve communications stress. A few examples:

The evolving character of the "new" company. Outmoded images persist long after the fact of change. Steel and paper producers develop into fabricators and marketers. Natural gas producers spread into manufacturing. Kresge, one of the oldest "5 & 10's," is now predominantly a discount store operation. How have new ventures and marketing thrusts, mergers and acquisitions, altered the nature of the business?

---

[1] The annual report in 1967 ranked first among 20 information sources as "very important" for appraising companies, with 95 percent of 1758 industry specialists citing it. *Opinion Research Corporation*, fifth biennial audit of financial analysts.

[2] See Chapter 63, "Financial Public Relations."

Capital needs for expansion. Where growth objectives dictate heavy plow-back of profits, investors should be advised. Normally, stockholders expect their dividends to keep pace with per share earnings.

Perspective on the earnings trend. A slowdown or downturn calls for unusual candor in discussing causes and prospects. Similarly, a temporary boost should be explained to avoid inflating future expectations. IBM, among others, has taken great pains to forewarn against continuance of extraordinary earnings gains.

Sales promotion. In their own interest, stockholders favor company overtures for their patronage. Such companies as General Motors, National Biscuit, National Distillers, RCA, Shulton—also some industrial producers—appeal to the owners for their buying dollars.

Legislative support. Utilities, railroads, and many other companies whose fortunes turn on regulatory or legislative decisions, invite the investor's active backing for their positions.

Management development. Knowledgeable investors shy away from the one-man show. Results of a concerted broadening effort may be the focal point for one year's report.

A rigorous selection of objectives contributes clarity and vitality to the year's report. In some respects a good annual report is like a good speech. It captures attention and excites interest, and at the same time it informs. In addition, it must serve a third function—a storehouse of facts neatly arranged for painless retrieval.

The journalistic challenge is to so structure the document that it intrigues and informs the quick reader, and also satisfies the professional investor's thirst for comprehensive detail.

How long should the report be?

The shorter the report is, the greater the percentage of shareowners that read some part. The longer it is, the more it costs to produce and mail.

Yet the short, bare-bones report fails to satisfy. Asked for their reactions, run-of-the-mill investors complain that it is "skimpy," "doesn't tell you much." Professionals get no help toward their desired "knowledge in depth" of operations, finances, plans, and the caliber of the men that run the company.

Do you seek to broaden the ownership family? Do you wish to attract institutional buying? Would you like to have brokers and investment advisory services write up your company and recommend the stock? If so, the eight-page document confined to financial statements and a brief President's Letter will not pull its weight.

A moderate-sized company concentrating in one product or service field may find 16 pages enough to say what needs to be said. A large, diversified company usually finds it must prune and clip to compress the story into 32 pages. The majority of reports of listed companies fall within these limits.

Structuring the report

It is well to bear in mind that the majority of investors read as they run. The businessman is trained to extract the meat from the nut, fast. The small shareholder skims the high spots because anything technical or complex is beyond his ken. A report is read not like a novel, but more like a news magazine.

One report that scored high in overall interest in a readership test serves an example. Based on those who opened the covers, reading of the 12 main sections ranged from 95 percent to 52 percent. Yet only 32 percent read each of the main sections. In another report test, only 9 percent read cover to cover.

In good part, stockholders depend on management to signal what deserves their attention. Once the key elements in this year's message have been decided upon, they can be underscored by the use of proven journalistic techniques:

Symbolize ideas on the cover, pictorially and reinforced with a theme or news headlines

Put the important events up front

Summarize financial data in simple and bold Highlights

Add prose interpretations of events in the short letter signed by the chief executive (alternatively in brief paragraphs next to the Highlights)

Sectionalize the report and index the sections

Place pictures and charts next to the text items they dramatize

Put formal financial statements at the back

Spotlight the parts "every stockholder should read" by employing—

Bold type
Ample white space
Color
Declarative news heads
Layman's language

If layman's language detracts from nobility of style or scientific aura, it serves the hard-to-achieve goal of communicating. In audience surveys among name-of-record shareholders, the reports of 14 companies ranged widely in effectiveness. In the case of the lowest performer, six in ten either had not read their recently received report or could recall nothing from their perusal. At the other extreme was the best performer; 62 percent not only claimed to have looked over the report but could describe something they had read. Many factors enter in, but certainly one of the major barriers is the strange tongue that financial experts speak.

Ways to bridge the semantics gap

A safe assumption is that less than half the company's owners understand most terms commonly used in traditional financial statements.

In a 1961 study among 240 men and women stockholders, less than one in ten could define, even partially correctly, such terms as *debentures, funded debt, equity capital, paid-in surplus, cash flow*. One in four could describe *bonds,* as distinguished from *stock.*

Standing out as familiar to 50 percent or more were: *profits* and *net profits, assets* and *liabilities, dividends,* and *labor costs.* Worth noting is that profits, the standard term among economists, has given way in reporting practice to the nicer sounding *earnings.* Stockholders find earnings confusing because it brings to mind wages and salaries and only 1 percent could define paid-in surplus.

At the root of the problem is an appalling ignorance of corporate affairs. Long range, nothing short of education in the economics of the firm will deal with it. But short range, there are many devices companies adopt to cut through the semantic underbrush. Some examples:

Common language headings.   Use these both in formal statements and simplified tables. Girard Trust, for instance, uses *operating income* in place of *revenues,* and net profits in place of *net earnings. Surplus* really is not; get rid of it. Use an explanatory phrase, or such labels as *reinvested profits* and *stockholders' investment.*

Summarizers.   The Highlights, Ten-Year Review, and Simplified Financial Statements are not bound by accountingese. The balance sheet, for example, can be recast to show: What We Own, What We Owe, (difference) Belongs to the Stockholders. In tests, this form proves far more understandable than the conventional long form.

The simplest of graphics.   Visuals supplant words. Graphs and charts are particularly effective to show trends: sales, per-share profits, dividends, expense ratios, capital expansion, sources of funds. Illustrative 1967 reports: International Mineral & Chemicals, General Electric, North American–Rockwell, Southwestern Public Service.

Glossary of financial terms.   This feature is helpful to stockholders, and especially valuable if reports are to be supplied to schools as teaching aids. Manufacturers National Bank of Detroit, for instance, gives over the entire last page of its 1967 report to definitions of banking terms.

What stockholders look for in annual reports

Investors invest money to make money, and are not very patient with side excursions. When a company attempts to embellish its image by leading off with trails blazed (or to be blazed) in scientific discovery, or high aims in public service, many a reader reacts, "Sounds nice, I suppose, but is it for real?"

First and foremost, the reader looks for an overview of the year's results. Below are six leading report features (from a list of 14) as determined by stockholders' expressed choices:

Feature	Importance Score*
Earnings and dividends for past year	3650
The company's financial position	2731
Operating problems for the near future	1271
Effect of taxes on earnings	886
Last year's operating problems	821
Long term expansion plans	691

* Maximum possible score is 4650, weighting first choice votes 5, second choice 4, third choice 3, fourth choice 2, and fifth choice 1.

No imaginative writer will be straight-jacketed by a mechanistic pattern. Happenings and causes vary widely in significance from industry to industry and from company to company. An expanding electric utility will give prominence to capital needs and resources; a manufacturing company which is generating ample funds internally will merely reassure the owners that no dilution of equity is contemplated.

Further, shareowner interest in reading can never be taken for granted. It must be aroused. Close to half of name-of-record stockholders approach reading under the stereotype that reports are dull. The artful writer thus faces the challenge of surmounting the communications deluge, if he is to hook and hold the shareowner's interest long enough to get across the salient points in the year's message. Profits constitute the initial pivot of interest, and the most dependable sustaining thread. A distinguishing mark of the more dynamic and exciting reports is the forthrightness with which top executives discuss profit successes and disappointments, foundations laid for earnings growth, and increasingly, when probabilities can be assayed, management's targets for annual growth rates.

Conveying a sense of direction

Most investors in established companies intend to hold for the long term. To evaluate the company's progress in perspective, they need to share management's aims and operating objectives.

The well-ordered report, therefore, is a recounting of events strung together on a chain of declared purpose.

A basic steel producer, with an eye to dividend security, may stress control of production costs. A retailer may well feature territorial expansion, or a shift to new types of outlets. A groundbreaker in a new technology will have little to say about current profits and less about dividends, but quite properly will discuss progress in research, in product development, and in gaining customer acceptance.

Whatever the connecting chain, the report will gain editorial force if all its major elements are fashioned to reinforce the core ideas. Not the least of these elements is the report cover.

The report cover can say something

Analysis of the 1941 covers of 250 prominent corporations brought out that 87% carried only the company name or the name and logotype—a waste of good space, or worse.

Reacting to these covers, investors most often said they conveyed nothing. Others got the impression of a company that is "old fashioned," "behind the times."

While name-only covers are on the way out, there is much groping and experimenting to find the best ways to use the cover area. Among the more imaginative is what might be called the artist's favorite, the abstract painting. This is arresting, perhaps, but generally confounding to stockholders, and in most cases a fine example of noncommunication.

The art form should be suited to the idea being projected. Among the styles that have demonstrated superior efficiency in projecting intended ideas or impressions:

> Vivid display of company products, preferably those familiar to the average citizen

> Literal scenes symbolizing the company's main fields of activity

> Collage of recognizcable scientific instruments, signaling "progressiveness," "research mindedness"

> Maps of transmission systems, or company plants and offices. World maps, for instance, do a good job of suggesting "operations international in scope"

> News headlines underscoring key developments or happenings

> Rising trend lines, in graph or pictorial representation

> Live, warm people: a stockholder's family, a consumer, an employee. The idealized worker, for example, quickly registers a company "interested in its employees," "good management-employee relations"—particularly appropriate if the report is distributed to employees.

Today virtually every magazine cover tantalizes the potential reader with clues to the good things inside. Why report designers neglect this journalistic technique is hard to fathom. The cover is the first thing the recipient sees. It can be utilized to capture attention, announce themes, punch home significant points. A good example is Federated Department Stores' 1967 report. The accompanying cover, reproduced in black and white, features the first and third main headlines in bright red, the second headline and the upper right block in vivid blue.

Federated Department Stores, Inc.
1967 Annual Report

1967: year of the cautious consumer

but net income up 8.6% on 7.7% sales gain; per share earnings rose 31 cents, continuing long-term trend, page 1

Growth from within

1.2 million square feet of department store space added in nine major markets; discount stores planned, page 4

Ralphs: new business for Federated

grocery pioneer joins Federated family; operates 52 quality supermarkets in greater Los Angeles, page 10

Highlights, the one-page fact summary

This is usually the best read feature of any report that contains one. It deserves care in its design.

Much of what appears in the text body is selective, and asserts management's view. The stark statistics supply validation. The Highlights page, together with the Long-Term Review, carry the chief burden of factual validation.

Tests among individual stockholders and security analysts have developed the following criteria for a high-performance Highlights page:

> Front position, adjacent to the President's Letter (relieving the Letter of boring recitations of routine figures)
>
> Restricted number of items, 10 or 12 at most
>
> Rounded figures (000 omitted, or millions to the nearest tenth)
>
> Visual clarity: large, bold type set off by generous white space
>
> Comparative data. Two years minimum. Trend is toward three, four, or five years to add perspective. Current year figures can be spotlighted by bolder type or color contrast.

A word of caution: overprinting on solid color background or on a dense photograph penalizes reading. If illustrations are supplied, set them apart from the tabulated data.

The president's letter

The chief executive's personal message is a comparative newcomer. A decade ago, less than half of the large companies used it. When they did, it was usually no more than a thumbnail version of the main report.

Today, in more advanced usage, it is a unique feature. It is a genuine expression of the president's views with his personality showing—direct, candid, honest in admitting stumbles, enthusiastic about the company, and often venturesome in stating management goals in quantitative terms.

Though the chief should say what he wants to say in his own manner, observing a few ground rules will increase the readership of the message and its impact.

> Place it at or near the beginning, next to the traffic-building Highlights
>
> Subdue or eliminate the formal salutation, and lead off with a direct statement or significant quote
>
> Keep the style crisp, informal, idiomatic
>
> Explain recent happenings, management's actions, and their meaning for the future
>
> Key the main points or subjects with indented running heads
>
> Inset a photo of the President (and the Chairman if he also signs)
>
> Hold it to one or two pages. A long letter loses its distinctive identity.

Sprucing up the main body of text

Lengthy, unbroken text discourages reading. If management aims at owner involvement through building an intimate knowledge of operations, skillful presentation is needed.

Most basic is Departmentalization—setting off and identifying each main section so that the searching reader can locate matters of foremost concern. Traditionally, this scheme has mirrored the organization chart with sections labeled Sales, Production, Research, Financial, etc. This division is logical, but pedestrian.

The excitement is in growth, which usually hinges on the exploitation of markets. Consequently, many market-minded companies are now ordering the main body of the report around product groups or customer classes. Wilson & Company, for its 1967 report, goes so far as to issue two documents—one a lyric, high-styled "Profile of Programmed Growth," the second, a conventional Financial Section.

Storytelling heads. A widely used simplification technique is informative news headlines by which management calls attention to important events. These replace the staid headings—Sales, Production, etc. A life insurance company, for example, might head the sections as follows:

Our Life Insurance Sales Set a New Record

Life Insurance in Force at a New High

Stepped Up Agent Training for Better Service to Policyholders

Our Investments Help Our Economy Grow

New Types of Policies Stretch Premium Dollars

Section head plus thumbnail summary. Set off each main section with an arresting title in large type, followed by a boldface copy block summarizing the main points of interest. This is standard practice in magazines which businessmen read, but is yet to be widely adopted in financial reporting.

Picture keys. A third interest getter is the symbolic photo. An oil company might insert a photo of a rig in the Cook Inlet to lead off the section on exploration, a new-style service station for the marketing section, and so on.

The formal financial statements

Though the majority of stockholders glance at them, only a minority claim they give them any serious attention.

The formal statements, therefore, are primarily for professionals and accounting sophisticates. To accommodate all their demands would suggest a report of the proportions of an SEC registration statement. Still, it is possible to supply more information than most companies do. Some general guides:

Include all major items the company is willing to divulge to inquiring security analysts

Group the items in sections, under simplified headings

Summarize the figures in each section using labels and amounts that agree with the items appearing in the Highlights and Long-Term Review

Relegate details to the explanatory notes, and expand these notes to answer all foreseeable questions. Include principles of consolidation; clear descriptions of company accounting practices, especially in controversial areas; any changes during the year and their quantitative effect; also pertinent information beyond the scope of the formal statements such as contingent liabilities, schedule of bond maturities; and conversions, warrants, and stock options.

The ideal pursued by financial executives is to present all significant information which is relevant to appraising the value of the investment. Just what is significant and relevant is, of course, a matter of judgment. But so long as "generally accepted accounting principles" afford wide latitude in the treatment of many items affecting net profits, companies must either furnish the data inputs which analysts require for calculating earnings on a uniform basis, or invite the imposition of a rigid regulatory code from outside.

The judicious use of pictures

Once considered an expensive frill, pictures have come to be recognized as one of the best tools of financial journalism.

Their power can be wasted, if they are sprinkled about hit or miss for decoration. Pictures are best used for dramatic emphasis, as integral parts of the report design.

Here are pointers evolved from readership research on picture performance:

Photographs are more powerful than sketches because they convey authenticity—the real thing

Tie in the picture and the picture caption to the adjacent text, to be read as a coherent unit

Where possible, include people. Consumers, employees, stockholders can add emotional warmth

Scenes familiar to readers in everyday life will pull better than machinery or apparatus

Run a big picture—a full page or two-page spread—to announce the main theme or an outstanding development. Examples: a new research laboratory, a revolutionary production process, an impressive store or plant[3]

Coach the photographer on the exact effect desired, and pretest selected shots to see that they register. Research on actual reports shows that many pictures miss the target.

A useful exercise is to assume that the reader gets his impressions from the visuals alone. What story will he likely come away with?

Should companies furnish division breakdowns?

The ideal which the SEC sets forth is full disclosure, on a voluntary basis. To the regulators, this means more liberality than at present. Currently, pressure is mounting on multi-industry companies to reveal financial results broken down by products, divisions, or other major segments.

The decision to divulge or not divulge is by no means confined to burgeoning conglomerates. In its June 1967 issue, *Fortune* sifted out the 46 most diversified large manufacturing companies. Less than half of these would be labeled conglomerates by the narrow definition: a company growing through acquisition of unrelated businesses. Included in the *Fortune* list are such companies as Du Pont, Ford, and IBM, as well as such conglomerates as Brunswick, Ogden, and U.S. Industries.

The rationale for demanding breakdowns appears particularly cogent with respect to companies composed of independently operated subsidiaries or divisions. Are the conglomerates, in fact, more open in disclosure?

For evidence, a comparative study of reporting practices in 1967 annual reports was undertaken for this *Handbook*. A backdrop of general corporate practice is available in the study by George Hobgood, Assistant Research Director of the Financial Executives Research Foundation: "Voluntary Disclosure in 1967 Annual Reports." Of the 457 corporations included, 48 percent showed breakdowns of gross revenues by two or more products or product groups, industrial markets, geographical markets, or organization divisions. Only 9 percent showed similar breakdowns of net income.

The present study is confined to multi-industry companies in the *Fortune* "500" lists, classified judgmentally, according to the foregoing definition, into "conglomerates" and "other diversified companies."

In sum, approximately half the conglomerates supply sales breakdowns to answer the investor's question, "What businesses are you in?"

---

[3] In the 1950's, General Electric featured a huge color photo of the Knolls Research installation, on the inside cover spread to page 1. Compared to previous year's feature made up of small shots, the number who looked at the page increased by two-thirds, and reading of the accompanying text by one-half.

This frequency is no greater than that for large companies generally, and is somewhat below the level of disclosure for big, highly diversified companies that are not engaged in acquisition programs. Conglomerates are, however, more inclined to reveal earnings by segments of the enterprise.

It should be noted that while some of the more glamorous conglomerates hide the hard facts under roseate clouds of verbiage, others are

Breakdowns: 1967 Reporting Practices

	60 Conglomerates		60 Other Diversified Companies	
	Sales	Earnings	Sales	Earnings
Report by two or more product or service groups, customer markets, domestic geographic divisions, or organizational divisions	37	15	40	4
Do not report as above, but do report sales by—				
Defense and space/Other	1	0	2	0
U.S./Foreign	1	2	1	7
Year of acquisition	2	3	0	0
Supply none of above breakdowns	19	40	17	49
Give financial statements of consolidated subsidiaries				
Income statements	6		1	
Balance sheets	6		0	

models of disclosure, supplying considerable detail on both sales and profits: e.g. Armour, Genesco, Kaiser Industries, Ling-Temco-Vought, National Distillers.

No prudent company will disclose information that truly aids competitors or stirs regulatory zeal. However, research has demonstrated that, as a rule, the better its investors know a company, the more confidence they have in it. Financial executives therefore may wish to reexamine traditional practices in furnishing breakdowns, with a view to cementing the loyalty of existing stockholders and attracting new ones. Then too, voluntary disclosure preserves that cherished flexibility for adapting reporting practices to the nature of the business.

Certainly the investment community is hungry for more information. In a survey conducted by Opinion Research Corporation in the second quarter of 1967 among 758 security analysts in 36 financial centers, 81 percent of the analysts declared they favor "an SEC regulation requiring companies to issue detailed reports of their earnings including a breakdown of earnings for separate divisions within the company."

Controlling report costs

Even among big companies with big press runs, production costs range widely, from 25¢ to $1.25 or more per report copy.[4]

Chief determinant of cost is volume: the smaller the run, the higher the cost per copy. Executives of modest-sized companies, therefore, may be particularly concerned with ways to control preparation and production costs. Some useful measures:

1. *To conserve executive time,* decide on the overall tenor and the main points to stress four to five months in advance of the final proof date. Postponing decisions until the first draft invites expensive delays.

2. *To save preparation cost,* give writers and graphic designers freedom to create within the outline of the year's communication objectives.

3. *To cut printing costs,* choose a printer wise in cost-saving methods. Sprightly, eye-appealing reports can be produced in two or three colors in place of four-color process, using tinted and textured papers, half pages, gate folds and inserts, distinctive and dramatic typefaces. And, after having set the printer's schedule, adhere to it!

4. *To reduce mailing costs,* consider the new light-weight opaque book papers. Enclose meeting notices, proxy requests, brochures. Test-weigh the package to hold it under ounce limits.

Economy need not stifle effectiveness. The companies that strive most aggressively to improve investor relations with broad-gauged programs do not as a rule go overboard on the annual report. Companies classified in this group in the Financial Executives Research Foundation study reported costs averaging $.50 per copy; for all others costs averaged $.60 per copy.

---

[4] For cost analyses by company size and by industry groups, based on companies in *Fortune* "500" lists, see the writer's, *Telling the Company's Financial Story;* Financial Executives Research Foundation, 1964; p . 53.

Financial public relations

Harold Burson and Anthony D. Hughes*

Every publicly held corporation today is engaged in financial public relations. Some participate only to the extent required by rules of the SEC and leading stock exchanges. Others—a growing number—see financial public relations as a key element in company expansion.

The difference depends on the way in which a company relates financial relations to broader business objectives. At one extreme are those whose only interest is in meeting the letter of the law, which requires that they provide annual reports, quarterly press releases on earnings, prompt announcement of dividend action and other important corporate news, and the conduct of an annual meeting for shareholders.

However, the strong trend today is toward making use of financial communications to achieve much broader, more businesslike objectives. Financial officers and other members of management are becoming increasingly concerned about the effect their communications efforts have on the financial community. More to the point, their interest is in the financial community's evaluation of the company—specifically as this is reflected in the market price of the company's shares.

There is growing awareness that share prices can have a decisive effect—either positive or negative—on far-reaching business decisions. For example, the price of a company's shares will affect its ability to raise capital, either debt or equity.

Whether the shares are relatively low or high in price can be an important factor in making the company vulnerable to a corporate raid, or can help protect it from one.

---

* Chairman, and Vice President–Financial Relations, respectively, Burson-Marsteller, New York.

The shares themselves, depending on the price, can be a valuable aid in the aggressive pursuit of acquisition opportunities.

Shares can also, through the use of stock options, give management a device for attracting and motivating key employees. In this instance, the long-range evaluation of the shares becomes of special importance.

For all these reasons, the effectiveness of a company's financial relations program is becoming of growing interest and concern to corporate management. However, to be effective, financial relations activities must be programmed toward specific objectives.

Financial relations is a fast-growing area of corporate communications. It is also one of the most sensitive.

Lack of sound organization planning or failure to understand the purposes and goals of financial relations can be damaging. And there can be severe penalties if the company does not know or understand its responsibilities with respect to the required disclosure of information.

This chapter will describe the basic elements of a sound progressive financial relations program aimed at the professional financial community. It will answer many questions which a corporate financial executive may well ask himself as he seeks the best possible communications program for his company. Some of the latest techniques will be described and guidelines suggested for disseminating significant corporate information.

Financial public relations objectives

Every publicly held corporation, at one time or another, wants something from the financial community. Most often it's money—for either debt or equity financing. But unlike bank financing, which is based on prevailing interest rates, equity financing is influenced to a great degree by the financial community's appraisal of the company. This is, of course, something much less tangible than interest rates. But it has great influence. It explains, for example, why glamour companies raise equity capital at a much lower rate than more mature, more slowly growing companies.

The money a company can raise by sale of shares is based to a large degree on the current market price of the company's shares. A capital-goods company's market price might approximate 9 to 10 times the amount it earns for each share outstanding. This ratio, commonly referred to as the price/earnings or P/E ratio, represents the way in which the market indicates its assessment of a company.

A company in electronics or communications (two of the fastest developing fields) might have a P/E ratio as high as 40. Clearly, it is in a much more advantageous position to raise money through equity financing than the capital-goods company.

One way for the capital-goods company to improve its P/E ratio could be to expand operations into the communications field. This approach might not be too practical.

It might be more realistic for the company seeking to raise capital on the most advantageous terms to consider first whether or not it is putting its best image forward.

Price/earnings ratios are not rigid

Price/earnings ratios, even within a single industry, are not rigid. Within the capital-goods industry, earnings ratios vary as widely as 8 to 12 times. Obviously, the company raising new capital would be much better off if its shares were rated at the 12-times level than at the 8. In fact, at 12-times earnings it could raise 50 percent more capital with the same amount of dilution as at the 8 multiple. This adds up to significant money.

There is no magic way to move from 8 to 12-times earnings. This will depend, to a significant extent, on the way the market evaluates the company. However, it is important to realize that such an evaluation is a variable—and is not completely beyond the influence of the company.

It may well be that the financial community knows a particular company very well and, on the basis of this knowledge, has come to the conclusion that the company's stock is not worth more than 8 times earnings. Often, though, low price/earnings ratios result from a lack of communication. For that reason, a company should try to determine very early the basis of the market's evaluation. Is it a fair evaluation? Is it based on thorough understanding of the company's present position and long-range goals? Or is it based on either lack of information or misunderstanding?

Researching investment attitudes

Finding the basis for the present share price is the starting point in a financial relations program. In some cases this might require merely a few contacts on Wall Street. But a sounder approach would be an in-depth audit of financial community attitudes to find out precisely how the professional investor and investment advisor view the company. This research, which usually forms the basis for any long-range communications program, is discussed later in this chapter.

But no matter how the company's image is evaluated on Wall Street, the fact is that it can significantly affect the raising of capital. That's reason enough to suggest that a well-planned financial relations program merits top-executive time and attention.

There are other compelling reasons for a financial relations program. For example, stock exerts tremendous leverage in the current avalanche of acquisitions. It can be used both ways—to acquire companies and to defend against being taken over.

The stock of the so-called glamour companies (those with very high P/E multiples) has become a valuable acquisition factor. Stock used as a form of cash gives the company an opportunity to offer a very high market price to purchase other companies without suffering any great dilution or giving away much equity. For example, a 50 P/E company that acquires a 15 P/E company would end up with higher earnings per share from the acquisition and quite possibly an increase in its market price as a result of the higher earnings.

Contrast this with the acquisition position of the capital-goods maker. At a 10 P/E ratio he is at a distinct disadvantage. To acquire the same company he has to give up considerably more equity. And what does he end up with? An immediate decrease in his earnings per share and possibly a decrease in his market price. That's a tough package to sell shareholders.

On a very simple basis, therefore, it is easy to see that a company's appraisal by the financial community can definitely affect its ability to make acquisitions with stock.

Stock price has also been mentioned as a defense against corporate raiding. One rule of thumb on raiding is that a company planning to make a tender generally expects to offer a price at least 20 percent higher than the most recent high for the other company's stock, and above its book value. For example, if a company's stock is selling at $50, and the most recent high was $60, the tender price would be $72 to $75. This might be considered enough to induce someone holding the stock at $50 to sell out quickly.

If, on the other hand, the company's stock is selling at $70, the potential raider might have to go as high as $90 a share. The difference between $70 and $90 might be enough to dissuade a would-be raider.

One conclusion might be that the higher your shares sell, the better off your company will be. There's some truth to this. It doesn't imply, however, that a company can easily or arbitrarily push its stock to any height. In the first place, the market just doesn't work that way. Even if a company could strongly influence the price of its stock, any rise unjustified by the company's current position and outlook would be quickly and sharply reversed. And no company wants a sudden drop in its shares, which brings with it other problems.

"Fair" market appraisal is communications goal

The objective, then, is to encourage the market to give the best possible appraisal to the company's shares consistent with its realistic short- and long-term outlook—in other words, a "fair" appraisal. On this basis, there is sufficient reason to encourage a well-planned financial communications effort.

If an industry group has a price/earnings range of 12 to 16, a financial relations program aimed at improving the price of the company's stock toward the upper range of the industry scale, assuming the company considers itself one of the best companies in the industry, would be realistic.

Another area in which share prices play a part is executive compensation. Stock options have become a rather sophisticated means of attracting and motivating key executives. However, they have been known to backfire.

Let's say a key employee is issued an option at the current market price of $40, exercisable within the next five years. The company shows modest improvement during the year but its stock declines in price, and, at the year-end, the stock is at $35. The employee holding the options at $40 might not consider them much of an incentive. True, he has four more years in which to exercise the options, and it might be presumed that the company will do well over that period. Nevertheless, at least psychologically, he is not likely to get very excited or be strongly motivated by the options until he can see some actual gain.

Stock options are most effective as motivating tools when a company is moving forward as a business, both in sales and earnings, and when this progress is reflected in the price of its shares. The executive feels rewarded when he helps make his company grow, and, as a result, sees his options grow along with it.

He understands, of course, that no company can successfully buck a general stock market trend. However, it does pay to assure him that the company is doing its best to get a fair evaluation in the current market place.

Other reasons for conducting a financial relations program are somewhat less compelling than those already cited. For example, it is possible to rank companies in a given industry according to their P/E ratios. This ranking says in effect that professional business analysts familiar with the industry have decided that companies at the higher P/E levels are the industry's most promising and those at the lowest levels are less attractive. These relative ratings are well known in the industry concerned as well as in the investment community. This means a company should be concerned with its rating both in terms of attracting investors and customers.

There's also the question of corporate ego. No company wants to be at the bottom of the rating list. For all these reasons, financial communications become an extremely important corporate project.

Defensive financial communications

There is also a defensive aspect to financial relations that is too often overlooked. In a free competitive economy, company sales and earnings are bound to fluctuate. The pattern in a cyclical industry may be quite volatile. Stock market prices tend to reflect, and in many cases anticipate, the trend of a company's sales and earnings in relation to the rest of the industry and the economy as a whole.

It can easily be seen, therefore, that since a program of full information is important for an accurate appraisal of a company on the way up, it is equally imperative to continue such a program during any temporary downturn. Analysts, accustomed to a steady flow of information, should not suddenly be left hanging when a company's earnings taper off momentarily. Rumors can be devastating to a company temporarily on the downside, even more so than when it is moving forward. Financial relations, then, must be a consistent, continuing effort.

Influences on share prices

Stock prices are determined by supply and demand within the stock market—who's willing to buy, who wants to sell, and for how much.

There are said to be more than 26 million buyers and sellers in the market today. The term investor, however, doesn't convey the wide range of interests among all those who invest.

At one extreme are the individuals. These are usually small investors who commit relatively small amounts directly into corporate securities on a long-term, continuing basis. At the other extreme are the traders. They see the stock market as something of a racetrack, and they change their bets almost daily.

This range of attitudes among individual investors is duplicated among large, institutional investors. There are high-performance funds looking for continuous turnover in their investments, trying for maximum gain in the shortest possible time. And there are the more conservative large investors—insurance companies, bank trusts, college endowment funds, etc.—which seek a combination of income, security and capital growth. Today, large institutional investors hold 40 percent of all listed shares and this percentage is growing.

There are, then, extremes in the sizes of investors and also in their approaches to investment.

As a practical matter, it is virtually impossible for a corporation to decide to attract a particular type of shareholder. It comes down to a question of the inherent nature of the company's securities. Is its stock considered an income stock, a growth stock, or something in between?

Understanding shareholder appeal

While a company can't effectively influence its shareholder breakdown, it should be aware of the type of shareholder it is most likely to attract so that management can have a reasonable understanding of how that shareholder is likely to act. For example, stocks attractive to high-performance funds tend to be at the higher price levels and tend to be more volatile. Stocks with broad, small-shareowner support tend to be more stable. While this latter condition may be desirable from an operating standpoint, it can also lead to lower share prices.

In influencing investors, the direct approach is not necessarily the most effective. Most investors, both small and large, are strongly influenced in their stock buying decisions by professional investment advisors.

It is a rule of the exchanges that each security salesman know his customer well and offer him advice on share purchases. As a result, when a small investor tells a security salesman he wants to buy a particular stock, he's likely to get the investment firm's appraisal of the stock—whether he wants it or not.

For example, a customer may ask for a particular chemical company and be advised that another chemical company would be a better investment. Of course, the customer may stay with his original choice. But he is quite likely to be influenced by his investment salesman/advisor.

This is also the pattern of major investment institutions. Since all institutions, including the banks, insurance companies, and pension funds, must purchase and sell their securities through exchange member firms, they also must pay commissions. Commissions on huge block orders can run very high. To compensate for this cost, large institutions require their brokerage firms to provide extensive, in-depth investment studies. This is even true with funds that have their own investment advisors on staff. They still look to the investment community for original ideas or for confirmation of their own decisions. As a result, investment firms put a considerable amount of time and talent into research to meet the needs of the major institutions.

A consideration of these factors makes it a lot easier to narrow the primary target for a company's financial relations program.

Narrowing the financial communications audience

The 26 million investors are an important target but not a primary target. Nor are the 200,000 or more professionals who work in the investment community—partners, salesmen, order clerks, traders and others.

Responsibility for researching and recommending stock sales and purchases rests with the security analyst. Today more than 12,000 registered security analysts provide the major flow of information within the financial community. This is the most significant single audience. However, a particular company can narrow it down even further.

Within the analyst fraternity are those who specialize in particular industries or in particular types of stock. For example, there are specialists in chemical stocks, steels, utilities, electronics, etc. And there are specialists in conglomerates and related diversified companies. Whatever the company's category, it can begin to narrow its analyst group to no more than 200 or 250 individuals. Identifying the analysts who can have the strongest influence on the purchase or sale of a company's shares is the single, most important objective of a successful financial public relations program.

Once a company has identified those analysts who can most directly affect its stock, it can then begin to plan its financial communications. The first step is to find out what they know about the company. In other words, what are the prevailing attitudes that lead the analysts to recommend that investors pay the current price for the company's shares?

A company must have this information before it can begin to communicate effectively. Communication involves either changing or reinforcing ideas. Obviously, it is essential to know what the ideas are before drafting a program designed to modify them.

Most often, this type of research proves the financial community doesn't have a clear or current understanding of the company. And *that* proves most companies don't communicate enough. When one considers the number of shares now being traded, it is easy to understand why the securities industry cannot research every company.

Security analysts are commission-motivated

A few stocks are on the security analyst's "must" or high-priority list. These are the very large companies and those that trade very actively. Both generate a considerable amount of commission income and, therefore, automatically demand attention. However, these two designations apply to very few companies. Most companies on a major exchange or in the over-the-counter market must compete for attention.

As this indicates, the most likely finding of attitude research is that the company is not well known. Specifically, some of its high points are either not clearly understood or not known at all. This is the simplest type of condition to correct. It requires only a broad, well-balanced information program.

The type of program required to change an erroneous attitude is more difficult. For example, analysts may feel that a particular company lacks management depth, either because of a lack of qualified people or because of failure in a "one-man show" to delegate authority properly. This, incidentally, is a fairly common complaint. Security analysts consider management depth and ability by far the most important corporate asset.

Some feel a good management will eventually do well under almost any conditions, whereas a poor management will falter sooner or later even under the best of conditions. For this reason, it's a strong negative point if the analyst has any question about the management of a company.

Other areas of common misunderstanding involve company competence in research, product innovation, marketing, and so on.

Identifying communications needs

Effective attitude research should enable a company to identify its specific communications needs and thus at least indicate how to mount a specific program.

The preferred approach in the financial community is in-depth research among key security analysts in a position to have the strongest influence on a company's stock—generally a sample of 100 or so. It consists of about an hour-long interview with each analyst. The company under study is first compared through a series of questions to a group of similar companies, on such points as product innovation, marketing, management, etc. Then the analyst is invited to comment specifically on the company itself and his relations with it. Such studies are conducted by a number of independent agencies.

Follow-up research is also recommended. While the ultimate effectiveness of a financial communications program might be represented by the relative position of the company's shares in the marketplace, it is also valuable from time to time to try to identify information gaps in the communications process. This does not require research as extensive as that suggested for an initial program. However, it is useful at intervals of 18 months or so to take a sounding among the most important analysts to see what communications problems still need to be considered.

Telling the story

With a clear understanding of prevailing financial community attitudes, a complete communications program can be planned.

A starting point is the annual report—the most widely recognized element in any financial relations effort.

A publicly held company is required to send each shareholder an audited financial report at the end of the year. This need be nothing more than the audited financial statements. But almost every company goes much further.

The typical annual report includes a letter from the president, a chronological rundown on events, some highlights of the year, and perhaps a review of each of the company's basic operations.

The trouble with most reports is that they don't contribute in any meaningful way to the company's total image. They are merely an explanation of what happened in the past twelve months—a stewardship report. The annual report should aim for much more.

Annual report objectives

For example, assume preliminary surveys had indicated that the stock market questioned the company's ability to generate new products from research, the annual report might focus specifically on the company's ability in this area.

If analyst surveys suggested some doubt about the company's management depth, the report might concentrate on this subject. In any case, a planned approach is necessary to develop a truly valuable, working report.

There are many ways in which annual reports are measured. Some are based on the graphics involved, others on the amount of financial information. From a purely business point of view, the report should be judged on the basis of whether or not it helped to improve or reinforce prevailing opinions about the company. Does it in fact zero in on and try to improve areas in which there is a communications gap?

The annual report is discussed in depth in Chapter 62, "Published Annual Reports."

Quarterly or interim reports are another often misused communications element.

Expanded quarterly reports

The SEC and the exchanges do not require companies to issue a quarterly report; the only requirement is that press releases on earnings be issued on a quarterly or semi-annual basis. Many publicly-held companies, nevertheless, print quarterly reports. But what do they say in them?

Typically, and this covers the majority of quarterly reports, they list the financial information previously covered in the press release, and include a president's letter that seldom tells more than the tables show in figures. It's difficult to understand why companies go to the expense. Why not simply mail the press releases?

However, there is a trend toward making much better use of these reports. Considered as part of a total and continuing flow of information to the investment community, they can be valuable vehicles for conveying additional information.

Telling the company's story once a year in the annual report is effective. Reinforcing some of the major points through expanded discussion in a quarterly report is even better. For this reason many companies are turning to an expanded form for their quarterly reports and are giving thought to providing much more information.

The annual report is used to discuss all the major corporate activities and objectives. The quarterly report would concentrate on one point at a time.

A well-planned program would include advanced scheduling of specific points to be made through the year in each of these documents.

Proxy statements

Proxy statements can also be made more informative, more readable and more valuable. There is, for example, a trend toward adding more information about directors. Professional investment advisors want to know the directors as well as management, and are particularly interested in their ability to make a contribution to the company.

Another trend is toward fuller explanation of proposals within the proxy.

Most shareholders are not qualified as readers of annual reports, quarterly reports, and other printed materials—in fact, studies indicate that they read very little of the material sent to them. A company should be most concerned, therefore, with its primary audience of influentials —the 250 or so professional investment advisors. They can be counted on to read almost anything. If the company designs its reports to influence these professionals, they will be in a position to spread the word to everyone else.

Special mailings

There are other opportunities to provide a continuing and valuable flow of information. One is through the mailing of special materials, speeches, article reprints and any other information which helps to support the programs and basic messages.

Many analysts feel that trade magazines are a primary source of information. They consider these publications often more reliable than the general business press. A good financial relations program will attempt to make use of this by first attempting to get its story told effectively in the trade press and, secondly, by seeing that reprints of such articles are brought to the attention of the financial community.

Speeches and speech reprints offer management the opportunity to present very specific messages on a first-person basis, in a controlled way. Finding appropriate speech platforms and making sure that the speeches then get into the right hands is also an important part of effective financial relations.

Shareholder correspondence

A final consideration in shareholder relations is correspondence, particularly correspondence beyond the routine "welcome" letters. It is advisable to establish a procedure for giving prompt—and not voluminous—answers to letters from shareholders.

Occasionally it is valuable to get a profile of shareholders to find out who they are, where they are, and why they became shareholders. This kind of information helps to pinpoint spheres of influence and to indicate the basis on which the company's shares are being marketed within the financial community. In other words, is the company being sold by the financial community as a long-term growth situation, a conservative income stock, or what?

Annual meetings

Annual meetings are a basic, though usually over-emphasized, element of financial relations. Some are big meetings with box lunches, gifts —the works. Others are almost nonexistent. Generally speaking, the size of the meeting depends on the type of company. Consumer product companies seem to attract more people than utilities, for example.

A company can attract some shareholders and professional investors to its meetings by holding them in convenient locations. Regardless of whether the turnout is large or small, however, the meeting should be planned in terms of the overall financial relations message the company wants to convey. In many respects, the meeting can be something of a verbal annual report, but with an added dimension. Since it is given in person, the message can be conveyed more informally. The audience can see the company's management and possibly see and touch its products. Finally, the meeting presents an opportunity for an exchange of views.

The most consistent visitors to annual meetings are the security analysts. For this reason alone, the meetings take on special significance. And since box lunches and gifts aren't likely to have any particular influence on the security analysts, they are of marginal value.

The annual meeting, then, like the annual and interim reports, the proxy statements, the speeches and article reprints, should be planned in terms of the specific points a company has found it needs to convey to the financial community in order to be properly appraised. On this basis, and this basis alone, can an effective communications program be drawn.

Special shareholder programs

Recently, shareholder relations have taken on a new significance, particularly for companies considered vulnerable to corporate raids. It has been found that shareholders do not necessarily rush to cash in their chips simply because another company makes a stock or cash tender offer for their company's shares. Such a thing as loyalty to management and the company still exists, though often irrationally. As a result, many companies are making renewed efforts to win shareholder support.

In addition to maintaining the normal flow of information to all shareholders, these new efforts include special attention for larger holders—those with 500 shares or more.

In some companies, any shareholder with 500 shares or more is contacted at least once a year by telephone by an officer of the company, "just to say hello." Typically, the conversation is designed to let the shareholder know he is important to the company and to keep him informed about recent company developments. The objective is to give each large shareholder a warm feeling about the company and its management and some personal identification.

Another approach is the establishment of regional shareholder meetings. These are not business meetings. In fact, they more closely resemble security analyst presentations. Selection of appropriate sites for regional meetings is based on the company shareholder breakdown. For example, if the company has a large number of shareholders in Ohio it might consider holding such a meeting in Cincinnati or Dayton. A letter would be sent to all shareholders within a reasonable distance of the town in which the meeting is to be held inviting them to attend. It would be billed simply as an opportunity to meet the management and discuss the company's current developments.

Another approach consistent with the intensified shareholder relations efforts, is the use of an occasional special letter from the president to shareholders. Shareholder readership of formally printed materials does not run very high. However, readership of personally directed letters is rather good. For this reason, an occasional special letter highlighting significant developments and pegged to some current action, can be an effective means of breaking through the communications barrier to set up a dialog between company president and shareholders.

While the basic purpose of the calls to large shareholders and the regional shareholder meetings is to establish a warm feeling, a second reason is to open up a channel of direct communication that can be used quickly if an urgent need ever exists. For example, if an actual tender offer is made, management can quickly move to the telephones and try to at least urge shareholders to hold up from making any decisions to sell their shares until after the board of directors has had a chance to meet and take action.

News handling

One of the most sensitive areas in financial relations is the handling of important corporate news.

Publicly held companies are required to reveal promptly and accurately any information which may materially affect security values or influence investor decisions.

Developments requiring prompt and accurate disclosure include annual and quarterly earnings, dividend action (or lack of action), mergers, acquisitions, stock splits, key management changes, major new products, contract awards, expansion plans and discoveries.

Companies must also disclose promptly any unfavorable information which may affect the public's appraisal of their stock.

Corporate news must be handled in proper perspective—that is, with restraint, good judgment and careful adherence to the facts. Projections must be soundly based, appropriately qualified, conservative and factual. However, excessive or misleading conservatism must be avoided.

Also to be avoided are overly optimistic forecasts, exaggerated claims and unwarranted promises.

There may be situations that require a company to withhold certain significant information, at least for the time being, to achieve a corporate objective. Such a case requires the company to use great discretion. Also, it should be prepared to issue an announcement immediately in the event of unusual market action or other indications of possible leak of information.

There are distinct advantages to keeping the company in the public's eye by maintaining a constant news flow. For this reason, the financial relations effort should be well coordinated with all other public relations activities.

Communications gap

For greatest effectiveness, general news and feature attention should be given to areas in which a communications gap is known to exist. For example, if analysts question the company's research depth, newspaper interviews of the company's research director or news releases on new research developments might help to change this attitude.

One of the most difficult questions confronting corporate management is whether or not to give earnings estimates to the press or to analysts. This becomes a matter of corporate policy which depends to a great extent on the company's ability to be reasonably reliable with its estimates. At the very minimum, a company should be aware of stock market estimates of the company's earnings, and should make sure that they are realistic.

Meeting with security analysts

Meeting security analysts is relatively easy. They welcome any opportunity to learn more about the companies they must follow.

There are 41 societies of security analysts around the country, all of which are members of the Financial Analysts Federation, and all of which invite regular presentations to their members by company management.

The largest, and most influential, is the New York Society of Security Analysts which has a company presentation at lunch five days a week and afternoon presentations on specific industries several times a week. In addition, the society occasionally arranges dinner meetings with major companies and tours of significant company plants. Most publicly held companies on the two major exchanges can expect an invitation to appear on the program of the New York Society every two or three years.

The other large societies are in Boston, Chicago, Los Angeles and San Francisco. These generally hold two meetings a week except in the summer months, when they close. Other societies around the country usually hold one meeting a week.

Formal presentations

Formal presentations to leading societies are generally handled by the company's chief executive or chief financial officer. The usual procedure is to have a brief luncheon, followed by a 20 minute presentation and 20 minutes of questions and answers. Copies of the speeches should be made available for distribution. The press should always be invited to cover the meetings and the information should be cleared for press releases as soon as the speech begins.

The formal presentations, however, represent a shotgun rather than a rifle approach to a company's primary audience. Reaching the more limited group of key analysts can best be handled in a variety of other ways:

1. *Through small group meetings.* Many of the industry specialists are organized into highly selective analyst groups. For example, there is an Electro/Science analyst group, an Electrical and Electronics analyst group, a Chemical Process Industry group, etc. These specialist panels will invite presentations by managements within their industries. You should learn the names of those covering your industry.
2. *Company-sponsored luncheons.* Another effective approach is to invite selected analysts, 10 or 12 at a time, to have lunch with management. Small meetings of this type enable key analysts to meet management on a very personal basis and to get to know the company more thoroughly.
3. *Plant tours.* One of the most dramatic ways to get across a complete company story is to actually bring 40 to 50 key analysts to the company's major headquarters, manufacturing or research facility for a one- or two-day thorough briefing and indoctrination. In this type of program, it is desirable to mix both social and business functions and to include a large representation from management. This enables the important analysts to get a better feel of the company.
4. *Personal visits.* Key analysts should also be encouraged to visit the company's chief financial officer on a personal basis from time to time for an updating on the company. It doesn't take many enthusiastic analysts to give a company very solid support in the financial community. For this reason, it is worth the personal attention that individual visits require.

All security analyst relations are designed to establish a large number of well informed investment influences within the financial community. However, analysts are not entitled to confidential information. The general rule to follow is to tell security analysts—and also news reporters—only as much as you would be willing to tell a shareholder or any other responsible person who might call.

Conclusion

Financial relations, properly planned and executed, can be a valuable aid to business expansion. The key is to identify gaps in investors' knowledge and understanding of the company and to plan a communications program to fill these gaps.

It starts with research among the professional investment advisors. It requires the application of specific communications objectives to such basic elements as the annual and quarterly reports, annual meetings and security analyst contacts. Every communications element must do a job, must work for the company by helping to tell the story. Finally, continuing success with financial relations depends on follow-up research to measure effectiveness.

Relations with government agencies

Daniel E. Lyons*

Since the 1930's when Congress found it necessary to adopt a series of new controls, the American financial executive has had to work more closely than ever with a number of government agencies and departments. Many of these were created especially to implement and watch over the new legislation. In numerous instances the large corporation has been forced to depend to a large extent upon the various actions and interpretations of the administration officials running these agencies. As a result, hundreds of companies have established offices or placed representatives in Washington to keep abreast of policies and changes while also guarding the welfare of their shareholders. Moreover, during the post-World War II period, many United States corporations became multinational companies with vast overseas operations so that today foreign investments contribute a substantial amount of earnings to their worldwide income.

It is principally for these reasons that the American financial executive should have a good understanding of the businessman's relations with such government agencies as the Securities and Exchange Commission, the Department of State, and the Department of Commerce, as well as with lobbying in general. This chapter is organized into four sections—one each for these major topics.

---

* Vice President—Finance, City Investing Company, New York.

Reporting to the Securities and Exchange Commission

The Securities and Exchange Commission was created by an act of Congress and is responsible, among other things, for the enforcement and administration of the following:

The Securities Act of 1933	The Securities and Exchange Act of
Public Utility Holding Com-	1934
pany Act of 1935	The Trust Indenture Act of 1939
The Investment Company Act	The Investment Advisors Act of
of 1940	1940

The Securities Act of 1933 provides for the disclosure in registration statements and prospectuses of the more important facts and information to assist prudent investors in making an intelligent decision whether or not to purchase securities offered and sold to the public through interstate commerce or the mails. The regulations specify several forms for use by different industries in the registration of various types of securities.

The Securities Act of 1934 provides for the registration of national securities exchanges, the securities listed on national securities exchanges, and brokers and dealers. In addition, the act requires registration of companies whose assets exceed $1 million and of any class of stock whose equity securities is held by at least 500 persons. Under the authority of this act, the Commission regulates various trading activities of brokers and dealers and the solicitation of proxies from the holders of listed securities. The Commission exercises its supervision largely through registration and reporting requirements.

The Public Utility Holding Company Act was passed by Congress in 1935 as a direct result of the financial difficulties of the Insull public utility holding companies. The act gives the Commission authority to bring about a simplification of the capital structure of electric and gas utility holding companies and a better geographical integration of the operating utility companies. These are commonly referred to as the "death sentence" provisions of the act. The Commission also has the power to regulate certain financial transactions of public utility holding companies. The Commission's objectives are accomplished by requiring the companies to file registration statements supplemented by annual reports.

The Trust Indenture Act of 1939, while a separate act passed by Congress, is in substance an amendment to the Securities Act of 1933. It provides, among other things, that debt securities cannot be offered for sale to the public unless they are covered by a trust indenture which conforms to specific standards. When debt securities are registered and issued under the Securities Act of 1933, certain additional information must be filed with the Commission to enable it to pass upon the adequacy of the trust indenture and the eligibility of the trustee designated thereunder. Similar provisions also apply to certain debt securities not required to be registered under the Securities Act of 1933.

Under the Investment Company Act of 1940, an investment company must register as such with the Securities and Exchange Commission before it can offer its stock for sale to the public under the Securities Act of 1933. Certain forms are specified in the regulations for registering under both acts.

Individuals engaged in the business of advising others with respect to security transactions must register under the Investment Advisors Act of 1940, and amendments are required to be filed with the Commission to keep the information current. The investment advisors must maintain certain organization and operating standards which have been established and must keep certain books and records.

Organization of the Securities and Exchange Commission

The Securities and Exchange Commission consists of five members appointed by the President of the United States with the consent of the Senate. One member is designated by the President to serve as chairman. The commission is assisted by a staff of professional employees consisting of lawyers, accountants, engineers, security analysts, and examiners, and by administrative and clerical employees. An organization chart for the Commission is shown in Exhibit 1.

The principal responsibility of the Division of Corporation Finance is to ascertain that the financial information presented to the public in connection with security offerings is complete and not misleading. The division also prescribes the kind of information to be included in proxy material and periodic reports. A director supervises this division, assisted by a number of examining sections, the office of the Chief Counsel, and the office of Chief Accountant. Each section, headed by a security analyst, is comprised of accountants, lawyers, and examiners, to whom are assigned various filings. When necessary or desirable, the sections may call upon engineers, geologists, statisticians, and other experts. Each section becomes familiar with all filings, amendments, periodic reports, etc., of companies assigned to it, and in that manner industry specialization is developed. In addition to registration statements, applications, periodic reports, etc. of registered and listed companies, this division also examines proxy statements and reports of trading in securities on the part of officers, directors, and principal holders. The staff also makes field investigations and conducts hearings in stop-order proceedings. The division is also in charge of drafting rules, regulations, and forms for registrations, reports, etc., and gives advice and guidance in the application and interpretation of statutes and rules and forms.

EXHIBIT 1
Securities and Exchange Commission

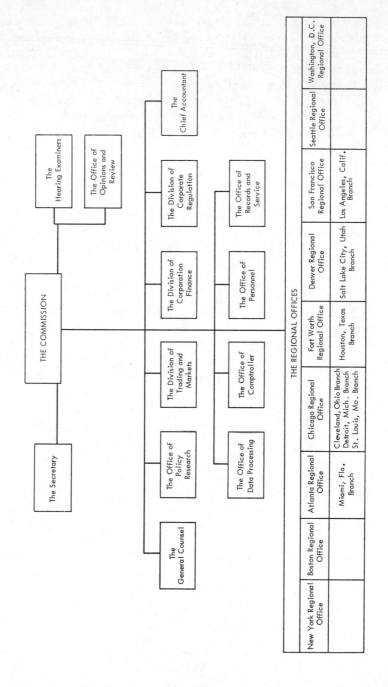

THE COMMISSION

The Secretary

The Hearing Examiners

The Office of Opinions and Review

The General Counsel

The Office of Policy Research

The Division of Trading and Markets

The Division of Corporation Finance

The Division of Corporate Regulation

The Chief Accountant

The Office of Data Processing

The Office of Comptroller

The Office of Personnel

The Office of Records and Service

THE REGIONAL OFFICES

New York Regional Office	Boston Regional Office	Atlanta Regional Office	Chicago Regional Office	Fort Worth Regional Office	Denver Regional Office	San Francisco Regional Office	Seattle Regional Office	Washington, D.C. Regional Office
		Miami, Fla. Branch	Cleveland, Ohio Branch Detroit, Mich. Branch St. Louis, Mo. Branch	Houston, Texas Branch	Salt Lake City, Utah Branch	Los Angeles, Calif. Branch		

The Chief Accountant is the principal advisor to the Securities and Exchange Commission on all matters relating to accounting and auditing, and is responsible for the execution of Commission policy in these areas. He supervises all the work of accountants assigned to examine financial data filed, and initiates and supervises studies relating to accounting and auditing. He confers with accounting authorities, professional organizations, public accountants, and officials of government. Some of his opinions are published by the Securities and Exchange Commission as "Accounting Series Releases."

Nature of filings with the Securities and Exchange Commission

The following are the more commonly used forms provided for under the Securities Act of 1933:

Form S–1 —general form for registration under this Act for which no other form is authorized or prescribed; the form that is used the most.

Form S–2 —for registration under the Act of commercial and industrial companies in the development stage.

Form S–3 —for registration under the Act of mining corporations in the promotional stage.

Form S–7 —for registration under the Act of securities of certain issuers to be offered for cash.

Form S–8 —for registration under the Act of securities to be offered to employees pursuant to certain plans.

Form S–9 —for registration under the Act of nonconvertible fixed interest debt securities.

Form S–11—for registration under the Act of certain real estate companies.

The following forms are the more commonly used forms provided for under the Securities Act of 1934:

Form 7–K—quarterly report for certain real estate companies with respect to distributions made to shareholders.

Form 8   —amendment to application or report.

Form 8–K—current report for issuers having securities registered on national security exchanges.

Form 9–K—semiannual reports for issuers having securities registered on a national security exchange.

Form 10   —general form of application for registration of securities on a national security exchange.

Form 10–K—general form of annual report.

Form 11–K—annual report of employees' stock purchase savings or similar plans.

The above is just a partial listing; there are other forms available.

REVIEW OF FILINGS BY THE SECURITIES AND EXCHANGE COMMISSION. Registration statements are filed at the main office of the Securities and Exchange Commission in Washington, D.C. and are logged in and given file numbers for identification and then assigned to examining sections for review. As previously indicated, the examining sections have attempted to obtain specialization in various industries by being assigned industry group registration statements. It takes an examining section from thirty to ninety working days to complete its review of a registration statement. The time lapse is dependent upon the work load of the section and familiarity of the section with the company filing. Initial filings naturally will usually take a longer time to clear through the section.

On November 21, 1968, the Securities and Exchange Commission issued Securities Act of 1933 Release No. 4934, which invited the cooperation of industry, the bar, underwriters, accountants, and other experts to assist the Commission's staff in processing the increased volume of registration statements filed under the Securities Act of 1933.

Until such time as the volume of filings will permit the normal procedure, an officer of the Commission's Division of Corporation Finance will make a cursory review of every registration statement filed and will make one of the following three decisions:

1. The registration statement is so poorly prepared or otherwise presents problems so serious that no further review will be made. Oral or written comments will not be issued, for to do so would delay the review of other registration statements which do not appear to contain comparable disclosure problems. Counsel will be notified.

2. Counsel shall be advised that the staff has made only a cursory review of the registration statement; no written or oral comments will be provided; and review by the staff, whether extensive, as is customary, or cursory as in this case, may not be relied upon in any degree to indicate that the registration is true, complete, or accurate. Particularly with respect to companies which have never before been subject to the registration process, counsel will be requested to furnish as supplemental information letters from the chief executive officer of the issuer, the auditors, and the managing underwriter on behalf of all underwriters. These letters shall include representations that the respective persons are aware that the staff has made only a cursory and not a customary review of the registration statement, which may not be relied upon in any degree to indicate that the registration statement is true, complete, or accurate, and are also aware of their statutory responsibilities under the Securities Act. Counsel will be advised that upon receipt of such supplemental information in satisfactory form, the staff will recommend clearance of the registration statement upon request, not earlier than 20 days after the date of original filing.

3. The filing will be subject to the regular review process.

Upon completion of the review, a "letter of comment," commonly referred to as a "deficiency letter," is issued by the Securities and Exchange Commission to the filing company. The letter usually contains requests for additional disclosures or clarification of information, or questions the treatment of various items in the body of the prospectus and the financial statements. In most instances, clarification of the comments and agreement with members of the Commission's staff as to the manner in which to satisfy these comments can be arrived at in telephone conversations. However, in more complicated situations it is not uncommon to request a conference with the Securities and Exchange Commission staff members to discuss their comments.

It is considered advisable, when there are problem areas, to meet with the appropriate members of the Commission's staff and to discuss, clarify, and come to an understanding as to the manner of treatment prior to the filing of a registration statement. When arranging such a meeting, it is most important that proper preparation be made; specifically, a memorandum which may be left with the staff should be prepared setting forth in detail the facts and problem areas so that the staff members can obtain a full understanding of the situation. At present, there is some delay in obtaining meetings with staff members because of their heavy work loads, and it may be more expeditious to set forth all the facts and problem areas in letter form to the Commission and obtain their suggestions and comments by letter or telephone.

Relations with the State Department

The Department of State plans and implements the course of action in our dealings with other nations, while in most countries of the world the functions of the State Department are performed by a foreign office under a minister of foreign affairs. In the United States these activities are the responsibility of the Department of State under the Secretary of State, who is the ranking member of the President's Cabinet. An organization chart for the department is shown in Exhibit 2.

Four chief advisors serve under the Secretary of State. The Under Secretary serves as his alter ego and acts for him in his absence. A second Under Secretary concentrates on political matters. Two Deputy Under Secretaries are specialists in political affairs and administration. The Secretary also is assisted by one or two ambassadors at large who serve as troubleshooters, undertaking assignments anywhere in the world; they also are advisers to the President. Currently, specialized units, most of which are headed by Assistant Secretaries, carry on the daily work of the Department. One of these units is broken into five geographic bureaus which are responsible for our relationships with the various regions of the world. These are the Bureaus of African Affairs, European Affairs, East Asian and Pacific Affairs, Inter-American Affairs, and Near Eastern and South Asian Affairs.

In 1968 the Department had about 7,500 American employees in the United States and an equal number stationed abroad. In addition, it employs approximately 10,000 foreign nationals at our overseas posts with 118 embassies and 160 other posts. From their posts abroad, members of the United States Foreign Service report to the State Department on foreign developments relating to the welfare and security of the American people. From the Department in Washington to the overseas posts go the instructions which guide our foreign service in carrying out America's foreign policy. Chief implementer of these instructions overseas is our ambassador to each country with which we have diplomatic

EXHIBIT 2
Department of State

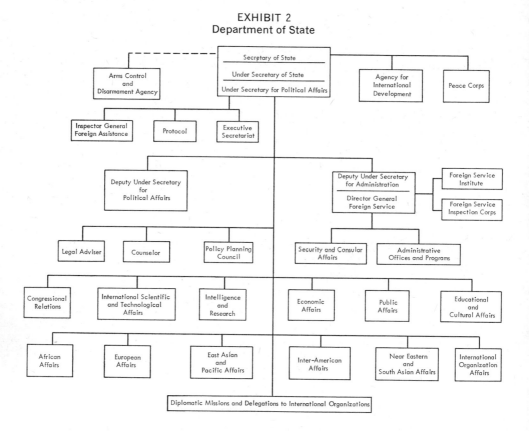

relations. To the ambassador falls the responsibility to negotiate agreements between the United States and the host country, to explain and disseminate official United States policy, and to maintain cordial relations with that country's government and people.

During the past few years organizational changes made both in Washington and overseas enable the Department to provide more effective assistance to United States business, significant of which was the creation of a position of Deputy Assistant Secretary for Commercial Affairs and Business Activities. Shortly before this, a new International Business Affairs Division was established. As a result, America's economic and commercial activities abroad have now been integrated in an effort to obtain the best possible use of our manpower on behalf of United States business.

Bureau of Economic Affairs

With the sharp increase in our foreign trade from $50 billion in 1962, when the Kennedy Round trade negotiations were authorized by Congress, to the 1968 and 1969 rates of approximately $65 billion, or a 30 percent gain, the emphasis of the Bureaus of Economic Affairs and International Business Affairs naturally was directed toward the trade relations of American businessmen. The Bureau of Economic Affairs formulates and implements policy regarding foreign economic matters of an interregional nature. In this connection it negotiates agreements, administers the Mutual Defense Assistance Control Act (known as the Battle Act), and clears assignments of officers to economic positions abroad.

Broken down by functions, the Bureau of Economic Affairs covers: (1) commercial affairs and business activities, (2) international monetary affairs, (3) international trade policy, (4) international resources and food policy, and (5) transportation and telecommunications. The commercial affairs and business activities provide the broadest liaison for the United States businessman with the outside world. It recommends and approves policy programs concerning all international commercial matters, restrictive business practices affecting American interests abroad, international aspects of industrial property rights, economic reporting policies and programs, and specific business problems confronting American business abroad. The Bureau of Economic Affairs comprises the Business Practices Division, the Foreign Reporting Division, and the International Business Affairs Division.

International Business Affairs Division

It is particularly the International Business Affairs Division created in 1965 that has grown in stature more recently in the eyes of the American businessman. Working closely with the State Department's Advisory Committee on International Business Problems, a group of leading businessmen formed in 1963, it has broadened the consultation program for senior foreign service officers and ambassadors who meet with business executives. These conferences are arranged in New York through the Business Council for International Understanding (BCIU), and in Chicago under the auspices of the Mid-America Committee. A major objective of these consultations is to acquaint the office with the problems faced by United States companies and to bring them into closer relationship with company executives who handle overseas relations. These conferences also provide an opportunity for American business executives to increase their knowledge of overseas situations and United States government policies.

American ambassadors abroad have been encouraged to hold regular formal meetings with local United States business representatives where conditions are unstable or the economy is undeveloped. A newly arrived business representative or a businessman who is traveling through a country quickly can obtain considerable assistance from overseas posts. The foreign service staffs supply up-to-date information on the local economy, the various government programs, and the organization of the local government.

Since trouble usually brings people together, our State Department officials can be of most assistance when they are informed early of situations that might develop difficulties later on. They regularly meet representatives of many important companies, the BCIU, and the United States Chamber of Commerce to find ways to bring the foreign service and United States business closer together. It is advisable for American businessmen to check in with local embassies or consular offices as soon as possible upon arriving in a foreign country. Officials of the foreign service frequently will provide the United States national with key information about local jurisdictions not generally known. Sometimes they will provide introductions to officers of local foreign governments or explain the best ways to cooperate with them. This can eliminate much red tape and save valuable time for the businessman in the end.

Office of International Trade Policy

Through the Office of International Trade Policy the Department of State develops policy recommendations and discharges responsibilities not only for trade, but also for economic defense and its related intergovernmental cooperation and security export controls, as well as administering the Mutual Defense Assistance Control Act. This office comprises the Office of International Trade, the General Commercial Policy Division, the Trade Agreements Division, the special Trade Activities and Commercial Treaties Division, and the Office of East-West Trade.

In handling the multilateral trade negotiations of the United States, the Department of State has major responsibilities in the field of tariff agreements. It actively participates in interagency consideration of trade and tariff questions and is particularly responsible for advising the Special Representative for Tariff Negotiations and the President on the foreign policy implications of proposed duty changes or other aspects of tariff negotiations with our trading partners. Since the inauguration of the Reciprocal Trade Agreements program in 1934, the authority to grant cuts in exchange for comparable reductions by others has been an important tool of foreign economic policy. Beginning in 1947, in the context of the multilateral General Agreement on Tariffs and Trade (GATT), a number of tariff negotiating conferences has been held. The last of these was the successful "Kennedy Round," signed in June, 1967; the Department of State actively participated in interagency consideration and coordination of United States positions for the Kennedy Round negotiations.

Through the General Agreement on Tariffs and Trade the United States endeavors to lower foreign nontariff barriers to our exports of agricultural and industrial products. These efforts have met with considerable success. Article XI of the GATT generally forbids the use of quantitative import restrictions. However, a major exception to this rule is contained in Article XII, which allows GATT contracting parties to maintain import quotas to protect their foreign exchange reserves in a period of balance of payments difficulty. Consultations have been held with many of the GATT countries under this article over the years since GATT came into being, and the United States has played a leading role in the conduct of the tariff negotiations.

The Organization for Economic Cooperation and Development (OECD) is essentially an organization for cooperation rather than operation. One of the primary objectives of United States membership in the organization has been to foster economic stability and growth among the developed countries by cooperating with other OECD countries on problems of mutual concern and international importance. In this context the United States sought to generate a favorable climate and favorable conditions for United States business and commercial activities abroad.

Activities in foreign offices

Through its diplomatic representatives abroad, the Department of State approaches foreign governments on a bilateral basis endeavoring to secure most-favored-nation treatment for exports and to obtain relaxation of import controls and other restrictions harmful to United States trade. Sometimes these approaches are strictly on a government-to-government basis. At other times the more formal provisions of Articles XXII and XXIII of the GATT are followed. For example, in 1966 discussions were held in Oslo on a number of agricultural import restrictions maintained by Norway. As a direct result of these consultations, on January 1, 1967, Norway removed and relaxed quantitative controls on many of the agricultural items in which American businessmen have substantial trade interest. Similarly, Article XXIII consultations have been held in recent years with France. They have been conducted through the American

Embassy in Paris and have resulted in a steady relaxation of import controls maintained on a number of agricultural items. Normally, in such consultations the Department of State representative or embassy or mission representative acts as chairman for the United States side. He receives important technical advice and assistance in the negotiations from representatives of other agencies.

In addition to its participation in efforts through such organizations as the GATT and the OECD to reduce specific quantitative and other restrictions which impede the flow of United States exports abroad, the Department of State plays an important daily role in efforts to expand United States and world trade on a nondiscriminatory basis. In some cases this means pointing out a government's obligations under its international commitments; in others it means appealing to good economic sense alone. Seeking the removal or reduction of bilateral trading arrangements and discriminatory or preferential import arrangements which harm our trade interest is literally the daily business of the Department of State. In providing instructions and guidance to the field in the execution of this policy, the Department receives helpful support from other Washington agencies.

The Department of State also has negotiated the important Treaties of Friendship, Commerce, and Navigation with 22 countries since the end of World War II. These treaty commitments confer upon the American businessman a very substantial body of economic privileges in foreign countries. Moreover, they are designed to assure to America's economic enterprises the ability to operate in a foreign country on a basis of true competitive equality with local concerns.

A foreign inquiry about purchasing an American product on credit terms often originates at one of our foreign offices, which transmits it to Washington for referral to United States exporters or to the Export-Import Bank. Later, if an export credit comes under serious consideration by the Export-Import Bank, that agency will seek the advice and assistance of the Department of State or the appropriate American embassy. The embassy may be asked to gather specific information relating to the loan for the Export-Import Bank or to perform a negotiating role on a government-to-government level. In Washington, the Department is represented in the weekly Export-Import Bank board meetings, where loan guarantee and insurance decisions are made, as well as on the interagency National Advisory Council on International Monetary and Financial Policies where all export credit policy questions are formally reviewed.

The American businessman who sets out to do business in Eastern Europe will find himself relying more heavily on our embassies than in most other areas of the world, particularly in Western Europe. This is due largely to the high degree of centralization and control, as well as the unfamiliar methods of trade in these economies. Because U.S. foreign policy favors increased East-West trade in nonstrategic goods, the State Department actively encourages a greater volume of trade and investment through its embassies. Here are some of the ways the embassy can promote American business in Eastern Europe:

1. It can assist American businessmen in making the initial contacts with appropriate members of the various state trading enterprises.
2. The foreign service can be helpful in the allocation of foreign exchange as the tendency of state trading groups to attempt to barter may confront the would-be trader or investor. The experience of embassy officers can be invaluable in coming up with a "package" agreeable to all.
3. Since the Eastern Europeans invariably ask for credit, the State Department can be of tremendous assistance in helping the businessman obtain financial information for guaranties or insurance under the restricted Export-Import Bank and FCIA programs on sales to Eastern Europe.
4. Such standard aids as trade lists, which can be obtained in routine fashion for most countries, are available for both Yugoslavia and Poland.
5. The State Department promotes American business in eastern Europe through active support of the Trade Mission Program of the Department of Commerce. Successful trade missions have been carried out in several Eastern European countries.

International claims

The Office of the Assistant Legal Adviser for International Claims is responsible for international claims of American nationals against foreign governments, and international claims of nationals of foreign governments against the government of the United States. It is also responsible for determining claims under various domestic laws of the United States.

Hundreds of claims are considered annually and disposed of by rejection on an individual basis or settlement through espousal, negotiation, or arbitration. Arbitration is resorted to only (1) when agreement cannot be reached through ordinary processes of diplomacy and the claim or claims are of sufficient importance to warrant arbitration, or (2) when the number of claims against a particular government to be settled is so large as to render impracticable settlement through other than the machinery of an organized tribunal with authority to hold hearings and to make final determinations on law and fact.

While the procedure with respect to the method of handling and settling international claims of the United States nationals does not follow established forms, the legality of the claims is dependent upon the responsibility of a foreign government under principles of international law.

Relations with the Commerce Department

The Department of Commerce is the business services arm of the government. Its objective is to work for the businessman by fostering, promoting, and developing the foreign and domestic commerce and the manufacturing and service industries of the United States. To fulfill this objective, the Commerce Department offers a multitude of services to aid the American businessman. An organization chart for the Department is shown in Exhibit 3.

The Commerce Department has set as a major purpose the preparation and dissemination of basic business, economic, scientific, demographic, and environmental information. Key programs include the promotion of foreign trade and increased travel to the United States, the overseeing of investments abroad, assuring fullest use of the nation's scientific and technical resources, and fostering development of the American Merchant Marine. One of the Department's newest missions is to assist in the economic development of communities and regions with lagging economies. It also administers the vital patent and trademark systems, regulates control over export of strategic materials, and performs materials priorities and mobilization functions.

The Secretary of Commerce is responsible for the administration of the functions and authorities assigned to the Department of Commerce by law. One of his most significant, and sometimes delicate, duties is advising the President on federal policy and programs affecting the industrial and commercial segments of the national economy. Although the Under Secretary of Commerce serves as the principal deputy of the Secretary, the businessman is concerned more with two of the five Assistant Secretaries. These two are the Assistant Secretary for Economic Affairs and the Assistant Secretary for Domestic and International Business. The former serves as the principal adviser to the Secretary on a broad range of economic matters, which includes coordinations and review of the economic research and statistical programs. As such, he is the Department liaison with the President's Council of Economic Advisers. He exercises policy direction and general supervision over the Bureau of Census and the Office of Business Economics.

It is the Assistant Secretary for Domestic and International Business who has the businessman's interest uppermost in his mind at all times. He serves as the principal adviser on all domestic and international aspects of industry, trade, investment, and related economic activities. The importance of his position to the businessman is emphasized in his direction and general supervision of the Bureau of International Commerce, the Business and Defense Services Administration, the Office of Field Services and the Office of Foreign Commercial Services.

EXHIBIT 3
Department of Commerce

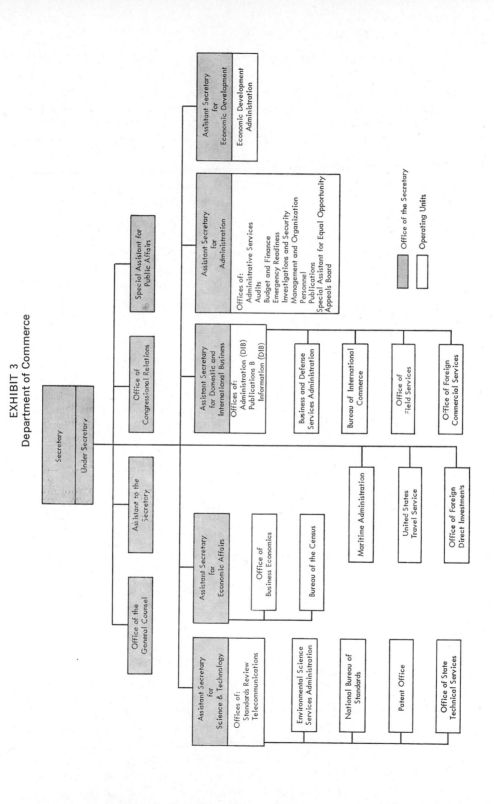

THE FIELD OFFICE. Although the principal Department of Commerce office in Washington is available for any businessman who needs help, it is the field office which usually is in daily contact with the individual or company from the start. In 1968, there were 42 field offices from Honolulu and Anchorage to Miami and Boston. Each field office is the prime contact point for the United States Department of Commerce in its own locality. It carries out the field programs of four major Commerce agencies—the Business and Defense Services Administration, Bureau of International Commerce, Office of Business Economics, and the Institute for Applied Technology. It also disseminates Census Bureau data and serves as a local information center for other Commerce agencies, including the National Bureau of Standards, United States Patent Office, United States Travel Service, and the Economic Development Administration. In addition, the field office advises and assists the business public in matters pertaining to the Agency for International Development (AID), the Export-Import Bank of Washington, and the Foreign Credit Insurance Association (FCIA).

PUBLICATIONS. For businessmen interested in selling to, buying from, or making proposals to the federal government, the Department of Commerce publishes the *Commerce Business Daily*. This includes requests for bids and proposals, procurement reserved for small business, prime contracts awarded, contractors seeking subcontract assistance, and upcoming sales of property (including real estate, machinery, equipment, and supplies). It also lists research and development leads and foreign government procurement in the United States.

To make the Commerce Department's facilities, reports, publications, and services even more accessible to United States businessmen, over 600 business organizations located in the 50 states and Puerto Rico are serving their areas as "cooperative offices" of the United States Department of Commerce. These organizations include local and state chambers of commerce, manufacturers' associations, and state and municipal development commissions. Each maintains close liaison with the field office serving its area. Business problems requiring counsel and assistance not available at a cooperative office are referred to the nearest field office of the Department.

Business and Defense Services Administration

Aside from the better known Office of Business Economics and the Bureau of the Census, where the businessman may quickly obtain statistics on practically any given economic subject, the influential Business and Defense Services Administration (BDSA) today probably handles more of the Department's major domestic functions than any other division. BDSA is the business services agency for the Commerce Department. Created to promote and develop the growth of United States industry and commerce and to prepare and execute plans for industrial mobilization readiness, its slogan is "working with business for business." Its industry and commodity specialists provide information, counsel, and assistance to 424 manufacturing, construction, distribution, and service industries. It presents the viewpoint of business in the councils of government. It counsels other federal agencies on business problems, develops recommendations for sound public policies relating to business, and supplies industrial information and analyses on which policy decisions are based.

As a "defense services" agency, the direct successor to the War Production Board of World War II and the National Production Authority of Korea, BDSA administers the system of priorities and allocations set up under the Defense Production Act to assure on-time production and delivery of military orders for United States military, atomic energy, and space programs. It allocates aluminum, copper, steel, and other materials to meet defense production requirements.

Working in the domestic and international business area of the Commerce Department, BDSA carries out a program to promote the progress of United States competitive private enterprise at home and abroad and to provide for industrial mobilization preparedness.

1. *Industrial and market reporting.* One of the major activities of BDSA is to report on domestic industries and markets. It provides statistics, compiles them in useful form, analyzes them, and forecasts industry trends. BDSA's annual year-end review and industrial outlook contains the kind of information United States industry needs for planning production, marketing, and capital investment. For example, the "United States Industrial Outlook for 1967," published annually by BDSA, reviewed the prospects in 78 different industries accounting for 60 percent of manufacturing, and the construction and wholesale and retail trades. It analyzed factors influencing demand, output, and foreign trade, and highlighted trends in the various industries.

BDSA also publishes six periodicals covering the chemicals, construction, containers and packaging, copper, printing and publishing, and pulp, paper, and board industries; a monthly *Marketing Information Guide;* market research data; and a variety of special industry studies and reports. It is also taking an increasingly active interest in consumer affairs matters, representing both business and the public in pricing, lending, cost-of-living, and other key consumer problems.

2. *Legislation and regulation.* BDSA also initiates and supports bills to expand business opportunities. It reviews some 800 legislative proposals a year to assess their potential effect on American industry and commerce or proposes government policies and regulations. If it sees roadblocks to United States economic growth, BDSA recommends

corrective action to reduce or eliminate the obstacles. For example, in 1966 it reviewed a bill which proposed a substantial increase in the minimum wage scale from $1.25 to $1.75 an hour. BDSA thought this would create financial burdens that could not be met by small business-men, especially those in distributive and service trades, and would also slow down economic growth. After a meeting with business, BDSA recommended that certain modifications be made in the proposed legisla-tion through adoption of a graduated scale.

3. *Government-business relations.* The agency solicits the views of business on government policies and programs and explains the govern-ment's position to business; assists on industry problems in government; enlists business participation in national economic and social programs, such as the President's program for summer employment of young peo-ple; and maintains liaison with some 2,100 business trade associations. It also regularly consults with industry on national stockpile activities so that the United States can plan for the orderly sales and distribution of surplus stockpile commodities without creating an adverse effect upon the economy and industry.

The federal government, as a large-scale buyer of goods and services, is a prime market for business. To enable more businessmen, especially small businessmen, to sell in this market, BDSA helped to develop a government procurement counseling conference program. The 27 confer-ences held in 1966 resulted in the development of 3,100 new supply sources for the Department of Defense, while prime contractors found 613 new subcontractors.

4. *Foreign trade support.* Another BDSA function is to advise indus-try and government on international business opportunities, market pros-pects abroad, commodity problems, and tariff questions. United States exporters can get from BDSA information on trade opportunities and world markets for products ranging from aluminum cable to welding equipment. Commercial officers in the United States foreign service report some 300 new trade leads to BDSA each week, and its commodity specialists call the opportunities to the attention of interested companies and industry trade associations.

BDSA also provides support for American commodity trade by con-tributing to the development of United States commercial policy. Spe-cialists in BDSA analyze the effect of tariff cuts on American industries and develop studies and recommendations on United States and foreign tariff questions to assist United States negotiators. Thus, for a number of years BDSA was actively involved in the work of the recently completed Kennedy Round.

5. *Industrial modernization.* American industry today is operating in an environment of constant change. New industries, new products, new markets are emerging. BDSA assesses the effect of these changes on individual industries, analyzes the impact of new materials, technology,

and management systems, and evaluates the consequences of changes in industrial practices. Through published studies, conferences, and personal contacts with business, it encourages more American productivity, employment, and profits. This area of activity is not of interest to the general businessman and, therefore, no further description of this activity is covered herein.

6. *Government services.* The Secretary of Commerce and agencies in the Commerce Department and elsewhere in the government rely on BDSA for assistance and advice on commodities, products, industries, and services. It prepared a number of reports for the Council of Economic Advisors and the President's Advisory Committee on Labor Management Policy, among others, with respect to price trends, strike impact, and productivity problems.

7. *Industrial mobilization.* In addition to administering the defense priorities and allocations system, BDSA mobilizes the nation's industry to meet a national emergency. BDSA assists industries in the development of standby survival, dispersal, and conversion plans, contributing toward the administration of the national stockpile program.

Other major activities and offices

Another domestic function of the Commerce Department rapidly gaining in importance in recent years is the economic development of states, regions, areas, districts, centers, and communities in the United States. The Department of Commerce, through the Assistant Secretary for Economic Development, is the liaison between the federal development programs for economically depressed areas and the local governments. As an outgrowth of the critical need to create new employment opportunities, the Economic Development Administration (EDA) was established in 1965 under the Public Works and Economic Development.

The primary purpose of EDA is the long-range economic development and programming for areas and regions of substantial and persistent unemployment and low income groups by creating new employment opportunities and expanding existing local facilities and resources. The activities include public works grants and loans, loans for industrial projects, working capital loan guarantees, technical planning, and research assistance, all of which benefit the businessman in the designated area.

The Maritime Administration. It also falls under the Department of Commerce, and has a particularly close relationship with American business. It administers the operating-differential and construction-differential subsidy programs and other government aids to merchant shipping authorized by law. Under these programs, the government pays the difference to shipping companies between certain costs of operating ships under United States flags as opposed to foreign competitive flags on essential foreign trade routes, and the difference between the costs of constructing ships in the United States rather than in foreign shipbuilding centers. In addition, the Maritime Administration insures mortgages and/or loans made by private lending institutions to finance the construction, reconstruction, and reconditioning of ships. It also investigates and determines ocean services, routes, and lines essential for the development and maintenance of the foreign commerce of the United States, and the type, size, speed, and other requirements of ships to provide adequate service on such routes.

The Patent Office.   This office administers the patent laws as they relate to granting of letters patent for inventions and the trademark laws as they relate to the registration of trademarks. It examines applications and grants patents when applicants are entitled to them under the law. The office publishes and disseminates patented matter, records assignment of patents, and maintains a search center consisting of United States and foreign patents and general reference literature. It also works closely with the State Department in the interests of American businessmen in relation to patent, trademark and copyright negotiations for Conventions in which the United States may participate.

The National Bureau of Standards.   This is another necessary segment of the Commerce Department's services. It is a focal point in the federal government for assuring maximum application of the physical and engineering services of the technology in industry and commerce. The Bureau conducts research and provides central national services for basic materials and technological measurements and standards, and assists in the transfer of technology. As one of the four departments within the bureau, the Institute for Basic Standards provides the basis within the United States for a complete and consistent system of physical measurement, coordinates this with other nations, and furnishes essential services leading to accurate and uniform physical measurements for the nation's industry and commerce.

The Bureau of International Commerce.   BIC has as its prime objective the increasing of America's exports. To carry out this objective, BIC (1) provides services and information to American businessmen to help them trade abroad; (2) operates overseas trade centers, sends trade missions abroad, stages commercial exhibitions at international trade fairs, and provides other marketing services to promote the sale of United States goods abroad; (3) works with other government agencies and international organizations to improve conditions for international trade and investment; (4) presents the views of traders and investors in governmental councils; and (5) works out policies and procedures to make doing business abroad simpler and more profitable. The bureau also administers the Export Control Act of 1949 to prevent the export of strategic and other United States materials in situations involving national security, foreign policy, and short supply.

The Bureau of International Commerce works closely with the Office of Foreign Commercial Services. The Office carries out the responsibilities of the Department of Commerce for participating with the Department of State in the management of economic and commercial program activities of the United States foreign service, providing support for all international programs of the department which involve worldwide representation of United States business interests through the unified foreign service, and obtaining business and reporting services from the overseas foreign service posts. It is these foreign service posts which deal on the spot with American businessmen traveling abroad who need assistance in meeting local problems.

The Office of Foreign Direct Investments. This office was established on January 1, 1968. Its purpose is to reduce substantially the outflow of funds for direct investment in foreign countries, in order to help correct the balance of payments deficit. Functions and activities of the Office include receiving, recording, reviewing, and reporting on applications for specific authorizations and exemptions from the regulations as filed by individual direct investors; receiving base period and quarterly reports; evaluating the adequacy of control techniques and measuring the economic consequences of restriction on overseas investment and the balance of payments; promoting and maintaining compliance with the provisions of the Executive order and implementing the regulations issued by the Secretary of Commerce; and keeping under continuous review and updating the regulations and written interpretations.

Lobbying—why and how

The congressman has to listen to the businessman, either to his trade association or his attorney, the two best known vehicles for making the congressman aware of the businessman's interests. Hundreds of legislative measures are introduced into the House or Senate hoppers each year that could affect the businessman's profits. Sometimes there is no legislation involved at all. It may simply be federal bureaucracy that is holding up the businessman's contact. But the right kind of politics could well protect the businessman's profits in both cases.

Your congressman wants to help you. He may know your partisan sentiments, but even if you did not support him in the past he does not want to antagonize a potential customer because he does not agree with him. However, your congressman also realizes it is impossible to help every constituent with his individual problem. On the other hand, he also is the first to admit it is difficult to turn down a request for assistance when it is presented on a collective scale. It is easier for him to avoid charges of collusion or discrimination when he supports an issue for many businessmen rather than for one corporation. This is why he will listen more receptively to a trade association.

The role of trade associations

Any trade association's legislative endeavors should be designed around an official policy adopted by the membership or by the elected or appointed authorities. Frequently the association's activities will give clear authority to the staff, committees, board of directors, or executive committee to handle legislative matters with little or no encumbrance. If the association's membership is unified on a specific issue affecting the industry concerned, it is advisable to have a printed policy. This can be distributed to congressmen, the administration and to the public in order to better identify the issue and the pros and cons behind it.

When the association's policy is controversial, it may be the task of the board of directors or governing body to establish the line of attack or defense. Sometimes it is preferable to resort to the membership for a referendum. Surveys show that when controversial policies do arise, the governing body makes the decision in about 60 percent of the cases. It is a generally accepted rule that, in order for trade associations to be successful in their lobbying efforts, they must have a well-organized and planned legislative program. The objectives of the specific industry and their contribution to the economy should be constantly brought to the attention of the federal and state legislatures. Usually this is most effectively accomplished through public affairs or government relations committees created within the association. These committees are assigned the important functions of (a) acting as a liaison between the industry and various government agencies, (b) recommending policies affecting legislation, (c) publishing industry recommendations, and (d) advising members and other committees of all legislation affecting the trade association's industry.

A study of a number of trade associations prepared by the Chamber of Commerce of the United States reveals there are four steps necessary in establishing an effective legislative committee. Briefly, these are as follows:

1. Obtain the proper authorization, usually from the association's governing board, to establish the committee.
2. Find a good organizer to be the chairman to guide the committee in the right direction.
3. Appoint committee members who have persuasive abilities and who are aware of legislative needs and procedures.
4. Limit the assignments of individual committee members to one or two projects by category.

The trade association's legislative activities must be guided by the Federal Regulation of Lobbying Act, which requires public disclosure of lobbying activities. It calls for registration and filing of reports by organizations or individuals subject to the act. However, the Supreme

Court has restricted activities under the law to so-called "direct lobbying." Generally, direct lobbying means direct communications with Congress or its members. "Indirect lobbying" is interpreted to be lobbying through general publicity.

Lobbying does not affect the tax-exempt status of an association. Under a ruling issued by the Internal Revenue Service in 1961, organizations classified as a "business league" may qualify for tax exemption even though their sole activity is influencing legislation germane to such interests. Moreover, the Internal Revenue Code does permit the deduction of dues and certain other payments to an organization such as a trade association.

Of the approximately 700 sizable trade associations in the United States, about one-half are concerned enough with the activities of the federal government to warrant maintenance of full-time headquarters or branches in Washington. Surveys repeatedly taken of American businessmen reveal that the trade association's most important work is to exercise its influence in government. Some of the greatest successes in influencing legislation have come from the major associations, whose budgets have become enormous and who have recruited some of the top executives in America to handle a delicate but necessary job.

USING THE GRASS ROOTS APPROACH.   Most associations encourage the so-called "grass roots" approach of combining the legislative committee's activities with the influence of as many members as possible in order to convince the legislatures that lobbying for a bill or on an issue embraces the entire industry. A card file of members of the association or participants in the industry having a close relationship with legislators is imperative. Personal letters and special bulletins marked "action requested" usually bring successful response. Associations find that the continuous urging of their members to contact their representatives frequently brings successful grass roots action.

However, the grass roots approach generally is supported by an organized program of personal contact with Washington senators and representatives by committee and industry members. Moreover, it is not unusual for state delegations to meet with their Congressional representatives to present the industry's viewpoint. National associations find it worthwhile to coordinate their lobbying position with state and local associations when the latter exist. This is particularly important during the opening weeks of Congress each year when thousands of lobbyists converge upon Washington. Trade associations frequently bring the members of their government relations or public affairs committees to Washington for briefing sessions with administration legislators and other officials. One of the basic requirements for successful lobbying campaigns is a good approach from the start. Proper procedure to enlist support is a necessity.

An experienced member of the Maryland House of Delegates has outlined 13 key points to be followed. These include: knowing your state, its principal industries, and the benefits of the proposed legislation to the general public; obtaining a good sponsor and determining the legislative committee to which the bill will be referred; meeting the chairman of the legislative committee and determining any opposition within the industry; requesting an opportunity to appear before the committee and selecting competent witnesses; providing the sponsor with facts and figures and analyzing the opposition; and finally, enlisting grass roots support.

Before resorting to the grass roots approach, one of the first steps in formulating a good lobbying campaign is to analyze the thinking of the other parties with potential interests in the subject to see if they are likely to be opposed to your stand. If there is opposition on their part, it is frequently possible to arrange a compromise that still might allow your group to obtain what it wants.

Compromise is not always possible. When it is, a compromising approach generally is the most effective way to deal with the situation. Bureaucrats try to avoid enemies, and would much prefer a compromise to a battle. Moreover, sometimes there is opposition within the membership of the organization itself because of differing interests. When this exists, trade associations tend to avoid the issue altogether, which is a weakness of a trade association.

Cooperation between trade associations also should be emphasized. Interassociation cooperation is known to have impressed Congress sufficiently in the past to govern their votes. Exchange of information and developing mutual areas of interest frequently develop strength in accomplishing goals. Moreover, specific assignments may be spread throughout the various cooperating associations. For instance, the association with the best contacts or technical or legal counsel should be assigned that particular responsibility. Each association should appoint one person whose task is to report the activities and actual progress to date regularly to the organizing associations.

Most trade associations which do not maintain an office in Washington rely upon a Washington representative to provide the necessary services connected with effective lobbying. Frequently the help of the Chambers of Commerce of the United States is enlisted. The Chamber's Association Service Department and Congressional Action Services Department have had considerable experience in assisting its members in the past.

WASHINGTON LAWYERS.   Probably the most effective way of achieving success when a trade association does not have a headquarters in Washington is to consult with a member of Washington's influential group of lawyer-lobbyists. The Washington lawyer is unique in that he not only represents his client in dealings with the federal government and before the courts, but he also usually is a skilled specialist in knowing how the federal machinery functions. Because of his inside contacts and his reputation (frequently he is a former outstanding government executive), the Washington lawyer normally is associated with Washington lobbying. In fact, most Washington lawyers are lobbyists.

A major reason for his close association with lobbying is that much of lobbying is related to enactment of new laws. It is easy for the Washington lawyer to include lobbying among his services since he has easy access to the legislators and their sessions. It is said that lobbying is "an honorable, justifiable and even essential part of the legislative process." Because laws regulate business, the lawyer regards it as his duty to bring to the attention of Congress his client's interests as a normal procedure. Lawyer lobbyists have found that they can represent their clients in the best manner when they work with congressional committees in the preparation of laws. Since the lawyer does have knowledge of the law, he frequently may be able to deal with the issue more effectively. Another source of his effectiveness is his understanding of the workings of the particular agency with which he was associated.

Testifying at legislative hearings

Although testifying at congressional hearings is a major function of the trade association, it is not always done through a trade association. More frequently than not, corporate executives testify on behalf of their own company. Sometimes they serve the dual purpose of testifying for their company as well as for the trade association. Corporate executives often are better witnesses than professional lobbyists. In some instances, they may be more credible than a lawyer-lobbyist, who may state what he is paid to say rather than what he believes.

Since the witness is the key to successful testimony, he should be chosen carefully to ensure the most rewarding testimony. The competent witness must be well-informed, persuasive, experienced before audiences, have a tolerant attitude and a thorough knowledge of his subject, know the exact position of each member of the legislative committee, and should be able to testify from first-hand experience. He should also use statistics, charts, tables, etc.

An important function of the trade association or a company's own Washington lobbyist is to provide advice to management concerning the company's action and the possible consequences of any steps taken when it is engaged, or is considering being engaged, in activities likely to result in government intervention.

Long regarded as the official sounding board in developing legislation, the hearings provide elected representatives and the public with sound information required to draft the best possible legislation. It is the duty of the association to provide Congress and the state legislatures with all the information relative to the proposed measure. Thus, it is vital that the trade association spend considerable time on studying, researching, conferring, and preparing accurate testimony.

When a witness performs well, the particular trade association should keep a file on him, supplying him with material regularly and appointing him to various committees. In this way, witnesses frequently become experts in their field, and the association has a strong aid to rely upon when needed. Since the decision of the legislature substantially depends upon the presentation of the industry's testimony, it is of prime importance that the testimony be prepared with ultimate care.

More than two thirds of all state and national associations ordinarily present testimony. When the trade association has decided to testify before a committee, it is beneficial to attend the hearings in advance and rehearse the testimony before presenting it. Other hints include being courteous and brief and staying with the subject. It is also helpful to know the identity of the committee members and invite questions at the end of the testimony.

The effectiveness of lobbying may be subject to question. Although influencing legislative action in Congress should not be the main function of a trade association, it should be a significant part of its program. Trade associations and lawyer-lobbyists obviously may be more successful with certain persons such as senators and congressmen who are predisposed to the businessmen's point of view. In recent years legislation has become an increasing influence on the operations of business. Therefore, it is necessary for the trade association and its members to keep current on legislative matters at all times. The membership should be informed of any action that may affect the industry, the economy, and the free enterprise system.

The Washington lobbyist, whether it is the trade association or the lawyer, has found that working with various government agencies, rather than against them, is the key to success. A successful program is not dependent upon whether an industry or a corporation hires a full-time lobbyist or uses the facilities of the trade association to accomplish its end. The lawyer may be better able to provide counsel on the especially thorny problems. However, the trade association generally is able to obtain more background information on legislation due to a larger staff and perhaps more contacts.

Industry recognizes the useful functions performed by lobbyists and, therefore, needs to use them. The lobbyist is accepted as the mode of the day, and his services are destined to become even more in demand as new legislation is required to guide our destinies.

Bibliography

Legislative Handbook for Associations. Washington, D.C.: Chamber of Commerce of the United States.

"Industries' Men in Washington," *Duns Review,* May, 1968.

"Washington's Influencial Lawyer-Lobbyists," *Duns Review,* January, 1968.

The Legislative Process, National Association of Manufacturers.

HUTCHISON, G. SCOTT, "Reactions to The Latent Lobby," *Harvard Business Review,* July–August, 1967.

You and Your Congressman, National Association of Manufacturers.

Corporate contributions

Henry L. Brown*

To give or not to give is no longer an essential question with most companies. The value to a company of making contributions to worthy causes is really no longer in dispute. Corporate giving is generally recognized as one of several important tools to help create a better environment for business under the free enterprise system.

What is, perhaps, of greater relevance currently is how to give, how much to give, and to whom. Equally important in many instances is establishment of a contributions system that answers these questions while providing maximum flexibility for creative giving and the ability to change direction without generating antagonism.

Definitions and legal restrictions

Perhaps the most meaningful description of a charitable contribution for purposes of this discussion is related to the requirements necessary for income tax exemption under current Federal law.

In general terms, a deductible charitable contribution is a gift to: (a) a state, territory, possession, or other political subdivision of the United States for public purposes; (b) a corporation, trust, community chest, fund, or foundation in the United States or its possessions operated exclusively for religious, charitable, scientific, literary, or educational purposes, or for the prevention of cruelty to children or animals; and (c) a post or organization of war veterans.

* Vice President–Corporate Public Relations, National Distillers and Chemical Corporation, New York.

The present Federal income tax law permits a corporation to take a tax deduction for charitable contributions paid within the taxable year. The amount which may be deducted is limited, however, to 5 percent of taxable income for the year. If charitable contributions exceed this 5 percent limitation, the excess can be carried forward and included in the computation of deductible charitable contributions for five succeeding years.

For corporations reporting taxable income on an accrual basis, a special elective rule makes it possible to deduct certain contributions paid after the close of the corporation's taxable year by meeting three requirements: (a) the company's board of directors must authorize a charitable contribution during the taxable year; (b) the contribution must be paid on or before the 15th day of the third month following the close of the taxable year; and (c) the corporation must report the deduction not later than the time it files its tax return for the year.

Payments made to political parties, committees, or candidates for public office, or for any other political use do not qualify as charitable contributions.

While these Federal income tax definitions seem clear, it is important to recognize here that state laws may limit the scope of coporate giving. The New Jersey statute, for example, authorizes charitable gifts which "will contribute to the protection of the corporate interest." However, the courts have generally liberalized their views as to the propriety of corporate giving to public charities and most states have equally liberal views.

There have been some instances of stockholder disapproval of corporate contributions expressed at company annual meetings, although the great majority of stockholders approve. The minority voice indicates the importance of effective control of the contributions function, with emphasis on corporate benefits.

Trends in contributions organization

Which group or individual in a company should be responsible for contributions decisions and administration? In actual practice, this would appear to be a function of company size, according to a study sponsored by the Chicago Chapter, Public Relations Society of America.[1]

In the smaller companies or firms ranging from 4 to 20 employees where there is obviously no need for group organization, the responsibility for contributions is most often taken by the president or senior partner. In a small percentage of these companies, the administrative officer undertakes the job, and in still fewer companies the finance officer or principal sales executive makes the decisions. The sales executive would seem the least objective candidate for the assignment since he is

---

[1] Leo J. Shapiro, *Company Giving* (Chicago, Ill.: Survey Press, 1960).

subject to pressures applied by customers and would risk alienating those whom he felt it necessary to turn down. In companies of somewhat larger size, ranging up to 100 employees, the president or chairman continues to dominate in administering the contributions function. There is a sharp reversal of this situation as we move up in size to companies of 500 employees. Here the practice is to assign the administration of contributions to the administrative officer or to the financial officer. In some of these middle-sized companies, executives such as the assistant to the president or the director of public relations take on the assignment.

In companies of major size employing more than 500, the top executive is responsible for contributions in a relatively small number of instances, with administrative and financial officers dominating, and public relations officers, presidential assistants, and personnel directors taking a more active part. Companies with upward of 10,000 employees very often have someone spending all or most of his time in administering the contributions program. These individuals often act as secretary to the contributions committee, or have titles such as manager or supervisor of contributions and memberships. In other instances the administrator is a full-time employee of a company-sponsored foundation.

As we range upward in company size we find the emergence of programming, and of the contributions committee or executive board concerned with contributions policy and decision. The contributions administrator becomes increasingly responsible for evaluating requests and progressively less responsible for actual contributions decisions. He spends his time assembling facts about the organizations from which requests are received and assessing the relationship of these facts to the contributions objectives of his company. He is often charged with responsibility for contributions and membership budgets and for all records relating to activity in these fields. The contributions committee relies heavily on the recommendations made by this individual in reaching its decisions.

The contributions committee

There are many advantages to formation of a contributions committee in medium-sized and larger companies. Group decisions represent viewpoints which are often more inclusive and objective than those made by an individual. The committee approach has definite internal benefits, since it is a means of keeping management people informed about contributions policy and actual activities. Very often membership decisions are also made by the same committee.

Some companies adopt a flexible approach to decisions through what might be termed a "floating" contributions committee. The contributions administrator, after the usual screening and evaluating, has requests reviewed by specialists in the area of the business most knowledgeable about and concerned with the projects in question. For example, an appeal involving a scientific program would be reviewed by appropriate technical people, a health or medical proposal by the company medical director, etc. This approach involves people with background and knowledge relating to the requests and does not waste the time of others who have neither the interest nor the competence to make effective judgments.

The more formal committee, variously called contributions and memberships committee, donations committee, or community relations committee, typically varies in size from three to eight members. In many companies committee membership devolves primarily on members of management, including such executives as president, vice president–finance, vice president–administration, vice president–divisional general manager, vice president–personnel, vice president–public relations, and vice president–sales. In other companies the committee members occupy lesser positions which might include the assistant to the president, assistant directors of personnel or public relations, and corporate secretary.

The contributions committee, whatever its official designation, is generally responsible for:

a) Approval of the annual contributions and memberships budgets.
b) Decisions on specific requests within limits imposed by the company's contributions and memberships policy.
c) Directing the activities of the contributions administrator in regard to recommendations, records, and files, and methods of keeping personnel at the local level informed of the company's contributions program and activities.
d) Suggesting means to improve the contributions function through special studies and research.
e) Reporting to and receiving the approval of the company's board of directors on contributions exceeding a specified amount (often $1,000 or more) and on the annual contributions and memberships budgets.

Item (e) is of particular importance in protecting the committee, particularly if it is composed of middle management people, from undue influence by sales executives under pressure from important customers for major contributions to organizations in which the customers have a personal interest. In other cases, there is considerable rivalry among members of a particular industry in contributing to "pet" charities. The heat is moderated when the committee can honestly tell the company executive pressing for a major gift for his "pet" philanthropy that his request will have to be approved by the company's board of directors.

Another device which has both positive and protective aspects for companies of any size is the statement of company contributions policy in printed form which can be used as a mailing piece when rejecting or reducing contributions requests. Many such printed policies are also designed to inform company personnel of contributions opportunities and limitations.

Statement of contributions policy

The basis of contributions policy is normally closely related to enlightened company self-interest. Provisions must be clearly stated in the light of the needs and interests of the business, whether immediate or long range. This is particularly important in protecting the company from contributions requests that do not promise benefits to the giver as well as to the recipient.

In the case of a major diversified company doing business nationally, the general contributions policy is stated as follows:

1. The theory by which contributions can be justified is that they bear a reasonable relation to the business affairs of the company, and usually bring direct or indirect benefits to our business. This does not mean that in all cases the relation must be measurable.

2. Ours is a national business. Hence, there must be a general pattern that governs our contributions in all parts of the country. We have to consider precedents carefully. We cannot very well give to certain types of organizations in one part of the country and not give to them in another. So, while every contribution request should be considered on its individual merits, nationwide consistency in our contribution policy is almost a necessity.

3. Because we must contribute in many different communities, we sometimes cannot make local contributions as large as those made by purely local businesses, especially those whose headquarters are located in the community.

4. We regard our first contributions responsibility as being to those communities in which we have manufacturing plants or other operations. Our products are distributed all over the United States. However, it would be an impossible financial burden for us to take part in the civic affairs of all the communities in which our products are sold.

5. The company favors having its management people take part in local community activities. However, company executives should bear in mind that if they accept important working assignments in fund-raising campaigns, the company is likely to be asked for a corporate contribution. Key management people should limit their participation to organizations where support falls within the established policy of the company. If there is any question of the organization's ability to qualify for company financial support, the management people concerned should check with the secretary of the contributions committee before accepting working assignments in fund-raising campaigns.[2] This qualification, of course, does not apply to activities of a personal nature where the company is not involved.

---

[2] A more recent policy decision now requires that all management personnel clear requests that they serve in fund-raising drives with the contributions committee. This enables busy executives to decline gracefully, without personal recriminations, if they wish to do so.

6. We follow a definite policy of not contributing to the operating expenses of agencies that are members of Community Chests or United Funds in cities where we have operations, since such operating funds are provided in large part from the Chests or Funds to which we contribute. Such agencies, however, are given permission by their Chest or Fund from time to time to seek capital funds, and in such cases their requests to us are given consideration on their merits and in the light of our contributions policy.

Summing up general policy, the first test we apply to all contributions requests is: Would it benefit the company directly or indirectly to give to the organization in question? Unless it can be demonstrated that it would, the contribution is generally not made.

The policy booklet then describes in some detail the types of contributions that are made, classified in six main categories: health, welfare, and relief; hospitals; public welfare; social betterment agencies; educational institutions, including scientific research foundations; and business organizations and trade associations. The last are not charitable organizations, per se, and contributions to them are in the nature of a business expense. The list includes chambers of commerce, local, state, and national; manufacturers' associations; and similar groups.

Equally important in this policy are the "contributions not made." These include political contributions, gifts to religious organizations of a sectarian or denominational nature, veterans' organizations, and "courtesy" advertising.

While the objectives and needs of other companies may be quite different from those behind the policy above, the benefits of printing and disseminating such a policy statement are obvious.

It is important to recognize that the contributions policy tends to change with changing conditions and that frequent review is both necessary and desirable. As changes are made, company people may be informed of them either directly or through the company publication.

The contributions budget

An essential element of the contributions program in a growing number of companies of all sizes is the contributions budget, usually prepared annually. Beyond the obvious advantage that such a budget, like all budgets, fixes the dollar amount of contributions beyond which the company will not go, there are other benefits. The contributions budget:

1. Enables the administrator to forecast cash needs rather exactly on a quarterly or monthly basis.
2. Provides the financial information needed for annual approval of the program by the company's board of directors.
3. Provides a comparison of contributions costs with other company expenditures.

4. Simplifies analysis of the trend and scope of the contributions program.
5. Serves as a basis for declining appeals.

Consideration of an annual budget requires the administrator and/or contributions committee to assess in advance the implications of the program for the ensuing year. After a budget system has been established, it enables those concerned to relate the size of future commitments to those of the past. For contributions pledged in payments extending over two or more years, the budget is also helpful.

Most contributions budgets are broken down into areas of giving which permit a realistic assessment of amounts designated for each area in terms of policy objectives and the size of the total program. In multi-plant or multi-division companies, the budget makes it easier for a balance to be maintained between headquarters giving and local support.

Smaller organizations which are also centralized may be able to conduct a sensible contributions program without a formal budget so long as contributions are carefully screened.

How to arrive at a reasonable size for the contributions budget will be discussed in a later section. Whatever the amount may be, the basis of budget preparation is the listing of proposed beneficiaries with the suggested amounts for each. The necessary data are often listed on specially designed forms. One large company uses two forms for budgetary purposes: Contributions and Memberships Budget Control (Form CM–1) and Solicitation Information Report (Form CM–2). The CM–1 form serves two purposes: (a) it supplies the information needed for annual budget purposes by plants and sales offices; and (b) it is used as a request for payment of budgeted contributions or memberships.

The items and amounts are listed on the CM–1 by the contributions administrator toward the end of each year and the forms are forwarded through divisional executives to plant and sales office locations, where the items are examined in the light of current local needs and objectives. Local officials eliminate listings which are no longer pertinent and add items which they wish to propose for new contributions. In regard to each new item, they are required to complete Form CM–2, which is returned with the CM–1 to the contributions administrator.

In the course of their return to headquarters, the CM–1 and CM–2 forms are approved by local management and by the divisional general manager. After review by the contributions administrator, they are submitted for approval by the corporate contributions committee at its annual budget meeting.

After final approval, the originals are returned through divisional management, to the local plant or sales office involved, and the budget goes into operation for the ensuing year.

EXHIBIT 1

Contributions and Memberships Budget Control
(Form CM–1)

Contributions and Memberships Budget Control								
Division Chemical	**Originating Plant or Office** Headquarters						**Date** Nov. 30, 1967	
CLASSIFICATION	TRANSACTION							
☒ Contribution(s) ☐ Membership(s)	☒ Annual Budget ☐ Individual Request				☐ Quarterly·Disbursement Record ☐ Annual Disbursement Record			
☐ Disbursement Request (Circle Payee & Amount Below)	SEND CHECK TO	☐ ORIGINATING PLANT OR OFFICE ☐ OTHER (Specify)						
Organization* (Double Space)	This Year's Payment	Next Year's Budget	Quarterly Disbursements				Annual Total	
			1st	2nd	3rd	4th		
American Legion	$500	$500	3/8/68					
Anti Defamation League	1,000	1,000						
Boy Scouts		500	2/27/68					
Catholic Charities	5,000	5,000		6/4/68				
Chemical Library	250	250						
Culinary Institute	500	500		4/1/68				
Federation of Jewish Philanthropies	5,000	5,000						
Future Farmers of America	500	500						

Goodwill Industries
  Final payement on 3-year
  pledge of $9,000
	3,000	3,000*						

Junior Achievement	1,000	1,000						
Memorial Hospital Fund		5,000		5/7/68				
National Art Museum		250	3/5/68					
United Cerebral Palsy Assoc.	1,000	1,000	1/2/68					
United Fund	3,500	4,000						
Discretionary Fund for Local Contribution	250	500						
APPROVALS	DISBURSEMENT RECORD FOR INDIVIDUAL REQUESTS							
Plant/Branch Manager (By/Date)	Public Relations Department (By/Date)							
Division General Manager (By/Date)	Sent to:							
Corporate Contributions Committee								

*For each organization not previously approved complete Solicitation Information Report CM-2

If a local manager wishes to suggest additional contributions during the course of the year, he submits the CM–2 for consideration by the contributions committee at its quarterly meetings.

Certain major plants and sales offices are granted so-called discretionary funds of a limited amount to take care of local requests of $50 or less.

EXHIBIT 2

Solicitation Information Report
(Form CM–2)

SOLICITATION INFORMATION REPORT

NAME OF ORGANIZATION_____

ADDRESS_____

_____

NATURE AND PURPOSE OF ORGANIZATION

  1. Will our contribution or lack of it have a material effect on Company community or public relations?

  2. Does the soliciting organization aid the community as a whole or are its benefits restricted to a limited group or groups?

  3. Does the organization have widespread acceptance and support?

  4. Are the leading companies in the community supporting this organization? If so, please list them and indicate amounts pledged, if this information can be obtained. (If more space is needed continue on reverse side.)

  5. Are important customers active in this solicitation?

  6. Would a contribution now obligate us for additional contributions in the future?

  7. Do you recommend support? If so, in what amount?

Submitted by_____

Location _____

Date _____

Disbursements of discretionary funds are reported each quarter to the contributions administrator.

In addition to the specific amounts budgeted and approved, it is useful to provide a contingency fund, or reserve, to take care of important solicitations not specifically anticipated, or to adjust contributions which were underestimated originally.

Self-defense aspects of contributions organization

Without a policy and without a budget, it is not easy to say no to solicitors for worthy causes. In fact, it can be not only embarrassing but, in some sales-related instances, damaging.

With a policy and a budget, the unpleasant task is made much easier. If the budget for the year has been completely subscribed, the aggressive solicitor can be refused quickly and with justification. If the company's policy is in written or printed form, it is an easy matter to indicate why the solicitor's organization does not qualify.

Solicitations received by telephone are ignored by a number of companies as not of pressing importance either to the solicitor or to the company.

If the contributions administrator is an expert in his field, he can often make public relations capital for his company by what might be termed a "creative" refusal. If he has studied a situation which does not conform to the company's policy or exceeds budgetary limitations, he can often be of help to the solicitor in suggesting where he might find a readier acceptance for his proposal.

Many requests for contributions may be declined by the use of form letters or paragraphs carefully worded to build good will, despite the necessity for saying no. A few examples follow:

EXAMPLE 1

As you may imagine, companies such as ours operating on a nationwide basis receive numerous requests for contributions to worthy causes from all parts of the country each week. Obviously, it is impossible for us to honor all of these requests.

At the same time, we have always felt a deep obligation as a corporate citizen to carry our fair share of the charitable burden.

These two factors have led to the concentration of our support in the communities where we have plants, offices, and significant numbers of employees, by contributions to United Funds and Community Chests in these areas. We have discontinued support to individual, independent agencies, except to the extent that they participate in United Funds.

We are particularly sorry that we can't help you and hope that you will understand the reasoning behind our decision.

EXAMPLE 2

This is in reply to your letter of December 11 regarding the Crusade of the New York City Division of your Society.

We certainly agree with your objective of holding fund-raising costs to a minimum. Unfortunately, however, we are not in a position to detach personnel from their regular duties for this work, worthy though it is. We have been forced to decline similar requests from other organizations engaged in fund-raising activities and, while you have our best wishes for a successful campaign, we regret that we cannot comply.

EXAMPLE 3

Our President has asked me to reply to your letter of March 29th regarding your university's five-year development campaign.

The problems you cite are, of course, similar in many educational institutions today and deserve the consideration of industry as well as of individuals. We in our company have a very keen interest in assisting education to the best of our ability but have not felt that we could make specific contributions to individual colleges or schools. We have been confining our gifts to scholarships and matching contributions when employees of our company make donations to the educational institutions of their choice. This takes about as much money as we feel we can properly allocate to educational purposes.

Although we are not able to comply with your request, I do appreciate your writing and hope that additional financial aid will be forthcoming as a result of your activities.

EXAMPLE 4

Your letter of September 30th about the Annual Bazaar of the Blessed Sacrament Academy on October 22, 23, and 24 is in behalf of such a worthy cause that it is difficult for us to refuse your request.

Unfortunately, as a national company doing business in every part of the United States, we receive so many similar requests that our budget committee handling matters of this kind some time ago came to the conclusion that it was impossible to comply with all of them. Since it would obviously not be fair to evaluate one against the other, we have regretfully discontinued such contributions.

I am particularly sorry that we cannot honor your request, and I hope that you will understand our position.

A somewhat more difficult situation arises when it is deemed necessary to lessen support to previously favored organizations, or to eliminate aid. The refusal or cutback may be laid to a change in company policy or to budgetary limitations, with emphasis on the previous help provided by the company.

In general, the harmful effects of refusal tend to be over-magnified. Actually, the public has very little idea of what a company gives, or to whom, and the fear of alienating customers by saying no to specific requests has little foundation in fact. The situation is analogous in some respects to that of the individual who supports some projects and not others, or who withdraws his support from one organization in favor of another. His friends do not desert him because of this. In fact, they, too, are subject to the same pressures and changes of opinion and in most instances they understand what is involved.

Solicitation for many charities and other types of organizations is often conducted by professional fund raisers. They bear no rancor for individual company decisions because they know that next month they may well be working for another organization and would hope to be warmly received on subsequent visits.

Foundations

With the passage of years, more and more companies have established charitable foundations through which contributions funds are channeled. Most company-sponsored foundations are simply convenient conduits for corporate funds intended for charitable purposes. In some few instances, the foundations are heavily endowed and make their contributions from tax-free income realized from their investments.

In setting up a foundation it is imperative to investigate thoroughly all the legal restrictions and obligations pertaining to trustees, financial advisors, custodians, and depositories, as well as those relating to the formation of the foundation itself. As to the last, the most common form of organization is incorporation under the laws of a particular state. These laws differ widely from state to state, and the guidance of legal counsel is indispensable.

It is wise to make the statement of purpose of the foundation as broad as possible, so that changes in scope and activities may be accomplished without difficulty.

Procedures to obtain tax exemption involve filing an affidavit with the District Director of Internal Revenue, together with a copy of the articles of incorporation, or trust instrument, a copy of the bylaws, and the latest financial statements. Tax-exempt status is confirmed by letter by the Treasury Department, if all conditions are met.

The primary function of most company foundations is to provide a means for the companies to stabilize their donations in spite of variable earnings. Gifts by companies to their foundations tend to be increased in good earnings years and decreased or eliminated in less favorable years. The existence of foundations enables companies to maintain their contributions programs on an even keel for a reasonable span of years despite financial vicissitudes.

A foundation may enable a company to distribute to a number of charities the value of property which, if directly given, would, almost of necessity, have to go to a single charity if equivalent tax advantages were to be derived. For example, a company may have property which is no longer deemed necessary in the conduct of its business. If such property were sold by the corporation, any gain involved would be subject to income tax and the cash available for gifts reduced by the tax. If the property were donated to the company's foundation and subsequently sold, no tax would be payable by the foundation, and the company would be entitled to a tax deduction equal to the fair market value of the property contributed. Proceeds of the sale could then be donated to one or more charities.

Foundations are sometimes helpful in regard to state laws. Some states, for example, permit deduction of charitable contributions for state tax purposes only when the gifts are made to charities within the state. By contributing to its own foundation incorporated within the state, a company secures exemption for its gifts, even though the ultimate recipients of foundation gifts are outside the state.

A foundation which qualifies for tax exemption cannot participate in a company's memberships program, and memberships have to be separately administered. In addition, since the foundation is incorporated and its charter is publicly available, the existence of a foundation tends to increase the number of requests received by a company. This is mitigated, however, by the policy statement and by budgetary procedures.

Determining recipients of corporate giving

The essence of corporate giving is determining who will receive corporate gifts.

In recent years there have been some interesting shifts in emphasis in company giving. Total philanthropy in the United States more than doubled in the decade between 1957 and 1966, and is now also a larger percentage of the gross national product. According to the Internal Revenue Service, corporate giving in the 10 years 1955–64 increased from $415 million to $729 million and in 1964 amounted to .115 percent of the GNP versus .104 percent in 1955.

In the last decade, while overall corporate contributions have shown steady growth, certain areas have received additional emphasis and others have diminished in interest. The principal beneficiary of this trend has been the field of education. In the mid-1950's, education received about 14 percent of corporate giving. It is now receiving at least 38 percent, a gain of about 170 percent. Health and welfare organizations, on the other hand, have suffered in almost direct ratio, receiving 42 percent of corporate giving today compared with 66 percent ten years ago. This does not mean that total funds going to health and welfare have declined, but simply that the category is getting a smaller percentage of the total.

A new and increasingly important area for corporate philanthropy, both in terms of need and of potential benefits, is minority-group advancement, particularly relating to the urban "crisis."

There are many ways in which minority-group programs are being moved forward, and specific information on them can be obtained from such organizations as The Urban League, the newly formed Urban Coalition, and from the National Association of Manufacturers and the Chamber of Commerce of the United States.

Another significant trend is the shift in emphasis away from traditional giving toward innovation. This is exemplified in the new consideration being given to cultural endeavors, and particularly the arts. The viewpoint taken by contributors is that investment in the arts is necessary to the life of a free society. Local considerations tend to have strong influence in decisions regarding contributions to the arts. If, as many believe, the success of a business is measured at least in part in terms of its contribution to a better life for the people, gifts to the arts can be justified. In addition, by judicious donations to the arts, a company can advance its self-interest in terms of its image and in marketing.

To date, business tends to favor organizations such as art museums and symphony orchestras serving large numbers of people. Increasing interest in the theatre and the dance in its many forms makes it probable that there will be a corresponding shift in contributions emphasis in the future.

Another trend affecting many companies is the increase in the number of capital appeals. Capital appeals tend to generate response in the form of pledges extending beyond a single year. The increase in the number of appeals has a cumulative effect on pledges simultaneously supported by a company.

How much to give

The ways in which companies determine how much they may properly give in any period of time are almost as numerous as the companies giving. Much depends on management attitudes toward philanthropy, past performance, existence of foundations, the pressure of customers, location, and, particularly, the nature of the business.

It is still helpful, however, to examine some averages compiled by the National Industrial Conference Board which permit general comparisons. The common denominator is company size, expressed in terms of numbers of employees, net income, and/or assets. Smaller companies tend to be more liberal in their giving than the largest companies. Companies with fewer than 1,000 employees averaged 1.27 percent of net income before taxes in contributions, while companies employing between 5,000 and 10,000 people averaged 1.03 percent. With assets as a base, companies of $100 million to $199 million were the most generous, with contributions of 1.29 percent of net income, closely followed by companies between $50 million and $100 million at 1.27 percent. Companies with assets exceeding $200 million averaged .63 percent of net income.[3]

Based on contribution per employee, company size is in almost directly inverse relationship to contributions, with the overall average for 536 companies being $28 per employee.

---

[3] John H. Watson, III, "Report on company contributions for 1965," in *Readings in Company Contributions* (New York: National Industrial Conference Board, 1967).

The fair-share concept

A measure of giving devised by fund raisers, and particularly the United Funds, is the so-called fair-share formula. One of the major United Funds bases its fair-share guide on three elements: the need factor, the responsibility factor, and the ability-to-give factor. The need factor in this instance is the figure determined as the total required from corporate donors. The responsibility factor is the number of company employees in the city divided into the total sought from corporate donors. The ability-to-give factor is the average company annual earnings per employee. To implement this fair-share system, a work sheet is provided which involves dividing three-year average company earnings by total employees to derive average earnings per employee. A table indicates a suggested gift range per local employee on the basis of the three-year average earnings per employee. When these figures are multiplied by the number of local employees, a fair-share gift range for the company is arrived at. A number of other steps are suggested to obtain from these figures the exact fair-share gift.

There is no doubt that fair-share formulas of this kind have some interest and value to companies in helping them to determine how much to give. However, they are seldom the determining factor in the size of the company's contribution.

A few companies appear to be moving slowly in the direction of support levels indicated by the formulas and some seem willing to follow suit if other companies take similar action.

Corporate practice

Determination of the size of donations is, in actual practice, a matter for individual judgment, influenced by such factors as earnings, sales, number of employees, type of facility, size of investment, location, what other companies are doing, amount expected from industry, the company's relative prominence in the community, employee gifts to the same charity, customer pressures, and expected public reaction.

Some contributions administrators use crude formulas to arrive at recommendations which their committees use as bases for discussion in reaching decisions. They include the following: a percentage of the campaign objective; a fixed amount per employee; a ratio of the company's profits and/or sales to its industry's quota; a percentage of pre-tax income; a specific amount per unit of community population; ratio of company's property tax to total property tax; ratio of employees and their families to community population multiplied by local campaign goal; ratio of employees to total area employment multiplied by the business campaign goal; and, in hospital drives, ratio of employee/dependent

patient-days to total hospital patient-days multiplied by the public subscription goal.

The companies most enthusiastic about formulas are multi-plant organizations which find them particularly helpful in developing an equitable plan of giving to health and welfare agencies and federated drives
in their various communities.

Group consultation

One commonly used method of arriving at a fair contribution to a
specific cause, particularly in a local situation, is comparison with other
companies in the community. This may take the form of direct consultation with the contributions administrators of other companies, or simply
the use by smaller companies of the contributions of a larger company as
a guide. In some instances, the dominant company in the community
serves as a guide for lesser companies. In other cases, a leading retail
establishment or bank is the bellwether.

A method of consultation which has gained favor in a number of
communities is through informal groups within an industry which meet
periodically, often at lunch, to discuss their obligations.

In a few larger cities more comprehensive groups, involving companies in many industries, discuss not only local obligations but what is
required in response to appeals from regional or national organizations.
These groups comprise the professionals of corporate giving and there is
much to be gained by individual companies in becoming associated with
such a group. Here, there is intensive discussion not only of specifics but
of corporate contributions philosophy. In addition, the validity of individual appeals and the effectiveness of various fund raising organizations
and charities are periodically evaluated.

Information bureaus

A competent contributions administrator has available a number of
sources for basic information on the organizations from which requests
are received. These include trade associations such as The National
Better Business Bureau and The National Information Bureau which
specializes in gathering information about non-profit organizations. Information on local agency drives is sometimes available from special
agencies in the community. Community leaders, particularly bankers and
clergymen, are often good sources of information.

Gifts other than dollars

Many corporations long involved in giving money have also become
interested in other forms of charity. Some of these involve the time and

effort of middle- and top-management people. As such they are subject to policy decision by the contributions committee or other management group involved in philanthropy. Should the company decide, as more and more are doing, that its people should be made available to help worthy causes, there are many ways to accomplish this.

In some instances, members of management are granted a reasonable amount of time off for public service, with pay. They may be aided by company secretarial and clerical help. Company equipment, including calculating and duplicating machines, computers, and automobiles, is also often on call.

There are a number of reasons for encouraging employee participation in fund drives, and some obvious drawbacks. The benefits include betterment of the community, resulting in an improved climate for business; feedback of local attitudes toward the company; increased prestige; greater acceptance of the company's views by local officials; improved ability to hire, keep, and develop superior people; and increased local business volume. Some companies, however, feel that employee participation is not helpful to the company, that it is a waste of time, and that in larger communities the help provided makes little or no impression.

The participation of individual financial executives in philanthropic activities is discussed in chapter 66, "Professional, Community, and Civic Activities."

Gifts in merchandise or services

A growing number of companies, particularly those in small and medium-sized communities, offer the use of facilities such as meeting rooms, cafeterias, projection rooms, and parking lots. Others provide aid by printing notices, display materials, or booklets.

In some circumstances, gifts in the form of products or equipment can serve useful purposes and actually provide more aid than cash. A case in point was the donation of building materials instead of money to a youth organization building-fund drive. The deduction taken on the books of the company for the materials was at prices current in the company's ordinary wholesale channels of trade, even though the inventory cost of the material was substantially lower. The charity also gained by receiving more of the essential building materials for its use than it would have been able to acquire at retail prices with a comparable cash contribution.

Companies making goods or equipment available to charitable or educational organizations follow numerous practices. In some instances the material or equipment is loaned to the organization. Sometimes it is sold to the charity at a reduced or nominal price. In the latter case, it is wise to clear the proposed arrangements with dealers or distributors.

In most instances, gifts of materials or equipment are not integrated with a company's formal contribution program. The availability of useful and acceptable material often depends on chance and this kind of help does not have the continuity and stability of cash contributions.

Memberships

An activity often closely related to contributions in administration is the growing field of company memberships in various special interest groups, roughly classified as business and trade associations. Such memberships are normally tax-deductible as business expenses. Many companies have found that, by centralizing administration of memberships with contributions, a much tighter rein can be held on funds which formerly had leaked out through individual expense accounts and local discretionary funds.

To draw a line between a membership and a contribution is often difficult. Some payments may actually be classified either way, depending on company policy. A case in point would be a payment to a metropolitan chamber of commerce which exceeds the base rate for individual membership in the organization, with the excess earmarked for its education committee.

In the past decade, corporate membership budgets have increased significantly and there is reason to believe they will continue upward in the future. This trend indicates the real need for competent control of memberships, including periodic reviews of the benefits of specific memberships.

Evaluation of company memberships is essentially a matter of communication with those in the company who are actively engaged in association work. Most companies encourage employee participation. Some will not join a trade or business organization unless employees take an active part in it. This gives the company a voice in association affairs and provides feedback on the effectiveness of its operations.

Reports from participating employees are often garnered on an informal basis although, with the rise in membership costs, some companies are now formalizing such reporting, asking their people to fill out corporate membership analysis questionnaires on an annual basis.

The decisions on memberships are assigned to individuals in some companies, but the trend seems to be for the contributions committee or a special memberships committee to take on the task.

The impact of government funds

In recent years there has been a massive flow of governmental funds into philanthropic areas in which companies are vitally interested. The Federal Government has been spending more and more for welfare, international activities, health, and scientific research since World War II.

With the great influx of federal funds, not to mention support to education, welfare, and health from state and local governments, what is the role of company giving?

Manning M. Patillo, president, The Foundation Library Center, New York, says, "I do not think private philanthropy is obsolete. We shall never reach the point at which all human problems disappear and there is nothing for private philanthropy to do. Indeed, if we are to maintain a free society, the role of the non-governmental donor is absolutely essential. But the very size and pervasiveness of governmental programs places a premium on expertness and precision in the private sector. The old crude and impressionistic methods of much of private philanthropy will no longer do. Private donors can make an important contribution only if they do their job very, very well.

"What is that job? To use private funds for creative problem solving. . . . What I am proposing is that we shift gradually from the prevalent notion of supporting the budgets of worthy organizations and institutions to the idea of defining problems which need to be solved, finding the people who can solve them, and then providing the means to get the job done."[4]

Creative problem solving through company contributions

The society in which our companies do business is beset by difficulties of many kinds. These problems are found not only in the big cities but in smaller communities everywhere. While the great outpouring of federal funds is bound to have some beneficial effect, bureaucracy and politically motivated pressures, plus the multiplicity of agencies involved, tend, at times, to confuse the issues. The result, in some instances, is virtually to negate the underlying good intentions.

In these areas a creative program of corporate philanthropy can help to an extent that exceeds the cash involved. Several of the leaders in company giving are setting aside increasing amounts of the corporate contributions budget for this kind of venturing.

For example: A major pharmaceutical company aids newly appointed educators in the fields of medicine, pharmacy, and mental health. The funds provided enable the new appointees to carry out innovative ideas for curriculum and physical facilities with a high degree of imagination and productivity. A watch manufacturer has established a school to teach disabled veterans the jewelry trade. These men return to their communities as productive citizens, supporting themselves in the jewelry business. A leading New England manufacturer, together with several other companies, offered management advisory services to its city gov-

---

[4] Manning M. Patillo, address given to the Management Seminar on Company Contributions, National Industrial Conference Board, Princeton, N.J., November 1, 1967.

ernment. The program provides the business skills needed to review operations of the city's hospitals, to study the pros and cons of machine accounting, and to assist in issuing contracts for consulting services.

The foundation of a major national retailer has initiated a number of projects in poorer areas, both rural and urban. In conjunction with land grant colleges, 4-H Clubs, Future Farmers of America, and other organizations, the foundation supervises rural improvement programs and teaches farming and homemaking techniques. In cities, the foundation, together with the General Federation of Women's Clubs, sponsors a community achievement contest seeking to encourage self-betterment projects. With the American Medical Association, the foundation supports a community medical assistance plan to help smaller communities acquire local medical facilities through which to attract doctors.

A large paper manufacturer assists public secondary schools in its plant communities. The program was devised after extensive research to develop an efficient way to help public secondary schools. Administrators of the school systems involved helped develop policy statements under which grants would be made. Money is provided to support special school projects which would not normally receive tax support, with special emphasis on problems of guidance and curriculum planning. The grants are intended as "seed money" to encourage projects which might later be tax-supported.

The list of creative company philanthropic projects is increasing day by day. Such ingenious ways of helping to solve pressing problems are beneficial both to the companies involved and to the communities in which they do business. They call for interest, imagination, and the type of business management which is standard in other corporate areas.

Conclusion

Corporate contributions planning and administration is fast coming of age. It is a field offering stimulating challenge, room for creativity, and the opportunity for both corporate and personal accomplishment.

This is what Dr. W. Homer Turner, vice president and executive director of the United States Steel Foundation, Inc., says of the creative corporate contributions worker: "You must come to be a first-class student of the major forces of change affecting your corporation and then assimilate, through good evaluation procedures, the new knowledge before final grant actions are taken. You must approach your task as would a genuine professional in any major professional field. You must think, act, feel, and look like a "pro"—and be one. You must have confidence in yourself and in your ideas for creative opportunity seeking.

"Above all, you must recognize the hallmarks of impending social shifts and divine ways in which your corporation . . . may add to human productivity—and thus to bettered institutions and enhanced general progress."[5]

Bibliography

The National Industrial Conference Board through its Company Donations Department does much useful work in the collection and dissemination of data relating to current practices in company giving. In addition, it conducts periodic management seminars on corporate contributions which are attended by contributions administrators from many parts of the country.

ANDREWS, F. EMERSON. *Legal Instruments of Foundations*. New York: Russell Sage Foundation, 1958.

CARR, ELLIOTT G.; MORGAN, JAMES F. & ASSOCIATES. *Better Management of Business Giving*. New York: Hobbs, Dorman & Company, Inc., 1966.

HELD, WALTER J. *The Technique for Proper Giving*. New York: McGraw-Hill Book Company, Inc., 1955.

SHAPIRO, LEO J. *Company Giving*. Chicago, Illinois: Survey Press, 1960.

WATSON, JOHN H. III. *Company Contributions Primer*, 2nd ed. New York: National Industrial Conference Board, 1963.

WEAVER, WARREN. *U.S. Philanthropic Foundations*. New York: Harper & Row, 1967.

Readings in Company Contributions. New York: National Industrial Conference Board, 1967.

---

[5] W. Homer Turner, "Some Guidelines for Creative Grant Making" (a working paper for the Management Seminar on Company Contributions, National Industrial Conference Board, Princeton, N.J., October 30, 1967).

Professional, community, and civic activities

Edgar Peske*

Today's financial executive lives in a vibrant, restless world. Revolutionary advances in communications, education, and technology place him front-center in a changing, dynamic environment. Last year's standard operating procedure has often become a study in obsolescence.

But it is not just business practice that has changed. There has been a transformation—almost a revolution—in big business' attitude towards social problems. Gone is the day when a corporation limited its social involvement to charitable contributions to "safe" causes. Gone, too, is the day when business justified each and every commitment in terms of "enlightened self-interest"—some immediate benefit to the company that could be measured in terms of profit and loss. Corporate responsibility to the community is more likely today to be measured in terms of moral principle and social conscience. Commitment is justified by the long-range view—business needs a healthy social environment in order to survive and prosper.

The man in demand

Reflected in this change is a new concept of the financial executive and his position. No longer does management consider him just the pallid watchdog of the corporation's funds. Today he is often the man in demand, who acknowledges environmental changes and the resulting

---

* Vice President and Treasurer, Illinois Bell Telephone Company, Chicago.

problems—in his business, in his community, in his conception of himself and his relations with others—and who seeks meaningful responses to these changes.

Finance and economics are basic to the viability of both business and society. He has to apply what he knows or there is no progress. He has to be up-to-date and creative or progress is minimal.

The financial executive has always had both administrative ability and financial expertise. But what can he contribute today to professional, civic and community activities?

First, and most obviously, he is the trained specialist whose knowledge and skills are needed to bring financial order to the goals of such activities. He must perform certain basic, creative functions to insure their growth and continuance.

Whether or not the financial executive should participate in community activities is hardly open to debate. Practically speaking, he must. Like any modern-day business leader, he must go outside his business to develop himself, to achieve personal satisfaction and hone his professional skills. Indeed, if he and the business he represents are to survive and prosper, he must often be a leader.

There is great demand for his financial expertise. Indeed, the supply will never approach the level of demand for it. But how does the executive accept social commitment; how does he best utilize his special knowledge?

He may ask himself, "Why take part in civic projects? The ordinary demands and responsibilities of my position keep me fully occupied."

Experience, in fact, proves that any financial executive, from a profit or non-profit organization, a small or large corporation, must be able to find time to apply his years of experience to community endeavors. Both his company and the community expect this of him. His personal dividend is that he continues to polish his administrative abilities and contributes to the betterment of the social environment in which his business operates.

What is available

Because of the executive's financial skill and experience, he often will find himself in a leadership role. And he will usually discover firsthand the positive impact of active participation on his career.

Once he accepts the idea of participation in professional, community and civic activities, the executive should review and evaluate the possibilities open to him. He should ask himself which activities will most fully and fruitfully occupy his time, talent, energy and professional skills.

Professional activity. This gives the executive an opportunity to meet his peers, develop broad knowledge of the problems and practices of others, become acquainted with the financial market places and the key groups so important to his personal success and that of his business. He develops on a close, personal basis valuable resources in the business and academic communities.

These activities are neither static nor pedantic. Rather they create the climate in which to exchange ideas, discuss common problems and share information about improved management techniques, new research and methodology.

Active involvement also provides a forum and a nucleus for action in dealing with contemporary business and social problems. For example, financial executives are uniquely well-qualified consultants on the money matters faced by all social and charitable institutions. A professional society might act as the clearing house to match requests for financial advice with members having the required expertise.

Professional societies include numerous regional, local and special-interest groups. They usually share several common characteristics:

> serve as a meeting place for representatives of government, business and universities to gather and share experiences, ideas and reactions;
>
> stimulate and disseminate financial research findings;
>
> foster professional competence and standards;
>
> provide counsel on social problems;
>
> provide the means for continuing formal education in finance and economics.

Let's look at a few examples of opportunities for professional activities.

In early 1968, a group of midwestern businessmen organized a national symposium dealing with pension and profit sharing funds. Experts from government, business and the universities discussed this subject at length. Their papers and discussion summaries were made available to the financial community—compiling for the first time comprehensive factual data on the subject. This symposium gave the executive an opportunity to participate in the planning and to contribute to the discussions.

Many times, the financial community has provided expert testimony to law-making bodies considering bills on such topics as aerospace, poverty, taxation and wage-and-price control. As a general rule, professional associations make any significant testimony available to their constituencies. This information is of great value because there is provided a sounding board for hearing both sides of a question. The executive is thereby equipped to make more solid judgments for his own company.

In many cases, the executive himself will be the authority and will give the expert testimony or author the paper.

Professional activities offer forums to discuss controversial and timely economic matters—a proposed tax increase, for example. An executive can rarely find time to audit a university course on current tax legislation. But he can be briefed on the latest developments in a series of lecture-discussions.

To remain competent, the executive must keep informed about his field. Professional activities serve as an exchange for new information and give him the chance to contribute knowledge and leadership to the field of finance.

Community and civic activities. By community activities we mean endeavors conducted within the area in which the business is located and the area in which the executive actually lives. Civic activities often present different types of problems, demand more time and expertise and include wider geographic areas and more diverse populations. They often have longer-range goals.

In a community activity, the executive is part of a grass roots action and can affect change and progress more directly. The related problems are microcosms of civic-related activities. And his reasons for community participation often differ from his reasons for engaging in civic activities.

The participant does not profit so directly or immediately when he serves on a national Association of Commerce and Industry committee rather than the local chapter committee. The activities' goals and concepts remain the same or similar, but their impact on the executive himself is different.

Is the executive's time so valuable he should not waste it serving on a local committee when he is needed in a city or state group? He may find that, all things considered, working with the local group best serves both his personal needs and those of his company.

Suppose his company owns a large department store in a transitional neighborhood. Nearby slums breed crime; vandalism and theft are increasing; retail sales are falling. Employees are reluctant to work there; new employees are difficult to attract. Other merchants in the neighborhood face the same problems of protecting their investment and earning a profit. So the affected merchants band together to deal with this blight. Sound financial expertise is vital to such a group.

At the same time, the National Alliance of Businessmen is studying means of finding meaningful employment for the "hardcore unemployed" of the city and region. The executive's company is in the Alliance and should be represented in the planning of its activities.

Obviously, this executive could profitably work with both groups. But what if his schedule does not permit this?

He sets out to determine priorities. Which is the more crucial activity? How much time will each require? What particular expertise and strengths can he and the other men in his organization offer?

Or take open-housing legislation. The executive has been asked to serve on a statewide advisory commission to study the subject and make recommendations to the governor. At the same time, an open-housing ordinance is being debated by his village council. Heated discussion has endangered passage of the ordinance. The outcome will affect values in his own community.

Shall his participation be state or local?

In this situation, ethical considerations are a factor as well as the best use of his financial talents. And he must consider all factors and implications before deciding.

What to choose

Let us turn our attention now to the types of activities available. They are professional, community or civic. All three seek definite objectives.

Activities run the gamut of purpose and function: the Sunday afternoon chamber music group, the American Legion, the Cub Scouts, the United Fund Appeal, church or synagogue, a university trusteeship, the Rotary Club or library board membership, etc. In each case, someone with financial acumen is needed.

Everyone in America is affected, directly or indirectly, by the crisis in the cities. Professional, civic and community activities coping with these problems can progress only if the community's financial leadership plays a major role.

Shall the financial executive work with a professional, civic or community group? Consider what each of the three types of activities has to offer. They are, of course, neither mutually exclusive nor inclusive.

In any community there are many sound organizations. All support worthy causes or seek to solve serious problems. Each appears worthwhile and might warrant participation. But the busy executive cannot get involved in every activity which needs help. He must carefully establish priorities for his participation. Far more requests will be made for his time than he can possibly satisfy.

So how does he choose? His criteria, of course, will include personal interests and skills, his company's welfare and society's needs. He has to ask himself questions like these:

Which activity will enhance the social environment of my firm?

Which will best use my own particular talents and strengths?

Which will increase my knowledge and professional contacts?

Which is most attractive to me personally?

Activities offering a chance to serve often have a short-term objective —such as costing-out a program proposal seeking foundation support.

Sometimes they look far ahead—like a businessmen's committee to project the city's needs for mass transportation.

Ten years ago, problems such as water pollution, ghetto unemployment and quality education were not considered direct concerns of the executive. Today he deals with such problems as matter-of-factly as he does with company concerns such as profit goals and capital-fund attraction. The social, economic and ethical aspects of these new needs overlap the domain of business.

So he must apply his criteria, lay out the alternatives clearly, foresee the consequences of a variety of choices, and *decide*. Often this is not a simple matter. Frequently, he will be guided by his company's policies and commitments.

Sometimes, of course, personal interest has much to do with the choice of involvement.

For instance, a man whose family has known the tragedy of muscular dystrophy may have a special desire to work with the Muscular Dystrophy Campaign. His unique talent can be put to work in several ways: organizing and directing a fund drive; arranging financial support for new treatment facilities; or assisting with the organization's financial affairs. Whatever he does, he will feel a personal stake in that activity's progress because of his family's involvement.

Or take the executive who believes his city needs to attract more attention to its rapid development as a financial center. He may prefer to spend his time actively promoting the city, perhaps taking the lead in organizing a group to accomplish the planning and implementation.

Sooner or later the executive has to ask: "Am I the logical person to work with this problem and the related activity?"

Financial experts are a heterogeneous group. Their training, experience, and knowledge are varied. They offer different basic strengths, needs and interests.

An executive may be knowledgeable about financial matters, but his particular talents may not be fully utilized in certain organizations. Take the man whose special field is taxation. He's asked to volunteer his services to a local orphanage. What the orphanage really needs is counsel in fund-raising. All things equal, the tax expert should seek to serve a local group with tax problems, and recommend to the orphanage a colleague who has special talents for fund-raising.

He must, in short, approach the choice of an activity with the same objectivity, information, and thought as he gives to his business decisions. And he also must be willing to make long-term personal commitments.

Continuity among their members and leaders is a problem which plagues all community activities. To be effective, the financial executive should become involved with the intention of working and contributing during the course of years. The contacts he makes, the knowledge he gains about the program's goals and needs come only with time. His financial advice and counsel accrue in value with each year of participation.

Let us examine a hypothetical situation. A certain executive, already operating on a tightly burdened time schedule, is approached to participate in three different activities. Should he assume any or all of the added responsibilities?

In one case, the executive is invited to take part in a Chamber of Commerce project to attract new sources of capital to the city. He would be working directly for the benefit of his corporation, because it plans to bid for part of that new capital to finance construction of a plant. So much is obvious.

Next, he is asked to organize a week-long regional workshop on computer innovations for statisticians. This workshop would disseminate information which could be valuable to his own company and others as well. Its effect is uncertain.

Then, he is asked to work for passage of a bond issue for a teacher pay raise. His actions could contribute to the general welfare of both his corporation and the community. The long-term effect might mean that students entering the labor force would be better trained employees.

The financial executive, his company and society are inextricably linked. But how does the executive determine what is directly related to his position and what is merely an adjunct? Should he try to stretch his time to include any or all of these activities? Should he concentrate exclusively on short-term community gains (the capital attraction program) or should he work on projects which improve society yet still accrue undefinable benefits to his company (the bond issue)?

In some situations, the executive will act on directives from higher management. In others, he will have to take the initiative and interpret the various values to his management. The entire thought process on determining priorities for participation will help him here.

Suppose our man has decided with which activities he will work. Probably it will be a group effort. Before he leads the group forward in any project, he should now determine the present status of the activity and its immediate and long-range goals.

Some activities—a natural resources preservation committee, for example—are probably in the early organizational stages. Others—like the Y.M.C.A.—have an established organization, but need help to implement existing programs.

What the job demands

Once the executive selects participation possibilities, he should ask himself: What must I learn in order to participate in this activity? While his particular strength lies in financial matters, he has to become familiar with all aspects of the activity.

For example, suppose the executive decides that his time could be best spent teaching basic finance to ghetto businessmen. He then has to prepare simplified, practical lesson plans and become familiar with the ghetto's economic and social problems—e.g. lack of capital, customer buying habits, untrained employees. The executive has to learn to communicate in the ghetto businessman's vernacular. Analogies he uses to explain basic finance to his teenage son might be meaningless to the ghetto businessman. He may have to establish rapport; in some cases, overcome hostility and mistrust. Much more would be expected of the executive than merely talking to a class several hours a week.

The executive should ask himself: What specific function is expected of me? Is my role one of planning, decision-making, consultation, or committee membership? He should then make certain all are compatible with the demands the activity will make of him.

It can happen that the financial executive volunteers with the impression that he will provide financial counsel, only to find he is expected to do leg-work and provide financial support.

Once he determines the functions and responsibilities he will incur, he should determine also how much time his involvement will require. Many executives make overly ambitious appraisals of their available time.

What blocks of time will the activity take? Does this activity require a weekly luncheon, frequent committee meetings, complicated arrangements, or does it offer flexibility in fulfilling his responsibilities? Can he afford to miss meetings if his position with his company requires him to be out of town a great deal?

He should chart the time which day-to-day and unplanned needs of his business position will require, the time which family and personal life must receive, and the time needed for the outside activity. Thus, the executive can quickly determine whether he should participate and to what extent.

A man's professional integrity and reputation are laid on the line when he accepts new responsibilities. He should try to do the best job possible, for his own sake as well as for the program's success. Lack of time can be the biggest deterrent. He should make a realistic appraisal of the time he has to offer and the time the activity requires.

Overburdened executives who attend six board meetings a week may offer little of substance to any of them. What they might contribute in meaningful counsel is diluted, because little time is available to read, study or plan for each meeting.

Sooner or later the businessman faces the anomaly of spending more time in extra-curricular activities than he does in handling the obligations of his position. Encouragement of activity participation by individual companies varies widely. The wise executive, before reaching the saturation point, must determine to what extent he has the backing and support of his own company.

After all, his position in the corporation is of prime concern, even if a certain level of participation in outside activities does make him more effective. He will reach an optimum point of participation—which is not always easy to recognize.

Executive talent is, in large part, the ability to delegate authority, to direct others in the execution of assigned tasks, and to make the best possible use of the talents of subordinates. In many cases, a financial officer is not being asked to take charge of a project in person. He is being asked to lend it his name and prestige, to provide able workers from his own organization, and to use his own executive talents in seeing that the job gets done. The executive is not necessarily one who *does* things; he is a man who *gets things done*. This principle is true not only for his strictly business activities but for his outside involvements as well.

Community activities require the same sort of careful planning, research, decision-making and executive direction that an executive uses in his own business. He should be careful to bring his business talents to his outside activities—otherwise he will waste both time and effort.

Consider this example. Twenty prominent businessmen recently toured a riot-torn area. They saw children playing in the streets among the burnt out ruins. One executive suggested that these kids should have a recreational center and proposed that the group undertake this project.

Now, the image of the youngsters splashing in a new swimming pool and playing basketball in a decent gymnasium captured the imagination of the group. But they allowed well-intentioned fervor to displace objective fact-finding. After they had spent much time and effort planning a center, they learned that several charitable groups had already elaborated plans and were raising funds for just such a facility.

On the other hand, a neighborhood day-care center was critically needed. On further investigation, the group learned that an existing grass roots group had staff and educational programs ready for the center, but lacked the management expertise to operate it. So the executives undertook to provide this form of help—but only after they had wasted much effort on the gym idea.

Benefits of involvement

After considering the rationale for participation and some possibilities for service, the executive might wonder, "What's in it for me?" Participation in activities benefits the individual executive, his company and society at large.

Professional success depends on many factors. And it is certainly important to keep abreast of developments, trends and the persons responsible for them. Professional activity is the common meeting ground for these ideas and persons.

Community and civic activities offer an opportunity to deal with a variety of social issues, many-faceted problems and rewarding personalities.

Often the financial executive in his role as a college trustee learns of research applicable to his company. He may spot a bright young man on a church finance committee and tap him as a business assistant. He can call on a colleague in another state for local information, because he has established a friendship at a national convention.

Few outside the profession think of the financial executive as a creative person; normally, creativity is associated with the arts. But many financial experts are truly creative. Managing an investment portfolio demands not just financial skill, but imagination and creativity as well. Participation in community and civic activities allows the executive to express himself creatively by organizing meetings, stimulating research, preparing plans of action, drafting proposals and solving complex problems. The activities provide an outlet to maximize his capabilities for the benefits of others.

A financial executive has long hours. Each year demands on him increase. In return, he reaps financial gain. But he needs the extra dividend of knowing that he is involved—the satisfaction that comes from an important job well done.

Participation brings new opportunities and experience. For example, the executive may organize a fact-finding task force within his company to handle a problem of force retention. If he is successful, he may be asked by the mayor to organize another task force—to determine mobster influence in the business community. To accomplish this, he would use his organizing ability and data-assembling facility. He would improvise, too, as he sought to uncover new information and acquire fresh insight.

As a result, the executive would not only perform a valuable community service but gain as well new perspectives about the city in which he lives and does business.

There are personal fringe benefits in participation. Common activities bring together executives of similar background and provide a strong basis for social fellowship. Doing business together and working together for common goals can be pleasant as well as profitable.

As to the company—the executive's participation adds lustre to the company's reputation. It makes the community a better place in which to do business, brings new information, experiences and contacts into the company, and makes him a more responsive, sensitive and better-informed businessman.

A company whose executives are civic and community leaders naturally has a good public image. Making the community a better place in which to do business is intelligent self-interest. If the economy is flourishing, if local government is moving ahead, if basic social services are available, business is likely to prosper.

Any executive must be aware of current events. He reads. He attends symposiums, meetings, briefings. He circulates within his own organization to be familiar with employees, products and services. Outside activities provide another excellent source of keeping informed and becoming familiar with what is new.

For example, serving on a hospital board of trustees gives the financial executive knowledge about community facilities, health problems and medical research. He does not simply contribute; he learns. Meetings of the Investment Analysts Society provide the opportunity to discuss market trends and to learn first hand the pros and cons of individual investment possibilities. If his company needs to provide testimony before a congressional subcommittee, he knows where to look for an expert.

A financial specialist can be narrow, and participation is a broadening experience.

There was a financial executive who never liked symphonic music. To him, a Brahms concerto was twenty-five minutes of silent suffering in a black tie. Then, his company offered his services to the symphony's fund drive for a new concert hall. He became involved. He began to listen, to question, to read music history. The fund-raising campaign lasted three years. His interest in and receptivity to music were heightened. He even began to enjoy Bach's harpsichord compositions! He learned to appreciate new things. And his new sensitivity made him a better executive.

Society benefits from corporate responsibility. Corporate executives have an important obligation to be leaders in society. And professional understanding of finance is certainly essential to fostering growth and alleviating the problems which thwart progress.

The risk of controversy

Today social involvement is seldom innocuous. The executive—along with his company—frequently sticks his neck out when he chooses an activist role.

Remember the group of businessmen who interested themselves in a critically-needed neighborhood day-care center? The project seems innocent enough. But it turned out to be as complicated as determining a new plant location, hiring personnel, and marketing a line of products. Certain community factions objected to the center's educational program, others to its governing body. Several businessmen participating came in for sharp criticism from fellow executives and company stockholders.

Another example. An executive living in a medium-sized city recently accepted membership on an open-housing council. His role was to bargain with leading realtors to get them to show homes on a non-discriminatory basis. He succeeded, but he angered many. He was criticized by home-owners and business colleagues. And a group of irate realtors tried to block the purchase of a choice land plot in which his company was interested. He had foreseen the personal animosity, but not the backlash on his company.

These circumstances are unique, but they do show that there are numerous risks in activism, especially in an urban-dominated society.

Of course, the financial executive might become embroiled in controversy even while serving on the school board, the church finance committee, the businessmen's group to attract new industry, or the society to preserve national landmarks. There are few innocuous involvements today.

There is another side, too, to the question of risks. What are the risks if the executive *fails* to assume leadership in such activities?

Who can doubt that our cities today are in a state of crisis? There is a growing consensus in the business community that social involvement has to be radical—that is, it must strike at the *roots* of urban unrest. There is a growing tendency in society at large to look to industry and business for the solution to society's problems—and to look to them as the last hope. The executive's personal conscience—and his company's corporate conscience—will not allow him to remain aloof simply in order to avoid controversy.

Not all social problems have strictly financial solutions, but all do have financial implications. The successful financial executive recognizes the problems, focuses on them and works to bring about solutions and stability even before someone else points out the obvious need.

For example, health care looms as an increasingly complex problem in this country. If this is of prime concern, the executive should not wait for an appointment to a hospital board or government advisory committee before gathering facts and seeking solutions. He did not rise to his position in his company by waiting for others to identify problems. He himself has assumed responsibility and initiated action.

Today, so many problems are already urgent that it may seem unwise to suggest anticipating even more activities. However, someone must assume responsibility. And the executive should be both a working leader and trendsetter.

Conclusion

The protean character of contemporary society is destroying many stereotypes. The financial executive cannot afford to seem just a glorified accountant—or an impressive wheeler-dealer—or an archconservative who thinks only of stocks, bonds, equity capital and the last line of the income statement. Today he must be on the move—moving with the rapid currents of social change. He may choose the nature of his involvement. But involved he must be. There is no choice about that.

Index

Index

1237

Coordinated Examination Program, 170, 172

Coordination in planning department, 474

Copeland Act, 215

Copyrights, 1032, 1037
amortization of costs, 1040

Corporate affairs, legal aspects of; *see* Legal function

Corporate contributions; *see* Contributions

Corporate objectives; *see* Objectives

Corporate organization; *see* Organization

Corporate readjustment of fixed assets, accounting for, 1023–24

Corporate strategy; *see* Strategy formulation *and* Strategy implementation

Corporation; *see* Organization

Correlation analysis, 419

Correspondence courses, 144

Correspondence with shareholders, 1169–70

Cost of capital, 887

Cost accounting
adjustment to responsibility accounting, 635
defined, 630
standard costs; *see* Standard costs

Cost accounting function in make or buy decisions, 290

Cost centers defined, 633

Cost control through published annual reports to stockholders, 1158

Cost estimating techniques
centralized method, 207
grass roots, 207

Cost of goods sold
direct costing methods, 655
last-in, first-out method of inventory valuation, 655; *see also* Last-in, first-out method of inventory valuation (LIFO)
profit measurement problems, 655–56

Cost-of-living indices, 74

Cost and profit forecasting, 420–24
bottom to top approach, 420–21
committed costs, 422
construction of, 421–23
evaluation, 423–24
income taxes, 422–23
long range, 421
managed costs, 422
miscellaneous revenue and expense, 422–23
nonvariable operating costs, 422
overhead costs, 422
performance reporting, 424
personnel related costs, 422
short range, 420–21

Cost and profit forecasting—*Cont.*
top to bottom approach, 421
variable operating costs, 421–22

Cost ratio forecasting, 421–22

Cost reduction analysis
investment decision, 368–70
lease decision, 367

Cost reductions
administrative costs, 706–8
electronic data processing, 520–21

Cost reimbursement contracts, 203–5

Costs
accounts receivable financing, 878
acquisition of fixed assets; *see* Fixed assets, accounting for
administrative; *see* Administrative costs
amortization of; *see* Amortization
borrowing, 876
capital budgeting request elements, 497–98
control of; *see specific types of costs*
controllability of, determination of, 635–36
determination of, effect of organization upon, 30–31
electronic data processing system
comparison of factors, 567–68
considerations for, 515–23, 540; *see also* Electronic data processing
feasibility, 513
executive compensation administration, 93–95
government contract
considerations in, 207–9
principles in, 209–10
inventory and inventory valuation; *see* Inventory costs *and* Inventory valuation
inventory management considerations, 783–85
long-term financing, 887–88
make or buy decisions, applicable to, 294–303
manufacturing; *see* Manufacturing costs
pension plans, 1074
product line profitability analysis, 323–24
professional services, considerations in use of, 251–52
reduction suggestions through internal audit, 234
reinstatement in accounting for intangible assets, 1038–39
research and development; *see* Research and development costs

Counsel; *see* Attorneys; General Counsel; *and* Legal function

Coupon accounts, 745; *see also* Consumer credit

This book has been set in 10 and 9 point Caledonia, leaded 2 points. Part numbers and titles and chapter numbers and titles are in 18 point News Gothic. The size of the type page is 27 x 46½ picas.